THE ROUTLEDGE HANDBOOK OF ARCHAEOLOGICAL HUMAN REMAINS AND LEGISLATION

Methodologies and legislative frameworks regarding the archaeological excavation, retrieval, analysis, curation and potential reburial of human remains differ throughout the world. As workforces have become increasingly mobile and international research collaborations are steadily increasing, the need for a more comprehensive understanding of different national research traditions, methodologies and legislative structures within the academic and commercial sector of physical anthropology has arisen. *The Routledge handbook of archaeological human remains and legislation* provides comprehensive information on the excavation of archaeological human remains and the law through over 50 individual country contributions from Europe, Asia, Africa, North America, South America and Oceania with an additional contribution on Antarctica.

More specifically, the volume discusses the following:

- What is the current situation (including a brief history, education and training) of physical anthropology in the country?
- What happens on discovering human remains? Who is notified? What is the protocol?
- Where is the cut-off point between forensic and archaeological human remains (e.g., 100 years, 50 years, 25 years)?
- What is the current legislation regarding the excavation of archaeological human skeletal remains? Is a licence needed to excavate human remains? Is there any specific legislation regarding the excavation of human remains, their transportation, study and reburial? Any specific legislation regarding human remains from churchyards and those from recent war graves?
- Are physical anthropologists involved in the excavation process?
- What methods of anthropological analysis are mostly used in the country? Are there any population-specific methods created in the country?
- Are there any particular ethical issues that need to be considered when excavating human remains in a particular country?

In addition, an overview of landmark anthropological studies and important collections is provided where appropriate, as well as a list of useful resources (e.g., institutions, government and museum websites).

The contributions are discussed in an introductory chapter by the editors, which establishes the objectives and structure of the book, setting it within a wider archaeological framework, and in a conclusion which summarizes the current European and worldwide trends and perspectives in the study of archaeological human remains. *The Routledge handbook of archaeological human remains and legislation* makes a timely, much-needed contribution to the fields of physical anthropology, osteoarchaeology and bioarchaeology combining information on the excavation of human remains and the legislation that guides it, alongside information on the current state of physical anthropology across several continents. It is an indispensable tool for archaeologists, anthropologists and other scientists involved in the excavation and study of human remains around the world.

Dr Nicholas Márquez-Grant is a Forensic Anthropologist and Archaeologist at Cellmark Forensic Services, Abingdon (UK) and a Research Associate at the Institute of Human Sciences, School of Anthropology and Museum Ethnography, University of Oxford. He has done considerable work on human skeletal remains from archaeological contexts ranging from the Neolithic to the 19th century and from a number of countries. He is also regularly involved in forensic work in the UK. He has taught biological anthropology since 2001 at the University of Oxford.

Dr Linda Fibiger is a physical anthropologist whose research interests include interpersonal violence and conflict in prehistoric Europe, Irish Early Christian Burials, and standards and practice in osteoarchaeology. She has published widely on commercial and research projects in Britain and Ireland, and is currently involved in a research project at the University of Cardiff on changing patterns of living in the earliest agricultural societies of central Europe.

THE UNIVERSITY OF
WINCHESTER

Martial Rose Library
Tel: 01962 827306

SEVEN DAY LOAN ITEM

To be returned on or before the day marked above, subject to recall.

THE ROUTLEDGE HANDBOOK OF ARCHAEOLOGICAL HUMAN REMAINS AND LEGISLATION

An international guide to laws and practice in the excavation and treatment of archaeological human remains

Edited by Nicholas Márquez-Grant and Linda Fibiger

Routledge
Taylor & Francis Group

LONDON AND NEW YORK

First published 2011
by Routledge
2 Park Square, Milton Park, Abingdon, Oxon OX14 4RN

Simultaneously published in the USA and Canada
by Routledge
270 Madison Avenue, New York, NY 10016

Routledge is an imprint of the Taylor & Francis Group, an informa business

British Library Cataloguing in Publication Data
A catalogue record for this book is available from the British Library

Library of Congress Cataloging-in-Publication Data
The Routledge handbook of archaeological human remains and legislation: an
international guide to laws and practice in the excavation and treatment of archaeological
human remains / edited by Nicholas Márquez-Grant and Linda Fibiger.
    p. cm.
  Includes bibliographical references and index.
1. Human remains (Archaeology)--Law and legislation. I. Márquez-Grant,
Nicholas, 1976- II. Fibiger, Linda. III. Title: Handbook of archaeological
human remains and legislation.
  K3791.R68 2010
  344'.094--dc22

                                                          2010020706

ISBN: 978-0-415-58857-7 (hbk)
ISBN: 978-0-203-83871-6 (ebk)

Typeset in Bembo by
Taylor & Francis Books
Printed and bound in Great Britain by
CPI Antony Rowe, Chippenham, Wiltshire

CONTENTS

Contents

Contents

Contents

Contents

Contents

ILLUSTRATIONS

Tables

Figures

CONTRIBUTORS

Abel Fortó García. Historical Research Unit, Cultural Heritage of Andorra, Andorra

Agnès Malevez. Directorate of Archaeology of the Public Service of Wallonia, Namur, Belgium

Albert R. Zink. EURAC-Institute for Mummies and the Iceman, Bolzano, Italy

Alexander Varzari. Molecular Genetics Department, National Centre of Reproductive Health and Medical Genetics, Chişinău, Moldova

Alexandra Buzhilova. Institute and Museum of Anthropology, Moscow State University, Moscow, Russia. Institute of Archaeology, Russian Academy of Sciences, Moscow, Russia

Amila Zukanović. Faculty of Dentistry, University of Sarajevo, Sarajevo, Bosnia and Herzegovina

Ana Luísa Santos. CIAS – Research Centre for Anthropology and Health, and Department of Life Sciences, University of Coimbra, Portugal

Andrej Starović. National Museum in Belgrade, Belgrade, Serbia

Anja Sindermann. Nothwang & Partner, Anthropological Service and Research Society (ADFG), Frankfurt, Germany

Anthony Pace. Superintendent of Cultural Heritage, Superintendence of Cultural Heritage, Valetta, Malta

Berit J. Sellevold. NIKU – the Norwegian Institute for Cultural Heritage Research, Oslo, Norway

Bernardo Arriaza. Institute of Advanced Research, University of Tarapacá, Arica, Chile

Bill White. Centre for Human Bioarchaeology, Museum of London, London, UK

Bisserka Gaydarska. Department of Archaeology, Durham University, Durham, UK

Carme Rissech. Anthropology Unit, Department of Animal Biology, University of Barcelona, Barcelona, Spain

Christiane Bis-Worch. National Museum of History and Art, Luxembourg

Cláudia Umbelino. CIAS – Research Centre for Anthropology and Health, and Department of Life Sciences, University of Coimbra, Portugal

Clive Finlayson. The Gibraltar Museum, Gibraltar. Department of Social Sciences, University of Toronto at Scarborough, Toronto, Canada

Constantine Eliopoulos. Department of Animal and Human Physiology, Faculty of Biology, National and Kapodistrian University of Athens, Athens, Greece. Research Centre in Evolutionary Anthropology and Palaeoecology, School of Natural Sciences and Psychology, Liverpool John Moores University, Liverpool, UK

Dario Piombino-Mascali. EURAC-Institute for Mummies and the Iceman, Bolzano, Italy

David Maynard. Landsker Archaeology Ltd, Llys Aeron, Hebron, Wales, UK

Denise Donlon. Shellshear Museum, Discipline of Anatomy and Histology, Sydney Medical School, University of Sydney, Sydney, New South Wales, Australia

Don Brothwell. Department of Archaeology, University of York, York, UK

Douglas H. Ubelaker. Department of Anthropology, Smithsonian Institution, Washington D.C., USA

Drahoslav Hulínek. Slovak Archaeological and Historical Institute (SAHI), Bratislava, Slovak Republic

Edi Shukriu. Faculty of Philosophy, University of Prishtina, Prishtina, Kosovo

Elisabeth Iregren. Department of Archaeology and Ancient History, Lund University, Lund, Sweden

Elisabeth Smits. Amsterdam Archaeological Centre (AAC), University of Amsterdam, Amsterdam, The Netherlands

Ernesto González Licón. Graduate School in Archaeology, National School of Anthropology and History, INAH, Mexico City, Mexico

Eugenio Aspillaga Fontaine. Department of Anthropology, Faculty of Social Sciences and Programme in Human Genetics, Faculty of Medicine, University of Chile, Santiago, Chile

Fanica Veljanovska. Museum of Macedonia, Skopje, Former Yugoslav Republic of Macedonia

Foni Le Brun-Ricalens. National Museum of History and Art, Luxembourg

Frédérique Valentin. CNRS, UMR 7041, Paris 1 and 10, Nanterre, France

Geneviève Yernaux. Directorate of Archaeology of the Public Service of Wallonia, Namur, Belgium

Guillaume de Védrines. Law Faculty, Université Paris 1 Panthéon – Sorbonne, Paris, France

Guðný Zoëga. Skagafjordur Heritage Museum, Minjahúsið, Iceland

György Pálfi. Department of Biological Anthropology, University of Szeged, Szeged, Hungary

Hallie Buckley. Department of Anatomy and Structural Biology, Otago School of Medical Sciences, University of Otago, Dunedin, New Zealand

Handan Üstündağ. Department of Archaeology, Anadolu University, Eskişehir, Turkey

Hildur Gestsdóttir. Institute of Archaeology, Reykjavík, Iceland

Ildikó Pap. Department of Anthropology, Hungarian Natural History Museum, Budapest, Hungary

Ilka Weidig. Nothwang & Partner, Anthropological Service and Research Society (ADFG), Frankfurt, Germany

Inmaculada Alemán. Laboratory of Anthropology, University of Granada, Granada, Spain

Inna Potekhina. Department of Bioarchaeology, Institute of Archaeology, National Academy of Sciences of Ukraine, Kiev, Ukraine

Ivana Medenica. Centre for Archaeological Research of Montenegro, Podgorica, Montenegro

Iwona Teul. Chair and Department of Normal and Clinical Anatomy, Pomeranian Medical University, Szczecin, Poland

Jean Krier. National Museum of History and Art, Luxembourg

Jeannot Metzler. National Museum of History and Art, Luxembourg

Jerome S. Cybulski. Canadian Museum of Civilization, Gatineau, Quebec

Jörg Orschiedt. Department of History, Chair for Prehistory, University of Leipzig, Leipzig, Germany

Judith Littleton. Department of Anthropology, University of Auckland, Auckland, New Zealand.

Juho-Antti Junno. Department of Archaeology, University of Oulu, Oulu, Finland

Juliette Michel. Oxford Archéologie Méditerranée, Mauguio, France

Karl Harrison. Cranfield Forensic Institute, Defence Academy of the United Kingdom, Shrivenham, Wiltshire, UK

Kim Quintelier. Flemish Heritage Institute (VIOE), Brussels, Belgium. Royal Belgian Institute of Natural Sciences (RBINS), Brussels, Belgium

Kimberly Brown. The Gibraltar Museum, Gibraltar

Kirsi O. Lorentz. Science and Technology in Archaeology Research Centre (STARC), The Cyprus Institute (CyI), Nicosia, Cyprus

Kirsti Paavola. Department of Art Studies and Anthropoloy, University of Oulu, Oulu, Finland

Konstantinos Moraitis. Department of Forensic Medicine and Toxicology, School of Medicine, National and Kapodistrian University of Athens, Athens, Greece

Korakot Boonlop. Princess Maha Chakri Sirindhorn Anthropology Centre, Bangkok, Thailand

Kristina Jennbert. Department of Archaeology and Ancient History, Lund University, Lund, Sweden

Laureen Buckley. Department of Forensic Medicine, c/o State Pathologist's Office, Dublin, Ireland

Lena Strid. Oxford Archaeology, Oxford, UK

Linda Fibiger. School of History and Archaeology, Cardiff University, Cardiff, Wales, UK

Lidija Tegako. Department of Anthropology and Ecology Institute of the History of the National Academy of Sciences of Belarus, Minsk, Belarus

Lourdes Márquez Morfín. Graduate School in Physical Anthropology, National School of Anthropology and History, INAH, Mexico City, Mexico

Lourdes Penados. Forensic anthropologist, Guatemala

Luca Bianconi. Grupporicerche, International Institute of Ligurian Studies, Genova, Italy

Luis Caro Dobón. Area of Physical Anthropology, University of León, León, Spain

Lumír Poláček. Institute of Archaeology, Academy of Sciences, Brno, Czech Republic

Maria Grazia Amore. Archaeologist, International Centre for Albanian Archaeology, Tirana, Albania

Marija Djurić. Laboratory for Anthropology, Institute of Anatomy, School of Medicine, University of Belgrade, Belgrade, Serbia

Marin Vodanović. Department of Dental Anthropology, School of Dental Medicine, University of Zagreb, Zagreb, Croatia

Marina L. Sardi. División Antropología, Museo de La Plata, Buenos Aires, Argentina

Mario Novak. Department of Archaeology, Croatian Academy of Sciences and Arts, Zagreb, Croatia

Mario Šlaus. Department of Archaeology, Croatian Academy of Sciences and Arts, Zagreb, Croatia

Marit Vandenbruaene. Flemish Heritage Institute (VIOE), Brussels, Belgium

Marja-Leena Kortelainen. Department of Forensic Medicine, University of Oulu, Oulu, Finland

Markku Niskanen. Department of Archaeology, University of Oulu, Oulu, Finland

Maryna Steyn. Forensic Anthropology Research Centre, University of Pretoria, Pretoria, South Africa

Matthew Spriggs. The Australian National University, Canberra, Australia

Maureen E. Marshall. Department of Anthropology, University of Chicago, Chicago, USA

Michael Pearson. Managing Director, Heritage Management Consultants, Canberra, Australia. Adjunct Professor of Cultural Heritage Management, University of Canberra, Australia

Michel Signoli. UMR 6578 CNRS-EFS-Université de la Méditerranée, Marseille, France. Committee of Specialist Experts of the Musée de l'Armée (CESMA), Musée des Invalides, Paris, France.

Michel Toussaint. Directorate of Archaeology of the Public Service of Wallonia, Namur, Belgium

Mile Baković. Centre for Archaeological Research of Montenegro, Podgorica, Montenegro

Milton Núñez. Department of Archaeology, University of Oulu, Oulu, Finland

Mirette Modarress. Department of Archaeology, University of Oulu, Oulu, Finland

Mongeda Khalid Magzoub Ali. National Corporation for Antiquities and Museums, Khartoum, Sudan

Mónica Sans. Department of Biological Anthropology, Faculty of Humanities and Educational Sciences, Institute of Anthropological Sciences, University of the Republic, Montevideo, Uruguay

Myriam Llorens-Liboy. Department of Prehistory and Archaeology, University of Granada, Granada, Spain

Najaf Museyibli. Institute of Ethnography and Archaeology, Academy of Sciences, Baku, Azerbaijan

Nancy Tayles. Department of Anatomy and Structural Biology, Otago School of Medical Sciences, University of Otago, Dunedin, New Zealand

Natthamon Pureepatpong. Oriental Avenue, New Road, Bangkok, Thailand

Nermin Sarajlić. Faculty of Medicine, University of Sarajevo, Sarajevo, Bosnia and Herzegovina

Nicholas Márquez-Grant. Cellmark Forensic Services, Abingdon, UK. Institute of Human Sciences, School of Anthropology and Museum Ethnography, University of Oxford, UK

Nils-Jörn Rehbach. Nothwang & Partner, Anthropological Service and Research Society (ADFG), Frankfurt, Germany

Olalla López-Costas. Area of Physical Anthropology, Faculty of Biology, University of Santiago de Compostela, Santiago de Compostela, Spain. Laboratory of Anthropology, University of Granada, Granada, Spain

Olga Sorokina. Department of Anthropology and Ecology Institute of the History of the National Academy of Sciences of Belarus, Minsk, Belarus

Paola Ponce. Department of Archaeology, Durham University, Durham, UK

Paulina Kubacka. Western Pomeranian Provincial Office for Protection of Historical Monuments, Szczecin, Poland

Pavel Jamnik. Counsellor at the Criminal Police, Ministry of the Interior, Ljubljana, Republic of Slovenia

Petr Velemínský. Department of Anthropology, National Museum, Prague, Czech Republic

Petra Leben-Seljak. Physical anthropologist, Slovenia

Philippe Charlier. University Hospital Raymond Poincaré (AP-HP / UVSQ), Garches, France. HALMA-IPEL, UMR 8164 CNRS, Lille 3 University, Lille, France. Department of Medical Ethics, Paris 5 University, Paris, France

Pia Bennike. Saxo Institute, Prehistoric Archaeology & Centre for Textile Research, University of Copenhagen, Copenhagen, Denmark

Radoslav Beňuš. Department of Anthropology, Comenius University, Bratislava, Slovak Republic

Ralph Regenvanu. Vanuatu National Cultural Council, Port Vila, Vanuatu

Rimantas Jankauskas. Department of Anatomy, Histology and Anthropology, Faculty of Medicine, Vilnius University, Vilnius, Lithuania. State Forensic Medicine Service, Vilnius, Lithuania

Rosine Orban. Biological Anthropology Research Group, Royal Belgian Institute of Natural Sciences (RBINS) and Université Libre de Bruxelles, Brussels, Belgium

Ruzan A. Mkrtchyan. Yerevan State University, Yerevan, Republic of Armenia

Salima Ikram. American University in Cairo, Cairo, Egypt

Senem Škulj. Forensic Anthropologist, Bosnia and Herzegovina

Sergiu Musteaţă. History Department, 'Ion Creangă' State Pedagogical University, Chişinău, Moldova

Sheila Maria Ferraz Mendonça de Souza. Department of Endemic Diseases 'Samuel Pessoa', National School of Public Health 'Sérgio Arouca', Foundation Oswaldo Cruz, Rio de Janeiro, Brazil

Shirley J. Schermer. Burials Program, Office of State Archaeologist, University of Iowa, Iowa City, USA

Siân Halcrow. Department of Anatomy and Structural Biology, Otago School of Medical Sciences, University of Otago, Dunedin, New Zealand

Sirpa Niinimäki. Department of Archaeology, University of Oulu, Oulu, Finland

Soňa Masnicová. Department of Criminalistics and Forensic Sciences, Academy of Police Forces, Bratislava, Slovak Republic

Sotiris Manolis. Department of Animal and Human Physiology, Faculty of Biology, National and Kapodistrian University of Athens, Athens, Greece

Stefan Flohr. Department of Biology, University of Hildesheim, Hilsdesheim, Germany

Stuart Bedford. College of Asia & the Pacific, The Australian National University, Canberra, Australia

Sylvia Deskaj. Department of Anthropology, Michigan State University, East Lansing, USA

Szilárd Sándor Gál. Mureş County Museum, Târgu Mureş, Romania

Tina Christensen. School of Human & Life Sciences, Roehampton University, London, UK

Tina Jakob. Department of Archaeology, Durham University, Durham, UK

Torbjörn Ahlström. Department of Archaeology and Ancient History, Lund University, Lund, Sweden

Ulrich Nothwang. Nothwang & Partner, Anthropological Service and Research Society (ADFG), Frankfurt, Germany

Ursula Wittwer-Backofen. Department of Anthropology, Faculty of Medicine, Albert-Ludwigs-University of Freiburg, Freiburg, Germany

Velissaria Vanna. Institute of Archaeology, University College London, London, United Kingdom

Wiesław Lorkiewicz. Department of Anthropology, Faculty of Biology and Environmental Protection, University of Łódź, Łódź, Poland

Willem Coenraad Nienaber. Forensic Anthropology Research Centre, University of Pretoria, Pretoria, South Africa

Yossi Nagar. Israel Antiquities Authority, Rockefeller Museum, Jerusalem, Israel

Zuzana Obertová. Institute of Legal Medicine, Uniklinikum Düsseldorf, Düsseldorf, Germany

FOREWORD

Human remains and society: a field in transformation

Professor Don Brothwell

DEPARTMENT OF ARCHAEOLOGY, UNIVERSITY OF YORK, UK

I should begin by saying that I think this survey is long overdue, and that the editors are to be applauded for gathering together such a detailed overall review. Personally, I see myself as an academic mongrel, but certainly with a lifetime interest in human remains. I am thus delighted to be able to support this worthwhile project with some personal thoughts on the matter.

In the first few decades of the 20th century, regional interest in studying human remains was varied, with a relaxed attitude to the movement of remains into collections in North America and Europe. For instance, the Egyptologist Sir Flinders Petrie arranged for the transportation of large Egyptian series back to Britain, and similarly Aleš Hrdlička transferred much Peruvian material to the USA. Interest in these remains varied of course, with some investigating the pathology, and others the osteometric variability.

Curatorial space was not the problem it is today, and in Britain the skeletal collections in London, Cambridge and Oxford became vast. The Second World War greatly changed the environment for human skeletal studies in Europe, and the shadow of Nazi racism fell across some of the work and I believe deterred a new generation of researchers into ancient skeletal remains. But within the past fifty years the situation has gradually changed, as more cemetery excavations in Europe and beyond have demanded specialist studies on human remains. It was in the late 1950s that I began to study early British skeletons, and found to my surprise that there was no current manual providing an up-to-date review on the range of information which could be derived from bones and teeth, and no good comment on relevant recording methodologies. It was for this reason that my *Digging up Bones* was produced in 1963, and I hoped that it would also provide information for the field archaeologist. Since then, the literature has greatly expanded, and of course there are many more research papers on bone and tooth biology, including the fields of electron microscopy, digital radiography, trace element chemistry, isotope analysis and DNA analysis. In this methodological explosion, new biases have appeared, while interest in osteometric variation has waned.

Another major change, very relevant to this publication, is that legislation relating to the excavation, curation and reburial of human remains has become politically more significant. This has been partly stimulated by tribal and religious groups who wish to have a say in the process as it relates to their own people. In some countries this has been a difficult time for those involved in the study of human remains, and indeed the osteoarchaeologist has become something of a second-class citizen. Legislation will continue to mature on this matter, and it is to be hoped that compromises in the future will allow sufficient time for the study of skeletal material. There is certainly a need for us to explain, at a public level, why there is value in studying such remains. It is also important to indicate clearly that a report on bones is only a first step in analysis, and, with new techniques or further funding, far more information may be obtained. So, wherever possible, curation rather than reburial is the ideal, and again the public at large needs to be told that reburial usually means accelerated decay in a modified burial environment, whereas museum curation prevents further decay.

While forensic archaeology and anthropology are usually seen at a public level as contributing to the resolution of criminal investigations, there is still work to be done in showing that these investigations have similar value in relation to earlier burials (say, those over 100 years old). My hope is that, although the situation is still changing and is by no means ideal, there will eventually be a greater public understanding of why human remains need to be studied. I really welcome this volume, and its discussion of the various current issues related to the excavation of human remains throughout the world.

Don Brothwell

NOTES FROM THE EDITORS

1) We are aware of the problem surrounding the name 'Macedonia', with some countries supporting the 'Republic of Macedonia', others rejecting the latter and preferring 'FYROM' or the 'Former Yugoslav Republic of Macedonia', and we have made the best compromise possible.
2) We have decided to list the name of each country in English, followed by the name commonly used within the country. e.g. Kosovo/Kosova.
3) We have included Russia and Turkey under Europe although they have a large land mass in Asia.
4) We have decided to use 'Oceania' to include both Australasia (e.g. Australia, New Zealand) and Vanuatu.
5) We have decided to use the format for continents with North America and South America as two separate continents. Central American countries thus fall under the continent 'North America'.
6) Puerto Rico is a territory of the US with Commonwealth Status, but we have included it as a chapter in the main body of the book.
7) Vatican City State, also a country, has been included as an Appendix since it only provides a very brief, but nevertheless informative, summary on archaeological human remains and legislation.

INTRODUCTION

Nicholas Márquez-Grant and Linda Fibiger

This volume is intended to provide the reader with information on legislative frameworks and methodologies regarding the excavation, analysis and curation of human skeletal remains in 59 countries and on every continent. The main motivation behind it is the editors' long-standing interest in how human osteoarchaeology and palaeopathology are practised and dealt with in different parts of the world, with the hope that collating this information in one volume will allow the reader – whether physical a anthropologist, osteoarchaeologist, anthropologist, heritage consultant, civil servant, commercial archaeologist, museum curator, university lecturer or student – to learn and benefit from experiences across the globe. There is currently much confusion about the protocols and policies governing the treatment of archaeological human remains both on and off site, and this has frequently hindered collaborative work between researchers in different countries. This volume offers potential collaborators from different geographical entities a starting point to connect with each other and share their experiences, helping the subject to grow and develop.

Our definition of the discipline of physical anthropology for the purpose of this volume is restricted to the study of human remains from primarily archaeological contexts; in other parts of the world the study of archaeological human remains may be better known as osteoarchaeology, bioarchaeology, osteology, historical anthropology and palaeopathology.

The objectives of this volume are:

1 To understand the current state of physical anthropology in each country and to evaluate different historical backgrounds and traditions;
2 To understand what requirements are necessary necessary to undertake an excavation in a particular country and provide information on requirements, protocols, governmental and educational institutions and any specific legislation;
3 To highlight country- or population-specific analytical methods of anthropological analysis;
4 To discuss future needs and potential recommendations.

We asked the contributors to answer a number of key questions on a country-by-country basis:

• What is the main legislation that governs the excavation, analysis and curation of human remains?
• What happens on discovery of human skeletal remains? Who needs to be contacted? What period do archaeological human remains encompass?

- What is the role of the osteologist/physical anthropologist on site?
- Is the osteological and paleopathological analysis of archaeological human skeletal remains compulsory?
- Can human remains be sent abroad for analysis?
- Are there any country- or population-specific methods for age-at-death and sex assessment, and stature computation?

Each chapter is divided into four sections which include: an introduction with a brief history of physical anthropology and an assessment of the current state of the discipline (education, training, research, etc.); a section on human remains and legislation; a summary of country- or population-specific analytical methods; and a conclusion providing a summary and reflections on the future of physical anthropology in that particular country. In addition, each chapter also includes a list of useful contacts and web addresses. We believe that this information provides a good starting point for anyone wanting to work or study collections in a particular country. There have been a number of challenges along the way and we have attempted to standardize each chapter as much as possible. At times, different traditions and frameworks resulted in some variation, and each chapter does represent the individual author's account of the situation in a particular country; but we hope that the most important information has been made available in each case.

Initially, the volume was meant to have a European focus, but it grew steadily into a much more extensive piece of work. Many more countries than actually feature in this volume were approached, but in a number of cases previous professional commitments or indeed economic or political circumstances prevented their participation. We hope that potential future editions will see contributions from many more African and Asian colleagues.

This volume would obviously not have been possible without the dedication and hard work of the individual authors, and we would like to express our sincere thanks to all of them. We would also like to thank Don Brothwell for his encouragement and for allowing us to include his thoughts on the current state and future perspectives of the discipline. Our thanks also go to the many colleagues who have put us in contact with potential authors, and to Dr Eileen Murphy, Dr Martin Smith and an anonymous reviewer for improving the aims and presentation of the volume. Special thanks also go to Dr Paola Ponce, who was a great help in coordinating the chapters on South America. We would also like to thank the Routledge editorial staff, particularly Matthew Gibbons, Lalle Pursglove, Amy Poynter-Davis and Megan Graieg, for their help throughout the editorial process. Nicholas Márquez-Grant would particularly like to thank his colleagues Julie Roberts, Sally Houghton and Steve Litherland for their support; and to express his gratitude for their support to Marina Khmelnitskaya and to his family (with special thanks to his mother Jennifer, father José, brother Carlos, nephew Izan and his grandparents) and friends. Linda Fibiger would like to thank Jamie Lewis for encouragement and support throughout the completion of this volume.

At this point, it may be appropriate to reflect on the fact that the study of archaeological human remains is and will continue to be a great privilege, allowing us a unique insight into lives gone past. Physical anthropology is a fascinating field of study, and this volume is a testament to its richness and diversity. Finally, we would like to give a special mention to Bill White, who wrote the UK chapter of this volume. Very sadly, Bill passed away in November 2010, shortly before its publication. We would like to pay tribute to the contribution Bill has made to osteoarchaeology in Britain. He will be missed by many.

Nicholas Márquez-Grant and Linda Fibiger

PART 1

Europe

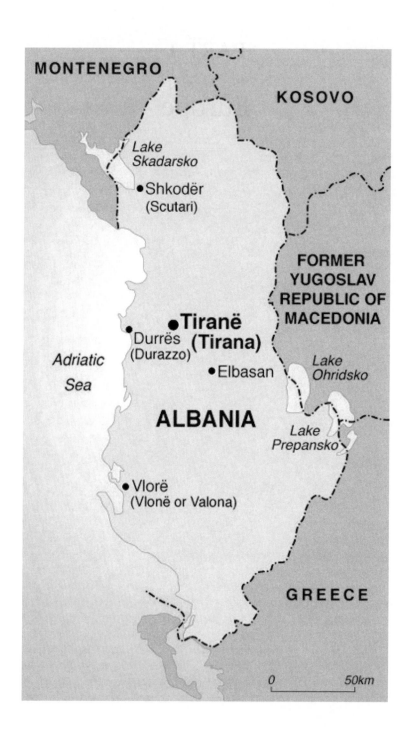

Albania/Shqipëria

Maria Grazia Amore

INTRODUCTION: A BRIEF HISTORY AND CURRENT STATE OF PHYSICAL ANTHROPOLOGY IN ALBANIA

Physical anthropology as a discipline began relatively late in Albania, after the Second World War. As with all other disciplines which arose and developed during this period, physical anthropology was based on Marxist theory, summarized by Engels as a science which made it possible to understand the transition from the morphology and physiology of the human being and its races to history. Central to anthropological studies became the issue of the ethnogenesis of the Albanian people.

Anthropological research on the Albanian living population, however, began in the last quarter of the 19th century, especially by foreign travellers such as François Pouqueville and scholars such as Carleton Coon and Renato Biasutti (Pouqueville 1805: 153–54; Coon 1950; Biasutti 1967: 332–34). Nevertheless their studies remained isolated and did not become part of a homogeneous scientific *corpus*. It was only in 1973 that the first anthropology department in the Institute of History was created, which in 1976 became part of the Centre of Archaeological Research of the Academy of Sciences (Qëndra e Kërkimeve Arkeologjike të Akademisë së Shkencave). The bases of Albanian anthropology at the time were the study of the physical characteristics of the modern population and a comparison of these to the skeletal material from past periods, in order to establish the origin, gradual formation, continuity and chronological development of the anthropological types in the country.

The first tasks of this research were to identify anthropological traits in particular areas of the country, and to begin a collection of skeletal remains pertaining to a wide chronological span, dating from the early Neolithic (sixth millennium BC) to the 19th century AD. The final goal was to demonstrate that modern Albanians were the direct descendants of the Illyrians, who played an important role in history, and that Albania was the centre of the Dinaric race, a subcategory of the Europid race (Dhima 1985: 5–6, 11–12, 15).

The methodology of the earlier studies consisted in measurements of the living population, mostly individuals from the north of the country where there was a higher degree of isolation. Due to lack of standardization, the results often varied from scholar to scholar because of the way the measurements were taken. Carleton Coon was the first scientist to include observations on the natural and social context which he considered as influencing human beings, especially in the early years of life (Coon 1950). Rudolf Virchow and Raphaël Zampa were the first scholars to focus on skull measurements, and Ernest-Théodore Hamy was the first one to take measurements of archaeological skulls found during the excavations in the cemetery of Koman, dated to between the sixth and eighth centuries AD (Virchow 1877: 769–819; Zampa 1886; Hamy 1900).

In the 1970s and 1980s Albanian scholars such as A. Ylli and B. Çipi wrote on the assessment of the age and sex of an adult individual on the basis of the ectocranial sutures (Ylli and Çipi 1973, 1975); however, the scholar who had collected data in a more systematic way was Aleksander Dhima. He had a medical background, and had specialized in anthropology through a Humboldt fellowship in Germany in the early 1980s. In his study, he collected data on living populations and on skeletal material from Antiquity to the Middle Ages. The objective of his work was to provide a general picture of the formation and transformation through time of the anthropological typologies of Albanians in order to contribute to the issue of the ethnogenesis of the Albanian population. To achieve this, he presented the anthropological data available for Albania, and he himself observed 1079 male and 668 female living individuals representative of the eight major regions of the country while also studying 201 mediaeval skeletons for comparison (Dhima 1985: 6–7). Among the living people of Albania, he observed individuals of three social categories: farmers, workers in state firms, and other professionals such as doctors and teachers, etc. The individuals in each of the three categories ranged between 19 and 60 years of age for men and between 18 and 55 years of age for women. Individuals with certain pathological conditions were excluded from his comparative study. The anthropometric measurements taken had as a reference internationally recognized standards such as those by Rudolf Martin and Henri-Victor Vallois. Skin colour was assessed using the scale developed by Felix von Luschan. The data were then statistically elaborated in the Centre of Mathematics of the Academy of Sciences in Tirana. Apart from the measurements and other observations, photographs of most individuals were also taken (Dhima 1985: 67–71). After his research, Dhima concluded that in all the Albanian regions there was a prevalence of the Adriatic anthropological physique (Dhima 1985: 146).

In the mediaeval skeletal sample, Dhima noticed more variation. The general picture was again that of a population with mostly Adriatic characteristics, but in some cases, Mediterranean, Alpine and Cromagnoid types were also observed. All the data were subsequently statistically analysed in order to assess the degree of homogeneity within the same series, and between the different series of the same and of different chronological periods and geographical regions. The statistical parameters used were those of Ronald Aylmer Fisher and Harold Hotelling (Dhima 1985: 203–9).

Dhima concluded that he supported the argument that the Albanian population had a consistent evolution from the Early Middle Ages (10th to 12th centuries AD) to modern times, with the Adriatic element as its anthropological substratum (Dhima 1985: 266). He reinforced this thesis with sporadic observations conducted during other archaeological excavations. He noticed, in fact, that the Adriatic element was present in the individual of the central grave of the Tumulus of Barç, dated to the late Bronze Age (13th century BC). Even the less prevalent types, such as the Mediterranean type, were present in the skeletons from Podgorie and Cakran, dated to the Neolithic period (late fifth millennium BC), and from the necropolis of Dyrrah dated between the fourth and second centuries BC. The Cromagnoid type was identified as being present in the individual of the central grave of the Tumulus of Piskovë, dated to the early Bronze Age (second half of the third millennium BC) (Dhima 1985: 231–32, 235).

Education and training

Physical anthropology in the country is currently underrepresented. There exists a course of physical anthropology in the Faculty of Biology at the University of Tirana, but no physical anthropologists collaborate with archaeologists. Since the 1990s, after the fall of the communist regime and with collaborations with foreign universities now possible, anthropological scholars from outside Albania have taken part in multidisciplinary teams undertaking archaeological excavations at various Albanian sites (Schepartz 2010; Stallo *et al.* 2010; Bejko *et al.* 2006; Papadopoulos *et al.* 2007).

ARCHAEOLOGICAL HUMAN REMAINS AND LEGISLATION

Archaeological legislation

The Law for Cultural Heritage (no. 9048, of 7 April 2003; updated with Law no. 9882 of 28 February 2008: MTKRS 2009) regulates all the issues concerning legislation regarding the protection, rights and duties of the institutions operating in the field of Cultural Heritage. Articles which deal with the archaeological activity include nos 33, 41, 42, 43, 44, 45, 46, 47, 48. These include information on excavations and conservation work. Archaeological activity at and protection of monuments fall under the National Council of Restoration (Këshilli Kombëtar e Restaurimeve), the Institute of Archaeology (Instituti Arkeologjik) for research excavations, and the Agency for the Archaeological Service (Agjencia e Shërbimit Arkeologjik) for rescue excavations.

In Albania, it is forbidden to excavate and to use metal detectors without authorization (Article 33). Investigations, test pits, and excavations in the entire territory of the republic of Albania are the monopoly of the Albanian State (Article 41). The Agency for the Archaeological Service is the principal institution, under the authority of the Cultural Heritage minister, and was created to undertake archaeological excavations and any other archaeological, architectural or historical studies which may be affected by urban planning or construction works of any kind. The structure and the personnel of the Agency for the Archaeological Service are approved by a decree of the prime minister according to proposals of the minister responsible for the Cultural Heritage. The National Council of Archaeology (Këshilli Kombëtar i Arkeologjisë) is an agency consisting of specialists of the respective fields who meet periodically with the ministry for the Cultural Heritage (Article 42). The activities mentioned in article 41 are undertaken by state and private agencies, local or foreign. These collaborations take place on the basis of bi- or multilateral agreements. Exclusively foreign institutions are forbidden to work independently in the country. In any case, collaborations are authorized by the National Council of Archaeology (Article 43).

Archaeological objects found during archaeological excavations are the property of the Albanian State (Article 44). Anybody who discovers, by chance, objects of Cultural Heritage have the duty to notify the local institution dealing with Cultural Heritage, the Agency for the Archaeological Service, or the regional directories of Cultural Heritage (Drejtoritë rajonale të kulturës kombëtare) within 20 days, stating the nature of the discovery and its location. After documenting the artefact, the commission created for this purpose by specialists of these different institutions assesses the value and future status of the object, as well as any compensation to the person(s) who discovered it (Article 45). In case of important discoveries, authorized personnel of the Agency for the Archaeological Service request any potential development work to stop immediately. Further actions are decided by the National Council of Archaeology no later than ten days from the interruption of the works (Article 46). In case of major projects such as the construction of roads, highways, airports, ports, industrial and residential complexes, during the process of planning and realization of the project investors are obliged to have the written approval from the National Council of Conservation and the National Council of Archaeology. Specialists evaluate the area and prepare a report. When important archaeological, ethnographical or architectural findings are expected, it is necessary for the construction project to change. All expenses for the investigation, documentation and any eventual changes in the project have to be covered by the investors (Article 47). In the case where archaeological excavation has to proceed all the archaeological expenses including the excavation and post-excavation analysis, restoration and conservation should be fully covered by the investors (Article 48).

HUMAN REMAINS AND LEGISLATION

The boundary between archaeological and forensic cases is 50 years. By experience, chance finds of skeletal material are notified to the local Cultural Heritage authorities. Human bones found outside modern cemeteries are investigated as archaeological finds.

As it is clear from the legislation illustrated above, there is no specific mention of human remains. It is implied, however, that archaeological human remains will be treated and stored in the same way as other archaeological finds, and therefore there is also no planning for reburial.

Excavating an ancient cemetery or necropolis does not require a different or additional permit from other archaeological monuments. The National Council of Archaeology has the right to establish particular requirements based on the nature of the proposed excavation, as well as to authorize sending any samples abroad, but there are no specific requirements in law.

The presence of a physical anthropologist in an archaeological project is not compulsory, but is certainly recommended. The anthropologist should assist and advise on excavation strategies and the lifting of human remains and then undertake any cleaning and analysis as well as advising on the appropriate storage of the remains.

METHODS OF ANTHROPOLOGICAL ANALYSIS

The methods of anthropological analysis for the assessment of age-at-death and sex include current methods taught in universities. In projects such as those carried out by the Albanian Rescue Archaeology Unit in the necropolis of Apollonia, at the prehistoric tumulus of Lofkënd, and in the Korça area (prehistoric tumulus of Kamenica and mediaeval cemetery of Rrembec), data have been collected on computerized recording forms adapted from the *Standards* of Buikstra and Ubelaker (1994).

CONCLUSION

In Albania, physical anthropology as a discipline began after the Second World War. The issue of the ethnogenesis of the Albanian people became central to anthropological studies. The National Council of Archaeology has the right to establish particular requirements based on the nature of the proposed excavation, as well as to issue permits to send samples abroad, but there are no specific requirements in the law. The presence of a physical anthropologist at an archaeological project is not compulsory, but is recommended.

For the first time in Albania, recent analyses and advances have included mitochondrial DNA (Bejko *et al.* 2006; Papadopoulos *et al.* 2007), stable isotope analyses (Stallo *et al.* 2010), and Accelerator Mass Spectrometry dating (Damiata and Southon 2010).

USEFUL CONTACTS

Agency for the Archaeological Service (Agjencia e Shërbimit Arkeologjik): Agjencia e Shërbimit Arkeologjik; Ministria e Turizmit, Kulturës, Rinisë dhe Sporteve; Rruga e Kavajës, 1001. Website: www.asha.gov.al

BIBLIOGRAPHY

Bejko, L., Fenton, T. and Foran, D. (2006) 'Recent advances in Albanian mortuary archaeology, human osteology, and ancient DNA', in L. Bejko and R. Hodges (eds) *New Directions in Albanian Archaeology,* Tiranë: International Centre for Albanian Archaeology Monograph Series No. 1.

Biasutti, R. (1967) *Razze e popoli della Terra, Vol II,* 4th edn, Torino: UTET.

Buikstra, J. E. and Ubelaker, D. H. (eds) (1994) *Standards for Data Collection from Human Skeletal Remains,* Fayetteville, AR: Arkansas Archaeological Survey Research Series No. 44.

Coon, C. S. (1950) *The Mountains of Giants. A Racial and Cultural Study of the North Albanian Mountain Ghegs,* Cambridge, MA: Peabody Museum of American Archaeology and Ethnology Cambridge (reprinted: Kraus Reprint New York, 1970).

Damiata, B. N. and Southon, J. (2010) 'Results of AMS Dating and stable-isotope analyses of skeletal remains: Tumuli 9 and 10, Apollonia (Albania)', in M. G. Amore *The Complex of Tumuli 9, 10, and 11 in the Necropolis of Apollonia,* Oxford: BAR International Series 2059 (I–II), International Centre for Albanian Archaeology Monograph Series No. 2.

Dhima, A. (1985) *Gjurmime Antropologjike për Shqiptarët,* Tiranë: Akademia e Shkencave e RPS ë Shqipërisë.

Hamy, E. T. (1900) 'Contribution à l'anthropologie de la Haute-Albanie', *Bulletin du Musée d'Histoire Naturelle,* 6: 268–72.

MTKRS (2009) *Ministria e Turizmit, Kulturës, Rinisë dhe Sporteve,* Website. Available online at www.mtkrs. gov.al (accessed 13 May 2009).

Papadopoulos, J. K., Bejko, L. and Morris S. P. (2007) 'Excavations at the prehistoric burial Tumulus of Lofkënd in Albania: a preliminary report for the 2004–5 seasons', *American Journal of Archaeology,* 111: 105–47.

Pouqueville, F. C. H. L. (1805) *Voyage en Morée, à Constantinopole et en Albanie, Vol. III,* Paris: Elibron Classic.

Schepartz, L. (2010) 'Bioarchaeology of Apollonia: Tumuli 9, 10, 11 and Appendixes 1, 2, and 3', in M. G. Amore, *The Complex of Tumuli 9, 10, and 11 in the Necropolis of Apollonia,* Oxford: BAR International Series 2059 (I–II), International Centre for Albanian Archaeology Monograph Series No. 2.

Stallo, J., Schepartz, L., Grimes, V. *et al.* (2010) 'Strontium isotope ratios and mobility reconstruction', in M. G. Amore, *The Complex of Tumuli 9, 10, and 11 in the Necropolis of Apollonia,* Oxford: BAR International Series 2059 (I–II), International Centre for Albanian Archaeology Monograph Series No. 2.

Virchow, R. (1877) 'Zur Kraniologie Illyriens', *Monatsbericht der Königlich Preussische Akademie der Wissenschaften zu Berlin* (1877): 768–803.

Ylli, A. and Çipi, B. (1973) 'Përcaktimi i moshës në bazë të studimit të suturave ekzokranike', *Bulletin i Universitetit e Tiranës (seria shkencat mjekësore),* 2: 21–35.

——(1975) 'Përcaktimi i seksit me anën e kafkës', *Bulletin i Universitetit e Tiranës (seria shkencat mjekësore),* 1: 45–53.

Zampa, R. (1886) 'Anthropologie Illyrienne', *Revue Anthropologique de l'Institut International d'Anthropologie,* 9: 625–48.

Andorra

Abel Fortó García

INTRODUCTION: A BRIEF HISTORY AND CURRENT STATE OF PHYSICAL ANTHROPOLOGY IN ANDORRA

The Principality of Andorra is a microstate with an area of 468 sq km and a population of 84,609 (2009 census), and hence a density of 180 inhabitants per sq km. This figure is the result of a population increase that began in the mid-20th century, mostly due to immigration. The population in the 13th and 14th centuries has been estimated at between 1,700 and 2,300 inhabitants (Gual and Puig 2005; Ros 2005), growing to about 5,500 in the 19th century.

In absolute terms, the number of excavated burials is quite low. However, considering the dimensions of the country, the volume of the population and the number of already excavated archaeological sites, the specific weight of such findings is quite significant. In fact, we only need to compare Andorra with nearby areas on both sides of the Pyrenees, Catalan and French, to see that the Principality occupies an outstanding position in terms of the number of archaeological interventions and the amount of information obtained about burials and human remains.

Since the very beginning of archaeological research in the Principality of Andorra (see note 2), the excavation of human remains has been constant enough to state that burials have been the most excavated archaeological feature in the country. A total of 13 different sites have revealed burials of various types and periods. Some human remains of unknown origin correspond to the recovery of archaeological materials during town-planning or building works in the early years of operation of the National Artistic Heritage (Patrimoni Artístic Nacional). Many of these human remains of unknown origin or archaeological context are kept in the warehouses of the Cultural Heritage of Andorra (Patrimoni Cultural d'Andorra or PCA).

The archaeological sites where burials have been found are varied in chronological terms (Table 2.1). There is a documented Neolithic cist (Yáñez *et al.* 2002), three Middle Neolithic cists (Llovera 1986), three Roman burials (two of them located inside a cave and in the same grave) (Guilaine and Martzluff 1995; Fortó and Maese 2008) and ten cemeteries from the mediaeval and post-mediaeval periods. From a quantitative point of view, taking into account the number of sites as well as the number of skeletons, mediaeval and post-mediaeval cemeteries are the most prominent, with a total of eight sites and about 650 individuals that have been excavated. These comprise individuals from the sixth to the 19th centuries AD, from five tombs (site

Table 2.1 Archaeological sites in Andorra yielding anthropological remains

Site	Anthropological study	DNA study	Radiocarbon dating	Early Neolithic	Middle Neolithic	Roman Period	Early Middle Ages	Late Middle Ages	Modern Age	Minimum number of individuals
Segudet		X	X	X						1
Feixa del Moro	X		X		X					3
Balma de la Margineda						X				2
Camp Vermell	X		X			X	X			5
Camp del Perot	X		X				X			42
Roc d'Enclar	X		X				X			50
L'Antuix	X						X			16
Sant Jaume d'Engordany	X						X	X		65
Santa Eulàlia d'Encamp	X						X	X	X	170
Santuari de Meritxell							X	X	X	34
Sant Joan de Caselles							X	X	X	204
Sant Martí de Nagol	X									6
Hort de l'Església	X		X					X		43

of Camp Vermell) to 204 tombs (site of Sant Joan de Caselles). The fact that these necropoli were generally associated with churches is the main reason why this type of site has been the most frequently excavated, since much refurbishing works are undertaken on these buildings.

Unfortunately, anthropological studies have not been able to keep up with the pace of excavation, so a significant number of the human remains have not yet been studied. In the early years of the PCA's operation, Dr Elisenda Vives was the palaeoanthropologist who carried out several studies and took part in excavations. Her work included the skeletal material from La Feixa del Moro (Llovera 1986), Santa Eulàlia d'Encamp (Juan *et al.* 1989), Sant Martí de Nagol (Vives 1990), La Balma de la Margineda (Guilaine and Martzluff 1995) and El Roc d'Enclar (Llovera *et al.* 1997). Vives's publications also include a study about Catalonian mediaeval populations with information on Andorra, specifically the sites of Sant Martí de Nagol and El Roc d'Enclar (Vives 1990).

After the departure of Dr Vives and in the subsequent absence of a physical anthropologist, the PCA has asked institutions or scientific groups from Catalonia to undertake the anthropological study of the human remains. These include anthropological studies from the sites of l'Antuix-Sant Jaume d'Engordany (Bosch 1993), El Camp del Perot (Agustí and Mestre 2001), Segudet (Malgosa *et al.* 2001), l'Hort de l'Església (Malgosa 2009) and El Camp del Vermell (Prats-Muñoz and Malgosa 2008). In fact, the contacts between PCA and the Biological Anthropology Unit of the Universitat Autònoma de Barcelona have strengthened anthropological research, especially of Andorran mediaeval populations and, focusing on previous works, the study of the human remains kept in the warehouses of the PCA, a recently excavated site called El Camp del Colomer de Juberri, radiocarbon dating and DNA analysis.

ARCHAEOLOGICAL HUMAN REMAINS AND LEGISLATION

Archaeological legislation

The peculiarity of the Principality of Andorra, which can be observed in its historical evolution and its institutional structure, is also present in the legislation on cultural heritage. The latter is a belated development, especially in comparison with its neighbouring countries, not taking place until the second half of the 20th century. The formulation of this legislation was closely linked to the development of archaeology in the Principality. The first edicts basically focused on regulating the archaeological activity and the export of archaeological findings and works of art (edicts of 1960 and 1970).[1] This link between legislation and the development of archaeology must be understood bearing in mind the beginning of Andorran archaeology,[2] motivated by scholarly interest in national history but also by the rising awareness of the value of cultural heritage and of its potential destruction, at a moment when Andorra experienced an economic boom and urban growth. As these scholars' intention was to preserve the Andorran cultural heritage, in 1960, coinciding with the first edict, the department of Patrimoni Cultural d'Andorra (PCA) was created, and became responsible for the management of heritage and with a unit specifically focused on archaeology.[3]

It was not until 1983 that the first law on the protection of the cultural and natural heritage was promulgated; however, this law did not have any specific reference to archaeological activity, so it was soon regarded as too generic and, consequently, inefficient. Years later, suggestions to change the law resulted in the current law on the cultural heritage of Andorra (2003). For the first time, a law contained a section that focused on archaeology, and there were plans to develop regulations on archaeological and palaeontological excavation. A draft of this regulation relating to archaeological and palaeontological work was finally completed in 2009, and is currently under consultation with the legal services of the Government of Andorra. It might seem that there has been an excessive delay, but the truth is that only in the last two or three years has the need for such a regulation become really imperative, due to the considerable rise in rescue and preventive archaeological excavation and the increasing participation of archaeological companies, freelance archaeologists, specialists and research groups from abroad; it has become impossible for all the staff at the Research Unit (URH) in Andorra to handle all archaeological activity in the country. Along these lines, it is worth mentioning that only in the last five years have excavations been directed by individuals external to the PCA's archaeological unit.[4]

Since the regulation of archaeological and palaeontological activities is still in its draft stages, the 2003 Heritage Law is at present the only legal text valid to regulate these activities; however, since the assessment of projects and excavation permits have followed this draft in recent years, the 2003 Heritage Law is somewhat generic concerning archaeological activities, with no specific mention of human remains, so for this reason the new draft considers human remains and a number of further changes.

One of the main problems in the 2003 Heritage Law lies in the fact that it came about from the point of view of archaeological heritage and not of archaeological activity. According to article 23 of the law, the definition of archaeological heritage states that it consists of 'the set of properties and goods, both on the surface and in the subsoil, which contribute to the knowledge of history and that need to be studied through archaeological methodology' [author's translation]. This definition has a broad meaning; the definition of archaeological heritage has an even broader one and the concept itself is quite difficult to define, especially since the development of modern and contemporary archaeology and even of landscape archaeology. Therefore it is almost impossible to establish clear boundaries between archaeological heritage, monuments, vernacular heritage and intangible heritage.

The new approach, a result of consulting many international treaties and conventions of heritage, introduces a broader view that understands archaeology as a 'set of specific techniques and procedures' with the goal of understanding 'past societies through the study of their remains, the traces they have left on the Earth or any kind of evidence of their existence or activities, whether they are on the surface, beneath the ground or underwater' [author's translation]. Moreover, this definition implicitly recognizes the multidisciplinary nature of the research, which means taking into account a range of studies and disciplines, such as physical anthropology.

HUMAN REMAINS AND LEGISLATION

Currently there is no legal distinction between archaeological and forensic human remains, so there is no specific protocol of action when such remains are fortuitously discovered. It is true that when this happens the finding should be reported to the police, who, in turn, should notify this to the department of forensic medicine, but in any case there is no requirement to report it to the department of Cultural Heritage. Although it is not a common occurrence, it should be taken into account in the future regulation of archaeological and palaeontological activities.

If we focus specifically on the excavation of archaeological human remains, they are included under the activity of open area excavation, meaning that they do not receive any kind of particular treatment or specific legislation; but in the case of a planned excavation in a cemetery area, the presence of a physical anthropologist in the excavation team is mandatory and that person will be in charge of the excavation of the human remains – or, at least, the anthropologist will be responsible for field supervision. In those cases where there is a small number of burials as part of a more complex site, or in cases where burials appear fortuitously during an excavation, it is possible to carry out the excavation without the presence of a physical anthropologist, provided that the research team has an established specific protocol for the excavation and recovery of human remains and, of course, authorization from the PCA. In both cases the subsequent anthropological study will be compulsory.

Since most of the time the study of human remains has been carried out abroad by foreign scholars, there is no doubt that human remains can be transported abroad. Likewise it is possible, with the necessary authorization from the Ministry of Culture, to carry out any kind of archaeometric studies including radiocarbon dating, although such studies may involve the destruction of the sample.

Once the anthropological study has been completed, the human remains are returned and stored permanently in the PCA warehouses, with a proper inventory and at a specific location (article 18), with the rest of the finds from the excavation.

METHODS OF ANTHROPOLOGICAL ANALYSIS

Due to the involvement of different and foreign research groups over the years, there are no national guidelines or recommendations, so a variety of methods have been used to conduct anthropological analyses (see Table 2.2).

CONCLUSION

The excavation of human remains in Andorra has been closely related to the development of archaeology in the country, hence cemeteries or isolated burials have been the most excavated kind of archaeological site or feature. Unfortunately the potential of this amount of data has not been fully exploited, since excavation was not typically followed by anthropological study. In recent years this trend has been corrected in a timely manner, so, today, the excavation of human remains is forbidden without further anthropological study.

A recent draft developed from the 2003 Heritage Law provides some benefit to the study of human remains and the role of the physical anthropologist. Hopefully, a standardized methodology in the future will enable the provision of population comparisons and the study of physical anthropology in Andorra, from prehistory to the post-mediaeval period.

USEFUL CONTACTS

More information is available through the Cultural Heritage of Andorra (Patrimoni Cultural d'Andorra) website at www.patrimonicultural.ad

ACKNOWLEDGEMENTS

I would like to thank Xavier Maese and Àlex Vidal from the Unitat de Recerca Històrica for their collaboration, and Violeta Cañigueral for help in translation.

Table 2.2 Anthropological methods used in Andorra, according to site

Site	Minimum number of individuals	Age estimation	Stature calculation	Sex determination	14C dating
Segudet	1	Meindl and Lovejoy 1985; Brothwell 1987; Gilbert and McKern 1973; Todd 1920	Martin and Saller 1957; Olivier 1960	Ferembach *et al.* 1980; Krogman and İşcan 1986	1
Feixa del Moro	3		Pearson 1898; Trotter and Gleser 1956		1
Balma de la Margineda	2				1
Camp Vermell	5	Crétot 1978; Ubelaker 1989; Scheuer and Black 2000; Rissech and Malgosa 2007; Alduch le Bagouse 1988		Ferembach *et al.* 1980; Krogman and İşcan 1986; Alemán *et al.* 1997; Safont *et al.* 2000; Schutkowski 1993	2
Camp del Perot	42		Pearson and Manouvrier (Olivier 1963)		
Roc d'Enclar	50	Ubelaker 1989; Brothwell 1981; Ferembach *et al.* 1979; Masset 1971	Martin and Saller 1957	Acsádi and Neméskeri 1970	4
L'Antuix	16		Pearson and Manouvrier (Olivier 1963)		
Sant Jaume d'Engordany	65	Brothwell 1981; Ferembach *et al.* 1979; Molleson 1986; Redfield 1970; Moorrees *et al.* 1963	Pearson and Manouvrier (Olivier 1963)		
Santa Eulàlia d'Encamp	170	Ubelaker 1978; Brothwell 1981; Ferembach *et al.* 1979; Masset 1971	Martin and Saller 1957	Acsádi and Nemeskéri 1970	
Sant Martí de Nagol	6	Ubelaker 1989; Brothwell 1981; Ferembach *et al.* 1979; Masset 1971	Martin and Saller 1957	Acsádi and Nemeskéri 1970	

NOTES

1 Some specialists have stated that, in a compilation of laws known as Manual Digest (written by Antoni Fiter, a local jurist, in 1748), there can be found the first legal regulation which refers, though only in part, to the protection of the cultural heritage. In my opinion, the meaning of 'cultural heritage' given to the sentence (Màxima 21; Fiter 1987: 500) is due to a misinterpretation of a word that in the text is used as a synonym of *usos i costums* (Catalan expression that means 'laws') but that has been understood as 'old or antique objects' by those specialists (Canturri *et al.* 1998).

2 The results of the excavation campaigns carried out in La Balma de la Margineda in 1959 and 1960 were published in 1960, first in the journal Andorra and, later, in Zephyrus, a journal of the University of Salamanca. Five years earlier, in 1955, the 'international courses of Andorra' were running, which brought about the opportunity of establishing contact with Dr Joan Maluquer de Motes who, apart from being a professor in archaeology at the University of Barcelona, was a disciple of the famous scholar Dr Pere Bosch Gimpera, and one of the most outstanding members of the second generation of the Catalan school of archaeology.

3 It was first called Patrimoni Artístic Nacional (PAN), but in 1993 its name changed to Patrimoni Cultural d'Andorra (PCA) with some novelty, such as the creation of the Unitat de Recerca Històrica (URH), which includes the archaeological unit.

4 Some of the more prominent examples would be: the three campaigns at the site of La Roureda de la Margineda (Andorra la Vella), carried out by the Catalan archaeological company Estrats SL between 2007 and 2009; the excavation of El Pont de la Margineda (Andorra la Vella), directed by the Catalan company Arkeòlik SCP in 2007; the research project of La Vall del Madriu (Sant Julià de Lòria, Escaldes-Engordany, Encamp), carried out by the Catalan institute ICAC (Institut Català d'Arqueologia Clàssica) between 2005 and 2009; and the archaeological surveys in the valley (Andorra la Vella, Sant Julià de Lòria, Escaldes-Engordany) carried out by the Grup de Recerca d'Alta Muntanya of the Universitat Autònoma de Barcelona in 2006 and 2007.

BIBLIOGRAPHY

Acsádi, G. and Neméskeri, J. (1970) *History of Human Life Span and Mortality*, Budapest: Akadémia Kiadó.

Agustí, B. and Mestre, A.M. (2001), 'Necròpoli de camp de Perot – 1991 (Sant Julià de Lòria, Andorra). Estudi antropològic', unpublished report.

Alduc-le Bagouse, A. (1988) 'Estimation de l'âge des non-adultes: maduration dentaire et croissance osseuses. Données comparatives pour deux nécropoles médiévales vas.normandes', *Actes des 3èmes Journées Anthropologiques. Notes et Monographies Techniques*, 24: 81–103. Paris: CNRS.

Alemán, I., Botella, M.C. and Ruíz, L. (1997) 'Determinación del sexo en el esqueleto postcraneal. Estudio de una población mediterránea actual', *Archivo Español Morfología*, 2: 7–17.

Bosch, J.M. (1993) *Engordany, la vida al solà. Segles II aC–XX dC*, Andorra la Vella: Ministeri d'Educació, Cultura i Joventut – Servei d'Arqueologia del Govern d'Andorra.

Brothwell, D.R. (1987) *Desenterrando huesos*, México: Fondo de Cultura Económica.

Buikstra, J.E. and Ubelaker, D.H. (eds) (1994) *Standards for Data Collection from Human Skeletal Remains*, Fayetteville, AR: Arkansas Archaeological Survey Research Series 44.

Canturri, P., Casal, N., Mas, D., *et al.* (1998) *Manual Digest. 250è aniversari. Catàleg de l'exposició*. Andorra la Vella: Ministeri de Turisme i Cultura.

Crétot, M. (1978) *L'arcade dentaire humaine (morphologie)*, Paris: Julien Prélat.

Ferembach, D., Schwidetzky, I. and Stloukal, M. (1980) 'Recommendations for age and sex diagnoses of skeletons', *Journal of Human Evolution*, 9: 517–49.

Fortó, A. and Codina, O. (2009) 'Poder, comunitats i territori. Una interpretació arqueològica de l'Andorra dels segles VI al XII', in M. Coma (ed.) *Andorra: un profund i llarg viatge. Catàleg de l'exposició*, Andorra la Vella: Govern d'Andorra.

Fortó, A. and Maese, X. (2008) 'Camp Vermell (Sant Julià de Lòria, Andorra): evidències d'hàbitat rural i activitat metal lúrgica a Andorra', in V. Revilla (ed.) 'Les vil les romanes a la Tarraconense. Implantació, evolució i transformació. Estat actual de la investigació del món rural en època romana (Lleida, 28 al 30 de novembre de 2007)', unpublished work.

Gual, V. and Puig, R. (2005) 'La població andorrana a l'època moderna', in E. Belenguer (ed.) *Història d'Andorra. De la prehistòria a l'edat contemporània*, Barcelona: Edicions 62.

Guilaine, J. and Martzluff, M. (1995) *Les excavacions a la Balma de la Margineda (1979–1991)*, Vol. I, Andorra la Vella: Ministeri de Cultura del Govern d'Andorra.

Juan, M., Llovera, X., Niño, V. et al. (1989) *Santa Eulàlia d'Encamp. Evolució històrica d'un edifici. Segles IX–XX*, Andorra la Vella: Govern d'Andorra.

Krogman, W.M. and İşcan, Y.M. (1986) *The Human Skeleton in Forensic Medicine*, Chicago: Charles C. Thomas.

Llovera, X. (1986) 'La Feixa del Moro (Juberri) i el Neolític Mig-Recent a Andorra', *Tribuna d'arqueologia*, 1985–86: 15–24.

Llovera, X., Bosch, J.M., Yáñez, C. *et al.* (eds) (1997) *Roc d'Enclar. Transformacions d'un espai dominant, segles IV – XIX*, Andorra la Vella: Ministeri de Cultura del Govern d'Andorra.

Malgosa, A. (2009) 'Estudi antropològic de les restes humanes de l'hort de l'Església (La Massana)', unpublished report.

Malgosa, A., Díaz, N., García, C. *et al.* (2001) 'Estudi antropològic de les restes humanes de la tomba de Segudet (Ordino)', unpublished report.

Martin, R. and Saller, K. (1957) *Lehrbuch der Anthropologie*, Stuttgart: Gustav Fischer.

Masset, C. (1971) 'Erreurs systématiques dans la détermination de l'âge par les mesures crânienes', *Bulletins et Mémoires de la Société d'Anthropologie de Paris*, 7: 85–105.

Molleson, T.I. (1986) 'Skeletal age and paleodemography', in A.H. Bittles and K.J. Collins (eds) *The Biology of Human Ageing*, Cambridge: Cambridge University Press.

Moorrees, C.F., Fanning, E.A. and Hunt, E.E. (1963) 'Formation and resorption of three deciduous teeth in children', *American Journal of Physical Anthropology*, 21: 205–13.

Olivier, G. (1963) *Pratique anthropologique*, Paris: Vigot.

Patrimoni Cultural d'Andorra (PCA) (1993) 'Recull de textos legislatius en matèria de Patrimoni Cultural i pautes per a l'elaboració de projectes de llei i reglaments sobre el patrimoni Cultural d'Andorra', unpublished report.

Prats-Muñoz, G. and Malgosa, A. (2008) 'Estudi antropològic de les restes humanes de Camp Vermell (Sant Julià de Lòria)', unpublished report.

Redfield, A. (1970) 'A new aid to aging immature skeletons: development of the occipital bone', *American Journal of Physical Anthropology*, 33: 207–20.

Rissech, C. and Malgosa, A. (2007) 'Pubis growth study: applicability in sexual and age diagnostic', *Forensic Science International*, 173: 137–45.

Ros, F. (2005) 'El poblament a Andorra', in E. Belenguer (ed.) *Història d'Andorra. De la prehistòria a l'edat contemporània*, Barcelona: Edicions 62.

Safont, S., Alesán, A. and Malgosa, A. (1999) 'Memòria d'excavació realitzada a la tomba del carrer nou, 12 (Sant Bartomeu del Grau, Osona)', unpublished report.

Scheuer, L. and Black, S. (2000) *Developmental Juvenile Osteology*, London: Academic Press.

Schutkowski, H. (1993) 'Sex determination of infant and juvenile skeletons. Morphognostic features', *American Journal of Physical Anthropology*, 90: 199–205.

Todd, T.W. (1920) 'Age changes in the pubic bone: I. The Male White pubis', *American Journal of Physical Anthropology*, 3: 285–334.

Ubelaker, D.H. (1989) *Human skeletal remains. Excavation, analysis, interpretation*, Washington, DC: Taraxacum.

Vives, E. (1990) *La població catalana medieval. Origen i evolució*, Capellades: Eumo editorial.

Yáñez, C., Malgosa, A., Burjachs, F. *et al.* (2002) 'El món funerari al final del V mil lenni a Andorra: la tomba de Segudet (Ordino)', *Cypsela*, 14: 175–94.

Armenia/Hayastan

Maureen E. Marshall and Ruzan A. Mkrtchyan

INTRODUCTION: A BRIEF HISTORY AND CURRENT STATE OF PHYSICAL ANTHROPOLOGY IN ARMENIA

Physical anthropology in Armenia is currently at a turning point, as recent work has started to turn towards bioarchaeological approaches. Armenia possesses a historically rich background of mortuary excavation and analysis of human remains, and has the potential to contribute important collections in the future. Combined with new techniques and methods of analysis, such collections will shed new light on the prehistory and history of ancient societies in the south Caucasus. Furthermore, the current diversity of collaborative international projects in Armenia is bringing different methods of analysis and epistemological traditions within physical anthropology into conversation. However, in order for these productive developments to be realized, several challenges in both the field and the laboratory must first be overcome.

The excavation of mortuary sites

The investigation of mortuary sites has a long history of research in the south Caucasus. In fact, the first excavations conducted in Armenia investigated mortuary sites, and since the late 19th century thousands of tombs have been excavated. In 1871, Alexander Yeritsov excavated 23 'pre-Christian' burials at the site of Akner in the Debed river canyon in northern Armenia (Smith *et al.* 2009: 12). Yeritsov was soon followed by Fredrich Bayern, who in 1882 excavated 86 burials at the Late Bronze and Iron Age (Table 3.1) cemetery at Redkin-Lager near Dilijan, and only a few years later by Jacques de Morgan who excavated 898 Iron Age burials near Alaverdi and Aktala in northern Armenia (Lindsay and Smith 2006: 168; Morgan 1889: 82). Bayern's (1885) publication worked to correlate materials across regional sites (Lindsay and Smith 2006: 168), while Morgan's (1889) publication situated the artefacts within the chronology of the Near East and the Mediterranean (Smith *et al.* 2009: 13). Morgan's publication also included several plan views and cross-sections of burial chambers and their inhumations, as well as sketches of two crania from Moçi-Yéri, located 3km north of Alaverdi (see Morgan 1889: 165). Yervand Lalayan also excavated several sites in the Sevan Basin, including Noraduz and Mrtbi Dzor (see Lalayan 1931). The crania from these excavations later formed part of a Sevan Basin collection that is discussed below. In many ways, these early reports set the basis for later

Table 3.1 Armenia: chronology

Time	Typological Period	Material Cultural Horizon
200 BC–300 AD	Iron IV	Artashat-Garni
600–200 BC	Iron III	Armavir-Tsaghkahovit
800–200 BC	Iron II	Lchashen-Metsamor 6, Urtartu
1150–800 BC	Iron I	Lchashen-Metsamor 4–5
1500–1150 BC	Late Bronze Age I–III	Lchashen-Metsamor 1–3
2400–1500 BC	Middle Bronze Age III	Karmirberd, Karmirvank, Sevan-Uzerlik
	Middle Bronze Age II	Trialeti-Vanadzor
	Middle Bronze Age I	Martkopi-Bendini
3500–2400 BC	Early Bronze Age	Kura-Araxes

publications of mortuary excavations, which tend to focus on *in situ* descriptions of the tombs, inhumations and associated objects.

At the turn of the century, archaeological investigations in Armenia were transformed by Nikolai Marr's research at the mediaeval Armenian capital of Ani (excavated 1892, 1893, 1904–17) (Smith 2005: 241). Marr and his students, most notably Toros Toramanyan and Ashkharbek Kalantar, conducted unsystematic regional surveys of the southern and western slopes of Mt. Aragats. They catalogued both settlement architecture and cemeteries (see Toramanyan 1942, 1948), several of which became sites of major excavations during the second half of the 20th century, including Horom, Metsamor, Oshakan and Shamiram. Following the disruption and tumult caused by the First World War and the incorporation of Armenia into the Union of Soviet Socialist Republics, archaeological institutions were reorganized and archaeological research proceeded under the developing framework of Marxist culture history (Smith *et al.* 2009: 16; see Trigger 1989: 214–25). A new generation of scholars working in the South Caucasus focused on major settlement sites. Some of the most notable projects included Evgenii Bayburtyan's 1936–38 excavations at Shengavit, Boris Piotrovskii's excavations at Karmir Blur starting in 1936, and Babken Arakelyan's work at Garni starting in 1949. These projects, along with Boris Kuftin's excavations at the Trialetti kurgans and at Beshtashen in Georgia, were fundamental to the development of a regional chronology (Kuftin 1941, 1946; Piotrovskii 1949). Starting in the late 1960s, Piotrovskii and Arakelyan's students, including Stepan Esayan, Arutyun Martirosyan, Telemak Khachatryan and Emma Khanzadyan, ushered in a period of large scale and long term excavations (Lindsay and Smith 2006: 175). These excavations included several major Middle/Late Bronze and Iron Age mortuary sites (Figure 3.1), including Artik (Khachatryan 1979), Elar (Khanzadyan 1979), Karashamb (Oganesyan 1992a; Oganesyan 1992b), Keti (Petrosyan 1989), Lchashen (Mnatsakanyan 1965), Lori Berd (Devedjyan 1981, 2006), Metsamor (Khanzadyan 1995), Oshakan (Esayan and Kalantaryan 1988), Shamiram (Areshyan 1977), Shirakavan (Torosyan *et al.* 2002), and Verin Naver (Simonyan 1979, 1984).

Archaeological research in Armenia was slowed down by the devastating 1988 earthquake, the collapse of the USSR, and the general socio-economic situation that resulted from these events. Nevertheless, intermittent excavation continued at several of the mortuary sites mentioned above, including Karashamb, Lchashen and Lori-Berd. During the late 1980s and the 1990s, new, larger scale excavations were conducted at the cemeteries of Horom (Badalyan and Aghekyan 1992) and Talin (Avetisyan and Muradyan 1991, 1994). Intermittent excavations of mortuary sites also continued at sites in the Sevan Basin, including Noraduz (Piliposyan 1991a),

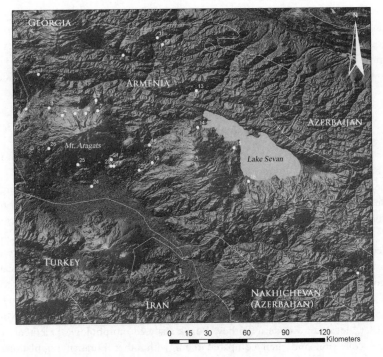

Figure 3.1 Major Bronze Age and Iron I mortuary sites in Armenia
  1) Keti, 2) Shirakavan, 3) Horom, 4) Artik, 5) Mantash, 6) Hnaberd, 7) Tsaghkahovit, 8) Gegharot, 9) Gegharot Kurgans, 10) Lori Berd, 11) Moçi-Yéri, 12) Akner, 13) Redkin Lager, 14) Lchashen, 15) Noraduz, 16) Nerkin Getashen, 17) Sisian, 18) Karashamb, 19) Elar, 20) Karmir Berd, 21) Verin Naver, 22) Sasunik, 23) Oshakan, 24) Metsamor, 25) Shamiram, 26) Talin.
Created by: M.E. Marshall.
Source: SRTM; Political Boundaries ESRI World Data 2008.

Mrtbi Dzor (Piliposyan 1991b) and Nerkin Getashen (Piliposyan and Hovhannisian 1991). Over the last ten years, Ashot Piliposyan's Sevan Basin excavations have also included tombs at Kanagegh (Piliposyan *et al.* 2002), Dari Glukh and Hatsarat. More regional approaches have produced catalogues of mortuary sites and descriptions of excavated tombs in Syunik (Xnkikyan 2002) and the southern shores of Lake Sevan (Biscione *et al.* 2002). Additionally, Ruben Badalyan and Pavel Avetisyan (2007) recently catalogued and published 40 new or previously poorly documented sites surrounding Mt Aragats.[1] Their corpus included a number of individual tombs, small scale mortuary excavations and occasional finds, including 19 Late Bronze Age and nine Iron I period cemeteries.

The 1990s also saw the introduction of long term international collaborative research projects in Armenia, including Project ArAGATS (the joint American-Armenian Project for the Archaeology and Geography of Ancient Transcaucasian Societies). In 1998 and 2000, Project ArAGATS conducted a systematic regional survey of the highlands overlooking the Tsaghka-hovit plain in central Armenia (Avetisyan *et al.* 2000; Badalyan *et al.* 2003). In addition to nine fortresses with Late Bronze Age components, the project identified 199 burial clusters spread along the northern slopes of Mt Aragats and the southern slopes of the Pambak range (with an overall estimation of 5,970 Late Bronze Age tombs within the Tsaghkahovit Plain) (Badalyan *et al.* 2003: 162; Smith *et al.* 2009: 396). Working within this context, Marshall conducted

21

excavations[2] at Tsaghkahovit Burial Cluster 12 as part of a dissertation research project broadly investigating Late Bronze Age social and political organization through a combined investigation of mortuary practices and everyday lived experiences. The combination of survey, intensive excavation and bioarchaeological analysis has allowed mortuary practices to be contextualized in relation to the fortress sites, as well as individual life histories to be placed within a local society and sphere of interaction.

Physical anthropology

While tied to the excavation of mortuary sites in many ways, the analysis of human remains in Armenia has a parallel but distinct history of research. In particular, physical anthropological investigations have centred on the study of ethnogenesis and craniology. After Morgan's 1889 publication of the sketches of crania from Moçi-Yéri, the first major contribution to physical anthropology is considered to be Viktor V. Bunak's 1927 publication *Crania Armenica*. Bunak was interested in the question of the genesis of the Armenoid cranial type, and from 1913 to 1917 undertook a physical anthropological research project, mainly in modern eastern Turkey. Similar to Marr,[3] Bunak followed the advancing front southwards from the Russian-Turkish border into 'Turkish Armenia' (Bunak 1927: 8). According to Bunak, he gathered a large collection of crania from Bingöl-Dağ, the central mountain range of the Armenian Highlands. More specifically, these crania belonged to the modern Armenian populations of Mush Snajak in Bitlis Vialet,[4] located in modern Turkey. Bunak analysed morphological elements and metric traits of the collection and then compared them with other Eurasian populations. He distinguished what he termed the 'Ponto-Zagros' cranial type (referred to by other authors as 'Armenoid race') (Bunak 1927: 47, 96). Bunak brought the collection to the Museum of Anthropology at Moscow State University (MGU), where the 150 crania were stored and catalogued (Bunak 1927: 9).[5] In 1929, Bunak went on to publish the craniological data from the excavations of Lalyan (see Lalyan 1931), which formed one of the first Soviet ancient physical anthropology collections. For some time this published information was used by other physical anthropologists as a reference or comparative data set, but was only listed under the general category of Iron Age Sevan Basin, Armenia. Mkrtchyan later collaborated with archaeologist Piliposyan to correct and specify the archaeological contexts for these crania.

While Bunak's interest in cranial types can be situated within the broader late 19th- and early 20th-century directions in physical anthropological research,[6] the focus on the development of ethnic types was carried into the period of Soviet scholarship and developed into a particular approach to physical anthropology. With Engels's work providing the theoretical basis or 'contours of science' (Alekseev 1989: 5), ethnogenesis served as the main subject of investigation for anthropology, ethnology and scholars in the humanities in general (Alekseev 1989: 13; Oshanin 1964: ix–x; Roginskii and Levin 1963: 6). The Soviet ethnographic approach to ethnogenesis focused on the reconstruction of the historical processes of the formation of particular ethnicities in space and time (Arutiunov and Bromley 1978; Oshanin 1964). Paleoanthropologists thus strove to understand the autochthonous development, migrations and diffusion of ethnic (or racial) types (see Alekseev 1989). Both modern populations and archaeological human remains were critical to this approach, as the comparison of the two allowed one 'to establish the history of the colonization of the territory [Central Asia] by various races' (Oshanin 1964: x). Thus, the Soviet comparative approach created an extensive collection of human remains that, when coupled with a detailed publication of measurements, created a spatially and temporally robust comparative data set for the analysis of metric variation throughout Eurasia.

Under this paradigm of ethnogenesis, Soviet anthropology maintained an interest in Armenia due to both its association with the Armenoid cranial type and its distinct modern 'ethnos'.[7] The next major phase of paleoanthropological research in Armenia occurred with Valerii P. Alekseev's visits to Armenia in the late 1960s and the subsequent 1974 publication of craniological materials from the Caucasus. Building on Bunak's morphological work, Alekseev further investigated ethnogenesis in the Caucasus with metric analyses of cranial series from the south and north Caucasus. He drew on Armenian collections from the History Museum of Armenia (*Haystani Patmutyan Tangaran*) in Yerevan and those housed at MGU. His data set included crania from Jrarat (4) and Shengavit (5) from the Eneolithic (now dated to the Early Bronze Age); Lchashen (100), Sevan (6), Tsamakaberd (10), Noraduz (15), and Artik (13) from the Bronze Age; and Garni (6) from the Late Antique Period (Roman or Iron IV) (Alekseev 1974, 84–101). For each of these collections, average as well as individual measurements were listed in tables. Alekseev then compared these data on metric traits with collections from Azerbaijan, Georgia and the north Caucasus. Based on these comparisons, Alekseev concluded that Armenoid cranial morphology had a Near Eastern origin (Alekseev 1974). Alekseev continued to use the data from Armenia to analyse, in widening and increasingly statistical analyses, the morphological and metric variation throughout Eurasia (see Alekseev and Gokhman 1984: 143–44, 162). Georgian scholar Abdushelishvili also compared craniometric means from Armenia to individual data from the Bronze Age in Georgia and the north Caucasus, and argued that there are distinct characteristics between the populations (Abdushelishvili 1982: 66).

The cranial collections from Armenia also played a key role in Soviet and post-Soviet ethnogenetic studies based on non-metric traits. Kozintsev (1988) compared non-metric traits from 65 populations throughout Eurasia, including Bunak's collection from Bingöl-Dağ. Movsesian (2005; Movsesian and Kochar 2004) used phylogenic tree and factor analyses to analyse non-metric traits from Bunak's collection, Alekseev's Sevan Basin materials, and materials from several newer excavations that again spanned the Early Bronze Age to the Iron Age. Movsesian's conclusions generally agreed with Alekseev's morphological and typological analyses, postulating the 'genetic integrity' of modern and ancient Armenian populations from the Bronze Age despite interpopulation ties between the Sevan Basin and other areas of Armenia during the Bronze Age and further variation in the Antique period (or Iron III and Iron IV) (Movsesian 2005: 209). Recent Armenian publications of human remains from other sites have begun to incorporate non-metric traits into this tradition (see Khudaverdyan 2008).

In comparing Bunak's and Alekseev's data sets of human remains with the major excavation sites discussed in the previous section, it should be noted that many of the most important Soviet reference collections of human remains do not necessarily match the most thoroughly published cemetery sites from Armenia. This disconnect reflects a historical separation of archaeological and physical anthropological analyses. This situation began to change during the late 1980s and 1990s when Alekseev's student, Ruzan Mkrtchyan, began working in Armenia. Mkrtchyan was trained in the Soviet tradition of physical anthropology at the Institute of Ethnology and Anthropology (IEA or Institut Etnologii i Antropologii) of the Russian Academy of Sciences (RAN or Rossiiskaya Akademiya Nauk) and has contributed some work to the field of ethnogenesis (see Alekseev and Mkrtchyan 1989; Mkrtchyan 2004), although she has mainly focused on demographic questions specific to Late Bronze and Iron I populations (see Mkrtchyan 2003, 2004) and has also begun to incorporate a bioarchaeological approach (see Mkrtchyan and Marshall 2009).

Collaboration between Mkrtchyan and Avetisyan (Avetisyan and Mkrtchyan 1994), Badalyan (Badalyan and Aghekyan 1992; Mkrtchyan 2004), and Piliposyan (Mkrtchyan, Piliposyan and Palikyan 1997) allowed for the concurrent excavation of tombs and analyses of skeletal materials that linked age and sex to mortuary treatments. Mkrtchyan also worked to situate Armenia's physical anthropological materials within the context of specific archaeological sites. After years of storage and examination by various researchers, the collections of crania studied by Alekseev were only partially or improperly labelled and catalogued. Working with Alekseev's publications[8] and the archaeologists' field notes, Mkrtchyan corrected the Armenia data set by re-measuring, matching and assigning the various collections from Armenia to their proper sites and tomb numbers, including 30 crania from Artik and the various smaller collections from the Sevan Basin.

In Soviet physical anthropology during the 1970s and 1980s, human evolution, population genetics, adaptation and human ecology came to play increasingly important roles as they were drawn on to substantiate the link between morphological and metric variation and processes of ethnogenesis (see Alekseev 1968; 1989; Alekseeva 1977; Alekseeva *et al.* 1977). These trends fed into a dramatic turn during the 1990s to the 'palaeo-ecological' approach that focused on human-environment adaptation, specifically concerned with palaeopathology, diet and other socio-cultural practices (see Alekseev 1993; Buzhilova 1995, 1998; Dobrovol'skaya 2005; Mednikova 2001).

In the last decade of research in Armenia there have been few major publications in physical anthropology, most notably Mkrtchyan's (2004) *Paleodemografiya Oromskogo Magil'nika*. In some ways this publication continued Alekseev's and Abdushelishvili's work with ethnic types; however, Mkrtchyan also introduced trends in palaeodemographic patterns as a new subject of analysis in physical anthropology in Armenia. In comparison to this work, the majority of recent research in Armenia is represented by brief reports or analyses. Some of these publications carry on the tradition of investigating ethnic questions in their description of metric or non-metric traits (Khudaverdyan 2006, 2008; Palikyan 2008). There have also been a few discussions on palaeopathological evidence (see Khudaverdyan 2005a, 2005b). However, such work has yet to be firmly grounded in a rigorous methodological and interpretive framework (see Mkrtchyan and Buzhilova 2006). Thus, while there is a nascent interest in the Russian palaeo-ecological and American bioarchaeological approaches, physical anthropology and archaeology in Armenia must surmount these research challenges, as well as others mentioned below, if they are to be integrated into a programme which aims to reconstruct ancient life and identify socio-cultural practices.

ARCHAEOLOGICAL HUMAN REMAINS AND LEGISLATION

Archaeological legislation

All excavation permit applications are granted by the Agency for the Preservation of Monuments, History and Culture (Patmutyan yev Mshakuti Hushardzanneri Pahpanutyan Gortsakalutyun), a branch of the Ministry of Culture, Republic of Armenia (Hayastani Hanrapetutyan Mshakuyti Nakhararutyan). Project directors then submit yearly reports on the site, excavation, and future plans to the agency.

HUMAN REMAINS AND LEGISLATION

There is no legislation in Armenia at present that is particular to the excavation and analysis of human remains. However, given the long history of the excavation of tombs and physical anthropological investigations, there are conventions and general guidelines that researchers follow. For example, church cemeteries established during the 19th century and later are not excavated, as the distinction of 'archaeological' materials is reserved for objects and sites dated prior to the 19th century. Human skeletal remains that are intrusive or from unclear contexts are often reburied. Tombs dated prior to the 19th century, including those from the Bronze and Iron Ages, are usually excavated by archaeologists with the same permit procedures as other excavation projects.

The preferred practice for excavating mortuary sites is to excavate a tomb until human remains are identified and then a physical anthropologist is called out to the site in order to excavate and remove the human remains. However, this model is starting to come under strain as the demand for physical anthropologists in the field continues, but there are few − if any − Armenian physical anthropologists who are currently excavating. Thus, despite the experience and familiarity of archaeologists with tombs, the current lack of physical anthropologists working in the field has left a gap in the practice of mortuary excavation.

This situation is further challenged by the varying nature of the interments themselves. Bronze and Iron Age burial practices range in terms of post-mortem treatment of the deceased (including tombs without bodies, possible cremation practices, interment of select body parts with different dismemberment practices, and complete inhumations). Thus an archaeologist never knows if a tomb will be devoid of human remains, have a straightforward and relatively easy to excavate single interment, or contain a complicated deposition of multiple individuals in various states of preservation. The combination of these post-mortem practices with varying soil matrices or environmental contexts often result in complex human taphonomy that must be teased apart and carefully analysed. Thus, depositional and post-depositional processes must be taken into account in order ultimately to build regional and chronological comparisons of mortuary practices. Such an analysis must begin with careful excavation designed to collect and record all possible data *in situ*, data that can then be used to reconstruct the deceased individual's deposition within the tomb as well as the deceased's life history (or osteobiography).

METHODS OF ANTHROPOLOGICAL ANALYSIS

Most physical anthropologists in Armenia were trained in Moscow, either at the Institute of Ethnology and Anthropology of the Russian Academy of Science (IEA RAS, formerly the Academy of Science of the USSR) or at MGU. Accordingly, methods for analysing human remains in Armenia are based on the Soviet tradition of physical anthropology, and developed in relation to the investigation of the genesis of historically and ethnographically known ethnic groups. These issues were mainly addressed through comparative morphological and metric analysis of human bones, particularly long bones and crania.

The main methods of analysis are based on Alekseev and Debets's 1964 *Kraniometriya* and Alekseev's 1966 *Osteometriya*. Alekseev and Debets drew on a number of contemporary sources in order to create a programme for measuring bones and calculating indices:

> В этой программе нужно, избегая неоправданного новаторства, отобрать наи-
> более ценное в массе предложенных в разное время приемов и методов и сос-
> тавить из них список, который одновременно не был бы чрезмерно громоздким
> и трудно реализуемым в практической работе, но в то же время охватывал бы
> все признаки, могущие быть полезными для антропологических целей.
>
> *(Alekseev and Debets 1964: 13)*

(This programme avoids unnecessary innovation by selecting and compiling a list of the most valuable techniques from the mass of methods that have been proposed at various times, so that it is not overly cumbersome and difficult to carry out in practice, but at the same time includes all of the features that may prove useful for anthropological purposes. [Author's translation])

Here Alekseev explained that the programme should be practical both in its ability to be carried out by researchers and in its application to anthropological questions. With these goals in mind, *Kraniometriya* defined guidelines for establishing age and sex, techniques for measuring and calculating skeletal indices, and criteria for recording descriptive elements (such as cranial form). Sex was determined through the combination of eight cranial morphological traits and 24 cranial measurements. These traits were derived from Vera I. Pashkova's (1961, 1963) own summaries of methods used to determine sex, age and stature from human skeletons. Citing both European and Russian sources, Pashkova listed 25 craniometric and 11 anatomical-morphological characteristics of the crania, morphological and metric characteristics of the pelvis (from Ivanov 1949; Zernov 1939; Tonkov 1953), and measurements of the humerus, femur, sternum, clavicle and hyoid in order to determine the sex from skeletal remains (Pashkova 1963: 18–30, 102–9).

In *Kraniometriya*, Alekseev based age on dental development (Gerasimov 1955; Zubov 1968) and individual cranial suture closure by examining specific landmarks on each individual suture (based on Simpson and Olivier, but also on Martin) (Alekseev and Debets 1964: 33). Stature estimations were based on Pearson (1898) and Trotter and Gleser (1958). Alekseev's measurements and indices are a shortened, or 'practical', version of Martin's (1928; Martin and Saller 1957) measurements, and in fact, in the Soviet tradition of physical anthropology, all measurements were published in tables according to their 'Martin number' and indices were listed according to the relationship between these Martin numbers. Thus, Alekseev's standardized method of recording and reporting age, sex and measurements facilitated comparison between skeletal populations and it is still the preferred method today of Armenian physical anthropologists (for examples, see Mkrtchyan 2004; Palikyan 2008).

Thus, on the one hand, Alekseev's standardized methods and Soviet physical anthropology succeeded admirably in compiling vast collections of palaeoanthropological material and established a robust approach to the analysis of metric variation. On the other hand, the Soviet tradition, by focusing resolutely on ethnic difference, did not develop the methods necessary for exploring the osteological signs of human–environment relations, behavioural practices and life histories, which can contribute to discussions of diachronic changes in health and diet, as well as the investigation of local societies and practices. While the palaeo-ecological approach to human remains has ushered in a suite of new analyses in Russia (see Alekseeva and Bader 2001), such approaches have yet to be applied to skeletal material in Armenia. Moreover, Soviet palaeoanthropology's particular emphasis on metrics has resulted in skeletal collections in Armenia that mainly consist of crania and sometimes long bones, and are thus fragmented and incomplete collections of individuals. It is only within the last few years that all bones, including the vertebrae and the bones of the hands and feet, have been retained, but these collections do not yet contain enough individuals for analyses that test statistical significance, which can be used to assess patterns within and between populations.

CONCLUSION

In 2008–9, the authors started a collaboration which originated in our work with Project ArAGATS and is based on the correlation of our data collection programmes with the goal of eventually using a combined database for the curation as well as the analysis of human remains.

In the course of our collaboration we inventoried the human skeletal remains at the Historico-Archaeological Museum-Reserve 'Erebuni' (Erebuni Museum) ('Erebuni' Patmahnagitakan Argelots-Tangaran) and several collections currently housed at the History Museum of Armenia in Yerevan. Collections at the new Bioarchaeology Laboratory at Erebuni Museum (Kensahnagituyan Laboratoriya, 'Erebuni' Patmahnagitakan Argelots-Tangaran) include several of the cranial collections discussed above (Nerkin Getashen, Noraduz, etc.) as well as recently excavated materials from Kanagegh, Dari Glukh and Hatsarat. For these newer collections we inventoried and recorded data according to the *Standards* (Buikstra and Ubelaker 1994) as well as Alekseev's programme, and also analysed pathological conditions and evidence of trauma. At the History Museum of Armenia we recorded pathological conditions and evidence of trauma from the Artik crania (30) and human remains from Horom (56). Our collaborative work highlighted the diverse and rich potential of bioarchaeological investigations in Armenia, which can provide one of the most productive and multifaceted sources for reconstructing ancient life, but it also made clear the amount of work that must be completed before such potentials can be realized.

At present, physical anthropology in Armenia faces challenges both at the excavation site and in the laboratory. It is critically important that physical anthropologists be present during the excavation of human remains. Moreover, the often complex nature of interments and human taphonomy requires close collaboration between the archaeologist and physical anthropologist in order to reconstruct mortuary practices (post-mortem treatment, deposition and post-depositional processes) and in order to create collections of individuals suitable for subsequent bioarchaeological analysis. Perhaps in the future, these two roles – archaeologist and physical anthropologist – can be combined so that there is one record to draw on for analysis and interpretation. Meanwhile, tombs continue to be excavated every year, some of which are small scale salvage projects resulting from construction projects or looting. Consequently, Armenia's mortuary record is under immediate threat from the current lack of physical anthropologists in Armenia working on excavations.

The second challenge to physical anthropology in Armenia comes from an equally serious need for a supporting system of storage resources and personnel in order to inventory, curate and preserve collections of human skeletal material. Currently, collections of human remains are stored at several locations, but are rarely given the same storage and preservation treatment as other archaeological objects. Careful curation and proper storage of human skeletal remains are critical to bioarchaeological investigations. Here, the standards and procedures developed in America with the passing of NAGPRA may serve as a guide to insure the survival of future collections for analysis (see Buikstra and Ubelaker 1994; Cassman *et al.* 2007; White 2000).

Both of these problems are further exacerbated by a lack of new students. While the scientific community as a whole in Armenia lost countless young scholars to the economic turmoil of the 1990s (Lindsay and Smith 2006: 178), in the last few years archaeology has once again begun to attract young students. However, there has not yet been a parallel influx of students in physical anthropology trained either abroad or within Armenia. As archaeological research in Armenia continues to develop and include topics such as diet and subsistence strategies based on faunal and botanical analyses (see Monahan 2004; Hovsepyan 2009), the potential for human remains to contribute to the reconstruction of ancient life is increasing exponentially. Given the broad spectrum of bioarchaeological research, a single skeletal collection can be repeatedly analysed from different perspectives. Moreover, the methods and techniques of bioarchaeology are constantly changing and developing in relation to the medical field and clinical research, meaning that researchers return to the same collections in order to evaluate new methods, test new techniques, compare results with other populations, and re-evaluate previous arguments and conclusions regarding the ancient life of a population. Consequently, well-preserved osteological collections may continue for years to serve as a valuable resource for social scientists working in Armenia. Furthermore, the current collaboration between Armenian archaeologists and diverse international scholars offers the rare potential for human skeletal collections to facilitate discussion, comparison and reflexivity amongst the global community of archaeologists and physical anthropologists.

USEFUL CONTACTS

Institute of Archaeology and Ethnography, 15 Charent St., Yerevan 375025, Republic of Armenia. Contact: Pavel Avetisyan (Director). Tel: (3741) 556896. Email: pavetisyan@sci. am. Website: www.sci.am/resorgs.php?oid=32& langid = 1/

Erebuni Museum, 38 Erebuni St., Yerevan – 020, Republic of Armenia. Tel: (3741) 458207.

History Museum of Armenia, Republic Square, Yerevan 375010, Republic of Armenia. Tel: (3741) 583861. Email: admin@historymuseum.am; museum@xter.net. Website: www.his-tory museum.am/history—en.htm/

Shirak Regional Museum, 118 Myasnikian St., Gyumri, Republic of Armenia. Tel: (3741) 22847. Email: Smuseum@web.am. Website: www.shirakmuseum.am/

Project ArAGATS. Website: www.aragats.net/

ACKNOWLEDGEMENTS

We would like to thank Ruben Badalyan at the Institute of Archaeology and Ethnography in Yerevan, who provided information on the excavation of mortuary sites in Armenia, as well as making helpful comments and corrections. Additionally, the paper benefited from insightful comments and questions from Adam T. Smith at the University of Chicago. Finally, we wish to extend our appreciation to Ashot Piliposyan and the Erebuni Museum staff for supporting our collaborative research.

NOTES

1 The corpus spans the Early Bronze to Iron I periods and includes the area encompassing Mount Aragats, the Shirak Basin, the Pambak Ridge, the Kasakh Valley and the northern part of the Ararat Plain.

2 Excavations were conducted under the auspices of Project ArAGATS in 2006 and 2008 at Tsaghkahovit Burial Cluster 12. In 2008 excavations were supported by a Fulbright-Hays DDRA grant.

3 See Smith *et al.* (2009) for a discussion of Marr's research.

4 Based on the location and Bunak's description, it is implicitly understood that these crania came from victims of the Armenian genocide (1915).

5 The cranial series is listed under Turkey, Bingol-Dag, Euphrates Valley, Armenian, collected by V.V. Bunak 1916–17, Numbers 71–82, 84–98, 100–219, 229, 8596, 8867 (Alekseeva and Epenburg 1979: 171).

6 For discussions of the debate surrounding physical types and race see Banton (1977), Boas (1911, 1940), Buikstra (2006), Caspari (2009), Cook (2006), Fforde (2004), Jones (1997), Stocking (1968, 1974, 1988).

7 Bromley defined 'ethnos' or, more specifically, 'ethnikos' as 'a historically formed aggregate of people who share common relatively stable specific features of culture (including language) and psychology, realization of their unity and distinctiveness from other similar aggregates of people as well as the self-nomination' (Bromley 1978: 18).

8 Alekseev's student R. Bubushyan (1973) originally measured the Artik crania, which were subsequently published in Alekseev's comparative work.

BIBLIOGRAPHY

Abdushelishvili, M.G. (1982) 'Antropologiya Kavkaza v bronzovom periode', *Materialy k Antropologii Kavkaza*, VIII. Tbilisi.

Alekseev, V.P. (1966) *Osteometriya*, Moscow: Nauka.

——(1968) 'K obosnovanniyu populyatsionnoi kontseptsii rasy', in A.A. Zubov, G.L. Khit and V.P. Alekseev (eds) *Problemy Evolutsii Cheloveka I Ego Ras*, Moscow: Nauka.

——(1974) *Proiskhozhdenie Narodov Kavkaza: Kraniologicheskoe issledovanie*, Moscow: Nauka.

——(1989) *Istoricheskaya Antropologiya I Etnogenez*, Moscow: Nauka.

——(1993) *Ocherki Ekologii Cheloveka*, Moscow: Nauka.

Alekseev, V.P. and Debets, G.F. (1964) *Kraniometriya: Metodika antropologicheskikh issledovanii*, Moscow: Nauka.

Alekseev, V. P. and Gokhman, I.I. (1984) *Antropologiya Aziatskoi Chasti SSSR*, Moscow: Nauka.

Alekseev, V.P. and Mkrtchyan, R.A. (1989) 'Paleoantropologicheskii material iz pogrebenii v Armenii I voprosy genezisa naseleniya kuro-arakskoi kul'tury', *Sovietskaya Etnografiya*, 1989: 127–34.

Alekseeva, T.I. (1977) *Geograficheskaya sreda I biologiya cheloveka*, Moscow: Nauka.

Alekseeva, T.I. and Bader, N.O. (eds) (2001) *Homo Sungirensis: Verkhnepaleoliticheskiy Chelovek: ekologicheskie I evolyutsionnye aspekty issledovaniya*, Moscow: Nauchniy Mir.

Alekseeva, T.I. and Epenburg, R.B. (1979) *Katalog Kraniologicheskikh I Osteologicheskikh Kollektsii Instituta I Muzeya Antropologii MGU (1865–1977)*, Moscow: Izdatel'stvo Moskovskogo Universiteta.

Alekseeva, T.I., Volkov-Dubrovin, V.P. and Pavlovskii, O.M. (1977) 'Antropologicheskie issledovanie v Zabaikal'e v svyazi s problemoi adaptatsii u cheloveka: morfologiya, fiziologiya i populyatsionnaya genetika' *Voprosy Antropologii*, 54: 36–37.

Areshyan, G.E., Kafadryan, K.K., Simonyan, H.E. *et al.* (1977) 'Arkheologicheskie Issledovaniya v Ashtarakskom I Nairiskom Raionakh Armyanskoi SSR', *Vestnik Obshchesvennikh Nauk*, 4: 77–93.

Arutiunov, S.A. and Bromley, Yu.V. (1978) 'Problems of Ethnicity in Soviet Ethnographic Studies', in R.E. Holloman and S.A. Arutiunov (eds) *Perspectives on Ethnicity*, The Hague: Mouton.

Avetisyan, P., Badalyan, R.S. and Smith, A.T. (2000) 'Preliminary Report on the 1998 Archaeological Investigations of Project ArAGATS in the Tsakahovit Plain, Armenia', *Studi Micenei ed Egeo-Anatolici*, 42: 19–59.

Avetisyan, P. and Mkrtchyan, R.A. (1994) 'Talini yerkatedaryan dambaranneri sotsial – joghovrdagrakan verlutsutyan porsz', *Hayastani Hanrapetutyunum 1991–1992 tt dashtayin hnagitakan ashkhatankneri ardyun-knerin nvvirvats gitakan nstashrdgan. Dgekutsumneri tezisner*, Yerevan: Hayastani Azgayin Akademiayi Haratarakchutyun.

Avetisyan, P. and Muradyan, F. (1991) 'Raskopki na Novostroykakh Talina', in *Tezisy Dokladov Nauchnoy Sessii, Posvyashchennoy Itogam Polevykh Arkheologicheskikh Issledovaniy v Respublike Armeniya (1989–1990)*, Yerevan: Hayastani Azgayin Akademiayi Haratarakchutyun.

——(1994) 'Rezultaty Raskopok Mogil'nika Talina v 1991 gg', in *Tezisy Dokladov Nauchnoy Sessii, Posvyashchennoy Itogam Polevykh Arkheologicheskikh Issledovaniy v Respublike Armeniya (1991–1992)*, Yerevan: Hayastani Azgayin Akademiayi Haratarakchutyun.

Badalyan, R.S. and Aghekyan, O.K. (1992) 'Raskopki Oromskogo Nekropolya (predvaritel'niy otchet o rabotakh 1987 goda)', in *Archaeological Works at New Buildings of Armenia (results of excavations 1986–1987)*, Yerevan: Institute of Archaeology and Ethnography.

Badalyan, R.S. and Avetisyan, P.S. (2007) *Bronze and Early Iron Age Archaeological Sites in Armenia I: Mt. Aragats and its Surrounding Region*, British Archaeological Reports International Series 1697, Oxford: Archaeopress.

Badalyan, R.S., Smith, A.T. and Avetisyan, P. (2003) 'The emergence of sociopolitical complexity in Southern Caucasia: an interim report on the research of project ArAGATS', in A.T. Smith and K.S. Rubinson (eds) *Archaeology in the Borderlands: Investigations in Caucasia and Beyond*, Los Angeles: Cotsen Institute of Archaeology at UCLA.

Banton, M. (1977) *The Idea of Race*, London: Tavistock.

Baybutyan, E.A. (1937) 'Problema krashennoy keramiki v Armenii', *Vestnik Instituta Istorii I Literatury AN Arm SSR*, 1937: 268–308.

Bayern, F. (1856) 'Untersuchungen über die ältensten gräber-und schatzfunde in Kaukasien', *Zeitschrift für Ethnologie*, Supplement: viii, 1–60.

Boas, F. (1911) 'Instability of Human Types', in G.W. Stocking (ed.); reprinted in *A Franz Boas Reader: The Shaping of American Anthropology 1883–1911* (1974), New York: Basic Books.

——(1940) *Race Language and Culture*, Chicago: University of Chicago Press.

Biscione, R., Hmayakyan, S. and Parmegiani, N. (eds) (2002) *The North-Eastern Frontier: Urartians and Non-Urartians in the Sevan Lake Basin*, Rome: CNR istituto do studi sulle civilta dell'Eegeo e del Vicino Oriente.

Bromley, Yu.V. (1978) 'On the typology of ethnic communities', in R.E. Holloman and S.A. Arutiunov (eds) *Perspectives on Ethnicity*, The Hague: Mouton.

Bubushyan, R.A. (1973) *Material'naya kul'tura i fizicheskiy tip naseleniya Armenii v epokhu bronzy*, Avtoreferat kand, Dissertatsii, Yerevan.

Buikstra, J.E. (2006) 'A historical introduction', in J.E. Buikstra and L.A. Beck (eds), *Bioarchaeology: The Contextual Analysis of Human Remains*, New York: Academic Press.

Buikstra, J.E. and Ubelaker, D.H. (eds) (1994) *Standards for Data Collection From Human Skeletal Remains*, Fayetteville, AR: Arkansas Archaeological Survey Research Series No. 44.

Buzhilova, A.P. (1995) *Drevnee Naselenie: Paleoantropologicheskie Aspekty Issledovaniya*, Moscow: Rossiiskaia Akademii Nauk.

——(1998) 'Paleopatalogiya v bioarkheologicheskikh rekonstruktsiyakh', in *Istoricheskaya ekologiya cheloveka: Metodika biologicheskikh issledovaniy*, Moscow: Rossiiskaia Akademii Nauk.

Bunak, V.V. (1927) *Crania Armenica: Issledovanie po antropologii perednei azii*, Moscow: MGU.

——(1929) 'Arkheologicheskie raskopki v Novobayetskom Uesde SSR Armenii' *Russkii Antropologicheskii Zhurnal*, 17: 3–4.

Caspari, R. (2009) '1918: three perspectives on race and human variation', *American Journal of Physical Anthropology*, 139: 5–15.

Cassman, V., Odegaard, N. and Powell, J. (2007) *Human Remains: Guide for Museums and Academic Institutions*, Lanham, MD: AltaMira Press.

Cook, D.C. (2006) 'The old physical anthropology and the New World: a look at the accomplishments of an antiquated paradigm', in J.E. Buikstra and L.A. Beck (eds) *Bioarchaeology: The Contextual Analysis of Human Remains*, New York: Academic Press.

Devedjyan, S.G. (1981) *Lori-Berd 1: Rezul'tati raskopok 1969–1973 gg*, Yerevan: Izdatel'stvo AN Armyanskoi SSR.

——(2006) *Lori-Berd 2*, Yerevan: Nairi.

Dobrovol'skaya, M.B. (2005) *Chelovek i Ego Pishcha*, Moscow: Nauka Mir.

Esayan, S.A. and Kalantaryan, A.A. (1988) *Oshakan 1: Osnovnie rezul'tati raskopok 1971–1983 gg*, Yerevan: Izdatel'stvo AN Armyanskoi SSR.

Fforde, C. (2004) 'Evolution, the great collections and the tenacity of "race"', in C. Fforde (ed.) *Collecting the Dead: Archaeology and the Reburial Issue*. London: Duckworth.

Gerasimov, M.M. (1955) *Vosstanovlenie litsa po cherepu*, Moscow: Nauka.

Hansen, G. (1953–54) *Die Altersbestimmung am proximalen Huemrus-und Femurende im Rahmen der Identifizierung menschlicher Skelettreste*, Wissenschaftl. Ztschr. D. Humboldt-Universität zu Berlin, Math-Naturw Reihe 3: 1–73.

Hovsepyan, R.A. (2009) *Polevye Kul'turi I Rasprostranennye Sornyaki Na Territorii Armenii v Period Neolita – Zheleznogo Veka*, Avtoreferat kand. Dissertatsii, Akaemiya Nauk.

Ivanov, G.F. (1949) *Osnovy normal'noi anatomii cheloveka*. Moscow: Medgiz.

Jones, S. (1997) *The Archaeology of Ethnicity: Constructing identities in the past and present*, London: Routledge.

Khachatryan, T.S. (1979) *Artikski Nekropol*, Yerevan: Izdatel'stvo Yerevansckogo Universiteta.

Khanzadyan, E. (1979) *Elar-Darani*, Yerevan: Izdatel'stvo AN Armyanskoi SSR.

——(1995) *Metsamor 2: La Necropole Volume 1: Les Tombes du Bronze Moyen et Recent*, Neuchâtel: Recherches et Publications.

——(2005a) 'Faktori Vneshnei Sredy v Obrazovanii Nozokomleksov Naseleniya Landjikskogo Nekropolya v Epokhu Rannei Bronzy', *Hin Hayastani Mshakuyte*, 13 :75–77.

——(2005b) *Atlas Paleopatologicheskih Nakhodok Na Territorii Armenii*, Yerevan: Van Aryan.

——(2006) 'O Meste Beniaminskoi Serii Na Antropologicheskoi Karte Kavkaza i Sopredel'nikh Territorii v Epokhu Antichnosti', in *Hay Azgabanutyan yev Hnagitutyan Khndirner*, Yerevan: Gitutyun.

——(2008) 'Kranioskopicheskaya i odontologicheskaya kharakteristika naseleniya Armenii v epokhu bronzi', *Hin Hayastani Mshakuyte*, 14: 333–41.

Kozintsev, A.G. (1988) *Etnicheskaya Kranioskopiya: Rasovaya izmenhivost' shvov cherepa sovremennogo cheloveka*, Leningrad: Nauka.

Kuftin, B. (1941) *Arkhelogicheskiye Raskopki v Trialeti I*, Tbilisi: Akademy Nauk Gruzinskii SSR.

——(1946) 'Prehistoric culture sequence in Transcaucasia', *Southwestern Journal of Anthropology*, 2: 340–60.

Lalayan, Y. (1931) *Dambanneri Peghumner Khorhrdayin Hayatanum*, Yerevan: publisher unknown.

Lindsay, I. and Smith, A.T. (2006) 'A history of archaeological practices in Armenia and the South Caucasus', *Journal of Field Archaeology*, 31: 165–84.

Martin, R. (1928) *Lehrbuch der Anthropologie* (2. Auflage). Jena: Fischer.

Martin, R. and Saller, K. (1957) *Lehrbuch der Anthropologie, Vol. 1*, Stuttgart: Gustav Fischer.

Mednikova, M.B. (1995) *Drevniw Skotovody Uzhnoi Sibiri: Paleoekologicheskaya Rekonstruktsiya po Dannym Antropolgii*, Moscow: Rossiiskaya Akademiya Nauk.

——(2001) *Trepanatsii u Drevnikh Narodov Evrazii*, Moscow: Nauchnyi Mir.

Mkrtchyan, R.A. (2003) 'Paledemografiya mogil'nika Nerkin Getashen', *Hayastani Hnaguyn Mshakuyte*, 3: 46–51.

——(2004) *Paleoantropolgiya Oromskogo Mogil'nika*, Yerevan: Institute of Archaeology and Ethnography, Republic of Armenia.

Mkrtchyan, R.A. and Buzhilova, A.P. (2006) 'Kritika na knigy Khudaverdyan, A. Yu. "Atlas Paleopatologicheskih Nakhodok Na Territorii Armenii.Yerevan, Van Aryan."', *Rossiiskaya Arkheologiya*, 4: 170–72.

Mkrtchyan, R.A. and Marshall, M.E. (2009) 'Hnamardabanakan nyuteri havakagrman yev fondavorman karevorutyune', in *Tangarani K'ar'avarum: UNESCO/ICOM azgayin treyning (dasentats-varzhank) HH tarngaranneri masnaget'neri hamar, 11–14 Hunis 2009t. Yerevan, Hayastan*, 82–85. Yerevan: Erebuni Museum.

Mkrtchyan, R.A., Piliposyan, A.S. and Palikyan, A.K. (1997) 'Kollektivnoe pogrebenie epokhi sredei bronzy Nerkin Getashena (sotsiokul'turnaya kharakteristika)', *Vestnik Obshchestvennikh Nauk*, 1.

Mnatsakanyan, A.O. (1965) 'Lchasheni mshakuyti zargatsman himnakan etapnery', *Istoriko-filologicheskiy zhurnal*, 2: 95–114.

Monahan, B.H. (2004). 'Faunal Remains from the Tsaghkahovit Plain', in *Mezhdunarodnaya Nauchnaya Konferentsiya «Arkheologiya, Etnologiya, Fol'loristika Kavkaza» Sbornik Kratkikh Soderzhanij Dokladov*, 99–100, Tbilisi: Nekeri.

Morgan, J.D. (1889) *Mission Scientifique Au Caucase: Études Archéologiques et Historiques*, Paris: E. Leroux.

Movsesian, A.A. (2005) *Feneticheskii analaiz v paleoantropolgii*, Moscow: Universitetskaya kniga.

Movsesian, A.A. and Kochar, N. (2004) 'On the origin of Armenians (in the light of non-metric traits data)', *Iran and the Caucasus*, 8: 184–97.

Oganesyan, V.E. (1992a) 'Raskopki Karashambskoje mogil'nika v 1987 g', in *Archaeological Works at New Buildings of Armenia (results of excavations 1986–1987)*, Yerevan: Institute of Archaeology and Ethnography.

——(1992b) 'A silver goblet from Karashamb', *Soviet Anthropology and Archaeology*, 30: 84–103.

Olivier, G. (1960) *Practique Anthropologique*, Paris: Vigot.

Oshanin, L.V. (1964) *Anthropological Composition of the Populations of Central Asia, and the Ethnogenesis of Its Peoples I*, Cambridge, MA: Peabody Museum.

Palikyan, A. (2008) 'Novii kraniologicjeskii material antichnoi epokhi s territorii shirakskoi ravini', *Hin Hayastani Mshakuyte*, 14: 343–45.

Pashkova, V.I. (1961) 'Kraniometriya kak odin iz metodov povyshenniya dostovernosti opredeleniya pola po cherepu', *Voprosy Antropologii*, 7: 95–101.

——(1963) *Ocherki Sudebnomeditsinskoi Osteologii: Opredelenie pola, vozrasta i posta po kostyam skeleta cheloveka*, Moscow: Gosudarstvennoe izdatel'stvo meditsinskoi literaturiy.

Pearson, K. (1898) 'On the reconstruction of the stature of prehistoric races', *Philosophical Transactions of the Royal Society*, 192A: 169–244.

Petrosyan, L.A. (1989) *Raskopki Pamyatnikov Keti I Voskeaska*, Yerevan: Akademij Nauk.

Piliposyan, A.S. (1991a) 'Peghumner Sevani Kolektori Noratusi Hatvatsum' in *Hayastani Hanrapetutyunum 1989–1990 tt.: Dashtayin Hnagitakan Ashkhatnkneri Argyunknerin Nvirvats Gitakan Natashrdgan*, Yerevan: Hayastani Gitutyunneri Akademiayi Hratarakchutyun.

——(1991b) 'Hetakhuzakan peghumner "Mrtbi Dzor" dambaranaghashtum', in *Hayastani Hanrapetutyunum 1989–1990 tt: Dashtayin Hnagitakan Ashkhatnkneri Argyunknerin Nvirvats Gitakan Natashrdgan*, Yerevan: Hayastani Gitutyunneri Akademiayi Hratarakchutyun.

Piliposyan, A.S. and Hovhannisian, V.E. (1991) 'Peghumner Nerkin Getashen Gyughum', in *Hayastani Hanrapetutyunum 1989–1990 tt.: Dashtayin Hnagitakan Ashkhatnkneri Argyunknerin Nvirvats Gitakan Natashrdgan*, Yerevan: Hayastani Gitutyunneri Akademiayi Hratarakchutyun.

Piliposyan, A.S., Mkrtchyan, R.A. and Kirakosyan, L. (2002) 'Kanageghi Damabaranadashti 1999t. Peghumner', *Hayastani Hnaguyn Mshakyut*, 2: 43–49.

Piotrovskii, B.B. (1949) *Arkheologiya Zakavkazya: S Drevenyshikh Vremen do I tys. do n.e*, Leningrad: Izdatelstvo Leningradskogo Gasudarstvennogo Ordena Lenina Universiteta.

Roginskii, Ya.Ya. and Levin, M. (1963) *Antropologiya*, Moscow: Vysshaya Shkola.

Simonyan, A.E. (1979) 'Raskopki mogil'nika Verin Naver', *Arkheologicheskie Otkrytiya* (1978): 524–25.

——(1984) 'Dva Pogrebeniya Epokhi Sredney Bronzy Mogil'nika Verin Naver', *Sovietskaya Arkhelogia*, 3: 122–35.

Smith, A.T. (2005) 'Prometheus Unbound: Southern Caucasia in Prehistory', *Journal of World Prehistory*, 19: 229–79.

Smith, A.T., Badalyan, R. and Avetisyan, P. (2009) *The Archaeology and Geography of Ancient Transcaucasian Societies. Volume 1: Regional Survey in the Tsaghkahovit Plain, Armenia*, Chicago: Oriental Institute Press.

Stocking, G.W. (1968) *Race, Culture, and Evolution*, Chicago: University of Chicago Press.

Stocking, G.W. (ed.) (1974) *A Franz Boas Reader: The Shaping of American Anthropology 1883–1911*, New York: Basic Books.

Stocking, G.W. (1988) 'Bones, bodies, and behaviour', in G.W. Stocking (ed.) *Bones, Bodies, and Behaviour*, Madison: Wisconsin University Press.

Tonkov, V.N. (1953) *Uchebnik Normal'noi Anatomii Cheloveka*, Leningrad: Medgiz.

Toramanyan, T. (1942) *Nyuter Haykakan Chartarapetutyan Patmutyan*, Yerevan: Haykakan SSR Gitowtyownneri Akademiayi.

——(1948) *Nyuter Haykakan Chartarapetutyan Patmutyan II*. Yerevan: Haykakan SSR Gitowtyownneri Akademiayi.

Torosyan, R.M., Khnkikyan, O.S. and Petrosyan, L.A. (2002) *Drevnij Shirakavan*, Yerevan: Izdael'stvo Gitutyun.

Trigger, B.G. (1989) *A History of Archaeological Thought*, Cambridge: Cambridge University Press.

Trotter, M. and Gleser, G.C. (1958) 'A re-evaluation of estimation of stature based on measurements of stature taken during life and long bones after death', *American Journal of Physical Anthropology*, 16: 79–123.

White, T.D. (2000) *Human Osteology*, London: Academic Press.

Xnkikyan, O.S. (2002) *Syunik During the Bronze and Iron Ages*, Barrington, RI: Mayreni.

Zernov, D.N. (1939) *Rukovodstvo po opisatel'noi anatomii cheloveka*, Moscow: Medgiz.

Zubov, A.A. (1968) Odontologiya: *metodika antropologicheskikh issledovani*, Moscow: Nauka.

Azerbaijan/Azərbaycan

David Maynard and Najaf Museyibli

INTRODUCTION: A BRIEF HISTORY AND CURRENT STATE OF PHYSICAL ANTHROPOLOGY IN AZERBAIJAN

Azerbaijan has a long and honourable tradition in the study of human remains (Goscharly *et al.* 2004). Arif Mustafayev and Mammadali Huseinov spent much time working on the Azykh Cave (Fizuli District) material which included the mandible of a Neanderthal female discovered in 1968 and was dated to approximately around 350,000 years ago (Lublin and Bosinski 1995). There has also been a strong tradition of using human material for evidence of ethnic movements within the modern populations. Unfortunately, much of this work has not developed over the past several decades due to lack of support and financial constraints.

This chapter is based on a case study that covers the experience of a recent pipeline project in Azerbaijan and the measures undertaken in relation to human remains. Full archaeological reports are in preparation for the work on the various sites (Maynard *et al.* forthcoming).

The BTC (Baku-Tbilisi-Ceyhan) pipeline project created a substantial archaeological project ahead of construction of the pipeline. Although the project extended for up to 1600km through Azerbaijan, Georgia and Turkey, the focus of this chapter is the 440km of the route through Azerbaijan (Figure 4.1).

Fieldwork in Azerbaijan took place between 2001 and 2005 and involved the excavation of over 50 sites. The work unearthed evidence from a range of periods, from the Chalcolithic through to the recent past. During the course of the work approximately 800 burials were located, all of which required appropriate treatment as stipulated by the laws of the Republic of Azerbaijan and international best practice for cultural heritage as defined by the International Lenders to the project.

The work was conducted by specialists from the Institute of Archaeology and Ethnography (IoEA), the Academy of Sciences, Baku, and British archaeologists. At the start of the fieldwork programme, it was recognised that the project would encounter human remains and there could be a potential for inadvertent negative reaction if correct procedures were not followed. Advice was taken from local community religious leaders and it was broadly agreed that, if pre-Muslim bodies were to be found, these could be treated as historical remains, but should be re-buried after archaeological and anthropological study.

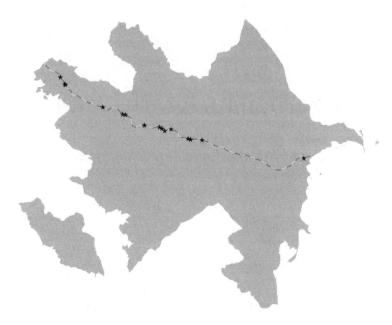

Figure 4.1 The BTC pipeline route through Azerbaijan highlighting the largest excavated sites

ARCHAEOLOGICAL HUMAN REMAINS AND LEGISLATION

Archaeological legislation

Normal archaeological features, including burials, are covered by the national legislation on the protection of cultural heritage, but the specific instances of disturbance of obviously Muslim burials from the more recent past is an issue of greater concern.

HUMAN REMAINS AND LEGISLATION

The modern nation of Azerbaijan is a largely Muslim state but with substantial representation of other religions. Throughout the Muslim era, Christian and Jewish communities have co-existed in various parts of Azerbaijan. Prior to the adoption of Islam, there was a strong Christian society in the Alban period, which was preceded by the Zoroastrian era from the last millennium BC. Details of the Bronze Age and Chalcolithic religious beliefs cannot be easily deduced. Examples of each of these religious and cultural groups were found in the excavations ahead of the pipeline.

Archaeological skeletons buried in the Muslim tradition that have been disturbed by development should be reburied immediately in a religious ceremony. It is known that there have been specific problems with existing cemeteries in Baku and the redevelopment that has occurred in recent years. It is not for this article to comment on the recent tensions and conflict. In 2007, during the construction of a stadium at Guba in the north of the country, numbers of bodies were discovered from a massacre of 1917.

Figure 4.2 Late Bronze Age grave 102 Zayamchai KP355, Azerbaijan

Figure 4.3 Antique jar grave burial Borsunlu Kurgan KP272, Azerbaijan

Case study

In the excavations carried out ahead of construction of the pipeline the following types of burial were found: inhumations where the bodies were extended (Muslim and Christian traditions); crouched inhumations with grave goods (Iron Age and Bronze Age; Figure 4.2); symbolic burials with pottery vessels but no evidence of human remains (Bronze Age); burials within large pottery vessels and usually accompanied by other vessels and ornaments (Antique period,

Iron Age and Chalcolithic); and burials in kurgan structures (mostly cairns or barrows) (Figure 4.3) and catacombs (Bronze Age). Several cases of late prehistoric skeletons were disarticulated and placed in secondary burials. There is no recorded evidence for the cremation of the body, which may be an observation of interest.

The Muslim tradition states that the burial should not be marked by grave markers and that any grave site should eventually return to its natural state. More recent Muslim traditions allow for the grave to be marked with a headstone and situated in family plots. This is a recent tradition, one which may be a result of influence from other faiths, and it has had an impact on the pipeline construction, since these more recent burials could not be disturbed. Because the earlier graves could not be identified in advance, several areas were inadvertently disturbed, such as areas Zayamchai, Seyidlar I and Girag Kasaman I. All had burials with recognizably Muslim characteristics and, after brief recording, the bodies were lifted and reburied with a religious ceremony in an adjacent burial area.

During the first part of the fieldwork, no human bone samples were retained. This was due to the generally poor condition of the bone and the lack of resources to transport and study the material. During the summer of 2005, a major late Christian or early Muslim cemetery was found at Chaparli. In view of the importance of the site and the quality of the bone, a decision was made to retain the human remains and to transport them to Baku for analysis. The anthropological analysis was undertaken by Kate Brayne (2007) as part of a training programme for IoAE staff. Subsequent programmes of human bone analysis have been led by the Smithsonian Institution for IoAE staff.

Unfortunately, as the human bone analysis was conducted after the excavations were completed, the results are not as conclusive as might be hoped for, but nevertheless some interesting features can be observed (see below).

METHODS OF ANTHROPOLOGICAL ANALYSIS

The lack of an appropriate methodology for the analysis and treatment of material from Azerbaijan, together with lack of resources and trained staff, does not help in the sympathetic treatment of this type of event. Where internationally recognized standards are used, they have been introduced by foreign scientists (see Brayne 2007).

Human skeletal material from a total of 49 individuals was studied from the Chaparli cemetery (KP335) of late Christian or early Muslim date. It was noted that 10.2 per cent of the population had evidence of a congenital absence of the third molar. This is not unduly high, compared with some populations, but 'could indicate that this community had close, stable genetic links and has not experienced wide scale incoming population movement' (Brayne 2007).

One other burial with interesting features was found in the excavation of the Borsunlu Kurgan (KP272). This was of a juvenile in the age range 12–18, buried in a large pottery vessel of the Antique period, dating to around 400BC. This individual presented dental caries and endocranial lesions.

CONCLUSION

This chapter has been based on a case study that covers the experience of a recent pipeline project in Azerbaijan. Excavations were carried out with the participation of the Institute of

Archaeology and Ethnography in Baku. The excavations brought about a number of ethical issues when excavating the remains and when dealing with Muslim graves.

Further support in the future will hopefully increase anthropological analysis of such rich graves and provide a further understanding of Azerbaijan's history.

USEFUL CONTACTS

Institute of Archaeology and Ethnography, Azerbaijan National Academy of Sciences. Website: www.science.az/en/archaeology/index.htm (accessed 7 July 2010).

BIBLIOGRAPHY

Brayne, K., (2007) 'Report on the Skeletal Assemblages from the Baku Tbilisi Ceyhan Oil Pipeline', unpublished report.

Goscharly, G., Maynard, D., Moore, R. *et al.* (2004) 'Excavations of Bronze Age Funerary Sites in Azerbaijan', *Antiquity*, 78. Available online at http://antiquity.ac.uk/Projgall/maynard/index.html (accessed 6 April 2010).

Lublin, V.P. and Bosinski, G. (1995) 'The earliest occupation of the Caucasus region', in W. Roebroeks and van Kolfschoten (eds) *The Earliest Occupation of Europe*, Proceedings of The European Science Foundation Workshop at Tautavel (France), 1993, Leiden: Leiden University Press.

Maynard, D.J., Taylor, P. and Museyibli, N. *(forthcoming)* 'Archaeological Excavations on the BTC Pipeline in Azerbaijan', *Internet Archaeology*.

Belarus/БЕЛАРУСЬ

Lidija Tegako and Olga Sorokina

INTRODUCTION: A BRIEF HISTORY AND CURRENT STATE OF PHYSICAL ANTHROPOLOGY IN BELARUS

Belarus, with a population of over ten million people, is situated in central Europe, to the west of the Eastern European Plain, on the watershed of the Black and Baltic seas. Such a location has played an important role in its ethnic history, creating a potential conflict of interests between the various ethnic groups of Europe.

According to anthropological analysis, it seems that Belarus had two significant migration waves: one coming from western Europe during the Bronze Age (end of the third to beginning of the second millennium BC), and another of Slavic tribes during the Iron Age (first century BC). The most ancient human remains discovered in the country are two ancient skeletons from the Bronze Age. The first discovery was made by M.M. Cherniavsky in 1962 during excavations of the second 2,000-year-old village near Krasnosel Volkovysk in the Grodno region. In 1980 A.G. Kalechits, during excavations of settlements in the Middle Dnieper culture in the Vetka district of Gomel region, found a male skeleton. Comparison of the two skeletons revealed differences in physical characteristics and two different 'types' in the Bronze Age. The first skeleton was a male individual from the site of Krasnoe Selo, Grodno Voblast (in the western part of Belarus), with a height of 170–75cm and with European facial characteristics. The second skeleton, dating from the Bronze Age, was found in the Rogachev district, Gomelskaia Voblast, and was shorter (c. 160cm) with some physical traits that appeared to be Mongoloid.

Further anthropological analysis has also provided an idea of the physical characteristics of ancient ethnic groups and the manifestation of sexual dimorphism and variability through the ages. I.I. Gokhman (1966) and S.I. Krutz (1976) explored ancient populations from the Mesolithic, Neolithic and Bronze Ages, and showed a predominance of brachycephalic skulls in Ukraine and possibly in Eastern Europe in general, a trend that seems to also continue in the mediaeval and modern populations of Belarus.

The beginning of research in physical anthropology at the Academy of Sciences of Belarus (Академии наук Беларуси) hit a milestone in 1926, when the Institute of Belarusian Culture (Институте Белоруской культуры) created the first scientific institution: the Anthropological Commission (Антропологическая комиссия). This commission served as a basis for the Department of Anthropology at the Academy of Sciences of Belarus. The activities of the department continued until 1941, when it was interrupted by the war. Research on the physical characteristics of the modern and ancient inhabitants of Belarus resumed in 1965, when the Institute of History, Ethnography and Folklore of the Academy of Sciences of the Republic of Belarus opened a Fellowship in Anthropology, and staff began conducting various studies of modern and ancient populations. I.I. Salivon undertook palaeoanthropological studies, and L. Tegako carried out research in odontology and dermatoglyphs (Salivon *et al.* 1976). These first studies were published as 'Essays on the Anthropology of Belarus' (Очерки по антропологии Белоруссии). In recent years, L. Tegako developed and implemented a comprehensive programme of research based on a set of standardized methods described in national and international textbooks. At present, comprehensive studies are continuing at the department of Anthropology and Ecology, Institute of the History of the National Academy of Sciences.

Training of specialists in anthropology was originally conducted at scientific institutions in Moscow, such as the N.N. Miklukho-Maklai Institute of Ethnology and Anthropology. After the Republic of Belarus was established as an independent state, postgraduate courses were taught at the Department of Anthropology and Ecology at the Institute of History of the National Academy of Sciences.

Skeletal collections

Today, the most significant cranial and osteological collections are held in the laboratory of the Department of Anthropology and Ecology, Institute of History, and in the Anatomical Museum of the Belorussian State Medical University. Other small and isolated findings are curated in regional museums.

The collection at the Department of Anthropology consists of about 500 crania and a number of other skeletal elements. One famous find is the well preserved skeleton of a male from the Bronze Age village of Krasnoselov.

ARCHAEOLOGICAL HUMAN REMAINS AND LEGISLATION

Archaeological legislation

Skeletal remains from archaeological contexts fall under the Law on the Protection of Historical and Cultural Heritage of the Republic of Belarus.[1] The law is periodically reviewed and edited in the light of current developments. Currently, anthropologists and archaeologists are guided by the law of the Republic of Belarus, registered in the National Register of Legal Acts of the Republic of Belarus (17.XII. 2006 N2/1195; Законом Республики Беларусь, зарегистрированным в Национальном реестре правовых актов Республики Беларусь). The law applies to moveable objects and immoveable manifestations of human creativity.

HUMAN REMAINS AND LEGISLATION

Human remains from archaeological contexts, with their antiquity and historical value, are stored in museums or special storage facilities. In some cases, there is reburial.

METHODS OF ANTHROPOLOGICAL ANALYSIS

In our team, determination of sex has been based on the manifestations of sexual dimorphism in the morphology of the skull and pelvis, the shape of the thorax, the robustness of the skeleton and the angle of the neck of the femur. We also have a number of distinguishing functions: for example, male ulnae are longer than 265mm and female ulnae shorter than 230mm. Age-at-death is assessed by examination of dental eruption, dental wear, ossification, cranial suture closure and degenerative changes in adults. Body height is determined by using the known formulae of Pearson (1898) and Trotter and Gleser (1952, 1958).

Overall, we use the reference works of Soviet authors (Alexeev 1966; Gerasimov 1955), Polish authors (Malinovski and Wolański 1988) and other foreign authors (e.g., White 2000). We also have some national reference books (Tegako and Marfina 2003).

CONCLUSION

The physical type of the ancient population of the Republic of Belarus, as well as the temporal variability of the physical type of the modern population, has attracted considerable interest from both a scientific point of view and that of the general public. Such research has been and continues to be carried out in Belarus with the increasing development of skeletal research, and the increasing accumulation and storage of skeletal collections. However, the evolution of the physical type of the ancient population is limited by the lack of skeletal data from a number of periods. The Bronze Age is represented by only one preserved skeleton, while a collection of over 400 skulls represents the historical periods from the 10th century onwards. Although the soil environment in which the skeletons may have been buried does not favour good preservation, nevertheless there are currently a number of excavations that may considerably increase the skeletal representativeness of some periods.

USEFUL CONTACTS

The National Academy of Sciences of Belarus (NASB). Website: http://nasb.gov.by/eng/index.php (accessed 7 July 2010).

NOTE

1 http://portal.unesco.org/culture/fr/files/25262/11061239243Belarusian_CH_law_EN.pdf/Belarusian_CH_law_EN.pdf

BIBLIOGRAPHY

Alekseeva T.I. (1973) *Etnogenez vostochnykh slavian po dannym antropologii*, Moscow: Moscow State University.
Alexeev V.P. (1966) *Osteometrija*, Moscow: Nauka.
Gerasimov, M.M. (1955) *Vosstanovlenie litsa po cherepu*, Mocow: Nauka.
Gokhman, I.I. (1966) *Naselenie Ukrainy v epokhu mezolita i neolita*, Moscow: Nauka.
Krutz, S.I. (1976) *Antropologicheskie osobennosti naseleniya srubnoi kul'tury territorii Ukrainy. Eneolit i bronzovyi vek Ukrainy*, Kiev: publisher unknown.

Malinovski, A. and Wolański, N. (1988) *Metody badán w biologii człowieka*, Warsaw: Państwowe Wydawnictwo Naukowe.

Pearson, K. (1898) 'Mathematical contributions to the Theory of Evolution. On the reconstruction of the stature of prehistoric races', *Philosophical Transactions of the Royal Society of London*, Series A, 192: 169–244.

Salivon, I.I., Tegako, L.I. and Mikulich, A.I. (1976) *Ocherki po antropologii Belorussii*, Minsk: Institut Iskustvovedenija, Etnografii i Folklera.

Tegako, L. and Marfina, O. (2003) *Prakticheskaya antropologiya*, Rostov-na-Donu: Feniks.

Trotter, M. and Gleser, G.C. (1952) 'Estimation of stature from long bones of American Whites and Negroes', *American Journal of Physical Anthropology*, 10: 463–514.

——(1958) 'A re-evaluation of estimation of stature based on measurements of stature taken during life and of long bones after death', *American Journal of Physical Anthropology*, 16: 79–123.

White, T.D. (2000) *Human Osteology*, 2nd edn, San Diego: Academic Press.

Belgium/België/Belgique/Belgien

Kim Quintelier, Agnès Malevez, Rosine Orban, Michel Toussaint,
Marit Vandenbruaene and Geneviève Yernaux

INTRODUCTION: A BRIEF HISTORY AND CURRENT STATE OF PHYSICAL ANTHROPOLOGY IN BELGIUM

For such a small country, Belgium has a complex structure. The fact that Belgium sits across the fault line which separates German and Latin cultures explains why the country has three official languages: Dutch, French and German. Belgium gained its independence from The Netherlands in 1830. Between 1970 and 1993, the country evolved into a federal structure through a number of state reforms. Today Belgium is a federal state made up of communities and regions. The redistribution of power took place along two lines. The first relates to language and cultural matters. As a result, three communities were established: the Flemish Community, the French Community and the German-speaking Community. They are empowered to deal with local matters (cultural affairs, sports, education, health, language, etc.). The second line of state reform was inspired by historical economic interests and resulted in the establishment of three regions: the Flemish Region, the Brussels-Capital Region and the Walloon Region. The regions' authority is confined to territorial matters (e.g., spatial planning, environment, agriculture, employment, economics and foreign trade). The country is further divided into ten provinces and 589 municipal councils (Figure 6.1). However, the federal state retains important powers, for example in the area of foreign affairs, justice, national defence, finance, social security and domestic affairs.

More information about Belgium can be found on its official web portal, www.belgium.be (accessed 7 July 2010).

Archaeological sites are considered to be places which can teach us about past human societies. Therefore archaeology belongs to the immovable heritage, as do monuments and landscapes. Consequently, this immovable heritage relates to spatial planning and is therefore a regional competence. On the other hand, the movable cultural heritage (such as archaeological artefacts in museums) is governed by the communities' Ministers of Culture.

Following the dissolution of the National Excavation Services (Nationale Dienst voor Opgravingen; Service National des Fouilles) in 1989, each of the country's three distinct regions developed its own archaeological legislation and institutions. Legal protection and awareness of the value of the archaeological heritage increased slowly in the different regions. The extent of the legal protection is however complicated by the complexity of federal regulations. At the international level, Belgium is slow at implementing European regulations for the protections of

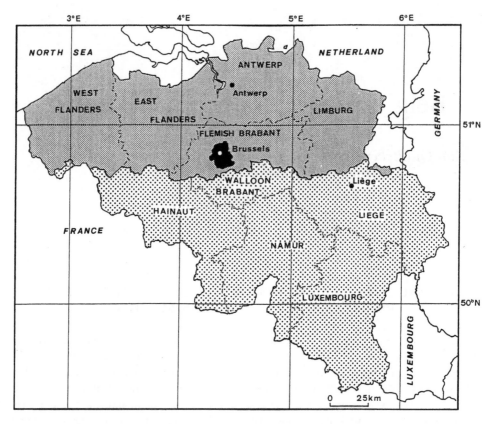

Figure 6.1 Map of Belgium illustrating the three different regions (the Flemish region in the north, the
Brussels-Capital region in the centre, and the Walloon region in the south of the country, and
their divisions according to provinces).
Source: A.-M. Wittek, AIDA

the archaeological heritage. For physical anthropology, the three regions are equal, with the
exception of the remains of First World War soldiers, since none of the regions have specific
legislation regarding archaeological human skeletal remains.

For the purposes of this article, the term 'physical anthropology' is limited to the study of
archaeological human skeletal remains, inhumations as well as cremation burials, in order to
obtain information about demographic trends and the health status of past populations. It should
also be noted that this article is limited to local/native excavated human skeletal remains and
will not cover the issue of non-native human skeletal collections in Belgian museums or other
institutions.

Belgium has a longstanding tradition regarding the study of fossil hominid remains or
palaeoanthropology (Leguebe and Orban 1984; Toussaint 1992, 2001; Toussaint *et al.* 2001a,
2001b; Toussaint and Pirson 2007). In the winter of 1829–30, physician P.-C. Schmerling discovered authenticated human fossils in different caves in the province of Liège, mainly in the
famous cave of Engis where he unearthed two calottes (the top part of a cranium). These finds
allowed Schmerling to understand and demonstrate that man had coexisted with large extinct
prehistoric mammals, but without going as far as to claim that fossil men were morphologically
different from modern humans. He also realized that the flint artefacts found in association

with human and animal bones were actually man-made. However, Schmerling's theories were not accepted during his lifetime. Almost a century later, after the discovery of the eponymous fossils in the Neander valley (Germany) in 1856 and the beginning of the debate about the evolution of mankind, the Engis juvenile skull was accepted as a Neanderthal fossil. In 1866, in the cave site of La Naulette (province of Namur), geologist E. Dupont found a fossilized human mandible in association with the remains of extinct animals, and this was considered to be the first anatomical evidence of the evolution of man. The discovery of prehistoric tools, animal bones from the Ice Age and two Neanderthal skeletons at Spy in 1886, and the publication of these finds, had a huge impact (Leguebe 1986). At that time, Belgium was one of the leading countries in the field of human palaeontology. Most of the researchers in those days were trained geologists. Currently, Belgium still has a handful of competent researchers in the field of fossil remains; most of them are based at the Royal Belgian Institute of Natural Sciences (RBINS) situated in Brussels and at the Directorate of Archaeology of the Public Service of Wallonia.

In the past, human skeletal remains found during archaeological excavations from various historical time periods were often treated as of secondary interest, compared to other archaeological artefacts such as pottery or metal objects. Frequently they were not even collected and were either disposed of after excavation or left in the depositories of museums or other institutions. There was an exception to this, however, at the end of the 19th century, with the publication of numerous articles focusing mainly on metrical data from historical cemeteries by, among others, V. Jacques and E. Houzé (Couttenier 2007). Scientific interest in historical skeletal collections began in 1936, when physician F. Twiesselmann established the department of Anthropology and Prehistory at RBINS. His objective was to foster opportunities for studying osteological material from modern man and prehistoric hominids within the context of their living environment, as materialized by the extensive collections of prehistoric tools and animal bones collected by E. Dupont (Twiesselmann 1954). Until some ten years ago, research carried out by Twiesselmann and his successors at RBINS, most of whom came from a biology background, was primarily focused on biometrical and statistical analyses (Orban 2010). The thousand or more skeletons from the Cistercian abbey of Koksijde/Coxyde (province of Western Flanders; Figure 6.2) are currently the largest historical collection held at RBINS (Orban and Vandoorne 2006). This collection has served as the basis for some 60 publications (Van Neer 1985; VIOE 2007–8); most of which concern osteometric and dental studies. Over the past thirty years there has been a shift within physical anthropological research in Belgium from biometry to 'reconstruction of life from the skeleton' and palaeopathological research, together with the implementation of modern scientific techniques performed on bone (e.g., isotope and trace element analysis in order to reconstruct diet and migration).

Palaeoanthropological and palaeopathological examinations were undertaken in the 1950s by physician P. Janssens, who worked as a freelance researcher for the national service of archaeological excavations on cremated remains dating from the Bronze Age to the Iron Age. During his lifetime, he published some 50 articles about cremated as well as inhumated remains; he also wrote a well known monograph on palaeopathology (Janssens 1970). However, his articles are often considered to be of only anecdotal interest, used to complement descriptions of the excavated archaeological remains.

In the Flemish Region, it was not until 1999 that physical anthropology was structurally integrated within archaeological research at the Flemish Heritage Institute. For the Brussels-Capital Region, the structural analysis of human remains began only in 2007. In the Walloon Region, anthropologists have been employed by the Directorate of Archaeology for the study of prehistoric remains since 1994, and for historical remains since 1995.

Today it is normal procedure to excavate, document and analyse skeletal material using scientific methods.

Education and training

No Belgian university offers specific academic education (at bachelor or master level) in physical anthropology. Even within the archaeological curriculum, not every university offers an introductory course on the subject. Currently, only the Université Libre de Bruxelles (ULB) and the University of Liège (ULg) teach basic principles for recording human remains. In the past, anthropological research and teaching was conducted at the University of Liège (until 1940) and at the University of Louvain-la-Neuve (from 1973 till 1994; Thoma 1985). The University of Ghent provided some lectures on the subject. Because of this lack of training, most researchers

Figure 6.2a

Figure 6.2b

Figure 6.2c Excavations at the Cistercian abbey at Koksijde/Coxyde, province of Western Flanders, Belgium
Note: a–b in 1948 (photos archives RBINS), C in 2002 (photo C. Polet, RBINS)

in anthropology have a background in archaeology, biology, forensic medicine or geology (palaeontology), or acquired their education at universities abroad.

Present-day human osteological research performed in Belgium is still too limited. Almost all human osteologists in Belgium (there are less than ten of them at the time of writing) are employed within scientific institutions such as RBINS, the Flemish Heritage Institute and the Directorate of Archaeology of the Walloon Region. Within universities, museums, provincial or municipal archaeological departments, no physical anthropologists are structurally active. The small number of active researchers is the result of the limited professional opportunities, for a variety of reasons. The most important is budgetary, coupled with the difficulty of processing archaeological excavations due to Belgium's complex archaeological legislative framework. Furthermore, the inclusion of natural sciences (e.g., archaeozoology, archaeobotany, etc.) within archaeological research is a recent development and has not yet been fully implemented. This is exacerbated by the lack of proper education and training in osteoarchaeological analysis. The latest development, at this stage only appearing in Flanders, is the increase of commercially organized research, where a physical anthropologist is employed by a private archaeological organization.

Since there is so little osteological investigation in Belgium, active researchers maintain close contacts with their international colleagues from other universities and institutions.

Skeletal collections

As for the available assemblages, osteological material from the prehistoric period comes almost exclusively from cave sites in the southern part of Belgium. Some cremation cemeteries are known, dating from the Bronze Age, Iron Age and the Roman period. The majority of human remains are excavated from Christian church cemeteries, cloisters and abbeys, dating from the early, late mediaeval and post-mediaeval period. Consequently, acquired osteological analysis of human bone expertise is based primarily on inhumations. Only a few researchers specialize in the analysis of cremated remains. Skeleton collections from the 19th and 20th centuries AD are scarce, including the only two identified Belgian skeletal assemblages of Schoten and Châtelet which are housed at RBINS (Orban and Vandoorne 2006; Polet *pers. comm.*). The Châtelet collection, derived from the province of Hainaut, consists of skeletons from unclaimed graves. It was begun in 2006 and the collection is still ongoing.

Royal Belgian Society of Anthropology and Prehistory

Belgium has one acknowledged society regarding the research of human skeletal remains, namely the Royal Belgian Association of Anthropology and Prehistory (www.srbap. naturalsciences.be) which was founded in 1882 and played an important role in the development of Belgian anthropology (Leloup and Orban 2009). This association unites professional and amateur researchers from home and abroad who are investigating prehistoric archaeology, physical anthropology, genetic anthropology and human palaeontology. The society manages several osteological and prehistoric collections, which are deposited at the RBINS.

ARCHAEOLOGICAL HUMAN REMAINS AND LEGISLATION

Archaeological legislation

Each year, many human skeletons are discovered during some kind of building work. In most cases archaeological research precedes large scale development projects (e.g., underground car parks or industrial estates) thanks to the European Convention on the Protection of the Archaeological Heritage (the Valetta Convention). Belgium's entire archaeological landscape is slowly but continually evolving. Although Belgium signed the Valetta Convention in 1992, it has not yet been ratified.

The excavation of archaeological sites requires a general excavation licence. To obtain this authorization, several conditions have to be met. The procedure for applying for this licence is different in each of Belgium's three regions.

Discovery of human remains

On Belgian territory, human skeletal remains are usually encountered in three ways: most of them are unearthed from archaeological sites; some are found by chance (e.g., during building work); and others may be the object of forensic investigation.

Should unexpected archaeological remains be found during excavation, regardless of their location or size, they must be reported. This has become compulsory in the three different regions following a decree relating to the protection of the archaeological heritage. In the Flemish Region, finds have to be reported within three days to the Agency of Spatial Planning and Immovable Heritage, Flanders. These finds have to be maintained, protected and made accessible for further archaeological research for ten days (cf. Decreet van 30 juni 1993 hou-dende bescherming van het Archeologisch Patrimonium or DAP). For the Brussels-Capital

Region, archaeological discoveries have to be reported to the owner of the site and to the Region within three days. The archaeological site and the artefacts must be preserved in their existing state, be protected from damage and destruction, and must to be available for research for a maximum period of 21 days (cf. Brussels Wetboek van de Ruimtelijke Ordening, abbreviated to BWRO, or Code bruxellois de l'aménagement du territoire, abbreviated to CoBAT, published in 2004). For the Walloon Region, each accidental archaeological find has to be reported to the Directorate General for Spatial Planning, Accommodation and Heritage, or to the municipality where the remains were found, also within three days. Within 15 days after declaration, an assigned person is sent to assess the discovery (cf. Code wallon de l'aménagement du territoire, de l'urbanisme, du patrimoine et de l'énergie or CWATUPE).

Should skeletal remains be found outside the context of an official excavation, the police have to be notified. The first step is to confirm whether the remains are human. The Ministry of Justice can request the assistance of a forensic anthropologist or pathologist. Should it be established that the mortal remains are not those of a soldier from the First or Second World Wars, or from previous conflicts, then the case is handled as suspicious. Should doubt remain as to the context surrounding the remains, the police will request the assistance of an archaeologist working in the nearest archaeological department to assess the situation. In cases of forensic concern, the 'Disaster Victim Identification' team (DVI) of Belgium's federal police is contacted in order to have the excavation performed by a forensic archaeologist. Recently, the DVI team added a forensic archaeologist to its team. Forensic archaeology or the application of archaeological principles, techniques and methodologies in legal context, is generally employed for the localization and recovery of buried human remains. Furthermore, when necessary it can also call upon the assistance of a forensic anthropologist. The Ministry of Justice can refer the analysis of human remains and other evidence to freelance experts (forensic pathologists, forensic anthropologists, forensic odontologists, forensic entomologists, etc.).

The decrees concerning archaeological heritage in Belgium do not mention a specific time-frame for archaeological monuments. However, archaeological monuments, in a broad sense, are supposed to provide evidence of past eras or civilizations – for which excavations and findings could supply useful information. Owing to this, recent skeletons are excluded, since excavation would not necessarily provide significant information about recent populations.

In Belgium, murder and manslaughter are barred by the statute of limitations after a maximum of thirty years. Consequently, there is a gap in the law for the period between the Second World War and legal involvement. In 2005, a decree proposal to amend article 21 of the Criminal Proceedings Code concerning this lapse of the criminal proceeding for specific crimes was submitted to the Belgian Senate. The decree proposed to bring Belgian legislation in line with international humanitarian rights where certain severe violations of law cannot be prescribed, such as murder, manslaughters, hostage taking, etc. The request lapsed in 2007 following the dissolution of the Chambers.

With the exception of human remains with a military background, Belgium lacks specific guidelines for the treatment of archaeological human remains, including excavation and post-excavation processing and analysis. The presence of a physical anthropologist on site is not compulsory in Belgium. In Flanders more specifically, the physical anthropologists of the Flemish Heritage Institute are informed by the Agency for Town and Country Planning and Immovable Heritage when human skeletons are found, and they will go on site when their assistance is requested.

This same Agency, in charge of policy execution, the preparation of protections and the management of 'immovable goods', provides a standard field recording form for documenting human skeleton remains, and this form is accessible to every archaeologist. On this recording form the state of preservation, the position and orientation of the skeleton are to be described, and several *in situ* measurements are to be taken. Disturbances, grave goods and grave contexts must be noted down as well. In Wallonia, skeletons are removed by physical anthropologists according to the techniques described by French field anthropologists (Duday *et al.* 1990; Bonnabel and Carré 1996). In the case of historical cemeteries, the outline of the bones and the burials are today usually computerized from digital pictures taken during excavation. This method has the combined advantage of taking very little time on site and storing the information immediately in a digital format.

Finally, most decrees relating to human remains concern graveyards and the disposal of corpses. Within Belgium's structure, this competence belongs to the regions. The current legal framework for the excavation of human remains is only applicable to operating cemeteries and relates to expiring concessions or when older graves have to be re-organized in order to make room for new interments. This means that secular law is generally aimed at regulating the manner in which human remains and tombstones have to be cleared from burial grounds. Current legislation determines, among other matters, the establishment and closure of cemeteries, the provision of burial concessions, burial rules, burial ornamentation, etc. An implementation ruling defines the guidelines for coffins, for the establishment and management of crematoria, cremation conditions, etc. Local municipal policy can further add to these rulings. According to the Belgian penal code, the damaging of graves, grave fences or tombstones is punishable by law. It is unlawful to remove or disturb human remains without proper legal authority.

Victims of war

Human remains from military conflicts are found on a regular basis (e.g., during the construction of new industrial building sites), particularly in the province of Western Flanders where numerous remains from the First World War (1914–18) have been preserved in the clay soil. Excavations in this soil demand extreme precaution because of the live explosives that are still buried in the landscape. Thus, archaeological excavations have frequently to be supervised by 'DOVO', a federal police team responsible for the clearance and destruction of explosive devices. They provide the archaeologists with advice on safety and the identification of explosives.

In 2004, following inquiries from town councils and police services relating to First World War (WWI) excavations, a manual was published giving guidelines and answers (Anon. 2004). These guidelines provide directions for the excavation and post-excavation treatment of WWI soldiers and it answers some of the questions posed by municipalities and the police. This manual can also be used for other military conflicts (Anon. 2004). It states that, when uncovering human skeletons, the police are to be notified, who would then, in turn, alert the War Graves Department of the Ministry of Defence. After these steps have been taken, an anthropological evaluation *in situ* may take place (Figure 6.3). The remains and associated artefacts (uniforms, badges, weapons, etc.) are collected by the police and stored in national military domains until they are interred in a military cemetery. If possible, the nationality of the soldier should be established, often by way of identification of their military equipment. In those cases, the War Graves Department will inform its foreign counterpart and will return the human remains and associated artefacts to that country for interment. If the nationality of the victim cannot be determined, inhumation will take place in a Belgian military cemetery. Only rarely is it possible to identify individuals by examination of their personal

Figure 6.3 During the construction of the A19 motorway in Belgium, several skeletal remains of First
World War soldiers were examined before their reburial
Source: VIOE

belongings or by DNA analysis. In cases where the individual has been identified, every effort is
made to notify the soldier's relatives (Anon. 2004).

Curation, treatment and transportation of archaeological human remains

After carefully documenting, measuring, drawing and photographing the archaeological burial
context, the bones are generally collected and transported to the archaeological laboratory. This
procedure is based on internationally recognized guidelines. There are no specific regulations in
Belgium, either for the excavation and recording of graves or for the transport of archaeological
human skeletal remains. Depending on their condition, the bones are washed and dried in the
laboratory. After this process, they are stored until they can be studied. Osteological analysis of
archaeological human skeletal remains is not compulsory and depends on the existing archaeological
interests. Some collections have still to be studied after decades of storage.

There are no specific legislation or guidelines concerning the treatment of human remains
after excavation and analysis. In principle, the owner of the remains is responsible for the
preservation, protection and related costs of the archaeological material (for the Flemish Region,
see article 4 of the DAP). It is expected that suitable storage will be provided which will
ensure the skeleton's physical integrity. In most cases the human remains are stored in archaeological or scientific depositories, where they will be kept available for future studies. The
type of container depends on the institution in charge of storing the skeletons, but usually
the remains are preserved in wooden or plastic boxes. If the excavated remains present only
limited research potential for the future (depending on the quality of preservation, the size of
the sample, the closeness of dating and the type of assemblage), they can be reburied or
cremated.

Although human skeletal remains can be used in exhibitions and for teaching or handling purposes for the general public, there are no specific regulations. Scientific and/or educational projects will encounter few problems, as long as the 'material' is treated with sufficient respect. Displays of human remains in museums or exhibitions are popular with the general public and are acceptable provided they follow the museum's deontological code guidelines. Based on the International Council of Museums (ICOM, www.icom.museum/ethics.html), it is stated that collections of human remains may only be acquired if they can be housed, maintained, researched and used securely and respectfully. Professional norms are observed and the concerns and persuasions of societies, ethical or religious groups to whom the 'objects' are related are to be taken into account (articles 2.5, 3.7. and 4.3 from the ICOM code of ethics for museums, 2006). In addition, article 9 of the Valetta Convention states that exhibiting archaeological objects, including human skeletal remains, to the general public should be encouraged.

Regarding the issue of ownership and whether a human skeleton can be transferred or sold, Belgian legislation provides no clear answer. Furthermore, there are no known judicial cases on this subject. Consequently, the following argumentation should be considered as a brainstorm exercise based on an internal jurist's memo drafted in 2004 following an enquiry to the Flemish Region's legal advisor from a physical anthropologist working for the Flemish Heritage Institute. According to the general ownership principles, one can only be the owner of an 'object' as defined by Belgian judicature as 'everything that exists, with the exception of the human individual' [authors' translation]. Assuming that a skeleton may no longer be qualified as a human being, it might therefore be defined as an object.

However, even as an object, this does not automatically imply that a skeleton is eligible for private appropriation. Organs and other body parts, of a living human being or of a corpse, are considered to be objects 'beyond business', and under no circumstances can they become the object of property transfers (article 1128 and 1598 of the Civil Code). This begs the question whether human bones should also be considered objects 'beyond business'. If so, this point of view would hamper the use of human skeletal remains for archaeological research.

Should a human skeleton be considered as a 'commercial' object (i.e., not 'beyond business'), then logically this would imply that efforts should first be made in order to identify any relatives or heirs. Should they be identified, it would then be up to them to decide what should happen to the skeleton. If no relative can be found, then article 522 of the Civil Code would apply. This states that the owner of a piece of land is also the owner of everything present in and above it. However, classifying an archaeological skeleton as an object is not the only option. Due to the absence of specific legislation there are alternative approaches to the issue. First of all, human skeletal remains could be classified as 'ownerless goods'. These are goods which have never been owned and, as such, according to articles 539 and 713 of the Civil Code, they belong to the State. Second, when the skeleton is found on private property it could be qualified as a 'treasure'. Belgian law defines the term 'treasure' as 'every hidden or buried object (not lost objects) discovered by chance and for which nobody can give proof of his or her right of ownership' [authors' translation] (article 716 of the Civil Code). Should the owner of an archaeological find be identified, then this person or his successor(s) is the legal owner(s). If there is no successor, the finder becomes the owner of the object by prescription. The period of limitation is laid down to 30 years (article 2262 of the Civil Code) with the exception of objects which are part of military equipment, such as a uniforms, badges and weapons. These objects remain the property of the State of which the soldier was a citizen. Should a treasure be found by an individual on his land, then he or she becomes the owner. Should the treasure be found on the property of a second party, then both the finder and the owner of the land are each entitled to a half of the treasure. Those who purposefully search for and discover a treasure on the property of a second party are not entitled to a half share, since the discovery was not accidental. This also applies to archaeologists who within the framework of their profession are seeking treasures. An archaeologist can never claim a share of the find, unless he has a prior agreement with the land's owner. This principle applies both for discoveries on private grounds and for those in the public domain. Artefacts, archaeological, natural historical, numismatic or other objects of scientific value or other rare and valuable objects discovered by excavation or demolition work are the property of the contracting authority. These objects are put at the disposal of local authorities.

Today, in Belgium, it would appear that in practice no distinction is made between different types of archaeological object. As a result, the same property rights apply to human skeletal remains as to pottery, with the exception of military objects as described earlier. In most cases in which human skeletal remains are found on private territory, they are donated by the owners to the archaeological services or to the scientific institutions involved with the excavation. In this case, a written agreement, with or without compensation, is signed between the two parties concerned. When the owner of a skeleton decides to keep his find, he has to ensure that he will take the necessary steps to preserve it. In the Flemish Region specifically, the authorities have the right to supervise and can even, as is stated in article 4 of the DAP, hold the owner responsible and liable to prosecution for damage or destruction of the archaeological heritage on his or her property.

Obviously, with such limited legislation, black market sale of human skeletal remains can never be totally avoided. From a Belgian legal point of view, there is nothing to prevent someone from owning a human skull. Naturally, from an ethical point of view, one could wonder if this is acceptable.

As demonstrated here, specific legislation for the proprietary rights of archaeological skeletal remains is currently lacking in Belgium, and only the introduction of a new law could resolve this issue. A comparative study of legal practices in other countries would be useful.

Further ethical considerations

For the purposes of future scientific research, Belgian national institutions store many thousands of remains, both from inhumation and cremation burials, spanning a time frame from prehistory to recent times.

There is no strong public opposition to the disturbance of ancient native human remains. To date, Belgium has been spared from the debate around the issue of human skeletal remains that has taken place, for example, in North America and Australasia, where there have been issues revolving around the reburial of skeletal collections. Nevertheless, the question of how to deal with human skeletal remains in Belgium from an ethical standpoint is open and is poorly documented. Most archaeologists consciously treat the dead with respect and try to avoid offending religious or secular sensibilities when dealing with human remains. However, standards of practice have yet to be clearly defined.

METHODS OF ANTHROPOLOGICAL ANALYSIS

Internationally recognized standards are used to analyse the skeletons. Most researchers use a combination of international techniques including Buikstra and Ubelaker (1994) and Dutour *et al.* (2005).

Following good argumentation, requests for the destructive analysis of human remains (C^{14} dating, stable isotope analysis, histology, ancient DNA, etc.) are usually granted. Although there are no specific guidelines, it can safely be assumed that all sampling is fully documented, measured and recorded prior to analysis.

CONCLUSION

During many years of research, Belgian palaeoanthropology achieved a valued international standard, especially with the studies of prehistoric remains including Neanderthal sites such as Engis, La Naulette, Spy, Walou and Scladina; and Mesolithic and Neolithic graves. At present, multiple international collaborations have been established and continue to develop towards research within the framework of new methodological studies using the most recent techniques in anthropology.

Although Belgian research broke new ground on prehistoric material, the study of historical skeletal assemblages from inhumation as well as cremation burials is still in its infancy. For Flanders specifically, the majority of published articles cover smaller (1–100 individuals) collections. Larger collections have already been analysed, but the results are still to be published. Demographical and palaeopathological analyses are consistently included in articles published by the Flemish Heritage Institute.

Specific future inquiries in the Flemish (www.onderzoeksbalans.be) and Brussels-Capital Region will involve social differentiations in human skeletal assemblages based on enforced palaeopathological investigation and stable isotope analysis. Continuing development of research in physical anthropology in Belgium should encourage opportunities for establishing general and comparative studies but at the same time requires collaboration between the three separate regions. At present, it could be argued that Belgian anthropology needs a more sustainable interaction between Dutch- and French-speaking researchers.

Gradually it becomes inconceivable to unearth human remains except by an osteologically trained archaeologist or with the assistance of a professional physical anthropologist. The general implementation of (human) osteological courses in archaeological education should therefore be a priority. As a result, the training of professional archaeologists would improve the quality of sepulchral excavations.

Finally, as discussed throughout this chapter, one of the major challenges for Belgian anthropology in the years to come will be the clarification of numerous legal aspects concerning human bones, both at a national and a regional level, and the creation of standardized guidelines on dealing with human remains.

USEFUL CONTACTS

Flemish Heritage Institute. Website: www.vioe.be (accessed 7 July 2010).
Royal Belgian Society of Anthropology and Prehistory. Website: http://srbap.naturalsciences.be (accessed 7 July 2010).
Royal Belgian Institute of Natural Sciences. Website: www.naturalsciences.be (accessed 7 July 2010).

ACKNOWLEDGEMENTS

The authors are grateful to the juridical services of the Flemish and Walloon Regions. We would like to thank J.-P. Beauthier, J. Lacroix, D. Roels, M. Vercauteren and our colleagues at the RBINS, VIOE and the Archaeology Department of the Brussels-Capital Region, for their comments and suggestions on earlier drafts of this article. We also thank Jennifer Schubert, Christiaan Iken and Liesbeth Van Camp for correcting the English manuscript.

BIBLIOGRAPHY

Anon. (2004) *Omgaan met bodemvondsten. Opgraving WOI*, Brugge.

——(2006) *ICOM code of ethics for museums*, Paris: Nory.

Belgian Federal Government (2009) *Portal Belgium*. Available online at www.belgium.be (accessed 10 March 2010).

Bonnabel, L. and Carré, F. (1996) *Rencontre autour de Linceul*, Compte rendu de la réunion du 5 avril 1996 tenue à Paris, Groupe d'Anthropologie et d'Archéologie Funéraire en Île-de-France et le Service régional de l'archéologie de Haute-Normandie, bulletin de liaison.

Buikstra, J.E. and Ubelaker, D.H. (eds) (1994) *Standards for Data Collection from Human Skeletal Remains*, Fayetteville, AR: Arkansas Archaeological Survey Research Series No. 44.

Couttenier, M. (2007) *Congo tentoongesteld. Een geschiedenis van de Belgische antropologie en het museum van Tervuren, 1882–1924*, Leuven: Acco.

Deweirdt, M. (2005) 'De bescherming van het archeologisch erfgoed', in *Het onroerend goed in de praktijk*. Mechelen: Kluwer.

Duday, H., Courtaud, P., Crubézy, E., *et al.* (1990) 'L'anthropologie «de terrain»: reconnaissance et interprétation des gestes funéraires', *Bulletin et Mémoires de la Société d'Anthropologie de Paris*, 2: 29–50.

Dutour, O., Hublin, J.-J. and Vandermeersch, B. (2005) *Objets et méthodes en paléoanthropologie*, Paris: Comité des Travaux Historiques et Scientifiques.

ICOM (2006) *Code of Ethics for Museums*. Available online at www.icom.museum/ethics.html (accessed 10 March 2010).

Janssens, P.A. (1970) *Paleopathology. Diseases and Injuries of the Prehistoric Man*, London: J. Baker.

Leguebe, A. and Orban, R. (1984) 'Paléontologie humaine', in D. Cahen and P. Hasaerts (eds) *Peuples chasseurs de la Belgique préhistorique dans leur cadre naturel*, Brussels: Institut royal des Sciences naturelles de Belgique.

Leguebe, A. (1986) 'Importance des découvertes de Néandertaliens en Belgique pour le développement de la paléontologie humaine', *Bulletin de la Société royale belge d'Anthropologie et de Préhistoire*, 97: 13–31.

Leloup, G. and Orban, R. (2009) 'Een archiefselectie lijst voor de Koninklijke Belgische Vereniging voor Antropologie en Prehistorie (KBVAP): nuttig voor verleden, heden en toekomst. Un tableau de tri des archives de la Société royale belge d'Anthropologie et de Préhistoire (SRBAP): utile pour le passé, le présent et le futur', *Anthropologica et Præhistorica*, 120: 203–17.

Orban, R. (2010) 'François Twiesselmann, Lila Defrise et André Leguebe: acteurs de l'émergence et du développement de l'Anthropologie à l'Institut royal des Sciences naturelles de Belgique (IRSNB) entre 1936 et 1989', *Bulletins et Mémoires de la Société d'Anthropologie de Paris*, 22 (3–4).

Orban, R. and Vandoorne, K. (2006) 'Les squelettes humains de Koksijde (Coxyde) et Schoten: deux collections remarquables conservées à l'Institut Royal des Sciences Naturelles de Belgique', in Y. Ardagna, B. Bizot, G. Boëtsch *et al.* (eds) *Les collections ostéologiques humaines: gestion, valorisation et perspectives*, Actes de la table ronde de Carry-le-Rouet (Bouches-du-Rhône, France), 25–26 avril 2003, Supplement Bulletin Archéologique de Provence 4: 79–84.

Royal Belgian Society of Anthropology and Prehistory (2000–2010) *Anthropologica et Praehistorica*. Available online at www.srbap.naturalsciences.be (accessed 10 March 2010).

Thoma, A.L. (1985) *Eléments de paléoanthropologie*, Louvain-la-Neuve: Université Catholique de Louvain.

Toussaint, M. (1992) 'The Role of Wallonia in the History of Palaeo-anthropology', in M. Toussaint (ed.) *Cinq millions d'années, l'aventure humaine*, Etudes et recherches archéologiques de l'Université de Liège, Liège: Université de Liège.

——(2001) *Les hommes fossiles en Wallonie. De Philippe-Charles Schmerling à Julien Fraipont, l'émergence de la paléoanthropologie*, Monograph Carnet du Patrimoine 33, Namur.

Toussaint, M., Orban, R., Polet, C., *et al.* (2001a) 'Apports récents sur l'anthropologie des Mésolithiques et des Néolithiques mosans', in N. Cauwe, A. Hauzeur and P.-L. van Berg (eds) *Prehistory in Belgium*, Special issue on the occasion of the XIVth Congress of the International Union for Prehistoric and Protohistoric Sciences, *Anthropologica et Praehistorica*, 112: 91–105.

Toussaint, M, Pirson, S. and Bocherens, H. (2001b) 'Neandertals from Belgium', in N. Cauwe, A. Hauzeur and P.-L. van Berg, (eds), *Prehistory in Belgium*, Special issue on the occasion of the XIVth Congress of the International Union for Prehistoric and Protohistoric Sciences, *Anthropologica et Praehistorica* 112: 21–38.

Toussaint, M. and Pirson S. (2007) 'Aperçu historiques des recherches concernant l'homme préhistorique dans le karst belge aux XIXe et XXe siècles: archéologie, géologie, paléoanthropologie, paléontologie, datations', in J. Evin (ed.) *Un siècle de constructions du discours scientifique en préhistoire. Actes du XXVIe Congrès préhistorique de France. Avignon, 21–25 septembre 2004. Volume 2*, Paris: Société Préhistorique Française.

Twiesselmann, F. (1954) 'Propos sur l'anthropologie', in *Volume jubilaire Victor Van Straelen (1925–1954)*, Bruxelles: Institut Royal des Sciences Naturelles de Belgique 2, 1063–98.

Van Neer, W. (1985) 'Antropologisch onderzoek over het grafveld der duinenabdij te Koksijde: een kritische literatuurstudie', *De Duinen*, 15: 39–57.

VIOE (2007–8) *Onderzoeksbalans Onroerend erfgoed Vlaanderen*. Available online at www.onderzoeksbalans. be (accessed 10 March 2010).

Bosnia and Herzegovina/Bosna i Hercegovina

Amila Zukanović, Nermin Sarajlić and Senem Škulj

INTRODUCTION: A BRIEF HISTORY AND CURRENT STATE OF PHYSICAL ANTHROPOLOGY IN BOSNIA AND HERZEGOVINA

The Republic of Bosnia and Herzegovina (BH) is divided for the purposes of administration into two entities (the Federation of Bosnia and Herzegovina, and Republika Srpska) and one district, Brčko. The Federation of Bosnia and Herzegovina consists of ten cantons, each with its own cantonal government. This division has led to legislative complexity in many areas, including the legislation governing archaeological sites, and thereby archaeological human remains.

As in many other countries, research on earlier (archaeological) human population samples has taken place within broader archaeological or palaeontological studies. Ćiro Truhelka, Radimsky Vaclav, Alojz Benac and Đuro Basler are some of the archaeologists who described findings of human remains during their exploration of archaeological sites in Bosnia and Herzegovina. Furthermore, V. Radimsky wrote instructions for archaeological excavation in caves, and protection and conservation procedures for any material including human remains in his book *Prehistoricka nalazišta* (Prehistoric Finds), published in 1891 in Sarajevo (Radimsky 1891).

Živko Mikić, an archaeologist and physical anthropologist, contributed significantly to research in the field of bioarchaeology. He investigated and described a large number of anthropological remains from many archaeological sites in the former Yugoslavia, mostly from prehistoric periods. Two of his books should be mentioned: Atlas osteopatoloških promjena na istorijskim populacijama Jugoslavije (Atlas of Osteopathologic Changes in Historical Yugoslav Populations) (Lovrinčević and Mikić 1989) and Visina i problem fizičke antropologije-prethistoriski periodi (Stature and Problems of Physical Anthropology in Yugoslavia – Prehistoric Periods) (Mikić 1981). In his work, Mikić also studied dental samples from archaeological sites, usually describing dental pathology. Palaeodontology, as a specific field of research in BH, does not have a long tradition. Development of palaeodontology in BH has been encouraged by the establishment of the International Association of Paleodontology (IAPO), which provides researchers with the possibility of sharing experiences, information and new ideas (Zukanović 2007).

There are at present no associations of physical anthropology in BH.

63

Education and training

Any courses in physical anthropology are taught either at the Faculty of Medicine and Faculty of Dentistry at the University of Sarajevo or at the Faculty of Natural Sciences and Mathematics (Department of Biology), also in Sarajevo. The former includes a few lectures on anthropology in human anatomy modules, although anthropology does not exist as a subject within the curriculum; the latter faculty includes a module in bioanthropology in the third-year undergraduate degree.

For the academic year 2008–9, a new department opened in the Faculty of Philosophy at the University of Sarajevo: the Department of Archaeology. In the third year of study anthropology is in the curriculum.

ARCHAEOLOGICAL HUMAN REMAINS AND LEGISLATION

Archaeological legislation

The UNESCO World Heritage Convention was ratified by the former Yugoslavia (and consequently also by Bosnia and Herzegovina, as one of its republics) in 1974. Bosnia and Herzegovina reaffirmed its ratification in 1993, when it also ratified the European Convention on the Protection of the Archaeological Heritage (Council of Europe, London, 1969); the revised Convention (Valletta 1992) was ratified by BH on 11 February 2009 and published in the Official Gazette of BH (International Agreements, no. 02/09).

The 1985 legislation in the Official Gazette of the Socialist Republic of Bosnia and Herzegovina (Službeni list Socijalističke Republike Bosne i Hercegovine) treats archaeological sites as part of the cultural heritage, which means that they are governed by the Law on the Protection and Use of the Cultural, Historical and Natural Heritage (Official Gazette of SR BiH nos 20/85 and 12/87). This law is still in force in the Federation of BH in those cantons that have not yet enacted their own heritage protection laws.

At the state level, covering both the Federation of Bosnia and Herzegovina and Republika Srpska, there is as yet no umbrella law governing the protection and use of the cultural and natural heritage (although a bill is currently before Parliament); but there is a set of rules on the safekeeping and use of technical, photographic and other documentation and records of pro-tected properties of the Institute for the Protection and Use of the Cultural, Historical and Natural Heritage of BH (Official Gazette of BH no. 3/97–21).

As part of the cultural heritage, archaeological sites are subject to entity and cantonal legislation. In the Federation of Bosnia and Herzegovina, the Law on the Protection and Use of the Cultural, Historical and Natural Heritage (Official Gazette of SR BiH nos 20/85 and 12/87) still applies, while in Republika Srpska the relevant law is the Law on Cultural Properties (Official Gazette of Republika Srpska no.11/95). The ministries responsible for the protection of heritage properties are the Federal Ministry of Culture and Sport (Federalno Ministarstvo kuture i sporta BiH) and the Ministry of Education and Culture of Republika Srpska (Ministarstvo prosvjete i kulture Republike Srpske) respectively.

At the cantonal level in particular, the legislation consists of a set of laws and by-laws per-taining to the way in which potential heritage properties are to be listed, the criteria for cate-gorizing heritage properties, heritage protection and the technical and personnel requirements for conducting archaeological investigations.

HUMAN REMAINS AND LEGISLATION

There is no legally defined line of demarcation between recent and archaeological remains. In practice, the 15th and 16th centuries AD are regarded as the limit for human remains to be regarded as archaeological, and any such remains are usually housed in the National Museum. Finds dating from after the 15th and 16th centuries are usually handed over to the local museum or left *in situ*.

Human remains, to the extent that they constitute archaeological finds, are therefore also regarded as heritage properties and are subject to the same legislation. Though the legislation does not explicitly refer to the way in which human remains are to be investigated, excavated, safeguarded and protected, it does govern archaeological investigations and the protection of archaeological finds, of which human remains form part.

It should be noted that in cases where the Commission to Preserve National Monuments (Komisija za Očuvanje Nacionalnih Spomenika), a state-level body, renders a decision designating an archaeological site as a national monument, in so doing it prescribes the measures for its protection and safekeeping, prohibits its export, and so on.

Under the terms of the basic provisions of the Regulations on the Technical and Personnel Requirements for Conducting Archaeological Investigations (Official Gazette of Sarajevo Canton no. 9/02; Službene novine Kantona Sarajevo), archaeological investigations may be conducted by natural persons and juristic entities of BH under the supervision of a qualified archaeologist, who should lead the investigation. Foreign natural persons and juristic entities may take part in archaeological investigations subject to the approval of the cantonal ministry responsible for culture. The cantonal heritage protection authority issues permits to conduct archaeological investigations for natural persons and juristic entities of BiH.

There is no requirement for an anthropologist to form part of the team in the case of archaeological investigations being conducted with a view to finding and identifying human remains. It is sufficient for the archaeological investigations to be led by a graduate in archaeology with experience in the organization and execution of archaeological investigations, acquired either in the field or from an appropriate specialist course.

The lead archaeologist maintains a daily works log in which all details of the investigative works are recorded, including the finding of any human remains. The natural person or juristic entity conducting the archaeological investigations is required to submit to the relevant ministry a report setting out the full results of the investigations.

Under the terms of the Heritage Protection Law applicable in Sarajevo Canton (Official Gazette of Sarajevo Canton no. 2/00), a listed heritage property may not be destroyed, altered or impaired, in whole or in part, nor may it be removed from the country without permission. With the exception of contemporary art works, heritage properties may not be removed permanently from the country. They may, however, be taken abroad temporarily, subject to a permit from the relevant ministry, which will specify the terms and conditions of their removal and the obligations of the owner of the property or any third party to whom the property has been entrusted for safekeeping, including, in particular, a guarantee that the property will be returned to the canton within the specified time, and will determine whether there is some other relevant reason for the removal of the property from the country. Before deciding whether to issue a permit, the ministry will obtain the opinion of the Cantonal Institute, which will set out the conditions for the removal of the property, the time limit for its return, and the obligations of the owner of the property or any third party to whom it has been entrusted for safekeeping.

Human remains and other archaeological finds uncovered on an archaeological site are to be left *in situ* after being recorded, unless they are to be subjected to further examination. In some cases, such remains are submitted for safekeeping and study to a local or national museum, depending on the type, age and importance of the finds.

Anthropological analysis of exhumed war victims

One of the consequences of the 1992–95 war in BH is the very large number of missing persons. 'Missing persons' is a euphemism introduced after the war to denote all those who were killed during the war but whose bodies have yet to be found. The search for missing persons began immediately after the war, and will continue for several decades. Some 30,000 persons are believed to have gone missing in BH (ICMP 2009); of these, the mortal remains of more than 10,000 are still unaccounted for.

It has become clear that DNA analysis, though a crucial element in determining identity, is not in itself sufficient to provide a definitive identity for all these mortal remains. The principal reason is that so many bodies were disposed of in mass graves. In secondary and tertiary mass graves in particular – which are to be found all over BH but especially in relation to the genocide in Srebrenica – the remains are frequently commingled (Honig and Both 1997; Rohde 1998; Skinner *et al.* 2002). In such cases it is possible only to match the DNA profile of samples from bones or teeth with the DNA profile of blood samples provided by relatives. One problem of the DNA-led identification system are childless brothers, who can't be differentiated by DNA.

These are the main reasons for the need to resort in each case, notwithstanding a positive DNA match, to other methods in order to arrive at a positive, definitive and official identification for a given set of skeletal remains. Every fact that it is possible to ascertain must be taken into account (e.g., witness statements on the place and circumstances of death, statements by the family on personal effects and clothing), and a careful comparison between the ante-mortem and post-mortem data must be conducted (Sarajlic and Skulj, pers. comm. 2005–9; Yazedjian *et al.* 2005). The basic post-mortem element of this comparison is an anthropological analysis of the mortal remains that have been exhumed, to determine the biological profile (Klonowski 1997).

Legislation governing forensic cases

Every case of exhumation, autopsy and identification of war victims in BH represents the detection and evidence of war crimes. Until 2003, investigations fell within the jurisdiction of the courts and their investigating judges. Since 2003, when new Criminal Codes and Criminal Proceedings Codes were adopted, the public prosecutor's office has jurisdiction over the entire investigative process. This means that exhumation, autopsy and identification orders are issued by a prosecutor, with the prior agreement of a preliminary proceedings judge.

The legislation of BH recognizes only forensic scientists to be qualified for such work, meaning that anthropologists do not yet have a place in the legal procedures applicable to forensic cases. The Criminal Code provides legislation regarding autopsy and exhumation.

METHODS OF ANTHROPOLOGICAL ANALYSIS

In the first few post-war years, the basic parameters of the biological profile (sex, age and stature) were identified mainly using methods developed for the American population (Brooks 1955; Brooks and Suchey 1990; Bruzek 2002; Buikstra and Ubelaker 1994; Giles 1964; Giles and Eliot

1963; İşcan *et al.* 1984; Katz and Suchey 1986; Lamendin *et al.* 1992; Lovejoy *et al.* 1985; McKern and Stewart 1957; Phenice 1969; Pietrusewsky 2000; Scheuer and Black 2000; Trotter and Gleser 1952; Todd 1920; Webb and Suchey 1985). The analysis of several thousand cases of mortal remains revealed that these methods were unsuitable for the Bosnian population. Intensive work on the biological profile of skeletal remains revealed that the standards obtained from American and other populations did not provide the exact information on the biological profile that was required here. A great many cases were also found in which the morphology of certain skeletal elements displayed wide variations between estimated and actual age. Over the past decade, as a result, a series of studies have been conducted which have generated new standards for the Bosnian population for determining age, stature and bone length ratios for the upper and lower limbs in order to verify which bones belong to which individual (Cihlarž and Kešetović 1997a, 1997b, 1996–97; Djurić *et al.* 2007; Jantz *et al.* 2008; Kimmerle *et al.* 2008; Prince and Konigsberg 2008; Ross and Konigsberg 2002; Sarajlić 2006; Sarajlić and Cihlarž 2007; Sarajlić *et al.* 2006a, 2006b, 2006c; Schaefer and Black 2005; Simmons 1999; Simmons *et al.* 1999; Skulj 2008). Though standards specific to the Bosnian population have been generated, any anthropologist or pathologist engaged in identifying war victims must be extremely cautious, since practice to date has shown that it is very common for individuals in the Bosnian population to display variations from these standards (Sarajlić *et al.* 2006a; Sarajlić 2006; Skulj 2008). It should also be borne in mind that ante-mortem data may not be wholly reliable, given the circumstances, and also that bodies may have been moved more than once from one mass grave to another in an attempt to conceal war crimes, so that the victims' mortal remains are often commingled and badly damaged. Another possible obstacle to the identification of victims is that they constitute a large number of people from a small population group. Of the 30,000 missing persons, 27,000 (90 per cent) were men aged 14–90+, and of this 27,000, 90 per cent were aged between 20 and 40, giving some 25,000 missing persons with similar biological characteristics. This problem came to light when attempting to identify victims from Srebrenica without the assistance of DNA analysis (Komar 2003).

It should also be noted that the studies with proposed standards relate to the 'Balkan' population, where the observation groups included skeletal material from several population groups in ex-Yugoslavia (Djurić *et al.* 2007; Kimmerle *et al.* 2008; Prince and Konigsberg 2008; Ross and Konigsberg 2002). A revision of some of the proposed standards generated by these studies on the Bosnian population shows that they display certain inconsistencies as regards the determination of age (Sarajlić *et al.* 2006a; Sarajlić 2006; Simmons 1999; Skulj 2008). In our view, the Balkan population is a broad concept, within which Kosovars, Croats, Serbs and Bosnians cannot be regarded as a single population. Although these groups all belong to a limited geographical area, they derive historically from different groups or tribes (Malcolm 1995). The population of BH, like the others referred to, should therefore be regarded as a distinct group, to be studied as such.

Unfortunately, despite the huge number of identified mortal remains that could generate new anthropological standards specific to the Bosnian population, the pace and number of identifications simply do not allow sufficient time for pathologists and anthropologists to conduct further studies with an attempt to generate more accurate standards to assist in the identification of victims.

For stature calculation Trotter and Gleser (1952) and Sarajlić *et al.* (2006d) formulae and standards are used.

CONCLUSION

BH laws and legislations do not fully cover all aspects dealing with human remains (archaeological or forensic), but it can be anticipated that the government will work on improvements on this issue. The government slowly takes steps to deal with the issue of missing persons at a state level, rather than at the complex cantonal level. Furthermore, it has to be noted that the BH government, with all its governmental bodies (courts, ministries, educational institutions, etc.), is relatively young and on a transitional path. This can be a factor that slows the legal processes related to archaeology and anthropology. It is inevitable that forensic anthropology practices have greatly improved in the development of policies and especially the generation of population-specific standards in the past decade. This has come as a result of constant dealing with the excavation and identification of huge numbers of missing persons from the Bosnian war. Moreover, it is foreseeable that, as the BH state continues to strengthen, it will improve the legislation regulating archaeology and anthropology.

LAWS AND BY-LAWS

For ease of reference, a list of the laws and by-laws relating to the cultural heritage in various parts of BH is given below:

Legislation of Bosnia and Herzegovina

- Rules on the Safekeeping and Use of Technical, Photographic and other Documentation and Records on Protected Properties of the Institute for the Protection and Use of the Cultural, Historical and Natural Heritage of BiH (Official Gazette of BiH no. 3/97–21).

Legislation of the Federation of BiH

- Law on the Protection and Use of the Cultural, Historical and Natural Heritage (Official Gazette of SR BiH nos. 20/85 and 12/87).

Legislation of Republika Srpska

- Law on Cultural Properties (Official Gazette of Republika Srpska no.11/95)

Cantonal legislation in the Federation of Bosnia and Herzegovina

- Sarajevo Canton: Heritage Protection Law (Official Gazette of SC, no. 2/00)
- Una-Sana Canton: Heritage Protection Law (Official Gazette of USC, no. 3/04)
- Zenica-Doboj Canton: Heritage Protection Law (Official Gazette of ZDC, no. 2/00)
- Western Herzegovina Canton: Law on the Protection and Use of the Heritage (Official Gazette of WHC, no. 6/99)
- Herzegovina-Neretva Canton: HNC Heritage Protection Law (Official Gazette of HNC, no. 2/06)
- Sava Valley Canton: The 1985 Law of SRBiH applies
- Tuzla Canton: The 1985 Law of SRBiH applies
- Bosna-Drina Canton: The 1985 Law of SRBiH applies
- Central Bosnia Canton: The 1985 Law of SRBiH applies
- Herceg-Bosna Canton: The 1985 Law of SRBiH applies

Criminal code

For further information concerning the criminal code of Bosnia and Herzegovina see:

- Criminal Code of Bosnia and Herzegovina: Official Gazette of BiH nos. 3/03, 32/03, 37/03, 61/04, 30/05, 53/06, 55/06 and 32/07.
- Criminal Proceedings Law of Bosnia and Herzegovina: Official Gazette of BiH nos. 3/03, 32/03, 36/03, 26/04, 63/04, 13/05, 48/05, 46/06, 76/06, 29/07, 32/07 and 58/08.

Note: identical laws have also been adopted in the Federation of Bosnia and Herzegovina, Republika Srpska and Brčko District.

USEFUL CONTACTS

Bosnia and Herzegovina Commission to Preserve National Monuments. Website: www.aneks8komisija.com.ba (accessed 7 July 2010).

Ministry of Culture and Sport of Federation of Bosnia and Herzegovina. Website: www.fmks.gov.ba (accessed 7 July 2010).

Republic Institute for Protection of the Cultural, Historical and Natural Heritage of the Republica Srpska. Website: www.heritagers.org (accessed 7 July 2010).

Institute for the Protection of the Cultural, Historical and Natural Heritage of Canton Sarajevo. Website: www.spomenici-sa.ba (accessed 7 July 2010).

Institute of Forensic Medicine and Forensic Toxicology, Medical Faculty, University of Sarajevo. Website: www.forensic-sarajevo.org (accessed 7 July 2010).

International Commission of Missing Persons (ICMP). Website: www.ic-mp.org (accessed 7 July 2010).

International Association for Paleodontology. Website: www.paleodontology.com (accessed 7 July 2010).

ACKNOWLEDGEMENTS

We would like to thank to Lidija Fekeža from the National Museum of Bosnia and Herzegovina for valuable suggestions and helpful comments.

BIBLIOGRAPHY

Brooks, S. and Suchey, J.M. (1990) 'Skeletal age determination based on the os pubis: a comparison of the Ascadi-Nemeskeri and Suchey-Brooks Methods', *Human Evolution*, 5: 227–38.

Brooks, S.T. (1955) 'Skeletal age at death: reliability of cranial and pubic age indicators', *American Journal of Physical Anthropology*, 13: 567–97.

Bruzek, J. (2002) 'A method for visual determination of sex, using the human hip bone', *American Journal of Physical Anthropology*, 117: 157–68.

Buikstra, J.E. and Ubelaker, D.H. (eds) (1994) *Standards for Data Collection from Human Skeletal Remains*, Fayetteville, AR: Arkansas Archeological Survey Research Series No. 44.

Cihlarž, Z. and Kešetović, R. (1996–97) 'Sudsko-medicinska ekspertiza posmrtnih ostataka žrtava Srebrenice u periodu', *Zbornik radova*, 1996–97: 278–82.

——(1997a) 'Sex determination by discriminant analysis of human crania' *Medicinski Žurnal*, 3: 16–24.

——(1997b) 'Sex estimation of human calvaria using morphological characters', *Acta Medica Saliniana*, 26: 61–64.

Djurić, M., Djonić, D., Nikolić, S., *et al.* (2007) 'Evaluation of the Suchey-Brooks method for aging skeletons in the Balkans', *Journal of Forensic Science*, 52: 21–23.

Giles, E. (1964) 'Sex determination by discriminant function analysis of the mandible', *American Journal of Physical Anthropology*, 22: 129–35.

Giles, E. and Elliot, O. (1963) 'Sex determination by discriminant function analysis of crania', *American Journal of Physical Anthropology*, 21: 53–68.

Honig, J.W. and Both, N. (1997) *Srebrenica: Record of a War Crime*, New York: Penguin Books.

ICMP (2009), International Commission on Missing Persons, Fact Sheets. Available online at www.ic-mp. org/wp-content/uploads/2009/02/fact-sheet-eng.pdf (accessed 5 July 2009).

İşcan, M.Y. (1984) 'Metamorphosis at the sternal rib end: a new method to estimate age at death in white males', *American Journal of Physical Anthropology*, 65: 147–56.

İşcan, M.Y., Loth, S.R. and Wright, R.K. (1984) 'Age estimation from the rib by phase analysis: white males', *Journal of Forensic Science*, 29: 1094–104.

Jantz, R.L., Kimmerle, E.H. and Baraybar, J.P. (2008) 'Sexing and stature estimation criteria for Balkan populations', *Journal of Forensic Science*, 53: 601–5.

Katz, D. and Suchey, J.M. (1986) 'Age determination of the male os pubis', *American Journal of Physical Anthropology*, 69: 427–35.

Kimmerle, E.H., Prince, D.A. and Berg, G.E. (2008) 'Inter-observer variation in methodologies involving the pubic symphysis, sternal ribs, and teeth', *Journal of Forensic Science*, 53: 594–600.

Kimmerle, E.H., Konigsberg, L.W., Jantz, R.L., *et al.* (2008) 'Analysis of age-at-death estimation through the use of pubic symphyseal data', *Journal of Forensic Science*, 53: 558–68.

Klonowski, E.E. (1997) *Uputstva za ekshumaciju i identifikaciju ljudskog skeleta*, Sarajevo: PHR.

Komar, D. (2003) 'Lessons from Srebrenica: the contributions and limitations of physical anthropology in identifying victims of War Crimes', *Journal of Forensic Sciences*, 48: 1–4.

Lamendin, H., Baccino, E., Humbert, J.F., *et al.* (1992) 'A simple techinque for age determination in adult corpses: the two criteria dental method', *Journal of Forensic Science*, 37: 1373–79.

Lovrincević, A. and Mikić, Ž. (1989) *Atlas of Osteopathologic Changes of the Historical Yugoslav Populations*, Sarajevo: Svjetlost.

Lovejoy, C.O., Meindl, R., Pryzbeck, T.R., *et al.* (1985) 'Chronological metamorphosis of the auricular surface of the ilium: a new method for the determination of adult skeletal age at death', *American Journal of Physical Anthropology*, 68: 15–28.

McKern, T.W. and Stewart, T.D. (1957) *Skeletal Age Changes in Young American Males Analyzed from the Standpoint of Age Identification*, United States Army: Headquarters Quartermaster Research and Development Command, Technical Report EP-45.

Malcolm, N. (1995) *Povijest Bosne, Kratki Pregled*, Sarajevo: Dani Sarajevo.

Mikić, Ž. (1981) *Stanje i problemi fizicke antropologije u Jugoslaviji – praistorijski periodi*, Sarajevo: Akademija nauka i umjetnosti BiH, Centar za Balkanološka ispitivanja.

Phenice, T.W. (1969) 'A newly developed visual method of sexing the os pubis', *American Journal of Physical Anthropology*, 30: 297–301.

Pietrusewsky, M. (2000) 'Metric analysis of skeletal remains: methods and applications', in M.A. Katzenberg and S.R. Saunders (eds) *Biological Anthropology of the Human Skeleton*, New York: Wiley-Liss.

Prince, D.A., Kimmerle, E.H. and Konigsberg, L.W. (2008) 'A Bayesian approach to estimate skeletal age-at-death utilizing dental wear', *Journal of Forensic Science*, 53: 588–93.

Prince, D.A. and Konigsberg, L.W. (2008) 'New formulae for estimating age-at-death in the Balkans utilizing Lamendin's dental technique and Bayesian analysis', *Journal of Forensic Science*, 53: 578–87.

Radimsky, V. (1891) *Prehistoricka nalazišta*, Sarajevo: Zemaljski Muzej.

Rohde, D. (1998) *Endgame: The Betrayal and Fall of Srebrenica, Europe's Worst Massacre Since World War II*, Boulder, CO: Westview Press.

Ross, A.H. and Konigsberg, L.W. (2002) 'New formulae for estimating stature in the Balkans', *Journal of Forensic Science*, 47: 165–67.

Sarajlić, N. (2006) 'Procjena starosti bosanske populacije muškog spola na osnovu faznih promjena sternalnih krajeva rebara', *Medicinski Arhiv*, 60: 343–46.

Sarajlić, N. and Cihlarž, Z. (2007) 'Diverse stature estimation formulae applied to a Bosnian population', *Bosnian Journal of Basic Medical Sciences*, 7: 136–39.

Sarajlić, N., Cihlarž, Z., Klonowski, E.E., *et al.* (2006a) 'Two criteria dental aging method applied on Bosnian population: formulae for each tooth group versus one formula for all teeth', *Bosnian Journal of Basic Medical Sciences*, 6: 78–83.

——(2006b) 'Stature estimation for Bosnian male population', *Bosnian Journal of Basic Medical Sciences*, 6: 62–67.

——(2006c) 'Odnosi dužina dugih kostiju gornjih i donjih ekstremiteta', *Acta Medica Saliniana*, 35: 71–76.

——(2006d) 'Diverse stature estimation formulae applied to a Bosnian population', *Bosnian Journal of Basic Medical Sciences*, 7: 136–39.

Schaefer, M.C. and Black, S.M. (2005) 'Comparison of ages of epiphyseal union in North American and Bosnian skeletal material', *Journal of Forensic Science*, 50: 777–84.

Scheuer, L. and Black, S. (2000) *Developmental Juvenile Osteology*, London: Academic Press.

Simmons, T. (1999) 'Revising age estimation standards for a Bosnian forensic population: clavicle, rib and pubic symphysis', *Paper presented at the American Association of Physical Anthropology Annual Meeting, Columbus, Ohio*.

Simmons, T., Tuco, V., Kešetović, R., *et al.* (1999) 'Evaluating Age Estimation in a Bosnian Forensic Population: "Age-at-stage" via Probit Analysis', *Paper presented at the Annual Meeting of the American Academy of Forensic Sciences, Orlando, Florida*.

Skinner, M.F., York, H.P. and Connor, M.A. (2002) 'Postburial disturbance of graves in Bosnia-Herzegovina', in W.D. Haglund and M.H. Sorg (eds) *Advances in Forensic Taphonomy: Method, Theory, and Archaeological Perspectives*, Boca Raton, FL: CRC Press.

Skulj, S. (2008) 'Skeletal methods for ageing the pelvic girdle in a Bosnian male population: analysis of Suchey-Brooks method on pubic symphyses and the Lovejoy Method on auricular surfaces', Unpublished MSc Thesis, University of Central Lancashire.

Todd, T.W. (1920) 'Age change in the pubic bone I: the male white pubis', *American Journal of Physical Anthropology*, 3: 467–70.

Trotter, M. and Gleser, G.C. (1952) 'Estimation of stature from long bones of American Whites and Negroes', *American Journal of Physical Anthropology*, 10: 463–514.

Webb, P.O. and Suchey, J. (1985) 'Epiphyseal union of the anterior iliac crest and medial clavicle in a modern multiracial sample of American males and females', *American Journal of Physical Anthropology*, 68: 457–66.

Yazedjian, L.N., Kesetovic, R., Boza-Arliotti, A., *et al.* (2005) 'The Importance of Using Traditional Anthropological Methods in a DNA-Led Identification System', *Paper presented at the Annual Meeting of the American Academy of Forensic Sciences, New Orleans, Louisiana*.

Zukanović, A. (2007) 'Paleodontology in Bosnia and Herzegovina – history and perspectives', *Bulletin of the International Association for Paleodontology*, 1: 18–20.

Bulgaria/БЪЛГАРИЯ

Bisserka Gaydarska

INTRODUCTION: A BRIEF HISTORY AND CURRENT STATE OF PHYSICAL ANTHROPOLOGY IN BULGARIA

It was until very recently that Eastern Europe was considered as the backyard of Europe. The dramatic changes in many East European countries, and in Bulgaria in particular, in the last two decades should not delude us about the political legacy of the recent past. This is not the place to discuss the particularities of the political regimes in Bulgaria after the Second World War, but it should be made absolutely clear that the development of any professional discipline cannot be divorced from its contemporary leading ideology, if is it to be understood correctly. This is particularly valid for the social sciences and humanities, with which *physical anthropology* (henceforth '*anthropology*') is affiliated by the nature of its source materials. This chapter aims to give a flavour of the development of anthropology in Bulgaria, the anthropological and archaeological practice, and provides recommendations for legislation and best practice. While in-depth analysis of the current state of Bulgarian anthropology is much needed, this chapter has the less ambitious task of presenting a short critical assessment.

Anthropology in Bulgaria has a history of 136 years, a fact which is quite impressive for a small country that only obtained its sovereignty in 1878 as a result of one of the 19th-century Russo–Turkish Wars. Not surprisingly, the first anthropologists involved with Bulgarian skeletal material (mainly skulls) were foreigners (e.g., Scheiber 1873; Virchow 1886). The first professional Bulgarian anthropologist was Krum Dronchilov (Yordanov 1999: 9) who, together with Stephan Vatev, is considered to be the founder of Bulgarian anthropology in the 1920s (Boev 1958: 153). The next 35 years saw the establishment of the new field, with attempts at theoretical advances and some measurement of the contemporary population, but with primary attention paid to the development of palaeoanthropology.

The political regime established in Bulgaria after the Second World War was highly ideological, and the imposition of politically driven agenda as research priorities in all public spheres was inevitable. For anthropology, such a priority was the linking of the ethnogenesis of the Bulgarians to the Slavs as the major component of the present anthropological type of the Bulgarian people (Boev 1958: 153). While following the official line to some extent or other in the majority of the investigations, the beneficial by-product of close examination of large amounts of skeletal material, from prehistory to the present day, cannot be underestimated. If the ideological message is filtered, there is much useful information in terms of measurements, different anthropological types, artificial skull deformation, trepanation, etc. State-funded research and the institutionalization of Bulgarian anthropology led to diversification and the creation of sub-disciplines such as morphology (dealing with the present population), statistics, the refinement of methodologies, serology, etc. Most importantly, it guaranteed the regular publication of investigations. As Figure 8.1 demonstrates, there was a flourishing period between 1970 and 1990. A good example of the quality of the research is the monograph written by Boev (1972) who systematized chronologically and spatially all the available palaeoanthropological data found to the south of the Danube, and related it to various historical (e.g., written sources) and archaeological (e.g., figurines, tomb decorations) sources in order to reconstruct a dynamic picture of local development, along with the influences of migration and diffusion. After the fall of the Berlin Wall, the decline in state funding is well reflected in the number of publications after 1990. Information about the development of anthropology in the last decade as measured by the number of publications is not easily available, a fact that clearly speaks for itself.[1]

The institutional basis of anthropology

The main institution currently responsible for performing all aspects of anthropological research in Bulgaria is the Institute of Experimental Morphology and Anthropology with Museum, at the Bulgarian Academy of Sciences or IEMAM-BAS (IEMAM 2008). The institute (formerly known as the Institute for Morphology) was founded in 1953, while the Museum, exhibiting a group of skeletons (including some palaeopathological specimens) and a series of skull reconstructions from past populations dating from the Neolithic to the National Uprising of 1876, is a new achievement that opened only in 2007. The section in IEMAM-BAS under the name

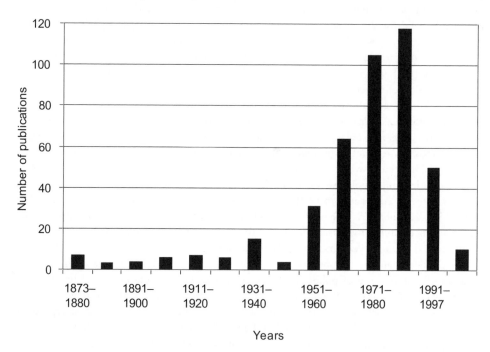

Figure 8.1 Publications on Bulgarian palaeoanthropology (1873–2008)

'Anthropology' conducts the anthropological investigations. The institute has had a fluctuating number of associated members over the years. A handful of specialists, mainly with medical backgrounds and some with degrees in biology, were involved in all aspects of analysis, including the study of the archaeological skeletal material as well as of the contemporary population by employing measurements. The peaks and troughs of the work of the few devoted palaeoanthropologists are evident from Figure 8.1. A recent epic effort of IEMAM-BAS, and in particular its anthropology section, was the publication of *Anthropology of the Bulgarian Population at the End of the 20th Century* (Yordanov 2006).

The second Bulgarian institution relevant to the present discussion is the National Institute of Archaeology and Museum, also at the Bulgarian Academy of Sciences (henceforth 'NIAM') (NIAM 2010). Among the different sections in NIAM, there is a group for interdisciplinary investigations that consists of archaeologists and specialists in archaeobotany, archaeozoology, geophysics and geodesy. Curiously, no human osteologist is employed either by this group or any other section of NIAM.

There are no formal agreements for cooperation between IEMAM and NIAM, and experience shows that arrangements are made either on a one-to-one basis (archaeologists approaching certain anthropologists) or according to preferential choices among the anthropologists.

Education and training

With very few exceptions, all of the practising anthropologists in Bulgaria have a medical or biological background. There is no tradition of physical anthropologists receiving any formal training or education in archaeology or history. Thus, their non-medical conclusions should be ideologically filtered or approached with care, especially if used to underpin the claims of leading archaeologists that are not always widely shared.

Since 1992, a single Honours degree course in Archaeology has been offered at Sofia University, with courses soon to follow at universities such as Veliko Turnovo University and the New Bulgarian University. At present, archaeology is taught in at least five universities. Part of the curriculum is a one- or two-semester course in physical anthropology, consisting of 45 hours of lectures and practical classes (for details of the curriculum, see www.clio.uni-sofia.bg/BG/pass/Antropologiya.pdf).

A general comparison between degree programmes in Britain and Bulgaria shows a possibility for progression from the first to the third year in Britain, in terms of the analysis of human skeletal remains, which is completely lacking in Bulgaria. A specialized Master's degree in human skeletal analysis in the UK is a requirement for working as an osteoarchaeologist or to go on to do a PhD in the subject. The undergraduate curriculum, with the opportunity for Master's-level specialization found at such universities as Durham, Sheffield, Bradford, Southampton and University College London in the UK is so far unparalleled in Bulgaria. This is probably why there is only one practising anthropologist in Bulgaria whose first degree was awarded in archaeology. From the seven PhDs awarded between 2003 and 2008 under the subject 'Anthropology',[2] there is only one archaeologist (Virtual Info Centre for PhD Students 2010), whose publication record reveals as much primary analysis of skeletal material as analytical interest (e.g., in mortality rates).

There are two handbooks in Bulgarian that are specifically targeted to aid archaeologists in their work with human bones. The first was published in 1996; the second makes some minor changes to the first edition and was published in 1999 (Yordanov 1996, 1999). Both can be summarized as modified and adapted versions of Bass's (1987) manual. While there are few ways of introducing the basics of human osteology, the two books suffice for their purpose and are a useful guide of what to do and what not to do during the excavation of human remains. However, they fail to provide up-to-date advances in physical anthropology for archaeologists that, even in the mid-to-late 1990s, were numerous and diverse and covered a wide area of practical and theoretical issues, including recording and recovering techniques, aspects of health and diet of past populations, dating and social interpretation (the most obvious examples are Ortner and Aufderheide 1991; Bush and Zvelebil 1991; Roberts and Manchester 1995; Larsen 1997; and Mays 1998, to mention but a few).

ARCHAEOLOGICAL HUMAN REMAINS AND LEGISLATION

Archaeological legislation

In order to perform any type of archaeological field investigation in Bulgaria, a permit issued by NIAM-BAS is required. After the end of each season, a full set of all the field documentation should be deposited in the NIAM-BAS archive. The regulations have tightened in recent years, so that an archaeologist may be refused a permit if he/she has failed to provide documentation from previous excavations (Ministry of Culture of Republic of Bulgaria 2010). Apart from NIAM-BAS, practising archaeologists are employed in more than 20 regional museums, the National History Museum, the National Institute for the Protection of Cultural Heritage, the Institute of Thracology-BAS and several Universities offering archaeology as a subject.

Depending on the scale and available funding of archaeological expeditions, the usual archaeological practice in Bulgaria is to hire workers to undertake manual labour and excavate with shovels and spades. Teams consisting only of professional archaeologists and students in archaeology are rare in the case of excavations; such teams are more readily associated with field surveys. Usually, archaeology students and professional archaeologists supervise and work alongside the local workers. However, it should be pointed out that, in large-scale rescue excavations, it is not uncommon for graves to be excavated by workers. Naturally, an on-the-spot assessment of the individuals' ability is made and only the best-trained and experienced workers are given such delicate tasks. One positive example for the workability of such arrangements is the prehistoric cemetery near the village of Durankulak (Todorova 2002), comprising 1,204 graves. Without an extra workforce of village labourers and school-children, the excavation would have been delayed by over ten years. If such a practice seems unacceptable for modern ethics in archaeology (Mays *et al.* 2004: 2), what can one say for the justification of the absence of an anthropologist during the excavation of skeletal remains (Yordanov 1999)? The actual wording in this amended good practice guide by Bass (1987) is 'in *some cases* the participation of a specialist anthropologist during archaeological investigations is compulsory' (Yordanov 1999: 153, present author's emphasis). Ultimately, the presence of an anthropologist during fieldwork is an exception and only usually found in sites of great significance, such as the famous Varna cemetery (Yordanov and Marinov 1978; Ivanov 1991; Higham *et al.* 2007); or where there is some personal agreement between the archaeological director and the anthropologist. No matter how disgraceful that may be in terms of ethics, it is explicable in terms of practicality since, in 2007 alone, for example, at least 65 sites containing human remains were excavated (AOR 2007). While it is inconceivable that an anthropologist would be present throughout each of the projects, some flexible scheme including visits to the site may be planned ahead, at least for sites where human remains are very likely to be encountered, such as in prehistoric barrows or mediaeval churches. Last, but not least, if the presence of an anthropologist proves to be impossible, mutual guarantees between archaeologists and anthropologists should ensure that the anthropological analysis will be performed in the future.

HUMAN REMAINS AND LEGISLATION

As already mentioned, there are no formal requirements or recommendations for excavating archaeological human remains, and there are only a few cases in which special arrangements should be made, such as in military or ethnic minority cemeteries.

In Bulgaria, as in other countries, the main principle in the excavation of human bones is to reveal the skeletal material within its archaeological context and record it fully before lifting. Afterwards, the human remains are treated in one of the following ways in Bulgaria:

- They are taken to an institution for further investigation. Sometimes they are kept in local museums, but most often they are taken to IEMAM-BAS;
- They are taken to an institution and then re-buried at a later date. This is usually the case for multiple burials in mediaeval churches and churchyards, or when rescue excavations are undertaken; or
- They are reburied immediately after excavation.

Reburials are usually performed in order to save space in local museums. Apparently, Orthodox priests attend some of these events. While the lack of anthropological studies as a result of immediate reburial lies with the professional conscience of the archaeologist responsible for the entire project, it should be said that the overall tendency is to seek anthropological analysis; and this is reflected in the fact that there are no important sites that have been left unstudied. A lack of resources and relevant forward planning are to be blamed for partial or incomplete anthropological study of skeletal remains. It is interesting to observe how many such cases there are in Bulgaria from information that can only be obtained from the archives of IEMAM-BAS and NIAM-BAS.

Ethical considerations

There are several documents that sanction and regulate who can perform archaeological excavations, how should the investigation be conducted, what should be done with immovable features and monuments and movable artefacts, where should artefacts be stored, etc. (Ministry of Culture of Republic of Bulgaria 2010). None of these documents mentions human bones.

One of the positive spin-offs of the opening of the borders in the last two decades, which has improved Bulgarian exposure to archaeological practice in other countries, is the gradual demand to introduce ethics into the excavation and post-excavation stages, as well as ethics in relation to the treatment of human bones. Nowadays, many Bulgarian archaeologists are taking good care of skeletal material and are actively looking for relevant experts to undertake anthropological research. It is already recognized that anthropological research is as important as any other type of archaeological study.

The professional code of practice (if such exists) of Bulgarian anthropologists is not publicly available; and, more to the point, one has never been formally communicated to the archaeological community.

Most of the excavated bones studied at IEMAM-BAS have been stored in the attic of the institute building,[3] where they were sorted according to individual graves and cemeteries in inadequate or inappropriate storage conditions. With the older excavated material, the paper containers in some cases did not survive the challenge of time; in others the information written on the bags and boxes did not survive. However, the long-planned concept of the present director of IEMAM-BAS for the creation of a national 'ossuary', a storage-place for the human remains of past populations, is close to realization, at which point we should expect great improvements in the storage conditions of human bones after excavation.

Of the many practical and ethical issues raised in the above account, priority is given to three major area: training, legislation and context.

Professionals with relevant training

It is obvious that there are not enough qualified specialists in the field of physical anthropology in Bulgaria. There are no such specialists in NIAM-BAS, while each of the specialists in IEMAM-BAS has a very tight schedule. In addition to the lack of a sustained research agenda for palaeoanthropology in the latter institution, there are very few young people joining the 'Anthropology' section of IEMAM-BAS, and even fewer who take the issues of palaeoanthropology at heart. As a consequence of the political and social situation in the last 20 years, the recent activities of IEMAM-BAS are angled more towards PR, to win publicity and to save the institute, and looking for popularity as much as basic science. While attracting public interest in the achievements of anthropology should be welcomed, it should not cast a shadow over crucial unsolved issues: the incorporation of all excavated bones of past populations in a national ossuary, an understaffed cadre of specialists, the modernization of equipment and the updating of methods and interpretations.

The recruitment of young people from different backgrounds, rather than only medical graduates, and their special training as anthropologists, should become a priority of both archaeologists and anthropologists. An increase in formal employment opportunities for anthropologists in each institution involved in archaeological studies (the above-mentioned museums and institutes) would be of benefit to anthropology as well as archaeology. Last, but not least, post-doctoral qualification and education abroad will secure a regular update of the most recent methodological advances and leading-edge research.

Legislation and standards

Another very necessary change is to standardize Bulgarian legislation, creating a code of ethics and professional practice in accordance with European standards. That would also involve changes in attitude towards excavated human remains and a re-thinking and re-structuring of present anthropological and archaeological practice – a process that may take some time to materialize.

A first step in this direction is a better coordination between archaeologists and anthropologists, which would lead to the involvement of anthropologists from the very beginning of the fieldwork, where recommendations can be provided with regard to correct excavation, storage and future study of the remains. Formal guidance for best practice of joint archaeo-anthropological fieldwork and further studies should be created following well established and recognized examples from abroad, such as BABAO (British Association of Biological Anthropology and Osteoarchaeology). A key role in the sense can be played by the Bulgarian Anthropological Society with more active promotion of its members' expertise.

Bulgarian anthropology in a modern context

There is always the dilemma of whether to assess a particular aspect of scientific development in the context of European or world development of the subject, or to emphasize its internal development, taking all local particularities into consideration. If the first stance is taken,

Bulgarian physical anthropology is far behind the present European standards in legislation, methodology, research potential of the study of human remains, social interpretations, etc. While, in other European countries, old data and interpretations are re-visited and scrutinized (e.g., the famous example of the Worth Park burial of a 'rape victim'), there seems to be no urge to do the same in Bulgaria. On the contrary, people continue to build on old and unchallenged theories and practice. If the second view is taken, the development and present state of Bulgarian physical anthropology does not differ much from the fate of the majority of other disciplines, whether academic or practical (e.g., biology or medicine, but especially archaeology). Building on a good pre-Second World War tradition (see Cholakov 1998) and relying on state funding during the Cold War (see Figure 8.1), the achievements of Bulgarian anthropologists were modest but perfectly suited for the purposes of contemporary archaeological practice. While both anthropology and archaeology have undergone significant intellectual and practical changes in the last two or three decades, these two fields remained broadly similar in Bulgaria. That is probably why at present more and more young Bulgarian archaeologists are using the expertise of foreign anthropologists (see, e.g., McSweeney 2008).

One way of breaking the present deadlock in Bulgarian anthropology is to turn towards project-based research that is funded by foreign sources. Such a turn would involve a radical change in the research agenda of both NIAM and IEMAM, which should not be considered as a threat but rather as a new opportunity for development. A crucial element in such development is the involvement of research students who, in the process of their professional training, can address multiple aspects of the still much unexplored potential of Bulgarian anthropological data.

METHODS OF ANTHROPOLOGICAL ANALYSIS

Apart from international recommendations (e.g., Buikstra and Ubelaker 1994), a reference textbook used in Bulgaria is Yordanov's publication (1999) which basically summarizes the methods described in Bass (1987).

CONCLUSION

This article does not seek to 'name and shame' the archaeologists and anthropologists who, willingly or unwillingly, have contributed to the present state of Bulgarian anthropology. It has the much more important task of raising awareness among archaeologists and anthropologists alike, and hopefully triggering some relevant response from people in positions of authority. There can be no doubt that change is needed, and that it will be a long and painful process. A key starting point to such a change is the introduction of legislation in accordance with modern ethical and research standards. The expansion the institutional base of anthropological research and especially the attraction of more young people (with different backgrounds, but preferably archaeologists) are two further crucial steps towards the transformation and modernization of Bulgarian anthropology.

ACKNOWLEDGEMENTS

I am indebted to Tatiana Stefanova, Petar Zidarov and Nikola Theodossiev for providing basic references and information, without which this chapter would not have been possible. Special thanks to Becky Gowland for her valuable advice on important issues of physical anthropology in Britain and her comments on earlier drafts. As always, I am grateful to John for his support and re-assurance each time I am faced with the painstaking effort of assessing the research situation in my homeland.

NOTES

1 Information for the last column in Figure 8.1 was found on the IEMAM-BAS official website, and it is likely the ten titles (only four of which are related to palaeoanthropology) for the last decade are far from an exhaustive list. However, I have decided to include this data since it reveals an important pattern of overall neglect of the role of modern technology and information that ultimately results in the incompatibility of maybe otherwise good Bulgarian anthropologists. In this particular case, very little is needed: an update (the most recent publication is from 2004), and links to more detailed bibliography.
2 The Bulgarian system of awarding a PhD is centralized, and the on-line database contains information from 1962 onwards. The very few PhDs listed under the subject of 'Anthropology' is indicative of the general lack of interest in that field, but may also mean that such a subject was differentiated in the last two decades and that practising anthropologists have degrees in other subjects.
3 There is a discrepancy between the electronically-published interview with Professor Yordanov in 2008 (www.duma.bg/2008/0408/010408/obshtestvo/ob-9.html), in which the word 'ossuary' is mentioned, and the reference to an existing 'ossuary' on the web page of the new Museum of Anthropology (www.iema.bas.bg/MuseumHistory.html).

BIBLIOGRAPHY

AOR (2007) *Arheologicheski otkritia i razkopki prez 2007*, Sofia: NIAM-BAS.
Bass, W.M. (1987) *Human Osteology: A Laboratory and Field Manual*, 3rd edn, Columbia, Mo: Missouri Archaeological Society.
Boev, P. (1958) 'Sostoianie antropologicheskoi nauki v Narodnoi Respublike Bolgarii', *Sovetskaya Etnografia*, 1: 153–57.
——(1972) *Die Rassentypen der Balkanhalbinsel und der Ostagaischen Insel-welt*, Sofia: BAS.
Buikstra, J.E. and Ubelaker, D.H. (eds) (1994) *Standards for Data Collection from Human Skeletal Remains, Proceedings of a Seminar at The Field Museum of Natural History*, Fayetteville, Ar: Arkansas Archeological Survey Research Series no. 44.
Bush, H. and Zvelebil, M. (1991) *Health in Past Societies*, BAR (International Series) 567, Oxford: Tempus Reparatum.
Cholakov, S. (1998) *Bibliografia na bulgarskata paleoantropologia*, Sofia: Agato.
Higham, T., Chapman, J., Slavchev, V., et al. (2007) 'New perspectives on the Varna cemetery (Bulgaria) – AMS dates and social implications', *Antiquity*, 81: 640–54.
IEMAM (2008) *Institute of Experimental Morphology and Anthropology with Museum*. Available online at www.iema.bas.bg (accessed 27 March 2010).
Ivanov, I. (1991) 'Der Bestattungsritus in der chalkolitischen Nekropole von Varna (mit einem Katalog der wichstigsten Gräber)', in J. Lichardus (ed.) *Die Kupferzeit als historische Epoche*, Saarbrücken: Saarland Museum.
Larsen, C.S. (1997) *Bioarchaeology: Interpreting Human Behaviour from the Human Skeleton*, Cambridge: Cambridge University Press.
McSweeney, K. (2008) 'The human remains from Tell Provadia-Solnitsata', in V. Nikolov (ed.) *Provadia-Solinitsata Prehistoric Salt-Production Center. The 2005–2007 Excavation Seasons*, Sofia: National Institute of Archaeology and Museum.
Mays, S. (1998) *The Archaeology of Human Bones*, London: Routledge.
Mays, S, Brickley, M and Dodwell, N. (2004) *Human Bones from Archaeological Sites: Guidelines for producing assessment documents and analytical reports*, Centre for Archaeology Guidelines, London: English Heritage/BABAO.

Ministry of Culture of Republic of Bulgaria (2010) *Home*. Available online at http://mc.government.bg/ page.php?p=141& s = 142& sp = 0& t = 0& z = 0 (accessed 27 March 2010).

NIAM (2010) *National Institute of Archaeology and Museum*. Available online at www.niam.bg (accessed 27 March 2010).

Ortner, D.J. and Aufderheide, A.C. (1991) *Human Paleopathology: Current Syntheses and Future Options*, Washington, DC: Smithsonian Institution Press.

Roberts, C. and Manchester, K. (1995) *The Archaeology of Disease*, 2nd edn, Gloucester: Sutton.

Scheiber, I. (1873) 'Tabelle mit Massen von 5 Bulgarien Schadeln', *Verh*, 94–97.

Todorova, H. (ed.) (2002) *Durankulak Band II. Die prähistorischen Gräberfelder*, Sofia: Anubis.

Taylor, T. (1993) 'Conversations with Leo Klejn', *Current Anthropology*, 34: 723–35.

Virchow, K. (1886) 'Anthropologie der Bulgaren', *Verh*, I: 112.

Virtual Info Centre for PhD Students 2010 *Home*. Available online at http://phd-center.bvu-bg.eu/index. php?Cmd=searchzasht (accessed 27 March 2010).

Yordanov, Y. (1996) *Naruchnik po antropologia za arheolozi*, Sofia: Sv. Kliment Ohridski.

——(1999) *Prakticheska antropologia za arheolozi*, Sofia: Dios.

——(ed.) (2006) *Antropologia na naselenieto na Bulgaria v kraia na XX vek (vuzrastova grupa 30–40 godini)*, Sofia: Akademichno izdatelstvo Profesor Marin Drinov.

Yordanov, Y. and Marinov, G. (1978) 'Antropologichesko prouchvane na kostnia material ot rannohalkolitni grobove do Varna', *Izvestia na Narodnia muzei Varna*, XIV: 94–103.

Croatia/Hrvatska

Mario Šlaus, Mario Novak and Marin Vodanović

INTRODUCTION: A BRIEF HISTORY AND CURRENT STATUS OF PHYSICAL ANTHROPOLOGY IN CROATIA

The beginnings of bioarchaeological research in Croatia are related to the palaeoanthropological studies carried out by Dragutin Gorjanović Kramberger at the end of the 19th and the beginning of the 20th century (Gorjanović-Kramberger 1899, 1906, 1913). His analysis of the Neanderthal skeletal material recovered from Hušnjakovo brdo near Krapina significantly contributed to the acceptance of the existence of fossil man, and thus, to the acceptance of the concept of the evolution of mankind. Gorjanović's multidisciplinary analysis of human, animal and stone artefacts recovered from Krapina were crucial, not only for the reconstruction of the anatomical features and the quality of life of the Neanderthal inhabitants of Croatia, but they also provided clues to some social characteristics of Neanderthal society. These analyses were part of the foundations of modern palaeoanthropology.

Bioarchaeological analyses of modern man in Croatia began after the Second World War with two major publications by Franjo Ivaniček. In these works Ivaniček presented the results of detailed palaeodemographic and craniometric analyses of the mediaeval sites of Bijelo Brdo (Ivaniček 1949) and Ptuj (Ivaniček 1951). Unfortunately these studies, although in many respects ahead of their time (for instance the anthropological analysis of the 11th–13th-century Bijelo Brdo site incorporated the results of animal bone and pollen analysis), were not noticed by the international scientific community, possibly because of the fact that they were written in Croatian. Twenty years later, Ivaniček's student Georgina Pilarić published several papers that focused on the craniometric characteristics of early mediaeval Croat populations (Pilarić 1967, 1968, 1969, 1974; Pilarić and Schwidetzky 1987).

A major qualitative and quantitative leap forward in Croatian physical anthropology and bioarchaeology began in the 1990s. It was enabled through the work of two extraordinary scientists: Pavao Rudan and Hubert Maver, who in 1977 founded both the Croatian Anthropological Society (Hrvatsko antropološko društvo), and the scientific journal *Collegium Antropologicum*. They organized numerous international scientific workshops including among them the annually held School of Biological Anthropology. Their work led to the founding of the first scientific and educational institution dedicated exclusively to anthropological research in Croatia: the Institute of Anthropology in Zagreb, established in 1992.

Today, bioarchaeological and physical anthropological analyses are performed in numerous Croatian scientific centres of excellence: the Institute of Anthropology, Department of Archaeology at the University of Zagreb; the Institute for Archaeology in Zagreb; the Department of Pathology and Forensic Medicine at the University of Split; the Department of Dental Anthropology at the School of Dental Medicine, University of Zagreb; and the Department of Archaeology at the Croatian Academy of Sciences and Arts. The results of the research undertaken by these institutions are published in international peer-reviewed journals of the highest quality, such as the *American Journal of Physical Anthropology*, *Homo*, *International Journal of Osteoarchaeology* and the *Journal of Forensic Sciences*. Scientists actively engaged in this field of science in Croatia today are: Ž. Bedić, J. Boljunčić, H. Brkić, Z. Hincak, I. Janković, M. Novak, P. Rajić Šikanjić, M. Šlaus, M. Vodanović, and V. Vyroubal.

Besides the tireless work of Pavao Rudan and Hubert Maver, additional impetus to the development of bioarchaeology in Croatia was given by the establishment of three undergraduate and two postgraduate courses in bioarchaeology at the universities of Zagreb and Zadar, and the founding of the osteological collection of the Croatian Academy of Sciences and Arts. Readers interested in a more detailed review of the history of physical anthropology/bioarchaeology in Croatia can get a better appreciation of it in the works of Rajić Šikanjić (2005) and Šlaus (2006).

Physical anthropology/bioarchaeology in Croatia today

The leading centre of bioarchaeological research in Croatia today is the Department of Archaeology at the Croatian Academy of Sciences and Arts in Zagreb where four scientists (Ž. Bedić, V. Vyroubal, M. Novak and M. Šlaus) are actively engaged in bioarchaeological studies of Croatian archaeological populations. These researchers study a wide range of topics including demography (Šlaus 2000, 2002, 2006), subadult stress (Šlaus 2008a), infectious diseases (Šlaus 2006; Šlaus and Novak 2007), dental pathology (Šlaus 2002; Vodanović *et al.* 2005) and bone trauma (Šlaus 2008a; Šlaus and Novak 2006). A list of the archaeological sites in Croatia at which anthropological/bioarchaeological studies have been carried out is presented in Table 9.1.

Skeletal collections and databases

The osteological collection of the Department of Archaeology at the Croatian Academy of Arts and Sciences in Zagreb is the largest collection of human skeletal material in Croatia. It currently holds skeletal material from more than 37 archaeological sites in Croatia dating from approximately 8,000 years BC to the eighteenth century AD, with a total number of over 5,500 skeletons. The collection holds approximately 150 skeletons dated to the prehistoric period, 600 skeletons from the Antique period, over 3,000 skeletons from the mediaeval period, and 1,750 skeletons from the Historic/Modern Age period. The numbers are approximations because the collection is growing, both through the addition of skeletons from newly discovered sites, and through the addition of skeletons from systematic excavations that have, in some cases, continued for over ten years.

In the osteological laboratory of the same department, skeletal material is processed through strictly defined procedures. First, the bones are cleaned under running water with soft brushes, dried, numerated and when necessary and possible reconstructed. Following this a complete inventory of all present bones, joint surfaces and teeth is made for each skeleton. After that, each individual skeleton is sexed, aged, and the available pathological and trauma data are collected and detailed taphonomic data are recorded, as is the potential presence of associated

Table 9.1 Archaeological sites in Croatia for which anthropological/bioarchaeological studies have been carried out

Site	Chronology	Type of analysis	Author(s)
Vukovar – Srednja škola	Neolithic	Demography, pathology	Šlaus 2002a
Vinkovci	Neolithic	Demography, DNA	Hincak *et al.*, 2007b
Josipovac – Gravinjak	Eneolithic	Pathology	Vlak *et al.*, 2009
Vučedol	Eneolithic	Demography, pathology	Šlaus 2002a
		Demography, artificial cranial deformation	Teschler-Nicola and Berner 1994
		Demography, DNA	Hincak *et al.* 2007b
Franjevac	Eneolithic	Pathology	Rajić Šikanjić *et al.* 2009
Bezdanjača	Bronze Age	Demography, pathology	Šlaus 2002a
		Lead concentration in human bone samples	Brajković *et al.* 1990
		Occipital bone analysis (qualitative and quantitative characteristics)	Boljunčić 1994/1995
		Anomalies – upper portion of the vault	Boljunčić 1991
		Blood types of ABO system	Petričević-Jagić *et al.* 1992
		Oval defect on frontal bone	Malez and Nikolić 1975
		Morphological characteristics of lower jaws	Percač 1993
Laganiši	Bronze Age	Demography, pathology	Rajić Šikanjić 2008
Nadin	Iron Age	Demography, pathology	Rajić Šikanjić 2006
Vinkovci – "NAMA"	Early Iron Age	Demography, pathology	Šlaus 2002a, 2003
Zvonimirovo – Veliko polje	Late Iron Age	Analysis of cremated human bones	Šlaus and Novak 2004
Šepkovčica	Antique period	Microscopic analysis of cremated human bones	Hincak *et al.* 2007a
Štrbinci	Late Antique period	Demography, pathology	Šlaus 1998, 2001, 2002a, 2008a; Šlaus *et al.*, 2004b, 2004c
Osijek	Late Antique period	Demography, pathology	Šlaus 2002a, 2008a; Šlaus *et al.*, 2004b
Zmajevac	Late Antique period	Demography, pathology	Šlaus 2002a, 2008a; Šlaus *et al.*, 2004b
Vinkovci	Late Antique period	Demography, pathology	Šlaus 2002a, 2008a; Šlaus *et al.*, 2004b
Treštanovačka gradina	Late Antique period	Craniometric analysis	Pilarić 1974
		Dental measurements	Kallay 1974
Vid	Late Antique period	Demography, pathology	Šlaus 2002b, 2004a, 2004b, 2008a
Kaštel Sućurac	Late Antique period	Demography, pathology	Šlaus 2008a
Zadar	Late Antique period	Demography, pathology	Šlaus 2008a
Split – Ad basilicas pictas	Late Antique period	Demography, pathology	Šlaus 1999, 2008a

(Continued on next page)

Table 9.1 (continued)

Site	Chronology	Type of analysis	Author(s)
Ferenci	Early Mediaeval period	Case of dental anomaly	Rajić Šikanjić and Meštrović 2006
Guran – Na križu	Late Antique/Early Mediaeval period	Case of perimortem trauma	Šlaus *et al.* 2007a
Novigrad	Late Antique/Early Mediaeval period	Demography, pathology, correlation: grave type and sex/age	Rajić and Ujčić 2003; Rajić Šikanjić and Ujčić 2003
Vinkovci	Early Mediaeval period	Demography, pathology	Šlaus 2002a; Šlaus *et al.* 2002
Jopićeva pećina	Early Mediaeval period	Case of artificial cranial deformation	Šlaus 2002a
Privlaka – Gornje njive	Early Mediaeval period	Demography, pathology, discriminant analysis of crania	Šlaus 1993, 1996a, 2002a, 2008a; Šlaus *et al.* 2002
Stari Jankovci	Early Mediaeval period	Demography, pathology, discriminant analysis of crania	Šlaus 1993, 2008; Šlaus *et al.* 2002
Buzet – Mejica	Early Mediaeval period	Dental pathologies	Dolinar and Vidovič 1974
Nin – Ždrijac	Early Mediaeval period	Demography, morphology and typology of crania	Štefančič 1995
Donje polje	Early Mediaeval period	Demography, pathology	Šlaus 2006, 2008a
Radašinovci	Early Mediaeval period	Demography, pathology	Šlaus 2006, 2008a
Glavice	Early Mediaeval period	Demography, pathology	Šlaus 2006
Velim – Velištak	Early Mediaeval period	Demography, pathology	Šlaus 2006, 2008a
Konjsko polje – Livade	Early Mediaeval period	Demography, pathology	Novak *et al.* 2008
Mravinci	Early Mediaeval period	Cranial measurements and indexes	Mikić 1990
Bijelo Brdo	Early Mediaeval period	Demography, craniometry, cranial measurements and indexes	Ivaniček 1949; Pilarić 1968
		Dental pathologies	Vodanović *et al.* 2004, 2005
		Sex determination based on morphology of the lower jaw and odontometrics	Vodanović *et al.* 2006, 2007
Vukovar – Lijeva Bara	Early Mediaeval period	Multivariate craniometric analysis	Pilarić and Schwidetzky 1987
Bribir	Early and Late Mediaeval period	Multivariate craniometric analysis	Pilarić and Schwidetzky 1987
Vinkovci	Early and Late Mediaeval period	Demography, pathology	Šlaus 2002a; Šlaus *et al.*, 2002
Daraž – Bošnjaci	Early and Late Mediaeval period	Demography, cranial measurements and indexes	Pilarić 1967
Lobor	Early and Late Mediaeval period	Demography, pathology	Šlaus 2002a; Šlaus *et al.* 2002
		Case of osteochondroma	Šlaus *et al.* 2000

Table 9.1 (continued)

Site	Chronology	Type of analysis	Author(s)
Sčitarjevo	Early and Late Mediaeval period	Demography, pathology	Šlaus 2002a; Šlaus *et al.* 2002
Đelekovec	Early and Late Mediaeval period	Demography, pathology	Šlaus 2002a; Šlaus *et al.* 2002
Stenjevec	Early and Late Mediaeval period	Demography, pathology	Šlaus 2002a, 2002c; Šlaus *et al.* 2002
Zvonimirovo – Veliko polje	Early and Late Mediaeval period	Demography, pathology	Boljunčić 1997a; Boljunčić and Mandić 1993
		DNA	Boljunčić 2007
Josipovo	Early and Late Mediaeval period	Demography, pathology	Boljunčić 1997b
Đakovo	Mediaeval period	Demography, pathology; craniometric differences between 2 phases	Šlaus 2002a; Šlaus and Filipec 1998; Šlaus *et al.* 2002
Danilo – Šematorij	Mediaeval period	Demography, pathology, multivariate craniometric analysis	Šlaus 1996b
Suhopolje – Kliškovac	Mediaeval period	Trauma analysis	Šlaus and Novak 2006
Ozalj	Mediaeval period	Perimortem trauma and occupational stress	Šlaus 1994
Ričice	Late Mediaeval period	Demography, pathology	Mikić 1988
Krbavsko polje	Late Mediaeval period	Trauma analysis	Šlaus 2008b
Dugopolje	Late Mediaeval period	Demography, subadult stress	Novak and Šlaus 2007
Nova Rača	Late Mediaeval period	Dental pathologies	Šlaus *et al.* 1997
		Sex differences in mortality profiles and stress levels	Šlaus 2000
Kamengrad	Late Mediaeval period	Demography, pathology	Šlaus 2002a
Zagreb – Sv. Franjo	Late Mediaeval period	Demography, pathology	Šlaus *et al.* 2007b
Tomaš	Late Mediaeval period	Demography, pathology	Šlaus 2002a
Koprivno – Kod križa	Early Modern period	Demography, pathology	Novak *et al.* 2007
		Subadult stress	Novak 2008
Crkvari – Sv. Lovre	Mediaeval/Early Modern period	Trauma analysis	Šlaus and Novak 2006
		Case of venereal syphilis	Šlaus and Novak 2007
Torčec	Mediaeval/Early Modern period	Demography, pathology	Šlaus *et al.* 2003b
Požega – Sv. Terezija	Modern period	Sex determination based on lower jaws	Vodanović *et al.* 2006

archaeological material or animal remains. Finally anthropometric and craniometric data are recorded.

Skeletal material may be sent for additional analyses (x-ray, DNA, CT, stable isotope analysis, etc.) to other institutions in Croatia, or other parts of the world if required. Once the analysis is completed, all bones are stored in individually marked boxes in the osteological collection of the Department of Archaeology of the Croatian Academy of Arts and Sciences.

Apart from the Department of Archaeology of the Croatian Academy of Sciences and Arts, bioarchaeological analyses are also conducted at the Institute of Anthropology in Zagreb by P. Rajić Šikanjić; the Institute of Archaeology in Zagreb (J. Boljunčić); the Department of Archaeology, Faculty of Philosophy, University of Zagreb (Z. Hincak); and the Department of Dental Anthropology, School of Dental Medicine, University of Zagreb (H. Brkić and M. Vodanović).

In terms of the popularity, interest from the general public and from the media for the results of bioarchaeological research, the situation in Croatia is specific. The high quality of the work undertaken by Croatian physical anthropologists in the identification and analysis of the cause of death of civilian victims of the 1991 war that followed the dissolution of the former Yugoslavia has highlighted both the importance of physical – in this context forensic – anthropology, and the importance of developing an osteological database.

The 1991 conflict between Croatia and Serbia caused extensive material destruction and loss of life. From 1991 to 1995 there were more than 14,000 war-related deaths in Croatia. Among these were a large number of civilians whose remains were subsequently recovered from 143 mass graves and a large number of individual inhumations. To identify and determine the cause of death of these individuals, a joint USA–Croatia forensic anthropology project was developed. In this project, forensic anthropologists from the Croatian Academy of Sciences and Arts (Hrvatske akademije znanosti i umjetnosti), and the Department of Forensic Medicine at the School of Medicine, University of Zagreb, together with forensic anthropologists from the Smithsonian Institution, Washington DC, and the University of Tennessee in Knoxville, developed a forensic anthropology database in which data were collected on age, sex, stature, metric characteristics, osteological and dental pathology, and on peri-mortem trauma and possible cause of death. The purpose of this database, modelled on the forensic database developed at the University of Tennessee, has been to:

1 Identify a basic and standard set of measurements, observations and definitions to ensure that data are comparable;
2 Store the data in a computer in such a way that particular subsets can be quickly accessed;
3 Provide up-to-date discriminant formulae for determining sex, estimating stature, and defining other traits useful for comparative research and forensic analysis.

The formation of this database has contributed to the high frequency of positive identifications of civilian victims of the 1991 conflict (85.7%), and has educated the Croatian public and media on the type of data that physical anthropological research can yield. This has carried on to bioarchaeological research, with results frequently featuring on TV shows and in newspaper articles.

An additional positive response following the formation of the forensic osteological database was the increased interest of scientists from related scientific fields, particularly archaeologists, for the preservation and analysis of human skeletal material. The vast majority of Croatian archaeologists today are aware of the usefulness of bioarchaeological analysis for reconstructing the living conditions and lifestyles of archaeological populations. However, because bioarchaeological analyses of human skeletal material from archaeological sites in Croatia are not legally required, physical anthropologists/bioarchaeologists still utilize every opportunity (workshops, lectures, science festivals, etc.) to emphasize the importance of these analyses. The result is that virtually all human bones found in archaeological sites in Croatia today are analysed.

The downside of this significantly increased interest for bioarchaeological research is that the large number of rescue archaeological excavations related to large state infrastructure projects such as the construction of highways, coupled with the relatively small number of active bioarchaeologists/physical anthropologists in Croatia, means that physical anthropologists are rarely able to stay on a site throughout its entire archaeological excavation. Bioarchaeologists are present on an archaeological site usually at the invitation of the archaeologist, and generally for a short period of time. This sometimes causes problems in terms of the recovery of the less well preserved skeletal remains. Apart from preliminary analyses of sex and age, physical anthropologists on archaeological sites assist in differentiating between human and animal remains, and between archaeological and potential forensic cases.

There are several professional associations in Croatia in which bioarchaeologists/physical anthropologists actively participate. The most important is the Hrvatsko antropološko društvo (Croatian Anthropological Society), which is a part of the European Anthropological Association. This association assembles not only bioarchaeologists/physical anthropologists but also experts and scientists from all branches of anthropology. Beside this association, almost all Croatian bioarchaeologists are active members of the Hrvatsko arheološko društvo (Croatian Archaeological Association), and actively participate in their annual congresses. The seat of the International Association for Paleodontology (IAPO) is at the Department of Dental Anthropology, School of Dental Medicine, in Zagreb. This is an association that deals with the research of the oral and dental health of ancient populations.

ARCHAEOLOGICAL HUMAN REMAINS AND LEGISLATION

There is no legislation that specifically regulates the excavation and treatment of human skeletal material found in archaeological sites in Croatia. The fate of newly discovered human remains in Croatia depends on the circumstances of their discovery. When the remains are discovered in archaeological excavations they are treated as any other archaeological finds. If human skeletal material is found accidentally (for instance, during construction works), a team consisting of forensic experts, physical anthropologists/bioarchaeologists and archaeologists is sent to the site to determine whether the discovered remains are from an archaeological context or represent a forensic case. If the bones are considered to be a forensic case they are transported to the pathology departments of a local hospital, or to the Departments of Forensic Medicine in Zagreb, Split, Rijeka or Osijek. When human bones are considered to be part of an archaeological context they are transported to the local museum, or to one of the institutions in which bioarchaeologists are active.

There is no regulation that determines when human remains are considered to be from archaeological contexts, and when they are considered to be part of a forensic investigation. A general rule is that human skeletal remains dated to the end of the 19th century are usually considered to be from archaeological contexts.

Because of atrocities committed during the Second World War and its immediate aftermath, mass graves with victims from this time period are sometimes uncovered. Although there have been several attempts to develop a governmental body that would holistically deal with these remains, from identifying the number, age and sex of the victims, through possible positive identification of some victims, to the reburial of the remains in one or several specific cemeteries, as yet nothing has transpired. At present, these remains are treated as forensic investigations in the sense that the remains are transported to and analysed in departments of forensic medicine – usually the department in Zagreb.

As previously noted, there is also the possibility of uncovering individual or mass graves related to the 1991 war in Croatia. In instances where there is any indication that this may be the case, the remains are handled by the 'Committee for Imprisoned and Missing Individuals'. This governmental body coordinates all procedures related to the recovery, transportation, storage and identification of these remains and treats them as forensic cases (Šlaus *et al.* 2007c).

Archaeological legislation

The 'Law on the protection and preservation of cultural goods', adopted in 1999 and revised in 2003, legally regulates archaeological research in the Republic of Croatia. Below are described the most important articles of this act that relate to archaeological excavations and the handling of archaeological findings, including human skeletal material.

According to article 2 of the Croatian 'Law on the protection and preservation of cultural goods', cultural goods include movable and immovable items of palaeontological, archaeological, and anthropological significance. Consequently, human skeletal remains recovered during archaeological research are considered archaeological findings. Article 6 of the same law cites the competent legal authorities responsible for the protection and proper handling of archaeological material found during excavations: conservation departments of the Ministry of Culture, and the Zagreb City Bureau for the protection of monuments of culture and the natural heritage. Article 47 describes the conditions that need to be satisfied in order to get approval for archaeological excavations:

> … approval may be issued only to legal and physical persons that meet the requirements of qualification for the performance of such works, and if the necessary material and technical resources to carry out the excavations, the conservation of sites, planning, and presentation of sites and the findings are provided.
>
> *Law on the protection and preservation of cultural goods, Article 47 (author's translation)*

Article 68 defines the procedure employed when archaeological material is sent abroad:

> … it may be temporarily sent abroad for purposes of exhibition, expertise, analysis, implementation of procedures for the protection and preservation, or other justifiable reasons, with the approval of the Croatian Ministry of Culture. The applicant for the temporary export shall at the request of the Ministry of Culture give a guarantee in case of damage, destruction or theft of cultural goods in the form of cash deposit in a bank in the full amount of the value of cultural goods, or some other appropriate guarantee. The Minister of Culture prescribes conditions for the temporary export of cultural goods.
>
> *Law on the protection and preservation of cultural goods, Article 68 (author's translation)*

The 'Regulations for archaeological research', adopted in 2005, describe in more detail the procedures for excavation, analysis, documentation and storage of archaeological material, including among them human skeletal material. Article 4 of the 'Regulations for archaeological research' prescribes the measures that have to be taken before the start of the excavation, such as obtaining the approval of the conservation departments of the Ministry of Culture, or the Zagreb City Bureau for the protection of monuments of culture and nature. The same article cites which documents must be provided by the applicant for authorization: a form for specific details on the director of the excavation; data on the type, methodology, location, time, scope, content, and goals of the research; data on the manager and individuals involved in the work; and data on the storage place that will be used for the recovered archaeological artefacts. Article 6 prescribes the necessary conditions that the professional manager of the archaeological research must satisfy: he or she must be a citizen of the Republic of Croatia, must have a BA in archaeology, must have at least 12 months' experience in archaeological excavations, and must have the approval of the Ministry of Culture. Article 10 prescribes the technical requirements and equipment that the professional manager is required to provide. Article 17 lays down the conditions that must be met if the material is to be exported outside the country:

> ... exporting the samples intended for analysis abroad is only possible with the approval of the Ministry of Culture and under the conditions prescribed by the Law on the protection and preservation of cultural goods. A professional manager must submit the application for export.
>
> *Regulations for archaeological research, Article 17 (author's translation)*

Article 18 addresses the issue of the publication of the excavated and analysed material and documentation.

HUMAN REMAINS AND LEGISLATION

The above information indicates the most important legal regulations in Croatia concerning issues of excavation and the handling of archaeological findings, including among them human skeletal material. So far, these legal provisions have worked well in practice, and there are no significant negative experiences. This does not mean, however, that in the near future the possibility of further elaboration of legal provisions that would better regulate the treatment of human skeletal material found during archaeological excavations should be ignored.

Skeletal material can be, and in fact almost routinely is, sent to other countries for additional analyses. Skeletal samples are frequently sent for C^{14} dating (for instance to the Leibniz–Labor für Altersbestimmung und Isotopenforschung in Kiel, Germany, or to the Beta Analytic Laboratory in Miami, USA). Bone and dental samples from the collection of the Department of Archaeology of the Croatian Academy of Sciences and Arts have also been sent for stable isotopes analysis to the Dorothy Garrod Laboratory for Isotopic Analysis at the Department of Archaeology, University of Cambridge.

So far no ethical issues have been raised by any religious or non-government groups that would impede the analysis of human skeletal material recovered from archaeological sites.

METHODS OF ANTHROPOLOGICAL ANALYSIS

Internationally recognized standards and methods for determining age and sex (for a more detailed list of these see, for example, Šlaus 2008a) are generally used in the bioarchaeological analysis of skeletal material from Croatia, although specific methods generated for Croatian archaeological populations are also utilized. These include discriminant functions for determining sex in mediaeval Croatian populations based on the dimensions of the femur and tibia (Šlaus 1997; Šlaus and Tomičić 2005), as well as discriminant functions for determining sex in modern Croats based on the dimensions of the femur (Šlaus *et al.* 2003a).

CONCLUSION

Croatia has a long history and tradition of research in physical anthropology dating from the end of the 19th century, and the exceptional palaeoanthropological studies carried out by Dragutin Gorjanović Kramberger on the Krapina Neanderthal remains. Bioarchaeological research of archaeological populations that inhabited Croatia significantly intensified at the end of the last century, when a new generation of bioarchaeologists/physical anthropologists working under the tutelage of Pavao Rudan and Hubert Maver emerged. The increased interest in bioarchaeological research in Croatia was additionally fuelled by a widespread interest in physical anthropology triggered by the role that Croatian physical anthropologists played in the identification of civilian victims of the 1991 war in Croatia.

Although the level of funding and equipment in Croatian bioarchaeological laboratories cannot be compared to that in more developed countries, the results that Croatian bioarchaeologists/physical anthropologists are able to achieve are of the same high standard achieved throughout European bioarchaeology/physical anthropology.

There is no specific legislation in Croatia prescribing the treatment of human skeletal remains recovered from archaeological contexts. Procedures that must be implemented prior to and during archaeological excavations, as well as procedures related to the handling of all archaeological material, including human skeletal remains, are regulated by the 'Law on the protection and preservation of cultural goods' and the 'Regulations on the archaeological research of the Republic of Croatia'. So far, there have been no significantly negative experiences, and the cooperation between Croatian archaeologists and bioarchaeologists/physical anthropologists is generally excellent. This does not mean, however, that more detailed legal provisions in the form of regulations that would standardize the process of excavation, transportation, analysis, presentation and publication of human skeletal remains should not be developed in the future.

USEFUL CONTACTS

Croatian Anthropological Society, Gajeva 5, 10 000 Zagreb. Email: petra@inantro.hr; ivor@inantro.hr.

Croatian Archaeological Society, Tomašićeva 6, 10 000 Zagreb. Email: jbalen@amz.hr.

International Association for Paleodontology, Gundulićeva 5, 10 000 Zagreb. Email: iapo@paleodontology.com. Website: www.paleodontology.com/

Institute of Anthropology, Gajeva 5, 10 000 Zagreb. Email: petra@inantro.hr; ivor@inantro.hr. Website: www.inantro.hr/

Department of Archaeology, Croatian Academy of Sciences and Arts, Ante Kovačića 5, 10 000 Zagreb. Email: mario.slaus@zg.htnet.hr.

Email: vyroubal@hazu.hr; mnovak@hazu.hr; zeljka.bedic@gmail.com. Website: www.info.hazu.hr/odsjek_za_arheologiju/

Institute of Archaeology, Divka Budaka 1D, 10 000 Zagreb. Email: jadranka.boljuncic@iarh.hr. Website: www.iarh.hr/

Department of Archaeology, Faculty of Philosophy, University of Zagreb, Ivana Lučića 3, 10 000 Zagreb. Email: zdhincak@inet.hr. Website: www.ffzg.hr/arheo/

Department of Dental Anthropology, School of Dental Medicine, University of Zagreb, Gundulićeva 5, 10 000 Zagreb. Email: vodanovic@sfzg.hr. Website: www.sfzg.hr/zda/

BIBLIOGRAPHY

Boljunčić, J. (1991) 'Anomalije na gornjim ljuskama zatiljnih kostiju dviju brončanodobnih čovječjih lubanja iz špilje Bezdanjače kod Vrhovina u Lici', *Rad Hrvatske akademije znanosti i umjetnosti*, 458: 131–42.

Boljunčić, J. and Mandić, Z. (1993) 'Antropološka analiza kosturnih ostataka iz srednjovjekovnog groblja Zvonimirovo kod Suhopolja (Hrvatska)', *Prilozi Instituta za arheologiju u Zagrebu*, 10: 131–48.

Boljunčić, J. (1994/1995) 'Analiza zatiljne kosti populacije ljudi iz brončanodobne nekropole u špilji Bezdanjači (Hrvatska)', *Prilozi Instituta za arheologiju u Zagrebu*, 11/12: 151–66.

——(1997a) 'Antropološka analiza ranosrednjovjekovnog groblja Josipovo (Ciganka)', in Ž. Tomičić (ed.) *Zvonimirovo i Josipovo – groblja starohrvatskog doba u Virovitičko-podravskoj županiji*, Zagreb – Virovitica: Institut za arheologiju u Zagrebu.

——(1997b) 'Antropološka analiza ranosrednjovjekovnog groblja Zvonimirovo – Veliko Polje', in Ž. Tomičić (ed.) *Zvonimirovo i Josipovo – groblja starohrvatskog doba u Virovitičko-podravskoj županiji*, Zagreb – Virovitica: Institut za arheologiju u Zagrebu.

——(2007) 'DNA analysis of Early Mediaeval individuals from Zvonimirovo burial site in northern Croatia: investigation of kinship relationships by using multiplex system amplification for short tandem repeat loci', *Croatian Medical Journal*, 48: 536–46.

Brajković, D., Malez, M., Bagi, Č., Kozar, S., Branica, M. and Knivald, G. (1990) 'Sadržaj olova u ljudskim kostima brončanodobne nekropole u spilji Bezdanjači kod Vrhovina (Lika, Hrvatska)', *Rad Jugoslavenske akademije znanosti i umjetnosti*, 449: 11–28.

Dolinar, Z. and Vidovič, M. (1974) 'Studija zobovja iz grobišča Buzet – Mejica', *Glasnik Antropološkog društva Jugoslavije*, 11: 47–53.

Gorjanović-Kramberger, D. (1899) 'Paleolitički ostaci čovjeka i njegovih suvremenika iz diluvija u Krapini', *Ljetopis Jugoslavenske akademije znanosti i umjetnosti*, 14: 90–98.

——(1906) *Der diluviale Mensch von Krapina in Kroatien. Ein Beitrag zur Paläoanthropologie*, Wiesbaden: Kreidel.

——(1913) *Život i kultura diluvijalnog čovjeka iz Krapine u Hrvatskoj*, Zagreb: Jugoslavenska akademija znanosti i umjetnosti.

Hincak, Z., Mihelić, D. and Bugar, A. (2007a) 'Cremated human and animal remains of the Roman period – microscopic method of analysis (Šepkovčica, Croatia)', *Collegium Antropologicum*, 31: 1127–34.

Hincak, Z., Drmić-Hofman, I. and Mihelić, D. (2007b) 'Anthropological analysis of Neolithic and Early Bronze Age skeletons – a Classical and molecular approach (East Slavonia, Croatia)', *Collegium Antropologicum*, 31: 1135–41.

Ivaniček, F. (1949) 'Istraživanje nekropole ranog srednjeg vijeka u Bijelom Brdu', *Ljetopis Jugoslavenske akademije*, 55: 111–44.

——(1951) *Staroslavenska nekropola u Ptuju – rezultati antropoloških istraživanja*, Ljubljana: Slovenska akademija znanosti in umetnosti.

Kallay, J. (1974) 'Antropološke mjere zubi iz nekropole', *Požeški zbornik*, 4: 152–59.

Malez, M. and Nikolić, V. (1975) 'Patološka pojava na prethistorijskoj čovječjoj lubanji iz pećine Bezdanjače u Lici', *Rad Jugoslavenske akademije znanosti i umjetnosti*, 371: 171–79.

Mikić, Ž. (1983) 'Antropološki prikaz srednjovekovnih stanovnika Ričica', in J. Jeličić (ed.) *Ričice – nekropole stećaka*, Split: Regionalni zavod za zaštitu spomenika kulture.

Mikić, Z. (1990) 'Antropološki profil srednjovekovne nekropole u Mravincima kod Splita', *Vjesnik za arheologiju i historiju dalmatinsku*, 83: 225–32.

Novak, M. and Šlaus, M. (2007) 'Učestalost i distribucija *cribrae orbitaliae* u kasnosrednjovjekovnoj populaciji iz Dugopolja', *Starohrvatska prosvjeta*, 34: 451–75.

Novak, M., Šlaus, M. and Pasarić, M. (2007) 'Bioarheološke osobine novovjekovne populacije s nalazišta Koprivno – Kod križa kraj Klisa', *Opuscula archaeological*, 31: 303–46.

Novak, M. (2008) 'Subadult stress in Early Modern Period (16th-18th century) skeletal sample from Koprivno – Kod križa near Klis, southern Croatia', in J. Boldsen (ed.) *Abstracts Book of the 16th Congress of the European Anthropological Association (28th-31st August, Odense – Denmark)*, Odense: University of Southern Denmark.

Novak, M., Vyroubal, V., Bedić, Ž. and Šlaus, M. (2008) 'Antropološka analiza groblja Konjsko polje – Livade u kontekstu drugih ranosrednjovjekovnih grobalja iz Dalmacije', *Starohrvatska prosvjeta*, 35: 211–39.

Perčač, S. (1993) 'Morphological characteristics of human lower jaws of the eneolithic population of the Bezdanjaca cave (Croatia)', *Rad Hrvatske akademije znanosti i umjetnosti*, 463: 81–90.

Petričević-Jagić, N., Brajković, D. and Bagi, Č. (1992) 'Utvrđivanje krvnih grupa sustava ABO na pre-thistorijskim ljudskim kostima iz spilje Bezdanjača (Lika, Hrvatska)', *Rad Hrvatske akademije znanosti i umjetnosti*, 463: 13–23.

Pilarić, G. (1967) 'Antropološka istraživanja starohrvatskog groblja u Daraž – Bošnjacima 1961. godine', *Arheološki radovi i rasprave*, 4/5: 419–43.

——(1968) 'Fenotipske značajke bjelobrdskih lubanja iz ranog srednjeg vijeka', *Arheološki radovi i rasprave*, 6: 263–91.

——(1969) 'Antropološka istraživanja slavenske populacije sa Baltinih Bara kod Gomjenice', *Glasnik Zemaljskog muzeja Sarajevo*, 24: 185–211.

——(1974) 'O lubanjama iz nekropole', *Požeški zbornik*, 4: 141–51.

Pilarić, G. and Schwidetzky, I. (1987) 'Vukovar und Bribir: Beitrag zur Anthropologie mittelalterlicher Sudslawen', *Homo*, 38: 1–15.

Rajić, P. and Ujčić, Ž. (2003) 'Anthropological analysis of the Late Roman/Early Medieval cemetery of Novigrad (Istria)', *Collegium Antropologicum*, 27: 803–8.

Rajić Šikanjić, P. and Ujčić, Ž. (2003) 'Antropološka analiza ranokršćanske/ranosrednjovjekovne populacije s groblja u Novigradu (Istra)', *Histria archaeologica*, 34: 103–9.

Rajić Šikanjić, P. (2005) 'Bioarchaeological research in Croatia – A historical review', *Collegium Antropologicum*, 29: 763–68.

——(2006) 'Analysis of human skeletal remains from Nadin Iron age burial mound', *Collegium Antropologicum*, 30: 795–99.

——(2008) 'Analiza ljudskog skeletnog materijala iz jame Laganiši', in D. Komšo (ed.) *Pećina Laganiši – Mjesto života i smrti*, Pula: Arheološki muzej Istre.

Rajić Šikanjić, P. and Meštrović, S. (2006) 'A Case of short-root anomaly in a female from Medieval Istria', *International Jorunal of Osteoarchaeology*, 16: 177–80.

Rajić Šikanjić, P., Janković, I. and Balen, J. (2009) 'Human skeletal remains from the prehistoric site of Franjevac, Eastern Croatia', *American Journal of Physical Anthropology*, 138 (Supplement): 334.

Šlaus, M. (1993) 'Cranial variation and microevolution in two early medieval age sites from Croatia: Privlaka and Stari Jankovci', *Opuscula archaeologica*, 17: 273–307.

——(1994) 'Osteological evidence for perimortem trauma and occupational stress in two medieval skeletons from Croatia', *Collegium Antropologicum*, 18: 165–75.

——(1996a) 'Demography and disease in the Early medieval site of Privlaka', *Opuscula archaeologica*, 20: 141–50.

——(1996b) 'Antropološka analiza kasnosrednjovjekovne populacije iz Danila Gornjeg kraj Šibenika', *Arheološki radovi i rasprave*, 12: 343–64.

——(1997) 'Discriminant function sexing of fragmentary and complete femora from medieval sites in continental Croatia', *Opuscula archaeologica*, 21: 167–75.

——(1998) 'Antropološka analiza osteološkog materijala', in B. Migotti (ed.) *Accede ad Certissiam – Antički i ranokršćanski horizont arheološkog nalazišta Štrbinci kod Đakova*, Zagreb: Hrvatska akademija znanosti i umjetnosti.

——(1999) 'Antropološka analiza kasnoantičke populacije s nalazišta Ad Basilicas Pictas', in F. Oreb., T. Rismondo and M.Topić (eds) *Ad Basilicas Pictas*, Split: Konzervatorski odjel Ministarstva kulture.

——(2000) 'Biocultural analysis of sex differences in mortality profiles and stress levels in the late Medieval population from Nova Rača, Croatia', *American Journal of Physical Anthropology*, 111: 193–209.

——(2001) 'Bioarchaeological research of the Štrbinci skeletal series', *Arheološki radovi i rasprave*, 13: 205–24.

——(2002a) *The Bioarchaeology of Continental Croatia. An analysis of human skeletal remains from the prehistoric to post-medieval periods*, BAR International Series 1021, Oxford: Archaeopress.

——(2002b) 'Rezultati antropološke analize ljudskog osteološkog materijala s nalazišta Narona – Erešove bare', *Vjesnik za arheologiju i historiju dalmatinsku*, 94: 205–15.

——(2002c) 'Demography and pathology of the medieval population from Stenjevec', *Opuscula archaeologica*, 26: 257–73.

——(2003) 'Anthropological analysis of human skeletal remains from the Hallstatt period "Vinkovci-Nama" site', *Opuscula archaeologica*, 27: 257–67.

——(2004a) 'Anthropological remarks on the graveyard', in E. Marin and M. Vickers (eds) *The Rise and Fall of an Imperial Shrine*, Split: Arheološki muzej Split.

——(2004b) 'Bioarheološka analiza ljudskog osteološkog materijala s nalazišta Narona–Augusteum', *Vjesnik za arheologiju i historiju dalmatinsku*, 96: 539–61.

——(2006) *Bioarheologija – demografija, zdravlje, traume i prehrana starohrvatskih populacija*, Zagreb: Školska knjiga.

——(2008a) 'Osteological and dental markers of health in the transition from the Late Antique to the Early Medieval period in Croatia', *American Journal of Physical Anthropology*, 136: 455–69.

——(2008b) 'Perimortem trauma from the 15th century battle on Krbava field in Croatia', in J. Boldsen (ed.) *Abstracts Book of the 16th Congress of the European Anthropological Association (28th-31st August, Odense – Denmark)*, Odense: University of Southern Denmark.

Šlaus, M. and Filipec, K. (1998) 'Bioarchaeology of the medieval Đakovo cemetery: Archaeological and anthropological evidence for ethnic affiliation and migration', *Opuscula archaeologica*, 22: 129–39.

Šlaus, M. and Novak, M. (2004) 'Zvonimirovo – Veliko Polje, nalazište Latenske kulture – analiza spaljenog ljudskog osteološkog materijala', *Obavijesti Hrvatskog arheološkog društva*, 2: 15.

Šlaus, M. and Tomičić, Ž. (2005) 'Discriminant function sexing of fragmentary and complete tibiae from medieval Croatian sites', *Forensic Science International*, 147: 147–52.

Šlaus, M. and Novak, M. (2006) 'Analiza trauma u srednjovjekovnim uzorcima iz Kliškovca i Crkvara', *Prilozi Instituta za arheologiju u Zagrebu*, 23: 213–28.

——(2007) 'Slučaj veneričnog sifilisa u novovjekovnom horizontu grobova kraj crkve Svetog Lovre u Crkvarima', *Prilozi Instituta za arheologiju u Zagrebu*, 24: 503–10.

Šlaus, M., Pećina-Hrnčević, A. and Jakovljević, G. (1997) 'Dental disease in the late medieval population from Nova Rača, Croatia', *Collegium Antropologicum*, 21: 561–72.

Šlaus, M., Orlić, D. and Pećina, M. (2000) 'Osteochondroma in a skeleton from an 11th century Croatian cemetery', *Croatian Medical Journal*, 41: 336–40.

Šlaus, M., Kollmann, D., Novak, S. and Novak, M. (2002) 'Temporal trends in demographic profiles and stress levels in medieval (6th-13th century) population samples from continental Croatia', *Croatian Medical Journal*, 43: 598–605.

Šlaus, M., Strinović, D., Škavić, J. and Petrovečki, V. (2003a) 'Discriminant function sexing of fragmentary and complete femora: Standards for contemporary Croatia', *Journal of Forensic Sciences*, 48: 509–12.

Šlaus, M., Novak, M. and Krznar, S. (2003b) 'Paleodemografska i paleopatološka analiza ljudskog osteo-loškog materijala s kasnosrednjovjekovnog nalazišta Torčec – Cirkvišće kraj Koprivnice', *Podravina*, 2: 37–48.

Šlaus, M., Pećina-Šlaus, N., Tomičić, Ž., Minichreiter, K. and Uglešić, A. (2004a) 'Skeletal evidence for neoplasms in Croatian archaeological series', in H.H. Grunicke (ed) *Proceedings of the 18th Meeting of the European Association for Cancer Research (3rd-6th June 2004), Innsbruck, Austria*, Innsbruck: European Association for Cancer Research, Innsbruck.

Šlaus, M., Pećina-Šlaus, N. and Brkić, H. (2004b) 'Life stress on the Roman limes in continental Croatia', *Homo*, 54: 240–63.

Šlaus, M., Novak, M. and Kollmann, D. (2004c) 'The Štrbinci skeletal series in context of other Late Antique skeletal series from continental Croatia', *Arheološki radovi i rasprave*, 14: 247–92.

Šlaus, M., Bedić, Ž. and Vyroubal, V. (2007a) 'Forenzično-antropološka analiza ljudskih kostiju iz groba 1 s nalazišta Guran – Na križu u Istri – Davno počinjeno ubojstvo i primjer kako postmortalna oštećenja mogu oponašati ubojstvo', in L. Bekić (ed.) *Zaštitna arheologija na magistralnom plinovodu Pula – Karlovac/Rescue archaeology on magistral gas pipeline Pula – Karlovac*, Zagreb: Hrvatski restauratorski zavod.

Šlaus, M., Novak, M., Bedić, Ž. and Vyroubal, V. (2007b) 'Antropološka analiza kasnosrednjovjekovnog groblja kraj crkve svetog Franje na Opatovini u Zagrebu', *Arheološki radovi i rasprave*, 15: 211–47.

Šlaus, M., Strinović, D., Pećina Šlaus, N., Brkić, H., Baličević, D., Petrovečki, V. and Cicvara Pećina, T. (2007c) 'Identification and analysis of human remains recovered from wells from the 1991 War in Croatia', *Forensic Science International*, 171: 37–43.

Šlaus, M., Novak, M., Vyroubal, V and Bedić, Ž. (2010) 'The harsh life on the 15th century Croatia-Ottoman Empire military border: analyzing and identifying the reasons for the massacre in Čepin', *American Journal of Physical Anthropology*, 141: 358–72.

Štefančič, M. (1995) 'Antropološka obdelava zgodnjosrednjeveških okostij iz grobišča Nin – Ždrijac (Severna Dalmacija)', *Arheološki vestnik*, 46: 291–325.

Teschler-Nicola, M. and Berner, M.E. (1994) 'Zur Anthropologie der endneolitischen Funde aus Vuče-dol', in *Die Neandertaler und die Anfange Europas. Katalog zur Sonderausstellung*, Eisenstadt: Burgerlandisches Landesmuseum.

Vlak, D., Janković, I. and Mihelić, S., (2009) 'Juvenile burial from the Eneolithic site of Josipovac-Gravinjak, Croatia', *American Journal of Physical Anthropology*, 138: 409–10.

Vodanović, M., Brkić, H. and Demo, Ž. (2004) 'Paleostomatološka analiza humanoga kraniofacijalnoga osteološkoga materijala sa srednjevjekovnog nalazišta Bijelo Brdo kraj Osijeka', *Vjesnik Arheološkog muzeja u Zagrebu*, 37: 251–61.

Vodanović, M., Brkić, H., Šlaus, M. and Demo, Ž. (2005) 'The frequency and distribution of caries in the mediaeval population of Bijelo Brdo in Croatia (10th-11th century)', *Archives of Oral Biology*, 50: 669–80.

Vodanović, M., Dumančić, J., Demo, Ž. and Mihelić, D. (2006) 'Determination of sex by discriminant function analysis of mandibles from two Croatian archaeological sites', *Acta Stomatologica Croatica*, 40: 263–77.

Vodanović, M., Demo, Ž., Njemirovskij, V., Keros, J. and Brkić, H. (2007) 'Odontometrics: a useful method for sex determination in an archaeological skeletal population?', *Journal of Archaeological Science*, 34: 905–13.

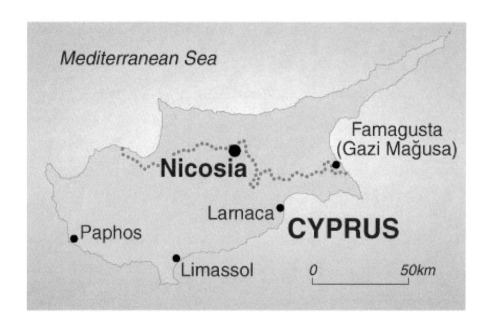

Cyprus/ΚΥΠΡΟΣ/Kibris

Kirsi O. Lorentz

INTRODUCTION: A BRIEF HISTORY AND CURRENT STATE OF PHYSICAL ANTHROPOLOGY IN CYPRUS

The foundations for research on archaeological human remains were laid relatively early in Cyprus (see, e.g., Virchow 1884), but the development of systematic, problem oriented research on the remains of Cypriot archaeological populations, as well as educational provisions and institutional infrastructures for physical anthropology and human bioarchaeology in Cyprus, are still in their infancy.

In addition to focusing on relevant legislation and practice, this chapter outlines some key historical developments as to physical anthropology in Cyprus, highlights some recent developments in cutting edge research, and draws attention to the importance of local human resources and infrastructure (including equipment, instrumentation and reference collections) to the future development of physical anthropology and human bioarchaeology in Cyprus.

This chapter focuses on archaeological human remains and does not include the legislation and practice regarding forensic work in Cyprus. For the purposes of this chapter, archaeological human remains are defined as any human remains that date before 1850 AD (see below, and the Antiquities Law of Cyprus). The oldest human remains discovered to date in Cyprus derive from the so called Cypro-PPNB period (c. 9900–7000 BC). Further information relevant to forensic anthropology in Cyprus can be found on the Committee of Missing Persons in Cyprus (CMP) webpage (CMP 2010), or by referring to the CMP Terms of Reference (1981) and the CMP Fact Sheet (2009).

Research on archaeological human remains has a relatively long history in Cyprus. Cypriot human skeletal remains first appear in scientific treatises as early as the 19th century (e.g., Virchow 1884), and the early part of the 20th century saw the publication of several treatises and reports focusing exclusively on Cypriot human remains, as well as some further comparative work (e.g., Buxton 1920a, 1920b, 1931; Fürst 1933; Guest 1936; Schaeffer 1935; Rix 1938; Rix and Buxton 1938). The majority of this early work had a tendency to focus exclusively on the human skull, in keeping with the research history of the discipline in general. After the Second World War, physical anthropological research activity on the island resumed, and J.L. Angel, R.-P. Charles and other scholars analysed and published several Cypriot human skeletal series during the mid-20th century (Angel 1953, 1955, 1961, 1964, 1966, 1967,

1969a, 1969b; Axmacher and Hjortsjö 1959; Charles 1960, 1962, 1963, 1964, 1966, 1967; Hjortsjö 1947; Kurth 1958; Rix 1950). During the 1970s some of these already established physical anthropologists continued their research activity on Cypriot skeletal series (see, e.g., Angel 1972a, 1972b, 1978; Charles 1970), and are joined by a number of new researchers (Longmore 1975; Schulte-Campbell 1979; Schwartz 1974; Walker 1975). During the 1980s the number of researchers analysing Cypriot skeletal series increased further (Domurad 1985, 1986a, 1986b, 1987a, 1987b, 1988; Cadogan and Domurad 1985; Downs 1982; Fischer 1986; Fischer and Norén 1988; Galloway 1985; Moyer 1984, 1985, 1989; Musgrave and Evans 1980; Schulte-Campbell 1983, 1986; Soliveres 1981), and a few of these scholars focused specifically on human dentition (Fischer and Norén 1988; Lunt 1980, 1985, 1989; Nyqvist 1980; Taramides 1983). While palaeopathological analyses of Cypriot skeletal series can be said to have begun with Angel's focus on porotic hyperostosis (Angel 1966, 1967, 1978), and continued with notes on dental palaeopathology in the 1980s (see, e.g., Lunt 1980, 1985, 1989), it is not until the 1990s that systematic problem oriented studies of postcranial palaeopathology in Cyprus begin to appear (Agelarakis 1997; Fox-Leonard 1997), together with reports on specific skeletal series (Agelarakis *et al.* 1998; Domurad 1992; Fessas 1990; Fox 1996, 1997; Herscher and Fox 1994; Le Mort 1994, 1995; Lunt 1994, 1995; Lunt and Watt 1998; Moyer 1997). While the necessary, detailed reporting on specific human skeletal series continues during the first decade of the 21st century (Crewe *et al.* 2005; Fox 2001, 2003a, 2003b, 2003c, 2006, 2007; Harper 2002; Lorentz 2001, 2004a, 2006a, 2007a, 2009a, 2009b, in press a; Lunt 2006; Lunt and Watt 2003; Moyer 2004, 2005, 2006, 2007; Parks *et al.* 2000, 2001; Parras 2006a; Schulte-Campbell 2003; Tucker and Clegget 2007), the new millennium sees the publication of further problem oriented and comparative studies on a variety of topics (Baker *et al.* 2007; Fox 2005; Harper, in press; Le Mort 2000, 2007, 2008; Lorentz 2002, 2003a, 2003b, 2006b, 2007b, 2009a, in press b, in press c; Parras 2004, 2006b), theoretically informed human bioarchaeology (Lorentz 2004b, 2005, 2008a, 2008b, 2008c, in press d) including *anthropologie de terrain* (Lorentz, in press d), syntheses (Harper 2008; Harper and Fox 2008), and studies employing state-of-the art scientific methodologies and techniques such as palaeoparasitology (Harter-Lailheugue *et al.* 2005) and strontium isotope analyses for investigating residential mobility (Lorentz *et al.*, forthcoming).

Development

The preceding sections briefly outline research history in Cyprus, providing a substantial body of bibliographic references covering over a hundred years of research. None of the physical anthropological analyses published to date have been conducted by a Cypriot researcher. Development of local analytical capabilities is a key step towards the protection of the remains of past Cypriot populations. This needs to involve the development of both infrastructure (instrumentation and physical facilities, as well as reference collections) and human resources. Harper and Fox (2008) note that:

> [T]he Archaeological Research Unit of the university [University of Cyprus] does not yet have trained anthropologists on staff, nor does the Department of Antiquities. The foundation of the Science and Technology in Archaeology Research Center (STARC) within The Cyprus Institute is a positive step ... Currently one of the [two] research coordinators is a bioarchaeologist.
>
> *(Harper and Fox 2008: 20)*

In September 2009 a research assistant with expertise in human bioarchaeology began work under the above-named research coordinator.

Education and training

There are no formal academic degrees in physical anthropology and/or human bioarchaeology available in Cyprus, although such degrees are available in the region (e.g. Greece, Turkey, Jordan and Israel). The few Cypriot students that have undertaken postgraduate level studies in human bioarchaeology and/or physical anthropology to date have conducted their studies in the UK, and in some cases in the USA. The undergraduate level course on Environmental Archaeology at the University of Cyprus usually includes a session on human bioarchaeology or physical anthropology. The Souskiou-Laona Human Bioarchaeology Field School,[1] which takes place annually in Cyprus (Figure 10.1), provides opportunities to learn excavation techniques relevant to the recovery of human remains, sampling protocols, as well as physical anthropological methods and techniques for laboratory analyses, and basic theoretical understanding of cutting-edge analytical approaches such as palaeoparasitology, a range of isotopic analyses, dating, dental histology and micro-sampling (LA-ICP-MS). The Souskiou-Laona Human Bioarchaeology Field School has been running since 2002, with 20 international postgraduate students (including Cypriots) participating in July 2009.

In addition to training students, facilitation of collaboration between colleagues is seen to be beneficial for the development of physical anthropology and human bioarchaeology in Cyprus. The Cyprus Ancient Population Project (CAPP) is an open research network of researchers focusing on archaeological human remains in Cyprus. Its period of coverage extends from the earliest prehistory to the historical period. CAPP aims to promote:

1 Preparation of the *Cyprus Human Skeletal Data Base* (a research resource for physical anthropologists, palaeopathologists and bioarchaeologists)
2 Symposia on human skeletal remains research in Cyprus (the first CAPP symposium 'New Approaches to Archaeological Human Remains in Cyprus' was held in Nicosia in September 2008), leading to the preparation of an up-to-date synthesis on current research on ancient Cypriot populations;
3 Comparative, problem oriented, collaborative analyses of ancient Cypriot skeletal populations based on network participants' work at various sites;
4 Training and placements for local Cypriot students and researchers, with view of promoting excellence in physical anthropology, palaeopathology and bioarchaeology in Cyprus.

Further aspects, responsive to the network participants' research vision, are developed through network discussions.

ARCHAEOLOGICAL HUMAN REMAINS AND LEGISLATION

Archaeological legislation

There is no legislation specific to archaeological human remains in Cyprus. Human remains are mentioned only in brief in the existing legislation governing Cypriot antiquities. The following legislation govern the treatment of Cypriot Antiquities: the Antiquities Law (Ο ΠΕΡΙ ΑΡΧΑΙΟΤΗΤΩΝ ΝΟΜΟΣ), and any subsequent amendments to this law. Material culture items and related remains that date before the year 1850 are defined as antiquities, and are thus governed by the Antiquities Law. For 'works of ecclesiastical or folk art of great archaeological

Figure 10.1 A Polish field school student analysing a pubic bone from the site of Souskiou-Laona, Cyprus

or artistic, or historical value, the year 1940 AD shall be taken into account in place of the year 1850 AD' (Antiquities Law, Section 2).

Human remains and legislation

The following sections are the only ones within the Cyprus Antiquities Law that directly mention human remains:

> Save with the permission in writing of the Director, no person shall, during any excavations destroy, damage, remove or conceal any antiquities or any human, animal or other remains discovered during such excavations.
> *(Antiquities Law, Part III, Section 18, Subsection 1; Control over antiquities, etc., discovered during excavations; 8 of 32 of 1973 and 3 of 166 of 1987)*

And:

> Any person who acts in contravention of any of the provisions of subsection (1) of this section shall be guilty of an offence and shall be liable to imprisonment not exceeding one year or to a fine not exceeding one thousand pounds or to both.
> *(Antiquities Law, Part III, Section 18, Subsection 2; Control over antiquities, etc., discovered during excavations; 8 of 32 of 1973 and 3 of 166 of 1987).*

In practice, an excavation permit from the Director of the Department of Antiquities of Cyprus covers the excavation and lifting of human remains, as well as any other remains and finds, and no separate permit or licence for the excavation and lifting of human remains is required. Current legislation does not stipulate or make provision for any compulsory ostelogical analysis of human remains.

Practice

The occasions when archaeological human skeletal remains are discovered in Cyprus can be divided into two very general categories: (1) planned excavations; (2) accidental discovery. In addition to these, looting of both prehistoric and later period burials and burial grounds has been unfortunately common in Cyprus. While severely disturbing human remains, looters mostly leave these remains within the disturbed burial feature or in the vicinity of it. The discovery of human remains during *bona fide* archaeological excavations is covered by the excavation permit granted by the Director of the Department of Antiquities of Cyprus, and excavation of human remains can proceed according to the normal procedure of each excavation project (see Antiquities Law Part III, Section 18, Subsections 1 and 2). In the case that archaeological human remains are discovered accidentally, for example during construction work (a lamentably frequent scenario in Cyprus), the Department of Antiquities needs to be informed immediately. In practice, in most cases, the developers and/or members of the public alert the police, who in turn contact the Department of Antiquities (F. Hadjichristofi and E. Zachariou, pers. comm. 2009). In cases where a tomb has been discovered accidentally, for example during construction work, and salvage excavation is required, the Department of Antiquities arranges for a guard to stay at the site overnight, and excavations usually begin the following morning, led by an archaeologist designated for the task by the Director of the Department of Antiquities or his/her deputy (one of the two Curators for Museums and Monuments). The team conducting the salvage excavation usually consists of an archaeologist, a technician and a draftsperson (F. Hadjichristofi and E. Zachariou, pers. comm. 2009). There are no positions currently in physical anthropology/osteoarchaeology at the Department of Antiquities, although occasionally a temporary member of staff at the Department of Antiquities has had some osteological training.

Excavation and lifting

The excavation and lifting of archaeological human remains in Cyprus is in most cases conducted by archaeologists and archaeological technicians or students of archaeology. Archaeological projects which have a physical anthropologist/human bioarchaeologist in the field are still quite rare. Recent exceptions to this state of affairs include the excavation projects at Khirokitia (Le Mort 1994, 2000, 2008), Souskiou-Laona (Crewe *et al.* 2005; Lorentz in press e, forthcoming), Kourion Amathous Gate Cemetery (Parks *et al.* 2000, 2001) and Polis (Baker *et al.* 2007). The relatively poor state of preservation and often highly fragile nature of the human remains uncovered in Cyprus calls for the presence of highly trained physical anthropologists in the field, from the very first moment of discovery. Some morphological and metric data will only be accessible in the field, despite the very best efforts in lifting and/or consolidation where appropriate/necessary, and some sampling protocols for human bioarchaeological analyses (e.g., for palaeoparasitology) can only be undertaken when the remains are first discovered and during the excavation that ensues. Further, detailed knowledge of human skeletal anatomy facilitates excavation, ensuring that the fragile remains are not damaged further at this stage. There is clearly a need for further training of both archaeologists and laboratory based physical anthropologists in field techniques specific to human skeletal remains.

Curation

After recovery, the finds and human skeletal remains are transferred to the relevant museum (the Cyprus Museum, or the relevant district museum) and the artefacts are entered into inventory books.

In practice, archaeological human remains in Cyprus may be temporarily curated in excavation storage facilities, field laboratories and research institutions while they are undergoing study, with the understanding that the permanent location for curation of the remains will be within the museums and storage rooms belonging to the Department of Antiquities: the Cyprus Museum in Nicosia, or the District Museums in Limassol, Larnaca and Paphos, as well as additional local museums such as the Kouklia Museum and any additional storerooms.

Archaeological human remains can be temporarily transferred for analysis to research institutions in Cyprus or abroad after an undertaking has been signed between the researcher who will conduct the analyses and a Department of Antiquities representative. Some skeletal series have been temporarily relocated for the purposes of study in research institutions in Cyprus (such as the Science and Technology in Archaeology Research Center of The Cyprus Institute) as well as abroad (such as the Wiener Laboratory, ASCSA, Athens). Many archaeological human skeletal series originating from Cyprus are currently in institutions located abroad, due to the legacy of previous practices of 'dividing' the finds deriving from foreign archaeological expeditions that took place in the early part of the 20th century. The division of finds was made between the Cyprus Museum and the institutions behind the foreign expeditions. There is a critical need for a comprehensive database, accessible to *bona fide* researchers, on the location of the various Cypriot skeletal series. The construction of such a database is one of the aims of CAPP.[2]

Reburial

Sporadic and unsystematic cases of reburial of archaeological human remains discovered in Cyprus have taken place in some cases, such as for example in the case of Toumba tou Skourou (Vermeule 1974). While not strictly reburial, in some cases where Christian burials of mediaeval date were discovered accidentally, and were not threatened by subsequent development, they were left where they were found (F. Hadjichristofi, pers. comm.).

METHODS OF ANTHROPOLOGICAL ANALYSIS

The osteological and palaeopathological analysis of Cypriot human remains mostly takes place in museum study rooms, as well as at the field bases of specific ongoing excavation projects.

Recently a few physical anthropologists have begun conducting preliminary field analyses on-site, followed by full analyses off-site. There are currently no dedicated laboratory facilities for analyses of archaeological human remains on the island, but the newly established Cyprus Institute and its Science and Technology in Archaeology Research Center may provide a way forward. Development of local analytical capabilities needs to involve both infrastructure (instrumentation and physical facilities, as well as reference collections; see, e.g., Eliopoulos *et al.* 2007) and human resources.

No Cyprus-specific methods have been developed as far as the author is aware, and international recommendations tend to be used (e.g., Buikstra and Ubelaker 1994), including those for the assessment of age-at-death, sex and stature.

CONCLUSION

Published physical anthropological research in Cyprus spans more than one hundred years. Problem oriented comparative research on archaeological human remains, with cutting-edge methodologies, is however still in its infancy. The Antiquities Law of Cyprus briefly mentions human remains, and in practice the recovery of archaeological human remains is covered by the excavation permit. In order for physical anthropology and human bioarchaeology to develop further in Cyprus, investment in local infrastructures and human resources is required.

USEFUL CONTACTS

Department of Antiquities of Cyprus. Website: www.mcw.gov.cy/mcw/da/da.nsf
Committee on Missing Persons in Cyprus (CMP). Website: www.cmp–cyprus.org
Science and Technology in Archaeology Research Center, The Cyprus Institute. Website: http://starc.cyi.ac.cy
Department of History and Archaeology, University of Cyprus: Website: www2.ucy.ac.cy/isa/index.html

ACKNOWLEDGEMENTS

The author acknowledges the assistance from the Department of Antiquities of Cyprus regarding the legislation and current practice concerning archaeological human remains, and in particular the assistance and clarifications received from the following members of staff at the Department of Antiquities Cyprus: Eftychia Zachariou (Archaeological Officer) and Fryni Hadjichristofi (Contract Archaeological Officer).

NOTES

1 The Souskiou-Laona Field School is directed by K.O. Lorentz, and in 2009 was jointly sponsored by the Cyprus Institute and the University of Edinburgh.
2 CAPP is coordinated by Dr Kirsi O. Lorentz, Science and Technology in Archaeology Research Centre (STARC), The Cyprus Institute.

BIBLIOGRAPHY

Agelarakis, A. (1997) 'Paleopathology and Its Contributions to the Decipherment of the Human Condition in Antiquity: The Case of Two Populations from Malloura in Cyprus', *Report of the Department of Antiquities of Cyprus*: 239–50.

Agelarakis, A., Kanta P. and Stampolides, N. (1998) 'The osseous record in the Western Necropolis of Amathous: an archaeo-anthropological investigation', in V. Karageorghis and N.C. Stampolides (eds) *Proceedings of the International Symposium: The Eastern Mediterranean, Cyprus-Dodecanese-Crete 16th-6th c. B.C., Rethymnon, Crete*, Athens: University of Crete and the A.G. Leventis Foundation.

Angel, J.L. (1953) 'The human remains from Khirokitia', in P. Dikaios (ed.) *Khirokitia*, London: Oxford University Press.

——(1955) 'The skulls', in J. Du Plat Taylor, 'Roman tombs at Kambi Vasa', *Report of the Department of Antiquities of Cyprus*, 1940–48: 68–76.

——(1961) 'Neolithic crania from Sotira', in P. Dikaios (ed.) *Sotira*, Philadelphia: University Museum, University of Pennsylvania.

——(1964) 'Osteoporosis: Thalassemia?', *American Journal of Physical Anthropology*, 22: 363–73.

——(1966) 'Porotic hyperostosis, anemias, malarias, and marshes in the prehistoric Eastern Mediterranean', *Science*, 153: 760–63.

——(1967) 'Porotic hyperostosis or osteoporosis symmetrica', in D. Brothwell and A.T. Sandison (eds) *Diseases in Antiquity*, Springfield, IL: Charles C. Thomas.

——(1969a) 'The bases of paleodemography', *American Journal of Physical Anthropology*, 30: 427–37.

——(1969b) 'Paleodemography and evolution', *American Journal of Physical Anthropology*, 31: 343–53.

——(1972a) 'Genetic and social factors in a Cypriote village', *Human Biology*, 44: 53–80.

——(1972b) 'Late Bronze Age Cypriotes from Bamboula', in J.L. Benson (ed.) *Bamboula at Kourion*, Philadelphia: University Museum, University of Pennsylvania.

——(1978) 'Porotic Hyperostosis in the Eastern Mediterranean', *Medical College of Virginia Quarterly*, 14: 1–16.

Axmacher, B. and Hjortsjö, C.-H. (1959) *Exam en anthropologique des crânes constituent la materiel préhistorique mis à jour à la suite des fouilles effectuées par les archéologues français à Iskender, Chypre*, Luna: Lunds Universitets Årsskrift.

Baker, B.J., Terhune, C.E. and Papalexandrou, A. (2007) 'Sew Long: a Seamstress buried at medieval polis', *American Journal of Physical Anthropology Supplement 132*: 67.

Buikstra, J.E. and Ubelaker, D.H. (eds) (1994) *Standards for Data Collection from Human Skeletal Remains, Proceedings of a Seminar at The Field Museum of Natural History*, Fayetteville, AR: Arkansas Archeological Survey Research Series No. 44.

Buxton, L.H.D. (1920a) 'The inhabitants of the Eastern Mediterranean', *Biométrica*, 13: 92–112.

——(1920b) 'The anthropology of Cyprus', *The Journal of the Royal Anthropological Institute of Great Britain and Ireland*, 50: 183–235.

——(1931) 'Künstlich deformierte Schädel von Cypern', *Anthropologischer Anzeiger*, 7: 236–40.

Cadogan, G. and Domurad, M.R. (1985) 'Maroni V', *Report of the Department of Antiquities of Cyprus*: 77–81.

Charles, R.-P. (1960) 'Observation sur les crânes de Chrysopolitissa'; in V. Karageorghis, 'Fouilles de Kition 1959', *Bulletin de Correspondence Hellenique*, 84: 583–88.

——(1962) *Le peuplement de Chypre dans L'Antiquité*, Paris: École Française d'Athènes.

——(1963) 'Note sure les restes humains d'Iskender', in J. Deshayes (ed.) *La Necropole de Ktima*, Paris: Librairie Orientaliste, Paul Geuther.

——(1964) 'Étude anthropologique de sujets d'Idalion', *Report of the Department of Antiquities of Cyprus*: 85.

——(1966) 'Étude des crânes de la tombe I de Karpasha', *Report of the Department of Antiquities of Cyprus*: 41–50.

——(1967) 'Étude des restes humains de tombe 31', in V. Karageorghis (ed.) *Excavations in the Necropolis of Salamis*, Nicosia: Department of Antiquities.

——(1970) 'Étude des restes humains des tombes de Cellarka necropole de Salamine (Chypre)', in V. Karageorghis (ed.) *Excavations in the Necropolis of Salamis II*, Nicosia: Department of Antiquities.

CMP (2010) *Committee of Missing Persons*. Available online at http://cmp-cyprus.org/ (accessed 6 April 2010).

Committee on Missing Persons in Cyprus (1981) *CMP Terms of reference*. Available online at www.cmp-cyprus.org/media/attachments/CMP/CMP docs/Terms_of_Reference_1981.pdf (accessed 6 April 2010).

——(2009) *CMP Factsheet April 2009*. Available online at www.cmp-cyprus.org/media/attachments/CMP/CMP docs/CMP Fact Sheets/CMP_Fact_Sheet&__]Apr09.pdf (accessed 8 July 2010).

Crewe, L., Lorentz, K.O., Peltenburg, E. *et al.* (2005) 'Treatments of the Dead: Investigations at Souskiou-Laona Chalcolithic Cemetery, 2001–4', *Report of the Department of Antiquities of Cyprus*: 41–68.

Domurad, M.R. (1985) 'The Human Remains', in D. Michaelides and M. Snyczer, *A Phoenician Graffito from Tomb 103/84 at Nea Paphos*, Report of the Department of Antiquities of Cyprus.

——(1986a) 'The populations of Ancient Cyprus', unpublished PhD thesis, University of Cincinnati.

——(1986b) 'The Human Remains', in E.J. Peltenburg, *Excavations at Kissonerga-Mosphilia 1985*, Report of the Department of Antiquities of Cyprus.

——(1987a) 'The Burials', in E.J. Peltenburg, *Excavations at Kissonerga-Mosphilia 1986*, Report of the Department of Antiquities of Cyprus.

——(1987b) 'The skeletal remains from Aghios Giorghios 1985', in M. Yon and O. Callot, *Nouvelles découvertes dans la nécropole ouest de Kition (Aghios Giorghios, époque classique)*, Report of the Department of Antiquities of Cyprus.

——(1988) 'The Human Remains', in D. Michaelides and J. Młynarczyk, *Tombs P.M. 2520 and P.M. 2737 from the Eastern Necropolis of Nea Paphos*, Report of the Department of Antiquities of Cyprus, Part 2.

——(1992) 'The population of Ancient Amathus', in V. Karageorghis, O. Picard and C. Tytgat (eds) *Études Chypriotes XIV: La nécropole D'Amathonte, tombes*, Nicosia: Department of Antiquities.

Downs, D. (1982) 'The Human Remains', in E. Peltenburg, 'Lemba Archaeological Project, Cyprus, 1979: Preliminary Report', *Levant*, 14: 51–52.

Eliopoulos, C., Lagia, A. and Manolis, S. (2007) 'A modern documented human skeletal collection from Greece', *Homo: Journal of Comparative Human Biology*, 58: 221–28.

Fessas, C. (1990) 'The Ayios Theodoros, Larnaca Skulls', in P. Flourentzos, *Excavations in an Archaic Necropolis at Ayios Theodoros*, Report of the Department of Antiquities of Cyprus.

Fischer, P.M. (1986) *Prehistoric Cypriot Skulls*, Göteborg: Paul Åströms Förlag.

Fischer, P.M. and Norén, J. (1988) 'Enamel defects in teeth from a prehistoric Cypriot population', *Ossa* 13: 87–96.

Fox, S.C. (1996) 'The human skeletal remains from Alassa-Ayia Mavri, Cyprus', in P. Flourentzos (ed.) *Excavations in the Kouris River Valley II*, Nicosia: Department of Antiquities.

——(1997) 'The human skeletal remains from Tomb 1, Mari Village, Larnaka District, Cyprus', in M. Hadjicosti, *The Family Tomb of a Warrior of the Cypro-Archaic I Period at Mari*, Report of the Department of Antiquities, Cyprus.

——(2001) 'The human skeletal remains from Kouklia-Eliomylia (KM 393, T. 125)' in S. Hadjisavvas, *An Enigmatic Burial at Kouklia-Eliomylia*, Report of the Department of Antiquities of Cyprus.

——(2003a) 'The human skeletal remains: a preliminary report', in M. Rautman, 'A Cypriot Village of Late Antiquity: Kalavasos-Kopetra in the Vasilikos Valley', *Journal of Roman Archaeology, Supplementary Series 52*.

——(2003b) 'Human Skeletal Remains', in S. Manning (ed.) *The Late Roman Church at Maroni Petrera*, Oxford: A.G. Leventis Foundation.

——(2003c) 'Human remains', E. Peltenburg (ed.) *Lemba Archaeological Project III.1 Excavations at Kissonerga-Mylouthkia 1977–1995*, Studies in Mediterranean Archaeology 70.4, Göteborg: Paul Åströms Förlag.

——(2005) 'Health in Hellenistic and Roman times: the case studies of Paphos, Cyprus and Corinth, Greece', in H. King (ed.) *Health in Antiquity*, London: Routledge.

——(2006) 'Human skeletal remains from the 1991 to 1998 seasons', in D. Frankel and J.M. Webb (eds) *Marki Alonia. An Early and Middle Bronze Age Settlement in Cyprus. Excavations 1995–2000*, Studies in Mediterranean Archaeology 123, Sävedalen: Paul Åströms Förlag.

——(2007) 'The Human Skeletal Remains from Psematismenos-Koliokremmos/Palia' in J.M. Webb, D. Frankel, S.W. Manning *et al.* (eds), *Psematismenos-Koliokremmos/Palia Tomb PKK/94*, Report of the Department of Antiquities of Cyprus.

Fox-Leonard, S.C. (1997) 'Comparative Health from Paleopathological Analysis of the Human Skeletal Remains Dating to the Hellenistic and Roman Periods, from Paphos, Cyprus and Corinth, Greece', unpublished PhD thesis, Department of Anthropology, University of Arizona.

Kirsi O. Lorentz

Fürst, C.M. (1933) *Zur Kenntnis der Anthropologie der Prähistorischen Bevölkerung der Insel Cypern*, Lund: Lunds Universitets Arsskrift.

Galloway, A. (1985) 'Report on the Skeletal Remains from the 1984 Excavations, Kourion City, Grid L 9', in D. Soren and T. Davis (eds) *Report of the Department of Antiquities, Cyprus*: 302–6.

Guest, E.M. (1936) 'The Human Remains', in P. Dikaios, *The Excavations at Erimi 1933–35. Final Report*, Report of the Department of Antiquities of Cyprus.

Harper, N.K. (2002) 'The human remains from Pegia-Pappara', in E. Raptou, E. Stylianou and E. Vassiliou, *The Hellenistic Tomb of Pegeia-Pappara*, Report of the Department of Antiquities of Cyprus.

——(2008) 'Shorts skulls, long skulls and Thalassemia: J. Lawrence Angel and the development of anthropology in Cyprus', *Near Eastern Archaeology*, 711: 111–19.

Harper, N.K. (in press) 'From typology to population genetics: biodistance in Cyprus', in A. Satraki and M. Iacovou (eds) *Proceedings of the 7th Postgraduates in Cypriot Archaeology Meeting, Nicosia, Cyprus*, British Archaeological Reports International Series.

Harper, N. and Fox, S. (2008) 'Recent research in Cypriot bioarchaeology', *Bioarchaeology in the Near East* (e-journal), 2008: 1–38. Available online at www.anthropology.uw.edu.pl/02/bne-02-01.pdf (accessed 8 July 2010).

Harter-Lailheugue, S., Le Mort, F., Vigne, J.-D., *et al.* (2005) 'Premières données parasitologiques sur les populations humaines précéramiques chypriotes (VIIIe et VIIe millénaires av. J. C.)', *Paléorient*, 31: 43–54.

Herscher, E. and Fox, S.C. (1994) *A Middle Bronze Tomb from Western Cyprus*, Report of the Department of Antiquities, Cyprus.

Hjortsjö, C.-H. (1947) *To the Knowledge of the Prehistoric Craniology of Cyprus*, Lund: Kungliga Humanistika Vetenskapssamfundets Årsberättelse.

Kurth, G. (1958) 'Zur Stellung den neolitischen Menschenreste von Khirokitia auf Cypern', *Homo*, 104: 213–26.

Le Mort, F. (1994) 'Les sepultures', in A. Le Brun, *Fouilles récentes à Khirokitia (Chypre 1988–1991)*, Paris: Éditions Recherche sur les Civilisations.

——(1995) 'Le peuplement de Chypre: Rapport des données anthropologiques', *Paléorient*, 212: 111–21.

——(2000) 'The Neolithic subadult skeletons from Khirokitia (Cyprus): taphonomy and mortality', *Anthropologie*, 38: 63–70.

——(2007) 'Artificial cranial deformation in the Aceramic Neolithic Near East: evidence from Cyprus', in M. Faerman, L.K. Horwitz, T. Kahana and U. Zilberman (eds) *Faces from the Past: Diachronic Patterns in the Biology of Human Populations from the Eastern Mediterranean. Papers in Honor of Patricia Smith*, Oxford: Archaeopress.

——(2008) 'Infant burials in Pre-Pottery Neolithic Cyprus: evidence from Khirokitia', in K. Bacvarov (ed.) *Babies Reborn: Infant/Child Burials in Pre- and Protohistory*, Oxford: Archaeopress.

Longmore, B. (1975) 'The dentition of the Philia-Drakos Site A Skulls', in M. Walker, 'Early Neolithic Skeletons from Philia Drakos, Site A (Cyprus)', *Australian Journal of Biblical Archaeology*, 2: 77–89.

Lorentz, K.O. (2001) *The Human Skeletal Remains from Tremithousa Tomb PM 3397*, Report of the Department of Antiquities of Cyprus.

——(2002) 'Cultures of physical modifications', in G. Muskett, A. Koltsida and M. Georgiadis (eds) *Symposium on Mediterranean Archaeology (SOMA 2002), University of Liverpool*, British Archaeological Reports International Series 1040, Oxford: Archaeopress.

——(2003a) 'Minding the Body: The Growing Body in Cyprus from the Aceramic Neolithic to the Late Bronze Age', unpublished PhD thesis, Department of Archaeology, University of Cambridge.

——(2003b) 'Cultures of Physical Modifications: Child Bodies in Ancient Cyprus', *Stanford Journal of Archaeology*, 2: 1–17.

——(2004a) 'Human Skeletal Remains from the Tomb TSR', in S. Bezzola (ed.) *Lucerne fittili dagli scavi di Palaepaphos (Cipro)*, Mainz am Rhein: Verlag Philipp von Zabern.

——(2004b) 'Age and gender in Eastern Mediterranean prehistory: depictions, burials and skeletal evidence', *Ethnographisch-Archäologische Zeitschrift*, 45: 297–315.

——(2005) 'Late Bronze Age burial practices: age as a form of social difference', in V. Karageorghis, H. Matthäus and S. Rogge (eds) *Cyprus: Religion and Society from the Late Bronze Age to the End of the Archaic Period*, Mohnesee-Wamel: Bibliopolis.

——(2006a) 'Human skeletal remains from the 1999 and 2000 seasons', in D. Frankel and J. Webb (eds) *Marki Alonia. An Early and Middle Bronze Age Settlement in Cyprus. Excavations 1995–2000*, Sävedalen: Paul Åströms Förlag.

——(2006b) 'Headshaping at Marki and its socio-cultural significance', in D. Frankel and J. Webb (eds) *Marki Alonia. An Early and Middle Bronze Age Settlement in Cyprus. Excavations 1995–2000*, Sävedalen: Paul Åströms Förlag.

——(2007a) 'Human skeletal remains from KA Tomb I', in F.G. Maier (ed.) *Ausgrabungen in Alt-Paphos auf Cypern*, Berlin: Verlag Philipp von Zabern.

——(2007b) 'Teeth as tools: Health and disease at Shahr-e Sokhte', in ICAR (ed.) *Proceedings of the 9th International Symposium of Iranian Archaeology*, Tehran, Iranian Center for Archaeological Research (ICAR). [in Farsi]

——(2008a) 'Crafting the Head: The Human Body as Art?', in J.M. Córdoba, M. Molist, M. Carmen Pérez, *et al.* (eds) *Proceedings of the Fifth International Congress on the Archaeology of the Ancient Near East*, Madrid: Universidad Autónoma de Madrid.

——(2008b) 'From bodies to bones and back: theory and human bioarchaeology' in H. Schutkowski (ed.) *Between Biology and Culture*, Cambridge, Cambridge University Press.

——(2008c) 'From Life Course to longue durée: Headshaping as Gendered Capital?', in D. Bolger (ed.) *Gender through Time in the Ancient Near East*, Walnut Creek: Altamira Press.

——(2009a) 'The Malleable Body: headshaping in Greece and the surrounding regions', in L. Schepartz, S.C. Fox and C. Bourbou (eds) *New Directions in the Skeletal Biology of Greece*, Princeton: American School of Classical Studies at Athens.

——(2009b) 'Human remains from Karmi', in J.M. Webb, D. Frankel, K. Eriksson, *et al.* (eds), *The Bronze Age Cemeteries at Karmi Palealona and Lapatsa in Cyprus. Excavations by J.R.B. Stewart*, Studies in Mediterranean Archaeology Volume CXXXVI, Savedalen: Paul Astroms Forlag.

Lorentz K.O. (in press a) 'Human remains recovered from the Larnaka-Liperti Tomb 128 sarcophagi A (alpha) and B (beta)', in P. Flourentzos (ed.) *Two Exceptional Sarcophagi from Larnaka*, Nicosia: Department of Antiquities Cyprus.

Lorentz, K.O. (in press b) 'Ubaid headshaping: negotiations of identity through physical appearance?', in R.A. Carter and G. Philip (eds) *The Ubaid and Beyond: Exploring the Transmission of Culture in the Developed Prehistoric Societies of the Middle East*, Proceedings of the International Conference on the Ubaid, Durham, 20–22 April 2006.

Lorentz K. O. (in press c) 'Parts to a whole: Manipulations of the body in prehistoric Eastern Mediterranean', in K. Rebay, M. L. S. Sørensen, and J. Hughes (eds.) *Body parts and wholes: Changing relations and meanings.* Oxford, Oxbow.

Lorentz, K.O. (in press d) 'Human bioarchaeology of the Cypriot Chalcolithic: analyses at Souskiou-Laona cemetery', in *Proceedings of the IV International Cyprological Congress.*

Lorentz, K.O. (forthcoming) 'Orderly Disposal: Human Remains at Chalcolithic Souskiou-Laona, Cyprus', in P. Karsgaard (ed.) *Death and Discard: The Transformations of Places, People, Animals and Things in the Ancient Near East, BANEA Monograph 2*, Oxford: Oxbow.

Lunt, D.A. (1980) 'Evidence of Tooth Extraction in a Cypriot Mandible of the Hellenistic or Early Roman Period, c. 150 B.C. to 100 A.D.', *British Dental Journal*, 173: 242.

——(1985) 'Report on the human dentitions', in E.J. Peltenburg (ed.) *Lemba Archaeological Project 1. Excavations at Lemba-Lakkous 1976–1983*, Studies in Mediterranean Archaeology 701, Göteborg: Paul Åströms Förlag.

——(1994) 'Report on the human dentitions from Souskiou-Vathrykakas, 1972', in F.G. Maier and M.-L. von Wartburg (eds) *Excavations at Kouklia (Palaipaphos). Seventeenth Preliminary Report: Seasons 1991 and 1992*, Report of the Department of Antiquities of Cyprus.

——(1995) 'Lemba Lakkous and Kissonerga Mosphilia: evidence from the dentition in Chacolithic Cyprus', in S. Campbell and A. Green (eds) *Archaeology of Death in the Ancient Near East*, Oxford: Oxbow.

——(2006) 'The human dentition', in E. Peltenburg (ed.) *The Chalcolithic Cemetery of Souskiou-Vathrykakas, Cyprus*, Cyprus: Department of Antiquities.

Lunt, D.A. and Watt, M.E. (1998) 'The human dentitions', in E. Peltenburg (ed.) *Lemba Archaeological Project Vol. II.1A: Excavations at Kissonerga-Mosphilia 1979–1992*, Göteborg: Paul Åströms Förlag.

——(2003) 'The dentitions' in E. Peltenburg (ed.) *The Colonisation and Settlement of Cyprus: Investigations at Kissonerga-Mylouthkia, 1976–1996*, Sävedalen: Paul Åströms Förlag.

Moyer, C.J. (1984) 'Report on the human skeletal remains from Amathonte, Cyprus' in P. Aupert and C. Tytgat, 'Deux tombes géométriques de la nécropole nord d'Amathonte', *Bulletin de Correspondence Hellenique*, 108: 649–53.

——(1985) 'The human skeletal remains', in I.A. Todd, *A Middle Bronze Age Tomb at Psematismenos-Trelloukkas*, Report of the Department of Antiquities of Cyprus.

——(1989) 'Human skeletal remains', in A.K. South, P. Russel and P. Schuster Keswani (eds) *Vasilikos Valley Project 3: Kalavasos-Ayios Dhimitirios II*, Jönsered: Paul Åströms Förlag.

——(1997) 'Human Remains from Marki-Alonia, Cyprus', *Report of the Department of Antiquities of Cyprus*: 111–18.

——(2004) 'Human skeletal remains', in I.A.Todd and P. Croft (eds) *Vasilikos Valley Project 8: Excavations at Kalavasos-Ayious*, Sävedalen: Paul Åströms Förlag.

——(2005) 'Human burials' in I.A. Todd (ed.) *Vasilikos Valley Project, 7: Excavations at Kalavasos-Tenta, 2*, Sävedalen: Paul Åströms Förlag.

——(2006) 'Human remains from LVII-1, context 963', in D. Frankel and J.M. Webb (eds) *Marki Alonia: An Early and Middle Bronze Age Settlement in Cyprus Excavations 1995–2000*, Sävedalen: Paul Åströms Förlag.

——(2007) 'Human skeletal remains', in I.A. Todd (ed.) *Vasilikos Valley Project 11: Kalavasos Village Tombs 52–79*, Sävedalen: Paul Åströms Förlag.

Musgrave, J.H. and Evans, S.P. (1980) 'By Strangers Honor'd: a statistical study of ancient crania from Crete, mainland Greece, Cyprus, Israel and Egypt', *Journal of Mediterranean Anthropology and Archaeology*, 1: 50–107.

Nyqvist, E. (1980) 'Human teeth from Kition', *Opuscula Atheniensia*, 13: 185–88.

Parks, D.A., Mavromatis, C.M. and Harper, N.K. (2000) 'Preliminary Report of Excavations at Kourion's Amathous Gate Cemetery, 1999', *Report of the Department of Antiquities of Cyprus*: 305–16.

——(2001) 'Preliminary Report of Excavations at Kourion's Amathous Gate Cemetery, 1999', *Report of the Department of Antiquities of Cyprus*: 232–45.

Parras, Z. (2004) *The Biological Affinities of the Eastern Mediterranean in the Chalcolithic and Bronze Age: A Regional Dental Non-Metric Approach*, Oxford: Archaeopress.

——(2006a) 'The human remains', in E. Peltenburg (ed.) *The Chalcolithic Cemetery of Souskiou-Vathrykakas, Cyprus*, Cyprus: Department of Antiquities.

——(2006b) 'Looking for immigrants at Kissonerga-Mosphilia in the Late Chalcolithic: a dental non-metric perspective of Chalcolithic and Early Bronze Age southwest Cyprus', in A.P. McCarthy (ed.) *Island Dialogues. Cyprus in the Mediterranean Network*, Edinburgh: University of Edinburgh Archaeology Occasional Paper 21.

Rix, M.M. (1938) 'Description of skeleton No. 2', in P. Dikaios, *The Excavations at Erimi 1933–35. Final Report*, Report of the Department of Antiquities of Cyprus.

——(1950) 'Cranial measurements', in E. Stewart and J. Stewart (eds) *Vounous 1937–1938: Field Report on the Excavations Sponsored by the British School of Archaeology at Athens*, Lund: Gleerup.

Rix, M.M. and Buxton, L.H.D. (1938) 'The anthropology of prehistoric Cyprus', *Man*, 38: 91–92.

Schaeffer, C.F.A. (1935) 'Crania Cypria Antiqua', *L'Anthropologie*, 45: 218–21.

Schulte-Campbell, C. (1979) 'Human skeletal remains', in I.A. Todd, *Vasilikos Valley Project, 1977–1978: An Interim Report*, Report of the Department of Antiquities of Cyprus.

——(1983) 'The human remains from Palaepaphos-Skales', in V. Karageorghis (ed.), *Palaepaphos-Skales, An Iron Age cemetery in Cyprus*, Konstanz: Universitätsverlag.

——(1986) 'Human skeletal remains', in I.A.Todd (ed.) *Vasilikos Valley Project 1: The Bronze Age Cemetery in Kalavasos Village*, Studies in Mediterranean Archaeology 71: 1, Göteborg: Paul Åströms Förlag.

——(1989) 'A Late Cypriot IIC tomb: Idalion tomb 1.76. Introduction and skeletal remains', in L.E. Stager and A.M. Walker (eds) *American Expedition to Idalion, Cyprus, 1973–1980*, Chicago: The Oriental Institute of the University of Chicago.

——(2003) 'The human skeletal remains', in S. Swiny, G. Rapp and E. Herscher (eds) *Sotira Kaminoudhia: An Early Bronze Age site in Cyprus*, Cyprus American Archaeological Research Center Monograph Series 4, Boston: American Schools of Oriental Research.

Schwartz, J.H. (1974) 'The human remains from Kition and Hala Sultan Tekke: a cultural interpretation', in V. Karageorghis (ed.) *Excavations at Kition I. The Tombs*, Nicosia: Department of Antiquities, Cyprus.

Soliveres, O.M. (1981) 'Étude des crânes du Cap Andreas-Kastros', in A. Le Brun, *Un site néolithique pré-céramique en Chypre: Cap Andreas-Kastros*, Récherche sur le grandes civilizations 5, Paris: Editions Recherche sur les Civilisations.

Taramides, G. (1983) 'The teeth of Neolithic Cypriots (5800–3000 B.C.)', *Odontostomatoloyiki Proozos*, 37: 213–18. [in Greek]

Tucker, K. and Clegget, S. (2007) 'Human remains from tomb 789', in D. Frankel and J.M. Webb (ed.) *The Bronze Age Cemeteries at Denia in Cyprus*, Sävedalen: Paul Åströms Förlag.

Vermeule, E. (1974) *Toumba tou Skourou: the Mound of Darkness: A Bronze Age town on Morphou Bay, Cyprus*, Boston: Harvard University, Museum of Fine Arts.

Virchow, R. (1884) *Über alte Schädel von Assos Und Cypern*, Berlin: Abhandlungen der Königlichen Akademie der Wissenschaften zu Berlin.

Walker, M. (1975) 'Early Neolithic skeletons from Philia-Drakos', Site A (Cyprus), *Australian Journal of Biblical Archaeology*, 2: 77–89.

Czech Republic/Česká republika

Petr Velemínský and Lumír Poláček

INTRODUCTION: A BRIEF HISTORY AND CURRENT STATE OF PHYSICAL ANTHROPOLOGY IN THE CZECH REPUBLIC

The beginning of the field of anthropology in the Czech territory dates to the second half of the 19th century. The first research in the field of skeletal anthropology also dates to this period. The authors of research at this time were naturally the archaeologists who uncovered skeletal remains. They considered the study of skeletons, and predominantly of skulls, to be 'complementary' to archaeological research. Thus, this did not involve a systematic study based on a precisely defined methodology. This state of affairs naturally reflected the situation in other European countries. The works of Edvard Grégr (1827–1907) and Jindřich Wankel (1821–97) are considered to be the oldest works dedicated to the study of past populations. Grégr's study 'Of human skulls generally and Slavonic skulls particularly' ('O lebkách člověčích vůbec a slovanských zvláště') was published as early as 1858. The subtext of this research, though, was partly political. At the time, Bohemia was part of the Austro-Hungarian Empire. The author was attempting to prove that Slavs represented the original settlers of the central European territory and thus indirectly to substantiate the right of the Czech nation to its own language and greater political independence from Vienna. Besides, a similar theme was subsequently tackled in other works.

Three men contributed fundamentally to the development of anthropology in the first half of the 20th century: Luboš Niederle (1865–1944), Bohumil Hellich (1851–1918) and Jindřich Matiegka (1862–1941). Luboš Niederle was the first associate professor of anthropology at Charles University in Prague (1892). Eventually, he left this field and dedicated himself solely to archaeology, where he proposed a system of Czech Prehistory which remains more or less valid today. Hellich analysed an extensive collection of skulls from the Museum of the Czech Kingdom (Muzeum království českého). The last to be named, Jindřich Matiegka, was definitely the greatest personality of Czech inter-war anthropology (Figure 11.1). In 1920, he founded at Charles University the first independent anthropological institute in Czechoslovakia. Together with Aleš Hrdlička, he also founded the journal *Anthropologie* (1923), and was editor-in-chief for nearly 20 years. At the beginning of the 1920s, he held the position of Dean at the Faculty of Natural Sciences. Apart from palaeoanthropology (*Homo predmostensis*) and 'historical' anthropology (regarding the physical character of the prehistoric populations of the Czech territory), his publications included studies from other areas of anthropology (somatic–anthropological philosophy, racial types). Matiegka also devoted himself to the examination of the remains of prominent personalities of Czech and European history (e.g., St Wenceslas, Wenceslas II, Wenceslas III, Comenius, Tycho Brahe) (see, e.g., Stloukal *et al.* 1999). His work on the Gravettian skeletons from Předmostí represents an especially exceptional study of that time.

The second anthropological university institute, The Institute of Anthropology, was founded in the years 1923–27 by Vojtěch Suk at the Masaryk University in Brno (Antropologický ústav, Masarykova Univerzita, Brno).

When we attributed to Matiegka a privileged position within Czech anthropology, we did not take into consideration Aleš Hrdlička (1869–1943). Hrdlička left Bohemia in his youth and spent the rest of his life in the USA. There, besides medicine, he graduated in anthropology and fundamentally influenced the development of this field in America. In Chicago, he founded probably the as yet most prestigious international anthropological journal, the *American Journal of Physical Anthropology*. He headed the Department of Anthropology at the Smithsonian Institution in Washington. During his career, he published more than 300 anthropological studies. He formulated the theory regarding the common origin and development of Man. Hrdlička supported the development of this field in Bohemia. As has been mentioned already, he was the co-founder of the journal *Anthropologie* and he initiated the foundation of the Museum

Figure 11.1 Jindrich Matiegka, founder of the Department of Anthropology in the Faculty of Science of Charles University, Czech Republic
Source: J. Matiegka/J. Maly

of Man (today the Hrdlička Museum of Man) at Charles University in Prague (see. e.g., Fetter *et al.* 1967).

Another eminent personality in Czech anthropology was archaeologist and palaeontologist Karel Absolon (1877–1960). In the 1920s and 1930s he directed research on many Moravian Palaeolithic sites and he collected a considerable amount of Palaeolithic finds from a number of sites (e.g., Býčí skála, Pekárna, Dolní Věstonice, Stránská skála, Šipka). Absolon founded the Department of Prehistory at the Moravian Museum in Brno. He also organized a large exhibition about the Evolution of Mankind at this museum (see, e.g., Malina *et al.* 2009).

After the Second World War, the development of anthropology in Bohemia was indirectly influenced by the systematic archaeological investigation of extensive burial grounds. In Communist Czechoslovakia, great attention was dedicated especially to Slavonic archaeology, partly characterized by localities of the early Mediaeval Great Moravian Empire (e.g., Staré Město near Uherské Hradiště, Mikulčice-Valy) and by the Mediaeval Premysl dynasty in Bohemia (e.g., Libice, Budeč). This fact was also naturally related to the attempt to support the ideal of 'Slavonic brotherhood' in association with the justification of political ties with the Union of Soviet Socialist Republics. This research uncovered dozens of burial grounds. One example is the Great Moravian settlement agglomeration at Mikulčice-Valy, where around 2,500 human graves have been discovered to date.

In the 1950s and 1960s several institutions were established in Bohemia focusing on the research of our ancestors. These mainly included the Department of Anthropology at the Institute of Archaeology of the Academy of Sciences of the Czech Republic in Prague (Archeologický ústav Akademie věd České republiky, Praha), the Anthropos Institute at the Moravian Museum in Brno (Anthropos, Moravské zemské museum, Brno) and finally the Department of Anthropology at the National Museum in Prague (Antropologické oddělení, Národní museum, Praha). Other anthropologists giving consideration to the study of methods of skeletal anthropology worked in the biological department of the Criminology Institute in Prague, which was founded in 1958.

At this time, within the research of past populations, three main trends gradually crystallized in Bohemia. These were:

1 Palaeoanthropology, which focused on processing the fossils of Neanderthals and Upper Palaeolithic Anatomically Modern Humans found in Moravia (Šipka, Kůlna, Dolní Věstonice, Pavlov, Předmostí, Stránská Skála), Bohemia (Zlatý kůň) and Slovakia (Gánovce, Šala) (research by Emanuel Vlček and Jan Jelínek);

2 Palaeodemography of prehistoric and historical burial grounds: the establishment and development of this new approach to the analysis of human skeletal remains was influenced by the discovery of large burial grounds. This method was based on the demographic characteristics of groups, based in turn on the calculation of so-called life tables (research by Milan Stloukal, Hana Hanáková, Jaromír Chochol, Miroslava Blajero and Vladimír);

3 Palaeopathology: the study of the health status of past populations (by Eugen Strouhal and Luboš Vyhnánek).

After the fall of the communist regime in 1989, no fundamental changes occurred in the Czech Republic with regard to the existence of institutions dedicated to skeletal anthropology. None the less, the adjustment of property-legal relations influenced the change in character of archaeological research. Rescue archaeology started unequivocally to predominate. This was also due to the construction and building boom in the Czech Republic. By contrast, planned and systematic research was reduced to a great extent. The research area of extensive burial grounds thus became sporadic. This fact, together with new trends in palaeodemography, led to the reduction of 'classical' palaeodemographic publications.

The aforementioned text represents only an outline of the history of physical anthropology focusing on the study of past populations. It cannot be stressed enough that the development of Czech anthropology always reflected the development of European and subsequently American anthropology.

Skeletal collections

The founding of the first 'collections' of human skeletal remains from archaeological research is associated in Bohemia with the early years of the National Museum at the beginning of the 19th century, when the so-called 'Patriotic Museum' was established. V. Krolmus from the Archaeology Board of the Czech Museum was one of the first to assemble and collect archaeological material. The principal section of his craniological collection came from J.E. Purkyně. One of the first anthropological studies in Bohemia, 'On human skulls and Slavonic skulls particularly' by Grégr in 1858, was based on this series. An extensive collection of skulls from various pre-historic periods was also assembled by archaeologist Jindřich Wankel (1821–97) who sold it towards the end of his life to the Naturhistorische Museum in Vienna (this collection included, for example, skeletons from the Hallstatt locality of Býčí skála). Further proof that anthro-pological finds were deposited and studied in the museum may also be found in Hellich's work from 1899, 'Prehistoric skulls in Bohemia from the Czech Kingdom Museum collection' ('Prehistorické lebky v Čechách ze sbírky Musea království Českého'). None the less, it proved impossible to establish an independent anthropological department in the museum since there was no anthropologist working there. L. Niederle attempted in 1889 unsuccessfully to establish such a department. This is one of the reasons why today we generally have no idea about what happened to these old 'collections'. A smaller part of the finds ended up in the Hrdlička Museum of Man at Charles University in Prague.

In the inter-war period, skeletal remains from archaeological research belonging to the Prehistory Department of the National Museum were assembled in the Institute of Anthropology of Charles University in Prague. None the less, only a small part of this material was preserved. A similar situation reigned in Moravia, where skeletons from archaeological research were usually deposited either in the University Institute of Anthropology in Brno or in the Department of Archaeology of the Moravian Museum. It may be presumed that some of these finds were also deposited in smaller district/city museums. As such institutions did not employ then, nor do they employ today, any anthropologists, these finds have not been underpinned.

Unfortunately, current revisions show that a great proportion of skeletal finds from research conducted up to the Second World War have not survived. This applies especially to research conducted in the 19th century.

After the Second World War, Czechoslovakia witnessed the previously described boom in archaeological research of extensive burial grounds, which also helped establish anthropological institutions. In the 1950s, the Natural Sciences Department was founded at the Institute of Archaeology of the Academy of Sciences in Prague. In the 1960s, the Anthropos Institute was established in the Moravian Museum in Brno, and, finally, in 1967 Emanuel Vlček founded the Department of Anthropology of the National Museum (Figure 11.2).

These institutions became the principal collection-forming institutions in the field of past population studies in the Czech Republic. A great majority of the skeletons uncovered during archaeological research were transferred to these institutions. At the beginning of the 1990s,

Figure 11.2 The building of the National Museum in Prague

after the change in the political system, the Prague Institute of Archaeology handed over its osteological collection to the National Museum. The legal and property changes that occurred in the 1990s led to an increase in the number of cases in which an archaeological institution failed to hand over uncovered human skeletal remains to collection-forming organisations and museums, and kept these stored in its own 'depositories'. The amendment of the Act on the Conservation of Monuments from 2005 relating to the ownership of archaeological finds, moreover, led to a number of skeletons being handed over to district and town museums. One shortcoming is the fact that these institutions usually do not employ anthropologists, therefore they lack professional and erudite administration of their anthropological collections. In the long-term prospect, there is a risk that burial grounds deposited in these institutions without anthropologists will fail to be entered into the Central Records of Collections of the Czech Republic (Centrální evidence sbírek České republiky) and thus may end up 'forgotten' for several decades from now. There is some analogy with the deposition of collections in the period before the First World War and eventually between the First and Second World Wars.

Thus today, in the Czech Republic, the largest collection of human skeletal remains of past populations is deposited in the National Museum in Prague (Figure 11.3). This collection includes around 25,000 skeletal remains including cremated remains dating from the Neolithic to the Modern Age. Most of the skeletons originate from archaeological research conducted on the territory of the Czech Republic. Burial grounds excavated and uncovered on the territory of Slovakia are also represented. It may be presumed that this is one of the largest osteological collections in Europe. Naturally, this collection is being constantly expanded, supported by the fact that the National Museum built a new, extensive natural science depositary at the turn of the millennium. The second largest collection of skeletons from archaeological research is deposited in the Moravian Museum, in Anthropos (Anthropos, Moravské zemské muzeum).

Figure 11.3 The osteological depository of the anthropology department, National Museum in Prague

It includes more than 10,000 skeletons. Finally, a smaller 'archaeological' osteological collection is stored at Hrdlicka Museum of Man in Prague.

Education and training

Until 1920, when the first university anthropology department in Czechoslovakia was founded, anthropology was taught at Charles University as part of Prehistory and Archaeology. Luboš Niederle was named the first associate professor of anthropology in 1892. The first independent Department of Anthropology at Charles University was established in 1920, following the founding of the Faculty of Natural Sciences. Until then, Natural Sciences was taught at the faculties of Philosophy and Medicine. The first head of this institution was Jindřich Matiegka. Soon after the establishment of the department in Prague, Vojtěch Suk founded the Institute of Anthropology (1923–27) at Masaryk University in Brno. This, however, was abolished after the Second World War and its employees were transferred to the zoology department. An independent Department of Anthropology (today known again as the Institute of Anthropology) was only restored in the 1990s. Both previously mentioned institutions remain the principal teaching centres today. Since the 1990s, 'osteological anthropology' is also taught at the Department of Biological Anthropology in the Faculty of Philosophy of the University of West Bohemia in Plzeň. It should be mentioned that the pivotal research theme of all these departments is currently the study of past populations, or bioarchaeology. Moreover, clinical anthropology has its tradition in Prague, and the past decades have also seen the development of human genetics. Sociocultural Anthropology is taught at the same time at Masaryk University. Physical anthropology, which focuses on sports medicine, is taught at the Department of Anthropology and Hygiene, College of Education, Palacký University in Olomouc, and at the Department of Functional Anthropology and Physiology, Faculty of Physical Training, also at Palacký University. Physical anthropology is also taught at the Department of Biology and

Ecological Studies in the Faculty of Pedagogy of Charles University in Prague and at the Department of Medical Anthropology of Institute of Anatomy, Faculty of Medicine, Masaryk University.

Thus, in the Czech Republic, Anthropology and Archaeology are studied independently: Anthropology usually at faculties of Natural Sciences; Archaeology at faculties of Philosophy. At the Faculty of Philosophy of Charles University, physical anthropology is classified as an optional subject. Students do, however, have the opportunity to attend lectures at several other faculties.

Thus, physical anthropology in Czechoslovakia, or rather in the Czech Republic, has a tradition in excess of 100 years, and has been unequivocally preferred to cultural anthropology. This fact has been conditioned by the European space, and later, naturally, also by the political system. Cultural anthropology was from an ideological point of view in conflict with the Communist regime and it was given space at universities only after the regime's fall. Today, it is taught at the Faculties of Philosophy of Charles University and the University of West Bohemia, and the Faculty of Humanities of Charles University.

ARCHAEOLOGICAL HUMAN REMAINS AND LEGISLATION

Archaeological legislation

In the Czech Republic, only the Institute of Archaeology of the Academy of Sciences of the address reference of website with the list of authorized organizations for executing of archaeological excavations. It means: Czech Republic is by law authorized to conduct archaeological research. This institution also voices pronouncements regarding the protection of archaeological heritage. The Ministry of Culture may, on request and in justified cases, authorize universities, museums or other organizations or qualified physical entities to conduct archaeological research following the agreement of the Academy of Sciences of the Czech Republic ('the authorized organization').

Currently, in the Czech Republic there are more than 100 institutions authorized to conduct archaeological research. 'State-run' institutions unequivocally dominate (the Institutes of Archaeology of the Academy of Sciences of the Czech Republic, the National Institutes for the Protection and Conservation of Monuments and Sites, the Institutes of Archaeological Monument Preservation, the Museums) over private institutions (the non-profit organizations, Archaia, Labrys, etc.).

Qualifications refer to the expertise and professional qualifications of the physical entity requesting an authorization or to the expertise and professional qualifications of the person requesting such authorization. This person must ensure professionalism during the conducted archaeological research and provide information on the equipment, laboratory apparatus and the necessary premises for the scientific processing and documentation of archaeological material, including the provisional storage of movable archaeological findings. Professional qualifications are demonstrated by meeting the achieved qualification requirement such as a university education from an accredited master's programme in the field of Social Sciences with specialization in archaeology and two years of professional experience. This means that only graduates in archaeology and not anthropology may direct archaeological research in the Czech Republic.

The authorized organization is required to announce to the Institute of Archaeology of the Academy of Sciences of the Czech Republic (Archeologický ústav Akademie věd České republiky) and the National Institute for the Protection and Conservation of Monuments and Sites (Národní památkový ústav), and eventually the province or town institutions, the beginning of archaeological research and to submit to them a report regarding the results of the work undertaken.

The institution that is to direct the archaeological research is required, before such research begins, to conclude an agreement with the owner of the property, outlining the conditions governing the research on such property.

If archaeological finds (including human skeletal remains) are uncovered accidentally, that is, they are not uncovered during the course of archaeological research, the authorized institution, either the nearest museum or the Institute of Archaeology of the Academy of Sciences of the Czech Republic, must be informed. This fact must be announced by the finder or by the person responsible for the work during which the finds were made (e.g., most often the investor of construction work). The site of these finds should be left unaltered until the arrival of archaeologists (usually within five working days), who will then decide the course to be followed. If archaeological finds are not reported, then a fine of up to several tens of thousands of Czech crowns may be imposed. If the findings occurred within a more extensive and costly construction enterprise, the investor usually considers whether the extent of financial losses due to delays of the construction work schedule will not exceed several times the potential fine. The danger of construction delays has thus, in the past, several times exceeded the threat of receiving a fine from the state. One such example in Prague was the failure to inform of the uncovering of a cemetery in the Wratislaw Palace at the beginning of the 1990s. It is presumed that more than 50 graves dating from the 11th to the 13th centuries were destroyed at that time.

Movable archaeological finds (including human skeletons) are, according to the Act on National Protection and Conservation of Monuments from the year 2005 (Zákon o státní památkové péči), the property of the district on whose territory they were uncovered. This does not apply if these finds are uncovered during research conducted by an organization belonging to a town. In such cases, they are the property of the given town. If they are uncovered during research conducted by state organizations, they become the property of the Czech Republic. Movable archaeological finds that are the property of districts are deposited in the given district's museum. If they are the property of the town, then they are deposited in the museum run by the given town or by another town or the relevant district. Finally, finds uncovered by state organizations are usually deposited in the museums run by the Ministry of Culture. They may also be deposited in other state organizations, if these keep and preserve collections. For example, an extensive collection related to two Gravettian localities, Dolní Věstonice (Figure 11.4) and Pavlov, which includes human fossils is deposited at the Department of Palaeolites and Palaeoethnology of the Institute of Archaeology of the Academy of Sciences in Brno. Under certain conditions, the Czech Ministry of Culture may call on the district or town to transfer the movable archaeological finds to the ownership of the state, that is, to hand them over to a state institution – most often the National Museum or the Moravian Museum.

The aforementioned rules form part of the Act on National Protection and Conservation of Monuments, which came into force in 1987. Some of its sections were later revised. Legislatively, archaeological research is in some cases also governed by the Act on Zoning and Building Regulations (i.e., the 'Building Act') (Zákon o územním plánování a stavebním řádu), the Act on Environmental Protection (Zákon o ochraně přírody a krajiny) or eventually, by 2002, the Charter for the Protection and Management of European Archaeological Heritage (Úmluva o ochraně archeologického dědictví Evropy).

HUMAN REMAINS AND LEGISLATION

In the case of finds involving isolated skeletal remains with no evidence of their dating, the issue of whether it is an 'archaeological' or a 'forensic' find becomes central. If the human skeletal

Figure 11.4 Three Upper Palaeolithic graves, DV13–DV15, discovered in Dolni Věstonice in South Moravia in 1987, the most recent find of human fossils within the Czech Republic
Source: B Klima

remains are older than 20 years, they are no longer considered to be important from the aspect of criminal law, on the basis that it is not possible to prove who, if anyone, had committed the crime. The legal statute of limitations regarding murder is 20 years.

It is the archaeologist who decides about the course of research, including whether it is necessary to invite an anthropologist in cases when skeletal remains are found. If systematic archaeological research is not considered, then the anthropologist is usually invited only in the case of more complicated findings of human remains or in the case of graves dating to older prehistoric periods. The participation of an anthropologist throughout the archaeological excavation is rare. This is given by the fact that anthropologists are only rarely employed by archaeological institutions undertaking rescue excavations. Skeletal remains are thus usually excavated by archaeologists or by volunteers working under the direction of an archaeologist. Thus, the anthropologist only receives the bones 'packed in crates'. It is needless to stress that the information which the anthropologist could retrieve from observations of the skeleton *in situ* is thus often lost.

The export of human skeletal remains from the Czech Republic is possible for research or exhibition purposes, but is more complicated from an administrative aspect. Export is approved and authorized by the Czech Ministry of Culture (Ministerstvo kultury České republiky). The skeleton should be part of a collection, registered with the aforementioned ministry (i.e., it must be recorded in the database of the Central Records of Collections of the Czech Republic). This also applies in cases where the owner of the collection is a private, non-museum institution. The means of transportation of human skeletal remains depends on the number of individuals involved. There are no exact, legally binding rules governing such export, only that the remains should be laid out respectfully during transport. Transport in clean, solid boxes/crates, with individual bones safely wrapped (e.g., in bubble wrap) is possible. This system was used to transport, for example, the skeletons from the La Tène period to Bibracte in France or Manching in Germany, which several years ago hosted the exhibition 'La Femme Dans Le Monde Celtique', in which the National Museum also participated.

In the case of human skeletal remains uncovered on Church property, decisions regarding their excavation are taken by the Church. There is no special legislation governing the approach to remains buried in churches. The same applies in the case of the skeletal remains of victims of war and conflicts that took place on the territory of the Czech Republic in the past. We refer here mainly to the victims of the First and Second World Wars, whose relatives could be located today. In the past decades, for example, the skeletal remains of German soldiers from the Second World War have been uncovered. These skeletons were transferred and piously buried in a new cemetery.

METHODS OF ANTHROPOLOGICAL ANALYSIS

The development of physical anthropology in the Czech Republic always reflected the developments in this field in Europe. This also fully applies to the development of the methods used. Since the beginning, anthropological research has been based on two basic methods or approaches: the metric evaluation of the body/skeleton; and the scopic evaluation of body/skeletal morphology. These approaches essentially remain the basis of anthropological research to date, the only difference being the application of 21st century techniques such as 3D imaging methods, enabling, for example, the analysis of bone geometry.

Logically, the 19th and the beginning of the 20th century may be considered in anthropology as the period of exploration and testing of suitable evaluation methods. Researchers used various means to describe skeletons, and their results were often not mutually comparable. For example, several craniometric schools arose (A.A. Retzius, A. Török, P.P. Broca) and a system for evaluating a number of morphological, descriptive traits was proposed (D. Blumenbach, W. Scheidt). The approach to the classification of Czech prehistory also developed and changed throughout this period. It need not be stressed enough that unification and integration of the methodology used always represents the basic prerequisite for the comparison of results.

Thus, the adoption of the 'International Craniometric Agreement' in Monaco in 1906, with the purpose of unifying craniometric methods, represents an event of fundamental importance for European anthropology. Rudolf Martin's first textbook, *Lehrbuch der Anthropologie in systematischer Darstellung*, was published five years later, in 1911. This included the dimensions, which researchers had agreed upon in Monaco, and which had been additionally numbered. This textbook and its later re-edition (e.g., Martin and Saller 1957, and later Knußmann 1988) became the fundamental textbooks of continental anthropology, including the Czech territory, in the 20th century. On the other hand, English-speaking countries took as their basis the book published by Aleš Hrdlička in 1920, *Practical Anthropometry*.

Naturally, from a methodological aspect, the situation regarding the evaluation of morphological traits was much more complicated. Multi-level graphic schemes for the evaluation of descriptive traits were proposed and elaborated from the 19th century until the 1960s (by, e.g., P.P. Broca, T. Dwight, R. Virchow, G. Sergi, E. Eickstedt, G. Acsádi and J. Nemeskéri). The attempt to specify and refine the evaluation of descriptive traits led to the expansion of the graphic schemes, with further levels, further possible 'manifestations' of traits being added. Some of these classification schemes included many levels (see, e.g., Michalski 1955). Logically, the subjective factor played an important role in the evaluation of traits, and the comparability of results among researchers was problematic. A detailed evaluation of morphognostic (descriptive morphological) traits was popular in the Czech Republic, mainly in the 1960s. It was a common component of the anthropological analysis of extensive burial grounds. In the next decade, this methodology (descriptive morphological traits) was gradually abandoned, or simpler, three-level schemes were used for the evaluation of descriptive traits. On the contrary, the epigenetic or discrete (non-metric) morphological traits got the attention of anthropologists. The compilatory work that standardized the recording of non-metric or epigenetic traits was published as late as 1989 (see, e.g., Hauser and De Stefano 1989).

After the Second World War, the excavation and uncovering of large burial sites led to the development of a new approach to the analysis of human skeletal samples: palaeodemography. Here, Czech anthropologists took as their basis mainly the studies of Hungarian and French anthropologists (G. Acsádi, J. Nemeskéri, N.G. Gejvall, J.P. Bocquet-Appel and C. Masset). In this context, the attempt to specify basic demographic characteristics (the sex of skeletons and estimated biological age-at-death) became the focus of interest of historic and naturally also of forensic anthropologists.

At the beginning of the 1970s, an international symposium dedicated to these two indicators was held in Prague. This resulted in an anthology of methodological contributions (Vlček 1971). The Prague meeting indirectly initiated the elaboration of the so-called European recommendation for the age and sex diagnoses from skeletons (Ferembach *et al.* 1979). This work, which included the contribution of Milan Stloukal from the National Museum in Prague, was translated into several international languages and in the 1980s it formed the basis of most demographic research in Europe. In the Czech workplace, Ubelaker's study on age estimation on the basis of dental mineralization was recognized (se, e.g., Ubelaker 1978). At the end of the 1990s, Stloukal was the editor of a more extensive anthropological textbook, a 'manual' for the study of human skeletons (Stloukal *et al.* 1999). Part of this textbook covers the subject of palaeodemography. This book is still used at many Czech/Slovak osteological workplaces.

In the 1990s, the accuracy and reliability of the applied methods cited in the 'European recommendations' started to be questioned and challenged, especially in France. More precisely, this mainly applied to the determination of the biological age of skeletons, where today the view that in adults it is only possible to estimate age with an accuracy of 20-year intervals is no longer accepted. In the case of determining sex in adults, only the pelvis is considered to be conclusive. If we wish to determine sex on the basis of other bones of the skeleton, we must first know the degree of sexual dimorphism of the population in question. This means that it is suitable to use the primary (Bruzek 2002) and secondary sexual diagnosis approach (Murail *et al.* 2005). Based on the above, sexually diagnostic discriminatory formulas have been proposed for the Eneolithic population of Bohemia (Černý 1999). Similarly, formulae have also been proposed for the Great Moravian population of the Early Middle Ages (Bruzek and Velemínský 2008).

Milan Stloukal participated in another work much respected throughout Europe, namely the estimation of the age of non-adult individuals on the basis of linear dimensions of the long bones. This study was conducted on the Great Moravian population from Mikulčice (Stloukal and Hanáková 1978).

Although the trend today is to unify the methodology of evaluation of individual biological indicators, at this present time institutions specializing in the analysis of human skeletons in the Czech Republic definitely lack a standardized methodology for their examination. As is already clear from the above text, the most ideal state reigns in the field of estimating basic demographic characteristics (i.e., sex and age).

In the case of other biological traits (e.g., stature, palaeopathology such as cribra orbitalia or enamel hypoplastic defects), the situation is more or less similar to that abroad, in that the same evaluation methodology is used by several institutions. For example in the National Museum in Prague stature was estimated most frequently on the basis of the following methods: Breitinger (1937), Bach (1965) and Sjøvold (1990). On the basis of the 20th century Czech population the regression equations proposed Černý and Komenda (1982).

CONCLUSION

The first research in the field of skeletal anthropology dates to the second half of the 19th century. From this date about 13 anthropological workplaces were found in the Czech republic, and out of these, six specialize in the study of past populations. Four men contributed fundamentally to the development of anthropology in the first half of the 20th century: Luboš Niederle, Bohumil Hellich, Jindřich Matiegka and Aleš Hrdlička. After the Second World War, the development of anthropology in Bohemia was indirectly influenced by the systematic archaeological investigations of extensive burial grounds. If we look back, then naturally the period of Communist Czechoslovakia generally represented a very propitious time for 'archaeology'. The private ownership of land/plots practically did not exist. The Archaeological Institute of the Czechoslovak Socialist Republic in the event of support from the Communist Party of the Czechoslovak Socialist Republic held practically unrestricted power when deciding on which research would be undertaken and which would not. As mentioned previously, this period is associated with a multitude of systematic, extensive area research. Interest mainly focused on early mediaeval localities such as strongholds and burial grounds. This was also due to the frequency of finds dating to this period in our territory. The fact that the Communist regime proudly declared the origins of Slavonic settlement and the origins of sta-tehood to be in its territory also played a role here. After the fall of the Communist regime in 1989, no fundamental changes occurred in the Czech Republic with regard to the existence of institutions dedicated to skeletal anthropology. None the less, the adjustment of property-legal relations influenced the change in character of archaeological research. Rescue archaeology started unequivocally to predominate. This was also due to the construction and building boom in the Czech Republic. By contrast, planned and systematic research was to a great extent reduced.

USEFUL CONTACTS

Addresses of anthropological departments in the Czech Republic

Czech Anthropological Society, Viničná 7 128 00 Praha 2. Website: http://anthropology.cz/ index.htm

Department of Anthropology and Human Genetics, Faculty of Science, Charles University, Viničná 7 128 00 Praha 2 Website: http://natur.cuni.cz/anthropology/

Department of Anthropology, Faculty of Science, Masaryk University, Kotlářská 2, 611 37 Brno. Website: http://anthrop.sci.muni.cz/

Department of Biological Anthropology, Faculty of Philosophy and Arts, University of West Bohemia, Sedláčkova 15 306 14 Plzeň. Website: www.ksa.zcu.cz/

Department of Anthropology, National Museum in Prague, Václavské nám. 68, 115 18 Prague 1. Website: http://www.nm.cz/prirodovedecke-muzeum/antropologie.php

Anthropos Institute, The Moravian Museum, Zelný trh 6, 659 37, Brno. Website: www.mzm.cz/mzm/oddeleni/ustav_anthropos.html

Hrdlicka Museum of Man, The building of Faculty of Science, Charles University, Viničná 7 128 00 Praha 2. Website: www.natur.cuni.cz/~hmc/

Department of the Archaeology of Landscape and Archaeobiology, Institute of Archaeology, Academy of Sciences of the Czech Republic, Letenská 4, 110 00 Prague 1. Website: www.arup.cas.cz/index.html

Department of Biology, Institute of Criminal Science, Prague, Police of the Czech Republic Bartolomějská 310/10, 110 00 Praha-Staré Město. Website: www.policie.cz/kriminalisticky ustav-praha.aspx

Department of Medical Anthropology, Institute of Anatomy, Faculty of Medicine, Masaryk University, Kamenice 3, 625 00 Brno. Websites: www.muni.cz/med/110514/people? lang=en/ and www.med.muni.cz/anatomie/

Department of Anatomy, 1st. Faculty of Medicine, Charles University, U nemocnice 3, 120 00 Prague 2. Website: http://anat.lf1.cuni.cz/internet.htm

Biology and Environmental Education Dept., Faculty of Education, Charles University in Prague, M.D. Rettigové 4, 116 39 Praha 1. Websites: www.pedf.cuni.cz/index.php?cat=kat edra&pid=01220/ and www.dyksoft.cz/kbev/Student/galery.php

Department of Anthropology and Hygiene, College of Education, Palacky University, Kříž kovského 8, 771 47 Olomouc. Tel.: +420 585 631 111, +420 587 441 111; website: www.upol.cz/fakulty/pdf/struktura/katedry-a-pracoviste/kaz

Department of Functional Anthropology and Physiology, Faculty of Physical Training, Palacký University, Křížkovského 8, 771 47 Olomouc. Website: www.upol.cz/fakulty/ftk/struktura/katedry-a-pracoviste/katedra-funkcni-antropologie-a-fyziologie/uvod

Anthropological journals

In the Czech Republic only one journal is published at present: *Anthropologie*. Many anthropological studies are also published in publications of other disciplines (most often of archaeology and medicine), eventually within the scope of multidisciplinary journals. Thematic monographies are edited also, generally by institutions. Below is a list of journals in which anthropological contributions from the area of bioarchaeology are published.

- *Anthropologie* (*International Journal of the Science of Man*), founded by Jindrich Matiegka and Ales Hrdlička in 1923. Its publication was interrupted in 1941 and was later resumed again in 1962 by Jan Jelinek.
- *Česká antropologie*, (*Journal of the Czech Anthropological Association*) (ISSN–0862–5085)
- *Journal of the National Museum (Prague)*, Natural History Series (ISSN: 1802–6842 (print), 1802–6850 (electronic))
- *Acta Musei Nationalis Pragae*, Series B, Historia Naturalis (ISSN: 0036–5343)

- *Studien zum Burgwall von Mikulčice*, papers of the Institute of Archaeology, Academy of Sciences of the Czech Republic, Brno
- *Acta Universitatis Carolinae*

Anthropological studies in the Czech language are published in the journals *Archeologické rozhledy*, *Archeologie středních Čech* and *Ve službách archeologie*.

Anthropological exhibitions

- Anthropos Institute, The Moravian Museum – 'The Story of Mankind' (Figure 11.5) and 'The Moravia of Prehistoric Hunters'. The exhibition describes human evolution. The Anthropos Institute was opened in 1962 by anthropologist Jan Jelinek. It continues on successful exhibition from the year 1928 what took place in the exhibition area in Brno (author: Karel Absolon). In 2006, the Institute was rebuilt and the new exhibition was opened. Contact: Anthropos Institute, Pisárecká 5, Brno, 602 00, tel. 543 248 391. Website: www.anthropos.cz/onas.html/
- National Museum in Prague: 'The Human Skeletons … '. The exhibition is dedicated above all to the methods of skeletal anthropology and palaeopathology (Figure 11.6). It was opened in 1992. Most of the exhibits derive from archaeologiocal excavations of early mediaeval sites. Contact: Národní Muzeum, Václavské náměstí 68, 115 79 Praha 1. Tel. +420 224 497 111; website: www.nm.cz/expozice-detail.php?f_id=14/
- Hrdlička Museum of Man: The exhibition on human evolution and human ontogeny, ethnography (e.g., the culture of African pygmies) and the health status of our ancestors. The Museum was found in 1931 (officially opened in 1937). The Museum is actually a

Figure 11.5 The exhibition of the Anthropos Institute of The Moravian Museum, 'The Story of Mankind'

Figure 11.6 The exhibition of the National Museum in Prague, 'The Human Skeletons ...'

university collection and is divided in two parts: museum exhibitions open to the public, and a depository for study purposes. There are about 4,000 exhibits stored here, including Hrdlicka's collection of facial mask casts and sculptures of heads of North American Indians, and Šebesta's collection of pygmy casts. Contact: Hrdlicka Museum of Man, The Faculty of Science Building, Charles University, Viničná 7 128 00 Praha 2. Website: www.natur.cuni.cz/~hmc/

- The Museum of the Department of Anatomy, 1st Faculty of Medicine, Charles University, is the museum for students of the Faculty of Medicine, the Faculty of Sciences and the scientific public and scientific community. There is a clinical cranial collection and also a 'spriti collection' of anatomical specimens. Website: http://anat.lf1.cuni.cz/muzeum.html/

Archaeological legislation

- The list of authorized organizations to carry out archaeological excavations (see. § 21 par.2, Act No. 20/1987 Col.) http://www.cz-museums.cz/amg/UserFiles/File/Legislativa/Opravn ene%20organizace.doc
- Acts in the Czech language is possible to download from web pages of the Association of Museums and Galleries of the Czech Republic. (see: http://www.cz-museums.cz/amg/ faces/web/deni_v_oboru/legislativa).
- Act No. 20/1987 Coll. on National Protection and Conservation of Monuments (Zákon č. 20/1987 Sb. o státní památkové péči) http://www.cz-museums.cz/amg/UserFiles/File/ Legislativa/l987_020_2008_2.doc
- Act No. 183/2006 Coll., on Zoning and Building Regulations (Zákon č. 183/2006 Sb., o územním plánování a stavebním řádu (changes: č. 68/2007 Sb., 191/2008 Sb., 223/2009

Sb., 227/2009 Sb., 345/2009 Sb., 379/2009 Sb.) http://www.cz-museums.cz/amg/UserFiles/File/Legislativa/stavebni%20zakon%20zm.%20227_2009.doc

- Charter for the Protection and Management of European Archaeological Heritage. (Úmluva o ochraně architektonického dědictví Evropy.) http://www.cz-museums.cz/amg/UserFiles/File/Deni%20v%2oboru/Legislativa/Úmluva%20o%20ochraně%20architektonického%20dědict ví%20Evropy.doc
- Regulation No. 187/2007 Coll., content and terms of town planning scheme with archaeological findings. (Vyhláška č. 187/2007 Sb., obsah a náležitosti plánu území s archeologickými nálezy.) http://www.cz-museums.cz/amg/UserFiles/File/Legislativa/01._pln_zn_n_187.07.doc

BIBLIOGRAPHY

Bach, H. (1965) 'Zur Berechnung der Körperhöhe aus den langen Gliedmassenknochen weiblicher Skelette', *Anthropol. Anz.* 29: 12–21.

Breitinger, E. (1937) 'Zur Berechnung der Körperhöhe aus den langen Gliedmassenknochen', *Anthropol. Anz.* 14: 249.

Bruzek, J. (2002) 'A method for visual determination of sex, using the human hip bone', *American Journal of Physical Anthropology*, 117: 157–68.

Bruzek, J. and Velemínský, P. (2008) 'Reliable sex determination based on skeletal remains for the Early Medieval Population of Great Moravia (9th–10th Century)', in P. Velemínský and L. Poláček (eds) *Anthropological and Epidemiological Characterization of Great Moravian Population in Connection with the Social and Economic Structure*, Studien zum Burgwall von Mikulčice VIII, Brno: Archaeological Institute of Academy of Science CZ, Brno 27.

Černý, M. and Komenda, S. (1982) 'Reconstruction of body height based on humerus and femur lengths (material from Czech lands)', in: V. Novotný (ed.) *Second Anthropological Congress of A. Hrdlička*, Universitas Carolina Pragensis: 475–80.

Černý, V. (1999) 'Anthropologie du Chalcolithique en Europe centrale: variabilité chronologique, géographique et dimorphisme sexuel', unpublished PhD thesis, L'Université de Bordeaux.

Ferembach, D., Schwidetzky, I. and Stloukal, M. (1979) 'Empfehlungen fur die Alters-und Geschlechtsdiagnose am Skelett', *Homo*, 30: 1–32.

Fetter, V., Prokopec, M., Suchý, J. *et al.* (1967) *Antropologie*, Praha: Academia.

Hauser, G. and De Stefano, G.F. (1989) *Epigenetic Variants of the Human Skull*, Stuttgart: E. Schweizerbartische Verlagsbuchhandlung.

Knußmann, R. (1988) *Anthropologie: Handbuch der Vergeichenden Biologie des Menschen I*, Stuttgart: Gustav Fischer Verlag.

Malina, J. *et al.* (2009) *Antropologický slovník*, Brno: Akademické nakladatelství CERM.

Martin, R. and Saller, K. (1957) *Lehrbuch der Anthropologie in systematischer Darstellung mit besonderer Berücksichtigung der anthropologischen Methoden. Band. I*, Stuttgart: Gustav Fischer Verlag.

Michalski, I. (1955) *Podstawy antropometrii*, Warszawa–Lódž: Wydawnictwo Naukowe PWN.

Murail, P., Bruzek, J., Houët, F. and Cunha, E. (2005) 'DSP: a probabilistic sex diagnosis tool using world-wide variation of pelvic bone measurements', *Bulletins et Mémoires de la Société d'Anthropologie de Paris*, n.s., t.17, 3–4: 167–176.

Sjøvold, T. (1990) 'Estimation of stature from long bones utilizing the line of organic corelation', *Human Evolution*, 5: 431–47.

Stloukal, M., Dobisíková, M., Kuželka, V., *et al.* (1999) *Antropologie. Příručka pro studium kostry*, Praha: Národní Museum.

Stloukal, M. and Hanáková, H. (1978) 'Die Länge der Längsknochen altschlawischer Bevölkerungen unter besonderer Berücksichtigung von Wachstumsfragen', *Homo*, 29: 53–69.

Ubelaker, D.H. (1978) *Human Skeletal Remains. Excavation, Analysis, Interpretation*, Chicago: Aldine Publishing Company.

Vlček, E. (ed.) (1971) *Symposium o určování stáří a pohlaví jedince na základě studia kostry*, Praha: Národní Museum.

North Sea
0
100km
Ålborg (Aalborg)
SWEDEN
DENMARK
Århus
(Aarhus)
København
(Copenhagen)
JUTLAND
FUNEN
ZEALAND
Esbjerg
Odense
BORNHOLM
GERMANY
LOLLAND
FALSTER

Denmark/Danmark

Tina Christensen and Pia Bennike

INTRODUCTION: A BRIEF HISTORY AND THE CURRENT STATE OF PHYSICAL ANTHROPOLOGY IN DENMARK

Despite the fact that Denmark is richly endowed with human skeletal material, physical anthropology has never been a separate and independent discipline as in many other European countries and in the USA. Full-time positions have not existed until recently and the very few that are available today are rather 'earmarked' by the Medical Faculty. Nevertheless Denmark has a long history of scientific inquiry into the physical (biological) nature of the human condition, especially palaeopathology.

The earliest anthropological study in Denmark was conducted by the anatomist Jacob Winsløw (1669–1760), who in 1722 published an extremely precise description of an Eskimo skull found in Western Greenland (Winsløw 1722). The tradition of 'craniology' first appeared in the late part of the 19th century and into the first decades of the 20th, resulting in large catalogues of skulls, many of which included prehistoric samples, such as, for example, the publication *Crania Groelandica* (Fürst and Hansen 1915).

At the beginning of the 20th century, however, a shift from mere 'craniology' to a more holistic approach was introduced, and between 1906 and 1915 all of the available prehistoric Danish skeletal material was catalogued and described by Hans Andreas Nielsen (1850–1932) (Nielsen 1906, 1911, 1915). This work was continued by the physician Kurt Bröste (1902–54) and his co-workers, who made a detailed study of Stone and Bronze Age skeletal material (Bröste *et al.* 1956). A similar work devoted to the study of Iron Age skeletal material followed in 1984 and was conducted by the anthropologist Berit Jansen Sellevold (Sellevold *et al.* 1984). A group of Danish scientists have been particular interested in skeletal material from Greenland. In 1949 the dentist Poul Overgaard Pedersen published his thesis on Eskimo dentition (Pedersen 1949) based on Greenlandic skeletal material. This was followed by a dissertation on 'The Eskimo Skeleton' by the physician and surgeon Jørgen Balslev Jørgensen (Jørgensen 1953), employing the traditional anthropometric procedures of the time. A colleague of Pedersen was the dental specialist Jens Jørgen Pindborg, who is probably best known for his book *Pathology of the Dental Hard Tissue* (Pindborg 1970). Also of interest from this period is the study by Ole Vagn Nielsen (1970) of Nubian skeletal material collected by workers during the Scandinavian expedition to the Sudan in 1963 (Bennike 1997).

During the 20th century, the collection of skeletal material held in Denmark increased considerably. Alongside the prehistoric remains already mentioned in the publications of Nielsen

(1906, 1911, 1915), Bröste *et al.* (1956) and Sellevold *et al.* (1984), new material was excavated and stored, and today a total of more than 20,000 human skeletons are housed in Denmark deriving from sites spanning a period of 10,000 years. With the exception of only a few collections, such as three leprosy cemeteries excavated by Møller-Christensen, most of the uncremated material is located either in Copenhagen (Panum Institute, University of Copenhagen) or in Odense (Institute of Forensic Medicine, University of Southern Denmark). The University of Southern Denmark houses only skeletal remains from the mediaeval time, whereas skeletons from all periods are stored at the University of Copenhagen. The skeletal material, however, is only deposited at the two locations and is legally owned by one of the 44 local Danish museums.

Palaeopathology in Denmark

Palaeopathology, the study of ancient diseases as reflected in the osteological remains, is a comparatively recent subject in Denmark. The skeletons of Norsemen from Greenland were among the first to be examined from this perspective – in 1924 by Frederik Carl Christian Hansen (1870–1934) (Hansen 1924). His conclusion that the extinction of the Norsemen in the 15th century was due to 'degeneration' was strongly criticised by the physician Knud Eyvind Fischer-Møller (1872–1942), who subsequently argued that the 'evidence of degeneration' reported by Hansen was accounted for either by changes in the skeleton due to the normal ageing process (such as osteoarthritis in the joints) or simply by changes directly attributable to postmortem deformation (Fischer-Møller 1942). Similarly, the physician Kristian Isager (1864–1943) was the first to make a study of palaeopathology on Danish mediaeval skeletons (Isager 1936). After the Second World War, Vilhelm Møller-Christensen (1903–88) emerged as a dominant figure in this field (Møller-Christensen 1978), and a major interest of his was the study of leprosy. During his tenure at the Museum of Medical History, University of Copenhagen, he established a separate museum, the Museum of Leprosy. In the 1980s and into the 1990s, the anthropologist of the Museum of Leprosy, Pia Bennike, developed this field of inquiry further (Bennike 1985, 1991). Research on palaeopathology has been and is continuously pursued in Denmark, reflected in a number of publications on differential diagnosis (Bennike 1999, 2003; Bennike and Ebbesen 1986; Lefort and Bennike 2007; Bennike *et al.* 1987, 2005) and the fact that a palaeopathology course at PhD level is offered biannually by Pia Bennike.

Education, training, current research and employment

Since the beginning of the 20th century the Laboratory of Biological Anthropology, a former sub-department of the Institute of Medical Anatomy at the University of Copenhagen, has been the primary focus of human skeletal research in Denmark. The founder, F.C.C. Hansen, was not a physical anthropologist but a professor of anatomy, and like many of the earlier pioneers in physical anthropology had no specific interest in developing the field of study as an independent discipline. The Laboratory of Biological Anthropology became affiliated to the Department of Medical Anatomy and later to the Department of Forensic Medicine. Consequently, it has not been possible to obtain an academic education as a physical anthropologist in Denmark, and interested students are forced to complete their studies abroad. Until now the only teaching activities in the discipline comprise two undergraduate courses at the University of Copenhagen and at the University of Southern Denmark, as well as a short international PhD course in palaeopathology using a comprehensive pathological collection from the 19th century stored in the Museum of Medical History (now the Medical Museion). The focus of the course at the University of Southern Denmark, however, lies mainly on the use of statistical models related to demographic, anthropometric and pathological conditions.

Although no permanent full-time position in physical anthropology was established in Denmark before 1995, P. Bennike and V. Alexandersen have, since the 1980s, continued the tradition established by F.C.C. Hansen and his successors with their ongoing study of Danish prehistoric skeletal remains and dentition, respectively, while several other researchers have worked periodically on a variety of different short-term projects. For example, in the late 1980s, the pathologist Jens Peder Hart Hansen conducted an interdisciplinary study of Eskimo mummies (Hansen and Gulløv 1989), and in the early 1990s Niels Lynnerup made a study of Norse skeletons from Greenland as a PhD project (Lynnerup 1998).

The introduction of new methods in the analysis of the health of past people also gained footing in Denmark. Scanning of bone mineral content has been used for a number of prehistoric bones to estimate the bone mass in various time periods (Bennike *et al.* 1993). Systematic CT scanning is often part of bog body studies (Lynnerup 2007). DNA analyses have been undertaken on some Danish material with unexpected results, which have been met with some scepticism by archaeologists (Melchior 2008; Melchior *et al.* 2008). Isotopes have been studied in almost all prehistoric bones from the Mesolithic/Neolithic, Iron Age and later periods (Fischer *et al.* 2007; Jørkov 2007). An ongoing study on strontium in Danish Vikings has already shown some promising, though still unpublished, results. Other studies involving the level of strontium on Mesolithic material have, however, been completed (Price *et al.* 2007), and a study of Carbon 14 dating of cremated bones has been successful (Olsen *et al.* 2008). A common denominator for all these studies is that they have overwhelmingly been conducted by researchers with backgrounds in archaeology, biology, medicine, dentistry or genetics. Current research in the major Danish anthropological institution, the Laboratory of Biological Anthropology in Copenhagen, increasingly focuses on issues linked to forensic anthropology and, since 2008, the Laboratory of Biological Anthropology no longer employs a physical anthropologist.

ARCHAEOLOGICAL HUMAN REMAINS AND LEGISLATION

Archaeological legislation

The excavation of human skeletal remains in Denmark falls under archaeology, and according to the Danish Museum Act, the Heritage Agency of Denmark holds overall responsibility for all archaeological excavations undertaken. In addition to the local museums, the National Museum and the respective archaeological institutes at the Universities in Copenhagen and Aarhus also conduct archaeological excavations. Any location in Denmark is in principle within a museum's 'area of responsibility'. Forty-four local museums deal with archaeology, and their geographical areas of responsibility are of variable size. Altogether, these institutions conduct approximately 800 archaeological excavations per year. The vast majority (around 90%) of the projects take place either prior to construction or on cultivated land where modern farm machinery has encountered ancient monuments.

HUMAN REMAINS AND LEGISLATION

Excavation of human skeletal remains in Denmark is always handled by one of the local museums or archaeological institutions, which are also the legal owners of the recovered skeletal material. It is not a legal requirement to have an anthropologist on site whenever archaeological human remains are recovered, and this only takes place if the excavation authorities, for example the responsible museum, require it.

In 2002, an agreement of cooperation was reached between the Faculty of Health and Science at the University of Copenhagen and the Heritage Agency. Part of the agreement appointed the Laboratory of Biological Anthropology in Copenhagen as the central anthropological institution in Denmark, and it is here that the majority of prehistoric and mediaeval skeletal remains from Denmark, Greenland and the Faroe Islands are held. However, if a foreign institution or museum wishes to borrow skeletal remains, for instance for display or research, the borrowing institution contacts the legal owner of the material, one of the 44 museums, for permission.

Ethical Issues

The current consensus on repatriation in Denmark considers two specific issues. First, the cultural heritage, including human material, must be preserved for posterity in accordance with the interests of the museums and science. Second, the special significance that material such as skeletons may have to the original culture is considered as well. Therefore, Denmark has in many cases chosen to meet requests for repatriation of human material, such as the case of the Inuits in Canada, Alaska and Greenland, including cases concerning reburial. However, a repatriation act *per se* does not exist in Denmark. Instead, each request is assessed and negotiated individually (Gabriel 2008).

Forensic anthropology

No formal education and training in forensic, biological or physical anthropology exists in Denmark, so medically trained people experienced in legal pathology and forensic medicine perform the duties of a forensic anthropologist. In Denmark, the cut-off point between archaeological entities and forensic evidence is not determined chronologically and distinction can be difficult, especially if only the skeletal material with no information regarding the burial environment is available. However, when skeletal remains are found in connection with, for example, construction works in older market towns, the authorities rely on the local museums' elaborate archives, which often point to the location of a historic cemetery or a prehistoric burial place on the finding spot or in the near vicinity (Lynnerup 1999).

METHODS OF ANTHROPOLOGICAL ANALYSIS

Almost all known and conventional international methods for studying human skeletal material are being used, such as those summarized in Acsádi and Nemeskéri (1970) and in Buikstra and Ubelaker (1994). It is worth mentioning that, although Trotter and Gleser (1958) is used for stature reconstruction, the biologist Jesper Boldsen has suggested new methods to estimate stature and age of adults from a statistical point of view, utilizing skeletal material recovered from mediaeval burial grounds (Boldsen 1984a, 1984b; Milner *et al.* 2000).

New methods such as CT scans, DEXA analysis, aDNA and isotopes are increasingly being employed in the analysis of the health of past people. The choice of methods may vary in relation to the condition of the material, the aim of the study, the technical availability and costs and the focus of the various research projects and interests.

CONCLUSION

Based on the summary of the field presented in this chapter, it is important that the osteological and palaeopathological traditions, which were started so many years ago in Denmark by pioneers of the discipline, are continued by younger scholars with a cultural understanding of both history and archaeology as well as an insight into diseases of the past rather than solely medical skills – although there is an evident need for close collaboration with scientists of various backgrounds.

USEFUL CONTACTS AND ADDRESSES

The Heritage Agency of Denmark (*Kulturarvsstyrelsen*), H.C. Andersens Boulevard 2, 1553 København V; Tel: +45 33 74 51 00; website: www.kulturarv.dk/english/home/

The National Museum (*Nationalmuseet*), Frederiksholms Kanal 12, 1220 København K; Tel: +45 33 13 44 11; website: www.nationalmuseet.dk/sw20374.asp/

BIBLIOGRAPHY

Acsádi, GY. and Nemeskéri, J. (1970) *History of Human Life Span and Mortality*, Budapest: Akadémiai Kiadó.

Bennike, P. (1985) *Palaeopathology of Danish Skeletons. A Comparative Study of Demography, Disease and Injury*, Copenhagen: Akademisk Forlag.

——(1991) 'Epidemiological aspects of palaeopathology in Denmark. Past, present, and future studies', in D. J. Ortner and C. Aufderheide (eds) *Human Paleopathology: Current Syntheses and Future Options*, Washington, DC: Smithsonian Institution Press.

——(1997) 'History of physical anthropology in Denmark. Past, present and future studies', in F. Spencer (ed.) *History of Physical Anthropology: an Encyclopedia*, Vol. I., London: Routledge.

——(1999) 'Facts or myths? A re-evaluation of cases of diagnosed tuberculosis in the past in Denmark', in G. Palfi, O. Dutour, J. Deák, *et al.* (eds) *Tuberculosis. Past and Present*, Szeged: Golden Book Publishers/ TB Foundation.

——(2003) 'Ancient trepanations and differential diagnosis: A re-evaluation of skeletal remains from Denmark', in T. Otto, H. Thrane and H. Vandkilde (eds) *Warfare and Society. Archaeological and Social Anthropological Perspectives*, Aarhus: Aarhus University Press.

Bennike, P., Bohr, H. and Toft, T. (1993) 'Determination of mineral content and organic matrix in bone samples using dual photon absorptiometry', *International Journal of Anthropology*, 8: 111–16.

Bennike, P., Bro-Rasmussen, F. and Bro-Rasmussen, P. (1987) 'Dislocation and/or congenital malformation of the shoulder joint. Observations on a mediaeval skeleton from Denmark', *Anthropologischer Anzeiger*, 45: 117–29.

Bennike, P. and Ebbesen, K. (1986) 'The bog find from Sigersdal. Human sacrifice in the early Neolithic', *Journal of Danish Archaeology*, 5: 85–115.

Bennike, P., Lewis, M.E., Schutkowski, H., *et al.*(2005) 'Comparison of child mortality in two contrasting medieval cemeteries from Denmark', *American Journal of Physical Anthropology*, 128: 734–46.

Boldsen, J.L. (1984a) 'A statistical evaluation of the basis for predicting stature from lengths of long bones in European populations', *American Journal of Physical Anthropology*, 65: 305–12.

——(1984b) 'Palaeodemography of two southern Scandinavian medieval communities', *Meddelanden från Lunds Universitets Historiska Museum*, 5: 107–15.

Bröste, K., Jørgensen, J.B., Becker, C.J., *et al.* (1956) *Prehistoric Man in Denmark. Vol. I-II. A study in physical anthropology*, Copenhagen: Munksgaard.

Buikstra, J.E. and Ubelaker, D.H. (eds) (1994) *Standards for Data Collection from Human Skeletal Remains*, Fayetteville, Ak: Archaeological Survey Research Series no. 44.

Fischer, A., Olsen, J., Richards, M., *et al.* (2007) 'Coast–inland mobility and diet in the Danish Mesolithic and Neolithic: evidence from stable isotope values of human and dogs', *Journal of Archaeological Science*, 34: 2125–50.

Fischer-Møller, K. (1942) 'The mediaeval Norse settlements in Greenland', *Antrophological investigations. Meddelelser om Grønland* 89: 2.

Fürst, C.M. and Hansen Fr. C.C. (1915) *Crania Groenlandica. A description of Eskimo crania*, Copenhagen: A.F. Høst and Son.

Gabriel, M. (2008) 'Repatiering af humant materiale', in N. Lynnerup, P. Bennike and E. Iregren (eds) *Biologisk Antropologi med Human Osteologi*, København: Gyldendal.

Hansen, Fr. C.C. (1924) 'Anthropologia Medico-Historica Groenlandiae Antiquae. I. Herjolfnes', *Meddelelser om Grønland,* 67: 293–547.

Hansen, J.P.H. and Gulløv, H.C. (eds) (1989) *The mummies from Qulakitsoq. Eskimos in the 15th century*, Meddelelser om Grønland, Man & Society Series 12, Copenhagen: Meddelelser om Grønland.

Isager, K. (1936) *Skeletfundene ved Øm Kloster*, Kobenhavn: Levin and Munksgaard.

Jørgensen, J.B. (1953) 'The Eskimo skeleton', *Meddelelser om Grønland*, 46: 1–154.

Jørkov, M.L.S. (2007) 'Drinking with the rich and dining with the poor in Roman Iron Age Denmark', unpublished PhD thesis, University of Copenhagen.

Lefort, M. and Bennike, P. (2007) 'Differential dignoses: leprosy, ergotism, treponematosis, sarcoidosis or smallpox', *International Journal of Osteoarchaeology*, 17: 337–49.

Lynnerup, N. (1998) 'The Greenland Norse', *Meddelelser om Grønland, Man & Society*, 24: 1–149.

——(1999) 'Retsantropologi', *Ugeskrift for Læger*, 26: 3983–87.

——(2007) 'Mummies', *Yearbook of Physical Anthropology*, 50: 162–90.

Melchior, L. (2008) 'Denmark's genetic past', unpublished PhD thesis, University of Copenhagen.

Melchior, L., Gilbert, M.T.P., Kivsild, T., *et al.* (2008) 'Rare mtDNA haplogroups and genetic differences in rich and poor Danish Iron-age villages', *American Journal of Physical Anthropology*, 135: 206–15.

Milner, G.R., Wood, J.W. and Boldsen J.L. (2000) 'Paleodemography', in M.A. Katzenberg and S.R. Saunders (eds) *Biological Anthropology of the Human Skeleton*, New York: Wiley-Liss.

Møller-Christensen, V. (1978) *Leprosy Changes in the Skull*, Odense: Odense University Press.

Nielsen, H.A. (1906) 'Bidrag til Danmarks forhistoriske befolknings (særligt stenalderfolkets) antropologi', *Aarbøger for nordisk oldkyndighed og historie (1906)*: 237–318.

——(1911) 'Yderligere bidrag til Danmarks stenalderfolks anthropologi', *Aarbøger for nordisk oldkyndighed og historie (1911)*: 81–205.

——(1915) 'Fortsatte bidrag til vort oldtidsfolks anthropologi. De sidste 5–6 aars skeletfund fra stenaldergrave og saerligt de sidste 10–12 aars skeletfund fra jernaldergrave', *Aarbøger for nordisk Oldkyndighed og Historie (1915)*: 275–337.

Nielsen, O.V. (1970) *The Nubian skeleton through 4000 years*, Copenhagen: Munksgaard.

Olsen, J., Heinemeier, J., Bennike, P., *et al.*. (2008) 'Characterisation and blind testing of radiocarbon dating of cremated bone', *Journal of Archaeological Science*, 35: 791–800.

Pedersen, P.O. (1949) 'The east Greenland Eskimo dentition', *Meddelelser om Grønland*, 142: 1–256.

Pindborg, J.J. (1970) *Pathology of the Dental Hard Tissue*, Philadelphia, PA: WB Saunders.

Price, T.D., Ambrose, S.H., Bennike, P., *et al.* (2007) 'The Stone Age graves at Dragsholm, Denmark: new dates, isotopes and other information'. *Acta Archaeologica*, 78: 193–219.

Sellevold, B.J., Hansen, U.L. and Jørgensen, J.B. (1984) *Iron Age man in Denmark: Prehistoric man in Denmark*, København: Kongelige Nordiske Oldskriftsselskab.

Trotter, M. and Gleser, G.C. (1958) 'A re-evaluation of estimation of stature based on measurements of stature taken during life and of long bones after death', *American Journal of Physical Anthropology*, 16: 79–123.

Trotter, M. (1970) 'Estimation of stature from intact long limb bones', in T.D. Stewart (ed.) *Personal Identification in Mass Disasters*, Washington: Smithsonian Institution Press.

Winsløw, J.J. (1722) 'Conformation particuliere du crane d'un sauvage de l'Amerique septentrionale' *Histoire de l'Academie Royale des Sciences Paris (1722)*: 322–24.

Finland/Suomi

Milton Núñez, Markku Niskanen, Marja-Leena Kortelainen,
Juho-Antti Junno, Kirsti Paavola, Sirpa Niinimäki
and Mirette Modarress

INTRODUCTION: A BRIEF HISTORY AND CURRENT STATE OF PHYSICAL ANTHROPOLOGY IN FINLAND

Finland is a relatively large country (c. 338,000 sq km) with a small population of only about 5.3 million. Its situation between the 60th and 70th parallels of latitude results in rather low temperatures and explains why the country was covered and eroded by the Scandinavian ice sheet during the Ice Age. As a result, Finland's soil, flora, fauna and human occupation cannot be older than 10,000–12,000 years. Although the cold temperature may help preservation, the young acid podzol soils contribute to the rapid decay of organic matter, including bone.

Until 1809 Finland was part of the Swedish Kingdom and, even though new laws were introduced during both the autonomous period (1809–1917) and the subsequent republican times, some of the current legislation affecting ancient human remains has its original roots in the Swedish period. Although it has never stood as a distinct discipline in Finland, much that can classify as physical anthropological research has been traditionally conducted mainly by medical doctors. It is only during the last few decades that the study of ancient human remains has begun to be carried out by anthropology-trained archaeologists.

Since physical anthropology was not regarded in the past as an independent discipline which was taught at Finnish universities, medical graduates were amongst the only ones capable of conducting some sort of anthropological research before the 1970s. A number of studies on the anthropology of the Finns were made, mainly by physicians during the late 19th and, particularly, the early 20th centuries (see, e.g., Retzius 1878; Westerlund 1900, 1902, 1904; Kajava 1924, 1925; Kajava and Finne 1926). These investigations were attempts to define the physical characteristics of the Finns and their regional variations within the country. They were, in other words, studies of race involving physical traits such as stature, cranial morphology, body proportions and pigmentation. Despite their somewhat skewed orientation, these early works are important because they involve data from thousands of individuals. Of particular significance was the work initiated by Professor Yrjö Kajava, who in the 1920s organized a series of regional anthropological studies that came to be published as various monographs between 1931 and 1957 (see Kajanoja 1971 and references therein). This work, conducted by medical doctors, concerned mainly living subjects, but a few researchers went as far as digging up skulls, especially from recent Lapland cemeteries, on rather dubious legal grounds. The research and results associated with the physical traits of the Finns have been summarized by Kajanoja (1971). In addition to the preoccupation with physical traits, Finnish researchers produced some valuable results in forensic anthropology, such as the work of Professor Antti Telkkä on long bone dimensions and the stature of adult and juvenile Finns (Telkkä 1950; Telkkä *et al.* 1962; Palkama *et al.* 1962; Virtama *et al.* 1962), Professor Pauli Kajanoja's use of discriminant functions for sexing Finnish crania (Kajanoja 1966), and the more recent research on differential shoulder development in tennis players (Kannus *et al.* 1995).

In the case of ancient human remains, anthropological analyses were carried out by a handful of physicians interested in the subject. The bones were excavated and retrieved by archaeologists, and the skeletal remains, or what was left of them, were usually delivered afterwards to the interested researcher for anthropological examination (see, e.g., Grönroos 1913; Pesonen 1939; Blomquist 1953).

This situation could perhaps be seen as the first of three developmental stages in the study of ancient human remains in Finland. The first stage began with the discovery of the Jettböle skeletal material on the Åland Islands in 1905 and lasted until the late 1960s.

The second stage is characterized by the presence of some physical anthropology-trained archaeologists. A few Finnish archaeological students, unhappy with the situation, travelled abroad in order to obtain training in human osteology. Upon their return they engaged in the anthropological analysis of human remains that were being excavated in Finland (see, e.g., Lahtiperä 1970; Formisto 1993). However, the apparently poor prospects of making a living by undertaking this kind of work in Finland forced most of these researchers to seek greener pastures abroad. This was not quite the case in the Åland Islands, where bone preservation is better and human remains are encountered more commonly than on the mainland. For this reason, it was not unusual that the reports of excavations conducted on the islands included an osteological report. In the mid-1980s, Milton Núñez, who had studied Physical Anthropology at the University of Calgary (Canada), was hired as a special researcher in the Archaeology Section of the Ålands Museum. This led to the anthropological analyses of newly and previously excavated ancient human remains from the archipelago (see, e.g., Núñez 1987, 1997; Núñez and Lidén 1994, 1997). This second stage came to an end in the late 1990s.

The third stage is marked by the introduction of significant changes in the university education of Physical Anthropology and the shift of the bulk of the research on ancient remains to the University of Oulu. In September 1994, Milton Núñez was offered a professorship with the purpose of creating a new Archaeology Department at the University of Oulu, in northern Finland. By September 1996 a new study programme had been designed and the newly admitted Oulu archaeology students faced a compulsory introductory course in Biological Anthropology.

Prior to this, in the 1970s and 1980s, the archaeology-inclined staff and students of the Oulu History Department had excavated a few mediaeval and early historical burial sites in northern Finland (see, e.g., Koivunen 1978, 1982; Paavola 1989). Although no thorough anthropological analyses were made, there were a few interesting articles by a team of researchers from the Oulu Odontology Department (see, e.g., Pirttiniemi and Heikkinen 1989; Pirttiniemi and Huggare 1989; Pirttiniemi *et al.* 1990). For a summary of this early anthropological work carried out by Oulu researchers see Niinimäki *et al.* (2009).

Interest on the subject of human remains increased in the 1990s with a series of investigations by Oulu archaeologists at various northern church sites. In 1997, there was the excavation of over 300 individuals buried in the vicinity of Oulu Cathedral dating to the 17th and 18th centuries. Fortunately, the Oulu parish was very understanding and kindly allowed the study of the skeletal material until 2006, when it was returned and reburied. The Oulu Cathedral material generated several master's theses and publications (see, e.g., Cózar *et al.* 2000; Ojanlatva *et al.* 2000; Maijanen 2006; Núñez *et al.* 2006; Núñez 2007).

Around the same time, Kirsti Paavola, who was undertaking her doctoral research on the traditions and practices of church burials, directed the inspection of the crypts of three churches situated within 100km of Oulu. This work revealed dozens of naturally mummified human remains (Joona *et al.* 1997; Ojanlatva *et al.* 1997; Paavola *et al.* 1997; Paavola 1998; Núñez *et al.* 2008). In connection with this work, Dr Paavola also dealt with the ethical issues involving human remains (Paavola 1995, 1998).

In 1997 Markku Niskanen moved to Oulu after having completed his PhD in Physical Anthropology at Washington State University. This brought more courses and research into the country, all of which resulted in master's and PhD theses and several publications on various research topics, often conducted with international cooperation. Currently, Dr Niskanen holds a Finnish Academy Researcher post at Oulu, and there are over €500,000 in external grants connected to Physical Anthropology projects with broad international links. Moreover, compulsory and selective courses on different aspects of physical anthropology are being offered, and a number of students are pursuing research in this discipline at both the master's and PhD levels. During this first decade of the new millennium, physical anthropology trained staff and students from Oulu have conducted research on various topics (e.g., human osteology, musculo-skeletal markers, palaeodemography, palaeoanthropology, palaeopathology and palaeodiet) and generated a number of publications (see, e.g., Núñez 2000; Jarva *et al.* 2001; Junno 2005; Núñez *et al.* 2005, 2006, 2009; Ruff *et al.* 2005; Torres Joerges 2005; Torres and Núñez 2005; Maijanen and Niskanen 2006, 2009; Niskanen 2006; Niskanen and Junno 2006, 2009; Garcia-Guixé *et al.* 2009; Junno *et al.* 2009; Maijanen 2009).

In recent years, the Archaeology Departments at the universities of Helsinki and Turku have also been engaged in the excavation of human remains, sometimes together with the local Forensic Departments, for example in the 2007 excavation of 19th-century Russian mass graves from Huuhtiniemi (a monograph is in the planning stage). As in Oulu, these activities have resulted in a few master's theses on physical anthropology topics and may lead to doctoral dissertations in the future.

ARCHAEOLOGIAL HUMAN REMAINS AND LEGISLATION

Archaeological legislation

The current Ancient Monuments Law (295/63) protects all prehistoric and historic monuments from being excavated, covered, modified, destroyed or damaged in any way without the permission of the National Board of Antiquities (*Museovirasto/Museiverket*).

HUMAN REMAINS AND LEGISLATION

We were surprised to find virtually no Finnish legislation concerning ancient human remains. This is not meant as a criticism. The system seems to function fairly well, even if there may be cases where the questions of jurisdiction and responsibility may not be obvious.

What happens when human remains are found in Finland? Much has to do with the nature of the remains and where the discovery takes place. If the remains come from a site not known to be related to prehistoric activity or a former historic cemetery, and they lack association with objects of obvious antiquity, the police should be informed. They will then decide whether the matter is of police concern or the responsibility of the National Board of Antiquities. If the police see it necessary, they will conduct an inquiry and attempt to determine the identity and cause of death according to Laws 459/73 and 948/73 (all current Finnish law texts can be accessed at www.Finlex.fi), which concern cause of death determination (*kuolemansyyn selvittämisestä/ utredande av dödsorsak*). There are six localities where autopsies may be performed for this purpose, including the Forensic Departments of the Universities of Helsinki, Oulu and Turku. The small population and fairly good records are of help in establishing the identity of the remains of Finnish nationals. It generally involves the selection of likely individuals from a relatively short list of missing persons and then checking them out using dental records and/or DNA analyses.

If the human remains occur at a known archaeological site or a former cemetery, the matter is generally reported to the National Board of Antiquities, either directly or via the police. The Board of Antiquities will then act according to what is prescribed in Law 63/295, known as the Ancient Monuments Law (*Muinaismuistolaki/Låg om fornminnen*). This law text dates to 1963, with a handful of minor modifications and additions made in subsequent decades. It follows earlier antiquities legislation from 1883, but the earliest antecedents for these two laws go back to a 1666 decree by the Swedish King (Figure 13.1). This ordinance, one of the earliest if not the first of its kind, proclaims the preservation of ancient monuments from heathen times, including graves.

The current Ancient Monuments Law (295/63) includes graves and cemeteries among the monuments listed in Law 295/63, but there is no specific mention of any skeletons or bones that may be found in such ancient graves or cemeteries.

A reason for this may be that bones from the prehistoric period (9000 BC-1200 AD) are seldom preserved in the acidic Finnish soils. Only in the more basic soils of the Åland archipelago (see, e.g., Grönroos 1913; Núñez and Lidén 1994) or under very exceptional conditions on

Figure 13.1 First page of the 1666 Swedish Royal Decree proclaiming the protection of all ancient monuments and antiquities in the kingdom

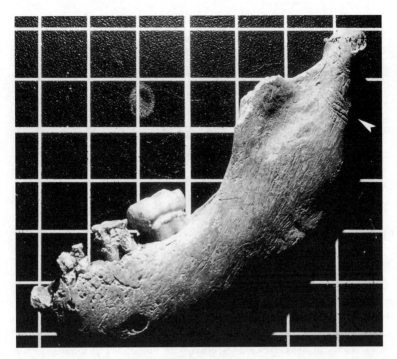

Figure 13.2 Fragment of a child's mandible with cut marks near the condyle, from the Neolithic site of Jettböle, Åland Islands

Figure 13.3 The articulated skeleton from a burial at the Neolithic site of Jettböle, Åland Islands, 1905
Source: Ålands Museum Archives

the Finnish mainland (see, e.g., Pesonen 1939; Blomquist 1953; Formisto 1993) have prehistoric human remains survived (Figures 13.2, 13.3 and 13.4). Whenever prehistoric human bones have been found, archaeologists have collected and stored them, though not necessarily subjected them to anthropological analysis.

The matter is slightly more complex with human remains from the late mediaeval or early modern period, which tend to be better preserved. If skeletons are found in an old Christian

Figure 13.4 Cranial remains from the bog site of Leväluhta, Ostrobotnia
Source: Heureka Science Centre

grave or cemetery no longer connected with a church, they fall within the jurisdiction of the National Board of Antiquities and are processed in the same manner as the prehistoric material (Figure 13.5). However, if the bones come from church land their fate is up to the parish in question (Figure 13.6). In the latter case there has been no conflict of interests in the past. The Board of Antiquities was not keen on taking the space-demanding bones into its crowded storage facilities and, moreover, there was no one interested in or capable of carrying out anthropological analyses. Consequently, the bones found under such circumstances have usually been reburied shortly after the excavations were over. This situation has changed somewhat in the last few decades with the increasing presence of physical anthropology-trained archaeologists in the country. Whenever asked, parishes have consented in most cases to loaning the skeletons for analysis for a few months or years prior to their reburial.

In general, access to the human remains by anthropologists is rather good, even if the material is not that abundant. The National Board of Antiquities seldom raises objections to their study. Obviously, a written petition describing the nature of the intended research is required, but this is to be expected and a mere formality. Depending on the nature and uniqueness of the specimen in question, it is also possible to obtain authorization for removing bone for analytical purposes (radiocarbon, stable isotope or DNA analyses), even to a foreign laboratory.

To our knowledge, there have been no claims or repatriations of human remains stored at the National Board of Antiquities. A possible exception may be some weak and unheeded voices for the return of the Neolithic skeleton from Jettböle (Figure 13.3) to the autonomous Åland Islands. On the other hand, in 1995 the Helsinki Department of Anatomy returned 57 Sami crania that had been removed from a cemetery in Inari, Finnish Lapland, in the early 20th century. This and similar repatriation events elsewhere, together with related ethics guidelines, have been recently summarized by Norwegian Professor Berit Sellevold (2009).

METHODS OF ANTHROPOLOGICAL ANALYSIS

Apart from following international recommendations (see, e.g., Ferembach *et al.* 1980; Buikstra and Ubelaker 1994), Finnish researchers have provided some methods for stature estimation

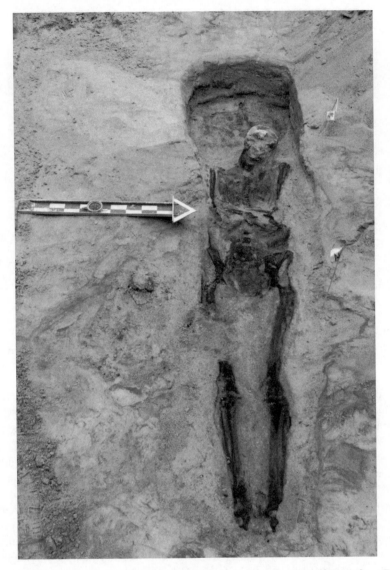

Figure 13.5 A frail but somewhat preserved east-facing skeleton from the town of Ii, northern Finland
Source: Titta Kallio-Seppä, National Board of Antiquities

(Telkkä 1950; Telkkä *et al.* 1962; Palkama *et al.* 1962; Virtama *et al.* 1962) and sex distinguishing functions (Kajanoja 1966) that may be considered when undertaking anthropological analysis.

CONCLUSION

There is no specific mention of either human remains or the role of physical anthropologists in the legislation concerning prehistoric and early historic sites in Finland. The National Board of Antiquities is responsible for all ancient sites and it delegates and/or gives permission for their

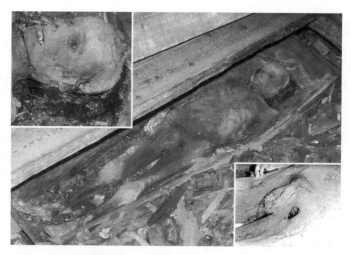

Figure 13.6 The mummified remains of a man who died in the 1840s in Keminmaa (latitude 66°N), northern Finland
Source: Kirsti Paavola

excavation to archaeology graduates. The anthropological analysis of human remains found at such sites is not compulsory. If the archaeologist responsible for the excavations has no anthropological training, he or she may ask a physical anthropologist to be present on site as the human remains are unearthed. Otherwise, if anthropologists wish to study the remains, they can generally do so once the material has been brought from the field to the processing or storage facility. Much depends on the area, the local availability of a physical anthropologist and the excavation budget. Though things are beginning to change, most excavation budgets do not include a provision for anthropological analysis.

Finally, it should be stressed that the advent of anthropology-trained archaeologists in the 1970s did not mean the end of anthropological research by scholars from other disciplines. Their work has continued, though in a much more diversified manner. There are, to name a few, the semi-popular palaeoanthropology books by the late Professor Björn Kurtén (1972, 1993), the works by Professors Reijo Norio (2000) and Jukka Vuorinen (2002, 2006) on Finnish diseases, the never-ending work carried out by the Forensic Departments of the Universities of Helsinki, Oulu and Turku (see, e.g., Sajantila 2003; Palo *et al.* 2007, 2009), and a great deal of research that falls within the realm of physical anthropology by scholars of various disciplines. The number of researchers involved is simply too long to list here.

Even if thesis research topics may be classified as purely Physical Anthropology, the degrees granted at Oulu are nevertheless in Archaeology. The question of Finnish master's and doctoral degrees in Physical Anthropology should still be seen as a possible future event, one which would definitely mark the beginning of a new, fourth stage in the development of the discipline in Finland.

USEFUL CONTACTS

National Board of Antiquities (*Museovirasto*), Nervanderinkatu 13, P.O. Box 913, FI-00101 Helsinki; tel. + 358 9 40 501; fax + 358 9 4050 9300; website www.nba.fi/en/

ACKNOWLEDGEMENTS

The authors wish to thank the Academy of Finland (grants 119268, 122623, 214370), the National Science Foundation (grant 0642297) and the University of Oulu for the funds that have made possible much of the physical anthropology research conducted at the Oulu Archaeology Department. We are also grateful to the National Board of Antiquities and the Autonomous Government of the Åland Islands and Museibyrån staff for access to their collections and archives, and the same applies to the parishes of Haukipudas, Keminmaa, Kempele and Oulu. Finally, we wish to thank Exhibition Manager Jaakko Pöyhönen of Heureka, the Finnish Science Centre, for kindly providing us with the photograph in Figure 13.4.

BIBLIOGRAPHY

Blomquist, H.E. (1953). *Über die aus dem 5.-6. Jahrhundert n. Chr. Stammenden Knochenfunde von Kjeldamäki. (im Kirchspiel Wöra, Süd-Ostbottnien, Finnland), Annales Academiae Scientiarum Fennicae*, Series A V, 36.

Buikstra, J.E. and Ubelaker, D. (eds) (1994) *Standards for Data Collection from Human Skeletal Remains*, Fayetteville, Ar: Arkansas Archeological Survey Research Series No. 44.

Cózar, P., López, I., Núñez, M., *et al.* (2000) 'Rasgos patológicos de una población de los siglos XVI-XVIII del norte de Finlandia (Oulu)', in L. Caro, H. Rodríguez, E. Sánchez, *et al.* (eds) *Tendencias actuales de investigación en la Antropología Física española*, León: Universidad de León.

Ferembach, D., Schwidetzky, L. and Stloukal, M. (1980) 'Recommendations for age and sex diagnoses of skeletons', *Journal of Human Evolution*, 9: 517–49.

Formisto, T. (1993) *An Osteological Analysis of Human and Animal Bones from Levänluhta*, Vammala: Vammala Kirjapaino.

Garcia-Guixé, E., Martínez-Moreno, J., Mora, R, *et al.* (2009) 'Stable isotope analysis of human and animal remains from the Late Upper Palaeolithic site of Balma Guilanyà, southeastern Pre-Pyrenees, Spain', *Journal of Archaeological Science*, 36: 1018–26.

Grönroos, H. (1913) 'Stenåldersskelettfynden vid Jettböle på Åland', *Finska Läkaresällskapets Handlingar*, 55: 393–407.

Jarva, E., Niskanen, M. and Paavola, K. (2001) 'Anatomy of a the late Iron Age inhumation burial from Hiukka at Nivankylä (Rovaniemi, Finnish Lapland)', *Fennoscandia Archaeologica*, 18: 27–49.

Joona, J.-P., Ojanlatva, E., Paavola, K., *et al.* (1997) 'Kempeleen kirkkohaudat', *Meteli No. 11*.

Junno, J-A. (2005) *The Use of Body Mass Prediction in Paleoanthropology. Defining Species and Mating Systems*, Oulu: Department of Arts and Anthropology.

Junno, J.-A., Niskanen, M., Nieminen, M.T., *et al.* (2009) 'Temporal trends in vertebral size and shape from medieval to modern-day', *PLoS ONE* 4: 1–5.

Kajanoja, P. (1966) 'Sex determination of Finnish crania by discriminant functions', *American Journal of Physical Anthropology*, 24: 29–33.

——(1971) 'A study in the morphology of the Finns and its relation to the settlement of Finland', *Annales Academiae Scientiarum Fennicae, Series AV No. 146*.

Kajava, Y. (1924) 'Über den Schultergürtel der Finnen', *Annales Academiae Scientiarum Fennicae, Series AV No. 2*.

——(1925) 'Antropologische Untersuchung des finnischen Volkes', *Anthropologischer Anzeiger*, 2/3: 228–53.

Kajava, Y. and Finne, J. (1926) 'Mitteilungen über die Körpergrosse des finnischen Mannes Ende des 18. und am Anfang des 19. Jahrhunderts', *Annales Academiae Scientiarum Fennicae, Series AV No. 25*.

Kannus, P., Haapasalo, H., Sankelo, M., *et al.* (1995) 'Effect of starting age of physical activity on bone mass in the dominant arm of tennis and squash players', *Annals of Internal Medicine*, 123: 27–31.

Koivunen, P. (1978) 'Ylikylän ja Nivänkylän arkeologiset tutkimukset 1978', *Faravid*, 2: 133–43.

——(1982) 'Keminmaan kirkonpaikan tutkimukset Valmarinniemellä kesällä 1981: alustava rapportti', *Faravid*, 5: 37–53.

Kurtén, B. (1972) *Not From the Apes*, New York: Vintage Books.

——(1993 [1986]) *Our Earliest Ancestors*, New York: Columbia University Press.

Lahtiperä, P. (1970) *Metallikautinen asutus Kokemäenjoen suussa II*, Pori: Satakunnan Museon Kannatusyhdistys.

Maijanen, H. (2006) 'Stature estimation for a 17th and 18th century Oulu population', *Studia Humaniora Ouluensia*, 1: 329–36.

——(2009) 'Testing anatomical methods for stature estimation on individuals from the W. M. Bass Donated Skeletal Collection', *Journal of Forensic Sciences*, 54: 746–52.

Maijanen, H. and Niskanen, M. (2006) 'Testing stature-estimation methods on medieval inhabitants of Westerhus, Sweden', *Fennoscandia Archaeologica*, 23: 37–46.

——(2009) 'New regression equations for stature estimation for medieval Scandinavians', *International Journal of Osteoarchaeology*, online, DOI:1002/oa.1071.

Niinimäki, S., Junno, J-H., Niskanen, M., et al. (2009) 'Ihmisjäänteiden tutkimuksen historiaa Oulun yliopistossa', in J. Ikäheimo and S. Lipponen (eds) *Ei kiveäkään kääntämättä*, Oulu: Pentti Koivusen Juhlakirjatoimikunta.

Niskanen, M. (2006) 'Stature of the Merovingian period inhabitants from Leväluhta, Finland', *Fennoscandia Archaeologica*, 23: 24–36.

Niskanen, M. and Junno, J-A. (2006) 'The reconstruction of body size and shape of the Paleolithic period Europeans', *Studia Humaniora Ouluensia*, 1: 310–20.

——(2009) 'Estimation of African apes' body size from postcranial dimentions', *Primates*, 50: 211–20.

Norio, R. (2000) *Suomi-neidon geenit. Tautiperinnön takana, juurillemme johtamassa*, Helsinki: Otava.

Núñez, M. (1987) 'Archaeology and anthropology of a mass grave in Tranvik, Sund, Åland Islands', *Fennoscandia Archaeologica*, 6: 51–66.

——(1995) 'Cannibalism on Pitted ware Åland?', *Karhunhammas*, 16: 61–68.

——(1997) 'Growth patterns in immature skeletal remains from medieval Kökar, Åland Islands', in H.S. Vuorinen and U. Vala (eds) *Vanhojen luiden kertomaa*, Helsinki: Helsinki University Press.

——(2000) 'Morbilidad y mortalidad en el Archipiélago de Åland 1749–90', in L. Caro, H. Rodríguez, E. Sánchez, et al. (eds) *Tendencias actuales de investigación en la Antropología Física española*, León, Universidad de León.

——(2005) 'Att tillreda en människa', in C. Bunte (ed.) *Arkeologi och naturvetenskap*, Lund: Krapperupstiffelse.

——(2007) 'Un tumor odontogénico en el maxilar de un adulto enterrado en el siglo XVIII en la catedral de Oulu, Finlandia', in J. Barca Durán and J. Jiménez Ávila (eds) *Enfermedad, muerte y cultura en las sociedades del pasado*, Cáceres, Universidad de Extremadura.

Núñez, M. and Botella, M. (2004) 'Indicios de canibalismo en el Archipiélago de Åland, Finlandia, hace 5000 años', in T. Varela (ed.) *Investigaciones en biodiversidad humana*, Santiago de Compostela: Universidad de Santiago de Compostela.

Núñez, M., Garcia, E., Lidén, K., et al. (2006) 'Diferencias dietéticas en torno al Mar Báltico (10000–10200 BP)', in A. Martínez-Almagro (ed.) *Diversidad Biológica y Salud Humana*, Murcia: Fundación Universitaria San Antonio.

Núñez, M., Garcia-Guixé, E., Liebe-Harkort, C., et al. (2009) 'Treponematosis en cráneos aborigines de Puerto Rico', in M. Polo-Cerdá and E. García-Prósper (eds) *Investigaciones histórico-médicas sobre salud y enfermedad en el pasado*, Valencia: Grupo Paleolab & SEP.

Núñez, M., Háber, M. and Garcia, E. (2006) 'Occurrence of suprainiac fossae in Iron Age and later crania from northern Finland', *Studia Humaniora Ouluensia*, 1: 321–28.

Núñez, M. and Lidén, K. (1994) 'Interpretación biocultural de una población subneolítica del archipiélago de Åland, Finlandia', in C. Bernis, C. Varea, F. Robles, et al. (eds) *Biología de las poblaciones humanas: problemas metodológicos e interpretación ecológica*, Madrid: Universidad Autónoma de Madrid.

——(1997) 'Taking the 5000 year old Jettböle skeleton out of the closet.' *Journal of Circumpolar Health*, 56: 30–39.

Núñez, M., Paavola, K. and Garcia-Guixé, E. (2008) 'The mummies of northern Finland', in P. Atoche Peña, C. Rodríguez-Martín and A. Ramírez Rodríguez (eds) *Mummies and Science. Proceedings of the VI World Congress on Mummy Studies*, Santa Cruz de Tenerife: Academia Canaria de Historia.

Núñez, M., Torres Joerges, X. and Botella López, M. (2005) 'Evidencia de malaria endémica en Finlandia durante 1750–1850', in A. Cañellas Trobat (ed.) *Nuevas Perspectivas del diagnóstico diferencial en Paleopatología*, Mahón: Universitat de les Illes Balears.

Ojanlatva, E., Koskela, T., Joona, J-P., et al. (1997) 'Haukiputaan kirkkohaudat', *Meteli No.13*.

Ojanlatva, E., Núñez, M., Cózar, P., et al. (2000) 'Incidence of palatine torus in a 16th-18th century population from Oulu, northern Finland', in L. Caro, H. Rodríguez, E. Sánchez, et al. (eds) *Tendencias actuales de investigación en la Antropología Física española*, León: Universidad de León.

Paavola, K. (1989) 'Hailuodon kirkkohaudat', *Faravid*, 12: 63–67.

——(1995) '"Maatumisrauha". Kemiaa ja eettisiä ongelmia', *Muinaistutkija*, 2/1995: 12–16.

——(1998) 'Kepeät mullat. Kirjallisiin ja esineellisiin perustuva tutkimus Pohjois-Pohjanmaan rannikon kirkkohaudoista', *Acta Universitatis Ouluensis B 28.*

Paavola, K., Ojanlatva, E., Joona, J-P., *et al.* (1997) 'Keminmaan kirkkohaudat', *Meteli No.14.*

Palkama, A., Virtama, P., and Telkkä, A. (1962) 'Estimation of stature from radiographs of long bones in children II. Children under one year of age', *Annales Medicinae Experimentalis et Biologiae Fenniae*, 40: 219–22.

Palo, J.U., Hedman, M., Söderholm, N., *et al.* (2007) 'Repatriation and identification of Finnish World War II Soldiers', *Croatian Medical Journal*, 48: 528–35.

Palo, J.U., Ulmanen, I., Lukka, M., *et al.* (2009) 'Genetic markers and population history: Finland revisited', *European Journal of Human Genetics*, 17: 1336–46.

Pesonen, N. (1939) 'Über die aus dem 6–7. Jahrhundert n.Chr. stammenden Knochenfunde der Opferquelle Leväluhta', *Sitzungsberichte der Finnischen Akademie der Wissenschaften* (1938): 54–69.

Pirttiniemi, P. and Heikkinen, T. (1989) '1400–1700-luvuilta peräisin olevien hailuotolaisäääkallojen hampaistotutkimuksia', *Faravid*, 12: 77–87.

Pirttiniemi, P. and Huggare, J. (1989) '1400–1700-luvuulla eläneiden hailuotolaisten kallon ja alaleuan muodon tarkasteluja', *Faravid*, 12: 69–75.

Pirttiniemi, P., Kantomaa, T. and Rönning, O. (1990) 'Relation of the glenoid fossa to craniofacial morphology, studied in dry human Lapp skulls', *Acta Odontologica Scandinavica*, 48: 359–64.

Retzius, G. (1878) *Finska kranier jämte några natur-och litteratur studier inom andra områden af finsk antropologi*, Stockholm: Central-tryckeriet.

Ruff, C.B., Niskanen, M., Junno, J-A., *et al.* (2005) 'Body mass prediction from stature and bi-iliac breadth in two high latitude populations, with applications to earlier high latitude populations', *Journal of Human Evolution*, 48: 381–92.

Sajantila, A. (2003) 'The history of the Sámi in the light of genetics', in J. Pennanen and K. Näkkäläjärvi (eds) *Siiddastallan: from Lapp communities to modern Sámi life*, Inari: Siida Sámi Museum.

Sellevold, B. (2009) *Etikk og gamle skjeletter. De nasjonale forskningsetiske komiteer.* Available online at http://etikkom.no/no/FBIB/Temaer/Forskning-pa-menneskelig-materiale/Menneskelige-levninger/Etikk-og-gamle-skjeletter/

Telkkä, A. (1950) 'On the prediction of human stature from the long bones', *Acta Anatomica*, 9: 103–7.

Telkkä, A., Palkama, A. and Virtama, P. (1962) 'Estimation of stature from radiographs of long bones in children. Children aged one to nine', *Annales Medicinae Experimentalis Biologiae Fenniae*, 40: 91–96.

Torres Joerges, X. (2005) 'Importancia de la viruela, gastroenteritis aguda y paludismo en Finlandia entre 1749 y 1850', *Acta Universitatis Ouluensis B 68*, Oulu: Oulu University. (Available http: http://herkules.oulu.fi/isbn9514279417/)

Torres, X. and Núñez, M. (2005) 'Morbidity and mortality in Finland based on parish death-cause registers from 1750–1850', *International Conference Life Courses in Context, Sydney. Section of the Commission for Historical Demography. D. Micro-data base and GIS-applications.* Available online at www.lifecoursesincontext.nl/sydney2005.html/

Virtama, P., Kiviluoto, R., Palkama, A., *et al.* (1962) 'Estimation of stature from radiographs of long bones in children III. Children aged from ten to fifteen', *Annales Medicinae Experimentalis et Biologiae Fenniae*, 40: 283–85.

Vuorinen, H. (2002) *Tauti(n)en historia*, Tampere: Vastapaino.

——(2006) *Tautinen Suomi 1857–1865*, Tampere: Tampere University Press.

Westerlund, F.W. (1900) 'Studier i Finlands antropologi I-II. Kroppslängden', *Fennia No. 18.*

——(1902) 'Studier i Finlands antropologi III. Huvudets form', *Fennia No. 20.*

——(1904) 'Studier i Finlands antropologi III. Ögon och hårfärg', *Fennia No. 21.*

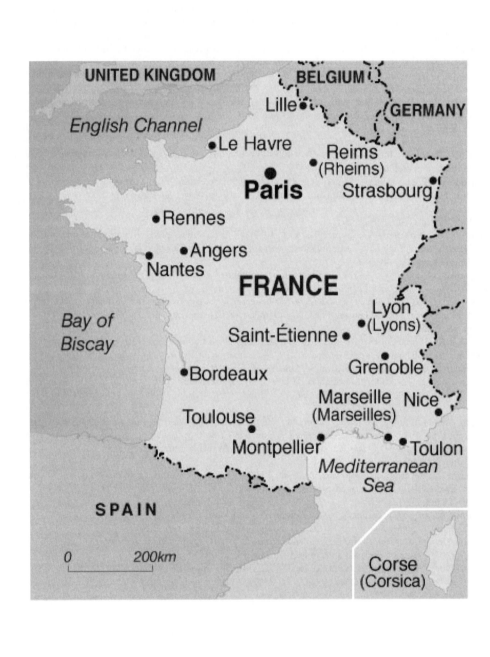

France

Juliette Michel and Philippe Charlier

INTRODUCTION: A BRIEF HISTORY AND CURRENT STATE OF PHYSICAL ANTHROPOLOGY IN FRANCE

At its inception, French anthropology primarily focused on the study of the biology and evolution of the human species. Research of skeletal remains takes its roots from the school of naturalism in Western Europe at the beginning of the 19th century. The publication of *Recherche sur les ossements fossiles* by Georges Cuvier (1820), was followed by the work of the Belgian researcher Philippe-Charles Schmerling with *Description des ossements fossiles à l'état pathologique provenant des cavernes de Lièges* (1835) and the German Philipp Franz Von Walther with *Ueber das Alterthum der Knochenkrankheiten* (1825). Both Schmerling and Von Walther proposed a scientific classification of human bones and identification of pathological lesions. However, an explicit definition of the discipline had not yet materialized, with additional branches of research, such as morphology, physiology and evolutionary theory adding to the confusion. Nevertheless, physical anthropology would be led by two major schools of thought, the French school supervised by Broca, and the English school by Virchow.

The Society of Anthropology of Paris (Societé d'Anthropologie de Paris) has been the template of the development of physical anthropology in France. This organization was created in 1855 by Paul Broca, surgeon and neurologist, who gathered together the leading experts of anthropology, ethnology, medicine, archaeology and other disciplines. Human skeletons were coming from different places: archaeological excavations in Paris (Baron Haussman's building work policies); in the rest of France following nationalist policies inspired by Napoleon III with the myth of Nos ancêtres les Gaulois ('Our Gaul Ancestors') where the Gauls are portrayed as strong warriors united to fight the Roman invaders; and in the colonies (Algeria, Antilles, Guyana, Cochinchina, Melanesia, New Caledonia, etc.). However, at this time only the skulls were studied and the rest of the skeleton was often barely analysed. It was believed that the skulls presented all the racial, physiological, psychological and pathological stigmas of the individual. The theory was backed by many metric indices (the cephalic index in particular). Another area of considerable interest at the time was the identification of trepanation (sometimes under the influence of Broca himself), or the association of skeletal abnormalities with contemporary illnesses (mainly syphilis and tuberculosis). The French physical anthropology school got rid of these racial stereotypes only at the end of the 1970s, when people such as Robert P. Charles

stopped practising (Charlier 2006; 2008a). In parallel, anthropology evolved towards archaeological anthropology with the excavation of many prehistoric sites, such as the excavation of
the Hypogeum II of Mournouards by André Leroi-Gouran in the 1950s, which publication
brought the basis for interpretation of burial contexts in France (Leroi-Gourhan *et al.* 1962).

Burial anthropology or field anthropology (anthropologie de terrain) emerged only in the
1970s under the leadership of Jean Leclerc, Claude Masset and Henri Duday (Duday and Masset
1987), and with the development of rescue archaeology in the 1980s. The anthropologists took
into account taphonomic changes, and even used these alterations in order to recreate the burial
context for the purpose of dating the remains and to understand the funerary practices. Since
the mid-1990s, field anthropology or burial archaeology evolved towards a multi-disciplinary
approach, including studies on ancient DNA, isotopes, entomological and parasitological remains,
palynology, carpology or anthracology in cremation burials.

Several anthropological laboratories direct their research in these new disciplines, but with
different focus. The Bordeaux school, which was at the origin of the development of burial archaeology with Henri Duday, directed its work towards human evolution, although more recently
towards palaeogenetic studies. At the end of the 1980s, they studied burnt and cremated remains.
The Marseilles school was originated at the end of the 1990s with Olivier Dutour, who is
particularly interested in the palaeopathological study of past populations. More recently with
Michel Signoli, the Marseilles school also focuses its work now on mass graves (sépultures de
catastrophe) in the context of plague epidemics and armed conflicts. The Toulouse school managed by Eric Crubézy ran significant works on the analysis of non-metric traits. The laboratory
now specializes in palaeogenetics. The Nice school, thanks to the joint effort of Luc Buchet and
Isabelle Séguy, focuses its effort on palaeodemography, following the methodology developed
by Claude Masset and Jean-Pierre Bocquet-Appel.

ARCHAEOLOGICAL HUMAN REMAINS AND LEGISLATION

Discovery of human remains

Every discovery of a corpse or human remains will lead to an inquiry. First, the remains have to
be dated. With some exceptions, every finding which is discovered more than 10 years after the
date of the crime is not subject to a criminal inquiry (article 706–47 of the Criminal Procedure
Code) and becomes an archaeological issue. Prosecution is proscribed after 10 completed years
since the date of the crime (20 years if the person was under 18 years old at the moment of
death), if no charges have been brought during that period of time. It is particularly critical to
determine precisely the age of the deceased and the age of the human remains. In practice, after
10 years (20 years for minors), human remains are not subject to criminal investigation. However, some crimes are without proscriptions, such as crimes against humanity or war crimes
(articles 211–1 to 211–13 and 213–15 of the Criminal Procedure Code). These include genocide, deportation, slavery, execution and torture, inspired by political, philosophical, ideological,
racial or religious justification.

In forensic medicine, every discovery of a corpse or human remains, except for skeletons
clearly found in an archaeological context, leads to an inquiry as mentioned in article 74 of the
Criminal Procedure Code (Code de Procédure Pénale): the person who discovers the corpse
must inform a police officer (officier de police judiciaire, or OPJ) who will go to the scene to
undertake an initial assessment and will inform the public prosecutor (procureur de la République).
Usually, the OPJ will be assisted by a coroner or, by default, by a competent doctor, who will

produce a report on the age of the remains and the possible reason for the death, as soon as possible and usually immediately after the post-mortem examination and within a maximum period of 8 days.

For older remains (i.e., those corresponding to a death older than 10 years), it is important to search for signs of violence (mutilation, physical abuse, torture, violent death, etc.) that may provide evidence of a crime against humanity or a war crime. The context in which the remains are found (e.g., a mass grave) as well as associated objects (clothes, coins, ammunition, etc.) may also provide further information in this regard.

Archaeological legislation

Archaeological excavation is conducted in two ways: 'preventive' or rescue excavation, and 'planned' or research excavation. The former involves archaeological excavation when there is a risk of destruction of the archaeological or historical heritage by new development (such as road schemes or building work). The second type has specific scientific research objectives and is usually conducted by university departments.

'Preventive' archaeology involves a desktop survey or DBA (desk based assessment) to evaluate the potential of the archaeology. If there is risk to the archaeology in the area, evaluation trenches are dug to assess the archaeological potential of the site. Excavations can be carried out by public and private companies that hold a licence issued by the regional governmental authority for culture, or DRAC (Direction Régionale des Affaires Culturelles). Archaeological evaluations and excavations are funded by the developer. The developing contractor, nevertheless, can ask for financial assistance from the FNAP (Fond National pour l'Archéologie Préventive) or a bonus granted by the state.

With regard to research excavations, a licence is not compulsory although an authorization request must be sent to the Regional Archaeological Department, or SRA (Service Régional de l'Archéologie). This authority oversees the application process prior to presenting it to one of the six interregional committees for archaeological research, or CIRA (Commissions Interrégionales de la Recherche Archéologique). Planned excavations may also receive financial assistance from the Ministry of Culture.

HUMAN REMAINS AND LEGISLATION

Human remains derived from archaeological contexts do not have any particular legal status. Indeed, Law no. 2001–44 (17 January 2001), relating to rescue archaeology, discusses in a general manner archaeological heritage or archaeological artefacts. The term 'human remains' is never mentioned. This law considers that human remains are absorbed into the main archaeological legislation, thus being considered as having the same status as an artefact. Consequently they seem to follow the same administrative and legal process, notably in terms of heritage protection and artefact property, as defined in the Law no. 41–4011 (27 September 1941), a law governing the regulation of archaeological excavation. However, the decree of 16 September 2004, relating to standards of inventory, archiving and storage of scientific documentation and of artefacts from archaeological evaluations and excavations, seems to include biological items recovered from archaeological fieldwork. This would be an implicit reference to human remains.

Further, there is no religious prescription regarding the excavation of human remains. Religious authorities are rarely involved in the excavation strategy or implementation. A gesture to involve these authorities by the Prefect of the Region (with the right to authorize excavations) could help to relieve tensions from current religious communities. Human remains can be re-interred, although no specific regulation exists, as they are considered as artefacts.

Contrary to other countries, therefore, it is not necessary to hold a particular licence to excavate archaeological human remains. Moreover, if ancient burials are discovered during archaeological excavation, there is no obligation to inform the authorities. Only a permit to excavate is compulsory, and this covers all archaeological remains present at the site. The licence is obtained from DRAC and is delivered under the authority of the Regional Prefect. The regional curators at DRAC supervise the excavation, with the help of CIRA, and, when the project is particularly significant, of the National Council for Archaeological Research, or CNRA (Conseil National de la Recherche Archéologique).

War graves

The excavation of the burials resulting from the two World Wars is a far more sensitive matter. This is due to the fact that they lie between the spheres of archaeology and forensic medicine. The excavation of soldiers fallen in the line of duty does not depend on the Ministry of Culture but on the Secretariat of War Veterans (Secrétariat des anciens combattants). These excavations are considered as an exhumation process, with the archaeological excavation perceived as a single step along this path.

Since 1915, every civil or military person killed as a result of a war conflict is entitled to be recognized as 'Dead for France' (Mort pour la France). If they have been found and identified, they must be given back to their families, and this process of repatriation or reburial should be paid for by the state as stated in legislative section D402 and D403 of the Code of Military Invalid Pensions and War Casualty Pensions (Code des pensions militaires d'invalidité et des victimes de guerres).

However, considerable losses of French and Allied soldiers during battle are interred together in national cemeteries (section L498 of the same Code), as in the case of Alain Fournier. Alain Fournier, a famous French author notable for his work *Le Grand Meaulnes*, was killed during a First World War campaign. His burial place was rediscovered along with that of 20 other soldiers in 1991 during an archaeological investigation (Boura *et al.* 1992). After a programme of research, the remains of the soldiers were reburied individually at a French cemetery. All state property or personal effects are returned to the Army or to families, rather than being retained in museums.

Post-excavation analysis and the treatment of human remains

All artefacts and human remains retrieved from the excavation are retained by the archaeological company for study. A report is presented to DRAC within two years of the end of the excavation. However, artefacts or human remains may be retained for further study for up to five years, after which these are submitted to the state. A decision is then made concerning their future. The artefacts may be curated in governmental archaeological storage facilities. However, according to the Code du Patrimoine (article L523–14 and L531–11), these artefacts (human remains would be here classified as an artefact) may be divided equally between the state and the owner of the land. If the state wishes to retain all artefacts, a compensation payment may be made to the landowner; however, placing a monetary value upon human remains is problematic to say the least. But if the decree of 16 September 2004 is taken into consideration, then the human remains seem to form a part of the scientific documentation and thus cannot be considered with the other artefacts.

Some facilities are specific for the storage of skeletal remains, thus creating new centres of study such as at Pessac (Gironde), the ostéothèque of the Centre de Recherches Archéologiques et Historiques Médiévales (CRAM) of the University of Caen (Basse-Normandie), the regional ostéothèque of the Faculty of Medicine of Marseilles or the ostéothèque of the departmental Archaeological Service of Val-d'Oise (SDAVO) (see Ardagna *et al.* 2006).

At present, no specific legislation exists concerning the disposal of human remains. A decision may be made regarding the non-curation of human remains, and in this case these may be deposited in a local ossuary. Unfortunately, there have been some examples of human remains and other artefacts that have been deposited in public waste sites. This should not be taken as a reflection of a lack of respect but because the disposal of human remains is only given the classification of an 'object' or 'artefact' in the French archaeological policy.

Human remains, and any samples, may be sent abroad for further analysis. An agreement is negotiated between the relevant authorities of the two countries. Occasionally an export declaration is required.

Ethical considerations

Recently, an exhibition of human remains called *Our Body, à corps ouvert* organized by the Chinese medical foundation Anatomical Sciences & Technologies in Hong Kong was subject to a ban in France on the basis of the law regulating corpses. (Ordonnance de référé du Tribunal de Grande Instance de Paris dated 21 April 2009; Arrêt de la Cour d'Appel de Paris du 30 avril.) It was clearly stated that ' ... the corpses and any parts are meant to be buried or incinerated or placed as part of a scientific collection of a public authority; ... the private retention of a corpse is illegal.' (Ordonnance de référé du Tribunal de Grande Instance de Paris rendue le 21 avril 2009.)

The court of Appeal of Paris (decision of the 30 April 2009) admits that this protection towards the human body (living or dead) does not exclude the utilization of corpse for scientific or pedagogic purposes. However, in the same court decision, the court opens the opportunity to museum and religious presentation of human remains: ' ... respect does not exclude the society to look at death and at the religious and non-religious rituals that surround it in different cultures. This allows the exhibition of mummies that are exhumed from their burials, to expose relics without provoking indignation or trouble to the public order'. This regulation may have come into being to avoid possible court claims against existing anatomical exhibits (for instance in the exhibition *Et la mort n'en saura rien* ... , where trophy-skulls were presented) or in specialized museums such as medical museums.

As a result of this scenario, researchers such as Henri Duday (2003) have suggested guidelines of professional and ethical conduct. Conferences have been organized to examine these proposals and create a code of conduct concerning the treatment of human remains (e.g., the International Symposium taken place in Quai Branly museum of Paris in February 2008: Des collections anatomiques aux objets de culture, conservation et exposition des restes humains dans les musées).

The International Council of Museums (ICOM) has announced many principles of ethics specific to human remains. Its principles have inspired the Charter International Unidroit, signed by France, which suggests the return of cultural items that were taken without authorization from the country of origin.

Display of human remains in museums

Within museum collections and archaeological excavations, human remains appear to have the same status as other artefacts, even though this has not been explicitly stated in the law. The absence of particular legislation for human remains, in both museum and archaeological collections, makes this a problem for the future management of these remains.

Law no. 2002–5 of 4 January 2002, concerning French museums (Musées de France), stipulates that museum collections includes any items which provide knowledge, education and pleasure to the public (article 1). So there is nothing to exclude human remains from museum collections, which are the purpose of medical museums for example. However, some natural history museums have exhibited human remains from France's recent colonial past that have shocked many people and institutions because of the lack of respect towards the human being and the absence of scientific aims in some of the exhibitions. These abuses have led some former French colonies to ask for the restitution of human remains conserved in museums. This is the case, for example, of the 'Hottentot Venus'.

Saartjie 'Sarah' Baartman (1789–1815) was one of the famous Khoikhoi women exhibited as attractions in the 19th century under the name 'Hottentot Venus'. She was born and lived in South Africa during the 19th century, prior to going to London and then to Paris, where she was exhibited for her overdeveloped buttocks. After her death in 1915, her body was studied at the French National Natural History Museum. Following a request from South Africa, her remains were repatriated in 2002, after a long controversy.

The debate concerned on the one hand the legislation on museum collections, and on the other the legislation on human remains. Indeed, Article 11 of Law no. 2002–5 regarding French museums states that 'French museum collections are imprescriptible' (Article L. 451.3), and that 'the items of French museums belong to the public domain and are inalienable' (Article L 451–55). According to this law, therefore, human remains in museums cannot be repatriated. But the law stipulates as well that a downgrading is still possible if it is validated by a specific commission in charge of the request for repatriation (Article L69–1).

Only a living human being is considered to have legal rights in French legislation. Indeed, the law on bioethics of 29 July 1994 was passed to protect human organ trafficking, as well as the regulation of the use of genetic studies in order to prevent abuse. These texts refer to the living and at no point make reference to the body of the deceased.

However, some of these articles have been paid much attention in relation to the repatriation of Saartijie Baartmaan's remains. Article 16–1 of the 'Civil Code' stipulates that 'everybody is entitled to have their body respected. The human body is inviolable. The human body, its elements and products cannot be subject to property law'. In this case any downgrading process is not necessary in order to repatriate these remains. Does this mean that the principle of alienation does not apply to human remains? If the repatriation of Saartijie Baartmaan's remains was clearly justified, however, the application of this law for all human remains may be alarming for medical and archaeological museum collections, and would have implications for research in the future.

METHODS OF ANTHROPOLOGICAL ANALYSIS

This section is a summary of the main osteological methods used in France, classified in three domains: burial archeology, paleodemography and pathology.

Funerary osteoarchaeology

Taphonomic analysis is well developed in France. It encompasses the state of preservation and condition of the remains and their position in the burial, as well as the position of the skeleton and of all its skeletal elements (Duday 2005: 164). With the development of rescue archaeology, Henri Duday developed a method known as 'Anthropologie de terrain' (field funerary archaeology) or 'Archaeothanatology'. His research still serves as a standard for the study and recording of osteological data on site (Duday 1995, 2005, 2009). The following section summarizes this methodology.

'Anthropologie de terrain'

We have already stated that the work of Henri Duday (1995, 2005, 2009) has been important in the recording of skeletons *in situ*. A number of additional publications present different disciplines and methods used commonly in burial archaeology in France, and their use is recommended when working in France: Duday and Masset (1987), Duday *et al.* (1990); Crubezy *et al.* (1990) and Castex *et al.* (1996). The research of J. McKinley in UK (1993, 2000, 2004) discusses cremation burials. Building on her methods for excavation by spit, sieving protocols and weight analysis, other methods have been presented and developed by Grévin (1990), Duday *et al.* (2000), Blaizot and Tranoy (2004) and Duday (2005, 2009).

Field osteoarchaeologists record the precise identity of each anatomical part, its exact position and orientation and its anatomical relationships with other bones and archaeological elements. An initial observation of the age, sex and measurements of long bones is carried out in the field, and subsequently developed in the laboratory – preservation permitting. All these critical data are recorded on specially designed skeleton sheets. Some of the terms used in France after Duday's work are the differences between primary and secondary burial, decomposition in a void or in a filled space, etc.; terms which the researcher should be familiar with when working in France.

Osteologists must record on site the location of every bone and register which side it lies on and if it has remained articulated or whether it has become disarticulated. They should also observe if the bones have moved from their original position and if they are located outside the initial volume of the corpse (i.e., volume before decomposition), or if they have remained in an unstable position (i.e., where bones should have moved during decomposition process, due to the law of gravity, but they haven't). All these data can provide useful information on the presence of primary or secondary burial, and on the use of a container such as a shroud or a coffin, when there is no artefactual preservation. The analysis performed on site is essential for the understanding of burial practices.

Methods of anthropological analysis

Estimation of subadult skeletal age is usually based on three methods: the tooth mineralization stage, using the method of Moorrees, Fanning and Hunt (1963a, 1963b) and Ubelaker (1989); bone measurements based on the works of Sundick (1978), Stloukal and Hanàkovà (1978) and Scheuer and Black (2000); and Birkner's (1980) method for age estimation from epiphyseal fusion. The age of fetuses and neonates is estimated from bone length, based on Fazekas and Kosa's (1978) method and adapted by French researchers (Duday *et al.* 1995; Sellier *et al.* 1997; Adalian 2001).

For estimation of adult age, where a burial includes a large number of skeletons, a probabilistic approach (Bayesian approach) can be used from cranial sutures (Masset 1982, 1989), although this method is inaccurate. The auricular surface of the pelvis is a better criterion for estimating adult skeletal age (Schmitt 2005).

Sex determination is based mainly on the pelvis which is the most distinguishing bone. Methods to estimate sex by the pelvis include those based on macroscopic observations (Bruzek *et al.* 1996, Bruzek 2002) and metric analysis (Murail *et al.* 2005).

Age and sex estimation is essential to establish palaeodemographic profiles. Ledermann's (1969) tables are commonly used for palaeodemographic analysis. C. Masset, as well as L. Buchet and I. Séguy have created mortality tables based on historical documentation which are considered to be more accurate than those tables derived from archaeological skeletal population (Buchet and Séguy 2002; Buchet *et al.* 2006).

Methods in stature estimation, include Trotter and Gleser's (1958) work as well as the tables devised by Olivier (1960, 1969) which are based on those by Manouvrier (1893).

Recording non-metric traits uses as a reference Hauser and De Stefano's (1989) work for the skull; Scott and Turner (1997) for the teeth; and Saunders (1978) for post-cranial skeleton. In addition, Eric Crubézy and Pascal Murail (Crubézy 1991; Crubézy and Sellier 1990; Crubézy *et al.* 1999; Murail 1996, 2005) have researched and published on non-metric traits in France.

French-language reference books for palaeopathology are those by Thillaud (1996) and Charlier (2008b).

CONCLUSION

The discovery of human remains more than 10 years after the point of death, has not concerned the French judicial system. These remains seem to have fallen into the archaeological domain.

The status of human remains in archaeological and museum collections appears a little blurred, as these terms are never explicitly written. But the decree of 16 September 2004 seems to incorporate them as part of scientific documentation, thus preventing any private ownership of human remains. If the absence of a particular law on human remains, in both museum and archaeological collections, reduces the constraints of osteological research, then certain abuse of this absence has led this approach to be questioned.

However, as the law states, the study of human remains can be undertaken when the aim of the research leads to knowledge and education (Law no. 2002–5 of 4 January 2002), and must always be done with respect towards the dead (Article 16-1-1 of the 'Civil Code').

In France, osteologists are usually involved in the archaeological excavation of human remains. As forensic doctors, they record and analyse the remains in order to determine the biological identity of the skeleton, as well as the different burial practices, in order to enlighten our understanding of the cultural aspect of the human past.

USEFUL CONTACTS

Main osteological laboratories in France

Laboratoire d'Anthropologie des Populations du Passé (LAPP) of Bordeaux (UMR or Unité Mixte de Recherche 5199), University of Sciences and Technologies, Bordeaux 1. Website: www.pacea.u-bordeaux1.fr/

Laboratoire d'anthropologie biologique of Toulouse (UMR 8555), University P. Sabatier, Toulouse 3. Website: www.anthropobiologie.cict.fr/

Laboratoire d'Anthropologie Bioculturelle of Marseille (UMR 6578), Université de la Mediterranée, Aix-Marseille 2, Faculty of Medicine. Website: www.anthropologie-biologique.cnrs.fr/

Muséum National d'Histoire Naturelle and Musée de l'Homme, Paris (UMR7194). Website: www.mnhn.fr/
Centre d'Etudes Préhistoire, Antiquité, Moyen-Age (CEPAM) of Valbonne (UMR 6130). Website: www.cepam.cnrs.fr/
Laboratoire d'Archéologie, Cultures et Sociétés of Dijon (UMR 5594), University of Bourgogne, Dijon. Website: www.artehis.cnrs.fr/
Service de Médecine Légale (Anthropologie et d'Anatomie/Cytologie Pathologiques), CHU R. Poincaré (AP-HP, UVSQ), F-92380 Garches.

Contact details of Laboratories and Researchers can be found online at www.cnrs.fr/

Rescue archaeology companies

Contacts can be found at online at www.culture.gouv.fr/culture/dp/archeo/pdf/operateur_agree.pdf/

INRAP (Institut National de Recherches Archéologiques Préventives). Website: www.inrap.fr/
Oxford Archéologie Méditerranée. Website: www.oamed.fr/

Main French anthropological journals

Biométrie Humaine et Anthropologie. Website: www.biom-hum.com/Revue.htm/
Bulletins et Mémoires de la Société d'Anthropologie de Paris. Website: http://bmsap.revues.org/
Populations et Sociétés
L'Homme
L'Anthropologie
Population

Anthropological associations and conferences (osteology and archaeology)

SAP (Société d'Anthropologie de Paris): organizes a conference every year since 1859. Website: www.sapweb.fr/
AFPP (Association Française de Paléopathologie et de Pathographie): organizes an international congress every two years, whose papers are published by De Boccard, Paris.
GAAF (Groupement des Archéologues et Anthropologues Funéraires): organizes a conference and several workshops every year. Website: http://gaaf.e-monsite.com/
GALF (Groupement des Anthropologistes de Langue Française): organizes a conference every second year since 1965.
GPLF (Groupement des Paléopathologistes de Langue Française): organizes a conference every year.
Les journées anthropologiques de Valbonne: organizes a conference every three years

Legal and ethic texts (websites)

www.legifrance.gouv.fr/
www.dalloz.fr/
www.culture.fr/sections/themes/archeologie/
www.culture.gouv.fr/nav/index-dt.html/
http://icom.museum/ethics_fr.html/

BIBLIOGRAPHY

Adalian, P. (2001) 'Evaluation multiparamétrique de la croissance fœtale: application à la détermination de l'âge et du sexe', unpublished doctoral thesis, Aix-Marseille II University, France.

Ardagna, Y., Bizot, B., Boëtsch, G., *et al.* (eds) (2006) *Les collections ostéologiques humaines: gestion, valorisation, perspectives*, Bulletin Archéologique de Provence, suppl 4, Aix-en-Provence: Association Provence Archéologie.

Beauthier, J.P. (2008), *Traité de médecine légale*, Bruxelles: De Boeck.

Birkner, R. (1980) *L'image radiographique typique du squelette*, Paris: Maloine.

Blaizot, F. and Tranoy, L. (2004) 'La notion de sépulture au Haut-Empire. Identification et interprétation des structures funéraires liées aux crémations', in L. Baray (ed.) *Archéologie des pratiques funéraires. Approches critiques*. Actes de la table ronde de BIBRACTE, 7–9 juin 2001. Collection Bibracte-9, Glux-en-Glenne.

Boura, F., Duday, H., Hervet, P., *et al.* (1992) 'Fouille archéologique d'une sépulture militaire de 1914: la sépulture collective de Saint-Rémy-la-Calonne (Meuse)', *Les Nouvelles de l'Archéologie*, 48/49: 56–70.

Bruzek, J. (2002) 'A method for visual determination of sex, using the human hip bone', *American Journal of Physical Anthropology*, 117: 157–68.

Bruzek, J., Castex, D. and Majo, T. (1996) 'Evaluation des caractères morphologiques de la face sacro-pelvienne de l'os coxal: approche pour une proposition d'une méthode de diagnose sexuelle', in D. Castex, P. Courtaud, P. Sellier, *et al.* (eds) *Les ensembles funéraires, du terrain à l'interprétation*, Actes du Colloque du GDR 742 du CNRS. *Bulletins et Mémoires de la Société d'Anthropologie de Paris*, 8.

Buchet, L., Dauphin, C. and Séguy, I. (eds) (2006) *La paléodémographie. Mémoire d'os, mémoire d'hommes*. Actes des VIIIe journées anthropologiques de Valbonne (juin 2003), Antibes: Editions APDCA.

Buchet, L. and Séguy, I. (2002) 'La paléodémographie aujourd'hui: bilan et perspectives', *Annales de Démographie Historique*, 1: 161–212.

Castex, D., Courtaud, P., Sellier, P., *et al.* (eds) (1996) *Les ensembles funéraires, du terrain à l'interprétation*, Actes du Colloque du GDR 742 du CNRS. *Bulletins et Mémoires de la Société d'Anthropologie de Paris*, 8.

Charlier, P. (2006) 'L'anthropologie grecque comme cheval de bataille: l'affrontement des écoles française et américaine dans l'étude des restes humains en Grèce (1943–85)', *European Review of History*, 13: 643–60.

——(2008a) 'Enseignement et recherche paléopathologique en France. Spécificités et bibliographie choisie', *Histoire des Sciences Médicales*, 42: 153–69.

——(ed.) (2008b) *Ostéo-archéologie et techniques médico-légales: tendances et perspectives. Pour un 'Manuel pratique de paléopathologie humaine'*, Paris: Editions de Boccard.

Crubézy, É. (1991) 'Caractère discrets et évolution: exemple d'une population nubienne: Missiminia (Soudan)', unpublished doctoral thesis, Bordeaux I University, France.

Crubézy, E. and Sellier, P. (1990) 'Caractères discrets et organisation des ensembles sépulcraux', *Bulletins et Mémoires de la Société d'Anthropologie de Paris*, 2: 171–78.

Crubézy, E., Duday, H., Sellier, P., *et al.* (eds) (1990) *Anthropologie et Archéologie: Dialogues sur les ensembles funéraires*. Actes du colloque de la Société d'Anthropologie de Paris au Musée d'Aquitaine. *Bulletins et Mémoires de la Société d'Anthropologie de Paris*, 2.

Crubézy, E., Telmon, N., Sevin, A., *et al.* (1999) 'Microévolution d'une population historique: étude des caractères discrets de la population de Missiminia (Soudann IIIe-VIe siècles)', *Bulletins et Mémoires de la Société d'Anthropologie de Paris*, 11: 197–213.

Duday, H. (1995) 'Anthropologie "de terrain", archéologie de la mort', in R. Joussaume (ed.) *La mort, passé, présent, conditionnel*, colloque du GVEP (La Roche sur Yon, June 1994). La Roche sur Yon: Groupe Vendéen d'Etudes Préhistoriques.

——(2003) 'Entre génétique et culture, la dualité patrimoniale des restes humains', in H. Rousso (ed.) *Le regard de l'Histoire. L'émergence et l'évolution de la notion de Patrimoine au cours du XXème siècle en France*, Paris: Éditions du Patrimoine.

——(2005) 'L'archéothanatologie ou l'archéologie de la mort', in O. Dutour, J.-J. Hublin and B. Vandermeersch (eds) *Objets et Méthodes en Paléopathologie*, Paris: Comité des Travaux Historiques et Scientifiques, Orientation et Méthodes No. 7.

——(2009) *The Archaeology of the Dead. Lectures in Archaeothanatology*, Oxford: Oxbow Books.

Duday, H. and Masset, C. (eds) (1987) *Anthropologie physique et archéologie. Méthodes d'étude des sepultures*, Paris: CNRS

Duday, H., Courtaud, P., Cruzéby, E., *et al.* (1990) 'L'anthropologie de terrain: reconnaissance et interprétation des gestes funéraires', *Bulletins et Mémoires de la Société d'Anthropologie de Paris*, 2: 29–50.

Duday, H., Laubenheimer, F., Tillier, A.-M. (1995) *Sallèles-d'Aude. Nouveau-nés et nourrissons gallo-romains'*, Paris: Les Belles Lettres, Annales Littéraires de l'Université de Besançon, 563, and Centre de Recherche d'Histoire Ancienne, 144, Série Amphores, 3.

Duday, H., Depierre, G and Janin, T. (2000) 'Validation des paramètres de quantification, protocoles et stratégies dans l'étude anthropologique des sépultures secondaires à incinération. L'exemple des nécropoles protohistoriques du Midi de la France', in Dedet, B., Gruat, P., Marchand, G., *et al.* (eds) *Archéologie de la Mort, Archéologie de la Tombe au Premier Age du Fer.* Actes du XXIe Colloque International de l'Association Française pour l'Etude de l'Age du fer, Conques-Montrozier, 8–11 mai 1997. Lattes: CNRS.

Fazekas, I.G. and Kòsa, F. (1978) *Forensic Fetal Osteology*, Budapest: Akadémiai Kiadō.

Grévin, G. (1990) 'La fouille en laboratoire des sépultures à incinérations: son apport à l'Archéologie', in Crubézy, É., Duday, H., Sellier, P., *et al.* (eds), *Anthropologie et Archéologie: Dialogues sur les ensembles funéraires. Bulletins et Mémoires de la Société d'Anthropologie de Paris*, 2.

Hauser, G. and De Stefano, G.F. (1989) *Epigenetic variants of the human skull*, Stuttgart: Schweizerbart.

Ledermann, S. (1969) *Nouvelles tables-types de mortalité*, Paris: Institut National des Études Démographiques, Travaux et Documents No. 53.

Leroi-Gourhan, A., Bailloud, G. and Brezillon, M. (1962) 'L'hypogée II des Mournouards', *Gallia Préhistoire*, 5: 23–133.

McKinley, J. I. (1993) 'Bone Fragment Size and Weights of Bone from Modern British Cremations and the Implications the Pyre Technology and Ritual', *Journal of Archeological Science*, 21: 339–42.

——(2000) 'The analysis of cremated bone', in M. Cox and S. Mays (eds) *Human Osteology in Archaeology and Forensic Science*, London: Greenwich Medical Media, 403–21.

——(2004) 'The human remains and aspects of pyre technology and cremation rituals', in H.E.M. Cool, *The Roman Cemetery at Brougham, Cumbria*, London: Britannia Monograph Series, 21: 283–309.

Manouvrier, L. (1893) 'La détermination de la taille d'après les grands os des membres', *Mémoires de la Société d'Anthropololgie de Paris*, 4: 347–402.

Masset, C. (1982) 'Estimation de l'âge au décès par les sutures crâniennes', unpublished doctoral thesis, Paris VIII University, France.

——(1989) 'Age estimation on the basis of cranial sutures', in M.Y. İşcan (ed.) *Age Markers in the Human Skeleton*, Springfield, IL: Charles C. Thomas.

Moorrees, C.F.A., Fanning, E.A. and Hunt, E.E. (1963a) 'Formation and resorption of three deciduous teeth in children', *American Journal of Physical Anthropology*, 21: 205–13.

——(1963b) 'Age variation of formation stages for ten permanent teeth', *Journal of Dental Research*, 42: 1490–1502.

Murail, P. (1996) 'Biologie et pratiques funéraires d'une population gallo-romaine rurale (Chantambre, Essonne)', Unpublished doctoral thesis, Université de Bordeaux I.

——(2005) 'Variations anatomiques non métriques: les caractères discrets', in O. Dutour, J.-J. Hublin and B. Vandermeersch (eds) *Objets et Méthodes en Paléopathologie*, Paris: Comité des Travaux Historiques et Scientifiques, Orientation et Méthodes No. 7.

Murail, P., Bruzek, J., Houët, F., *et al.* (2005) 'DSP: a tool for probabilistic sex diagnosis using worldwide variability in hip bone measurements', *Bulletins et Mémoires de la Société d'Anthropologie de Paris*, 17: 167–76.

Olivier, G. (1960) *Pratique anthropologique*, Paris: Vigot.

——(1969) *Pratical Anthropology*, Springfield, IL: Charles C. Thomas.

Saunders, S.R. (1978) *The Development and Distribution of Discontinuous Morphological Variation of the Human Infracranial Skeleton*, Ottawa: National Museums of Canada, Archaeological Survey of Canada, paper No. 81.

Scheuer, L. and Black, S. (2000) *Development Juvenile Osteology*, London: Academic Press.

Schmitt, A. (2005) 'Une nouvelle méthode pour estimer l'âge au décès des adultes à partir de la surface sacropelvienne iliaque', *Bulletins et Mémoires de la Société d'Anthropologie de Paris*, 17: 89–102.

Scott, G.R. and Turner, C.G. II (1997) *The Anthropology of Modern Human Teeth. Dental Morphology and its Variation in Recent Human Populations*, Cambridge: Cambridge University Press.

Sellier, P., Tillier, A.-M. and Bruzek, J. (1997) 'A la recherche d'une référence pour l'estimation de l'âge des foetus, nouveau-nés et nourrissons des populations archéologiques européennes', *Anthropologie et Préhistoire*, 108: 75–87.

Stloukal, M. and Hanàkovà, H. (1978) 'Die länge der Längsknochen altslawischer Bevölkerungen. Unter besonderer Berücksichtigung von Wachstumsfragen', *Homo*, 29: 53–69.

161

Sundick, R. (1978) 'Human skeleton growth and age determination', *Homo*, 29: 228–49.

Thillaud, P.L. (1996) *Paléopathologie humaine*. Sceaux: Kronos B.Y. Editions.

Trotter, M. and Gleser, G.C. (1958) 'A re-evaluation of estimation of stature based on measurements of stature taken during life and of long bones after death', *American Journal of Physical Anthropology*, 16: 79–123.

Ubelaker, D.H. (1989) *Human skeletal remains: excavation, analysis, interpretation*, 2nd edn, Washington DC: Taraxacum.

Germany/Deutschland

Jörg Orschiedt, Ursula Wittwer-Backofen and Stefan Flohr

INTRODUCTION: A BRIEF HISTORY AND CURRENT STATE OF PHYSICAL ANTHROPOLOGY IN GERMANY

This chapter briefly summarizes the history, present situation, and prospects of physical anthropology in Germany. More comprehensive accounts on this issue were previously published by other authors (Hoßfeld 2005, Schwidetzky 1988, 1992, Spiegel-Rösing and Schwidetzky 1982, Spencer 1997).

Roots of German physical anthropology 1861–1933

The year 1861 can be regarded as the beginning of an institutionally organized physical anthropology in Germany. In this year the first meeting of German physical anthropologists took place in Göttingen, arranged by Karl Ernst von Baer and Rudolf Wagner, following the example of French scholars who had constituted the Société d'Anthropologie de Paris in 1859. However, even prior to this date other scientists had already worked on topics that are today considered part of the discipline of 'physical anthropology'. One of the most prominent scholars in this field was Johann Friedrich Blumenbach (1752–1840), who in Germany is sometimes referred to as the 'father of anthropology' (Schwidetzky 1982: 77) although he did not call himself an anthropologist but rather a scientist studying the 'natural history of man'.

The 1861 meeting aimed to achieve the establishment of a professional society for promoting scientific exchange and the standardization of anthropometric methods. However, this aim was not to be accomplished before 1870. In 1866, the anatomist Alexander Ecker from the University of Freiburg founded the '*Archiv für Anthropologie*', which was issued until 1943. This journal was the second anthropological journal worldwide and became the publication organ of the Deutsche Gesellschaft für Anthropologie, Ethnologie und Urgeschichte (Deutsche Gesellschaft für Anthropologie, DGA, for short) that was finally established in 1870. Around that time also some other more local societies were founded, including the Berliner Gesellschaft für Anthropologie, Ethnologie und Urgeschichte (BGAEU) in 1869 that still exists today. They all formed a loose confederation under the umbrella of the DGA.

From the first meeting of the DGA in 1861 it took 25 years before anthropology became established as a distinct subject at German universities (Schwidetzky 1982: 86). The first chairs and institutes of Anthropology were established at the Universities of Munich (1886), Leipzig (1889) and Berlin (1900). Most anthropological institutes were, however, founded during the time of the Weimar Republic (1919–33).

It took many years to establish physical anthropology as a discrete discipline and an independent academic profession. Initially, many positions were filled by anatomists who also studied morphological variation in humans. However, the scope of anthropological research was clearly broader than that of pure anatomy, as is made clear by the titles of the societies. Thus, anthropological research also addressed questions related to the fields of ethnography, prehistory and later human evolution.

The other aim of the 1861 meeting, to establish standardizations of anthropometric methods, developed gradually. The need for this emerged with the interest in classifying human populations. This research led to the typological concept of human races. The skull especially became a central topic of interest (Schmutz 2006). Starting already in the 18th century, large collections of human skulls from all over the world were gathered in several Institutes, such as the Alexander Ecker collection in Freiburg, the Rudolf Virchow collection in Berlin and the Blumenbach collection in Göttingen. They served the documentation of human variability and the definition of distinct regional groups. The effort towards establishing anthropometric standards culminated in the 'Frankfort agreement' of 1882 in which – amongst others – the 'Frankfort plane' was defined.

Another important topic of early physical anthropology in Germany was the reception of Darwin's theory of evolution. Among the members of the DGA, opinions were strongly divided. One of the most famous opponents of Darwin's theory was the pathologist Rudolf Virchow, whereas other scientists such as Ernst Haeckel, Alexander Ecker and Herrmann Schaaffhausen supported Darwin's concept. Kindled by the 1856 discovery of the Neanderthal type specimen, much of the debate centred on the existence of 'diluvial man'. By the end of the 19th century, Darwin's theory had gained wide acceptance among German physical anthropologists.

The foundation of the journal *Zeitschrift für Morphologie und Anthropologie* in 1899 by Gustav Schwalbe underscores an increasing role of German anthropological research on an international level. Another highlight was the publication of the influential textbook *Lehrbuch der Anthropologie* by Rudolf Martin in 1914 that summarizes morphometric and osteometric standards for anthropological research. Martin's collection of standards was, and still is, widely used, the volume being updated several times – by Martin himself (1927), by Karl Saller in the third edition (1957), and completely revised and expanded by Rainer Knußmann in 1988. In 1924, another professional journal, the *Anthropologischer Anzeiger*, was founded by Rudolf Martin. This journal is still being published, is currently undergoing a process of re-organization, and will in future be published under the new name *Journal of Biological and Clinical Anthropology*.

The huge interest in Germany's prehistory in the late 19th and the early 20th centuries led to increasing scientific activity in the fields of physical anthropology and archaeology. The findings of the famous fossils from the Feldhofer Grotto in the Neanderthal in 1856 and the Mauer mandible in 1907, in particular, gave important impulses for palaeoanthropological research. These increased research activities culminated in publications such as 'Die Urgeschichte des Menschen' (1892) by Moritz Hoernes and 'Die Deutsche Vorgeschichte' by Gustav Kosinna (1912).

German physical anthropologists in the first half of the 20th century

Typological classification of skulls was used by physical anthropologists as a tool to define and separate human 'races'. This approach culminated in the distinction of small groups such as the 'Reihengräbertypus' described in detail by Alexander Ecker (1865) and the '*Homo alpineus*' (including the subspecies '*H.a.tirolensis*' according to Frizzi 1907). The latter 'taxon' was described first by Karl von Linné and later in the late 19th century 're-discovered' by Lapouge, Retzius and von Baer (Schmutz 2006, 189). Arranging human 'races' in a hierarchic order, and the concept of eugenics ('*Rassenhygiene*'), both date back long before the Nazi period. At German universities these topics were lectured during the beginning of the 20th century, as is documented, for example, for the University of Jena (Zimmermann 2006). The aforementioned work of Kosinna was often regarded as a precursor of Nazi ideology. Like the works of Eugen Fischer – for example the 'Rehobother Bastards' publication of 1913 – and other physical anthropologists of the time, Kosinna's ideas are closely linked to '*Rassen-hygiene*' and the concept that more or less valuable human individuals exist. This concept, which was extended from individuals to 'races', was later used by the Nazis to legitimize their practice of euthanasia of handicapped people and the genocide of the European Jews and Roma.

An increasing importance of physical anthropology as a scientific discipline is indicated by the foundation of the Kaiser Wilhelm Institut für Anthropologie, menschliche Erblehre und Eugenik in Berlin in 1926. The first director of this institute was Eugen Fischer, who played a leading role among the scientists supporting the racial laws and delivering alleged 'scientific' arguments for the national socialist racial policy. Eugen Fischer also headed the Deutsche Gesellschaft für physische Anthropologie (DGPA) that was founded in Freiburg in 1925. The society was renamed the Deutsche Gesellschaft für Rassenforschung (German society for racial research) in 1937. During this period, university departments of physical anthropology existed in Berlin, Breslau, Frankfurt, Göttingen, Hamburg, Heidelberg, Kiel, Köln, Leipzig, München and Tübingen. Although research was dominated by racial and taxonomic issues, there were also major advances in palaeoanthropology in the 1920s and early 1930s. The publication of the late Middle Pleistocene Ehringsdorf skull by Franz Weidenreich in 1928 and his studies on *Homo erectus* in Zhoukoudian in 1935–40 were of major importance. Weidenreich was removed from his chair at the Anthropological Institute in Frankfurt and had to leave Germany in 1935 as a victim of the *Rassengesetze* (racial laws). Among others, the publication of Hans Weinert and Fritz Berkhemer on the Steinheim skull, and the works of Gustaf Heinrich Ralph von Koenigswald on Ngangdong and Sangiran, were of great importance within this period. After 1933, the dominance of racial issues within research in physical anthropology in Germany increased dramatically. The Kaiser Wilhelm Institute played a major role in research and the administration of the racial and eugenic policy of the Third Reich. For some anthropologists, the fixation of the Nazi government on racial issues provided the basis for a scientific career (Preuß 2006, 103). Only few anthropologists refused to follow the Nazi ideology, the most prominent being Karl Saller, who was forced to leave his Chair at the University of Munich in 1935. Eugen Fischer took on responsibility for eugenic reports used to 'justify' the sterilization of mentally ill or retarded persons. The involvement of physical anthropologists in the genocide of the European Jews and members of other ethnic groups, as well as the killing of mentally ill or retarded persons, was not discussed in detail after the end of the Second World War. The prevalent view was that no physical anthropologist had directly contributed to the crimes against humanity by the Nazi regime, but that several researchers had contributed indirectly through their work. This opinion was justified by the fact that no scientist was accused or sentenced by law in the post-war period. As a consequence of this there was a far-reaching personal continuity of physical anthropologist in university institutions (Kröner 1998, Hoßfeld 2005, Preuß 2006), a fact that was heavily criticised in more recent years.

After the Second World War

The post-war period was dominated by the re-orientation of physical anthropologists in the two separate German states. Physical anthropology in the German Democratic Republic (GDR) started with the Arbeitsgruppe Anthropologie der biologischen Gesellschaft der DDR, founded in 1959. In 1961, the Journal *Mitteilungen der Sektion Anthropologie der biologischen Gesellschaft der DDR* was founded. Major centres of research in Eastern Germany were Jena and Berlin. Abroad, cooperation was focused on other socialist countries, and contacts with colleagues from Western countries were reduced to a minimum, leading to an uncoupling from international developments.

In West Germany, several institutes were closed, the most prominent being the Kaiser Wilhelm Institute in Berlin. Anthropological departments remained at the Universities in Frankfurt, Freiburg, Hamburg, Kiel, Munich and Tübingen; however, the number of staff positions at these institutions was reduced. In the 1960s and early 1970s, the institutes at Göttingen, Giessen, Braunschweig, Ulm and Bremen were founded. The professional society for anthropologists was re-founded in 1948 under the name Deutsche Gesellschaft für Anthropologie (DGA). At the same time, the new journal *Homo* was founded and the *Zeitschrift für Morphologie und Anthropologie* was restarted as well. The *Anthropologischer Anzeiger* resumed its appearance in 1956. In the 1960s, the DGA and the Deutsche Gesellschaft für Konstitutionsforschung united and constituted the Gesellschaft für Anthropologie und Humangenetik (GAH). The growing field of human genetics was welcomed as a promising new discipline, helping to overcome the largely morphology-based typological thinking that had prevailed for so long in physical anthropology. Population genetics revealed the variability of human populations, leading to an expansion of population thinking into the anthropological field. However, the close connection between physical anthropology and human genetics got more and more lost with the expansion of the latter as a scientific subject of its own. This left physical anthropology with the task of defining its field of study and overcoming the historical burden of the Nazi period. An important step in the separation process was the recommendation of the German Council of Science and Humanities for the development of universities in 1960. Human genetics was regarded as being a field of science with future potential and thus worth supporting, whereas physical anthropology came off much less well. The trend for human genetics to separate from physical anthropology resulted in the foundation of the Deutsche Gesellschaft für Humangenetik (GfH) in 1987.

Physical anthropology was reorganized after the German reunification by fusion of the two anthropological societies in 1992 into the Gesellschaft für Anthropologie (GfA). Another society, the Gesellschaft für Archäozoologie und Prähistorische Anthropologie (GAPA), which covers archaeological, archaeozoological as well as anthropological topics, was founded in 1994. The GAPA publishes proceedings of their meetings held every two years as *Beiträge zur Archäozoologie und Prähistorischen Anthropologie*.

Archaeology is one of the classic neighbour disciplines of physical anthropology in Germany. Recently, cooperation between the two disciplines has been increasing due to the growing importance of natural sciences in archaeology and the more comprehensive interpretation of findings in a bioarchaeological context. However, a close institutional connection between the two disciplines never existed in Germany (Eggert 1995: 33; Orschiedt 1998).

Commonly, there is no institutional implementation of a physical anthropologist (or osteoarchaeologist) within the State Offices except in the federal state of Baden-Württemberg. At German universities, the two disciplines are typically strictly divided and often belong to different faculties. A new development that may help to overcome this institutional separation is the formation of interdisciplinary research groups, as for instance at the University of Tübingen or in the case of the State Collection of Anthropology and Palaeoanatomy of Bavaria, which is under custody of the Anthropological Chair of the University of Munich.

Physical anthropology in Germany today

The interdisciplinary approach that connects physical anthropology with other fields of research provides a comprehensive picture of human evolutionary history and the reconstruction of living conditions of past human populations, as well as interactions of past and present human populations with their environment. This is at the same time a great chance and a challenge for physical anthropology, as there is a need to define core competencies for physical anthropology in an interdisciplinary setting. This core is the human individual and the human population, as they are affecting and being affected by their respective environments.

Since the 1980s, the number of anthropological institutes in Germany is declining, and several universities decided to cancel their physical anthropological curricula. The institutes in Berlin, Frankfurt (Main), Giessen, Braunschweig, Bremen and Kiel were closed, while other chairs were integrated into larger departments of zoology or pre-clinical medicine.

Academic institutions and research institutes

Currently, active research and/or teaching in physical anthropology takes place at the universities of Freiburg, Göttingen, Hamburg, Hildesheim, Jena, Mainz, Munich, Potsdam and Tübingen. However, the future of some of the mentioned institutions is bleak. During the last years, non-university institutions dealing with anthropological questions were founded or expanded. Here, the Max Planck Institute for Evolutionary Anthropology in Leipzig (EVA), the Senckenberg Museum in Frankfurt (Main), and the Neanderthal Museum in Mettmann deserve special mentioning. Additionally there are anthropologists working in small units outside of universities and scholars of neighbouring fields dealing with anthropological questions.

ARCHAEOLOGICAL HUMAN REMAINS AND LEGISLATION

Archaeological legislation

The responsibility for the archaeological heritage, including human remains, lies with the particular State Offices for Historical Monuments. There are no detailed regulations for the treatment of human remains during the post-excavation phase. Usually the remains are stored as archaeological finds and are treated in the same manner as other archaeological finds. They are protected by the Denkmalschutzgesetz which covers all archaeological finds embedded in the soil, the so called Bodenfunde. Reburial is not usual except in some cases of excavations within churches or their graveyards or more recent finds up to the 20th century, but this is not consistently done. In cases of more recent finds of human remains which cannot easily be attributed to historical periods, a forensic investigation of the post-mortem interval (Liegezeit) is carried out to exclude the possibility of a crime. Usually after an exposure time of more than 30–50 years, no investigations will be started, the case will be closed, and the remains are handed over to the State Offices for Historical Monuments who will decide on storage, possible analysis or reburial.

HUMAN REMAINS AND LEGISLATION

So far, no laws exist in Germany which regulate that human remains from archaeological excavations have to be investigated. Thus, generally and with only a few exceptions, only a low budget or no budget at all for the investigation of the remains is available in Offices for Historical Monuments, except in the case of special projects supported by grants from the Deutsche Forschungsgemeinschaft (DFG) or other funding institution.

METHODS OF ANTHROPOLOGICAL ANALYSIS

Recent textbooks are helpful in defining the topics and methods of current physical anthropology as a whole (Grupe *et al.* 2004) or of some its sub-disciplines such as palaeoanthropology (Henke and Rothe 2000; Henke and Tattersall 2007) and prehistoric anthropology (Herrmann *et al.* 1990). A large and widely recognized collection of standards for the investigation of living humans and of skeletal human remains was the already mentioned handbook edited by Knußmann (1988). Currently, a commonly used guide of methods and protocols for the investigation of human skeletal remains does not exist. However, in the course of an increasing globalization in scientific communities, many German physical anthropologists apply techniques and procedures according to international standards.

CONCLUSION

Currently, physical anthropology in Germany, as elsewhere in the world, is characterized by a wide methodological spectrum, including molecular genetics, analysis of stable isotopes, and various morphological approaches including the use of modern imaging systems. However, related ethical questions are also discussed, such as for example the use of historical skeletal collections and their sometimes problematic mode of acquisition and unclear provenance.

Compared with the role of physical anthropology in the English-speaking world, and in the United States in particular, physical anthropology in Germany is presently of only minor importance regarding both its representation as a separate discipline at Germany's universities and its role in scientific debate. Large fields like forensic anthropology that are prominent in the USA are not fully established in Germany. In the future, the closing of institutes and the decline in the teaching of physical anthropology and its methods will probably have a serious impact on neighbour disciplines such as archaeology. However, great efforts are made by the GfA to strengthen the profile of anthropology in Germany, and the position of this discipline at German universities. An important aspect for future endeavours to strengthen physical anthropology in Germany might be the enormous public interest in anthropological issues.

USEFUL CONTACTS

Gesellschaft für Anthropologie (GFA). Website: www.gfanet.de/ (with various links to anthropological institutions in German speaking countries)
Gesellschaft für Archäozoologie und Prähistorische Anthropologie e.V. (GAPA). Website: www.gapa-kn.de/

Berliner Gesellschaft für Anthropologie, Ethnologie und Urgeschichte (BGAEU). Website: www.bgaeu.de/

ACKNOWLEDGEMENTS

The authors are grateful to Prof. Dr. Uwe Kierdorf for his useful comments on the manuscript.

BIBLIOGRAPHY

Ecker, A. (1865) *Crania Germaniae Meridionalis Occidentalis*, Freiburg i.Br: Wagner'sche Buchhandlung.

Eggert, M.K.H. (1995) 'Anthropologie, Ethnologie und Urgeschichte. Zur Relativierung eines forschungsgeschichtlichen Mythologems', *Mitteilungen der Berliner Gesellschaft für Anthropologie, Ethnologie und Urgeschichte*, 16: 33–38.

Fischer, E. (1913) *Die Rehobother Bastards und das Bastardierungsproblem beim Menschen*, Jena: Gustav Fischer.

Frizzi, E. (1907) 'Über den sogenannten "*Homo alpinus*"', *Korrespondenzblatt der Deutschen Anthropologischen Gesellschaft*, 38: 1–4.

Grupe, G., Christiansen, K., Schröder, I., *et al.* (2004) *Anthropologie. Ein einführendes Lehrbuch*, Berlin: Springer.

Henke, W. and Rothe, H. (2000) *Stammesgeschichte des Menschen. Eine Einführung*, Berlin: Springer.

Henke, W. and Tattersall, I. (eds) (2007) *Handbook of Paleoanthropology*, Berlin, Heidelberg; New York: Springer.

Herrmann, B., Grupe, G., Hummel, S., *et al.* (1990) *Prähistorische Anthropologie. Ein Leitfaden der Feld-und Labormethoden*, Berlin: Springer.

Hoernes, M. (1892) *Die Urgeschichte des Menschen*, Wien: Hartlebens Verlag.

Hoßfeld, U. (2005) *Geschichte der biologischen Anthropologie in Deutschland*, Stuttgart: Franz Steiner.

Knußmann, R. (ed.) 1988. *Anthropologie. Handbuch der vergleichenden Biologie des Menschen*, Stuttgart, New York: Gustav Fischer.

Kosinna, G. (1912) *Die deutsche Vorgeschichte, eine hervorragend nationale Wissenschaft*, Leipzig: Curt Kabitzsch Verlag.

Kröner, H.-P. (1998) *Von der Rassenhygiene zur Humangenetik. Das Kaiser-Wilhelm-Institut für Anthropologie, menschliche Erblehre und Eugenik nach dem Kriege*, Stuttgart, Jena, Lübeck, Ulm: Gustav Fischer.

Martin, R. (1914) *Lehrbuch der Anthropologie*, Jena: Gustav Fischer.

——(1927) *Lehrbuch der Anthropologie*, 2nd edn, Jena: Gustav Fischer.

Martin, R. and Saller, K. (1957) *Lehrbuch der Anthropologie*, 3rd edn, Stuttgart: Gustav Fischer.

Orschiedt, J. (1998) 'Anthropologie und Archäologie. Interdisziplinarität – Utopie oder Wirklichkeit?', *Archäologische Informationen*, 21: 33–39.

Preuß, D. (2006) '"Zeitwende ist Wissenschaftswende"? Egon Freiherr von Eickstedt und die Neuanfänge der "Breslauer Tradition" in Leipzig und Mainz 1945–50', in D. Preuß, U. Hoßfeld and O. Breidbach (eds) *Anthropologie nach Haeckel*, Stuttgart: Franz Steiner Verlag.

Schmutz, H.-K. (2006) 'Vermessene Nation. Eine Skizze der imagologischen Anthropologie nach 1860', in D. Preuß, U. Hoßfeld and O. Breidbach (eds) *Anthropologie nach Haeckel*, Stuttgart: Franz Steiner Verlag.

Schwidetzky, I. (1982) 'Die institutionelle Entwicklung der Anthropologie', in I. Spiegel-Rösing and I. Schwidetzky (eds) *Maus und Schlange. Untersuchungen zur Lage der deutschen Anthropologie*, München, Wien: R. Oldenbourg.

——(1988) 'Geschichte der Anthropologie', in R. Knußmann (ed.) *Vergleichende Biologie des Menschen. Lehrbuch der Anthropologie und Humangenetik I/1*, Stuttgart: Gustav Fischer.

——(1992) *History of Biological Anthropology in Germany*. International Association of Human Biologists: Occasional papers. Vol. 3/4, Newcastle upon Tyne: IAHB.

Spencer, F. (ed.) (1997) *History of Physical Anthropology Vol. 1*, New York, London: Garland.

Spiegel-Rösing, I., Schwidetzky, I. (eds) (1982) *Maus und Schlange – Untersuchungen zur Lage der deutschen Anthropologie*, München, Wien: R. Oldenbourg.

Zimmermann, S. (2006) 'Rassenhygiene in Forschung und Lehre an der medizinischen Fakultät Jena vor 1933', in D. Preuß, U. Hoßfeld and O. Breidbach (eds) *Anthropologie nach Haeckel*, Stuttgart: Franz Steiner Verlag.

Greece/ΕΛΛΑΔΑ

Constantine Eliopoulos, Konstantinos Moraitis, Velissaria Vanna and Sotiris Manolis

INTRODUCTION: A BRIEF HISTORY AND CURRENT STATE OF PHYSICAL ANTHROPOLOGY IN GREECE

As early as the sixth century BC, human physiology and medicine were fields that had drawn the interest of philosophers and practitioners such as Democedes, Alkmaeon and Hippocrates. During the Roman era Galen of Pergamum was the scientist whose work influenced anatomy for a number of centuries to come. What sets Galen apart from others were his dissections on monkeys, a practice that gave him the power to correct and redefine many aspects of anatomy, neurology, osteology and pathology (Nutton 1973).

In Modern Greece, the father of physical anthropology is considered to be Klon Stephanos (1854–1915), a medical doctor educated in France. His work, and his friendship with Paul Broca, the famous French surgeon and physical anthropologist, had been very important in his research interests. After coming to Greece in 1885 to study archaeological skeletons from Arcadia, he established the Anthropological Museum at the University of Athens a year later. Along with his contemporaries Michael Apostolides and Georgios Neophytos, also physicians by training, he was engaged in analysing skeletons recovered from archaeological excavations (Agelarakis 1995). After the death of Stephanos in 1915, Ioannis Koumaris became the director of the Anthropological Museum and the first professor of physical anthropology in Greece, at the University of Athens. As a medical doctor, Koumaris had been trained for a short period in Berlin. In the 1960s he invited back to Greece Aris Poulianos, who conducted palaeontological studies at the Petralona cave in northern Greece (Agelarakis 1997; Poulianos 1983). Poulianos was an anthropologist educated in the USA and the Soviet Union, and served on the Directing Committee of the newly founded University of Patra. After the fall of the dictatorship in Greece (1967–74), Poulianos was able to establish the Ephorate of Palaeoanthropology and Speleology under the auspices of the Ministry of Culture (Poulianou 2006). Until that time, anthropology in Greece had focused on providing evidence of the biological continuity between the ancient Greeks and the modern inhabitants of the country (Roberts *et al.* 2005).

Among the international scholars, J.L. Angel, an academic with an interest in the history of the eastern Mediterranean, undertook a number of studies in the middle of the 20th century on Greek skeletal collections. His interest initially was on population movement, but this was later replaced by work on palaeopathology (Angel 1944, 1946, 1964, 1967). Another very important work on palaeopathology is that of Grmek (1983), who combined information from written sources with skeletal data in an attempt to reconstruct the health profile of the ancient Greeks.

In the past 40 years, other anthropologists have emerged in Greek academia, some educated locally and some who have been trained abroad, mainly in Germany and North America. The vast majority of these scholars have a background in either medicine or biology. They include Konstantinos Zafeiratos, Theodoros Pitsios, Nikolaos Xirotiris, Paris Pavlakis, Antonios Bartsiokas and Sotiris Manolis. Currently, there are many students who are conducting doctoral studies in anthropology in Greece, in addition to those who are educated in other countries. It is also noteworthy to mention that there are anthropologists of Greek descent who live and work abroad. Among them are two of the better known physical anthropologists in the USA: Anagnosti Agelarakis and George Armelagos.

Largely due to the fact that a number of scholars have been trained abroad, thus creating a link for collaborations between institutions from Greece and other countries (see, e.g., Lagia 1993; Triantaphyllou 1998, 2000; Tsaliki 2003, 2004; Vanna 2005, 2007), research in physical anthropology in Greece has grown significantly in recent years. Another important factor is the increasing awareness among archaeologists in the country of the value of information that can be obtained through anthropology. In addition, foreign archaeological schools have been established in Greece and, along with universities from a number of different countries, they conduct excavations every year at sites throughout the country.

Greek institutions are also actively involved in the Global History of Health Project, led by Ohio State University in the USA. This project is aimed at documenting and interpreting the history of human health in Europe from the late Palaeolithic period to the 20th century (Steckel *et al.* 2009). Another contribution of Greek physical anthropology is the hosting of the 16th Paleopathology Association Meeting which took place in 2006 in Santorini, Greece.

Today, some of the most important research units in Greece include:

- *Laboratory of Anthropology, Department of History and Ethnology, Democritus University of Thrace*
  The Laboratory of Anthropology of the Department of History and Ethnology was established in 1993 and its facilities are located on the campus in the city of Komotini. Its present director is Professor Dr N. Xirotiris, a medical doctor. The laboratory is mainly oriented to physical anthropology in areas such as human evolution, dermatoglyphics, biochemical genetic markers and anthropometric traits (Xirotiris 1980; Chlorokosta *et al.* 2006). However, the laboratory has close ties with socio-cultural anthropology, human ecology and demography, in an effort to follow the North American model of a holistic approach. Indicative of the scope of the laboratory is the fact that it includes research groups in biochemistry, osteology, dermatoglyphics, demography and genealogy.
- *The Anthropological Museum of the National and Kapodistrian University of Athens*
  One of the basic aims of the Anthropology Museum has been to advance the discipline by producing scientific knowledge. This knowledge is the result of research undertaken mainly on skeletal material excavated from various archaeological sites throughout Greece. Another important goal of the museum is the dissemination of scientific results to a diverse audience that includes both academics and the general public. In line with these aims, the museum has participated in a number of archaeological excavations and studies of palaeoanthropological finds that include those of Western Mani, Athens and Rhodes (Pitsios 1994).
- *Department of Animal and Human Physiology, Faculty of Biology, National and Kapodistrian University of Athens*
  The department is actively engaged in bioarchaeological research on several skeletal collections housed at its facilities. Much of the effort of the Biological Anthropology Research

Unit (BARU) is focused on the biocultural adaptation of populations from the geographical area of Greece in the last 10,000 years (Manolis and Neroutsos 1997). History of health and disease, morphological variation, interactions between human biology and culture are all issues that BARU investigates (Lagia *et al.* 2007). In addition to the skeletons of archaeological origin, the department also houses a modern skeletal collection known as the Athens Collection (Eliopoulos *et al.* 2007; see below). One of the first attempts to bridge the gap between physical anthropology and archaeology in Greece was a seminar entitled 'Anthropology for Archaeologists' that was held at the department in 2001. It is hoped that similar seminars will take place in the future, so that the two disciplines can come closer together, as both will benefit from such efforts. In addition, the department conducts studies on the variability of modern Greeks by collecting and analysing data from university students and schoolchildren. These data include dermatoglyphics, stature and other body proportions and are useful for research on trends in growth and comparisons with other populations (Manolis and Neroutsos 1995).

- *Forensic Anthropology Unit, Department of Forensic Medicine and Toxicology, National and Kapodistrian University of Athens (UoAFAU)*
  The Forensic Anthropology Unit is currently involved in research projects involving forensic anthropology, human taphonomy and identification. These include the forensic evaluation of skeletal trauma with regard to the timing of injuries and marine taphonomy (Moraitis 2003, 2006; Moraitis and Spiliopoulou 2006). The staff at the unit also supervises undergraduate and postgraduate research projects in a wide range of topics related to forensic anthropology.

- *Ephorate of Palaeoanthropology and Speleology*
  The objective of this institution of the Greek Ministry of Culture is the investigation of caves dating back to the Palaeolithic. In addition, it has undertaken many studies of open-air sites in association with local archaeological services, foreign schools and universities. Some of the Ephorate's most important sites include the caves of Theopetra, Franchthi and Alepotrypa (Papathanasiou 2000; Stravopodi *et al.* 1999). Interdisciplinary research is emphasized in this institution, where scientists of different backgrounds integrate excavation data to produce studies that are aimed at promoting archaeological science in Greece.

- *Wiener Laboratory, American School of Classical Studies at Athens*
  Since its foundation in 1992, the Wiener Laboratory has carried out numerous successful projects in areas such as physical anthropology, zooarchaeology, geoarchaeology and environmental studies. Through annual fellowships and scholarships, a number of Greek and foreign researchers of different specialties are attracted to the laboratory. During the academic year knowledge is disseminated through workshops, seminars and lectures. In addition, publications such as the 'Occasional Wiener Laboratory Series' (OWLS) promote archaeological and anthropological research in Greece (Fox 2005; Schepartz *et al.* 2009). The laboratory also serves as an important resource for the Greek archaeological authorities.

Skeletal collections

In addition to the skeletons of archaeological origin, the Department of Animal and Human Physiology, Faculty of Biology, National and Kapodistrian University of Athens houses a modern skeletal collection known as the Athens Collection. This collection consists of 225 well–documented skeletons of individuals who lived during the 20th century and who died between 1960 and 1996 (Eliopoulos *et al.* 2007). Information, such as sex, age, occupation and cause of death, is derived from death certificates. The collection has been used for several research projects, seminars and workshops.

Physical anthropology associations

The Hellenic Anthropological Association (HAA) was founded in Athens in 1924 by Ioannis Koumaris, then director of the Anthropological Museum of the University of Athens. Its establishment was a catalyst for the development of the discipline in Greece. Through the regular publication of the proceedings of the HAA, physical anthropology was promoted and recognized by members of the Greek academic community. With the death of Dr Koumaris in 1970, the activities of the HAA were halted for a number of years, but recently the association has been reactivated and is again in the forefront of anthropological research (Agelarakis 1997). It has organized two international anthropological conferences (2003 and 2006) and a third conference was held in 2009 for the celebration of the 200 years since the birth of Charles Darwin.

The Anthropological Association of Greece (AAG) was established in 1971 by Aris Poulianos. Its basic aims are the recognition of anthropology and the protection of the Greek cultural heritage. In order to achieve these goals, it is open to other disciplines related to anthropology such as ethnology, linguistics, archaeology, palaeontology and geology. Much of the research effort of the AAG has been focused on the Petralona cave in northern Greece, where the remains of an archaic *Homo sapiens* have been discovered. The association has been actively participating in international conferences and it is a member of the European Anthropological Association (Poulianou 2006).

Museums of physical anthropology

Klon Stephanos founded the Anthropological Museum in Athens in 1886, as part of the Medical School of the University. As a director until his death in 1915, he put together the first skeletal collections of the museum, derived from archaeological excavations. In addition, Stephanos was the first to conduct systematic anthropological studies on the inhabitants of modern Greece (Pitsios 1994). The current director of the museum, Theodoros Pitsios, is engaged in research of prehistoric sites, mainly in the Peloponnese. One of the most important projects of the museum is the palaeoanthropological research at Areopolis, Laconia, which started in 1980 and has brought to light an important and novel space of human habitation for Greece, dating back to the Early and Middle Pleistocene (Pitsios and Liebhaber 1995).

In 1981 the Anthropological Museum of Petralona opened its doors to the public for the first time. Exhibits include mainly prehistoric finds from the Petralona cave such as human remains, stone and bone tools, dating back to 700,000 BC. The museum has a conference room, geological and palaeoanthropological conservation workshops, as well as a library, and it can accommodate up to 30 researchers at the same time (Poulianos 1995).

Education and training

There is no Department of Physical Anthropology at any of the universities in Greece today. The most relevant scientific entity is the Department of History and Ethnology at the Democritus University of Thrace, where there is an anthropological laboratory. Some of the courses taught there include the evolution of the species, ethology and evolution of primates, demography and palaeoanthropology.

Physical anthropology is also taught as an individual course in three biology departments at the Universities of Athens, Thessaloniki and Patra. Individual courses in physical anthropology are also offered at the School of Medicine and Faculty of Geology and Geoenvironment of the University of Athens. Another relevant course is taught at the Department of Mediterranean Studies, University of the Aegean, where archaeometry of skeletal materials is the focus.

The UoAFAU Medical School offers seminars on forensic anthropology for final-year medical students and hands-on training for residents in forensic medicine. The unit has plans to integrate a forensic anthropology course in the syllabus for the 2010–11 academic year.

ARCHAEOLOGICAL HUMAN REMAINS AND LEGISLATION

Archaeological legislation

The Hellenic Ministry of Culture (www.culture.gr/war/index_en.jsp) is the main governmental body responsible for issuing and administering policies on cultural heritage in Greece. The Central Service of the Ministry controls work of the regional services, known as 'Ephorates', and secures their funding. The Ephorates approve and control building activities and public construction projects carried out in archaeological areas. Their role encompasses the identification, study, excavation and protection of monuments, in addition to educational programmes and related events for the promotion of cultural values to the public. Finally, they are responsible for archaeological museums belonging to the state (Government Gazette 146/A/2003, 2243; Council of Europe 2009).

Systematic excavations can be conducted by: the Ephorates of Antiquities (Εφορείες Αρχαιοτήτων); (b) Greek scientific, research or educational organizations and institutions, specializing in the field of archaeological or palaeontological research; and (c) foreign archaeological missions or schools established in Greece. The latter are allowed to manage a maximum, per year, of three systematic excavations or other archaeological research, and another three in cooperation with the competent authorities of the Ministry of Culture (Government Gazette 153/A/2002, 3017). Rescue excavations can only be carried out by the Ministry of Culture; the director is appointed by the Ministry and has to have at least three years of experience in archaeological excavations (Government Gazette 153/A/2002, 3018).

Excavation permits

The permit is granted by the Minister of Culture upon recommendation of the Central Archaeological Council (Κεντρικό Αρχαιολογικό Συμβούλιο). The interested institution has to submit documentation proving: (a) that there is strong evidence suggesting the existence of an archaeological site; (b) the professionalism and reliability of the organization or institution that will undertake the excavation; (c) the experience and the scientific authority of the director; (d) the interdisciplinarity of the scientific team; (e) the experience of the team members in the conservation, protection and publication of the finds; (f) the sufficiency of the technical infrastructure; and (g) the adequacy of the budget for the excavation, conservation and publication of the finds. In addition, the importance of the excavation and the expected contribution to scientific knowledge should be demonstrated (Government Gazette 153/A/2002, 3017).

The director of the excavation should have a minimum of five years of experience in excavations and at least two scientific publications on excavation or on finds from an excavation.

The duration of each excavation is specified in the permit but cannot in any case exceed five years. For its extension a new decision is required which again cannot exceed the five-year limit (Government Gazette 153/A/2002, 3018). The directors of systematic excavations have exclusive rights to publish the results of their research, as long as they abide by the time limits specified by the law (Government Gazette 153/A/2002, 3019).

The director of an excavation or other archaeological research should submit the following to the Ministry of Culture: (a) an initial presentation for publication, which must include a list of the finds recovered and drawings of the immovable monuments revealed, within two years from the commencement of the excavation; (b) reports on the progress of the excavation every two years; and (c) a final publication within five years from the completion of the excavation. For rescue excavations: (a) a final report, list of finds, photographs and drawings should be submitted within nine months; and (b) a final publication within six years from completion (Government Gazette 153/A/2002, 3019).

HUMAN REMAINS AND LEGISLATION

In Greece, human remains that are recovered during construction activities or from sites that are not currently undergoing an archaeological excavation are reported to the police. In this case, the discovery of human remains is first treated as a crime scene in order to rule out any recent criminal activity. According to the Code of Penal Procedure a forensic investigation is carried out only after the issue of a written order by a judicial authority (Michalodimitrakis and Tsatsakis 1997). Once police authorities have been informed, a forensic pathologist, who is responsible for investigating and certifying the cause of death, and in some cases a forensic anthropologist, will attend the scene to confirm that the remains are human and to determine whether they are recent or archaeological. If the forensic pathologist and anthropologist determine that the remains are of forensic importance, they will immediately proceed with the investigation involving their recovery. Subsequent to the recovery, the remains are submitted to a mortuary facility for a post-mortem examination. The UoAFAU is the only academic institution in Greece that offers specialized services in the field of forensic anthropology (Moraitis *et al.* 2000). Since 1999, the UoAFAU investigates cases that involve the identification of decomposing, skeletonized, fragmentary or burned human remains. The techniques used in the Forensic Anthropology Unit are aimed primarily at establishing the identity of an individual, initially by determining sex, age, ancestry and stature, and then by determining skeletal features that may be unique. In addition, forensic anthropologists of the unit might be called upon to advise the forensic pathologist on the evaluation of skeletal trauma, and to offer an opinion on the post-mortem interval and possibly the cause and manner of death.

In those cases where the forensic scientists determine that the reported remains are not of forensic concern, the regional Ephorate of Antiquities is notified. However, although certain chemical dating methods have been applied in the past (Vass *et al.* 1992; Castellano *et al.* 1984), the distinction between forensic and archaeological bone is still problematic. In Greece, this distinction is heavily based upon experience of the forensic anthropologist in evaluating the state of preservation of the recovered bones and the contextual information. In the final conclusion regarding the time since death, Article 111 of the Greek Penal Code, which states that 'the statute of limitations of capital offences or life felonies is 20 years', is also considered. In case of archaeological bones, their approximate dating is based upon the judgement of the archaeologist who is called on site. Unfortunately, in Greek Law 3028/2002 on the 'Protection of Antiquities and Cultural Heritage in General' (Government Gazette 153/A/2002) there is no provision for the protection of material remains, including human remains, from before the establishment of the independent Greek state (1830). Thus, legislation on this topic needs to be modified since human remains are a very commonly encountered type of archaeological material in Greece.

Human remains from archaeological contexts

As far as the legislation regarding human remains from archaeological contexts is concerned, there is an enormous void in the regulations currently in force. In fact, there is no legal framework specific to human remains or any special reference in the relevant Law 3028/2002 on the 'Protection of Antiquities and Cultural Heritage in General', which covers all the monuments that are part of the country's cultural heritage (Government Gazette 153/A/2002). The law, which was enacted in 2002 and applies to all parts of the country, was voted by the Greek Parliament, and the agency responsible for enforcing it is the Ministry of Culture (Government Gazette 153/A/2002, 3003).

Ancient monuments or antiquities, subject to Law 3028/2002, are defined as all cultural objects, either immovable or movable, that date to the prehistoric, ancient, Byzantine and post-Byzantine times up to 1830; as well as caves and palaeontological remains, for which there is evidence that they are associated with human presence (Government Gazette 153/A/2002, 3003). Monuments that date to the years after 1830 are protected by law only if they are included 'on the statutory list of buildings of special interest drawn up by the Minister of Culture' (Council of Europe 2009). A property not listed can still be declared as a modern cultural heritage monument even if it dates to less than one hundred years, as long as there is adequate justification proving its cultural, architectural, social, historical or scientific significance (Government Gazette 153/A/2002, 3003–4; Council of Europe 2009). Although cultural objects are not specifically named in the law, the term is used to describe testimonies of the existence of human activity. Human remains coming from archaeological contexts are thus regarded as 'cultural objects' and, more specifically, as portable monuments. Immovable monuments, on the other hand, are specified in the Law 3028/2002 (Government Gazette 153/A/2002, 3003) and include cemeteries. The excavation, recovery, protection and study of human remains, therefore, fall under Law 3028/2002, and all issues related to their treatment are subject to the same legislative controls as any other ancient monument.

Church remains that belong to the country's heritage are treated as any other cultural object. More specifically, the Church, according to its Constitution Charter (Government Gazette 146/A/1977), collaborates with the State for the protection of all cultural objects, immovable or portable, that constitute its patrimony. Protection of this patrimony is subject to Law 3028/2002 and is implemented by the Services of the Hellenic Ministry of Culture (Council of Europe 2009). Human remains from palaeontological sites are the responsibility of the Ephorate of Palaeoanthropology – Speleology and are also subject to Law 3028/2002 (Government Gazette 146/A/2003, 2260).

In archaeological excavations, the director should facilitate access to the site for specialists (Government Gazette 153/A/2002, 3017), but there is no mention in the law about the compulsory presence of an anthropologist or bioarchaeologist during the excavation and recovery of human remains.

Study and export of archaeological material

The Ministry of Culture should facilitate access to archaeological finds, in order for specialists to study them and, subsequently, to publish the results of their research, provided that a permit is granted by the archaeologist who has the exclusive rights to publication. Scholars may be given access to the excavation material in cases where the time limits for publication mentioned above have been exceeded by the director of the excavation (Government Gazette 153/A/2002, 3019 and 3022).

Archaeological human remains (including bone, teeth, mummified tissue and cremated remains) are considered cultural objects, since according to the Greek Law 3028/2002 (Government Gazette 153/A/2002) any physical evidence of human life or activity is characterized as a cultural object. According to this law, the export of archaeological remains from Greece is prohibited unless a permit is obtained from the Directorate of Conservation of Ancient and Modern Monuments of the Ministry of Culture for temporary museum exhibition or scientific research. In such cases, the permit holder requesting an export of bone samples shall provide the following information in writing: (a) justification of the need for the export permit; (b) a detailed list and count of all samples to be exported; (c) a description of arrangements for shipping the archaeological bone samples; and (d) a detailed schedule for the return of the archaeological bone samples to the location where the collection of origin is curated. The law also states that permission for the export of human skeletal material may be given if the analyses to be conducted cannot take place in Greece due to lack of technological expertise or equipment.

METHODS OF ANTHROPOLOGICAL ANALYSIS

Physical anthropologists working in Greece employ internationally accepted standards of analysis. There are two different schools of thought regarding the selection of methods employed. The first is that of a European educational background which primarily use the standards proposed by the European Anthropological Association (Ferembach *et al.* 1980). The second follows the methods recommended by Buikstra and Ubelaker (1994). These latter standards are believed to include the methods that are most widely used in the world today. Some of the most popular textbooks on physical anthropology recommend these standards (see, e.g., Ubelaker 1989; Bass 1995; Mays 1998; Burns 1999). The popularity of these methods can also be inferred from the fact that, in studies where standards for age-at-death and sex determination are tested, researchers select these methods (Klepinger *et al.* 1992; Dudar *et al.* 1993; Rogers and Saunders 1994; Galera *et al.* 1998; Osborne *et al.* 2004). According to current trends that call for population-specific standards in physical anthropology, a recent study has examined the applicability of these methods on Greek skeletal populations (Eliopoulos 2006). The findings of this research indicate that, while some of the traits used for sex determination and age estimation may apply to Greek skeletons, others do not. There is therefore a need to develop methods that will accurately describe the skeletal expression of sex and age on skeletons from this part of the world. Some early local standards were those of Eliakis *et al.* (1966) who conducted research that produced stature formulae specifically for Greeks. However, this early attempt has not gained acceptance among anthropologists in Greece, who have been using Western standards (see, e.g., Trotter and Gleser 1952).

CONCLUSION

Physical anthropology in Greece has certainly made some steps forward in the past years; however, its status is far from being equivalent to those of other Western countries. The main reason for this is the lack of regular and close co-operation between archaeologists and anthropologists. The potential value of human remains is not fully appreciated by all members of the archaeological community in Greece. Activities such as anthropology seminars, lectures and workshops aimed specifically at raising awareness among Greek archaeologists may rectify this situation. Additionally, a change in archaeological laws to include provisions for the participation of anthropologists during excavations will lead to skeletal collections that are better recovered, documented and curated. This in turn will create the necessary conditions for interdisciplinary projects that will obtain the maximum amount of information from archaeological excavations. Only through such well-informed investigations is it possible to make interpretations that describe past societies in an accurate manner.

USEFUL CONTACTS

The Hellenic Anthropological Association (HAA). Website: http://anthrop.med.uoa.gr/index.htm/

The Anthropological Association of Greece (AAG). Website: www.aee.gr/

The Anthropological Museum of the National and Kapodistrian University of Athens. Website: http://anthropology-museum.med.uoa.gr/

Department of History and Ethnology at the Democritus University of Thrace. Website: www.he.duth.gr/

Wiener Laboratory, American School of Classical Studies at Athens. Website: www.ascsa.edu.gr/index.php/wiener-laboratory/

The Hellenic Ministry of Culture. Website: www.culture.gr/war/index_en.jsp/

ACKNOWLEDGEMENTS

The authors wish to thank archaeologists Ms Maria Konioti, Dr Eleni Psathi and Dr Anastasia Papathanasiou, for the very useful information they provided us regarding the current status of archaeological excavations in Greece.

BIBLIOGRAPHY

Agelarakis, A. (1995) 'An anthology of Hellenes involved with the field of physical anthropology', *International Journal of Anthropology*, 10: 149–62.

——(1997) 'Greece', in F. Spencer (ed.) *History of Physical Anthropology. An Encyclopedia, Vol. 1*, New York and London: Garland Publishing.

Angel, J.L. (1944) 'A racial analysis of the ancient Greeks: an essay on the use of morphological types', *American Journal of Physical Anthropology*, 2: 329–76.

——(1946) 'Race, type and ethnic group in ancient Greece', *Human Biology*, 18: 1–32.

——(1964) 'Osteoporosis: thalassemia?', *American Journal of Physical Anthropology*, 22: 369–74.

——(1967) 'Porotic hyperostosis, anemias, malarias and marshes in the prehistoric eastern Mediterranean', *Science*, 153: 760–63.

Bass, W.M. (1995) *Human Osteology: A Laboratory and Field Manual*, 4th edn, Columbia, MO: Missouri Archaeological Society.

Buikstra, J.E. and Ubelaker, D.H. (eds) (1994) *Standards for Data Collection from Human Skeletal Remains*, Fayettville, AR: Arkansas Archaeological Survey Research Series No. 44.

Burns, K.R. (1999) *Forensic Anthropology Training Manual*, New Jersey: Prentice Hall.

Castellano, M.A., Villanueva, E.C. and von Frenckel, R. (1984) 'Estimating the date of bone remains: a multivariate study', *Journal of Forensic Sciences*, 29: 527–34.

Chlorokosta, G., Hatzisavva, K. and Xirotiris, N.I. (2006) 'Metsovo: an anthropological approach', *International Journal of Anthropology*, 21: 61–78.

Council of Europe. (n.d.) European Heritage Network. Available online at www.european-heritage.net/sdx/herein/ (accessed 5 May 2009).

Dudar, J.C., Pfeiffer, S. and Saunders, S.R. (1993) 'Evaluation of morphological and histological adult skeletal age-at-death estimation techniques using ribs', *Journal of Forensic Sciences*, 38: 677–85.

Eliakis, C., Eliakis, C.E. and Iordanidis, P. (1966) 'Sur la détermination de la taille d'après la mensuration des os longs', *Annales de Médecine Légale*, 46: 403–21.

Eliopoulos, C. (2006) 'The creation of a documented human skeletal collection and the application of current aging and sexing standards on a Greek skeletal population', unpublished PhD thesis, University of Sheffield.

Eliopoulos, C., Lagia, A. and Manolis, S.K. (2007) 'A modern, documented human skeletal collection from Greece', *HOMO-Journal of Comparative Human Biology*, 58: 221–28.

Ferembach, D., Schwidetzky, I. and Stoukal, M. (1980) 'Recommendations for age and sex diagnoses of skeletons', *Journal of Human Evolution*, 9: 517–49.

Fox, S.C. (2005) 'Health in Hellenistic and Roman times. The case studies of Paphos, Cyprus and Corinth, Greece', in H. King (ed.) *Health in Antiquity*, New York: Routledge.

Galera, V., Ubelaker, D.H. and Hayek, L.C. (1998) 'Comparison of macroscopic cranial methods of age estimation applied to skeletons from the Terry collection', *Journal of Forensic Sciences*, 43: 933–39.

Greek Penal Code. (n.d.) *Article 111, Paragraph 2*.

Government Gazette of the Hellenic Republic (Εφημερίς της Κυβερνήσεως της Ελληνικής Δημοκρατίας). *A 153/2002*.

Grmek, M.D. (1983) *Diseases in the Ancient Greek World*, Baltimore: Johns Hopkins University Press.

Klepinger, L.L., Katz, D., Micozzi, M.S., *et al.* (1992) 'Evaluation of cast methods for estimating age from the os pubis', *Journal of Forensic Sciences*, 37: 763–70.

Lagia, A. (1993) 'Differential diagnosis of the three main types of anemia (Thalassemia, Sickle Cell Anemia, Iron Deficiency Anemia) from the skeleton based on macroscopic and radiographic skeletal characteristics', unpublished MSc thesis, University of Bradford.

Lagia, A., Eliopoulos, C. and Manolis, S.K. (2007) 'Thalassemia: macroscopic and radiological study of a case', *International Journal of Osteoarchaeology*, 17: 269–85.

Manolis, S.K. and Neroutsos, A. (1995) 'Secular changes in body formation of Greek students', *Human Evolution*, 10: 199–204.

——(1997) 'The Middle Bronze Age burial of Kolona at Aegina island, Greece: study of the human skeletal remains', in I. Kilian-Dirlmeier (ed.) *Das Mittelbronzezeitliche Schachtgrab von Agina*, Mainz am Rhein: Verlag Philipp Von Zabern.

Mays, S. (1998) *The Archaeology of Human Bones*, London: Routledge.

Michalodimitrakis, M. and Tsatsakis, A.M. (1997) 'The changing status of forensic medicine in Greece', *Journal of Clinical Forensic Medicine*, 4: 159–62.

Moraitis, K. (2003) 'The contribution of forensic anthropology in the development of diagnostic criteria for the determination of timing of skeletal injuries through the assessment of their particular morphological characteristics', unpublished PhD thesis, University of Athens. [in Greek]

——(2006) 'Taphonomic alterations on bones of forensic interest', in A. Kalofoutis, N. Papadopoulos, C. Spiliopoulou, *et al.* (eds) *Festschrift in Honour of Professor Antonis Koutselinis*, Athens: Parisianou Editions. [in Greek]

Moraitis, K. and Spiliopoulou, C. (2006) 'Identification and differential diagnosis of perimortem blunt force trauma in tubular long bones', *Forensic Science, Medicine, and Pathology*, 2: 221–29.

Moraitis, K., Spiliopoulou, C. and Koutselinis, A. (2000) 'Forensic anthropology: a new scientific branch in the service of justice', *Police Review* (2000): 756–59. [in Greek]

Nutton, V. (1973) 'The chronology of Galen's early career', *The Classical Quarterly. New Series*, 23: 158–71.

Osborne, D.L, Simmons, T.L. and Nawrocki, S.P. (2004) 'Reconsidering the auricular surface as an indicator of age at death', *Journal of Forensic Sciences*, 49: 1–7.

Papathanasiou, A. (2000) 'Bioarchaeological inferences from a Neolithic ossuary from Alepotrypa Cave, Diros, Greece', *International Journal of Osteoarchaeology*, 10: 210–28.

Pitsios, T. (1994) 'The museum of anthropology at the University of Athens: history and reconstruction of the museum', *Anthropologia*, 2: 5–17.

Pitsios, T. and Liebhaber, B. (1995) 'Research conducted at the site of Apidima and the surrounding region-Taenarios man', *Acta Anthropologica*, 1: 175–79.

Poulianos, A. (1983) 'Faunal and tool distribution in the layers of the Petralona Cave', *Journal of Human Evolution*, 12: 743–46.

Poulianos, N. (1995) 'La Grotta e l'Uomo di Petralona', unpublished PhD thesis, Anthropological Institute of Florence.

Poulianou, D. (2006) *Aris N. Poulianos: Changes in his Life and Work*, Athens: Anthropological Association of Greece. [in Greek]

Roberts, C.A., Bourbou, C., Lagia, A., *et al.* (2005) 'Health and disease in Greece', in H. King (ed.) *Health in Antiquity*, New York: Routledge.

Rogers, T. and Saunders, S. (1994) 'Accuracy of sex determination using morphological traits of the human pelvis', *Journal of Forensic Sciences*, 39: 1047–56.

Schepartz, L.A., Fox, S.C. and Bourbou, C. (eds) (2009) *New Directions in the Skeletal Biology of Greece*, *Hesperia Supplement 43*, Athens: American School of Classical Studies at Athens.

Steckel, R.H., Larsen, C.S., Walker, P., *et al.* (2009) 'The European Project: introduction to goals, materials and methods', *Presented at the 78th Annual Meeting of the American Association of Physical Anthropologists, March 31 – April 4, 2009, Chicago, Illinois, USA*.

Stravopodi, E., Manolis, S.K. and Kyparissi-Apostolika, N. (1999) 'Paleoanthropological findings from Theopetra Cave in Thessaly. A preliminary report', in G.N. Bailey, E. Adam, E. Panagopoulou, *et al.* (eds) *The Palaeolithic Archaeology of Greece and Surrounding Areas*, Proceedings of the ICOPAG Conference, September 1994, Athens: British School at Athens Studies 3.

Triantaphyllou, S. (1998) 'Prehistoric populations from northern Greece: a breath of life for the skeletal remains', in K. Branigan (ed.) *Cemetery and Society in the Aegean Bronze Age*, Sheffield: Sheffield Academic Press.

——(2000) 'Prehistoric Makrigialos: a story from the fragments', in P. Halstead (ed.) *Neolithic Society in Greece*, Sheffield: Sheffield Academic Press.

Trotter, M. and Gleser, G.C. (1952) 'Estimation of stature from long bones of American whites and Negroes', *American Journal of Physical Anthropology*, 10: 463–514.

Tsaliki, A. (2003) 'Evidence of platycnemia 5000 B.P. at Sifnos, Greece', *British Association of Biological Anthropology and Osteoarchaeology (BABAO) Annual Review*, 4: 13–14.

——(2004) 'Spine pathology and disability at Lesbos, Greece', *Palaeopathology Association Newsletter*, 125: 13–17.

Ubelaker, D.H. (1989) *Human Skeletal Remains: Excavation, Analysis, Interpretation*, 2nd edn, Washington DC: Taraxacum.

Vanna, V. (2005) 'Biological status differences between a Hellenistic and a modern skeletal population from Greece', *Papers from the Institute of Archaeology*, 16: 90–94.

——(2007) 'Sex and gender related health status differences in ancient and contemporary skeletal populations', *Papers from the Institute of Archaeology*, 18: 114–47.

Vass, A.A., Bass, W.M., Wolt, J.D., *et al.* (1992) 'Time since death determinations of human cadavers using soil solution', *Journal of Forensic Sciences*, 37: 1236–53.

Xirotiris, N.I. (1980) 'The Indo-Europeans in Greece. An anthropological approach to the population of the Bronze Age', *Journal of Indo-European Studies*, 8: 201–10.

Hungary/Magyar Köztársaság

Ildikó Pap and György Pálfi

INTRODUCTION: A BRIEF HISTORY AND CURRENT STATE OF PHYSICAL ANTHROPOLOGY IN HUNGARY

Biological anthropology or physical anthropology (in Hungarian: embertan), is a science dealing with the study of the evolution and the variations of hominids. In Hungary, historical anthropology is responsible for analysing the human remains discovered during archaeological excavations; thus we will focus primarily on historical anthropology in this chapter.

The first initiatives of Hungarian anthropology can be found at the end of the 17th and the beginning of the 18th centuries, among others in the writings of János Apáczai Csere, a leading Protestant scholar and writer, and in the works of Mátyás Bél, a Lutheran pastor and polymath. The first Hungarian writing in the field of anthropology was published in 1807 by György Fejér, under the title of *Antropológia vagyis az ember ismertetése* ('Anthropology or the Study of Man'). Sámuel Scheiber had an outstanding role in the foundation of Hungarian anthropology, as well as in the intellectual preparation of the International Conference on Hungarian Pre-history held in Budapest in 1876. He suggested the establishment of an association, a university department and a museum of anthropology in his works *Pro Memoria* and '*Hon*' ('Homeland'). That conference had a decisive effect on the further development of anthropology in Hungary (Table 17.1). In 1878 the National Association of Archaeology and Anthropology was founded.

The Institute of Anthropology of the University of Budapest was established in 1881, and was the fourth institute of its kind in Europe. Its leader was Professor Aurél Török, who acquired his knowledge in anthropology by attending Paul Broca's courses. He even planned the creation of a university collection and the foundation of an anthropological association. The anthropological research founded on the groundwork of natural sciences was continued in the 1930s. Lajos Bartucz, who was Aurél Török's student and would later become his successor as head of department, summarized in his book *A magyar ember* ('The Hungarian Man'), published in 1938, the results that had been reached by then in the field of Hungarian anthropological research. In 1936 Bartucz became the acting director of the Museum of Ethnography and in 1938 he became the director of the museum. In the mid-1930s, the collection of findings deriving from excavations was also assisted by the leading board of the capital city. They entrusted the Budapest Institute of Anthropology with the examination of the findings, report writing and funding for the completion of the analysis. As a matter of fact, the obligation to write a report

Table 17.1 Milestones in the history of physical anthropology in Hungary

Year	Events
1802	Foundation of the Hungarian National Museum (Magyar Nemzeti Múzeum), Budapest
1807	First Hungarian book on anthropology: *Antropológia vagyis az ember ismertetése* ('Anthropology or the Study of Man') by Gy. Fejér
1821	Foundation of the Hungarian Academy of Sciences, Budapest
1847	The Department of Ethnography became independent from the Hungarian National Museum, and is named Museum of Ethnography
1872	Interim Committee for Historic Monuments (MIB)
1876	International Conference on Hungarian Prehistory, Budapest
1878	Foundation of the Hungarian Archaeological and Anthropological Society (Magyar Régészeti és Művészettörténeti Társulat), Budapest
	Aurél Török visited the World Exhibition and International Anthropological Congress in Paris and met Paul Broca.
1881	Foundation of the Anthropological Department at the University of Budapest (Head: A. Török)
	Topinard's book, *Anthropologia*, was translated into Hungarian.
1882	*AnthropológiaiFüzetek* (*Journals of Anthropology*, Periodical) (Török issued one volume)
1883	Foundation of the Anthropological Museum, Anthropological Laboratory within the Hungarian National Museum
1890	*Grundzüge einer systematischen Kraniometrie* was published by A. Török
1922	Anthropological Section under the Hungarian Ethnographic Society
1923	*AnthropológiaiFüzetek* (*Journals of Anthropology*, Periodical) (Recommenced by L. Bartucz)
1930	The Anthropometric Laboratory was founded (within the College of Physical Education, Budapest) (Head: M. Malán)
1938	*A magyar ember* ('The Hungarian Man') was published by Bartucz
1940	Foundation of the Anthropological Department at the University of Szeged (Head: L. Bartucz)
	Systematic collection of human skeletal remains.
1940–1945	Anthropological Institute at the University of Kolozsvár, Transylvania (part of Hungary at that time) (Head: M. Malán)
1945	Foundation of the Department of Anthropology within the Natural History Museum
1950	Foundation of the Department of Anthropology at the University of Szeged
1952	Foundation of the Anthropological Committee at the Department of Biology of the Hungarian Academy of Science
	Foundation of the Hungarian Biological Society, Section of Anthropology
1954	*BiológiaiKözlemények – Pars Anthropologica* (Periodical)
1956	*AntropológiaiKözlemények – Pars Anthropologica* (Periodical)
	Crania Hungarica (Periodical) (until 1961; later *Anthropologia Hungarica*)
1961	*Anthropologia Hungarica* (Periodical) (until 1992)
1957	Foundation of OMF (National Inspectorate of Historic Monuments) within the Ministry of Building Construction
1958	Foundation of the Archaeological Institute of HAS
1966	*Prehistoric Trephining and Grave Finds relating to the History of Medicine* (Book by L. Bartucz)
1970	*History of Human Life-Spain and Mortality* (Book publishedbyG. Acsádi and J. Nemeskéri)
1974	*HumanbiologiaBudapestiensis* (Periodical by O. Eiben)
1999	Initiation of three-year postgraduate courses in anthropology/human biology (Department of Anthropology, Eötvös Loránd University). The courses were offered in three consecutive years.
	Human Biology. Development: Growth and Maturation (Book by E. Bodzsár)

Table 17.1 (continued)

Year	Events
2001	Human Biology. *Evolution of Hominids* (Book by G. Gyenis)
2003	Human Biology. *Development: Growth and Maturation* (Book by E. Bodzsár)
	Human Biology. *Biology of Aging: Puberty* (Book by E. Bodzsár)
2004	Human Biology. *Practical Manual* (Book by Bodzsár and Zsákai)

can be considered as the renewal of the decree issued in the time of Török. Anthropological research was already fairly extensive in those years. In 1930 Mihály Malán set up the Anthropometric Laboratory at the Budapest College of Physical Education.

The second Institute of Anthropology was founded in 1940 at Horthy Miklós University of Szeged. Lajos Bartucz was appointed as the head of the institute, whose main purpose was the collection and study of human remains deriving from excavations, as well as the examination of the living Hungarian population. Following the Second World War, the Departments of Anthropology at both Budapest and Szeged were directed by Bartucz until 1959. The research profile of the Budapest Department was expanded and changed. In addition to the analysis of human remains obtained from the excavations, the study of body growth and maturation and the examination of the characteristic features of the living adult population were thrust into the limelight.

The third Hungarian Department of Anthropology was founded around 1947 at Kossuth Lajos University of Debrecen. The organizing duties of the department were carried out by Mihály Malán, who set up two anthropological institutes during his tenure of almost half a century. He established a scientific school, where he initiated and directed the first body growth monitoring that led to the realization of the growth reference rate in Hungary. Between 1970 and 1984, János Nemeskéri was the head of the department. He supervised the scientific activity of the group, which was carried out in the fields of demogenetics and palaeodemography. Since the year 1991, research in historical anthropology was taken up again under the direction of László Szathmáry. Nowadays the department is run within the frames of the Department of Evolutionary Zoology and Human Biology of the University of Debrecen. Their main research areas are the following: the monitoring of body growth, the study of the characteristic features and population genetics of the living adult populations in Hungary, an historical anthropology.

Although the outlines of an anthropological collection started to unfold in the mid-1930s, the fourth Hungarian Institute of Anthropology was not established until 1945. This was the Department of Anthropology of the Natural History Museum, within the framework of the Hungarian National Museum (later the Natural History Museum), then from 1992 the Hungarian Natural History Museum (Magyar Természettudományi Múzeum). The aim of the institute was, and still is, the collection and storage of human remains obtained from archaeological excavations. The first leader and organizer of this focus was János Nemeskéri. The foundation of the Department of Anthropology of the Hungarian Natural History Museum was a milestone in the history of Hungarian anthropology. This institute became so important that it has been shaping the position of Hungarian anthropology ever since. Nemeskéri was succeeded as director by Tibor Tóth (1965–90) and then by Ildikó Pap (1990–present). Today the main research areas of the department are still the fields of historical anthropology and palaeopathology.

The Anthropological Theme Committee of the Hungarian Academy of Sciences was established in 1958, and has been functioning under the name of Anthropological Committee (Magyar Tudományos Akadémia Antropológiai Bizottság) since 1970. It figures among the most important tasks of the board to take a stand on the issues of the politics of science, the ethics of science, and other crucial questions concerning the field of anthropology.

This brief review of the history of physical anthropology was based on the works of Bartucz (1948), Nemeskéri (1961), Tóth (1971, 1981, 1990), Eiben (1988), Farkas (1988, 1991, 2000a) and Farkas and Dezső (1994).

Hungarian anthropology in the 20th century

The situation of Hungarian biological anthropology and of research in the different sub-disciplines was reviewed at the Conference of Hungarian Anthropologists, organized in 2000. The results were published in the 44th volume of *Acta Biologica Szegediensis* (2000). In his article, *The Past of the Hungarian Anthropology and Future Objectives*, Farkas (2000b) outlined the history of the establishment of university institutes, collections, scientific associations and periodicals, listed the places and fields of research of Hungarian anthropology, and formulated future objectives. He gave a chronological list of all Hungarian congresses and conferences related to anthropological research.

Kordos presented the new results of Hominoid research in the Carpathian Basin (Kordos 2000); Éry offered a brief and selected review of palaeoanthropological research in Hungary by means of chronologically listed studies containing new trends, methods and observations (Éry 2000); Zoffmann attempted to sketch the anthropological characteristics of the populations that had inhabited the Carpathian Basin throughout the years of prehistoric times (Zoffmann 2000); Fóthi (2000) outlined the history and results of the anthropological analysis of the population of the Central Danube Basin ranging from the Roman Period to the ninth century AD; and Szathmáry (2000) provided a summary of the anthropological research on the history of ancient Hungarians populating the Carpathian Basin from the 10th through to the 13th century. In addition, Marcsik and Pap (Marcsik and Pap 2000) reviewed the palaeopathological research in Hungary; and Kocsis (2000) revised the results of the palaeostomatological research. Bodzsár (2000a, 2000b) and Farkas (2000a) presented the results of the anthropological research of living populations. In addition, the outcomes of dermatoglyphic studies were described by Gyenis (2000), and those on population genetics were reviewed in the works of M. Pap (Pap, M. 2000). The role of anthropometry in competitive sport was outlined by Mészáros *et al.* (2000); while the results of the anthropological studies of people living with disabilities in Hungary were outlined in the article by Buday (2000). Kósa (2000) focused on the role of anthropological material in forensic medicine. Susa (2000) summarized the identification of Hungarian historical personalities and gave details about those who had died as martyrs and those that had been exhumed from mass graves.

On palaeopathological research, a detailed overview has been provided by Marcsik and Pap (2000) and Pálfi *et al.* (in press).

Forensic medicine and forensic anthropology in Hungary

The Decree of the Governor's Board of 22 November 1793 stated that the Medicina Forensis and the Politica Medica (Medical Administration) should be taught as a major subject at an independent department of the University of Pest. In 1827 it was added to the curriculum as the independent subject of Forensic Medicine, and and has remained so ever since. The predecessor of the Institute of Forensic Medicine at the Faculty of Medicine of Semmelweis University in Budapest was the Institute of Judicial Medicine, which started operating in 1886. In 1953, the name of the institute was changed from Institute of Judicial Medicine to Institute of

Forensic Medicine because the Court of Justice was not used any more or the names of courts were modified.

The Research Institutes for Forensic Sciences (ISZKI, Igazságügyi Szakértői és Kutató Intézetek) were founded by the Minister of Justice in 1992. Their predecessors were the ten regional forensic bureaus, established in Budapest and in the country by Government Decree no. 29/ 1964 (XI. 23). Government Directive no. 1/2006 (IK2) records that the name of the Office of Forensic Experts Institutes was changed on 1 January 2006 to Research Institutes for Forensic Sciences (ISZKI). The organization and operation of the Research Institutes for Forensic Sciences is determined by the Organizational and Operational Rules, described in Directive no. 2/2006 (IK3) of the Ministry of Justice. According to the decision of the Minister of Justice, since January 2000 a group of experts has been in operation to assist the practice of the Tribute Act in connection with the individuals who died between 1945 and 1962 in uncertain conditions and were then buried in unmarked graves. The forensic anthropologist experts of the group (from 2000, headed by Éva Susa, director general of the Research Institutes for Forensic Sciences) have been working on the exhumation and identification of those remains at the Budapest Institute of Forensic Medicine (one of the ten forensic bureaus) since the change of the regime in 1989.

The current state of Hungarian anthropological collections

Human remains that derive from archaeological excavations are stored in national and regional (county) museums, as well as in Hungarian university departments, such as the Department of Anthropology of the Hungarian Natural History Museum in Budapest, and the Department of Biological Anthropology of the University of Szeged, among others. The anthropological collections of the local county museums comprise in total approximately 30,000 to 40,000 specimens (individual skeletons), dating from the Neolithic period to the Late Middle Ages. The majority of these collections contain specimens appearing in the inventory registers of Székesfehérvár, Veszprém, Pécs and Miskolc. In certain Hungarian museological institutions, due to the lack of anthropological experts, the supervision of the collections is assured by archaeologists or curators specialized in ethnography.

In Hungary, physical anthropology is essentially based on two human osteological collections, one in Budapest (Table 17.2) and one in Szeged (Table 17.3).The two big collections house fossil finds of hominids and remains of historic human populations who used to live in the territory of Hungary. They both comprise more than 70,000 specimens (individual skeletons) from the Neolithic to the Modern Ages.

Table 17.2 Development of the collection of the Department of Anthropology, Hungarian Natural History Museum, Budapest

Year	Number of specimens
1847	The Hungarian National Museum and later the independent Department of Ethnography housed skulls gained from archaeological excavations already at the time of its construction
1883	974 skulls
1886	1500 skulls, 25 skeletons, 70 endocasts, 40 brain endocasts
1894	10,000 skulls, 1000 skeletons
2010	Middle and Upper Palaeolithic remains
	40,000 specimens from the postglacial populations of the Middle Danube Basin.
	300 mummies (Egyptian and from the Mummy Collection of Vác)
	Facial reconstructions collections (70 specimens)

Table 17.3 Development of the collections of the Department of Biological Anthropology, University of Szeged, Hungary

Year	Number of specimens
1940	Ferenc Móra, director of the Museum of Szeged, handed over to Lajos Bartucz, Professor of Anthropology, about 3000 skulls unearthed in the archaeological excavations around Szeged. This laid the foundations of the anthropological collection of Szeged
1965	In addition to the initial 3000 skulls, the collection comprised about 10,000 skeletons gained from archaeological excavations. It includes another 1600 skeletons, the so-called depository collection of the Department of Anthropology of the Hungarian Natural History Museum, Budapest
2010	30,000 specimens from the Neolithic Age to the 17th century AD

Department of Anthropology, Hungarian Natural History Museum, Budapest

As early as 1802, at the time of its construction, the Hungarian National Museum had already housed some anthropological material. The Department of Ethnography became independent from the National Museum in 1847 and was named the Museum of Ethnography thereafter. The skull collection of the National Museum was relocated as well. When Aurél Ponori Török, the first Hungarian anthropologist, was appointed as the head of the Department of Anthropology in Budapest, he underlined the necessity of having in the establishment an anthropological museum 'so that anthropological exploration can take roots in our country' (Farkas 1988). It was János Jankó, ethnographer and director of the Museum of Ethnography at that time, who set up the osteological collection, when he encouraged the establishment of an independent osteological collection within the museum. 'The duties of this Laboratory include the collection of anthropological finds of the peoples who used to live in the territory of our country, the exploration of the past anthropological history of our folks and the study of our recent population' (Farkas 1988). The findings from some exotic expeditions also enriched the collection.

In 1945, András Tasnádi-Kubacska, mandatory director of the Natural History Museum, suggested in a petition addressed to the Ministry of Health and Education the establishment of a fifth department, the Department of Anthropology, in the museum: 'We would like to put the Department investigating mankind in its own place, into the discipline of biological sciences.' He delegated a secondary school teacher, János Nemeskéri. The department was acknowledged in 1945, the official opening date of the Department of Anthropology. During its history, the department was located in a succession of places in Budapest; it moved to its present home in the Ludoviceum Building in 1999.

The Department's main task is the scientific research of its rich collection of fossil hominids and skeletal remains from historic populations, which is representative in both time and space; as well as the exhibition of our achievements. The department is the foundation of the Hungarian historical anthropological research. Its collections range from Neolithic finds to Modern Pre-Industrial material, and include the Middle and Upper Palaeolithic Collection, the Post-Pleistocene Collection, the Aurél Török Collection, the Egyptian Collection, the 19th-century Mummy Collection of Vác, the Facial Reconstruction Collection and the Archive Photo Collection. The Department has a Laboratory of Molecular Anthropology, suitable for ancient human DNA analysis. Due to the continuous curatorship and fortunate circumstances, the arrangement, the storage and the inventory system of the collections are outstanding in the Ludoviceum Building.

The collections appearing in the inventory record comprise more than 27,000 individuals, but the department houses approximately 15,000 un-inventoried individuals, too. The department also stores 265 mummies from the 18th century, which is the Mummy Collection of Vác. The entries are searchable by inventory books and an up-to-date database. Information on the collections, the catalogues and the database is available in printed and digital forms (Makra and Pap 2006; Makra 2007a, 2007b, 2009a, 2009b; Merkl *et al.* 2008). The material is available for study. For more details on admission and loan, the head of the department should be contacted.

Department of Anthropology, University of Szeged

The historical anthropological collection of Szeged can take pride in its approximately 70 years of existence. When Lajos Bartucz became head of the Department of Anthropology at Szeged, his friendship with many leading archaeologists (especially with writer Ferenc Móra) initiated the systematic collection not only of archaeological artefacts but also of human remains deriving from excavations. By the mid-1950s, the osteological collection of the department in Szeged had already been composed of 3000–4000 finds (individual skeletons) dating from various archaeological time periods. A most significant development of the collection began around the end of the 1950s when the department got hold of the human skeletons recovered during the excavations of Ottó Trogmayer, archaeologist and former director of the Szeged Museum, as well as from excavations by other archaeologists in the southern and eastern regions of Hungary. The Szeged collection has been increasing significantly in the past 50 years, and reached a total of around 30,000 specimens (individual skeletons) by the turn of the millennium.

The main purpose of the Szeged collection within the university was the progression of university research for undergraduate and postgraduate courses. The specimens, covering about 7000 years from the Neolithic Age to the 18th century AD, form an internationally well-known collection, which outgrew the university's walls by the end of the 1980s and became an internationally renowned research base.

However, the expansion and the increase in the number of specimens has caused considerable hardship since the beginning of the millennium. First, the randomly chosen and inappropriate university storage rooms (empty cellars and other depository premises) are of neither adequate quality nor appropriate size, thus at present the collection cannot be expanded; second, the Department of Anthropology of the University of Szeged, consequently the museological institution of the collection, does not provide a post for a curator; third, there is neither a curator nor a conservator to maintain the collection, so this task is carried out by the three professors and the students of the department, which can only be a temporary solution. The University of Szeged and its partner institutions are working on a rapid and solid solution to all three problems. Although the department also houses approximately 3000–4000 remains which have not been inventoried, most of the specimens are searchable by means of the inventory books. The computerized inventory is currently being prepared, a process which could be facilitated significantly by the employment of a curator. The material is available for study but, since part of the collection is being moved to a new location, all professional visits have to be preceded by thorough coordination. For further details on accessing the material, the head of the department should be contacted.

Education and training

Department of Anthropology, Eötvös Loránd University

Eötvös Loránd University is the oldest and largest university in Hungary. It was founded in 1635 in Nagyszombat (today Trnava, Slovakia). The College of Law was added in 1667 and the

College of Medicine began in 1769. Upon the request of its founder, the university was moved to Buda in 1777, and then in 1784 it moved to its final location in Pest. It was known as the University of Budapest (Budapesti Tudományegyetem) until 1921, when it changed to Pázmány Péter University. The university received its current name, Eötvös Loránd University, in 1950 after the physicist Loránd Eötvös (http://www.elte.hu/en/elte_brief_history).

The Department of Anthropology was established as one of the Institutes of the University of Budapest in 1881. Aurél Török was appointed the first professor of the department and he began to teach courses and deliver lectures immediately. In his university courses, Török made use of Topinard's manual, which he and G. Pethő had translated into Hungarian and published in 1881. His main purpose was to study the origins of the Hungarian people by employing the methods of palaeoanthropology and ethnical anthropology.

In 1940 Lajos Bartucz was appointed professor at the Department of Anthropology of the University of Szeged. First he combined his Szeged duties with lectures in Budapest. Later, in 1959, he left the University of Szeged and was appointed professor of anthropology at the Department of Anthropology of Eötvös Loránd University in Budapest.

Ottó Eiben directed the work of the department from 1965. Due to his efforts, the educational and research activities of the department were consolidated in the early 1970s. Research has been pursued mainly on the growth and development of children, variations in human physique and human population genetics. In addition to the somatometric, ergonometric, auxological and epidemiological laboratories suitable for anthropological research on living people, the department has a historico-anthropological laboratory as well. In 1996 Gyula Gyenis became the head of the department. At present, and since 2005, the department chair is Éva Bodzsár. The main research topics are the growth and maturation of Hungarian youth, variations of human physique and body composition. In 2001, the department moved to the new campus of the Faculty of Science, on the Buda side of the capital city (http://ludens.elte.hu/~anthrop/tortenet_e.html)

Department of Biological Anthropology, University of Szeged

The University of Szeged is one of the most distinguished universities in Hungary and in Central Europe. It is located at Szeged in southern Hungary. The university was founded in Kolozsvár (today Cluj-Napoca, Romania) in 1872, and moved to Szeged in 1921. The Medical School was separated from the University in 1952 and an independent institution was established. In 1962 the University took the name of 'József Attila' (JATE). In 2000, all the institutions were unified under the name of the University of Szeged. The University of Szeged has never had a unified campus; its buildings are rather scattered across the city (www.sci.u-szeged.hu).

The Department of Anthropology was established in 1940 at Horthy Miklós University, Szeged, which was the previous title of the University of Szeged. Lajos Bartucz, a full-time professor, became the department head, as we have already mentioned. The department survived the events of the Second World War, suffering no harm at all. The fact that Bartucz acted as the Dean of the Faculty of Mathematics and Natural Sciences between 1943 and 1946 showed a sign of recognition to anthropology as well. In the post-war years, graduate courses to train biology teachers were improved so much that this resulted in the upswing of other degree courses in the training of biological anthropologists. To ensure high quality education, Bartucz wrote several university manuals, the first books published in Hungarian containing supplementary material for MA students of anthropology (since at that time Bartucz also taught at the Department of Anthropology of Budapest University, the same manuals were uniformly used at both universities). In those years, the research work done in the departments of anthropology was already giving prominence to the study of bone remains gained from archaeological excavations, the results of which were later used by Bartucz in his excellent book on palaeopathology (Bartucz 1966).

After Bartucz's appointment in Budapest in 1960, Pál Lipták became the Department Chair in Szeged. Professor Lipták succeeded in reinforcing the administrative unity of the department, and he wrote and published in 1969 the first manual of biological anthropology in Hungarian, entitled *Embertan és Emberszármazástan* (Biological Anthropology and Human Genealogy). In 1980, Gyula Farkas took over the direction of the department from Professor Lipták (let us mention here that, at that time, there were nine full-time colleagues appointed in the department, which had not happened before and has not taken place since). Making use of the continually expanding anthropological collection in the possession of the Szeged Department of Anthropology, its professors further developed its research profile of historical anthropology, which was completed by human biological analyses based on the examination of living populations, under the direction of Gyula Farkas. Historical anthropology also served as the source of palaeopathological research, which has become the main research profile of the department since 1997, the year Antónia Marcsik took over its direction. In 2007, György Pálfi succeeded Antónia Marcsik as Department Chair and has directed the department since then. Pálfi and his colleagues carefully follow the traditional line of palaeopathological research. In their international and interdisciplinary research, they concentrate primarily on the palaeoepidemiology of specific infectious diseases.

Department of Evolutionary Zoology and Human Biology, University of Debrecen

The University of Debrecen is a university located in the north-eastern part of Hungary. Higher education began in Debrecen with the foundation of the Calvinist College of Debrecen in 1538. Over the centuries it has been one of the key institutions of higher education in Hungary. In 1918, the first new medical school building was opened, and the original medical school campus was completed in 1927. In 1952 the Faculty of Arts, Humanities and Social Sciences and the Faculty of Natural Sciences were united as Lajos Kossuth University. The newly formed universities – the Medical University, the University of Agriculture and Lajos Kossuth University – continued to co-exist as three separate institutions up until 2000, when the disjointed former University of Debrecen was once again united (http://www.unideb.hu/portal/en/node/19).

Education in biological anthropology take place in the Department of Evolutionary Zoology and Human Biology. The traditional research profile of the group concerns the disciplines of evolution (Miklós Kretzoi), palaeoanthropology (Andor Thoma) and population biology (Mihály Malán, János Nemeskéri and László Szathmáry). Their most noteworthy research topics are the following: genetic polymorphism and structure of human populations, population genealogy and migration, palaeoecology, osteological and biometric analysis of skeletal populations, anthropological examination of mentally disabled children, and dermatoglyphic research.

Professionals in the field of anthropology

Most of the experts dealing with historical anthropology in Hungary have a college or university MA degree, and many of them lecture on biology. According to their educational background, some members of the profession are archaeologists, physicians or chemists. After their graduation with MA, MSc or MD degrees, they tend to follow postgraduate courses in order to acquire all the biological and anthropological skills necessary to work as physical anthropologists. In the autumn of 1990, the Department of Anthropology of Eötvös Loránd

University offered for the first time, under the direction of Ottó Eiben, a three-year post-graduate courses on anthropology and human biology, which enabled students to graduate on three occasions with a second degree of anthropology and human biology.

Since 1990, graduate students have had the opportunity of taking up fully accredited doctoral degree programmes at Hungarian universities. After graduating with a PhD degree, those who want to reach a higher scientific degree may work towards the so-called degree of the Doctor of the Hungarian Academy of Sciences.

The number of experts dealing with historical anthropology or osteoarchaeology in Hungary is close to 20, while there are about 250 archaeologists (though the number of active archaeologists working at excavations is lower). Most of the anthropologists work in museums, university institutions, and at the Archaeological Institute of the Hungarian Academy of Sciences. Since 2009, some experts have been employed by the Field Service for Cultural Heritage (now Hungarian National Museum, National Cultural Heritage Protection Centre).

ARCHAEOLOGICAL HUMAN REMAINS AND LEGISLATION

Archaeological legislation

Act LXIV of 2001, the law on the protection of our cultural heritage (2001/LXIV; Codes on cultural heritage) declares that all findings in the ground, under water and in caves constitute the property of the state both before and after their excavation. In Hungary, all traces of human existence dating from the times before 1711 that help us understand the history of mankind are considered cultural heritage. Besides the national regulations, Hungary has signed and ratified all major International Conventions on the protection of cultural heritage (the 1954 Hague Convention, applicable since 1956, the 1970 UNESCO Convention, applicable since 1979, and the UNIDROIT Convention, applicable since 1998).

In 2005 a revision and addition were made to the existing law. The amended version of Act 2001/LXIV became Act 2005/LXXXIX, which settles the question of the protection of our cultural heritage. Archaeological excavations can be executed by the museums assigned to this duty and also by the museums possessing archaeological collections from different sites. Other institutions that can take part in excavations in Hungary are the following: universities with departments of archaeology, the Archaeological Institute of the Hungarian Academy of Sciences, the National Office of Cultural Heritage (Kulturális Örökségvédelmi Hivatal) and the Hungarian National Museum, National Cultural Heritage Protection Centre (Magyar Nemzeti Múzeum, Nemzeti Örökségvédelmi Központ, NÖK (until August 1, 2010 Field Service for Cultural Heritage)). The director of the excavation must be an archaeologist with a university degree or qualifications gained in the required field of specialization. Furthermore, the archaeologist should be hired as a public servant or civil servant, or should have a contractual job with the institution assigned to excavate. The team working at the excavation may be composed of an anthropologist, a geophysicist, an illustrator, a photographer, a conservator, an archaeozoologist and an archaeobotanist. The law does not oblige the presence of an anthropologist during archaeological excavations. The archaeological excavation (except for rescue excavations) may be carried out exclusively by the authorization (Decree 16/2001, X.18.) of the Ministry of National Cultural Heritage (Nemzeti Kulturális Örökség Minisztériuma, from 2010 Ministry of National Resources/Nemzeti Erőforrás Minisztérium). The formal consent is issued by the National Office of Cultural Heritage.

The National Office of Cultural Heritage was founded in 2001, in accordance with the relevant legislation (Act LXIV of 2001, on the Protection of Cultural Heritage), and renewed in 2008 (its predecessors, OMvH: National Office for the Protection of Historic Monuments and

KÖI: Directorate of Cultural Heritage in charge of archaeology and movable items, merged in 2001). The regulatory and structural conceptions provide a legal framework which corresponds to recent European trends. The National Office of Cultural Heritage is a governmental organization under the professional supervision of the Ministry of Education and Culture and is headed by the Chairman, who is appointed by the Minister. According to legal regulations, The National Office of Cultural Heritage is the administrative authority of first instance for historic monuments, archaeological sites and the movable cultural heritage (www.koh.hu/english.html).

HUMAN REMAINS AND LEGISLATION

Remains dating before 1711 are considered cultural heritage. Remains of individuals who died after 1711 fall outside the framework of archaeology. Remains younger than 25 years can be considered forensic cases.

In Hungary, the idea of the recovery of human bone remains occurred for the first time in 1876, at the International Conference on Hungarian Prehistory, Budapest. Article no. 1881/XXXIX was the first article to regulate buildings found on the surface or buried in the ground. This ancient monuments act was among the first laws of its kind in Europe. The article of 1881 (1881/XXXIX.) was completed in 1929 by the protection of anthropological relics. Article no. XIX of 1922 regulates the autonomy and the personnel of our largest national public collections. However, the systematic recovery and preservation of human bone remains did not become conventional until the 1940s. The decree of 1949 (signed by the President, thus equivalent to a law) declared all archaeological findings in Hungarian territory to be state property, regardless of the depth of deposition.

The legislative background, imposing regulations on the recovery of human bone remains, serves as the legislative framework of the collections with scientific objectives. In addition to observing the rules, a number of other ethical and practical aspects are also considered, which will determine the methods of recovery and preservation after common deliberations. During the collection, maintenance, registration and scientific processing of the human remains, the fact that the remains are those of individuals who were once alive must be considered.

Human bone remains preserved in anthropological collections have come to light as the result of archaeological excavations (Act LXIV of 2001, the law on the cultural heritage).

The remains of individuals who died after 1711 fall outside the framework of archaeology. Regarding the deceased, the governing laws to be applied are the acts on cemeteries and burials (1999. XLIII) of the Civil Code. These laws set the rules about the remains, declare that a decent burial is a human right, and regulate the protection of the memory of the deceased.

Decree no. 145 /1999 (X.1.) provides the execution of Act no. XLIII of 1999, that is the Act on Cemeteries and Burials. On the other hand, it is Decree no. 146 /1999 (X.1.) that regulates the organization and tasks of the National Enshrine Committee. In certain cases, the validation of state ownership may come up against serious obstacles. After the change of regime in 1999, the county and city museums, but not the national museums, became the property of the local authorities. That is to say, the findings unearthed through excavations constitute the property of the Hungarian State exclusively until the moment that they are taken over by the museums of the territorial jurisdiction. From that moment, the findings become the property of the local authorities in question. However, there is contradiction between the two laws: according to the first law, the unearthed findings constitute the property of the state; but by contrast, the law carried into effect after the change of regime proclaims that the local authorities have the right to dispose of the findings after their excavation.

Legislation in museology

The registration of anthropological findings takes place in accordance with the 20/2002 (X.4.) Ministerial Decree of the Ministry of National Cultural Heritage, which sets the registry rules of the museological institutions. The decree delineates the substantial requirements of the registry of cultural goods kept and exposed in museological institutions. It also sets the rules for the computerized inventory record, regulates the inventory stock book and the register, both based on computerized data, the catalogue card system and the description card system; as well as the preparation and storage of the registry tools.

The inventory record of cultural goods is needed for minimum collection accountability. The inventory is indispensable for keeping records of the results revealed through their scientific definition and the continually expanding and changing knowledge related to these items. Furthermore, it is essential for protection and security, as well as for further research, educational, intellectual and cultural refinement purposes. By virtue of the ministerial decree, the museological institution keeps record of its anthropological collection, which had previously gone through scientific registration, in special anthropological of registry books. The traditional registration is obligatory, although the computerized inventory record is not yet regulated by the decree. However, almost every museum with an anthropological collection has some kind of computerized database. The IT requirements and principles concerning the hardware and software authorized in museological institutions for registry purposes are summarized in the information material issued on the basis of section (1) in § 55 of Act no. IX of 1987, in accordance with the 20/2002 (X.4.) Ministerial Decree of the Ministry of National Cultural Heritage.

In Hungary, almost all the institutions possessing anthropological collections have some kind of computerized database. Nevertheless, no unified anthropological data processing programmes are used. In the Department of Anthropology of the Hungarian Natural History Museum, the so-called 'MNYR' electronic registry system, developed by the Ministry of Education and Culture, is in use (www.okm.gov.hu/kultura/muzeumi-nyilvantartasi/muzeumi-nyilvantartasi). The conditions and rules of borrowing and interchanging cultural objects are also regulated by laws and decrees. The conditions of borrowing cultural objects within the country or abroad, either with the aim of exposition or with any other purpose, were modified and made stricter by Act no. CXL of 1997, amended in 2009. Both skeletal and mummified human remains can be transported abroad with the aim of exhibition or research in accordance with the law issued in 2009 and with the enforcement of the law effective since 1 January 2010. Table 17.4 summarizes the milestones in Hungarian legislation regarding the cultural heritage.

METHODS OF ANTHROPOLOGICAL ANALYSIS

Historical protocol for recovery, curation, maintenance and investigation of anthropological material deriving from archaeological excavations

The necessity for the regulation and standardization for the recovery, analysis and curation of archaeological human remains occurred in the field of the Hungarian biological anthropology a long time ago. In 2008, the Committee of Anthropology (CA) from the Section of Biological Sciences of the Hungarian Academy of Sciences (SBS, HAS) appointed a team to provide advice on a Historical Anthropological Protocol. The recommendations were drawn up by this working group, named the 'Ad hoc Historical Anthropological Protocol Committee', comprised of physical anthropologists and curators from the Department of Anthropology at the

Table 17.4 Milestones in the legislation concerning cultural heritage and anthropology in Hungary

Year	Events
1802	Foundation of the Hungarian National Museum, Budapest
1872	Interim Committee for Historic Monuments (MIB)
1876	International Conference on Hungarian Prehistory, Budapest
1881	1st law: 1881/XXXIX: Article no. 1881 (XXXIX), the first article to regulate edifices found in the ground or on the surface.
	Foundation of MOB (National Committee for Historic Monuments)
1919	National Office for Historic Monuments – only for a transitory period during the Hungarian Republic of Councils
1922	Anthropological section within the Hungarian Ethnographic Society
1922	Article no.XIX regulating the autonomy and the personnel of our largest national public collections. www.1000ev.hu/index.php?a=3&param=7530
1929	The article of 1881 (1881/XXXIX) was amended in 1929 by Article no. XI, which set rules about the protection of anthropological relics
1940	Foundation of the Anthropological Department at the University of Szeged (Head: L. Bartucz)
1940	Systematic collecting of human skeletal remains
1945	Foundation of the Department of Anthropology within the Natural History Museum
1950	Foundation of the Department of Anthropology at the University of Szeged
1954	Hungary signed and ratified the 1954 Hague Convention (applicable since 1956)
1957	Foundation of OMF (National Inspectorate of Historic Monuments) within the Ministry of Building Construction
1964	3rd law: Act of 1964/III on Building Activities and Construction
1967	Ministerial Decree: 1967. I. 31 (ÉM) laying down the detailed regulation of monument conservation
1970	Hungary signed and ratified the 1970 UNESCO Convention (applicable since 1979)
1992	Transformation of OMF into OMvH, the National Office for the Protection of Historic Monuments (Országos Műemlékvédelmi Hivatal)
1993	Foundation of the National Cultural Fund
1997	4th law: Act of 1997/LIV on Monument Preservation
1997	Act no. CXL of 1997 on Museological Institutions, Public Library and Cultural Facilities
1998	Hungary signed and ratified the UNIDROIT Convention
1999	Codes on Cemeteries and Burials (1999. XLIII). The laws in question set the rules about remains, declare that a decent burial is the human right of every individual, and regulate the protection of the memory of the deceased
1999	Decree no.145/1999 (X.1.) assures the enforcement of Act no.XLIII of 1999 – Codes on Cemeteries and Burials. Decree no.146/1999 (X.1.) regulates the organization and tasks of the National Enshrine Committee.
	A methodological guide on the maintenance of cemeteries, burial grounds, burial monuments of heroes, located in the National Graveyard
2001	5th law: 2001/LXIV on Codes on Cultural Heritage
	Establishment of KÖH (Kulturális Örökségvédelmi Hivatal) – National Office of Cultural Heritage, incorporating OMvH and KÖI (Directorate of Cultural Heritage in charge of archaeology and movable items)
2002	Ministerial Decree no. 20/2002 (X.4.) of the National Cultural Heritage Ministry (NKÖM) on the Regulations of the Registers of Museological Institutions.
	Information about the IT requirements concerning the hardware and software authorized in museological institutions for registry purposes

(Continued on next page)

Table 17.4 (continued)

Year	Events
2004	Human Tissue Act of 2004
2004	ICOM Code of Ethics for Museums, Seoul
2004	Hungary's accession to the EU
2005	Amendment of Act no. 2001/LXIV by Act no. 2005/LXXXIX on the Protection of the Cultural Heritage
2009	Amendment of Act no. CXL of 1997. It amends, among others, the conditions of borrowing and transporting cultural goods with the aim of exhibition abroad or for any other purpose. § 54 (2) of the Constitution of the Republic of Hungary on the Tribute Act

Hungarian Natural History Museum, the Department of Anthropology at the Faculty of Science, Budapest University, and from the Department of Biological Anthropology, University of Szeged.

The Protocol consists of: guidance for the exploration, maintenance and registration of human remains in museums and other museological institutions possessing anthropological collections; and recommendations for the general anthropological examination of human remains. The Protocol was read and approved by the Committee of Anthropology in 2009, and was published in the same year (Pap and Pálfi 2009; Pap *et al.* 2009).

The Historical Anthropological Protocol has a list of suggested references for anthropological analysis. Besides the internationally recognized standards, there are several methods used specifically for the analysis of human skeletal remains including the methods of Éry *et al.* (1963) for ageing and sex assessments; the methods applied in forensic foetal osteology (Fazekas and Kósa 1978); those of Bernert *et al.* (2007) for the biological age estimation of children by means of bone measurements based on the historical populations of the Carpathian Basin; and finally the formulae provided by Bernert (2005a, 2008) for the calculation of body height on the basis of the extremities of individuals living in different historical periods in the Carpathian Basin. An anthropological programme package is partly used to make a database and partly for statistical analysis (Bernert 2005b).

The Historical Anthropological Protocol is recommended for the recovery, curation, maintenance and anthropological investigation of the anthropological material deriving from archaeological excavations in Hungary.

CONCLUSION

Although the beginning of Hungarian anthropological research goes back to the end of the 19th century, the examination of human remains explored in archaeological excavations began in the mid-20th century. The research is essentially based on the two large skeletal collections which comprise more than 70,000 skeletons from the Neolithic period to the present day. These include those held in Budapest at the Department of Anthropology, Natural History Museum, and in Szeged at the Department of Anthropology, University of Szeged.

Besides the detailed and multidisciplinary examinations, research focuses on general trends in human health through time. Since the year 2000, significant activity has been observed in Hungarian palaeopathological research, which has become increasingly multidisciplinary and thus necessitates the development of international cooperation. Within the principal research projects in human palaeopathology, the main topics are the palaeoepidemiology of specific infectious diseases, leprosy, tuberculosis, syphilis, and the palaeopathology of neoplastic diseases.

Apart from so-called 'classical' or 'traditional' Hungarian palaeopathology, based essentially on the study of ancient skeletal materials, the past decade has also been characterized by the development of the study of palaeopathology in mummies from Budapest. Most of these research projects are multidisciplinary, and in cooperation with Hungarian and foreign institutes and researchers. New techniques such as palaeoradiology, palaeohistology, geometric morphometry and aDNA analysis are applied.

USEFUL CONTACTS

Ministry of Education and Culture. Website: www.okm.gov.hu/

Hungarian Academy of Sciences, Section VIII of Biological Sciences. Website: www.mta.hu/ index.php?id=406&type=0/

Department of Biological Anthropology, Faculty of Sciences, Eötvös Loránd University, Budapest. Website: ludens.elte.hu/~anthrop/index_e.html/

Department of Anthropology, University of Szeged. Website: www.sci.u-szeged.hu/embertan/

Department of Anthropology, Hungarian Natural History Museum. Website: www.mttm.hu/ modules.php?name=Tar-Ember/

Museums in Hungary. Website: www.ace.hu/ceicom/hungary/vlmp.html/; www.museum.hu/ index_en.php/; www.ace.hu/ceicom/hungary/hunliste.html/

Hungarian Biological Society, Section of Anthropology. Website: www.mbt.mtesz.hu/tisztsegvi selok_adatai.htm/

ICOM Hungarian National Committee. Website: www.ace.hu/icom/

Hungarian Scientific Research Found (OTKA). Website: www.otka.hu/index.php?akt_ menu=991&set_lang=991/

Archaeological Institute of the Hungarian Academy of Sciences, Budapest. Website: www. archeo.mta.hu/

National Office of Cultural Heritage (KÖH). Website: www.koh.hu/english.html/

Association of Hungarian Archaeologists. Website: www.regeszet.org.hu/

HNM National Cultural Heritage Protection Centre NÖK. Website: http://www.mnm-nok. gov.hu/

ARCHEOCOMP Association. Website: www.ace.hu/

Institute of Archaeology, Faculty of Humanities, Eötvös Loránd University, Budapest. Website: http://btk.elte.hu/regeszet.intezet.aspx/; www.regeszettudomany.hu/

Department of Forensic Medicine, Semmelweis University. Website: www.igaz.sote.hu/

ICOMOS Association of Hungarian National Committees. Website: www.icomos.hu/

Research Institutes for Forensic Sciences. Website: www.iszki.hu

BIBLIOGRAPHY

Bartucz, L. (1948) *Alföldi Tudományos Gyűjtemény* (*Az Alföldi Tudományos Intézet Évkönyve, Szeged*), 2 (1946–47): 329–32.

——(1966) *A praehistorikus trepanáció és orvostörténeti vonatkozású sírleletek*, Medicina: Budapest.

Bernert, Zs. (2005a) 'Kárpát-medencei történeti népességek végtagarányai és testmagassága (Rate of the limbs and the stature of the historical populations of the Carpathian Basin)', in Z. Korsós (ed.) *IV. Kárpát-medencei Biológiai Szimpózium (Proceedings of the 4th Biological Symposium of the Carpathian Basin.)*, Budapest: Magyar Biológiai Társaság.

——(2005b) 'Paleoantropológiai programcsomag (Microprograms to the evaluation of the anthropological data gained from the historical anthropological series)', *Folia Anthropologica*, 3: 71–74.

——(2008) 'Data for the calculation of body height on the basis of extremities of individuals living in different historical periods in the Carpathian Basin', *Annales Historico-naturales Musei Nationalis Hungarici*, 100: 385–97.

Bernert, Zs., Évinger, S. and Hajdu, T. (2007) 'New data on the biological age estimation of children using bone measurements based on historical populations from the Carpathian Basin', *Annales Historico-naturales Musei Nationalis Hungarici*, 99: 199–206

Bodzsár, É. (2000a) 'A review of Hungarian studies on growth and physique of children', *Acta Biologica Szegediensis*, 44: 139–53.

——(2000b) 'Studies on sexual maturation of Hungarian children', *Acta Biologica Szegediensis*, 44: 155–65.

Buday, J. (2000) 'Anthropological studies of the disabled in Hungary', *Acta Biologica Szegediensis*, 44: 167–73.

Eiben, O. (1988) 'History of human biology in Hungary', *International Association of Human Biologists, Occasional papers*, 2(4): 1–75. Newcastle upon Tyne: International Association of Human Biologists.

Éry, K. (2000) 'Palaeoanthropological research in Hungary', *Acta Biologica Szegediensis*, 44: 81–86.

Éry, K., Kralovánszky, A. and Nemeskéri, J. (1963) 'Történeti népességek rekonstrukciójának reprezentációja (A representative reconstruction of historic populations), *Anthropológiai Közlemények*, 7: 41–90.

Farkas, Gy. (1988) 'A magyar antropológia története kezdettől 1945-ig (Die Geschichte der Antropologie in Ungarn von den Anfängen bis 1945)', *Móra Ferenc Múzeum Évkönyve*, 1987: 81–118.

——(ed.) (1991) *Papers of the Scientific Sessions in Szeged (Hungary), 1990 – 50th Anniversary of the Department of Anthropology in Szeged*, Szeged–Ulm: Szeged University.

——(2000a) 'Paleoanthropological research in Hungary', *Acta Biologica Szegediensis*, 44: 81–86.

——(2000b) 'The past of Hungarian anthropology and future objectives', *Acta Biologica Szegediensis*, 44: 61–69.

Farkas, Gy. and Dezső, G. (1994) *A magyar antropológia története a kezdetektől napjainkig* (The history of the Hungarian anthropology from the beginnings till our days), Szeged: JATEPress.

Fazekas, I. and Kósa, F. (1978) *Forensic Fetal Osteology*, Budapest: Akadémiai Kiadó.

Fóthi, E. (2000) 'Anthropological conclusions of the study of Roman and Migration periods', *Acta Biologica Szegediensis*, 44: 87–94.

Gyenis, Gy. (2000) 'A short history and some results of the dermatoglyphic studies in Hungary', *Acta Biologica Szegediensis*, 44: 135–38.

Kocsis, S.G. (2000) 'Results of the paleostomatological researches', *Acta Biologica Szegediensis*, 44: 109–22.

Kordos, L. (2000) 'New results of Hominoid research in the Carpathian Basin', *Acta Biologica Szegediensis*, 44: 71–74.

Kósa, F. (2000) 'Application and role of anthropological research in the practice of forensic medicine', *Acta Biologica Szegediensis*, 44: 179–88.

Makra, Sz. (2007a) *A Magyar Természettudományi Múzeum Embertani Tárának leltározott szakanyaga (Inventorised anthropological material of the Department of Anthropology, Hungarian Natural History Museum)*, [CD-ROM: ISBN 978-963-9877-00-9], Budapest: Foundation of the Hungarian Natural History Museum.

——(2007b) *Anthropological collection of the Department of Anthropology, Hungarian Natural History Museum* [CD], Budapest: Foundation of the Hungarian Natural History Museum.

——(2009a) 'A Magyar Természettudományi Múzeum Embertani Tárában őrzött avar kori temetők leletkatalógusa' (Catalogue of the human remains coming from the Avar Period series, stored in the Department of Anthropology, Hungarian Natural History Museum), *Folia Anthropologica*, 8: 93–118.

——(2009b) 'A Magyar Természettudományi Múzeum Embertani Tárában őrzött, 2009-ig leltározott avar kori temetők leletkatalógusa' (Catalogue of the human remains from the Avar Period, inventoried until 2009, and stored in the Department of Anthropology, Hungarian Natural History Museum), unpublished manuscript, Hungarian Natural History Museum.

Makra, Sz. and Pap, I. (2006) 'The anthropological collections and the electronic registration in the Department of Anthropology, the Hungarian Natural History Museum', in Z. Újlaki Pongrácz (ed.) *16th Conference of the young researchers of the migration*. Available online at www.nhmus.hu/modules/Tar-Ember/pdf/makra-pap.pdf (accessed 6 April 2010).

Marcsik, A. and Pap, I. (2000) 'Paleopathological research in Hungary', *Acta Biologica Szegediensis*, 44: 103–08.

Merkl, O., Grabant, A., Makra, Sz., et al. (2008) 'Complete list of papers published in the Annales historico-naturales Musei nationalis hungarici between 1903 and 2007', *Annales historico-naturales Musei nationalis hungarici*, 100: 95–244. Available online at www.nhmus.hu/modules/Tar-Ember/pdf/merkl-grabant-makra-peregovits-soltesz.pdf (accessed 6 April 2010).

Mészáros, J., Mohácsi, J., Szabó, T., *et al.* (2000) 'Anthropometry and competitive sport in Hungary', *Acta Biologica Szegediensis*, 44: 189–92.

Nemeskéri, J. (1961) 'Fifteen years of the Anthropological Department of the Hungarian Natural History Museum (1945–60)', *Annales historico-naturales Musei nationalis hungarici*, 53: 615–39.

Pálfi, Gy., Pap, I. and Marcsik, A. (in press) 'A short history of paleopathological research in Hungary', in J.E. Buikstra and C. Roberts (eds) *History of Paleopathology*. Oxford University Press.

Pap, I. and Pálfi, Gy. (2009) 'A történeti embertani anyagok kezelését és elsődleges feldolgozását szabályozó egységes protokoll megteremtésének szükségessége, alkalmazási viszonyai és az azokkal kapcsolatos általános javaslatok', (necessity, practice and recommendations of standard historical anthropological protocol for regulation of recovery, curation, caring and anthropological investigations of the anthropological material, as well as relevant general recommendations), *Anthropológiai Közlemények*, 50: 101–4. Available online at www.nhmus.hu/modules.php?name=Tar-Ember&newlang=english (accessed 6 April 2010).

Pap, I., Fóthi, E., Józsa, L., *et al.* (2009) 'Történeti embertani protokoll – A régészeti feltárások embertani anyagainak kezelésére, alapszintű feldolgozására és elsődleges tudományos vizsgálatára (Historical Anthropological Protocol for recovery, curation, caring and preliminary anthropological investigations of the anthropological material deriving from archaeological excavation)', *Anthropológiai Közlemények*, 50: 105–23. Available online at www.nhmus.hu/modules.php?name=Tar-Ember&newlang=english (accessed 6 April 2010).

Pap, M. (2000) 'Population genetic research in Hungary', *Acta Biologica Szegediensis*, 44: 129–33.

Susa, É. (2000) 'Identification of Hungarian historical persons', *Acta Biologica Szegediensis*, 44: 175–78.

Szathmáry, L. (2000) 'Observations on anthropological research concerning the period of Hungarian conquest and Arpadian age', *Acta Biologica Szegediensis*, 44: 95–102.

Topinard, P. (1881) *Az anthropológia kézikönyve*. Trans. G. Petrovics and A. Török, Budapest: Királyi Magyar Természettudományi Társulat Kiadó, Természettudományi Könyvkiadó–Vállalat. 19. sorozat.

Tóth, T. (1971) 'Twenty-five years (1945–70) of the Anthropological Department Hungarian Natural History Museum', *Anthropologia hungarica*, 10: 5–10.

——(1981) 'The Anthropological Department in the history of Hungarian anthropology', *Anthropologia hungarica*, 17: 109–21.

——(1990) 'The beginning of modern trends in Hungarian anthropology. In memoriam of J. Nemeskéri (1914–89)', *Anthropologia hungarica*, 21: 5–10.

Visy, Zs. and Nagy, M. (eds) (2003) *Hungarian Archaeology at the Turn of the Millennium*. Budapest: Ministry of National Cultural Heritage and Teleky László Foundation. Available online at www.regeszet.org.hu/images/angol/a_000.pdf (accessed 6 Apr 2010).

Zoffmann, K.Zs. (2000) 'Anthropological sketch of the prehistoric population of the Carpathian Basin', *Acta Biologica Szegediensis*, 44: 75–79.

Iceland/Ísland

Guðný Zoëga and Hildur Gestsdóttir

INTRODUCTION: A BRIEF HISTORY AND CURRENT STATE OF PHYSICAL ANTHROPOLOGY IN ICELAND

Although the excavation and curation of archaeological human remains in Iceland can be traced back to the latter part of the 19th century (Gestsdóttir 2004), the origins of physical anthropological research in Iceland are usually considered as starting with the work of Jón Steffensen in the cemetery excavation at Skeljastaðir in south-western Iceland in 1939, which was the first large-scale systematic archaeological excavation of a Christian cemetery in Iceland (Steffensen 1943). Steffensen was a medical doctor and professor of anatomy and biophysics at the University of Iceland. All the analysis of archaeological skeletal remains recovered in Iceland between 1939 and Steffensen's death in 1991 were carried out by him. Steffensen published widely during his career, not only anthropological material, but also in medicine and history (Magnússon 1992). Although not trained in the field, he also took part in several of the burial excavations carried out during that period, including the rescue excavation of the cemetery associated with the Bishopric of Skálholt in 1954–58. His report of the skeletons there focused heavily on the identification of individuals, based not only on coffin inscriptions, but also on comparisons of crania to portraits and location within the cemetery (Steffensen 1988). This reflects the focus within early archaeological excavations in Iceland, which were frequently on the identification of individuals and locations mentioned in documentary sources, in particular the Icelandic Sagas.

Earlier publications prior to those written by Jón Steffensen on the analysis of archaeological skeletal remains do exist. In addition to brief comments on isolated skeletal finds by medical doctors, for example that by Guðmundur Björnsson on the skeletal remains from two Viking Age burials (Bruun 1903), the earliest physical anthropological analysis is Hooton's publication in the first issue of the *American Journal of Physical Anthropology* on the study of the mostly commingled human remains recovered by Vilhjálmur Stefánsson in 1905 at the early cemetery sites of Álftanes and Haffjarðarey in southern and western Iceland (Hooton 1918). However, Jón Steffensen's involvement in the excavation at Skeljastaðir marked the start of systematic analysis of archaeological skeletal remains in Iceland.

Iceland was first settled in the late ninth century AD, as supported by archaeological and documentary evidence (cf. Karlsson, 2001; Roberts *et al.* 2003), which means that it is the youngest settlement in Europe. Burials in Iceland are usually divided into two probably over-simplified groups: pre-Christian Viking inhumations and Christian inhumations. The Viking burials vary from single to multiple inhumations, dating from the latter part of the ninth century to the middle of the 11th century AD (Eldjárn 2000). The Christian cemeteries vary in size from small family or farm based plots to larger parish churches, and are frequently seen to be dated post AD 1000, which is the official date for the conversion of Icelanders to Christianity (Karlsson, 2001) – although recent excavations of earlier cemeteries indicate earlier dates for some of these Christian sites (Zoëga and Traustadóttir 2007).

Current state of physical anthropology

Prior to the 1990s all excavations of burials were rescue excavations, either because of erosion or due to development (Gestsdóttir 2004). This has changed in the past few decades with the advent of research excavations of both pre-Christian Viking burials and Christian cemeteries. Examples include the Viking-age boat burial from Litlu Núpar in Northern Iceland (Roberts 2009) and the cemetery associated with the mediaeval cloister at Skriðuklaustur in East Iceland (Kristjánsdóttir 2008).

Today the authors of this chapter are the only professional osteoarchaeologists working in Iceland. Our background is very similar, having started out with a degree in archaeology before specializing with a master's degree in osteoarchaeology. We are both currently working on our respective doctoral theses. There are also, however, visiting physical anthropologists who take part in specific projects, for example the late Dr Phillip Walker who was involved in the still-ongoing research excavations at the site of Hrísbrú in southern Iceland (Byock *et al.* 2005). Despite the small size of the discipline in Iceland, the research which is being carried out on Icelandic skeletal material today is however very diverse, including, for example: research on the cemetery associated with the hospital at Skriðuklaustur (Kristjánsdóttir 2008; Zoëga 2008; Pacciani 2006); the work on the trial excavations of cemeteries in Skaftártunga in southern Iceland to look at fluoride poisoning as a result of the catastrophic volcanic eruption of Laki in 1783–84 (Gestsdóttir *et al.* 2006; Stone 2004); and work on projects involving the palaeopathological analysis of curated material (Gestsdóttir in print), the palaeopathology of the hospital at Skriðuklaustur monastery (Zoëga 2007), strontium isotope analysis of dental enamel to study the colonization of Iceland (Price and Gestsdóttir 2006) and DNA analysis to study the genetic origin of Icelanders (Helgason *et al.* 2009).

Physical anthropology is taught as a partial Bachelor of Arts degree within the anthropology department at the University of Iceland, although the focus is not on the human skeleton but rather on human evolution and aDNA, and it does not include any archaeological approaches. There is a single undergraduate course in osteology taught in the archaeology department by author H.G. and a zooarchaeologist.

ARCHAEOLOGICAL HUMAN REMAINS AND LEGISLATION

Archaeological legislation

The current central authority dealing with archaeological remains is the Archaeological Heritage Agency of Iceland (Fornleifavernd ríkisins). The Agency is responsible for the protection of archaeological monuments and sites in Iceland and the issuing of permits for archaeological research (www.fornleifavernd.is/index.php?pid=55).

The Agency operates according to the current legislation relating to Icelandic archaeological heritage management, the National Heritage Act (þjóðminjalög) no. 107. The Act was passed by the Icelandic Parliament in 2001 and is currently under extensive revision and parliamentary review. Thus any discussion here is subject to possible change, although some changes introduced in the new laws are discussed.

HUMAN REMAINS AND LEGISLATION

Specific regulations regarding the excavation and treatment of human remains have not, as yet, been issued by the Agency. Any research involving the excavation of human archaeological remains falls under the general definition of archaeological excavations. Under the archaeological Heritage Act of 2001 the definition of archaeological remains is all surface and subsurface remains of ancient structures constructed or altered by man (þjóðminjalög no. 107/2001) if such remains are 100 years or older. The new heritage laws that are currently under review, however, define archaeological and artefactual remains as structures and artefacts dating before 1900. Younger remains can also be specifically protected. Individual graves and graveyards of both Pre-Christian and Christian origin are included in the list of protected archaeological sites included in the law's text. Human remains, however, are defined as artefacts and, as for archaeological remains, they have to be over 100 years old if they are to be protected by the laws.

Permits for excavation are only issued to experienced archaeologists who have submitted a suitable research plan with guaranteed funding. The excavator must also obtain a statement from the National Museum guaranteeing that all finds will be treated by its department of conservation; and finally a permit has to be obtained from the pertinent landowners. There are no specific instructions in place for the excavation of human bones and no formal recording forms to be used.

The laws for cemeteries, burial and cremation (No. 36 from 1993[1]) deal with the treatment and disposal of recent human remains and the commission and decommission of Christian cemeteries, most of which will be at least partly protected by the Heritage Act. According to the law, graves are guaranteed protection for 75 years,[2] after which the graves can be reused or granted further protection. However, graves are only protected under the Heritage Act of 2001 if they are 100 years or older. This leaves an awkward gap of 25 years where protection is not granted. All cemeteries that have been formally decommissioned, however, fall automatically under the protection of the heritage laws regardless of the age decree.

If human remains are encountered within a grave that is being dug in a functional cemetery, the bones are to be reburied in the same spot or, alternately, disposed of in a crematorium where applicable.[3] Outside of functional cemeteries, however, discovery of buried human remains are most frequently treated as an archaeological find upon discovery. The same can be said for partially exposed or eroded material, except in those cases, of course, where obvious signs of modernity can be observed. No legislation is in place which specifically states the protocol for the formal handling of such remains other than the aforementioned heritage laws where the Heritage Agency is supposed to be informed of any unexpected finds of archaeological remains. The remains are examined by a representative of the Heritage Agency and further excavation or treatment of the site is then decided upon. The presence of an osteologist is not required during an excavation or the subsequent handling of human skeletal remains. The skeletons are treated as finds and are to be handed over to the Heritage Agency and subsequently stored in the skeletal storage facility at the National Museum or other museums if adequate storage requirements are met. If there is any suspicion that it might be more recent than the required 100 years, the find is reported to the police, but as a rule the police are not notified of perceived archaeological skeletal finds.

The definition of 'forensic' *vs.* 'archaeological' remains can be interpreted on the borderline of 100 years, although under future heritage legislation forensic criteria would be extended to any remains dating after 1900. For forensic purposes there is a formal ID committee commissioned by the Ministry of Justice and Ecclesiastical affairs. The committee does not include a forensic anthropologist or a trained osteologist. In a regulation pertaining to the ID committee from March 2009 it is stated that Chief of Police have a duty to report to the National Commissioner of the Icelandic police if the remains of an unknown body have been found.[4] This regulation does not specify the treatment of a possible archaeological find but it seems to refer to discernibly more recent remains, victims of accidents or natural disasters.

The exportation of human skeletal material is controlled by the Museum Council of Iceland under the current laws of exportation of cultural material to other countries (No. 105/2001). In order for such materials to be exported for research purposes an application has to be made to the Council, which will view the application in light of its working policies. In order to obtain a permit, one has to submit information on who is responsible for the exportation, a detailed description of the material in question, how it is going to be transported, who will be responsible for it abroad and when and how the material will be coming back into the country. The permits are granted for one year.[5] To our knowledge, there have been few instances of major transportation of skeletal material in recent years, but any samples taken for scientific analysis such as AMS dating and DNA analysis are subject to the same application process.

Ethical considerations

There are no specific Icelandic laws or codes of ethics dealing specifically with the treatment of archaeological skeletal material, but the treatment of skeletons encountered in cemeteries still in use has already been discussed above. Archaeologists are also bound by the ethical code set by the Association of Icelandic Archaeologists on the professional treatment of archaeological materials and publication. As with all other archaeological materials, skeletons are ultimately stored in museum storage facilities, and their treatment falls under the various sections dealing with culturally sensitive material in the Code of Ethics for Museums agreed upon by the International Committee of Museums (ICOM).[6]

As stated before, throughout the 1100 years of Icelandic history there have only been two major religions with associated burial contexts: Pre-Christian pagan religion and Christianity. These were practised to a great extent by the same people, as opposed to separating them into two distinct religious communities. The old Nordic pagan religion was superseded by Christianity by a universal decree around the year 1000 AD, and has remained the dominant religion until the present day. Both religions, however, are practised in the country today. Modern day Icelanders are, for the most part, descended from the earliest settlers and are, as such, a fairly homogenous group in terms of both genetic makeup and religious background. There has been limited discussion on the ethics of human bone excavation and research outside the archaeological community, and in general such research is favourably viewed and although alternate views can be found, they tend to be of a more personal individual nature as opposed to a more systematic opposition. This may, to some extent, be attributed to a fairly liberal view of religion and religious practices, but also partly due to the inherent Icelandic interest in family lineages and personal history. A part of the explanation may also be that as a small, close knit society spread out over a large island with a short history of urbanization, a fair number of people have come in contact with human bones or followed media stories of such finds, for instance through agricultural work or road construction. Archaeology also tends to be fairly well reported in the national media, especially during the summer months.

METHODS OF ANTHROPOLOGICAL ANALYSIS

As already stated, the field of osteoarchaeolgy in Iceland is far too small for any nationwide approach to analysis to be considered, and there has been no work in the way of developing specific Icelandic standards. This is caused by the small size of the field, as well as the type of collections available, as most of them are no larger than around 30 to 70 skeletons, i.e., not large enough to use to develop standards. The small size of the field has also meant that frequent collaborations with specialists from other fields in Iceland and abroad are set up – medical doctors, geneticists and geologists; which means that the emphasis from these disciplines can be seen in the work carried out within the field.

There is no specific legislation on how to deal with archaeological skeletal remains; they are classed as artefacts, and so the methodology used during excavation and analysis is decided on by the individual undertaking the work. The basic osteological analysis carried out in Iceland tends to follow the standards presented by Buikstra and Ubelaker (1994). Stature is calculated by applying the methods of Trotter and Gleser (see, e.g., Trotter and Gleser 1958) to long bone measurements.

The central database of human skeletal remains, which is housed at the National Museum, contains all excavated human remains in Iceland, whether they are curated in the National Museum or not. The database is also based on the *Standards* of Buikstra and Ubelaker (1994). There are approximately 1000 skeleton numbers recorded in the National Museum database, although more detailed information is required to identify these numbers, as either complete skeletons, skeletal fragments or commingled skeletal remains are likely to be present.

CONCLUSION

The field of osteology is small in Iceland, and osteological research tends to be a multi-disciplinary approach. Human remains considered as forensic fall under a specific set of regulations, but no official distinction exists of what constitute forensic human remains. In general, any human remains deemed to be a 100 years old or less fall into the category of forensic. At the time of writing this article (2009) there are no specific laws or regulations regarding ancient human remains or their handling, but the law environment is currently undergoing considerable revision and is subject to major change in the near future.

USEFUL CONTACTS

The National Museum of Iceland (þjóðminjasafn Íslands), Suðurgata 41, 101 Reykjavík, Iceland. Tel: +354–5302200. Website: www.natmus.is/

The Archaeological Heritage Agency of Iceland (Fornleifavernd ríkisins), Suðurgata 39, 101 Reykjavík, Iceland. Tel: +354–5556630. Website: www.fornleifavernd.is/

Hildur Gestsdóttir, Institute of Archaeology, Bárugata 3, 101 Reykjavík, Iceland. Tel: +354–5511033.

Guðný Zoëga, Fornleifadeild Byggðasafns Skagfirðinga ('Skagafjordur Heritage Museum'), Minjahúsinu, Aðalgötu16b, Pósthólf 57, 550 Sauðárkrókur. Tel: +352–453 5097.

NOTES

1 See www.althingi.is/lagas/nuna/1993036.html (accessed 23 May 2009).

2 See article 29 of the cemetery laws, available online at www.althingi.is/lagas/nuna/1993036.html (accessed 23 May 2009).

3 See the 24th article of the Heritage Act, available online at www.althingi.is/lagas/136a/2001107.html (accessed 25 May 2009).
4 See www.reglugerd.is/interpro/dkm/WebGuard.nsf/printview/0ca4a4f88e4cae8a00257598005c49b4? OpenDocument (accessed 23 May 2009).
5 See www.safnarad.is/utflutningur_menningarverdmaeta/umsoknir_um_leyfi_til_utflutnings_menningarver dmaeta/ (accessed 23 May 2009).
6 See sections 2.5, 3.7 and 4.3 of the ICOM Code of Ethics for Museums, available online at http://icom.museum/ethics.html (acccessed 2 June 2009).

BIBLIOGRAPHY

Buikstra, J.E. and Ubelaker D.H. (eds) (1994) *Standards for Data Collection from Human Skeletal Remains*, Fayetteville, AR: Arkansas Archaeological Survey Research Series No.44.
Bruun, D. (1903) 'Nokkrar dysjar frá heiðni', *Árbók Hins íslenkzka fornleifafélags* (1903): 17–30.
Byock, J., Walker, P., Erlandsson, J., et al. (2005) 'A Viking Age Valley in Iceland: The Mosfell Archaeological Project', *Medieval Archaeology*, XLIX: 194–218.
Eldjárn, E. (2000) *Kuml og haugfé*, 2nd edn, Reykjavík: Mál og menning.
Gestsdóttir, H. (2004) 'Mannabein í þúsund ár', in Björnsson, Á. and Róbertsdóttir, H. (eds) *Hlutavelta tímans*, Reykjavík: National Museum of Iceland.
——(2009) 'Sögur af beinagrindum', *Árbók Hins íslenzka fornleifafélags* (2008–2009): 123–141.
Gestsdóttir, H., Baxter, P. and Gísladóttir, G.A. (2006) *Fluorine poisoning in victims of the 1783–84 eruption of the Laki fissure, Iceland*, Reykjavík: Reports of the Institute of Archaeology.
Helgason, A., Lalueza-Fox, C., Ghosh, S., et al. (2009) 'Sequences from first settlers reveal rapid evolution in Icelandic mtDNA Pool', *PloS Genetics*, 1: 1–10.
Hooton, E.A. (1918) 'On certain Eskimoid characters in Icelandic skulls', *American Journal of Physical Anthropology*, 1: 53–76.
Karlsson, G. (2001) *Iceland's 1100 Years*, London: Hurst and Company.
Kristjánsdóttir, S. (2008) *Skriðuklaustur: evrópskt miðaldaklaustur í Fljótsdal*, Skriðuklaustur: Gunnarsstofnun.
Magnússon, þ. (1992) 'Prófessor Jón Steffensen. Minningarorð', *Árbók Hins íslenzka fornleifafélags* (1991): 5–10.
Pacciani, E. (2006) 'Anthropological description of skeletons from graves no. 4, 62,63,65,66,67 and 68 at Skriðuklaustur Monastery', in Skriðuklaustursrannsókna, S. (ed.) *Steinunn Kristjánsdóttir*, Reykjavík: Skriðuklaustursrannsóknir.
Price, T.D. and Gestsdóttir, H. (2006) 'The first settlers of Iceland: an isotopic approach to colonisation', *Antiquity*, 80: 130–44.
Roberts, H.M. (2009) 'Journey to the dead. The Litlu-Núpar boat burial', *Current World Archaeology*, 32: 36–41.
Roberts, H.M, Snæsdóttir, M., Mehler, N., et al. (2003) 'Skáli frá Víkingaöld í Reykjavík', *Árbók Hins íslenzka fornleifafélags* (2000–2001): 219–34.
Steffensen, J. (1943) 'Knoglerne fra Skeljastaðir i þjórsárdalur', in M. Stenberger (ed.) *Forntida gårdar i Island*, Copenhagen: Ejnar Munksgaard.
——(1975) *Menning og meinsemdir*, Reykjavík: Ísafoldarprentsmiðja.
——(1988) 'Líkamsleifar', in K. Eldjárn, H. Christie and J. Steffensen (eds) *Skálholt. Fornleifarannsóknir 1954–1958*, Reykjavík: Lögberg.
Stone, R. (2004) 'Iceland's Doomesday scenario?', *Science*, 306: 1278–81.
Trotter, M. and Gleser, G.C. (1958) 'A re-evaluation of estimation of stature based on measurements of stature taken during life and of long bones after death', *American Journal of Physical Anthropology*, 16: 79–123.
Zoëga, G. and Traustadóttir, R. (2007) 'Keldudalur – a sacred place in Pagan and Christian times in Iceland', in U. Fransson, M. Svedin, S. Bergerbrant, et al. (eds) *Cultural Interaction Between East and West: Archaeology and Human Contacts in Northern Europe*, Stockholm: Stockholms universitet.
Zoëga, G. (2007) *Fornmeinafræðileg greining fimm beinagrinda frá klausturkirkjugarðinum á Skriðu*, Research reports of the Skagafjörður Heritage Museum 2007/61, Skagafjörður: Skagafjörður Heritage Museum.
——(2008) 'Sjúkdómar á miðöldum', in H. Lárusson and S. Kristjándóttir (eds) *Skriðuklaustur evrópskt miðaldaklaustur í Fljótsdal. Greinasafn Skriðuklaustursrannsókna*, Skriðuklaustur: Gunnarsstofnun.

Atlantic Ocean

NORTHERN IRELAND

IRELAND

Galway

Dublin

Dún Laoghaire

Irish Sea

Limerick

Cork

0   100km

Ireland/Éire

Laureen Buckley

INTRODUCTION: A BRIEF HISTORY AND CURRENT STATE OF PHYSICAL ANTHROPOLOGY IN IRELAND

Anthropological studies in Ireland have a relatively short history. Prior to 1985 only two studies of large groups of skeletal human remains had been carried out. These studies – Howells's (1941) analysis of 200 Early Christian and Mediaeval burials from Gallen Priory, Co. Offaly, and McLoughlin's (1938) study of 372 Early Christian burials from Castleknock, Co. Dublin, concentrated mainly on metrical analysis and morphological traits of the skull. There are detailed skull and long bone measurements presented, along with various skeletal indices. The Castleknock report in particular deals with groups of individual bones rather than individual skeletons. The report on Gallen Priory places a lot of emphasis on skull types, although data for dental pathology is also given. A large part of the discussion of the reports concentrates on the racial origins of the population. Palaeopathology was barely mentioned, but age and sex ratio of the populations were provided.

From the 1950s onwards skeletal reports consisted mainly of short statements by Professors of Anatomy appended to the archaeological report, listing the number of individuals, their age and sex. Archaeologists assumed that this was all that could be done with human remains, and took little interest in them. The remains of humans from past populations were not considered part of the archaeology. In fact, until the late 1980s, when skeletons were found they were generally considered to interfere with the archaeology.

The potential of human skeletal studies was highlighted at a meeting of the Association of Young Irish Archaeologists in 1972 (Scott 1973) at which Dr Maura Delaney gave a paper on the subject. This aroused the interest of archaeologists and resulted in a detailed study of 88 skeletons from Tintern Abbey, Co. Wexford (O'Donnabháin 1985). This was the first major skeletal report from Ireland with a detailed analysis of human burials covering demography, dentition, palaeopathology, etc.

Since that time several reports for the assemblages from individual sites have been produced. A talk to the Irish Association of Professional Archaeologists (now the Institute of Archaeologists of Ireland) by the present author in 1996 emphasized the need for osteoarchaeologist involvement at an early stage in the excavation process. Over a period of time the presence of at least one if not more osteoarchaeologists on cemetery excavations, or even

211

excavations where only one or two skeletons were found, became the norm. A detailed skeletal report also became standard, although the upsurge in infrastructure development in Ireland from the 1990s onwards meant that there was too much work to cope with for the few osteoarchaeologists working and there was little time for research or an overall assessment of the various individual reports produced. In fact, to date, the only review of the data was carried out by Power in 1993 using published data to attempt to reconstruct the health of Irish prehistoric populations. The amount of skeletal material and data from the analysis has increased tremendously since then, but as yet it has not been synthesized, although some effort was made to include Irish data in Roberts and Cox's (2003) work on Health and Disease in Britain. The National Roads Authority was established in 1993 and came into effect in 1994 as Ireland was about to embark on a widespread and ambitious programme of infrastructural road building. This meant the development of large tracts of land, all of which had to be assessed for archaeology with excavations carried out where necessary. This generated a lot of work for osteoarchaeologists both on site and in the post-excavation analysis. All the newly qualified osteoarchaeologists had almost full employment for a number of years; however, it was felt that research in the bioarchaeology field was lacking at this stage. In particular there was very little interest in or analysis of post-mediaeval remains, including those from the famine period, 1845–49, and 19th-century crypt burials. Most of the short reports published between the 1950s and the 1980s concentrated on prehistoric burials or early mediaeval burials.

In 1999 the Heritage Council of Ireland, at the request of the National Museum of Ireland, commissioned a report on all aspects of human remains. The report, published in 2002, examined all the issues concerned with burial archaeology, including ethical and legal issues, and consulted widely with different sections of the community, including archaeologists, osteoarchaeologists, institutions such as the National Museum of Ireland, and representatives of the main churches (O'Sullivan *et al.* 2002). An important point raised in the report was the shortage of osteoarchaeologists at that time, and the lack of osteoarchaeological training in Ireland. Most individuals with this career in mind followed structured courses mainly at British universities, although it was possible to carry out independent research in the field at Irish universities. In 2001 the first post in the field of bioarchaeology had been established at University College, Cork (UCC) when Barra O'Donnabháin was appointed. Since 2004 Dr O'Donnabháin has been running a taught master's course in bioarchaeology, with his students carrying out a small research project as part of the course. Research projects are also carried out at Queen's University Belfast (QUB) under the supervision of Dr Eileen Murphy, senior lecturer in osteoarchaeology. Osteoarchaeology forms part of the BSc and BSc (Hons) in Applied Archaeology at the Institute of Technology, Sligo.

Research

The NRA also started an ambitious plan of research associated with QUB and the Institute of Technology, Sligo. Instead of a normal bone report depending on one person's observations it was possible to have a multi-disciplined research team. This was the start of serious programmes of research in this field in Ireland. The research is centred on a large population of 1300 individuals from the Mediaeval period. This is all funded by the NRA and has provided studentships for a Master's degree and PhD research. Already there are plans to take the research further, influenced by the results of the initial study (McCarthy 2009).

The downturn in economic fortunes at the end of 2007 meant severe cutbacks in development generally, including road building. This meant widespread job losses in archaeology, including in osteoarchaeology. However, a setback can be seen as a new opportunity and osteoarchaeologists with years of practical experience are now using this as an opportunity to carry out doctoral and post-doctoral research. Jonny Geber at QUB is examining famine period burials, a neglected area of research in Ireland. At UCC Linda Lynch is also carrying out extensive research on post-mediaeval burials. There are also several PhD projects ongoing at UCC on mediaeval and post-mediaeval Irish populations, and University College Dublin (UCD) has also expanded its doctoral research area to include bioarchaeology. Parallel to this, the Heritage Council has provided funding through its INSTAR (Irish National Strategic Targeted Archaeological Research) programme for work on a synthesis of information gathered over the years on prehistoric populations. After years of generating data from basic bone reports, this era is giving us all a chance to think about the information, to write overviews of the past populations in Ireland, and to extend research to attempt to answer the questions generated.

Professional associations

To provide a forum for the growing number of osteoarchaeologists, the Irish Association for Professional Osteoarchaeologists (IAPO) was set up in 2006. The aim was to provide seminars and discussion opportunities for any osteoarchaeologist of any nationality in Ireland, whether they were employed in the development sector, academics, or students.

ARCHAEOLOGICAL HUMAN REMAINS AND LEGISLATION

Archaeological legislation

Archaeological excavation in Ireland is covered by the National Monuments Acts (1930–94). Without going into too much detail, this means that all archaeological excavation has to be licensed to qualified archaeologists only. The licensing system is carried out by the Department of Environment, Heritage and Local Government (DoEH&LG), which consults the National Museum of Ireland regarding licence applications. Since the mid-1990s a system of first-time licence interviews has been in operation. Applicants who have the appropriate field experience up to supervisor or assistant director level are requested to present themselves to a panel and face questions that cover their ability to assess terrain, testing procedures, excavation procedures, artefact identification, archaeological interpretation and knowledge of specialists and specialist techniques. The interview panel consists of representatives from DOEH&LG as well as the National Museum of Ireland and a non-archaeological administrator. Candidates who do not meet the standard required are given a letter advising them of areas where they need to do more training or reading. The interview can be re-taken as many times as necessary. The successful applicants must apply for a licence for each site they want to excavate. This has to be accompanied by a method statement and an undertaking that sufficient funds have been secured for the excavation and all post-excavation works necessary. Under Section 26 of the 1930 National Monument Act, as amended in 1994, the minister of DOEH&LG is required to consult the director of the NMI before making a decision. The excavation licence number is then issued by the DOEH&LG. These authorities can visit the excavations at any time to inspect the work, health and safety arrangements, and the security of the site archive. Standard licence conditions require that a preliminary report be sent to both DOEH&LG and the National Museum within six weeks of the finish of the excavation.

HUMAN REMAINS AND LEGISLATION

Discovery of human remains

The discovery of human remains is governed by the Coroner's Act 1962. While archaeological remains are not specifically covered in this Act, it is within Common Law tradition that the coroner has legal possession of remains until their archaeological context is established. It was recommended by O'Sullivan *et al.* (2002), following an opinion given by Dr Brian Farrell, Dublin City Coroner, that, wherever human remains are found, even on a known burial ground or archaeological site, they should be reported to the coroner. A new Coroner's Bill has been prepared, although it has not been enacted yet. This will specify further the circumstances in which remains must be reported. There is a coroner for each of the 26 counties in the Republic of Ireland, with the larger counties having two or more coroners. Although the phone numbers of the coroners are available in the telephone directory under the Department of Justice, in practice it is usually easier to telephone the Gardai (the police) and ask them to inform the coroner. The coroner has to satisfy himself that the remains are ancient and not of recent origin. Individual coroners take action as they see fit. If the remains are found in the course of a licensed archaeological excavation, the coroner may canvass the opinion of the archaeologist on whether the bones are ancient, or will ask the Gardai to visit the site and ascertain whether the remains warrant investigation. Once it has been established to the satisfaction of the coroner that the remains are ancient and not of forensic interest, responsibility reverts to the archaeological authorities, The National Museum of Ireland and DOEH&LG. Statutory procedures for dealing with ancient human remains come under the terms of the National Monuments Acts (1930–94). As ancient remains are archaeological objects within the meaning of the Acts, the discovery of ancient human remains must be reported as soon as possible to the National Museum of Ireland. Archaeological objects found in the course of a licensed archaeological excavation are exempt from this requirement, although the conditions covering the excavation licence would require preparation of a report on the excavation. In practice many archaeologists report unusual finds, including human remains, to the National Museum of Ireland during the course of an excavation. The method statement is adjusted if necessary, an osteoarchaeologist, if not already present, is consulted, and excavation proceeds under the archaeological licence. The discovery of large numbers of skeletons may make a developer rethink and modify his plans in consultation with DOEH&LG, so as to avoid them if possible. Indeed it is the written policy, *Framework and Principles for the Protection of the Archaeological Heritage* (DAHGI 1999), of DOEH&LG to recommend preservation 'in situ' for all archaeological material, including skeletal material, where possible.

Single burials or unexpected burials are often found, not as a result of archaeological excavation, but as a result of natural forces, e.g., a storm or high tide suddenly eroding a sand dune on the coast or, as frequently happens, landscaping work carried out privately. These might well herald the discovery of a new archaeological site, but the coroner will inform the Office of the State Pathologist and request that they investigate. The pathologist may visit the scene or consult with an experienced osteoarchaeologist or anthropologist. If the burials are established as ancient, then the National Museum is informed. The National Museum will then decide how to proceed.

At the time of writing, new legislation has been proposed to replace the National Monuments Acts, and this includes clarifying the role of the coroner in dealing with human remains of archaeological interest. It may be some years before this comes to fruition and the Act comes into law.

Excavation of human remains

There is no special licence for the excavation of human remains. This is because human remains are defined as archaeological objects under the National Monuments Acts, and as such only require an archaeological excavation licence. However, before a licence is granted, a method statement must be agreed with DOEH&LG as well as with the National Museum of Ireland. There is also an undertaking on the licence application that the services of an osteoarchaeologist will be used if human remains are found, and the osteoarchaeologist has to be named on the application. To avoid the problem of osteoarchaeologists being named without their knowledge, an agreement in writing from the named osteoarchaeologist should be included with the licence application. However, this is not a statutory requirement.

In Ireland there are no ethnic groups that must be consulted prior to the excavation of human remains. The Heritage Council report found, after wide consultation, that the general public supported archaeology, including the excavation and analysis of human remains. However, it is expected that all individuals working with human remains will show them the utmost respect and dignity. Under the National Monuments Act 1994 and the National Cultural Institutions Act 1997, the final deposition of human remains is at the discretion of the National Museum of Ireland. Preference is for permanent curation as recommended by the Heritage Council, but consultation with local communities is also a strong consideration. The policy of the National Museum is to treat each case on its merits, and if there is strong local interest the Museum will consider the option of reburial.

Transport of human remains

The guidelines for the transport of human skeletal remains have been outlined by the IAI and, although they are voluntary, they again concentrate on respect for the remains and their safekeeping. Transport of skeletal remains abroad is subject to the agreement of the National Museum, and requires a 'licence to export an archaeological object' which is only issued by the National Museum. The Museum will issue transport conditions, but will usually require that the remains are brought back within a specified period.

Remains that include flesh usually require transport in exhumation coffins or, for smaller body parts, transportation in bio-transport containers.

Exhumation

Exhumation is generally reserved for recent remains, known individuals, or remains where soft tissue is likely to be present. A special exhumation order is required from the local county council. The local Director of Community Care and Medical Officer of Health must issue a certificate to say that the exhumation can be carried out without danger to public health or breach of public decency, but it is the local council that gives or rejects the request for the exhumation. Sometimes this is required if a recent cemetery has to be cleared or if the remains are of a known individual. A usual requirement is that the remains are reburied or cremated within 48 hours of the exhumation. Some sites will require a combination of exhumation order and archaeological licence, and O'Sullivan and Killgore (2003) advise caution and applying for an exhumation order if work is being carried out on Church grounds and there is the slightest possibility of disturbing recent remains. Exhumation is covered by Section 4 of the Local Government (Sanitary Services) Act 1948, as amended by Section 4 (2) and the Second Schedule of the Local Government Act 1994.

Anthropological analysis and sampling of human skeletal remains

Any test on archaeological objects that requires the modification, total or partial destruction of the objects necessitates further licensing from the National Museum. As human remains are archaeological objects, they will require a 'licence to alter' if any destructive test is to be carried out. This includes the taking of samples for radiocarbon dating of ancient bone, isotope analysis, scanning electron microscopy or any other test not yet devised. Furthermore, if the tests are to be carried out outside Ireland, then a 'licence to export' must also be applied for. Samples taken to Northern Ireland require an export licence. The National Museum requires that the results of scientific tests are reported to them and a copy is placed on file.

METHODS OF ANTHROPOLOGICAL ANALYSIS

Anthropological methods for the excavation of human skeletal remains

Guidelines for the excavation of archaeological remains have been issued by the National Monuments Service which was part of the Department of Arts, Heritage, Gaeltacht and Islands (DAGHI) in 1999. Also in 1999 the human remains sub-committee of the Irish Association of Professional Archaeologists produced guidelines for the excavation, handling, storage and analysis of human remains (Buckley *et al.* 1999). When this body became the Institute of Archaeologists of Ireland (IAI), these guidelines were incorporated into the Institute's codes of conduct for the excavation of human remains. The codes of conduct are available from the IAI website.

The Heritage council report in 2002 gives recommendations for the analysis and presentation of osteoarchaeological reports. However, it also stated that this was already occurring in published reports. To briefly summarize, a report should give an introduction which includes excavation details, archaeological summary, preservation and mode of interment of the remains and a statement of the aims of the report. The methods used should be outlined and the results should include demographic data, metric and non-metric data, skeletal anomalies and pathological conditions. The report should be accompanied by a catalogue of the burials.

Anthropological analysis in the laboratory

Osteoarchaeologists in Ireland follow the methods in *Standards* (Buikstra and Ubelaker 1994) for sexing and ageing individual skeletons. The Irish Association of Professional Osteoarchaeologists (IAPO) has produced a simplified recording sheet to try to standardize the recording of skeletal material in Ireland. The list of measurements to be taken and non-metric traits to be recorded is shorter than that given in *Standards*, but it was thought that those listed were the least ambiguous, and inter-observer error would be at a minimum. *Standards* was influenced by the fact that most skeletons excavated in America have to be reburied by law. Different circumstances exist in Ireland where, at the moment, almost every skeleton is retained by the National Museum. However, if there is a request or possibility that skeletons would be reburied, then more detailed recording than the IAPO form would be required.

Publication

Publication of skeletal reports in Ireland is still variable. There appeared to be a change in the mid-1990s when joint publications between osteoarchaeologist and archaeologist appeared, giving prominence to the skeletal remains from the excavation (Halpin and Buckley 1995).

However, these turned out to be rarities and skeletal reports were designated to appendices once more. Although the appendices will usually consist of the full skeletal report, in some instances only a summary of the report is published. It is not unknown for appendices to consist of a CD in the back of the publication. In one case the skeletal report was only available as a download from the publisher (Marshall and Walsh 2005). On the positive side, publication of full site reports including all the specialists reports as individual books are becoming more common in recent years. The NRA is a regular publisher of archaeological reports based on excavation work carried out in the previous year. Recently a number of themed publications have been produced by various authors and academics as well as the NRA. These include skeletal reports and discussions of the social context (Fibiger, 2008, Fibiger *et al.* 2008). Interesting case studies on palaeopathology are usually either published in *Archaeology Ireland* or the *Palaeopathology Association Irish Section Newsletter*. This newsletter was first published in 2000, with two issues in the first year and one issue each year thereafter. The newsletter also provides information on research or finished theses at universities and colleges, completed skeletal analysis arising from development, and recent publications.

Databases

Every year a record of excavation licences issued and summary reports of the excavations are published in the *Excavations Bulletin*, edited by Isobel Bennett. The publication is funded by DOEH& LG and, while it is not a statutory requirement to produce a summary report, it can lead to the refusal of an excavation licence if directors do not keep up to date with their reports. The excavations are organized by county, and there is no separate category for sites containing human remains, although this was a recommendation of the Heritage Council's 2002 report. However, a search through this publication, which is now available on-line, will discover those sites with human remains. The NRA's website also has a database of excavated sites, but this only includes those funded by the NRA. A search of the database will provide details of sites that contained human remains.

Recently the heritage council has funded a number of projects with the intention of producing overviews and knowledge from the vast amount of data derived from various archaeological excavations carried out during the 'Celtic Tiger' boom years. Some of these projects relate to human remains, and one of the beneficiaries is the People of Prehistoric Ireland project. This project is not yet complete, but will include a searchable database for skeletal sites by period and area of the country.

CONCLUSION

The National Museum of Ireland has always had a policy of allowing research on its collections, including the skeletal collections. Various research projects on material in their care have been carried out over the years. Recently, with the help of the Heritage Council, the Museum has undertaken a project to ensure that all their past burial excavations are published (Cahill and Sikora in press) with a full skeletal analysis of the material (Buckley in press). As well as skeletal remains, the National Museum has a collection of bog bodies. In the last few years the Museum has undertaken a large research project on Iron Age bog bodies. This project involved several international specialists with all possible aspects of analysis addressed, including environmental analysis, pathology, isotope analysis, and the examination of hairstyles and finger prints. This research will shortly be published in a monograph. The future of bioarchaeology in Ireland looks exciting.

ACKNOWLEDGEMENTS

The author wishes to gratefully acknowledge, with thanks, the help of Mr Sean Kirwan of DOEH&LG, for reading and advising on legal technicalities in this publication.

USEFUL CONTACTS AND ADDRESSES

Institutions

The National Museum of Ireland, Kildare Street, Dublin 2 (queries and correspondence to be addressed to the Duty Officer). Website: www.museum.ie/
National Monuments Service, Department of Environment Heritage and Local Government, The Customs House, Dublin 1. Website: www.environ.ie/
The Heritage Council of Ireland, Aras na hOldhreachta, Church Lane, Kilkenny. Website: www.heritagecouncil.ie/
Institute of Archaeologists of Ireland, Merrion Square, Dublin 2. Website: www.iaireland.ie/
National Roads Authority, St Martin's House, Waterloo Road, Dublin 4. Website: www.nra.ie/archaeology/

Colleges

The Queen's University Belfast, University Road, Belfast BT7 1NN. Website: www.qub.ac.uk/
Institute of Technology, Ash Lane, Sligo. Website: www.itsligo.ie/
Department of Archaeology, Connolly Building, University College Cork. Website: www.ucc.ie/
University College Dublin, Bellfield Campus, Dublin 4. Website: www.ucd.ie/
University College Galway. Website: www.ucg.ie/
People of Prehistoric Ireland project. Website: www.qub.ac.uk/sites/INSTARpeopleofprehisto ricIreland/

FURTHER READING

Major publications

Excavations Bulletin. A yearly publication with summary results of all the licensed excavations in Ireland, even where no archaeology was found. The most recent publication is I. Bennet, '*Excavations 2005: Summary accounts of archaeological excavations in Ireland*', Dublin: Wordwell (2008). Available online at www.excavations.ie/
The Journal of Irish Archaeology. The journal of the Institute of Archaeologists of Ireland, produced yearly. It contains very useful overview articles on all aspects of Irish Archaeology.
Archaeology Ireland. A quarterly magazine designed to give quick access to results. Content varies from news of new sites with limited reports, overviews of certain monument or site types, interesting osteoarchaeology articles, and news of conferences and book reviews.
NRA publications. These are produced yearly, based on the previous year's conferences, and are designed to give a narrative version of sites excavated rather than full site reports and plans. Photographs are usually to an excellent standard.
Mediaeval Dublin Series. Volumes in this series (at volume IX at the time of writing: Duffy 2008) often include full archaeological reports on excavations that have taken place in the city of Dublin.

There is useful content of historical papers also. Reports on human skeletal remains have occasionally been published, either individually or as part of archaeological reports (Buckley 2003; Coughlan 2003).

Themed books

Underworld: Death and Burial in Cloghermore Cave, Co. Kerry, by M. Connolly, F. Coyne, and L.G. Lynch, Dublin: Wordwell (2005).
The Archaeology of Life and Death in the Boyne Floodplain: The linear landscape of the M4, by N. Carlin, L. Clarke and F. Walsh, NRA Scheme Monographs 2, Dublin: The National Roads Authority (2008).
Deviant Burial in the Archaeological Record, by E. Murphy, Oxford: Oxbow (2008).

BIBLIOGRAPHY

Buckley, L.A. (2003) 'Health status in Medieval Dublin: analysis of the skeletal remains from the Abbey of St. Thomas the Martyr', in S. Duffy (ed.) *Medieval Dublin IV,* Dublin: Four Courts Press.
——(in press) 'Chapter 8, General Survey of the Osteoarchaeology' in M. Cahill and M. Sikora (eds) *Breaking Ground, Finding Graves – Reports on excavation of burial by the National Museum of Ireland 1927–2009,* Dublin: Wordwell.
Buckley, L.A., Murphy, E. and Donnabhin, B. (1999) *Irish Association for Professional Archaeologists Technical paper No 1: The Treatment of Human Remains,* Dublin: IAPA.
Buikstra, J.E. and Ubelaker, D.H. (eds) (1994) *Standards for Data Collection from Human Skeletal Remains,* Fayetteville, AR: Arkansas Archaeological Survey Research Series No. 44.
Cahill, M. and Sikora, M. (in press) *Breaking Ground, Finding Graves – Reports on excavation of burial by the National Museum of Ireland 1927–2009,* Dublin: Wordwell.
Coughlan, T. (2003) 'Excavations at the medieval cemetery of St. Peter's Church, Dublin', in S. Duffy (ed.) *Medieval Dublin IV,* Dublin: Four Courts Press.
Delaney, M. (1974) 'The Examination of Bone from an Archaeological Viewpoint' in B. Scott (ed.) *Perspectives in Irish* Archaeology, Belfast: Association of Young Irish Archaeologists.
Duffy, S. (ed.) (2003) *Medieval Dublin IV,* Dublin: Four Courts Press.
——(ed.) (2008) *Medieval Dublin IX,* Dublin: Four Courts Press.
Fibiger, L. (2008) 'Human skeletal remains', in N.L. Carlin, L. Clarke and F. Walsh, '*The archaeology of life and death in the Boyne floodplain*', CD Appendix, Dublin: NRA.
Fibiger, L., Carlin, N. and Kinsella, J. (2008) 'The social and economic context of the enclosures', in N.L. Carlin, L. Clarke and F. Walsh, '*The archaeology of life and death in the Boyne floodplain*', Dublin: NRA.
Halpin, A. and Buckley, L.A. (1995) 'The Dominican Priory, Drogheda, Co. Louth', *Proceedings of the Royal Irish Academy,* 95C: 5–252.
Howells, W.W. (1941) 'The Early Christian Irish: the skeletons at Gallen Priory', *Proceedings of the Royal Irish Academy,* XLVIC: 103–219.
McCarthy, D. (2009) 'Ballyhanna Research Project 2009 update', *Seanda,* 4: 22–27.
McLoughlin, E.P. (1938) *Castleknock Skeletal Material,* Dublin: Stationery Office.
Marshall, J.W. and Walsh, C. (2005) *Illaunloughan Island. An Early Medieval Monastery in County Kerry,* Dublin: Wordwell.
O'Donnabháin, J.F. (1985) 'A study of the human remains from Tintern Abbey, Co. Wexford', unpublished MA thesis, National University of Ireland.
O'Sullivan, J., Hallissey, M. and Roberts, J. (2002) *Human Remains in Irish Archaeology. Legal, Scientific, Planning and Ethical Implications,* Kilkenny: The Heritage Council of Ireland.
O'Sullivan, J. and Killgore, J. (2003) *Human Remains in Archaeology,* Kilkenny: The Heritage Council of Ireland.
Power, C. (1993) 'Reconstructing patterns of health and dietary change in Irish prehistoric populations', *Ulster Journal of Archaeology,* 56: 9–17.
Roberts, C. and Cox, M. (2003) *Health and Disease in Britain: From Prehistory to the Present Day,* Thrupp, Gloucester: Sutton Publishing.
Scott, B.G. (ed.) (1973) *Perspectives in Irish Archaeology,* Belfast: Association of Young Irish Archaeologists.

Italy/Italia

Dario Piombino-Mascali and Albert R. Zink

INTRODUCTION: A BRIEF HISTORY AND CURRENT STATE OF
PHYSICAL ANTHROPOLOGY IN ITALY

Italy is a land with a long and flourishing history. Through the ages, it was home to several human groups, which through invasions, movements and expansion often found an ideal place to settle. The extremely heterogeneous geographic variability and the complex peopling of the peninsula make it an ideal place for bioarchaeological investigations aimed at reconstructing the lives and lifestyles of past human groups, which can integrate and complete the strong 'traditional' approach in archaeological research, based on written sources and on material culture.

The origins of Italian physical anthropology date back to the early and mid-19th century, when a new interest in prehistoric and early historical populations promoted a number of cemetery excavations, occasionally including observations on human remains (see, e.g., Delle Chiaie 1854). While most emphasis was clearly put on material culture (an issue present even today) it was in this period that some scholars began to develop an interest in human remains, creating the first collections of skulls and skeletons (Chiarelli and D'Amore 1997). However, the official recognition of physical anthropology as a scientific discipline occurs only after the National Unification (Chiarelli 2003). Following the diffusion of Darwin's ideas, whose work was translated into Italian by Giovanni Canestrini in 1864, the value of bioanthropological research was recognized, thanks especially to the activities of physician Paolo Mantegazza (Correnti 1980–81). It was he who created the first chair of anthropology at the University of Florence in 1869, which was followed by the creation of a society, the Museo Nazionale di Antropologia ed Etnologia (1869), and of the first specialized journal, the *Archivio per l'Antropologia e la Etnologia* (1871), which is still published today. Later on, in 1893, Giuseppe Sergi created another significant institution, the Società Romana di Antropologia, which in 1937 was renamed the Istituto Italiano di Antropologia. The proceedings of the society were later published as *Rivista di Antropologia* (1911), a journal which in 2004 changed its name to the *Journal of Anthropological Sciences*, one of today's most prestigious Italian periodicals in the field. The great impulse given to archaeological research was clearly related to the desire of investigating the origins of Italians (Guidi 1988; Killgrove 2005). For this reason, research was mainly on morphological type, aimed at investigating affinities and differences among populations through the study of craniometry (see, e.g., Sergi 1899–1900; Giuffrida-Ruggeri 1904; Genna 1933–34; Sergi 1933–34), a theme that was maintained until much later (Corrain and Capitanio 1968; Passarello and Alciati 1969; Pardini *et al.* 1982; Lombardi-Pardini *et al.* 1984).

After the Second World War, metric studies began to decline, slowly accompanied by new focuses (see, e.g., Maxia and Cossu 1950). In this respect, a great contribution was provided by Antonio Ascenzi, a pathologist with a vivid interest in physical anthropology. Ascenzi played an important role, because he was the first one to apply microscopic techniques to ancient human bones, and successfully demonstrated the presence of haemoglobin fragments in historic and pre-historic remains, also contributing to the study of anaemia in ancient times (Ascenzi 1964; Ascenzi 1983; Ascenzi *et al.* 1991). However, it was only during the 1960s and 1970s that an increased emphasis in understanding health conditions and the reconstruction of lifestyles of past populations developed (see, e.g., Messeri 1962; Grilletto 1973; Ascenzi and Balistreri 1977; Ascenzi 1979), and eventually became established in the 1980s (see, e.g., Repetto *et al.* 1988; Rubini and Coppa 1991; Rubini *et al.* 1990). Key figures of this period were physical anthropologist Francesco Mallegni and pathologist Gino Fornaciari, the first ones to emphasize the bioanthropological importance of other aspects including stress, disease and demography (see, e.g., Fornaciari and Mallegni 1981; Fornaciari and Mallegni 1989), thus widening the 'classical' approach to a thorough appreciation of human remains (see, e.g., Minellono *et al.* 1980; Fornaciari *et al.* 1981; Fornaciari and Mallegni 1986; Repetto *et al.* 1988). This trend eventually flourished in the 1990s (see, e.g., Germanà and Fornaciari 1992; Minozzi *et al.* 1994; Moggi-Cecchi *et al.* 1994; Sonego and Scarsini 1994; Fornaciari 1997; Scattarella *et al.* 1997). Another relevant figure is clearly Luigi Capasso, a physician by training who has worked as a physical anthropologist since the early 1980s (see, e.g., Capasso and Piccardi 1980). Capasso's important work not only comprises the palaeodemographic and palaeopatho-logical study of several large populations, most notably that of Herculaneum (Capasso *et al.* 2000; Capasso 2001), but also the establishment of the *Journal of Paleopathology* (1987), the Società Italiana di Paleopatologia (1995) and the Museo di Storia delle Scienze Biomediche (1998), an institution devoted to anthropological and palaeopathological research and education.

Other notable bioarchaeologists of the last three decades include Gaspare Baggieri, Maria Giovanna Belcastro, Silvana Borgognini-Tarli, Cristina Cattaneo, Alfredo Coppa, Gianfranco De Stefano, Fiorenzo Facchini, Vincenzo Formicola, Ezio Fulcheri, Roberto Macchiarelli, Mauro Rubini, Vito Scattarella and Sandro Sublimi-Saponetti, all of whom have contributed to the development of present-day physical anthropology.

Physical anthropology/bioarchaeology today: current research

Although it may not always be the case, archaeologists seem to involve physical anthropologists more regularly during and after excavations to allow a more accurate recovery, inventory and study of skeletal materials (see Bonghi Jovino 1999). Active research on human remains is performed at the Universities of Bologna, Chieti, Lecce, Pisa, Turin, Udine and Venice. Beyond academia, other important bioarchaeological centres consist of the Service of Anthropology at the Archaeological Superintendence of Latium (Servizio di Antropologia della Soprintendenza per i Beni Archeologici del Lazio) in Tivoli, and the anthropology laboratory at the Museo Preistorico Etnografico 'L. Pigorini' of Rome, both active since 1986. The latter is also the seat of the Servizio Tecnico per le Ricerche Antropologiche e Paleopatologiche, created in 1992 by the Ministry of Cultural Heritage in order to document, study and curate archaeological human remains. Finally, private companies producing bone reports include the Anthropozoologica of Livorno (see, e.g., Bedini and Bertoldi 2006a and 2006b), and the Società Ricerche Archeologiche of Bressanone (see, e.g., Conzato and Rizzi 2008).

Current investigations touch a wide range of topics, such as palaeodemography (see, e.g., Capasso *et al.* 2000; Cucina *et al.* 2006), palaeopathology (Salvadei *et al.* 2001; Belcastro *et al.* 2007), biodistance studies (Rubini and Mogliazza, 2005; Coppa *et al.* 2007; Rubini *et al.* 2007), palaeodiet by employing stable isotope analysis (Giorgi *et al.* 2005; Scarabino *et al.* 2006; Fornaciari 2008; Tafuri *et al.* 2009) and even biomolecular archaeology (Vernesi *et al.* 2004). Some significant international collaborations are also worth mentioning (see, e.g., Rothschild *et al.* 2004), especially those regarding a direct comparison between grave goods and skeletal remains (Robb *et al.* 2001; Tafuri *et al.* 2009).

As far as mummified human remains are concerned, impressive scientific investigations were performed by the Universities of Pisa, Genoa and Turin, focusing on histology, immunology, immunohistochemistry, molecular biology and imaging studies (see, e.g., Fornaciari 2006; Fulcheri 2006; Cesarani *et al.* 2009). In addition, since 2007 a new impetus in mummy research was provided through the creation of the Institute for Mummies and the Iceman, a centre hosted by the European Academy of Bolzano (EURAC) entirely devoted to the study of preserved bodies through non-invasive techniques (see, e.g., Piombino-Mascali 2009; Piombino-Mascali *et al.* 2009; Zink 2009).

Anthropological associations

As mentioned, there are two long-established, historical anthropological societies in Italy, Mantegazza's Società Italiana di Antropologia ed Etnologia of Florence, created in 1871, and Sergi's Istituto Italiano di Antropologia of Rome, created in 1893 (Chiarelli and D'Amore 1997; Chiarelli 2003). Both still actively promote the study of physical anthropology and support scientific research through congresses and publications. Beyond these institutions, the 1970s saw a new associational impulse in anthropology. In fact, two other important scientific societies came into existence: the Unione Antropologica Italiana founded by Brunetto Chiarelli, Melchiorre Masali and Gianfranco Alciati in 1976; and the Federazione delle Istituzioni Antropologiche Italiane, created in 1977 by Raffaello Parenti, Pietro Messeri and Luigi Brian. Both societies were involved in educational and scientific activities, as well as in the organization of meetings. In 1995 they merged into one society, the Associazione Antropologica Italiana, which is still considered the premier anthropological society of Italy. Finally, another remarkable association is the Associazione Antropologica Abruzzese, which promotes research activities in biological anthropology, and the publication of a journal and occasional monographs.

Museum collections

As far as bone collections are concerned, human remains recovered on Italian territory and available for investigation are usually present in either Superintendences or Universities, many of which may possess historical collections and museums. A primary list of the latter should include the following: Museo di Storia Naturale, Sezione di Antropologia ed Etnologia and Museo Fiorentino di Preistoria 'Paolo Graziosi' of Florence; Museo Preistorico Etnografico 'L. Pigorini' and Museo di Antropologia 'Giuseppe Sergi' of Rome; Museo di Antropologia of Bologna, Naples and Padua; Museo di Antropologia ed Etnografia of Turin; and Museo di Anatomia Umana of Modena.

Education and training

According to the academic classification established by the Ministry of University and Scientific Research, physical anthropology is a discipline pertaining to biological sciences (area 05), where it is listed together with its related subjects as a BIO-08 sector (Cabasino 2005). Therefore, according to such categorization, teaching and research within this field should only be expected in science faculties. However, from the 1990s onwards, individual modules on physical anthropology or bioarchaeology have progressively appeared in several faculties of arts and humanities. In fact, most archaeology courses, which are now termed 'scienze dei beni cultur-ali', do include the study of human remains, focusing on aspects regarding their correct excava-tion, handling and conservation. Accordingly, a number of manuals regarding the archaeology of human remains was also published to favour education (Borgognini-Tarli and Pacciani 1993; Mal-legni and Rubini 1994; Canci and Minozzi 2005; Rubini 2008; Fornaciari and Giuffra 2009). Postgraduate courses founded in the last decade include an MSc course in the biological anthro-pology of the Mediterranean area, which has been offered by the University of Florence since 2000; and an MA course in the bioarchaeology and archaeology of human settlement, which was offered by the University of Bologna for the academic year 2004–5 (Associazione Antropologica Italiana 2005). In 2009 a joint course was offered by the Universities of Pisa, Bologna and Milan in bioarchaeology, palaeopathology and forensic anthropology. However, some of the above-mentioned classes are not always offered annually. As far as PhD courses are concerned, they are available in biology departments, such as Bologna, Cagliari and Rome which also enable spe-cialization in physical anthropology, while a PhD programme exclusively devoted to anthro-pological sciences is provided by the University of Florence. Furthermore, since 2001 the University of Pisa has offered an archaeology doctoral programme in 'palaeoanthropology and pathocoenosis', focusing on the bioarchaeology of once-living peninsular human groups (Asso-ciazione Antropologica Italiana 2005). In 2008 the University of Chieti created a new PhD course in biomedical sciences which includes the subject of 'anthro-palaeopathology'. However, only a limited number of positions is available and competition is generally very high.

It is interesting to note that, notwithstanding the recent availability of anthropological train-ing in departments of archaeology, the official requirements to gain a 'public' position within the field still lie in a biomedical training (Cabasino 2005).

ARCHAEOLOGICAL HUMAN REMAINS AND LEGISLATION

Archaeological legislation

All permissions regarding excavations fall under the Soprintendenza ('Superintendence'). There are several Soprintendenze which cover either one province or perhaps several provinces; such is the case, for example, of one Soprintendenza to cover the provinces of Salerno, Avellino, Benevento and Caserta.

The legislation which operates regarding the cultural heritage is the so-called Codice Urbani (Decree no. 42, issued on 22 January 2004; and subsequent modifications contained in the Decrees no. 156 and no. 157, issued on 24 March 2006; and Decrees no. 62 and no. 63, issued on 19 March 2008). This Codice Urbani incorporates the historical legislation produced during the Fascist period, regarding historical and artistic goods (Law no. 1089, issued on 1 June 1939) and landscapes and natural assets (Law no. 1497, issued on 29 June 1939) as well as the fol-lowing disposition comprising both cultural and natural assets: Decree no. 490, issued on 29 October 1999 (Alibrandi and Ferri 1988; Giuliani 1992; Rubini *et al.* 1994).

It is important to note that the present law does not specifically mention human remains (Article 10), but includes an exemplary list of assets which, due to their specific interest (his-torical, artistic, archaeological, ethnographic, or regarding palaeontology, prehistory and primi-tive populations), can be incorporated in the protected category, as the definition of 'archaeological goods' is non-specific to the types of artefacts or material. In this way, the kind of goods which are protected by the law is substantially open and adaptable. Another important aspect of the current legislation is the decentralization of the protection of cultural heritage, its curation and valorization, previously controlled by the State. It is now under the umbrella of the local authorities, including regions, provinces and city councils. This implies that investigations rest under the discretion of superintendences and museums. Additionally, it is worth mentioning that even those remains which are found inside churches are controlled under the Soprintendenza. It is clear that skeletal or mummified human remains inside a church belong to the church and not to the Italian State; but they must still be protected by the State in cooperation with the local religious authorities as if they were public heritage (Article 9; see also Decree no. 571, issued on 26 September 1996).

As far as the temporary export of human remains for research purposes is concerned, this may only be allowed for a limited period of time, provided the study and analysis cannot be carried out on Italian territory (Article 67).

Of relevance to the study of human remains is also Law no. 78, issued on 7 March 2001, aimed at protecting the historical heritage dating from the First World War, which may be applied to the human remains of soldiers, thus contributing to their recovery and possible identification (Nicolis 2007).

HUMAN REMAINS AND LEGISLATION

In case of the accidental discovery of human remains, the Italian State relies upon the regulations of the mortuary police established in 1990 (Decree no. 285, issued on 10 September 1990); later referred to each regional and local authority in order to better apply the norms to different local contexts (Decree no. 112, issued on 31 March 1998). According to this 1990 decree, the discoverer shall inform the mayor, who in turn will inform the competent judiciary authority, the Italian police, and the Department of Health. Providing the judge does not find elements which require further investigation (e.g., homicide), the Department of Health will commission a forensic medical professional to examine the remains and produce a report, which will be submitted to the mayor and to the same judiciary authority in order to authorize burial in a communal cemetery. If an archaeological interest in the remains is understood, then the legislation which operates is that regarding the cultural heritage – that is, the above-mentioned Codice Urbani.

Case study: the Iceman

The Iceman (Figure 20.1), one of the most famous preserved bodies, was found on Thursday 19 September 1991 in the Ötztal Alps, South Tyrol, Italy. Soon after the mummy was recovered, rumours spread that it had actually been found on the Italian side of the border and not, as originally thought, on Austrian soil.

In accordance with the 1919 Treaty of St Germain-en-Laye between Austria and the Allied powers, the Austrian–Italian border was drawn along the watershed between the Inn and Etsch valleys. In the area of the Tisenjoch, however, the glacier made it difficult to establish the exact location of the watershed (Fleckinger 2005). A new survey of the border carried out on 2 October 1991 clarified the matter. It turned out that the discovery had been located 92.56m from the border in South Tyrol, therefore in Italy. Although the site where the mummy was recovered drains towards the Inn Valley (i.e., towards the north), the boundary established after the First World War remains valid under international law.

The province of South Tyrol therefore claimed property rights but entrusted the finds as a whole to Innsbruck University until scientific examinations could be completed. The South Tyrolean

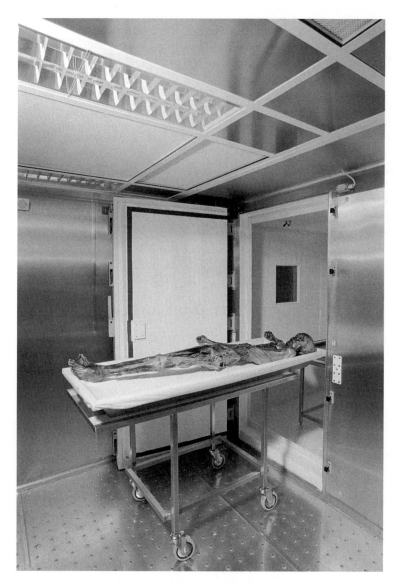

Figure 20.1 The Iceman in front of the door of the cooling cell
Copyright: South Tyrol Museum of Archaeology (www.iceman.it)

authorities also gave permission for the Institut für Ur-und Frühgeschichte der Universität Innsbruck, Austria, to carry out further archaeological investigations at the scene (Figure 20.2).

Shortly after transportation to the Institut für Gerichtsmedizin, the body was moved to the Institut für Anatomie, where it was stored until 16 January 1998. On that date, the body was finally transported to Bolzano, Italy, where a brand-new museum, the Museo Archeologico dell'Alto Adige, due to be opened on 28 March 1998, was created to curate the mummy and its precious equipment (Fleckinger 2005). There, a special cell (Figure 20.3) with controlled parameters of temperature (-6°C) and relative humidity (98%) was created for the conservation of this unique human finding (Samadelli 2004).

Figure 20.2 The site of the discovery in the Ötztal Alps, South Tyrol, Italy
Copyright: South Tyrol Museum of Archaeology (www.iceman.it)

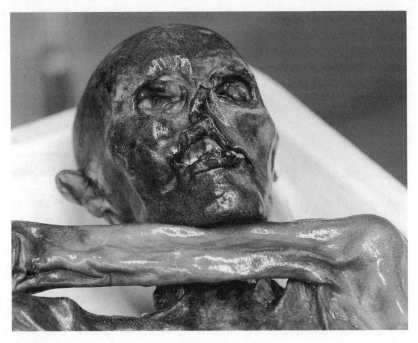

Figure 20.3 Close-up of the Iceman from South Tyrol, Italy
Copyright: South Tyrol Museum of Archaeology (www.iceman.it)

METHODS OF ANTHROPOLOGICAL ANALYSIS

Due to the lack of appropriate standardized methods developed for Italian populations, anthropologists employ recommended international standards such as, for example, the recent guidelines by Buikstra and Ubelaker (1994) and Brickley and McKinley (2004) which include methods of age and sex determination; these are replacing the once popular 'old' recommendations of Ferembach *et al.* (1977–79), established during the European Anthropologists' Workshop. Recently, however, valuable and promising tests of the accuracy of anthropological ageing determination methods have been performed on an Italian identified collection (Hens *et al.* 2008). With regard to stature, this varies according to investigator, although most people use the formulae suggested by Trotter and Gleser for white Americans (Trotter and Gleser 1958). In this respect, it is also worth mentioning the work of Formicola (2003), who suggested that the formulae for Black Americans are more appropriate in the case of Palaeolithic specimens. Significant standardized methodologies recommended by Italian research groups include the recording of markers of occupational stress (see, e.g., Mariotti *et al.* 2004; Donatelli and Scarsini 2006), though it remains difficult to predict their positive adoption by other scholars involved in the study of human remains.

CONCLUSION

The situation described above offers a bright picture of the progress and current research in physical anthropology and bioarchaeology. Indeed, Italy offers a rich and precious background for investigators, and research units and departments deserve financial and scientific support for this expanding field of study. However, some problems which require being addressed still remain (Piombino-Mascali *et al.* 2008). First of all, from a methodological viewpoint, it should be mentioned that the adoption of appropriate standardized methods for handling, recording and studying human remains is somewhat lacking. This makes it extremely difficult to make comparisons among different populations – an issue even more complex than the long-complained-of intra- and interobserver differences – with consequences on the significance of the results. Second, some 'population-based' analyses are *just* too small to provide a significant contribution, if any at all, in palaeodemography and palaeoepidemiology (see Piombino-Mascali 2007 for a discussion); this could be viewed, to some extent, as frustrating, especially if one considers the enormous potential and the unique opportunities for research that our wide skeletal collections represent. Furthermore, as of today, no accessible resource database of Italian skeletal collections has ever been produced, except for that regarding fossil remains (Alciati *et al.* 2005). The availability of such a resource is much more than desirable, because it would allow scholars to plan specific research projects and answer hypothesis-driven questions on ancient lives and lifestyles.

Beyond the merely methodological issues, it should also be pointed out that the current legislation is too non-specific when it comes to human remains, and future emendations will be mandatory to guarantee an 'official' involvement of physical anthropologists and bioarchaeologists in the analysis of human remains, from excavation to curation. Additionally, Italian legislators should also face the complete lack of an equivalent of NAGPRA, as Christian groups might feel uncomfortable in allowing a permanent retention of human bones without any control on reburial.

Clearly, physical anthropology has significantly improved in the past 30 years, but the contribution of Italy to this intriguing field of research can still grow in the near future, allowing a deeper understanding of our past which is so important for our cultural history.

USEFUL CONTACTS

Associazione Antropologica Italiana, c/o Dipartimento di Genetica, Biologia dei Microrganismi, Antropologia, Evoluzione, Università degli Studi di Parma, Viale G.P. Usberti 11/a, 43100 Parma. Website: http://aai.unipr.it/

Società Italiana di Antropologia ed Etnologia, c/o Laboratori di Antropologia, Dipartimento di Biologia Evoluzionistica 'L. Pardi', Università degli Studi di Firenze, Via del Proconsolo 12, 50122 Firenze. Website: www.unifi.it/dbalan/

Istituto Italiano di Antropologia, c/o Dipartimento di Biologia Animale e dell'Uomo, Università di Roma 'La Sapienza', Piazzale A. Moro 5, 00185 Roma. Website: www.isita-org.com/

Istituto Italiano di Paleontologia Umana, Piazza Mincio 2, 00198 Roma. Website: www.isipu.org/

Istituto per le Mummie e l'Iceman, Accademia Europea di Bolzano (EURAC), Viale Druso 1, 39100 Bolzano. Website: www.eurac.edu/

Istituto Italiano di Preistoria e Protostoria, Via S. Egidio 21, 50122 Firenze. Website: www.iipp.it/

Ministero per i Beni e le Attività Culturali, Via del Collegio Romano 27, 00186 Roma. Website: www.beniculturali.it/

Servizio Tecnico per le Ricerche Antropologiche e Paleopatologiche, c/o Museo Nazionale Preistorico Etnografico 'L. Pigorini', Piazzale G. Marconi 14, 00144 Roma. Website: www.pigorini.arti.beniculturali.it/

Associazione Antropologia Abruzzese, c/o Museo di Storia delle Scienze Biomediche, Università degli Studi 'G. D'Annunzio', Piazza Trento e Trieste, 66100 Chieti. Website: www.unich.it/museo/

BIBLIOGRAPHY

Alciati, G., Pesce Delfino, V. and Vacca E. (2005) 'Catalogue of Italian fossil human remains from the Palaeolithic to the Mesolithic', *Journal of Anthropological Sciences*, 84 (Supplement).

Alibrandi, T. and Ferri, P.G. (1988) *Il Diritto dei Beni Culturali. La Protezione del Patrimonio Storico-Artistico* Roma: Carocci.

Ascenzi, A. (1964) 'Microscopia e osso preistorico', *Rivista di Antropologia*, 51: 5–21.

——(1979) 'A problem in palaeopathology. The origin of thalassemia in Italy', *Virchows* Archiv A, 384: 121–30.

——(1983) 'Problemi di paleopatologia', in 'L'Uomo di Saccopastore e il suo ambiente', *Rivista di Antropologia*, 62 (Supplement): 99–122.

Ascenzi, A. and Balistreri, P. (1977) 'Porotic hyperostosis and the problem of origin of thalassemia in Italy', *Journal of Human Evolution*, 6: 595–604.

Ascenzi, A., Bellelli, A., Brunori, M., *et al.* (1991) 'Diagnosis of thalassemia in ancient bones: problems and prospects in pathology', in D.J. Ortner and A.C. Aufderheide (eds) *Human Paleopathology: Current Syntheses and Future Options*, Washington, DC: Smithsonian Institution Press.

Associazione Antropologica Italiana (2005) 'Le Scienze Antropologiche in Italia', *International Journal of Anthropology*, 1 (Supplement).

Bedini, E. and Bertoldi, F. (2006a) 'Paleobiologia e tradizioni culturali dei primi gruppi di origine germanica stanziati in Piemonte: i Goti', *Anthropos & Iatria*, 10: 40–42.

——(2006b) 'Paleobiologia e tradizioni culturali dei primi gruppi di origine germanica stanziati in Piemonte: i Longobardi', *Anthropos & Iatria*, 10: 44–48.

Belcastro, M.G., Rastelli, E., Mariotti, V., *et al.* (2007) 'Continuity or discontinuity of the life-style in central Italy during the Roman Imperial Age-Early Middle Ages transition: diet, health and behavior', *American Journal of Physical Anthropology*, 132: 381–94.

Bonghi Jovino, M. (1999) 'Aspetti e problemi dell'Archeologia da Campo, acquisizioni, prospettive e considerazioni teoriche e metodologiche', in R.F. Docter and E.M. Moormann (eds) *Classical Archaeology towards the Third Millennium: Reflections and Perspectives*, Proceedings of the XVth International Congress of Classical Archaeology, Amsterdam, July 12–17, Amsterdam: Allard Pierson Series.

Borgognini-Tarli, S.M. and Pacciani, E. (1993) *I resti umani nello scavo archeologico. Metodiche di recupero e studio*, Roma: Bulzoni.

Brickley, M. and McKinley, J. (2004) *Guidelines to the Standards for Recording Human Remains*, Institute of Field Archaeology Paper No. 7, Reading: Institute of Field Archaeologists.

Buikstra, J.E. and Ubelaker, D.H. (eds) (1994) *Standards for Data Collection from Human Skeletal Remains*, Fayetteville, AR: Arkansas Archaeological Survey Research Series No. 44.

Cabasino, E. (2005) *I mestieri dei patrimonio. Professioni e mercato del lavoro nei beni culturali in Italia*, Milano: Franco Angeli.

Canci, A. and Minozzi, S. (2005) *Archeologia dei resti umani. Dallo scavo al laboratorio*, Roma: Carocci.

Capasso, L. (2001) *I fuggiaschi di Ercolano. Paleobiologia delle vittime dell'eruzione vesuviana del 79 d.C.*, Roma: 'L'Erma' di Bretschneider.

Capasso, L., Capasso, L., Caramiello, S., *et al.* (2000) 'Paleobiologia della popolazione di Ercolano (79 d.C.)', *Recenti Progressi in Medicina*, 91: 288–96.

Capasso, L. and Piccardi, M. (1980) 'La grotta dello Scoglietto: un probabile centro nosocomiale dell'antica Età del Bronzo in Toscana', *Rivista di Scienze Preistoriche*, 35: 165–81.

Cesarani, F., Martina, M.C., Boano, R., *et al.* (2009) 'Multidetector CT study of gallbladder stones in a wrapped Egyptian mummy', *RadioGraphics*, 29: 1191–94.

Chiarelli, B. (2003) 'L'Antropologia come storia naturale dell'Uomo', in B. Chiarelli (ed.) *Dalla Natura alla Cultura. Principi di Antropologia Biologica e Culturale. Vol. 1*, Padova: Piccin.

Chiarelli, B. and D'Amore, G. (1997) 'Italy', in F. Spencer (ed.) *History of Physical Anthropology: an Encyclopedia. Vol. 1*, New York: Garland Publishing.

Conzato, A. and Rizzi, J. (2008) 'Rio di Pusteria e il suo vaso di Pandora. L'ossario della cappella San Floriano: banca dati paleopatologica on-line', *Antrocom*, 4: 99–103.

Coppa, A., Cucina, A., Lucci, M., *et al.* (2007) 'The origins and spread of agriculture in Italy: a dental nonmetric analysis', *American Journal of Physical Anthropology*, 133: 918–30.

Corrain, C. and Capitanio, M. (1968) 'I resti scheletrici umani nelle tombe neolitiche del Passo di Corvo (Foggia)', *Archivio per l'Antropologia e la Etnologia*, 98: 16–24.

Correnti, V. (1980–81) 'L'antropologia fisica in Italia', *Rivista di Antropologia*, 61: 21–40.

Cucina, A., Vargiu, R., Mancinelli, D., *et al.* (2006) 'The necropolis of Vallerano (Rome II-III century A.D.): an anthropological perspective of the ancient Romans in the Suburbium', *International Journal of Osteoarchaeology*, 16: 104–17.

Delle Chiaie, S. (1854) *Cenno notomico-patologico sulle ossa umane scavate in Pompei*, Napoli: Filiatre Sebezio.

Donatelli, A. and Scarsini, C. (2006) 'Proposta di un metodo per il rilievo delle entesopatie', *Archivio per l'Antropologia e la Etnologia*, 136: 151–81.

Ferembach, D., Schwidetzky, I. and Stloukal, M. (1977–79) 'Raccomandazioni per la determinazione dell'età e del sesso sullo scheletro'. *Rivista di Antropologia*, 60, 5–51.

Fleckinger, A. (2005) *Ötzi, the Iceman. The full facts at a glance*, 2nd edn, Bolzano: Folio.

Formicola, V. (2003) 'More is not always better: Trotter and Gleser's equations and stature estimates of Upper Paleolithic European samples', *Journal of Human Evolution*, 45, 239–43.

Fornaciari, G. (1997) 'Paleopatologia di gruppi umani a cultura etrusca: il caso di Pontecagnano, Salerno (VII–IV secolo a.C.)', in G. Maetzke (ed.) *Aspetti della cultura di Volterra etrusca fra l'Età del Ferro e l'Età Ellenistica e contributi della ricerca antropologica alla conoscenza del popolo etrusco. Atti del XIX Convegno di Studi Etruschi ed Italici, Volterra 15–19 Ottobre 1995*, Firenze: Leo S. Olschki.

——(2006) 'Le mummie aragonesi in San Domenico Maggiore di Napoli', *Medicina nei Secoli*, 18: 843–64.

——(2008) 'Food and disease at the Renaissance courts of Naples and Florence: a paleonutritional study', *Appetite*, 51: 10–14.

Fornaciari, G., and Giuffra, V. (2009) *Lezioni di paleopatologia*, Genova: ECIG.

Fornaciari, G. and Mallegni, F. (1981) 'Alimentazione e paleopatologia', *Archeologia Medievale*, 8: 353–68.

——(1986) 'Su un gruppo di inumati della necropoli di Cornus. Aspetti antropologici, paleopatologici e paleonutrizionali', in M. Pani-Ermini (ed.) *L'Archeologia Romana e Altomedievale nell'Oristanese, Atti del Convegno di Cuglieri (22–23 Giugno 1984)*, Taranto: Scorpioneo.

——(1989) 'Nuovi metodi e prospettive della Paleoantropologia di Età Storica', Atti Secondo Congresso Internazionale Etrusco, Firenze 26 Maggio – 2 Giugno 1985, *Studi Etruschi*, 3 (Supplement): 1445–80.

Fornaciari, G., Mallegni, F., Bertini, F., *et al.* (1981) 'Cribra orbitalia and elemental bone iron in the Punics of Carthage', *Ossa*, 8: 63–77.

Fulcheri, E. (2006) 'Le malattie dei santi alla luce della fede e nelle evidenze paleopatologiche', *Medicina nei Secoli*, 18: 815–30.

Genna, G.E. (1933–34) 'Elementi eneolitici cromagnonoidi nel Lazio', *Rivista di Antropologia*, 30: 235–62.

Germanà, F. and Fornaciari, G. (1992) *Trapanazioni, craniotomie e traumi cranici in Italia dalla Preistoria all'Età Moderna*, Pisa; Giardini.

Giorgi, F., Bartoli, F., Iacumin, P., *et al.* (2005) 'Oligoelements and isotopic geochemistry: a multi-disciplinary approach to the reconstruction of the paleodiet', *Human Evolution*, 20: 55–82.

Giuffrida-Ruggeri, V. (1904) 'La capacità del cranio nelle diverse popolazioni italiane antiche e moderne', *Atti della Società Romana di Antropologia*, 10: 240–78.

Giuliani, S. (1992) 'Das Verfahren bei menschlichen Funden von archäologischem Interesse nach italie-nischem Recht', in F. Höpfel, W. Platzer and K. Spindler (eds) *Der Mann im Eis, Band 1*, Veröffentlichungen der Universität Innsbruck 187, Innsbruck: Eigenverlag der Universität Innsbruck.

Grilletto, R. (1973) 'Caries and dental attrition in the Early Egyptians as seen in the Turin Collections', in D.R. Brothwell and B.A. Chiarelli (eds) *Population biology of the Ancient Egyptians*, London: Academic Press.

Guidi, A. (1988) *Storia della Paletnologia*, Roma-Bari: Laterza.

Hens, S.M., Rastelli, E. and Belcastro, M.G. (2008) 'Age Estimation from the Human Os Coxa: A Test on a Documented Italian Collection'. *Journal of Forensic Sciences*, 53: 1040–43.

Killgrove, K. (2005) 'Bioarchaeology in the Roman World', unpublished MA thesis, Department of Classics, University of North Carolina.

Lombardi-Pardini, E.C., Polosa, D. and Pardini, E. (1984) 'Gli inumati di Pontecagnano (Salerno) (VII-VI secolo a.C.)', *Archivio per l'Antropologia e la Etnologia*, 114: 3–62.

Mallegni, F. and Rubini, M. (1994) *Recupero dei materiali scheletrici umani in archeologia*, Roma: CISU.

Mariotti, V., Facchini, F. and Belcastro, M.G. (2004) 'Enthesopathies – Proposal of a Standardized Scoring Method and Applications'. *Collegium Anthropologicum*, 28: 145–59.

Maxia, C. and Cossu, D. (1950) 'Ricerche anatomiche e radiografiche dei segni del morbo di Cooley nei crani sardi dal periodo neolitico a quello medievale-moderno', *Annali Italiani di Pediatria*, 3: 415–16.

Messeri, P. (1962) 'Aspetti abnormi e patologici nel materiale scheletrico umano dello Scoglietto (Età del Bronzo)', *Archivio per l'Antropologia e la Etnologia*, 92: 129–59.

Minellono, F., Pardini, E. and Fornaciari, G. (1980) 'Le sepolture epigravettiane di Vado all'Arancio (Grosseto)', *Rivista di Scienze Preistoriche*, 35: 1–44.

Minozzi, S., Canci, A., Borgognini-Tarli, S.M., *et al.* (1994) 'Stress e stato di salute in serie scheletriche dell'età del Bronzo', *Bullettino di Paletnologia Italiana*, 85: 333–48.

Moggi-Cecchi, J., Pacciani, E. and Pinto-Cisternas, J. (1994) 'Enamel hypoplasia and age at weaning in 19th century Florence, Italy', *American Journal of Physical Anthropology*, 93: 299–306.

Nicolis, F. (2007) 'Ghiacciai: un patrimonio culturale da salvaguardare. Nuove prospettive per l'archeologia', *Bollettino SAT*, 60: 43–46.

Pardini, E., Innocenti, F., Fulgaro, A., *et al.* (1982) 'Gli inumati di Pontecagnano (Salerno)(V-IV secolo a. C.)', *Archivio per l'Antropologia e la Etnologia*, 112: 281–329.

Passarello, P. and Alciati, G. (1969) 'Esame antropologico di un gruppo di crani della necropoli bizantina di Modica', *Rivista di Antropologia*, 56: 67–80.

Piombino-Mascali, D. (2007) 'Pontecagnano: Studio bioculturale degli indicatori di stress in una popolazione etrusco-campana', unpublished PhD thesis, Università di Pisa.

——(2009) *Il Maestro del Sonno Eterno*. Palermo: La Zisa.

Piombino-Mascali, D., Aufderheide, A.C., Johnson Williams, M., *et al.* (2009) 'The Salafia method rediscovered', *Virchows Archiv*, 454: 355–57.

Piombino-Mascali, D., Messina, A. and Sineo, L. (2008) 'La bioarcheologia umana: problematiche e prospettive', *International Journal of Anthropology* (Numero Speciale): 307–12.

Repetto, E., Canci, A. and Borgognini-Tarli, S.M. (1988) 'Indicatori scheletrici e dentari dello stato di salute nel campione dell'Età del Bronzo di Toppo Daguzzo, Basilicata', *Rivista di Antropologia*, 66 (Supplement): 89–112.

Robb, J., Bigazzi, R., Lazzarini, L., *et al.* (2001) 'Social "status" and biological "status": a comparison of grave goods and skeletal indicators from Pontecagnano', *American Journal of Physical Anthropology*, 115: 213–23.

Rothschild, B.M., Coppa, A. and Petrone, P.P. (2004) '"Like a virgin": absence of rheumatoid arthritis and treponematosis, good sanitation and only rare gout in Italy prior to the 15th century', *Reumatismo*, 56: 61–66.

Rubini, M. (2008) *Elementi di paleopatologia, Atlante*, Roma: CISU.

Rubini, M., Andreini, L. and Coppa, A. (1990) 'Gli inumati della grotta Vittorio Vecchi di Monte Fulcino (Sezze, Latina; media Età del Bronzo, XVII-XIV sec. a.C.)', *Rivista di Antropologia*, 68: 141–63.

Rubini, M., Andreini, R. and Mori, G. (1994) 'Recupero, restauro e conservazione di materiali scheletrici in archeologia', in F. Mallegni and M. Rubini (eds) *Recupero dei materiali scheletrici umani in archeologia*, Roma: CISU.

Rubini, M. and Coppa, A. (1991) 'Studio antropologico sugli inumati della necropoli arcaica di Riofreddo (Lazio, VI sec. a.C.)', *Rivista di Antropologia*, 69: 153–66.

Rubini, M. and Mogliazza, S. (2005) *Storia delle Popolazioni Italiane dal Neolitico a Oggi. I nuovi orientamenti dell'Antropologia*, Roma: Soprintendenza per i Beni Archeologici del Lazio.

Rubini, M., Mogliazza, S. and Corruccini, R.S.T. (2007) 'Biological divergence and equality during the first millennium BC in human populations of central Italy', *American Journal of Human Biology*, 19: 119–31.

Salvadei, L., Ricci, F. and Manzi, G. (2001) 'Porotic hyperostosis as a marker of health and nutritional conditions during childhood: studies at the transition between imperial Rome and the Early Middle Ages', *American Journal of Human Biology*, 13: 709–17.

Samadelli, M. (2004) *The Chalcolithic Mummy – Volume 3. In Search of Immortality*, Schriften des Südtiroler Archäologiemuseums 4, Bolzano: South Tyrol Museum of Archaeology.

Scarabino, C., Lubritto, C., Proto, A., *et al.* (2006) 'Paleodiet characterisation of an Etrurian population of Pontecagnano (Italy) by Isotope Ratio Mass Spectrometry (IRSM) and Atomic Absorption Spectrometry (AAS)', *Isotopes for Environmental and Health Studies*, 42: 151–58.

Scattarella, V., Sublimi-Saponetti, S., Selvaggi, A., *et al.* (1997) 'Indicatori scheletrici e dentari di stress e attività occupazionali della Necropoli di Via Marche a Taranto (VI-IV sec. a.C.)', *Antropologia Contemporanea*, 20: 217–19.

Sergi, G. (1899–1900) 'Crani preistorici della Sicilia', *Atti della Società Romana di Antropologia*, 6: 3–13.

——(1933–34). 'La necropoli di Vetulonia'. *Rivista di Antropologia*, 30, 373–91.

Sonego, F. and Scarsini, C. (1994) 'Indicatori scheletrici e dentari dello stato di salute e delle condizioni di vita a Pontecagnano (Salerno) nel VII-V sec. a.C.', *Bullettino di Paletnologia Italiana*, 85: 449–73.

Tafuri, M.A., Craig, O.E. and Canci, A. (2009) 'Stable isotope evidence for the consumption of millet and other plants in Bronze Age Italy', *American Journal of Physical Anthropology*, 139: 146–53.

Trotter, M. and Gleser, G.C. (1958) 'A pre-evaluation of estimation of stature based on measurements of stature during life and of long bones after death', *American Journal of Physical Anthropology*, 16: 79–123.

Vernesi, C., Caramelli, D., Dupanloup, I., *et al.* (2004) 'The Etruscans: a population-genetic study', *American Journal of Human Genetics*, 74: 694–704.

Zink, A.R. (2009) 'Molecular detection of infectious diseases in ancient Egyptian mummies', in A. Wieczorek, W. Rosendahl and H. Wiegand (eds) *Mumien und Museen*, Remmagazin Sonderveröffentlichung 2, Mannheim: REM.

Kosovo/Kosova

Shirley J. Schermer, Edi Shukriu and Sylvia Deskaj

INTRODUCTION: A BRIEF HISTORY AND CURRENT STATE OF PHYSICAL ANTHROPOLOGY IN KOSOVO

Kosovo became an independent state on 17 February 2009. After NATO intervention, Kosovo had been under UN protectorate (UNMIK) since June 1999. After independence, the European Union Rule of Law Mission in Kosovo (EULEX) has provided assistance and support to the Kosovan authorities. Malcolm (1998) provides a comprehensive history of the years preceding this.

Kosovo's past, the war and the disruptions caused by it, made the recovery from the war to be directed less toward the cultural heritage. In Kosovo, as a part of the former Yugoslavia and under Serbian control, physical anthropology has not been sufficiently institutionalized for decades. A few human remains studies were done, but they were mainly concentrated on Slavic mediaeval bones to prove the presence of Slavs in Kosovo. With independence, Kosovo will finally be able to use its rich cultural heritage and have the opportunity for further studies in physical anthropology.

The first archaeological excavations in Kosovo were conducted by Austrian soldiers during the First World War in an Illyrian cemetery in Neprebishte, the vicinity of Theranda/Suhareka. The Museum of Kosovo marked the beginning of institutional research of archaeological sites in 1949 (Shukriu 2004: 11). The number of archaeologically investigated sites and the number of human remains found since the first systematic archaeological excavations in 1951 are quite large (Table 21.1; Figure 21.1). Although human remains number more than 3000, studies in physical anthropology are still few.

In the past, some studies were carried out, such as the craniometric analyses conducted by Pittard (1920) on Balkan populations and by Ž. Gavrilović (1964) on the mediaeval human remains from Artana (Novoberda). The mediaeval necropolis of Vermica near Prizren (Figure 21.2) yielded around 450 graves, excavated in 1974–75 by Albanian archaeologist Edi Shukriu and Serbian archaeologist Aleksandar Bačkalov, supervised by two Serbian archaeologists from Prishtina and Belgrade. In 1978 Hungarian anthropologist Janos Nemeskéri (Budapest) studied the human remains of the Vermica mediaeval cemetery. The study was organized by the Institute for the Protection of Monuments in the Municipality of Prizren (Instituti për Mbrojtjen e Monumenteve, Komuna e Prizrenit), under the direction of Muhamed Shukriu. The osteological methods employed in the study followed Lengyel (1963, 1968) and Acsádi and

Table 21.1 Archaeological sites in Kosovo where human remains have been found

Bronze Age Inhumations	Iron Age Tumulusnecropoli	Iron Age Urn graves	Roman and Early Byzantine period Necropoli	Mediaeval period
Bernica	Baja e Pejes	Bernica	Gjonaj	Artana (Novoberdo)
Grashtica	Llashtica (Vllashtica)	Grashtica	Gjytet (Dubovc)	Graboc
Perceta (Perceva)	Komoran		Gllamnik	Kuline near Banje
Qëndresan (Gllareva)	Moglica		Karagac	Matican
Rugova	Neprebishte		Komoran	Rezala
Ujz	Perceta (Perceva)		Municipium DD	Vermica
	Porodime		Tupec	
	Rogova		Ulpiana	
	Romaja		(Northern	
	Shiroka		Necropolis, Fusha e	
			Cerkezit tumulus,	
			Cernica tumulus)	

Source: from Shukriu (2004)*

*The human remains from these sites are mainly curated at the Museum of Kosovo or the Institute for Protection of Monuments of Kosovo, both in Prishtina. The MNI represented by these remains is approximately 3000.

Nemeskéri (1970). The Vermica osteological material also was submitted for analysis to the Albanian anthropologist Aleksandër Dhima, but no additional information is available. During this same time period, anthropologist Nemeskéri and archaeologist G. Gabričević (Belgrade) excavated the grave of Ymer Prizren (1819–85, Head of the Albanian Prizren League) in Ulqin. The results of this work are found in several unpublished documents (Batalli 1978; Lengyel 1978; Nemeskéri 1978).

A total of fifty skeletons from the site Mali Vogël (Mala Planina), part of the large urban complex in Artana (Novoberda), were analysed and published by Ž. Gavrilović (1964: 145–47). Archaeological excavations were made intermittently between 1952 and 1970, and more than 900 individual graves and family tombs in the cathedral church and churchyard were investigated.

Only mediaeval graves were anthropologically analysed and published by Serbian anthropologist Živko Mikić (1982, 1983, 1984a, 1984b, 1992, 1994, 1997, 2006). Due to Mikić's concentration on Slav human remains, 122 mediaeval skeletons found in Kosovo have been analysed. His anthropological analyses were done according to the method of E. Breitinger (1937).

Twenty-one mediaeval graves were investigated at Ploshe in Gjonaj, near Prizren, in 1978, with the anthropological analysis conducted in 1980 (Mikić 1984a: 115–22). The necropolis dated from the tenth to the thirteenth century. Seventy graves were archaeologically investigated at Kuline, near the village of Banje in Kolasin of Iber, in 1978, and anthropologically analysed (Mikić 1984b: 50–53). The necropolis dated to between the 13th and 18th centuries.

Forty-two graves were archaeologically investigated at the Greek Cemetery site in Rezala (Kolashin) in 1978 and anthropologically analysed (Mikić 1984b: 45–49). The necropolis dated between the 13th and 17th centuries. Fifty-eight sepulchral features with 59 skeletons were found at Breg in Matiçan, near Prishtina. One hundred and twelve graves were excavated between 1969 and 1973 by Vojislav S. Jovanović (1988: 17). The necropolis dated from the ninth to the eleventh century.

The human remains and artefacts are held at the Museum of Kosovo (Muzeu i Kosovës), National Museum (Narodni Muzej) in Belgrade, the Institute for Protection of Monuments of

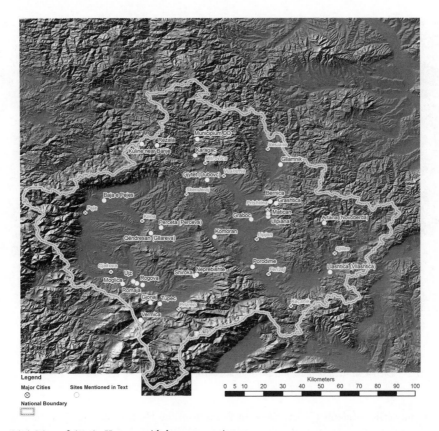

Figure 21.1 Map of sites in Kosovo with human remains

Kosovo (Instituti për Mbrojtjen e Monumenteve të Kosovës), the Institute for the Protection of Monuments of the Municipality of Prizren, and the Institute for the Protection of Monuments of the Municipality of Prishtina (Instituti për Mbrojtjen e Monumenteve – Komuna e Prishtinës). A special small building was built near the original site for long-term storage of the human remains from the Vermica necropolis.

Physical anthropology in Kosovo today

'The phase preceding the occupation of Kosovo, the occupation itself and the war that followed (1981–99), were the most unfortunate periods for Kosovo archaeology and Albanian archaeologists' (Shukriu 2004: 13). Although the Vermica site was excavated jointly by Albanian and Serb archaeologists in 1974–75, this site was used by the Serbs in 1981 to accuse Albanians of being destroyers of the graves of 'Slavs'. Political motivation drove the emphasis on analysis of mediaeval graves to prove the presence of Slavs in Kosovo. Thus, in many cases, the skeletons found in prehistoric tumuli were ignored.

Occupation, oppression and war have taken a toll on all aspects of life in Kosovo. Even prior to the past few decades, anthropology as a discipline was very much lacking. Except for some anthropological analyses between the years 1975–80 and since 2006, no other steps have been taken in this field. No academic courses or formal training of students exist. In attempts to increase the awareness of physical anthropology studies, co-author Schermer gave a lecture in

237

Figure 21.2 Palaeo-Christian basilica and mediaeval necropolis at Vermica, Kosovo

2007 to university students ('What We Can Learn from the Human Skeleton') at the request of co-author Shukriu, professor at the University of Prishtina. In February 2008, Dr Shukriu, with the support of Schermer, the University of Iowa and OMPF, offered a proposal for the development of a Department of Anthropology at the University of Prishtina. Driving this proposal are the large number (more than 3000) of human remains in Kosovo requiring osteological analysis and the need for Kosovo-educated and trained physical anthropologists.

ARCHAEOLOGICAL HUMAN REMAINS AND LEGISLATION

Archaeological legislation

The Law on Cultural Heritage of the former Yugoslavia did not mention physical anthropology at all. The Institute for Protection of Monuments of Kosovo was the institution under that former law with the authority to give permission for archaeological excavations. The authors looked at Kosovo's newly-developed laws dealing with heritage: the 2006 Law on Cultural Heritage (Ligi për trashëgiminë kulturore); the 2004 Law on Construction (Ligji për ndërtim); the 2003 Law on Spatial Planning (Ligji për planifikim hapësinor); the 2008 sub-law Regulation on Procedure for Archaeological Excavations/Investigations (Regullore mbi procedurat për gërmimet/hulumtimet arkeologjike); and the 2009 Law on the Department of Forensic Medicine (Ligji për Departamentin e Mjekësisisë Ligjore). Physical anthropology and human remains in an archaeological context are not specifically mentioned in any of them.

To get a better overview of the current understanding of laws, practices and problems, the authors prepared a questionnaire (see Table 21.2) and sent it out to numerous agencies, institutions and individuals within Kosovo. Responses were received from the following: Luan Gashi, archaeologist-anthropologist, Institute for Protection of Monuments of Kosovo; Dr. Enver Rexha, Director/historian and Milot Berisha, archaeologist, Institute of Archaeology (Instituti i Arkeologjisë); the Institute for Protection of Monuments – Prizren; Sali Shoshaj, head of the Prishtina office of Cultural Heritage without Borders (CHwB) (Trashëgimia Kulturore Pa Kufij); Birte Brugmann, former consultant to CHwB; Kersti Berggren, Swedish

Table 21.2 Questionnaire sent to agencies, institutions and individuals in Kosovo

Questionnaire for current law and practices in Kosovo
1   What are the laws, regulations and protocols regarding human skeletal remains in Kosovo?
2   What periods do archaeological human remains encompass? Is the antiquity of the remains a factor in which laws, regulations or protocols are applicable?
3   Is a licence needed to excavate the remains? If so, how does one get the necessary licence?
4   What happens on the accidental discovery of human skeletal remains? Is there a law or regulation that covers this? Who needs to be contacted? What is the role of the UNMIK Office of Missing Persons and Forensics?
5   Is the presence of an osteologist/physical anthropologist required on a site when human remains are excavated? What is the role of an osteologist/physical anthropologist on site?
6   Are there laws or regulations concerning what happens to the human remains once they are excavated?
7   Is the osteological analysis of archaeological human skeletal remains compulsory?
8   Can human remains be sent abroad for analysis?
9   Are human remains reburied? If so, where and by whom? Or are the remains curated at a facility? If so, in a central repository? Individual agencies or museums? Can human remains be displayed in museum exhibits?

Historical practices in Kosovo
The editors of the volume are interested in knowing some background information on physical anthropology in each country, such as a few basic historical facts or milestones, how long physical anthropology has existed as a discipline, whether specialized associations and academic courses exist, the current state of the discipline, any special case studies, and perhaps a note on population-specific methods for stature, age and sex.
1   What were the laws, regulations and protocols in the past for dealing with human remains, both intentional excavation and accidental discoveries?
2   What is the history of physical anthropology as a discipline in Kosovo?
3   What is the history of any specialized associations and academic courses related specifically to human osteology or physical anthropology in Kosovo?
4   Are there any population-specific methods for stature, age and sex? If so, please provide the relevant references.

5   Can you provide information on a specific excavation of human remains or accidental discovery:
      a. When did this occur?
      b. Who was in involved in the project?
      c. Where did the excavation occur, at a known archaeological site or other location?
      d. Antiquity of the remains?
      e. Any special permits or permission required?
      f. What happened to the remains after they were excavated?
      g. Was an osteological report published? If so, please provide the reference.
      i. Where are the remains now?

National Heritage Board, who previously worked with CHwB in Kosovo; and Valérie Brasey, formerly with the UNMIK Office of Missing Persons and Forensics (OMPF), Prishtina, and currently with the European Union Rule of Law Mission (EULEX) in Kosovo. Their questionnaire responses are used throughout the following sections.

The general provisions of the Law on Cultural Heritage 2006 (Section 1.3) state: 'The Cultural Heritage within this Law shall include: architectural, archaeological, movable and spiritual heritage regardless of the time of creation and construction, type of construction, beneficiary, creator or implementer of a work.' Types of archaeological heritage are defined in the law as follows:

7.1 'Archaeological Heritage' is composed of immovable and movable objects as defined in Article 2.3 of this Law;

7.2 'Immovable archaeological objects' are monuments, settlements, structures constructed by human hand and stratigraphic composition;

7.3 'Movable archaeological objects' are finds unearthed during archaeological excavations or accidental finds, which are expression and evidence of human creativity.

The types of 'movable heritage' include 'objects or parts of objects found during archaeological excavations or accidental discoveries' (Law on Cultural Heritage 9.1). Although human remains are not specifically mentioned, they are considered to be included. The law also states that movable heritage older than 100 years shall be automatically put under protection (Section 9.6).

The law also provides legal protections for cultural heritage including 'movable heritage.':

4.10 Each legal and physical person has duty of care to safeguard the integrity of Cultural Heritage if he/she is owner, possessor or occupier of this Cultural Heritage;

4.11 Any legal or physical person who damages Cultural Heritage regardless of their ownership relationship to it, shall be fined or sanctioned based on the Penal Code of Kosovo, the Law on Minor Offences and according to Article 11 of this Law;

9.8 All objects or parts of objects found during archaeological excavations or accidental discoveries shall be the property of Kosovo according to Article 7.10.

Throughout the Law on Cultural Heritage and its sub-laws, the term 'competent institution' is used rather than naming a specific agency. In her questionnaire response, Kersti Berggren, of the Swedish National Heritage Board, who previously worked with CHwB in Kosovo, shared the following from her involvement (along with many others) with the completion of the Kosovo Heritage Law during 2008:

> When the sub laws were drafted we used the name 'Ministry responsible for … ' and 'Competent Institution' to leave open for changes in the administrative/institutional structure. There is an urgent need for institutional reform in Kosovo, and to start that work should be the next step after the law has been approved.
>
> *(Kersti Berggren, pers. comm., 2009)*

Permission requirements for excavation

Every excavation requires an excavation permit from a competent institution. Several sections of the Law on Cultural Heritage and regulations focus on the requirements for permission to excavate archaeological sites:

7.20   Archaeological excavation can only be carried out with the written permission of the Competent Institution. The decision regarding this permission shall be given within 30 days from the date of the request;

7.21   Institutions or physical or legal persons can only be permitted to carry out archaeological excavation by licence according to criteria concerning professional standards and supervision to be determined by a sub-legal act based on this Law;

7.22   A licensee for archaeological excavation shall submit a report of the excavation, including photographic material, sketches, drawings, plans, topographic material, cartographic and other scientific and professional material obtained during excavations, as well as any archaeological discoveries to the Competent Institution within one year of the commencement of the archaeological excavation;

7.23   Criteria on documentation and recording of archaeological investigation and discoveries found during archaeological excavations shall be specified by a sub-legal act to this Law;

7.24   The right to publication of the archaeological investigation shall lie with the possessor of the licence for the archaeological excavation for four years. After this time, the right to publish is open to other licensed archaeologists;

9.5   According to this Law, movable objects, component parts of the Cultural Heritage, historical compounds, religious buildings, shall be under protection and they cannot be removed from the natural context of the site where they are situated, without a written permission by the Competent Institution.

CHwB assists primarily with the conservation and restoration of historic and more contemporary buildings and has supported only a few archaeological projects in Kosovo (CHwB 2004). In those cases, they rely on local archaeologists to obtain the necessary permission and permits. It is assumed that similar organizations working in Kosovo also rely on local archaeologists. As the relevant institution is not specified in the Law on Cultural Heritage or the new regulations, a special commission had to be formed by the Ministry of Culture for the 2008 excavations in Ulpiana. This special, one-time commission was formed at Dr Shukriu's request and, by order of the Minister of Culture, consisted of the Head of the sector of heritage at the Ministry and two representatives of heritage institutions of the Ministry.

In 27 February 2009, the Kosovo Council for Cultural Heritage (Këshilli i Kosovës për Trashëgimi Kulturore) was formed, with seven professional members voted by Parliament. The Law on Cultural Heritage provided for the formation of this council in sections 4.8 and 4.9:

> The Kosovo Council for the Cultural Heritage is a body which will be established by the Assembly of Kosovo who will determine the objects of its activity in the field of cultural heritage … The Kosovo Council for the Cultural Heritage will identify necessary financial support measures for the Cultural Heritage for each year to the Assembly of Kosovo in compliance with this law. The Kosovo Council for the Cultural Heritage cooperates with the competent institutions that act in the field of cultural heritage.
>
> *(Law on Cultural Heritage 2009, Sections 4.8 and 4.9)*

The Law on Cultural Heritage is the main state authority on cultural heritage in Kosovo, and co-author Shukriu was elected to head it, acknowledging that there is a lot of work to be done to put things in place. The members of the Kosovo Council for the Cultural Heritage (KCCH), in consultation with lawyers, prepared and adopted the Regulation of KCCH. Efforts are underway to secure funding, budget and staff from Parliament. One of the roles of KCCH will be to identify the appropriate 'competent institution' in specific situations.

HUMAN REMAINS AND LEGISLATION

Although the Law on Cultural Heritage does not specifically mention human remains, Section 7.8. does state: 'Accidental archaeological discoveries should be notified within three days to the Competent Institution'. It also states:

7.6 If during construction works an archaeological discovery is made, the discoverer or investor shall inform the Competent Institution immediately, but not later than the following day from the time of discovery. The Competent Institution has the right to immediately stop the initiated development works and will undertake an evaluated study and rescue archaeology on site for a limited period of time to be determined by a sublegal act based on this Law. Development works can only recommence following the express permission in writing by the Competent Institution;

7.9 All archaeological finds and those unearthed from archaeological excavations are property of Kosovo;

7.10 Authorities in charge of any public work are required to comply with the provision of articles 7.4 to 7.9 inclusive.

Until summer 2009, skeletal remains of recent war victims fell exclusively under the jurisdiction of the Office of Missing Persons and Forensics (OMPF). This office was created in 2002 by the United Nations Mission in Kosovo (UNMIK). Missing persons, as a result of the conflict and its aftermath, numbered 5602 in 2002; in 2008 they numbered 1938. In response to the questionnaire, Valérie Brasey, formerly with OMPF, wrote:

> OMPF is dealing with exhumations performed in the frame of the judicial process and in view of performing an autopsy to determine cause of death and identity. Therefore, all exhumations performed by our office are done on the basis of an Order from the relevant judicial authority. The law governing the exhumations performed to identify and determine the cause of death of the remains is the Kosovo Code of Criminal Procedures (art 186 – 189) (UNMIK 2003).
>
> In case there is an accidental discovery of bones, the Police secure the place. If OMPF is informed by the police that bones are found on the surface, we send an anthropologist to have a look at the bones and we bring them to the morgue only if we believe that they may belong to victims of the 98–99 conflict. However, often the police bring directly the bones to the morgue. If they are buried (for instance, accidental discovery of bones by someone digging the soil to build a house), a Court Order is requested and the place is then exhumed by OMPF.
>
> *(Valérie Brasey, pers. comm., 2009)*

A new law passed and approved in July 2009, entitled *Law on the Department of Forensic Medicine* (Law No. 03/L-137), establishes a new Department of Forensic Medicine (DFM) within the Ministry of Justice. The OMPF will be incorporated into this new department. The DFM as the competent public authority will be responsible, among other duties, for 'managing and maintaining a forensic system based on international recognized standards and European best practices to provide forensic medical services, teaching, and outreach services for missing persons' (Article 3). The Forensic Medical-Anthropology and Archaeology Section is one of the sections that will be established under the Division of Forensic Medicine (Article 4).

Under Article 6, the authority of the DFM shall include 'exclusive authority to perform exhumations pursuant to the Criminal Procedure Code of Kosovo and exclusive authority to determine the sex, race, stature, age, and cause of death of the mortal remains of an unidentified person, whenever possible.' Article 8 provides the details of continued European Union Rule of Law Mission in Kosovo (EULEX) participation. EULEX experts at the DFM shall 'monitor, mentor and advise the local experts at the Department, while working in mixed teams' and 'work closely with the local authorities to develop the local capacity'.

Among the definitions provided in Article 2 are the following:

- 'Forensic Anthropology' is a discipline for the application of physical anthropology standard scientific techniques to identify mortal remains and to assist in the medical investigation in the judicial process.
- 'Biological anthropological profile' is a procedure that consists of a physical examination of mortal remains, performed by a forensic anthropologist, with the aim of suggesting the age, sex, origin, stature, and unique features of the victim.
- 'Forensic Archaeology' means the application of archaeological methods to assist in locating, exhuming, and recording mortal remains to assist in the medical investigation in the judicial process.

The role of the osteologist/physical anthropologist

Kosovo currently does not have laws or regulations requiring the presence of a physical anthropologist on site when human remains are excavated, nor is there a requirement to undertake osteological analysis of archaeological human skeletal remains. The preferred procedures when skeletons are excavated by archaeologists would be to document, photograph, draw and then take the remains to the Museum of Kosovo, Institute for Protection of Cultural Monuments of Kosovo, or other regional heritage institution. However, responses to the questionnaire reflect some of the frustrations resulting from a lack of regulations.

Since all cemetery and/or skeletal remains present opportunities for studying various archaeological periods, the presence of an osteologist/physical anthropologist should be mandatory so that the *in situ* context, description of the cemetery and estimations of age and sex can be determined, and archaeological, historical and morphological characteristics profiled.

Although not required by law, co-author Shukriu and the French professor Jean-Luc Lamboley (Université de Grenoble/Université Lyon 2, France) invited a physical anthropologist, Luan Gashi, to their Ulpiana excavations when they identified a human skeleton *in situ*. They plan to issue an invitation again during future excavations at the site. The hope is that Kosovo and the KKCH will develop specific regulations concerning osteological analyses.

Treatment of human remains once excavated

One section of the Law on Cultural Heritage pertinent to materials recovered from archaeological excavations includes:

9.12. Measures regarding the conservation, protection and preservation of the Movable Heritage under protection shall be undertaken by the Competent Institution according to a sub-legal act based on this Law which will set out the proper criteria and necessary equipment for its protection and preservation, and necessary preventive and safety measures concerning damage, decomposition, destruction or loss.

Responses to the questionnaire provided examples of how recent finds of human remains were handled. In December 2004, 11 graves were discovered in the village of Graboc in the region of Fushe Kosova. This find involved Professor Dr Jahja Drancolli (historian, Institute of Archaeology) and Fatmir Peja (archaeologist, Museum of Kosovo), with additional assistance from others. Age-at-death and sex of the remains remain unknown, due to the lack of anthropological experts present at the site. The remains were reburied after they were documented, drawn (CorelDraw) and photographed. In the event that these remains would be accidentally rediscovered, Milot Berisha wrote a short text in Albanian, Serbo-Croatian, English and German, with information regarding the remains. This short text was placed in a jar and buried with the remains.

Luan Gashi reported that the discovery of human remains occurs quite often. These are mainly accidental finds, and provide rich osteological information. In September 2008, Gashi was involved with the accidental discovery at the Church of Grashtica of more than ten skeletons of various ages at the time of death. Most of the archaeological material is from the Early Christian period. The Ministry of Culture gave authorization for the excavation. The skeletons are now housed at the IMMK and are protected in a cleared area, following standard European norms. Gashi hopes to publish the results once excavations and osteological analyses are complete.

Human remains were displayed for the first time in an exposition in Prishtina entitled 'ULPIANA VITA', mounted by Luan Gashi in 2007. The remains are now curated at the Institute for the Protection of Cultural Monuments of Kosovo.

Human remains as well as artefacts can be sent abroad for analysis after completing the documentation and acquiring the necessary permission.

The Law on Cultural Heritage, Section 9.23, indicates that an 'object of Movable Heritage under protection may be temporarily circulated outside of Kosovo in limited circumstances for the purposes of conservation, restoration and exhibition'. This has to have the 'written permission of the Minister according to a sub-legal act based on this Law which will set out the criteria for guaranteeing the safety and protection of such an object.'

Questionnaire responses indicated the benefit of creating professional ties with foreign countries, as they may provide more appropriately equipped laboratories and additional osteological experts to assist in the study of human remains. The research potential in Kosovo for human osteology and archaeology is tremendous. The University of Prishtina is open to international collaborative research and student and faculty exchanges, such as the formal memorandum of agreement with the University of Iowa signed in 2007.

METHODS OF ANTHROPOLOGICAL ANALYSIS

Because Kosovo does not have any anthropologists, preferred osteological methods follow those of Czarnetzki (1971, 1983, 1992), Czarnetzki *et al.* (1997), Graw *et al.* (1999), Norén *et al.* (2005), van Vark *et al.* (1990) and Wittwer-Backofen *et al.* (2008).

CONCLUSION

The spirit and determination of the people of Kosovo is impressive. The passage of cultural laws and the formation of the Kosovo Council for Cultural Heritage are major steps towards the protection of cultural resources. As the KCCH becomes fully operationalized, attention should be given to addressing the role that physical anthropology should play in the future and to developing regulations and protocols to ensure that this critical aspect of cultural heritage becomes an integral part of archaeological research.

USEFUL CONTACTS

Museum of Kosovo, Miladin Popovic, Prishtina, Kosovo.

BIBLIOGRAPHY

Acsádi, G. and Nemeskéri, J. (1970) *History of Human Life Span and Mortality*, Budapest: Akadémiai Kiadó.

Batalli, F. (1978) 'Ekzaminimi i shkakut të vdekjes së Ymer Prizrenit /Examination of the cause of death of Ymer Prizreni', Institute of Forensics, Medicine Faculty, Prishtina, unpublished document, Institute for the Protection of Monuments – Municipality of Prizren.

Breitinger, E. (1937) 'Zur Berechnung der Körperhöhe aus den langen Gliedmassenknochen', *Anthropological Anzeiger*, XIV: 249–74.

CHwB (2004) *Cultural Heritage without Borders*. Available online at http://chwbkosovo.org/ (accessed 26 March 2010).

Czarnetzki, A. (1971) 'Metrische Merkmale der langen Extremitätenknochen im Populationsvergleich', *Homo*, 31: 221–27.

——(1983) 'Methoden der Paläanthropologie', in R.C.A. Rottländer (ed.) *Einführung in die naturwissenschaftlichen Methoden in der Archäologie*, Archaeologica Venatoria 6, Tübingen: Institut für Vorgeschichte der Universität Tübingen.

——(1992) 'Contribución a una crítica metodológica', *Trabajos de Prehistoria*, 49: 400–06.

Czarnetzki, A., Graw, M. and Haffner, H.T. (1997) 'Methode zur Untersuchung des Margo supraorbitalis als Kriterium zur Geschlechtsdiagnose – Reliabilität und Validität', *Rechtsmedizin*, 7: 121–26.

Gavrilović, Ž. (1964) *Kraniometrijska ispitivanja srednjevekovnog coveka sa Novog Brda u Srbiji*, Beograd: Glasnik Antropološkog društva Jugoslavije.

Graw, M., Czarnetzki, A. and Haffner, H.T. (1999) 'The form of the supraorbital margin as a criterion in identification of sex from the skull: investigations based on modern human skulls', *American Journal of Physical Anthropology*, 108: 91–96.

Jovanović, V.S. (1988) *Arheološka istraživanja srednjovekovnih spomenika i nalazišta na Kosovu*, Beograd: Naučni skupovi SANU vol. XLII.

Lengyel, I. (1963) 'Application of biochemical methods to biological reconstruction', *Zeitschrift für Morphologie und Anthropologie*, 54: 1–56.

——(1968) 'Biochemical aspects of early skeletons', in D. Brothwell (ed.) *The Skeletal Biology of Earlier Human Populations*, London: Pergamon.

——(1978) 'Rezultati Laboratorijskog istrazivanja i bioloska rekonskrukcija kosti Ymera Prizreni (Results of the laboratory studies and biological reconstruction of the individuality of Ymer Prizreni)', unpublished document, Institute for the Protection of Monuments – Municipality of Prizren.

Malcolm, N. (1998) *Kosovo: A Short History*, London: Macmillan.

Mikić, Ž. (1982) 'Heiratsgrenzen und Bevölkerungsmischung zwischen Einheimischen und slawischen Zuwanderern in Jugoslawien', *HOMO*, XXXIII (Mainz–Göttingen): 134–49.

——(1983) 'Medieval necropolis ðonaj near Prizren and its anthropological relation to the corresponding neighbouring series', *Godišnji Zbornik Medicinskog Fakulteta*, 29: 147–52.

——(1984a) 'Antropološke karakteristike srednjovekovne nekropole Djonaj kod Prizrena', *Glasnik Muzeja Kosova*, XIII/XIV: 115–22.

——(1984b) 'Beitrag zur Anthropologie spätrömischer bis zum spätmittelaltericher Bevölkerungen Jugoslawiens', *Godišnjak Centra za balkanološka ispitivanja Akademija Nauka i Umetnosti Bosnje i Hercegovine*, XXII: 45–53.

——(1992) '*Antropološka struktura stanovništva Srbije*', Catena mundi, II, 840–50.

——(1994) 'Beitrag zur Anthropologie der Slawen aug dem mittleren und westlichen Balkan', *Balcanica*, XXV: 99–109.

——(1997) *Sloveni na Balkanu – Uporedna antropološka analiza*, Centar za arheološka istraživanja Filozofskog Fakulteta vol. 17, Beograd: Srejovicu.

——(2006) 'Anthropological Traces of Slav Presence in Kosovo and Metohija', *Balcanica*, XXXVI: 39–50.

Nemeskéri, J. (1978) 'Rezultati istrazivanja i antropoloska rekonstrukcija individualiteta Ymera Prizreni (Results of the studies and anthropological reconstruction of the individuality of Ymer Prizreni)', unpublished document, Institute for the Protection of Monuments – Municipality of Prizren.

Norén, A., Lynnerup, N., Czarnetzki, A., *et al.* (2005) 'The lateral angle: a method for sexing using the petrous bone', *American Journal of Physical Anthropology*, 128: 318–23.

Pittard, E. (1920) *Les peuples des Balkans: recherches anthropologiques dans la Péninsule des Balkans, spécialement dans la Dobroudja*, Genève.

Shukriu, E. (2004) *Ancient Kosova*, Prishtina: Museum of Kosova.

UNMIK (2003) *Provisional Criminal Procedure Code of Kosovo*. Available online at www.unmikonline.org/regulations/2003/RE2003–26.pdf (accessed 26 March 2010).

van Vark, G.N., Steerneman, A.G.M. and Czarnetzki, A. (1990) 'Some notes on the definition and application of nonmetrical skeletal variables', *Homo*, 40: 133–36.

Wittwer-Backofen, U., Buckberry, J., Czarnetzki, A., *et al.* (2008) 'Basics in paleodemography: a comparison of age indicators applied to the Early Medieval skeletal sample of Lauchheim', *American Journal of Physical Anthropology*, 137: 384–96.

Lithuania/Lietuva

Rimantas Jankauskas

INTRODUCTION: A BRIEF HISTORY AND CURRENT STATE OF PHYSICAL ANTHROPOLOGY IN LITHUANIA

The formation of the principal anthropological traditions in Europe took place in the 19th century. Many anthropological institutes were established at that time, and started the collection and systematization of palaeoanthropological, and mostly craniological, samples. The main goal of such research was to examine parallels between 'racial' and 'ethnic' history. Under the influence of these traditions, before the First World War, J. Tałko-Hrynciewicz and J. Basana-vičius started the creation of a Lithuanian craniological collection. After the First World War, this was continued by J. Žilinskas in Kaunas and M. Reicher at Vilnius University. After the war, the first Lithuanian anthropological publications appeared (Pavilonis and Česnys 1974: 87).

During the Second World War and the post-war turmoil, the core of these cranial collections was still present, and, after encouragement from archaeologists, the systematic collection of new samples and analysis of materials took place in the 1960s. According to recent regulations, all human remains excavated in Lithuania are deposited at the Department of Anatomy, Histology and Anthropology at the University of Vilnius. Currently, about 15,000 skeletons or skeletal fragments dated from the Mesolithic to early modern times have been catalogued. On the basis of these materials, the extensive studies of Česnys on craniometry, non-metric traits, palaeode-mography, osteometry and stature reconstruction (Česnys and Urbanavičius 1978: 195; Česnys 1982: 407; 1986: 349; 1987: 9; 1988: 75), studies by Balčiūnienė on dental morphology, odon-tology and the pathology of the masticatory apparatus (Česnys and Balčiūnienė 1988; Balčiū-nienė 1996: 277) and by Jankauskas on the morphology of the vertebral column (Jankauskas 1992, 1994a) were undertaken.

Recently, attempts have been made to apply modern techniques and methods to bioarch-aeological studies. Recent case studies of skeletons follow the osteobiographic approach. Indi-vidualized descriptions are developed and serve as an initial database for further interpretation. Some of them are of greater significance in establishing the history of disease, and others shed light particularly on specific regions and historical contexts. Evidence of trauma (Jankauskas 1994a: 12; Teegen *et al.* 1997: 469), non-specific and specific infections such as tuberculosis (Jankauskas 1998: 357; 1999: 551); molecular analyses (Faerman *et al.* 1997: 205; Faerman and Jankauskas 2000: 57), treponematoses (Jankauskas 1989: 481; 1994b: 237), metabolic disorders and endocrine disturbances (Jankauskas 2003: 289), dental disease (Palubeckaitė and Jankauskas 2006: 165), and diseases of the ear (Sakalinskas and Jankauskas 1991: 127) have been reported. Most of these findings are included in regular site reports for archaeologists as annexes or descriptive chapters (Jankauskas 2005: 95). Analysis and interpretation of such evidence enables palaeopathologists to reconstruct the life of an individual and in some cases to investigate the cause of death.

As Lithuania has historically been the battleground of great powers, mass graves left by foreign armies have been uncovered and their skeletal remains examined, such as the mass graves of Napoleonic soldiers (Signoli *et al.* 2004: 219; Palubeckaitė *et al.* 2006: 355) and graves with German soldiers from the First World War (Jankauskas *et al.* 2007: 122).

International collaborations have also been facilitated by applying modern molecular techniques of analysis to detect pathogens, such as the agents of typhus and trench fever (Raoult *et al.* 2006: 112). Contributions of Lithuanian skeletal data into the general database of the Global Health History Project are another example of such international collaboration.

Other studies have focused on population health. Peculiarities of child growth in the past have been assessed (Šereikienė and Jankauskas 2004: 226). Another research trend relates to the investigation of non-specific markers of 'stress'. Pilot studies on Lithuanian skeletal material have revealed certain biological and demographic parallels in dental enamel hypoplasia and fluctuating asymmetry (Palubeckaitė and Jankauskas 2000: 133; 2001: 207; Palubeckaitė *et al.* 2002: 189).

Other research topics have provided results about the lifestyle of the Baltic Mesolithic and Neolithic populations (Butrimas and Jankauskas 1998: 219; Jankauskas and Palubeckaitė 2006: 149; Palubeckaitė and Jankauskas 2006: 165), their nutrition (Antanaitis-Jacobs *et al.* 2009: 12), ancient DNA analyses (Bramanti *et al.* 2009: 137), first millennium AD communities (Jankauskas 2002: 129), and mediaeval and post-mediaeval urban populations (Jankauskas and Urbanavičius 1998: 465).

The first works on forensic anthropology in Lithuania appeared in the late 1960s (Nainys 1972). Earlier exhumations of mass graves from the Second World War, palaeoanthropological work, and examination of the remains of some prominent people encouraged research in osteology. During three decades, professor J.V. Nainys, his students and followers, carried out a great number of studies on the human skeleton, elaborating original methods for sex, stature and age estimation on almost all bones (for a summary, see Garmus and Jankauskas 1993: 5; Garmus 1993, 1996). The exhumation, subsequent analysis and identification of post-war (1944–47) KGB victims from the Tuskulėnai site in Vilnius were a challenge and employment of those methods proved their validity in most cases (Jankauskas *et al.* 2005: 70).

To sum up, Lithuanian physical anthropology has a longstanding tradition in both bioarchaeology and forensic anthropology, and the contribution is recognized in the country and internationally. Significant archaeological skeletal collections can serve generations of future researchers. Traditionally, scholars with degrees in medicine were and still are working in this field, although recently there is a tendency to recruit young researchers from biology and archaeology.

ARCHAEOLOGICAL HUMAN REMAINS AND LEGISLATION

Archaeological legislation

As Lithuania joined the European Convention on the Protection of the Archaeological Heritage (Valetta, 16.I.1992) on 9 November 1999, national legislation is arranged in concert with this convention. The Department of Cultural Heritage under the Ministry of Culture has authority to implement protection and regulation for the use and investigation of all archaeological sites.

Cemeteries are considered as the sites of public respect of unmovable cultural heritage. As human remains of the past are also considered to be archaeological finds, their excavation is conducted by state research institutions and researchers who have been granted a licence. Licences are issued on the basis of qualifications (including former research). As a rule, a Master's degree in archaeology is a minimum prerequisite for applying for such a licence. The presence of a physical anthropologist on the site is not compulsory; in practice, only in cases of numerous burials or 'important' burial sites are anthropologists sub-contracted by the archaeologist managing the site.

HUMAN REMAINS AND LEGISLATION

There is no formal borderline between 'forensic' and 'archaeological' human remains. In the forensic setting, cases over 50 years old are considered to be closed. However, the sites of the Holocaust and the executions that took place after the Second World War are still under the legislation for criminal proceedings although they are older than 50 years. The gap between graves traditionally considered to be of archaeological interest (containing grave goods – in Lithuania – up to the seventeenth century) remains poorly defined.

When human remains are discovered, the police or, when there is no doubt that the remains are archaeological, the local authorities dealing with the cultural heritage are informed. Both institutions further process the case according to their regulations. Police (or other legal authorities) as a rule start a case of identification, submitting finds to the Institute of Forensic Medicine with a 'standard' set of questions to be answered: Are the finds human? If human, how many individuals are present? What are their age and sex? Are there any signs of violence? How old are the finds? etc. According to these answers they will take appropriate action. If the cultural heritage officers deal with the case, the site becomes protected according to the cultural legislation and, if necessary, an excavation is carried out. Unfortunately, coordination between these two institutions does not always work in the best way.

There is no specific legislation for human remains found in Christian (Roman Catholic, Russian Orthodox, Lutheran, Calvinist) churches and churchyards, so the general legislation applies. However, ethical issues of particular ethnic and/or religious groups in Lithuania are considered where applicable. The Jewish community as well as the local Muslim and Karaite communities have strong objections against excavation or disturbance of their historical cemeteries. Such investigations are performed only in the case of absolute necessity (e.g., on a construction site) and the remains are processed in consideration of the wishes of the religious or community authorities.

Once excavated, archaeological human remains are transported to the laboratory of the Department of Anatomy, Histology and Anthropology at Vilnius University. There are no special formal regulations concerning their transportation and further research. Bones are cleaned, conserved (if necessary) and investigated according to the standard protocols of the laboratory. There are no objections to transportation of these samples abroad for research. Some years ago, samples had to be declared in the Customs Office for temporary export of archaeological finds after a formal permission had been granted from the Department of Cultural Heritage. Recently, as Lithuania has joined the Schengen area, skeletal remains can be transported within the EU at least with a formal declaration issued by the University that these artefacts contain no infectious or poisonous substances and have only scientific (non-commercial) value.

METHODS OF ANTHROPOLOGICAL ANALYSIS

Laboratory studies start with the slow drying and cleaning of bones with soft brushes; washing is only undertaken in exceptional cases. If necessary, minimal conservation with PBMA xylene/ acetone solution is performed, which is a procedure in our recommendations for the conservation of archaeological finds. After filling in the inventory sheets indicating the presence or absence of particular bones, sex and age determination is undertaken based on the Recommendations of the Workshop of European Anthropologists (Ferembach *et al.* 1980). In Lithuania, a set of original population-specific forensic anthropological methods have been developed and validated, for example for sex and stature determination from the humerus and femur (Nainys 1972), the tibia and fibula (Garmus 1974: 8; 1989: 8), the radius and ulna (Nainys and Anusevičienė 1984: 60). For age estimation, priority is given to changes of the pubic symphysis with the methods described by Buikstra and Ubelaker (1994) as reference. However, as the pubic bone is characterized by poor preservation, additional criteria (skull suture closure, degenerative changes of the vertebral column and synovial joints, dental attrition, etc.) are referred to as well. For cremated bone, methods described by Gejvall (1981) and Van Vark (1975: 47) as modified by Zviagin (2007) are used.

Routine osteometric or craniometric analysis is performed according to Martin and Saller (1957). Pathological changes of bone and teeth are documented during routine macroscopic observation. For palaeopathological diagnosis, several reference books (e.g., Ortner and Putschar 1985) are used.

Records are kept in paper form; some data are recorded onto spreadsheets. Both the skeletal samples as well as the records are accessible to other researchers.

CONCLUSION

Until recent times, physical anthropology in Lithuania was understood as an almost entirely medical science, although since its very beginnings at the onset of the 19th century various social aspects were also taken into account. Stereotypes about anthropology as a science dealing solely with skull measurements and their typology and, to a lesser extent, regularities of child growth and maturation were imprinted in society by the charisma of numerous prominent scientists and personalities before and after the First World War, and were further developed after the Second World War.

The importance of skeletal studies is recently being considered as twofold: for medicine and human biology, when experimental studies with human beings are limited due to various reasons; and for studies of past societies, these analyses can unveil various aspects of the past. During the last few decades, a biocultural approach has increasingly been applied, as it enables more reliable results to be obtained in studies of population history with the collaboration of anthropologists and archaeologists on the palaeodemography, palaeoepidemiology and palaeoecology and genetic relationships of past populations.

Other promising fields are forensic anthropology (mostly with regard to the identification of skeletal remains) and the population genetics of past populations. The need for closer collaboration with social and cultural anthropology, especially in bioarchaeology (hypothesis testing and application of theories in research of past populations) becomes increasingly more evident. Another need is the application of advanced laboratory techniques (imaging, chemical, physical, palaeogenenetic), which in turn requires the need for international collaboration as Lithuania, being a small country with limited resources, cannot afford to have separate laboratories with expensive equipment.

USEFUL CONTACTS

Department of Anatomy, Histology and Anthropology, University of Vilnius (Anatomijos, histologijos ir antropologijos katedra, Vilniaus Universiteto Medicinos Fakultetas) Čiurlionio 21, Vilnius. Website: www.aha.mf.vu.lt/index.html/

State Forensic Medicine Service (Valstybinė teismo medicinos tarnyba), Didlaukio g. 86E, LT – 08303 Vilnius. Website: www.mruni.eu/tmi/en/

BIBLIOGRAPHY

Antanaitis-Jacobs, I., Richards, M., Daugnora, L., *et al.* (2009) 'Diet in early east Baltic prehistory and the new Lithuanian stable isotope evidence', *Archaeologia Baltica*, 12: 12–30.

Balčiūnienė, I. (1996) 'The odontological characteristics of Lithuanian Balts and their roots', in K. Jones-Bley and M.E. Huld (eds) *The Indo-Europeanization of Northern Europe*, Washington, DC: Journal of Indo-European Studies Monograph No. 17.

Bramanti, B., Thomas, M.G., Haak, W., *et al.* (2009) 'Genetic Discontinuity Between Local Hunter-Gatherers and Central Europe's First Farmers', *Science*, 326 (5949): 137–40.

Buikstra, J.E. and Ubelaker, D.H. (eds) (1994) *Standards for Data Collection from Human Skeletal Remains*, Fayetteville, AR: Arkansas Archeological Service Research Series No.44.

Butrimas, A. and Jankauskas, R. (1998) 'Mesolithic and Neolithic graves in Lithuania: data on the transition from foraging to food production', in M. Zvelebil, R. Dennell and L. Domanska (eds) *Harvesting the Sea, Farming the Forest: the Emergence of the Neolithic Societies in the Baltic Region*, Sheffield: Sheffield Archaeological Monographs 10.

Česnys, G. (1982) 'Changes in body stature of Lithuanians during millennia A.D.', In *2nd Anthropological Congress of Aleš Hrdlička*, Praha: Charles University.

——(1986) 'On the craniology of the Balts', in W. Bernhard and A. Kandler-Pálsson (eds) *Ethnogenese Europäischer Völker*, Stuttgart: Springer-Verlag.

——(1987) 'Paleodemography of Iron Age man in Lithuania', *Historická demografie*, 11: 9–20.

——(1988) 'The variability of discrete cranial traits in the East Baltic area and adjacent territories', *Homo*, 38: 75–97.

Česnys, G. and Balčiūnienė, I. (1988) *Senųjų Lietuvos gyventojų antropologija*, Vilnius: Mokslas.

Česnys, G. and Urbanavičius, V. (1978) 'Materials on the historical demography of Lithuania in the 14th–18th cc', *Anthropologie*, 16: 195–203.

Faerman, M. and Jankauskas, R. (2000) 'Paleopathological and molecular evidence of human bone tuberculosis in Iron Age Lithuania' *Anthropologischer Anzeiger*, 58: 57–62.

Faerman, M., Jankauskas, R., Gorski, A., *et al.* (1997) 'Prevalence of human tuberculosis in a Medieval population of Lithuania studied by ancient DNA analysis', *Ancient Biomolecules*, 1: 205–14.

Ferembach, D., Schwidetzky, I. and Stloukal, M. (1980) 'Recommendations for age and sex diagnoses of skeletons', *Journal of Human Evolution*, 9: 517–49.

Garmus, A. (1974) 'Opredelenije pola po metričeskim priznakam kostej goleni', *Sudebno-medicinskaja ekspertiza*, 26: 8–10.

——(1989) 'Žmogaus ūgio nustatymas pagal jo blauzdos kaulų ilgį', *Sveikatos apsauga*, 24: 8–11.

——(1993) *Pelvic Bones in Forensic Medicine*, Vilnius: Baltic Medico-Legal Association.

——(1996) *Lithuanian Forensic Osteology*, Vilnius: Baltic Medico-Legal Association.

Garmus, A. and Jankauskas, R. (1993) 'Methods of person's identification from skeleton in Lithuania', *Medicina Legalis Baltica*, 3–4: 5–21.

Gejvall, N.-G. (1981) *Determination of burned bones from prehistoric graves*, Ossa letters No.2, Solna: Osteological Research Laboratory, University of Stockholm.

Jankauskas, R. (1989) 'On the origin and antiquity of syphilis', *Current Anthropology*, 30: 481–82.

——(1992) 'Degenerative changes of the vertebral column in Lithuanian paleoosteological material', *Anthropologie*, 30: 109–19.

——(1994a) 'Variability of vertebral column measurements in Lithuanian paleopopulation', *International Journal of Anthropology*, 9: 137–51.

——(1994b) 'Syphilis in Eastern Europe: historical and paleopathological evidences', in O. Dutour *et al.* (eds) *L'origine de la syphilis en Europe. Avant ou apres 1493?, Actes du colloque international de Toulon, 25–28 Novembre 1993*, Toulon: Centre archéologique du Var – Éditions Errance.

——(1995) 'Traumatic lesions in human osteological remains from Neolithic Lithuania', in V. Kazakevičius and R. Sidrys (eds) *Archaeologia Baltica*, Vilnius: Institute of Lithuanian History.

——(1998) 'History of human tuberculosis in Lithuania: possibilities and limitations of paleoosteological evidences', *Bulletin et Mémoires de la Société d'Anthropologie de Paris*, 10: 357–74.

——(1999) 'Tuberculosis in Lithuania: paleopathological and historical correlations', in Gy. Pálfi *et al.* (eds), *Tuberculosis: Past and Present*, Budapest and Szeged: Golden Book and Tuberculosis Foundation.

——(2002) 'Anthropology of the Iron Age inhabitants of Lithuania', in P. Bennike, E.B. Bodzsar and C. Susanne (eds), *Ecological aspects of past human settlements in Europe (Biennial Books of EAA 2)*, Budapest: Eotvos University Press.

——(2003) 'The incidence of Diffuse Idiopathic Skeletal Hyperostosis and Social Status Correlations in Lithuanian Skeletal Materials', *International Journal of Osteoarchaeology*, 13, 289–93.

——(2005) 'Anthropologische Bestimmungen (Skeletal Inventory, Age, Sex and Pathologies of Marvelė sample)', in M. Bertašius (ed.), *Marvelė. Ein Gräberfeld Mittellitauens/Bd I*, Kaunas: Kauno technologijos universiteto Humanitarinių mokslų fakulteto Kultūros projektų centras.

Jankauskas, R., Barkus, A., Urbanavičius, A., *et al.* (2007) 'Military stature variation during the 19th century: Napoleonic versus German soldiers of World War', *Papers on Anthropology (Tartu)*, 16: 122–31.

Jankauskas, R., Barkus, A., Urbanavičius, V., *et al.* (2005) 'Forensic archaeology in Lithuania: the Tuskulėnai mass grave', *Acta Medica Lituanica*, 12: 70–74.

Jankauskas, R. and Palubeckaitė, Ž. (2006) 'Palaeopathological review of Zvejnieki sample. Analysis of cases and considerations about subsistence', in L. Larsson and I. Zagorska (eds) *Back to the Origin: New research in the Mesolithic-Neolithic Zvejnieki cemetery and environment, northern Latvia*, Lund: Almqvist & Wiksell International.

Jankauskas, R. and Urbanavičius, A. (1998) 'Diseases in European Historical Populations and Their Effects on Individuals and Society', *Collegium Antropologicum*, 22: 465–76.

Martin, R. and Saller, K. (1957) *Lehrbuch der Anthropologie in systematischer Darstellung*, Stuttgart: Fischer Verlag.

Nainys, J.V. (1972) *Identifikacija ličnosti po proksimalnym kostiam konečnostei*, Vilnius: Mokslas.

Nainys, J.V. and Anusevičienė, O.V. (1984) 'Nekotoryje anatomo-antropologičeskije osobennosti kostej predplečja', *Archiv anatomii, gistologii i embriologii*, 86: 60–68.

Ohio State University (2002) *The global history of health project*. Available online at http://global.sbs.ohio-state.edu/ (accessed 15 March 2010).

Ortner, D.J. and Putschar, W.G.J. (1985) *Identification of Pathological Conditions in Human Skeletal Remains*, Washington: Smithsonian Institution Press.

Palubeckaitė, Ž. and Jankauskas, R. (2000) 'Inter-population differences on linear enamel hypoplasias in two Lithuanian and Danish medieval and early modern samples', *Papers on Anthropology (Tartu)*, 9: 133–41.

——(2001) 'Fluctuating Asymmetry in Two Lithuanian and Danish Medieval and Early Modern Samples', *Papers on Anthropology (Tartu)*, 10: 207–21.

——(2006) 'Dental status of Zvejnieki sample as reflection of early ontogenesis and activities in adulthood', in L. Larsson and I. Zagorska (eds), *Back to the Origin: New research in the Mesolithic-Neolithic Zvejnieki cemetery and environment, northern Latvia*, Lund: Almqvist & Wiksell International.

Palubeckaitė, Ž., Jankauskas, R. and Boldsen, J. (2002) 'Enamel hypoplasia in Danish and Lithuanian Late Medieval / Early modern samples: a possible reflection of child morbidity and mortality patterns', *International Journal of Osteoarchaeology*, 12: 189–201.

Palubeckaitė, Ž., Jankauskas, R., Ardagna, Y., *et al.* (2006) 'Dental status of Napoleon's Great Army's (1812) mass burial of soldiers in Vilnius: childhood peculiarities and adult dietary habits', *International Journal of Osteoarchaeology*, 16: 355–65.

Pavilonis, S. and Česnys, G. (1974) 'An Essay on the History of Anthropology in Lithuania', *Anatomischer Anzeiger*, 135: 87–96.

Raoult, D., Dutour, O., Houhamdi, L., *et al.* (2006) 'Evidence for Louse-Transmitted Diseases in Soldiers of Napoleon's Grand Army in Vilnius', *The Journal Of Infectious Diseases*, 193: 112–20.

Sakalinskas, V. and Jankauskas, R. (1991) 'An Otological Investigation of Lithuanian Skulls', *International Journal of Osteoarchaeology*, 1: 127–34.

Šereikienė, I. and Jankauskas, R. (2004) 'Lithuanian children's growth in the past – an updated medieval sample', *Papers on Anthropology (Tartu)*, 13: 226–38.

Signoli, M., Ardagna, Y., Adalian, P., *et al.* (2004) 'Discovery of a mass grave of Napoleonic period in Lithuania (1812, Vilnius)', *Comptes Rendus Palevol*, 3: 219–27.

Teegen, W.-R, Schultz, M. and Jankauskas, R. (1997) 'A shortened and deformed humerus from early modern Lithuania (16th/17th century AD): an unusual case of amputation in childhood?', *Journal of Anatomy*, 191: 469–73.

Van Vark, G.N. (1975) 'The investigation of human cremated skeletal material by multivariate statistical methods, II. Measures', *Ossa*, 2: 47–68.

Zviagin, V.N. (2007) *Opredelenije prižiznennych somatičeskich razmerov tela čeloveka pri sudebno-medicinskoj ekspertize skeletirovannych i sožžennych ostankov*, Moscow: publisher unknown.

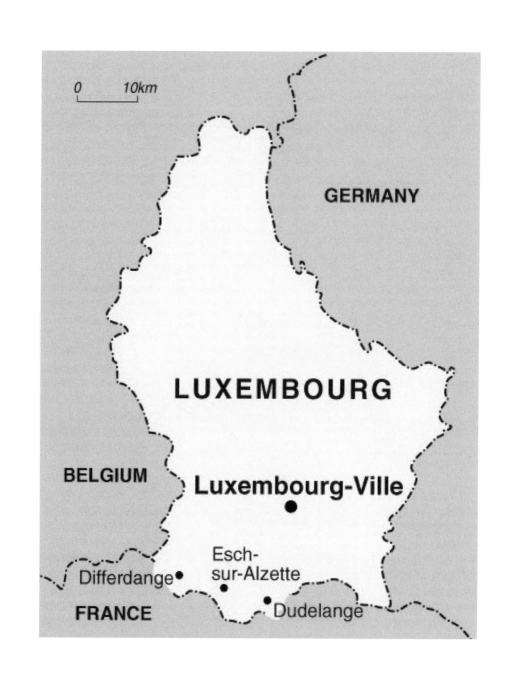

GERMANY

LUXEMBOURG

BELGIUM

Luxembourg-Ville

Esch-
sur-Alzette

Differdange

Dudelange

FRANCE

0   10km

Luxembourg

Ilka Weidig, Christiane Bis-Worch, Nils-Jörn Rehbach,
Ulrich Nothwang, Anja Sindermann, Jean Krier, Foni Le Brun-Ricalens
and Jeannot Metzler

INTRODUCTION: A BRIEF HISTORY AND CURRENT STATE OF PHYSICAL ANTHROPOLOGY IN LUXEMBOURG

As one of Europe's smallest countries, Luxembourg does not have any physical anthropologists. Subsequently, excavation of historical human remains is done by archaeologists, while modern skeletons with potential criminal implications fall under the care of the police and, if there is an indication of a crime, the public prosecutor.

A fairly high number of skeletons (about 1000 individuals) have been studied or are currently under study (Table 23.1). However, many of these studies have not been published yet. In addition, there are about 300 individuals, mostly cremated, from Roman, Iron Age or even older sites that have been studied and published. These have also been listed in Table 23.1.

ARCHAEOLOGICAL HUMAN REMAINS AND LEGISLATION

Archaeological legislation

In Luxembourg, a number of laws concerning human remains exist, and are available online in French. These concern legislation regarding transportation, burial and cremation (Service Central de Legislation 2009a) and the use of bodies or body parts for scientific purposes (Service Central de Legislation 2009b, 2009c); however, these all refer to 'fresh' human remains; no specific legislation regarding skeletal human remains exists.

Upon the discovery of skeletal human remains, the first step is to identify preliminarily whether the remains are archaeological or more recent (forensic) in nature. This differentiation is initially handled very pragmatically, based on the context in which the remains are found, the presence or absence of dental fillings, together with additional information such as jewellery, clothing, position of the bones and so forth. Human remains of possible modern origin (i.e., younger than 80 years) are the responsibility of the Luxembourg police. Archaeological human remains are the sole responsibility of the Musée National d'Histoire et d'Art (MNHA).

If human remains might belong to First and Second World War soldiers, the International Tracing Service (ITS) of the International Committee of the Red Cross (ICRC) will be informed. For the remains of US soldiers, the American Military Cemetery in Hamm is the

Table 23.1 Sites with human remains within Luxembourg

Site	Type of site	Chronology	n=approximate number of individuals	Studied by	Publication
Altwies Groufbirg	Merovingian cemetery	6th–7th century AD	app. 20		
Altwies 'op dem Boesch'	Two graves from the Bell-Beaker culture (Glockenbecherkultur)	3820 ± 40 BP (279B) and 3680 ± 40 BP (383B)	3	Service public de Wallonie, Belgium	Toussaint *et al.* 2002
Bartringen-Bourmicht	Merovingian cemetery situated in ruins from the late Roman period	Merovingian, 5th–7th century AD	12	Giessen University, Germany	Teegen *et al.* 2003
Berdorf-Kalekapp I	Isolated finds		at least 1	MNHA	under study
Berdorf-Schnellert	Grave in context of a pseudo-megalithic monument	4180 ± 40 BP (1) 4120 ± 40 BP (2)	2	MNHA, Service public de Wallonie, Belgium	Valotteau and Toussaint 2004
Berdorf-St. Mathieu	Cave	3880 BP ± 50 a	1	MNHA, only dated/not studied	Valloteau *et al.* 2008
Bertrange-Tossenberg	Cemetery of Gallo-Roman settlement (vicus) of Mamer	Roman, 1st–5th century AD	56 (including 54 cremations)	Giessen University, Germany	Kunter 2003
Clemency	Aristocratic grave	app. 60 BC	1 cremation	Giessen University, Germany	Kunter 1991
Diekirch-Deiwelselter	Grave in context of megalithic (?) monument	5320 ± 40 BP (1), 4310 ± 50 BP (2)	2	MNHA, F. Chenal (France)	Chenal and Valotteau (in prep)
Fentingen	Church	10th–15th century AD	44	ADFG, Germany	Rehbach *et al.* 2005
Feulen	Cemetery	1st century BC	109 graves (107 studied)	Giessen University, Germany	Kunter 2006
Givenich	Manor house with chapel	11th/12th–15th century AD	68	ADFG, Germany	Rehbach *et al.* 2009, Weidig *et al.* 2009
Goeblange-Nospelt	Cemetery	50 – app. 10 BC	14 graves (11 cremations studied)	INRAP, France	Le Goff 2009
Grevenmacher	Cemetery with church	8th – early 15th century	app. 350 (partially cremated)	Tübingen University, Germany	under study, Obertova *et al.* 2008, Trautwein 2007
Heffingen-Atsebach	Isolated finds under rock ledge	5010 ± 80 BP	2	Musée National d'histoire naturelle Luxembourg (MNHNL)	Heuertz 1969, Spier 1993

Table 23.1 (continued)

Site	Type of site	Chronology	n=approximate number of individuals	Studied by	Publication
Heffingen-Loschbour	Mesolithic burial and cremation under rock ledge	7960 ± 40 BP (cremation) 7205 ± 50 BP (burial)	2 (including 1 cremation)	MNHNL, Service public de Wallonie, Belgium	Heuertz 1969, Toussaint *et al.* 2009
Heffingen-Schléd	Iron Age grave under rock ledge	2490 ± 40 BP	1	MNHA, MNHNL	Heuertz 1969, Valloteau 2009
Hersberg-Bourlach	Iron Age grave	2450 ± 40 BP	1	MNHA	Valloteau *et al.* 2009, Valloteau 2009
Larochette-Manzebaach	Isolated find, 'grave' under rock ledge	3860 ± 40 BP (1), 3820 ± 40 BP (2)	1?, 2 bones were dated	MNHA, only dated, not studied	Valloteau *et al.* 2008
Luxemburg-Hospice civil	Former convent	Baroque, late 16th century – 1792 AD	27	ADFG, Germany	Nothwang *et al.* 2004; Rehbach *et al.* 2007
Luxemburg-Neumünster	Cemetery and monastery	13th–18th century, majority 14th–15th century AD	800 (175 studied)	Amsterdam University, Netherlands	d'Hollosy and de Meulenmeester 1999
Luxemburg-St. Esprit	Convent	12th–17th century, majority 15th century AD	>300	ADFG, Germany	under study; Nothwang *et al.* 2006; Rehbach and Bis-Worch 2006; Rehbach and Nothwang 2007; Rehbach *et al.* 2007, Rehbach and Nothwang in press
Mersch	Cemetery with church	mediaeval			
Oetrange-Kakert	Isolated finds in cave/diaclase	4980 ± 40 BP (1), 5040 ± 50 BP (2), 4950 ± 40 BP (3)	app. 6	MNHA, MNHNL	Heuertz 1969, Valloteau *et al.* 2008
Oetrange-Schlaed	Isolated find under rock ledge		1	MNHNL	Heuertz 1969
Pettange-Moersdorf	Isolated find, early Iron Age	appr. 800 BC	1	MNHNL	Heuertz 1969
Remerschen-Schengerwis	Iron age grave in a silo	Iron Age	1		
Titelberg-Lamadeleine Plon	Cemetery of an Iron Age and Roman settlement	1000 BC – 1st century AD	85 (including 79 cremations)	I. Villemeur, France	Villemeur 1999
Walsbillig-Karelslé	Isolated finds in a grotto	5060 ± 40 BP (1 of 2)	2	MNHA, only dated, not studied	Valloteau *et al.* 2008

official contact in Luxembourg. In the past, several searches for crashed American military air-craft have been carried out by the JPAC (Joint Prisoner of War/Missing in Action Accounting Command, Hawaii). A German military cemetery for Second World War soldiers is located at Sandweiler. Additional human remains from the two World Wars, as well as from previous European wars, are buried at the old garrison cemetery in Clausen. Upon the discovery of remains of German soldiers, the Volksbund Deutsche Kriegsgräberfürsorge e.V. at the military cemetery at Sandweiler should be contacted.

HUMAN REMAINS AND LEGISLATION

Historical or archaeological remains are excavated by the MNHA or persons subcontracted by the MNHA. During excavation, the presence of a physical anthropologist is not legally required. As the MNHA employs a physical anthropologist in special cases only, there is often no physical anthropologist present during excavation. The excavation teams of the MNHA comprise scientists with a university degree in archaeology as well as archaeological technicians; similar qualifications are necessary for subcontractors.

Once excavated, the human remains are subsequently stored at the MNHA. In some cases, the remains are later reburied. As there is no physical anthropologist at the MNHA (or in Luxembourg in general), the scientific study of the human remains is subcontracted to physical anthropologists in other countries. So far, studies on Luxembourg human remains have been conducted by German, French, Dutch and Belgian researchers (see Table 23.1). The analysis of the remains is undertaken in the scientists' home institution. In order to transport skeletal human remains out of Luxembourg within the European Union, a special permit from the MNHA is necessary.

METHODS OF ANTHROPOLOGICAL ANALYSIS

Human remains from the mediaeval and modern ages in Luxembourg mainly derive from inhumations, while at the majority of older sites there is a predominant presence of cremation burials. Accordingly, different methods have been used to study the human remains.

The published anthropological studies include estimation of sex, age, stature, and the identi-fication of dental and skeletal pathologies and anatomical variations. The estimation of sex, age and stature are based on internationally recognized methods. Sex estimation mainly employs the methods covered in Bass (1971), Brothwell (1972) and Ferembach *et al.* (1979). In addition, some authors consider bone robustness and measurements of the femur and the head of the radius (Black 1978; Berrizbeittia 1989; Di Bennardo and Taylor 1979). The sex of infants and subadult individuals is usually estimated based on the methods of Schutkowski (1993) or Majo (1996).

A number of methods are used to estimate age, using both cranial and postcranial skeletal elements. Methods based on cranial elements include suture closure (see, e.g., Masset 1989; Masset *et al.* 1990; Meindl and Lovejoy 1985; Nemeskéri *et al.* 1960; Rösing 1977) and dental wear (see, e.g., Lovejoy 1985; Miles 1962, 1963). Postcranially, the clavicle (Szilvássy 1980), the thoracic region (Loth and İşcan 1989), and the *os coxa* including both the auricular surface (*facies auricularis*) and the pubic symphysis (*facies symphysialis*) have been employed (Brooks and Suchey 1990; Bruzek 1991, 1992a, 1992b; Bruzek *et al.* 1996; Gilbert and McKern 1973; Lovejoy *et al.* 1985; McKern and Stewart 1957; Meindl *et al.* 1985; Murail *et al.* 1999; Nemeskéri *et al.* 1960;

Todd 1920). Different methods of age estimation are used for subadults, depending upon their age. Age estimation for children includes study of tooth development (see, e.g., Hodacová 1977; Moorrees *et al.* 1963; Ubelaker 1978), epiphyseal fusion (see, e.g., Brothwell 1972; Ferembach *et al.* 1979; Owings-Webb and Suchey 1985) and long bone length (see, e.g., Stloukal and Hanáková 1978). The age of prenatal and perinatal children is estimated based on long bone length, using Scheuer *et al.* (1980) for prenatal children and Fazekas and Kósa (1978) for perinatal children.

Stature estimation is carried out using the formulae of Cleuvenot and Houët (1993), Olivier *et al.* (1978), Trotter and Gleser (1958) or the formulae by Pearson (1899), the latter being adapted for non-accelerated populations (Rösing 1988).

For cremated human remains, specific standards are used. These include methods detailed by Binford (1972), Buikstra and Swegle (1989), Dokladal (1969), Duday (1987), Gaillard (1960), Gejvall (1963), Hermann (1976), Holck (1987), Krogman (1978), MacLaughin and Bruce (1985), Malinowski and Porawski (1969), McKinley (1993), Rösing (1977), Schutkowski (1991), Schutkowski and Hummel (1987), Van Vark (1974), Wahl (1982, 1983, 1988a, 1988b, 1996), and Wahl and Henke (1980).

CONCLUSION

As the institution responsible for all archaeological excavations in Luxembourg, enquiries concerning human skeletal remains should be directed to the MNHA or to the authors of the relevant publications. At the moment, the MNHA homepage (Musée National d'Histoire et d'Art) contains only general information about the collections and is in French only; however, the MNHA maintains a database on excavation sites which is planned to be available online in the future.

USEFUL CONTACTS

Musée National d'Histoire et d'Art, Marché-aux-Poissons, L-2345 Luxembourg. Website: www.mnha.public.lu/

BIBLIOGRAPHY

Bass, W. (1971) *Human Osteology. A Laboratory and Field Manual of the Human Skeleton*, Columbia, MO: Missouri Archaeological Society.
Berrizbeittia, E.L. (1989) 'Sex determination with the head of the radius', *Journal of Forensic Sciences*, 14: 1206–13.
Binford, L.R. (1972) 'Analysis of cremation from three Michigan sites', in L.R. Binford (ed.) *An Archaeological Perspective*, New York: Seminar Press.
Bis-Worch, C. (2008) 'Zu den Ausgrabungen des Nationalmuseums auf der Escher Gleicht – Bilanz der Jahre 2002 bis 2006', *Empreintes Annuaire du Musée National d'Histoire et d'Art*, 1: 85–91.
Black, T.K. (1978) 'A new method for assessing the sex of fragmentary skeletal remains: femora shaft circumference', *American Journal of Physical Anthropology*, 48: 227–32.
Brooks, S. and Suchey, J.M. (1990) 'Skeletal age determination based on the os pubis: a comparison of the Ascádi-Nemeskéri and Suchey-Brooks method', *Human Evolution*, 5: 227–38.
Brothwell, D.R. (1972) *Digging up Bones: The Excavation, Treatment and Study of Human Skeletal Remains*, London: British Museum (Natural History).

Bruzek, J. (1991) 'Fiabilité des procédés de détermination du sexe à partir de l'os coxal. Implications à l'étude du dimorphisme sexuel de l'homme fossile', unpublished PhD thesis, IPH Paris.

——(1992a) 'La diagnose sexuelle à partir du squelette: possibilité et limites', *Archéo-Nil*, 2: 43–51.

——(1992b) 'Fiabilité des fonctions discriminantes dans la détermination sexuelle de l'os coxal. Critiques et propositions', *Bulletins et Mémoires de la Société d'Anthropologie de Paris*, 4: 67–104.

Bruzek, J., Castex, D. and Majo, T. (1996) 'Evaluation des caractères morphologiques de la face sacro-pelvienne de l'os coxal. Proposition d'une nouvelle méthode de diagnose sexuelle', *Bulletin de la Société d'Anthropologie de Paris*, 8: 491–502.

Buikstra, J.E. and Swegle, M. (1989) 'Bone modification due to burning: experimental evidence', in R. Bonnichsen and M.H. Sorg (eds) *Bone modification*, University of Maine, Orono: Centre for the studies of the first Americans, Institute for Quaternary Studies.

Cleuvenot, E. and Houët, F. (1993) 'Proposition de nouvelles équations d'estimation de statures applicables pour une sexe indéterminé, et basées sure les échantillons de Trotter et Gleser', *Bulletins et Mémoires de la Société d'Anthropologie de Paris*, 5: 245–53.

d'Hollosy, M. and de Meulemeester, J. (1999) 'Le cimetière de Saint-Jean et l'étude des squelettes', in L. Baray (ed.) *Le Passé recomposé, Archéologie urbaine à Luxembourg, Catalogue d'exposition du Musée national d'histoire et d'art*, Luxembourg: Musée National d'Histoire et d'Art.

Di Bennardo, R. and Taylor, J.V. (1979) 'Sex assessment of the femur: a test of a new method', *American Journal of Physical Anthropology*, 50: 635–37.

Dokladal, M. (1969) 'Über die heutigen Möglichkeiten der Personenidentifizierung aufgrund von verbrannten Knochen', in M. Dokladal (ed.) *Aktuelle Kriminologie*, Hamburg: Kriminalistik-Verlag.

Duday, H. (1987) 'La quantification des restes humains. Applications à l'étude des sépultures à incinération out des différentiels autres que la conservation', *Actes de la Table-ronde de la RCP 742 du CNRS. Saint-Germain-en-Laye*: 17–21.

Fazekas, I.G. and Kósa, F. (1978) *Forensic Fetal Osteology*, Budapest: Akadémiai Kiadó.

Ferembach, D., Schwidetzky, I. and Stloukal, M. (1979) 'Empfehlungen für die Alters-und Geschlechtsdiagnose am Skelett', *Homo*, 30: 1–32.

Gaillard, J. (1960) 'Détermination sexuelle d'un os coxal fragmentaire', *Bulletins et Mémoires de la Société d'Anthropologie de Paris*, 11 (série I): 255–67.

Gejvall, N.-G. (1963) 'Cremations', in D.R. Brothwell and E. Higgs (eds) *Science in Archaeology*, London: Thames & Hudson.

——(1981) 'Determination of burned bones from prehistoric graves', *Ossa Letter*, 2: 1–13.

Gilbert, B.M. and McKern, T.W. (1973) 'A method for aging the female os pubis', *American Journal of Physical Anthropology*, 38: 31–38.

Hermann, B. (1976) 'Neuere Ergebnisse zur Beurteilung menschlicher Brandknochen', *Zeitschrift für Rechtsmedizin*, 77: 191–200.

Heuertz, M. (1969) *Documents préhistoriques du territoire luxembourgeois – Le milieu naturel l'homme et son ouvre, fasc. 1*, Luxembourg: Publication du Musée d'Histoire Naturelle et de la Société des Naturalistes Luxembourgeois.

Hodacová, Z. (1977) 'Determination of the dental age on osteological material of immature individuals', *Anthropologie Brno*, 15: 111–15.

Holck, P. (1987) *Cremated Bones*, Oslo: Universitetet i Oslo.

Krogman, W.M. (1978) *The Human Skeleton in Forensic Medicine*, Springfield, IL: Charles C. Thomas.

Kunter, M. (1991) 'Bestimmung der Leichenbrandreste von Clemency', in J. Metzler et al. (eds) *Clemency et les tombes de l'aristocratie en Gaule Belgique*, Dossiers d'Archéologie du Musée national d'Histoire et d'Art No. 1, Luxembourg: Musée national d'Histoire et d'Art.

——(2003) 'Anthropologische Untersuchung der beiden Skelette vom Tossenberg sowie der Leichenbrände an der Universität Giessen', *Den Ausgriewer*, 13: 34–35.

——(2006) 'Kapitel 8.1. Anthropologische Analyse der menschlichen Leichenbrände aus dem Brandgräberfeld von Feulen, Luxembourg', in S. Schendzielorz (ed.) *Feulen, ein spätlatènezeitlich-frührömisches Gräberfeld in Luxemburg*, Dossiers d'Archéologie du Musée national d'Histoire et d'Art No. 9, Luxembourg: Musée National d'Histoire et d'Art.

Le Goff, I. (2009) '4.1. l'Homme', in J. Metzler and C. Gaeng (eds) *Goeblange-Nospelt, une nécropole aristocratique trévire*, Dossiers d'archéologie du Musée national d'Histoire et d'Art No. 13, Luxembourg: Musée National d'Histoire et d'Art.

Loth, S.R. and İşcan, M.Y. (1989) 'Morphological assessment of age in the adult: the thoracic region', in M.Y. İşcan (ed.) *Age Markers in the Human Skeleton*, Springfield, IL: Charles C. Thomas.

Lovejoy, C.O. (1985) 'Dental wear in the Libben population: its functional pattern and role in the determination of adult skeletal age at death', *American Journal of Physical Anthropology*, 68: 47–56.

Lovejoy, C.O., Meindl, R.S., Pryzbeck, T.R., *et al.* (1985) 'Chronological metamorphosis of the auricular surface of the ilium: a new method for the determination of adult skeletal age at death', *American Journal of Physical Anthropology*, 68: 15–28.

MacLaughin, S.M. and Bruce, M.F. (1985) 'A simple univariate technique for determining sex from fragmentary femora: its application to a Scottish Short Cist Population', *American Journal of Physical Anthropology*, 67: 413–17.

Majo, T. (1996) 'Réflexions méthodologiques liées à la diagnose sexuelles des squelette non-adultes', *Bulletins et Mémoires de la Société d'Anthropologie de Paris*, 8: 481–90.

Malinowski, A. and Porawski, R. (1969) 'Identifikationsmöglichkeiten menschlicher Brandknochen mit besonderer Berücksichtigung ihres Gewichts', *Zacchia*, 44: 1–19.

Masset, C. (1989) 'Age estimation on the basis of cranial sutures', in M.Y. İşcan (ed.) *Age Markers in the Human Skeleton*, Springfield, IL: Charles C. Thomas.

Masset, C., de Castro, E. and Almeida, M.E. (1990) *Âge et sutures craniennes*, Cattana: Atti del Academia Mediterranea delle Scienze.

McKern, T.W. and Stewart, T.D. (1957) *Skeletal Age Changes in Young American Males, Analysed From the Standpoint of Identification*, Natick, MA: Headquarter QM Research Dir. Command, Technical Report EP.

McKinley, J.I. (1993) 'Bone fragment size and weights of bone from modern British cremations and the implications for the interpretation of archaeological cremations', *International Journal of Osteoarchaeology*, 3: 283–87.

Meindl, R.S. and Lovejoy, C.O. (1985) 'Ectocranial suture closure: a revised method for the determination of skeletal age at death based on the lateral-anterior sutures', *American Journal of Physical Anthropology*, 68: 57–66.

Meindl, R.S., Lovejoy, C.O., Mensforth, R.P., *et al.* (1985) 'A revised method of age determination using the os pubis with a review and tests of accuracy of other current methods of pubic symphyseal aging', *American Journal of Physical Anthropology*, 68: 29–45.

Miles, A.E.W. (1962) 'Assessment of the ages of a population of Anglo-Saxons from their dentitions', *Proceedings of the Royal Society of Medicine (London)*, 55: 881–86.

——(1963) 'The dentition in the assessment of individual age in skeletal material', in D.R. Brothwell (ed.) *Dental Anthropology*, Oxford: Pergamon.

Moorrees, C.F.A., Fanning, E.A. and Hunt Jr., E.E. (1963) 'Age variation of formation stages for ten permanent teeth', *Journal of Dental Research*, 42: 1490–1502.

Murail, P., Bruzek, J., and Braga, J. (1999) 'A new approach to sexual diagnosis in past populations. Practical adjustments from Van Vark's procedure', *International Journal of Osteoarchaeology*, 9: 39–53.

Musée National d'Histoire et d'Art (2009) *Musée National d'Histoire et d'Art: Collections*. Available online at www.mnha.lu (accessed 15 May 2009).

Nemeskéri, J., Harsányi, L. and Ascádi, G. (1960) 'Methoden zur Diagnose des Lebensalters von Skelettfunden', *Anthropologischer Anzeiger*, 24: 70–95.

Nothwang, U., Rehbach, N.-J., Flohr, S., *et al.* (2004) 'Die Gräberserie "Hospice civil": Eine Bestandsaufnahme aus dem Barock', *Bulletin d'information du Musée national d'histoire et d'art*, 17: 67–68.

Nothwang, U., Rehbach, N.-J. and Rauschmann, M.A. (2006) 'Eine Obduktion aus der Zeit um 1600 aus Luxemburg', in N. Benecke (ed.) *Beiträge zur Archäozoologie und prähistorischen Anthropologie*, Langenweißbach: Beier & Beran.

Obertova, Z., Menninger, M., Wahl, J., *et al.* (2008) 'Die "Traufkinder" von der Nordseite der Kirche "10" in Grevenmacher (Luxemburg) – anthropologische Auswertung der Skelettreste', *Empreintes Annuaire du Musée National d'histoire et d'art*, 1: 92–99.

Olivier, G., Aaron, C., Fully, G., *et al.* (1978) 'New estimations of stature and cranial capacity in modern man', *Journal of Human Evolution*, 7: 513–18.

Owings-Webb, P.A. and Suchey, J.M. (1985) 'Epiphyseal union of the anterior iliac creast and medial clavicule in a modern multiracial sample', *American Journal of Physical Anthropology*, 68: 457–66.

Pearson, K. (1899) 'Mathematical contributions to the theory of evolution. V. On the reconstruction of the stature of Prehistoric Races', *Philosophical Transactions Royal Society Series A*, 192: 169–245.

Rehbach, N.-J. and Bis-Worch, C. (2006) 'Das Kloster St. Esprit in Luxemburg und seine Toten', in N. Benecke (ed.) *Beiträge zur Archäozoologie und prähistorischen Anthropologie*, Langenweißbach: Beier & Beran.

Rehbach, N.-J. and Nothwang, U. (2007) 'Ein Fall von Polydaktylie aus dem Spätmittelalter', in N. Benecke (ed.) *Beiträge zur Archäozoologie und prähistorischen Anthropologie*, Langenweißbach: Beier & Beran.

——(2009) 'Syphilis in einem frühneuzeitlichen Nonnenkloster in Luxemburg', in N. Benecke (ed.) *Beiträge zur Archäozoologie und prähistorischen Anthropologie*, Langenweißbach: Beier & Beran.

Rehbach, N.-J., Nothwang, U. and Flohr, S. (2005) 'Die menschlichen Skelettfunde aus Fentingen – Ein Vorbericht', *Bulletin d'information du Musée national d'histoire et d'art*, 18: 70–72.

Rehbach, N.-J., Nothwang, U. and Weidig, I. (2007) 'Veränderungen der Bestattungskultur aus anthropologischer Sicht am Beispiel eines Frauenordens aus Luxemburg', *Archäologie der frühen Neuzeit. Mitteilungen der Deutschen Gesellschaft für Archäologie des Mittelalters und der Neuzeit*, 18: 56–58.

Rehbach, N.-J., Nothwang, U., Weidig, I., *et al.* (2009) *Abschlussbericht zur anthropologischen Untersuchung einer Givenicher Skelettserie aus dem 8.-15. Jahrhundert*, Frankfurt: ADFG.

Rösing, F.W. (1977) 'Methoden und Aussagemöglichkeiten der anthropologischen Leichenbrandbearbeitung', *Archäologie und Naturwissenschaften*, 1: 53–80.

——(1988) 'Körperhöhenrekonstruktion aus Skelettmaßen', in R. Knussmann (ed.) *Anthropologie. Handbuch der vergleichenden Biologie des Menschen*, Stuttgart: Verlag Gustav Fischer.

Scheuer, J.L., Musgrave, J.H. and Evans, S.P. (1980) 'The estimation of late fetal and perinatal age from limb bone length by linear and logarithmic regression', *Annals of Human Biology*, 7: 257–65.

Schutkowski, H. (1991) 'Experimentelle Befunde an Brandknochen und ihre Bedeutung für die Diagnose von Leichenbränden', *Archäologische Informationen*, 14: 206–18.

——(1993) 'Sex determination of infant and juvenile skeletons: I. Morphognostic features', *American Journal of Physical Anthropology*, 90: 199–205.

Schutkowski, H. and Hummel, B. (1987) 'Variabilitätsvergleich von Wandstärken für die Geschlechtszuweisung an Leichenbränden', *Anthropologischer Anzeiger*, 45: 43–47.

Service Central de Legislation (SCL) (2009a) *Cadavres humains*. Available online at www.legilux.public.lu/leg/textescoordonnes/compilation/recueil_lois_speciales/CADAVRES.pdf (accessed 15 May 2009).

——(2009b) *Mémorial du Grand-Duché de Luxembourg No. 61 Loi du 17 novembre 1958 concernant l'autopsie, le moulage, ainsi que l'utilisation de cadavres humains dans un intérêt scientifique ou thérapeutique*. Available online at www.legilux.public.lu/leg/a/archives/1958/0061/a061.pdf (accessed 15 May 2009).

——(2009c) *Mémorial du Grand-Duché de Luxembourg A – No. 98 Loi du 25 novembre 1982 réglant le prélèvement de substances d'origine humaine*. Available online at www.legilux.public.lu/leg/a/archives/1982/0098/a098.pdf (accessed 15 May 2009).

Spier, F. (1993) 'Un site du Mésolithique moyen à Ettelbruck-Haardt', *Bulletin de la Société Préhistorique Luxembourgeoise, Revue interrégionale de Pré et Protohistoire*, 14: 91–106.

Stloukal, M. and Hanáková, H. (1978) 'Die Länge der Längsknochen altslawischer Bevölkerungen – Unter besonderer Berücksichtigung von Wachstumsfragen', *Homo*, 29: 53–69.

Szilvássy, J. (1980) 'Age determination on the sternal articular face of the clavicle', *Journal of Human Evolution*, 9: 609–10.

Teegen, W.-R., Kreutz, K., Diegmann, J., *et al.* (2003) 'Meningeale Veränderungen in der merowingerzeitlichen Adelsnekropole von Bartringen (Luxemburg) – I. makroskopische Untersuchungen', in N. Benecke (ed.) *Beiträge zur Archäozoologie und prähistorischen Anthropologie* 4, Stuttgart: Wais & Partner.

Todd, T.W. (1920) 'Age changes in the pubic bone', *American Journal of Physical Anthropology*, 3: 285–334.

Toussaint M., Brou, L., Le Brun-Ricalens, F., *et al.* (2009) 'The Mesolithic site of Heffingen-Loschbour (Grand Duchy of Luxembourg), A yet undescribed human cremation possibly from the Rhine-Meuse-Schelde culture: anthropological, radiometric and archaeological implications', in P. Crombé *et al.* (eds), *Chronology and Evolution within the Mesolithic of North-West Europe*, Proceedings of an International Meeting, Brussels, May 30th-June 1st 2007, Cambridge: Cambridge Scholars Publishing.

Toussaint, M., Le Brun-Ricalens, F. and Hauzeur, A. (2002) 'Les deux sépultures campaniformes d'Altwies – "Op dem Boesch" (Grand-Duché de Luxembourg): méthodologie, données anthropologiques préliminaires et essai de caractérisation des pratiques sépulcrales', *Bulletin de la Société Préhistorique Luxembourgeoise*, 23–24: 249–84.

Trautwein, B. (2007) 'Anthropologische Auswertung einer Stichprobe aus dem Brandknochengemenge von Grevenmacher (Luxemburg)', unpublished Master's thesis, University of Tübingen.

Trotter, M. and Gleser, G.C. (1958) 'A re-evaluation of stature based on measurements of stature taken during life and of long bones after death', *American Journal of Physical Anthropology*, 16: 79–123.

Ubelaker, D.H. (1978) *Human Skeletal Remains: Excavation, Analysis and Interpretation*. Washington, DC: Smithsonian Institute Press.

Valotteau, F. (2004) 'Monument mégalithique (?) de Diekirch-«Deiwelselter»', *Rapport interne d'Archéologie programmée du Service d'archéologie préhistorique, no. 6*, Musée national d'histoire et d'art, Luxembourg, multigraphié, 68.

Valotteau, F. and Chenal, F. (2010) 'Étude anthropologique et datation radiocarbone des squelettes néolithiques découverts en 1892 au Deiwelselter de Diekirch', *Bulletin de la Société Préhistorique Luxembourgeoise*, 29: 179–88

Valotteau, F., Le Brun-Ricalens, F., Löhr, H., *et al.* (2008) 'Le Bassin mosellan luxembourgeois et allemand au cours des IVème et IIIème millénaires' in M.-H. Dias-Meirinho *et al.* (eds), *Les industries lithiques taillées des IVème et IIIème millénaires en Europe occidentale*, Actes du colloque international de Toulouse, 7–9 avril 2005, British Archaeological Reports S1884, Oxford: Archaeopress.

Valotteau, F., Toussaint, M., Chenal, F., *et al.* (2009) 'Une sépulture du premier Âge du Fer sous abri-sous-roche à Hersberg (commune de Bech): une redécouverte 94 ans après', *Empreintes*, 2: 22–31.

Valotteau, F., Toussaint, M. and Le Brun-Ricalens, F. (2000) 'Le pseudo-dolmen du Schnellert, commune de Berdorf (Grand-Duché de Luxembourg): état de la question à l'issue de la campagne de fouille 2000', *Bulletin de la Société Préhistorique Luxembourgeoise*, 22: 131–61.

Van Vark, G.N. (1974) 'The investigation of human cremated skeletal material by multivariate statistical methods. I. Methodology', *Ossa*, 1: 63–95.

Villemeur, I. (1999) 'L'Homme', in J. Metzler *et al.* (eds) *Lamadelaine – une nécropole de l'oppidum du Titelberg*, Dossier d'Archeologie du Musée National d'Histoire et d'Art No. 4, Luxembourg: Musée National d'Histoire et d'Art.

Wahl, J. (1982) 'Leichenbranduntersuchungen. Ein Überblick über die Bearbeitungs-und Aussagemöglichkeiten von 1Brandgräbern', *Prähistorische Zeitschrift*, 57: 2–125.

——(1983) 'Zur metrischen Altersbestimmung von kindlichen und jugendlichen Leichenbränden', *Homo*, 34: 48–54.

——(1988a) *Süderbrarup. Ein Gräberfeld der römischen Kaiserzeit und Völkerwanderungszeit in Angeln. II. Anthropologische Untersuchungen*. Offa-Bücher Neumünster Neue Folge 64.

——(1988b) 'Osteologischer Teil. A. Menschenknochen', in J. Wahl And M. Kokabi (eds) *Das römische Gräberfeld von Stettfeld I*, Forschungen und Berichte zur Vor-und Frühgeschichte in Baden-Württemberg, Band 029, Stuttgart: Theis.

——(1996) 'Erfahrungen zur metrischen Geschlechtsdiagnose bei Leichenbränden', *Homo*, 47: 339–59.

Wahl, J. and Henke, W. (1980) 'Die Pars petrosa als Diagnostikum für die multivariat-biometrische Geschlechtsbestimmung von Leichenbrandmaterial', *Zeitschrift für Morphologie und Anthropologie*, 70: 258–68.

Weidig, I., Sindermann, A., Rehbach, N.-J., *et al.* (2009) 'A medieval skeletal series from Givenich (Luxembourg) and its pathologies', in N. Benecke (ed.) *Beiträge zur Archäozoologie und prähistorischen Anthropologie 7*, Langenweißbach: Beier & Beran.

KOSOVO

SERBIA

BULGARIA

Kumanov

Skopje

FORMER YUGOSLAV
REPUBLIC OF
MACEDONIA

Prilep

Bitola

GREECE

ALBANIA

0   100km

FYRO Macedonia/Makedonija

Fanica Veljanovska

INTRODUCTION: A BRIEF HISTORY AND CURRENT STATE OF PHYSICAL ANTHROPOLOGY IN MACEDONIA

Research in physical anthropology in the Former Yugoslav Republic of Macedonia began alongside the first archaeological excavations. The first anthropological investigations were carried out in the 1930s. B. Šljivič, professor of anatomy at the Faculty of Medicine in Belgrade, conducted analyses of the scanty skeletal remains discovered at the Iron Age necropolis in Trebeništa near Ohrid, which was subject to excavation between 1930 and 1933 (Schlyvitch 1935).

After the Second World War there was no legal obligation to recover, collect and curate skeletal remains. Nevertheless, there were many examples of professional conduct by archaeologists excavating cemeteries. In the absence of trained experts in the country, anthropologists from other republics of the former Yugoslavia or further abroad were engaged in anthropological research.

In the 1950s, during several years of archaeological excavations at the mediaeval necropolis in Demir Kapija, anthropologist Z. Dolinar (Republic of Slovenia) became involved. Complete anthropological analysis was not carried out, however, although the skeletal material was recovered, carefully packed and stored in the Archaeological Museum in Skopje.

Somewhat similar was the destiny of the skeletal material from Stobi, one of the most important ancient towns in Macedonia, which was discovered in the frames of the international Yugoslav–American research project carried out at this site between 1970 and 1976. US anthropologist A. Wesolowsky was involved as part of the excavation team. The first palaeopathological study of human remains from Stobi was written by Wesolowsky (1973, 1975).

Another international project brought about the discovery of skeletal remains at the Neolithic settlement Anzabegovo near Sveti Nikole (1960, 1969–70). These were chronologically the earliest skeletal finds in Macedonia, and were examined by two Hungarian anthropologists, J. Nemeskéri and L. Lengyel. Besides the standard anthropological examinations, palaeoserological and chemical analysis were also carried out for the purpose of identifying the sex and age of the skeletons (Nemeskéri and Lengyel 1976).

A paper by B. Miszkiewicz (Poland) dealing with the anthropological structure of mediaeval populations in Macedonia was published in the 1970s (Miszkiewicz 1972). In the 1980s anthropologists Ž. Mikič (Serbia) and M. Štefančič (Slovenia) worked in Macedonia. At that time the number of published work on skeletal remains from different archaeological periods (the Iron Age, Antiquity and the Middle Ages) increased considerably owing to their intense research (Mikič 1981, 1984, 1987; Štefančič 1985, 1988). In the 1980s, the Archaeological Museum in Skopje began its continual collection and treatment of skeletal remains discovered during archaeological excavations in Macedonia up to the present day.

The oldest discovered skeletons in Macedonia are from the Neolithic (6100 BC), while the most recent ones date from the 19th century. Apart from the Palaeolithic, Mesolithic and Eneolithic, for which no skeletal remains have been discovered so far, all other periods have provided human remains. Several skeletal assemblages dating from prehistoric and historic periods have been analysed so far (Table 24.1).

The most scantily documented period is the Neolithic, although some new discoveries have taken place in recent years (Veljanovska 2006a). Skeletons in inhumation and cremation burials have been recorded from the Bronze Age (Veljanovska 2005a, 2008); while the most significant Iron Age palaeo-Balkan group in Macedonia, the Paeonians, are represented by several hundreds of skeletons discovered in four necropoli in the Vardar Valley (Veljanovska 1990a, 1991a, 1992, 1994, 1996). The bulk of the anthropological remains, however, come from Antiquity (Veljanovska 1990b, 1991b, 1993, 1995a, 1995b, 1999a, 2002, 2003, 2006b, 2006c) and the Middle Ages (Veljanovska 1989, 2001a, 2001b, 2001c, 2004a, 2005b, 2006a, 2007).

Specific analyses have been carried out in palaeodemography (Veljanovska 1999b), epigenetic and anthropogenetic processes (Veljanovska 2000, 2005a) as well as in palaeopathology (Veljanovska 1999c).

For the purpose of raising awareness of the discipline, including pathological changes in bone and facial reconstruction, several archaeological exhibitions have taken place (Veljanovska 2004b) (Table 24.1). A great number of finds has been published in professional journals.

Most of the anthropological analyses in Macedonia have been undertaken at the Anthropological Cabinet of the Museum of Macedonia. The Cabinet employs a full-time anthropologist, as well as a junior associate and a skeletal finds conservator. The activities of the Anthropological Cabinet are organized by adhering to the Law on Museums. Skeletal finds have been divided into three collections here: craniological, palaeopathological and a teaching collection. These collections include all skeletal remains discovered in archaeological excavations carried out by the Museum of Macedonia. The craniological collection comprises 400 crania from 40 archaeological sites dating from different periods. The palaeopathological collection consists of 2000 specimens, dating mostly from Antiquity. All skeletons have been documented and are logged into a special inventory book. There is also photo-documentation of every cranium, as well as every palaeopathological specimen and elements with particular epigenetic variations. The anthropological documentation is, however, much more extensive, since it also embraces data on over 12,000 individual skeletons that have been studied and interpreted so far, and they come from research conducted in all museums in Macedonia. In other words, the entire anthropological evidence that has been discovered in Macedonia in the past 25 years has been subject to anthropological study, and has been documented.

Since 2005, physical anthropology is being taught at undergraduate and post-graduate level in the department of Archaeology at the Faculty of Philosophy of the University of St Cyril and Methodius in Skopje. The course includes osteology, sex and age-at-death identification, osteometry, morphology, palaeopathology, as well as excavation techniques and conservation of skeletal finds; and there is also a course on the anthropology of past populations in Macedonia.

The Association of Physiologists and Anthropologists of Macedonia (Здрузение на физиолози и антрополози на Македонија) was established in 2004, but there is no single specialized anthropological journal in the country.

Table 24.1 Larger skeletal series from Macedonia: chronology, number of skeletons and researcher

Period/Site	Chronology	Number of skeletons	Researcher
Neolithic	*Early–Late Neolithic*	*37*	
Anzabeg., Sveti Nikole	6100–5000 BC	34	Nemes.-Lengyel.,76
2nd millennium BC	*15th–11th century BC*	*104*	
Vodovrati, Veles	13th–12th century BC	15	Вељановска, 2000
Ulanci, Veles	13th–11th century BC	69	Вељановска, 2000
Caska, Veles	Late Bronze–Early Iron Age	12	Вељановска, 08
1st millennium BC	*8th–3rd century BC*	*223*	
Bucinci, Skopje	7th–6th century BC	15	Вељановска
Varvara, Skopje	8th–4th century BC	24	Вељановска, 2000
Govrlevo, Skopje	Iron Age	15	Вељановска
Dedeli, Valandovo	7th–6th century BC	26	Вељановска, 94
Lisucin Dol, Marvinci	7th–5th century BC	28	Вељановска, 2000
Suva Reka, Gevgelija	7th–6th century BC	42	Mik, 81/Вељан, 94
Trebenista, Ohrid	7th–4th/3rd century BC	22	Štefančič, 85
Antiquity	*2nd century BC– 6th century AD*	*3340*	
Deboj, Ohrid	1st century BC – 3rd/4th century AD	145	Mikič, 84/ Вељан.
Marvinci, Valandovo	2nd/1st century BC – 3th century AD	367	Вељановска, 06
Opila, Kriva Palanka	4th–6th century AD	156	Вељановска, 2000
Skupi, Skopje	1st–6th century AD	432	Вељановска, 2000
Stobi, Veles	2nd century BC – 5th/6th century AD	2078	Вељановска, 2000
Middle Ages	*7th–19th century AD*	*8440*	
Teatar, Ohrid	10th–12th century AD	327	Вељановска
Dunje, Prilep	9th–11th century AD	97	Вељановска, 2000
Kale, Vinica	12th century AD	147	Вељановска, 2000
Opila, Kriva Palanka	10th–11th century AD	363	Вељановска, 2000
Radolista, Struga	9th–11th century AD	116	Mikič, 84
Sv. Erazmo, Ohrid	7th–11th century AD	124	Štefančič, 88
Vodoca, Strumica	9th–19th century AD	527	Вељановска
Grad.-Kale, Skopje	19th–20th century AD	154	Вељановска
Kale, Skopje	late mediaeval period	147	Вељановска
Morodvis, Kocani	9th–19th century AD	562	Velova
Orta Dzam., Strumica	12th–17th century AD	456	Вељановска, 2000
Plaosnik, Ohrid	9th–19th century AD	4530	Вељан.,07/Velova
Sv.15 Tiv., Strumica	late mediaeval period	180	Вељановска
Crkviste., D.Kapija	9th–15th century AD	476	Вељановска, 01
TOTAL: 70 sites	7th millennium BC – 19th century AD	12,145	

ARCHAEOLOGICAL HUMAN REMAINS AND LEGISLATION

Archaeological legislation

In Macedonia, studies of human skeletal remains are undertaken in museums. For this reason the legal framework regulating this issue falls under the Law on Cultural Heritage, the Law on Museums and the Book of Regulations on Archaeological Excavations. According to this legislation, human bones discovered in excavations have the same treatment as any other archaeological find. Any authorizations are controlled by the Cultural Heritage Protection Office (Управа за заштита на културното наследство).

HUMAN REMAINS AND LEGISLATION

The discovery of archaeological human bones during construction works must be reported by the construction company to the Cultural Heritage Protection Office, other heritage protection institutes or museums. Physical entities do not have such a legal obligation, yet they often are reported anyway and usually to the museum if not to the police. There is no official borderline between forensic and archaeological remains in Macedonian legislation.

Human remains can be excavated by authorized personnel (i.e., by archaeology graduates). Anthropologists are members of the research team. The role of the anthropologist in the field is to recover and pack the skeletal remains after they have been documented, photographed and drawn by the archaeologists.

The law does not specifically impose an obligation to carry out anthropological analysis. In practice, the incorporation of an anthropologist in the fieldwork team depends largely on the finances allocated for a given excavation campaign and, to some extent, on the availability of anthropologists. If the budget is scanty, the skeletons are lifted by archaeologists and sent to appropriate institutions (e.g., to a museum) for analysis once the excavation campaign has been completed.

Skeletal finds can be taken outside the country by adhering to the same regulations as archaeological finds. This requires a permission issued by the Cultural Heritage Protection Office.

Unfortunately, Macedonian legislation does not impose an obligation to store human remains from archaeological contexts. As a result of this, skeletal remains are sometimes reburied after the post-excavation analysis has been completed. Reburial also takes place when labels for the skeletons have been damaged or in cases where the series are very big and there is no appropriate place for their storage in regional museums. Remains are usually reburied in the same cemetery in which they have been discovered, and the location of the burial is marked on a plan of the site.

METHODS OF ANTHROPOLOGICAL ANALYSIS

The age-at-death and the sex of the deceased are determined according to the recommendations by Ferembach *et al.* (1979). Osteometry, including stature estimation, uses as a reference the work of Martin and Saller (1957, 1959), and the tables of Breitinger (1938) and Bach (1965). In any case, regarding stature estimation, the bone measurements are published wherever possible, which leaves open the possibility of applying any other method to those measurements.

CONCLUSION

In the near future there are plans for amendments in the legislation (to ensure the compulsory participation of an anthropologist in excavations), as well as ensuring greater protection of anthropological finds. For the time being, a proposal has been submitted for anthropological specimens to be assigned the status of cultural heritage, which would impose an obligation for their curation and protection.

ACKNOWLEDGEMENTS

This contribution was translated into English by Nada Andonovska.

USEFUL CONTACTS

Cultural Heritage Protection Office, Republic of Macedonia Ministry of Culture. Website: http://uzkn.gov.mk/default_en.html/

Macedonian Academy of Sciences and Arts (MANU). Website: www.manu.edu.mk/

Museum of Macedonia, Skopje (Muzej na Makedonija Arheoloski, Etnoloski i Istoriski), Curciska bb, 1000 Skopje. Tel: + 389 (91) 116 044; Email: musmk@mpt.com.mk

BIBLIOGRAPHY

Bach, H. (1965) 'Zur Berechnung der Korperhohe aus der langen Gliermassenknochen weiblicher Skelette' *Anthropologischer* Anzeiger, 29: 12–21.

Breitinger, E. (1938) 'Zur Berechnung der Korperhohe aus der langen Gliedmassenknochen mannlicher Skelette', *Anthropologischer* Anzeiger, 14: 249–74.

Ferembach, D., Schwidetzky, I. and Stloukal, M. (1979) 'Empfehlungen fur die Alters-und Geschlechtsdiagnose am Skelett', *Homo*, 30: 1–32.

Martin, R. and Saller, K. (1957). *Lehrbuch der Anthropologie, Vol I*, Stuttgart: Fischer Gustav Verlag.

——(1959). *Lehrbuch der Anthropologie, Vol II*, Stuttgart: Fischer Gustav Verlag.

Mikič, Ž. (1981) *Stanje i problemi fizičke antropologije u Jugoslaviji-praistoriski periodi*, Sarajevo: ANU BiH.

——(1984) 'Beitrag zur anthropologie spatromischer bis spatmittelalterlischer bevolkerung Jugoslawiens', *Godišnjak Centra za balkanološka ispitivanja ANU BiH*, 22: 5–109.

——(1987) 'Telo sina despota Jovana Dragusina u poloskom manastiru', *Zograf*, 18: 44–45.

Miszkiewicz, B. (1972) 'Z Badan nad struktura antropologiczna Macedonii', *Materialy i* Prace *Antropologiczne*, 83: 335–40.

Nemeskéri, J. and Lengyel, L. (1976) 'Neolithic skeletal finds', in M. Gimbutas (ed.) *Neolithic Macedonia as reflected by excavation at Anza, southeast Yugoslavia*, Los Angeles: Institute of Archaeology, University of California.

Schlyvitch, B. (1935) 'Knochenfunde in einem prahistorichen Grab bei Trebenischte', *Zeitschrift für Morphologische Anthropologie*, 37: 259–74.

Štefančič, M. (1985) 'Ilirskite skeleti od grobovite Tri Čequsti kaj Trebeništa', in P. Kuzman (ed.) *Tri Čequsti i Vrtuqka, Trebeništa 1972*, Ohrid: publisher unknown.

——(1988) *Ranosrednjovekovni skeleti nekropole Sv. Erazmo kod Ohrida*, Etnoantropološki problemi-Monografije No. 5, Belgrade: Department of Ethnology and Anthropology, University of Belgrade.

Velova, M. (2008) 'Antropološka serija Morodvis i profil sredwevekovnog stanovništva Istočne Makedonije', unpublished Master's thesis, University of Belgrade.

Veljanovska, F. (1989) 'Akropola-Žegligovski Kamen, antropološka analiza', *Macedoniae Acta Archaeologica*, 10: 259–76.

——(1990a) 'Slučaen naod na skelet od elezno vreme vo Skopje-antropološka analiza', *Macedoniae Acta Archaeologica*, 11: 228–31.

——(1990b) 'Skeletot od Episkopskata bazilika vo Stobi', *Macedoniae Acta Archaeologica*,11: 233–39.

——(1991a) 'Obid za antropološko definirawe na Pajonite', *Macedoniae Acta Archaeologica*, 12: 251–62.

——(1991b) 'Ranoantički skeleti od Ždanec-Skopje', *Macedoniae Acta Archaeologica*, 12: 265–72.

——(1992) 'Kremirani skeletni ostatoci od Klučka-Hipodrom, Skopje (rano 'elezno vreme)', *Macedoniae Acta Archaeologica*, 13: 281–86.

——(1993) 'Docnoantički skeleti od Gradište-Gradec, Gostivar', *Kulturno nasledstvo*, 16: 47–53.

——(1994) 'Antropološko definirawe na Pajonite', *Kulturno-istorisko nasledstvo na R. Makedonija*, 33: 116.

——(1995a) 'Docnoantički skelet od skopsko', *Zbornik*, 1: 239–44.

——(1995b) 'Antički skeleti od Zgropolsko Kale', *Zbornik*, 1: 245–58.

——(1996) 'Antropološki karakteristiki na Pajoncit', *Makedonsko Nasledstvo*, I-2: 25–36.

——(1999a) 'Docnoantički skeletni naodi od Zapadnata nekropola na Ž.egligovski Kamen-Kumanovo', *Muzejski Glasnik*, 5–6: 16–23.

——(1999b) 'Paleodemografski karakteristiki na naselenieto na Makedonija od bronzeno vreme do sreden vek', *Macedoniae Acta Archaeologica*, 15: 401–14.

——(1999c) 'Pojava na impaktirani zabi kaj antičkoto naselenie na Stobi', *Macedoniae Acta Archaeologica*, 15: 385–99.

——(2000) *Antropološki karakteristiki na naselenieto na Makedonija od neolit do sreden vek*, Kulturno-istorisko nasledstvo na Republika Makedonija No. 43, Skopje: Republički zavod za zaštita na spomenicite na kulturata.

——(2001a) *Antropološki karakteristiki na srednovekovnoto naselenie od Crkvište, Demir Kapija*, Skopje: Muzej na Makedonija.

——(2001b) 'Identifikacija na skeletnite ostatoci na Tole-Paša', *Zbornik-Istorija*, 2: 39–42.

——(2001c) 'Docnosrednovekovni antropološki naodi od Grobišta-Sred Selo, Pepelište', *Kulturno Nasledstvo*, 26–27: 51–64.

——(2002) 'Antropološki naodi od lokalitetot Drezga-Lopate, Kumanovo', *Muzejski Glasnik*, 4: 85–103.

——(2003) 'Antropološki karakteristiki na naselenieto od rimsko vreme vo Makedonija', *Starohristijanskata arheologija vo Makedonija* (2003): 273–301.

——(2004a) 'Srednovekovni skeletni naodi od Čukarka, Očipala-Delčevo', in M. Jovanov, M. Maneva and F. Veljanovska (eds) *Čukarka – rimski tumul, srednovekovna nekropola*, Monumenta Macedonia 9, Skopje: Makedonska Civilizacija.

——(2004b) *Čovekot vo praistoriskite i istoriski epohi vo Makedonija*, interactive multimedia CD, Skopje: Muzej na Makedonija.

——(2005a) 'Skelet od bronzeno vreme od Markova Sušica (skopsko)', *Zbornik*, 2: 79–81.

——(2005b) 'Antropološki karakteristiki na srednovekovnata populacija od Trnče-Pepelište, Negotino', *Zbornik*, 2: 195–217.

——(2005c) 'Praistoriskoto naselenie od Vardarski Rid', *Vardarski Rid T1*: 401–12.

——(2005d) 'Antropološkiot aspekt na etnogenetskite procesi vo Makedonija od bronzeno vreme do sreden vek', *Macedoniae Acta Archaeologica*, 16: 349–65.

——(2006a) 'Antropološki karakteristiki na srednovekovnite skeletni naodi od reonot na Palikurska bazilika vo Stobi', *Kulturno Nasledstvo*, 30–31: 20–28.

——(2006b) *Antičkoto naselenie od Marvinci-Valandovo*, Skopje: Muzej na Makedonija.

——(2006c) 'Skeleti od docnoantička cista kaj Bukovič, Skopsko', *Kulturno Nasledstvo*, 30–31: 31–36.

——(2007) 'Preliminarni antropološki sogleduvawa za srednovekovnoto naselenie od Plaošnik-Ohrid', *Kulturno Nasledstvo*, 32–33: 15–55.

——(2008) 'Praistoriski antropološki naodi od Čaška-Veles', *Macedoniae Acta Archaeologica*, 18: 431–37.

Wesolowsky, A. (1973) 'Burial customs in the West Cemetery', *Studies in the Antiquities of Stobi*, 1: 97–137.

——(1975) 'The Pathology of Human Remains from Stobi', *Studies in the Antiquities of Stobi*, 2: 143–61.

Malta

Anthony Pace

INTRODUCTION: A BRIEF HISTORY AND CURRENT STATE OF PHYSICAL ANTHROPOLOGY IN MALTA

Many ancient burial places in Malta have remained conspicuous since antiquity. The ubiquitous presence of ancient burial sites in the Maltese landscape, and especially the high concentration of Christian catacombs in Rabat, just outside Mdina or Melite, as it was known in Antiquity, meant that knowledge of these monuments persisted. The island's toponomy, mostly Mediaeval Arabic in origin, is full of references to burial places, while catacombs frequently attracted the curious and the antiquarians. A full-size anthropomorphic sarcophagus of Hellenistic Punic origin was a well-known part of a 17th-century Cabinet of Curiosities (Abela 1647). By the 19th century, Punic cremation urns adorned many private collections, several rock-cut chamber tombs were explored and often thoroughly rifled, while vedutisti and scholars carried out the first surveys of the major catacomb labyrinths at Rabat (Becker 1913; Caruana 1898). Though a long-known curiosity, ancient burials were mostly sought for artefacts. Human remains were never examined or recorded.

The discovery of the Ħal Saflieni Hypogeum in 1902 (Zammit 1926; Pace 2000) marked an important turning point in the study of Maltese antiquities. This subterranean prehistoric cemetery of Neolithic age (c. 4000–2500 BC) brought home the need for more organized excavation and recording techniques, as well as the need to establish a central authority in the form of a museum of Maltese antiquities. Until 1902, antiquities belonging to public collections formed part of the national library, and therefore still resembled a Cabinet of Curiosities in character. The excavators of the Hypogeum, Fr Manuel Magri SJ (1851–1907) and Sir Themistocles Zammit (1864–1935), were acutely aware of the importance of the prehistoric cemetery for studies of Maltese prehistory. Overall results of the site's excavation and policy-setting decisions now appear uneven at a distance of over a century since the monument was first discovered. The fragility of the bone material and the poor conditions of the deposits prevented a satisfactory retrieval of human remains or a proper recording of burials (Zammit *et al.* 1912). Zammit estimated that at least 7000 individuals had originally been buried at the site, though his counting methodology was never clearly described. Only seven skulls were retrieved, some in a fragmented state. In one of the subterranean chambers, a pile of sieved soil was left for visitors to view; in another chamber, Zammit left an unexcavated burial deposit for future generations of scholars to study if at all necessary. The protection of this small deposit foreshadowed modern concerns with the extent to which archaeological sites and cemeteries should be excavated. Over-excavation is sadly a hallmark of archaeology: it is short-termist and results in the depletion of valuable reference resources.

This period also saw the discovery of Bur Mgħeż, a natural cave cemetery used during the Neolithic, a unique cremation cemetery of the Early Bronze Age (Zammit 1916), and two very large human molars exhibiting a form of taurodontism from Għar Dalam (Despott 1917, 1918, 1923). Once again these discoveries were unevenly treated and recorded. Coming hot on the heels of the Ħal Safieni discovery, the discovery of Bur Megħeż was a missed opportunity. The subterranean cavern was poorly recorded and inadequately described (Tagliaferro 1911). Ceramic remains from the cave later showed that the site was certainly used for inhumations during the Tarxien Phase of Maltese prehistory (3000–2500 BC). Given its size, the cave may have contained a high density of human remains, comparable perhaps to that experienced at Ħal Saflieni a few years earlier. The site was unfortunately quarried away. A small number of human teeth from Bur Megħeż are housed at Malta's National Museum of Archaeology and a few have been traced to the Natural History Museum in London.

In 1913 the megalithic building site of Tarxien (c. 3600–2500 BC and 2500–1500 BC) was brought to the attention of Zammit, who began to excavate the monument in 1915. Though the site was contemporary with the Ħal Safieni cemetery and Bur Megħez burial cave, its original purpose and function were not related to inhumations, as was the case with other contemporary megalithic sites which were all constructed between 3600 and 2500 BC. However, Tarxien stands out in Maltese prehistory: at the end of the Maltese Late Neolithic, several chambers of the building and other enclosures were used as a cremation cemetery by a metal-using community. This deposit commonly referred to as the Tarxien Cemetery, a period dated to about 2500–1500 BC (Maltese Early Bronze Age), contained remains of numerous cremation burials. Zammit's description unfortunately lacks accuracy. The boundaries of the cremation deposits were never established properly; a distinction between cremation areas and actual places of burial was not established; cremation urns were not adequately described and have not been identified since the excavation; and distinct cremation burials and accompanying funerary embellishments, such as votive bowls and copper daggers, were not recorded in any detail. No deposits were conserved *in situ* and no samples of any significant use to the study of human remains were collected. Since the excavation of this extensive prehistoric deposit, no comparable cremation cemetery has been encountered on the islands.

At Għar Dalam the discovery of taurodont-like molars inspired much interest in a possible Maltese Palaeolithic (Keith 1924). However, the cave's archaeological layers were disturbed and the nature of the teeth – to this day a matter of controversy – has never been adequately explained, even more so with similar features having been noted in modern people (Mangion 1962). Worthy of note is the lack of evidence for pre-Neolithic human presence in Malta, which is a reflection, perhaps, of the current state of field research rather than of the certainty of such an absence.

The discovery of the Ħal Safieni Hypogeum in 1902 opened a period of exploration and excavation across the Maltese islands which came to an end shortly before Zammit's death in 1935. Within three decades, many of Malta's major prehistoric and historical sites were noted and in many cases thoroughly excavated. The period led to a slightly more systematic description of tombs and graves, which at a minimum were individually announced in the Museum Annual Report. Zammit published a number of reports on his excavations of tombs in the Museum Annual Reports, and synthesized available information in a short paper on the subject (Zammit 1910). The development of the investigation into prehistoric burial places has been synthesised by A. Pace (Pace 1992, 2000). Today we know of over 480 burial sites from the Museum Annual Reports, from Zammit's field notes and from sporadic 19th-century references. But apart from Zammit's field notes, which sometimes depicted light sketches or schematic figures of human remains, the bulk of what should have been a formidable repertoire of human remains went unrecorded. Many of the sites have not survived.

Apart from the intense interest in archaeological discoveries throughout Malta and Gozo, the first three decades of the 20th century also saw pioneering anthropological studies. Works by Bradley (1912), Dudley Buxton (1922), Zammit *et al.* (1912), examined various osteological features of the limited range of skeletal remains known at the time. Such studies compiled measurements and other important reference data, and attempted to incorporate knowledge of Malta's ancient human remains into broader syntheses of world anthropology. Though such studies have been superseded by modern anthropological theory and practice, their value lies in the early reference data that they contain.

During the past 65 years or so Maltese archaeology has adopted contemporary techniques and advances in osteoarchaeology and anthropological studies. The output of osteoarchaeological studies has been uneven with regard to novelty, some work simply revisiting pre-Second World War material, other studies focusing on Punic material, and other more recent studies dealing with the Neolithic cemetery at the Xagħra Circle, Gozo (c. 4000–2500 BC for the Neolithic deposits). In the early 1960s, J.J. Mangion revisited the case of taurodontism in the Għar Dalam teeth, arguing that this phenomenon was also observed in modern humans (Mangion 1962). The matter surfaced again with much controversy in recent years. A. Mifsud and G. Savona-Ventura (Mifsud and Mifsud 1997; Savona-Ventura and Mifsud 1999) challenged views of a number of scholars who, they believed, denied a Neanderthal presence in Malta. Mifsud and Savona-Ventura re-assessed the stratigraphy of the Għar Dalam Cave and argued that this denial was the result of a mistaken interpretation of the original contexts in which the molars were found (Savona-Ventura 1998: 5–12). They also argued that an error on the part of Sir Kenneth Oakley led to the assigment of a Neolithic date to the molars (Savona-Ventura and Mifsud 1999: 19). In 1972, J.L. Pace, Professor of Anatomy at the University of Malta's Medical School, presented a small display of figurines and skeletal remains to discuss anatomical features of prehistoric human beings in the archipelago (Pace 1972). The exhibition catalogue reflected older paradigms of race and migration of human beings from North Africa, an aspect which is more of a historiographic rather than a scientific importance. This study was followed by those of Schwidetzky (1978) on human remains from the Ħal Safieni Hypogeum and Schwidetzky and Ramaswamy (1980) on a selection of human remains from Punic rock-cut chamber tombs.

Since the late 1980s, the number of scientific excavations increased exponentially across the archipelago. Improved recording techniques and the increase in number of professional Maltese archaeologists have led to a larger number of cemeteries being examined and recorded. These excavations have addressed different periods, burial rites and archaeological contexts, with a broad chronological frame ranging from the Late Neolithic, the Punic period, the Late Roman and Byzantine periods, as well as the Early Modern period. On Gozo, the Xagħra Circle prehistoric cemetery provided a wealth of human bone material, including a significant number of complete articulated skeletons from the Maltese Late Neolithic, dated to between 4000 and 2500 BC (Malone *et al.* 2009); while the recent excavation of prehistoric tombs at Kercem, also in Gozo, by the Superintendence of Cultural Heritage have yielded another three complete skeletons of the period 3000–2500 BC. Punic and Roman period tomb recordings have increased, so that the Superintendence now possesses a larger repertoire of securely-contexted inhumation and cremation burials from these periods in comparison to the number of similar assemblages noted up to the First World War. During this period the Museums Department (1902–2003) and the Superintendence of Cultural Heritage (established in 2003) also excavated a small number of highly significant Early Christian catacombs, which have yielded an important repertoire of human remains dating up to the end of the seventh century. Of interest are a number of Late Mediaeval and Early Modern burial contexts representing old chapel cemeteries.

Since the Second World War several important advances have been made in the fields of archaeology, anthropology and osteoarchaeology. These disciplines are now part of mainstream higher education in Malta (e.g., in Archaeology departments), while several researchers also follow postgraduate training abroad. Contemporary excavation techniques and laboratory procedures have become well-established standards throughout the country. If not available locally, laboratory testing and analyses (e.g., palaeodietary analysis; Richards *et al.* 2001) are carried out abroad. The Museums Department and its replacement, the Superintendence of Cultural Heritage, have consolidated post-excavation approaches and rationalized the archiving of old and more recent skeletal material. Future plans will focus on the creation of a national database of existing ancient skeletal material. At the time of writing, the Superintendence of Cultural Heritage is reviewing osteoarchaeology and anthropology policies with a view to establishing a firm research framework for a more systematic cataloguing and study of ancient human remains.

ARCHAEOLOGICAL HUMAN REMAINS AND LEGISLATION

Archaeological legislation

Archaeological fieldwork has been governed by specific legislation since 1910. The most recent statute is the Cultural Heritage Act or Att Dwar il-Patrimonju Kulturali,[1] enacted in 2002 to replace the 1925 Antiquities Protection Act. In this long legal tradition, very much influenced in part by Italian legislation and by British law, all activities related to the treatment of archaeological sites and deposits have been governed by single laws. In Malta there are therefore no separate laws that regulate the excavation of archaeological human remains and their subsequent treatment. The Cultural Heritage Act of 2002 defines cultural heritage very broadly to cover a range of movable or immovable remains or objects, which are earth-bound, or geological, built monuments, deposits, collections, works of art and intangible entities.

HUMAN REMAINS AND LEGISLATION

There have rarely been instances where the distinction between ancient and modern human remains posed problems. Recognizable ancient settings, normally well-known forms of rock-cut tombs, Christian catacombs or graves, are in themselves sufficient to exclude police and magisterial intervention. In such cases, ancient human remains are treated as part of the archaeological record and, therefore, subject to the provisions of the Cultural Heritage Act (CAP 445). As antiquities, ancient human remains are therefore protected by the special powers of the state as expressed in the Act. Offences involving antiquities are subject to severe fines or imprisonment on successful prosecution at the Court of Magistrates. The involvement of forensic experts, police or an enquiring magistrate in case of crime involving ancient human remains is however not excluded, as will be necessary in the case of modern disturbance of ancient graves. In such cases investigations will focus on violations against cultural heritage legislation.

In cases of accidental discovery, normally during development, human remains immediately fall under the jurisdiction of the Superintendent of Cultural Heritage if they are noticeably ancient. The Superintendent normally intervenes by suspending any on-going works in order to enable a full anthropological excavation of the remains. Where possible, developers and engineers are requested to redesign any building foundations in order to mitigate impacts on burial monuments. In such cases, the Superintendent immediately transmits his position to the Malta Environment and Planning Authority (Awtorità ta' Malta dwar l-Ambjent u l-Ippjanar or MEPA). In cases of highly sensitive areas of archaeological value, a monitor reporting to the Superintendent is appointed to oversee the development. Where burials are encountered, these are excavated according to established standards of stratigraphy and archaeological practice. Osteoarchaeologists are often called in either to advise on the retrieval of bone material or to excavate human remains. Invariably, the Superintendent conducts all excavations of ancient human remains, and in any case, excavation of any kind is subject to his surveillance, control and accessibility. The Superintendent has the power to intervene on any excavations and to rescind any permits.

Excavated ancient human remains are the property of the state. The Cultural Heritage Act defines an antiquity as being older than 50 years. There are cases where this cut-off date is not sufficient to justify archaeological excavations of human remains. This is the case with church and functioning public cemeteries, which are governed by burial and sanitary laws. In public cemeteries, the Superintendent may intervene to protect old funerary monuments, but not to examine or handle human remains.

In the rare instances of forensic circumstances, human remains are the immediate responsibility of the police and enquiring magistrates, as the case may be. Even in those cases of uncertainty as to the age of human remains, forensic considerations take precedence over cultural ones. In cases involving magisterial or police inquiries, forensic examinations are undertaken independently and prior to any non-criminal investigations. An inquiring magistrate is empowered to seek the advice of the Superintendence of Cultural Heritage or an independent archaeologist regarding the possible cultural nature of human remains. In magisterial inquiries, field investigations and related scientific examinations have to be communicated in the first instance to the inquiring magistrate.

In the Cultural Heritage Act of 2002 there is no specific mention of ancient or 'archaeological' human remains. The assumption is that, unless of a very recent nature, or unless found in designated Church or public cemeteries, and if discoveries are clearly archaeological, human remains are considered ancient and archaeological. Human remains of a more recent nature are governed by sanitary regulations and in some cases by police law.

The Cultural Heritage Act lays down a series of regulations concerning excavation and conservation. Definitional clauses, in Article 2, explain the meaning of 'cultural heritage', and specifically define the terms 'exploration', 'investigation' and 'surveillance' as those measures that define archaeological activity. More importantly, the act assigns the regulation and licensing of all archaeological activity to the Superintendent of Cultural Heritage (Article 7d), who also has exclusive right to excavate on land and sea according to Article 43. The study of human remains in an archaeological context is therefore regulated by these statutory provisions. In the case of sample extraction from human remains held in collections, the approval of the Superintendent of Cultural Heritage (Sovrintendent tal-Patrimonju Kulturali) is also required. Through this legal framework, standards of data capture and recording, as well as excavation techniques and methods, are imposed *a priori* by the Superintendent of Cultural Heritage.

In cases where issues of cultural heritage converge with the management of modern cemeteries, the regulations of the Cultural Heritage Act are augmented by those of the Code of Police Laws (CAP 10), the Burials Ordinance (CAP 17) and the Addolorata Cemetery Ordinance (CAP 18). The last two laws refer to the establishment of 'The Santa Maria Addolorata

Cemetery', a central government-owned burial ground built between 1862 and 1868, managed by the island's Health Department in conformity with police laws governing burials. Because of its concentration of historic monuments, the cemetery is subject to the provisions of the Cultural Heritage Act in matters concerning monument conservation. Similarly, the modern expansion of old village cemeteries, now governed by the Code of Police Laws, often requires coordination with the Superintendence of Cultural Heritage, as well as planning development permission, on account of antiquities located within or near the cemeteries. Two recent cases are the expansion of the cemetery of Rabat, which involved the excavation of Punic, Roman and Mediaeval remains, and that of Luqa where a series of Bronze Age silos dating to between 1500 and 1750 BC were encountered during recent extension development projects. In such cases of overlapping jurisdiction involving modern cemeteries, the Cultural Heritage Act is deemed to cover archaeological features, whereas police and sanitary legislation have overriding governance of inhumations and human remains.

Handling, treatment and display of human remains

If during the 19th and early 20th centuries little regard was given to the handling of human remains, there is today a growing concern about delicate issues of display. Three inter-related concerns – handling, display and reburial – are central to the treatment of ancient human remains in Malta.

Generally, handling of human remains is limited to specialists. Limited handling is followed during site excavation, and supervision by qualified personnel is mandatory. If possible, especially in the case of special discoveries, a qualified osteoarchaeologist is required to conduct excavations or to direct the removal of human remains.

Post-excavation handling is allowed in the case of *bona fide* researchers, preferably those trained in a medical discipline or anthropologists.

The removal of ancient human remains from Maltese national territory, whether for permanent or temporary purposes, requires authorization from the Superintendent of Cultural Heritage. Applications are considered on their own particular merits. In most cases, applications are considered for scientific research purposes. In such cases, applications must be accompanied by a clear method statement concerning the proposed treatment of the human remains, highlighting especially the use of destructive or state-altering research methods and their justification.

Contemporary museum ethics are today responding to community concerns on the display of skeletal remains. Although there are no specific rules to govern such displays, a general rule of thumb is to minimize exposure of skeletal remains and to focus on the educational value of human bone material. Controlled exposure reduces conservation problems and reflects sensitivity to cultural or religious sentiments on displayed human remains. Malta is fortunate in that it has never received ancient human remains from foreign countries, and is therefore not liable to repatriation claims.

Human remains management policy and ethical issues

The treatment of ancient human remains is not free of contestation and requires a long-term ethical commitment in policy development. Though, in purely functional terms, ancient burials represent the disposal of the dead in contexts that in the main were perhaps intended to be permanent, the modern disciplines of archaeology and heritage view ancient human remains differently. In almost all cultures, burials are also considered to be matters of the strictly personal and sacred, with legislation very often providing protection and management frameworks in recognition of this fact. At the same time, however, improved scientific and anthropological approaches have, since the Second World War, advanced the importance of human remains as a source of bio-medical and cultural information on humankind. Considered in the full breadth of human evolution and history, this principle is one that cannot be easily ignored. Indeed, Maltese law reflects more a sense of general public interest and genuine inquisitiveness rather than contestation. In this, the passage of time greatly reduces emotive factors that often fuel demands for reburial in the case of proven ancestry. In addition the full potential of ancient human remains studies for present and future generations has still not been fully realized or recognized either in global bio-medical terms or in terms of public policy and rule of law.

Nevertheless such considerations do not eliminate contestation on religious, cultural or ethical grounds. In such cases the 50-year cut-off date for defining an antiquity in terms of age according to the Cultural Heritage Act will not resolve issues of contestation. Central to this problem are the principles of property, kinship and lineage, and how these are sometimes conditioned by religious and cultural sentiments.

Legally, the Cultural Heritage Act renders ancient human remains state property by virtue of their archaeological nature and context. This means that, in spite of possible religious or cultural claims over ancient human remains found anywhere on Maltese territory, such claims are not superior to state policy and necessary authorizations. Nevertheless Malta does recognize and acknowledge cultural and religious requests, such as those concerning display or reburial. Such requests are considered carefully with respect to a number of considerations broadly falling into two categories, both representing a dilemma for heritage authorities: on the one hand, a reserve of ancient human remains is of great value for academic and scientific research, each study contributing to the great whole of knowledge of human evolution; on the other hand, contestations on religious or cultural grounds, though motivated by non-scientific beliefs, are often an inevitable practicality reflecting contemporary socio-religious needs. There is, in this, a tension between potential advances made in the realm of human knowledge and past on the one hand, and a degree of disrespect of religious beliefs. However old, burials in formal facilities or cemeteries were not meant to be intentionally disturbed by scientific excavation or accidental destruction. The treatment of ancient human remains represents a strong divide between the sacred and the profane, the latter representing archaeology and science, as well as instances of accidental destruction. This does not mean that scientific approaches to handling human remains are necessarily disrespectful. On the contrary, it can be safely argued that osteoarchaeology today has devised very high standards, in some respects even clinical requirements, and cautionary respect in the handling of human remains. In matters of reburial claims, Malta therefore adopts a cautionary approach based on best practice, religious guidance and ethical standards. Though extremely rare and publically inconspicuous, issues of reburial are addressed on a case-by-case basis, without recourse to precedent. In principle, after scientific objectives are advanced, reburial is not at all discounted provided that conservation standards are adhered to.

Although reburial issues are unusual in Malta, in the special cases where requests for reburial have been made, these have been treated with the utmost care and discretion. A recent request by a religious group advanced the principle that human bones are to remain untouched, and graves unopened. Such positions are opposed to scientific examination. While the Maltese state is not averse to reburial, authorities are also conscious of the scientific value of ancient human remains. Religious claims often do not leave much space for considering scientific interest or the contribution that human remains can make to humankind's history.

METHODS OF ANTHROPOLOGICAL ANALYSIS

In the field

Archaeological excavations are carried out to high standards of stratigraphic analysis and recording. The Cultural Heritage Act recognizes the importance of international instruments, treaties and conventions concerning the proper use and conservation of national or world cultural property. These and national standards and conditions govern all excavation on Maltese territory. Documentation is national property and for the most part recorded on special sheets belonging to the Superintendence of Cultural Heritage.

There are no local standards specific for the Maltese population. Osteoarchaeological studies are carried out to accepted standards and according to a number of well-established international examination methods (see, e.g., Buikstra and Ubelaker 1994). In recent years, the presence of local osteoarchaeologists has meant that retrieval during field excavations can be undertaken by trained professionals.

In the laboratory

In general, more than one method is used to examine skeletal remains. For age assessment of adults from dental wear Miles (1962) and/or Richards and Miller (1991) are followed; for ectocranial suture closure the work of Meindl and Lovejoy (1985). Methods applied to the pelvis for age assessment are those of Brooks and Suchey (1990) and Lovejoy *et al.* (1985), together with Buckberry and Chamberlain (2002). İşcan and Loth (1986) are used when employing ribs. For foetal remains and subadult individuals up to the age of about fifteen years old, age assessment is based on long bone measurements following Scheuer *et al.* (1980), Gowland (1998), Hoppa (1992), and Hoppa and Gruspier (1996); and on the ossification and epiphyseal fusion following the reference work of Schwartz (1991), Scheuer and Black (2000), and Webb and Suchey (1985) among others. Where possible, age determination based on dental remains follow Smith (1991), Moorrees *et al.* (1963), Deutsch and Peer (1982), and Liversidge *et al.* (1993).

For the determination of sex in adult individuals, various morphological traits of the pelvis and the skull are employed following Schwartz (1991), Ferembach *et al.* (1980), Krogman and İşcan (1986), Phenice (1969), and Loth and Henneberg (1996). For stature Trotter (1970), Steele (1970), Feldesman *et al.* (1990), and Fully's (1956) method are followed. For the assessment of 'musculoskeletal-stress-markers' (MSM) the criteria of Hawkey and Merbs (1995) are followed.

National database

At the time of writing, the Superintendence of Cultural Heritage is drawing up plans for a national database and repository of ancient human remains. Data derived from excavations and from the study of skeletal remains are documented in the national inventory which is managed by the Superintendence of Cultural Heritage. The national database will bring together records of skeletal remains from a wide span of time covering the Neolithic, Phoenician-Punic, Roman, Late Roman, Islamic, Mediaeval and Early Modern periods.

The underlying principle behind the national database is the creation of a consolidated archive for research and reference. Given their size and relative isolation from the European continent, the Maltese islands offer unique opportunities to study a physically contained set of ancient human remains. Though the islands were never totally isolated, they do provide a secure retrieval context which can be compared with ancient human remains found in neighbouring places and elsewhere in the Mediterranean. Maltese archaeology has provided a very broad span of retrieval contexts, albeit ones that are no longer securely linked in time. These contexts comprise Neolithic burials (4000–2500 BC), the Maltese Early Bronze Age of the Tarxien cremation cemetery (2500–1500 BC) of which nothing remains, the Phoenician and Punic period (750–218 BC), Roman, Late Roman and Byzantine remains (218 BC – 870 AD), Islamic, Mediaeval and Early Modern burials (870 AD to the 18th century). Though incomplete and uneven in terms of quantitative or qualitative representation for every period, this range offers a unique data set.

The national database of human ancient remains will also inform authorities and researchers on the extent to which future archaeological excavations are to be carried out. An underlying concern is the depletion of valuable archaeological resources and unique data sources of ancient human remains, especially given the small territorial size of the archipelago and, therefore, the higher probability of loss of these non-renewable resources. The database will therefore provide a policy framework for the sustainable care and proper use of ancient human remains.

CONCLUSION

Although the first few decades of the 20th century meant the discovery of a considerable number of sites and human remains, the scientific excavations have also increased exponentially since the 1980s, especially at prehistoric, Punic and Roman sites. During these last decades the Superintendence of Cultural Heritage has also excavated a number of highly significant Early Christian catacombs, and a number of Late Mediaeval and Early Modern burial contexts representing old chapel cemeteries.

The number of human remains yet to be studied is therefore significant and this will be the focus of osteoarchaeologists in the future. The development of a database and a repository of human remains from archaeological sites will provide a great source of information on Malta and of the central Mediterranean in general.

ACKNOWLEDGEMENTS

I would like to thank His Excellency Dr Ugo Mifsud Bonnici, Bernardette Mercieca, and Charles Mifsud for their valuable comments and suggestions.

USEFUL CONTACTS

Superintendence of Cultural Heritage, 173, St Christopher Street, Valletta, VLT 2000, Malta. Website: www.culturalheritage.gov.mt/

NOTE

1 The laws in Malta are bilingual in English and Maltese, and are enacted in both languages in the House of Representatives.

BIBLIOGRAPHY

Abela, G.F. (1647) *Della Descrittione di Malta Isola nel Mare Siciliano con le sue Antichita'*, *ed altri notitie*, Malta: Paolo Bonacota (facsimile copy Midsea Books Ltd, Malta, 1984)

Becker, E. (1913) *Malta sotterranea: Studien zur Altchristlichen und Juedischen Sepulkralkunst*, Strassburg: J.H. Ed. Heitz; trans. Katrin Fenech (2009) *Malta sotterranea: studies of its early Christian and Jewish sepulchral art*, Malta: Midsea Books.

Bradley, R.N. (1912) *Malta and the Mediterranean Race*, London: T. Fisher Unwin.

Brooks, S. and Suchey, J.M. (1990) 'Skeletal age determination based on the Os Pubis: a comparison of the Ascádi-Neméskeri and Suchey-Brooks methods', *Human Evolution* 5: 227–38.

Buckberry, J.L. and Chamberlain, A.T. (2002) 'Age estimation from the auricular surface of the ilium: a revised method', *American Journal of Physical Anthropology*, 199: 231–39.

Buikstra, J. and Ubelaker, D. (eds) (1994) *Standards for Data Collection from Human Skeletal Remains*, Fayetteville, AR: Arkansas Archaeological Survey Research Series No. 44.

Caruana, A.A. (1898) *Ancient Pagan Tombs and Christian Cemeteries in the Islands of Malta Explored and Surveyed from the Year 1881 to the Year 1897*, Malta: Government Printing Office.

Despott, G. (1917) 'The excavations conducted at Ghar Dalam (Malta) in July, 1916', *Report of the Meeting of the British Association for the Advancement of Science*, 86: 294–302.

——(1918) 'Excavations conducted at Ghar Dalam (Malta) in the Summer of 1917', *The Journal of the Royal Anthropological Institute of Great Britain and Ireland*, 48: 214–21.

——(1923) 'Excavations at Ghar Dalam (Dalam Cave), Malta', *The Journal of the Royal Anthropological Institute of Great Britain and Ireland*, 53: 18–35.

Deutsch, D. and Peer, E. (1982) 'Development of enamel in human fetal teeth', *Journal of Dental Research*, 61: 1543–51.

Dudley Buxton, L.H. (1922) 'The Ethnology of Malta and Gozo', *The Journal of the Royal Anthropological Institute of Great Britain and Ireland*, 52: 164–211.

Feldesman, M.R., Kleckner, J.G. and Lundy, J.K. (1990) 'Femur/stature ratio and estimates of stature in mid- and late-Pleistocene fossil hominids', *American Journal of Physical Anthropology*, 83: 359–72.

Ferembach, D., Schwidetzky, I. and Stloukal, M. (1980) 'Recommendations for age and sex diagnoses of skeletons', *Journal of Human Evolution*, 9: 517–49.

Fully, G. (1956) 'Une nouvelle méthode de détermination de la taille', *Annales de Médecine Légale*, 35: 266–73.

Gowland, R. (1998) 'The Use of Prior Probabilities in Ageing Perinatal Skeletal Remains: Implications for the Evidence of Infanticide in Roman Britain', unpublished Master's thesis, Department of Archaeology and Prehistory, University of Sheffield.

Hawkey, D. and Merbs, C. (1995) 'Activity-induced musculoskeletal stress markers (MSM) and subsistence strategy changes among Hudson Bay Eskimos', *International Journal of Osteoarchaeology*, 5: 324–38.

Hoppa, R.D. (1992) 'Evaluating human skeletal growth: an Anglo-Saxon example', *International Journal of Osteoarchaeology*, 2: 275–88.

Hoppa, R.D. and Gruspier, K.L. (1996) 'Estimating diaphyseal length from fragmentary subadult skeletal remains: implications for palaeodemographic reconstructions of a southern Ontario ossuary', *American Journal of Physical Anthropology*, 100: 341–54.

İşcan, M.Y. and Loth, S.R. (1986) 'Determination of age from the sternal rib in white females: a test of the Phase Method', *Journal of Forensic Sciences*, 29: 990–99.

Keith, A. (1924) 'Neanderthal Man in Malta', *The Journal of the Royal Anthropological Institute of Great Britain and Ireland*, 54: 251–60.

Krogman, W.M. and İşcan, M.Y. (1986) *The Human Skeleton in Forensic Medicine*, 2nd edn, Springfield, IL: Charles C. Thomas.

Liversidge, H.M., Dean, M.C. and Molleson, T.A. (1993) 'Increasing human tooth length between birth and 5.4 years', *American Journal of Physical Anthropology*, 90: 307–13.

Loth, S.R. and Henneberg, M. (1996) 'Mandibular ramus flexure: a new morphologic indicator of sexual dimorphism in the human skeleton', *American Journal of Physical Anthropology*, 99: 473–85.

Lovejoy, C.O., Meindl, R.S., Pryzbeck, T.R., *et al.* (1985) 'Chronological metamorphosis of the auricular surface of the ilium: a new method for the determination of adult skeletal age at death', *American Journal of Physical Anthropology*, 68: 15–28.

Malone, C., Stoddart, S., Bonanno, A., *et al.* (2009) *Mortuary Customs in Prehistoric Malta. Excavations at the Brochtorff Circle at Xaghra (1987–94)*, Cambridge, McDonald Institute.

Mangion, J.J. (1962) 'Two cases of taurodontism in Modern Jaws', *British Dental Journal*, 113: 309.

Meindl, R.S. and Lovejoy, C.O. (1985) 'Ectocranial suture closure: a revised method for the determination of skeletal age at death based on the lateral-anterior suture', *American Journal of Physical Anthropology*, 68: 57–66.

Mifsud, A. and Mifsud, S. (1997) *Dossier Malta Evidence for the Magdalenian*, Malta: Proprint Company Limited.

Miles, A.E.W. (1962) 'Assessment of the ages of a population of Anglo-Saxons from the dentitions', *Proceedings of the Royal Society of Medicine*, 55: 881–86.

Moorrees, C.F.A., Fanning, E.A. and Hunt, E.E. Jr. (1963) 'Age variation of formation stages for ten permanent teeth', *Journal of Dental Research*, 42: 1490–1502.

Pace, A. (2000) *The Ħal Saflieni Hypogeum 4000 BC–2000 AD*, Malta: Museums Department.

——(1992) 'The development of megalithic structures, mortuary facilities and site location patterning during the Maltese Late Neolithic and Early Bronze Age. Some reconsiderations', unpublished MPhil dissertation, University of Cambridge.

——(2000) 'The Prehistoric Hypogeum at Ħal Saflieni', in A. Pace (ed.) *The Ħal Saflieni Hypogeum 4000 BC–2000 AD*, Malta: Museums Department.

Pace, J.L. (1972) *The Anatomical Features of Prehistoric Man in Malta – Royal University Open Day Exhibition 19–20 May 1972*, Malta: University of Malta.

Patriquin, M.L., Steyn, M. and Loth, S.R. (2005) 'Metric analysis of sex differences in South African black and white pelves', *Forensic Science International*,147: 119–27.

Phenice, T.W. (1969) 'A newly developed visual method of sexing the pubis', *American Journal of Physical Anthropology*, 30: 297–301.

Richards, L.C. and Miller, S.L.J. (1991) 'Relationships between age and dental attrition in Australian aboriginals', *American Journal of Physical Anthropology*, 84: 159–64.

Richards, M.P., Hedges, R.E.M., Walton, I., *et al.* (2001) 'Neolithic diet at the Brochtorff Circle, Malta', *European Journal of Archaeology*, 4: 253–62.

Savona-Ventura, C. and Mifsud, A. (1998) 'Għar Dalam Cave – A review of the cave floor stratigraphy', *Ix-Xjenza*, 3: 5–12.

——(1999) *Prehistoric Medicine in Malta*, Malta: Proprint Company Limited.

Scheuer, L. and Black, S. (2000) *Developmental Juvenile Osteology*, London: Academic Press.

Scheuer, J.L., Musgrave, J.H. and Evans, S.P. (1980) 'Estimation of late fetal and perinatal age from limb bone length by linear and logarithmic regression', *Annals of Human Biology*, 7: 257–65.

Schwartz, J.H. (1991) *Skeleton Keys*, New York: Oxford University Press.

Schwidetzky, I. (1978) *Report on the human remains from the Hypogeum of Ħal Saflieni, Malta*, Malta: Typescript in the collection of the National Museum of Archaeology, Valletta.

Schwidetzky, I. and Ramaswamy, S. (1980) 'Human remains from Punic shaft graves in Malta. I. Physical anthropology', *Journal of Mediterranean Anthropology and Archaeology*, 1: 108–38.

Sinclair, G.G. (1924) 'Ghar Dalam and the Eurafrican land bridge', *Journal of the Royal Anthropological Institute*, 54: 261–75.

Smith, B.H. (1991) 'Standards of human tooth formation and dental age assessment', in M.A. Kelly and C.S. Larsen (eds) *Advances in Dental Anthropology*, New York: Wiley-Liss.

Steele, D.G. (1970) 'Estimation of stature from fragment of long limb bones', in T.D. Stewart (ed.) *Personal Identification in Mass Disasters*, Washington, DC: Smithsonian Institution.

Tagliaferro, N. (1911) 'Prehistoric burials in a cave at Bur-Meghez, near Mqabba, Malta', *Man*, 11: 147–50.

Trotter, M. (1970) 'Estimation of stature from intact long bones', in T.D. Stewart (ed.) *Personal Identification in Mass Disasters*. Washington, DC: Smithsonian Institution.

Webb, P.A. and Suchey, J.M. (1985) 'Epiphyseal union of the anterior iliac crest and medial clavicle in a modern multiracial sample of American males and females', *American Journal of Physical Anthropology*, 68: 457–66.

Zammit, T. (1910) 'The Maltese rock tombs', *The Antiquaries Journal*, 8:

——(1916) 'The Ħal Tarxien Neolithic Temple, Malta', *Archaeologia*, 67:127–44.

——(1926) *The Ħal Saflieni Neolithic Hypogeum at Casal Paula*, Malta: Government of Malta.

Zammit, T., Peet, T.E and Bradley, R.N. (1912) *The Small Objects and the Human Skulls Found in the Hal Saflieni Prehistoric Hypogeum at Casal Paula, Malta*, Malta: Government Printing Press.

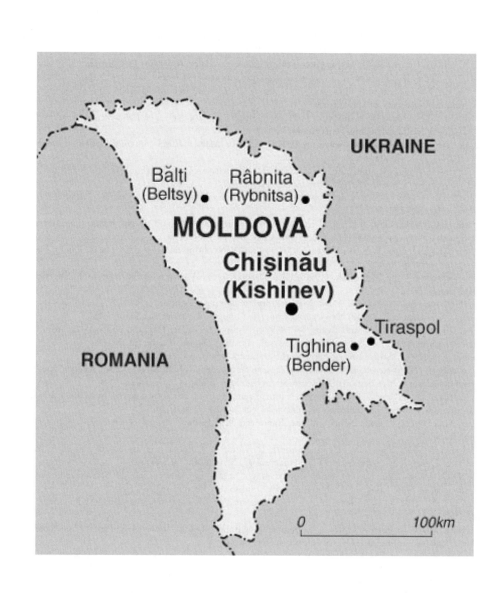

Moldova

Sergiu Musteață and Alexander Varzari

INTRODUCTION: A BRIEF HISTORY AND CURRENT STATE OF PHYSICAL ANTHROPOLOGY IN MOLDOVA

Moldova is one of the few European countries where the majority of anthropological studies have been conducted by foreign anthropologists: by Russian, Ukrainian and Romanian researchers. This is explained by the lack of local qualified specialists during a long period of time.

The first palaeoanthropological studies in Moldova were conducted by the Romanian anthropologist Alexandru Donici, who studied a series of skulls dated to Scythian (7th–3rd C. BC) times (Donici 1935). Some materials from excavations carried out in the late 19th century in Transdniestria, dated to the Bronze, Iron and Middle Ages, were studied by the Russian anthropologist Georg Debets (Debets 1948).

An important contribution to our perception of the physical appearance of the ancient population in Moldova was made by the Russian researcher Marina Velikanova. She conducted detailed studies (morphological and demographic) of palaeoanthropological collections of different historical periods, starting from the late Eneolithic (3000–3500 BC) and ending in the late Middle Ages (17th–18th C.). The results of these studies were published in her monograph 'Palaeoanthropology of the Prut-Dniester River Basin' (Velikanova 1975).

In the 1990s, palaeoanthropological finds from Moldova were studied mainly by Ukrainian anthropologists Serghei Segheda, Ludmila Litvinova and Svetlana Kruts. Since 1999, a Moldovan anthropologist and geneticist, Alexander Varzari, has been contributing to these palaeoanthropological studies. Together with Ukrainian and Russian colleagues, he has minutely studied the Neolithic burial ground Sakarovka I (Kruts *et al.* 2003), as well as two skeletons from Eneolithic and Hallstatt burials in Tatarauca Noua (Varzari and Pezhemskii 2003; Varzari *et al.* 2005).

Besides studies on skeletal remains, research on the physical variations in the modern population have been carried out in Moldova. The first anthropological description of Moldovans was done by Russian anthropologist S.A. Shluger (Shluger 1936). Just before the Second World War, studies in Moldova (Bessarabia) were conducted by Romanian anthropologist Olga Nekrasov (Necrasov 1940). During the Soviet period, somatic variations in Moldovans were studied by Russian anthropologist Rachel Levman (Levman 1950) and Ukrainian researcher Vasili Dyachenko (Dyachenko 1965). Dyachenko's research, besides Moldovans, also included

Ukrainians, Gagauzes and Bulgarians. Later, dermatoglyphic patterns were studied in the same ethnic groups by the Russian anthropologists Henrietta Khit' and Natalia Dolinova (Khit' and Dolinova 1990). Their colleague Natalia Khaldeeva described odontological variations in Moldovan dentition (Zubov and Khaldeeva 1989). A vast range of serologic and molecular genetic markers have been analysed in various ethnic groups living in Moldova, mainly by Alexander Varzari (Varsahr), with support from Russian and German researchers (Varsahr *et al.* 2001, 2003; Varzari *et al.* 2007, 2009). Studies in this field are still ongoing.

Education and training

A course of lectures on physical anthropology, totalling 30 academic hours, encompassing evolutionary anthropology, population anthropology and human morphology, is only taught to History students at the High Anthropological School (Высшая антропологическая школа – the official name of the private university). However, there are no institutions in Moldova that provide qualifications in physical anthropology. An absence of a scientific anthropological base in the country is determined, first of all, by the poor economic situation and low income of the population and, consequently, the preference of young people to enter specialisms that yield more income, such as business and law.

Anthropological studies in Moldova

Table 26.1 contains brief information on skeletal remains that have been analysed. Since there were no local expert anthropologists in Moldova for a long period of time, the remains were usually transported abroad (mainly to Moscow) for anthropological analysis. Among the anthropological collections held in Moldova, although they have not yet been analysed, it is worth highlighting the collection at Tiraspol University 'Taras Shevchenko', which consists of materials from burial grounds dating to the late Eneolithic (Usatov type of Cucuteni-Tripolye culture) and the Iron Age (Scythians, Getae).

ARCHAEOLOGICAL HUMAN REMAINS AND LEGISLATION

Archaeological legislation

In the Republic of Moldova, the legislation concerning the protection of cultural heritage is very general. There are a few laws which deal with certain elements of the heritage. They include: The Law on the Protection of Monuments (Legea privind ocrotirea monumentelor, nr. 1530-XII, 1993), The Law of the Republic of Moldova on Culture (Legea Republicii Moldova despre cultură 1999), The Law of the Republic of Moldova on Archives (Legea privind Fondul Arhivistic al Republicii Moldova 1992), and the Law on Museums. Other legal requirements are addressed in the Civil Code,[1] Criminal Code,[2] Customs Code,[3] Administrative Violations Code,[4] Tax Code,[5] Land Code,[6] Forests Code,[7] Underground Resources Code,[8] etc. The archaeological heritage, as well as the historical architectural and monumental heritage, movable and immovable, is not treated separately. Moldovan laws address value, nature reserves and memorial parks, graves and cemeteries, archaeological and architectural monuments, and landscapes. State institutions are under an obligation to protect this heritage.[9] The decisions of state bodies for the protection of monuments, concerning the recording, study, evaluation, preservation and restoration of monuments, are extended to all individuals and legal entities.[10]

Table 26.1 Anthropological material from Moldova

Cemetery (site name)	Culture or ethnic group	Historical period, dates	Number of subjects analysed	Place where the material is stored	Source of information
Sakarovka I	Mariupol culture	Late Neolithic, 4800–5100 BC	22	National Museum of History of Moldova	Krutz *et al.* (2003)
Solonceni	Cucuteni-Trypillian culture, early period	Ealy Eneolithic, 4100–4800 BC	1	MAE	Gokhman (1958)
Vykhvatintsy	Cucuteni-Trypillian culture, Vykhvatintsy type	Late Eneolithic, 3100–3500 BC	13	IMA	Velikanova (1975)
Tatarauca Noua XV	Cucuteni-Trypillian culture, Gordinesti type	Late Eneolithic, 3100–3500 BC	1	IEA	Varzari and Pezhemsky (2003)
Calfa	Srubna (Timber-grave) culture	Late Bronze Age, 1400–1500 BC	13	IEA	Velikanova (1975)
Badragii Vechi	Noua culture	Late Bronze Age, 1300–1400 BC	23	IEA	Velikanova (1975)
Glinjeni II	Saharna-Solonceni (Thracians)	Early Iron Age (Hallstatt), 10th–9th C. BC	165	National Museum of History of Moldova	Litvinova (1995)
Tatarauca Noua XV	Chernolessk culture	Early Iron Age (Hallstatt), 8th C. BC	1	IEA	Varzari *et al.* (2005)
Bessarabia (combined collection)	Scythians	6th–3th C. BC	77	Material is lost	Donici (1935)
Bocani	Sarmatians	2nd–3rd C. AD	11	IEA	Velikanova (1975)
Budesti	Chernyakhov culture	2nd–4th C. AD	37	IMA	Velikanova (1975)
Malaiesti	Chernyakhov culture	2nd–4th C. AD	13	IMA	Velikanova (1975)
Baltati	Chernyakhov culture	2nd–4th C. AD	4	IEA	Velikanova (1975)
Branesti	Slavs	10th–11th C.	50	IEA	Velikanova (1975)
Hansca-Limbari	Raducaueni culture (supposedly Turkic speakers)	11th–12th C.	40	IEA	Velikanova (1975)
Orheiul Vechi	Golden Horde	14th C.	70	IEA	Velikanova (1993)
Orheiul Vechi	Moldovans/Romanian	15th C.	47	IEA	Velikanova (1993)
Orheiul Vechi	Moldovans/Romanian	16th–17th C.	74	IEA	Velikanova (1993)
Varatic	Moldovans/Romanian	17th–18th C.	116	IEA	Velikanova (1975)

IEA: N.N. Miklukho-Maklai Institute of Ethnology and Anthropology, Russian Academy of Sciences, Moscow
MAE: Peter the Great's Museum of Anthropology and Ethnography, Russian Academy of Sciences, St. Petersburg
IMA: Institute and Museum of Anthropology, Moscow State University, Moscow

The law also provides for better accounting and hence preservation of monuments by the creation of a National Register of Monuments, which is in the process of creation.

Archaeological sites are defined in Moldovan national legislation in very general terms. They are included under the definition of 'sites', along with other man-made productions, under the category of cultural and natural monuments protected by the state: 'Sites: works of man or oeuvres resulting from joint actions by man and nature, as well as *areas that include archaeological sites* carrying national or international values from a historic, aesthetic, ethnographic or *anthropologic* viewpoint' (The Law on the Protection of Monuments no. 1530-XII, 22 June 1993, Article 1, 3 (c)) [author's emphasis].

The Moldovan national legislation defines movable and immovable monuments by using general archaeological terms along with specific terms such as 'tumuli', 'stone steles', 'isolated ancient tombs', 'fortifications', 'ancient roads', etc. The national legal framework does not discriminate between 'forensic' and 'archaeological', or distinguish between forensic and archaeological human remains (but these should be at least 100 years old). Thus, the legislation defines the following as immovable goods:

> Natural objects that have geological, biological, zoological, anthropological, archaeological, ethnographic, historic value, as well as buildings, constructions, *monuments in burial grounds*, works of monumental and architectural art, *tumuli*, stone steles, *isolated ancient tombs*, fortifications, ancient roads, old bridges and mediaeval aqueducts
> *(The Law on the Protection of Monuments no. 1530-XII, 22 June 1993, Article 2 (2)*
> *[author's emphasis])*

Further on, under 'ensembles of monuments', the law underlines the term 'ensembles of archaeological sites' and attempts to list its component elements. The following are considered ensembles of monuments in the form of immovable goods:

> Natural territories and landscapes, archaeological ensembles and sites which comprise small earthen fortresses, non-fortified settlements (hillocks, ancient settlements, prehistoric settlements, grottos, caves, *tumuli tombs*, *cemeteries*, strata carrying archaeological value), ensembles of monuments with a historic, archaeological or memorial value (memorials, *burial grounds*) that comprise *anthropological objects*, earth mounds, stone steles, *isolated ancient tombs*, ancient defence ditches, ethnographic objects, ensembles and reservations of urban and rural architecture (cities, urban centres, neighbourhoods, squares, streets, fortresses, monasteries, parks, natural landscapes carrying objects of architecture).
> *(The Law on the Protection of Monuments no. 1530-XII, 22 June 1993, Article 2 (3)*
> *[author's emphasis])*

The exercise of property rights over monuments is also governed by the laws of the Republic of Moldova.[11]Thus, the national legislation clearly stipulates that the privatization of objects representing the national cultural heritage is forbidden,[12] while illegal transactions are null and shall be subjected to liability as provided by the Civil Code.[13] This legal environment does not, however, exclude the right to private ownership of monuments[14] or to their use,[15] but the right to their use is definitely limited by the protection measures of the European Convention.[16] At the same time, in order to maintain the integrity of monuments, their owners, regardless of their legal status, are under an obligation to take measures towards protecting the monuments.[17] It is up to local and central public authorities to oversee the monument protection measures.[18]

Moldovan laws state that historic monuments, archaeological artefacts and the treasures that may be discovered therein, are protected.[19] Individuals and legal entities who, in the course of any type of work, discover archaeological remains that may be defined as monuments, are under an obligation to cease work and inform the local authority on whose territory the vestiges are found, as well as the Ministry of Culture, in writing, within 48 hours, with an aim to protect and preserve them.[20] Thus, the owner of the land on which archaeological remains are found is obliged to ensure their integrity and, if needed, to permit research and preservation activities, including on human remains.[21] At the same time, state institutions are obliged to organize preservation and restoration works[22] and to compensate the owner of the land with equivalent property or with money for the damage done or for land taken into the public domain.[23]

Unfortunately, liability for the violation of legal provisions receives little enforcement and the application of sanctions is rare. However, the national law contains a number of provisions concerning illegal actions leading to damage to or destruction of historic monuments. Thus, individuals and legal entities that have damaged a monument or its protected area shall restore both the monument and its protected area to its initial state, and if this is not possible, they shall provide compensation for the damage as stipulated by law; any officials and employees who are responsible for such damage are materially liable as per law.[24] In this respect, the Code on Administrative Contraventions states that:

> The violation of rules for the protection and use of monuments of history and culture shall result in a warning or fine being applied to individuals in an amount of up to ten minimal salaries or a warning or fine applied to officials of up to 20 minimal salaries.
>
> *(The Law on the Protection of Monuments no. 1530-XII, 22 June 1993, Article 9 (2))*

The amount of the fine and the other sanctions, as well as the level of compensation, are set by Courts of Law, based on the degree to which the monument is damaged or destroyed, according to assessments performed by specialists.[25] At the same time, the Criminal Code of the Republic of Moldova provides for special penalties for the intentional destruction or damage of historical or cultural monuments or natural sites:

> The intentional destruction or damage of historical or cultural monuments or objects of nature, which are under state protection, shall be punished by a fine from 500 to 3000 conventional units or by unpaid community work to be performed from 180 to 240 hours, while legal entities shall be punished by a fine from 3000 to 5000 conventional units and withdrawal of the right to practice a certain activity.
>
> *(The Criminal Code of the Republic of Moldova, Article 221)*

Concerning the desecration of graves:

> (1) The desecration, by any means, of a grave, a monument, a funeral urn or a body, as well as the seizure of goods found in or on the grave, shall be punished by a fine of up to 300 conventional units or by unpaid community work from 180 to 240 hours, or by imprisonment of up to 2 years.
> (2) The same actions committed:
>   a) by two or more people;
>   b) based on hostility or social, national, racial or religious hatred shall be punished by a fine from 400 to 600 conventional units, or by unpaid community work from 180 to 240 hours, or by imprisonment up to five years.
>
> *(The Criminal Code of the Republic of Moldova, Article 222 on the Desecration of Graves)*

Cultural heritage management

The preservation and use of the national cultural heritage is established by the Government in agreement with the Parliament and in accordance with the laws of the Republic of Moldova.[26] The Ministry of Culture is the national official body responsible for the listing, preservation and evaluation of monuments:

> (1) The responsibility for the destruction, loss, unauthorized sale, delay in salvage, protection, preservation and restoration of monuments lies with the Ministry of Culture of Moldova, as well as with the owners.
>
> *(The Law of the Republic of Moldova on Culture, 5 August 1999, Article 55)*

Moldovan legislation requires special authorization to be secured by a person wishing to carry out excavations. The Archaeology Commission of the Ministry of Culture (Comisia Arheologică a Ministerului Culturii) is authorized to evaluate projects relating to archaeological research and to recommend to the Ministry of Culture the issuing of permits to reputable and qualified individuals or archaeologists. Thus, only with this authorization does one obtain the right to commence or develop the archaeological investigation of a site or of its human remains. The members of the Archaeology Commission have the right to supervise and control the works.

The permit for archaeological investigations is the legal document aimed at preventing illicit excavations and is meant to compel the holder to use the methods and techniques of scientific investigation.

After the fieldwork, every researcher is required to submit a written report to the Archaeology Commission, which should include a description of the place and period of excavation, methodology, results, etc. The report should be accompanied by plans, figures, photographs and other illustrations. Before submitting the report to the Commission, it has to be reviewed by two qualified archaeologists. According to the national and international rules, archaeologists are obliged to publish the results of the excavation as soon as possible. The excavation results must be available to the public within five years after the excavation. In most cases, this rule does not work, because 'reputable archaeologists' maintain some kind of 'monopoly' on the publication of the results.

HUMAN REMAINS AND LEGISLATION

As we can see, Moldovan legislation does not contain special laws on human remains. But the laws quoted do, directly or indirectly, refer to funerary remains. According to national law, it is forbidden to undertake certain activities on archaeological sites without special authorization. Anyone who has discovered archaeological remains by chance, including human remains, is obliged to inform the state institutions within 48 hours. All human remains are declared by law to be part of the national cultural heritage and the law stated above therefore applies in a similar way to the excavation of cemetery sites and human remains.

There is no legal requirement to have an anthropologist on site, but if a cemetery or isolated grave is being investigated, the human remains should be analysed by a local anthropologist or transported abroad for research purposes. Transportation abroad must be done according to the Ministry of Culture and Customs Department rules, as they are applied for artefacts from museums used for national and international exhibitions. The most important issue in this case is that they should be insured.

The national legislation does not mention any ethical issues to be considered (e.g., the rights of religious groups, tribal groups, etc.) for human remains found in churches and churchyards.

METHODS OF ANTHROPOLOGICAL ANALYSIS

Anthropological studies of skeletal remains in Moldova have been conducted in accordance with the standard references accepted in the Russian anthropological school (Alexeev and Debets 1964; Alexeev 1966).

Methods employed on the skull are described in detail by Alexeev and Debets (1964) and include the following:

- Age determination of adults from teeth, by Gerasimov (1955);
- Age determination of children from teeth, by Altukhov (see Alexeev and Debets 1964; Pashkova 1963) and Nikitiuk (1960);
- Estimation of age from cranial suture closure according to Alexeev and Debets (1964);
- Sex determination through cranial morphology, by Pashkova (1963);
- Measurements and the calculation of indices according to Martin (1928);
- Descriptive analysis of cranial morphology, by Alexeev and Debets (1964).

The method of study of the postcranial skeleton is described in detail by Alexeev (1966) and includes:

- Age determination in children and adolescents, by Nikitiuk (1960) and Pashkova (1963);
- Age determination in adults, by Hansen (1953–54) and Rokhlin (1936);
- Sex determination, by Alexeev (1966), Pashkova (1963) and Dobriak (1960);
- Measurements and the calculation of indices according to Alexeev (1966);
- Body height determination from bones using the formulae of Debets (see Alexeev 1966), Dupertuis and Hadden (1951), Manouvrier (1893), Pearson (1899) and Trotter and Gleser (1952).

Palaeopathological analysis of human remains, as well as analysis of markers of mechanical stress, from the Neolithic burial ground Sakarovka I was conducted in accordance with the recommendations developed by Buzhilova (Buzhilova *et al.* 1998).

CONCLUSION

In the Republic of Moldova the legislation concerning cultural heritage preservation is not fully developed, which makes its interpretation difficult and liable to bias. It is not enough just to create a legal framework; what is also required is a change in attitude. In order to improve the degree of protection granted to the archaeological heritage of Moldova, a number of specific steps are required at the national and local levels in the fields of legislation, administrative, scientific and education.

NOTES

1 Civil Code of the Republic of Moldova, no. 1107-XV of 6.06.2002, MO no. 82–86, 22.06.2002.
2 Criminal Code, no. 985-XV of 18.04.2002, MO no. 128–29, 13.09.2002.
3 Customs Code, no. 1149-XIV of 20.07.2000, MO no.160–62, 23.12.2000.
4 Administrative Violations Code of 29 March 1985.
5 Tax Code, no. 1163-XIII of 24.04.97, MO no. 62, 18.09.1997.
6 Land Code, no. 828-XII of 25.12.91, republished in MO no. 107, 04.09.2001.

7 Forests Code, no. 887 of 21.06.96, MO no. 4–5, 16.01.1997.
8 Underground Resources Code, no. 1511-XII of 15.06.93, MO no. 11, 30.11.1993.
9 Article 59, The Land Code of the Republic of Moldova, The Law of the Republic of Moldova No. 828-XII of 25 December 1991.
10 Article 6, The Law on the Protection of Monuments, no. 1530-XII, 22 June 1993.
11 Article 8, The Law on Property, 22 January 1991.
12 Article 17 (4), The Law of the Republic of Moldova on Culture, in MO, 5 August 1999, no. 83–86, p. I, art. 401.
13 Article 9 (2), The Law on the Protection of Monuments, no. 1530-XII, 22 June 1993.
14 Ibid., Article 7 (6).
15 Ibid., Article 9 (1). The monuments on one's property may be sold, donated or alienated with a mandatory notification to state bodies for the protection of monuments. The state has the right of first refusal in the sale/purchase of monuments; see Articles 13–16.
16 Article 4, 5, European Convention for the Protection of Archaeological Heritage.
17 Ibid., Article 13.
18 Ibid., Article 15.
19 Article 32, The Land Code of the Republic of Moldova, Law of the Republic of Moldova No. 828-XII of 25 December 1991.
20 Article 20, The Law on the Protection of Monuments.
21 Article 32, The Land Code of the Republic of Moldova.
22 Article 25 (2), The Law on the Protection of Monuments.
23 Article 32, The Land Code of the Republic of Moldova.
24 Ibid., Article 53.
25 Article 54, The Law on the Protection of Monuments.
26 Article 17 (1), The Law of the Republic of Moldova on Culture, in MO, 5 August 1999, no. 83–86, p. I, art. 401.

BIBLIOGRAPHY

Alexeev, V.P. (1966) *Osteometry. Methods of Anthropological Research*, Moscow: Nauka [in Russian].
Alexeev, V.P. and Debets, G.F. (1964) *Craniometry. Methods of Anthropological Research*, Moscow: Nauka [in Russian].
Buzhilova, A.P., Kozlovskaia, M.V., Lebedinskaia G.V., *et al.* (1998) *Historical Ecology of Humans. Methods of biological studies*, Moscow: Staryi Sad [in Russian].
Debets, G.F. (1948) *Palaeoanthropology of the USSR (Trudi Instituta Etnografii. Novaya seria 4)*, Moscow–Leningrad: USSR Academy of Sciences [in Russian].
Dobriak, V.I. (1960) *Forensic Medical Examination of the Skeletonized Body*, Kiev: Gos. Med. Izd-vo USSR [in Ukrainian].
Donici, A. (1935) 'Crania Scythica', *Memoriile Secţiunii Ştiinţifice. Academia Română*, X (Mem. 9): 289–339.
Dupertuis, C.W. and Hadden, J.A. (1951) 'On the reconstruction of stature from long bones', *American Journal of Physical Anthropology*, 9: 15–53.
Dyachenko, V.D. (1965) *The Anthropological Composition of the Ukrainian People*, Kiev: Naukova Dumka [in Ukrainian].
Gerasimov, M.M. (1955) *Facial Reconstruction from the Cranium (Trudi Instituta Etnografii. Novaya seria 28)*, Moscow: USSR Academy of Sciences [in Russian].
Gokhman, I.I. (1958) 'A child's skull from the early Trypillian settlement Luka-Ustinskaia', *Sovetskaia Antropologia (Soviet Anthropology)*, 4: 127–32 [in Russian].
Hansen, G. (1953–54) 'Die Altersbestimmung am proximalen Humerus und Femurende im Rahmen der Identifizierung menschlicher Skelettreste. Wissenschaftliche Zeitschrift der Humboldt Universitat zu Berlin', *Mathematisch-naturwissenschaftliche Reihe*, 3: 1–73.
Khit', G.L. and Dolinova, N.A. (1990) *Racial Differentiation of Humankind (Dermatoglyphic data)*, Moscow: Nauka [in Russian].
Kruts, S.I., Buzhilova, A.P. and Varzari, A.M. (2003) 'The anthropological material from the Neolithic cemetery Sakarovka I', *Rossiiskaia Arkheologiia (Russian Archaeology)*, 3: 104–18 [in Russian].
Levman, R.S. (1950) 'Anthropological types of the native population of the Moldavian SSR (to the problem of the ethnogeny of Moldavians)', unpublished PhD thesis, Institute of Ethnography, Moscow [in Russian].

Litvinova, L.V. (1995) 'Anthropological material from Early Hallstatt ash-pit on Glinjeni II fort's citadel. Glinjeni II', in N.V. Goltsova and M. Kaşuba (eds) *Multilayer Site in Middle Dniester basin*, Tiraspol: Mako [in Russian].

Manouvrier, L. (1893) 'La détermination de la taille d'après les grands os des membres', *Mémoires de la Societé d'Anthropologie de Paris*, 4: 347–402.

Martin, R. (1928) *Lehrbuch der Anthropologie*, Jena: Gustav Fischer Verlag.

Necrasov, O.C. (1940) *Le Problème de l'origine des Gagaouz. Et la Structure Anthropologique de ce Groupement Ethnique*, Iaşi: Institutul de Arte Grafice 'Brawo'.

Nikitiuk, B.A. (1960) 'Definition of human age from the skeleton and teeth', *Voprosy Antropologii*, 3: 118–29 [in Russian].

Pashkova, V.I. (1963) *Sketches on Forensic Osteology: Determining Sex, Age and Height from Human Skeleton Bones*, Moscow: Medgiz [in Russian].

Pearson, K. (1899) 'Mathematical contribution to the theory of evolution: on the reconstruction of the stature of prehistoric races', *Philosophical Transactions of the Royal Society*, 192: 169–244.

Rokhlin, D.G. (ed.) (1936) *Rentgenoosteology and Rentgenoanthropology*, Moscow–Leningrad: Biomed-giz [in Russian].

Shluger, S.A. (1936) 'Materials on anthropology of Moldovans', *Anthropological Journal*, 4: 461–66 [in Russian].

Trotter, M. and Gleser, G.C. (1952) 'Estimation of stature from long bones of American Whites and Negroes', *American Journal of Physical Anthropology*, 10: 463–514.

Varsahr (Varzari), A.M., Dubova, N.A. and Kutuyev, I.A. (2003) 'Serological researches in the South of Moldavia in connection with the problem of the ethnogeny of the Gagauzes, the Moldavians and the Bulgarians', *Anthropologischer Anzeiger*, 61: 395–411.

Varsahr (Varzari), A.M., Scheil, H.G. and Schmidt, H.D. (1999) 'Blood group and serum protein polymorphisms in a population group of Moldavians', *Anthropologischer Anzeiger*, 64: 51–58.

Varsahr (Varzari), A.M., Spitsyn, V.A., Bychkovskaya, L.S., *et al.* (2001) 'To the research of the gene pool of the Gagauz population of Moldavia', *Anthropologischer Anzeiger*, 59: 11–17.

Varzari, A., Kharkov, V., Stephan, W., *et al.* (2009) 'Searching for the origin of Gagauzes: inferences from Y-chromosome analysis', *American Journal of Human Biology*, 21: 326–36.

Varzari, A.M. and Pezhemskii, D.V. (2003) 'Palaeoanthropological material from the Late Trypillian comlex Tatarauca Noua XV', *Revista Arheologică*, new series 1: 381–87 [in Russian].

Varzari, A.M., Pezhemskii, D.V. and Larina, O.V. (2005) 'Paleoanthropological material from the Late Chernoles Complex Tatarauca Noua XV', in E. Sava *et al.* (eds) *Interferenţe Cultural-Cronologice în Spaţiul Nord-Pontic*, Chişinău: Academy of Sciences of Moldova [in Russian].

Varzari, A., Stephan, W., Stepanov, V., *et al.* (2007) 'Population history of the Dniester-Carpathians: evidence from Alu markers', *Journal of Human Genetics*, 52: 308–16.

Velikanova, M.S. (1975) *Palaeoanthropology of the Prut-Dniester River Basin*, Moscow: Nauka [in Russian].

Zubov, A.A. and Khaldeeva, N.I. (1989) *Odontology in Modern Anthropology*, Moscow: Nauka [in Russian].

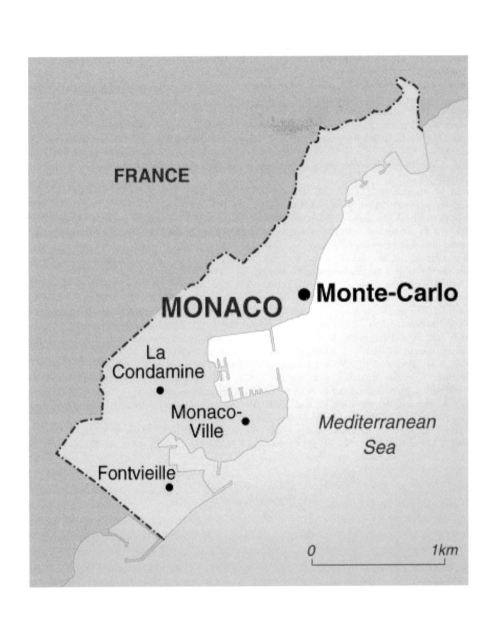

Monaco

Luca Bianconi

INTRODUCTION: A BRIEF HISTORY AND CURRENT STATE OF PHYSICAL ANTHROPOLOGY IN MONACO

The Principality of Monaco is a small country with an area approximately 1.97 sq km and a population of c. 33,000 inhabitants, many of whom are not native to Monaco. It lies on the Mediterranean coast, in the middle of the Riviera between France and Italy, and this geographic position has made this country a popular place in history for international meetings between people from Monaco, France, Italy and many more countries. Human settlement in this area dates back to prehistory (Simone 1993), and the roots of the Grimaldi family (the traditional rulers of the Principality) lie in the Late Middle Ages when the Principality was ruled by the House of Grimaldi (De Rosa 2007). Since 8 January 1297, Monaco has maintained its independence (Costanzo 2006).

The history of the country is strictly connected to the history of the Grimaldi family and it is mainly thanks to its rulers that the country has rapidly become an important economic and research centre. One of the branches of research that has a long and important tradition in Monaco (see, e.g., Landwerlin 1986) is that of anthropology. The ruling family has generously supported research in anthropology during the last two centuries.

Unfortunately this short chapter is just a brief summary of the Principality's regulations and laws on cultural heritage, as far as it is based mostly on bibliographical research and a very short number of brief interviews of researchers who have visited Monaco for their research.

The tradition of anthropological research began in 1846 when Prince Florestan I began to document the exploration of the Grimaldi caves (the so called 'Balzi Rossi' – in Italy, but very close to Monaco: Graziosi 1976). These Grimaldi caves, located partly on a red rock cliff (hence the name 'Balzi Rossi'), were a suitable shelter for prehistoric communities that left behind rich burials and a huge quantity of artefacts, and at least one painting (depicting a horse). The most ancient evidence of human activity (stone tools) and human presence (a female human bone) in these caves dates back to 200,000–150,000 years ago.

It was thanks to the intervention of Princes Florestan and Albert I that this archaeological complex was saved from bad excavations and modern building works. Prince Albert I gave the study of this site and material to famous archeologists including Verneau, Boule and Cartailhac. Since then and until the present day, many institutions (e.g., Istituto Italiano di Paleontologia

Umana and Istituto Internazionale di Studi Liguri) have intervened in different missions and have studied the site and its materials.

This work has recovered a total of 16 skeletons, all dated to the Upper Palaeolithic (see Formicola *et al.* 2004), among which the most famous are:

- Two children buried with seashells, from the 'Grotta dei Fanciulli';
- An adult individual with a rich supply of lithic lames and seashells, also from the 'Grotta dei Fanciulli';
- A very interesting burial with two individuals (an elderly woman and a young woman), also from the 'Grotta dei Fanciulli';
- The skeleton of an adult individual, covered in red ochre, and a supply of lithic tools and seashells, from the 'Grotta del Caviglione';
- The burial of three individuals found in a grave and covered in ochre, with a number of artefacts, from the 'Barma Grande'.

This site is also famous for the beautiful carved prehistoric statuettes that have been discovered. Following in Prince Florestan footsteps, his grandson Albert I in 1883 also started exploring the Grimaldi caves, partially excavating them and making important discoveries during his archaeological campaigns between 1895 and 1902.

At the beginning of the 20th century, three important events took place in Monaco in relation to anthropology: the foundation in 1902 of the Anthropological Museum; the hosting of the XIIIth International Congress of Prehistoric Archaeology and Anthropology (XIIIème session du Congrès international d'Anthropologie et d'Archéologie préhistorique) in 1906; and finally the publication of two monographs in 1906, one on the Grimaldi caves and the other on Altamira's cave.

The international congress in 1906 led to the 'International Craniometric Agreement' which standardized cranial measurements and became the base of standards, and is still the basis of much work today.

In the years following 1906, from an anthropological point of view, the importance of Monaco and the interest in its collections increased. This interest also led The Prince Albert of Monaco Foundation (Fondation Prince Albert Ier de Monaco: www.fondationiph.org/) to become strongly involved in the foundation of the Institut de Paléontologie Humaine, established in Paris in 1920.

Another important step in anthropological research in the Principality was the publication in 1954 of the first issue of the archaeological and anthropological journal *Bulletin du Musée d'Anthropologie Préhistorique de Monaco*. The museum publishes this journal annually, and its main topics are anthropology and prehistoric archaeology. It is a very important source of documentation on many aspects of archaeology in Monaco and the regions surrounding the Principality.

No less important was a second congress hosted in the country in 1959, the XVIth French Prehistoric Congress (XVIème session, Congrès Préhistorique de France).

The 1960s saw a number of anthropological studies being undertaken. Legoux (1962, 1963) published on the dentition of some of the skeletons from the Grimaldi Caves, while Barral and Charles (1963) published on cranial morphology, and Charles (1964) on the human skeletal remains from the cave Bas-Moulins. De Lumley (1962) published at this time a palaeopathological study, too, from his examinations of individuals from the cave of Castellar. A number of physical anthropological studies have followed since then, including the studies by De Lumley (1972), Olivier and Mantelin (1974) and Formicola (1988, 1991).

Throughout the latter half of the 20th century a number of excavations involving specialists from Monaco and abroad have taken place, the results of which are usually published in the museum's bulletin. One example of these activities was the excavations in the 1970s of the Upper Palaeolithic site of Loreto (Basilicata, Italy) by a team from the Museum of Monaco.

The Prehistoric Anthropology Museum of Monaco (Musée d'Anthropologie Préhistorique de Monaco)

The most important institution related to anthropology in Monaco is the Prehistoric Anthropology Museum, which is a very important centre of archaeological research for the whole Riviera, including archaeological research in Italy and France. The Anthropological Museum leads scientific research as well as excavations and publications. The Museum curates a number of skeletons and grave goods from all around the Principality, in particular those discovered in the Grimaldi caves.

The Museum was founded by Prince Albert I in 1901 with the specific aim of preserving the anthropological relics and finds discovered within or near the Principality, such as at 'Balzi Rossi'.

The collections of the Museum embrace some of the most significant stages in mankind's evolution, from Australopithecus to Cro-Magnon, and with artefacts from the Palaeolithic to the Bronze Age deriving from a number of prehistoric sites in Monaco: the Spélugues cave, the caves of Saint-Martin, the cave of the Bas-Moulins, the site of Castelleretto and – the most famous – the cave of l'Observatoire (see, e.g., Chaix and Desse 1982, 1983, 1991; Onoratini *et al.* 1999), located in the *Jardin Exotique*, close to the Anthropological Museum.

The museum holds collections that were recovered during a history of anthropological research in the Principality lasting more than 160 years. As an institution, it has always been strongly linked to the archaeological and historic interest and support of Monaco's princes. The Museum has undertaken a number of excavations in Monaco and the surrounding regions in France and Italy. Some of the sites that museum staff have investigated include Pendimoun (Castellar), the Repaire caves (Roquebrune), the caves of Bas-Moulins (Monaco), Barriera (La Turbie) and the Observatoire (Monaco), and in Grimaldi, the caves Prince, Cavillon and Barma Grande (Barral 1954). The Museum has also undertaken excavations abroad, for example in Mongolia (Mission Archéologique Monaco–Mongolia).

The present situation

As far as the author is aware, there are officially no physical anthropologists in Monaco. However, the Principality has attracted a number of researchers from abroad to study the collections of the Anthropological Museum. Some of the most important anthropologists who have worked in collaboration with the Museum publish often in the 'Bulletin'. In 2004 an international scientific committee was created at the Museum with Yves Coppens as president.

It is also important to underline that the Fondation Prince Albert Ier de Monaco is a major sponsor of the Institut de Paléontologie Humaine in Paris, one of the most ancient research institutes in France and partly established with financial investment from Monaco's rulers (Haurel 2000–2001). The Foundation was also a major sponsor in the excavations undertaken by René Neuville in the Qafzeh cave in Israel. Neuville's work there started in 1934 and, in collaboration with M. Stekelis, he discovered the remains of five individuals from the

Mousterian levels (Vandermeersch 2002). In addition, the Ministère d'État funds a number of archaeological excavations in other countries, such as in Croatia.[1]

ARCHAEOLOGICAL HUMAN REMAINS AND LEGISLATION

Archaeological legislation

There are a number of international conventions and national laws on the protection and preservation of the cultural heritage within the Principauté de Monaco (they can be found mainly online at www.unesco.org/culture/natlaws/index.php). The international conventions include:

- 1958 Convention for the protection of cultural heritage and goods in case of conflicts;
- 1977 Bilateral agreement Franco–Monegasque;
- 1979 Convention about the protection of world cultural and natural heritage;
- 1983 Convention about international expositions;
- 1994 European cultural convention;
- 1999 Convention for the protection of archaeological heritage;
- 2003 European convention for the protection of the audiovisual heritage; together with this convention's Protocol.

National laws relating to cultural heritage and archaeology in general are:

- Law no. 814 of 27 January 1964, which regulates the recovery and management of cultural maritime wrecks;
- A 1970 publication of Monaco's general rules and conditions (Cahier des Clauses et Conditions Générales de Monaco: CCCG), which regulates the course of works for building contractors and states (in Article 24) the obligation of constructors to notify the discovery of any potential archaeological remains to the Directeur des travaux (Director of Works). The state will compensate the discoverer;
- Law no. 1.141 of 28 June 1991 and Law no. 1.014 of 29 December 1978, both related to the public sale of cultural goods;
- Law no. 1.198 of 27 March 1998, related to the discovery, recovery and preservation of maritime wrecks. Here, the discovery should be notified within 24 hours to the Direction des Affaires Maritimes. The finds can be claimed by the legitimate owner within one year and one day, but can later be sold by the state. Chapter 2 of this law is of interest from an archaeological point of view, since the value and importance of the find is calculated for the state by an appointed person of proven experience and competence, chosen by the Ministre d'État (Minister of State). If the owner of such a find is unknown, it becomes the property of the state. The discoverer of such a find will be remunerated;
- Law no. 1.277 of 22 December 2003, related to public exhibitions of cultural heritage;
- Law proposal, 4 June 2008, in particular Articles 31–33;

This last proposed law is of interest in relation to the discovery, excavation, recovery and protection of any kind of goods related to the Cultural Heritage. This law is thus related to archaeological excavations and to the recovery of archaeological finds. It also creates a committee for the protection of the national heritage (Comité de protection du patrimoine national), which is the body responsible for Monaco's cultural heritage.

HUMAN REMAINS AND LEGISLATION

Since, in Monaco's legislation, human remains do not appear to be distinguished from other archaeological findings, the writer supposes that human remains are subject to the same rights as any other archaeological artefact. There appears to be no legal reference to the necessity for the presence of a physical anthropologist in an archaeological excavation where human remains are discovered.

There is a form to accompany the export of cultural goods; this seems to be a standard for the European Community, and was designed by the Direction Générale des douanes et droits indirects. The form requires the exported material to be dated and described, and accompanied with a photograph.

There are at present no ethical issues with the excavation of human remains, though such remains tend not to be from recent centuries. Human remains are displayed in the Anthropological Museum.

METHODS OF ANTHROPOLOGICAL ANALYSIS

There are no specific methods for the study of human skeletal remains in Monaco. Anthropological analysis is usually undertaken by foreign researchers, especially from France, and their methods are appropriate for the region of Monaco.

A number of articles on methods in anthropology have been published in the Museum's bulletin. In volume 19 of the bulletin there are a number of articles devoted to growth and development, including, for example, articles on dental age assessment (Demirjian 1973–74).

CONCLUSION

This chapter is based almost exclusively on bibliographical research, and it is hoped that further information can be provided in the future from a number of interviews, and by further understanding the implications of human remains in legislation and in society.

USEFUL CONTACTS

Most of the information related to the Anthropological Museum of Monaco can be obtained at the Museum's website: www.map-mc.com/

NOTE

1 Such as the project on the 'Ljubic Cave'; see www.cooperation-monaco.gouv.mc/315Coop/ wwwnew.nsf/1909!/x3Gb?OpenDocument&3Gb/

BIBLIOGRAPHY

Barral, L. (1954) *La Grotte Barriera, Un Gisement Eneolithique dans les Alpes-Maritimes*, Monaco: Publications du Musée d'Anthropologie Préhistorique de Monaco.

Barral, L. and Charles, R.-P. (1963) 'Nouvelles-donées anthropométriques et précisions sur les affinités systemátiques des "Negroïdes de Grimaldi"', *Bulletin du Musée d'Anthropologie Préhistorique de Monaco*, 10: 123–40.

301

Chaix, L. and Desse, J. (1982) 'Les bouquetins de l'Observatoire (Monaco) et de Baoussé Roussé (Grimaldi, Italie). Première partie', *Bulletin du Musée d'Anthropologie Préhistorique de Monaco*, 26: 41–74.

——(1983) 'Les bouquetins de l'Observatoire (Monaco) et de Baoussé Roussé (Grimaldi, Italie). Seconde partie', *Bulletin du Musée d'Anthropologie Préhistorique de Monaco*, 27: 21–49.

——(1991) 'Les bouquetins de l'Observatoire (Monaco) et de Baoussé Roussé (Grimaldi, Italie). Troisième partie', *Bulletin du Musée d'Anthropologie Préhistorique de Monaco*, 34: 51–73.

Charles, R.-P. (1964) 'L'ossuaire des Bas-Moulins, Principauté de Monaco', *Bulletin du Musée d'Anthropologie Préhistorique de Monaco*, 11: 127–54.

Costanzo, P. (2006) *La costituzione del Principato di Monaco*, Torino: Giappichelli.

De Lumley, M.-A. (1962) 'Les lésions osseuses de l'homme de Castellar (A.-M)', *Bulletin du Musée d'Anthropologie Préhistorique de Monaco*, 9: 191–205.

——(1972) 'L'os iliaque anténéandertalien de la grotte du Prince (Grimaldi, Ligurie Italienne)', *Bulletin du Musée d'Anthropologie Préhistorique de Monaco*, 18: 89–112.

De Rosa, R. (2007) *I Grimaldi signori di Monaco. Storia di una dinastia*, Parma: La Rupe Mutevole.

Demirjian, A. (1973–74) 'Importance de l'âge dentaire comme indice de maturité', *Bulletin du Musée d'Anthropologie Préhistorique de Monaco*, 19: 107–24.

Formicola, V. (1988) 'The male and female in the Upper Paleolithic burials from Grimaldi caves (Liguria, Italy)', *Bulletin du Musée d'Anthropologie Préhistorique de Monaco*, 31: 41–48.

——(1991) 'Le sepolture paleolitiche dei Balzi Rossi', *Le Scienze*, 280: 76–85.

Formicola, V., Pettit, P.B. and Del Lucchese, A. (2004) 'A direct AMS radiocarbon date on the Barma Grande 6 Upper Paleolithic Skeleton', *Current Anthropology*, 45: 114–18.

Graziosi, P. (1976) I Balzi Rossi, Bordighera: Istituto Internazionale di Studi Liguri.

Haurel, A. (2000–01) 'Varia. La creation de l'Institut de Paléontologie humaine par le prince Albert Ier. Une étape vers l'institutionnalisation de la préhistoire', *Bulletin du Musée d'Anthropologie Préhistorique de Monaco*, 41: 49–62.

Landwerlin, J.-F. (1986) 'Varia. La contribution monégasque à la recherche en Préhistoire', *Bulletin du Musée d'Anthropologie Préhistorique de Monaco*, 29: 99–123.

Legoux, P. (1962) 'Étude odontologique des Enfants dits de Menton, de la grotte des Enfants, Grimaldi (Italie). Fouilles de E. Rivière (1874–75)', *Bulletin du Musée d'Anthropologie Préhistorique de Monaco*, 9: 109–70.

——(1963) 'Étude odontologique de la race de Grimaldi', *Bulletin du Musée d'Anthropologie Préhistorique de Monaco*, 10: 63–122.

Olivier, G. and Mantelin, F. (1974) 'Nouvelle reconstitution du crâne de l'adolescent de Grimaldi', *Bulletin du Musèe d'Antropologie Prèhistorique de Monaco*, 10: 123–39.

Onoratini, G., Simon, P. and Simone, S. (1999) 'Mise en évidence du Protoaurignacien à la grotte de l'Observatoire (Monaco)', *Bulletin du Musée d'Anthropologie Préhistorique de Monaco*, 40: 43–56.

Simone, S. (1993) 'Varia. Prèhistoire de Monaco', *Bulletin du Musée d'Anthropologie Préhistorique de Monaco*, 36: 59–63.

Vandermeersch, B. (2002) ' La fouille de Qafzeh', *Bulletin du Centre de recherche français de Jérusalem*, 10: 65–70.

Montenegro/Crnq Gora

Mile Baković and Ivana Medenica

INTRODUCTION: A BRIEF HISTORY AND CURRENT STATE OF PHYSICAL ANTHROPOLOGY IN MONTENEGRO

The history of physical anthropology in Montenegro is closely connected to the Department of Physical Anthropology at the University of Belgrade. Since Montenegro was a part of Yugoslavia from 1918 until it declared independence in 2006, problems concerning physical anthropology were generally solved at the federal level.

The founder and the only expert in the field of physical anthropology in Montenegro to date was Božina M. Ivanović (1931–2002), a professor in the Department of Biology at the University of Montenegro's Faculty of Natural Sciences and Mathematics. His studies were dedicated to the origin of human populations in Montenegro and their development from prehistory to modern times.

Currently there are no experts in physical anthropology in Montenegro and no appropriate academic course either. For a brief period of time there was a course in physical anthropology held at the Department of Biology at the University of Montenegro, but it was soon to become only a part of the lecture course in genetics.

ARCHAEOLOGICAL HUMAN REMAINS AND LEGISLATION

Archaeological legislation

Archaeological excavations in Montenegro are performed in accordance with the Law on Protection of Cultural Monuments (Zakon o zaštiti spomenika kulture, Sl. list RCG, br. 47/91, 17/92, 27/94) and the Code on Conditions and Ways of Performing Archaeological Excavation and Research (Pravilnik o uslovima i načinu na koji se mogu vršiti arheološka istraživanja i iskopavanja spomenika kulture, Sl. list RCG, br. [55/92]).

In order to perform archaeological research and excavations it is necessary to obtain a licence from the Republic Institute for Protection of Cultural Monuments. The excavation director must be an archaeologist with a minimum of three years work experience. This is an obligatory prerequisite for the field supervisor as well, and if necessary, depending on the complexity of the site, other experts of appropriate specialities may also be involved.

When systematic archaeological excavations are performed, the excavation director is an archaeologist specialized in that particular period to which the archaeological site is assigned, while if the site is multi-layered, a professional team is formed, consisting of specialists for each of the periods. Depending on the type of site and its complexity, participation and cooperation of other experts of appropriate specialties (architects, anthropologists, geologists, palaeontologists, palaeobiologists, etc.) is provided.

Currently, mostly rescue archaeological excavations are undertaken in Montenegro. All necessary analyses, including DNA and radiocarbon dating, are performed abroad.

HUMAN REMAINS AND LEGISLATION

The existing legislation does not contain precise stipulations concerning the obligation of preserving human or non-human (animal) skeletal remains. Osteological material discovered during archaeological excavation is treated as an archaeological find and museum material and, as such, comes under the Law on Museums (Zakon o muzejskoj djelatnosti, Sl. list SRCG, br. 26/77, 30/77, 33/89, Sl. list RCG, br. 48/91, 17/92, 27/94) and the Code on Conditions of Protection and Preservation of Museum Material (Pravilnik o bližim uslovima o očuvanju i održavanju muzejskog materijala, Sl. list SRCG, br. 39/81). These contain regulations that apply to the preservation of the geological and palaeontological museum material and material made of bone, including protection from the source of light, maximum air humidity of 65 per cent, maximum temperature of 20° C, protection of the material from chemical influences and dust, etc.

The legislation allows museum material to be sent abroad for analysis with a licence or authorization from the Ministry of Culture, based on the opinion of the Republic Institute for Protection of Cultural Monuments of Montenegro. Anthropological material is in this case treated as any other archaeological material or geological sample.

Some related laws, such as the Law on Cemeteries (Zakon o grobljima, Sl. list SRCG, br. 04/62, 09/62, 10/65, 27/94), deal indirectly with the protection of skeletal remains, by stating that a cemetery may be excavated and used for other purposes thirty years (or earlier, in case of important social reasons) after it has been pronounced out of use by the municipal parliament; and that the transfer of skeletal remains from one tomb to another is allowed only under conditions defined by the Ministry of Health.

In practice, it is up to the researcher (archaeologist, anthropologist, etc.) to evaluate if the discovered skeletal material should be preserved and, as far as we know, over the last twenty years archaeologists have been regularly depositing and preserving human skeletal remains, particularly ones that come from prehistoric times, the Roman Era, or the Early Middle Ages.

The oldest sample on which anthropological analyses have been performed comes from the skeletal remains found at the site of Kuće Rakića, dated to the Eneolithic Period (Ivanović and Pravilović 1994). Skeletal remains from the 18th and 19th centuries, after technical and photographic documenting (in some cases anthropological analysis is performed as well), are reburied in appropriate tombs at the site, or in the place designed particularly for that purpose.

METHODS OF ANTHROPOLOGICAL ANALYSIS

No methods exist specifically for populations from Montenegro, although internationally recognized methods and those used in neighbouring countries may be used.

CONCLUSION

Since there is no specific legislation for human skeletal remains in Montenegro, protection of osteological material depends mostly on the professional ethics of the researcher and on some related laws that may be applied.

When it comes to the analysis of skeletal remains, the absence of appropriate institutions in this country makes it most likely that the past practice of relying on the assistance of foreign experts will continue in the future.

USEFUL CONTACTS

National Museum of Montenegro (Narodni Muzej Crne Gore). Website: www.mnmuseum.org/infoE.htm/

Centre for Archaeological Research (Centar za arheološka istraživanja), Crne Gore, 81000 Podgorica, Crna Gora

BIBLIOGRAPHY

Ivanović, B.M. and Pravilović, M.Đ. (1994) 'Osteološki nalazi – Tumul iz Zetske ravnice', *Glasnik Odjeljenja prirodnih nauka CANU*, 10: 265–78.

Netherlands/Nederland

Elisabeth Smits

INTRODUCTION: A BRIEF HISTORY AND CURRENT STATE OF PHYSICAL ANTHROPOLOGY IN THE NETHERLANDS

In the second half of the 20th century, physical anthropological research was mainly performed at the 'Institute of Anthropobiology' (the Huizinga Institute, which was part of the medical faculty in Utrecht) until it closed down at the beginning of the 1990s. Archaeologists have however increasingly recognized the importance of physical anthropological research in recent decades. The field attracts a growing number of students, and the interest of the media and the general public has increased enormously in the last ten years. Nowadays it is a normal procedure that skeletal material is properly excavated, documented and investigated. The examination of cremated remains has also become a standard part of archaeological projects.

Physical anthropology is included in the archaeological and forensic educational curricula at the universities of Leiden and Amsterdam. The amount of physical anthropological research and the institutional incorporation is restricted. A reason for this is the scarcity of human skeletal remains, especially from prehistoric periods, due to the poor state of preservation caused by the Dutch soil. Better preserved and more abundant are skeletal remains from historical periods. Many Bronze Age, Iron Age and Roman cemeteries with cremation burials have been excavated.

Graves from various periods are addressed in a handbook on Dutch archaeology by Louwe Kooijmans *et al.* (2005). Archaeological excavations have grown exponentially in the last 15 years, thus leading to the discovery of several Mesolithic and Neolithic sites with human skeletal remains.

The late Mesolithic sites at Hardinxveld-Giessendam have yielded burials and scattered human bones (Smits and Louwe Kooijmans 2001; Louwe Kooijmans and Smits 2001). Cemeteries and isolated human bones have been recovered from the middle Neolithic sites of Ypenburg (Baetsen 2008) and Schipluiden (Smits and Louwe Kooijmans 2006).

Much of the research is incorporated in state-funded research programmes, as well as through commercial archaeological projects. Physical–anthropological research focuses on the demographic size and composition, health, composition of the diet, the heterogeneity of the different burial populations by means of isotope research, and the variety of traditions in the burial ritual (e.g., a NWO (Nederlandse Organisatie voor Wetenschappelijk Onderzoek) funded project entitled: 'From Hardinxveld to Noord-Hoorn'; see Smits *et al.* 2010; Smits and van der Plicht

2009). Early Mediaeval research is incorporated in the NWO-funded Servatius project of the Amsterdam Archaeological Centre (AAC). Large skeletal series from Maastricht are under investigation.

Several dissertations have been published in which physical-anthropological and archaeological data have been integrated. Examples include studies of Bronze Age burial mounds (Lohof 1991; Theunissen 1999). The investigation of a few thousand cremation burials originating from four Roman cemeteries forms the topic of the NWO-funded research (Smits 2006). Central theme in this dissertation is the physical-anthropological study of four burial populations from the northern frontier region of Germania Inferior dating from the first to the third centuries AD. Cemeteries with cremation graves from the Iron Age and Roman period in the southern Netherlands have been published by Hiddink (2003); while the dissertation of Panhuysen (2005) presents the physical-anthropological results of two populations from early mediaeval Maastricht.

Collections from later periods include several large post-mediaeval series dating mainly from the 17th and 18th centuries. These are usually skeletons from churches and churchyards, such as those deriving from Pieterskerk in Leiden (Maat 1982), Broerekerk in Zwolle (Clevis and Constandse-Westermann 1992), St Laurens in Alkmaar (Baetsen 2001) and s-Hertogenbosch (Maat *et al.* 2002).

Universities in Amsterdam, Leiden and Groningen offer Bachelor's and Master's programmes in Archaeology. Courses in physical anthropology are provided by the Universities of Leiden and Amsterdam. Forensic anthropology is included in the Master in Forensic Science degree at the University of Amsterdam.

Since 1983 the Dutch Association of Physical Anthropology (Nederlandse Vereniging voor Fysische Antropologie or NVFA) aims to promote knowledge of the physical anthropology and to encourage and coordinate activities in this area. The association has about 60 members. A great diversity of specializations exists between the members of the group and includes specialists in forensic anthropology, evolutionary biology, osteoarchaeology, and growth and development. Several meetings, lectures and excursions are organized every year and further information on the history and development of Dutch physical anthropology can be found in its newsletter.

ARCHAEOLOGICAL HUMAN REMAINS AND LEGISLATION

Archaeological legislation

Various organizations under the auspices of the Ministry of Education are responsible for the archaeological heritage in the Netherlands. The laws that protect the cultural heritage are based on the European Convention on the Protection of the Archaeological Heritage known as the Valetta Convention of 1992.

The governmental organization concerned with the protection of archaeological sites and monuments is the RCE (Rijkdienst voor het Cultureel Erfgoed). This institution serves as a centre which provides information and advice, but also assesses policies. The RCE is the institution that issues the permits for excavation.

The Netherlands are divided into 12 provinces and each province occupies the position between the national government and the local municipality. The provinces are responsible for mapping archaeological sites, which is important with regards to planning matters. There are c. 40 municipalities (they are mainly cities), and each municipality has an archaeological department within the local authorities. These departments who manage the archaeological remains form part of a union called the Convent voor Gemeentelijk Archeologen or CGA.

Commercial businesses are involved in all aspects of archaeological research. Only certified corporations are allowed to operate in the commercial archaeological market. In principle, most archaeological projects can be performed by foreign European companies if they comply with the regulations and possess a permit to excavate in the Netherlands; such a permit must be obtained from the RCE (Rijkdienst voor het Cultureel Erfgoed). Quality control has been defined in the KNA (Kwaliteitsnorm Nederlandse Archeologie); these are guidelines to ensure quality standards are maintained in Dutch archaeology. Many of these businesses are part of a union, the VOiA (Vereniging voor Ondernemers in de Archeologie). Archaeological practice and its regulations are supervised by the RIA institution (Rijks Inspectie Archeologie). The KNA is regularly evaluated and monitored by the SIKB (Stichting Infrastructuur Kwaliteitsborging Bodembeheer).

In addition to universities, companies, museums and other institutions, more than 2500 volunteers (amateur archaeologists) are members of the Archaeological Society of The Netherlands, or AWN (Archeologische Werkgemeenschap voor Nederland). The members are in regional departments which cover the whole country and participate where possible in archaeological work.

Excavations can be carried out by the different certified organizations (governmental, municipal, commercial, universities).

HUMAN REMAINS AND LEGISLATION

Before excavations are performed on a known archaeological site, the site is evaluated according to defined criteria. The first question raised is whether an archaeological monument is worth preserving. An assessment of its value will proceed and this evaluation will be based on its aesthetic and historical value (Deeben *et al.* 1999). The following phase is to evaluate of the physical quality of the site or monument. and this covers aspects of physical integrity and preservation. The archaeological context is taken into account so that, for example, a Pleistocene inhumation that does not contain any skeletal remains but in which the silhouette of the corpse is visible will be assigned a high score, while the absence of skeletal material in graves from the Holocene where human remains are to be expected will result in a low score. Therefore, part of the criteria are rarity, research potential and context value or group value. This latter aspect concerns the archaeo-region in which relations with other archaeological sites and/or landscape characteristics provide more research possibilities on a larger scale. Only when a site is threatened with destruction (e.g., by construction work, or poor preservation due to the conditions of the soil) will it be excavated. When human skeletal remains are discovered by chance, the above evaluation system is not possible because no decisions could have been made beforehand.

When human remains are discovered accidentally, they will often be brought to the police. A coroner will decide whether to contact a physical anthropologist and/or the Dutch Forensic institute (NFI). Archaeological specimens are considered to be those older than 50 years. When archaeological human remains are discovered unexpectedly in an ongoing excavation, a physical anthropologist will be contacted for supervision and/or excavation on site as defined by the regulations. A physical anthropologist has to fulfil the following criteria in order to be able to undertake this role: possess a Master's degree in Archaeology, Science or Medicine with demonstrable knowledge of physical anthropology; possess knowledge of the regulations and protocols (Willems and Brandt 2004); have three years of demonstrable experience in physical anthropological research in north-western Europe, together with publications.

Procedures on the excavation of grave structures have been defined in cooperation with physical anthropologists in the Netherlands. They are described in the KNA (Willems and Brandt 2004) and provide a number of guidelines which are given in the following section on anthropological methods.

With regard to whether human remains can be transported abroad for research purposes, the national funeral law only concerns recently deceased persons; there is no legislation for the transportation of archaeological human remains.

Finally, some ethical considerations relate to the topic of the reburial of skeletons which originate from mediaeval and post-mediaeval churches. Reburial often means 'dumping' all the bones in one communal grave pit, thereby destroying the integrity of the individuals. Preservation *ex situ* is preferred because the collection will be available for future research.

METHODS OF ANTHROPOLOGICAL ANALYSIS

Procedures on the excavation of grave structures have been defined in cooperation with physical anthropologists in the Netherlands. They are described in the KNA (Willems and Brandt 2004) and, alongside the recommendations by Smits (2002), they provide a number of guidelines for the excavation and recording of graves and human skeletal remains, as well as sampling strategies, the treatment of human remains, and analysis. These include standard excavation practices such as measurements of the remains, recording at a minimum scale of 1:10; leaving a transverse section in ring-ditches; half-sectioning a cremation burial, lifting it *en bloc* and sieving its contexts with a 2-mm mesh. Smits (2002) also provides guidelines for the excavation and lifting of human remains in different degrees of preservation. Important, however, is that the physical-anthropological recording should take place as far as possible in the field by a specialist. There is also very useful information on conservation of specimens and, although these guidelines may be basic, they are nevertheless included in the same document and will provide standardization in the country.

After excavation, the material will be temporary stored for a period of no more than two years following the excavation of the remains before storage at a final depot. Within this period, the material should also be analysed and the results published. Finally, digital data should be deposited according to the system of Data Archiving and Networked Services (DANS).

Laboratory analysis

Anthropological analysis should include an inventory of skeletal elements, the determination of age-at-death and sex where possible. Metric and non-metric variation as well as pathological changes in the skeleton should also be documented where present. The description of cremated remains should in addition include data about the weight, the fragmentation and the degree of combustion (through an assessment of colour). The most used methods for these procedures in the Netherlands are included in Table 29.1.

Skeletal material is dated by radiocarbon dating. The sex, age, height and pathology of the studied individuals form the basis for inferences on the demography and health of past populations. Isotope research has been applied during recent years to investigate diet (carbon and nitrogen stable isotopes) and provenance (strontium, oxygen, lead), and thereby have contributed to studying the processes of Neolithization and migratory patterns. In conjunction with

Table 29.1 Overview of the most used methods of anthropological analysis in the Netherlands

Feature	Methods used
Age-at-death (subadults)	Dental development (e.g., Ubelaker 1978)
	Ossification and epiphyseal union (e.g., Ferembach *et al.* 1980; Scheuer and Black 2000)
	Long bone measurements (e.g., Maresh 1955)
Age-at-death (adults)	The complex method (WEA 1980)
	Auricular surface (Lovejoy *et al.* 1985)
	Pubic symphysis (Brooks and Suchey 1990)
	Fourth rib (İşcan *et al.* 1984, 1985), mainly for forensic applications
	TCA (tooth cementum annulation) (Wittwer-Backofen 2004), mainly for forensic applications
	Attrition (Brothwell 1981)
Sex (adults)	Skull and pelvis (WEA 1980)
	Robustness of the post-cranial skeleton and metrical data (different methods)
Stature	Long bone measurements (Breitinger 1937, for north European male populations; Trotter and Gleser 1958, 1970, for males and females of different race)
Pathology	Reference textbooks (Ortner 2003; Roberts and Manchester 1995; Rogers and Waldron 1989)
	Methods: macroscopic, microscopic, radiological
Epigenetic traits	Non-metrical traits, cranium and post-cranial skeleton (Berry and Berry 1976; Brothwell 1981; Buikstra and Ubelaker 1994)

the archaeological context, grave type and grave gift traditions in burial archaeology are studied. Data on gender and age are important to examine the social and cultural aspects of the burial ritual within a population and/or between geographical and chronological differences. DNA analyses have been carried out with the aim of establishing genetic relationships and hereditary diseases.

CONCLUSION

Physical anthropology has witnessed a growing interest and, during recent decades has led to more research, mainly due to the new European Legislation treaty. However, being a small country, education, training and research possibilities in the Netherlands are limited. Especially when multidisciplinary analyses which incorporate chemical and aDNA facilities and expertise are needed, we are dependent on collaboration with colleagues abroad. Recent publications have invoked more interest, and hopefully this will lead to the further development of opportunities for the study of human remains.

USEFUL CONTACTS

University of Amsterdam, Faculty of Humanities, Archaeological Centre,
Turfdraagsterpad 9, 1012 XT Amsterdam. Contacts: Dr E. Smits and Dr R. Panhuysen. Tel +31 (0)20 525 5839, Fax +31 (0)20 525 5831, email e.smits@uva.nl; r.panhuysen@gmail. com. Website : www.hum.uva.nl/archeologie/

Dutch Association for Physical Anthropology (NVFA). Website: www.nvfa.nl/

Rijksdienst voor het Cultureel Erfgoed (RCE), Smallepad 5, 3811 MG Amersfoort, Tel 033 421 7 421, Fax 033 42 17 799, Email info@cultureelerfgoed.nl. Website: www.culture elerfgoed.nl/

Data Archiving and Networked Services (DANS), Postbus 93067, 2509 AB Den Haag, Tel 070 3494450, Fax 070 3494451, Email info@dans.knaw.nl. Website : www.dans.knaw.nl/

BIBLIOGRAPHY

Baetsen, S. (2001) *Graven in de Grote Kerk. Het fysisch-antropologisch onderzoek van de graven in de St. Laurenskerk van Alkmaar.* Alkmaar: Rapporten Alkmaarse Monumentenzorg en Archeologie 8.

——(2008) 'Het grafveld', in J.M. Koot, L. Bruning and R. A. Houkes (eds) *Ypenburg-locatie 4. Een nederzetting met grafveld uit het Midden-Neolithicum in het West-Nederlandse Kustgebie*, Leiden: Hazenberg Archeologie BV.

Berry, A.C. and Berry, R.J. (1976) 'Epigenetic variation in the human cranium', *Journal of Anatomy*, 101: 361–79.

Breitinger, E. (1937) 'Zur Berechnung der Korperhöhe aus den langen Gliedermassenknochen', *Anthropologische Anzeiger*, 14: 249–74.

Brooks, S.T. and Suchey, J.M. (1990) 'Skeletal age determination based on the os pubis: comparison of the Acsádi-Nemeskéri and Suchey-Brooks methods', *Journal of Human Evolution*, 5: 227–38.

Brothwell, D.R. (1981) *Digging up Bones*, London/Oxford: British Museum (Natural History).

Buikstra, J.E. and Ubelaker, D.H. (eds) (1994) *Standards for Data Collection from Human Skeletal Remains*, Fayetteville, AR: Arkansas Archaeological Survey Research Series No. 44.

Clevis, H. and Constandse-Westermann, T. (1992) *De doden vertellen. Opgravingen in de Broerenkerk te Zwolle 1987–1988.* Kampen: Stichting Archeologie IJssel/Vechtsreek.

Deeben, J., Groenewoudt, B.J.D., Hallewas, P., *et al.* (1999) 'Proposals for a practical system of significance evaluation in archaeological heritage management', *European Journal of Archaeology*, 2: 177–99.

Hiddink, H.A. (2003) *Het grafritueel in de Late IJzertijd en de Romeinse tijd in het Maas-Demer-Scheldegebied, in het bijzonder van twee grafvelden bij Weert.* AIVU Amsterdam (Zuidnederlandse Archeologische Rapporten 11).

İşcan, M.Y., Loth, S.R. and Wright, R.K. (1984) 'Age estimation from the rib by phase analysis: white males', *Journal of Forensic Science*, 29: 1094–104.

——(1985) 'Age estimation from the rib by phase analysis: white females', *Journal of Forensic Science*, 30: 853–63.

Lohof, E. (1991) 'Grafritueel en sociale verandering in de Bronstijd van Noordoost-Nederland', unpublished PhD thesis, University of Amsterdam.

Louwe Kooijmans, L.P. and Smits, E. (2001) 'Menselijke skeletresten', in L.P. Louwe Kooijmans (ed.) *Hardinxveld-Giessendam, De Bruin. Een jachtkamp uit het Laat-Mesolithicum en het begin van de Swifterbant-cultuur, 5500–4450 v. Chr.*, Amersfoort: Rapportage Archeologische Monumentenzorg 88.

Louwe Kooijmans, L.P., van den Broeke, P.W., Fokkens, H., *et al.* (eds) (2005) *The Prehistory of the Netherlands*, Amsterdam: Amsterdam University Press.

Lovejoy, C.O., Meindl, R.S., Pryzbeck, T.R., *et al.* (1985) 'Chronological metamorphosis of the auricular surface of the ilium: a new method for the determination of age at death', *American Journal of Physical Anthropology*, 68: 15–28.

Maat, G.J.R. (1982) 'Boerhaave en zijn tijdgenoten, en de betekenis van hun lichaamslengte (een fysisch-antropologisch onderzoek van begravenen in de Pieterskerk te Leiden)', *Nederlands Tijdschrift voor de Geneeskunde*, 126: 705–12.

Maat, G.J.R., Mastwijk, R.W. and Jonker, M.A. (2002) 'Citizens Buried in the "Sint Janskerkhof" of the "Sint Jans" Cathedral of 's-Hertogenbosch in the Netherlands ca. 1450 and 1830–58 AD', *Barge's Antropologica 8*, Leiden: Barge's Antropologica.

Maresh, M.M. (1955) 'Linear Growth of Bones of Extremities from Infancy through Adolescence', *American Journal of Disease of Children*, 89: 752–43.

Ortner, D.J. (2003) *Identification of Pathological Conditions in Human Skeletal Remains*, 2nd edn, San Diego: Academic Press.

Panhuysen, R.G.A.M. (2005) 'Demography and health in early medieval Maastricht. Prosopographical observations on two cemeteries', unpublished PhD thesis, University of Utrecht.

Roberts, C. and Manchester, K. (1995) *The Archaeology of Disease*, Ithaca, NY: Cornell University Press.

Rogers, J. and Waldron, T. (1989) 'Infections in paleopathology: the basis of classification according to most probable cause', *Journal of Archaeological Science*, 16: 611–25.

——(1995) *A Field Guide to Joint Disease in Archaeology*, Chichester: John Wiley and Sons.

Scheuer, L. and Black, S. (2000) *Developmental Juvenile Osteology*, London: Academic Press.

Smits, E. (2002) 'Menselijke skeletresten', in A. Carmiggelt and P.J.W.M. Schulten (eds) *Veldhandleiding archeologie*, Zoetermeer: College voor de Archeologische Kwaliteit.

——(2006) 'Leven en sterven langs de limes', unpublished PhD thesis, University of Amsterdam.

Smits, E. and Hiddink, H.A. (1998) 'Het onderzoek van crematieresten', in N. Roymans, A. Tol and H.A. Hiddink (eds) *Opgravingen in Kampershoek en de Molenakker te Weert. Campagne 1996–1998*, Amsterdam: Zuidnederlandse archeologische rapporten 5.

Smits, E. and Louwe Kooijmans, L.P. (2001) 'De menselijke skeletten', in L.P. Louwe Kooijmans (ed.) *Archeologie in de Betuweroute. Hardinxveld-Giesendam Polderweg. Een mesolithisch jachtkamp in het rivierengebied (5500–5000 v. Chr.)*, Amersfoort: Rapportage Archeologische Monumentenzorg 83.

——(2006) 'Graves and human remains', in L.P. Louwe Kooijmans and P.F.B. Jongste (eds) *Schipluiden – A Neolithic settlement on the Dutch North sea coast c. 3500 cal BC*, Leiden: Analecta Praehistorica Leidensia 37–38, University of Leiden.

Smits, E., Millard, A.R., Nowell, G., et al. (2010) 'Isotopic investigation of diet and residential mobility in the Neolithic of the Lower Rhine Basin', *European Journal of Archaeology*, 13–1: 5–31.

Smits, E. and van der Plicht, J. (2009) 'Mesolithic and Neolithic human remains in the Netherlands: physical anthropological and stable isotope investigations', *Journal of Archaeology of the Low Countries*, 1–1: 55–85.

Theunissen, E.M. (1999) 'Midden-Bronstijdsamenlevingen in het zuiden van de Lage landen'. Een evaluatie van het begrip 'Hilversum-cultuur', unpublished PhD thesis, University of Leiden.

Trotter, M. (1970) 'Estimation of stature from intact limb bones', in T.D. Stewart (ed.) *Personal identification in Mass Disasters*, Washington DC: Smithsonian Institution.

Trotter, M. and Gleser, G.C. (1958) 'A re-evaluation of estimation of stature based on measurements of stature taken during life and of long bones after death', *American Journal of Physical Anthropology*, 16: 79–123.

Ubelaker, D.H. (1978) *Human Skeletal Remains: Excavation, Analysis and Interpretation*, Chicago, IL: Aldine Publishing Company.

Willems, W.J.H. and Brandt, R.W. (2004) *Dutch Archaeology Quality Standard*, The Hague: Rijksinspectie voor de Archeologie. Available online at www.sikb.nl/upload/documents/archeo/knauk.pdf/

Wittwer-Backofen, U., Gampe, J. and Vaupel, J.W. (2004) 'Tooth cementum annulation for age estimation: results from a large known-age validation study', *American Journal of Physical Anthropology*, 123: 119–29.

Workshop of European Anthropologists (1980) 'Recommendations for age and sex diagnosis of skeletons', *Journal of Human Evolution*, 9: 517–49.

Norway/Norge

Berit J. Sellevold

INTRODUCTION: A BRIEF HISTORY AND CURRENT STATE OF PHYSICAL ANTHROPOLOGY IN NORWAY

The systematic excavation, investigation and storing of ancient skeletal remains in Norway began more than 150 years ago when the Society for the Preservation of Ancient Monuments in Norway (Fortidsminneforeningen) made the first archaeological investigations in an ancient monument in 1851. The first skeletal parts to be salvaged for future scientific study were two skulls from the mediaeval Cistercian monastery ruins at Hovedøya in Oslo. These skulls were the first 'archaeological' finds of human remains to be incorporated in the growing skeletal collection at the newly established University of Oslo.

For more than a century, anthropological studies in Norway were carried out by practitioners of medicine who embraced the prevailing anthropological objectives and methods in Europe. Physical anthropological activities in Norway in the 20th century may be roughly subdivided into three periods, according to the chief interests of the scientific community (Næss and Sellevold 1990).

'The anthropological period'   During the first half of the 20th century, anatomists at the University of Oslo were active in physical anthropology, collecting skeletons, mostly skulls from churchyards all over the country, in order to get material for their research. The principal physical anthropologist during this period was Professor of Anatomy Kristian Emil Schreiner, who was head of the Department of Anatomy at the University from 1908 to 1945. His chief aim in physical anthropology was to provide a craniological description of the Norwegian prehistoric and mediaeval populations, and of Norway's indigenous ethnical minority group, the Sami, thus continuing in the tradition of his predecessors in Norwegian anthropology in the 19th century. Schreiner's major works appeared between 1927 and 1946: the comprehensive report on the Viking Oseberg skeletons (Schreiner 1927); two comprehensive publications on Norwegian prehistoric and mediaeval skulls, *Crania Norvegica* (Schreiner 1939, 1946); and three publications on Sami skeletal remains, *Zur Osteologie der Lappen (Bd 1 and Bd 2)* (Schreiner 1931, 1935) and *Further Note on the Craniology of the Lapps* (Schreiner 1945). Schreiner systematized the anthropological collection, and greatly enlarged it, both by encouraging churchyard diggers to send him skulls from abandoned graves and by organizing excavations of his own. Schreiner died in 1954, and in the late 1970s the anthropological collection was named 'The Schreiner Collection' in his honour.

'The antiquarian period' Between the Second World War and the middle of the 1980s, the excavation of skeletal remains was carried out by antiquarians, first and foremost by the Directorate for Cultural Heritage (Riksantikvaren). The aim of the excavations was not to collect material and data for skeletal research but to rescue skeletal remains which were uncovered in connection with road and building construction works, mainly in the mediaeval towns (Oslo, Tønsberg, Bergen and Trondheim). During these years, there were few research projects involving human skeletal remains, and skeletal finds were often reburied. In the 1970s, skeletal finds from archaeological investigations began to pose problems, chiefly due to a lack of interest in physical anthropology among the anatomists. In 1986, the Schreiner Collection was closed to new finds when the 'Archaeological Interim Committee' decided to discontinue the general practice of depositing finds in the collection. From then on, human skeletal remains were deposited in the repositories of the five archaeological museums in Oslo, Bergen, Trondheim, Tromsø and Stavanger.

'The archaeological period' This period continues to date. Since the end of the 1980s, archaeologists have taken responsibility for skeletal remains that are uncovered during archaeological investigations. There have been many extensive excavations in the mediaeval towns which have yielded a large number of skeletal finds from numerous churchyards. Unique and well preserved skeletal material has also been disinterred in connection with restoration projects in the mediaeval wooden stave churches. In 1986, a report on the state of human osteology in Norway was commissioned by the Archaeological Interim Committee (Brendalsmo *et al.* 1986). As a result of this, an Osteology Working Group and a Physical Anthropological Work Unit were established on 1 January 1990 by the Directorate for Cultural Heritage and the five archaeological museums. The Work Unit should participate in excavations of graves and skeletons, take part both in the planning of the investigations and in the fieldwork, and carry out skeletal analyses. The Work Unit was responsible for finds from the whole country. Initially, the Work Unit was located at the Museum of Antiquities at the University of Oslo (now The Cultural Historical Museum), but when NIKU – the Norwegian Institute for Cultural Heritage Research – was established in 1994, the Work Unit was closed down. Its functions were transferred to the Osteoarchaeology Laboratory of the new institute (NIKU). The Osteology Working Group ceased to function in 1994.

The current state of physical anthropology

At the present time, there are two scientists working in physical anthropology in Norway. At NIKU, a full-time position as senior research scientist in the Osteoarchaeology Laboratory is held by an osteoarchaeologist. In the Schreiner Collection of the Institute of Basal Medical Sciences/the Department of Anatomy of the University of Oslo, a part-time position as head of the collection is held by a professor of anatomy.

Archaeologists may submit skeletal finds to NIKU or to the Schreiner Collection for analysis. The methods of anthropological analysis follow internationally recognized standards. While the Schreiner Collection is focused on palaeopathology, NIKU's Osteoarchaeology Laboratory is mainly concerned with osteoarchaeology and interdisciplinary analyses. Both institutions collaborate with other institutions with regard to specialized investigations such as radiocarbon dating, ancient DNA analysis and trace element analysis. The Schreiner Collection functions as a repository for the skeletal remains of the Museum of Cultural History at the University of Oslo. NIKU does not have a skeletal collection, and after completion of the analyses, the finds are deposited for storage and curation in one of the five archaeological museums.

Physical anthropology is not an academic discipline in Norway. The archaeological institutes at the universities of Oslo, Bergen, Trondheim and Tromsø occasionally invite guest lecturers to give an introduction to physical anthropology to their students. Archaeology students who have wanted to focus on physical anthropology in their studies have gone to other countries to take courses in human osteology, mostly to the universities of Lund, Stockholm and Gotland in Sweden but also to universities further abroad such as in the United Kingdom. A few archaeology students have done graduate work in Norway, focusing their graduate research on skeletal remains and related issues. Some of these graduate students have received guidance in osteoarchaeology at NIKU, while others, with an interest in palaeopathology, have received guidance at the Schreiner Collection. An aDNA laboratory has recently been established at the Centre for Ecological and Evolutionary Synthesis (CEES) at the Institute of Biology, University of Oslo.

Human remains in Norway

The Ice Age in Norway ended between 11,000 and 9000 years ago. There are no human remains from the time before this. The earliest human remains are from the Mesolithic (in Norway defined as *c.* 9500 to *c.* 4000 BC): only four finds have been securely dated to this period. Likewise, very few finds have survived from the Neolithic (*c.* 4000 to *c.* 1750 BC) and the Bronze Age (*c.* 1750 to *c.* 500 BC). From the Neolithic there are both unburnt and cremated finds; from the Bronze Age, there are only cremated remains. From the Iron Age (*c.* 500 BC to *c.* 1050 AD), there are finds of both unburnt and cremated human remains (Holck 1986), but the finds are still comparatively few in number. For example, from the last part of the Iron Age, i.e. the Viking period (*c.* 800 to *c.* 1050 AD), there are less than 150 finds of unburnt skeletons, although a somewhat larger number of cremated remains. Most of the skeletal remains in the museums and collections are from historic periods including the Middle Ages (*c.* 1050 to 1537 AD) and the post-mediaeval (post-Reformation) period (1537 AD to the present). All mediaeval and post-mediaeval human remains are unburnt.

There are at present no comprehensive records of human osteological material from archaeological sites in Norway, but work is underway at NIKU to establish a national register of skeletal finds. In 2000, a preliminary survey established that there are at least 5000 finds of cremated skeletal remains from prehistoric sites, stored alongside other archaeological finds in the archaeological museums in Oslo, Bergen and Trondheim. There are more than 7000 finds of unburnt skeletal remains from prehistoric, mediaeval and post-mediaeval archaeological contexts (Sellevold 2000). Of the unburnt remains, around 5500 are in the Schreiner Collection at the University of Oslo, around 1000 are in the Museum of Natural History and Archaeology, NTNU, Trondheim, around 500 are in the Bergen Museum, University of Bergen, around 100 are in the Tromsø University Museum, and around 100 are in the Museum of Archaeology, University of Stavanger.

Among the unburnt remains, only around 400 finds are from prehistoric sites. Most of the unburnt skeletal remains are from the mediaeval and post-mediaeval periods and have been disinterred in connection with the extensive archaeological investigations in the mediaeval and post-mediaeval towns and church sites which have been carried out by the Directorate for Cultural Heritage (Riksantikvaren) since the late 1950s.

Case study: the Søgne find (Hummervikholmen)

Søgne is a small community on the southern coast of Norway, close to the city of Kristiansand. In 1994, fairly well preserved, although fragmented, skeletal remains were discovered in the sea, at a depth of *c*.1 m, in a small inlet on the tiny island of Hummervikholmen in the Søgne archipelago.

The remains were ^{14}C-dated to between 7910 and 7600 BC and 7290 and 6860 BC, that is, to the Mesolithic period. The dating of the find was a sensation: it was the earliest find of human remains in Norway (Sellevold and Skar 1999; Østmo and Hedeager 2005).

There are extremely few human remains from the Norwegian Mesolithic. So far, only four finds have been securely dated to this period, all from the southern part of Norway. In addition to the Søgne find, there is the find from Bleivik in Rogaland (7950 ±110 BP) (Sellevold and Skar 1999), from Skipshelleren in Hordaland (*c.* 6000 BP) (Sellevold and Skar 1999), and from Svarthola on Jæren in Viste in Rogaland (*c.* 6300 BC) (Østmo and Hedeager 2005: 371). The scarcity of finds is due to several factors, not least the nature of the soil in southern Norway. Skeletal finds from mediaeval and post-mediaeval churchyards are generally fairly well preserved in the calciferous soils of most cemeteries, but outside the cemeteries, the soil in most of southern Norway does not preserve bone at all well, and very few finds of unburnt pre-historic skeletons have been made in this part of the country. In the case of the Søgne find, the watery location of the bones in the calciferous seabed had ensured the preservation of the remains.

The Søgne assemblage consists of fragmented remains of at least three, but possibly as many as five, individuals: an almost complete but damaged skull, with the lower jaw missing; a fragment of the frontal bone of another skull; another skull fragment (occipital bone) from a third individual (which has a younger date than the other two skulls); a relatively well preserved left femur and a damaged left tibia. All bone fragments are from adult individuals and, so far, only females have been identified in the assemblage. The most complete skull is of a 35–40-year-old female.

The skull is robust, just like the skulls of other Scandinavian Mesolithic females. It is of medium breadth relative to its length, with a high upper face and rather low, rectangular eye sockets. The masticatory apparatus had been in vigorous use, and the attachment areas of the masticatory muscles are well developed. Analysis of the ∂^{13}C-signature yielded a value of -13.4%. This comparatively very high level means that 86% of the diet consisted of marine elements. The pattern of dental attrition is a helicoidal pattern typical of hunter-gatherers (Smith 1984). The enamel around the edges of the occlusal dental surfaces is chipped, which can be evidence of the presence of hard particles in the food. In addition to normal functioning, the dentition had most probably also been used as an auxiliary tool. There were slight to moderate defects in the enamel (linear enamel hypoplasia) on several dental crowns, resulting from arrested enamel formation during periods of disease, malnutrition and/or famine when the female was between two and four years old. In 1998, Robin Hennessy and colleagues at University College London made a reconstruction of the head and face of the best preserved skull, based on computerized tomographic scanning. In connection with an exhibition of the Søgne find at the Museum of Cultural History at the University of Oslo in 1999, a three-dimensional model of the reconstructed head and face was created by a computer-guided knife which cut out the head in polystyrene foam. Other analyses of the skeletal remains from Søgne are still in progress.

Case study: the Hamar Cathedral cemetery

Not far north of Oslo, the small picturesque town of Hamar is situated on the eastern shore of Lake Mjøsa, the largest lake in Norway. Hamar was an important political, economic and religious centre in the Middle Ages. Now a small market town, it was the administrative centre of the episcopal see of Hamar, with amongst others the bishop's residence and fortress, and a cathedral. Shortly after the Reformation in 1537 AD, the bishop's manor, the fortress and the cathedral fell into ruin. In 1991 and 1992, the construction of a spectacular protective glass building over the ruins of the cathedral necessitated archaeological excavations in the adjoining cemetery. A wide trench encircling the cathedral ruins was opened and investigated, yielding relatively well preserved skeletal remains of around 1000 individuals, partly from undisturbed graves, partly from disturbed graves, represented by commingled skeletal parts.

A physical anthropologist (osteoarchaeologist) was attached to the project from the very beginning, ensuring a controlled and well documented lifting of the skeletal remains. The skeletal assemblage comprised the remains of both young and old males, of elderly females, and of children of all ages, including prematurely born babies. The males were tall and well developed: more than 25 per cent of the males had been remarkably tall, with calculated statures over 180 cm, a few even over 190 cm (Sellevold 2001).

Among the questions posed to the archaeological and anthropological team was whether the cathedral churchyard had functioned solely as a cemetery for the ecclesiastical community, or if it had also functioned as a churchyard for the lay community, since no parish church had been identified in mediaeval Hamar. The skeletal investigations showed that the demographic profile of the cemetery assemblage was neither typical of a parish churchyard nor of a purely ecclesiastical churchyard. There was a majority of males; only a quarter of the adult skeletons were female. Less than 25 per cent of all individuals were children or subadults. Among the males, there were comparatively many young individuals, while a majority of the females were middle-aged or old.

Interdisciplinary studies of the churchyard's stratigraphic layers, the organization of the graves and the skeletal remains established that the cathedral cemetery had been used by members of the ecclesiastical community as well as by the lay community. The studies also showed that regulations and guidelines for burial according to social class, given in the ecclesiastical sections of the mediaeval provincial law Eidsivatingsloven, had been followed. Not unexpectedly, some of the graves contained remains of men of the church (bishops, canons and priests) identified by religious and other objects found associated with the skeletons. These men were buried in prestigious locations in the churchyard, close to the church building or even inside the church. Some graves contained men who had been killed in battle by fatal sharp blade injuries or by crossbow arrows. These men may have been soldiers in the bishop's personal army. The presence of lay persons in the churchyard is evidenced by the remains of women and children. Some of the lay persons may have been corrodarians at the cathedral: a few of the old women had suffered long lasting illnesses and had yet survived into old age. They must have received good care and attention throughout many years. The locations of the graves of women and children in the prestigious areas of the churchyard east of the chancel and south of the nave indicate an elevated social status for these lay persons. It is suggested that the churchyard, in addition to functioning as a churchyard for the clergy and members of the bishop's household, may also have functioned as a churchyard for a 'social parish', that is, for members of the aristocracy of the Hamar diocese. It is known that the high clergy were recruited from the aristocracy. Lay relatives of the priests and canons of the cathedral may have chosen to be buried in the cathedral churchyard near their kinsmen. Hereditary traits in the skeletons suggest that several individuals may have been related to each other.

The interdisciplinary analyses of the mediaeval Hamar cathedral skeletal assemblage have demonstrated the great source value of skeletal remains in cultural historical studies, and have established physical anthropology as a promising venue for future interdisciplinary projects.

ARCHAEOLOGICAL HUMAN REMAINS AND LEGISLATION

Archaeological legislation

The Cultural Heritage Act

The Act of 9 June 1978 No. 50, Concerning the Cultural Heritage (The Cultural Heritage Act) is Norway's most important piece of legislation with regard to archaeological human skeletal finds. According to this act, monuments and sites earlier than 1537 AD, Sami monuments and sites older than 100 years, and ship-related finds (that is, boats and parts of boats as well as everything on board the boat) older than 100 years are automatically protected, including 'burials of any kind, singly or in groups, such as burial mounds, burial cairns, burial chambers, cremation burials, urn burials, coffin burials, churchyards and their enclosures, and sepulchral monuments of all kinds' (1978). The Ministry of the Environment may issue protection orders, for example for post-Reformation structures and sites which are of value from the point of view of cultural history, such as graves and cemeteries.

International conventions and agreements

In 1995, Norway ratified The Valletta Treaty (also called The Malta Convention), which aims to protect the European archaeological heritage 'as a source of European collective memory and as an instrument for historical and scientific study. All remains and objects and any other traces of humankind from past times are considered elements of the archaeological heritage'. This includes human remains and graves. For the most part, Norwegian laws contain the necessary legal provisions for enacting the contractual obligations of the Valletta Treaty.

Norway has also ratified other international agreements, such as the Geneva Convention which protects war graves 'eternally', and various UNESCO conventions. In addition to agreements which have been ratified, Norway has also put into practice guidelines given in agreements which have not been ratified.

HUMAN REMAINS AND LEGISLATION

The legal basis for the protection of human remains, graves and cemeteries in Norway is given in, principally, the Cultural Heritage Act and in the Burial Act and its regulations (Sellevold 2009). According to Section 105 of the Norwegian Constitution, privately owned sites which contain single graves or cemeteries are legally protected.

The Burial Act

The Act of 7 June 1996 No. 32, Concerning churchyards, cremation and burial (The Burial Act), is relevant in connection with archaeological human remains since a substantial number of extant Norwegian churchyards contain both automatically protected remains and remains that have no legal protection (1996). According to Section 8 of the Burial Act, a grave may be used for a new burial 20 years or more after the last burial if the cemetery regulations do not stipulate a longer period of protection. Section 8 of the Burial Act also stipulates that when a cemetery or churchyard is abandoned, it shall be protected for at least 40 years after the last burial. An abandoned area of the cemetery or churchyard must be totally excavated prior to new use. The

Act stipulates that the human remains should be placed in a common grave in a churchyard or cemetery. The Cultural Heritage authorities should be consulted before such an excavation takes place.

According to Section 2 of the Burial Act, human remains found at the bottom of the sea or elsewhere in nature are said to be in what constitutes a so-called 'natural' grave. The remains must only be disturbed in order to move them to a churchyard or cemetery for burial.

Graves and skeletons from prehistoric times and the Middle Ages are automatically protected by the Cultural Heritage Act, and recent graves and human remains are protected by the Burial Act. This leaves a large number of churchyards and a substantial portion of human remains and graves without legal protection. Most of the skeletons and graves from the period after the Reformation in 1537 AD lack legal protection. A survey done in 2006 revealed that Norwegian museums and collections hold more than 2000 finds related to graves and skeletons from the post-Reformation years, deriving from more than 200 localities, and that such finds are continually being uncovered. The absence of guidelines for treating and curating these finds without legal protection constitutes an ethical as well as a practical problem, both for the authorities and for the scientific community. There is a very clear need for guidelines for the treatment and curation of these finds (Sellevold 2009).

Discovery, excavation and recovery of human remains

The treatment and handling of human remains depends on whether or not the remains have legal protection. The handling of finds that do not have legal protection has varied over the years. The archaeological museums are neither required to excavate, nor to store, legally unprotected finds. If disinterred, legally unprotected finds may be summarily reburied without any documentation, or they may be excavated, documented and reinterred in a churchyard, or deposited underneath a church. But legally unprotected finds *may* also be treated in the same way as legally protected finds. The treatment of such finds is decided by the institution in charge of the investigation.

Expected finds

Most human remains are disinterred in connection with planned archaeological excavations. When plans are made for construction works on sites where it is known or expected that graves and skeletal remains will be disturbed, the builder or the building owner will be notified in advance. If the finds are in the legally protected category, a responsible archaeological unit must design a project plan for excavating, documenting and collecting the remains. After disinterment, an archaeological museum will curate the finds in accordance with the provisions of the Cultural Heritage Act. If the finds do not have legal protection, an archaeological investigation is not mandatory, but this situation may be changed in the (near) future. The Directorate for Cultural Heritage is seeking to establish guidelines that will protect material which is presently outside the legal framework.

Unexpected finds

In the case of accidental discoveries of human remains, the police are usually the first to be notified. If the date of decease is thought to be less than 20 years, the find becomes a forensic case. A physical anthropologist may or may not be asked to examine the remains (there are no established protocols for such cases). If the remains are older than 20 years, the police will notify the proper administrative authorities and the site is secured. The site is assessed, and all the remains *in situ* are recorded. If necessary, an archaeological museum will be called in. If the finds are legally protected, archaeologists will be called in to excavate and lift the material, and the finds will be taken to the museum repository where they will be curated.

Only archaeologists are authorized to excavate human remains. There is no obligation to have a physical anthropologist as a regular part of an excavating team but the teams often include an archaeologist who has had training in (human) osteology. In recent years, a physical anthropologist or osteoarchaeologist has been attached to larger projects, especially in the case of churchyard investigations.

Post-excavation treatment of human remains

Physical anthropological investigations of archaeological human remains may be commissioned by the museum or the institution which is responsible for an excavation or survey, or by the Directorate for Cultural Heritage. Central and local government administrative units may also commission osteological analyses of finds that are made during, for example, construction works. Osteological (physical anthropological) analysis of archaeological human remains is not compulsory.

There has been a restrictive practice with regard to sending human remains abroad for analysis. A few students have applied for permission to take assemblages abroad in connection with studies at foreign universities, but permission has so far not been granted.

Ethical considerations

It is our duty to safeguard the cultural heritage for our descendants. Human remains from archaeological contexts are singular cultural historical documents and a most important source of knowledge about our ancestors and about the past. Analysis of the skeletal remains provides a basis for reconstructing and understanding past populations, their ways of life and their living conditions. To the general public, however, disturbing the peace of the grave is a very sensitive issue, and disturbing churchyards is especially problematic. The treatment and handling of human remains, including research involving skeletal material, necessitates conscious ethical approaches.

In a recent report, aspects of administrative ethics and research ethics are discussed in relation to Norwegian law and international agreements. In the report, examples are given which demonstrate some ethically problematic situations especially with regard to human remains and graves that do not have legal protection, such as mediaeval cemeteries or post-mediaeval cemeteries that are still in use today and which contain both automatically protected and non-protected material (Sellevold 2009).

Ethical considerations are especially important with regard to the human remains of ethnic groups. Norway has an indigenous ethnic population group, the Sami. The history of the treatment of the Sami by the Norwegian authorities and the Norwegian ethnic majority population is a sensitive issue, characterized by injustices and infringements. The transgressions also involved the skeletal remains of the Sami people. Between *c.* 1850 and *c.* 1940 AD, scientists plundered Sami burial grounds and churchyards in Finnmark (the northernmost part of Norway) in search of skulls for their research, against the strongly voiced protests of the local communities. The skulls were transported to Oslo and deposited in the anthropological collection (now the Schreiner Collection) of the University of Oslo. The (unburnt) remains of more than 1000 Sami individuals are still kept in the Schreiner Collection (Kyllingstad 2004; Schanche 2002).

In the late 1980s, there was a bitter fight over two skulls in the Sami collection. The skulls of two men, Mons Somby and Aslak Hætta, had come into the anthropological collection in 1854, following an uprising by the Sami in Kautokeino, Finnmark, against the Norwegian authorities (Zorgdrager 1997). Somby and Hætta, who were the leaders of this uprising, were tried and convicted. They were sentenced to death by decapitation and were executed in 1854. Their headless bodies were buried outside the churchyard fence at Kåfjord church, and their heads were sent to Oslo and placed in the anthropological skull collection.

In a letter to the Department of Anatomy in 1985, Niilas Somby requested the return of the skull of his grandfather's brother, Mons Somby, to the family for burial. The Department of Anatomy refused to surrender the skull, and a legal struggle ensued. The question of repatriation was not resolved until 1997 when the grandchildren of Aslak Hætta joined Niilas Somby and demanded the release of their own grandfather's skull. The Department of Anatomy still refused to surrender the skulls. After a legal debate between the Sami parliament, the University of Oslo, and the Ministry of Church, Education and Research, the university administration finally ordered the Department of Anatomy to yield up the two skulls for burial. The burial took place in November 1997 (Sellevold 2002).

The question of whether or not to repatriate all of the Sami skeletal remains is not resolved. The Sami remains are still kept in the Schreiner Collection, but access to, and research on, Sami remains is strictly regulated. The remains are now protected by a set of rules and guidelines which have been set out by the Norwegian government in collaboration with the Sami authorities and the University of Oslo (Lønning *et al.* 1998; Holand *et al.* 2000). Any type of handling and research involving Sami human remains must be approved first of all by the Sami Parliament of Norway, then by the University of Oslo, and finally by the Skeletal Remains Committee.

Besides the Sami, there are minority population groups in Norway from cultural spheres which are often quite different from the Norwegian cultural sphere. There may be important historical and religious differences between the cultural practices of these minority groups and Norwegians with regard to burials. So far, no guidelines or regulations concerning the handling and treatment of human remains from minority groups have been established.

The Skeletal Remains Committee

In 2007, 'The National Committee for Evaluation of Research Involving Human Skeletal Remains' (The Skeletal Remains Committee) was established as a sub-committee of The National Committee for Research Ethics in the Social Sciences and the Humanities. The need for establishing an independent national committee arose in connection with questions concerning the storage of, and research on, the Sami human remains in the Schreiner Collection at the University of Oslo, and the potential demand for repatriation of this material.

The Skeletal Remains Committee is an advisory committee. Its mandate is to evaluate the ethical aspects of all proposed research projects involving human remains (intact skeletons, parts of skeletons, cremated remains or any other human material) which are now deposited in museums and other institutions, as well as research projects involving material which will come to light in archaeological and other investigations in the future. The mandate of the Committee also covers research on human remains from coffins and sarcophagi which have never been interred, but which have been kept, for instance, in church crypts. The Committee bases its decisions on the rules and regulations of the Cultural Heritage Act, the Burial Act and other Norwegian laws as well as the ethical guidelines for research in international treaties and conventions which have been ratified by Norway, such as the Valletta/Malta

Treaty and ICOM's Code of Ethics. The Committee is working on establishing a set of ethical guidelines of its own.

METHODS OF ANTHROPOLOGICAL ANALYSIS

The methods of anthropological analyses follow internationally recognized standards (e.g., Buikstra and Ubelaker 1994). There are no specifically Norwegian methods. For example, in NIKU's Osteoarchaeology Laboratory, statures are calculated according to Trotter and Gleser (1952, 1958).

CONCLUSION

The systematic excavation, investigation and storage of ancient skeletal remains in Norway has a long tradition spanning more than 150 years. Physical anthropologists today are based at NIKU and at the University of Oslo. When human remains are encountered during the course of an archaeological investigation, archaeologists may submit skeletal finds to NIKU or to the Schreiner Collection at the University of Oslo for analysis.

The legal basis for the protection of human remains comes under, generally speaking, the Cultural Heritage Act and the Burial Act. Due to a number of ethical issues, the Skeletal Remains Committee was established in 2007 to provide some further guidelines about the research, treatment, handling, storage and reburial of human remains.

USEFUL CONTACTS

Riksantikvaren – The Directorate for Cultural Heritage, PO Box 8196 Dep., NO-0034 Oslo, Norway. Visiting address: Dronningensgate 13, Oslo. Tel +47 22 94 04 00, Fax +47 22 94 04 04, Email postmottak@ra.no. Website: www.riksantikvaren.no/English//

The Museum of Cultural History, University of Oslo, PO Box 6762 St. Olavsplass, NO-0130 Oslo, Norway. Visiting address: The Historical Museum, Frederiksgate 2, Oslo. Tel +47 22 85 19 00, Fax +47 22 85 19 38, Email postmottak@khm.uio.no. Website: www.khm.uio.no/om/kontakt_eng.html/

Bergen Museum, University of Bergen, PO Box 7800, NO-5020 Bergen, Norway. Visiting address: Harald Hårfagresgate 1, Bergen. Tel +47 55 58 00 00, Fax +47 55 58 93 64, Email post@bm.uib.no. Website: http://bergenmuseum.uib.no/fagsider/osteologi/index.htm/

Tromsø University Museum, University of Tromsø, NO-9037 Tromsø, Norway. Visiting address: Lars Thøringsvei 10, Tromsø. Tel +47 77 64 40 00, Fax +47 77 64 49 00, Email postmottak@uit.no. Website: http://uit.no/tmu/152?Language=en/

The Museum of Natural History and Archaeology, Norwegian University of Science and Technology (NTNU), NO-7491 Trondheim, Norway. Visiting address: Erling Skakkes gate 47, Trondheim. Tel +47 73 59 21 45, Fax +47 73 59 21 36, Email post@vm.ntnu.no. Website: www.ntnu.no/moreonMuseum/

The Museum of Archaeology, University of Stavanger, NO-4036 Stavanger, Norway. Visiting address: Peder Klows gate 30 A, Stavanger. Tel +47 51 83 26 00, Fax +47 51 84 61 99, Email post-am@uis.no. Website: http://am.uis.no/

The Schreiner Collection, University of Oslo, Avdeling for anatomi, PO Box 1105 Blindern, NO-0317 Oslo, Norway. Visiting address: Domus Medica, Sognsvannsveien 9, Oslo. Tel

+47 22 85 11 50, Fax +47 22 85 12 78, Email delarkiv-mr@labmed.uio.no. Website: www.uio.no/sok?la=en& enhet = 131020/

NIKU – The Norwegian Institute for Cultural Heritage Research, PO Box 736 Sentrum, NO-0105 Oslo, Norway. Visiting address: Storgaten 2, Oslo. Tel +47 23 35 50 00, Fax +47 23 35 50 01, Email kundeservice@niku.no. Website: www.niku.no/

The Skeletal Remains Committee, Norway, PO Box 511 Sentrum, NO-0105 Oslo, Norway. Visiting address: Prinsens gate 18, Oslo. Tel +47 23 31 83 00, Fax +47 23 31 83 01, Email post@etikkom.no. Website: www.etikkom.no/Vart-arbeid/Hvem-er-vi/Skjelettutvalget/

BIBLIOGRAPHY

Brendalsmo, A.J., Müller, I.H.V. and Næss, J.-R. (1986) *Spørsmål vedrørende osteologi i norsk arkeologi. Med spesiell vekt på bevaring av det humanosteologiske kildemateriale*, Oslo: The Archaeological Interim Committee.

Buikstra, J.E. and Ubelaker, D.H. (eds) (1994) *Standards for Data Collection from Human Skeletal Remains* Fayetteville, AR: Arkansas Archeological Survey Research Series No. 44.

Holand, I., Lynnerup, N., Schanche, A., et al. (2000) *Vurdering av den vitenskapelige verdi av De Schreinerske Samlinger ved Instituttgruppe for medisinske basalfag. Det medisinske fakultet, Universitetet i Oslo. Innstilling fra en internasjonal vitenskapelig komité nedsatt av Det akademiske kollegium 7. sept. 1999*, Oslo: Universitetet i Oslo.

Holck, P. (1986) *Cremated Bones. A Medical-Anthropological Study of an Archaeological Material on Cremation Burials. Antropologiske skrifter nr. 1*, Oslo: Anatomisk Institutt, Universitetet i Oslo.

Kyllingstad, J.R. (2004) *Kortskaller og langskaller. Fysisk antropologi i Norge og striden om det nordiske herremennesket*, Oslo: Scandinavian Academic Press/Spartacus Forlag AS.

Lønning, I., Guhttor, M., Holme, J., et al. (1998) *Innstilling fra Utvalg for vurdering av retningslinjer for bruk og forvaltning av skjelettmateriale ved Anatomisk institutt*. Oslo: Universitetet i Oslo.

Ministry of Culture and Church Affairs (1996) The Burial Act (Lov av 7. juni 1996 nr. 32 Gravferdsloven: Lov om kirkegårder, kremasjon og gravferd). Oslo.

Ministry of the Environment (1978) The Cultural Heritage Act (Lov om kulturminner av 1978 nr 50). Oslo.

Næss, J.-R. and Sellevold, B.J. (1990) 'Graver fra historisk tid. Vitenskapelig kilde og forvaltningsproblem', *Collegium Medievale*, 1990/s: i-xl.

Østmo, E. and Hedeager, L. (eds) (2005) *Norsk arkeologisk leksikon*, Oslo: Pax Forlag A/S.

Schanche, A. (2002) 'Saami skulls, anthropological race research and the repatriation question in Norway', in C. Fforde, J. Hubert and P. Turnbull (eds) *The Dead and their Possessions. Repatriation in principle, policy and practice*, One World Archaeology Series 43, London: Routledge.

Schreiner, K.E. (1927) *Menneskeknoklene fra Osebergskibet og de andre norske jernalderfund*, Oslo: Anatomisk Institutt.

——(1931) *Zur Osteologie der Lappen. 2. Band*, Oslo: Institutt for sammenlignende kulturforskning.

——(1935) *Zur Osteologie der Lappen. 1. Band*, Oslo: Institutt for sammenlignende kulturforskning.

——(1939) *Crania Norvegica. Bd. 1 (Middelalder)*, Oslo: Institutt for sammenlignende kulturforskning.

——(1945) *Further Note on the Craniology of the Lapps*, Oslo: Institutt for sammenlignende kulturforskning.

——(1946) *Crania Norvegica. Bd. 2 (Jernalder)*, Oslo: Institutt for sammenlignende kulturforskning.

Sellevold, B.J. (2000) 'Menneskelige skjelettrester som historisk kilde: Muligheter, problemer, metode', in A. Dybdahl (ed.) *Osteologisk materiale som historisk kilde*, Senter for middelalderstudier, NTNU, Trondheim: Tapir Akademisk Forlag.

——(2001) *From Death to Life in Medieval Hamar. Skeletons and Graves as Historical Source Material*, Acta Humaniora 109, Oslo: Unipub Forlag.

——(2002) 'Skeletal remains of the Norwegian Saami', in C. Fforde, J. Hubert and P. Turnbull (eds) *The Dead and their Possessions. Repatriation in principle, policy and practice*, One World Archaeology Series 43, London: Routledge.

——(2009) Om retningslinjer for håndtering og forvaltning av skjelett-og gravfunn fra nyere tid. Rapport til Riksantikvaren. NIKU Rapport 32. (English abstract.) Oslo: NIKU – the Norwegian Institute for Cultural Heritage Research. Available online at www.niku.no/archive/niku/publikasjoner/NIKU% 20Rapport%20pdf/Rapport_32_retningslinjer_handtering_skjelett_gravfunn.pdf/

Sellevold, B.J. and Skar, B. (1999) 'The First Lady of Norway', in G. Gundhus, E. Seip and E. Ulriksen (eds) *NIKU 1994–1999. Kulturminneforskningens mangfold. NIKU Temahefte* 31, Oslo: NIKU – the Norwegian Institute for Cultural Heritage Research.

Smith, B.H. (1984) 'Patterns of molar wear in hunter-gatherers and agriculturalists', *American Journal of Physical Anthropology*, 63: 39–56.

Trotter, M. and Gleser, G. (1952) 'Estimation of stature from long bones of American Whites and Negroes', *American Journal of Physical Anthropology*, 10: 463–515.

——(1958) 'A re-evaluation of estimation of stature based on measurements of stature taken during life and long bones after death', *American Journal of Physical Anthropology*, 16(1): 79–124.

Zorgdrager, N. (1997) *De rettferdiges strid. Kautokeino 1852. Samisk motstand mot norsk kolonialisme*, Nesbru: Norsk Folkemuseum og Vett og Viten AS.

Poland/Polska

Wiesław Lorkiewicz, Iwona Teul and Paulina Kubacka

INTRODUCTION: A BRIEF HISTORY AND CURRENT STATE OF PHYSICAL ANTHROPOLOGY IN POLAND

The origins of physical anthropology as a discipline in Poland date back to the late 18th and early 19th centuries, when anthropological issues were first made the subject of lectures and texts published by scholars belonging to the university circles in Vilnius. First of all, one should mention the outstanding medical doctor, naturalist and philosopher Jędrzej Śniadecki (1768–1838) who authored two works on man: *Teoria jestestw organicznych* ('Theory of Organic Beings') and *O fizycznym wychowaniu dzieci* ('On Physical Education of Children') (Malinowski 1985). In 1807, botanist Józef Jundziłł introduced to Polish science the definition of anthropology after Johann Friedrich Blumenbach as a discipline investigating the biology of man in relationship to his bio-cultural environment (Piontek 1997). Eleven years later the first Polish anthropological text-book was published under the title *Antropologia czyli o własnościach człowieka fizycznych i moralnych* ('Anthropology – on the Physical and Moral Properties of Man') by medical doctor Józef Jasiński, who also came from the Vilnius province. Interest in anthropology surfaced also in other centres of scientific study, which was reflected in an 1824 work published by Wawrzyniec Surowiecki, a professor of linguistics at the University of Warsaw. His *Śledzenie początków narodów Słowiańskich* ('Enquiry into the Origin of the Slavic Nations') touched upon, among others, the geographical differentiation of the physical features of the Slavic peoples (Jasicki *et al.* 1962).

The second half of the 19th century saw the rise of anthropology to the status of a fully-fledged scientific discipline in Poland. It was taught at the Jagiellonian University (JU) in Cracow, first by Józef Majer, and then by Izydor Kopernicki, who also established the first Chair of Physical Anthropology at a Polish university. It was the second Chair of Anthropology in Europe, after the Parisian one, which had been established by Paul Broca (Bielicki *et al.*, 1985). In 1874, in Cracow, the Anthropological Commission was founded (at the Academy of Learning, the predecessor of today's Polish Academy of Sciences), which invited all people interested in anthropology, and which was responsible, for example, for collecting data on the population of south-eastern Poland. Beginning in 1877, the Commission published its own journal entitled *Zbiór wiadomości do antropologii krajowej* ('Collection of Studies for National Anthropology'), the first Polish periodical devoted to anthropology, which later changed its name to *Materiały Antropologiczne, Archeologiczne i Etnograficzne* ('The Anthropological, Archaeological and Ethnographic Materials') (Piontek 1997).

After Kopernicki's death in 1891 and closing the Chair of Anthropology at the JU, for 17 years no anthropological institution existed in partitioned Poland. In spite of that, a number of works were published by Polish medical doctors who were interested in anthropology. They described the anthropometric characteristics of various ethnic groups, the influence of different aspects of the socioeconomic environment on human physical development (e.g., height, head form), and also presented analyses of human skeletal remains excavated during pioneering archaeological works.

The period of modern anthropology in Poland started with the creation of anthropological institutes in Warsaw (1905), Cracow (1908) and Lviv (1913), and soon after World War I also in Vilnius (1919) and Poznań (1921). They covered all the areas of anthropology as it was understood at the time. A description of the diversity and history of people in the Polish lands is given by Julian Talko-Hryncewicz, who restored the Chair of Anthropology in Cracow (at the JU), which specialized in growth processes and undertook the first longitudinal studies on physical development. A number of achievements in comparative anatomy (Edward Loth) and sports anthropology (Jan Mydlarski) were made by the Warsaw institutions: the Anthropological Unit at the Museum of Industry and Agriculture, which was later transformed into the Institute of Anthropological Sciences; and the Anthropological Unit at the Central Institute of Physical Education. Under the direction of Jan Mydlarski, the first major anthropological survey of the Polish population in the interwar period was conducted on over 80,000 Polish soldiers. The study encompassed not only anthropometric data, but also eye and hair colour as well as AB0 blood group (Bielicki *et al.* 1985). The Anthropological Unit of the University of Poznań (UP) soon became an important research centre on physiological anthropology, skeletal biology, palaeopathology and physical development. Its director, Adam Wrzosek, played a major role in establishing the Polish Anthropological Society in 1925, whose official journal was the *Przegląd Antropologiczny* (*Anthropological Review*), started in 1926. However, the most prominent anthropological institution in interwar Poland was the Department of Anthropology and Ethnology at the John Casimir University in Lviv, established by Jan Czekanowski. He was one of the students of the German anthropologist Rudolf Martin and began work in 1907 at the Prussian Museum in Berlin, and then took part in a two-year expedition to Central Africa led by Duke Adolf Friedrich of Mecklenburg (Bielicki *et al.* 1985). Czekanowski created the so-called Polish Anthropological School, together with other renowned Polish anthropologists of the time (some of whom had also been educated by Martin). The School introduced pioneering taxonomic methods, including the first biological distance measure, a method for sorting the matrixes of these distances as well as a racial typology based on them. The School broke new ground in research into relationships between human populations and reconstructing the history of ethnic groups, and soon attained an international reputation.

This period of dynamic development in Polish anthropology was interrupted by the outbreak of the Second World War, which caused great damage to it, most tragically through the death of many outstanding young researchers. However, the initial problems resulting from the loss of some of the collections, scattered research teams and administrative changes due to new national borders were soon overcome. After the Second World War, new chairs and departments of physical anthropology were established at the faculties of natural science of universities, at physical education academies and at other higher education institutions.

The current state of the discipline

A complete description of the current state of anthropology in Poland, its main interests and achievements could not possibly be contained in this chapter. Thus, it seems appropriate to give only some examples of research directions in contemporary Polish anthropology (more complete details are contained in the following sources: Bielicki and Charzewski 1995; Bielicki *et al.* 1985; Malinowski 1979; Piontek 1997). The most prominent anthropological studies are conducted at the Institute of Anthropology of the Polish Academy of Sciences (PAN) in social anthropology, which is understood in Poland as studying populations in terms of the biological results of the social stratification, secular trends, and indicators of individual biological condition (so-called epidemiological auxology). These issues also enjoy great popularity in other academic centres in Poland and thus have been studied in depth with respect to the Polish population, based on data obtained in mass cross-sectional examinations of children and adolescents as well as conscripts, out of which the earliest go back to the 19th century. The PAN Institute of Anthropology is also currently focused on research into evolutionary anthropology. Polish anthropology has substantial achievements in the field of auxology (or ontogenetic anthropology), especially in terms of analysis of individual development paths at the progressive stage of ontogenesis, and genetic and environmental factors influencing human physical growth (e.g., the PAN Institute of Anthropology in Wrocław, the Institute of Anthropology in Poznań). This research is based on, among other things, the results of longitudinal studies, including twin studies, conducted by several units. Internationally recognized studies into broadly understood human ecology, involving all the aspects of biological development and its conditioning, are conducted by, for example, the PAN Department of Human Ecology in Warsaw and the Institute of Anthropology in Poznań. A very important practical result of auxological studies are up-to-date growth standards published periodically by most anthropological units, which make it possible systematically to monitor children's physical growth. Over the past several years, dental anthropology has become a significant field of anthropological inquiry in Poland, which was reflected in the organization of the 13th Symposium on Dental Morphology in 2005 (the Department of Anthropology in Łódź). At the same time, techniques of molecular biology research, especially analysis of aDNA from skeletal remains (the Department of Anthropology in Łódź in collaboration with the Department of Molecular Biology of the Medical University in Łódź) and bone chemistry palaeodietary studies (the Department of Anthropology in Cracow), have gained greater popularity in anthropology. Polish anthropology has also greatly contributed to kinesiology (anthropomotorics) including the relation between the type of body build and motor fitness, predisposition to various sports disciplines, or the influence of physical training on the somatic features.

The scientific organization of Polish anthropologists is the Polish Anthropological Society (Polskie Towarzystwo Antropologiczne or PTA) with headquarters in Wrocław (up-to-date information about the Society, its activity and local branches can be found at www.pta.uni. wroc.pl). Right now, it has approximately 330 members (not only anthropologists, but also researchers pursuing other disciplines dealing with man), and 11 branches attached to universities. The official journal of the Society is *The Anthropological Review*, which has been published since 1926. The journal is issued annually, and since 1997 it has been publishing only articles in the English language. Furthermore, the PAN Institute of Anthropology in Wrocław and the Institute of Anthropology in Poznań publish monographs (mostly in Polish). Every two years, the PTA organizes nationwide scientific conferences (the most recent at the time of writing took place in Łódź in September 2009).

The brief description given above of the current state of physical anthropology in Poland purposefully omits one of the main fields in this discipline, namely, the study of human remains excavated during archaeological works. As it is of great relevance to the main subject of this book, it is presented in more detail later in the chapter. Skeletal biology (which is also known in Poland as historical anthropology or anthropology of skeletal populations) is one of the major areas of anthropological research in Poland, due to both its long traditions and its current popularity, which is reflected in the great number of researchers and publications in this field. An important factor here is also the availability of skeletal material owing to close cooperation with archaeologists. The first anthropological descriptions of human remains, uncovered accidentally or excavated by amateur archaeologists, date back to the 19th century. The main object of interest then was skulls, which were characterized by means of the basic indexes and descriptive features consistent with contemporary knowledge of the morphology of ancient human populations. A great breakthrough in that kind of research was the creation of theoretical foundations and methods of analysis of intra- and inter-population variation of man by the Polish Anthropological School in the 1920s. Together with later modifications that adapted them to craniological research, these theories and methods provided archaeologists with simple and clear information about the anthropological structure of populations identified with particular archaeological cultures, forming a basis for fundamental, synthetic works concerning the ethnogenesis of European peoples, and in particular of Slavs. Thanks to them, physical anthropology gained a standing equal to that of linguistics and archaeology in terms of solving ethnogenetic issues. At that time, however, focusing on these issues, anthropologists mostly limited their studies to the examination of skulls. Still, in the 1930s, some works concerning post-cranial skeletons were published concerning, for example, the reconstruction of the body height of early mediaeval inhabitants of central Poland. As early as the 1920s, Polish anthropologists started to study cremated human remains from prehistoric and early historical burial grounds and created special research methods for that purpose. Thus it was possible to bridge the gap in the reconstructed picture of the biology of ancient human populations that had resulted from the fact that, for a period of about three thousand years (from the beginning of the Bronze Age to approximately the tenth century AD), cremation rites prevailed in the area of what is Poland today. The issues described here continue to be explored by modern anthropology of prehistoric populations in Poland. On the basis of results from experimental cremations of animal and human bones, the methods of study of cremated human remains were improved, especially in terms of determining the sex, age and living stature of individuals (in this case the Trotter and Gleser method was used).

The rejection of the typological concept of race led to an initial stagnation in ethnogenetic research. However, nowadays, studies in this field are conducted with the use of modern statistical analysis, on the basis of the metric and the non-metric traits of the skull and teeth, and of aDNA (e.g., research into the anthropological variation of peoples representing various Neolithic cultures of Central Europe and the ethnogenesis of the Slavs). Studies of skeletal series invariably focus on the markers of stress and deprivation and pathological conditions, which makes it possible to reconstruct changes in the biological condition of ancient populations and their connection with the evolution of human culture and social organization. The mechanism of the development of deprivation markers is also being investigated (e.g., the influence of Harris lines on the morphology of long bones). Large, territorially homogeneous skeletal series, which well document the continuity of populations in some regions from the early Middle Ages to the 19th century, make it possible to examine secular and micro-evolutionary changes, for instance in terms of body height or skull form (the brachycephalization process).

The health of ancient populations is also widely studied, which has led to numerous publications. Moreover, one of the anthropological centres has a permanent palaeopathological exhibition and Polish researchers have taken part in the Global History of Health Project. The analysis of aDNA is also used on an increasingly wide scale to determine sex (especially that of children) and kinship, and to solve some of the key ethnogenetic problems. Furthermore, they are used to verify palaeopathological diagnoses and find genetic predisposition to some illnesses in ancient populations (palaeoepidemiology). Another issue is trace element and isotope analysis of human bones, for reconstructing both prehistoric diet and migration events.

The above-mentioned studies are based on skeletal series owned by major anthropological institutions, which are their property or are on loan from archaeological institutions. So far, very little skeletal material has been found in Poland that dates back to pre-Neolithic time. While the oldest archaeological sites containing artefacts related to human activity in the form of stone implements and animal bones come from about 500,000 years BP (they probably should be connected with the archaic *Homo sapiens*), the oldest finds of human skeletal fragments date back to the Upper Palaeolithic (in 2010, a report on the discovery of the first Neanderthal specimen in Poland, preliminarily dated to 49,000 BP, was published). There are not many Mesolithic finds of this kind, either. A greater number of skeletal series date from the early Neolithic, that is, to approximately 5500 years BC (in total, several hundred skeletons well enough preserved to enable anthropological examination). This is not only due to the greater sedentarism of agriculturalists but is also a consequence of soil properties usually more favourable for the preservation of bones in the environments which were preferred by these peoples. In the area of present-day Poland, the early Neolithic series represent allochthonous populations, given the mechanism of agricultural dispersal in north-central Europe. Archaeological sites with human remains from the beginning of the Bronze Age to approximately the tenth century AD in Poland include mostly cremation burials grounds. Many of them were readily examined by the archaeologists due to ample grave goods belonging to particular cultures, but the cremated bone remains were not always subject to anthropological study. The most numerous skeletal series in possession of anthropological institutions come from the Middle Ages. A good example is the early mediaeval (tenth to 14th centuries) skeletal series from Ostrów Lednicki, an island on Lednickie Lake in north-central Poland, one of the most important centres of power in early mediaeval Poland. The site was excavated as early as the 1930s. It is hard to determine exactly the number of historical and prehistoric skeletons in Polish anthropological collections, but it is probably well over 10,000.

Education and training

Nowadays, the main academic centres of physical anthropology in Poland (chairs or departments) which have a significant part of their research activity focused on human skeletal remains are located in Poznań (the only anthropological institute in Poland), Wrocław, Cracow, Łódź, Toruń, and Warsaw (where the Department of Historical Anthropology is attached to a Humanities faculty). Anthropological research is also conducted by individual scientists occupying chairs of anatomy at medical universities. The institute that continues in the tradition of the first anthropological centres in Warsaw is now the Institute of Anthropology of the Polish Academy of Sciences (PAN) in Wrocław. Chairs and departments which entirely or at least partly deal with biological anthropology (mostly auxology) are also present at universities in Szczecin, Lublin, Rzeszów, Kielce, and the Pedagogical Academy in Słupsk. Finally, there are a number of anthropological departments at Academies of Physical Education in Gdańsk, Katowice, Cracow, Poznań, Warsaw, and Wrocław. The main centres teaching physical anthropology, which in Poland is conducted within studies at biological departments, are the universities in Poznań, Wrocław, Cracow, Łódź, Toruń, and Szczecin.

ARCHAEOLOGICAL HUMAN REMAINS AND LEGISLATION

Archaeological legislation

In order to carry out excavation works at a recognized archaeological site it is necessary to obtain a permit from the Province Conservator of Monuments. The procedure for issuing such permits and the required qualifications of persons authorized to carry out such work are determined by the Decree of the Minister of Culture, as of 9 June 2004, concerning conservation, restoration, construction and other works conducted on registered monuments as well as archaeological research and search for hidden or lost movable historic monuments. Thus, a permit may be granted to a person having archaeological professional qualifications, that is, a person who at least has completed graduate studies in an archaeological department, holds a MA degree in archaeology, and has completed a traineeship in field research. No additional permits or licences are required in Poland to excavate human bone remains at archaeological sites, nor it is compulsory by law to employ anthropologists at such sites (or to conduct osteological analysis).

HUMAN REMAINS AND LEGISLATION

In Poland there are no clearly defined time frames that would distinguish between 'archaeological' and 'non-archaeological' human remains with respect to the possibility of subjecting them to archaeological or anthropological examination. Obviously, contemporary cemeteries managed by local civil or church authorities are a separate case. Anthropologists themselves suggest that, for ethical reasons, excavations in such places should be limited to indispensable rescue works. As far as historical and prehistoric cemeteries are concerned, there are no objections on the part of church authorities, as the prevailing Roman Catholic religion in Poland does not forbid conducting archaeological or anthropological works. However, research work conducted in Jewish cemeteries is subject to strict regulation: every such case requires the approval of the local Jewish community. Thus, in the context of problems arising in many countries with respect of the excavation and examination of human bone remains, the almost exclusively native character of osteological collections in Poland proves to be very comfortable. With only one exception (the osteological collection of the PAN Anthropological Unit), Polish collections do not contain skeletal series from non-European cultures.

What is the legal status of human bone remains in Poland and what are the regulations concerning their uncovering in archaeological works and their subsequent examination? First of all, human remains are legally protected by the Polish Penal Code, which defines the penal responsibility for the desecration of a human corpse, human remains or a burial site. Article 262, §1 of the Code reads: 'Every person who shall desecrate a human corpse, remains or grave shall be fined or subject to restriction of freedom or imprisonment for up to two years.' This responsibility holds irrespective of the place where the corpse is situated, and includes its unlawful removal from the grave. By contrast, human remains uncovered during archaeological excavations have the status of historic objects and are protected by the Act on Preservation and Care of Historic Monuments of 23 July 2003. In accordance with this Act, cemeteries are subject to protection as immovable monuments while burial grounds and barrows are archaeological monuments. Consequently, such human remains have a different legal status, which is reflected in the Act on Cemeteries and Burying the Dead, which expressly stipulates that its regulations on the exhumation and transportation of human corpses do not apply to archaeological excavation works concerning graves and burial grounds located outside contemporary cemeteries protected by this Act.

What action should be taken in accordance with the existing law in the case of the discovery of human skeletal remains? There are two possible situations: accidental discoveries made in the process of various earthworks which require explanation (for instance, whether they are related to a crime), and discoveries made during scheduled excavation works at identified archaeological sites. In the first case, the character of the discovery, its circumstances and any objects found with the remains can be helpful in choosing the adequate institution, which should be notified. The key question is to determine the time that elapsed from the individual's death to the time of discovery of the remains. If there is a presumption that the skeletonized remains belonged to a contemporary individual and attempts should be made to determine the cause and manner of death and to identify the person, then the police must be notified, in accordance with the Penal Code (the time limit for forensic human remains is stipulated in the regulations of the Polish Penal Code concerning the period of prescription for crimes against life: murder may not be prosecuted 30 years after the event, although this limitation does not apply to crimes against humanity and war crimes). Further procedures depend on police regulations, and the remains are submitted for examination to a forensic doctor. Such cases are obviously not of great interest to anthropologists concerned with bioarchaeology, although they may be appointed expert witnesses by the prosecutor (in addition to a forensic doctor, whose opinions on the cause of death have a legally binding character) in order to answer some of these questions, including such basic problem as whether the bones are human.

Due to the tragic events of the Second World War and the following decade, many unknown graves, including mass graves, related to war crimes committed at that time continue to be found. Institutions competent to deal with such discoveries are the Main Commission for the Prosecution of Crimes against the Polish Nation and its local branches (the Commission is part of the Institute of National Remembrance). Such discoveries are usually followed by a prosecutor's investigation involving the examination of the human remains by a forensic doctor, and sometimes by an anthropologist as an additional expert. Since in Poland, as in English-speaking countries, there is an increasing interest in the application of archaeological methodology and field research methods in forensic sciences (sometimes the term 'forensic archaeology' is used), archaeologists are often employed to conduct excavations at this kind of site. That, in turn, usually entails the involvement of an anthropologist, due to close cooperation between representatives of both disciplines. Thus one of the authors of this text has been involved on many occasions in exhumation and anthropological-forensic work (e.g., in the examination of the mass graves in Katyń, Russia, resulting from one of the greatest crimes against the Polish prisoners of war committed during the Second World War).

The procedures upon the discovery of human remains of presumed historical or prehistoric significance (possible objects of antiquity, according to the Polish law) are stipulated by the above-mentioned Act on the Preservation and Care of Historic Monuments. Measures to be taken are the same as in the case of the discovery of other objects thought to be antiquities: the suspension of any works that might lead to damaging them, the securing of the bones and the place of their discovery, and the notification of the Province Office for the Protection of Historic Monuments or its local branch appropriate for a given area. The Province Conservator of Monuments is obliged, within a specified time of the receipt of such notification, to conduct an inspection of the find and, if its significance is confirmed, make a decision concerning the necessary archaeological works. The status of human bones as objects of antiquity decides the proprietary issue: they are part of national heritage and, as such, the property of the State. As a consequence, disposal thereof (e.g., taking them abroad for exhibition or examination) is conditional upon permission of the Province Conservator of Monuments. The age of bone remains is not the only criterion for classifying them as objects of antiquity. On the one hand, in Poland mediaeval and older skeletal remains are automatically treated as objects of antiquity. On the other hand, the definition of an object of antiquity as possessing 'historic, artistic or scientific value' makes it possible to classify even later remains as antiquities (obviously the notion of 'artistic value' does not apply here).

Excavations at a prehistoric or historical burial ground are carried out just like any other type of archaeological exploration. As anthropologists working in Poland have mainly graduated from faculties of biology (as was mentioned, education in physical anthropology in Poland is conducted at biological departments), they are not authorized to carry out excavations on their own. Fortunately, research practice makes up for what the authors of this article perceive as some deficiencies in the Polish law. First of all, archaeologists should acquire the basic qualifications for exploring uncovered human skeletons as part of university studies involving elements of physical anthropology. Furthermore, archaeologists, in order to ensure the best results of their exploration, usually undertake collaboration with an anthropologist, as they are aware that they may thus obtain invaluable information. What is more, the Conservator of Monuments himself may require (but does not have to) the archaeologist who applies for a permit to cooperate with an anthropologist in order to ensure that the human bones to be explored will be properly taken care of.

In the case of discovery of human remains that are not of much interest to any of the above-mentioned institutions (e.g., they do not meet the criteria for objects of antiquity or are not found in an area subject to a conservator's supervision), and their presence at the site of discovery stands in conflict with the area development plan, the remains should be removed to a regular cemetery. This issue is regulated by the Act on the Interment of Human Dead and the Maintenance of Cemeteries as well as by the Regulation on the Disposal of Dead Bodies and Human Remains, and anthropologists are involved in exhumations almost only in extraordinary situations.

Ethical issues

Although, for the above-mentioned reasons, Polish research institutions have not been required to return or rebury any of the human skeletal remains they possess, anthropologists themselves are striving to establish some procedures related to the access, storage and examination of the material. The proposals of Polish anthropologists were presented at a special session devoted to ethical issues in anthropology during the 16th Congress of the European Anthropological Association in Odense in 2008 (at the so-called Ethics Round Table). According to them, the key issues in the approach to human remains are the notions of ethnic, religious and individual remembrance (Krenz-Niedbała 2008). If the first two factors are at play, any examination of human remains should be consulted with relevant communities representing a given ethnic or religious group. In the case of individual remembrance, bone remains, after examination, should be interred according to the rites adopted in the descendants' society. No planned excavations should take place in contemporary cemeteries, except for necessary rescue works. The focus is also on creating adequate, dignified conditions for the storage of human remains and to replace real human bones with models for teaching purposes, if possible.

METHODS OF ANTHROPOLOGICAL ANALYSIS

Physical anthropology in Poland is clearly oriented towards the methods of research used in Western Europe and the USA. This is reflected in the wide application of internationally recognized standards in anthropological analysis of human skeletal remains, such as the methods for determining sex and age-at-death proposed by Ferembach *et al.* (1980) and Szilvássy (1988). With regard to the reconstruction of living stature, the choice of a method depends on its usefulness for particular remains. For instance, the very popular method of Trotter and Gleser (for white peoples) generally does not seem to be well-suited to prehistoric and historical skeletons, as it tends to overstate the reconstructed values. Another popular method is that of Pearson, despite the reservations concerning the method's source material and statistical analysis. An increasing popularity is enjoyed by the method developed by the Czech antrhopologist Vančata (1996), which better reflects the actual variance of body height in human populations.

CONCLUSION

Anthropological research based on human skeletal remains has a long tradition in Poland. Despite some aforementioned deficiencies in this regard in Polish legislation (particularly in relation to the lack of requirements of the presence of a trained physical anthropologist on archaeological sites with human skeletal remains), the current state of the discipline and the prospects for its future development can be described as very promising. Owing to all these measures, one may expect that research into ancient human populations, whose results are usually met with great interest in Poland, will continue to thrive in the future with no hindrances, encouraging only positive fact-finding attitudes rather than unnecessary controversies.

USEFUL CONTACTS

Polish Anthropological Society (Polskie Towarzystwo Antropologiczne: PTA). Website: www. pta.uni.wroc.pl/

BIBLIOGRAPHY

Bielicki, T. and Charzewski, J. (1995) 'Antropologia w Polsce: problematyka, osiągnięcia, zagrożenia, perspektywy', *Wychowanie Fizyczne i Sport*, 2: 3–16.
Bielicki, T., Krupiński, T. and Strzałko, J. (1985) *History of physical anthropology in Poland*, International Association of Human Biologists, Occasional Papers 1(6), Newcastle: University of Newcastle.
Ferembach, D., Schwidetzky, I. and Stloukal, M. (1980) 'Recommendations for age and sex diagnosis of skeletons', *Journal of Human Evolution*, 9: 517–49.
Jasicki, B., Panek, S., Sikora, P., *et al.* (1962) *Zarys antropologii*, Warszawa: PWN.
Krenz-Niedbała, M. (2008) 'Ethics Round Table – dyskusja nad etyką pracy ze szczątkami ludzkimi, Odense 2008', in B. Jerszyńska (ed.) *Współczesna antropologia fizyczna. Zakres i metody badań, współpraca interdyscyplinarna*, Poznań: Wyd. Sorus.
Malinowski, A. (1979) 'The present state of Polish anthropology', *Collegium Anthropologicum*, 3: 265–69.
——(1985) 'Zarys historii antropologii', in A. Malinowski and J. Strzałko (eds) *Antropologia*, Warszawa-Poznań: PWN.
Piontek, J. (1997) 'Poland', in F. Spencer (ed.) *History of Physical Anthropology. An Encyclopedia*, New York and London: Garland Publishing.
Szilvássy, J. (1988) 'Alterdiagnose am Skelett', in R. Knußmann (ed.) *Anthropologie. Handbuch der vergleichenden Biologie des Menschen*, Stuttgart: Gustav Fischer.
Vančata, V. (1996) 'Major patterns of early hominid evolution: body size, proportions, encephalisation and sexual dimorphism', *Anthropologie (Brno)*, 34: 313–28.

Portugal

Cláudia Umbelino and Ana Luísa Santos

INTRODUCTION: A BRIEF HISTORY AND CURRENT STATE OF PHYSICAL ANTHROPOLOGY IN PORTUGAL

Portugal has a considerable number of human archaeological skeletal series that cover a vast time span. Despite the high number of Palaeolithic sites, those with human skeletal remains are very scarce. The Middle Palaeolithic is represented by few human bones derived from the Almonda carstic system, namely the Oliveira Cave, and by some teeth recovered from the Figueira Brava (Arrábida), Columbeira (Bombarral) and Lapa da Rainha (Lourinhã) caves attributed to one individual per site from the species *Homo neanderthalensis* (Cruz and Cunha 2007–8). A similar situation is observed in the Upper Palaeolithic, which is represented by only seven sites with human remains, mostly teeth and long bone fragments; with the exception of the almost complete skeleton from Lagar Velho (Leiria), known as the 'Lapedo child', approximately four or five years old and dated from 24,500 BP (Zilhão and Trinkaus 2002). Pertaining to the Mesolithic there are the renowned Muge and Sado shell middens, with more than 400 skeletons, making them one of the largest Mesolithic collections in the world (Cunha *et al.* 2003). There is a good skeletal representation from the Neolithic to the modern era, as in the majority of European countries. The large, identified, modern skeletal collections gathered since the end of the 19th century should also be highlighted, however (Cardoso 2006; Rocha 1995).

The history of physical anthropology in Portugal has been researched on several occasions by different researchers (Cardoso 2006; Cunha 1982; Cunha 2002, 2007; Lubell and Jackes 1997; Oliveira 1997; Tamagnini 1947; Tamagnini and Serra 1942). Its beginnings can be traced back to the second half of the 19th century. The well-known shell middens at Muge, dated from the end of the Mesolithic, are some of the first sites that were excavated in Portugal and one of the most noteworthy to this day. The archaeological work during this period was mainly carried out under the responsibility of scientists who belonged to the Comissão de Trabalhos Geológicos (Commission for Geological Works), also known as the Comissão Geológica Portuguesa, and later, in 1918, by Serviços Geológicos de Portugal (Raposo and Silva 1996). The first Comissão Geológica Portuguesa (Portuguese Geological Commission), created in 1849 in Lisbon, was responsible for the geological and mineralogical exploration in the country and was under the umbrella of the Academia das Ciências de Lisboa (Raposo and Silva 1996). Soon after, in 1857, this structure was reorganized and subordinated to the Direcção-General de Trabalhos Geodésicos, having as first director Carlos Ribeiro (1813–82), assisted by Francisco A. Pereira da Costa (1809–89) and Joaquim F. Nery Delgado (1835–1908) (Lubell and Jackes 1997; Raposo and Silva 1996). These three individuals were responsible for the emergence of pre-historic studies in Portugal (Raposo and Silva 1996) and according to António Xavier da Cunha, an important Portuguese anthropologist, they should be considered as 'the first Portuguese anthropologists, although self-taught in anthropological science' (Cunha 1982: 7). Ribeiro was a senior military officer and a geologist; Pereira da Costa graduated in Natural Philosophy and Medicine; and Nery Delgado was a military engineer (Cunha 1982).

In 1863, Carlos Ribeiro, with the purpose of collecting data for a geological map of Portugal, identified the first shell midden from the Tagus valley, Arneiro-do-Roquete, also named Quinta da Sardinha (Cardoso and Rolão 1999–2000; Gonçalves 1986). In the same year, one of the three most famous Muge shell middens, Cabeço da Arruda, was discovered and Moita do Sebastião and Cabeço da Amoreira were identified and excavated a year later (Rolão 1999; Umbelino 2006). Pereira da Costa (1865) was responsible both for the first publication on human remains and for the first paper about the Muge shell middens (Umbelino 2006). Two years later, Nery Delgado (1867) brought out the news about the Cesareda caves: Casa da Moura, Lapa Furada and Cova da Moura (Raposo and Silva 1996). In 1880, Sebastião Estácio da Veiga (1828–91), with a background in mine engineering, published his archaeological discoveries in Mértola as well as five volumes on the Algarve region, which included anthropological information (Santos 2007).

One major subject of analysis at the end of the 19th century that most fascinated the scientific community, and especially Carlos Ribeiro, was the eventual presence of the 'Tertiary Man' in Portuguese territory. The discovery of 'eólitos' (silex with shape and size that were interpreted as stone artefacts made by ancient populations dated from the Miocenic and Pliocenic (Bicho, 2006)) from the Ota region, had Ribeiro as one of its most committed defenders. This polemic matter, associated with the international credibility gained by the Comissão Geológica through their archaeological work, led to IXe Congrès International d'Anthropologie & d'Archéologie Préhistorique in Lisbon in 1880. This international congress attracted delegates from 19 countries, and its programme included a visit to the Muge sites (Raposo and Silva 1996; Santos 2007). The proceedings from this meeting were published in 1884 (*Compte rendu de la 9ème session du Congrès International d'Anthropologie et d'Archéologie préhistorique (Lisboa, 1880)*), including the main results from several excavations that had taken place in Portugal, including information on the Muge shell middens. After the death of Carlos Ribeiro, a group of students from Oporto influenced by his work created in 1887 the 'Carlos Ribeiro' Society (Guimarães 1995).

Two fundamental figures in archaeology and anthropology were the physicians José Leite de Vasconcelos (1858–1941) and Mendes Corrêa (1888–1960), both of whom will be mentioned later in the text. At the end of the 19th century and beginning of the 20th, the influence of the French school was undeniable, attested to not only by the language used to publish the scientific articles produced by Portuguese researchers but also by the number of French researchers working with Portuguese material, such as Émile Cartailhac (1845–1921), Georges Hervé (1855–1932), Henry Breuil (1877–1961), Henri-V. Vallois (1889–1981), Abbé Jean Roche (1913–2008) and Denise Ferembach (1924–94). They focused mainly on human variation, with a major typological focus on metric analysis for racial classification, following the established anthropological current of the time (Cartailhac 1886; Hervé 1899; Mendes Côrrea 1917, 1919, 1923, 1936; Paula e Oliveira 1884, 1886; Vallois 1930). With regard to palaeopathology, the first publications dealt largely with single cases (Santos 1999/2000; Santos and Cunha, to be submitted), including trepanations from the Neolithic period, namely the site of Casa da Moura and Furninha Caves (Delgado 1884) and from other prehistoric sites (Vasconcelos 1897, 1913).

Other foreigner scholars who undertook some important work in Portugal were the Leisners, the German Georg Leisner (1870–1960) and his American wife Vera (1885–1965), the Russian Georges Zbyszewski (1935–99), and the Germans Konrad Spindler (1939–2005) and Gretel Gallay.

Education and training

The year 1857 is considered by Leite de Vasconcelos (1933: 66) as the beginning of 'the scientific study of Anthropology' in Portugal; he stated that prior to that only 'single observations, usually subjective ones, made by physicians, chorographers, historians, travellers, etc., on physical, physiological, pathological and psychic traits' were made. Physical Anthropology as a discipline was official taught for the first time in Portugal at the Faculty of Philosophy, University of Coimbra, in 1885 and supported by the Natural History Museum which had had an educational or outreach section since 1886–87 (Areia and Rocha 1985: 14). Bernardino Machado (1851–1944) was responsible for its creation under the name of 'Anthropology, Human Palaeontology and Prehistoric Archaeology' (Anthropologia, Paleontologia Humana e Archeologia Préhistórica) (Areia and Rocha 1985; Cunha 1982; Tamagnini 1947). It was physician Henrique Teixeira Bastos (1861–1943) who became the first Professor of Anthropology (Tamagnini and Serra 1942: 5). He taught cranial capacity, race, monogenism and polygenism, as well as the 'tradition of the first populations' dating back to the Stone, Bronze and Iron Ages (Areia and Rocha 1985: 28–32). Through this programme, the scientific development of anthropology and archaeology at that time was recognized. After Bernardino Machado's resignation for political reasons, in 1907 Eusébio Tamagnini became Professor of Anthropology and director of the Gabinete de Antropologia, later called the Museu e Laboratório Antropológico – Instituto de Antropologia, until 1950 when he retired (Cunha 1982: 18). His successors José Antunes Serra from 1950 to 1953, and later Alberto Xavier da Cunha until 1963, kept the programme running (Areia and Rocha 1985). Between 1963 and 1972 there was no professor assigned to Anthropology, and the discipline was taught by biologists Susana Almeida Santos and Francisco Ferrand de Almeida, who gave great emphasis to the latest discoveries in human evolution (Areia and Rocha 1985). As a consequence of the revolution in April 1974, there were some changes in the way the university was organized, and it is at this time that anthropology teaching became an option, namely for biology students. It became compulsory once more in 1977 with the General Anthropology course. From 1975 until 1983, other related disciplines such as Human Palaeontology arose in 1983. In the following decade there was an increase in the number of students and disciplines within the scientific area of Anthropology. This increase led to the creation of the degree in Anthropology in 1992, thanks to the efforts of Manuel Laranjeira Rodrigues de Areia and the collaboration of Maria Augusta Rocha and other members of staff. These scholars taught a different perception compared to other courses that already existed in Portugal, with a strong emphasis on the relationship between the biological component and the social and cultural ones. For the first time, physical anthropologists received an education in human osteology, evolution, genetics, ecology, primatology, palaeopathology, palaeodemography and funerary anthropology, in addition to the social and cultural component; this made this university education unique in Portugal. Until then, physical anthropologists came from a variety of backgrounds, mostly from the fields of Biology and Archaeology. At the beginning of the 1990s, there was a re-emergence of anthropological studies focusing on skeletal biology and palaeopathology (Cunha 2002).

Eugénia Cunha played an important role in the creation of a Master's degree course in Human Evolution which started in 1998. In 2007, with the Bologna Declaration, the course was entitled Master in Evolution and Human Biology. According to Cunha (2007: 13), this Master's degree course has been sought after by 'anthropologists, biologists, archaeologists and undergraduate students with other backgrounds who try, therefore, to initiate or complement their academic formation in this domain'. Nowadays, where biological anthropology is concerned, besides the subjects already mentioned, others have been introduced including paleodiet, oral pathology and forensic anthropology. In addition, the University of Coimbra also offers a PhD in Anthropology with specializations in Biological Anthropology, Cultural Anthropology and Forensic Anthropology. Nine Portuguese researchers have completed their doctoral thesis in physical anthropology (Cardoso 2005; Cardoso 2008; Cunha 1994; Fernandes 2008; Garcia 2007; Santos 2000; Silva 2002; Umbelino 2006; Wasterlain 2006) and the number of doctoral students is constantly increasing.

In Lisbon, the history of Anthropology is associated with the creation of the Escola Politécnica de Lisboa in 1837 (Almaça 2000), where anthropology is taught in the field of Compared Anatomy, Physiology and Zoology (Cunha 1937, in Cardoso 2006). Later, in 1905, the Zoology Section of the National Museum of Lisbon, which was associated with the Escola Politécnica, was renamed the Museu Bocage (Cardoso 2006).

In 1911, after the universities' reform, the teaching of Anthropology as a discipline began at the universities of Lisbon and Oporto (Cunha 1982). The Escola Politécnica and its Museums were incorporated in the Faculty of Sciences at the University of Lisbon (Cunha 1937, in Cardoso 2006). The creation of Anthropology in Lisbon was not accompanied by a Department or section for teaching and research in Anthropology, as had occurred in Coimbra and Oporto (Xavier da Cunha 1982). For Ferreira (1908, in Cardoso 2006), the donation of the Ferraz Macedo Identified Skeletal Collection, with more than 1000 skulls and 200 skeletons, also played an important role in the creation of this discipline in Lisbon. According to Ferreira (1928), Macedo was the first Portuguese anthropologist; however, he was not well known and recognized, and was the butt of humour due to his devotion to craniology to the point that he received the nickname 'o Ferraz das caveiras' (the Ferraz of the skulls).

Researchers that have been considered by Xavier da Cunha (1982) as precursors of Anthropology in Lisbon are Oliveira Martins (1845–94), Eduardo Burnay (1853–1924), Francisco de Arruda Furtado (1854–87) and António Aurélio da Costa Ferreira (1879–1922), among others. Francisco António Pereira da Costa (1808–89) was another important scholar, lecturer at the Escola Politécnica and, as mentioned earlier, author of one of the first detailed anthropological analysis of a human skeletal sample from Cabeço da Arruda (Costa 1865). Eduardo Burnay (1853–1924) was also a teacher at Escola Politécnica de Lisboa and in 1880 wrote a thesis entitled 'Craniology as the basis of anthropological classification' (Da craneologia como base da classificação antropológica). António Aurélio da Costa Ferreira (1879–1922), a student of Bernardino Machado, was the first researcher at Museu Bocage with a background in anthropology, having published several papers on the osteological collection of Ferraz de Macedo (Cardoso 2006; Tamagnini 1947); while the first teacher of anthropology was Baltazar Machado da Cunha Osório (1855–1926), who kept this position until 1926 (Cardoso 2006; Cunha 1982).

One scholar who should not be forgotten and who undertook a considerable amount of study in physical anthropology is physician Manuel Bernardo Barbosa Sueiro (1894–1974). He began his research at the Ferraz Macedo Collection in 1918, and six years later he assumed the post of teaching assistant (Segundo Assistente de Antropologia) of Anthropology in the Faculty of Sciences (Moura 1986). Not until 1966 was Anthropology once again taught by a specialist in this area, Maria Emília de Castro e Almeida, until 1976 when she headed the Centro de

Antropobiologia do Instituto de Investigação Científica Tropical (Cardoso 2006). In 1978, a fire almost destroyed the building and the Ferraz Macedo Collection, as well as other specimens. Only around 40 skulls and a few post-cranial bones survived (Cardoso 2006). Later, in 1981, Maria Cristina Neto, assistant teacher in palaeoanthropology, together with Luís Alves Lopes, started a new skeletal collection from several cemeteries from Lisbon, which was taken over by Hugo Cardoso in 2001 (Cardoso 2006b). In Lisbon, nowadays, the degree in Anthropology is taught at ISCTE (Instituto Superior de Ciências do Trabalho e da Empresa) and is strictly dedicated to Social and Cultural Anthropology, while at the New University of Lisbon and at the Technical University of Lisbon, the degrees have biological anthropology including primatology.

In Oporto, Oliveira Martins (1845–94) went against the mainstream by criticising the conclusions made by Broca based on craniometrical studies. In the first half of the 19th century, Câmara Sínval from the Medical Chirurgical School published on physical anthropology (Guimarães 1995). Also from Oporto, physician José Leite de Vasconcelos founded in 1893 the Museu Etnográfico Português in Lisbon, nowadays under the name of Museu Nacional de Arqueologia. Albeit moving to Lisbon, he remained in contact with members from the Escola de Antropologia do Porto (Guimarães 1995). In Oporto, physical anthropology was taught at the Academia Politécnica and the Escola Médico-Cirúrgica do Porto (Guimarães 1995). The discipline of Anthropology was created in 1912 with the physician Mendes Côrrea as its chair (Cunha 1982; Lubell and Jackes 1997). This researcher, among others, founded in Oporto the Portuguese Society of Anthropology and Ethnology (Sociedade Portuguesa de Antropologia e Etnologia) in 1918 (Cardoso 1999).

Mendes Côrrea undertook research on the Muge shell middens, and this subject was discussed during the XVe Congrès International d'Anthropologie & d'Archéologie Préhistorique in the IVe Session de l'Institute International d'Anthropologie (1931), which took place in Coimbra and Oporto. Like Carlos Ribeiro, Mendes Côrrea almost 50 years later still defended the existence of the 'Tertiary Man' and the importance of cephalic index in the race definition.

After 1919, Anthropology in Oporto became part of the Natural and Historical Sciences (Ciências-Histórico-Naturais). Ten years later the department's name changed to Instituto de Antropologia da Faculdade de Ciências da Universidade do Porto. This institute later took the name of its former director Mendes Côrrea to call itself the Instituto de Antropologia Dr. Mendes Côrrea (Guimarães 1995), and is now the Museu de História Natural da Faculdade de Ciências da Universidade do Porto (Umbelino 2006). A fire in the 1970s resulted 'in the loss, and loss of identification, of a number of specimens' (Lubell and Jackes 1997: 835). Some of the Muge material is still housed there.

More recently, the University of Évora has started teaching physical anthropology in a course entitled Introduction to Biological Anthropology for the degrees in Biology and Archaeology. At the University of the Azores and the University of Madeira, biological anthropology is also taught.

Publications

According to Xavier da Cunha (1982: 18), several journals in Lisbon have published articles that are anthropological in nature: *Comunicação dos Serviços Geológicos de Portugal, Archivos de Anatomia e Antropologia, Boletim da Sociedade Portuguesa de Ciências Naturais, Trabalhos da Academia das Ciências de Portugal, Boletim da Sociedade de Geographia de Lisboa, Arquivos do Museu Bocage, Secção de Antropologia da 'Revista de História da Sociedade Portuguesa de Estudos Históricos'* and *Boletim do Instituto de criminologia de Lisboa*. Others are *Revista Lusitana* and *O Arqueólogo Português*, both founded by Leite de Vasconcelos, and *Portugália*.

A main journal published between 1914 and 1982 by the Institute of Anthropology (later Department of Anthropology) at the University of Coimbra was *Contribuições para o Estudo da Antropologia Portuguesa*. In 1983 this journal was renamed *Antropologia Portuguesa* and continues today. The great majority of works printed in *Contribuições para o Estudo da Antropologia Portuguesa* were on physical anthropology, namely anthropometric studies: 44 out of 64 published issues by authors such as Maria Augusta Neto, Maria Helena Morais and Maria Augusta Rocha. Before the journal was established, research undertaken by students was published in a volume entitled *Trabalhos de alumnos*, created in 1904. Of the 25 volumes of *Antropologia Portuguesa* (www.uc.pt/en/cia/publica/), special issues on the topics of physical anthropology (volume 13, 1995) and palaeopathology (volume 19, 2002) have been published.

In 1919, the Portuguese Society of Anthropology and Ethnology started to publish the journal *Trabalhos da Sociedade Portuguesa de Antropologia e Etnologia*, retitled in 1947 *Trabalhos de Antropologia e Etnologia* which is the current title today.

The archaeological site at Mértola, (Campo Arqueológico de Mértola or CAM) has published a relevant journal called *Arqueologia Mediaeval* since 1992. The CAM was created in 1978 as result of the recognition of the important archaeological remains at the site evidencing a continuous occupation of the city that goes back to at least the Phoenicians and Carthaginians, with the oldest evidence dating back to the Neolithic period.

In Lisbon, among the works developed by the former IPA (Instituto Português de Arqueologia) was the publication of the journal *Trabalhos de Arqueologia* which published several studies and results from excavations at which human remains were recovered. Other journals in archaeology that often publish papers in anthropology are *Al-Madan*, *Conimbriga*, *Promontoria* and *Xelb*.

Anthropological collections

Since the 19th century, Coimbra students have benefited from the existence of the Human Identified Osteological Collections and Archaeological series at the university. Bernardino Machado begun the Medical School Collection of 585 human skulls acquired from the Medical Schools at Lisbon, Oporto and Coimbra. Other identified collections include those started by Tamagnini and are 'The International Exchange' (Colecção de Trocas Internacionais) with 1,075 skulls, and the 'Identified Skeletal Collection' (Colecção de Esqueletos Identificados), comprising 505 skeletons, both deriving from the Cemitério Municipal da Conchada in Coimbra (Rocha 1995). These collections have been object of numerous studies (Cunha and Wasterlain 2007; Rocha 1995; Santos 2000; Santos and Roberts 2001).

ARCHAEOLOGICAL HUMAN REMAINS AND LEGISLATION

Archaeological legislation

In order to carry out archaeological excavations in Portugal, the archaeologist should submit an authorization request for archaeological work to IGESPAR, IP (Instituto de Gestão do Património Arquitectónico e Arqueológico, or IP), which must first include the type of intervention: either a) a programmed investigation with a maximum duration of four years and integrated within a research project; b) a project of study to evaluate how a site or monument should be classified if it is in the process of classification; c) preventive excavation prior to any construction work by public or private companies or institutions, whether in a rural, urban or submerged environment; or

d) rescue excavation of archaeological sites that are in danger of partial or total destruction due to human or natural action. Besides including information on the location and nature of the site, the name of any landowners and their authorization for the work must be submitted too, together with a financial plan, information regarding the storage facilities where the material will be kept after the excavation, an archaeological strategy, the team members involved in the project, any literature review on the site if applicable, and a time schedule (which is mandatory).

The IGESPAR is an institution belonging to the Ministry of Culture (www.igespar.pt/) that regulates the architectural and archaeological heritage and was established in 2007 as a consequence of the integration of three institutions: IPPAR (Instituto Português do Património Arquitectónico), IPA (Instituto Português de Arqueologia) and part of the assignments of the former DGEMN (Direcção-Geral dos Edifícios e Monumentos Nacionais).

HUMAN REMAINS AND LEGISLATION

The presence of a physical anthropologist in excavations began in the late 1980s, although not on a regular basis. As Cunha (2002: 263) wrote: 'for many years the human skeletons had a marginal role in archaeology'. Basically, it depended on the director of the archaeological excavation whether or not to consider a physical anthropologist. One of the Portuguese archaeologists who first understood the importance of having a physical anthropologist on site was Rui Parreira, who initially worked with physical anthropologist Teresa Fernandes (nowadays a teacher at the University of Évora) in 1986 at the excavation of the convent Flor da Rosa in Crato (Cunha 2007; Santos 1999/2000). In 1989, anthropologist Eugénia Cunha started the systematic excavation of a mediaeval necropolis at Fão (Cunha 1994). This was followed by several other partnerships with archaeologists all over the country.

On 15 July 1999, and thanks to the efforts made by IPA (Instituto Português de Arqueologia) and namely by its director at the time, archaeologist João Zilhão, a decree was published demanding that a physical anthropologist must be present whenever human bones are identified in archaeological contexts. The decree states that: 'The cemetery excavation, where presumably anthropological material will be found, will only be authorized if the promoting team has guaranteed the cooperation of specialists in physical anthropology'[1] (Diário da República, I-A série, de 15 de Julho de 1999, Decreto-lei no 270/99, Art. 8°: 4414). In the past, IPA ensured the presence of a specialist in physical anthropology during archaeological work involving human remains (Duarte 2003). The post-excavation analysis, however, regrettably never became a full reality. Nowadays, with the closure of IPA, more frequently than is desirable there is no physical anthropologist involved in fieldwork.

Strongly influenced by the publication of this decree, there was an increase in the number of researchers in this area. This fact was naturally accompanied by a higher number of Master and undergraduate-level theses, produced mainly by the students from the Department of Anthropology at the University of Coimbra and from the University of Évora. Some of these researchers started to work freelance, writing hundreds of unpublished technical–scientific reports which have been archived at IGESPAR (Instituto de Gestão do Património Arquitectónico e Arqueológico).

Osteological assemblages, after they have been analysed, are generally housed in museums, universities or municipal facilities.

In Portugal, reburial is not common (Cunha 2006). Only lately there are accounts of a number of reburials of human skeletal remains found within churches and that are relatively recent in date.

METHODS OF ANTHROPOLOGICAL ANALYSIS

In the field

The recovery of human remains from archaeological contexts usually follows the recommendations given by Brothwell (1981), Bass (1987), Ubelaker (1989) and Buikstra and Ubelaker (1994). The usual practice in Portugal after the skeletal remains have been exposed *in situ* is, therefore, to record by coordinates the body and any inclination of bone elements. After a plan is drawn, preferentially at 1:10 or 1:20 scale, and the remains photographed, filling in an anthropological field recording form is recommended. There is no standardization in Portugal concerning the form and/or the data to retrieve during fieldwork. Nevertheless, there are some published recording forms, such as the form created by Caria Mendes for his study of a necropolis (Mendes 1989). The archaeological field school at Mértola has also developed its own recording forms. In 1991/1992, Santos and co-authors published a two-page form that has since been used regularly. On one page there is space for general information, such as place, date, the acronym of the site, coordinates, dating elements, type of soil and grave, grave measurements, any photographs and drawings that have been undertaken, the orientation according to cardinal directions of the bones, the position of the upper and lower limbs, etc. On the second page, there is space to record several bone measurements to be taken on site, particularly when the state of bone preservation is poor. Cidália Duarte, member of CIPA (Centro de Investigação em Paleoecologia Humana), a branch of IPA, published in 2003 a recording form for excavation and osteometric data in the field.

Laboratory analysis

Once the human osteological material arrives at the laboratory, it is cleaned and if necessary reconstruction is attempted. Labeling of the material is also undertaken with name of site, year of excavation and skeleton number. If commingled bones are present, they are all sequentially numbered and an inventory is made. After this treatment stage, the skeletal analysis can commence.

First the individual sex and age-at-death is determined, and afterwards the individual's morphology and pathological lesions are evaluated. The recommendations by Buikstra and Ubelaker (1994) are usually followed. In addition, sex determination is assessed, by following Bruzek's (2002) method based on the morphological traits of the innominate bones; as well as Ferembach *et al.*'s (1980) method for skull and pelvic morphological traits. Some metric parameters also aid in sex determination, such as the diameter of the femoral head (Wasterlain 2000) and the length of the foot bones, the calcaneous and talus (Silva 1995). These two latter methods are commonly applied since they were developed from the Identified Skeletal Collections of the University of Coimbra, which is a Portuguese sample. However, in order to compare the results with foreign studies, other methods have sometimes to be applied.

In the case of age-at-death for juvenile, subadult or non-adult individuals, Scheuer and Black (2000) is the reference book that is used. The epiphyseal fusion stages by Ferembach *et al.* (1980) and MacLaughlin (1990) are also commonly useful. Age-at-death estimation in adults is much more difficult to establish. Some of the methods used for adult skeletons are those developed by Masset (1982), Lovejoy *et al.* (1985), Brooks and Suchey (1990), and some more recent developments of these methods, like Igarashi *et al.* (2005).

For morphology, metric and non-metric traits are assessed. Stature is calculated by employing the formulae from Olivier *et al.* (1978) and Byers *et al.* (1989), and from Portuguese studies such as Mendonça (2000) and Santos (2002). Robustness and other indexes are evaluated in reference to Olivier and Demoulin (1984). Non-metric traits are evaluated according to the descriptions in Finnegan (1978), Saunders (1978) and Hauser and De Stefano (1989).

Pathological lesions are evaluated macroscopically and with a magnifying lens, although radiological analyses are performed when required and where possible. For radiological analysis, much assistance has been granted in the past by the centre Clínica Universitária de Imagiologia – Hospitais da Universidade de Coimbra. A differential diagnosis is always sought.

The above procedures are common in Portugal, namely among CIAS (Research Centre for Anthropology and Health: www.uc.pt/en/cia) members who belong to the group 'Anthropology of Past Populations', fully committed to the study of human remains from Mesolithic to recent times, as well as committed to developing methodologies for palaeodemographic and palaeopathological analysis.

CONCLUSION

In the 19th and part of the 20th centuries the same scientist may have performed both archaeological and anthropological analysis. The occupation of these earlier scholars varied from physician and engineer to army officer, but all had in common a fascination for past culture and past populations. This trend started to change during the second half of the 20th century, and in the last two decades anthropological studies have been conducted mainly by qualified physical anthropologists, thanks to the teaching of the discipline at a number of Portuguese universities and as a result too of the legislation regulating archaeological activity. The need is evident for close collaboration between anthropologist, archaeologist and other professionals, from the planning stages of the fieldwork, through to the interpretation of the results, the eventual conservation and curation of the site and its materials and any dissemination of the information to the general public (Santos 1999/2000).

The results of excavations and laboratory studies undertaken in Portugal or on Portuguese materials have been published in national and international journals, and continue to be so, in the scientific areas of anthropology and archaeology. Several of these publications arise from the collaboration between archaeologists and physical anthropologists, which certainly benefits both disciplines.

The standardization of the excavation procedure and the laboratory analysis, as well as tight control of the regulation requiring the presence of a specialist in physical anthropology, are some of the goals that Portugal needs to achieve in the near future.

USEFUL CONTACTS

IGESPAR (Instituto de Gestão do Património Arquitectónico e Arqueológico). Website: www.igespar.pt/
CIAS (Research Centre for Anthropology and Health), University of Coimbra. Website: www.uc.pt/en/cia/

ACKNOWLEDGEMENTS

We thank Ana Gonçalves for her help with documentation and to the editors for their suggestions and English revision.

NOTE

1 'A escavação de necrópoles onde se presume venha a ser encontrado espólio antropológico só será autorizada caso a equipa promotora tenha garantida a colaboração de especialistas em antropologia física.'

BIBLIOGRAPHY

Almaça, C. (2000) *Museu Bocage: ensino e exibição*, Lisboa: Museu Bocage.

Areia, M.L. and Rocha, M.A.T. (1985) 'O Ensino da Antropologia', in Museu e Laboratório Antropológico (ed.) *Cem anos de Antropologia em Coimbra: 1885–1985*, Coimbra: Museu e Laboratório Antropológico.

Bass, W.M. (1987) *Human Osteology: A Laboratory and Field Manual*, Columbia, MO: Missouri Archaeological Society.

Bicho, N.F. (2006) *Manual de Arqueologia pré-histórica*, Lisboa: Edições 70.

Brothwell, D.R. (1981) *Digging Up Bones. The Excavation, Treatment and Study of Human Skeletal Remains*, London: British Museum.

Brooks, S. and Suchey, J.M. (1990) 'Skeletal age determination based on the os pubis: a comparison of the Acsádi-Neméskeri and Suchey-Brooks methods', *Human Evolution*, 5: 227–38.

Bruzek, J. (2002) 'A method for visual determination of sex, using the human hip bone', *American Journal of Physical Anthropology*, 117: 157–68.

Buikstra, J. and Ubelaker, D. (eds) (1994) *Standards for Data Collection from Human Skeletal Remains*, Fayetteville, AR: Arkansas Archaeological Survey Research Series No. 44.

Burnay, E. (1880) *Da craneologia como base da classificação antropológica*, Coimbra: Imprensa da Universidade.

Byers, S., Akoshima, K. and Curran, B. (1989) 'Determination of adult stature from metatarsal length', *American Journal of Physical Anthropology*, 79: 275–79.

Cardoso, F.A. (2008) 'A portrait of gender in two 19th and 20th century Portuguese populations: a palaeopathological perspective', unpublished PhD thesis, Durham University.

Cardoso, H.F.V. (2005) 'Patterns of growth and development of the humana skeleton and dentition in relation to environmental quality: a biocultural analysis of a sample of 20th century Portuguese subadult documented skeletons', unpublished PhD thesis, McMaster University.

——(2006a) 'Elementos para a história da Antropologia Biológica em Portugal: o contributo do Museu Bocage (Museu Nacional de História Natural, Lisboa)', *Trabalhos de Antropologia e Etnologia*, 46: 47–66.

——(2006b) 'The Collection of Identified Human Skeletons housed at the Bocage Museum (National Museum of Natural History) in Lisbon, Portugal', *American Journal of Physical Anthropology*, 129: 173–76.

Cardoso, J.L. (1999) 'O Professor Mendes Côrrea e a Arqueologia Portuguesa', *Al-madan*, 8: 138–56.

Cardoso, J.L. and Rolão, J.M. (1999–2000) 'Prospecções e escavações nos concheiros mesolíticos de Muge e Magos (Salvaterra de Magos): contribuição para a história dos trabalhos arqueológicos efectuados', *Estudos Arqueológicos de Oeiras*, 8: 83–240.

Cartailhac, M.E. (1886) 'Époque Néolithique', in M.E. Cartailhac (ed.) *Les Ages Préhistoriques de l'Espagne et du Portugal*, Paris: Reinwald Librairie. *Compte rendu de la 9ème session du Congrès International d'Anthropologie et d'Archéologie préhistorique (Lisboa, 1880)*. 1884. Lisbonne, Typographie de l'Académie Royale des Sciences.

Cruz, C. and Cunha, E. (2007–8) 'Os vestígios osteológicos humanos do Paleolítico Português: revisão bibliográfica e análise dos dados', *Antropologia Portuguesa*, 24–25: 75–93.

Cunha, A.X. (1982) 'Contribution à l'Histoire de l'Anthropologie Physique au Portugal', *Contribuições para o Estudo da Antropologia Portuguesa*, 11: 5–56.

Cunha, E. (1994) 'Paleobiologia das populações medievais portuguesas: os casos de Fão e S. João de Almedina', unpublished PhD thesis, Universidade de Coimbra.

——(2002) 'Antropologia Física e Paleoantropologia em Portugal: um balanço', *Arqueologia & História*, 54: 261–72.

——(2006) 'La conservation des series "séculaires" de Coimbra: quelques réflexions', *Bulletin Archéologique de Provence*, 4: 91–95.

——(2007) 'Antropologia Biológica em Portugal: uma retrospectiva dos últimos 25 anos', *Al-madam*, 15: 113–15.

Cunha, E., Cardoso, F. and Umbelino, C. (2003) 'Inferences about Mesolithic life style on the basis of anthropological data. The case of the Portuguese shell middens', in L. Larsson *et al.* (eds) *Mesolithic on the Move*, Papers presented at the Sixth International Conference on the Mesolithic in Europe, Stockholm, Oxford: Oxbow Books.

Cunha, E. and Wasterlain, S. (2007) 'The Coimbra identified osteological collections', in G. Grupe and J. Peters (eds) *Skeletal Series and Their Socio-Economic Context*, Documenta Archaeobiologiae 5, Rahden/Westf: Verlag Marie Leidorf GmbH.

Delgado, M.J.FN. (1884) 'La grotte de Furninha a Peniche', *Compte rendu de la 9ème session du Congrès International d'Anthropologie et d'Archéologie préhistorique (Lisboa, 1880)*, Lisbon: Typographie de l'Académie Royale des Sciences.

Duarte, C. (2003) 'Bioantropologia', *Trabalhos de Arqueologia*, 29: 263–96.

Fernandes, T. (2008) 'A população Medieval de S. Miguel de Odrinhas (Sintra): caracterização biológica', unpublished PhD thesis, Universidade de Évora.

Ferembach, D., Schwidetzky, I. and Stloukal, M. (1980) 'Recommendation for age and sex diagnoses of skeletons', *Journal of Human Evolution*, 9: 517–49.

Finnegan, M. (1978) 'Non-metric variation of the infracranial skeleton', *Journal of Anatomy*, 125: 23–37.

Garcia, S. (2007) '*Maleitas do corpo em tempos Medievais: indicadores paleodemográficos, de stresse e paleopatológicos numa série osteológica urbana de Leiria.*', unpublished PhD thesis, Universidade de Coimbra.

Gonçalves, A.A. (1986) 'Inéditos de Rui Serpa Pinto sobre as escavações arqueológicas de Muge', *Trabalhos de Antropologia e Etnologia*, 26: 211–29.

Guimarães, G. (1995) 'A Escola de Antropologia do Porto e os estudos Pré-históricos em Portugal', *Revista de Ciências Históricas*, 10: 59–78.

Hauser, G. and De Stefano, G.F. (1989) *Epigenetic Variants of the Human Skull*, Stuttgart: Schweizerbart'sche Verlagsbuchhandlung.

Hervé, G. (1899) 'Populations Mésolithiques et Néolithiques de l'Espagne et du Portugal'. *Revue Mensuelle de L'École d'Anthropologie de Paris*, 9: 265–80.

Igarashi, Y., Uesu, K., Wakebe, T., *et al.* (2005) 'New method for estimation of adult skeletal age at death from the morphology of the auricular surface of the ilium', *American Journal of Physical Anthropology*, 128: 324–39.

Lovejoy, C.O., Meindl, R., Pryzbeck, T., *et al.* (1985) 'Chronological metamorphosis of the auricular surface of the ilium: a new method for the determination of adult skeletal age at death', *American Journal of Physical Anthropology*, 68: 15–28.

Lubell, D. and Jackes, M. (1997) 'Portugal', in F. Spencer (ed.) *History of Physical Anthropology: An Encyclopedia*, London: Garland Publishing.

MacLaughlin, S.M. (1990) 'Epiphyseal fusion at the sternal end of the clavicle in modern Portuguese skeletal sample', *Antropologia Portuguesa*, 8: 59–68.

Masset, C. (1982) 'Estimation de l'âge au décès par les sutures crâniennes', unpublished PhD thesis, University of Paris VII.

Mendes, J.C. (1989) 'Guia de estudo bioantropológico de uma necrópole', *Arquivo de Anatomia e Antropologia*, 40: 187–92.

Mendes Côrrea, A.A. (1917) 'À propôs des caractères inférieurs de quelques crânes préhistoriques du Portugal', *Archivo de Anatomia e Antropologia*, 3: 221–37.

——(1919) 'Origins of the Portuguese', *American Journal of Physical Anthropology*, 2: 117–45.

——(1923) 'Nouvelles observations sur l'Homo Taganus, Nob.', *Revue Anthropologique*, 33: 570–78.

——(1936) 'A propósito do "Homo Taganus". Africanos em Portugal', *Boletim da Junta Geral do Distrito de Santarém*, 43: 5–23.

Mendonça, M.C. (2000) 'Estimation of height from the length of the long bones in a Portuguese adult population', *American Journal of Physical Anthropology*, 112: 39–48.

Moura, M. (1986) 'Homenagem da cidade de Lisboa a dois mestres da Medicina Portuguesa', *Arquivos de Reumatologia e doenças ósteo-articulares*, 8: 237–46.

Oliveira, A.M. (1997) 'O contributo da Antropologia Física em Portugal como ciência inter e transdisciplinar: uma possível síntese histórica até finais do século XIX', *Revista de Guimarães*, 107: 243–83.

Olivier, G., Aaron, G., Fully, G., *et al.* (1978) 'New estimations of stature and cranial capacity in modern man', *Journal of Human Evolution*, 7: 513–18.

Olivier, G. and Demoulin, F. (1984) *Pratique Anthropologique*, Paris: Université de Paris VII.

Paula e Oliveira, F. (1884) 'Notes sur les ossements humains qui se trouvent dans le Musée de la Section Géologique de Lisbonne', *Compte rendu de la 9ème session du Congrès International d'Anthropologie et d'Archéologie préhistorique (Lisboa, 1880)*, Lisbon: Typographie de l'Académie Royale des Sciences.

——(1886) 'Les ossements humains du Musée Géologique a Lisbonne', in M.E. Cartailhac (ed.) *Les Ages Préhistoriques de l'Espagne et du Portugal*, Paris: Reinwald Librairie.

Raposo, L. and Silva, A.C. (1996) '*A linguagem das coisas: ensaios e crónicas de Arqueologia*', Mem Martins: Publicações Europa-América.

Rocha, M.A. (1995) 'Les collections ostéologiques humaines identifiées du Musée Anthropologique de l'Université de Coimbra', *Antropologia Portuguesa*, 13: 7–38.

Rolão, J.M. (1999) 'Del Würm final al Holocénico en el Bajo Valle del Tajo (Complejo Arqueológico Mesolítico de Muge)', unpublished PhD thesis, Universidad de Salamanca.

Santos, A.L. (1999/2000) 'Os caminhos da paleopatologia: passado e desafios', *Antropologia Portuguesa*, 16/17: 161–84.

——(2000) 'A skeletal picture of tuberculosis: macroscopic, radiological, biomolecular, and historical evidence from the Coimbra Identified Skeletal Collection', unpublished PhD thesis, Universidade de Coimbra.

——(2007) 'Estácio da Veiga e os primórdios da Antropologia Física', Actas do 4º Encontro de Arqueologia do Algarve (Silves, 24 e 25 de Novembro de 2006), *Xelb*, 7: 239–48.

Santos, A.L. and Cunha, E. (to be submitted for publication) Portuguese development in Paleopathology: an outline history, in J.E. Buikstra, C.A. Roberts and S.M. Schreiner (eds), *The History of Palaeopathology: Pioneers and Prospects*, New York and Oxford: Oxford University Press.

Santos, A.L., Cunha, C., Dâmaso, N., *et al.* (1991/1992) 'Ficha antropológica: a utilizar na escavação', Antropologia Portuguesa, 9–10: 67–68.

Santos, A.L. and Roberts, C. (2001) 'A picture of tuberculosis in young Portuguese people in the earlier 20th century: a multidisciplinary study of the skeletal and historical evidence', *American Journal of Physical Anthropology*, 115: 38–49.

Santos, C.M.G.C. (2002) 'Estimativa da estatura a partir dos metatársicos', unpublished MA thesis, Universidade de Coimbra.

Saunders, S.R. (1978) *The Development and Distribution of Discontinuous Morphological Variation of the Human Infracranial Skeleton*, Archaeological Survey of Canada 81, Ottawa: National Museum of Man.

Scheuer, L. and Black, S. (2000) *Developmental Juvenile Osteology*, London: Academic Press.

Silva, A.M. (1995) 'Sex assessment using the calcaneus and talus', *Antropologia Portuguesa*, 13: 107–19.

——(2002) 'Antropologia funerária e paleobiologia das populações portuguesas (litorais) do Neolítico final-Calcolítico', unpublished PhD thesis, Universidade de Coimbra.

Tamagnini, E. (1947) 'Les études anthropologiques et ethnologiques en Portugal', *Man*, 47: 55–57.

Tamagnini, E. and Serra, J.A. (1942) Subsídios para a história da Antropologia Portuguesa, Coimbra: Mémória apresentada ao Congresso da Actividade Científica Portuguesa (Coimbra 1940).

Ubelaker, D.H. (1989) *Human Skeletal Remains: Excavation, Analysis, Interpretation*, Washington DC: Taraxacum.

Umbelino, C. (2006) 'Outros sabores do passado: as análises de oligoelementos e de isótopos estáveis na reconstituição da dieta das comunidades humanas do Mesolítico final e do Neolítico final/Calcolítico do território português', unpublished PhD thesis, Universidade de Coimbra.

Vallois, H.-V. (1930) 'Recherches sur les ossements Mésolithiques de Mugem', *L'Anthropologie*, 40: 337–89.

Vasconcelos, J.L. (1897, 1913) *Religiões da Lusitania na parte que principalmente se refere a Portugal*, Lisboa: Imprensa Nacional.

——(1933) 'Etnografia Portuguesa', in *Lisboa, Imprensa Nacional de Lisboa, XVe Congrès International d'Anthropologie & d'Archéologie Préhistorique 1931*, Paris: Librarie E. Nourry.

Veiga, S.P.M.E. (1880) *Memoria das antiguidades de Mertola: observadas em 1877 e relatadas*, Lisboa: Imprensa Nacional.

Wasterlain, R.S.N. (2000) 'Morphé: análise das proporções entre os membros, dimorfismo sexual e estatura de uma amostra da colecção de esqueletos identificados do Museu Antropológico da Universidade de Coimbra', unpublished MA thesis, Universidade de Coimbra.

Wasterlain, R.S.N. (2006) 'Males da boca: estudo da patologia oral numa amostra das colecções osteológicas identificadas do Museu Antropológico da Universidade de Coimbra: finais do séc. XIX inícios do séc. XX', unpublished PhD thesis, Universidade de Coimbra.

Zilhão, J. and Trinkaus, E. (eds) (2002) *Portrait of the Artist as a Child: The Gravettian Human Skeleton from the Abrigo do Lagar Velho and its Archeological Context*, Trabalhos de Arqueologia 22, Lisboa: Instituto Português de Arqueologia.

Romania/România

Szilárd Sándor Gál

INTRODUCTION: A BRIEF HISTORY AND CURRENT STATE OF PHYSICAL ANTHROPOLOGY IN ROMANIA

The science of physical anthropology can be recognized as having begun in 1859 by Pierre Paul Broca with the organization of the first Anthropological Society in Paris. The activity of Broca had primary influence in spreading anthropology to other European countries.

In Romania, in the region of Transilvania, which was part of the Austro–Hungarian empire, lived the first important scientist in anthropology, Aurel Török.[1] In 1867 Török was promoted as Professor at the Department of Physiology, Histology, Biophysics and Forensic Medicine at the Faculty of Medical-Surgery in Cluj Napoca. In 1872, by establishing the Ferencz József University in Cluj Napoca, he became University Professor in Histology and Pathology. At this time he had contact with the world of physical anthropology.

In 1878 Török took part in the Paris World Expo and there he met Paul Broca for the first time. In 1880 Török started a collaboration with the Institute where Broca was based and he participated in the 5th World Anthropological Society in Budapest, Hungary.

During the First World War anthropological studies were neglected and only began to attract more attention just after 1930. In 1920[2] Transilvania was annexed to Romania and the anthropological activity was carried out in three centres, namely Bucharest (led by F.R. Rainer), Cluj Napoca (led by V. Papilian) and Iaşi (led by I. Botez and later O. Necraşov).

In 1926 the School of Anthropology was founded in Bucharest. The founder of the institute was Francisc I. Rainer, who undertook studies in embryology and histology. Rainer started collecting skulls from different periods and regions, and this material was the basis of the Museum and Institute of Anthropology in Bucharest. The collection has now 6300 skulls and approximately 3000 of these have been entirely catalogued (age, sex, pathological observations). In 1940 the Institute of Anthropology 'Francisc I. Rainer' was established within the Faculty of Medicine at the Romanian Academy.

In 1930 the Anthropology and Palaeoanthropology Department within the Faculty of Science was founded in Iaşi by I.C. Botez, who had studied physical anthropology in Berlin. Unfortunately after 1938 the department was dissolved but Botez's student, Olga Necraşov, who came from a German anthropological tradition, moved to Bucharest where she lectured voluntarily on anthropology at the Centre of Anthropological Studies (Centrul de Studii

Antropologice). In 1933, the Anthropological Society in Cluj-Napoca was founded by V. Papilian[3] and C. Velluda, with the assistance of E. Racoviţă.[4]

In 1937 in Bucharest the 17th International Congress of Anthropology and Prehistoric Archaeology took place, organized by V. Papilian and N. Minovici. It was an important event with the participation of many scientists from all over the world, including Professor Pittard, a Swiss anthropologist from the University of Geneva who had undertaken numerous studies on race and the evolution of man.

In 1940 the Institute of Anthropology was opened within the Faculty of Medicine in Bucharest, and 1954 saw the first anthropological yearbook, entitled 'Probleme de Antropologie' (Issues in Anthropology).

The 1960s saw the creation of the Centre of Anthropological Research (Centrul de Cercetări Antropologice) of the Romanian Academy in 1963. In 1964 Olga Necraşov, a member of the Romanian Academy, was promoted director of the anthropological centre and during her directorship two periodicals were started, *Studii şi Cercetări de Antropologie* (*Studies and Research in Anthropology*) and *Annuaire Roumain d'Anthropologie*. The main focus of the Centre of Anthropological Research was physical anthropology, demography and palaeodemography, and cultural anthropology. The research projects were carried out in cooperation with the Institute of Archaeology and involved the study of human remains from the Late Palaeolithic, the Neolithic, the Iron Age, the Bronze Age and the mediaeval period.

In 1974, the Centre of Anthropological Research was dissolved and transformed into the Laboratory of Anthropology (Laboratorul de Antropologie), a Department of the Institute of Pathological Anatomy 'Victor Babeş' (Institutul de Anatomie Patologică 'Victor Babeş').

After the Revolution of 1989, Victor Sahleanu became the director of the Laboratory of Anthropology from 1990 until his death in 1997. This post was then taken over by Cristian Glavce.

In 2007 the Laboratory of Anthropology became the Institute of Anthropology 'Francisc I. Rainer'[5] (according to G.D.[6] no. 1754/2006, published in the Official Journal of Romania-Monitorul Oficial-no. 5/4 January 2007).[7]

Education and training

In Romania it is possible to identify at least two important periods in the field of physical anthropology: the inter-war period distinguished by the work of I. Botez[8] and Francisc I. Rainer;[9] and the period between 1960 and 1970 with Olga Necraşov as the predominant figure.

In the Communist period, anthropology was not officially taught as a major subject in universities (e.g., in schools of medicine) and after the revolution of 1989 this attitude was still present. In most universities in Romania students cannot learn physical anthropology, morphology, palaeopathology, palaeodemography or palaeoepidemiology.

Although there are anthropological research centres in Bucharest and Iaşi (unfortunately this is not resolved in Transilvania), there are no specific student programmes in physical anthropology, and research on anthropology only takes place in the doctoral or PhD programmes (within the Faculty of Biology); most research projects, in any case, tend not to be connected with archaeological human remains. In Cluj Napoca at the Babeş-Bolyai University, Faculty of Biology and Geology, students have no physical anthropology degree programmes. The major programmes are experimental biology, ecology, mineralogy and palaeontology.

At the Institute of Anthropology 'Francisc I. Rainer' there are two research programmes. One of these looks at the anthropological characteristics of prehistoric and historic communities (historical or cultural anthropology); and the other looks at the anthropological characteristics of the present population of the Romanian territory, with a biological, psychological and medical focus.

ARCHAEOLOGICAL HUMAN REMAINS AND LEGISLATION

Archaeological legislation

According to the Archaeological Standards and Procedures by Order of the Ministry of Culture no. 2392/September 9 2004 (Ordonanța Ministerului Culturii și Cultelor nr. 2392/06.09.2004 privind instituirea Standardelor și Procedurilor Arheologice din România) and the Code of Conduct of the European Association of Archaeologists from 27 September 1997, researchers can find several methods for excavating, storing, analysing and restoring archaeological materials (e.g., pottery, stone, animal and human skeletal remains). Archaeological excavation is controlled by an authorized person from the Archaeological Registry of Romania, having achieved Expert level in archaeological research.[10]

HUMAN REMAINS AND LEGISLATION

A clear delimitation between archaeological and forensic human remains does not exist, although for archaeological excavations the most timely point is the Second World War.[11] This period can be considered the borderline between forensic and archaeological human remains. There are exceptions to this borderline, however, such as in the case of human rights violations. In April 2009 three skeletons were exhumed, victims of Communism in 1949. Three peasants were executed by Security Officers from Bistrița (Cluj county). The exhumation was organized by the Institute of Investigation for Crimes of Communism in Romania (IICCR).[12] These human remains have been examined from the point of view of forensic medicine to find out the circumstances surrounding their deaths and they will then be reburied in the Orthodox Christian tradition.

In Romania there is no specific physical anthropological legislation or regulation for implementing methods of collecting, transporting, storing and analysing human skeletal material. Relevant laws are the Criminal Procedure Code and Regulations for Implementing the Provisions of Ordinance no. 1/2000 regarding the organization and activity of forensic institutions, so this legislation is applicable only to recent skeletal remains.

In archaeological exhumations (e.g., when excavating a cemetery) there must be present an authorized person from the Archaeological Registry from Romania (Registrul Arheologilor din România), the archaeologist will have submitted a petition to the Ministry of Culture and Religious Affairs (Ministerul Culturii și Cultelor Religioase), and the director of the archaeological project must have a certain rank in the Archaeological Council (Comisia Națională de Arheologie).

In accidental findings of human remains, the authorities are notified and the lifting of the remains is carried out in the presence of a prosecutor and a police officer. However, if archaeological artefacts are discovered associated with the body, then an archaeologist must be informed. This moment is very important, since there are methodical differences in exhumation: a forensic expert takes photos of the 'crime scene' and describes the location of the skeleton; while an archaeologist specialized in osteology takes photos, draws the grave with the skeleton, describes the skeleton's orientation, depth of bones, and describes artefacts in the grave (position, depth) among others. If the bones are mixed up or commingled, the presence of pathologists, anthropologists and osteologists is necessary.

After emptying the graves, the contents are packed for transportation. In Romania it is obligatory to transport the human remains in a funerary car, authorized by the forensic expert (Law no. 104 from March 27 2003 considering the legal transportation of human remains in Romania, published in the Official Journal of Romania 222/April 3 2003 – Legea nr. 104 din 27 martie 2003, privind manipularea cadavrelor umane şi prelevarea organelor şi ţesuturilor de la cadavre în vederea transplantului, M.O. 222/3 aprilie 2003). The following documents are needed: certificate of death, authorization for inhumation and authorization from 'Sanepid', the institution regulating sanitary conditions. On the other hand, transportation of human remains from archaeological excavations requires an authorization from the museum or individual who directed the excavation and a contract from the institute that will examine and store the archaeological materials. In Romania forensic experts use one small paper bag for human remains and another for the deceased's personal effects. The anthropologist uses one paper bag for the skull (it is very fragile), one paper bag for the postcranial skeleton and small boxes for artefacts.[13]

If it is considered that DNA analysis is needed, the bone fragments are collected according to the sampling procedures of the DNA laboratory.

Specific legislation for human remains found in churches and churchyards

In Romania there are two important laws relating to human remains and graves in churches, churchyards, civil war cemeteries, world war cemeteries, etc.: Law no. 422 from 2001 July 24 2001 (published in Official Journal of Romania no. 407/July 24 2001) and Law no. 379 from 23 September 2003 (published in Official Journal of Romania no. 700/October 7 2003) consider that cemeteries in use until the 19th century and war memorials are historical monuments, and therefore fall under the protection of the Ministry of Culture and Religious Affairs. According to the laws, human remains are excavated by archaeological teams, authorized by the Archaeological Registry and examined by an anthropologist.

METHODS OF ANTHROPOLOGICAL ANALYSIS

During analysis of human skeletal remains, anthropologists in Romania include the measurements of postcranial bones and the skull, and examination of physical characteristics, including age, sex and ancestry, in their routine anthropological analysis.

For the analysis of teeth and to understand the morphology and evolution of teeth, examination of occlusion and genetic variations is undertaken (Sjøvold 1990: 432).

Age-at-death estimation is based on three criteria: long bone length and skeletal and dental maturity, degenerative changes in the skeleton, and dental wear. The different age groups generally used, and the appropriate methods for each age interval, are listed below:

- Infant (*Infans* I-II): dental development, skeletal maturity and long bone dimensions (Stloukal and Hanáková 1978: 54);
- Juvenile (*Iuvenis*): skeletal maturity;
- Adult (*Adultus* and *Senilis*): the method of Nemeskéri, Harsányi and Acsádi (Nemeskéri et al. 1960) is employed. This includes Todd's 1920 method to age the pubic symphysis and the method of Meindl and Lovejoy (1985) on cranial suture closure.

Unfortunately, for adults, only a 5-year (±2 years) interval is possible, since human variation, due to a number of factors including geography, cultural, dietary and pathology among others, makes age determination difficult.

For sex determination, anthropologists in Romania follow the morphological method of Hungarian anthropologists Kinga Éry, Alán Kralovánszky and János Nemeskéri (Éry *et al.*, 1963). The advantage of this method is that values for criteria employed in sex determination could be expressed mathematically. With this in mind, 22 landmarks on the skeleton are observed and the 'sexual index' is represented by one of the following categories: -2 to -1.1 (hyperfeminine), -1 to -0.4 (feminine), -0.4 to +0.4 (indifferent); +0.4 to +1.0 (masculine), and +1.0 to +2.0 (hypermasculine).

For the calculation of stature several methods employing long bones are used in Romania, according to Sjøvold (1990), Pearson and Rösing (1988) and Zsolt Bernert (2005).

In pathological analysis, macroscopic and bio-molecular methods are used. It is possible to group the nosologic alterations after Steinboch's classification: traumatic changes, non-specific infections, specific infections, haematological and metabolic anomalies, disease of the joints and other diseases. Reference books used for traumatic changes include the work of Ortner and Putschar (1981), for non-specific infections, reference is to the work of László Szatmáry (Szatmáry and Marcsik 2006),[14] for non-specific infections the work carried out by A. Ion (2008) and A. Marcsik (Szatmáry and Marcsik 2006) respectively.

In palaeodemography the method of Zsolt Bernert[15] (Palaeoanthropological Programme Pack)[16] is employed, taking into consideration the general conditions of the samples and their nature.

CONCLUSION

Physical anthropology plays an important role in Romanian archaeological research programmes today. The interdisciplinary approach has won an important place in archaeological activity by introducing the 'New Archaeology' in Romania. In most archaeological excavations today, it is fundamental that the anthropological data is integrated with other disciplines, including geology, palaeozoology, palaeobotany, etc. Nevertheless, there is a major problem in research: the lack of communication between archaeological institutes and anthropological laboratories; and the lack of funding. At present, Romanian scientists are undertaking a few collaborative research programmes including that at Porolissum-Zalău[17] and the Neolithic settlements at Lumea Nouă-Alba Iulia.[18] In most cases, archaeological centres are oriented automatically to contacting anthropological institutions from the West, neglecting collaboration with anthropologists from Romania, which is an issue that needs to improve in the future.

USEFUL CONTACTS

Institutul de Arheologie şi Istoria Artei Cluj Napoca (Institute of Archaeology and History of Art Cluj Napoca), Str. C. Daicoviciu 2, 400020 Cluj-Napoca. Email: iaiacluj@yahoo.com
Muzeul Naţional de Istorie a Transilvaniei, Cluj Napoca (National Museum of Transilvania, Cluj Napoca), Strada C. Daicoviciu 2, 400020 Cluj-Napoca.
Institutul de Antropologie 'Franisc I. Rainer' Bucureşti (Institute of Anthropology 'Franisc I. Rainer', Bucharest), Str. Eroii Sanitari nr. 8, sect. 5, Bucharest. Email: franciscrainer@ yahoo.com.

Institutul de Arheologie (Institute of Archaeology, Iaşi), Str. Lascar Catargi, nr.18, CP 164,700107 – Iasi.

Universitatea Babeş-Bolyai Cluj Napoca, Facultatea de Biologie şi Geologie (Babeş-Bolyai University, Faculty of Biology and Geology), Str. Mihail Kogalniceanu nr. 1 RO-400084, Cluj-Napoca. Website: www.ubbcluj.ro/

CIMEC – Institutul de Memorie Culturală, Bucureşti (Institute for Cultural Memory. The Gateway to Romanian Cultural Heritage), P-ţa Presei Libere no. 1. Box. 33–90, Bucharest. Website: www.cimec.ro/

NOTES

1 Török was a 19th-century doctor, university professor and anthropologist. He graduated at PhD level in Medicine in Vienna.

2 The Treaty of Trianon was the peace treaty concluded at the end of the First World War by the Allied Powers on the one side, and Hungary, seen as a successor of Austria–Hungary, on the other.

3 Papilian was a doctor, writer and university professor. He founded the Society of Biology and the Society of Anthropology in Cluj Napoca.

4 Emil Racoviţă was a biologist and speleologist who founded the world's first Institute of Speleology in 1920.

5 Reiner Osteological Collection and Collection of Ethnographical and Anthropological Photographies (Colecţia osteologică Reiner, Colecţia de fotografii etnografie şi antropologice). Reiner Catalogue, Anastasia Publisher, 2001, Bucharest (winner of C. I. Parhon Romanian Acadamy Reward, 2002).

6 Government Direction

7 With its establishment in 1991, Monitorul Oficial R.A. was entitled to carry on the task of publishing the official journal of Romania, which had initially been released in 1832. Since its first number, this paper began to produce a concise chronicle of the main historical, political and cultural events, which contributed to the progress and foundation of the modern Romanian state.

8 Major articles by Ion Botez: 'Étude morphologique et morphogénique du squelette du bras et de l'avant-bras chez les primates', Paris, 1926; Curs de Antropologie generală, Iaşi, 1936.

9 Francisc I. Reiner was a famous anatomist, anthropologist, and member of the Romanian Acadamy. His important book was: *Romanian Encyclopedic Dictionary* (Dicţionar Enciclopedic Român), Politica publisher, Bucharest, 1962–64.

10 Adopted methodology in archaeological excavations. www.cimec.ro. Order by the Ministry of Culture and Religious Affairs, no. 2103/2003. Ordinul Ministrului Culturii şi Cultelor nr. 2103/2007 pentru aprobarea Metodologiei privind coordonarea activităţii de cercetare arheologică în siturile arheologice declarate zone de interes naţional.

11 Chronicle of Archaeological Research (Cronica Cercetărilor Arheologice) 2004, Site code: 136535.02.

12 Felseghi 2009, nr. 1324. Ziua de Cluj. Securist 'bântuit' de victimele de acum 60 de ani.

13 Balazs Mende, anthropologist from the Laboratory of Archaeogenetics in Budapest (Institute of Archaeology, Budapest) has designed a good system of excavating and storing human remains, although he has not published these methods.

14 László Szatmáry is University Professor at the University of Debrecen, Department of Evolutionary Zoology and Human Biology, Hungary.

15 Zsolt Bernert is curator and anthropologist at the Hungarian Natural History Museum, Department of Anthropology, Budapest. Bernert's research area is the post-Pleistocene Collection/Avar Age.

16 The Palaeoanthropological Programme Pack by Zsolt Bernert contains research methods for palaeodemography, post-cranial metric calculations, stature and craniometric calculations.

17 Research Project directed by Professor Nicolae Gudea, Dr Cristian Găzdac, Szilamér Pánczél, Ágnes Găzdac and Loránt Vass: 'Fenomenologia spatiului şi antopologiei funerare. Necropola Porolissum'. Financial assistance by UEFISCU, code 516.

18 M. Gligor, M. Breazu and S. Varvara have undertaken archaeological research at the Neolithic settlement *from* Alba Iulia. Research Project by CEEX (Contract no 2-CEX 06-11-25/31.07.06).

BIBLIOGRAPHY

Acsádi, G. and Nemeskéri, J. (1970) *History of Human Life Span and Mortality*, Budapest: Akadémiai Kiadó.

Alekszejev, V.P. and Debec, G.F. (1964) *Kraniometrija*, Moscow: Nauka.

Bernert, Z. (2005) 'Paleoantropológiai programcsomag', *Folia Anthropologica*, 3: 71–75.

Éry, K., Kralovánszki, A. and Nemeskéri, J. (1963) 'Történeti népességek rekonstrukciójának reprezentációja', *Anthropológiai Közlemények*, 7: 41–90.

Ion, A. (2008) 'Oseminte umane descoperite în aşezări din arealul culturii Gumelniţa', *Studii de preistorie*, 5: 109–29.

Marcsik, A., Molnár, E. and Szathmáry, L. (2006) 'The antiquity of tuberculosis in Hungary: the skeletal evidence', *Memórias do Instituto Oswaldo Cruz*, 101 (Supplement II): 67–71.

Martin, R. and Saller, L. (1957) *Lehrbuch der Anthropologie*, Stuttgart: Gustav Fischer Verlag.

Mays, S. (1998) *The Archaeology of Human Bones*, London: Routledge.

Meindl, R.S. and Lovejoy, C.O. (1985) 'Ectocranial suture closure: a revised method for the determination of skeletal age at death based on the lateral-anterior sutures', *American Journal of Physical Anthropology*, 68: 57–66.

Miles, E.A.W. (1963) 'The dentition in the assessment of individual age in skeletal material', in D.R. Brothwell (ed.) *Dental Anthropology*, Oxford: Pergamon Press.

Nemeskéri, J., Harsányi, L. and Acsádi, G. (1960) 'Methoden zur Diagnose des Lebensalter von Skeletfunden', *Anthropologischer Anzeiger*, 24: 103–15.

Ortner, D.J. and Putschar, W.G.J. (1981) *Identification of Pathological Conditions in Human Skeletal Remains*, Washington DC: Smithsonian Institution Press.

Rösing, F.W. (1988) 'Körperhöhenrekonstruktion aus Skelettmaβen', in R. Knussmann (ed.) *Anthropologie, Band I*, Stuttgart: Gustav Fischer Verlag.

Sjøvold, T. (1990) 'Estimation of stature from long bones utilizing the line of organic correlation', *Journal of Human Evolution*, 5: 431–47.

Stloukal, M. and Hanáková, H. (1978) 'Die Lange der Längsknochen altslawischer Bevölkerungen unter besonderer Berücksichtigung von Wachstumsfragen', *Homo*, 29: 53–69.

Szatmáry, L. and Marcsik, A. (2006) 'Symbolic trephinations and population structure', *Memórias do Instituto Oswaldo Cruz*, 101: 129–32.

Ubelaker, D.H. (1984) *Human Skeletal Remains: Excavation, Analysis, Interpretation*, revised edn, Washington DC: Taraxacum.

White, T.D. (2000) *Human Osteology*, 2nd edn, San Diego, CA: Academic Press.

Russia/РОССИЯ

Alexandra Buzhilova

INTRODUCTION: A BRIEF HISTORY AND CURRENT STATE OF PHYSICAL ANTHROPOLOGY IN RUSSIA

The first scientific anthropological institutions and societies were established in Russia at the end of the 1850s. The development of physical anthropology in the country as a new branch of Science shows a long period of development, starting with a growing interest in association with the beginning of collection of osteological and ethnological samples.

The anthropological research in the country proceeded in two basic directions: the research on physical variation in the populations of the large Russian territories; and the development of theoretical concepts about the origin of modern humans. This latter subject occupied an important place in the studies of Russian philosophers and naturalists. More specific questions relating to physical anthropology mainly remained in the field of interests of physicians and anatomists.

In the history of the development of Russian physical anthropology a special place is occupied by the report of Moscow University professor I.F. Vensovich, delivered on the occasion of the 50th anniversary of the University in 1805. Vensovich strictly differentiated between anthropology (in a wider meaning of this term) and physical anthropology. In his opinion, physical anthropology embraced studies about humans, including body composition, physical activity, and morphological and physical changes during illness. He underlined that physical anthropology was not a part of medicine because it had other purposes (Levin 1960).

Another university professor, A.L. Lovetsky, contributed considerably to the popularization of physical anthropology at Moscow University. He was the author of the university textbook *The Physiology or Anthropo-Biology*, published in 1835. Lovetsky was also an author of the first anthropological manual in Russia, published by Moscow University in 1838 under the title *Guidebook to Knowledge of Tribes of Mankind* ... (Chtetcov 2004).

Later in 1864 the Society of Enthusiasts of Natural Sciences was founded at Moscow University. It came about due to the initiative of the extraordinary professor of Moscow University and Director of the Zoological Museum, A.P. Bogdanov. Anthropological topics were the most important in the activity of the new Society. Already on 4 November 1864 the Anthropological Department was divided and therefore re-structured. Anthropological, ethnographic and archaeological studies embraced the interests of the Department, which reflected the founders' viewpoint on anthropology as a complex science about the physical characteristics of Man and his culture. One of the main purposes of the Society was to collect anthropological, archaeological and ethnological samples (Buzhilova 2009). With great enthusiasm the members organized and participated in archaeological and ethnological expeditions in different areas of Eurasia.

The first collections

The history of creating the first scientific anthropological and medical collections is inseparably linked with the activity of the Russian Tsar Peter the Great. In 1698, while in Holland, Peter the Great attended the anatomy lectures of a well-known anatomist, F. Ruysch. As a result, Tsar Peter bought the collection of embalmed samples. A large part of this collection presented various morphological deviations from human anatomical norms.[1] In Russia, Peter published a Decree to replenish this collection, which ordered people to deliver human, animal and bird 'monsters' to the Kunstkamera in St Petersburg (a new museum established for the exposition of such specimens) (Nartov 1891).

The next Decree of Peter was dated 13 February 1718 and supported archaeological research by remunerating any 'antique things' which could be found in the ground or underwater. He ordered the protection of the mediaeval Bulgarian fortress in southern Russia. He asked the archaeologist Messerschmitt to travel all over Siberia to gather and buy antiques from local populations, who had found numerous archaeological silver and golden rarities. All the findings were conveyed directly to the Kunstkamera (Nartov 1891).

The organization and regulation of the collections under the patronage of a Russian Tsar was the first experience of legislative practice in Russia. After the special Decree of Peter the First, entrance to the Kunstkamera became free for the public (Rybak 2005). During that time, collections from different fields of archaeology, ethnology and anthropology were enlarged and housed in the Museum. In 1741–45 two volumes were published and these formed a Catalogue of the Kunstkamera Collections (Musei Imperialis Petropolitani) (Gokhman 1980).

The onset of regular collections of osteological specimens for scientific purposes in Russia is connected with the name of Karl von Baer. In 1814, after graduating from the medical faculty of Derpt University (today Tartu University, Estonia), von Baer spent three years in Austria and Germany studying natural sciences. These became his main interest, and von Baer abandoned medicine, totally devoting himself to scientific research. In 1842 he became a member of the Russian Academy of Sciences and head of the Academy's Department of Anatomy. By that time, Karl Maksimovich Baer (which is how he presented his name in Russia) worked in St Petersburg. Soon, under his initiative, the Department had been renamed the Department of Anthropology. In the collections of the Department there was a famous set of anatomical specimens accumulated by Tsar Peter and a small series of skulls from occasional Russian archaeological excavations.

Thanks to many years of Baer's scientific activity, the academic community in Russia was interested in developing a new science. As a result, in 1858 the number of skulls in the osteological collection increased to almost 400 (Levin 1960; Gokhman 1980). It became the basis of the numerous anthropological and archaeological collections of today's Museum of Anthropology and Ethnology of the Russian Academy of Sciences in St Petersburg. Simultaneously, Baer published some works, which were important for the development of physical anthropology in the country (Gokhman 1980).

It is important to note that there were no special legal grounds for the collection of archaeological and anthropological materials at that time, except for the few decrees of Tsar Peter the

Great in the 17th and 18th centuries. Nevertheless, the Decree of the Russian Academy of Sciences, which recorded the foundation of special scientific museums on the basis of the Kunstkamera in 1836, promoted active collecting of archaeological and anthropological data in Russia (Table 34.1).

The Russian Imperial Archaeological Commission opened in 1859. The members mainly studied the archaeological sites in Southern Russia. The Archaeological Society was founded in 1864 in Moscow, and it became famous due to its active organization of archaeological congresses in different Russian towns. The diffusion of this new science promoted the gathering of archaeological and osteological material for collections in numerous areas of Russia, and especially in a number of local universities.

At the same time, in 1864 in Moscow, the University's Society of Enthusiasts of Natural Sciences formed the Anthropological Department on the initiative of A.P. Bogdanov. This date also became a milestone in the legislation regarding the collection of museum samples. From 1864 the regional reform of the Russian government led to the government's management of local museums of natural history, including the organization and preservation of their collections.

In 1867, with the idea of propagating the discipline, Bogdanov organized in Moscow an exhibition about anthropology and ethnography. Later, the materials that had been exhibited became the basis of the collection of the newly opened Ethnographic Museum in Moscow.

Thanks to Bogdanov, in 1876 the sub-Faculty of Anthropology started at Moscow University from private donations. A part of the anthropological collection, which had been

Table 34.1 The chronology of events related to anthropological collections in the 17th to 19th centuries

Year	Event
1714	Foundation of Russia's first museum (the Kunstkamera, St Petersburg). Decree of Peter the First
1782	First provincial museum in Russia (Irkutsk, Siberia)
1791	Museum of Natural History, Moscow University
The beginning of the XIXth century	Archaeological museums in the Black Sea region, period of the so-called 'archaeological boom'
1836	Decree of the Russian Academy of Sciences regarding the creation of special scientific museums on the basis of the Kunstkamera
1859	Russian Imperial Archaeological Commission was established
1863	Society of Enthusiasts of Natural Sciences was founded at Moscow University
1864	Moscow Archaeological Society was founded
1864	Anthropological Department, the Society of Enthusiasts of Natural Sciences, Moscow University, was created
1867	Ethnographic Exhibition in Moscow. Founding of the Ethnographic Museum in Moscow
1872	Polytechnic Exhibition in Moscow. Founding of the Polytechnic Museum in Moscow
1872	Founding of the Imperial Russian Historical Museum in Moscow
1879	Anthropological Exhibition in Moscow
1883	Founding of Anthropological Museum at Moscow University
1887	VIIth Archaeological Congress in Yaroslavl. The declaration about new status of Russian Museums (as Public Museums, not only Private ones) presented by P.S. Uvarova
1889	Special exhibition 'Human skulls and skeletons' in the Kunstkamera, St Petersburg

made from material collected on the expeditions of the Society, became the property of the Department.

D.N. Anuchin (the scholar and a follower of Bogdanov) assisted Professor Bogdanov in the organization of the department. Later he participated in the opening of the Russian section of the Anthropological Exhibition in Paris in 1878. The best samples of archaeological and anthropological findings from the latest archaeological excavations and ethnological expeditions in Russia were presented there. After that, Anuchin and Bogdanov organized the Anthropological Exhibition in Moscow, which was opened in April 1879 (Buzhilova 2009).

The Anthropological Exhibition in Moscow reflects a major stage in the development of physical anthropology in Russia. At this time a lot of anthropological and archaeological collections, gathered by Bogdanov and his colleagues from Moscow University, became the material from which the Exhibition was created. A special building was rented in the centre of Moscow near the Kremlin (nowadays the exhibition centre is called the 'Manezh')[2]. The building was first used as a traditional *manège* for horses and the place where soldiers were trained in equestrianism. The *Manège* was large enough to hold an entire infantry regiment (over 2000 soldiers) as well as an invited audience. Since 1831 it has served as an exhibition hall. For example, in 1867 Hector Berlioz and Nikolai Rubinstein performed at the *Manège* before a crowd of 12,000. Thus, in 1879, the building became the centre of performance of anthropology in Russia. In the Exhibition there were sections from the anthropological, archaeological, palaeontological, ethnological and medical departments. The impressive construction, which architect V.N. Korneev, sculptor I.I. Sevrugin and horticulturist F.I. Demur were invited to help build, allowed the public, for example, to enter a forest (with real plants and trees), to see reconstructed palaeontological animals, to observe the highland panorama with original Bronze Age dolmens (they were conveyed to Moscow from the northern Caucasus), or to see a full-scale model of a Russian mediaeval kurgan (burial mound). The craniological part of the Exhibition included about 3000 skulls. The Exhibition was popular and remained open for about six months.

From 29 July to 3 August 1879 the International Anthropological Congress took place in Moscow University, resulting in about 30 outstanding foreign anthropologists and archaeologists visiting the Exhibition.

After the closing of the Exhibition, the Anthropological Museum was opened at Moscow University. It housed archaeological, anthropological and ethnological materials from the Exhibition. Zoological and palaeontological samples became part of the Zoological Museum at Moscow University. Stone Age archaeological series went to the then newly opened Imperial Russian Historical Museum in Moscow. A number of specimens went to the sub-Faculty of Anthropology of Moscow University and served as teaching materials. At that time different exhibitions were opened in the Kunstkamera in St Petersburg. In 1889 a new building of the Museum was opened with the exhibition 'Human skulls and skeletons', which became one of the most exceptional exhibitions in the activity of the Kunstkamera (Buzhilova 2009). All these events opened new ways for further development of physical anthropology in the country.

We have to pay attention to the direct legal regulations regarding the preservation of anthropological and archaeological collections in museums. Regulations regarding archaeological excavation at a legislative level did not exist in the Russian empire. There were many regulations for local museums; the few Decrees of Peter the Great regulated the problems of gathering and curating collections of ancient material. At the VIIth Archaeological Congress in 1887 P.S. Uvarova presented a Declaration regarding the new status of Russian museums. According to the declaration, a museum must be an official body, whose collections should be of national property; and this is the reasons why collections cannot be sold or transferred from one department to another (Rybak 2005).

Thus, museum laws, which regulated the preservation, investigation and popularization of cultural values, did not represent a strict system at the end of the 19th century. The elements of regulation of museum rights had been dispersed, and it was not the independent branch of jurisprudence in Russia.

Modern tendencies towards collections of human remains and physical anthropology research

Archaeology and anthropology in Russia, as everywhere else, rapidly changes, expanding the scope of the research interests, developing new methods, including interdisciplinary approaches, striving for greater accuracy and detail in the historical reconstruction. The gradual accumulation of new archeological and anthropological materials is the focus of many research questions, such as the environmental conditions in which people lived and everyday life.

Some changes have been noted in the organization of collections of anthropological remains. First, in the 19th century anthropological collections mainly comprised skulls, not skeletons. The mid-1930s saw a tendency to collect all the human remains from excavations and at this time it became a tradition to collect so-called thematic collections: palaeopathological, urban populations, nomads, skulls with artificial deformation and so on.

Interest in examples of ancient diseases led to the first Russian palaeopathological skeletal collections being established, including that held at the Museum of Age and Pathological Osteology of Modern and Ancient Populations in the Department of Roentgen and Radiology of the First Leningrad I.P. Pavlov Medical Institute (today St Petersburg Medical University). Founded in the 1930s by Professor D.G. Rokhlin, the Museum held both exhibition areas and scientific collections. The Museum also provided resources for students of constitutional anatomy and Roentgen-anatomy, particularly examples of bone and joint disease. Its exhibits and collections have provided materials for monographs, funded research, theses, and several hundred articles (summarized in Rokhlin 1964).

Due to Rokhlin's interest in history, the tradition of developing case histories of famous historical persons through palaeopathological investigation developed in Russia (Rokhlin 1940; Rokhlin and Maikowa-Stroganowa 1935). Studies of the remains of Grand Duke Yaroslav I the Wise and Grand Duke Andrei Bogolubsky made Rokhlin's name popular in Russian archaeology and history. Duke Yaroslav I (c. 980–1054) was thrice Grand Prince of Novgorod and Kiev, uniting the two principalities (Eastern Europe) under his rule. During his lengthy reign, Kievan Rus' reached a zenith of cultural development and military power. Roentgenological investigation of his remains showed a healed infection in the right hip joint, which affected Duke Yaroslav I during childhood, as Rokhlin pointed out. The scientist described healed trauma and spinal pathology, and he suggested possible evidence of horseriding on the basis of occupational stress markers, thus pioneering the study of occupational stress (Rokhlin 1965). Duke Andrei I of Vladimir, commonly known as Andrey Bogolyubsky (c. 1111–74) was a Prince of Vladimir-Suzdal lands (after 1157). Increased princely authority and conflict with outstanding persons led to a plot against Bogolyubsky, and he was killed in 1174 AD. Examination of bone trauma showed that the story about his death, which had been written in the Ipatiev annals, was erroneous. The mediaeval writer noted an amputation of the right hand, but in fact Rokhlin found a lot of cut marks on the left humerus and forearm bones (Rokhlin 1965). Later the observations by Rokhlin were confirmed by a special historical study by Russian historian A.V. Artcikhovsky (Buzhilova 2009). Rokhlin (1965: 292) discussed the general health of the Grand Duke from his anthropological observations which 'depict the peculiar appearance and behaviour of a given individual with convincing exactness'.

The main results of Rokhlin's palaeopathological research are summarized in his monograph *Diseases of Ancient Humans: Human Bones of Various Epochs – Normal and Pathologically Changed* (Rokhlin 1965). It was the first Russian book in which the reader could find the history of palaeopathology, and explore differential diagnoses for certain bacterial infections, arthropathies, malformations, traumas and neoplasms using radiographic imaging. This book was immensely popular, not only among scientists, but also among the general public. Subsequently, many physicians and physical anthropologists became interested in palaeopathology during the 1970s and 1980s.

During the last decade, papers devoted to problems of anthropology have become more numerous in Russia. Authors, mainly physical anthropologists, have different interests but, in general, they may be considered due to their integrated focus upon cultural and biological questions. Following much earlier Russian emphasis upon interdisciplinary study, anthropologists today use osteological and archaeological data to reconstruct the history of different ancient cultural groups who occupied a wide area of the modern Eurasian territory of Russia.

Among the impressive results of recent field work in Russian archaeology are the Early Palaeolithic sites in the north Caucasus, the study of multi-layer stratified Upper Paleolithic sites in the Altai region, Siberia, the excavation of 'frozen graves' of the Pazyryk culture in the territory of Mongolia, the excavation of 'royal' Sarmatian burial mounds in the southern Urals and funerary complexes of the Hun in the territory of Buryatia and Mongolia, the study of ancient Russian fortifications of Novgorod (Ryurikov), the discovery of mass graves from the tragic Mongol destruction of Yaroslavl in 1238, and the study of mediaeval wooden buildings in Moscow's Kremlin (Egoreichenko *et al.* 2009).

The most visible phenomenon, which characterizes the present situation of archaeology in Russia, is the rapid growth of field research due to the rise of new investment into projects. From 1994 the number of licences for excavations has increased threefold. Almost every University in Russia has an osteological collection, which is used for scientific and training purposes.

ARCHAEOLOGICAL HUMAN REMAINS AND LEGISLATION

Archaeological legislation

After the Social Revolution of 1917 the status of historical monuments and museum collections changed. The Decree of the new government dated 13 July 1918 proclaimed that, after the confiscation of property from the Russian Emperor, it would become the property of the Russian Socialist Soviet Federal Republic. A later Decree from 5 October 1918 regulated the registration and preservation of the collections and cultural monuments in the country. At that time the government initiated the first state registration of all collections in museums and others departments, as well as registration of their properties (Rybak 2005).

In Petrograd (nowadays St Petersburg) on 19 April 1919, the Decree of the People's Commissars of the new Government formed the Russian Academy of the History of Material Culture (RAHMC). RAHMC was established on the basis of the disbanded Imperial Archaeological Commission, which was the main archaeological organization of pre-revolutionary Russia. In 1937 the RAHMC became a member of the Academy of Sciences of the USSR and changes its name to the Institute of History of Material Culture (IHMC). Later two academic Institutes were created on the basis of it: the Institute of Archaeology of the Russian Academy of Sciences (RAS) in Moscow and the Institute of History of Material Culture in Leningrad (nowadays St Petersburg).

The structure of the Institute of Archaeology in Moscow and the Institute of History of Material Culture in St Petersburg was organized according to chronological or cultural-historical principles (Stone Age Department, Bronze Age Department, etc.). A special place in the structure of the Institute of Archaeology in Moscow was the Department of Field Investigations, which was responsible for the regulation of scientific fieldwork and supervision of the professional quality of archaeological field investigations throughout Russia.

In recent years, as archaeological fieldwork in Russia has considerably increased, the activity of the Department and of a Council of Experts, which provides the expertise to help submit yearly reports of archaeological fieldwork, has become particularly important. All excavation reports are archived at the Institute of Archaeology, RAS. This centralized system for collecting and archiving documents started in the middle of the 19th century thanks to the activity of the Imperial Archaeological Commission. Today this work is closely coordinated by the State Department 'Rossvyazokhrankultura'.

HUMAN REMAINS AND LEGISLATION

There is no specific legislation regarding the excavation of human remains. Every archaeologist who plans to start an excavation, for example of a cemetery, has to receive an 'open list for excavation', a licence needed to legalize an archaeological excavation in Russia. The Department of Field Investigations regulates the number of them every year. After the excavation has been completed, archaeologists have to send the excavation report to the Department of Field Investigations of the Institute of Archaeology, Moscow, before the start of the following season (usually in May). At the same time, the archaeologist works with different specialists to study artefacts and osteological materials. After the preliminary study is completed, the archaeologist is responsible for transporting the collection to the regional museum. In some cases, human remains may be submitted to the Osteological stores of the Institute and Museum of Anthropology of Moscow University, the Anthropological Department of the Kunstkamera, the Historical State Museum, the Hermitage, etc. If the archaeologist responsible for the excavation does not submit the report in time, he will not be able to apply for another licence until the report has been submitted.

Therefore some efforts exist to preserve the archaeological heritage of Russia and to develop effective approaches to the protection of archaeological monuments. The work is particularly relevant in the present situation, where there are at times illegal excavations by 'antiquity hunters' and building activities in historical places which have destroyed ancient monuments (Makarov 2005).

In recent years, the Institute of Archaeology of RAS has organized numerous rescue excavations in ancient historic towns, and has provided precious information on the preservation of ancient monuments. During rescue excavations the most qualified scientists (archaeologists, anthropologists, zoologists and so on), who specialize in specific periods, have coordinated the projects. The excavations have become sources of new materials that characterize the cultures and history of towns and rural settlements of Russia. After the completion of the rescue excavations the archaeological material would be submitted to the local museum in the region where the excavation has taken place. The same regulation applies to other archaeological departments of the Russian Academy of Sciences. Osteological assemblages from local excavations are to be curated in local museums or in local universities.

After the publication of the European Convention in 1992 on the protection of objects of archaeological heritage (ETS no. 143; Rybak 2005), archaeological data are considered a resource of European collective memory and the tool of historical and scientific investigation. Russia, as well as other European countries, took part in this 1992 Convention.

Legislation in the fields of conservation, management, promotion and public protection of cultural heritage (historical and cultural monuments) of the Russian Federation are based on the provisions of the Constitution, Civil Code of Russia and Federal Law 'Objects of cultural heritage (monuments of history and culture) of RF nations' (June 25 2002 no. 73-FZ). The title of the aw in its original language is Федеральный закон от 25 июня 2002 г. N 73-ФЗ 'Об объектах культурного наследия (памятниках истории и культуры) народов Российской Федерации'. Today, archaeologists are active participants in the new edition of Federal Law in Russia when considering anthropological and archaeological collections.

In 2007 in San Diego, California, members of the Institute of Archaeology of the Russian Academy of Sciences (Nikolaj Makarov), the Archaeological Institute of America (Jane C. Waldbaum and Brian Rose) and the German Archaeological Institute (Ortwin Dally) signed the agreement known as the 'Joint Statement of Principle on the Protection of Archaeological Sites, Monuments and Museums' in which it was declared that monuments, archaeological sites and museums are irreplaceable parts of the common heritage of humanity. The document states:

> Their extraordinary value as records of humanity's past history imposes a moral obligation on governments and peoples to protect and conserve them ... All nations should ratify and consistently respect the provisions embodied in the 1954 Hague Convention on the Protection of Cultural Property in the Event of Armed Conflict, and its First and Second Protocols, regarding the protection of cultural heritage during armed conflict and military occupation. Protection of sites, monuments, and museums requires the participation of the political, economic, and policing agencies of governments, as well as of non-governmental organizations, individuals, and the private sector. The German Archaeological Institute, the Institute of Archaeology of the Russian Academy of Sciences, and the Archaeological Institute of America urge governments and individuals to endorse these objectives and to work actively to realize them.
>
> *Joint Statement of Principle on the Protection of Archaeological Sites 2007*

METHODS OF ANTHROPOLOGICAL ANALYSIS

Determination of the age and sex of skeletons is achieved by standard methods which take into account various morphological criteria (Pashkova 1963; Alexeev and Debetc 1964; Alexeev 1966; Bass 1995). Specific measurements of bones are taken to estimate the sex of adults and the age of children (Ubelaker 1978; Bass 1995). The standard measurements are taken on skulls and on long bones to study diversity of ancient populations (Alexeev and Debetc 1964; Alexeev 1966). The length of long bones is used to calculate stature according to the formulae developed by M. Trotter and G.C. Gleser, G. Olivier and Russian anthropologists V.V. Bunak and G.F. Debetc (Alexeev 1966). The general state of bones, dentition and indicators of physical stress are investigated for osteoarthropathies and infections, tumours and metabolic disorders (Cohen and Armelagos 1984; Ortner and Putschar 1985; Buzhilova 1998). Traumata and injuries are analysed using methods particular to forensic anthropology, so as to distinguish them from *post-mortem* damage produced by degradation characteristic of a process of diagenesis (destruction of bones by physical and chemical agents). This part of the study is conducted according to methods of differential diagnosis, including macro- and microscopic observation (see, e.g., Dobryak 1960; Pashkova 1963).

CONCLUSION

In recent years, research on archaeological human remains has increased. This is partly the result of individuals, institutions and legislation both governing the protection of human remains and ensuring that archaeological excavations are conducted during construction work. In addition, famous discoveries, the anthropological tradition – which is probably one of the oldest in Europe – and the exhibitions have helped popular awareness. Following this long tradition, efforts exist to preserve the archaeological heritage of Russia and to develop effective approaches to the protection of ancient sites and monuments.

Following much earlier Russian emphasis upon interdisciplinary study, anthropologists today analyse archaeological human remains to reconstruct the lifestyles of past populations and to enhance the understanding of anthropological diversity in ancient times.

USEFUL CONTACTS

Russian Academy of Sciences (Росси́йская акаде́мия нау́к). Website: www.ras.ru/

Institute of Archaeology of the Russian Academy of Sciences, Moscow. Website: www.archaeolog.ru/

Institute of Archaeology and Ethnography of the Siberian Branch of the Russian Academy of Sciences. Website: www.archaeology.nsc.ru/

Institute for the History of Material Culture of the Russian Academy of Sciences. Website: www.archeo.ru/eng/

Archaeological portal of Russia. Website: www.archaeology.ru/

Peter the Great Museum of Anthropology and Ethnography (Kunstkamera), Russian Academy of Sciences. Website: www.kunstkamera.ru/

Institute and Museum of Anthropology of Moscow State University. Website: www.antropos.msu.ru/

State Hermitage Museum. Website: www.hermitagemuseum.org/

Vladimir and Suzdal museum reserve. Website: www.museum.vladimir.ru/

The Museum of History of Moscow. Website: www.museum.ru/moscow/about.htm/

Archaeological Museum of Kazan State University. Website: www.ksu.ru/archeol_en/

NOTES

1 A considerable part of this collection is still housed at this Museum (Kunstkamera) in St Petersburg. In recent years a special exhibition has been on display at the Museum.

2 Moscow Manezh was erected from 1817 to 1825 by the Russian architect Joseph Bové, who decorated it in its Neoclassical exterior, a number of Roman Doric columns enclosing bays of arch-headed windows in a blind arcade, painted white and cream yellow.

BIBLIOGRAPHY

Alexeev, V.P. (1966) *Osteometry. A Method of Anthropological Study*, Moscow: Nauka. [in Russian]

Alexeev, V.P. and Debetc, G.F. (1964) *Craniometry. A Method of Anthropological Study*, Moscow: Nauka. [in Russian].

Bass, W.M. (1995) *Human Osteology. A Laboratory and Field Manual*, 4th edn, Columbia, MO: Missouri Archaeological Society.

Buzhilova, A.P. (1998) 'Paleopathology in Bio-Archaeological Reconstruction', in A. Buzhilova, M. Kozlovskaya and M. Mednikova (eds) *Historical Human Ecology*, Moscow: Staryi Sad. [in Russian].

——(2009) 'Palaeopathology in Russia: historical background', *Vestnik MGU. Antropologia*, 1: 27–34.

Chtetcov, V.P. (2004) *The Cradle of Russian Anthropology*, Moscow: Moscow University Press. [in Russian].

Cohen, M.N. and Armelagos, G. (eds) (1984) *Paleopathology at the Origins of Agriculture*, New York: Academic Press.

Dobryak, V.I. (1960) *Forensic Medicine in the Investigation of Human Remains*, Kiev: Medicina. [in Russian].

Egoreichenko, A.A., Kalinin, V.A. and Gaidukov, P.G. (2009) 'II (XVIII) Archaeological Congress in Suzdal, 2008', *Rossiskaya arkheologia*, 3: 171–91.

Gokhman, I.I. (1980) '*Craniological Collections of the Museum of Anthropology and Ethnology and the Importance of Them to Anthropological Study*', Leningrad: Museum of Anthropology and Ethnology. [in Russian]

Levin, M.G. (1960) *Issues About the History of Anthropology in Russia*, Moscow: Academy of Sciences of USSR. [in Russian]

Makarov, N.A. (2005) 'The round table "Preservation of an archaeological heritage of Russia" in the Federation Council of Federal Meeting of the Russian Federation', *Rossiaskaya arkhaeologia*, 1: 5–6.

Nartov, A. (1891) *The Stories About Peter the Great*, St. Petersburg: Ya. Grey. [in Russian]

Ortner, D.J. and Putschar, W.G.J. (1985) *Identification of Pathological Conditions in Human Skeletal Remains*, Washington, DC: Smithsonian Institution Press.

Pashkova, V.I. (1963) *Sketches of forensic osteology. Determination of sex, age and stature basing on bones of human skeleton*, Moscow: Publishing House of Medical Literature. [in Russian].

Rokhlin, D.G. (1940) 'The anatomy and roentgen study of remains of Grand Duke Yaroslav Mudry', *Short reports of Institute of History of Material culture*, 7: 7–11. [in Russian]

——(1964) 'The Museum of Age and Pathologic Osteology of Modern and Ancient Populations of the USSR, Department of Roentgenology and Radiology, Leningrad I.P. Pavlov 1st Medical Institute', *Archives of Anatomy, Histology and Embriology*, 46: 105–8. [in Russian]

——(1965) *Diseases of Ancient Men (Bones of the Men of Various Epochs – Normal and Pathological changed)*, Leningrad: Nauka. [in Russian]

Rokhlin, D.G. and Maikowa-Stroganowa, W.S. (1935) 'Roentgen-anthropological study of remains of Grand Duke Andrei Bogolubsky', *Problemy istorii dokapitalisticheskich obshestv*, 9–10: 17–25. [in Russian]

Rybak, K.E. (2005) *The Museum Law (The International and Legal Aspects)*, Moscow: Yurist. [in Russian].

Ubelaker, D.H. (1978) *Human Skeletal Remains. Excavations, Analysis, Interpretation*, Chicago, IL: Adline Publishing Company.

Serbia/Srbija

Marija Djurić and Andrej Starović

INTRODUCTION: A BRIEF HISTORY AND CURRENT STATE OF PHYSICAL ANTHROPOLOGY IN SERBIA

Archaeology as a scientific field in the Balkans and specifically in Serbia has a long and illustrious tradition. It is well legislated, follows – for the most part – actual standards in methodology and has produced fascinating archaeological information. However, the study of human skeletal biology did not follow the strengths of archaeological research in the area. The discipline is relatively new, with its own methodology dependent on individual researchers involved. In this brief overview of history and current practices in the field in Serbia, we are going to concentrate on both the current advances and areas that still need improvement in this domain.

Archaeological sites are valuable sources of information about our past that are destroyed in the very process of excavation. This fact requires careful balancing of the need to excavate archaeological sites in order to get as much scientific information as possible with the necessity to preserve sites and protect them from destruction. In general, control over the archaeological resources is always dependent on current scientific development, funding issues, and the local strategy of the community. Skeletal remains, as part of this general archaeological issue, are bound by the same constraints and require the same approach. In essence, if the excavation of the remains is not followed by their thorough anthropological analysis, documentation, and proper curation, they cannot contribute to the improvement of our knowledge of past populations. Unfortunately, one or all of these aspects in the treatment of human remains from archaeological contexts is often lacking in Serbia.

Skeletal remains have been excavated from a large percentage of archaeological sites in Serbia. When conducting research for this chapter we quickly perceived that, to even attempt to assess the total number of skeletons excavated from different sites, we were confronted with substantial uncertainty. Despite the fact that many archaeological reports and papers indicated the presence of buried individuals at the site, bioarchaeological information, if present at all, is commonly limited to basic age and sex data, and often published as appendices to archaeological papers and monographs. Furthermore, many archaeologically collected human remains from the past (excavated bones or chance finds) have not been reported at all, and others have been mentioned without any precise information on the number or composition of the skeletal sample. This is not limited to published papers, but extends to the 'grey literature' as well. When we tried to

Table 35.1 Archaeological recovery of human remains *vs.* anthropological analysis in Serbia (according to data assessment and estimation made by the authors)★

Period	Archaeological sites containing human remains	Sites with published anthropological reports	Number of recorded individuals in anthropological published reports	Estimated total number of individuals
Prehistoric	185	33	1056	c. 4500
Classical	94	7	696	>22,000
Mediaeval	>250	36	3177	>15,000
TOTAL	>529	76	4929	>47,000

★ Sites from Kosovo and Metohija are included

review the official report files at the Serbian Ministry of Culture, the Institute for the Protection of Cultural Heritage, and the National Museum in Belgrade, we were not able to assemble a reliable list of all the excavated human remains and the minimum number of individuals per site. In order to create the best possible estimate, we have included in Table 35.1 information gathered from the interviews with archaeologists and physical anthropologists who either excavated or curated the collections.

The drastic discrepancy between the number of archaeologically recorded human remains (excavated or discovered as chance finds) on one side, and analysed and/or published anthropological data on the other, is the result of obvious insensitivity of the researchers towards the importance of skeletal material in furthering the interpretation of our past. Generally, for decades archaeologists were not aware of the potential of anthropological analysis towards our understanding of the past. This was supported by the attitude of anthropologists who, particularly in the case of cemeteries from the Classic period, were predominantly focused on determining the different anthropological types of Balkan populations. Moreover, many published reports on cemeteries, especially from the context of ruined mediaeval churches or monastery graveyards, do not actually have any relevant osteological data, except for the number of graves and the number of individuals that had been buried. Such types of grave regularly do not include grave goods, so in written reports authors would mention skeletal remains only in a 'binary style' (either *there was* or *there was not*). As a result of this, we now have a significant discrepancy between recovered and analysed skeletons, and a kind of blurred picture about the number and distribution of human remains from different archaeological periods in Serbia.

The very first findings of human skeletal remains from the ancient past in Serbia go back to the end of 18th century, reported briefly in popular magazines by non-experts. An extraordinary chance find of human skull from Belgrade, dating from the Middle Pleistocene, was described by Đ. Jovanović (Stefanović 2007). At the end of the 19th century, with the rise of scientific archaeology, the number of archaeologically excavated graves and necropoli with more descriptive information increased. Many Roman necropoli had already been excavated and/or identified at this time, but little attention was paid to the human remains. As early as 1908, Serbian ethnographer T. Đorđević, in his article 'Unknown graveyard in Žagubica', insisted that it was important to study burials and skeletal remains since they were often the only source of information on what people looked like and how they lived in ancient times (Đorđević 1909). In keeping with the 'culture history paradigm', the types of burial ritual, the size and shape of the graves, and the nature of the grave goods were described and analysed, in order to create a proper typological and chronological sequence.

Several ethnographers and geologists – J. Žujović, S. Trojanović (PhD in Anthropology at Heidelberg University in 1885), J. Cvijić, V. Dvorniković and J. Erdljanović – all from the late 19th and early 20th centuries, were important for the development of physical anthropology as a discipline in the study of past populations (see historical overview in Djurić-Srejić 1995). Following European scientific trends of the time, Serbian anthropologists were predominantly interested in population-specific traits, and the origin and migrations of different ethnic groups, while some research was devoted to diet, health and biological adaptation.

The 1950s witnessed a growing awareness of the importance of skeletal remains for the study of past populations. However, due to the lack of trained local specialists, most of the analyses were undertaken by foreign scholars. The anthropological assemblages of Lepenski Vir and Vlasac were studied by Nemeskéri and his team (Nemeskéri 1969; Nemeskéri and Szathmary 1978); while Mokrin was studied by Farkas and Liptak (1971). S. Živanović, a Serbian anthropologist who worked at the time at Saint Bartholomew's Hospital in London, investigated numerous skeletal series, focusing mainly on palaeopathology (*cf.* Živanović 1976, 1982).

About that time, the first association whose aim was to promote the science of anthropology, the 'Anthropological Society of Yugoslavia', was formed in 1959. The local scientific, political and social context of the time forced the Society to abandon its primary goal, and to focus its attention upon collecting anthropometric data and providing a standard and statistical descriptions of the 'Yugoslav' population. Its role further developed towards more practical goals: anthropometric data of schoolchildren was collected in order to describe current secular trends in growth and development; from adults to provide adequate anthropometric information of the military-age population for the design and sizing of military clothing, protective and personal equipment; and to incorporate anthropometric characteristics into a wide variety of industrial designs. These visions guided the Society for years, as can be clearly seen from annual meetings and articles in the Society's journal (*Glasnik antropološkog društva Jugoslavije*: Yugoslav Anthropological Society's Herald). The Society continues to exist, but in 2007 it changed name to the Society of Anthropologists of Serbia (Društvo antropologa Srbije).

General trends in anthropological studies made their way into Serbian anthropology too, and the focus on biometrics, typology and racial history was clearly abandoned by the early 1990s. The new scholars emphasized contemporary trends in anthropology, an interdisciplinary approach and a more modern scientific methodology. Reflecting the attitude of a new generation of scientists who brought modern research design into physical anthropology, the Serbian Anthropological Association (Srpsko antropološko društvo) was established in 1997. Nevertheless, despite the wide diversity of professionals included in this organization, little was done to strengthen the network between scientists of biological and cultural background.

Education and training

The academic development of physical anthropology has been strongly influenced by the traditional European division of anthropology into physical and social (ethnology). There are few opportunities in Serbia for individuals who wish to become physical anthropologists. Since 1985 the Department of Archaeology at the Faculty of Philosophy in Belgrade offers only one basic course in biological anthropology in the core curriculum for students of archaeology. Additionally, since 2005, three elective courses for students of archaeology or ethnology were included. During the 1990s the Petnica Science Centre, a non-governmental educational institution founded to help and support young people with demonstrated interest in science beyond the school curricula, offered very attractive courses in physical anthropology that have emphasized a multidisciplinary scientific methodology. A lack of job opportunities further decelerated the academic promotion and development of the discipline. At present, only two academic positions are available for biological anthropologists at the Faculty of Philosophy. Other bioanthropologists teach in anatomy, dentistry and human biology, or work on part-time contracts with the Institute of Archaeology. Many of them have left the country.

One centre has provided informal education in bioanthropology since 1995. The Laboratory for Anthropology, a research department of the Institute of Anatomy, School of Medicine, University of Belgrade (Figure 35.1) was founded for the purpose of providing a research facility for the study of human remains from both archaeological and forensic contexts (Institute of Anatomy University of Belgrade 2006). The main research interests are in palaeopathology, forensic anthropology, dental anthropology and bone structural analysis. The laboratory strongly supports interdisciplinary and collaborative research, and many of the activities conducted within the laboratory could only be possible with the assistance of other university departments, as well as with the increasingly active role of Serbian museums. Its growing importance was also recognized in 2009 when the University of Belgrade introduced a new PhD programme in skeletal biology, with bioanthropology as one of the main streams. The programme is based at the Laboratory for Anthropology. It involves faculty members from other departments, and several academics from other countries as well. Reflecting the need for such a programme not only in Serbia but in South and Central Europe in general, the courses are offered in English.

Figure 35.1 Work in progress. Laboratory for Anthropology, Institute of Anatomy, School of Medicine, University of Belgrade, Serbia
Documentary photograph: A. Janovic

Case studies

In order to illustrate the apparent incoherence in the general strategy in the recovery and treatment of human remains from the past in Serbia, two case studies are presented below, both involving systematic fieldwork projects with large series of human skeletal material. They will illustrate two different ways of dealing with skeletal remains. The first case refers to a site from the Mesolithic–Neolithic transitional period where bones have been preserved and stored for future analysis; the second, an assemblage from the Late Iron Age/Roman period which was reburied just after a preliminary anthropological analysis, thus disabling any further research on this material.

Case Study 1: The Iron Gate research project

In the early 1960s, large dams were scheduled to be constructed in the area known as the 'Iron Gates' which covers the Danube gorge, between the modern Serbian city of Kladovo and across the river from the Romanian city of Turnu Severin. Practically, in this area an artificial lake had to be constructed as well as two hydroelectric power plants: Đerdap 1 and 2 ('Đerdap' is the Serbian name for 'Iron Gates'). This forthcoming ambitious engineering project included an archaeological evaluation of the area. For the first time in the history of Serbian archaeology there was an opportunity to mobilize an entire archaeological community from the former Yugoslavia to work there, as well as some experts from abroad. More than 500 sites from different periods were recorded, from the Late Pleistocene to the present. It was then common, in the late 1960s, to have several dozen archaeological teams working on large and small scale excavations simultaneously.

Starting from 1965, new and amazing discoveries took place there. The settlement of Lepenski Vir, explored by D. Srejović and his team, brought to world archaeology a valuable contribution regarding the question of the origin of the Neolithic in Europe. Practically, the complete area of that prehistoric settlement was excavated, and more than 50 dwellings and more than 80 graves were unearthed (Srejović 1979: 49). In total, remains of around 170 individuals were discovered, although not all of them belonged to the Lepenski Vir culture. The majority of skeletons belonged to a sensitive transitional period between the traditional Mesolithic and the upcoming Neolithic (Figure 35.2). Buildings with recognizable features (trapezoidal bases flanked with stone slabs and covered with reddish ground limestone, rectangular stone hearths and imaginatively sculpted boulders) became the 'trademark' of Lepenski Vir. Besides the architectural and artistic importance of the site, Lepenski Vir also became well-known for its complex funeral rituals. A total of 82 graves of infants and adults of both sexes were archaeologically recorded. A variety of funerary treatments relating to rituals and burials were present: primary skeletal burials (unflexed or with semi-flexed knees); and secondary partial burials (disarticulated, selected bones, sometimes slightly burnt; see, e.g., Srejović 1973: 197; Roksandić 1999).

Not only Lepenski Vir itself, but some 20 different sites belonging to prehistoric cultures have been discovered in 1965–70 in the region of the Iron Gates. On the Serbian side of the river Danube, the most important ones are Padina, Hajdučka Vodenica (cf. Jovanović 2004), and Vlasac (Srejović and Letica 1978). Similar settlements on the riverbanks yielded 84 (Vlasac), and 37 (Padina) burials. Altogether with other Serbian and Romanian sites, the so-called Iron Gates Series was represented by more than 250 remains of adult individuals from the Mesolithic and Neolithic period. Most of the anthropological research in the Iron Gates Gorge was based on comparisons of metric data for the two sites that had yielded larger numbers of measurable cranial remains, namely Vlasac and Lepenski Vir (Nemeskéri and Lengyel 1978; Nemeskéri and

Figure 35.2 Dragoslav Srejović in the field season in 1968 at Lepenski Vir, Serbia, lifting a skull – Burial 7/ II-b in House 21
Source: Archaeological Collection, Belgrade University

Szathmary 1978a, 1978b, 1978c). Nemeskéri's research was very influential and remains one of the most comprehensive studies of the Vlasac material. The first synthesis on the Iron Gates material comes from Mikić (1980a). The findings of both Nemeskéri and Mikić were strongly influenced by Srejović 's (1969) initial claim that the neolithization of the region was a process resulting from the indigenous intensification of plant use and domestication in the region (Roksandić 1999). Padina and Hajdučka Vodenica were very briefly treated by Živanović (1975a, 1975b) and most of the conclusions were based on the archaeological interpretation of the sites.

Why should this particular case study be important for the purpose of our chapter? The Iron Gates anthropological collection presents one of the rare cases in Serbia today that is still completely preserved and stored. The Faculty of Philosophy of the University of Belgrade, in the frame of its Archaeological Collection, formed the Anthropological Collection (Antropološka zbirka, not yet formally established), which consists mostly of the skeletal remains from the Iron Gates. Although, at the time, the collection was not formally established as a distinctive scientific unit, in 1998 an agreement was reached between the National Museum in Belgrade, the Archaeological Institute and the Faculty of Philosophy to bring together all the skeletal remains from the Iron Gates gorge. This agreement was facilitated by a Wenner-Gren grant that enabled cleaning, restoration and conservation of the remains and purchase of proper storage boxes (Roskandić, pers. comm.). Although the collection is divided into two separate units, the bioanthropological documentation is thoroughly collected and can be accessed upon request. The material is preserved and can be (though less often than desirable) accessible to other researchers.

Since the mid-1990s there has been an increased interest in reinterpreting and re-evaluating the Lepenski Vir culture. New generations of scholars have re-examined the basic data from the excavations in order to test Srejović's original conclusions. His final interpretation suggested that the culture of Lepenski Vir was an autochthonous manifestation of the Mesolithic in the region, without any relevant influences from (or contacts with) 'newcomers' (*cf.* Srejović 1979). But, two main questions remained uncertain: time (absolute dating) and people (their origin). Several thorough re-analyses of the material culture have been made so far (Antonović 2006; Borić 2002; Perić and Nikolić 2004; Radovanović 1996). Furthermore, different studies of the human bones have yielded valuable new data about the date and the palaeodemographic nature of the

Iron Gates gorge population in the Lepenski Vir culture. Thus, around 120 new AMS dates from the human bone samples settled the sensitive phase I/II (with trapezoidal buildings and sculpted boulders) right on the transitional Mesolithic/Neolithic period (Bonsall *et al.* 1997; Borić 2008). Several aspects of the anthropological series were examined (Roksandić 2000; Jackes *et al.* 2008; Roksandić *et al.* 2006) examining population structure, demography and violence in the series. A number of articles on stable isotopes and trace elements also examined the dietary patterns of the individuals comprising the assemblage. A relatively new method (strontium isotope analyses) applied to human bone samples suggested that at least some people at Vlasac and Lepenski Vir were not born in the Danube Gorges (Borić 2008: 21 *et pass*) (see Figure 35.3). The anthropological analysis combined with isotope analyses (Borić *et al.* 2004; Bonsall *et al.* 1997) has provided a more thorough picture of the changes occurring in the process of neolithization in the region.

This case study represents one of the better scenarios in Serbia, as the material has been preserved enabling researchers to use the series towards a better understanding of past human populations. The case study presented below shows a different, and unfortunately a not uncommon occurrence.

Case Study 2: Necropoli from the Imperial cities of Viminacium and Sirmium

Two important archaeological micro-regional areas of the Balkans from Roman times are Sirmium, which was the capital of the Roman province of Pannonia Inferior, and Viminacium, which was the ancient capital city of the province of Moesia Superior. The presence of both cities was archaeologically known by the end of the 19th century and the very first scientific explorations were conducted almost simultaneously on both sites in the middle of the 20th century.

More than 80 different archaeological sites at Sirmium have been documented so far. Among the imperial courts and palaces, a circus, temples and shrines, and other administrative and commercial buildings, several necropoli have been uncovered. In fact, graves have been found in approximately 50 sites belonging to different archaeological and historical periods, but only some were identified as Roman *senso stricto* (Miladinović, pers. comm.).[1] One of the burial sites,

Figure 35.3 Serbia: burial 32a from Lepenski Vir
Source: Archaeological Collection, the Belgrade University (after Borić 2008)

with around 60 individuals, was excavated and later scarcely analysed by S. Živanović (Milošević 2001; Popović 2003). After 50 years of archaeological excavations at Sirmium, where thousands of graves have been identified and explored, it is only in the last few years that appropriate anthropological studies have been undertaken on the collection, with important questions addressed including the palaeodemographic structure (cf. Miladinović 2005, 2006b, 2008).

Another case to point out is that relating to the necropoli of Viminacium, possibly the largest-ever excavated Roman graveyard in Europe. More than 13,000 individuals have been unearthed to date. Viminacium started as a military camp in the first century AD, and developed eco-nomically over the next few centuries due to its geopolitical position. At the beginning of the second century AD the emperor Hadrian promoted Viminacium to the level of *municipium*, and soon after it became the capital of Upper Moesia, one of the most important provinces of the Late Empire. After the rule of Gordian III, there was a mint in Viminacium. As a powerful commercial centre, from the fourth century onwards it became an archdiocese as well.

At the end of the 19th century M. Valtrović and M. Vasić started to investigate Viminacium's military camp. But it was not until the 1970s when archaeological excavations began in the area as a result of an initial plan in 1973 to build a thermo-electric power plant for which huge open-air coalmines had to be developed. The excavations have been running continuously until the present day. Although a number of graveyards have formed around the urban centre in almost 500 years, there are two sites that have been the most systematically explored southward from the city: Pećine and Više grobalja. More than 13,000 graves have been excavated and one third of these are cremation burials (M. Radović, pers. comm.). As far as the archaeological records demonstrate, very large cemeteries exist northward and westward from the city, as well. Therefore, the estimated quantity of buried individuals in the area considerably surpasses the quantity of 13,000 individuals. In this regard, the skeletal collections at Viminacium could be viewed as the largest anthropological series ever collected from a territory which once belonged to the Roman Empire. In addition, the earliest graves belong to the pre-Roman Celtic period (the site of Pećine), and there are also important series from the period of the 'Great Migration' (Gepids and Ostrogoths) as well as Mediaeval Slavic (11th to 16th centuries).

During the excavations, especially in the field seasons 1975–88, the system of preliminary anthropological recording was established. Only a few of anthropological observations (age, sex, obvious palaeopathological lesions) were conducted at the time. Some palaeodemographic and palaeosociological interpretations based on the findings from Viminacium have been conducted so far (cf. Mikić 1980b, 1988). Brief anthropological reports about each grave still exist, but the human remains were deliberately re-buried.[2]

Bearing in mind the many possibilities for re-analysing skeletal material using modern tech-niques, it is unfortunate to have missed such an opportunity on these remains. Several inter-esting questions have already arisen, such as the very heterogeneous palaeodemographic profile which included Europeans and Asians, people of African origin, military officers from Italy, and local Balkan tribes (cf. Mikić 1980b), pathology, diet, ancient medicine and surgery. Unfortunately, these questions are now unable to be answered with regard to the skeletal material.

Forensic anthropology in Serbia

Although forensic pathologists in Serbia still play the most authoritative role in forensic cases, physical anthropologists (medical doctors from the Laboratory for Anthropology, School of Medicine) are increasingly involved in the forensic application of their expertise. When unmarked burials or human skeletal remains are found as a result of building construction, agricultural activities or accidentally, the police (under the authority of the District Court) are notified and take the remains to the Department of Forensic Medicine. The first job of the anthropologist is to suggest if the remains are archaeological or of forensic (medico-legal) significance. Clear distinction between these two categories is not stated in the current legal documents, so it is up to a court to estimate the potential forensic importance of each case. The question addressed to anthropologists is related to estimation of time since death and requires (in addition to knowledge of a variety of factors influencing the process of decomposition) careful examination of the remains for the presence of soft tissue, the state of soft tissue preservation, the characteristics of bones including weight, colour, humidity, the amount of grease or adipocere remaining, sun bleaching and cracking, etc. Of course, any personal effects and any other evidence such as dental fillings are considered. Anthropologists are expected to make a skeletal inventory, to assess age, sex, ancestry, stature, and other distinguishing characteristics of the individual, as well as to assess the presence of any ante-mortem, peri-mortem or post-mortem trauma on the skeleton. Thus, the anthropologists (since they are medically trained) may assist the pathologist in the determination of cause and manner of death. In the past decade the remains of more than 100 unknown individuals were examined in the Forensic Department of the School of Medicine in Belgrade, involving the participation of anthropologists. The majority of contemporary cases have been identified using biological profiles made by anthropologists and DNA data extracted in the Forensic Department's recently founded DNA laboratory.

The investigation of mass graves in the former Yugoslavia has been conducted within a nexus of forensic, humanitarian, and political challenges and has included many Serbian experts. Involvement of physical anthropologists in practical forensic work brought new professional requirements, particularly in mass grave exhumations. Working as part of a forensic team presented its own challenge and implied that, besides the traditional knowledge of osteology, anthropologist had to deal with considerable issues of taphonomy, radiology, DNA analysis, surveying and remote sensing techniques, international law, human rights, etc. Our forensic work started in Kosovo in 1998, at the beginning of the Kosovo crisis, when during the conflict between the Serb Security Forces and the Kosovo Liberation Army the police discovered corpses in an advanced state of decomposition in the region between the villages of Glođane and Jablanica. For the first time in Serbia, a forensic team was formed comprised of three forensic pathologists and one anthropologist (MD) from the School of Medicine, University of Belgrade.

ARCHAEOLOGICAL HUMAN REMAINS AND LEGISLATION

Archaeological legislation

In Serbia practically there is no legal regulation specific to the treatment of ancient human remains. Regulations in the 'Law of Cultural Goods' (formally accepted in 1996, and still in use) mention only indirectly 'remains of ... the grave findings and others' (Article 20), defining the archaeological site (Kljaić and Kljaić 1996: 17). This means that practically any human remains in any state of preservation (skeletal or otherwise), even those that are very ancient and significant for understanding the human past, are not to be observed as a sort of cultural heritage. Mention of 'the grave findings and others' in the context of legal treatment of archaeological work only really refers to grave artefacts.

Central Serbian institutions dedicated to the protection of the cultural heritage in the area of archaeology are the National Museum in Belgrade (movable cultural objects), and the Institute for the Protection of Cultural Monuments of Serbia (non-movable objects). Besides these two, more than 170 regional/local museums and 15 regional/local institutes for the protection of cultural monuments exist. Another legal document (Kljaić and Kljaić 1996: 151–57) strictly defines the responsibilities and tasks of the museums and institutes, according to 'the sort of art and history objects and the territorial aspects'. In spite of the fact that any single type of artefact and/or natural object is listed specifically, neither the National Museum in Belgrade, nor the Ethnographical Museum (or at least the Museum of Natural History) is responsible for ancient human remains. Only if we strive to clarify the strict definition of the National Museum's responsibilities could we find the formulation 'documentary materials'.[3]

Although the actual law is not old (about a decade at the time of writing), the majority of Serbian professionals are not satisfied with it. As far as the present authors are aware, several versions of a new (and more modern) law dealing with the protection of cultural heritage have been written; but none of those versions offers an accurate vision of the treatment of the human material remains from the past. Even if the standards from European legal praxis and UNESCO's documents are taken into account, cultural heritage is usually artefact-based.

HUMAN REMAINS AND LEGISLATION

The only possible legislative regulations that could treat ancient human remains (indirectly) are found in the current 'Law of the Graveyards'; but in this law there is no mention of archaeologically discovered remains, or, at least, remains 'from the past'.

There is no special legal regulation related to basic practical questions of the archaeological recovery of human remains. For example, when an archaeological team wishes to excavate a graveyard a written project has to be submitted to the Ministry of Culture with all required general conditions satisfied. A permanent special commission estimates the proposal and gives written authorization for the excavation to take place with all conditions precisely listed. However, the conditions that applicants should fulfil are fairly general, with no specific reference to the 'nature' of the archaeological site to be excavated (e.g., building, graveyard).

Having had the opportunity to look at one of the authorizations, the present authors found the following: 'Authors are due to follow all the procedures and methodology of a scientific excavation … with field expertise including a physical anthropologist … and, to ensure further anthropological analysis of skeletal (and other) material' [authors' translation]. Furthermore, the archaeologists must 'send a final report to the Ministry'. However, what would happen if all artefacts are analysed and systematized and the final report is sent, but the anthropological analysis has not been completed yet? Practically, nothing. We assume that the reason for this is that human remains from the legal point of view are not classed as artefacts, and so, indirectly, they are not part of the cultural heritage. No museum or institution is going to ensure that the analysis of human remains is undertaken, so, in the end, it is down to the researcher's personal interest and responsibility to figure out the fate of excavated human material.

This reflects that the physical remains of humans from the Serbian past remain 'isolated' from the analysis, treatment, and preservation of the cultural heritage.

METHODS OF ANTHROPOLOGICAL ANALYSIS

Recovery of human remains from forensic contexts

Positive experience in regarding strategy and methodology used by archaeologists has stimulated forensic professionals to include a small group of skilled archaeologists in their multidisciplinary teams. The discovery of a large mass grave (five grave pits) near Batajnica, a few miles northwest of Belgrade, led in 2001 and 2002 to the authors' [M.D. and S.A.] involvement in the exhumation, analysis and identification of the deceased. The recovery operation of the remains was challenging due to the complexity of site, the large number of bodies and body parts, the commingling of remains, partial burning and the presence of a large quantity of artefacts. Valuable help and assistance was provided by archaeologists and monitors from the International Commission on Missing Persons (ICMP). In addition, in 2001, an exhumation was conducted in the mass grave on the north bank of Derventa River close to its junction with Lake Perućac, near Bajina Bašta in western Serbia. The investigation at the site was conducted by military pathologists from Belgrade Military Medical Academy, and assistance in forensic anthropology was provided by one of the present authors [M.D.].

Based on these experiences, a study has been provided to compare two basic methods of mass grave excavation, the 'pedestal' and 'stratigraphic' methods, in order to define which method allows for the exhumation of more complete bodies and recovery of the smaller bones that invariably become disarticulated and lost in the soil matrix during excavation (Tuller and Djurić 2006). It is now recommended that, when planning an excavation, the stratigraphic method should be preferred if circumstances allow.

Anthropological analysis in the laboratory

The role of the forensic anthropologist in these cases was to confirm if the remains were human, the minimum number of individuals, their sex, approximate age, and stature (Skinner *et al.* 2003). Special attention was paid to dental characteristics and skeletal traces of diseases suffered in life that could be used to help identify the victims. Therefore, a lot of radiographies, including panoramic radiography, were taken and analysed in the radiology department at the School of Dentistry. All this experience profoundly influenced the research interest of the Laboratory for Anthropology at the School of Medicine, University of Belgrade, for almost an entire decade. Identification of victims provided an opportunity for the forensic anthropologists to evaluate their *post-mortem* findings of classical markers of identity in comparison with ante-mortem information.

Although it became evident that identification of mortal remains from mass graves was moving away from a reliance on classical markers of identity (particularly age-at-death, sex, stature, dental status, pathology and personal effects) to a DNA-based system, in order to help courts and families to accept a formal, legal decision of identity, the comparison of classical anthropological markers of identity to a DNA-based identification has been necessary. While, theoretically, there should be good correspondence between the two methods of identification, in some instances the results may differ as a function of both the quality of ante-mortem data and the methodological weaknesses of classical markers of identity. Several studies were conducted in order to evaluate the reliability of classical anthropological methods in forensic work (Djurić 2004; Djurić *et al.* 2005, 2007a, 2007b). It was demonstrated that sex determination from pelvic bones was very reliable, as were age-at-death estimates from pelvic (Suchey's and Brooks's method) and rib standards (İşcan's method) for young to middle-aged adults. The uncertainty intervals for age-at-death in older adults underlined the need to create local population-specific standards. Stature was assessed using all limb bones, with ultimate reliance being placed on the femur plus the tibia or fibula and applying the formulae of Trotter and Gleser (1958). With a broader uncertainty interval of ±5cm, a 76.6 per cent reliability was reached.

Of all identification markers, dental status performed most poorly due to the lack of ante-mortem data. Finally, the frequency of post-mortem tooth loss was analysed relative to post-mortem interval in several skeletal samples, excavation methods, age distribution, and presence of bone loss associated with periodontal disease (Djurić *et al.* 2004). The results indicate that the degree of alveolar bone loss significantly affected both ante-mortem and post-mortem tooth loss and that the frequency of post-mortem tooth loss has the strongest correlation to time since death.

CONCLUSION

Anthropology in Serbia has had apparently no systematic development in either a scientific or an educational sense. In the period after the Second World War, the discipline was under ideological pressures stemming from the local political context, but later it received the influence of German and then British and American anthropological schools. The abundance of skeletal material from archaeological sites, and recently from the forensic context due to the presence of political conflict in the 1990s, created the opportunity to analyse large skeletal series, and to form research teams that gained considerable experience. The development of physical anthropology in Serbia was based on the enthusiasm of individual researchers. However, the lack of a proper place for anthropology in the educational system, as well as the poor legal regulation in relation to skeletal remains, has led to a series of flaws in anthropological work. Moreover, the discipline does not provide a promising outlook for young researchers seeking employment or research funding in the future. Our opinion is that establishing an institution that specializes in physical anthropological research in Serbia will be beneficial for further development of the discipline, particularly in terms of creating a working environment promoting a thorough biocultural approach in the interpretation of skeletal remains.

USEFUL CONTACTS

Republicki zavod za zastitu spomenika kulture (Institute for the Protection of Cultural Monuments of Serbia), Radoslava Grujica 11, 11000 Beograd, Yugoslavia. Tel. (+ 381) 11 2454 786; fax (+ 381) 11 344 1430. Website: www.heritage.sr.gov.yu/

National Museum in Belgrade, Trg Republike 1a, 11000 Beograd. Tel. (+381) 11 33 060 00; fax (+381) 11 2627 721; email: pr@narodnimuzej.rs. Website: www.narodnimuzej.rs/code/navigate.php?Id=1/

Anthropological Society of Serbia (Antropološko društvo Srbije). Website: www.antropoloskod rustvosrbije.com/odrustvu.html/

Laboratory for Anthropology, Department of Anatomy

School of Medicine, University of Belgrade. Tel. (+381) 11 26 86 172; fax (+381) 11 26 86 172; email: anthropologylab.bg@gmail.com; marijadjuric5@gmail.com. Website: www.anthropology lab-bg.com//

NOTES

1 N. Miladinović is a bioanthropologist who is conducting a wide-ranging study of skeletal remains from Sirmium.

2 This information was also obtained from upcoming anthropologist M. Radović who has explained that, as far as she is aware, after the basic anthropological analysis had finished, all the bones were reburied in a huge collective pit.

3 As the official lawyer from the National Museum in Belgrade explained to the authors, human skeletal remains could be recognized as 'documentary material'.

BIBLIOGRAPHY

Antonović, D. (2006) *Stone Tools from Lepenski Vir*, Cahiers des Portes de Fer Monographies 5, Belgrade: Institute of Archaeology.

Bonsall, C., Lennon, R., McSweeney, K., *et al.* (1997) 'Mesolithic and early Neolithic in the Iron Gates: a palaeodietary perspective', *Journal of European Archaeology*, 5: 50–92.

Bonsall, C., Cook, G., Lennon, R., *et al.* (2000) 'Stable isotopes, radiocarbon and the Mesolithic-Neolithic transition in the Iron Gate', *Documenta Praehistorica*, 27: 119–32.

Bonsall, C., Cook, G., Hedges, R., *et al.* (2004) 'Radiocarbon and stable isotope evidence of dietary changes from the Mesolithic to the Middle Ages in the Iron Gates: new results from Lepenski Vir', *Radiocarbon*, 46: 293–300.

Borić, D. (2002) 'The Lepenski Vir conundrum: reinterpretation of the Mesolithic and Neolithic sequences in the Danube Gorges', *Antiquity*, 76: 1026–39.

——(2008) 'Kultura Lepenskog Vira u svetlu novih istraživanja (The Lepenski Vir Culture in the Light of New Research)', *Glasnik SAD*, 24: 9–48.

Borić, D., Grupe, G., Peters, J., *et al.* (2004) 'Is the Mesolithic-Neolithic subsistence dichotomy real? New stable isotope evidence from the Danube Gorges', *European Journal of Archaeology*, 7: 221–48.

Đorđević, T. (1909) 'Neznano groblje u Žagubici', *Starinar za 1908*: 161–71.

Djurić-Srejić, M. (1995) *Uvod u fizičku antropologiju drevnih populacija*, Beograd: Zavod za udžbenike i nastavna sredstva.

Djurić, M. (2004) 'Anthropological data in individualization of skeletal remains from a forensic context in Kosovo – a case history', *Journal of Forensic Science*, 49: 464–68.

Djurić, M., Rakočević, Z. and Tuller, H. (2004) 'Factors affecting postmortem tooth loss', *Journal of Forensic Science*, 49: 1313–18.

Djurić, M., Rakočević, Z. and Đonić, D. (2005) 'The reliability of sex determination of skeletons from forensic context in the Balkans', *Forensic Science International*, 147: 159–64.

Djurić, M., Đonić, D., Nikolić, S., *et al.* (2007a) 'Evaluation of the Suchey–Brooks method for aging skeletons in the Balkans', *Journal of Forensic Science*, 52: 21–23.

Djurić, M., Dunjić, D., Đonić, D., *et al.* (2007b) 'Identification of victims from two mass-graves in Serbia: a critical evaluation of classical markers of identity', *Forensic Science International*, 172: 125–29.

Farkas, Gy. and Liptak, P. (1971) 'Antropološka istraživanje nekropole u Mokrinu iz ranog bronzanog doba', in M. Girić (ed.) *Mokrin II. Dissertations and Monographies XI*, Beograd: SADJ.

Institute of Anatomy, University of Belgrade (2006) *Anthropology Lab Belgrade*. Available online at www.anthropologylab-bg.com/ (accessed 26 March 2010).

Jackes, M., Roksandic, M. and Meiklejohn, C. (2008) 'The Demography of the Djerdap Mesolithic/Neolithic Transition', in C. Bonsall, I. Radovanović and V. Boroneanţ (eds) *Iron Gates Gorge in the Mesolithic: New Perspectives*, Oxford: Archaeopress.

Jovanović, B. (2004) 'Padina and Hajdučka Vodenica: Sites of the Lepenski Vir Culture in the upper and lower Gorges of the Iron Gates', in Secrétariat du Congrès (ed.) *Section 7: Le Mésolithique/The Mesolithic … Acts of the XIVth UISPP Congress, University of Liège, Belgium, 2–8 September 2001*, Oxford: Archaeopress.

Kljaić, M. and Kljaić, Nj. (1996) *Pravni sistem zaštite kulturnih dobara u Srbiji* [Legal System of the Protection of Cultural Goods in Serbia]', Belgrade: Službeni glasnik.

Mikić, Ž. (1980a) 'O antropološkim tipovima u antičkim nekropolama Viminacijuma', *Starinar*, 31: 117–22.

——(1980b) 'Anthropologische Typen der Djerdap (Eisernen-Tor)-Serie', in J.K. Kozlowski and J. Machnik (eds) *Problémes de la néolithisation dans certaines régions de l'Europe*, Krakow: Polska Akademia Nauk, Oddizial w Krakowie.

——(1988) 'Rezultati epigenetske obrade masovnog groba broj 4924 sa antičkog Viminacijuma (Stari Kostolac)', *Glasnik Antropološkog društva Jugoslavije*, 25: 19–34.

Miladinović, N. (2005) 'Paledemografska struktura i problematika srednjovekovne nekropole u Sremskoj Mitrovici', unpublished MA thesis, Faculty of Philosophy, University of Belgrade.

——(2006a) *Metodologija utvrđivanja polne pripadnosti skeleta sa arheoloških nalazišta*, Sremska Mitrovica: Blago Sirmijuma.

——(2006b) 'Fizičko-antropološka analiza osteološkog materijala iz germanskih grobova sa lokaliteta 85 u Sremskoj Mitrovici', *Glasnik SAD*, 22: 409–34.

——(2008) 'Polna i starosna struktura dečijih individua sahranjenih na srednjovekovnoj nekropoli na lokalitetu 85 u Sremskoj Mitrovici', *Glasnik SAD*, 24: 445–56.

Milošević, P. (2001) *Arheologija i istorija Sirmijuma*, Novi Sad: Matica srpska.

Nemeskéri, J. (1969) 'Stanovništvo Lepenskog Vira', in D. Srejović (ed.) *Lepenski Vir*, Beograd: Srpska književna zadruga.

Nemeskéri, J. and Lengyel, I. (1978) 'The results of paleopathological examinations', in M. Garašanin (ed.) *Vlasac 2. Geology – Biology – Anthropology*, Belgrade: Serbian Academy of Sciences and Arts.

Nemeskéri, J. and Szathmary, L. (1978a) 'Anthroposcopic and epigenetic variation', in M. Garašanin (ed.) *Vlasac 2. Geology – Biology – Anthropology*, Belgrade: Serbian Academy of Sciences and Arts.

——(1978b) 'Analysis of the variation of quantitative traits', in M. Garašanin (ed.) *Vlasac 2. Geology – Biology – Anthropology*, Belgrade: Serbian Academy of Sciences and Arts.

——(1978c) 'Taxonomical structure of the Vlasac Mesolithic population', in M. Garašanin (ed.) *Vlasac 2. Geology – Biology – Anthropology*, Belgrade: Serbian Academy of Sciences and Arts.

——(1978d) 'Methodics Applied in the Research of the Vlasac Mesolithic Anthropological Series', in M. Garašanin (ed.) *Vlasac 2. Geology – Biology – Anthropology*, Belgrade: Serbian Academy of Sciences and Arts.

Perić, S. and Nikolić, D. (2004) 'Stratigraphic, cultural and chronological characteristics of the pottery from Lepenski Vir – 1965 Excavations', in S. Perić (ed.) *The Central Pomoravlje in Neolithization of South-East Europe. The Neolithic in the Middle Morava Valley* 1, Belgrade: Archaeological Institute.

Popović, V. (2003) *Sirmium – grad careva i mučenika. Sabrani radovi o arheologiji i istoriji Sirmijuma*, Sremska Mitrovica: Blago Sirmijuma.

Radovanović, I. (1996) *The Iron Gates Mesolithic*, Archaeological Series 11, Ann Arbor: International Monographs in Prehistory.

Roksandić, M. (1999) 'Transition from Mesolithic to Neolithic in the Iron Gates gorge: Physical anthropology perspective', unpublished PhD thesis, Simon Fraser University.

——(2000) 'Between foragers and farmers in the Iron Gates Gorge: physical anthropology perspective. Djerdap population in transition from Mesolithic to Neolithic', *Documenta Praehistorica*, 27: 1–100.

Roksandić, M., Djurić, M., Rakočević, Z., *et al.* (2006) 'Interpersonal violence at Lepenski Vir Meso-lithic/Neolithic complex of the Iron Gates Gorge (Serbia-Romania)', *American Journal of Physical Anthropology*, 129: 339–48.

Skinner, M., Alempijević, Đ. and Djurić, M. (2003) 'Guidelines for international forensic bio-archaeology monitors of mass grave exhumations', *Forensic Science International*, 134: 81–92.

Srejović, D. (1969) *Lepenski Vir – nova praistorijska kultura u Podunavlju*, Beograd: Srpska književna zadruga.

——(1973) *Lepenski Vir. Eine vorgeshichtlishe Geburtsstätte europäischer Kultur*, Bergisch Gladbach: Nomen.

——(1979) 'Protoneolit – kultura Lepenskog vira', in A. Benac (ed.) *Praistorija jugoslavenskih zemalja* II, Sarajevo: 'Svjetlost' and ANU BiH.

Srejović, D. and Letica, Z. (1978) *Vlasac. Mezolitsko naselje u Đerdapu I: arheologija*, Belgrade: Serbian Academy of Sciences and Arts.

Stefanović, S. (2000) 'Arheološki istražene i antropološki obrađene nekropole na tlu Srbije', unpublished MA thesis, University of Belgrade.

——(2007) 'Nalaz fosilne lobanje iz 1890. godine – beogradski neandertalac?', *Petničke sveske (Petnica Papers)*, 62: 58–65.

Trotter, M. and Gleser, G.C. (1958) 'A re-evaluation of estimation of stature based on measurements of stature taken during life and of long bones after death', *American Journal of Physical Anthropology*, 16(1), 79–123.

Tuller, H. and Djurić, M. (2006) 'Keeping the pieces together: Comparison of mass grave excavation methodology', *Forensic Science International*, 156: 192–200.

Živanović, S. (1975a) 'Mesolithic population in Đerdap region', *Balcanica*, 6: 1–9.

——(1975b) 'Note on the anthropological characteristics of the Padina population', *Zeitschrift für Morphologie und Anthropologie*, 66: 161–75.

——(1976) 'Cromagnon in the Iron Gate Gorge of the Danube', *Nature*, 260: 518.

——(1982) *Ancient Diseases: The Elements of Palaeopathology*, London: Methuen.

Slovakia/Slovenská Republika

Radoslav Beňuš, Soňa Masnicová, Zuzana Obertová and
Drahoslav Hulínek

INTRODUCTION: A BRIEF HISTORY AND CURRENT STATE OF PHYSICAL ANTHROPOLOGY IN SLOVAKIA

Human skeletal remains represent frequent finds in archaeological research. Skeletal remains in Slovakia are most frequently found in the form of inhumations in graves from the Stone Age to modern times. During the Early and Late Bronze Age, however, the prevailing burial practice was for cremated remains. In addition, artificially worked bones are rare but very valued finds at archaeological sites. Such bones may have served as cult objects as was most probably the case with the Bronze Age cult mask made from the facial region of a human skull from the site of Silica, Majda-Hraškova Cave (Furmánek *et al.* 1991: 293; Vlček and Kukla 1959). A special type of anthropological find is attributed to religious practices in the form of human sacrifices, and possibly cannibalism. The evidence for such practices has been found in settlements, for instance in a Bronze Age cult pit near the entrance to the fortification in Spišský Štvrtok (Jakab 1978) or cult objects from the settlements Nižná Myšla (Bronze Age) (Furmánek and Vladár 1995; Furmánek *et al.* 1991: 293–94; Jakab *et al.* 1999; Vladár 1977) and Smolenice-Molpír (Hallstatt Period) (Dušek 1974; Dušek and Dušek 1984). Skeletal burials can also be encountered within houses or in their close proximity. There are also some prehistoric sites with non-piously interred human bodies with signs of cuts and blows that might sometimes be related to cannibalism (Ambros 1971; Furmánek *et al.* 1991: 294).

Some finds of human remains in archaeological contexts can be related to unexpected or catastrophic death without ensuing burial. One such find is the travertine casting of the neurocranium of a Proto-Neanderthal (105,000 BC) from Gánovce near Poprad (Vlček 1955; Vlček 1958). Another example of these finds is the skeletal remains of victims of wars and interpersonal conflicts. The latter group consists of skeletal remains of victims killed as a result of a military or other conflict. In recent years, archaeological surveys have focused mainly on the exploration of battlefields of the First and Second World Wars (Beeman 2006; Bursa and Ušiak 2004).

Physical anthropology is a relatively young discipline in Slovakia. It was introduced in the period between the First and Second World Wars mainly by medical doctors (e.g., Zdenko Frankenberger and Alojz Ján Chura) who dedicated themselves to anthropological research. The first specialized institute was the Department of Anthropology and Genetics which was founded by Jindřich Antonín Valšík in 1957 at the Comenius University in Bratislava. At that time, research mainly focused on developmental anthropology and human variability. At present, the research interests cover a broader spectrum, including developmental anthropology, anthropological genetics, ergonomics, forensic anthropology and, last but not least, historical anthropology. The scientists specialized in the latter research topic are Milan Thurzo, Silvia Bodoriková and Radoslav Beňuš, in cooperation with Soňa Masnicová (Department of Criminalistics and Forensic Sciences, Police Academy of the Slovak Republic). Their research focuses mainly on population studies of skeletal remains from archaeological rescue excavations. Their research therefore covers conventional anthropological analyses including age and sex estimation of skeletal remains, as well as metric analysis, palaeopathology and kinship studies. Recently, an extensive project with a focus on the health status of Early Mediaeval populations (Beňuš *et al.* 1999; Bodoriková *et al.* 1999; Bodoriková and Urminský 2002; Masnicová and Beňuš 2001, 2003; Obertová and Thurzo 2008; Thurzo *et al.* 2002), and a project on the health status of sub-adults from the Bronze Age through to modern times were completed (Beňuš *et al.* 2008). The second anthropological facility in Bratislava was also founded by J. A. Valšík. In 1963 the Department of Anthropology of the Slovak National Museum (Slovenské národné múzeum) was established. The current director is Alena Šefčáková, and her research interests lie particularly in the field of palaeoanthropology (Sládek *et al.* 2002; Šefčáková *et al.* 2001; Velemínská *et al.* 2008).

Another anthropological research institute is the Archaeological Institute of the Slovak Academy of Sciences (Archeologický ústav Slovenskej akadémie vied, or AÚ SAV) in Nitra. At this institute, Emanuel Vlček started his career as an anthropologist in 1951. At that time, the institute was called the State Archaeological Institute and was located in Martin. During his work in Nitra, Vlček described the cast of the neurocranium of a classic *Homo neanderthalensis* as well as the frontal bone of the Neanderthal skull from Šaľa (Vlček 1955, 1958, 1968). At present, Július Jakab is the leading physical anthropologist at the Archaeological Institute (Jakab 1989; Jakab 2005; Jakab *et al.* 1999). In Nitra, there is also the Department of Zoology and Anthropology that was founded in 1995 at University of Constantine the Philosopher. Mária Vondráková, Monika Martiniaková and Branislav Kolena work here in the fields of physical anthropology, palaeopathology and osteology (Bauerová *et al.* 2007; Martiniaková *et al.* 2007).

Two of the smaller anthropological institutes are the Department of Biology at the University of Prešov and the Department of Biology and Ecology at Matej Bel University in Banská Bystrica. At the former, the research focuses mainly on the ethnogenesis, somatic characteristics and health of the Romani people. At the latter, Petra Selecká is active in the field of historic anthropology (Selecká 2006).

Among the mentioned academic facilities, only the Department of Anthropology of Comenius University in Bratislava offers specialized courses in skeletal anthropology. These are namely: anthropological methods including morphology, osteometrics, aging and sexing of human skeletal remains, estimation of ancestry, field research; as well as palaeopathology, human morphology, palaeoanthropology, dental anthropology and taphonomy.

Since 1966, the Slovak Anthropological Society (Slovenská antropologická spoločnost, or SAS) is active in Slovakia uniting anthropologists and experts from related disciplines, particularly medical doctors. Since 1998, the Society has published the journal *Slovenská antropológia* ('Slovak Anthropology').

ARCHAEOLOGICAL HUMAN REMAINS AND LEGISLATION

Archaeological legislation

An 'archaeological site' is defined by Article 2(6) of the Cultural Heritage Monuments Act No. 49/2002 Coll. (Zákon o ochrane pamiatkového fondu) as a topographically definable unit with surface or buried archaeological finds in their original archaeological context. Records on archaeological sites are kept by the Archaeological Institute of the Slovak Academy of Sciences in the Central Register of Archaeological Sites (Centrálna evidencia múzejných zbierkových predmetov) of the Slovak Republic. Consequently the Monuments Board and the Ministry of Culture (Ministerstvo kultúry) of the Slovak Republic can declare an archaeological site as a cultural heritage monument or cultural heritage area (Article 41(1) of the Cultural Heritage Monument Act No. 49/2002 Coll.).

Current Slovak legislation does not distinguish between the types of finds from archaeological sites, hence human skeletal remains are considered to be archaeological finds and are protected by the respective legislative. This is especially defined in Act No. 49/2002 Coll. On the protection of monuments and historic sites (hereafter as the 'Cultural Heritage Monuments Act') and Act No. 115/1998 Coll. On museums and art galleries and on the protection of objects of museum value and art gallery value.

According to Article 2(5) of the Cultural Heritage Monuments Act No. 49/2002 Coll., an archaeological find is any movable object or immovable feature that provides evidence of the life of mankind and related activities from the oldest era to modern times whether it is located in the earth, on the ground or underwater. According to Article 40(5) of the Cultural Heritage Monuments Act No. 49/2002 Coll., archaeological finds are in the ownership of the Slovak Republic. Article 2(6) regulates the protection of movable archaeological finds through Act No. 115/1998 Coll. on museums and galleries and on the protection of objects of museum value and art gallery value.

According to Article 2(2) of Act No. 115/1998 Coll. anthropological remains as well as other objects found at archaeological sites are objects of museum value that shall be professionally documented and maintained in a museum as museum collection objects. Article 11 of the Act No. 115/1998 Coll. distinguishes three types of museums: national, regional and local; but only national museums and the Slovak National Museum (established by the central body of the state administration, or the Ministry of Culture of the Slovak Republic) are allowed to acquire archaeological finds for their collections. This regulation is explained by the fact that regional museums established by self-governing regions and local museums established by municipalities cannot acquire archaeological finds, since these are in the property of the state (Article 4(5) of the Act No. 115/1998 Coll.).

In Appendix No. 5 of Act No. 115/1998 Coll. the categories of objects of museum value are listed and among these 'archaeological objects older than 50 years, which are products of excavations and troves in the ground or underwater, archaeological sites, archaeological collections' are listed. Hence skeletal remains older than 50 years old are classified as objects of museum value.

Archaeological excavation

Until 2009, 29 national and private organizations received an authorization for archaeological research by the Ministry of Culture of the Slovak Republic. The Monuments Board of the Slovak Republic and the Archaeological Institute of the Slovak Academy of Sciences in Nitra hold the dominant position in Slovakia. In the private sector, the dominant position is held by the Slovak Archaeological and Historical Institute or SAHI (Slovenský archeologický a historický inštitút). This organization conducts archaeological research both on Slovak territory and abroad.

Legal entities can obtain an authorization for archaeological excavation from the Ministry of Culture of the Slovak Republic if they ensure archaeological research through natural persons with special professional qualification (Article 36(3) of the Cultural Heritage Monuments Act No. 49/2002 Coll.). The qualification is defined by the Article 35(3–7) of the Cultural Heritage Monuments Act No. 49/2002 Coll. Specific conditions are stated in Article 35(5) of the Cultural Heritage Monuments Act No. 49/2002 Coll. where:

> A special professional qualification for the purposes of this Act can be obtained by a natural person with a university education in the respective field and through passing specialized exams that demonstrate theoretical and special professional knowledge on cultural heritage monuments and historic sites and who has at least three-year practice in the field of historic research and has no criminal record.
> *Article 35(5) of the Cultural Heritage Monuments Act No. 49/2002 Coll.*

The qualification in a respective field is regulated by Article 2(1) of Regulation No. 16/2003 Coll. implementing the Act on the protection of monuments and historic sites where 'Qualification in the respective field shall mean graduate level university education in the field of a) visual art history, b) architecture, c) urban planning, d) archaeology or e) any other related field completed by a final state examination.' The list of authorized natural persons is published by the Ministry of Culture in its official Journal (Article 35(8) of the Cultural Heritage Monuments Act No. 49/2002 Coll.). The Archaeological Committee acts as an advisory body in decisions of issuing authorization for archaeological research (Article 7 of the Cultural Heritage Monuments Act No. 49/2002 Coll.).

'Archaeological research' is defined in Article 36(1) of the Cultural Heritage Monuments Act No. 49/2002 Coll. as a set of professional activities aimed at searching for, identifying, documenting and preserving archaeological finds and archaeological sites, as well as searching for and collecting movable archaeological finds on the ground, in the earth or under the water. In practice, rescue excavation is a common type of archaeological research. This kind of research is regulated by Article 37 of the Cultural Heritage Monuments Act No. 49/2002 Coll.:

1   Rescue research must be carried out during the preparation for building constructions and other economic activities in areas where cultural heritage values and archaeological finds are likely to be endangered;
2   Rescue research is an advanced measure carried out to preserve archaeological and other historic finds anticipated on the ground, in the earth, under the water or within the structure of a building;
3   The Monuments Board shall decide on the necessity to carry out rescue research on a proposal by the building authority, the Regional Monuments Board or on its own initiative. In the case of rescue archaeological research, the Monuments Board shall issue a decision after the delivery of an opinion from the Archaeological Institute. The Monuments Board shall send the decision on conducting the archaeological research to the building authority without delay.
4   In cases where the builder or entity that shall execute the decision referred to in section 2 is unable for objective reasons to appoint an authorized person, the Ministry shall appoint the person authorized to carry out conservation on a proposal from the Monuments Board. If this concerns rescue archaeological research, the Monuments Board shall submit a proposal to the Ministry after receiving an opinion from the Archaeological Institute.

Before and during any research activities, the conditions for conducting an excavation shall be met according to Article 39 of the Cultural Heritage Monuments Act No. 49/2002 Coll. This

Article specifies the duties of the persons with an authorization to conduct archaeological research as well as of the owner of the immovable property. Article 39(4) of the Cultural Heritage Monuments Act No. 49/2002 Coll. states that research shall be carried out in accordance with respective international conventions, in compliance with contemporary scientific knowledge, and using suitable, preferably non-destructive, methods of investigation. Article 39(6) of the Cultural Heritage Monuments Act No. 49/2002 Coll. prohibits unauthorized research and excavation in cultural heritage monuments, in historic sites and sites with archaeological finds as well as unauthorized collection and relocation of movable finds or their search using metal detectors. Article 39(7) of the Cultural Heritage Monuments Act No. 49/2002 Coll. obliges any person carrying out a survey or an excavation to take measures to prevent damage, devaluation, destruction or theft of the finds. Article 39(8–9) of the Cultural Heritage Monuments Act No. 49/2002 Coll. obliges the involved persons to process the professional knowledge gained through the investigation in research and documentation. The contents of such documentation from archaeological research are regulated by Article 7(7) of Regulation No. 16/2003 Coll.

HUMAN REMAINS AND LEGISLATION

Any discovery of human skeletal remains, except for finds made during an ongoing archaeological investigation, should be reported to the police. The police will secure the place of discovery and provide for professional examination of the remains. The officers will subsequently contact a legal expert from the field of legal medicine, or less often from the field of anthropology. First of all, the expert will be asked to estimate the post-mortem interval (the time of death) of the individual. The context in which the remains are found should be taken into consideration in the decision on the forensic relevance of the find. A comprehensive anthropological analysis of the remains represents a crucial step in the estimation of the post-mortem interval as well as in the evaluation of the context in which the remains were found. The expert can also give advice on other natural scientific methods that can be applied either directly on the respective find or on other finds discovered within the same context. If the expert estimates the age of the remains to be more than 30 years old (the limitation period for crimes is 30 years; Article 87(1) of the Act No. 300/2005 Coll. The Criminal Code), the remains are transferred to legal entities that are authorized to conduct archaeological research (Article 36(2) of the Cultural Heritage Monuments Act No. 49/2002 Coll.).

In recent years, a great number of anthropological finds in Slovakia has been uncovered during rescue excavations. For instance, 80 graves from the La Tène period were uncovered during the rescue excavation due to the construction of the commercial centre in Levice (Nitra region) (Samuel 2007). During the rescue archaeological research in Nitra-Dolné Krškany, 18 objects, four graves and five skeletons in a cult pit dated to the Late Bronze Age were uncovered. The skeletons were placed in atypical positions, suggestive of human sacrifice (Ruttkay 2004; Jelínek 2007). The Slovak Archaeological and Historical Institute (SAHI) conducted a preliminary rescue archaeological excavation at the location of Vydrica in the vicinity of the Bratislava Castle. This research actually met the criteria of a systematic archaeological research since the location, from a scientific point of view, was explored to the maximum possible extent. Although the site was considered to be a settlement area, skeletal remains dated to the La Tène and Early Mediaeval period were uncovered (Štefanovičová et al. 2008).

In Slovakia, there is no legislative norm that would regulate the presence of an anthropologist at the location where human skeletal remains have been uncovered. Neither is the anthropologist obliged to write an anthropological report on skeletal remains from an archaeological excavation. In recent years, however, Slovak archaeologists are aware of the advantages resulting from the cooperation with anthropologists, particularly considering their presence during the excavation of human skeletal remains. Moreover, during the evaluation of the applications for conducting archaeological research the Archaeological Council takes into consideration if, in addition to the professional qualification of the natural persons, interdisciplinary cooperation, among others with an anthropologist, is included.

In addition to the forensically relevant finds of human skeletal remains the anthropologist is most commonly invited to excavations of skeletal remains within the scope of an archaeological intervention. After uncovering the skeletal remains, archaeologists clean the find for documentation purposes. After the archaeological documentation is finished the anthropologist provides advice on the excavation procedure considering the circumstances of the find and collection of all bones and ossified tissues. The presence of the anthropologist is particularly important in cases of multiple graves with commingled or superimposed skeletal remains. In such cases the experience of the anthropologist with skeletal remains can guarantee that individual bones are correctly assigned to respective individuals. According to Article 40(3) of the Cultural Heritage Monuments Act No. 49/2002 Coll., only an authorized person using methods of archaeological research shall collect and relocate an archaeological find from its original context.

Skeletal remains from archaeological sites are defined as objects of museum value (Act No. 115/1998 Coll.), hence their export is regulated by Article 16 of this Act. According to this Article, export of a collection object can be permanent or temporary. For the purpose of anthropological analysis, presentation, exhibition, scientific research and restoration of human skeletal remains from Slovak archaeological sites, a temporary export may be allowed for the duration of three years (Article 16(2) of the Act No. 115/1998 Coll.). According to this Article, the permission for temporary export of a collection object (see section below) is issued by the institution or by the archaeologist who discovered the find. Objects from archaeological sites, including human skeletal remains, are owned by the central body of the public administration, or the Ministry of Culture of the Slovak Republic. According to Article 16(9) of the Act No. 115/1998 Coll., a museum or gallery is obliged to obtain insurance, or to provide other guarantees that are necessary to prevent destruction, damage or theft of the collection object for the duration of the temporary export, and to ensure the eventual return of the collection object to its institution of origin.

A proforma of the application form for permission of temporary export of a collection object is given in Appendix 4 of Act No. 94/2008 Coll., amending Act No. 115/1998 Coll. on museums and galleries and on protection of objects of museum or gallery value as amended by later regulations.

In addition to national legislation, the export of cultural goods outside the EU is regulated by the Council Regulation (EEC) No. 3911/92 and the Commission Regulation (EEC) No. 752/93 on the export of cultural goods.

Curation of human remains in museums

The protection of archaeological finds is regulated by the Act No.115/1998 Coll. Article 23 says that the Ministry shall issue generally binding legal regulations that establish details of the professional administration of collection specimens. This obligation was fulfilled by the Ministry of Culture by issuing Regulation No. 342/1998 Coll. on professional administration in museum and gallery collections. According to Article 1, this Regulation lists details of: a) professional administration of museum collection objects and gallery collection objects (hereafter, 'collection objects'); and b) protection of collection objects in case of emergency events and during a period of armed readiness of the state. Article 4 of Act No. 115/1998 Coll. regulates the acquisition of collection objects; Article 5 the chronological record keeping of collection objects; and Article 6 the cataloguing of collection objects. According to Article 7(1) of the Regulation No. 342/1998 Coll., a museum or gallery is also allowed to keep professional records in electronic form. In 2003, the Central Register of Museum Collection Items (CEMUZ) has been introduced (CEMUZ 2010) and is coordinated by the Slovak National Museum.

Protection and security of buildings and premises where collection objects are deposited is defined in Article 9 of Regulation No. 342/1998 Coll. Article 10 of Regulation No. 342/1998 Coll. regarding professional protection of collection objects, stating that a museum shall provide for basic treatment, conservation, preservation and restoration of a collection object immediately after its acquisition. According to Article 10(2) of Regulation No. 342/1998 Coll., any professional treatment and conservation of a collection object shall be documented by photography and script, and this shall include: a) the forename and surname of the person who carried out the professional treatment; b) the method and procedure of conservation, preservation and restoration; and c) the date of treatment, and the signature of the person that carried out the professional treatment. Article 11 of the Regulation No. 342/1998 Coll. defines the professional location of collection objects in depositories, as well as the necessary structural, climatic, technical and security equipment for individual types of material groups. The museum director is authorized to organize the operation of the depository, the system of acquisition, exclusion, deposition and administration of collection objects, as well as access to the depository. According to Article 11(5) of the Regulation No. 342/1998 Coll., any collection object shall be kept under an individual registration number that consists of a characterizing letter, sequence number and the year of deposition. Registers are balanced by the year-end by giving the count of collection objects, and signed by the employee in charge.

Temporary transfer of collection objects is regulated by Article 12(1) of Regulation No. 342/1998 Coll. stating that collection objects may be temporarily transferred for the purposes of: a) examination by an expert and scientific evaluation, b) professional treatment, c) presentation, particularly exposition and exhibition, d) cultural and educational activities, e) study and scientific research. For the duration of the transfer, protection and security of the collection object shall be guaranteed. All necessary measures shall be taken to prevent damage, devaluation, loss, theft or exchange of collection objects (Article 12(4) of Regulation No. 342/1998 Coll.).

METHODS OF ANTHROPOLOGICAL ANALYSIS

Age-at-death is estimated using multiple indicators, including dental development (Ubelaker 1987), dental attrition (Lovejoy 1985), suture closure (Masset 1989; Meindl and Lovejoy 1985), and morphological changes of the pubic symphysis and the iliac auricular surface (Hanihara and Suzuki 1978; Lovejoy *et al.* 1985). In general, the European recommendations of Ferembach *et al.* (1979) are followed in the estimation of age-at-death.

The sex of the individuals is determined using dimorphic features of the pelvis, cranium and long bones (Acsádi and Nemeskéri 1970; Brůžek 2002; Černý and Komenda 1980; Ferembach *et al.* 1979; İşcan and Derrick 1984; Loth and Henneberg 1996; Phenice 1969).

For palaeodemographic analysis, life tables are constructed following Hermann *et al.* (1990).

The methods for recording metric and non-metric traits are derived from the standard publications on physical anthropology (Buikstra and Ubelaker 1994; Dobisíková *et al.* 1999; Hauser and De Stefano 1989; Herrmann *et al.* 1990; Knussmann *et al.* 1988; Martin and Saller 1957;

Piontek 1985). Stature in adults is currently estimated according to Sjøvold (1990), although in older publications the authors followed Manouvrier (1894), Breitinger (1937) and Bach (1965).

In general, pathological conditions are identified following Ortner and Putschar (2003) and Aufderheide and Rodriguez-Martin (1998). In case of some pathological lesions, such as osteoarthrosis (Schultz 1988), specialized publications are consulted.

CONCLUSION

In Slovakia, there is no special legislative act that regulates the handling of human skeletal remains from archaeological sites. Similarly, there is no law that regulates the presence of the anthropologist on site during an archaeological excavation of human remains. Consequently, there is no obligation to conduct anthropological analysis or to include an anthropological report to the archaeological documentation. From the legislative perspective, human skeletal remains from archaeological sites are archaeological finds (according to Act No. 49/2002), or objects of museum value (according to Act No. 115/1998 Coll.). Additional relevant acts are: Act No. 387/2001 amending Act No. 115/1998 Coll. on museums and galleries and on the protection of objects that are of value to a museum or gallery, and the amendment of Act No. 563/1991 Coll. on accounting as amended by later regulations; Act No. 94/2008 Coll. amending Act No. 115/1998 Coll. on museums and galleries and on the protection of objects of value for museums or galleries as amended by later regulations as well as implementing Regulations No. 342/1998 Coll. on the professional administration of specimens or objects from museum and gallery collections, and the Regulation No. 16/2003 Coll. implementing the act on the protection of cultural heritage monuments. Slovakia as a member state of the European Union also follows the revised version of the European Convention on the Protection of Archaeological Heritage (Valletta, 16 January 1992). For the Slovak Republic, this Convention came into effect on 1 May 2001 based on the Article 14(5) published in the Collection of Laws of the Slovak Republic Article 141, No. 344/2001.

Temporary export of osteological material is nationally regulated by the Act No. 115/1998 Coll. and the Act No. 94/2008 Coll., as well as internationally by the Council Regulation (EEC) No. 3911/92 and the Commission Regulation (EEC) No. 752/93 on the export of cultural goods.

USEFUL CONTACTS

Department of Anthropology, Comenius University (Bratislava). Website:
www.fns.uniba.sk/fileadmin/user_upload/editors/biol/kan/uvodna.html/ (in Slovak); www.
    fns.uniba.sk/?about/; www.fns.uniba.sk/index.php?id=2362/
Department of Zoology and Anthropology, Constantine the Philosopher University (Nitra).
    Website: www.kza.fpv.ukf.sk/ (in Slovak); www.en.ukf.sk/
Department of Biology and Ecology, Matej Bel University (Banská Bystrica). Website: http://
    vzdelavanie.fpv.umb.sk/bioeko/ (in Slovak); www.umb.sk/index.php?module=articles&
    id=238&language=2/
Department of Biology, University of Prešov (Prešov). Website: www.unipo.sk/
Department of Criminalistics and Forensic Sciences, Police Academy of the Slovak Republic
    (Bratislava). Website: www.akademiapz.sk/index.php?articleID=1005/ (in Slovak)

Slovak National Museum. Website: www.snm.sk/?lang=eng&section=home&org=0/
Archaeological Institute of Slovak Academy of Sciences. Website: www.archeol.sav.sk/
Slovak Archaeological and Historical Institute. Website: www.sahi.sk/
Slovenská antropológia (journal of the Slovak Anthropological Society) – abstracts in English.
   Website: www.fns.uniba.sk/fileadmin/user_upload/editors/biol/kan/slovenska_antropologia.html/
The Ministry of Culture of the Slovak Republic. Website: www.culture.gov.sk/en/
The Monuments Board of the Slovak Republic. Website: www.pamiatky.sk/pamiatky/en/

BIBLIOGRAPHY

Acsádi, G. and Nemeskéri, J. (1970) *History of Human Life Span and Mortality*, Budapest: Akadémiai Kiadó.
Ambros, C. (1971) 'Ein Beitrag zur Frage der Anthropophagie in den bronzezeitlichen Siedlungen der Slowakei', *Acta Facultatis Rerum Naturalium Universitatis Comenianae – Anthropologia*, 17: 1–14.
Aufderheide, A.C. and Rodriguez-Martín, C. (1998) *The Cambridge Encyclopedia of Human Paleopathology*, Cambridge: Cambridge Universty Press.
Bach, H. (1965) 'Zur Berechnung der Körperhöhe aus den langen Glidmassenknochen weiblicher Skelette', *Anthropologischer Anzeiger*, 29: 12–21.
Bauerová, M., Luptáková, L., Omelka, R., *et al.* (2007) 'The state of bone preservation is related to successful genetic sex determination of medieval skeletal remains from Dubovany cemetery, Slovakia', *American Journal of Physical Anthropology*, 132 (Supplement): 44.
Beeman, L.A. (2006) *Autentický denník stíhacieho pilota z II. svetovej vojny (The Authentic Diary of the Fighter Pilot from WW II)*, Banská Bystrica: Press group.
Beňuš, R., Masnicová, S. and Lietava, J. (1999) 'Intentional cranial vault deformation in a Slavonic population from the medieval cemetery in Devín (Slovakia)', *International Journal of Osteoarchaeology*, 9: 267–70.
Beňuš, R., Masnicová, S., Dörnhöferová, M., *et al.* (2008) 'Prevalencia prejavov nešpecifického stresu v starobronzovej populácii z lokality Branč (okr. Nitra) [The prevalence of non-specific stress indicators in Early Bronze Age population from Branč (district Nitra, Slovakia)]', *Slovenská antropológia*, 11: 10–16.
Bodoriková, S., Siváková, D. and Veselá, S. (1999) 'Dentition state of the Slav-Avar population of Šebastovce (Eastern Slovakia)', *Journal of Human Ecology*, 10: 131–35.
Bodoriková, S. and Urminský, J. (2002) 'Late medieval skeletal remains from the townhall of Trnava (West Slovakia): archeological evidence and anthropological analysis', *Anthropologie (Brno)*, 40: 165–75.
Breitinger, E. (1937) 'Zur Berechnung der Körperhöhe aus den langen Glidmassenknochen weiblicher Skelette', *Anthropologischer Anzeiger*, 14: 249–74.
Brůžek, J. (2002) 'A method for visual determination of sex, using the human hip bone', *American Journal of Physical Anthopology*, 117: 157–68.
Buikstra, J.E. and Ubelaker, D.H. (eds) (1994) *Standards for Data Collection from Human Skeletal Remains*, Fayetteville, AR: Arkansas Archeological Survey Research Series No. 44.
Bursa, S. and Ušiak, P. (2004) 'Havárie "furmanov" počas SNP v banskobystrickom okrese', *Bystrický permon*, 2: 10.
CEMUZ (2010) *Centrálny Múzejných Katalóg Zbierok*. Available online at www.cemuz.sk/ (accessed 6 April 2010).
Černý, M. and Komenda, S. (1980) 'Sexual diagnosis by the measurement of humerus and femur', *Sborník prací Pedagogické Fakulty University Palackého v Olomouci – Biologie*, 2: 147–67.
Dobisíková, M., Kuželka, V., Stloukal, M., *et al.* (1999) *Antropologie. Příručka pro studium kostry*, Praha: Národní Muzeum.
Dušek, M. (1974) 'Der junghallstattzeitliche Fürstensitz auf dem Molpír bei Smolenice', in B. Chropovský (ed.) *Symposium zu Problemen der jüngeren Hallstattzeit in Mitteleuropa*, Bratislava: VEDA.
Dušek, M. and Dušek, S. (1984) *Smolenice – Molpír. Befestigter Fürtensitz der Hallstattzeit. Vol. I*, Nitra: AÚ SAV.
Ferembach, D., Schwidetzky, I. and Stloukal, M. (1979) 'Empfehlungen für die Alters-und Geschlechtsdiagnose am Skelett', *HOMO – Journal of Comparative Human Biology*, 30: 1–32.
Furmánek, V., Veliačik, V. and Vladár, J. (1991) *Slovensko v dobe bronzovej*, Bratislava: VEDA.
Furmánek, V. and Vladár, J. (1995) 'Opferpraktiken in der Bronzeit in der Slowakei', *Pravěk (N.Ř.)*, 5: 109–26.

Hanihara, K. and Suzuki, T. (1978) 'Estimation of age from the pubic symphysis by means of multiple regresion analysis', *American Journal of Physical Anthropology*, 48: 233–40.

Hauser, G. and De Stefano, G.F. (1989) *Epigenetic Variants of the Human Skull*, Stuttgart: E. Schweizerbart'sche Verlagsbuchhandlung.

Herrmann, B., Gruppe, G., Hummel, S., *et al.* (1990) *Prähistorische Anthropologie. Leitfaden der Feld-und Labormethoden*, Berlin: Springer-Verlag.

İşcan, M.Y. and Derrick, K. (1984) 'Determination of sex from the sacroiliac. A visual assessment technique', *Florida Scientist*, 47: 94–98.

Jakab, J. (1978) 'Intentional interference on the skeletons of the Otomani People found at the Cultic Objekt in Spišský Štvrtok', *Anthropologie (Brno)*, 16: 139–41.

——(1989) 'The anthropologigal analysis of the differences among the Early Medieval sets of the territory of Slovakia on the basis of non-metrical skeletal traits', *Slovenská Archeológia*, 37: 105–50.

——(2005) 'ŠAĽA II: documentation and description of a Homo sapiens neanderthalensis find from Slovakia', *Anthropologie (Brno)*, 53: 325–30.

Jakab, J., Olexa, L. and Vladár, J. (1999) 'Ein Kultobjekt der Otomani-kultur in Nižná Myšľa', *Slovenská archeológia*, 47: 91–127.

Jelínek, P. (2007) 'Žehnajúci mŕtvy', *Historická Revue*, 7–8: 66.

Knussmann, R., Schwidetzky, I., Jürgens, H.W., *et al.* (eds) (1988) *Anthropologie. (Band I. Wesen und Methoden der Anthropologie)*, Stuttgart: Gustav Fischer Verlag.

Loth, S.R. and Henneberg, M. (1996) 'Mandibular ramus flexure. A new morphologic indicator of sexual dimorphism in the human skeleton', *American Journal of Physical Anthropology*, 99: 473–85.

Lovejoy, C.O. (1985) 'Dental wear in the Libben population. Its pattern and role in the determination of adult skeletal age at death', *American Journal of Physical Anthropology*, 68: 47–56.

Lovejoy, C.O., Meindl, R.S. and Przybeck, T.R. (1985) 'Chronological metamorphosis of the auricular surface of illium. A new method for the determination of adult skeletal age at death', *American Journal of Physical Anthropology*, 68: 15–28.

Manouvrier, L. (1894) 'La détermination de la taille d'aprés les grands os des membres', *Memoires de la Société d'Anthropologie de Paris*, 4: 347–402.

Martin, R. and Saller, K. (1957) *Lehrbuch der Anthropologie. In systematischer Darstellung mit besonderer Berügsichtigung der anthropologischen Methoden*, Stuttgart: Gustav Fischer Verlag.

Martiniaková, M., Grosskopf, B., Omelka, R., *et al.* (2007) 'Histological study of compact bone tissue in some mammals: a method for species determination', *International Journal of Osteoarchaeology*, 17: 82–90.

Masnicová, S. and Beňuš, R. (2001) 'Atresia of an external acoustic meatus in an individual from historical Bratislava (Slovakia)', *Anthropological Science*, 109: 315–23.

——(2003) 'Developmental Anomalies in Skeletal Remains from the Great Moravia and Middle Ages Cemeteries at Devín (Slovakia)', *International Journal of Osteoarchaeology*, 13: 266–74.

Masset, C. (1989) 'Age estimation on the basis of cranial sutures', in İşcan, M.Y. (ed.) *Age Markers in the Human Skeleton*, Springfield, IL: Charles C. Thomas.

Meindl, R.S. and Lovejoy, C.O. (1985) 'Ectocranial suture closure: a revised method for the determination of skeletal age at death and blind tests of its accuracy', *American Journal of Physical Anthropology*, 58: 57–66.

Obertová, Z. and Thurzo, M. (2008) 'Relationship between cribra orbitalia and enamel hypoplasia in the early medieval Slavic population at Borovce, Slovakia', *International Journal of Osteoarchaeology*, 18: 280–92.

Ortner, D.J. and Putschar, W.G.J. (2003) *Identification of Pathological Conditions in Human Skeletal Remains*, San Diego, CA: Academic Press.

Phenice, T.W. (1969) 'A newly developed visual method of sexing the os pubis', *American Journal of Physical Anthropology*, 30: 297–301.

Piontek, J. (1985) *Biologia populacji pradziejowych*, Poznań: Wydawnictwo naukowe Uniwersytetu im. Adama Mickiewicza.

Ruttkay, M. (2004) 'Záchranný výskum v Nitre – Dolných Krškanoch', In *Archeologické výskumy a nálezy na Slovensku v roku 2003*, Nitra: AÚ SAV.

Samuel, M. (2007) 'Nová polykultúrna lokalita v Leviciach', in *Archeologické výskumy a nálezy na Slovensku v roku 2005*, Nitra: AÚ SAV.

Šefčáková, A., Strouhal, E., Němečková, A., *et al.* (2001) 'Case of metastatic carcinoma from end of the 8th–Early 9th century Slovakia', *American Journal of Physical Anthropology*, 116: 216–29.

Štefanovičová, T., Jelínek, P., Kovár, B., *et al.* (2008) 'Predbežná správa z archeologického výskumu bratislavského podhradia – Vydrice', *Zborník SNM – Archeológia*, 102: 249–54.

Schultz, M. (1988) 'Paläopathologische Diagnostik', in R. Knussmann *et al.* (eds) *Anthropologie (Band I. Wesen und Methoden derAnthropologie)*, Stuttgart: Gustav Fischer Verlag.

Selecká, P. (2006) 'Zdravotný stav chrupu dospelých jedincov zo slovanského pohrebiska v Tvrdošovciach (okr. Nové Zámky), (Dentition state in adult individuals from Slavic cemetery at Tvrdošovce (district Nové Zámky), Slovakia', *Slovenská antropológia*, 9: 67–75.

Sjøvold, T. (1990) 'Estimation of stature from long bones utilizing the line of organic correlation', *Human Evolution*, 5: 431–47.

Sládek, V., Trinkaus, E., Šefčáková, A., *et al.* (2002) 'Morphological affinities of the Šaľa 1 frontal bone', *Journal of Human Evolution*, 43: 787–815.

Thurzo, M., Šefčáková, A., Katina, S., *et al.* (2002) 'Dental disease as an indicator of ecological factors in Medieval skeletal population from Slovakia', in P. Bennike *et al.* (eds) *Ecological Aspects of Past Human Settlements in Europe. Biennial Books of EAA. Volume 2*, Budapest: Eötvös University Press.

Ubelaker, D.H. (1987) 'Estimating age at death from immature human skeletons: an overview', *Journal of Forensic Sciences*, 32: 1254–63.

Velemínská, J., Brůžek, J., Velemínský, P., *et al.* (2008) 'Variability of the Upper Palaeolithic skulls from Předmostí near Přerov (Czech Republic): craniometric comparison with recent human standards', *HOMO – Journal of Comparative Human Biology*, 59: 1–26.

Vladár, J. (1977) 'Zur Problematik der befestigten Siedlungen der ausgehenden ältern Bronzezeit in der Slowakei', in O.H. Frey and H. Roth (eds) *Festschrift zum 50-jährigen Bestehen des Urgeschichtlichen Seminars*, Marburg: Gludenbach.

Vlček, E. (1955) 'The fossil man of Gánovce, Czechoslovakia', *Journal of the Royal Anthropological Institute*, 85: 163–71.

——(1958) 'Die Reste des Neanderthalmenschen aus dem Gebiete der Tschechoslowakei', in G.H.R. Koenigswald (ed) *Hundert Jahre Neanderthaler*, Utrecht: Kemink en Zoon.

——(1968) 'Nález pozůstatků neandertálce v Šali na Slovensku', *Anthropozoikum*, 5: 105–24.

Vlček, E. and Kukla, J. (1959) 'Halštatské kultovní masky z lidských lebek z Hraškovy jeskyně z Kilenc-fa v Jihoslovenském krasu', *Památky archeologické*, 50: 507–56.

The Acts

Council Regulation (EEC) No. 3911/92 On the export of cultural goods. *Official Journal of the European Union L* 395, published on 31 December 1992 (corrigendum: *Official Journal of the European Union L* 267, published on 19 October 1996).

Commission Regulation (EEC) No. 752/93 laying down provisions for the implementation of Council Regulation (EEC) No. 3911/92 on the export of cultural goods *Official Journal of the European Union L* 77, published on 30 March 1993.

Act No. 115/1998 Coll. On museums and art galleries and on the protection of objects of museum value and art gallery value. *The Slovak Republic Law Digest* 42, published on 29 April 1998. Available online at www.culture.gov.sk/uploads/Oj/fB/OjfBEogOxkja4EheF_1oEw/act_museumgal.pdf

Act No. 49/2002 Coll. On protection of monuments and historic sites ('Cultural Heritage Monuments Act'). The Slovak Republic Law Digest 23, published on 2 February 2002. Available online at www.culture.gov.sk/uploads/xY/Mm/xYMmsZWmfFw_TlpSSK7MFQ/act_protection_of_monuments.pdf

Act No. 300/2005 Coll. The Criminal Code. The Slovak Republic Law Digest 129, published on 2 July 2005.

Regulation No. 342/1998 Coll. On expert administration of the museum collection items and gallery collection items. *The Slovak Republic Law Digest* 135, published on 17 September 1998.

Regulation No. 16/2003 Coll. Implementing the act on protection of cultural heritage monuments. *The Slovak Republic Law Digest* 8, published on 16 January 2003.

Slovenia/Republika Slovenija

Petra Leben-Seljak and Pavel Jamnik

INTRODUCTION: A BRIEF HISTORY AND CURRENT STATE OF PHYSICAL ANTHROPOLOGY IN SLOVENIA

Slovenia is a small country with just about two million inhabitants; its territory is situated between the Adriatic Sea and the Alps. Even today, it represents an important traffic crossroad, connecting the East and the West, the North and the South of Europe. Throughout History various tribes settled on this territory. However, in the seventh century AD they were overtaken by Slavic tribes. Nowadays Slovenia is an ethnically homogenous country, with its own language which was used in written form since at least about the year 1000 AD. The language belongs to the group of South Slavic languages and has numerous characteristics of the West Slavic group. Slovenia was for the majority of its history linked with Central Europe, since it was a part of the Austro–Hungarian Empire for nearly 1000 years. After the fall of the empire in 1918, Slovenia associated itself with the South Slavic nations and became part of Yugoslavia. After the death of President Josip Broz Tito, the federation of six republics with different historical and cultural backgrounds started to crumble. In 1991, Slovenia was the first to become an independent state. From 1 May 2004 it has been a part of the European Union.

Physical anthropology in Slovenia

Physical anthropology has a rather long tradition in Slovenia, similar to its neighbouring central European countries. Its beginnings go back to the end of the 19th century with the interest of experts of various nationalities and backgrounds (Bögel-Dodič 1989; Vlahović 1989). Among these first scholars were the Austrian archaeologist Szombathy, who made the first anthropological analysis of skeletons found in Slovenia (Szombathy 1879); and the Austrian anatomist Carl Toldt (1912), who wrote about the characteristics of skulls from old Slavic cemeteries including six Slovenian sites.

The true development of physical anthropology as an independent science in Slovenia started after the Second World War with the work of the first Slovenian professional anthropologist, Božo Škerlj, born in 1904. Škerlj graduated in biology and geography in 1926 in Ljubljana and achieved his doctoral degree in 1927 in Prague, under the mentorship of Jindrich Matiegka, with the field of natural sciences and anthropology as his primary topics and sociology and philosophy as secondary subjects. With the aid of a Rockefeller scholarship, he travelled abroad in numerous European states and the USA, where he obtained additional knowledge. In the year 1952, he became an honorary member of the Royal Anthropological Society of Great Britain and Ireland. He was a humanist and a man with broad horizons, dealing with all branches of anthropology, from evolution and osteoarchaeology to ontogenesis, biological types and cultural anthropology. He left behind an enormous opus, including 15 books and over 200 scientific and popular science articles and papers. In 1946, he established the chair of anthropology at the University of Ljubljana and thus established the grounds for the Slovenian anthropological profession (Bögel-Dodić 1996). After his death in 1961 the chair was taken by his former assistant Zlata Dolinar Osole, whose main interests were human genetics. Her contemporary, Vida Brodar, studied mainly twins and worked mostly as an expert witness for courts in relation to cases on paternity. Professor Osole trained four anthropologists before her retirement in 1988. Unfortunately, her supposed successor Anton Pogačnik died prematurely; while Metka Bögel left the profession. Only two researchers remained at the University. Marija Štefančič, who specialized in the field of osteoarchaeology and investigated the skeletons found in the former Yugoslavian republics of Macedonia and Croatia (Štefančič 1980, 1988, 1995), became Head of Anthropology whereas her assistant Tatjana Tomazo-Ravnik dedicated herself to the field of auxology.

Despite the very long tradition, Slovenian physical anthropology nowadays faces a crisis. There are many experts declaring themselves as anthropologists; however, they are social and cultural anthropologists and not physical anthropologists. Currently there are only two physical anthropologists actively working in Slovenia and both are specialized in the field of human skeletal analysis. Marija Štefančič is now professor at the Biology Department of the Biotechnical Faculty of the University of Ljubljana. The faculty provides the study of physical anthropology at postgraduate level. It is also possible to take an interdisciplinary postgraduate course in anthropology, jointly run by the Biotechnical Faculty, the Faculty of Arts and the Faculty for Social Sciences at the University of Ljubljana. The other physical anthropologist is one of the present authors, Petra Leben-Seljak, now an independent researcher but who until 1996 was employed at the University of Ljubljana as an assistant and researcher under the mentorship of Professors Osole and Štefančič. Working freelance is the only way to work in the profession since there are no posts for physical anthropology in Slovenia. Since osteological analysis of archaeological assemblages is not compulsory by law, archaeological institutions do not employ anthropologists full-time and only require their assistance on certain rescue excavations.

Anthropological analyses of human skeletons in Slovenia

Anthropological analyses of individual sites

This section reviews the anthropological studies on assemblages from archaeological sites, listed chronologically according to period. Those studies prior to 1990 include mostly data about sex, age and anthropometry. After this date, the majority of studies contain, in addition, data about teeth, epigenetic traits, palaeopathology and occupational stress markers. These analyses have been carried out within the anthropological research projects financed by the Research Agency of the Republic of Slovenia (Agencija za raziskovalno dejavnost Republike Slovenije or ARRS).

So far, no human skeletons have been found at Palaeolithic sites. Two isolated findings, a human cranium (Hincak and Štefančič, 2006) and two teeth (Štamfelj *et al.* 2004) have been dated to the Mesolithic period. Neolithic sites with human remains are also quite rare and mainly comprise a few bones scattered at the bottom of caves. These remains belong to a number of incomplete skeletons, such as the ones at the Koblarska cave site (Jamnik *et al.* 2002). Some sporadic findings in the Ljubljana marsh belong to the Eneolithic period: one skull (Štefančič 1985), the remains of two skeletons (Štefančič 1992) and teeth of a child (Leben-Seljak 2004a); and a complete male skeleton from Šibernica Cave at Bled (Leben-Seljak, unpublished).

The cremation urns at the gravesite of Dobova in Brežice (Piontek *et al.* 1975) belong to the Late Bronze Age. Graves with urns were prevalent also during the Iron Age period. Inhumations in discrete graves were rare in this period (Dolinar-Osole 1956; Angel 1968) and, besides, the bones were hardly preserved due to the destructive activity of the acidic soil in the Dolenjska area, which was the centre of the Halstatt culture. There is almost no data about the population during the Roman period as the investigation of the large gravesite at Ptuj, dating back to the third and fourth centuries AD, only started in the year 2005 (Leben-Seljak, unpublished). Most probably the three individual skeletons found at various locations also belong to the Roman period (Leben-Seljak 1996a, Breščak *et al.* 2002). From the Migration period (fifth to sixth centuries AD), a number of sites have been excavated, but unfortunately the skeletal series were small and/or badly preserved. The majority of these skeletons come from different sites and, by archaeological and historical definition, represent the Romanized indigenous population: Pristava I at Bled (Škerlj 1953; Leben-Seljak 1996b); Ajdna (Leben-Seljak 1995, 1996b), Vrajk (Leben-Seljak 2003), Rifnik (Leben-Seljak 2006), part of Puščava (Leben-Seljak 2004b) and Tonovc Castle (Leben-Seljak, in press). On two locations, apart from the indigenous population, there were also the remains of people from various Germanic tribes, mostly Langobards and Goths: Dravlje by Ljubljana (Tomazo-Ravnik 1975) and Lajh at Kranj (Kiszely 1979, 1980; Leben-Seljak, unpublished). The intentionally deformed skulls are typical of these two sites, and also of the only skeleton discovered so far of a Hun (Figure 37.1). Occupational stress markers show that this male individual was a horserider and also that most probably he used his upper incisors to prepare the string of his bow (Leben-Seljak 2002, 2004c).

In Slovenia, the historians regard the Early Middle Ages (from the seventh to the tenth centuries AD) the same as the beginning of the old Slavic settlement. This period has been studied in the best possible way from the archaeological and anthropological point of view. Shortly after the Second World War, extensive systematic excavations were carried out at two large gravesites: Pristava II in Bled (Škerlj and Dolinar 1950) and Ptuj (Ivaniček 1951). Due to advances in knowledge and understanding of the period, it would be necessary to review the skeletal material, but unfortunately the skeletons were lost. During the same period, Škerlj also published the analysis of three skeletons from Ljubljana (Škerlj 1950); while his assistant processed a smaller gravesite at Turnišče near Ptuj (Dolinar 1951, 1953; Dolinar and Štefančič 1973). The next anthropological analysis of the Middle Ages would not start until after 1986. Approximately 500 skeletons from the necropolis at Kranj (Leben-Seljak 1991) and 47 skeletons from Bodešče (Štefančič and Leben-Seljak 1992) were analysed. Bodešče was included also in the analysis of two Late Roman and nine Early Middle Age gravesites in the area of Bled, providing a total of 475 skeletons (Leben-Seljak 1996b). Apart from these, data on two small skeletal series were also published (Leben-Seljak 2001a; Tomazo-Ravnik 1979); while data on 220 skeletons from Središče (Leben-Seljak 2001b; Štefančič *et al.* 2008) was only published in the form of a short contribution.

Other anthropological analyses

There have been relatively few comparative analyses due to the poor state of preservation of the skeletal remains and the relatively small samples sizes. Marija Štefančič (1990) has researched temporary changes of the cranial index in Slovenia. As a part of the master's and doctoral degree

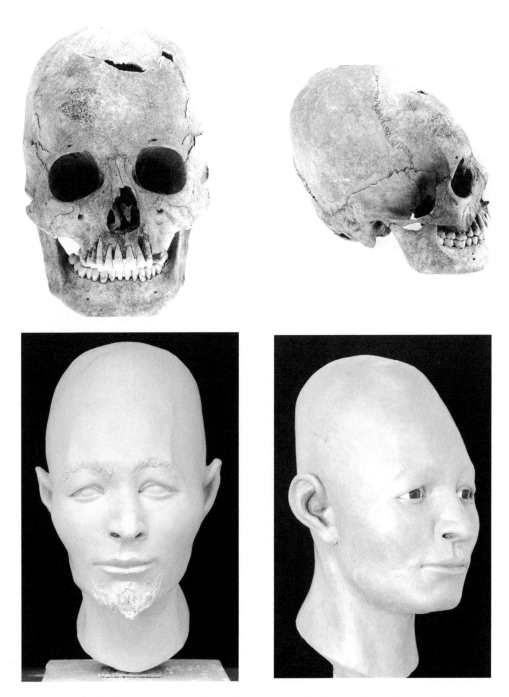

Figure 37.1 The skeleton of a Hun warrior, male, approximately 21 years of age, discovered in Slovenia
Facial reconstruction was carried out by Ágnes Kustár, PhD, Magyar Természettudományi
Múzeum, Hungary.
Source: Photos of skeleton, I. Lapajne, SAZU, Ljubljana; Photo of reconstruction: Boštjan Podvršič,
Ljubljana

406

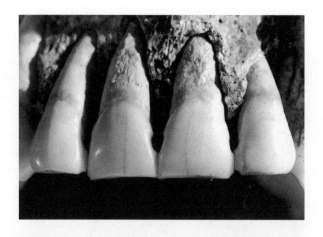

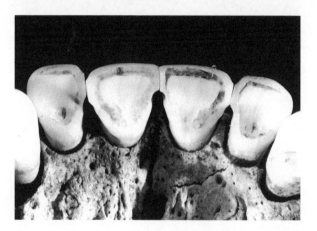

Figure 37.1 (continued)

theses, two palaeodemographic analyses have been produced (Leben-Seljak 1996c; Leben-Seljak and Štefančič 1999), as well as a short comparative analysis of morphological characteristics between populations (Leben-Seljak 2000). Very little is known about teeth, limited to some knowledge of dental caries and ante-mortem tooth loss. These data are included in more recent analyses of individual sites and also considered in some older studies by stomatologist Valter Krušič (1954, 1969, 1971a, 1971b). There has been only one comparative analysis on dental caries so far (Leben-Seljak and Štefančič 2001) and one Slovenian study on the morphological characteristics of teeth (Štamfelj 2004; Štamfelj *et al.* 2006).

Palaeopathological findings are rare, with the exception of healed fractures and the usual degenerative changes of the spinal column. More uncommon are isolated cases of athero-sclerosis (Figure 37.2), growth disturbance (Figure 37.3), traces of sawing (Figure 37.4) and a case of craniotomy (or cranial autopsy) from the end of the 18th century (Leben-Seljak 2005).

Among methodological studies, these include a comparison of hip morphology and muscu-lature in Neanderthal and modern man (Bajd 1996), the study on the lateral asymmetry of long limb bones (Čuk *et al.* 2001) and the attempt of the identification of the skulls related to the

Figure 37.2 Calcified deposits of fat in the blood vessel walls of the aorta and abdominal arteries, found in the grave of an extremely robust and muscular male of approximately 50 years of age, found in Slovenia

Source: Petra Leben-Seljak

family of the counts of Celje (Zupanič Slavec 2004). DNA analysis of archaeological material has not been carried out yet; and other chemical analyses are also very rare (Ogrinc 1999).

Forensic anthropology

In compliance with the law, forensic cases fall under the competence of the Forensic Institute of the Medical Faculty of the University of Ljubljana. Anthropology was included in this field of forensic work only in 2006, when the systematic excavations of war gravesites began to be carried out by the Commission of the Government of the Republic of Slovenia. One of the present authors participated in six excavations (Leben-Seljak 2007), the most interesting being the case of Konfin I (Leben-Seljak 2008). According to some archived documents it was suspected that 88 prisoners of war in a convoy were killed near Konfin on 24 June 1945, the victims being mostly Slovenian collaborator home guards, and these included some wounded persons who had been hospitalized in Ljubljana (Jamnik 2008c). Their bodies were thrown into a 45m-deep pit and the entrance to it was mined. During the excavation, commingled skeletal remains were brought up from the pit and examined at the site. As individualization of the skeletons was not possible, the anthropological analysis was made under the system employed for ossuary skeletal samples, based on innominates, femora and clavicles. The number, sex and age of the victims corresponded to the archive documents (Figure 37.5), their alleged identity was confirmed also by the identification of pathological changes, among which prevailed trauma in the healing phase, which had been inflicted about two to three months before death (Figure 37.6). With the aid of hospital archive documents it was possible to match bones showing trauma on five victims with actual persons, an identification that was later confirmed by DNA analysis (Zupanič Pajnič 2008).

Figure 37.3a

ARCHAEOLOGICAL HUMAN REMAINS AND LEGISLATION

Archaeological legislation

The Cultural Heritage Protection Act of Slovenia (Zakon o varstvu kulturne dediščine) (Official gazette of RS, No. 16–485/2008) regulates the material cultural heritage, which includes also human skeletal remains. The Act defines in detail the protection system, the methods of dealing with these issues, the issuing of permits and the competencies of individual legal and natural persons in the field, undertaking conservation and documentation work on the cultural heritage. The relations among the institutions for the protection of the cultural heritage, i.e. the institutions, conservation centres and museums, are defined in detail.

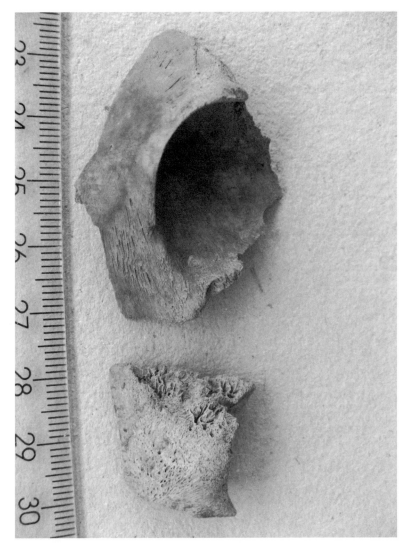

Figure 37.3b Skeletal remains of two newborns, the left one showing signs of growth disorder, from Koper-
    Rektorat, Slovenia, 2005, Late Roman Period
Source: Petra Leben-Seljak

HUMAN REMAINS AND LEGISLATION

The boundary between forensic and archaeological cases is not specific, but there are suggestions that it ought to be 50 years. In relation to mass graves, it depends on the circumstances,
but in the case that the persons suspected of killing the people are still alive, then it becomes a
forensic or legal case.

In relation to archaeological remains, although the Cultural Heritage Protection Act does not
quote exactly the work and role of physical anthropologists, it does define the intervention,
protection, documenting and conservation of archaeological remains, and therefore indirectly
includes their role regarding archaeological human remains.

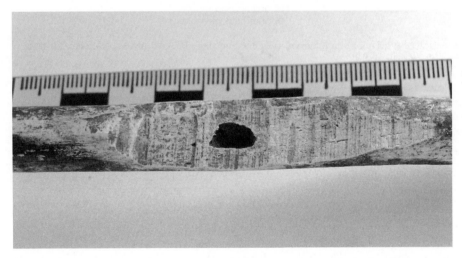

Figure 37.4 Humerus and radius from Krška jama, Slovenia (Late Bronze Age), showing traces of peri-
mortem sawing
Source: Pavel Jamnik

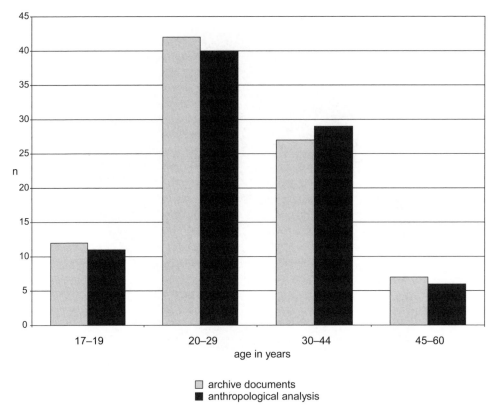

Figure 37.5 Mass grave Konfin I, Slovenia, 2006. Comparison of age structure
Source: Petra Leben-Seljak

Table 37.1 Mass grave Konfin I, Slovenia, 2006. Comparison of trauma and state of healing

Trauma	Bone	Anthropology	Archives
		n	*n*
Fractures	ribs	2	0
	humerus, r.	1	1
	ulna, r.	1	0
	femur, r.	4	4
	femur, l.	2	2
	tibia, r.	3	2
	tibia, l.	4	1
	fibula	3-5	1
Amputations	femur, r.	1	1
	crus, r.	1	1
	crus, l.	2	2
Shot wounds	innominate	2	max. 6

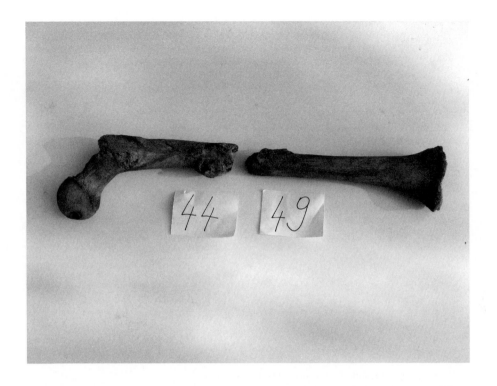

Figure 37.6a and b Mass grave Konfin I, Slovenia, 2006. Cases of fracture (37.6a) and amputation (37.6b)

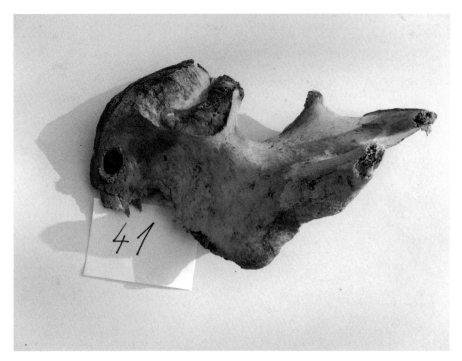

Figure 37.6c Mass grave Konfin I, Slovenia, 2006. Gunshot wound
Source: Petra Leben-Seljak and Pavel Jamnik

The inclusion of anthropological experts during the excavation of human skeletal remains in Slovenia is present in two types of investigation. The first one relates to archaeological research, since the presence of a physical anthropologist has been a long-term practice, and it would be impossible to imagine a professional excavation without such a presence. The second type of work involves the need for an anthropologist in the investigation of the mass graves in Slovenia dating from the end of the Second World War. The latter refers to the alleged 'clandestine graves and places of execution', which enter into the sphere of archaeological work but also into the field of forensic crime scene investigation. Specific field legislation regulates both types of investigation; however, in the future it will be necessary to provide more detail regulation in relation to dealing with human skeletal remains.

In Slovenia, the archaeological evaluation or preliminary archaeological investigations in advance of construction work prevail. These works are carried out to record and protect as much as possible the archaeological sites. The contractor carrying out the construction work shall engage the anthropologist in preventive or rescue archaeological excavations where human remains are present. The Cultural Heritage Protection Act states that the preliminary archaeological investigation includes also the post-excavation study and archiving of the archaeological material, and this is important for anthropological work. In theory, this will allow the involvement of an anthropologist in the post-excavation phase.

The Cultural Heritage Protection Act defines in detail the ownership, curation and cataloguing of archaeological remains, including human remains. Thus, the archaeological findings or archaeological remains that are movable or are found by anyone on the surface, underground or in the water, remain the property of the state. The inventorying of movable cultural heritage, which also includes archaeological remains, is implemented by the state and by authorized museums. Some unresolved questions regarding the storage and inventorying arise with excavated skeletal remains from late mediaeval and modern times (e.g., from abandoned cemeteries) although even in such cases where skeletal remains may be the focus of anthropological analysis, generally speaking the attitude is that they are of no true scientific importance for archaeologists. In cases like these the competent museums, to which these archaeological remains belong, can arrange with local communities for their reburial within a cemetery or in a protected area where the construction work is taking place. However, the act and legislation in general do not indicate the exact time limit regarding when and which human skeletal remains have to be reburied, and which ones to inventory and to curate in a competent museum institution.

Sending human skeletal remains abroad for analysis or further post-excavation work should comply with the Cultural Heritage Protection Act. There are two different concepts relating to the transportation of archaeological remains across the State border. 'Transfer' refers to the physical movement of movable heritage from the Republic of Slovenia to another EU Member State or a Member State of the European Economic Community. 'Export' means the physical movement of movable heritage from the Republic of Slovenia to a country which is not an EU Member State or a Member State of the European Economic Community. The conditions for 'transfer' or 'export', and the time limits, are defined in Article 45 of the Protection of Cultural Heritage Act, which also indicates issuing of permanent or temporary 'transfers or 'exports.

Alleged post-war mass graves

After the beginning of the process of democratization in the late 1980s, the question was raised in Slovenia of how to approach the investigation and identification of alleged victims of the communist regime, buried mostly in 1945–46 in mass graves. A database has already been compiled listing 588 clandestine graves (Ferenc 2008). According to some estimates, some of the graves contain several thousand bodies (Ferenc 2007). The Cultural Heritage Protection Act, passed in 2008, enumerates in its Article 3, among the archaeological remains, 'the issues connected with mass graves, defined by the regulations on war gravesites … '. However, due to the nature and context of these war graves, they cannot be dealt with solely within the frame of the Cultural Heritage Protection Act and only from an archaeological approach (Jamnik 2008a).

It was the Slovenian Police who started the fieldwork in the 1990s, namely the search and verification of war gravesites. It was expected that exhumations would have to be carried out, since it would be impossible to establish how many victims were buried and who they were without excavation. In order to retrieve as much information as possible to help the reconstruction of the event that led to the death and burial of the deceased, the first exhumation was carried out under the principles of forensic anthropology and archaeology in Slovenia in 2003 at the war gravesite at Jelenci, near Šmarjeta in Dolenjska.

The War Gravesites Act (Zakon o vojnih grobiščih) (Official Gazette of RS, No. 65/2003) was passed in 2003. According to Article 28 of the Act:

> For the registered alleged war gravesites, where the existence of human mortal remains was not proved, but the suspicion of their existence is founded, the Ministry may issue a permission for the implementation of procedures for the establishment of the existence of a war gravesite. Before the issue of such permission, the Ministry shall inform the Police and the Public Prosecution Service.
>
> *War Gravesites Act (Zakon o vojnih grobiščih), Article 28, paragraph 7*

This Act opened a legal possibility to check the existence of war graves, the locations of which were known only approximately or were even unknown although their existence seem to have been proven through other evidence. Thus, the only confirmation of a gravesite was to carry out evaluation trenches or test drilling.

The Commission of the Government of the Republic of Slovenia (Komisija Vlade Republike Slovenije za reševanje vprašanj prikritih grobišč) considered at its fourth session the 'Progress of the execution of test drilling and excavation' (Minutes of the Commission, Official Gazette of RS, 17400–422/2005–10 of 25 January 2006). The methodology originated as a result of past experience in exhumations, ordered by the court for actual criminal offences, based on the Criminal Procedure Act (Official Gazette of RS, No.96/2004), as well as a result of experience undertaking archaeological work. Basic guidelines for an accepted methodology of work are:

> Test drilling is carried out at alleged war gravesites where: the location of the burial site of the victims is unknown; where it is necessary to measure the size of the gravesite (e.g. anti tank trenches, bomb craters, caves); or at places where oral tradition indicates the gravesite and where the site survey has been inconclusive.
>
> The test drilling is made by machine or manual digging and the trench should be 1 x 1m or 0.5 x 2m in dimensions and to the depth of the skeletal remains.
>
> Upon discovery of the first skeletal remains all work must stop and the presence of an anthropological or forensic expert is required. The expert can then provide an opinion as to whether the remains are human and, if they are, an expert anthropological opinion on the age, sex, pathology and peri-mortem trauma.
>
> *Jamnik 2008b*

Excavation is carried out under forensic, archaeological and anthropological methods of work, using the appropriate excavation and recording techniques (e.g., photography, recovery of objects, etc.). Following improvement in forensic sciences, it is also necessary to secure samples for DNA analysis. The anthropologist should also give an expert opinion on the skeletal remains and any possible evidence of peri-mortem trauma.

METHODS OF ANTHROPOLOGICAL ANALYSIS

Regarding methodology, the standards used follow the 'European' recommendations of Ferembach *et al.* (1980); as well as the work of Martin and Saller (1957), Hillson (1996), İşcan and Kennedy (Kennedy 1989), Krogman and İşcan (1986), Cox and Mays (2000), Katzenberg and Saunders (2000), and Scheuer and Black (2000) among others. There are no specific methods for Slovenian populations nor is there a reference skeletal collection from which to develop them.

For stature calculation one of the present authors (PL-S) uses the old Manouvrier method because of its simplicity and the poor state of Slovenian skeletal material. This method is also appropriate for measurements *in situ.*; and it enables comparison with data from older studies. PL-S has also used the methods of Pearson and of Breitinger-Bach: these two methods underestimate and overestimate the calculation obtained from Manouvrier's method by 1–2 cm and by about 3–4 cm respectively. The same is true for Trotter and Gleser's method, proposed by USA forensic anthropologists, and which have given results 1–4 cm taller for the deceased from mass graves.

Non-metric traits are usually recorded in the skull according to Hauser and De Stefano (1989) and a number of references are used for palaeopathological analysis (see, e.g., Aufderheide and Rodríguez-Martín 1998).

Case study: the Hun warrior

Methods used are exemplified by the anthropological analysis of the skeleton of a Hun warrior from the fifth century AD. This skeleton was analysed immediately (Leben-Seljak 2002, 2004d, in press) since it represents the first evidence of the presence of Huns on Slovenian territory. A summary of this analysis, which is much more extensive, is provided below.

The skeleton, Ptuj–ŠC 2000, grave no. 50, was found in September 2000 during archaeological excavations of a Late Roman Period necropolis in Ptuj. The skeleton was buried in an abandoned Roman lime-kiln and was classified by grave-goods as the burial of a Hun warrior from the fifth century AD. The skeleton was in fairly good condition, the skull and the majority of postcranial bones were whole, only the part below the knees including feet was missing. Macroscopic and anthropometric anthropological analysis was done by employing standard methods.

The skeleton undoubtedly belongs to a male who died in his early twenties (Acsádi and Nemeskéri 1970; Brothwell 1972; Chiarelli 1980; Krogman and İşcan 1986; Hillson 1996; Scheuer and Black 2000). The degree of sexualization is rather low due to the more feminine features of the frontal bone and non-prominent muscular attachments, but sexual traits on the pelvis are hypermasculine. It is not possible to provide a cause or manner of death for this individual.

The skeleton has an artificially deformed skull (for a more detailed interpretation and a discussion see Leben-Seljak, in press) which is of a typical circular fronto-occipital type and would have been caused by the application of a circular band in early childhood (see Stloukal 1965; Aufderheide and Rodríguez-Martín 1998: 34–36). In Slovenia such skulls are reported at two sites: Lajh in Kranj (Kiszely 1979, 1980) and Dravlje near Ljubljana (Tomazo-Ravnik 1975).

Although the inter-orbital projection method of Gill and Hughes places the skull into the Caucasoid group, it also shows some Mongoloid anthroposcopic features such as unmarked masculine sexual traits, rounded orbits, broad zygomatic bones with inferior zygomatic projection, wide ramus of mandible, elliptic palate with straight suture and six-cusped lower first molar (Gill 1997).

Stature was 163 cm, calculated by a variety of different methods (Manouvrier, Dupertius and Hagen, Shitai, Stevenson, and Trotter and Gleser) for Caucasoid and Mongoloid groups, and the individual had a relatively gracile body composition.

This young man seems to have been right-handed (Steele 2000). Some pathological conditions include Schmorl's nodes and some osteoarthritis on vertebrae and ribs (Resnick and Niwayama 1978; Rogers and Waldron 1994). There a number of features, in addition, that may suggest horse-riding activities (Pálfi and Dutour 1996; Larsen 1997: 175). These include superior extension of the acetabulum, posterior extension of femoral head to the neck and torsion of the femoral distal end, as well as marked muscular attachments for m. gluteus maximus and m. gastrocnemius medialis (see Tortora and Grabowski 2003). Tooth wear (Figure 37.1) is another anomaly since the lingual surfaces of all four upper incisors show horizontal and lightly slanting grooves seen from the front as small holes between the incisors, and likely reflect use of the teeth as tools (Larsen 1997: 258–62; Kennedy 1989; Hillson 1996: 251).

CONCLUSION

We have tried to represent all subjects connected with physical anthropology in Slovenia, beginning with the history and current state of this scientific field. A review of all analysed skeletal material has been included for the sake of the present author PL–S's colleagues, bioarchaeologists and forensic anthropologists. Also the section on legislation should be of use to the present author PJ's colleagues in criminology and other fields.

USEFUL CONTACTS

Slovenian Archaeological Society. Website: www.arheologija.si/
Slovenian Anthropological Society. Website: www. drustvo-antropologov.si/
Slovenian National Museum. Website: www. narmuz-lj.si/
Department of Biology, Biotechnical Faculty, University of Ljubljana. Website: www.bf.uni-lj.si/;
  home page of the Chair of Anthropology at the Department of Biology: www.antropologija.net/

BIBLIOGRAPHY

Acsádi, G. and Nemeskéri, J. (1970) *History of Human Life Span and Mortality*, Budapest: Akadémia Kiádo.
Angel, L. (1968) 'Human skeletal remains from Slovenia', *Bulletin of American School of Prehistoric Research*, 25: 75–108.
Aufderheide, A.C. and Rodríguez-Martín, C. (1998) *The Cambridge Encyclopedia of Human Paleopathology*, Cambridge: Cambridge University Press.
Bajd, B. (1996) 'Primerjava funkcionalne odvisnosti oblike kolčnice in delovanja srednje zadnjične mišice pri modernem človeku in neandertalcu', *Anthropological notebooks*, 4: 109–20.
Bögel-Dodič, M. (1989) 'Nekaj misli o antropologiji na Slovenskem', *Glasnik Antropološkog društva Jugoslavije*, 26: 13–18.
——(1996) 'Profesor dr. Božo Škerlj (1904–61)', *Anthropological notebooks*, 4: 9–13.
Breščak, D., Lovenjak, M., Verbič, T., *et al.* (2002) 'Nov poznoantični grob z Zidanega Gabra na Gorjancih', *Arheološki vestnik*, 53: 223–32.
Brothwell, D.R. (1972) *Digging Up Bones*, London: British Museum (Natural History).
Čuk, T., Leben-Seljak, P. and Štefančič, M. (2001) 'Lateral asymmetry of human long bones', *Variability and Evolution*, 9: 19–32.
Chiarelli, A.B. (ed.) (1980) 'Recommendations for age and sex diagnoses of skeletons', *Journal of Human Evolution*, 9: 517–49.
Cox, M. and Mays, S. (eds) (2000) *Human Osteology in Archaeology and Forensic Science*, London: Greenwich Medical Media.
Dolinar, Z. (1951) 'Antropološki rezultat o okostju bojevnika s Turnišča pri Ptuju', *Arheološki vestnik*, 2: 31–39.
——(1953) 'Antropološka obdelava nekropole Turnišče pri Ptuju', *Razprave 1 razreda III:* 271–303, Slovenian Academy of Science (SAZU).
Dolinar-Osole, Z. (1956) 'Ilirska okostja iz gomile v Volčjih njivah', *Arheološki vestnik*, 7: 131–36.
Dolinar, Z. and Štefančič, M. (1973) 'Die Anthropologische bearbeitung der Skelette Nr. 1 und Nr. 2 aus der Nekropole in Turnišče bei Ptuj', *Balcanoslavica*, 2: 89–93.
Ferembach, D., Schwidetzky, I. and Stloukal, M. (1980) 'Recommendations for Age and Sex Diagnoses of Skeletons', *Jour. Hum. Evol.* 9, 517–49.
Ferenc, M. (2007) 'Vmesno poročilo o sondiranju v nekdanjem protitankovskem jarku v Teznem 8. in 9. avgusta 2007', unpublished report.
——(2008) 'Topografija evidentiranih grobišč', in J. Dežman (ed.) *Poročilo Komisije Vlade Republike Slovenije za reševanje vprašanj prikritih grobišč 2005–2008*, Ljubljana: Družina.
Gill, G.W. (1997) 'Craniofacial criteria in the skeletal attribution of race', in K.J. Reichs (ed.) *Forensic Osteology: Advances in the Identification of Human Remains*, Springfield, IL: Charles C. Thomas.
Hauser, G. and De Stefano, F. (1989) *Epigenetic Variants of the Human Skull*, Stuttgart: E. Schweizerbartsche Verlagsbuchhandlung.
Hillson, S. (1996) *Dental Anthropology*, Cambridge: Cambridge University Press.
Hincak, Z. and Štefančič, M. (2006) 'Anthropological analysis of the cranium', in A. Gaspari (ed.) *Zalog near Verd, Stone Age hunters' camp at the western edge of the Ljubljansko barje*, Ljubljana: Založba ZRC SAZU, Opera Instituti Archaeologici Sloveniae 11.
Ivaniček, F. (1951) *Staroslavenska nekropola u Ptuju*, Ljubljana: Slovenska akademija znanosti in umetnosti, Dela 1. razreda 5.
Jamnik, P. (2008a) 'Prikrita množična grobišča v Sloveniji. Koliko je arheološkega dela pri izkopih grobišč in ugotavljanju njihovega obstoja?', *Prispevki za novejšo zgodovino*, 48: 173–86.

——(2008b) 'Metodološki okviri izvedbe sodno odrejenih ekshumacij ter sondiranj in prekopov, izvedenih v okviru vladne komisije', in J. Dežman (ed.) *Poročilo Komisije Vlade republike Slovenije za reševanje vprašanj prikritih grobišč 2005–2008*, Ljubljana: Družina.

——(2008c) 'Ugotavljanje identitete žrtev iz brezna pri Konfinu I v arhivskih virih', in J. Dežman (ed.) *Poročilo Komisije Vlade Republike Slovenije za reševanje vprašanj prikritih grobišč 2005–2008*, Ljubljana: Družina.

Jamnik, P., Leben-Seljak, P., Bizjak, J., *et al.* (2002) 'Koblarska jama na Kočevskem – prazgodovinsko grobišče in kultni proctor: antropološka analiza skeletnih ostankov z opisom pridatkov', *Arheološki vestnik*, 53: 31–49.

Katzenberg, M.A. and Saunders, S.R. (eds) (2000) *Biological anthropology of the human skeleton*, New York: Wiley-Liss.

Kennedy, K.A.R. (1989) 'Skeletal markers of occupational stress', in M.Y. İşcan and K.A.R. Kennedy (eds) *Reconstruction of Life from the Skeleton*, New York: Wiley-Liss.

Kiszely, I. (1979) *The Anthropology of the Lombards, Part I*, Oxford: British Archaeological Reports International Series 61(i).

——(1980) 'Kratka antropološka karakterizacija grobišča iz langobardske dobe v Kranju', in V. Stare (ed.) *Kranj, nekropola iz časa preseljevanja ljudstev*, Ljubljana: Narodni Muzej Slovenije, Katalogi in monografije 18.

Krogman, W.M. and İşcan, M.Y. (1986) *The Human Skeleton in Forensic Medicine*, Springfield, IL: Charles C. Thomas.

Krušič, V. (1954) *Karies pri starih Slovanih*, Ljubljana: Slovenska akademija znanosti in umetnosti, Dela 4. razreda 6.

——(1969) 'Karies pri Ilirih, živečih na ozemlju današnje Slovenije', *Zobozdravstveni vestnik*, 24: 145–58.

——(1971a) 'Karies pri Langobardih, živečih na ozemlju današnje Slovenije', *Zobozdravstveni vestnik*, 26: 137–51.

——(1971b) 'Karies pri narodih, živečih na Slovenskem, gledan skozi prizmo tisočletij', *Arheološki vestnik*, 22: 225–36.

Larsen, C.S. (1997) *Bioarchaeology: Interpreting Behavior from the Human Skeleton*, Cambridge: Cambridge University Press.

Leben-Seljak, P. (1991) 'Antropološka analiza srednjeveških skeletov iz Kranja', unpublished Master's thesis, University of Ljubljana.

——(1995) 'Antropološka analiza poznoantičnih skeletov z Ajdne nad Potoki', *Jeseniški zbornik*, 7: 237–50.

——(1996a) 'Antropološka analiza dveh poznoantičnih skeletov iz Ljubljane in s Ptuja', *Ptujski zbornik*, 6: 395–404.

——(1996b) 'Antropološka analiza poznoantičnih in srednjeveških grobišč Bleda in okolice', unpublished PhD thesis, University of Ljubljana.

——(1996c) 'Paleodemografska analiza nekropole pri farni cerkvi v Kranju', *Anthropological notebooks*, 4: 95–107.

——(2000) 'Etnogeneza Slovencev: rezultati antropoloških raziskav', in R. Bratož (ed.) *Slovenija in sosednje dežele med antiko in karolinško dobo*, Ljubljana: Narodni Muzej Slovenije, Situla 19.

——(2001a) 'Antropološka analiza staroslovanskih skeletov z Malega gradu v Kamniku', *Arheološki vestnik*, 52: 379–84.

——(2001b) 'Spolna in starostna struktura srednjeveškega grobišča Središče ob Dravi', in *3. Škerljevi dnevi: zbornik povzetkov*, Ljubljana: Društvo antropologov Slovenije.

——(2002) 'A Hun skeleton with intentionally deformed skull from Ptuj', *Collegium Antropologicum*, 26 (suppl.): 119–20.

——(2003) 'Antropološka analiza poznoantičnega grobišča na Vrajku v Gorenjem Mokronogu', *Arheološki vestnik*, 54: 397–420.

——(2004a) 'Anthropological analysis of teeth from the Hočevarica site', in A. Velušček (ed.) *Hočevarica, an eneolithic pile dwelling in the Ljubljansko barje*, Ljubljana: Založba ZRC SAZU, Opera Instituti Archaeologici Sloveniae 8.

——(2004b) 'Antropološka analiza skeletov s Puščave nad Starim trgom pri Slovenj Gradcu', *Arheološki vestnik*, 55: 527–64.

——(2004c) 'The skeleton of a Hun warrior from Ptuj', in *Programme and abstracts: man between autonomy and the environment*, Ljubljana: Društvo antropologov Slovenije.

——(2005) 'Dokaz o obdukciji izpred 200 let'. *Gea*, 15(8): 42.

——(2006) 'Antropološka analiza poznoantične skeletne serije z Rifnika', *Arheološki vestnik*, 57: 427–55.

——(2007) 'Anthropological analyses of post-war mass graves in Slovenia', in G. Starc (ed.) *Life in the Time of Conflicts: Book of Abstracts*, Ljubljana: Slovene Anthropological Society.

——(2008) 'Antropološke analize povojnih grobišč: Konfin I', in J. Dežman (ed.) *Poročilo Komisije Vlade Republike Slovenije za reševanje vprašanj prikritih grobišč 2005–2008*, Ljubljana: Družina.

——(in press) 'Okostje hunskega bojevnika s Ptuja: antropološka analiza', *Arheološki vestnik*.

Leben-Seljak, P. and Štefančič, M. (1999) 'Adult mortality and biodynamic characeristics in the Early Middle Ages population at Bled, Slovenia', *Variability and Evolution*, 7: 65–77.

——(2001) 'Dental caries in skeletal samples from northeastern Slovenia', *Anthropological notebooks*, 7: 84–99.

Martin, R. and Saller, K. (1957) *Lehrbuch der Anthropologie I*, Stuttgart: Gustav Fischer Verlag

Ogrinc, N. (1999) 'Stable isotope evidence of the diet of the Neolithic population in Slovenia – a case study: Ajdovska jama', *Documenta praehistorica*, 26: 193–200.

Pálfi, G. and Dutour, O. (1996) 'Activity-induced skeletal markers in historical anthropological material', *International Journal of Anthropology*, 11: 41–55.

Piontek, J., Tomazo-Ravnik, T. and Štefančič, M. (1975) 'Antropološka obdelava grobov kasne bronaste dobe iz Dobove pri Brežicah', in F. Stare (ed.) *Dobova*, Brežice: Posavski muzej.

Resnick, D. and Niwayama, G. (1978) 'Intervertebral disk herniations: cartilaginous (Schmorl's) nodes', *Radiology*, 126: 57–65.

Rogers, J. and Waldron, T. (1994) *A Field Guide to Joint Disease in Archaeology*, Chichester: John Wiley & Sons.

Scheuer, L. and Black, S. (2000) *Developmental Juvenile Osteology*, London: Academic Press.

Škerlj, B. (1950) 'Kostni ostanki treh staroslovanskih grobov, izkopanih na dvorišču SAZU v Ljubljani', *Arheološki vestnik*, 1: 146–55.

——(1953) 'Srednjeveška okostja z Bleda, izkopana leta 1949', *Razprave 1. razreda SAZU*, 3: 313–55.

Škerlj, B. and Dolinar, Z. (1950) 'Staroslovanska okostja z Bleda', in J. Kastelic and B. Škerlj (eds) *Slovanska nekropola na Bledu*, Ljubljana: Slovenska akademija znanosti in umetnosti, Dela 1. razreda 2.

Štamfelj, I. (2004) 'Analiza morfoloških značilnosti in bolezenskih sprememb stalnih zob in čeljustne kosti na skeletnem gradivu iz 10. – 15. stoletja (Središče ob Dravi)', unpublished Master's thesis, University of Ljubljana.

Štamfelj, I., Cvetko, E., Bitenc-Ovsenik, M., *et al.* (2004) 'Identification of two human deciduous incisors excavated from archaeological sites in Mala Triglavca and Viktorjev spodmol', in I. Turk (ed.) *Viktorjev spodmol and Mala Triglavca*, Ljubljana: Založba ZRC SAZU, Opera Instituti Archaeologici Sloveniae 9.

Štamfelj, I., Štefančič, M., Gašperšič, D., *et al.* (2006) 'Carabelli's trait in Contemporary Slovenes and inhabitants of a medieval settlement (Središče by the Drava River)', *Collegium Antropologicum*, 30: 421–28.

Steele, J. (2000) 'Skeletal indicators of handedness', in M. Cox and S. Mays (eds) *Human Osteology in Archaeology and Forensic Science*, London: Greenwich Medical Media.

Štefančič, M. (1980) 'Demography of Early Middle Ages necropolis St. Erazmo near Ohrid', *Collegium Antropologicum*, 4: 213–20.

——(1985) 'Antropološka analiza lobanje z Ljubljanskega barja', *Poročilo o raziskovanju paleolita, neolita in eneolita v Sloveniji*, 12: 75–79.

——(1988) *Ranosrednjovekovni skeleti nekropole Sv. Erazmo kod Ohrida*, Beograd: Etnoantropološki problemi – monografije 5.

——(1990) 'Changes in the cephalic index in Slovenia from the Iron Age to the present', *Sborník Národního Muzea v Praze*, 46: 202–5.

——(1992) 'Skeletni ostanki koliščarjev z Ljubljanskega barja', *Poročilo o raziskovanju paleolita, neolita in eneolita v Sloveniji*, 20: 127–34.

——(1995) 'Antropološka obdelava zgodnjesrednjeveških okostij iz grobišča Nin-Ždrijac (Severna Dalmacija)', *Arheološki vestnik*, 46: 291–325.

Štefančič, M. and Leben-Seljak, P. (1992) 'Antropološka analiza staroslovanskega grobišča Dlesc pri Bodeščah', *Arheološki vestnik*, 43: 191–203.

Štefančič, M., Tomazo-Ravnik, T. and Leben-Seljak, P. (2008) 'The anthropological analysis of skeletons from the Medieval cemetery Središče by the Drava river (Slovenia)', in *16th Congress of the European Anthropological Association*, Odense: University of Southern Denmark.

Stloukal, M. (1965) 'Künstlich deformierte Schädel von Vyškov', *Anthropologischer* Anzeiger, 29: 250–60.

Szombathy, J. (1879) 'Die Skelette aus den Gräbern von Roje bei Moräutsch', in C. Deschmann and F. Hochstetter (eds) Prähistorische Ansiedlungen und Begräbnissstätten in Krain, Wien: Abgedruckt aus dem XLII Bande der Denkschriften der Mathematisch-naturwissenschaftlichen Classe der Kaiserlichen Akademie der Wissenschaften.

Toldt, C. (1912) 'Die Schädelformen in den österreichischen Wohngebieten der Altslawen – einst und jetzt', *Mitteilungen der Anthropologischen gesellschaft in Wien*, 42: 247–80.

Tomazo-Ravnik, T. (1975) 'Antropološka obdelava osteološkega gradiva', in M. Slabe (ed.) *Dravlje: grobišče iz časov preseljevanja ljudstev*, Ljubljana: Narodni Muzej Slovenije, Situla 16.

——(1979) 'Staroslovansko grobišče v Zgornjem Dupleku', *Arheološki vestnik*, 30: 489–96.

Tortora, G.J. and Grabowski, S.R. (2003) *Principles of Anatomy and Physiology*, 10th edn, New Jersey: Johns Wiley & Sons.

Vlahović, P. (1989) 'Slovenija u svetlu istorijske antropologije', *Glasnik Antropološkog društva Jugoslavije*, 26: 5–11.

Zupanič Pajnič, I. (2008) 'Preliminarno poročilo molekularno-genetske identifikacije okostij iz grobišča pri Konfinu I', in J. Dežman (ed.) *Poročilo Komisije Vlade Republike Slovenije za reševanje vprašanj prikritih grobišč 2005–2008*, Ljubljana: Družina.

Zupanič Slavec, Z. (2004) *New Method of Identifying Family Related Skulls: Forensic Medicine, Anthropology, Epigenetics*, Wien: Springer.

Spain/España

Nicholas Márquez-Grant, Carme Rissech, Olalla López-Costas,
Inmaculada Alemán and Luis Caro Dobón

INTRODUCTION: A BRIEF HISTORY AND CURRENT STATE OF PHYSICAL ANTHROPOLOGY IN SPAIN

Physical anthropology as a scientific discipline in Spain can be considered as starting in the 1860s under the influence of the French anthropologist Paul Broca (for further detailed information on its beginnings in Spain see Reverte Coma 1991). The year 1865 saw the creation of the Spanish Anthropological Society (Sociedad Española de Antropología) with several famous scholars such as Pedro González de Velasco and Ángel Pulido Fernández. In 1885 the Museum of Natural History in Madrid (Museo de Historia Natural de Madrid) was founded. In 1892, the museum's founder Manuel Antón y Ferrándiz, who had trained in Paris, took the first Chair of Anthropology in the Science Faculty of the Central University of Madrid (Universidad Central de Madrid). In 1894, Dr Federico Olóriz y Aguilera (see Arquiola 1981) carried out work on cephalic indices in Spain, publishing his famous work entitled *Distribución geográfica del índice cefálico en España*. In 1921, the Spanish Society of Anthropology, Ethnology and Prehistory was founded (Sociedad Española de Antropología, Etnología y Prehistoria). The end of the 19th century and first half of the 20th century saw many famous scholars including Hoyos Sáinz, Telesforo de Aranzadi, Francisco de las Barras de Aragón, José Pons and Santiago Alcobé. In México, a Spanish immigrant, Juan Comas, published *Manual de Antropología Física* (Comas 1959), followed by an English translation in 1960 (*Manual of Physical Anthropology*). In 1973 a number of Spanish physical anthropologists had created a Biological Anthropology group (Grupo de Antropología Biológica) within the Spanish Society of Natural History. In the same year, in order to improve the activity in the field of physical anthropology, a meeting was organized at the University of Seville between 30 January and 3 February (I Reunión de Antropólogos Españoles). This meeting gathered together Spanish social, cultural and biological anthropologists to discuss research and teaching. The success of this meeting led to a second meeting in Segovia in November of 1974 (II Reunión de Antropólogos Españoles) with an attendance of more than 200 scientists. While in the first meeting only one person, José Pons from the University of Barcelona, provided the vision of Biological Anthropology in Spain (Jiménez 1975), the second meeting saw an increase in the number of biological anthropologists. This considerable number motivated the organization of the first Spanish Anthropology Congress (I Congreso Español de Antropología) in Barcelona in 1977. The first symposium of Biological

Anthropology (I Simposio de Antropología Biológica de España) was hosted by the Universidad Complutense de Madrid between 28 and 31 March 1978, with both national and international participants; and the conference proceedings were published in 1979 (Garralda and Grande 1979). On 30 March 1978 the Spanish Society for Biological Anthropology (Sociedad Española de Antropología Biológica, or SEAB) was founded under the presidency of José Pons, although it only received official recognition on 4 December 1979. The first committee meeting in 1978, nevertheless, addressed the following issues: the creation of a publication (*Boletín de la Sociedad Española de Antropología Biológica*) with the first issue published in 1980; the hosting of a congress (Congreso de Antropología Biológica de España) every two years and the publication of the conference proceedings (*Actas y Comunicaciones*). In 1987, the Spanish Palaeopathological Society was founded (Asociación Española de Paleopatología) and is currently a very active and dynamic society (see Etxeberria 2009). Also of relevance is the foundation in 2006 of the Spanish Association of Forensic Anthropology and Odontology (Asociación Española de Antropología y Odontología Forenses or AEAOF).[1]

On 16 November 2006, the Spanish Society for Biological Anthropology changed its name from SEAB to SEAF (Sociedad Española de Antropología Física) and its journal became the *Revista Española de Antropología Física* or *REAF* (Figure 38.1). The conferences are every two years and at the time of writing the most recent one took place in Alcalá de Henares in 2009, with a number of international and national participants (Figure 38.2). Information on publication trends of the Society and its journal, which is a reflection of biological anthropology in Spain, can be found in the work of Vizcaíno *et al.* (2009), which reviews 1185 works published in conference proceedings from 1978 to 2005.

When biological anthropology is considered overall, then the discipline in Spain sees considerable research in human growth and nutrition, palaeoanthropology, dermatoglyphs and population genetics among other aspects. Palaeopathological research is extensive, as well as osteological research in relation to developing techniques for age and sex determination. Although more traditional studies such as craniometric analysis are still carried out today, many scholars are increasingly working on ancient DNA studies (e.g., Sampietro *et al.* 2005; Lalueza-Fox *et al.* 2005, 2009), trace element analysis (e.g., Safont *et al.* 1998; Subirà and Malgosa 2005) and stable isotope analysis (e.g., García-Guixé *et al.* 2006, 2009; Márquez-Grant *et al.* 2003) and within an increasing international network and a multidisciplinary and biocultural approach. Studies on mummies are also a focus of attention (e.g., González Antón *et al.* 1992; Isidro Llorens *et al.* 2006).

Skeletal collections in Spain

The oldest documented skeletal collections in Spain are the 1885 pathological collection of the University of Granada and the Olóriz Collection (Colección Olóriz) of the Anatomical Museum of the Universidad Complutense de Madrid. The pathological collection of the University of Granada was started by Dr Duarte from pathological cases at the Hospital Clínico of Granada University. The collection includes a considerable number of skeletal elements with a number of documented pathological conditions, including cranial malformation, syphilis, leprosy, tuberculosis, neoplasms and trauma. These human remains belonged to persons who were being treated but who later died in the hospital. The majority of these remains are accompanied by plaster casts which show the external symptoms that the disease had left on the body. The Olóriz collection was created by anatomist Dr Olóriz. It originally comprised 2250 documented skulls from different regions of Spain, although this number has been reduced today (database available online at www.ucm.es/info/museoana/Colecciones/Craneos/index.htm).

Since the 1980s, four more collections came into being. In 1985 Dr Francisco Pastor started the Valladolid collection at the Anatomical Museum of the University of Valladolid. This is

Figure 38.1 Front cover of the *Journal of the Spanish Society of Physical Anthropology* (REAF)
Source: Sociedad Española de Antropología Física

comprised of more than 100 documented individuals. In Granada, Dr Miguel Botella and Dr Immaculada Alemán began a collection of 489 complete skeletons in a good state of preservation and with information on age, sex and cause of death. Of these, 283 are skeletons of immature individuals less than ten years of age. The University of Granada also has a forensic collection of documented samples with traumatic peri-mortem injuries. Dr José Antonio Sánchez Sánchez created a documented collection, which is at the Universidad Complutense de Madrid; while in Barcelona Dr Carme Rissech and Dr Assumpció Malgosa created the UAB (Universitat Autònoma de Barcelona) collection with known age and sex information among other details (see Rissech and Steadman 2010).

There are many historical collections held in museums and institutions. These include the University of Leon's collection of over 2000 skeletons from 40 populations from the region of Castilla y León (Caro *et al.* 2008). Worthy of mention, too, are the human remains curated at the Museo Reverte Coma (or Museo de Antropología Forense, Paleopatología y Criminología) in Madrid, with a variety of crania from mediaeval times, a pathological collection and an

Figure 38.2 Attendees at the 2009 conference of the Spanish Society of Physical Anthropology in Alcalá de
    Henares, Madrid
Source: Sociedad Española de Antropología Física

interest in forensic anthropology among other sections (Reverte Coma 1991; www.museorever
tecoma.org).

Education and training

In 2000, Physical Anthropology in Spain was officially recognized as a subject (Área de Con-
ocimiento) within the Spanish university system, and is now compulsory within the Bachelor of
Science degree (formerly known as Licenciatura and soon to be known as Grados) in Biology.
Today, it is taught as a subject in biology or medicine at the universities of Barcelona (Central,
Autónoma and Pompeu Fabra), Granada, León, Madrid (Complutense, Autónoma and Alcalá),
Murcia, Oviedo, País Vasco, Salamanca, Santiago de Compostela, Valencia, Vigo and Zaragoza.
Thus, physical anthropologists in Spain tend to derive from a biological and medical back-
ground. More recently, thanks to the creation of Master's degree courses, many students
attending are those with an archaeological background.

   The subject has also been included in the fields of anatomy and comparative pathology, social
anthropology, archaeology, ecology, physical education and sport studies, genetics, forensic
medicine, palaeontology and zoology.

   Finally, although the subject of forensic anthropology is mainly within Forensic Medicine,
the Ministry of Education in Spain follows the UNESCO classification of the subject within
physical anthropology in science (Biology, Life Sciences) rather than medicine or forensic
medicine (Etxeberria 2001). The majority of practicing forensic anthropologists in Spain are
actually practising forensic pathologists (médico forense) who have specialized in forensic
anthropology. Usually, forensic anthropologists with a medical background and undertaking

modern casework tend to be attached to a governmental institution (e.g., Escuela de Medicina Legal or Instituto Anátomico Forense, both in Madrid). Additionally, both the National Police (Policía Nacional) and the Civil Guard (Guardia Civil) and other regional forces (e.g., Ertzaintza in the Basque Country) have their own team of forensic anthropologists. Aside from the armed forces, there are a number of anthropologists (especially at the universities of Pais Vasco, Granada and Madrid) that undertake casework and are expert witnesses.

ARCHAEOLOGICAL HUMAN REMAINS AND LEGISLATION

Archaeological legislation

Spain is divided into 17 autonomous regions (Comunidades Autónomas). In addition, there are two Spanish autonomous cities, Ceuta and Melilla, which are located in North Africa.

Archaeological work in Spain falls under the 1985 Ley del Patrimonio Histórico Español (Law of Spanish Historical Heritage). The law refers to any movable or unmovable artefacts, relics or structures (bienes muebles e inmuebles) that are of artistic, historical, palaeontological, archaeological, ethnographic, scientific or technical interest. It refers to documentary sources, archaeological sites, natural sites, gardens and parks of an artistic, historical or anthropological value, whether buried, on the surface or underwater. All sites or monuments that can be preserved will be listed as protected (e.g., Bien de Interés Cultural, or BIC).

This 1985 law provides general specifications established by the Spanish Government. However, the excavation licence (permiso de excavación), and more specific legislation regarding archaeological work, curation, archiving, post-excavation work, etc. has been transferred to the different regional governments that control the archaeological work and provide authorization for excavation and survey. Although all regions run directly under the general Ley del Patrimonio Histórico Español, they will also have their own regional laws. The authorization from a regional or local governmental institution (e.g., Consejería, Consell, Consellería or Saila, depending on the regional language) is required for any archae-ological activity to take place in that region, whether it is an excavation, an evaluation, a watching brief, an underwater exploration or the study of cave paintings. In the case of research projects, the interested party will have to provide a research proposal, identify the area to be excavated, provide a timeline for the project, information relating to team members, and will need consent from the landowner. With regard to rescue excavations or watching briefs, it is the regional government that will request that the construction company employs an archaeologist.

This regional or local authority obliges all archaeologists to submit the artefacts, human remains or any other environmental samples to the museums once they have been clearly catalogued, washed and labeled. These artefacts (no washing or labeling required for human remains) need to be inventoried and analysed, after which a final report is sent to the regional governmental institution (the council). The deadline to submit all the records, inventory and report is usually two years from the end of the excavation. The site director cannot usually direct another site if the report from his or her previous site has not been submitted.

It is the regional government that has the power to authorize or cause to cease archaeological work. In order to apply for an excavation permit, including the excavation of archaeological sites including human remains, the project director will have to present a proposal to the heritage or cultural authorities of the regional government where the excavation is to take place, since it is this regional institution which has the power to authorize or cause to cease archaeological work.

In Catalonia for example, the legislative framework for archaeology can be found in the official bulletin (DOG) for this region, which addresses the legislation regarding research excavations of archaeological or palaeontological interest. In the case of a research project, the proposal to apply for an excavation licence (permiso de excavación) requires information on the research project, the CVs of the director and the team, a likely timetable for the work, the support of a recognized institution and details on artefact conservation. The director should demonstrate experience and have a relevant degree, usually a degree in History (Licenciatura en Historia). Approval from the landlord is also required. The licence is only applicable for one intervention so that a separate licence is required for each campaign if applicable. The director of the excavation will be responsible for writing the report and cataloguing the materials within one year. Any permits required by foreign researchers or institutions must have the support of a known institution in their country. The project should also have at least one Spanish co-director.

To summarize, although the national law provides a legal framework, each region (Comunidad Autónoma) will develop its own legislation within the limits of the Spanish law, and will have total control of archaeological work and the protection of sites and monuments in that particular region. An exception to this are the lands or sites that are part of the National Heritage (Patrimonio Nacional) or that belong to the Ministry of Defence (Ministerio de Defensa). Due to this regional autonomy, therefore, it is necessary for archaeologists to check the regional legislation in order to follow specific requirements (see Arrizabalaga Valbuena 1997; Querol and Martínez 1996).

HUMAN REMAINS AND LEGISLATION

When human remains are randomly discovered, the police should be contacted, who will then inform the judge (juez de instrucción). The judge will decide what to do with the situation and who needs to attend the scene. The first person to attend the scene may be the forensic pathologist (médico forense). If the remains are skeletonized and likely to be archaeological, the pathologist would normally inform the judge, who will call for a government archaeologist (e.g., from the council) to attend the scene. If the archaeologist is called first to the site and confirms the remains as archaeological, it is still necessary on occasion to await the visit of the coroner, judge or forensic pathologist, after which a rescue excavation will be carried out.

The border between archaeological and non-archaeological remains unclear. In Galicia, the Heritage Law (Lei do Patrimonio Cultural de Galicia) and the decree relating to archaeological activity (Decreto 199/1997 de 10 de Julio) to establish a period of 100 years to consider something as archaeological. This applies to most regions. In certain other regions or instances, the law may indicate that sites of archaeological interest and under special protection will only have to be 50 years or older. The remains of the dead from the Civil War (1936–39) fall between archaeological and forensic. Moreover, the Criminal Code in Spain (Código Penal Español, Articles 131, 132 and 133; and Ley Orgánica 10/1995 de 23 de noviembre) stipulates a time limitation of 20 years for a homicide. However, the time frame commences from the time the police start searching for the suspect. In reality, it depends on the context in which the remains have been found. Human remains with no signs of violence or evidence of foul play appearing in a non-crime related context (contexto no judicial) and of a date, for example, of some 30 years, will be of no criminal or archaeological interest. In this case it is the judge who decides whether or not to close the case.

There is no specific legislation for the excavation of archaeological human remains and therefore they fall under the general heritage and excavation regulations.[2] There are also no specific differences between the palaeontological finds (e.g., the important archaic *Homo* finds from Atapuerca) and human remains from more recent archaeological contexts. Nevertheless, there are sometimes specific mentions of bones and human remains within this general legislation. In Andalucía, emphasis has been placed on human remains and a number of anthropologists are currently attempting to ensure that more specific requirements are stated. In the region of Cantabria, there is mention of bones ('los útiles, *huesos*, cerámicas, metales', emphasis ours) indicating they must be deposited in the regional museum within six months from the end of fieldwork.

At present, there is no legal obligation for an anthropologist to be on site, but this is certainly very strongly recommended by most institutions and national anthropological and palaeopathological associations. An exception may be the Dirección Xeral de Patrimonio de la Xunta de Galicia or the Galician Cultural Department, which may oblige the archaeological team to include a physical anthropologist in an excavation. Since 2007 the government of the region of Galicia (Xunta de Galicia) in the northwest of Spain, and the physical anthropology unit of the University of Santiago de Compostela, have a contract which enables the participation of the university anthropologist(s) in excavations carried out by archaeological companies. This allows for recording and methodological standardization across the region and government funding to undertake post-excavation analysis of the human remains (see, e.g., López-Costas 2008).

Regarding human remains from churches and churchyards, there is still a debate surrounding the excavation of human remains from Catholic grounds. In Christian cemeteries and burials within Catholic churches, permission needs to be sought from the Catholic Church (Iglesia Católica). Usually, the regional government will approve the excavation by liaising and informing the Church. In these cases, for example when the work involves excavating burials in a church nave, a mixed committee with regional government and Church representatives will approve, coordinate and inspect the work to be undertaken.

With regard to exhumations in cemeteries, the law (BOE) with its own regional bulletins (e.g., BOJA for Andalucia), has a section (Chapter V) relevant to the use of corpses and human remains for teaching and research purposes. These remains can derive from individuals who have voluntarily offered to donate their body, or human remains not claimed by relatives or, on the contrary, for which the donation has been approved by a relative; and always ensuring that the victim is not part of a criminal investigation. In these case, transportation of the bodies (e.g., from the cemetery to a Medical Faculty) should ideally be done in a hearse. The skeletal collection from the Autonomous University of Barcelona (UAB) mentioned previously and created in 1996–97, was the result of an agreement between the Biological Anthropology Unit of the Autonomous University of Barcelona and the Granollers City Hall (Granollers, Barcelona) with the aim of having a reference collection in Catalonia (Rissech and Steadman 2010). Granollers City Hall granted permission to collect the remains of individuals that had not been claimed by their families and that were destined for a communal ossuary in the cemetery. In Spanish cemeteries, the dead are usually buried in niches (cavities constructed in walls within the cemetery) and the possession of a niche can last for a number of years, after which they can be rented for renewable periods of five years. Non-payment of rent results in the loss of rights and the existing remains are exhumed by the town hall and taken to a common ossuary.

Finally, authorization for transportation of archaeological human remains will be sought from the local cultural or heritage authorities (e.g., regional government) and the director of the excavation. The authorization may be in the form of a letter stating the number of human remains, the place they are going to and the type of analysis to be undertaken. If the materials have been deposited in a museum, it is the museum director who would provide the authorization. Sometimes there is a requirement that remains to be transported must be insured (e.g., for any loss or damage).

Civil War graves

The Spanish Civil War (1936–39) and the dictatorship that followed (1939–75) resulted in thousands of mass graves. Since December 2007, there is legislation (Ley de Memoria Histórica)[3] regulating exhumations in order to recover and identify the deceased. The legislation indicates that collaboration must be present between the governmental institutions, the landowners and the relatives or legal representatives of the deceased. Generally speaking, this includes the requirement to have authorization from relatives or the legal representatives of the deceased, authorization of the governmental institutions in relation to excavation or survey taking into consideration the National Heritage Law, authorization from the Health administration (Mortuary Police or Policía Sanitaria Mortuaria), and authorization from the landlord that will allow excavation of the grave (see also, e.g., Polo Cerdá 2009).

This legislation, however, also depends on the different regions in Spain since each region may have its own specific legislation.[4] In this state bulletin there is also reference to the maps that are available with the location of some Civil War graves, and the bulletin also provides information regarding the transportation of the remains according to the legislation established by the Mortuary Police.

One government draft, written by Spanish forensic anthropologists under the coordination of Dr Francisco Etxeberria, provides some recommendations (Etxeberria Gabilondo 2004).[5] It is a draft in which other specialists in Spain have collaborated and provides some guidelines regarding how to proceed in order to investigate mass graves from the Civil War. For example, it states that if there are conflicting interests between the different relatives or legal representatives of the deceased, it will be the local authority that will decide on either a complete, partial or non-opening of the grave. In addition, the proposal recommends that the following steps be undertaken: the creation of an ante-mortem database for the victims and prior archival research; archaeological investigation – location and nature of the grave, planning of resources, costs and time required; authorization – written consent from the relatives of the victims and authorization from the local authorities; archaeological excavation – ensuring a fieldwork diary is kept and all necessary recording is undertaken, that the site has security measures, and the need to inform the judge, the police and the local authorities when remains have been found; and forensic examination – identification of the victims, and cause and manner of death where possible. When identification has been possible, the remains will be sent to the relatives and then reburied in a cemetery. Moreover, this proposal recommends the collaboration between different specialists (forensic pathologists, archaeologists, anthropologists, historians, etc.) as well as a close liaison with the families and the Civil War associations (e.g., Asociación para la Recuperación de la Memoria Histórica, www.memoriahistorica.org; and El foro por la Memoria, www.foroporlamemoria.info).

Ethical considerations

There have been a number of cases where there is a significant concern regarding the display and excavation of human remains. Although these cases are few, they nevertheless suggest that legislation is necessary in order to address these concerns.

Repatriation cases are rare in Spain and the first case of repatriation involved a 19th-century African body displayed in a local museum (Museu Darder, Banyoles) which was repatriated in the 1990s (Jaume *et al.* 1992). With regard to excavations, problems arose during the excavation in 1996 of 16th-century Jewish graves in Valencia (Jiménez and Mata 2001; Endere 2000). In this case, the town hall and the regional government had initially decided to return the remains to the Israeli Community in Spain so they could be reburied in a Jewish cemetery in Barcelona prior to any anthropological study. The archaeologists who directed the excavation complained to the Citizen's Bureau (Defensor del Pueblo) and in 1998 the authorities decided to overrule their initial decision and they considered the cemetery as part of the archaeological heritage and therefore protected under heritage law (Ley del Patrimonio Histórico Español). Similar problems were present in 2007 during the excavation of the Mediaeval Jewish cemetery of Les Roquetes in Tàrrega (Barcelona) and the regional government's decision was to have the remains returned to the Jewish community in Spain after a brief and rapid anthropological study. It was recognized at the time that there was a need for protocols in case similar future situations arose (for further information, see Jiménez and Mata 2001).

Mediaeval Islamic graves have been excavated and continue to be excavated, but one must be sensitive and consider the community in which the remains have been found. A large Islamic cemetery in Ávila, in the centre of Spain, with thousands of tombs dated to the 13th and 14th centuries AD, was excavated and in this case the archaeologists went to the authorities to actually have the area protected under heritage law, but their attempt was unsuccessful and construction works continued (see Gallego Anabitarte 2003).

Regarding the exhumations of Civil War graves, the relatives of those who have disappeared must be considered as well as their desire or otherwise to exhume and identify their deceased relatives.

It is also worthy of mention that a number of museum exhibitions including human remains have received positive feedback from the community. Examples of two recent exhibitions are Apocaliptica. Els rastres de la mort a través de la història, segles XVI-XVIII (Generalitat de Catalunya 2008), and Esquelets Malalts. Una visió de la malaltia a través del temps at the Museu Egipci de Barcelona (www.museuegipci.com) in 2009, with over 150 palaeopathological specimens. In 2010 in Valencia another exhibition has taken place, entitled Restes de Vida, Restes de Mort, at the Museu de Prehistòria de Valencia (www.museuprehistoriavalencia.es).

METHODS OF ANTHROPOLOGICAL ANALYSIS

International guidelines are followed in Spain, and these include Ferembach *et al.* (1980), Brothwell (1987), Buikstra and Ubelaker (1994), Bass (1995) and Brickley and McKinley (2004). However, anthropological methods developed from Spanish populations and neighbouring Portuguese and French populations are also employed and should be used in any anthropological analysis.

The completeness of a skeleton is commonly measured with the 'preservation index' (Índice de preservación), which is a formula modified by Safont (Safont *et al.* 1999) based on the work of Walker *et al.* (1988). Age estimation in sub-adult individuals follows internationally recognized charts for dental development (e.g., Ubelaker 1999; Crétot 1978; Schour and Massler 1941). For foetal skeletal development, the methods devised by Castellana and Kósa (1999) and Kósa and Castellana (2005) are also employed. Those methods developed also for sub-adult age estimation by Rissech and colleagues (Rissech *et al.* 2001, 2003, 2008; Rissech and Malgosa 2005, 2008; Rissech and Black 2007; Ríos *et al.* 2008) and other Spanish scholars (e.g., González-Martín 1999) are also applicable since they have been created from Spanish or Iberian populations.

Age estimation methods for adult skeletons, such as those on the pubic symphysis and auricular surface, have been tested on Spanish osteological collections (Corcione 2008; Powoanda 2008). These tests have revealed that the methods devised by Lovejoy *et al.* (1985), Buckberry and Chamberlain (2002), Todd (1921) and Brooks and Suchey (1990) provide an approximate accuracy of under 30%, 86% and 71% respectively, although this also depended on the wide age ranges used. The method devised by Brothwell (1987) on dental wear is the most widely used method when dental wear is considered; while the method devised by Miles (1963) is much less known and thus has been used less often. In addition, the 1995 method of Kvaal and colleagues to assess age from the dentition on living individuals has proved to be inaccurate and its use is not recommended for Iberian populations (Landa *et al.* 2009). More recently, new methods for age estimation on the first rib (Garamendi *et al.* 2007) and the acetabulum (Rissech *et al.* 2006, 2007) have had some success. Finally, when considering age categories, there is variation and, although debatable and perhaps controversial, many of the published works include the following age categories: perinates (36–40 weeks gestation), neonates (up to 12 months), Infant I (1–6 years), Infant II (7–12 years), Juvenile (13–20 years); while the adult categories are divided into 20–40 years, 40–60 and >60 years.

Spanish methods for sex determination include post-cranial discriminant functions (López-Bueis *et al.* 1995; Alemán *et al.* 1997; Trancho *et al.* 1997, 2000; Rissech and Malgosa 1997; Safont *et al.* 2000). Bruzek's (2002) method on pelvic morphology on French and Portuguese samples has also been employed in Spain.

Metric data is usually obtained following Martin and Saller (1957) but some national laboratories have also compiled their set of measurements to take (e.g., Robledo Acinas *et al.* 2008). When stature is estimated, Lalueza-Fox (1998) has indicated that the formulae by Trotter and Gleser (1952, 1958) for 'American Whites' are the least reliable, and that Pearson's (1898) method, widely used in Spain, appears to be the most reliable. Other methods employed are French (e.g., Manouvrier 1893; Olivier 1960) and Portuguese (Mendonça 2000). Trotter and Gleser's (1952, 1958) formulae for 'American Blacks' may be applicable in Mediterranean populations due to similar limb proportions.

General reference books that are popular include those by Reverte Coma on medical anthropology (Reverte Coma 1981) and forensic anthropology (Reverte Coma 1991). Other anthropological publications may also provide some useful information (see, e.g., Isidro and Malgosa 2003; Campillo and Subirà 2004; Villalaín Blanco and Puchalt Fortea 2000). A book on taphonomy has also been published by Spanish scholars (Botella *et al.* 2000). General works of reference in palaeopathology include the publications by D. Campillo which set some national recommendations and may aid recording and reporting (with correct Spanish terminology) of palaeopathological cases (e.g., Campillo 1983, 2001, 2007). The work of Aufderheide and Rodríguez-Martín (1998) has many references to pathological cases from Spain, and similarly the *Atlas Handbook of Paleopathology* (Baxarias and Herrerín 2008). Recommendations for oral palaeopathology have been given by Chimenos and colleagues (Chimenos *et al.* 1999). In 2007, the congress of the Spanish Palaeopathology Association included a workshop aimed at creating a working group for recommendations on report writing in biological anthropology and palaeopathology (González Martín *et al.* 2009).

The analysis of cremated human bone

In Spain, the study of cremated bone stems mainly from the work of J.M. Reverte Coma (e.g., 1981, 1991). His influential work, alongside protocols devised by F. Gómez-Bellard (1996), should be taken into account. National bibliography and the standard method to record and present cremated bone data which is usually very standardized in Spain has been summarized by Polo Cerdá and García-Prósper (2007) and is accessible at www.uv.es/paleolab. There is still a need, however, to standardize the terminology for cremation burials and cremation-related contexts.

Comparative material

There are a number of bibliographical reviews which are useful if undertaking work in Spain and provide work to be used as comparative data and a number of classic sites (e.g., La Torrecilla). These can be found in the journal of the Spanish Society of Physical anthropology (*REAF*) and the society's conference proceedings. Dr F. Etxeberria has also compiled a considerable amount of Spanish publications (Etxeberria 2007; see also Trancho *et al.* 1995, 1997).

CONCLUSION

Physical anthropology in Spain has had an active tradition since the 19th century. While most researchers have a biological or medical background, the creation of Master's degree courses has led to training of scientists from other fields.

When archaeological excavations are to be conducted, legislation falls under the national heritage law but also under regional law. It is the regional government that will have specific requirements and will authorize the excavation. There are a number of methods developed for Spanish populations and these have demonstrated a good level of accuracy. Some of these have been published in Spanish, but the most recent ones can be easily found in international journals. There is a need for guidelines and standardization in Spain. It would be useful to see national recommendations, especially relating to the recording and presentation of osteological results.

Biomolecular studies have seen an increase recently, as too have the creation of some databases and new societies. In addition, palaeoanthropological sites such as those at Atapuerca or El Sidrón have attracted a number of international scholars. It would only be fair to say that physical anthropology in Spain is thriving, with new generations of scholars re-shaping the field within a wider international network.

USEFUL CONTACTS

The Spanish Society of Physical Anthropology or SEAF (Sociedad Española de Antropología Física) is a good point of contact (www3.unileon.es/seaf). Other societies of relevance are the Spanish Palaeopathology Association (Asociación Española de Paleopatología; www.ucm.es/info/aep/), Dr Francisco Etxeberria's website from Sociedades de Ciencias Aranzadi (www.aranzadi-zientziak.org/index.php?id=97), the website of Grupo Paleolab (www.uv.es/paleolab) and the forensic anthropology and odontology association website (Asociación Española de Antropología y Odontología Forense; www.freewebtown.com/aeaof/). Every university department has its website, too, and information on each can be found under the Faculty of Sciences and departments of biology. Other smaller associations include the Catalano-Balearic Palaeopathological Association (Associació Catalano-Balear de Paleopatologia; email: paleopatologia@gmail.com). All the information on legislation can be found on the government's official website, www.boe.es.

ACKNOWLEDGEMENTS

We thank the archaeologist Jaime Almansa Sánchez for his help with regard to archaeological legislation in Spain. Author O.L.C. thanks the support of F.P.U. scholarship and the Dirección Xeral de Patrimonio Cultural de la Xunta de Galicia while co-writing this chapter. The authors would also like to thank the endless list of colleagues who helped us with queries, bibliography and very useful information that helped us improve this article.

NOTES

1 For information on the development of forensic anthropology in Spain please refer to the work of Reverte (1991) and Prieto (2008).
2 In the region of Andalucia, a draft was submitted in November 2009 to the Cultural governmental body (Consejería de Cultura) to amend the archaeological legislation to favour the recovery, study and treatment of human remains and the role of the osteoarchaeologist (I. López Flores, pers. comm). Discussions are still ongoing.
3 http://leymemoria.mjusticia.es/paginas/es/ley_memoria.html (bulletin BOE of 27 December 2007).
4 For example, a protocol for exhumation in the region of Andalucia has already been published in the governmental bulletin for the region (BOJA, no. 190: 8–12, dated 7 September 2009). In Catalonia, for example, it is not necessary to get authorization from the relatives of the deceased and a grave can be opened as long as the judge, the Civil Guard (Guardia Civil) and the local administration have been informed; and usually it is the governmental institution, the Generalitat, that undertakes the work. In the region of Aragon, mass graves are classified in different categories depending on the deceased (e.g., whether they are soldiers killed in action, civilians killed in combat or during explosions, etc.).
5 www.foroporlamemoria.info/excavaciones/panorama_organizativo_antropo_patolo.htm.

BIBLIOGRAPHY

Alemán, I., Botella, M. and Ruiz, L. (1997) 'Determinación del sexo en el esqueleto postcraneal. Estudio de una población mediterránea actual', *Archivo Español de Morfología*, 2: 7–17.
Arquiola, E. (1981) 'Anatomía y antropología en la obra de Olóriz', *Acta Hispanica ad Medicinae Sicentiarumque Historiam Illustrandam*, 1: 165–77.
Arrizabalaga Valbuena, A. (1997) 'El marco jurídico de la actividad arqueológica: legislación estatal y autonómica', in M.M. Macías López and J.E. Picazo Sánchez (eds) *La Enfermedad en los Restos Humanos Arqueológicos: Actualización Conceptual y Metodológica*, Actas del IV Congreso Nacional de Paleopatología (San Fernando, 2–5 Octubre 1997), Cádiz: Universidad de Cádiz, Servicio de Publicaciones.
Aufderheide, A.C. and Rodríguez-Martín, C. (1998) *The Cambridge Encyclopedia of Human Paleopathology*, Cambridge: Cambridge University Press.
Baxarias, J. and Herrerín, J. (2008) *Handbook Atlas of Paleopathology*, Zaragoza: Libros Pórtico.
Bass, W.M. (1995) *Human Osteology: A Laboratory and Field Manual*, 4th edn, Columbia, MO: Missouri Archaeological Society.
Botella, M., Alemán, I. and Jiménez (2000) *Los huesos humanos. Manipulación y alteraciones*, Barcelona: Bellaterra.
Brickley, M. and McKinley, J.I. (2004) *Guidelines to the Standards for Recording Human Remains*, Institute of Field Archaeology Paper no. 7, Reading: Institute of Field Archaeologists.
Brooks, S. and Suchey, J.M. (1990) 'Skeletal age determination based on the os pubis: a comparison of the Acsádi-Neméskeri and Suchey-Brooks methods', *Human Evolution*, 5: 227–38.
Brothwell, D.R. (1987) *Desenterrando huesos*, México: Fondo de Cultura Económica.
Bruzek, J. (2002) 'A method for visual determination of sex, using the human hip bone', *American Journal of Physical Anthropology*, 117: 157–68.
Buckberry, J.L. and Chamberlain, A.T. (2002) 'Age estimation from the auricular surface of the ilium: a revised method', *American Journal of Physical Anthropology*, 119: 231–39.
Buikstra, J. and Ubelaker, D. (eds) (1994) *Standards for Data Collection from Human Skeletal Remains*, Fayetteville, AR: Arkansas Archaeological Survey Research Series No. 44.

Campillo, D. (1983) *La Enfermedad en la Prehistoria: Introducción a la Paleopatología*, Barcelona: Editorial Salvat.

——(2001) *Introducción a la paleopatología*, Barcelona: Bellaterra.

——(2007) *La trepanación prehistórica*, Barcelona: Bellaterra.

Campillo, D. and Subirà, M.E. (2004) *Antropología Física para arqueólogos*. Barcelona: Editorial Ariel SA.

Caro, L., López, B. and Fernández, M.E. (2008) 'Estudio antropológico de la necrópolis medieval de San Miguel de Gormaz (Soria)', in *San Miguel de Gormaz. Plan integral para la recuperación de un edificio histórico*, Valladolid: Junta de Castilla y León, Consejería de Cultura y Turismo.

Castellana, C. and Kósa, F. (1999) 'Morphology of the cervical vertebrae in the fetal and neonatal human skeleton', *Journal of Anatomy*, 194: 147–52.

Chimenos, E., Safont, S., Alesán, A., *et al.* (1999) 'Propuesta de protocolo de valoración de parámetros en paleodontología', *Gaceta Dental: Industria y Profesiones*, 102: 44–52.

Comas, J. (1959) *Manual de antropología física*, México: Fondo de Cultural Económica.

——(1960) *Manual of Physical Anthropology*, Springfield, IL: Charles C. Thomas.

Corcione, M.A. (2008) 'Valoración de tres metodologías clásicas para la estimación de la edad adulta, aplicadas a dos colecciones documentadas de la península ibérica', unpublished Master's thesis, Universidad Autònoma de Barcelona.

Crétot, M. (1978) *L'arcade dentaire humaine (Morphologie)*, 10th edn, Paris: Julien Prélat.

Endere, M.L. (2000) 'Patrimonios en disputa: acervos nacionales, investigación arqueológica y reclamos étnicos sobre restos humanos', *Trabajos de Prehistoria*, 57: 5–17.

Etxeberria, F. (2001) 'Antropología Forense en el marco de las Ciencias Forenses', paper presented at the Primeras Jornadas Iberoamericanas de Ciencias Forenses (20–22 June 2001), Madrid: Universidad Complutense.

——(2007) *Bibliografía de las investigaciones sobre Paleopatología en España. Actualización 2007*, Donostia-San Sebastián: Aranzadi Zientzi Elkartea/Sociedad de Ciencias Aranzadi.

——(2009) 'La paleopatología, una ciencia dinámica en España. Orígenes y expectativas', in M. Polo Cerdá and E. García-Prósper (eds) *Investigaciones Histórico-Médicas sobre Salud y Enfermedad en el Pasado*, Actas del IX Congreso Nacional de Paleopatología (Morella, 26–29 Septiembre de 2007), Valencia: Grupo Paleolab y Sociedad Española de Paleopatología.

Etxeberria Gabilondo, F., (2004) 'Panorama organizativo sobre antropología y patología forense en España. Algunas propuestas para el estudio de fosas con restos humanos de la Guerra Civil española de 1936', in E. Silva, A. Esteban, J. Castan y P. Salvador (eds) *La Memoria de los Olvidados. Un Debate sobre el Silencio de la Represión Franquista*, Valladolid: Ámbito Ediciones.

Fazekas, G.I. and Kósa, F. (1978) '*Forensic fetal osteology*', Budapest: Akademiai Kiadó.

Ferembach, D., Schwidetzky, I. and Stloukal, M. (1980) 'Recommendations for age and sex diagnoses of skeletons', *Journal of Human Evolution*, 9: 517–49.

Fuller, B., Márquez-Grant, N. and Richards, M.P. (in press) 'Investigation of diachronic dietary patterns on the islands of Ibiza and Formentera, Spain: evidence from carbon and nitrogen stable isotope ratio analysis', *American Journal of Physical Anthropology*.

Gallego Anabitarte, A. (2003) 'Arqueología y derecho: hallazgos, jurisprudencia, legislación, carta arqueológica y planeamiento', *Revista de Derecho Urbanístico y Medio Ambiente*, 200: 41–133.

Garamendi, P.M., Landa, M.I., Alemán, I., *et al.* (2007) 'Osificación del cartílago costal de la primera costilla en relación con la edad. Aplicaciones en la estimación forense de la dad', *Cuadernos de Medicina Forense*, 13: 243–53.

Garcia-Guixé, E., Richards, M.P. and Subirà, M.E. (2006) 'Palaeodiets of humans and fauna at the Spanish Mesolithic site of El Collado', *Current Anthropology*, 47: 549–56.

Garcia-Guixé, E., Martínez-Moreno, J., Mora, R., *et al.* (2009) 'Stable isotope analysis of human and animal remains from the Late Upper Palaeolithic site of Balma Guilanyà, southeastern Pre-Pyrenees, Spain', *Journal of Archaeological Science*, 36: 1018–26.

Garralda, M.D. and Grande, R.M. (eds) (1979) *Actas del I Simposio de Antropología Biológica de España*, Madrid: Sociedad Española de Antropología Biológica.

Gómez-Bellard, F. (1996) 'El análisis antropológico de las cremaciones', *Complutum* (Extra), 6: 55–64.

González Antón, R., Rodríguez Martín, C. and Estévez González, F. (1992) 'Bioantropología de las momias guanches', *Munibe* (Supplement): 51–61.

González-Martín, A. (1999) 'Infancia y adolescencia en la Murcia musulmana. Estudio de restos óseos', unpublished PhD thesis, Universidad Autónoma de Madrid.

González Martín, A., Herrasti Erlogorri, L. and Campo Martín, M. (2009) 'Grupo de trabajo para la creación de unas recomendaciones sobre la elaboración de "El informe en bioantropología y paleopatología"', in M. Polo Cerdá and E. García-Prósper (eds) *Investigaciones Histórico-Médicas sobre Salud y*

Enfermedad en el Pasado, Actas del IX Congreso Nacional de Paleopatología (Morella, 26–29 Septiembre de 2007), Valencia: Grupo Paleolab y Sociedad Española de Paleopatología.

Isidro, A. and Malgosa, A. (eds) (2003) *La enfermedad no escrita*, Barcelona: Editorial Masson.

Isidro Llorens, A., Malgosa Morera, A., Esteban, J., *et al.* (2006) 'Examen endoscópico de una momia egipcia: valoración de los resultados', *Medicina Clínica*, 127: 622–25.

Jaume, D., Pons, G., Palmer, M., *et al.* (1992) 'Racism, archaeology and museums: the strange case the stuffed African male in the Darder Museum, Banyoles (Catalonia), Spain', *World Archaeological Bulletin*, 6: 113–18.

Jiménez, A. (1975) *Primera reunión de antropólogos españoles*, Sevilla: Universidad de Sevilla.

Jiménez, J.L. and Mata, C. (2001) 'Creencias religiosas *versus* gestión del patrimonio arqueológico: el caso del cementerio judío de Valencia', *Trabajos de Prehistoria*, 58: 27–40.

Kósa, F. and Castellana, C. (2005) 'New forensic anthropological approachment for the age determination of human skeletons on base of the morphometry of vertebral column', *Forensic Science International*, 147 (Supplement): 69–74.

Lalueza-Fox, C. (1998) 'Stature and sexual dimorphism in ancient Iberian populations', *Homo*, 49: 260–72.

Lalueza-Fox, C., Sampietro, M.L., Caramelli, D., *et al.* (2005) 'Neandertal evolutionary genetics; mitochondrial DNA data from the Iberian Peninsula', *Molecular Biology and Evolution*, 22: 1077–81.

Lalueza-Fox, C., Gigli, E., De la Rasilla, M., *et al.* (2009) 'Bitter taste perception in Neanderthals through the analysis of the TAS2R38 gene', *Biology Letters*, 5: 809–11.

Landa, M.I., Garamendi, P.M., Botella, M.C., *et al.* (2009) 'Application of the method of Kvaal et al. to digital orthopantomograms', *International Journal of Legal Medicine*, 123: 123–28.

López-Bueis, I., Robledo, B., Roselló, G.J., *et al.* (1995) 'Funciones discriminantes para la determinación sexual de la tibia en una serie española de sexo y edad conocida', in J.M. Nieto and L. Moreno (eds) *Avances en antropología ecológica y genética*, Zaragoza: Universidad de Zaragoza.

López-Costas, O. (2008) 'Resumen anual ano 2008 do proxecto "Antropoloxía dos restos óseos humanos de Galicia […]"', unpublished report, Dirección Xeral de Patrimonio Cultural da Xunta de Galicia.

Lovejoy, C.O., Meindl, R., Pryzbeck, T., *et al.* (1985) 'Chronological metamorphosis of the auricular surface of the ilium: a new method for the determination of adult skeletal age at death', *American Journal of Physical Anthropology*, 68: 15–28.

Manouvrier, L. (1893) 'La détermination de la taille d'après les grands os des membres', *Mémoires de la Société d'Anthropolologie de Paris*, 4: 347–402.

Márquez-Grant, N., Fuller, B. and Richards, M.P. (2003) 'Análisis de patrones de dieta en restos humanos de la isla de Ibiza a partir del contenido de los isótopos estables de carbono, nitrógeno y azufre', in A. Aluja, R. Nogués and A. Malgosa (eds) *Antropología y Biodiversidad*, Actas del XII Congreso de la Asociación Española de Antropología Biológica, Barcelona: Universitat Autònoma de Barcelona.

Martin, R. and Saller, K. (1957) *Lehrbuch der Anthropologie*, 3rd edn, Stuttgart: Gustav Fischer Verlag.

Mendonça, M.C. (2000) 'Estimation of height from the length of long bones in a Portuguese adult population', *American Journal of Physical Anthropology*, 112: 39–48.

Miles, A.E.W. (1963) 'The dentition in the assessment of individual age in skeletal material', in D.R. Brothwell (ed.) *Dental Anthropology*, Oxford: Pergamon.

Olivier, G. (1960) *Pratique anthropologique*, Paris: Vigot.

Olóriz, F. (1894) 'Distribución geográfica del índice cefálico en España, deducida del examen de 8.368 varones adultos', report presented at the Congreso Geográfico Hispano-Portugués-Americano (19 October 1892, Madrid), Madrid: Universidad Complutense.

Pearson, K. (1898) 'Mathematical contributions to the Theory of Evolution. On the reconstruction of the stature of prehistoric races', *Philosophical Transactions of the Royal Society of London*, Series A, 192: 169–244.

Polo Cerdá, M. (2009) 'Métodos internacionales empleados para la identificación de restos óseos humanos', I Seminario de Antropología Forense en el Marco de los Derechos Humanos, *Revista d'Estudis de la Violència*, 8. Available online at www.icev.cat/antropologiaforense.pdf/

Polo Cerdá, M. and García-Prósper, E. (2007) 'Propuesta de recogida de datos bioantropológicos en los estudios de cremaciones romanas', in F.J. Barca Durán and J. Jiménez Ávila (eds) *Enfermedad, Muerte y Cultura en las Sociedades del Pasado*, Cáceres: Universidad de Extremadura.

Powoanda, A. (2008) 'A comparison of pelvic age-estimation methods on two modern Iberian populations: bioarchaeological and forensic implications', unpublished Master's thesis, New York University.

Prieto, J.L. (2008) 'La antropología forense en España desde la perspectiva de la medicina forense', *Cuadernos de Medicina Forense*, 53–54: 189–200.

Querol, M.A. and Martínez, B. (1996) *La gestión del patrimonio arqueológico en España*, Madrid: Alianza Editorial.

Reverte Coma, J.M. (1981) *Antropología Médica I*, Madrid: Editorial Rueda.

——(1991) *Antropología Forense*, Madrid: Ministerio de Justicia, Centro de Publicaciones.

Ríos, L., Weisensee, K. and Rissech, C. (2008) 'Sacral fusion as an aid in age estimation', *Forensic Science international*, 180: 1–9.

Rissech, C. and Black, S. (2007) 'Scapular development from neonatal period to skeletal maturity. A preliminary study', *International Journal of Osteoarchaeology*, 17: 451–64.

Rissech, C. and Malgosa, A. (1991) 'Importancia relativa de la longitud del pubis y la anchura del ilion en el estudio del dimorfismo sexual de los coxales', *Boletín de la Sociedad. Española de Antropología Biológica*, 12: 29–43.

——(1997) 'Sex prediction by discriminant function with central portion measures of innominate bones', *Homo*, 48: 22–32.

——(2005) 'Ilium growth study: applicability in sexual and age diagnostic', *Forensic Science International*, 147: 165–74.

——(2008) 'Pubic growth study: applicability in sexual and age diagnostic', *Forensic Science International*, 173: 137–45.

Rissech, C. and Steadman, D. (2010) 'The demographic, socio-economic and temporal contextualisation of the Universitat Autònoma de Barcelona Collection of Identified Human Skeletons (UAB Collection)', *International Journal of Osteoarchaeology*, DOI: 10.1002/oa.1145.

Rissech, C., Estabrook, G.F., Malgosa, A. and Cunha, E. (2006) 'Using the acetabulum to estimate age at death of adult males', *Journal of Forensic Science*, 51: 213–29.

——(2007) 'Estimation of age-at-death for adult males using the acetabulum, applied to four Western European populations', *Journal of Forensic Science*, 52: 774–78.

Rissech, C., García, M. and Malgosa, A. (2003) 'Sex and age diagnosis by ischium morphometric analysis', *Forensic Science International*, 153: 188–96.

Rissech, C., Sañudo, J.R. and Malgosa, A. (2001) 'Acetabular point: a morphological and onthogenetics study', *Journal of Anatomy*, 198: 743–48.

Rissech, C., Schaefer, M. and Malgosa, A. (2008) 'Development of the femur – Implications for age and sex determination', *Forensic Science international*, 180: 111.e1–111.e7.

Robledo Acinas, M.M., Sánchez Sánchez, J.A., Labajo González, E., *et al.* (2008) 'Protocolo de antropología forense de la Escuela de Medicina Legal de Madrid', *Revista de la Escuela de Medicina Legal*, 8: 31–37.

Safont, S., Malgosa, A., Subirà, M.E., *et al.* (1998) 'Can trace elements in fossils provide information about palaeodiet?', *International Journal of Osteoarchaeology*, 8: 23–37.

Safont, S., Alesán, A. and Malgosa, A. (1999) 'Memñoria de l'excavació realitzada a la tomba del C/ Nou, 12 (Sant Bartomeu del Grau, Osona)' *Antropologia física* (Inèdita: dipositada a l'arxiu del Servei d'Arqueologia de la Generalitat de Catalunya).

——(2000) 'Sex assessment on the basis of long bone circumference', *American Journal of Physical Anthropology*, 113: 317–28.

Sampietro, M.L., Caramelli, D., Lao, O., *et al.* (2005) 'The genetics of Pre-Roman Iberian Peninsula: a mtDNA study of Ancient Iberians', *Annals of Human Genetics*, 69: 535–48.

Scheuer, L. and Black, S. (2000) *Developmental Juvenile Osteology*, London: Academic Press.

Schour, I. and Massler, M. (1941) 'The development of the human dentition', *Journal of the American Dental Association*, 28: 1153–60.

Subirà, M.E. and Malgosa, A. (2005) 'The effect of cremation on the study of trace elements', *International Journal of Osteoarchaeology*, 3: 115–18.

Todd, T.W. (1921) 'Age changes in the pubic bone', *American Journal of Physical Anthropology*, 4: 1–70.

Trancho, G.J., Robledo, B. and López-Bueis, I. (1995) *Investigaciones antropológicas en España. Base de datos bibliográfica (1861 referencias)*, Madrid: Universidad Complutense.

——(1997) *Investigaciones antropológicas en España. Base de datos bibliográfica. Actualización 1997*, Madrid: Universidad Complutense.

Trancho, G.J., Robledo, B., López-Bueis, I., *et al.* (1997) 'Sexual determination of the femur using discriminant functions. Analysis of a Spanish population of known sex and age', *Journal of Forensic Science*, 42: 181–85.

Trancho, G.J., López-Bueis, I., Robledo, B., *et al.* (2000) 'Diagnóstico sexual del radio mediante funciones discriminantes', in L. Caro *et al.* (eds) *Tendencias actuales de investigación en la Antropología Física española*, León: Universidad de León.

Trotter, M. and Gleser, G.C. (1952) 'Estimation of stature from long bones of American Whites and Negroes', *American Journal of Physical Anthropology*, 10: 463–514.

——(1958) 'A re-evaluation of estimation of stature based on measurements of stature taken during life and of long bones after death', *American Journal of Physical Anthropology*, 16: 79–123.

Ubelaker, D. (1999) *Human Skeletal Remains. Excavation, Analysis, Interpretation*, 3rd edn, Washington: Taraxacum.

Villalaín Blanco, J.D. and Puchalt Fortea, F.J. (2000) *Identificación antropológica policial y forense*, Valencia: Tirant Lo Blanch.

Vizcaíno, E., Monroy, D. and González, A. (2009) 'La historia de la Sociedad Española de Antropología Física a través de sus publicaciones: análisis de los trabajos recogidos en las actas de los Congresos de la SEAF (1978–2005)', *Revista Española de Antropología Física*, 29: 33–40.

Walker, P.L., Johnson, J.R. and Lambert, P.M. (1988) 'Age and sex biases in the preservation of human skeletal remains', *American Journal of Physical Anthropology*, 76: 183–88.

Arctic
Ocean

0   250km

SWEDEN

NORWAY

FINLAND

Umeå

Sundsvall

Gävle

Uppsala

Västerås

Eskilstuna

Stockholm

Örebro

Linköping

Norrköping

ESTONIA

Göteborg
(Gothenburg)

Jönköping

Borås

DENMARK

Helsingborg

Lund

Malmö

Baltic
Sea

LATVIA

LITHUANIA

Sweden/Sverige

Torbjörn Ahlström, Elisabeth Iregren, Kristina Jennbert and Lena Strid

INTRODUCTION: A BRIEF HISTORY AND CURRENT STATE OF PHYSICAL ANTHROPOLOGY IN SWEDEN

Human osteology (or bioarchaeology or physical anthropology) in Sweden is closely associated with zooarchaeology. Due to limited work opportunities, an exclusive specialization in either field is not realistic, and most osteologists working in Sweden analyse both human and animal remains. Osteology can be studied at three universities, and several field archaeologists have some basic knowledge on the subject.

The development of human osteology in Sweden from the 19th century until today is not straightforward. Several anatomists analysed archaeological skeletal remains with the aim of describing the sex and age of the deceased, and, if present, noting any palaeopathological findings. Unfortunately, the anatomists often worked detached from the archaeological context, merely exercising an anatomical interest. Several anatomists, however, worked from a broader perspective that ultimately established human osteology as an academic discipline.

Sven Nilsson (1787–1883) deserves to be mentioned as one of the pioneers of the study of human skeletal remains from archaeological contexts. In his major opus, *The Aborigines of the Scandinavian North* (Nilsson 1838–43), he advocated the use of morphological variation in human crania to identify the identity of the original inhabitants of the Scandinavian peninsula, whereas the artefacts could be used to address the cultural level. In a sense, Nilsson's studies are contextual, intertwining both skeletal remains and the archaeological record. Later anatomists such as Anders Retzius (1796–1860), Gustaf Retzius (1842–1919) and Carl Fürst (1854–1935) continued studying archaeological human remains with an underlying agenda of racial identification, using skull morphology, such as the cephalic index, to establish a racial history of the country. Fürst, however, also demonstrated the use of human skeletal remains to address archaeological and historical questions. Fürst worked with Mesolithic and Neolithic skeletal remains, scalping, trephinations, the palaeopathology of tuberculosis and leprosy. Another salient feature of his scientific production is the analysis of historical persons, such as Saint Bridget of Sweden, and the kings Magnus ladulås and Karl XII.

Important to the further development of the discipline was another professor of anatomy from Lund University, Carl-Herman Hjortsjö (1914–78). His scientific work embraces 305 publications, of which 65 are devoted to physical anthropology. He developed an anthropological interest early in his career and published data on skeletal remains that derived from Swedish international expeditions. A significant landmark in the development of the field transpired in 1951, when Hjortsjö, along with the zoologist and osteologist Nils-Gustaf Gejvall (1911–91), established 'The Swedish Expedition for Archaeological Anthropology' (Svenska expeditionen för arkeologisk antropologi). In the same spirit as Carl Fürst, Hjortsjö and Gejvall continued with studies on famous people in Swedish history, such as King Erik XIV, Saint Bridget of Sweden and the privateer Lars Andersson Gathe (Casparsson *et al.* 1962; Bygdén *et al.* 1954; Hjortsjö and Sandklef 1957). Thus, 'The Swedish Expedition for Archaeological Anthropology' provided significant contributions to the field, aroused public interest in osteological studies, and, more importantly, provided a constructive network between Hjortsjö and Gejvall. Up until the establishment of the Expedition, Gejvall had established himself as an archaeozoologist. It was under the tuition and supervision of Hjortsjö that Gejvall embarked upon his doctoral work in human osteology, including his study of the mediaeval population from Västerhus, in the province of Jämtland.

In 1960, Gejvall presented his thesis, 'Westerhus. Mediaeval Population and Church in the light of Skeletal Remains', at the Department of Anatomy at Lund University (Gejvall 1960). This work is remarkably prescient, using skeletal remains to answer a diverse array of questions pertaining to the mediaeval way of life. He describes different diseases among the adult individuals, and, along with demographic and stature data, he discusses the health of individuals buried in the cemetery. Prior to the work on Västerhus, Gejvall's main contribution to osteology was to develop methods for analysing cremated human bones, which he pioneered (Gejvall 1947; Sahlström and Gejvall 1948. Translated to English in Gejvall 1981). In 1968, Gejvall pursued his osteological research on a more permanent basis with the inauguration of the Osteological Research Laboratory at the Royal Palace Ulriksdal, Solna (Osteologiska forskningslaboratoriet i Ulriksdal; today known as Osteoarkeologiska Forskningslaboratoriet). Funds for the laboratory had been made available by the Wallenberg Foundation, with facilities supplied by King Gustaf VI Adolf, an ardent archaeologist with training from Uppsala University. The laboratory was attached to the Department of Archaeology, Stockholm University. Subsequently, Gejvall provided both graduate and undergraduate courses in historical osteology, embracing both animal and human bones. The laboratory became a melting pot for medical doctors, zoologists and archaeologists undertaking research on prehistoric and historic skeletal samples. He also started the international journal *Ossa*.

The Osteological Research Laboratory fostered the future generations of osteologists in Sweden. Well-known osteologists include Torstein Sjøvold and Ebba During. The subject became popular and was established as part of the archaeology departments at the University of Lund in 1991 by Elisabeth Iregren, and at the University College of Gotland in 1998 by Ebba During. Following the tradition established by Gejvall, the education in osteology involves both human and animal bones.

Education and training

Today, these three departments provide education at undergraduate and postgraduate levels. Doctoral studies can be pursued at the departments of Stockholm and Lund. However, due to funding problems in the Faculty of Arts overall, there are very few PhD students. This has been criticised in a recent evaluation of the education in archaeology by the Swedish National Agency for Higher Education (2009), arguing that the paucity of lecturers with a PhD and the paucity of PhD students may compromise the quality of the research.

In 2008, collaboration with Danish anthropologists resulted in the production of a textbook in human osteology (Lynnerup *et al.* 2008). The book comprises an extensive range of subjects, including human evolution, isotope analysis, DNA and forensic anthropology. Many examples are taken from the Scandinavian countries.

ARCHAEOLOGICAL HUMAN REMAINS AND LEGISLATION

Archaeological legislation

The Swedish legislation is not written specifically with regard to human skeletal remains. Therefore, human bones are related to ancient sites, which are protected by the law. In order to excavate an ancient site you must have authorization from the County Administrative Board (Länsstyrelsen) in the area of interest. Each of Sweden's 21 counties functions as representative of the state and has specialists that are responsible for protecting and looking after the cultural environment and ancient remains.

Concerning the cultural environment and ancient sites, the County Administrative Board mainly makes use of two laws: the Heritage Conservation Act and the Environmental Code. The central authority for cultural environment conservation in Sweden, the National Heritage Board in Stockholm, assists the County Administrative Board to implement the laws. Local and regional museums and the Archaeological Excavations Departments of the National Heritage Board do most of the field work due to infrastructural investments and other kinds of land exploitations. The law regulates the handling of archaeological finds and the processing for permission to excavate an ancient site.

HUMAN REMAINS AND LEGISLATION

Swedish legislation says nothing explicit about skeletal remains. However, the law protects contexts where human skeletal remains are likely to be found, and mentions among other things graves, grave fields, churchyards, settlements, occupation layers and ruins. To excavate an ancient site, it is necessary to get permission from the County Administrative Board, not as an individual person but in collaboration with an archaeological department or museum. It is also necessary to explain the reasons for the excavation, the funding, and the research focus as well as the plans to present the results.

Obviously, if human skeletal remains are discovered inadvertently, the Criminal Investigation Department should be contacted. However, if the context is within a supposed ancient or archaeological site, then the County Administrative Board must be informed.

The application of Swedish law

In practice human skeletal remains, when excavated at an ancient site, are regarded as ancient finds. According to the law, ancient sites are remains of human activities from prehistoric or historic times, which have been abandoned in perpetuity. According to the interpretation of the law, older graves in churchyards still in use should not be interpreted as ancient sites. As a consequence, churchyards as well as older Christian graves are protected by the Law of Cultural Heritage. Abandonment in perpetuity is an important criterion in the protection and handling of human skeletal remains (Trotzig 1995). Human remains buried, for example, during the mediaeval period but located in churchyards that are still in use are protected by criminal law if these graves are violated (Gregow 2009).

The basic regulation for the protection of Sweden's heritage is a registration of all monuments and finds in a central survey in connection with the National Property Map (Fastighetskartan). Besides prehistoric graves and grave fields, abandoned burial sites dated to historical times (including cholera and plague graveyards) and churchyards associated with abandoned churches and monasteries or mediaeval towns and villages are registered (Trotzig 1995; Riksantikvarieämbetet 2009). The Swedish registration is unique in a European perspective, as it presents all kinds of ancient sites that are known in Sweden today.

Osteological expertise is considered to be a guarantee of quality, and a condition to get permission to excavate human remains. In order to provide the best assessment for the selection, treatment and perhaps reburial of skeletal material, both archaeological and osteological expertise are recommended during this process of evaluation.

Practice

Swedish excavation regulations do not require the presence of an osteologist on site when human remains are anticipated, nor is it compulsory to carry out analyses of human remains. However, since osteology is a long-established academic discipline (see above), excavation units are fully aware of the scientific value of skeletal remains, and subsequently the study of human remains is usually included in excavation and post-excavation budgets. Furthermore, field archaeologists who have studied osteology at various levels are relatively common, and are often employed on sites where human remains are expected.

There is no official system of tender for osteological analysis. Some units employ osteologists to analyse human and animal remains for them, whereas others use the services of freelance osteologists, or osteologists connected to other units or universities. Bones are rarely sent abroad for analysis, due to the large number of osteologists in Sweden.

Curation of skeletal material in Sweden

Due to Swedish legislation and intense land exploitation, the quantity of excavated archaeological material in our country is vast. In Sweden, all finds belong to the state and are usually stored in state museums or similar scientific institutions. The Museum of National Antiquities in Stockholm is where the largest skeletal collection is curated, comprising around 108 tons of animal and human bones (Historiska Museet 2009). Very large amounts of human and animal bones are also stored in the Lund University Historical Museum and the Museum of Cultural History in Lund. We believe that tens of thousands of skeletons, mainly from the mediaeval period, are curated in Sweden.

A development of a national standard for storing human remains is in progress. At present, depending on the protocols of the unit and the receiving museum, the bones are either stored in plastic bags or wrapped in acid-free tissue paper in paper boxes, which are then placed in large museum-size boxes for storage. The provenance of human remains (i.e., site code and context number) is usually labelled in ink on the bones.

Human skeletons are on display in many exhibitions in Sweden: for instance, the world-famous museum of the warship *Vasa* in Stockholm, and the three museums mentioned above. Visitors are often very interested in the life of their ancestors and the burial traditions from different times (Nilsson Stutz 2008: 93). Regarding the *Vasa*, it should be noted that the ship and exhibitions have gained attention from new perspectives since the dreadful sea catastrophe of the ferry *Estonia* in the Baltic Sea in 1994 (Olsson and Nyberg 2000, cf Iregren 2004).

Early discussions, regulations and actions regarding the handling of human skeletons

Due to the absence of specific mention of skeletal remains in the law, curators at the National Museum of Antiquities felt a need for more detailed guidelines for archaeologists, osteologists and curators. For some years the question was debated in museums and in Swedish journals (Iregren 1981). In 1983 the National Museum of Antiquities and the Central Board of Antiquities published guidelines for the curation of skeletal material from archaeological sites (Riksantikvarieämbetet 1983). The main conclusion was that scientifically important material should be preserved, be available for research and should not be reburied. However, neither skeletons from sunken ships nor remains of Sámi or other indigenous groups were included. This has been criticised by Sámi representatives in Norway (Iregren 2002; Schanche 2002), but the National Museum of Antiquities and the Central Board of Antiquities have not issued any new guidelines so far. In 1990, a meeting was organized at the County Administrative Board in Malmö to discuss the question of retaining or reburial, as the issue had occasionally been raised. The majority of the talks have been published and these now act as guidelines (Iregren and Redin 1995).

Although the legal basis for human remains from archaeological sites in Sweden is curation of skeletal material in museums for exhibitions and research, some reburials and cases of repatriation to other countries have taken place. When studying the documentation, it is difficult to find consistency in the arguments. There is also considerable variation at the administrative level at which decisions are taken.

Table 39.1 lists reburial cases found in the archives of the National Museum of Antiquities and the Historical Museum of Lund University. The Ethnographical Museum in Stockholm has been much involved in repatriation, but their cases and outcomes have not been included here. The background of a few of their collections containing human remains is presented in a recent volume from the Swedish osteologists' journal, *Benbiten* (Hallgren 2009; Hedberg 2009; Helgesson Kjellin 2009).

Ethical considerations regarding reburial of archaeological skeletal material

In Sweden, prior to the late 1980s, mediaeval and post-mediaeval skeletons in churches were not always excavated nor retained. On some occasions, the anthropologist or anatomist determined age and sex of the deceased while standing at the edge of the trench and looking down at the skeleton *in situ* as, for ethical reasons, the excavator did not want to disturb the burial (B. Sundnér, pers. comm.). It was not regarded as necessary to investigate the burials in any detail osteologically, although they were properly documented archaeologically. Similar situations have also occurred since.

A comparable case occurred in 2001 regarding excavations in Bro church (Table 39.2, No. 8), where the County Administrative Board of Gotland did not want to move the skeletons beneath the floor. The osteologist argued, though, that the many child skeletons were of interest and should be analysed. As a compromise, the County Administrative Board decided that the skeletons could be analysed and then reburied. For reburial, the individual skeletons were laid to rest in plastic boxes and positioned in their original places in the church. It is, however, uncertain what will happen to the skeletons from a taphonomic point of view. For instance, re-examination of the reburied individuals from the warship *Vasa* showed that they had suffered heavy taphonomic deterioration while being kept in plastic bags in a crypt (During and Kvaal 2000).

Concerns about the issue of reburial in Sweden can be categorized into two different groups: mediaeval and post-mediaeval skeletons from archaeological excavations; and skulls and skeletons of various dates deriving from indigenous groups. Pre-Christian graves in Sweden have not yet become a source of dispute. This might happen if Asatru believers grow sufficiently in

Table 39.1. Reburial cases concerning human remains originally from anatomical collections in Sweden, now curated in museums

Museum	Town	Origin	No. of individuals	Decision by whom	Decision	Reason	Present situation
Lund University Historical Museum	Lund	Jewish	1 skull	Head of Lund University (2005)	To the Jewish congregation of Malmö	Religious or cultural bonds	Buried in Malmö Jewish burial ground
Lund University Historical Museum	Lund	Aborigines	2 skulls	Swedish government (2008)	To Australia		
Museum of National Antiquities	Stockholm	Lycksele, Västerbotten (assumed to be of Sámi ethnicity)	1 skull	Swedish government, following suggestion by Museum of National Antiquities (2009)	To the Sámi parliament	From an anatomical collection. The skull is not a typical part of the Museum collections.	Buried
Museum of National Antiquities	Stockholm	Hawaii	5 skulls	Suggestion from Museum of National Antiquities to government (2009)	To Hawaii	The skulls do not belong to areas of collection according to state regulations. Receivers are legitimate and serious. Repatriation is suggested.	Awaiting governmental decision

Table 39.2. Reburial cases concerning human remains from Swedish archaeological sites

No.	County	Parish	Site	No. of individuals	Anthropological analysis	Decision by whom	Decision	Reason	Present situation
1	Lappland	Tärna	Vilasund 70:2	c. 25	Alexandersen (1986) (teeth only)		Partially retained. The rest reburied?	Poorly preserved	5 mandibles retained at School of Dentistry, Umeå university
2	Västmanland	Västerås	Dominican monastery	c. 2000	Holm (unpublished)	RAÄ-SHMM (1964)			Stored in Västerås town hall. Accessible.
3	Stockholm		Vasa (warship)	c. 25	Gejvall unpublished; Düring and Kvaal (2000)		Reburied in plastic bags for 26 years in the Navy Cemetery in Stockholm		Analysed again. Severe damage to the skeletons. Some individuals on exhibit in the Vasa museum.
4	Södermanland	Björnlunda		14	Sten (1987)	RAÄ-SHMM, Director of Central Heritage Board (1989)	To parish	Not an abandoned monument	In wooden coffins, accessible in the church
5	Öland	Källa		48	Sjøvold (1990a)	RAÄ-SHMM, Director of Central Heritage Board (1990)	To parish	Promise to parish during excavation	In boxes, accessible in the church
6	Skåne	Bonderup	Bonderup church	3	Iregren (2002)	Swedish government (1993)	To Lund University Historical Museum	Museum curation considered best for preservation	
7	Lappland	Tärna	Soivengella	1	Hallgren and Gejvall (1961)	Director of Museum of National Antiquities (2002)	To Sámi village for reburial		Reburied in same mediaeval monument

(Continued on next page)

Table 39.2. (continued)

No.	County	Parish	Site	No. of individuals	Anthropological analysis	Decision by whom	Decision	Reason	Present situation
8	Gotland	Bro	Bro Church		Gustafsson (2004)	Gotland County Administrative Board in discussion with Bro parish (2001)	Reburial in church		In plastic boxes, accessible underneath the floor boards of the church
9	Northern Sweden (mediaeval assemblages)			c. 40		Suggestion from Museum of National Antiquities to government (2009)	Deposition/ loan to Ájtte Sámi museum	Presumed to be Sámi. Important resource for information on human life and history. State property	
10	Norrbotten*	Karesuando	Rounala church ruin	12		Suggestion from Museum of National Antiquities to government (2009)	To be retained	Uncertain of ethnic affiliation	

*Note that while the remains from Rounala Church ruin were excavated from an ancient monument, they formed part of the anatomical collections from Uppsala University

RAÄ-SHMM: Riksantikvarieämbetet och Statens Historiska Museer (Central Heritage Board and the National Historical Museums)

numbers to result in a situation similar to that in the USA (Nilsson Stutz 2008: 92–93). An increase in believers does not necessarily have to result in an increase in reburial requests; however, for the latter to be regarded as serious, the number of believers probably would need to increase.

The reburial issues regarding the first group are usually started by congregations, often in the countryside, where local people seem to feel direct bonds to mediaeval Christian burials, though of Roman Catholic origin. In some instances the parish priest or the church council take an active role (Table 39.2, Nos 4, 5 and 6). In these cases the arguments are based on culture, traditions and often on Christian belief. In general, mediaeval and post-mediaeval graves seem to engage local people more than older graves. A recent example of this are the 18th- and 19th-century burials from the cathedral of Linköping, where reburial has been discussed but post-poned so far through the dedicated work of Caroline Arcini, osteologist at the Central Board of Antiquities (C. Arcini, pers.comm). The longest discussion was related to Västerhus in Jämtland, where on several occasions the priests demanded that the collections be reburied. Archaeologists and anthropologists by contrast, however, claim that this is one of the most important skeletal populations from the mediaeval period in Sweden. The result of these discussions is that the material has been permanently stored in the National Museum since 1989. A new research volume was recently published on this assemblage (Iregren *et al.* 2009).

A much debated case in the media has related to the three skeletons of mediaeval children in Bonderup church, near Lund (Table 39.2, No. 6). The parish council wanted a reburial and the Department of Archaeology at Lund University, as a compromise, suggested a burial in the church as opposed to in the ground. Since mediaeval child skeletons from rural sites are relatively scarce, the conditions proposed by the archaeologists and osteologists were that the material should be kept safe and at a proper temperature and moisture environment and with the possibility of access for researchers. The Director of the National Board of Antiquities decided that the material should belong to the regional museum. The parish made legal complaints but, in the end, the Swedish government agreed with the Director of the National Board of Antiquities.

Reburial and repatriation of human remains from anatomical collections

The second group concerns museum collections that have been claimed through ethnic affilia-tion by certain groups. The questions have arisen from the indigenous groups in Scandinavia, the Sámi, with regard to skeletal material that has been stored in archaeological museums as well as in anatomical institutes. In addition, other ethnic groups from other parts of the world have claimed certain specimens too.

One case, much debated in 2005, was the burial of a skull collected in 1879 and curated at the Anatomical Institute of Lund University (Table 39.1, No. 1). This skull, belonging to a male from a Jewish family, had been on display at the Museum of Cultural History in Lund alongside a skull of a Sámi female and a skeleton of a Roman male. The exhibition, shown in three Swedish towns, dealt with prejudices, racism and races from the time of Carl Linnaeus up to present day. The display had the support of congregations, museums and organizations, and there were no objections whatsoever from the public visitors either.

The Jewish congregation of Malmö later decided to claim the skull for burial. The *rector magnificus*, head of Lund University, decreed that the congregation was an appropriate recipient, pointing to religious, cultural and ethnic bonds as reasons for burial. Elisabeth Iregren, osteol-ogist at the university, disputed this decision and asked the Parliamentary Ombudsman to check for the legal aspects. After investigation, the Parliamentary Ombudsman criticised the rector of the university since he was not allowed to transfer state property to another owner. Neither was he allowed to create standard rules for similar decisions, which he claimed that he wanted to. Instead, it was the task of the Swedish government to create such a policy. On another occasion, two skulls from Australia were repatriated from Lund University. The university then suggested that the government should make the decision (Table 39.1, No. 2).

Regarding the Sámi, we have long known that there are the remains of a few individuals with known ethnic background in Swedish museums. In 1984 an inventory was made in connection with the South Sámi project. Recently, Sametinget, the Sámi parliament, decided to make an inventory of Sámi artefacts and human remains in many museums in Europe. A report on the Swedish museums was made available in 2007 by Ájtte, the Swedish Mountain and Sámi museum (Kouljok 2007).

The first reburial at the request of a Sámi organization (a siida, approximately the equivalent of a village) took place in 2002 (Table 39.2, No. 7). The decision was made by the Director of the National Museum of Antiquities and behind this decision was the opportunity to undertake an anthropological examination before reburial. Archaeologists debated the fact that the reburial took place in the same burial place, a stone chamber, and they have been concerned about the potential for destruction and plunder by passing tourists.

Further, the Sámi parliament in Sweden has requested that the Museum of National Antiquities repatriate Sámi human remains that are kept in their collections. To help with the decision, the museum asked several Swedish research institutions their views on the Sámi skeletons in museums and their scientific value. The directors of the museum also had meetings with representatives of the Sámi parliament during 2007 and 2008. In 2009, the suggestions for a decision were handed over to the Swedish government. The museum had suggested that one skull of presumably Sámi origin (Table 39.1, No. 3) should be handed over to the Sámi parliament, as it originated from the anatomical collection of Uppsala university and was not a typical possession of this archaeological museum. Reburial of the skull was proposed, as its symbolic value is very significant to the Sámi and at the same time it was judged to be of low scientific value. A different suggestion has been put forward for other skeletal remains of possible Sámi origin from Northern Sweden (Table 39.2, Nos 9 and 10). Since the Sámi origin of some of these remains cannot be proven and, legally, the ownership of these latter remains cannot be transferred from the museum, the museum has suggested that these remains should not be repatriated. However, the Museum of National Antiquities is willing to lend or to make depositions, for instance to Ájtte, the Swedish Mountain and Sámi museum in Jokkmokk.

Another case is pending regarding five skulls from Hawaii (Table 39.1, No. 4). The Museum of National Antiquities suggests that the government repatriate these to Hui Malama I Na Kupuna O Hawaií Nei, a group caring for the ancestors of Hawaii. The arguments are that the skulls do not belong to the defined working area of the museum, as they were not found in Sweden. Moreover, the remains have not been used for research or exhibitions since they arrived at the museum in 1997. No decision has, so far, been taken by the government.

Future development

In 2005, the Social Democratic government decided that an inventory should be performed in museums and institutions where individuals of indigenous groups were kept. This inventory was rapidly undertaken but has not yet been summarized by the Ministry of Culture. The former Minister of Culture, Leif Pagrotsky, stated in 2007 that the second step would be an evaluation of the collections in order to be able to make wise decisions on repatriation (L. Pagrotsky, pers. comm.). The new centre-right coalition government has not started any discussion or evaluation of the results of the inventory, or at least this has not been publicly made known.

However, after taking office the new Minister of Culture, Lena Adelsohn Liljeroth, said in a public interview that the Sámi ought to have their ancestors returned.

In several debates and interviews in the Swedish media during 2006 and 2007, Lund University osteologist and co-author of this chapter Elisabeth Iregren has suggested that a cross-scientific committee should be formed. Both Norwegian and Finnish authorities have gained good results from such boards. In Finland, archaeologists, anthropologists, theologians, lawyers and Sámi representatives have taken part in the discussions and evaluations. In both countries the committees have reached consensus: the collections are now in the possession of Sámi authorities, which have the mandate to decide the fate of the collections, including who will be allowed to perform research. Both countries have so far decided that Sámi remains should not be reburied (Universitetet i Oslo 2000; Söderholm 2002). Our view is that Sweden should learn from its neighbouring countries and create a similar group to evaluate the Swedish situation and our collections.

It is evident from Tables 39.1 and 39.2 that the decisions of burial/reburial are taken at many different administrative levels in Swedish society. Since there is no law that provides guidelines, and only a few formal rules, this is very unsatisfactory for the outcomes. Further, from a legal standpoint this situation puts an organization or individual that initiates a claim for the reburial of human remains at risk of becoming victims of uncertainty regarding the legal rights.

It is clear from the table that many of the reburied skeletal collections have been neither studied properly nor published. This is astonishing, as osteology has been taught in Swedish universities since the late 1960s. Despite the availability of qualified osteologists, interest and funding have not been directed towards employing them. The absence of research is particularly problematic since this has been used as an argument for repatriation (Table 39.1, No. 4). Considering the scarcity for funding for osteological research in Sweden and the amount of material collected, this seems a very dangerous point of contention. Furthermore, a serious scientific argument against reburial is that we must be open to several interpretations. A collection can be studied both now and later from a number of disciplines and with many methods (Nilsson Stutz 2008: 90). A close collaboration between scholars and the groups of concern is also of great importance.

METHODS OF ANTHROPOLOGICAL ANALYSIS

Several standard works, such as Buikstra and Ubelaker (1994), Bass (2005), Brothwell (1981) and the Workshop of European Anthropologists (1980) are used for analysis. For the calculation of stature, Sjøvold (1990a) is often used, since these formulae don't distinguish between different sexes or ethnicities. However, many osteologists also use Trotter and Gleser (1952, 1958). Assemblages commonly used for reference include the Neolithic burials at Ajvide (Persson and Persson 1997; Molnar 2008) and the mediaeval burials at Helgeandsholmen (Jacobzon and Sjögren 1982), Lund (Arcini 1999) and Västerhus (Gejvall 1960; Iregren *et al.* 2009).

USEFUL CONTACTS

The County Administrative Board. Website: www.lansstyrelsen.se/lst/

Fornminnessök (Survey of Ancient Sites), The National Heritage Board. Website: www.raa.se/cms/fornsok/start.html/

Kulturminneslagen (The Law of Cultural Heritage) (1988: 950). Available online at www.riksda gen.se/Webbnav/index.aspx?nid=3911&bet=1988:950/

The National Heritage Board. Website: www.raa.se/cms/en/

BIBLIOGRAPHY

Arcini, C. (1999) *Health and disease in early Lund. Osteo-pathologic studies of 3,305 Individuals Buried in the First Cemetery area of Lund 990–1536*, Archaeologica Lundensia Investigationes de antiqvitatibus urbis Lundae VIII, Lund: Medical Faculty of Lund University.

Alexandersen, V. (1986) *Odontologiske undersøgelser af skeletmateriale fra gravfeltet på Vivallen i Funäsdalen*, Sörsamiska Projektet Report 5, Östersund: Jämtlands läns museum.

Bass, W.M. (2005) *Human Osteology: A Laboratory and Field Manual*, (5th edn), Missouri: Missouri Archaeological Society.

Brothwell, D.R. (1981) *Digging Up Bones* (3rd edn), Natural History Museum. Oxford: Oxford University Press.

Buikstra, J.E. and Ubelaker, D.H. (eds) (1994) *Standards for Data Collection from Human Skeletal Remains*, Fayetteville, AR: Arkansas Archeological Report Research Series No. 44.

Bygdén, A., Gejvall, N.A. and Hjortsjö, C.-H. (1954) *Heliga Birgittas reliker*, Lund: Gleerups förlag.

Casparsson, R., Ekström, G. and Hjortsjö, C.-H. (1962) *Erik XIV: en historisk, kulturhistorisk och medicinsk-antropologisk undersökning i samband med gravöppningen 1958 i Västerås domkyrka*, Stockholm: Norstedts förlag.

During, E.M. and Kvaal, S.I. (2000) 'Tafonomiska aspekter på osteologisk och odontologisk åldersbedömning', *Tandläkartidningen*, 92: 48–56.

Gejvall, N.-G. (1947) 'Bestämning av brända ben från forntida gravar', *Fornvännen*, 47: 39–47.

——(1960) *Westerhus. Medieval Population and Church in the light of Skeletal Remains*, Monograph 43, Stockholm: Kungliga Vitterhets-, historie- och antikvitetsakademien.

——(1981) 'Determination of burnt bones from prehistoric graves', *Ossa Letters*, 2: 1–13.

Gregow, T. (ed) (2009) *Brottsbalken*, Sveriges Rikes Lag. Stockholm: Norstedts Juridik: ch. 16, para. 10.

Gustafsson, E. (2004) 'Benen i Bro kyrka. En studie av ett omblandat medeltida skelettmaterial', unpublished postgraduate dissertation in archaeo-osteology, University College of Gotland.

Hallgren, B. and Gejvall, N-G. (1961) 'Lapska gravar i Arjeplog. Med preliminära skelettbestämningar', *Fornvännen*, 56: 191–200.

Hallgren, C. (2009) 'Rasbiologi i Australien, Eric Mjöbergs och Aboriginernas skilda världar', *Benbiten*, 1: 29–34.

Hedberg, A.S. (2009) 'En "indianvän" på "grafplundring" – Erland Nordenskiölds insamlande av mänskliga kvarlevor', *Benbiten*, 1: 19–24.

Helgesson Kjellin, K. (2009) 'Kranier i missionärers samlingar: Karl Edvard och Selma Lamans insamling av mänskliga kvarlevor i de båda Kongostaterna under 1900-talets början', *Benbiten*, 1: 25–28.

Historiska Museet (2009) *Sök i Historiska museets samlingar*. Available online at http://mis.historiska.se/mis/sok/sok.asp (accessed 23 July 2009).

Hjortsjö, C.-H. and Sandklef, A. (1957) *Lars Gathenhielms vittnesbörd. En medicinsk-antropologisk och en kulturhistorisk undersökning*, Göteborg: Nautic.

Iregren, E. (1981) 'Välsignade magasin. Dokumentation och förvaring av ben', *Kulturminnesvård*, 1: 18–25.

——(2002) 'Hur bevara samernas biologiska historia?', in *Vem äger kulturarvet? anföranden vid konferens om återföringsfrågor vid Ájtte, svenskt fjäll-och samemuseum 6–8 juni 2000*, Douddaris 20, Rapportserie från Ájtte, svenskt fjäll-och samemuseum, Jokkmokk: Ájtte.

——(2004) Humans in wrecks. An ethical discussion on marine archaeology, exhibitions and scuba diving. Karlsson, H. (red.), *Swedish Archaeologists on Ethics*, Lindome: Bricoleur.

Iregren, E. Alexandersen, V. and Redin, L. (eds) (2009) *Västerhus. Kapell, kyrkogård och befolkning*, Stockholm: Kungliga Vitterhets-, historie-och antikvitetsakademien.

Iregren, E. and Redin, L. (eds) (1995) *I Adams barn … En diskussion om etiska aspekter på museiförvaring och återbegravning av medeltida skelettmaterial*, Report series: University of Lund, Institute of Archaeology 55, Lund: Institute of Archaeology, University of Lund.

Jacobzon, L. and Sjögren, J. (1982) 'Människor i stadens utkant – Helgeandshusets kyrkogård berättar om liv och död', in G. Dahlbäck (ed.) *Helgeandsholmen. 1000 år i Stockholms ström*, Stockholm: LiberFörlag.

Kouljok, S. (2007) *Recalling Ancestral Voices – Repatriation of Sámi Cultural Heritage*, Jokkmokk: Ájtte.

Lynnerup, N., Bennike, P. and Iregren, E. (2008) *Biologisk antropologi med human osteologi*, Copenhagen: Gyldendal.

Molnar, P. (2008) *Tracing Prehistoric Activities: Life Ways, Habitual Behaviour and Health of Hunter-Gatherers on Gotland*, Theses and papers in osteoarchaeology 4, Stockholm: Department of Archaeology and Classical Studies, University of Stockholm.

Nilsson Stutz, L. (2008) 'Caught in the middle – an archaeological perspective on repatriation and reburial', in M. Gabriel and J. Dahl (eds) *Utimut: Past Heritage-Future Partnerships: Discussions on Repatriation in the 21st Century*, Copenhagen: International Work Group for Indigenous Affairs and Greenland National Museum & Archives.

Olsson, T. and Nyberg, I. (2000) *Efter det oväntade. En dokumentation av seminariet När tillvaron rämnar, Göteborgs stadsmuseum, våren 2000*, Göteborg: Göteborgs stadsmuseum.

Persson, E. and Persson, O. (1997) 'The osteo-anthropological analysis of skeleton material from Hablingbo and Ajvide, excavation seasons 1983–86, 1992–95', in G. Burenhult (ed.) *Remote Sensing. Applied Techniques for the Study of Cultural Resources and the Localization, Identification and Documentation of Sub-surface Prehistoric Remains in Swedish Archaeology. Vol. I. Osteo-anthropological, Economic, Environmental and Technical Analyses*, Theses and Papers in North-European Archaeology 13a, Stockholm: Department of Archaeology, University of Stockholm.

Riksantikvarieämbetet (1983) *Omhändertagande, förvaring och återbegravning av forntida och medeltida skelettmaterial*, Underrättelser från Riksantikvarieämbetet och Statens historiska museer 1983 (7), Stockholm: Riksantikvarieämbetet and Statens historiska museer.

——(2009) *Fornminnessök*. Available online at www.raa.se/cms/fornsok/start.html (accessed 23 July 2009).

Sahlström, K.E. and Gejvall, N.-G. (1948) *Gravfältet på kyrkbacken i Horns socken, Västergötland*. Handlingar 60.3. Stockholm: Kungliga Vitterhets-, historie- och antikvitetsakademien.

Schanche, A. (2002) 'Museer, genstander, rettigheter', in *Vem äger kulturarvet?: anföranden vid konferens om återföringsfrågor vid Ájtte, svenskt fjäll-och samemuseum 6–8 juni 2000*, Duoddaris 20, Rapportserie från Ájtte, svenskt fjäll-och samemuseum, Jokkmokk: Ájtte.

Swedish National Agency for Higher Education (2009) *Beslut om ifrågasättande av examensrätter efter fördjupade granskningar av utbildningar inom arkeologi*. Available online at www.hsv.se/download/18.1dbd1f9a120d72e05717ffe2358/643-4487-07+beslut+arkeologi.pdf (accessed 23 July 2009).

Sjøvold T. (1990a) 'Estimation of stature from long bones utilizing the line of organic correlation', *Human evolution*, 5: 431–47.

——(1990b) *Beträffande skeletten från Källa ödekyrka, Öland*, Unpublished report. Stockholm: Statens Historiska Museum.

Söderholm, N. (2002) 'Den anatomiska bensamlingen vid Helsingfors universitet', unpublished Master's dissertation. Helsinki, Helsingfors University, Institutionen för kulturforskning

Sten, S. (1987) *Osteologisk analys*, Dnr 5786/85 unpublished report, Stockholm: Statens Historiska Museum.

Trotter, M. and Gleser, G. (1952) 'Estimation of stature from long bones of American Whites and Negroes', *American Journal of Physical Anthropology*, 10: 463–515.

——(1958) 'A re-evaluation of stature based on measurements of stature taken during life and of long bones after death', *American Journal of Physical Anthropology*, 16: 79–125.

Trotzig, G. (1995) 'Bonderup och Björnlunda – Kulturminneslagen tillämpad', in E. Iregren and L. Redin (eds) *I Adams barn …* , Lund: University of Lund, Institute of Archaeology.

Universitetet i Oslo (2000) *Vurdering av den vitenskapelige verdi av De Schreinerske Samlinger ved Instituttgruppe for medisinske basalfag*, Oslo: Det medisinske fakultet, Universitetet i Oslo.

Workshop of European Anthropologists (1980) 'Recommendations for age and sex diagnoses of skeletons', *Journal of Human Evolution*, 9: 517–49.

Turkey/Türkiye

Handan Üstündağ

INTRODUCTION: A BRIEF HISTORY AND CURRENT STATE OF PHYSICAL ANTHROPOLOGY IN TURKEY

The study of human remains recovered from archaeological excavations was started in Turkey by German researchers in the late 19th century. The first reports on ancient human skeletons were only concerned with cranial morphology. German researchers such as Rudolf Virchow (1882, 1884, 1896) and Felix von Luschan (1911) were among those who studied ancient skulls from various archaeological sites in order to describe the cranial types of the early inhabitants of Turkey.

The history of Turkish anthropology started in 1925, following the foundation of the Republic of Turkey after the fall of the Ottoman Empire. The Republic of Turkey was founded by Mustafa Kemal Atatürk along secular and modernist lines. The desire to Westernize Turkey at this time led to the foundation of modern institutions as well as new universities including modern scientific disciplines such as anthropology.

The Turkish Anthropological Research Centre (Centre des Recherches Anthropologiques de la Turquie) was first established in 1925 as a subdivision within the Istanbul University Medical School (Istanbul Darülfünunu Tıp Fakültesi). In the same year, the first issue of the Turkish Anthropological Journal (*Revue Turque d'Anthropologie*) was published. The aim of this research centre and the journal was to collect the anthropological works that had been undertaken or were being undertaken in Turkey and to train young researchers (Kansu 1940). These first Turkish researchers believed that the science of (physical) anthropology was the key to identifying the place of the Turks among the ethnic/racial groups in the world (Kansu 1940). Between 1925 and 1929, skulls were collected from Turkish-Islamic cemeteries in Istanbul and they were measured at the Research Centre.

In 1927, Şevket Aziz Kansu, who was a medical assistant at Istanbul University Medical School, was sent to the Anthropological Institute in Paris by the government to acquire an anthropological education. He studied at Broca's Anthropological Laboratory at École des Hautes Études with Professor G. Papillaut. He returned to Turkey with a Diplôme des Sciences Anthropologiques in 1929 and worked as an assistant professor at the Istanbul University Medical School until 1933. At that time the Anthropological Research Centre moved to the Faculty of Sciences of Istanbul University. Kansu worked in the new Anthropological Institute until 1935 and taught several anthropology courses.

Mustafa Kemal Atatürk's encouragement had a significant influence on the development of anthropology. In 1935 a unique Language, History and Geography Faculty (Dil ve Tarih, Coğrafya Fakültesi) was established at Ankara University under the direction of Atatürk. One of his main goals was to determine the historical, cultural and biological/racial identity of the Turkish nation. Disciplines such as anthropology, archaeology and philology were ideal to construct a scientific basis for this goal. The establishment of this faculty at Ankara University and the beginning of archaeological excavations at this time provided a new direction for Turkish anthropology.

After the new Language, History and Geography Faculty was established in Ankara, the Anthropological Institute moved to join the Faculty with its full staff, materials and equipment. It became a proper Anthropology Department divided into physical and cultural anthropology. The division of physical anthropology had also a laboratory, where skeletal remains were curated. The activities of the Anthropological Institute focused on studying human remains found in archaeological excavations; palaeontological surveys and the examination of fossils; searching for prehistoric sites and collecting and analysing stone tools.

The government encouraged the education in Europe and in the USA for some young anthropologists at this time. The aim was to build the Anthropology Department in Ankara with well-educated young scholars. In 1934 Muzaffer Süleyman Şenyürek was sent to Harvard University to study with Professor Earnest Hooton. In 1935 Seniha Tunakan was sent to the University of Berlin to study with Professor Eugéne Fisher. Afet Inan, who was the head of the Turkish Historical Institute at that time, also participated in Eugéne Pittard's courses at the University of Geneva. It should be emphasized that both Seniha Tunakan and Afet Inan were women, which shows that women were playing an important role in the establishment of anthropology in Turkey.

The participation of Turkish anthropologists in archaeological excavations in Turkey began in 1930. First, Şevket Aziz Kansu joined the excavations at Alişar directed by the Oriental Institute of the University of Chicago. After him, Muine Atasayan joined the excavations at Alacahöyük as the first Turkish female anthropologist.

In 1937 an enormous process of anthropometric research was undertaken under the direction of Atatürk, in which 64,000 people from all over Turkey were measured by numerous medical staff and teachers (Inan 1947). The aim of the study was to determine the racial characteristics of the Turkish population. This traditional study meant the beginning of a new phase in Turkish anthropology, when anthropological research declined. Between this time and the 1980s, research on human skeletal remains was mainly descriptive (Çiner 1965; Şenyürek 1952; Tunakan 1971). The main objective was to describe the cranial types. There are few exceptional examples, including for example a study on longevity and life expectancy of the ancient inhabitants of Anatolia (Şenyürek 1947), a study on mandibular condyle osteoarthritis in the ancient Anatolians (Bostancı 1973), and a study on the mandibular paleopathology of the ancient Anatolians (Alpagut 1979).

After the 1980s, bioanthropologists began to study specific issues in osteology, such as the frequency of *torus mandibularis* (Alpagut 1980), stature (Güleç 1989) and the health status of ancient Anatolians (Özbek 1988a). It seems like this modern bioarchaeological approach reached Turkey in the 1980s. However, researchers preferred to publish in local periodicals and usually in Turkish until the 2000s. An increase in international publications has occurred in recent years (e.g. Duyar and Erdal 2003; Erdal 2006, 2008; Eroğlu and Erdal 2008; Eroğlu 2010; Güleç *et al.* 2007; Güngör *et al.* 2007; Koca Özer *et al.* 2006; Özbek 2001, 2005; Özer *et al.* 2006; Özer and Katayama 2006; Öztunç *et al.* 2006; Uysal 2006a, 2006b; Üstündağ-Aydın and Guidotti 2001).

European and American researchers in Turkey

After the German researchers who studied skulls from excavations in Turkey, an American anthropologist, W.M. Krogman, examined skulls found in Alişar Höyük excavations and studied their relationship to other populations (Krogman 1937).

J.L. Angel was also interested in skeletal remains from Turkey, as he was undertaking research in Greece. His first study in Turkey was on the human bones found during the excavations at Troy conducted by the University of Cincinnati between 1932 and 1938. He studied the bones during the summer of 1938 in the Archaeological Museum at Istanbul. He also studied the cranial types and compared them to other skulls found in Turkey and Greece. Later he studied the skeletal remains from Babaköy (1939), Karataş (1970) and Çatalhöyük (1971). In one study, Angel (1979) examined the prevalence of osteoarthritis in prehistoric (Kalinkaya, Central Anatolia) and Byzantine (Kalenderhane Camii, Istanbul) populations.

D. Brothwell (1986) made a detailed examination of human bones found during excavations at Saraçhane in Istanbul dating to the Byzantine period.

M. Schultz did several palaeopathological studies on human bones found at excavations in Boğazkale/Hattuşa (1986), Pergamon (1989), and Ikiztepe (1989). Some of his studies were undertaken alongside Turkish scholars (Schultz and Alpagut 1989; Schultz and Güleç 1989).

U. Wittwer-Backofen is another German anthropologist who studied human bones from İkiztepe/Samsun (Wittwer-Backofen 1986, 1988a), Boğazkale/Hattuşa (Wittwer-Backofen 1987) and Lidar (Wittwer-Backofen 1988b).

Researchers E. Reuer and S. Fabrizii-Reuer, from Austria, studied the human skeletons found in Ephesos (Reuer and Fabrizii-Reuer 1990; Fabrizii-Reuer 1994).

Researchers T. Molleson and P. Andrews, from the UK, have studied the skeletons of the Neolithic site of Çatalhöyük (Molleson *et al.* 1996, 2004, 2005; Andrews *et al.* 2005; Andrews and Bello 2006). Cowgill and Hager (2007) published an article on the same skeletal series.

Researchers from the USA and Italy published a palaeopathological study on Roman-Byzantine human skeletal remains from Elauissa Sebaste in southern Turkey (Paine *et al.* 2007).

Richards *et al.* (2003) studied stable isotope evidence for diet at Çatalhöyük. Another stable isotope study at a Neolithic site, Nevalli Çori, was published in 2006 by German researchers (Lösch *et al.* 2006). An example of ancient DNA research is Matheson and Loy's study (2001).

The current status of human bioarchaeology in Turkey

The Anthropology Department within the Language, History and Geography Faculty at Ankara University has today three sub-divisions: palaeoanthropology, physical anthropology and social anthropology (Ankara University 2009). All of these divisions have graduate and under-graduate schools. Bioarchaeological research on human skeletal remains has been undertaken by researchers at the subdivision of palaeoanthropology lead by professors Berna Alpagut, Erksin Güleç, and Ayla Sevim Erol at present (see, e.g., Alpagut 1986; Sevim 1998; Güleç *et al.* 2007). Ayla Sevim Erol is also the founder of the Forensic Anthopology Comission of the Turkish Forensic Science Society. Associate professor İsmail Özer has also researched on human bioarchaeology (see, e.g., Özer *et al.* 2006; Özer and Katayama 2006). Associate professor Ayhan Ersoy is mainly interested in palaeoanthropology. Researchers in the subdivision of physical anthropology such as Professor Galip Akın and associate professors Timur Gültekin and Başak Koca Özer are mainly interested in issues such as somatometry, anthropometry, growth and obesity, but they also publish on human bioarchaeology (see, e.g., Koca Özer *et al.* 2006; Güngör *et al.* 2007). Doctoral student Işın Günay, who is undertaking bioarchaeological research, is a TUBITAK (Turkish Academy of Sciences) research fellow (Günay *et al.* 2007).

The second anthropology department in Turkey which has bioanthropology oriented research was established in 1976 at Hacettepe University in Ankara (Hacettepe University 2009). The department has only a graduate school. In the department, two professors have strengths in human bioarchaeology. Professor Metin Özbek is Head of Department and did his master's degree at the University of Paris VII and his PhD at the University of Bordeaux I in France on skeletons from Byblos, Lebanon. His research areas are dental anthropology, palaeopathology and artificial cranial deformation. He is especially interested in Neolithic skeletal series from Turkey. Özbek has several publications in French (e.g. Özbek 1984, 1988b, 1991), but also in English (Özbek 2001, 2002, 2005). Professor Yılmaz Selim Erdal is a researcher in dental anthropology and palaeopathology on various skeletal series from Turkey (e.g. Erdal and Duyar 1999; Duyar and Erdal 2003; Erdal 2006, 2008). Research associates Gülfem Uysal (Uysal 2006a, 2006b) and Ömür Dilek Erdal (Erdal 2007), and doctoral students Ali Metin Büyükkarakaya and Özge Yıldız are doing human bioarchaeology oriented studies.

In the 1990s several new universities were founded in Turkey as a result of a new policy intended to help Turkey join the European Union. Four anthropology departments were established in these new universities. An anthropology department was established in 1995 in Cumhuriyet University, Sivas, with one associate professor, Ayşen Açıkkol, who is interested in human bioarchaeology and zooarchaeology (Güleç *et al.* 2004). An assistant professor, Pınar Gözlük Kırmızıoğlu (Gözlük 2005), and research assistant Ayhan Yiğit focus their research on human bioarchaeology. There is also an assistant professor, Gülüşan Özgün Başıbüyük, who is interested in anthropometry and growth.

An anthropology department was also established in 1998 at Mustafa Kemal University, Hatay. There is one assistant professor, Serpil Eroğlu, with a research interest in human bioarchaeology (Eroğlu and Erdal 2008; Eroğlu 2010).

The Department of Anthropology in Yüzüncü Yıl University, Van, was founded in 2003. There is one assistant professor, Cesur Pehlevan (Güleç *et al.* 2004), whose research area is palaeoanthropology and bioarchaeology. Research assistants Hakan Yılmaz, Nevin Şimşek and Ismail Baykara are interested in bioarchaeology. Yener Bektaş is undertaking research on growth.

A new anthropology department was founded at Ahi Evran University in Kırşehir in 2008. Assistant professor Ahmet Cem Erkman, who is employed in the department, is doing research on dental anthropology.

The youngest anthropology department was established in 2009 at Mehmet Akif Ersoy University in Burdur. There are two assistant professors, F. Arzu Demirel and Z. Füsun Yaşar, who are interested in bioarchaeology.

There are four human bioarchaeologists employed in archaeology departments in Turkey. Assistant professor Handan Üstündağ has been employed since 1995 in the Archaeology Department at Anadolu University, Eskişehir, with a research interest in human osteology and palaeopathology (Üstündağ-Aydın and Guidotti 2001). Başak Boz is assistant professor in the Archaeology Department at Trakya University, Edirne. She is interested in dental anthropology and especially dental microwear in Neolithic skeletons (Molleson *et al.* 1996, 2005; Andrews *et al.* 2005). Ercan Nalbantoğlu is employed in the Archaeology Department at Çukurova University, Adana, as assistant professor. His main interest is human bioarchaeology (Öztunç *et al.* 2006). Derya Atamtürk Duyar works in the Archaeology Department at Gaziantep University, also with a research interest is human bioarchaeology (Atamtürk and Duyar 2008).

Professor İzzet Duyar, who has carried out numerous bioarchaeological as well as physical anthropological studies, is employed in the Sociology Department at Gaziantep University (see, e.g., Erdal and Duyar 1999; Duyar and Erdal 2003).

There is only one bioarchaeologist, Asuman Alpagut, employed in the Museum of Anatolian Civilizations. Songül Alpaslan Roodenberg (Alpaslan Roodenberg 2008) and Yasemin Yılmaz are independent bioarchaeologists.

Associations, meetings, periodicals and databases

There are as yet no associations in Turkey for bioarchaeologists, physical anthropologists or palaeoanthropologists.

Monographs or edited volumes are not the preferred publication type for bioarchaeologists in Turkey, although they are quite common in archaeology. Most of the bioarchaeological papers have been published in periodicals. In 1964, a new anthropology journal was launched in place of the older *Turkish Anthropology Journal*, which consisted of 22 volumes published between 1925 and 1939. This new *Anthropology Journal* published 13 volumes until 1998; and after a four-year break, it resumed publication in 2002 and continues today. The journal includes physical anthropology, palaeoanthropology and bioarchaeology as well as social anthropological research articles. The articles are mainly in Turkish.

An 'Excavation Results Meeting' took place in 1979 in Ankara with the purpose of collecting together all the archaeological activities and results by the Ministry of Culture. In 1983 'Survey Results' and in 1985 'Archaeometry Results' sessions added to this meeting. The first bioarchaeological paper presented in the survey session was in 1985, and bioarchaeological studies have since then been presented in both the survey and the archaeometry sessions until 1988. After 1988 bioarchaeological studies only belong to the session on 'Archaeometry Results'. The meeting is called today the 'International Excavation, Survey and Archaeometry Symposium in Turkey'. It is the biggest annual meeting for archaeology and related disciplines such as bioarchaeology. Most of the bioarchaeology researches in Turkey are published in the symposia books entitled *Arkeometri Sonuçları Toplantısı*.

There is also a National Biological Anthropology Meeting (Ulusal Biyolojik Antropoloji Sempozyumu), which first took place in 1996 in Ankara. The second meeting was in 2000 and the third one was in 2008, again in Ankara. At the time of writing, the next meeting is scheduled for 2010, once again in Ankara.

There are also other journals which publish bioarchaeological papers such as *Belleten*, *Hacettepe Üniversitesi Edebiyat Fakültesi Dergisi* ('Hacettepe University Faculty of Humanities Journal') and *Ankara Üniversitesi Dil ve Tarih-Coğrafya Fakültesi Dergisi* ('Ankara University Faculty of Language, History and Geography Journal').

A standardized osteological database does not exist yet in Turkey.

Laboratories and collections

There are collections of human skeletons curated mainly in the anthropology departments of Ankara University and Hacettepe University, Ankara.

The skeletal collection in Ankara University includes approximately 3000 human skeletons. The largest group comes from mediaeval cemeteries such as Karagündüz (Van), Tepecik (Elazığ), Dilkaya (Van), and Topaklı (Nevşehir). There are also around 700 skulls dated to Ottoman period.

The skeletal collection in Hacettepe University consists of approximately 7500 skeletons from 30 different archaeological sites. Most of the sites comprise between 30 and 100 individuals; but six sites provide more than 250 individuals. The largest assemblages come from a Bronze Age population from İkiztepe (Samsun) and a Byzantine population from Iznik (Bursa).

There is also a small skeletal collection in the Archaeology Department at Anadolu University, Eskişehir.

ARCHAEOLOGICAL HUMAN REMAINS AND LEGISLATION

Archaeology and legislation

The Ministry of Culture and Tourism, General Directorate of Cultural Heritage and Museums, has the responsibility and the authority for the preservation and conservation of the cultural and national heritage at a national and international level. Apart from the protection of architectural heritage, this General Directorate also carries out studies such as archaeological excavations, documentation and restoration of cemeteries, restoration of monuments, conservation projects, exhibitions, the landscape design of the museums, and similar activities.

The current legislation which concerns movable and immovable cultural and natural property to be conserved and the obligations and responsibilities of individual and corporate bodies is the Legislation for the Conservation of Cultural and Natural Property (Kültür ve Tabiat Varlıklarını Koruma Kanunu), which is Law 2,863 of 23 July 1983 in the Oficial Gazette. This legislation aims to define the movable and immovable cultural and natural property to be conserved; regulates the relevant procedures and activities; and assigns responsibilities for the organization in charge of the project and takes operational decisions (Part 1, Article 1).

The legislation is divided into seven parts. Part 1 includes Articles 1 to 5, which define the aim and content of the law and provide definitions of terms such as 'cultural property', 'natural property', and 'archaeological site'. Part 2 includes Articles 6 to 22, which concerns the immovable cultural and natural properties and their conservation. Part 3 includes Articles 23 to 34, which concerns movable cultural and natural properties and their conservation. Part 4 includes Articles 35 to 50, which concerns the procedures, permissions and prohibitions of doing any research, evaluation, excavation, and treasure hunting. Part 5 includes Articles 51 to 63, which concerns the establishments, duties, authorities and the procedures of the Superior and Regional Conservation Councils of Immovable Cultural and Natural Property. Part 6 includes Articles 64 to 75, which concerns prizes for finding cultural properties and penalties for breaking the law regarding cultural and natural properties. Part 7 includes Articles 76 to 78, which includes some additional information.

Part 1 (Page 3, Article 4) defines the obligations for those who find any cultural and natural property:

> Those who discover movable or immovable cultural and natural property and those who know or learn that such property exists on the land they own or use are obliged to notify the nearest museum directorate or, Village Headman in villages or, Territorial Administrative Governors in other places within three days. If such property is found in military zones, high rank commanders should be informed. Administrators who receive notification or are already informed about such property within their precincts are responsible for taking preliminary measures for their protection and safety. Village Headmen (Muhtar) need to notify the nearest administrator then have to notify the Ministry of Culture and Tourism and the nearest museum directorate within ten days via letter. The notified Ministry and museum directorate act according to this Legislation and perform the designated operations as soon as possible.
>
> *Law 2,863, Part 1, page 3, Article 4*

In Part 1, Article 5 states that 'All movable and immovable cultural and natural property that is to be conserved and found or to be found on property belonging to the state, public institutions or private institutions and individuals is considered as a state property' [author's translation].

In this legislation the scope of Part 3, which deals with the movable cultural and natural properties, and Part 4, which deals with the procedures, permissions and prohibitions of doing any research, and excavating are of interest to physical anthropologists or bioarchaeologists. In Part 3, Article 23 (amended by the Legislation dated 17 June 1987, no. 3,386), movable cultural and natural properties are defined as:

> All kinds of cultural and natural properties that belong to geological, prehistoric or historic periods and that have documentary significance in terms of geology, *anthropology*, prehistory, archaeology and art history reflecting the social, cultural, technical and scientific characteristics and levels of their periods. All kinds of *animal or plant fossils*, *human skeletons*, flints (sleeks), obsidians, all kinds of bone or metallic tools, encaustic tile, ceramic, similar pots and pans, statues, figures, tablets, cutters, defenders and striking weapons, icons, glass objects, ornaments, etc.
>
> *Law 3,386, Part 3, Article 23*

In Part 3, and also in an amended Article 24 (17 June 1987), the preservation of the movable cultural and natural properties is described as 'movable cultural and natural properties to be conserved which are state properties, shall be preserved in the museums and evaluated by the state' [author's translation].

In Article 32, prohibition on taking properties out of Turkey is described:

> Movable cultural and natural property that has to be preserved inside the country cannot be taken out of the borders. However, taking into consideration national benefit, such property can be temporarily sent outside the country for exhibitions on condition that all security measures are taken and insurance is provided by the host state and the favourable decision of a commission to be set up by the Ministry of Culture and Tourism, consisting of the directors of the departments of archaeology and art history at universities is obtained and the concession of the Cabinet upon the request of the Ministry of Culture and Tourism is procured.
>
> *Law 3,386, Part 3, Article 32*

The rules for taking photographs and films, casts and copies of movable and immovable cultural property are defined in Article 34:

> Permission of the Ministry of Culture and Tourism has to be procured for photographs and films, casts and copies of movable and immovable cultural property to be taken for educational, scientific and presentative purposes in excavation sites and museums attached to the Ministry of Culture and Tourism. Procedures relating to such documentation are designated by regulation.
>
> *Law 3,386, Part 3, Article 34*

Getting permission to study, undertake evaluations and excavation is defined in Part 4, Article 35:

> The privilege to conduct studies, evaluations and excavations to find movable and immovable cultural and natural property within the scope of this legislation belongs to

461

the Ministry of Culture and Tourism. Permission to execute such studies can be granted to scientifically and financially Turkish and foreign recognized groups and institutions by the Ministry of Culture and Tourism, permission to make evaluations and excavations can be granted by the concession of the Cabinet upon the request of the Ministry of Culture and Tourism.

Law 3,386, Part 4, Article 35

The transfer of archaeological material from the excavation site to the museum is defined in Article 41 as follows:

At the termination of excavation work each year, all movable cultural and natural property to be found at excavations is handed over to state museums designated by the Ministry of Culture and Tourism. Human and animal skeletons and fossils to be found at full excavations and test excavation soundings can be handed over to natural history museums, universities or related Turkish scientific institutes with the consent of the Ministry of Culture and Tourism. All movable cultural property to be found at excavations and soundings pertaining to military history is handed over to military museums by the Ministry of Culture and Tourism with the consent of the Office of the Commander-in-Chief of the Army.

Law 3,386, Part 4, Article 41

Publication Rights is defined in Article 43 as follows:

In accordance with the provisions of the Law on Intellectual and Artistic Works numbered 5846, Publication Rights of the properties, found in excavation, test excavation and research activities, belong to the actual directors carrying out the excavation, test excavation and research for the committees and institutions which are granted the permits for these activities. Head of the excavations, at the termination of each excavation, is obliged to submit a scientific report to the Ministry of Culture and Tourism.

Law 3,386, Part 4, Article 43

HUMAN REMAINS AND LEGISLATION

Unfortunately there is no 'official' chronological boundary between a forensic and an archaeological skeleton in Turkey. Usually if a skeleton or an old cemetery is found, the local museum is informed. It is the archaeologist who decides if it is archaeological or forensic, according to the grave type and any artefacts that may provide a clue to the date of the burial.

There is no specific legal arrangement for the excavation of cemeteries. Cemeteries can be excavated as part of an archaeological site, or separately. Excavations of archaeological sites are determined by the regulations of the 'Legislation for the Conservation of Cultural of Cultural and Natural Property'.

There are no standard procedures for excavating human remains. If human remains are found in an archaeological excavation, it is the director's responsibility to offer a bioarchaeologist to study the skeletal remains. Human bioarchaeologists usually work in the field to excavate human bones on their own or with the archaeologists. Bioarchaeologists may study the remains in a simple temporary field laboratory, which is usually built at the site, or they may transport the bones to a university laboratory.

Most Turkish bioarchaeologists are employed at universities. There are no bioarchaeologists employed to produce osteological reports on excavated skeletal series (in archaeological projects done by Turkish researchers). Graduate students also take part in archaeological excavation projects and carry out their osteological examination in the field or in the university laboratories.

The most serious problem for bioarchaeologists in Turkey is the attitude of archaeologists. In many archaeological excavations, human remains are neither collected nor do archaeologists pay any attention to them. Even if they are collected, there are major methodological problems in the excavating and recording processes. The storage conditions of human skeletons in excavation depots as well as in museums are usually poor. As there are no bioanthropologists or human bone curators employed at the museums (except for one in the Museum of Anatolian Civilizations in Ankara), human remains are usually not stored in museums. This is the reason why human remains are usually transferred to university laboratories. The transfer of human as well as animal bones to the university laboratories is permitted.

The procedure for the laboratory analysis of material found in excavations, including human remains, is defined in Article 18 and Article 19 of the 'Licence for Excavation and Test Excavation to be Performed in Relation to Cultural and Natural Property' of the Ministry of Culture and Tourism, General Directorate for Cultural Property and Museums. Article 18 defines the procedure of sending samples for laboratory analysis as follows:

> Samples of the finds identified during the excavation, test excavation and cleaning to be sent for laboratory analysis shall be examined within the framework of the Law numbered 2863 as amended by the Law numbered 3386 by a commission to be formed by the relevant Museum Directorship. Should the request be found appropriate, three copies of the protocol, report and official cover letter shall be prepared by the Museum Directorate. One copy shall remain at the relevant museum, one copy submitted to the relevant authorities and one copy sent to the General Directorate.
>
> *Licence for Excavation and Test Excavation to be Performed in Relation to Cultural and Natural Property, Article 18*

An equal procedure is defined in Article 19 with regards to the procedures for transferring samples to universities, which do not have an inventory quality and are usually classified as study material only.

Ethical aspects of archaeological human remains such as reburial of excavated bones have not been an issue of debate in Turkey at all.

METHODS OF ANTHROPOLOGICAL ANALYSIS

No standard methodology exists in Turkey. There are two sex discriminant studies from Turkey using the scapula (Özer *et al.* 2006) and the femur (Özer and Katayama 2006). Researchers usually use both the Pearson and the Trotter and Gleser formulae for stature estimation. There is a formula developed for the modern Turkish population, which is also used, though not commonly (Sağır 2000).

CONCLUSION

The establishment of biological anthropology as a scientific discipline was an outcome of the new Turkish Republic after the fall of the Ottoman Empire. In the 1920s and 1930s it was believed that the discipline could be key to determining the biological/racial identity of the Turkish nation. Based on this idea, institutions and researchers were generously supported by the government. However 'racial identity' lost its value in the changing political climate in Turkey after the 1940s. That led to a long quiet period until the 1990s. In the 1990s several new universities and some new anthropology departments were established in Turkey. At the same time, some bioarchaeologists began to be employed in archaeology departments. This led to a slight rise in the development of bioarchaeology in Turkey. Although the history of Turkish anthropology started in the 1920s, the discipline became isolated from the international arena until the 2000s. Before the 2000s, mainly deterministic studies were published, usually in local journals. Today, there are more research papers from Turkey published in international journals, and Turkish researchers are joining international associations.

However, some basic things are still missing in Turkey, such as a national biological anthropology association, a standardized methodology, an osteological database, and a biological anthropology journal of international standard. It can be said that bioarchaeology in Turkey is still developing and it is more open to the international arena today than ever before.

USEFUL CONTACTS

Ankara University Faculty of Language, History and Geography. Website: www.dtcf.ankara. edu.tr/antropoloji.html/
Hacettepe University Anthropology Department. Website: www.antropoloji.hacettepe.edu.tr/

ACKNOWLEDGEMENTS

I would like to thank to Dr F. Arzu Demirel from Mehmet Akif Ersoy University, Dr Ali Umut Türkcan from Anadolu University and Işın Günay from Ankara University for their help.

BIBLIOGRAPHY

Alpagut, B. (1979) 'Some paleopathological cases of the ancient Anatolian mandibles', *Journal of Human Evolution*, 8: 571–78.
——(1980) 'Anadolu Neoltik toplumunda torus mandibularis', *Antropoloji*, 9: 77–91.
——(1986) 'The human skeletal remains from Kurban Höyük (Urfa Province)', *Anatolica*, 13: 149–74.
Alpaslan Roodenberg, S. (2008) 'The Neolithic cemetery', in J. Roodenberg and S. Alpaslan Roodenberg (eds) *Life and Death in a Prehistoric Settlement in Northwest Anatolia. The Ilıpınar Excavations, Volume III. With contributions on Hacılartepe and Menteşe*, Leiden: Nederlands Instituut Voor Het Nabije Oosten.
Andrews, P. and Bello, S. (2006) 'Pattern in human burial practices', in R. Gowland and C. Knüsel (eds) *Social Archaeology of Funerary Remains*, Oxford: Oxbow.
Andrews, P., Molleson, T. and Boz, B. (2005) 'The human burials at Çatalhöyük', in I. Hodder (ed.) *Inhabiting Çatalhöyük: Reports from the 1995–1999 Seasons*, Cambridge: McDonald Institute for Archaeological Research and the British Institute of Archaeology at Ankara.
Angel, J.L. (1939) 'The Babaköy skeleton', *Archiv für Orientforschung*, 13: 28–31.
——(1951) *Troy. The Human Remains. Supplemantary Monograph 1*, New Jersey: Princeton University.

——(1970) 'Appendix: Human skeletal remains at Karataş', *American Journal of Archaeology*, 74: 253–59.

——(1971) 'Early Neolithic skeletons from Çatal Höyük: demography and pathology', *Anatolian Studies*, 20: 77–98.

——(1979) 'Osteoarthritis in Prehistoric Turkey and Medieval Byzantium', *Henry Ford Hospital Medical Journal*, 27: 38–43.

Ankara University (2009) *Faculty of Language, History and Geography*. Available online at www.dtcf.ankara. edu.tr/antropoloji.html (accessed 17 March 2010).

Atamtürk, D. and Duyar, I. (2008) 'Adramytteion (Örentepe) İskeletlerinde Ağız ve Diş Sağlığı', *Hacettepe Üniversitesi Edebiyat Fakültesi Dergisi*, 25: 1–15.

Bostancı, E. (1973) 'Osteo-arthritis on the condylar process, the variation of the fovea capitulum mandibulae of the ancient Anatolians. Osteo-paleopathology study', *Antropoloji*, 6: 57–87.

Brothwell, D. (1986) 'The human bones', in R.M. Harrison (ed.) *Excavations at Saraçhane in Istanbul, Vol.1, The Excavations, Structures, Architectural Decoration, Small Finds, Coins, Bones, and Molluscs*, New Jersey: Princeton University.

Cowgill, L.W. and Hager, L.D. (2007) 'Variation in the development of postcranial robusticity: an example from Çatalhöyük, Turkey', *International Journal of Osteoarchaeology*, 17: 235–52.

Çiner, R. (1965) 'Altıntepe (Urartu) iskeletlerine ait kalıntıların tetkiki', *Belleten*, 24: 225–44.

Duyar, I. and Erdal, Y.S. (2003) 'A new approach for calibrating dental caries frequency of skeletal remains', *Homo*, 54: 57–70.

Erdal, Ö.D. (2007) 'Eklem hastalıkları ve yaşam biçimi arasındaki ilişkiler: Anadolu Neolitik topluluklarından örnekler', *Hacettepe Üniversitesi Edebiyat Fakültesi Dergisi*, 24: 77–93.

Erdal, Y.S. (2006) 'A pre-Columbian case of congenital syphilis from Anatolia', *International Journal of Osteoaechaology*, 16: 16–33.

——(2008) 'Occlusal grooves in anterior dentition among Kovuklukaya inhabitants (Sinop, Northern Anatolia, 10th century AD)', *International Journal of Osteoarchaeology*, 18: 152–66.

Erdal, Y.S. and Duyar, I. (1999) 'A new correction procedure for calibrating dental caries frequency (Brief Communication)', *American Journal of Physical Anthropology*, 108: 237–40.

Eroğlu, S. and Erdal, Y.S. (2008) 'Why did the frequency of palatine torus increase in the ancient Anatolian populations?', *HOMO – Journal of Comparative Human Biology*, 59: 365–82.

Eroğlu, S. (2010) 'Variations in the form of the hypoglossal canal in ancient Anatolian populations: Comparison of two recording methods', *HOMO – Journal of Comparative Human Biology*, 61: 33–47.

Fabrizii-Reuer, S. (1994) 'Die menschlichen Skelette aus den Hanghäusern von Ephesos', *Anzeiger der phil.-hist. Klasse der Österreichischen Akademie der Wissenschaften*, 130. Jahrgang 1993: 25–40.

Gözlük, P. (2005) 'Karagündüz toplumunun paleodemografik açıdan incelenmesi', *Antropoloji*, 20: 75–105.

Güleç, E. (1989) 'Paleoantropolojik verilere göre eski Anadolu bireylerinin boy açısından incelenmesi', *Arkeometri Sonuçları Toplantısı*, 5: 147–60.

Güleç, E., Açıkkol, A. and Pehlevan, C. (2004) 'Eski Anadolu insanlarında ağız ve diş sağlığı', *Antropoloji*, 16: 33–51.

Güleç, E., Gültekin, T., Özer, İ., et al. (2007) 'A brief overview of bio-anthropological analysis of human skeletal remains from Anatolia: Early Neolithic to Ottoman Empire', *International Journal of Anthropology*, 22: 3–4.

Güngör, K., Sağır, M. and Özer, İ. (2007) 'Evaluation of the gonial angle in the Anatolian populations: from past to present', *Collegium Antropologicum*, 31: 315–19.

Günay, I., Teke, H.Y., Bilge, Y., et al. (2007) 'Kelenderis Kentinde Bulunan Bir İskelette Saptanan Otitis Media Olgusunun Değerlendirilmesi', *Adli Tıp Bülteni*, 12: 32–35.

Hacettepe University (2009) *Anthropology department*. Available online at www.antropoloji.hacettepe.edu.tr (accessed 17 March 2010).

Inan, A. (1947) *Türkiye Halkının Antropolojik Karakterleri ve Türkiye Tarihi*, Ankara: T.T.K. Basımevi.

Kansu, Ş.A. (1940) *Türk Antropoloji Enstitüsü Tarihçesi / Historique de l'institut turc d'anthropologie*, Istanbul: Maarif Matbaası.

Krogman, W.M. (1937) 'Cranial types from Alishar Hüyük and their relations to other racial types, ancient and modern, of Europe and Western Asia', in H.H. von der Osten (ed.) *The Alishar Hüyük, Seasons of 1930–32, part III, XXX*, Chicago: Oriental Institute.

Koca Özer, B., Güleç, E., Gültekin, T., et al. (2006) 'Implications of dental caries in Anatolia: from hunting–gathering to the present', *Human Evolution*, 21: 215–22.

Lösch, S., Grupe, G., Peters, J. (2006) 'Stable isotopes and dietary adaptations in humans and animals at pre-pottery Neolithic Nevalli Çori, southeast Anatolia', *American Journal of Physical Anthropology*, 131: 181–93.

Luschan, F. von. (1911) 'The early inhabitants of Western Asia', *Journal of the Royal Anthropological Institute of London*, 41: 221–44.

Matheson, C.D. and Loy, T.H. (2001) 'Genetic sex identification of 9400-year-old human skull samples from Çayönü Tepesi, Turkey', *Journal of Archaeological Science*, 28: 569–75.

Molleson, T., Boz, B., Nudd, K., *et al.* (1996) 'Dietary indications in the dentitions from Çatal Hüyük', *Arkeometri Sonuçları Toplantısı*, 11: 141–50.

Molleson, T., Ottevanger, J. and Compton, T. (2004) 'Vatiation in Neolithic teeth from Çatalhöyük (1961–64)', *Anatolian Studies*, 54: 1–26.

Molleson, T., Andrews, P. and Boz, B. (2005) 'Reconstruction of the Neolithic people of Çatalhöyük', in I. Hodder (ed.) *Inhabiting Çatalhöyük: Reports from the 1995–1999 Seasons*, Cambridge: McDonald Institute for Archaeological Research and the British Institute of Archaeology at Ankara.

Özbek, M. (1984) 'Étude anthropologique des restes humains de Hayaz Höyük', *Anatolica*, 11: 155–70.

——(1988a) 'Çayönü insanları ve sağlık sorunları', *Arkeometri Sonuçları Toplantısı*, 4: 121–52.

——(1988b) 'Culte des chanes humains à Çayönü', *Anatolica*, 15: 127–37.

——(1991) 'Étude anthropologique de L'Enfant de Cafer Höyük (Neolithique, Turquie)', *Cahiers de L'Euphara*, 5–6: 151–59.

——(1995) 'Dental pathology of the Pre-pottery Neolithic residents of Çayönü, SE Turkey', *Rivista di Anthropologia*, 73: 99–122.

——(2001) 'Cranial deformation in a non-adult sample from Değirmentepe (Chalcolithic, Turkey)', *American Journal of Physical Anthropology*, 115: 238–44.

——(2002) 'Anthropological analysis of the Öküzini human remains', *Études et recherches archeologiques de L'Université de Liège*, 96: 353–65.

——(2005) 'Skeletal pathology of a high-ranking official from Thrace (Turkey, last quarter of the 4th century BC)', *International Journal of Osteoarchaeology*, 15: 216–25.

Özer, İ. and Katayama, K. (2006) 'Sex determination using the femur in an ancient Anatolian population', *Anthropologischer Anzeiger*, 64: 389–98.

Özer, İ., Katayama, K., Sağır, M., *et al.* (2006) 'Sex determination using the scapula in Medieval skeletons from East Anatolia', *Collegium Antropologicum*, 30: 415–19.

Öztunç, H., Yoldas, O. and Nalbantoglu, E. (2006) 'The periodontal disease status of the historical population of Assos', *International Journal of Osteoarchaeology*, 16: 76–81.

Paine, R.R., Vargiu, R., Coppa, A., *et al.* (2007) 'A health assessment of high status Christian burials recovered from the Roman–Byzantine archaeological site of Elaiussa Sebaste, Turkey', *HOMO-Journal of Comparative Human Biology*, 58: 173–90.

Reuer, E. and Fabrizii-Reuer, S. (1990) 'Some medieval inhabitants of coastal Asia minor Excavations at Selcuk-Ephesos', *Rivista di Antropologia*, 68: 363–68.

Richards, M.P., Pearson, J.A., Molleson, T., *et al.* (2003) 'Stable isotope evidence of diet at Neolithic Çatalhöyük, Turkey', *Journal of Archaeological Science*, 30: 67–76.

Sağır, M. (2000) 'Uzun kemik radyografilerinden boy formülü hesaplaması', 'unpublished PhD thesis', Institute of Social Sciences, Ankara University.

Schultz, M. (1987) 'Der Gesundheitszustandt der frühmittelalterlichen Bevölkerung von Boğazkale/ Hattuşa', *Araştırma Sonuçları Toplantısı*, 4: 401–9.

——(1989) 'Osteologische Untersuchungen an den Spätmittelalterlichen Skeleten von Pergamon. Ein vorläufiger Bericht', *Arkeometri Sonuçları Toplantısı*, 4: 111–14.

——(1990) 'Erkrankungen des Kinderalters bei der frühbronzezeitlichen Population von Ikiztepe (Türkei)', in F. Andraschko and W. R. Teegen (eds) *Gedenkschrift für Jürgen Driehaus*, Mainz: Zabern Verlag.

Schultz, M. and Alpagut, B. (1989) 'Die Bedeutung der Anämie bei Prähistorischen Bevölkerungen, Dargestellt an einem Kinderschädel aus Beyköy', *Arkeometri Sonuçları Toplantısı*, 4: 103–6.

Schultz, M. and Güleç, E. (1989) 'Die Bedeutung Entzündlicher Schädelerkrankungen für die Kinder-sterblichkeit in der vor-und frühgeschichte, dargestellt an einem Schädel aus dem Friedhof von Dilkaya/ Van', *Arkeometri Sonuçları Toplantısı*, 4: 107–9.

Schultz, M. and Schmidt-Schultz, T. (1995) 'Krankheiten des Kindesalters in der mittelalterlichen Popu-lation von Pergamon. Ergebnisse einer paläopathologischen Untersuchung', *Istanbuler Mitteilungen des Deutschen Archäologischen Instituts*, 44: 181–201.

Şenyürek, M. (1947) 'A note on the duration of life of the ancient inhabitants of Anatolia', *American Journal of Physical Anthropology*, 5: 55–66.

——(1952) 'A study of the human skeletons from Kültepe, excavated under the auspices of the Turkish Historical Society. The skeletons from the excavation season of 1948', *Belleten*, 16: 323–43.

Sevim, A. (1998) 'Eski Anadolu toplumlarında gözlenen bir paleopatolojik doku bozukluğu: porotic hyperostosis', *Antropoloji*, 13: 229–44.

Tunakan, S. (1971) 'Malatya-Aslantepe iskeletleri', *Antropoloji*, 1: 1–7.

Uysal, G. (2006a) 'An early Byzantine case of Eagle's syndrome in Turkey', *Paleopathological Newsletter*, 135.

——(2006b) 'The occurrance and age distribution of Harris Lines in Turkey', *International Journal of Anthropology*, 21: 193–201.

Üstündağ-Aydın, H. and Guidotti, A. (2001) 'Anthropologische Untersuchung der Skelette von Metropolis und Alaşehir, Westtürkei', *Archaeologia Austriaca. Beiträge zur Paläanthropologie, Ur-und Frühgeschichte Österreichs*, 84–85: 187–93.

Virchow, R. (1882) *Alttrojanische Gräber und Schädel*, Berlin: Abhandlungen der Königlichen Akademie der Wissenschaften zu Berlin.

——(1884) *Uber alte Schädel von Assos und Cypern*, Berlin: Abhandlungen der Königlichen Akademie der Wissenschaften zu Berlin. Physik. Klasse.

——(1896) 'Funde aus dem nordwestlichen Phrygien und von Salonik', *Zeitschrift für Ethnologie (Berlin)*, 28: 123–26.

Wittwer-Backofen, U. (1986) 'Anthropologische Untersuchungen der Nekropole Ikiztepe/Samsun', *Araştırma Sonuçları Toplantısı*, 3: 421–28.

——(1987) 'Anthropologische Untersuchungen des Byzantinischen Friedhofs Boğazköy/Hattusa', *Araştırma Sonuçları Toplantısı*, 4: 381–99.

——(1988a) 'Paleodemography of the early Bronze age cemetery of Ikiztepe/ Samsun', *Araştırma Sonuçları Toplantısı*, 5: 175–89.

——(1988b) 'Anthropological study of the skeleton material from Lidar', *Araştırma Sonuçları Toplantısı*, 5: 191–201.

Ukraine/УКРАЇНА

Inna Potekhina

INTRODUCTION: A BRIEF HISTORY AND CURRENT STATE OF PHYSICAL ANTHROPOLOGY IN UKRAINE

As in many European countries, the history of physical anthropology in Ukraine began in the second half of the 18th century when the first works about the physical features of the local population were published. From the very beginning, physical anthropology was integrated with palaeoanthropology and ethno-historical anthropology. The earliest pages of the history of Ukrainian anthropology were connected with Professor M. Maksymovych, the first Rector of Kiev University, who published a paper on the question of human origin in 1831. Further contribution to physical anthropology in Ukraine was made by P. Chubynsky, who was awarded the golden medal in Paris after he published, between 1872 and 1879, seven volumes on the different local groups including physical anthropological data.

An important scholar in the foundation and development of Ukrainian physical and ethnic anthropology was Hvedir Vovk (Fedor Volkov, 1847–1918), a prominent representative of European science who emigrated from Ukraine to France because of his political democratic views. Vovk successfully defended his dissertation, 'The skeletal changes of the foot in primates and human races', at the University of Sorbonne in 1905 and was awarded the great medal of P. Broca and the annual prize of E. Goddard. While in France, Vovk, with the support of his French colleagues, managed to organize anthropological research with Ukrainian material. He continued his researches at St Petersburg University, and his analyses resulted in his fundamental works on the physical characteristic of different groups among the Ukrainian population (Vovk 1908; Volkov 1916). In Soviet time his works were forbidden, but in the post-Soviet period they received their due recognition.

In the 1920s and 1930s, followers of Vovk's ideas (O. Alesho, M. Rudnitsky, I. Rakivsky and S. Rudenko) founded anthropological scientific societies at the universities of Kiev, Kharkiv, Odessa, Dnipropetrovsk and Lviv. These universities began to accumulate skeletal collections. At this time Ukrainian anthropology made progress, but its normal development was restricted by Stalin's purges with regard to anthropological research. After the Second World War, no anthropological centres remained in Ukraine, since some scholars were killed during the war or died in Stalin's camps, some ceased their research in order to avoid prosecution, and others emigrated to the West.

A new phase began in the mid-1950s when the Anthropology Group was established in Kiev at the Institute of Art, Folklore and Ethnography at the Academy of Sciences of the USSR. From this time onwards, regular expeditions collected anthropological materials, including skeletal collections from archaeological excavations. The first volume of the journal *Anthropological Materials of Ukraine* (Матеріали з антропології України) was published in 1955. A new generation of Ukrainian anthropologists with both historical and biological backgrounds (E.I. Danilova, V.D. Dyachenko, G.P. Zinevich, S.I. Kruts, R.A. Starovoitova, S.P. Segeda and I.D. Potekhina) worked in collaboration with the best representatives of the Russian anthropological school and colleagues from Latvia, Lithuania, Georgia and other Republics. Their research on the origin, evolution and physical characteristics of the ancient and contemporary populations of Ukraine resulted in numerous articles and monographs (Danilova 1965; Dyachenko 1965; Gokhman 1966; Konduktorova 1973; Kruts 1972; Starovoitova 1979; Zinevich 1967).

In the 1970s the Anthropology Group moved to the Institute of Archaeology, Academy of Sciences of the USSR, where it was transformed into the Palaeoanthropology Section. The participation of anthropologists in archaeological excavations in the steppes of Ukraine resulted in the analysis of numerous skeletal remains from isolated burials, cemeteries and burial mounds (kurgans) of different historical periods dating from the Palaeolithic to the Late Mediaeval period (Danilova 1979; Dyachenko 1986; Kruts 1984; Pokas 1987; Potekhina 1983, 1990; Telegin and Potekhina 1987).

After the collapse of the Soviet Union the situation in East European anthropology, including Ukrainian anthropology, significantly changed. Important new processes took place in the scientific community, and in particular among those studying the prehistoric populations of Eastern Europe. Scholars from Ukraine and other former Soviet Republics took the opportunity to discuss the problems of Eastern European prehistory freely without ideological limitations. Foreign scholars received easy access to anthropological collections from the territory of south-eastern Europe, including Ukraine, and started to undertake analysis of skeletal materials. Researchers all over the world were able to discuss their problems not only at international conferences, but also by participating in joint research projects. Scholars today are invited to undertake research on Ukrainian archaeological and anthropological collections from the different historic periods, which are among the richest in Europe. A good examples of such collaboration is the participation of Ukraine in the Global History of Health Project, an international research programme aiming to reconstruct and interpret human health based on the study of ancient skeletons from around the Globe. Another example of collaboration is the work undertaken abroad regarding radiocarbon dating and stable isotope analysis providing, respectively, new chronologies and dietary reconstruction of prehistoric populations and cultures (Haeussler and Potekhina 2001; Lillie and Richards 2000; Lillie *et al.* 2009; Potekhina and Telegin 1995).

Logically, all these circumstances in combination have enabled substantial progress in our understanding of the ethnic-cultural processes, biocultural adaptation and other aspects of human history. Although the number of publications has increased in recent years, the general results differ much from those that were expected. Many of the recent publications seriously contradict the established pillars of previous studies conducted ten or twenty years ago. Very often the reason for such disagreement lies in the underestimation of the complicated processes of historical development, such as cultural interactions and mass migrations of the populations of Eastern Europe. The success of future collaboration may be guaranteed if researchers specializing in European and regional archaeological, cultural, historical and physical anthropology work together to avoid the misfortunes of some of the projects carried out in the post-Soviet period.

Currently all Ukrainian anthropologists are concentrated in Kiev at the Department of Bioarchaeology of the Institute of Archaeology, National Academy of Sciences of Ukraine. Besides physical anthropology, scholars are working on the problems of the origin of the population, population genetics, genetic relations, palaeopathology, palaeodemography, and bioarchaeological reconstructions of the ancient populations of the Mesolithic and Bronze Age (Potekhina 1998a, 1998b, 1999), the Iron Age and the Early Mediaeval period (Nazarova 2006; Litvinova 2000; Rudich 1999), and of the time of the Ancient Russ (Kozak 2000, 2005; Kozak and Potekhina 2002; Potekhina and Kozak 1999; Rudich 2002). Currently, theoretical and practical classes in physical anthropology are taught by I.D. Potekhina and O.D. Kozak in the National University 'Kiev-Mohyla Academy'.

Ukrainian skeletal collections

Skeletal collections are housed in the anthropological stores of the Department of Bioarchaeology, Institute of Archaeology, Kiev. They comprise skulls and post-cranial bones from approximately 20,000 burials. Different periods and cultures from East Europe dating from the Epipaleolithic through to the Late Mediaeval period are represented by these collections. The populations that comprise the collections derive from a variety of ecological environments and different socio-economic status. The skeletons have rather good preservation, they have been fully documented archaeologically, and have been analysed for age-at-death and sex determination.

The Late Mesolithic and Neolithic periods are represented by over 320 crania and many more post-cranial elements. The remains were obtained from 12 Late Mesolithic-Neolithic cemeteries from the East European Steppe zone, in the Dnieper River Basin region, and belong to the Dnepr-Donets cultural community. Collections from seven Neolithic cemeteries, Yasinovatka, Dereivka, Nikol'sky, Osipovka, Vasil'evka V, Mar'evka and Kapulovka, are stored in Kiev, at the Institute of Archaeology of Ukraine, and another five (Vilnyanka, Vovnigi 1 and 2, Vasil'evka 2, Hospitalny Hill) in Moscow and St Petersburg. According to the recent radiocarbon dates from the Oxford and Kiev laboratories, these cemeteries date from the seventh through to the fifth millennia BC. The Neolithic skeletons from the Dnieper Rapids region belong to the massive, hypermorphic, proto-Europeans (Potekhina 1998b). Their economy was based upon the exploitation of a hunter-gatherer regime, where fish was an important component of the economy. According to the results of recent stable isotope analyses, these populations consumed protein-dominated diets (Potekhina 2000; Lillie and Richards 2000).

Radiocarbon dating of human, faunal and fish skeletal remains from a number of the Dnieper Rapids cemeteries has demonstrated the presence of a radiocarbon reservoir effect during the Neolithic-Eneolithic periods. The data suggests that the radiocarbon reservoir effect is only evident during these periods, and not in the earlier Epipalaeolithic-Mesolithic periods, prompting the suggestion that the effect is associated with elevated fish consumption, and possibly even linked to shifting hydrological regimes in the Black Sea region (Lillie *et al.* 2009).

These Early Neolithic collections are today very important in the current discussion of the question of the Neolithization of Eastern Europe. Recently, a suggestion was made that the populations of the Dnieper-Donets culture may have been focusing on a cereal/grain-intensive subsistence economy as early as the seventh century BC (Jakobs 1994). The arguments were based on stable isotopes, palaeopathological evidence and comparative analysis of skeletal remains of the Mesolithic and Early Neolithic populations. The results are interesting, although this new model contradicts the generally accepted notion about the time and place of agricultural dispersions in the Old World, especially taking into account that the first cultivated cereals were first brought by representatives of the Bug-Dniester and Linear Pottery cultures who appeared in the North Pontic region no earlier than the fifth millennium BC (Potekhina and Telegin 1995).

The Ukrainian Eneolithic period is represented in our collections by human skeletal remains from the Trypillia and Usatovo cultures as well as from the cemeteries of Igren and Dereivka II, which belong to the Sredny Stog culture (Telegin *et al.* 2001). The collections are not numerous, but they are rather interesting because they represent the first farmers and steppe cattle-breeders in Eastern Europe. Besides, the bearers of Sredny Stog culture made an important impact into the development of the world civilization by domesticating and saddling a horse as early as the fourth millennium BC. The steppe of the north-western Black Sea Littoral is represented by the collection from the Eneolithic cemetery of Mayaki that is attributed to the Usatovo culture. It is characterized by the expansion of cattle-breeding at the beginning of the third millennium BC. In general, the Eneolithic collections include both the massive proto-European and more gracile Mediterranean anthropological groups (Potekhina 1983, 1990).

Bronze Age populations are represented in the collections by the burial-mounds of the Pit Grave, Catacomb, Srubnaya and Poly-shafted Ware cultures. The collections of the Pit Grave culture represent the heterogeneous population of the second half of the third millennium BC. They originate from the steppe zone and a partially wooded steppe in Ukraine. People of the Pit Grave culture had a cattle-breeding economy and belonged to the robust East Mediterraneans with very narrow and high faces (Kruts 1972). The mixed type of economy – both pastoral and farming – characterizes the Catacomb culture. Materials from about 100 burials are available from Catacomb steppe zone cemeteries, dated to the first half of the second millennium BC. The skulls are very robust and broad-faced. Besides, there is the combined collection of 50 skeletons from the steppe burial-mounds, or kurgans, of the Srubnaya culture (Kruts 1972). People buried in these kurgans were pastorals and lived in the 18th to 16th centuries BC. A total of 90 skeletons of the half-sedentary and half-nomadic tribes of the Poly-shafted Ware culture represent the Late Bronze Age and also come from the Dnieper Basin region. It is worth mentioning also that there are 60 skeletons of the Tshinetskaya culture from a partially wooded steppe and wooded area from the Middle Dnieper region, Kiev district (16th to 12th centuries BC).

In the Iron Age, the Scythians, a stock-breeding tribe, populated the steppe zone north of the Black Sea. The general number of Scythian skeletons from the different regions of Ukraine is about 700. The Scythian remains that are stored may be classified into three large groups. The first group includes 100 burials from the left bank of the Dnieper River (Zaporozh'e and Kherson districts). The second group includes 50 skeletons from the territory on the right bank of the Dnieper; and the third group of 30 skeletons originates from the north-west Black Sea Littoral. In addition, 300 skeletons of the Scythian culture are available and derive from the Mamaj-Gora kurgan in the Lower Dnieper region (Litvinova 2007). There are also two collections of this time period from the Crimean peninsula. They represent the rural population of Zolotoye and Ak-Tash and comprise a total of approximately 70 skeletons.

The Antique Period is represented with numerous skeletal remains from towns once colonized by the Greeks in the territory of the north Black Sea Littoral and the Crimean peninsula. The material dating from the first to the fourth centuries from Olviya, Berezan', Khersones and other sites demonstrate the heterogeneity of the population (Nazarova 2006). Skeletons of the Chernyakhov culture, also present in the collection, represent agriculturalists from the third to fifth centuries from different regions in Ukraine (Rudich 1999).

The mediaeval collections are the most numerous and representative. They originate from the steppe and wooded zones, as well as from Crimea, and represent both rural and urban populations dating between the tenth and 17th centuries AD (Kozak 2000; Litvinova 2000; Pokas 1987; Rudich 2002). In addition, the stores contain skeletal material from Late Mediaeval nomads from the territory of the Dnieper Basin steppe, the Azov Sea Littoral and the north Crimea.

ARCHAEOLOGICAL HUMAN REMAINS AND LEGISLATION

Archaeological legislation

As an emerging country, Ukraine did not have a national legal framework until 1991. Legislation effective on the territory of Ukraine before 1991 consisted in a limited number of legislative acts from the USSR. Thus, the Ukrainian legislative framework regulating aspects related to physical anthropology is very young, and after more than 15 years of independence we are still in the process of lawmaking.

The requirements determined by the laws 'On the Protection of Cultural Heritage' and 'On the Protection of Archaeological Heritage' (hereinafter referred to as the 'Law') and other regulations are explained below.

The law 'On the Protection of Cultural Heritage' is focused on legal, social and economic measures of cultural heritage protection. It determines the state organs (government, central and local executive) responsible for the protection of archaeological materials. The law declares that the cultural heritage located in the territory of Ukraine is protected by the state. Its protection is considered to be priority for the government. Until now this provision, however, has been no more than a simple declaration since there is no mechanism to enforce it. At the same time there were some attempts to envisage a legal framework required to enforce the law by adoption of several legislative acts.

According to Article 10 of the Law, only archaeologists with relevant practical experience are entitled to conduct scientific investigations of the archaeological heritage. Archaeological excavations and research of human remains may be carried out provided that there is authorization from the executive organ for the protection of cultural heritage. In order to get this permit it is required that an official document (an 'open letter') is issued by the Institute of Archaeology of the National Academy of Sciences of Ukraine (hereinafter, 'Institute of Archaeology'). Archaeological research conducted without an 'open letter' and permit of the authorized organ is deemed illegal. The 'Criminal Code of Ukraine' sets forth sanctions for conducting illegal archaeological excavations. According to the Institute's regulations, archaeologists conducting fieldwork must submit a scientific report to the Institute of Archaeology after the excavation has been completed and before the following excavating season. Archaeological and anthropological reports are archived at the Institute of Archaeology.

The archaeologist to whom the 'open letter' has been granted and who therefore has authorization must direct the archaeological excavation. The archaeological project must be undertaken, however, by the Institute of Archaeology, scientific institutions of the National Academy of Sciences of Ukraine, departments of archaeology, state universities or museums that have archaeologists among their staff.

It is the Institute of Archaeology that is the only scientific institution in Ukraine to issue permits for archaeological and anthropological research on national territory. It organizes and arranges all kinds of scientific research of the 'archaeological heritage', and develops, approves and introduces scientific methodology for anthropological research, providing expertise, issuing reports and ensures the appropriate storage facilities for the human remains.

HUMAN REMAINS AND LEGISLATION

It was not until 2000 that Ukraine adopted the first law determining general principles for the treatment of human remains. This law was the first step on the way to create a framework in this area. Although the law contains no direct reference to human remains, the definition of the term 'cultural heritage' includes burial mounds, cemeteries, kurgans and other places of burial. Therefore, it would be logical to assume that under this law, skeletal remains (found in such 'burial mounds, cemeteries, kurgans ... ') are subject to legal protection.

The first direct reference to human skeletal remains as an object of legal protection is given by the law On the Protection of Archaeological Heritage which was adopted by parliament in 2004. What does the term 'archaeological heritage' mean? Its definition is quite vague, but it includes sites, buildings, complexes and territories created by Man that have archaeological, anthropological and ethnographical significance. 'Archaeological heritage' would cover skeletal remains as an object of legal protection. The law determines the principles and requirements of scientific research of the archaeological heritage, sets requirements for reporting and establishes other responsibilities for those undertaking the research.

Provisions of the law On the Protection of Archaeological Heritage are further developed in the legal act of the local legal force: Regulations on methodology of archaeological research and the reporting procedure (hereinafter referred to as 'Regulations') approved in 2008 by the Scientific Council of the Institute of Archaeology, National Academy of Sciences of Ukraine. This document was an attempt to fulfil the existing gaps in legislation regarding the procedure following the discovery of human remains, any research undertaken on them and their protection. It is worth highlighting, however, that some provisions of the Regulations which establish responsibilities for those conducting research can hardly be enforced in conditions of an imperfect legal environment. Regulations refer mostly to the procedure of archaeological research, expertise and reporting, while details of anthropological research are not given much attention.

Scientific information obtained during research on human skeletal remains is subject to intellectual property law protection. The Civil Code of Ukraine adopted in 2003 and the laws On Scientific and Technical Information and 'On Copyright and Related Rights' determine the protection of such information as an object of intellectual property.

Excavation, recovery, research and storage

If human skeletal remains are discovered during excavations, the presence of an anthropologist is required. Human skeletal remains are collected from the site according to the anthropologist's recommendations. The recovery of human skeletal remains is subject to the remains being recorded by drawings, plans, photography and video. Burial information such as the position of the skeleton and any grave goods should be recorded. The results of the anthropological analysis should be attached to the scientific archaeological report.

Human skeletal remains recovered during archaeological excavations are state property. They are subject to registration according to the methodology approved by the authorized central executive organ on the protection of the cultural heritage (in Ukraine this organ is represented by the Ministry of Culture). Human skeletons shall be preliminary preserved, transferred and stored at the Institute of Archaeology, museums, universities or other state institutions that have adequate conditions for their storage. Such institutions need to be mentioned in the 'open letter' and the respective permit.

To summarize, therefore the main responsibilities of the scientists conducting archaeological research and dealing with anthropological materials, according to the law and regulations are: to record the remains *in situ* by means of drawings, plans, photography and video recording; to ensure appropriate storage of the remains after excavation; to submit a report on the results of the research; and to transfer all the material (including human skeletal remains) to an authorized institution.

Ethical considerations

Legislation does not cover the procedure of reburial of human skeletal remains collected during archaeological excavations. It is required that such a procedure is developed and included in the national legislation. This recommendation would help to avoid reburial claims of certain communities; in our experience we have received such claims from Tatars in Crimea, and from a church community during analysis of the skeletons from the Kyiv Uspensky cathedral. In these cases the anthropological study was conducted and, after samples obtained for dating and stable isotope analysis had been collected, members of these communities were able to rebury the skeletons.

Transfer of human skeletal remains across the customs border of Ukraine

Issues related to transfer of human skeletal remains abroad are determined by the 'Customs Code of Ukraine' dated 2002 and the Ukrainian law 'On the Transfer of Cultural Values Across the Border'.

The law 'On Transfer of Cultural Values across the Borders of Ukraine' determines the procedure of how the cultural values may be moved across the Ukrainian customs border. Are human skeletal remains covered by the definition of 'cultural values'? Are they subject to regulation by such a law? In order to understand whether any specific customs restrictions exist regarding human skeletal remains it is necessary to find answers to the abovementioned questions.

Cultural values are objects of tangible and intangible culture having artistic, historical, ethnographical and scientific meaning and subject to storage, replication and protection under Ukrainian legislation; they include objects related to scientific events and the development of society, rare collections and samples of flora and fauna, mineralogy, anatomy and anthropology, etc. In the exhaustive list of cultural values, anthropological samples are missing. At the same time the language of the law seems to contradict its spirit. The spirit of the law proves that anthropological samples must be recognized as a cultural value. Therefore, this inconsistency creates a legislative gap in this area.

What happens at the border in reality? Human skeletal remains may be subject to customs control. They are subject to compulsory state expertise based on which the respective organ within one month decides whether cultural values may be transferred abroad or not. If the decision is positive, an authorization is issued supporting the transfer of human skeletal remains across the customs border. Without such a certificate, human skeletal remains may not be transferred abroad. In order to obtain a certificate the applicant must submit to the respective authority a copy of agreement with the receiving party.

Scientific information and intellectual property

Scientific information obtained during archaeological research is considered to be intellectual property and thus subject to intellectual property law protection. Information is considered to be subject to protection of intellectual property law if it was received as a result of archaeological research, created as a result of an effort or is subject to such protection under the contract. The law states that the scientist who has conducted the research has an exclusive right to publish scientific information during five years after the date when the research was completed.

METHODS OF ANTHROPOLOGICAL ANALYSIS

In their research, Ukrainian anthropologists use the internationally recognized standards (Bach 1965; Breitinger 1938; Dupertius and Hadden 1951; Martin and Saller 1957; Ortner 2003; Trotter and Gleser 1958; etc.) as well as those commonly accepted nationally (Alekseev and Debets 1964; Alekseev 1966). In Ukraine, textbooks on anthropology have been published by S.P. Segeda (1995, 2001).

CONCLUSION

The definitions of the terms 'cultural heritage' and 'archaeological heritage' do not directly indicate that they cover human skeletal remains. These definitions are too vague and unclear. Human skeletal remains must be protected under the Laws of Ukraine 'On the Protection of Cultural Heritage' and 'On the Protection of Archaeological Heritage'.

It is unclear whether human skeletal remains are covered by the definition of 'cultural values'. This is important in order to understand if they are subject to any customs restrictions under the Law of Ukraine 'On Transfer of Cultural Values across the Borders of Ukraine'. It is questionable whether human remains may be freely transferred abroad without any formalities (obtaining a certificate, etc.). Thus, it would be recommended to amend the law with consideration of the abovementioned.

Most legislative provisions of the Regulations setting forth the responsibilities of archaeologists conducting archaeological research and anthropologists dealing with human remains can hardly be enforced. There is no enforcement mechanism that mentions that archaeologists must invite anthropologists in case human remains are discovered. In order to make this and some other provisions legally enforcible (and not just declarative norms) it is necessary that the respective local legal acts are developed and adopted by the Institute of Archaeology.

Finally, ethical aspects for the treatment of human skeletal remains are not covered by the Ukrainian legislation either. It would be highly required that they become a part of our legislation.

USEFUL CONTACTS

Ukranian Academy of Sciences. Website: www.nas.gov.ua/Pages/default.aspx/

BIBLIOGRAPHY

Alekseev, V.P. (1966) *Osteometriya. Metodika antropologicheskih issledovaniy*, Moskva: Nauka.
Alekseev, V.P. and Debets, G.F. (1964) *Kraniometriya. Metodika antropologicheskih issledovaniy*, Moskva: Nauka.
Bach, H. (1965) 'Zur Berechnung der Körperhöhe aus den langen Gliedmaßenknochen weiblicher Skelette', *Anthropologischer Anzeiger*, 29: 12–21.
Breitinger, E. (1938) 'Zur Berechnung der Körperhöhe aus den langen Gliedmaßenknochen', *Anthropologischer Anzeiger*, 14: 249–74.
Danilova, E.I. (1965) *Evolyutsiya Ruki v Svyazi s Voprosami Antropogeneza*, Kiev: Naukova dumka.
——(1979) *Evolyutsiya Ruki*, Kiev: Vyshcha shkola.
Dupertius, C.W.J. and Hadden, A. (1951) 'On the reconstruction of stature from long bones'. *American Journal of Physical Anthropology*, 9: 15–54.
Dyachenko, V.D. (1965) *Antropologichny sklad ukrains'kogo narodu*, Kyiv: Naukova dumka.
——(1986) 'Antropologichesky sostav srednevekovykh vostochnykh slavyan', in *Problemy evolyutsionnoy morfologii cheloveka i ego ras*, Moskva: Nauka.
Gokhman, I.I. (1966) *Naselenie Ukrainy v epokhi mezolita i neolita*, Moskva: Nauka.
Haeussler, A. and Potekhina, I. (2001) 'North Pontic populations in the Mesolithic-Neolithic: osteological, dental, subsistence, and cultural factors', *American Journal of Physical Anthropology, Annual Meeting Issue 2001: Supplement 32: 74*.
Jakobs, K. (1994) 'Reply to Antony "On subsistence changes at the Mesolithic-Neolithic Transition"', *Current Anthropology* 35, 52–59.

Konduktorova, T.S. (1973) *Antropologiya naseleniya Ukrainy mezolita, neolita i epokhi bronzy*, Moskva: Nauka.

Kozak, A.D. (2005) 'Naselenie Kieva X–XIII vv. po dannym antropologii', *Avtoreferat dissertatsii na soiskanie nauchnoy stepeni kandidata istoricheskikh nauk*, Kiev: Institut Archeologii NAN Ukrainy.

Kozak, O.D. (2000) 'Antropologichny sklad ta morfofiziologichny rysy naselennya Serednyogo Podniprovya', *Arkheologiya*, 1: 67–81.

Kozak, O.D. and Potekhina, I.D. (2002) 'Meshkantsi "grada Volodymyra" za danymy antropologii', *Arkheologiya*, 1: 113–29.

Kruts, S.I (1972) *Naselenie teritorii Ukrainy epohi medi-bronzy*, Kiev: Naukova Dumka.

——(1984) *Paleoantropologicheskie issledovaniya Stepnogo Pridneprovia*, Kiev: Naukova Dumka.

Lillie, M.C. and Richards, M.P. (2000) 'Stable isotope analysis and dental evidence of diet at the Mesolithic-Neolithic transition in Ukraine', *Journal of Archaeological Science*, 27: 965–72.

Lillie, M., Budd, C., Potekhina, I., et al. (2009) 'The radiocarbon reservoir effect: new evidence from the cemeteries of the middle and lower Dnieper basin, Ukraine', *Journal of Archaeological Science*, 36: 256–64.

Litvinova, L.V. (2000) 'Naselenie Nizhnego Podneprovya XIII–XIV (po materialam mogil'nika Mamaj-Surka)', *Stepi Evrazii v epokhu srednevekovya* I, Donetsk: Donetsky Gosudarstvenny Universitet.

——(2007) 'Demograficheskaya struktura naseleniya skifskoy kul'tury (po materialam mogil'nika Mamay Gora)', *Vestnik antropologii*, 15: 292–99.

Martin, R. and Saller, K. (1957) *Lehrbuch der Anthropologie in systematischer Darstellung*, Stuttgart: Gustav Fischer Verlag.

Nazarova, T.A. (2006) 'Tavry v sostave naseleniya antichnogo Khersonesa', *Vestnik antropologii*, 14: 68–73.

Ortner, D.J. (ed.) (2003) *Identification of Pathological Conditions in Human Skeletal Remains*, San Diego, California: Academic Press.

Pokas, P.M. (1987) 'Do antropologii serednyovichnogo naselennya baseinu r. Psel', *Arkheologiya*, 58: 94–98.

Potekhina, I.D. (1983) 'O nositelyah kul'tury Sredni Stog II po antropologicheskim dannym', *Sovetskaya arheologiya*, 1: 144–54.

——(1990) 'Naselennya usativs'koi kul'tury za danymy antropologii', *Arheologiya*, 2: 56–67.

——(1998a) 'South Eastern influences on the formation of the Mesolithic to Early Eneolithic populations of the North Pontic Region: the evidence from anthropology', in L. Domanska and K. Jacobs (eds) *Beyond Balkanization*, Baltic-Pontic Studies, 5: 26–31.

——(1998b) 'Ancient North Europeans in the Mesolithic-Neolithic Transition of Southeast Europe', in M. Zvelebil et al. (eds) *Harvesting the Sea, Farming the Forest. The Emergence of Neolithic Societies in the Baltic Region*, Sheffield: Sheffield Academic Press.

——(1999) *Naselenie Ukrainy v epokhi neolita i rannego eneolita po antropologicheskim dannym*, Kiev: Institut Archeologii NAN Ukrainy.

Potekhina, I.D. and Kozak, O.D. (1999) 'Antropologichni doslidzhennya pokhovan' v 'Uspens'komu Sobori Kyevo-Pechers'koyi Lavry', *Lavrs'ky al'manakh*, 2: 87–97.

Potekhina, I.D. and Telegin, D.Y. (1995) 'On the dating of the Ukrainian Mesolithic-Neolithic Transition', *Current Anthropology*, 36: 823–26.

Rudich, T.A. (1999) 'Do pytannya pro antropologichny sklad naselennya chernyahivs'koi kul'tury na terytorii Serednyogo Podniprovya', *Arkheologiya*, 4: 64–75.

——(2002) 'Antropologichesky sostav naseleniya Kieva po materialam raskopok drevnerusskogo khristianskogo mogil'nika na teritorii Starokievskoy gory', *Tserkovnaya arkheologiya yuzhnoy Rusi*, Simferopol.

Segeda, S.P. (1995) *Osnovy antropologii*, Kyiv: Lybid'.

——(2001) *Antropologiya*, Kyiv: Lybid'.

Starovoitova, R.A. (1979) *Etnicheskaya genogeografiya Ukrainskoy SSR*, Kiev: Naukova dumka.

Telegin, D.Y. and Potekhina, I.D. (1987) *Neolithic Cemeteries and Populations in the Dnieper Basin*, British Archaeological Reports International Series 383, Oxford: Archaeopress.

Telegin, D.Y., Nechitaylo, A.L., Potekhina, I.D., et al. (2001) *Srednestogovskaya i Novodanilovskaya Kul'tury Eneolita Azovo-Chernomorskogo Regiona*, Lugansk: Shlyakh.

Trotter, M. and Gleser, G.C. (1958) 'A re-evaluation of estimation of stature based on measurements of stature taken during life and of long bones after death', *American Journal of Physical Anthropology*, 16: 79–123.

Volkov, F. (1916) 'Antropologicheskie osobennosti ukrainskogo naroda',in *Ukrainski narod v ego proshlom i nastoyashchem*, Petrograd: Petrogradsky Universitet.

Vovk, H. (1908) 'Antropometrychni doslidy ukrayinskogo naselennya Galychyny, Bukovyny i Ugorshchyny', in *Materialy do ukrayinsko-ruskoi etnologii. V. 10*, Lviv.

Zinevich, G.P. (1967) *Ocherki paleoantropologii Ukrainy*, Kiev: Naukova dumka.

Atlantic
Ocean

SCOTLAND

SHETLAND

ORKNEY

Edinburgh
Glasgow

North
Sea

NORTHERN
IRELAND

UNITED
KINGDOM

Belfast

Bradford Leeds Kingston
upon Hull

IRELAND

Liverpool Manchester

Sheffield
Stoke-on-Trent

Nottingham

Wolverhampton

Leicester

Birmingham Coventry

WALES ENGLAND

Cardiff

Bristol London

0   100km

English Channel

The United Kingdom

Bill White

INTRODUCTION: A BRIEF HISTORY AND CURRENT STATE OF PHYSICAL ANTHROPOLOGY IN THE UNITED KINGDOM

The United Kingdom has a rich and unique history of anthropology and antiquarian exhumation of the ancient dead (on its own territory, and throughout the former British Empire).

A number of contributory factors need to be considered. Until the 20th century, the recovery of human remains by archaeology or otherwise was chiefly the work of amateurs, even of *dilettanti*. There was a long history comprised chiefly of antiquarian curiosity, only partly relieved by the actions of nascent anthropologists (former anatomists, physicians and zoologists) who made valuable contributions to human knowledge. Furthermore, the existence of Britain as the seat of an empire of worldwide influence gave its anthropologists a significant global focus. In law, initially, treatment of the ancient dead was the subject of Common Law but actual legislation was introduced not as a reaction to over-zealous archaeologists but to circumvent commercial grave robbing which, in the 19th century, was supplying medical schools with cadavers for dissection. In much the same way, the Human Tissue Act (2004) was introduced to prevent pathologists retaining body samples without consent, a practice apparent, for example, at Alder Hey Hospital, Liverpool. Here in the 21st century there have been notable changes in the law, some of which have not yet been fully worked through.

Unlike certain other countries in Europe (France, Germany, Greece and so on) Britain lacked significant hominin fossils for study and anatomical comparison. This was because the glacial advances of the Quaternary repeatedly scoured the British Isles and destroyed skeletal remains from earlier periods. Indeed it is significant that any notable fossil remains found subsequently have all been from the very south of the country, which had been least subject to the weight and movement of the ice: Barnfield Pit, Swanscombe, Kent (400,000 years BP) and Boxgrove Quarry, West Sussex (500,000 BP). Indeed, Britain's 'Missing Link', the notorious find from Piltdown in East Sussex, was also from the south of the country. The enthusiastic and uncritical reception given to the Piltdown claim was explicable in that the British Empire could now boast of a potential ancestor to rival La Chapelle-aux-Saintes or Cro-Magnon in France and Steinheim or Mauer in Germany, say. Fortunately, and to their credit, some of Britain's physical anthropologists were sceptical, rather than chauvinistic, and they made their names through their tenacity in devising scientific tests capable of demonstrating that this 'fossil ancestor' was a forgery (Sir Wilfrid Le Gros Clark 1895–1971; Kenneth Oakley 1911–81).

479

Meanwhile skeletons of anatomically modern humans came to the fore. British Palaeolithic sites that have produced human skeletal remains are: Paviland Cave, Swansea (discovered in 1822), whose 'Red Lady' skeleton is actually male (*c.* 24,000 BP) and Kent's Cavern, Devon (1914). British Mesolithic skeletons are extremely rare: one site to mention is Gough's Cave, Cheddar (1903), dated to 11,820 ±120 BP – 12,380 ±130 BP (Roberts 2009: 41).

The huge resources available through the British Empire brought correspondingly large collections of human remains to institutions such as The British Museum (with the Natural History Museum incorporated until 1963), the Hunterian Museum in Glasgow and the Hunterian Museum at the Royal College of Surgeons of England, the Royal College of Surgeons of Edinburgh, the Duckworth Laboratory in Cambridge and the Henry Wellcome Collection in London, among others. Physical anthropologists who were representatives of this phase included Professor Frederick Wood-Jones (1879–1954) and the Australian Sir Grafton Eliot Smith (1871–1930), who worked on human remains from historic Egypt and Sudan, in particular. Others of great significance in the field included Sir Arthur Smith Woodward (1864–1946) and the Scottish Sir Arthur Keith (1866–1954). During this period there was a great emphasis on the importance of cranial shape and measurements made on the skull. These studies flourished during the unfortunate period of concern with eugenics (Roberts 2009: 7), but when the dust settled a vast array of materials for the study of human evolution and diversity remained. British anthropologists have always been in the forefront of evolutionary studies.

In the early 20th century British archaeology was still in its relative infancy, therefore studies on large samples of the indigenous population had to use the contents of church charnel houses and ossuaries. Those at Rothwell, Northamptonshire, were studied by Sharp (1870) and those at Hythe, Kent, by Stoessinger and Morant (1924). Meanwhile, large numbers of human remains were being encountered during extensive building development and infrastructure projects, with the remains sometimes explained away as mass burials in 'Plague Pits'. This was true of the crania studied by MacDonell (1904, 1906), whereas the remains examined by Beatrix Hooke (1926) were from Farringdon Street, London, and therefore probably from St Bride's Lower Churchyard. The remains found during the extension of Spitalfields Market during the 1920s were not Roman, as claimed, but were almost certainly from the Augustinian Priory and Hospital of St Mary Spital, East London (Morant and Hoadley 1931; Thomas *et al.* 1997). The large samples from London were re-examined by Professor Karl Pearson (1857–1936) of University College London, who initiated statistical studies on human bones. He did not merely measure crania but was also concerned with measuring long bones and addressing the problem of living stature reconstruction using dry bones (Pearson and Bell 1919).

The English antiquary

In Britain, antiquarian curiosity was always tenacious and many exhumations occurred during the 16th to 19th centuries. This was not yet archaeology, but casual opening of the known tombs of the famous. Thus, in Britain the tombs of saints, the nobility and royalty were opened, usually out of sheer curiosity or to obtain a relic of the burial as a souvenir (Celoria 1966). Royal tombs involved included the Plantagenet monarchs from King John to Edward I, then Queen Katherine Parr and so on. Rarely was there an excuse given, as in the exhumation of the skeleton of King Robert Bruce III in order to confirm that he died a leper (Pearson 1926). Given a free rein, curious antiquaries were able to proceed to exhume the bodies of almost all the monarchs of the Dynasties of Lancaster and York (White 1985). Likewise, the tomb of Henry VIII in St George's Chapel, Windsor, was opened and a metacarpal bone was removed from one of his hands to make the handle for a knife (Longford 1985). Alongside these generally disrespectful exhumations, prehistoric burials and later cemeteries alike were at the mercy of the amateur wielding a spade. Fortunately, early scholars managed to rescue such material for distinguished studies (Davis and Thurman 1865; Brothwell 2000: 4)

The study of ancient human remains

As indicated above, in the 18th and 19th centuries the typical expert who examined disinterred human remains was the anatomist. However, in the 20th century the emphasis was shifting rather to considerations of the health and disease of the deceased. Hence, increasingly, the retired or still active physician or dentist readily found a place in these studies. Here we begin to hear first mention of the modern names in UK anthropology, osteology and palaeopathology: Don Brothwell, Keith Manchester, Theya Molleson, Juliet Rogers, Tony Waldron, Calvin Wells and others (Roberts 2009: 8–11). Subsequently, UK universities began to offer courses in anatomy and anthropology as adjuncts of archaeology, and seven such establishments offered higher degrees in palaeopathology, bioarchaeology or a related discipline. The impressive body of research generated through the archaeology of human remains has led to the seminal publication *Health and Disease in Britain from Prehistory to the Present Day* (Roberts and Cox 2003); owing to subsequent further research and publications, there is already the perceived need for a new edition of the book.

Although the Anatomical Society of Great Britain and Ireland had a long and venerable history and the British Association for Human Identification (BAHID) fills the role for forensic archaeologists and forensic anthropologists, it became clear during the late 20th century that there was no professional body in the UK capable of properly representing biological (i.e. physical) anthropologists, human osteologists and bioarchaeologists. Following a conference at the University of Bournemouth in 1998 the British Association for Biological Anthropology and Osteoarchaeology (BABAO) was set up. The timing was right for a system of "Guidances" for good practice in the treatment and analysis of human bones to be put in place. These would apply to those conducting research in academia but equally to lone anthropologists working freelance. In the USA there had already been for ten years recommendations for minimum standards of skeletal data collection (Buikstra and Ubelaker 1994). In the UK a different situation prevailed in that far fewer skeletons were considered to be at risk of repatriation and/or reburial because they were predominantly of obvious UK origin. Nevertheless a BABAO Working Group devised a set of minimum standards for their study (Brickley and McKinley 2004). Similar guidelines for best practice in writing human bone reports were also in place (Mays *et al.* 2002). Today BABAO holds an annual conference but also has a standing committee, to which urgent matters affecting human bioarchaeology can be referred. BABAO has agreed on a Code of Ethics for those working with human remains (BABAO 2008).

The recognition that the excavation of human remains is a special area of archaeology, with its own priorities, problems and challenges, also led to consultation on the issue of best practice. The Church of England and English Heritage, two of the bodies most concerned with the archaeological excavation of cemeteries in England and Wales, issued the draft of potential guidance on cemetery excavations and invited comments from interested parties. The document, as amended, was issued in 2005 as *Guidance for Best Practice for Treatment of Human Remains Excavated from Christian Burial Grounds in England* (English Heritage/Church of England 2005). Following this, an advisory panel was constituted to provide advice on all aspects of the archaeology of burial grounds of Christian date (the Advisory Panel for the Archaeology of Christian Burial Grounds in England or APACBE). Their published *Guidance for Best Practice* gives case studies and flow charts to help advisors and clients alike to go through a step-by-step resolution of contentious issues.

These initiatives have all been made against a background of unusual interest by HM Government in the United Kingdom. As the result of a meeting in 2001 between the respective Prime Ministers of the UK and the Commonwealth of Australia, an agreement was made that Britain would expedite the repatriation to Australia of the skeletal remains of the latter's indigenous peoples from public and private collections. The political process continued with the setting up of a working group on human remains in museum collections by the Cultural Property Unit of the Department of Culture, Media and Sport (DCMS). The working group was charged to examine all aspects of the care, safe keeping, legal status and requests for return of human remains curated within the publicly funded museums and galleries of England and Wales (DCMS 2003). One of the findings was that there were 132 UK institutions that among them held the remains of about 61,000 individuals (DCMS 2003: 11). Both of these figures are now known to be vast underestimates and paid no heed to the skeletal holdings in some pathology museums, university departments and commercial archaeological units. They also, by definition, ignore the position in Scotland (Historic Scotland 1997), Northern Ireland and the Irish Republic (O'Sullivan and Killgore 2003). Although the DCMS committee produced a flawed and biased report, slanted heavily towards the repatriation of human remains of overseas origin and paying only lip service to the research value of such collections, the consultation process that followed finally produced useful guidelines (DCMS 2005). The new document, *Guidance for the Care of Human Remains in Museums*, contained a requirement for a museum to make an inventory of its holdings of human remains available publicly: 'Museums should have a policy to compile and make public an inventory of their holdings of human remains. This should include known information about the date and provenance of the remains and their exact nature and the circumstances of their acquisition.' (DCMS 2005: 22).

Two other actions flowed from the various consultation processes and the DCMS action. Previously, the UK national museums in particular had been constrained from de-accessioning human remains by law but were now allowed to de-accession those remains of people who had died less than 500 years previously (Human Tissue Act 2004). Also an advisory group had been set up by DCMS as the Human Remains Advisory Panel (HRAS). However, after only a single claim for repatriation had been referred, HRAS was found to be flawed and was dissolved in favour of the Advisory Panel on the Archaeology of Burials in England (APABE) for future references (White 2009).

It must be emphasized that the above discussion concerns guidance only, i.e. it lacks the force of law. In what follows, the highly complex question of the legal position of human remains will be explored further.

ARCHAEOLOGICAL HUMAN REMAINS AND LEGISLATION

Archaeological legislation

Planning Policy Guidance No. 16

Planning Policy Guidance No. 16 (PPG16), issued in November 1990, sets out the Secretary of State's policy on archaeological remains on land and how they should be preserved or recorded, both in an urban setting and in the countryside (Department of the Environment 1990). It was issued by the then Department of the Environment (DoE) on behalf of English Heritage, and provides guidance for local planning authorities, property owners, developers, archaeologists, amenity societies and the general public. English Heritage (or the 'Historical Buildings and

Monuments Commission of England') is a quasi-national government organization (i.e., not part of government but funded by it) and was set up in 1983. Its equivalent in Wales is Cadw. Effectively, PPG16 established the principle that developers should fund archaeological work on sites that they are proposing to develop (McCracken and Phillpotts 1995). Broadly, it was intended to show that the disparate needs of development and of archaeology could none the less be reconciled.

PPG16 was published against a background of government encouragement of an internal market in British archaeology, with English Heritage promoting competitive contract archaeology. It was therefore no longer the practice for archaeology contracts to be awarded automatically to professional organizations with a good track record. Instead, it was to be understood that archaeological projects ought to be put out to tender, the developer having the right to choose the cheapest tender, if desired. PPG16 makes the presumption that the best course of action normally would be preservation *in situ*. However, in practice, so far as burial grounds are concerned the Disused Burial Grounds (Amendment) Act's recourse to clearance of the burials by exhumation usually prevails, with the development going ahead. This has yet to be fully tested by a development requiring the clearance of burials from the cemetery of a minority religion.

HUMAN REMAINS AND LEGISLATION

Over most of British history, the main legal constraint on what might be done with human remains was the Common Law. A major principle of UK Common Law is that 'there is no property in a corpse'. Thus, in the UK a dead human body cannot be owned; likewise it cannot be stolen. A paradox of this is that it is not illegal to buy and sell human bodies, body parts, skeletons, mummies, etc., provided that they were not obtained illegally. Internet trafficking in human remains occurs, and when BABAO is made aware of examples the vendor is challenged about the morality of the sale. Mailing of human remains through the UK postal system is illegal, however. Moreover, the law also comes into play with regard to human burials, and in England and Wales it is an offence under Common Law to exhume a human body without lawful authority, or it is contrary to Ecclesiastical Law if human remains are removed from consecrated ground without a Faculty of Ordinary being granted by the diocesan court (Garratt-Frost 1992).

Thus, burial and exhumation of bodies were for a long time regulated by Common Law and Ecclesiastical Law, but not always satisfactorily, as we have seen. A major change came in the 19th century when there was the pressing need to deal with the activities of 'Resurrection Men'. Whereas in countries such as Italy and the Netherlands anatomy and dissection were extremely well developed, in the UK these activities were hampered by the dearth of human corpses for legal experimentation. It was true that the death penalty for homicide included the handing over of a murderer's body to anatomists for dissection, but the number of capital criminals available failed to meet the demand of the medical schools. Accordingly, bands of 'Resurrection Men' went about the country disinterring freshly-dead corpses to meet this shortfall. Edinburgh was particular notorious because of the wild excesses of the Burke and Hare exhumation teams (Parker Pearson 1999: 181). The *Anatomy Act* of 1832 relieved the pressure on UK schools of medicine by making available those corpses of the pauper inhabitants of Public Workhouses whose relatives had not claimed the body. Subsequently, other legislation was passed, affecting exhumation in England and Wales, whether accomplished for archaeology or for other purposes.

The predominant pieces of legislation involved are British Parliamentary Acts: the 'Burial Act' of 1857, the 'Disused Burial Grounds Act' of 1884 and (as amended by) the 'Disused Burial Grounds (Amendment) Act' of 1981 (Spoerry 1993: 23). For nearly 150 years up to 2007 it appeared quite clear that the exhumation of bodies was covered by the former Act (unless regulated by another piece of legislation) and the provision that dealt with archaeology was Section 25:

> Except in the cases where a body is removed from one consecrated place of burial to another by faculty granted by the ordinary for the purpose; it shall not be lawful to remove any body, or the remains of any body, which may have been interred in any place of burial without licence under the hand of one of Her Majesty's Principal Secretaries of State, and with such precautions as such Secretary of State may prescribe as the condition of such licence; and any person who shall remove any such body or remains, contrary to this enactment, or who shall neglect to observe the precautions prescribed as the condition of the licence for removal, shall, on summary conviction before any two justices of the peace, forfeit and pay for every such offence a sum not exceeding [level 1 on the standard scale]
>
> *Burial Act of 1857, Section 25*

A 'Burial Licence', issued under Section 25 of the 1857 Act, was a single page *proforma* signed by Her Majesty's Principal Secretary of State for the Home Office (i.e., the government department of the interior). It might bear several conditions to the effect that, for instance:

- The removal of the human remains from the original deposit should be accomplished with due care and attention to decency and respect;
- The ground or deposit from which the remains are being lifted should be screened from public gaze during these operations;
- The remains, if of scientific interest, should be transferred for specialist study;
- The remains, if of sufficient scientific importance, should be retained in archival storage or, if not, should be conveyed to a burial ground in which interments may legally take place and there be re-interred.

The 'Disused Burial Grounds Act' of 1884 and 1981 provides protection for human remains within former burial grounds under threat of development. Section 2(1) states that no building shall be erected upon a disused burial ground unless any human remains have first been removed and cremated or re-interred in accordance with the provisions of the Schedule of the Statute.

Another statute that comes into play is the 'Pastoral Measure' of 1983. Under Section 65 and Schedule 6 the removal of human remains (and tombstones, etc.) from a redundant church and/ or 'any land set apart and consecrated for the purpose of burials' is covered, unless the said buildings and/or burial ground are outside the jurisdiction of the Church of England or by planning and development legislation (see below). In every case, Section 25 of the 'Burial Act 1857' continues to apply (Garratt-Frost 1992: 8).

Ancillary legislation with a bearing on the exhumation of human remains in England and Wales

The acquisition of a burial ground, consecrated or unconsecrated, for the purposes of building development is allowed for in the following pieces of Planning and Development legislation:

the 'Town and Country Planning Act' of 1990, the 'Local Government, Planning and Land Act' of 1980, the 'New Towns Act' of 1981 and the 'Housing Act' of 1988 (Garratt-Frost 1992: 4–5). The property must then be used for the purpose for which it was acquired, first satisfying the obligation for the removal and subsequent re-interment of the pre-existing human remains. It is a requirement that a notice be placed in local newspapers, specifying the exhumations planned. Potentially, any relatives of the deceased then have a period of not less than one month from the date of the newspaper notice to announce their intention to re-inter the body of their ancestor or close relative. This re-interment is required to be accomplished within two months (Garratt-Frost 1992: 5–6).

The situation in Scotland and Northern Ireland

Scottish Law is entirely different in that the 'Burial Act 1857' and the 'Disused Burial Grounds (Amendment) Act 1981' have no force in Law. Also the Faculty issued by a bishop is not recognized. The exhumation of human bodies is chiefly governed by Common Law. However, guidance is difficult because of the conflicting decisions that have been made by judges. The expectation under Common Law is that, once buried a human body will never be exhumed (the 'right of sepulture'). There are certain exceptions, from considerations of necessity or 'expediency', for example if the burial was in ground within which there was no right of burial, such as in the cases where the deceased held no title to the land or had acquired no right to be buried there. Finally, even if a warrant has been obtained from the Sheriff Court to disinter the body there is no guarantee that the exhumation will take place, as the 'right of sepulture' takes precedence and may be invoked at any stage to thwart exhumation.

Some principles and objectives for Scottish remains are to ensure that the following occur (Parker-Pearson 1999: 189; Historic Scotland 1997):

- The lawful and respectful treatment of human remains by staff and contractors;
- The remains are not needlessly damaged, disturbed or destroyed at protected monuments;
- The remains are carefully excavated and removed prior to damaging developments;
- Decisions are made only after proper study, recognizing that the remains of late mediaeval/ modern Christians will occasionally be reburied but that certain minority religious groups instead demand immediate burial; also that the views of the local community, if any, be taken into account.

In Scottish Law, any place where human remains have been interred is considered a burial place, even if it is not consecrated ground (Spoerry 1993). A buried body's 'right of sepulture' means that the disturbance of a burial is a criminal act. The most recent case was in 2004. Teenage boys broke into a vault in Greyfriars churchyard, Edinburgh, removed a 17th-century skull and were prosecuted under this legislation. This was inarguably correct use of the law but, unfortunately, the 'right of sepulture' may interfere with graveyard archaeology in that it has been considered that archaeologists have no right to excavate human remains in Scotland (Parker Pearson 1999: 183).

In Northern Ireland the situation is different yet again. If human remains buried for more than 50 years are uncovered then the Environment and Heritage Service of Northern Ireland has to be informed of the fact. If they are in a known burial ground belonging to a District Council then there has to be compliance with the 'Burial Ground Regulations (Northern Ireland) 1992' and Section 11 (4) of the 'Coroners Act (Northern Ireland) 1959' (Roberts 2009: 27).

Actions required upon the discovery of human remains in the UK

Research excavations, i.e. speculative archaeological excavations or those required to resolve a specific question or problem, are comparatively rare in the UK. Instead, what normally happens is that archaeological excavations are necessary in advance of property development or re-development, or of infrastructure projects of varying size. Accordingly, they tend to be by nature 'rescue' or 'salvage' archaeology. The various archaeological units operating in the area of the building development will then engage in competitive tendering for the archaeological contract. In the year 1991, over 80 per cent of excavations involving human remains were by nature 'rescue' or 'salvage' archaeology rather than research-driven; the current proportion is likely to be higher still (Roberts 2009: 17–18).

If there is a reasonable expectation that human remains would be encountered during archaeological excavation then a 'Burial Licence' under Section 25 of the 'Burial Act 1857' is to be applied for. If human remains are encountered unexpectedly it is still possible to obtain a Burial Licence retrospectively. If the archaeological operations are wholly intended to involve moving human remains from one piece of consecrated ground to another it is sufficient to apply for a Faculty of the Ordinary from a bishop of the diocese.

In Scotland, on encountering a buried body the main action required is to inform the police or the Procurator Fiscal. In England and Wales there are additional circumstances in which the Coroner has to be informed if human remains are found or are to be disturbed. If the remains are less than 100 years old then the holding of a Coroner's Inquest to determine cause of death may be appropriate. However, in practice, if it can be demonstrated that the remains are of a person who died at least 50 years previously, then an Inquest is likely to be unnecessary (Spoerry 1993: 23). This is because even if the death was homicide the perpetrator and any adult witnesses may now be dead (or very old and with unreliable memory), or they may have been children at the time, therefore their testimony may be perceived as of lesser value. Quite often an archaeologist has been able to convince the police and the Coroner that death occurred more than 100 years previously, in which event a costly investigative process can be circumvented and a 'Burial Licence' under Section 25 of the 'Burial Act' applied for instead.

Private Acts of Parliament

The lengthy discussion of the legal position above has not fully exhausted the law as it affects buried human remains, as it is always possible that great corporations will promote private Acts of Parliament designed to be all-encompassing of a major infrastructure project. This was last seen in full operation in primary legislation: the 'Channel Tunnel Rail Link Act' of 1996 (CTRL 1996). Initially, there was a reasonable working relationship among the engineering team, the exhumation professionals and the archaeologists, the latter mounting a watching brief, with stopping powers, as well as excavating part of the area of the cemetery at St Pancras Station. However, behind the scenes there were perceptions that the work of construction was falling behind schedule. Consequently, there occurred the summary eviction of the archaeology team from the site, exhumation being accelerated by machining out the burials with a mechanical excavator, without archaeological supervision (Sayer 2009: 200). It is clear that exhumation was now proceeding without due regard for decency, dignity and respect but, of course, such niceties had been overridden by the arrogance inherent in the wording of the Act of Parliament, which was passed solely for the specific purpose of railway construction. Fortunately, this unacceptable practice was reversed following a huge volume of complaints made by the Church of England, English Heritage, the Council for British Archaeology, BABAO, The British Archaeological Trust (RESCUE), the local press and the general public (Sayer 2009) The disrespectful practices ceased and archaeology resumed. However, this is but one of several unacceptable acts by an exhumation contractor and serves to illustrate that large infrastructure projects, organized under specific Acts of Parliament, in the future will bear the same sort of risks that the wording of an Act can circumvent the normal considerations of decency and respect, unless there is active scrutiny during the Committee stages as they pass through the Lords and Commons.

The Department of Constitutional Affairs

In the year 2005 the responsibility for all aspects of buried human remains was transferred suddenly (albeit briefly) to the government Department of Constitutional Affairs (DCA). This alteration was not in force for long enough for it to have a direct impact on the issuing of 'Burial Licences' under Section 25 of the 'Burial Act 1857' and these continued to be issued with as much regularity as hitherto.

During its short term of tenure the DCA carried out a widespread public consultation on the future of human burials and burial grounds in the UK. The major concern was the shortage of land that would be available for burial in the future and questions were asked about the re-use of existing cemeteries, including whether deep excavation for vertical integration of new burials was an acceptable practice. In addition, questions on cognate subjects were asked, including 'Exhumation or disturbance after burial'. The DCA findings here were that:

> The Government believes that it is right to continue to protect buried human remains from unauthorised disturbance. Where statutory provision has been made for remains to be exhumed or removed, it is important that the remains should be treated at all times with dignity and respect, however old the remains might be. The Government believes that disturbance may be justified only in limited circumstances:

- In the interests of justice (for example, exhumation on the order of a Coroner)
- For personal reasons by the next-of-kin of the deceased
- On grounds of public health or nuisance
- In the public interest (in connection with site developments which have public or other planning consent)
- For scientific purposes (e.g. for archaeological research) or
- For other exceptional reasons (the case for exhumation for the purpose of re-use of old graves is discussed [later])

> (Department of Constitutional Affairs 2006).

The comment made here was that 'the existing approach of single exhumations was generally supported, with most in favour of central licensing arrangements'. Also: 'In the light of responses received, there would seem to be general agreement that the current grounds for disturbing buried remains are widely accepted and that there is no strong argument to make major changes' (Department of Constitutional Affairs 2006: 33).

The legal position today: the Ministry of Justice

Although the short period whereby the DCA held responsibility for the Coroner's Office involved a smooth transfer of power, no-one was prepared for the complications that ensued when responsibility, in turn, passed to the Ministry of Justice (MoJ). Its first act was to publish a new policy on Burial Law in the 21st century, based on the UK Government's response to the consultation carried out earlier by the DCA (Ministry of Justice 2007a). This provided a false sense of security in that it reproduced the above earlier guidance by the DCA, including the justification of exhumation for scientific research, and the desirability of a centralized licensing arrangements (Ministry of Justice 2007a: 11). However, in its next publication the MoJ drew upon the expertise of its unique staff of lawyers to announce a major change in the regularization of exhumation under the parliamentary Acts (Ministry of Justice 2007b). Among these was that the availability of a 'Burial Licence' under the 1857 'Burial Act' was no longer the 'default' position. Most cemeteries that were subject to archaeological interest were not now regarded as 'in use', therefore exhumation did not require a Section 25 Licence (Sayer 2009: 201). The operative term 'any place of burial', familiar for 150 years, was now re-defined: 'places of burial which are recognized as such on the surface of the land and where the "place" in question has not passed, in surface terms, into other use'. Thus, archaeologists who informed the Ministry of Justice that they had uncovered human remains met the blanket statement that neither a 'Licence' under the 1857 Act nor directions under the 1981 Act were required in order to excavate human remains. 'There is no statutory impediment to … proceeding to excavate … remains and no requirement for any human remains … to be reinterred … [although] under Common Law it is a criminal offence to offer indignities to the remains of the dead' (Gallagher 2008). In the confused atmosphere that this engendered, there was even a belief that excavated human remains had to be re-buried within a two-month period. However, this was based on a misunderstanding; in fact, the two-month time limit under the 'Disused Burial Grounds *(Amendment)* Act 1981' refers to the need to report re-interment of the human remains after the said reburial has in fact occurred. Following representations from English Heritage, the Church of England and representative archaeological bodies, the MoJ agreed to resolve this very confusing break with exhumation tradition. Their response took the form of a statement from the Coroner's Unit: 'Burial Law and Archaeology' issued in April 2008:

> In the light of a further review of the burial legislation in relation to the archaeological excavation of human remains and as an immediate first stage of reform the MoJ proposes to proceed on the following basis with immediate effect:
>
> - To assist archaeologists in making applications for exhumation licences or directions, a new form designed to collect the minimum information required is now available upon request.
> - During the course of the year, as a second stage of reform, consideration, will be given to amending existing burial ground legislation so that it can be more responsive to 21st century needs. The aim will be in particular to allow otherwise lawful and legitimate activities, such a the archaeological examination of human remains, to proceed without the constraints of legislation not designed to deal with such issues and with retrospective effect as far as possible. In taking this forward, the MoJ aims to continue to work closely with the Department of Culture, Media and Sport, English Heritage and relevant professional bodies.
> - Any archaeologist wishing to seek assistance in any case is invited to contact the MoJ on 020 7210 0035.
>
> Burial Law and Archaeology, April 2008

Annexed 'Frequently asked Questions' included:

> 'Will the MoJ always require a firm date and details of arrangements for re-interment?'
> 'No. If no firm arrangements are proposed in the application, a time limit, normally up to two years, will be specified in a licence or direction.'

Also:

'Will it be possible to extend a time limit for re-interment if research has not ceased?'
'Yes, if circumstances make this reasonable. Apply to the MoJ (before the expiry date).'

There is no prospect in the near future of the 1857 and 1981 'Burial Acts' being repealed nor of new primary legislation being put in their place. However, recently Andrew Tucker, an official in the Coroners and Burial Division of the Ministry of Justice, has taken the trouble to spell out the proposed remedial action. The solution would appear to be secondary legislation taking the form of a Legislation Reform Order (LFO). Thus, a range of amendments to the law will be in the 'Provisions' to be considered by a Committee of Members of Parliament. The first actions, once again, will be to put the proposals in the public domain for consultation. These will include draft model LFOs. Also, views will be invited on facilitating the exhumation of human remains for archaeological purposes and retention of the remains for analysis, research and display, etc. Apparently there is scope to ensure that unlicensed exhumations are limited to 'those undertaken, or under the direction of, members of suitable self-regulating professional bodies' (Tucker 2009). Another possible proposal is that the age (i.e., the date) of the humans remains should be taken into account, such that perhaps no licence would be required to exhume remains more than 200 years old (although, of course, they would be subject to the usual conditions of decency, respect and care). The consultation phase later in 2009 was accompanied by an Impact Assessment dealing with the costs and benefits of the new arrangements. Implementation in law should follow in 2010 but at the time of writing (April 2010) this has yet to be accomplished.

METHODS OF ANTHROPOLOGICAL ANALYSIS

A BABAO Working Group devised a set of minimum standards for the study of human remains (Brickley and McKinley 2004). Similar Guidelines for Best Practice in writing human bone reports were also in place (Mays *et al.* 2002).

CONCLUSION

Anthropology in the UK has long since reached maturity and is thriving under the umbrella term of 'Human Bioarchaeology'. By contrast, the legislation covering the archaeological excavation of human remains was in force for a very long time but recent reinterpretation of the statutes gave rise to some anomalies. It is felt that no new Acts of Parliament are required but, instead, secondary legislation will ensure that Burial Licences are issued centrally and that their attached conditions will allow the possibility of analysis, retention and display (Tucker 2009). Advice on the excavation of burial grounds will be expanded to cover all religious denominations, not only nominally Christian (White 2009: 29).

USEFUL CONTACTS

Advisory Panel for the Archaeology of Burials in England. Website: http://www.britarch.ac.
uk/churches/human remains/

Association of Diocesan and Cathedral Archaeologists. Website: www.dca.gov.uk/corbur/buria
01htm/

British Association for Biological Anthropology and Osteoarchaeology. Website: www.babao,
org.uk/

English Heritage. Website: www.english-heritage.org.uk/

Institute of Field Archaeology. Website: www.archaeologists.net/

Ministry of Justice. Website: www.justice.gov.uk/

Department of Culture, Media and Sport. Website: www.culture/gov/uk/global/publications/
archive.2003/your report2003.htm/

Church of England. Website: www.cofe.anglican.org/about/builtheritage/

BIBLIOGRAPHY

BABAO (2008) *Ethics and Standards*. Available online at www.babao.org.uk/index/ethicsandstandards
(accessed 3 August 2009).

Brickley, M. and McKinley, J.I. (2004) *Guidelines to the Standards for Recording Human Remains*, Institute of
Field Archaeology Paper No. 7, Reading: Institute of Field Archaeologists.

Brothwell, D. (2000) 'Studies on skeletal and dental variation; a view across two centuries', in M. Cox
and S. Mays (eds) *Human Osteology in Archaeology and Forensic Science*. London: Greenwich Medical
Media.

Buikstra, J.E. and Ubelaker, D.H. (eds) (1994) *Standards for Data Collection from Human Skeletal Remains*,
Fayetteville, AR: Arkansas Archaeological Survey Research Series No. 44.

Celoria, F. (1966) 'Burials and archaeology: a survey of attitudes to research', *Folklore*, 77: 161–83.

CTRL (1996) 'Channel Tunnel Rail Link Act'. Available online at: www.opsi.gov.uk.Acts/acts1996/
ukpga_1996 (accessed 3 August 2009).

Davis, J.B. and Thurman, J. (1865) *Crania Britannica: Delineation and Descriptions of the Skulls of Aboriginal
and Early Inhabitants of the British Isles*, London: Taylor and Francis.

Department of Constitutional Affairs (DCA) (2006) *Burial Law and Policy in the 21st Century*, London: DCA.

Department of Culture, Media and Sport (DCMS) (2003) *The Report of the Working Group on Human
Remains*, London: DCMS.

——(2005) *Guidance for the Care of Human Remains in Museums*, London: DCMS.

Department of the Environment (DoE) (1990) *Planning Policy Guidance: Archaeology and Planning No 16
('PPG16')*, London: DoE.

Emery, P.A. (2007) 'Cracking the code: biography and (reconstructed) stratigraphy at St Pancras burial
ground', in S.R. Zakrzewski and W. White (eds) *Proceedings of the Seventh Annual Conference of the British
Association for Biological Anthropology and Osteoarchaeology*, British Archaeological Reports International
Series No 1712, Oxford: Archaeopress.

English Heritage/Church of England (2005) *Guidance for Best Practice for Treatment of Human Remains
Excavated from Christian Burial Grounds in England*, Swindon: English Heritage.

Gallagher, S. (2008) 'Protecting the dead: exhumation and the Ministry of Justice', *Web Journal of Current Legal
Issues*, 5. Available online at: http://webjcli.ncl.ac.uk/2008/issue5/gallagher5.html (accessed 3 August 2009).

Garratt-Frost, S. (1992) *The Law and Burial Archaeology*, Institute of Field Archaeology: Technical Paper
no. 11, Birmingham: Institute of Field Archaeology.

Historic Scotland (1997) *The Treatment of Human Remains in Archaeology*, Historic Scotland Operational
Paper No. 5, Edinburgh: Historic Scotland.

Hooke, B.G.E. (1928) 'A third study of the English skull, with special reference to the Farringdon Street
crania', *Biometrika*, 18: 1–33.

Longford, E. (1985) *The Oxford Book of Royal Anecdotes*, Oxford: Oxford University Press.

McCracken, S. and Phillpotts, C. (1995) *Archaeology and Planning in London: Assessing the Effects of PPG16*,
London: Standing Conference on London Archaeology.

MacDonell, W.R. (1904) 'A study of the variation and correlation of the human skull, with special reference
to English crania', *Biometrika*, 3: 191–244.

——(1906) 'A second study of the English skull, with special reference to Moorfields crania', *Biometrika*, 5:
88–104.

Mays, S., Brickley, M. and Dodwell, N. (2002) *Human Bones from Archaeological Sites: Guidelines for Producing Assessment Documents and Analytical Reports*, Swindon: English Heritage Centre for Archaeology Guidelines.

Ministry of Justice (MoJ) (2007a) *Burial Law and Policy in the 21st Century: the Way Forward*, London: MoJ.

——(2007b) *Excavation of Buried Human Remains: Interim Guidance and Procedures for Archaeologists and Developers*, London: MoJ.

Morant, G.M. and Hoadley, M. (1931) 'A study of the recently excavated Spitalfields crania', *Biometrika*, 23: 191–248.

O'Sullivan, J. and Killgore, J. (2003) *Human Remains in Irish Archaeology*, Dublin: Heritage Council.

Parker-Pearson, M. (1999) *The Archaeology of Death and Burial*, Stroud: Sutton.

Pearson, K. (1926) 'The skull of Robert the Bruce, King of Scotland 1274–1324', *Biometrika*, 18: 253–72.

Pearson, K. and Bell, J.R. (1919) *A Study of the Long Bones of the English Skeleton*, Cambridge: Cambridge University Press.

Roberts, C. (1984) 'Analysis of some human femora from a medieval charnel house at Rothwell parish church, Northamptonshire, England', *Ossa*, 9–11: 119–34.

——(2009) *Human Remains in Archaeology: a Handbook*, Practical Handbooks in Archaeology No. 19, York: Council for British Archaeology.

Roberts, C. and Cox, M. (2003) *Health and Disease in Britain from Prehistory to the Present Day*, Stroud: Sutton.

Sayer, D. (2009) 'Is there a crisis in British burial archaeology?' *Antiquity* 83: 199–205.

Sharp, S. (1870) 'The Rothwell crypt and bones', *Archaeological Journal*, 27: 56–59.

Spoerry, P. (1993) *Archaeology and Legislation in Britain*, Hertford: RESCUE, the British Archaeological Trust.

Stoessiger, B.N. and Morant, G.M. (1932) 'A study of the crania in the vaulted ambulatory of St Leonard's church, Hythe, Kent', *Biometrika*, 24: 135–202.

Thomas, C., Sloane, B. and Phillpotts, C. (1997) *Excavations at the Priory and Hospital of St Mary Spital, London*, MoLAS Monograph No. 1, London: Museum of London Archaeology Service.

Tucker, A. (2009) 'Burial law reform and archaeology', *The Archaeologist*, 72: 30.

White, W. (1985) 'Changing burial practice in late medieval England', in J. Petre (ed.) *Richard III: Crown and People*, Upminster: Richard III Society and Yorkist History Trust.

——(2009) 'An advisory panel for the archaeology of all burials in England?', *The Archaeologist*, 72: 28–29.

PART 2

Rest of the world

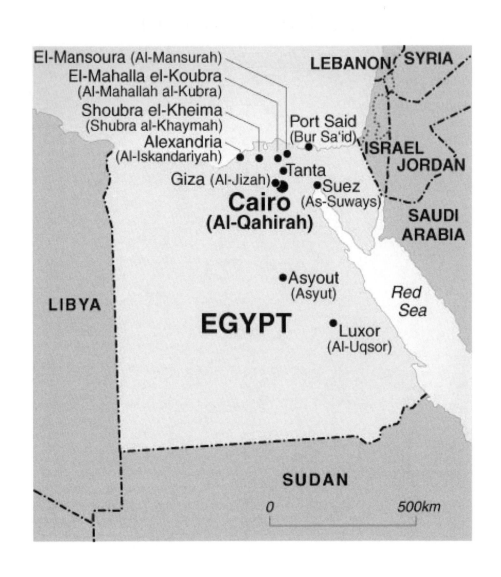

Egypt/Misr

Salima Ikram

INTRODUCTION: A BRIEF HISTORY AND CURRENT STATE OF PHYSICAL ANTHROPOLOGY IN EGYPT

In Egypt, the abundance of human and animal remains, both as skeletons and as mummies, provides a rich source of information concerning the ancient Egyptian culture, environment and people. These have been intermittently studied in the past, and have become a focus of attention from the middle of the 20th century onward. A study of skeletal material provides the same sort of data as it does anywhere else: age, sex, disease; and additionally, depending on sample size, relationship, epidemiological or population studies can be executed. Holistic studies of mummies yield information about technology, disease, diet, medical science, aesthetics (cosmetics, tattooing and hairstyles), religious beliefs and customs, diachronic change in mummification technology, specific materials used in manufacturing mummies, embalming ateliers, trade, social and religious divisions, and the environment of ancient Egypt.

The history of the study of human remains in Egypt is varied, with little rigorous scientific work being carried out until the 20th century, although an increasing number of medical-style autopsies were carried out on mummies in the second half of the 19th century (Ikram, in press). These included examination by X-rays, with the first royal mummy (Thutmose IV) being X-rayed by Dr Khayrat in 1903 (Smith 1912: iii–iv).

Interest in human remains increased during the early years of the 20th century (Smith and Dawson 1924). Mummies, defleshed mummies (skeletons), and skeletal remains were examined by doctors primarily, as well as by anthropologists. Generally, small samples were examined, although, on occasion, larger cemetery studies were instituted, such as the 6000 bodies excavated and examined by G.E. Smith, W. Dawson, and F.W. Jones (Smith and Wood-Jones 1910), in the hope of a broader understanding of a population, rather than the medical history of one specific individual. With the advent of palaeopathology, tissue samples from mummies were analysed to identify organs as well as to isolate diseases (Ruffer 1921).

Initially, human remains were studied primarily by medical examiners: doctors, anatomists and (palaeo)pathologists. These scholars, as one might expect, were trying to identify diseases, establish dietary patterns, in addition to establishing the sex and age of the body. Anthropologists were also involved with the study of human remains, but to a lesser extent. Anthropologists (some as early as 1844) were subjecting ancient Egyptians' skulls to craniometric analysis to identify and better understand and identify racial characteristics on the skeleton. It was not until the latter half of the 20th century that physical anthropologists entered the fray as members of excavation teams to work on skeletal remains.

Mummies and skeletons have not been treated in the same way; one has tissue, the other, not. Thus, a variety of technologies, mainly adopted from the medical profession, have been used to study the former in particular, while the latter is examined in a standard manner (sex, age, disease), depending on the scientists' training, inclination, access to the bones, and time. For mummies, additional analysis includes tissue sampling to identify diseases, CT-scans (computed tomography), MRI (magnetic resonance imaging), and ultrasound imaging whenever possible. Diseases such as malaria, schistosomiasis, tuberculosis, and trichinosis (Deelder *et al.* 1990; Nehrlich and Zink 1999; Miller *et al.* 1994: 31–32, 1992) have been identified from mummies. Stable isotope analysis is used on bone or tooth enamel in an effort to better understand ancient diets. Mummification materials have been isolated and identified using gas chromatography and mass spectrometry (Buckley and Evershed 2001; Buckley *et al.*1999, 2004: 294–99). Currently DNA work is also being carried out on mummified remains, particularly the royal mummies. This work is spearheaded by the Director General of Antiquities, Dr Zahi Hawass. Currently, permission for DNA work is restricted to Egyptian-led groups of scientists and the analysis itself is carried out primarily in Egypt.

Who studies human remains?

Currently the majority of scholars working on human remains are from outside of Egypt (Europe, Britain, the United States), although in the earlier part of the 20th century significant work was carried out by Ahmed el-Batrawi, who was a doctor and anatomist, as well as an anthropologist who worked and published extensively on ancient Egyptian human remains. The anatomical collection of ancient remains made by Douglas Derry and el-Batrawi formed the basis of the teaching and research collection of the Qasr el-Aini hospital in Cairo, which tends to train doctors rather than physical anthropologists. Anatomists from that institution have carried out some work on the material, but interest has, on the whole, been negligible.

Recently, the number of Egyptians who are interested in the study of human remains is increasing slowly. Some of the growing number of specialists are drawn from the medical profession, though the majority are coming from an archaeological background. Field schools with special components dedicated to physical anthropology, such as that of the Ancient Egypt Research Associates (AERA), are training a core group of employees of Egypt's Supreme Council of Antiquities in the excavation, identification and analysis of human remains, a task that is also being taken up by other archaeological training missions.

Non-Egyptian specialists have always dominated the field. In the early years of the subject, the majority of people came from a medical tradition. By the mid-20th century and onward, specifically trained physical anthropologists study human remains, bringing whatever training they have obtained in their home countries to Egypt, and applying it to the material here. Some differences have been noted in the literature with regard to ageing based on tooth-wear, as ancient Egyptians' teeth are worn down at a faster rate than those of other groups, probably due to the amount of grit in their bread (Duhig 2009).

ARCHAEOLOGICAL HUMAN REMAINS AND LEGISLATION

Archaeological remains are generally defined as being found in archaeological zones and clearly being buried for more than 100 years. There are, no doubt, some exceptional cases, but generally bodies found within a stratified archaeological context are designated as ancient remains.

Archaeological legislation

There is no set legislation regarding the excavation of human remains, although there are stringent rules regarding archaeological excavation. For excavations, permits must be obtained through the Supreme Council of Antiquities (SCA), which has a vetting process (for details see the SCA website, www.sca-egypt.org/, and the website of the American Research Center in Egypt, www.arce.org/, which outlines the procedure for applicants).

If a cemetery is being excavated, physical anthropologists are part of the team. If they are not present at the time of excavation, they come to study the material during a subsequent season. In addition to getting permits from the SCA, team-members are vetted by the Egyptian Security Service. In some instances, an Egyptian expert will be assigned to work with the foreign specialists.

HUMAN REMAINS AND LEGISLATION

Ethics

Currently there are no ethical issues in play regarding the excavation of Pharaonic or pre-Pharaonic remains. Some early Coptic Christian cemeteries (i.e., those still being used as burial grounds or with active family plots) are excluded from excavations, as are any cemeteries that have only been in use for 150–300 years or so.

There is some sensitivity with regard to the display of human remains. In the 1970s, the Royal Mummies were taken off display in the Egyptian Museum in Cairo, but have subsequently been returned to the public forum with new display cases and refurbished rooms. It is possible that they, together with other human remains, might be removed from the public eye in the future.

Export

No remains can leave Egypt under current Egyptian law. It is possible, but not easy, to obtain export permits for samples for scientific study, but this is uncommon.

METHODS OF ANTHROPOLOGICAL ANALYSIS

Standard anthropological analysis of human remains is used by most physical anthropologists, varying somewhat depending on each scholar's training and background. For measurements, many people use the North American standards, in addition to any other methods used on Egyptian material that has produced usable data (this varies, depending on the opinion of each scholar). Currently, the stature formula in use by the majority of people working in Egypt is that published by Raxter *et al.* (2008).

CONCLUSION

Currently there is an increase of interest in and care devoted to human remains. A series of conferences in 2010 in Egypt, sponsored by Egyptian and foreign institutions, have targeted practical and theoretical concerns regarding the collection, care and study of human remains. Local universities, such as the American University in Cairo, are increasing their training in Bioarchaeology, and it is hoped that this initiative will be picked up by the state universities.

USEFUL CONTACTS

The Supreme Council of Antiquities, 3 el-Adel Abu Bakr Street, Zamalek, Cairo, Egypt. Website: www.sca-egypt.org/
Department of Biological Anthropology, National Research Centre, Cairo, Egypt.
American Research Center. Website: www.arce.org/

BIBLIOGRAPHY

Buckley, S.A., Clark, K.A. and Evershed, R.P. (2004) 'Complex organic chemical balms of Pharaonic animal mummies', *Nature*, 431: 294–99.

Buckley, S.A. and Evershed, R.P. (2001) 'Organic chemistry of embalming agents in Pharaonic and Graeco-Roman mummies', *Nature*, 413: 837–41.

Buckley, S.A., Stott, A.W. and Evershed, R.P. (1999) 'Studies of organic residues from Ancient Egyptian Mummies using high temperature-gas chromatography-mass spectometry and sequential thermal desorption-gas chromatography-mass spectometry and pyrolysis-gas chromatography-mass spectrometry', *Analyst*, 124: 443–52.

Deelder, A.M., Miller, R.L., De Jonge, N., *et al.* (1990) 'Detection of antigen in mummies', *Lancet*, 335: 724–25.

Duhig, C. 2009. '"They are eating people here!" Paleopathology and living conditions in th First Intermediate Period', S. Ikram and A. M. Dodson (eds) *Beyond the Horizon: Studies in Egyptian Art, Archaeology, and History in Honour of Barry J. Kemp* 1–2. Cairo: Supreme Council of Antiquities. 45–88.

Ikram, S. (in press) 'Physical anthropology and mummies', in I. Shaw and J. Allen (eds) *Oxford Handbook of Egyptology*, Oxford: Oxford University Press.

Miller, R., Ikram, S., Armelagos, G.J., *et al.* (1994) 'Diagnosis of *Plasmodium falciparum* infections in mummies using the rapid manual ParaSight [TM] F test', *Transaction of The Royal Society of Tropical Medicine and Hygiene*, 88: 31–32.

Miller, R.L., Armelagos, G.J., Ikram, S., *et al.* (1992) 'Palaeo-epidemiology of Schistosoma infection in Mummies', *British Medical Journal*, 304: 555–56.

Nehrlich, A.G. and Zink, A. (1999) 'Detection of tuberculosis in an Ancient Egyptian population and the estimation of its frequency', *Journal of Paleopathology*, 11: 86.

Raxter, M.H., Ruff, C., Azab, A., *et al.* (2008) 'Stature estimation in Ancient Egyptians: a new technique based on anatomical reconstruction of stature', *American Journal of Physical Anthropology*, 136: 147–55.

Ruffer, M.A. (1921) *Studies in the Paleopathology of Egypt*, Chicago: University of Chicago.

Smith, G.E. (1912) *The Royal Mummies* (CCG), Cairo: Institut Français d'Archéologie Orientale.

Smith, G.E. and Dawson, W.R. (1924) *Egyptian Mummies*, London: Allen and Unwin.

Smith, G.E. and Wood-Jones, F. (1910) *Report on the Human Remains. The Archaeological Survey of Nubia. Report for 1907–8*, Cairo: Institut Français d'Archéologie Orientale.

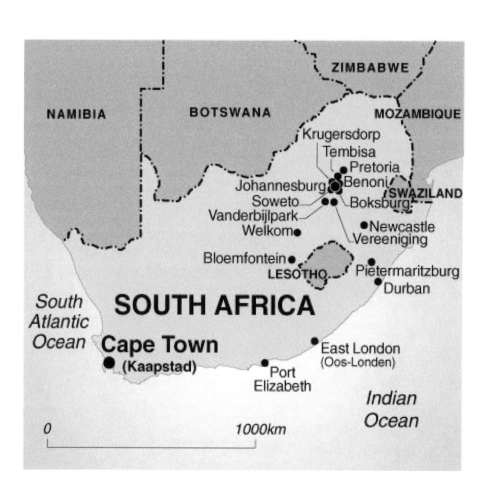

Republic of South Africa

Willem Coenraad Nienaber and Maryna Steyn

INTRODUCTION: A BRIEF HISTORY AND CURRENT STATE OF PHYSICAL ANTHROPOLOGY IN SOUTH AFRICA

South Africa has a long and proud history in physical anthropology, although the bulk of past research has focused on palaeoanthropology. However, as a result of the long time depths, wealth of archaeological sites and also the increasing numbers of remains found in forensic contexts, research into more recent skeletal material has gained considerable momentum.

Historically South Africa followed the British system with regard to the training and education of physical/biological anthropologists, resulting in the fact that most physical anthropologists are trained in medical faculties, or sometimes enter the discipline through the biology route. Therefore there tends to be a somewhat artificial barrier between archaeologists and physical anthropologists, with little cross-over between the two disciplines.

Due to the unique burial practices in this part of the continent, there are very few large archaeological skeletal collections from any specific site. Extensive formal burial grounds are rare, and it seems that in local Iron Age contexts it frequently happened that men were buried in the cattle kraal, while women and children were interred under hut floors or in living areas (Huffman 2007: 55). Most collections from particular sites are therefore small and resulted from accidental discovery. Notable exceptions here were the remains from the Mapungubwe and K2 sites (AD 900 – 1300) (Fouché 1937; Gardner 1963; Meyer 1998), but these skeletons were all repatriated and reburied (Nienaber *et al.* 2008). A catalogue of all archaeological skeletons housed in various collections across the country was published by Morris (1992a), although this needs to be updated.

In contrast to the relative paucity of remains from archaeological contexts, South Africa has some of the best modern skeletal collections in the world. The two most well-known collections are the Raymond Dart Collection at the University of the Witwatersrand (Dayal *et al.* 2009) and the Pretoria Bone Collection housed at the University of Pretoria (L'Abbé *et al.* 2005). These collections are unique, since they are both still growing due to the addition of recent, modern skeletons. This is very important, since research results based on these collections are not influenced by secular trend. Both these collections are large, and are frequently used by national and international researchers.

Education and training

Due to the historical divisions between archaeology and physical anthropology, very few archaeologists will independently study remains found during the course of their research. Similarly, few physical anthropologists will conduct archaeological excavations, and will usually only handle referred remains. This often leads to a loss of integration between context and biological characteristics and in some cases the results of analyses are merely attached to archaeological reports as appendices. There are, however, several upcoming multidisciplinary research centres that include both these professions in excavations and analysis, and several of the established physical anthropologists are willing to assist archaeologists with fieldwork that concerns human remains and on-site analysis; and even *in situ* analysis is not unheard of.

All of the established centres for physical anthropology in South Africa, especially those based at the University of Pretoria and the University of Cape Town, have close ties and a long association with both the South African Police Service (SAPS) and the heritage resources authorities. Most often, skeletonized remains from forensic settings are referred to these centres for specialist analysis for the purposes of identification. Several of the professional physical anthropologists also regularly act as specialist witnesses in court cases that involve human remains. Professionals from these centres also regularly assist the South African Heritage Resources Agency (SAHRA) in the rescue of inadvertently discovered human remains of cultural, historical and archaeological origin. In some cases this arrangement is formalized by Memoranda of Understanding and even long-term consultation appointments between the institutions involved.

Because there are so few physical anthropologists in the country, there are no specific biological anthropological departments or professional associations. Most professionals are associated with one of the larger universities, and are members of international associations such as the American Association of Physical Anthropologists or the Anatomical Society of Southern Africa.

ARCHAEOLOGICAL HUMAN REMAINS AND LEGISLATION

Archaeological legislation

Emerging politically from a long and oppressive colonial past with the democratization of the country in 1994, South African legislation was reviewed, transformed and modernized for almost all aspects of government. However, some minor acts, ordinances and regulations were retained from previous governments and re-instituted as part of the new dispensation. Due to the relative youth of many pieces of legislation cutting across different spheres of society, some problems exist with the integration of different sets of legislation governing various activities.

Some legislative functions are also delegated to provincial level, where it is not interpreted uniformly and where it is applied at different levels of competency by civil servants who, although having the same compliance functions, often work in different departments in different provinces. Thus, while in one province a function is fulfilled by the head of a government department, and in some cases even a member of the provincial executive, the same function is delegated to a clerk in a different department in others. This leads to various problems, especially when activities are occurring concurrently in more than one province.

Legislation applicable to archaeology was one of the areas totally transformed by new legislation with the promulgation of the National Heritage Resources Act (Act 25 of 1999) (NHRA). This new act replaced previous legislation largely inherited from British colonial rule (where government had a strong decision-making and regulatory role) with a framework that is democratic and with a strong focus on community participation and heritage stewardship. By, among other things, vesting ownership of heritage resources in the national community, emphasizing the importance of oral traditions and for the first time requiring heritage impact assessments for any new development, this act also transformed archaeology in South Africa in several meaningful ways. These aspects required a new approach and major re-organization of archaeological practice. The nature of archaeology means it functions across various aspects of society, even more so with the introduction of the concept of heritage impact assessment, requiring in-depth integration with other legislation that regulates mining and industry, water resources, environmental management, national parks, infrastructure development and civil rights. Integration is still ongoing and in many cases has not been achieved in full.

The ambit of the NHRA recognizes that heritage is a non-renewable resource and empowers communities to cherish, develop and conserve their heritage. It aims to define cultural identity as the foundation of nation building and to rectify past injustice by deepening the understanding of cultural diversity through research, sustained utilization and custodianship.

The legislated National Estate includes: objects, places, structures, landscapes and geographical features of cultural significance, those which are related to oral traditions, are archaeological or palaeontological in nature, as well as certain burial grounds and graves and sites of significance in the history of slavery. In broad terms, any of the above heritage resources older than 100 years are defined as archaeological or palaeontological depending on their age. Other defined categories of protection include, among others, sites of military importance older than 75 years, buildings and built structures older than 60 years, certain graves and burial grounds older than 60 years and different classes of shipwrecks and aspects of the 'Struggle' history of South Africa. Any action impacting on any of the above requires a permit issued by the South African Heritage Resources Agency or SAHRA, established by the NHRA as the compliance agency for heritage resources. The abovementioned heritage resources are also indicative of the requirements for heritage impact assessment coupled to a system of grading of resources at different levels of significance which informs the mitigation requirements where resources of this nature are affected.

SAHRA functions as the national compliance agency, with some responsibilities specifically delegated. For instance, graves and burial grounds indicated in the NHRA fall under the jurisdiction of the Burial Grounds and Graves Unit, while archaeology, meteorites, palaeontology and heritage objects also have a specific unit (AMPHOB Unit) to oversee and manage these specific resources. The NHRA also makes provision for Provincial Heritage Resources Agencies (PHRAs). Currently the establishment of PHRAs for different provinces and the delegation of functions to PHRAs are at different stages of implementation. For the Western Cape Province and KwaZulu-Natal, fully functional PHRAs exist, and for the other provinces various interagency agreements regulate functions that are fulfilled by SAHRA on behalf of the PHRA. SAHRA also has regional offices in some provinces, and some functions are delegated regionally. In effect, all regulatory and compliance functions for all heritage resources that are not of national significance (which fall under SAHRA) are undertaken at provincial level where fully functioning PHRAs have been established. This makes for a very complex and confusing compliance structure; for example, all graves under the ambit of the NHRA are managed by the SAHRA Burial Grounds and Graves Unit, apart from graves older than 1570 in the Western Cape Province, which falls under Heritage Western Cape, and all graves in KwaZulu-Natal Province, which falls under 'Amafa' (AkwaZulu Natali/Heritage KwaZulu Natal).

Structures older than 60 years related to the built environment in Gauteng are handled by the Gauteng PHRA, while all other heritage resources in the province are handled by SAHRA on an agency basis.

To simplify, any archaeological excavation, conservation measure or utilization affecting any of the heritage resources identified in the NHRA requires a permit issued by SAHRA, the relevant PHRA or one of the established SAHRA units. SAHRA has a good and regularly updated website, and the staff are always well informed and willing to assist with compliance enquiries when contacted. An enquiry with SAHRA will, in almost all cases, indicate the correct responsible agency and will inform the prospective archaeologist of the correct procedures and forms needed to obtain a permit.

Permits are issued on application using standard forms to qualified archaeologists with a *bona fide* research interest in the site or object in question. Permit applications are vetted by a permit committee consisting of other professional archaeologists, historians, heritage resources managers, academics and persons from civil society democratically nominated and appointed for a four-year term. Usually it is required that applicant archaeologists have at least an honours degree in archaeology, be professionally employed as an archaeologist and have some relevant experience in the field applicable to the permit application. Depending on the site and nature of the research, protocols and conservation management plans for the proposed work may also be required. In all cases there is a strong emphasis on community participation in research on heritage resources, and proof of consent from local communities and the details of community consultations are often required.

South African National Parks (SANParks) has a policy in place for research in national parks. Since they are the landowner, and since landowner permission is required before an SAHRA permit for archaeology can be issued, their requirements must be adhered to before permission is given.

HUMAN REMAINS AND LEGISLATION

Probably the most wide-ranging legislative aspect of archaeology is where it involves human remains. Although, archaeologically, these finds are ecofacts (albeit with high cultural, religious and ethical significance) and can be grouped with other archaeological objects of the same age and from similar contexts on a practical level, legally they are human remains and all actions that involve them must also comply with other legislation applicable. Therefore, although archaeological human remains are handled within the sphere of archaeology, various other legal requirements must be adhered to.

The NHRA identifies the following categories of human remains, whether they form part of formal collections or as incidentally discovered remains, or in burial grounds and graves:

- Human remains older than 100 years, which are defined as archaeological;
- 'Victims of Conflict' that include:
  - Persons who died in the present territory of the Republic of South Africa as a direct result of any war or conflict [the act requires regulations to list these but none has been published to date] excluding those covered by the Commonwealth War Graves Act (Act 8 of 1992) [effectively, persons who were citizens of Commonwealth Countries other than South Africa who died in South Africa after 4 August 1914];
  - Members of the forces of Great Britain and the former British Empire who died on active duty in the present territory of the Republic of South Africa before 4 August 1914;
  - Persons that were exiled from the present territory of the Republic of South Africa and died outside of South Africa during the Anglo–Boer War (1899–1902);
  - Certain persons who died in the 'liberation struggle' [the act requires regulations to list such persons but none have been published to date] in the present territory of the Republic of South Africa and outside South Africa.

- Ancestral graves;
- Persons of royal descent and traditional leaders;
- Individuals indicated by the Minister of Arts and Culture in notices in the Government Gazette;
- Historical graves and burial grounds.

Graves are defined as the place of burial as well as the contents, headstone or any other marker and any other structure on, or associated with such a place.

Under the provisions of the NHRA, a SAHRA permit is therefore required for any action affecting a burial ground, grave or human remains (including the handling and housing thereof) older than 100 years; that of a victim of conflict, a person of royal descent or a traditional leader, and those from historical and ancestral graves, as well as any grave or burial ground older than 60 years which is situated outside a formal cemetery administered by a recognized local authority. In addition to the normal requirements for an archaeological excavation permit, the following requirements must be met in applications involving any of the above:

- The applicant must illustrate a concerted effort to trace and identify any person or community with an interest in the grave, burial ground or remains. This should be done by means of documentary and archival research, a process of public participation and social consultation and the placing of site and newspaper notices;
- If any interested parties are identified, their permission for the exhumation of the remains or any action affecting the graves must be obtained and an agreement as to the requirements for exhumation, the research on and the re-interment of, or any other arrangement for the long-term storage of the remains must be met.

In addition to this, SANParks have their own requirements for human remains in national parks, as reflected in their policy. This broadly entails obtaining the permission of and arranging for the participation of communities with an interest in the park in question. This varies somewhat in content between different parks, due to the diverse nature of communities sur- rounding parks or with interests in the heritage resources included in some parks. These requirements are usually addressed when a prospective researcher requests permission for archaeological excavations from SANParks as landowner.

If the grave or burial ground in question is that of a member of the military forces of a Commonwealth Country other than South Africa, permission must be obtained from the Commonwealth War Graves Commission (CWGC).

The handling, storage and transport of human remains, whether they be of archaeological or recent origin, is further regulated by the Graves and Dead Bodies Ordinance (Ord 7 of 1925; re-instituted by Proclamation 109 of 17 June 1994), the Exhumations Ordinance (Ord 12 of 1980), and either the Human Tissues Act (Act 65 of 1983 as Amended) or the National Health Act (Act 61 of 2003). With the promulgation of the Health Act, not all of the sections of the Human Tissues Act were repealed, and since this process is ongoing these acts must be used in conjunction with each other. In addition, graves and human remains in municipal cemeteries are regulated by the applicable Municipal By-Laws.

For practical purposes the following is required to legally excavate and handle human remains:

- Notices advertising the proposed exhumation of graves must be placed in a local newspaper in English and one of the common additional official languages of the area. These notices must invite possible objections to the proposed exhumation. A period of two weeks must be allowed for comments;

- Site notices similar in content to the newspaper notices must be placed at the site and should remain in place for a period of 60 days;
- A concerted effort to identify and contact persons or groups with an interest in the graves must be undertaken through documentary and archival research, public participation and social consultation. The process must be documented and this record must accompany the application;
- If any interested parties are identified, their permission for the proposed action must be obtained in an agreement that states the preferred place of reburial or mode of long-term retention of the remains and the cultural and/or religious requirements that must be met. The applicant must assist the group in question to meet the agreed requirements;
- If the grave is located in a National Park the requirements of the SANParks policy must be met;
- The permission of the Premier of the Province, or the delegated official, must be obtained;
- A permit from the Provincial Department of Health must be obtained;
- Permission of the Municipality from where the remains are exhumed and where they will be reburied must be obtained. The second is usually included in the process of obtaining new burial plots for re-interment. If the graves in question are not located in the jurisdiction of a Municipality but in an area under a Traditional Authority, permission from said authority is required;
- The permission of the landowner where the remains are to be exhumed as well as where the remains will be buried is required;
- If the agreement allows for the remains to be placed in a collection, the permission of the head of the institution that houses the collection must be obtained. If the agreement with the interested parties allows for the study of the remains before re-interment, this implies temporary storage which also requires the permission of the head of the institution involved;
- An SAHRA permit must be obtained for graves and remains listed above, in short for graves older than 100 years, older than 60 years if located outside the jurisdiction of a municipality, and for other graves of cultural significance irrelevant of their age (note that this may vary between provinces);
- Permission from the Commonwealth War Graves Commission must be obtained for any graves under their administration;
- The local South African Police Services must be notified of the exhumation seven days prior to the action;
- Only a certified funeral undertaker, or an institution with a similar legal status and facilities, is legally allowed to handle, transport and store human remains. South African medical schools legally have this status.

The export of human remains for study outside of South Africa is also regulated by a permit system and will require compliance with both the NHRA as well as the relevant Department of Health requirements on communicable diseases control. Permits can be applied for to SAHRA for both the temporary export as well as export for destructive analysis (e.g., dating) in conjunction with the institution holding the remains.

Inadvertently discovered human remains

The requirements set out in the previous section are readily applied to graves that are identified beforehand and that are excavated as part of a planned process. It is, however, problematic when graves are discovered during the course of archaeological research, or inadvertently during construction activities. Human remains are also often exposed by natural agents and are then reported to the authorities. The rescue procedure currently employed by the SAHRA Burial

Grounds and Graves Unit entails a speedy process of application which is usually granted with the requirement of full retrospective social consultation with the aim of identifying the interested parties and arranging the re-interment of the rescued remains, i.e. the remains are rescued with the consent of the legislated authority and the rest of the process is then completed.

If human remains are uncovered during the course of archaeological work, this usually entails that excavations affecting the burial must be stopped. SAHRA should then be consulted and, depending on the situation, the remains are either covered and left *in situ*, exposed (but not removed) and studied *in situ*, or fully excavated and studied with the consent and participation of the interested parties. It is, therefore, advisable that, if it is foreseen that any archaeological research will uncover human remains, an agreement with the interested parties and a permit for burials be obtained beforehand.

For human remains inadvertently discovered in other situations, the legal requirement is that all activities affecting the burial must be stopped and that the discovery must be reported to the SAPS and SAHRA. The status of the remains is then ascertained. If they are found to be forensic in nature (nominally younger than 60 years and perceived to be those of the victim of crime or a person who has died of unnatural causes), recovery by the Provincial Forensic Pathology Services in conjunction with the SAPS is mandated. If the remains are of cultural, historical or archaeological origin, recovery is usually facilitated by SAHRA by means of a Rescue Permit, as described above.

Ethical considerations

Normally an application for the excavation of graves purely for research purposes would not be considered by the compliance agencies. Archaeologists refrain from conducting excavations with the express aim of finding and exhuming human remains for study purposes, but the principle of recovering the maximum amount of data, where this does not contravene the rights of interested parties, is well established. The principle that biological data such as lifestyle and demographic information will add to a better understanding of the archaeological record is well entrenched.

ASAPA members are also ethically bound by the ICOMOS Charter and the UNESCO 1970 Charter.

Standards in archaeology

There are no legally mandated standards of minimum practice for archaeology in South Africa, apart from SAHRA guidelines on reports for Heritage Impact Assessments. Most South African archaeologists, however, are members of the Association of Southern African Professional Archaeologists (ASAPA) that has minimum standards of practice. All members are ethically bound to adhere to these. These minimum standards and the ASAPA code of conduct are based on the conservation ethic, with the stewardship concept as the prominent theme, and, with regard to human remains, on respect for the remains themselves as well as for the customs, beliefs and practices of persons and communities with an interest in the remains.

METHODS OF ANTHROPOLOGICAL ANALYSIS

South Africa has a very diverse society, with people from African (Khoesan and Black African), European, and even some Eastern Asian/Mongoloid descent. This, coupled with the fact that modern remains are available and accessible, has led to a wealth of research with regard to population-specific analyses of skeletons. Most of these results find application in forensic cases, but they can be applied in archaeological contexts. Care should, however, be taken to take factors such as possible secular trends and the changing composition of societies into account.

Research results applicable to South Africans specifically are available for age determination, sex determination, assessment of ancestry and calculation of stature. These are also summarized in a CD-Rom program ('Forensic Anthropology') which is available from the Department of Anatomy at the University of Pretoria. As far as age determination is considered, specific data are available, amongst others, for sternal ends of ribs (Oettlé and Steyn 2000) and dental maturation sequences (Phillips 2008).

Papers on sex determination include both morphological aspects (e.g. De Villiers 1968a on the skull; Loth and Henneberg 1996 on the mandible; Patriquin *et al.* 2003 on the pelvis) and metrics (e.g. Steyn and İşcan 1997 and Asala 2001 on the femur; Steyn and İşcan 1999 on the humerus; Barrier and L'Abbé 2008 on the forearm; Patriquin *et al.* 2005 on the pelvis; Kieser and Groeneveld 1986, Steyn and İşcan 1998, Franklin *et al.* 2005 on the skull; and Dayal *et al.* 2008 and Franklin *et al.* 2008 specifically on the mandible). Some publications also employ geometric morphometrics in shape assessments (e.g. Steyn *et al.* 2004; Oettlé *et al.* 2005; Franklin *et al.* 2007). Data are even available for some of the less frequently used bones such as the patella (Dayal and Bidmos 2005) and foot bones (Bidmos and Asala 2003; Bidmos and Asala 2004; Bidmos and Dayal 2004).

Similarly, a number of papers were published with regard to determination of ancestry using the morphological (De Villiers 1968b) and metric characteristics of the skull (İşcan and Steyn 1999; Franklin *et al.* 2007) and even the pelvis (Patriquin *et al.* 2002). To our knowledge, only one paper was published with regards to ancestry in juvenile remains (Steyn and Henneberg 1997).

Population-specific formulae are available for calculation of stature of both black (Lundy and Feldesman 1987) and white (Dayal *et al.*, 2008) South Africans. Published work also includes less frequently used bones (Bidmos and Asala 2005; Bidmos 2006; Ryan and Bidmos 2007) and fragmentary bones (Chibba and Bidmos 2007). Some information on stature in general can be found in Steyn and Smith (2007).

The papers quoted above mostly refer to the South African population of European and African descent, and the list is by no means complete. Much less has been published on skeletal identification of the Stone Age hunter-gatherers of South Africa (Khoesan peoples). These groups are not very sexually dimorphic, and it can therefore be difficult to determine their sex. Craniometric data have been published by Morris (1992b) and Ribot (2004) among others, with information on stature, robustness and lifestyle provided by authors such as Pfeiffer and Sealy (2006). Wilson and Lundy (1994) also published a paper on reconstruction of stature in the Khoesan.

CONCLUSION

Most current research on human remains from archaeological sites takes place following the accidental disturbance of human graves or burial sites. These human remains are frequently found as a result of development or sometimes in forensic contexts. This results in the fact that skeletal analyses are frequently required, and that much research is done continuously in order to improve the quality of the assessments. It is advocated that population-specific standards are used as far as possible.

At present, it is unlikely that archaeological projects with the aim of excavating and studying human remains will be approved. There are, however, ongoing large projects where graves are located as part of heritage resource management projects, and graves and human remains are frequently found by accident. There are, therefore, many opportunities to study human remains, and often these cases are scientifically extremely interesting.

USEFUL CONTACTS

Association of Southern African Professional Archaeologists (ASAPA). Website: www.asapa.org.za/
Anatomical Society of Southern Africa (ASSA). Website: www.assa.uct.ac.za/
Commonwealth War Graves Commission. Website: www.cwgc.org/
Forensic Anthropology Research Centre (FARC), Department of Anatomy, School of Medicine, Faculty of Health Sciences, PO Box 2034, Pretoria 0001, South Africa. Tel: +27(0)12 319 2244. Website: www.be.up.co.za/farc/
Pretoria Bone Collection (Department of Anatomy, University of Pretoria). Contact: Dr E.N. L'Abbé. Email: ericka.labbe@up.ac.za
Raymont Dart Collection (Department of Anatomical Sciences, University of the Witwatersrand). Contact: Brendon Billings Email: Brendon.billings@wits.ac.za
South African Heritage Resources Agency (SAHRA), PO Box 4637, Cape Town 8000, South Africa. Tel: +27(0) 21 462 45021. Website: www.sahra.org.za/
SAHRA Burial Grounds and Graves Unit, PO Box 87552, Houghton 2041, South Africa. Tel: +27(0) 11 403 0683. Website: www.sahra.org.za/
SANParks. Website: www.sanparks.org/

BIBLIOGRAPHY

Asala, S.A. (2001) 'Sex determination from the head of the femur of South African whites and blacks', *Forensic Science International*, 117: 15–22
Barrier, I.L.O. and L'Abbé, E. (2008) 'Sex determination from the bones of the forearm in a modern South African sample', *Forensic Science International*, 179: 85.e1–85.e7.
Bidmos, M.A. (2006) 'Adult stature reconstruction from the calcaneus of South Africans of European descent', *Journal of Clinical Forensic Medicine*, 13: 247–52.
Bidmos, M.A. and Asala, S.A. (2003) 'Discriminant function sexing of the calcaneus of the South African Whites', *Journal of Forensic Science*, 48: 1213–18.
——(2004) 'Sexual dimorphism of calcaneus of South Africa Blacks', *Journal of Forensic Science*, 49: 446–50.
——(2005) 'Calcaneal measurement in estimation of stature of South African blacks', *American Journal of Physical Anthropology*, 126: 335–42.
Bidmos, M.A. and Dayal, M.R. (2004) 'Further evidence to show population specificity of discriminant function equations for sex determination using the talus of South African Blacks', *Journal of Forensic Science* 49: 1165–70.
Chibba, K. and Bidmos, M.A. (2007) 'Using tibia fragments from South Africans of European descent to estimate maximum tibia length and stature', *Forensic Science International*, 169: 145–51.
Dayal, M.R. and Bidmos, M.A. (2005) 'Discriminating sex in South African Blacks using patella dimensions', *Journal of Forensic Science*, 50: 1294–97.
Dayal, M.R., Kegley, A.D.T., Strkalj, G., *et al.* (2009) 'The history and composition of the Raymond A. Dart Collection of Human Skeletons at the University of the Witwatersrand, Johannesburg, South Africa', *American Journal of Physical Anthropology*, 140 (2): 324–35.
Dayal, M.R., Spocter, M.A. and Bidmos, M.A. (2008) 'An assessment of sex using the skull of black South Africans by discriminant function analysis', *Homo*, 59: 209–21.

Dayal, M.R., Steyn, M. and Kuykendall, K.L. (2008) 'Stature estimation from bones of South African whites', *South African Journal of Science*, 4: 124–28.

De Villiers, H. (1968a) 'Sexual dimorphism of the skull of the South African Bantu-speaking Negro', *South African Journal of Science*, 64: 118–24.

——(1968b) *The Skull of the South African Negro*, Johannesburg: Witwatersrand University Press.

Fouché, J.F. (1937) *Mapungubwe, Ancient Bantu Civilization on the Limpopo*, Cambridge: Cambridge University Press.

Franklin, D., Freedman, L. and Milne, N. (2005) 'Sexual dimorphism and discriminant function sexing in indigenous South African crania', *Homo*, 55: 213–28.

Franklin, D., Freedman, L., Milne, N., *et al.* (2007) 'A geometric morphometric study of population variation in indigenous southern African crania', *American Journal of Human Biology*, 19: 20–33.

Franklin, D., O'Higgins, P., Oxnard, C.E. *et al.* (2008) 'Discriminant function sexing of the mandible of indigenous South Africans', *Forensic Science International*, 179: 84e1–84e5.

Gardner, G.A. (1963) *Mapungubwe: Vol II*, Pretoria: J.L. Van Schaik.

Huffman, T.N. (2007) *Handbook to the Iron Age. The Archaeology of Pre-Colonial Farming Societies in Southern Africa*, Scottsville: University of KwaZulu-Natal Press.

İşcan, M.Y. and Steyn, M. (1999) 'Craniometric determination of population affinity in South Africans', *International Journal of Legal Medicine*, 112: 91–97.

Kieser, J.Y. and Groeneveld, H.T. (1986) 'Multivariate sexing of the human viscerocranium', *Journal of Forensic Odontostomatology*, 4: 41–46.

L'Abbé, E.N., Loots, M. and Meiring, J.H. (2005) 'The Pretoria Bone Collection: A modern South African skeletal sample', *Homo*, 56: 197–205.

Loth, S.R. and Henneberg, M. (1996) 'Mandibular ramus flexure: a new morphologic indicator of sexual dimorphism in the human skeleton', *American Journal of Physical Anthropology*, 99: 473–85.

Lundy, J.K. and Feldesman, M.R. (1987) 'Revised equations for estimating living stature from the long bones of the South African Negro', *South African Journal of Science*, 83: 54–5.

Meyer, A. (1998) *The Archaeological Sites of Greefswald*, Pretoria: University of Pretoria.

Morris, A. (1992a) *A Master Catalogue: Holocene Human Skeletons from South Africa*, Johannesburg: Witwatersrand University Press.

——(1992b) *The Skeletons of Contact. A Study of Protohistoric Burials from the Lower and Orange River valley, South Africa*, Johannesburg: Witwatersrand University Press.

Nienaber, W.C., Keough, N., Steyn, M., *et al.* (2008) 'Reburial of the Mapungubwe human remains: an overview of process and procedure', *South African Archaeological Bulletin*, 63: 164–75.

Oettlé, A.C., Pretorius, E. and Steyn, M. (2005) 'Geometric morphometric analysis of mandibular ramus flexure', *American Journal of Physical Anthropology*, 128: 623–29.

Oettlé, A.C. and Steyn, M. (2000) 'Age estimation from sternal ends of ribs by phase analysis in South African blacks', *Journal of Forensic Science*, 45: 1071–79.

Patriquin, M.L., Loth, S.R. and Steyn, M. (2003) 'Sexually dimorphic pelvic morphology in South African whites and blacks', *Homo*, 53: 255–62.

Patriquin, M.L., Steyn, M. and Loth, S.R. (2002) 'Metric assessment of race from the pelvis in South Africans', *Forensic Science International*, 127: 104–13.

Patriquin, M.L., Steyn, M. and Loth, S.R. (2005) 'Metric analysis of sex differences in South African black and white pelves', *Forensic Science International*, 147: 119–27.

Pfeiffer, S. and Sealy, J. (2006) 'Body size among Holocene foragers of the Cape Ecozone, southern Africa', *American Journal of Physical Anthropology*, 129: 1–11.

Phillips, V.M. (2008) 'Dental maturation of South African children and the relation to chronological age', unpublished PhD thesis, University of the Western Cape.

Ribot, I. (2004) 'Differentiation of modern sub-Saharan African populations: craniometric interpretations in relation to geography and history', *Bulletins et Mémoires de la Société d'Anthropologie de Paris*, 16: 143–65.

Ryan, I. and Bidmos, M.A. (2007) 'Skeletal height reconstruction from measurements of the skull in indigenous South Africans', *Forensic Science International*, 167: 16–21.

Steyn, M. and Henneberg, M. (1997) 'Cranial growth in the prehistoric sample from K2 at Mapungubwe (South Africa) is population specific', *Homo*, 48: 62–71.

Steyn, M. and İşcan, M.Y. (1997) 'Sex determination from the femur and tibia in South African Whites', *Forensic Science International*, 90: 111–19.

——(1998) 'Sexual dimorphism in the crania of the mandibles of South African whites', *Forensic Science International*, 98: 9–16.

——(1999) 'Osteometric variation in the humerus: sexual dimorphism in South Africans', *Forensic Science International*, 106: 77–85.

Steyn, M., Pretorius, E. and Hutten, L. (2004) 'Geometric morphometric analysis of the greater sciatic notch in South Africans', *Homo*, 54: 197–206.

Steyn, M. and Smith, J.R. (2007) 'Interpretation of ante-mortem stature estimates in South Africans', *Forensic Science International*, 171: 97–102.

Wilson, M.E. and Lundy, J.K. (1994) 'Estimated living statures of dated Khoisan skeletons from the South-Western coastal region of South Africa', *South African Archaeological Bulletin*, 49: 2–8.

LIBYA

EGYPT

SAUDI ARABIA

Port Sudan

Red Sea

CHAD

Khartoum North

ERITREA

Omdurman

Khartoum

Kassala

El-Gezira

Gedaref

Kosti

El-Obeid

Nyala

SUDAN

ETHIOPIA

CENTRAL AFRICAN REPUBLIC

DEMOCRATIC REPUBLIC OF THE CONGO

UGANDA

KENYA

0   1000km

Sudan/السودان

Tina Jakob and Mongeda Khalid Magzoub Ali

INTRODUCTION: A BRIEF HISTORY AND CURRENT STATE OF PHYSICAL ANTHROPOLOGY IN SUDAN

Sudan has a rich and diverse cultural heritage, deriving from its unique location and history. Sudan is situated in north-eastern Africa, sharing borders with nine other countries (Eritrea, Ethiopia, Kenya, Uganda, Democratic Republic of the Congo, Central African Republic, Chad, Libya and Egypt) and the Red Sea. The country is dominated by the river Nile, with its two tributaries – the Blue Nile and the White Nile. With an area of more than 2.5 million sq. km, Sudan is Africa's largest country, and its geography ranges from arid and semi-arid deserts in the north and central areas to savannahs and tropical rainforests in the south. Sandstorms occur, especially during the summer months, and high temperatures, easily exceeding 40°C, in combination with summer rains, may restrict archaeological excavations to the 'cooler' months between October and March.

Due to its unique geographical location, Sudan has been described as a corridor linking the Arab world, the Mediterranean and equatorial Africa (Adams 1977), and this is reflected in the number and diversity of its archaeological remains, ranging from the Pleistocene period to 100 years ago. Sudan attracted travellers and archaeologists in the 18th and 19th centuries, but many of their observations concentrated on exploring parallels between the cultural remains of Sudan and those of its northern neighbour, dynastic Egypt, in line with the prevailing Egyptocentric view (Adams 1998). This contributed to the majority of excavation taking place in Nubia, the northern part of Sudan, with many archaeologists viewing the country as a cultural extension of Egypt (Török 1997). Politically, Sudan was ruled by Egypt as part of the Ottoman Empire, and since 1898, as Anglo-Egyptian Sudan, the country remained under foreign rule until its independence in 1956. As a consequence of the colonial administration, Sudan was opened up for archaeological research to foreign missions, exploring pyramids and temples, as well as prehistoric and historic settlements and cemeteries.

In 1903, Sudan's first Antiquities Service was established and two years later the Antiquities and Museums First Ordinance began to regulate archaeological work under the guidance of J.W. Crawfoot. The post of Commissioner for Archaeology and Anthropology was held by British archaeologists A.J. Arkell (1938–48), P.L. Shinnie (1948–55) and the French archaeologist J. Vercoutter (1956–60), who all directed archaeological excavations in Sudan. Shinnie was also responsible for drafting the second Antiquities Ordinance of 1952, which set out clear definitions of objects and monuments covered by the Ordinance.

With the Sudanization of government posts in 1960, the first Sudanese Commissioner for Archaeology, T.H. Thabit, was appointed and subsequently joint surveys and fieldwork projects between Sudanese and foreign archaeologists began to increase. Today, Sudan has five university departments teaching archaeology and a large number of museums which curate and display the cultural heritage of Sudan. The National Museum of Sudan in Khartoum was already established in 1904 and today houses the majority of archaeological finds, but a number of regional museums exist across the country or are being planned.

Due to the considerable time depth of human occupation and the vast geographical area, there is no straightforward archaeological chronology of Sudan's prehistoric and historic periods. However, the main periods, especially for Upper Nubia, have already been defined in the earlier part of the 20th century and are still largely valid today. Nevertheless, many dates have changed over time and might continue to do so with the development of even more exact scientific dating methods. Table 45.1 gives an overview of the chronological framework and associated sites, especially cemeteries, but due to the large number of archaeological sites this has to remain incomplete. Many of the cemeteries were in use over considerable amounts of time, for example skeletons from Qustul date to the Neolithic, Meroitic and post-Meroitic periods.

The study of human remains derived from the territory of modern-day Sudan has a long history, dating back to the 19th century. Here an overview of the main archaeological

Table 45.1 Overview of chronological periods and some archaeological sites in Upper Nubia and Central Sudan

Chronology (BC/AD)	Upper Nubia	Central Sudan
Before 8000	Upper Palaeolithic (? Jebel Sahaba)	Pre-Mesolithic (Al-Khiday 2)
8000–6000	Mesolithic (Wadi Halfa 6-B-36, El-Barga)	Mesolithic (Khartoum Hospital, Saggai 1, Shabona, Al-Khiday 1)
6000–5500	Early Neolithic (El-Barga)	Late Mesolithic (Kabbashi, 10-W-4)
5500–5000	?	
5000–4500	Middle Neolithic (Kadruka 13, 18	Early Neolithic (Shaheinab, El-Ghaba, Kadero)
4500–4000	and 21, R12, Kerma Site 8, Multaga)	
4000–3500		Late Neolithic (Es-Sour; El-Kadada, until 3400
3500–2600	Pre-Kerma (Kerma Site 1, 21; Saï 8-B-52A)	BC; Shaqadud, after 3000 BC)
2600–1500	Kerma (early, middle and classic periods; Saï 8-B-51, Kerma, Buhen)	(Khasm el-Girba)
1500–1100?	Late Kerma (Tombos, Kerma, Soleb, Mirgissa)	?
?1100–?800	Kingdom of Kush	Kingdom of Kush
?800–300	Napatan (Kerma, Kawa, Jebel Barkal, Nuri, El-Kurru)	Napatan (Meroe, Jebel Moya)
300 BC–c.AD 350	Meroitic (Abri, Soleb, Aksha)	Meroitic (Meroe, Geili, Gabati)
c.AD 350–550	Post-Meroitic (Ballana, Qustul, Sesibi, Meinarti)	Post-Meroitic (Akad, Al-Hobagi)
AD 500–1500	Mediaeval (Faras, Old Dongola, Kulubnarti)	Mediaeval (Soba, Sennar)

Source: Based on Edwards 2004; Reinold 2000; Salvatori and Usai 2008; Welsby 1996, 2002

excavations that resulted in the recovery of human remains is given, together with a review of changing research paradigms.

Physical anthropologists of the 19th and early 20th centuries were almost exclusively concerned with determining the racial origins of indigenous populations, and in this vein S.G. Morton (1844) collected and studied human skulls by concentrating on measurements to determine racial differences between groups living along the river Nile, including in Nubia. With the First Nubian Survey (1907–11) along the river to the south of the First Cataract, in response to the raising of the high dam at Aswan, approximately 10,000 skeletons from different time periods were discovered (Reisner 1910). These excavations and subsequent studies of some of the human remains laid the groundwork for further research and helped to demonstrate the abundance of human skeletal remains from this geographical area. Based on differences in material culture and grave construction, Reisner defined several chronological groups, namely A-Group, C-Group, Meroitic, X-Group and Christian, all supposedly representing waves of racially distinct immigrants, from either the north or the south. Although racial affinities formed an important aspect of the study, palaeopathological analyses, for example of fractures (Wood Jones 1910) and dental diseases were also presented (Elliot Smith and Wood Jones 1910). Elliot Smith and Wood Jones, both anatomists with an interest in mummies and skeletal remains, together with D.E. Derry, recorded 'some six thousand bodies' (Elliot Smith and Wood Jones 1910: 263), but, due to time constraints, it was impossible to study all the human remains recovered and many have now been lost. Unfortunately, despite detailed lists and descriptions, data presentation does not allow the calculation of crude or absolute prevalence rates and only the presence or absence of certain diseases can be tentatively verified, although many of the diagnoses are rather ambiguous.

Reisner's work continued in northern Sudan with excavations at the settlements and cemeteries of Kerma, El-Kurru, Jebel Barkal and Nuri. From 1913 to 1915 Reisner led a joint team from Harvard University and Boston Museum of Fine Arts working at Kerma, the first capital of the kingdom of Kush (Reisner 1923), with ongoing excavation since 1973, directed by C. Bonnet of the University of Geneva. Close to the settlement lies a vast cemetery with an estimated 30,000 individuals, of which only a fraction have been recovered. Believed to be the remains of the ruling male elite, their scarified queens and 'slaves', earlier studies, once again, concentrated on racial affinities (see, e.g., Collett 1933; Simon 1989), while more recent research focused on a wider range of topics, such as cranial injuries (Filer 1992), fractures (Judd 2002, 2004, 2008), diet (Thompson *et al.* 2008), as well as possible health differences between social groups (Buzon and Judd 2008).

A second Archaeological Survey of Nubia (1929–34) directed by W.B. Emery and L.P. Kirwan became necessary with a further enlargement of the Aswan Dam (Emery and Kirwan 1935). Similar to the first survey, rescue work was concentrated on the Egyptian part of Nubia and, again, large numbers of human remains were recovered. The initial study by the anatomist A. Batrawi (1935), based on craniometric analysis, also concluded that different cultural periods equated with different 'racial' types, thus confirming previous research. However, more than a decade later, Batrawi (1946: 131) concluded that changes in Nubian cultural groups and migrations of different races were not linked, since he was unable to find any morphological differences between populations of different time periods. Nevertheless, he held on to the accepted concept of different races and their 'admixture' being visible in the cranial remains of Nubian skeletons, in keeping with the prevailing interest in the discovery of the origins of the Egyptian peoples.

Outside Lower Nubia, one of the largest excavations on the African continent was initiated by Sir Henry Wellcome, who oversaw four seasons (1910–13) of work at Jebel Moya, site 100.

Situated 30 km to the west of the Blue Nile near the modern city of Sennar, more than 3000 skeletons were found, but apparently only one-fifth of the site had been excavated (Addison 1949). Unfortunately, the site records and index cards are largely useless due to measurement errors and problems with sex estimation (Mukherjee *et al.* 1955). The human remains were transported to London, but subsequently most have been damaged or were lost altogether and today fewer than 100 crania, 139 mandibles and a few post-cranial remains are preserved (Irish and Konigsberg 2007). Mukherjee and co-workers (Mukherjee *et al.* 1955) used statistical methods to assess population differences derived from cranial measurements, and metrical methods to revise the original sex estimations. Comparing their assessment of cranial morphology with studies by Elliot Smith and Wood Jones (1910) and Batrawi (1935), they came to the conclusion that no morphological differences were visible in populations from Upper Nubia and Jebel Moya. However, more recently, Irish and Konigsberg (2007) employed non-metric dental traits to establish that the individuals from Jebel Moya were a distinctive population that did not closely resemble other Sudanese samples.

In central Sudan, Arkell's discovery of human remains during a rescue excavation at Khartoum hospital (Arkell 1949) was the first to be attributed to a pottery-bearing Mesolithic period. The skeletal analysis by Derry (1949) concluded that the two skeletons that were complete enough to be assessed were of 'Negroid' origin, based on visual examination of 'typical' morphological traits such as prognathism. Regrettably, these skeletons now seem to be lost (L. Schepartz, pers. comm.), thus making it impossible to re-evaluate one of the earliest examples of human skeletal remains from Sudan.

Probably the best known archaeological rescue campaign in northern Sudan was launched by UNESCO in 1960, in response to the inevitable flooding of the area south of Aswan caused by yet another enlargement of the Aswan High Dam. Between 1960 and 1969 more than 60 international teams, backed by generous funding, worked along the banks of the Nile in Lower Egypt and Upper Nubia to document and excavate archaeological structures. Their work resulted in an unprecedented number of human remains from different archaeological time periods being discovered and becoming available for study. Due to the sheer number of skeletons and mummified individuals, not all were analysed in depth, but an impressive body of publications addressing old and new research questions now exists. The two most intensely researched areas comprise Wadi Halfa, close to the border with Egypt, where cemeteries of Mesolithic, Meroitic, post-Meroitic and Mediaeval date have been excavated, as well as the area known as the 'belly of rocks' (Batn-al-Hajjar), with its Meroitic, post-Meroitic and Mediaeval graves. Studies by G.J. Armelagos, D.S. Carlson, D.L. Greene and D.P. Van Gerven indicated that *in situ* adaptation, not migration, was responsible for subtle differences in cranial morphology (Carlson and Armelagos 1971; Carlson and Van Gerven 1977). These researchers also concluded that certain features, such as large teeth, massive mandibles and prominent cranial muscle attachment sites observed in the Mesolithic people of Wadi Halfa were probably indicative of heavy chewing stresses, not 'racial' affiliation, and the loss of these traits in subsequent populations demonstrated a softer diet (Carlson 1976; Greene and Armelagos 1972; Greene *et al.* 1967). Nevertheless, many researchers were still concerned with establishing various degrees of racial admixture and comparisons of supposedly different racial groups by employing cranial morphology (see, e.g., Strouhal 1971). Studies of non-metric cranial and dental traits added a further dimension (see, e.g., Greene 1966, 1972; Berry and Berry 1967), and, interestingly, the post-cranial skeleton was discovered to be of scientific value, with a number of studies on sub-adult long bone growth (Armelagos *et al.* 1972), cortical and trabecular properties, thus shifting the focus of research towards palaeopathological questions (Armelagos 1968, 1969; Burrell *et al.* 1986; Nielsen 1970; Carlson *et al.* 1974). In addition, the large number of well preserved individuals made the construction of life-tables and palaeodemographic analyses a rewarding task (Swedlund and Armelagos 1969). More recently, many of the skeletal and partially mummified populations from these rescue excavations have been re-studied, using newly developed methods and specific research questions (see, e.g., Alvrus 1997, 1999; Kilgore *et al.* 1997; Wapler *et al.* 2004).

More than 30 years after the international efforts to save the monuments of Nubia, the National Corporation for Antiquities and Museums (NCAM) made a similar appeal for archaeologists to investigate approximately 170 km of the Nile valley near the Fourth Cataract prior to the construction of a large hydroelectric dam, known as the Merowe Dam. Despite many archaeological teams responding to this call, their work in the Fourth Cataract area has received comparatively little international coverage, compared to the attention devoted to the UNESCO-backed endeavour of the 1960s. Nevertheless, a large number of archaeological sites were excavated before being inundated by the rising waters, many of them cemeteries dating to the Kerma and Christian periods, and the study of the large number of well preserved skeletal remains holds great potential for future research projects (Jakob 2007).

Other research in the Northern Dongola Reach (Irish 2008; Judd 2001, 2008) and further north on the Island of Saï (Murail *et al.* 2004) focused on prehistoric populations, and the same can be observed in areas north and south of Khartoum, where large cemeteries dating to the Neolithic, Mesolithic and pre-Mesolithic periods are studied (Reinold 2007; Usai and Salvatori 2005).

So far, the oldest find of human skeletal remains comes from Singa near the Blue Nile, where a calvaria is now dated to a minimum of 133,000 years (McDermott *et al.* 1996; Spoor *et al.* 1998). Sudan may also provide one of the earliest examples of violence, as seen in the skeletons from Jebel Sahaba (Anderson 1968), but their upper Palaeolithic date as never been confirmed by modern radiocarbon dating. Despite a growing number of prehistoric skeletons, most bioarchaeological research concentrates on Christian cemeteries, due to the excellent preservation of skeletal and naturally mummified human remains and the large numbers of individuals, including non-adults, which allow for statistical testing of observations. Since many cemeteries were in use over considerable amounts of time, comparative diachronic studies are possible, thus enhancing our knowledge of morphological and pathological changes over time. Bioarchaeological research reflects the concentration of archaeological excavations and rescue projects along the Nile Valley, although areas away from the river, such as the Wadi Howar in the north-west (e.g. Jesse and Keding 2002; Simon *et al.* 2002) and eastern regions near Kassala (Fattovich 1995; Manzo 2004), have been investigated. However, very little archaeological research has taken place in the south and west (but see recent work by Abd el-Rahman 2006a, 2006b), although much anthropological data has been collected by ethnologists of the previous centuries (Edwards 2007).

Collections of human remains

Collections of human remains from Sudan are curated at various universities and museums across the world, including the British Museum (London), the Duckworth Collection of the Department of Biological Anthropology (Cambridge), the Laboratory for Biological Anthropology at the University of Copenhagen, the Centre d'Anthropobiologie at the Université Paul Sabatier (Toulouse), the Peabody Museum of Archaeology and Ethnology at Harvard University (Cambridge, MA), the University of Colorado (Boulder) and the University of Arizona (Tempe). However, a comprehensive and regularly updated list of all human remains collections is urgently needed to facilitate further research on skeletal and mummified remains. Such a list, with details of available collections and their location, would also ensure that the same easily accessible populations are not used repeatedly, a practice that would inevitably lead to some damage or even loss of skeletal elements. A fully indexed bibliography of bioarchaeological studies in Sudan and Egypt has been compiled by J.G. Rose (1996); its particular strength lies in the inclusion of publications in languages other than English, thus providing a comprehensive overview of studies on human remains. More recently, a list of archaeological work, including research on human remains in Nubia (and Egypt) has been published by UNESCO (2000) and is available online.

ARCHAEOLOGICAL HUMAN REMAINS AND LEGISLATION

Archaeological legislation

Since 1991, the former Antiquities Service was restructured and became the National Corporation for Antiquities and Museums (NCAM). NCAM's responsibilities encompass the regulation of all archaeological surveys and excavations, the preservation and scientific study of Sudan's archaeological and ethnographical heritage and its curation and presentation in museums.

Anyone who wishes to excavate in Sudan, including individuals and institutions from foreign countries, has to apply for a licence by writing to the General Director of NCAM, stating their institutional affiliation, the geographical area they wish to work in and the nature of the proposed work (survey, evaluation or trial trenches, excavation); no special licence is necessary for the excavation of ancient cemeteries. If permission is granted, a curriculum vitae of all team members and copies of their passports need to be submitted, together with a list of previous archaeological work conducted by the licence holder. A new licence currently costs $1000 and is valid for one year, with a renewal fee of $500 and an additional fee of $250 payable to NCAM for subsequent years. Licences are granted providing the applicant can demonstrate adequate scientific competence, including previous publications of archaeological work, and all fieldwork, post-excavation research and publications are financially covered (OPA 1999, chapter III, section 23a, b, c). Furthermore, normal visa regulations for travelling to Sudan apply, and details of visa application procedures can be obtained from embassies and consulates of the Republic of the Sudan.

The excavation of cemeteries

The excavation licence requires the holder to excavate all archaeological remains and structures found within their concession area, regardless of their archaeological age, with the exception of modern cemeteries and buildings or land under cultivation. Sharia law, implemented in northern and central Sudan, forbids the disturbance of Islamic graves, and it is prudent to seek local knowledge to establish the potential presence of such graves within a concession area. All foreign excavation teams are joined by an NCAM inspector, who reports directly to NCAM and ensures that all obligations of the excavation licence are observed.

HUMAN REMAINS AND LEGISLATION

There seems to be no clear-cut borderline between archaeological and forensic cases with regards to human remains, and it may not always be easy to establish the age of skeletal elements, especially from non-archaeological contexts. For example, when human skeletal remains were discovered on the premises of the British embassy in Khartoum in January 2009, the police declared them to be more than 300 years old. However, it appears that no archaeological or scientific analysis took place to establish the chronological age of the bones. According to newspaper reports, the remains probably represented three individuals and were thought to be reburied to conform to Islamic laws (Sudan Tribune 2009).

In 1999, a new antiquities law, based on the 1952 Second Antiquities Ordinance, was passed by parliament. This Ordinance for the Protection of Antiquities (OPA 1999) defines antiquities as 'anything surviving from the ancient civilizations or past generations' and 100 or more years old, including 'some human, animal and botanical remains', if they are considered by NCAM to be of national importance (OPA 1999, section 3). This definition of human remains as antiquities stands in contrast with the previous ordinance, which included all human and animal remains dated prior to 1340 AD.

Although OPA 1999 (chapter III, section 25b) requires the presence of specialists in, for example, archaeology, architecture, survey and excavation, there is no legal obligation for a physical anthropologist to be present during excavation. However, most field directors have realized the benefits of having the expertise of a bioarchaeologist on site, and additionally, many NCAM inspectors have acquired significant experience in excavating human remains from different funerary contexts.

In accordance with OPA 1999 (chapter III, section 28), ownership of all excavated antiquities rests with the government, but samples of human remains may be exported for analysis (radiocarbon, stable isotope or DNA) and human remains can be exported for scientific study only with a licence issued by NCAM. All costs for the licence, packing and transport have to be met by the licence holder. Licences can be issued for indefinite curation of human remains in foreign countries, or can be temporary, and, again, the licence holder is responsible for all incurred costs. Exporting human remains and any other archaeological materials without a licence is illegal and will be punished by imprisonment of three years and/or a fine (OPA 1999, chapter III, section 31).

In addition, one has to be aware of country-specific regulations for the import of human remains; for example, in Britain the import of biological materials, including soils from non-EU countries, is regulated by the Department for Environment, Food and Rural Affairs (DEFRA), and it is imperative that human remains are thoroughly cleaned of any adhering soil prior to import to the UK. Import of human remains from Sudan to the United States of America is restricted due to a US embargo on goods from Sudan, but licences for temporary study may be obtained; skeletal remains imported before the embargo was put in place in 1997 are not affected.

METHODS OF ANTHROPOLOGICAL ANALYSIS

Almost 30 years ago, Strouhal (1981: 241) lamented the lack of training for physical anthropologists in Sudanese universities, despite the large number of well preserved human remains from archaeological excavations, and unfortunately the situation has not yet changed, but first publications on human remains by Sudanese researchers trained abroad are now emerging (Taha el-Ata and Mohamed Adam 2007). Bioarchaeological methods used in published reports vary according to the educational background of researchers, with most North American and British bioarchaeologists relying on methods outlined by Buikstra and Ubelaker (1994). Other bioarchaeological methods include the recommendations for age and sex estimation made by the Workshop of European Anthropologists (Ferembach *et al.* 1980). Stature calculation mainly employs regression equations developed by Trotter and Gleser (1952, 1977), although increasing awareness of problems with measurements of the tibia made by the original researchers has been voiced (Jantz 1992; Jantz *et al.* 1994). Alternatively, measurements of the femur alone can be used, but for this skeletal element a higher standard deviation has to be accepted. Other regression equations have been published by Robins and Shute (1986). Since these were developed to calculate stature for predynastic Egyptian populations, they may be more appropriate to determine the living stature of Sudanese individuals than the more widely used Trotter and Gleser formulae, developed on Americans of African origin.

CONCLUSION

Sudan is one of the countries with probably the largest number of archaeologically derived human remains. Over its long history of scientific research, starting with descriptive studies and the overlying question of racial affinities to determine population movements, more recent work has developed a much wider range of research agenda, including palaeopathological studies and morphological aspects, and much of this work is now tied in with archaeological studies to form a more holistic discipline. While this research is almost exclusively done by bioarchaeologists from foreign countries, it should now be a priority to train Sudanese researchers to enable them to perform bioarchaeological studies in Sudan, to ensure that the vast amount of human remains will be analysed. The ever increasing number of construction projects threatens more and more archaeological sites in this quickly developing country, and as a consequence more human skeletal remains will be excavated. Only their detailed study will answer many of the yet unresolved archaeological questions.

USEFUL CONTACTS

There are currently no anthropological societies in Sudan, but information and contact details of the National Corporation for Antiquities and Museums (NCAM) and a list of all current excavations in Sudan can be found through the following link to the NCAM website: www.agenziaitalianaeg.com/ncam/index.htm/

In Britain, the Sudan Archaeological Research Society (SARS) is dedicated to the study of Sudanese archaeology. Information on their activities, publications and conferences can be accessed online at www.sudarchrs.org.uk/

BIBLIOGRAPHY

Abd el-Rahman, M.F. (2006a) 'El-Frai: a new Meroitic habitation site in ed-Damer', *Sudan & Nubia*, 10: 102–3.
——(2006b) 'Gheresli: a post-Meroitic activity centre in the Blue Nile region', *Sudan & Nubia*, 10: 104–9.
Adams, W.Y. (1977) *Nubia: Corridor to Africa*, London: Allen Lane.
——(1998) 'The misappropriation of Nubia', *Sudan Studies*, 21: 1–9.
Addison, F. (1949) *Jebel Moya*, Oxford: Oxford University Press.
Alvrus, A. (1997) 'Trauma to the teeth and jaws: three Nubian examples', *Journal of Paleopathology*, 9: 5–14.
——(1999) 'Fracture patterns among the Nubians of Semna South, Sudanese Nubia', *International Journal of Osteoarchaeology*, 9: 417–29.

Anderson, J.E. (1968) 'Late Paleolithic skeletal remains from Nubia', in F. Wendorf (ed.) *The Prehistory of Nubia, Vol. 2*, Dallas: Fort Burgwin Research Center.

Arkell, A.J. (1949) *Early Khartoum*, London: Oxford University Press.

Armelagos, G.J. (1968) 'Paleopathology of three archaeological populations from Sudanese Nubia', unpublished PhD thesis, University of Colorado.

——(1969) 'Disease in ancient Nubia', *Science*, 163: 255–59.

Armelagos, G.J., Mielke, J., Owen, K.O., *et al.* (1972) 'Bone growth and development in prehistoric populations from Sudanese Nubia', *Journal of Human Evolution*, 1: 89–119.

Batrawi, A.M. (1935) *Report on the Human Remains, Mission Archaeologique de Nubie*, Cairo: Government Press.

——(1946) 'The racial history of Egypt and Nubia: part II', *Journal of the Royal Anthropological Institute*, 75: 131–56.

Berry, A.C. and Berry, R.J. (1967) 'Epigenetic variation in the human cranium', *Journal of Anatomy* 101: 361–379.

Buikstra, J.E. and Ubelaker, D. (eds) (1994) *Standards for Data Collection from Human Skeletal Remains*, Fayetteville, AR: Arkansas Archeological Survey Research Series No. 44.

Burrell, L.L., Maas, M.C. and Van Gerven, D.P. (1986) 'Pattern of long bone fractures in two Nubian populations', *Human Evolution*, 1: 495–506.

Buzon, M.R. and Judd, M.A. (2008) 'Investigating health at Kerma: sacrificial versus non-sacrificial burials', *American Journal of Physical Anthropology*, 136: 93–99.

Carlson, D.S. (1976) 'Temporal variation in prehistoric Nubian crania', *American Journal of Physical Anthropology*, 45: 467–84.

Carlson, D.S. and Armelagos, G.J. (1971) 'Problems in racial geography', *Annals of Geography*, 61: 630–32.

Carlson, D.S., Armelagos, G.J. and Van Gerven, D.P. (1974) 'Factors influencing the etiology of cribra orbitalia in prehistoric Nubia', *Journal of Human Evolution*, 3: 405–10.

Carlson, D.S. and Van Gerven, D.P. (1977) 'Masticatory function and post-Pleistocene evolution in Nubia', *American Journal of Physical Anthropology*, 46: 495–506.

Collett, M. (1933) 'A study of twelfth and thirteenth dynasty skulls from Kerma (Nubia)', *Biometrika*, 25: 254–84.

Derry, D.E. (1949) 'Report on the human remains', in A.J. Arkell (ed.) *Early Khartoum*, London: Oxford University Press.

Edwards, D.N. (2004) *The Nubian Past*, London: Routledge.

——(2007) 'The archaeology of Sudan and Nubia', *Annual Review of Anthropology*, 36: 211–28.

Elliot Smith, G. and Wood Jones, F. (1910) *The Archaeological Survey of Nubia. Report for 1907–1908. Vol. II: Report on the Human Remains*, Cairo: National Printing Department.

Emery, W.B. and Kirwan, L. (1935) *The Excavations and Survey Between Wadi es-Sebua and Andinan*, Cairo: Government Press.

Fattovich, R. (1995) 'The Gash Group. A complex society in the lowlands to the East of the Nile', *Actes de la VIIIe Conférence Internationale des Etudes Nubiennes, vol. I, Cahiers de Recherches de l'Institut de Papyrologie et d'Egyptologie de Lille*, 17: 191–200.

Ferembach, D., Schwidetzky, L. and Stloukal, M. (1980) 'Recommendations for age and sex diagnoses of skeletons', *Journal of Human Evolution*, 9: 517–49.

Filer, J.M. (1992) 'Head injuries in ancient Egypt and Nubia: a comparison of skulls from Giza and Kerma', *Journal of Egyptian Archaeology*, 78: 281–85.

Greene, D.L. (1966) 'Dentition and biological relationship of some Meroitic, X-Group and Christian populations from Wadi Halfa, Sudan', *Kush*, 14: 284–88.

——(1972) 'Dental anthropology of early Egypt and Nubia', *Journal of Human Evolution*, 1: 315–24.

Greene, D.L. and Armelagos, G.J. (1972) *Mesolithic Populations from Wadi Halfa*, Department of Anthropology Research Reports no. 1, Amherst: University of Massachusetts.

Greene, D.L., Ewing, G.H. and Armelagos, G.J. (1967) 'Dentition of a Mesolithic population from Wadi Halfa, Sudan', *American Journal of Physical Anthropology*, 27: 41–55.

Irish, J.D. (2008) 'Dental morphometrics analyses of the Neolithic human skeletal sample from R12: characterization and contrasts', in S. Salvatori and D. Usai (eds) *A Neolithic Cemetery in the Northern Dongola Reach: Excavations at Site R12*, Sudan Archaeological Research Society Publications no. 16, British Archaeological Reports International Series 1814, Oxford: Archaeopress.

Irish, J.D. and Konigsberg, L. (2007) 'The ancient inhabitants of Jebel Moya redux: measures of population affinity based on dental morphology', *International Journal of Osteoarchaeology*, 17: 138–56.

Jakob, T. (2007) 'Value and future potential of human skeletal remains excavated at the Fourth Cataract', *Sudan & Nubia*, 11: 43–47.

Jantz, R.L. (1992) 'Modification of Trotter and Gleser female stature estimation formulae', *Journal of Forensic Sciences*, 28: 1094–104.

Jantz, R.L., Hunt, D.R. and Meadows, L. (1994) 'Maximum length of the tibia: how did Trotter measure it?', *American Journal of Physical Anthropology*, 93: 525–28.

Jesse, F. and Keding, B. (2002) 'Death in the desert – burials in the Wadi Howar region (eastern Sudan)', in Jennerstrasse 8 (ed.), *Tides of the Desert – Gezeiten der Wüste*, Cologne: Heinrich-Barth-Institut.

Judd, M.A. (2001) 'The human remains', in D.A. Welsby (ed.) *Life at the Desert Edge. Seven Thousand Years of Settlement in the Northern Dongola Reach, Sudan*, Sudan Archaeological Research Society Publication no. 7, British Archaeological Reports, International Series 980 (II), Oxford: Archaeopress.

——(2002) 'Ancient injury recidivism: an example from the Kerma period of ancient Nubia', *International Journal of Osteoarchaeology*, 12: 89–106.

——(2004) 'Trauma in the city of Kerma: ancient versus modern injury patterns', *International Journal of Osteoarchaeology*, 14: 34–51.

——(2008) 'The human skeletal analysis', in S. Salvatori and D. Usai (eds) *A Neolithic cemetery in the Northern Dongola Reach: excavations at Site R12*, Sudan Archaeological Research Society Publications No 16, British Archaeological Reports International Series 1814, Oxford: Archaeopress.

Kilgore, L., Jurmain, R.D. and Van Gerven, D.P. (1997) 'Palaeoepidemiological patterns of trauma in a medieval Nubian skeletal population', *International Journal of Osteoarchaeology*, 7: 103–14.

Manzo, A. (2004) 'Late antique evidences in SE Sudan', *Sudan & Nubia*, 9: 75–83.

McDermott, F., Stringer, C., Grün, R., *et al.* (1996) 'New Late-Pleistocene uranium–thorium and ESR dates for the Singa hominid (Sudan)', *Journal of Human Evolution*, 31: 507–16.

Morton, S.G. (1844) *Crania Aegyptiaca: Or, Observations on Egyptian Ethnography, Derived from Anatomy, History, and the Monuments*, Philadelphia: J. Penington.

Mukherjee, R., Rao, C.R. and Trevor, J.C. (1955) *The Ancient Inhabitants of Jebel Moya (Sudan)*, Occasional Publications of the Cambridge University Museum of Archaeology and Ethnology III, Cambridge: Cambridge University Press.

Murail, P., Maureille, B., Peresinotto, D., *et al.* (2004) 'An infant cemetery of the Classic Kerma period (1750–1500 BC, Island of Saï, Sudan)', *Antiquity*, 78: 267–77.

Nielsen, O.V. (1970) *Human Remains. Metrical and Non-metrical Anatomical Variations*, The Scandinavian Joint Expedition to Sudanese Nubia vol. 9, Stockholm: Scandinavian University Books.

OPA 1999. Ordinance for the Protection of Antiquities. Available online at www.wipo.int/tk/en//laws/pdf/sudan_antiquities.pdf (accessed 4 February 2009).

Reinold, J. (2000) *Archéologie au Soudan: les civilisations de Nubie*, Paris: Éditions Errance.

——(2007) *La nécropole néolithique d'el-Kadada au Soudan central – Volume 1: les cimetières A et B (NE-36-O/3-V-2 et NE-36-O/3-V-3) du kôm principal*, Paris: Éditions Recherche sur les Civilisations.

Reisner, G.A. (1910) *The Archaeological Survey of Nubia. The Report for 1907–1908*, Cairo: National Printing Department.

——(1923) *Excavations at Kerma I-III/IV-V*, Harvard African Studies V, Cambridge, MA: Peabody Museum of Harvard University.

Rose, J.C. (1996) *Bioarchaeology of Ancient Egypt and Nubia: A Bibliography*, British Museum Occasional Paper no. 112, London: British Museum.

Robins, G. and Shute, C.C.D. (1986) 'Predynastic Egyptian stature and physical proportions', *Human Evolution*, 1: 313–24.

Salvatori, S. and Usai, D. (2008) *A Neolithic Cemetery in the Northern Dongola Reach: Excavations at Site R12*, Sudan Archaeological Research Society Publications no. 16, British Archaeological Reports International Series 1814, Oxford: Archaeopress.

Simon, C. (1989) 'Les populations Kerma – evolution interne et relations historiques dans le contexte égypto-nubien', *Archéologie du Nil Moyen*, 3: 139–47.

Simon, C., Menk, R. and Kramar, C. (2002) 'The human remains from Wadi Shaw (Sudan) – a study of physical anthropology and palaeopathology', in Jennerstrasse 8 (ed.) *Tides of the Desert – Gezeiten der Wüste*, 257–76. Cologne: Heinrich-Barth-Institut.

Spoor, F., Stringer, C.B. and Zonneveld, F. (1998) 'Rare temporal bone pathology of the Singa calvaria from Sudan', *American Journal of Physical Anthropology*, 107: 41–50.

Sudan Tribune (2009) 'Sudanese workers uncover skeletons from British embassy', *Sudan Tribune*, 14 January 2009. Available online at: www.sudantribune.com/spip.php?article29883 (accessed 20 February 2009).

Strouhal, E. (1971) 'Evidence for the early penetration of Negroes into prehistoric Egypt', *Journal of African History*, 12: 1–9.

——(1981) 'Current state of anthropological studies on ancient Egypt and Nubia', *Bulletins et Mémoires de la Société d'Anthropologie de Paris*, 8: 231–49.

Swedlund, A.C. and Armelagos, G.J. (1969) 'Une recherche in paleo-demographie: la Nubia Soudanaise', *Annales: Economies, Societies, Civilizations*, 24: 1287–98.

Taha el-Ata, H. and Mohamed Adam, H. (2007) 'Report on the human skeletal material from Akad', *Sudan & Nubia*, 11: 107–11.

Thompson, A.H., Chaix, L. and Richards, M.P. (2008) 'Stable isotopes and diet at ancient Kerma, upper Nubia (Sudan)', *Journal of Archaeological Science*, 35: 376–87.

Török, L. (1997) *The Kingdom of Kush: Handbook of the Nabatan-Meroitic Civilization*, Leiden: Brill.

Trotter, M., and Gleser, G.C. (1952) 'Estimation of stature from long bones of American Whites and Negroes', *American Journal of Physical Anthropology*, 10: 463–514.

——(1977) 'Corrigenda to "Estimation of stature from long limb bones of American Whites and Negroes" Am. J. Phys. Anthrop. (1952)', *American Journal of Physical Anthropology*, 47: 355–56.

UNESCO (2000). 'Nubia bibliography up to 2000: List of archaeological missions in Nubia'. Available online at: http://unesdoc.unesco.org/images/0015/001501/150176E.pdf (accessed 10 April 2009).

Usai, D. and Salvatori, S. (2005) 'The IsIAO Archaeological Project in the El Salha area (Omdurman South, Sudan): results and perspectives', *Africa* (Roma), 60: 474–93.

Wapler, U., Crubézy, E. and Schultz, M. (2004) 'Is cribra orbitalia synonymous with anemia? Analysis and interpretation of cranial pathology in Sudan', *American Journal of Physical Anthropology*, 123: 333–39.

Welsby, D.A. (1996) *The Kingdom of Kush*, London: British Museum Press.

——(2002) *The Medieval Kingdoms of Nubia*, London: British Museum Press.

Wood Jones, F. (1910) 'Broken bones and dislocations', in G. Elliot Smith and F. Wood Jones (eds) *The Archaeological Survey of Nubia. Report for 1907–1908. Vol. II: Report on the Human Remains*, Cairo: National Printing Department.

Canada

Jerome S. Cybulski

INTRODUCTION: A BRIEF HISTORY AND CURRENT STATE OF PHYSICAL ANTHROPOLOGY IN CANADA

Physical anthropology in Canada has a history that dates back to the middle of the 19th century (Melbye and Meiklejohn 1992; Popham 1950). The modern era in human osteology, with its emphasis on population variability in quantitative and discrete morphological traits, biological distance analysis and palaeopathology, began in the 1960s (Meiklejohn 1997; Melbye 1982). That decade also saw an incipient awareness of ethical issues surrounding the excavation and study of human remains, an awareness which became commonplace in the 1970s and has generally directed osteological studies on into the 21st century. While various forms of legislation have been enacted within Canada, it is the guiding principles of physical anthropology and archaeology themselves that have enabled progress in these disciplines.

The vast majority of archaeological sites, a few of which may be as old as 10,000 to 15,000 years, are in the presently or formerly occupied lands of indigenous peoples known today as First Nations (equivalent to Native Americans or American Indians in the USA), Inuit and Inuinnaq (equivalent to Eskimo in Alaska), and Métis (individuals of mixed First Nations and European parentage). Other sites are European or Euro-Canadian in origin and include pioneer cemeteries, towns and villages, early European settlements, and military fortifications.

Osteological site reports were the foundation of human skeletal studies in the 1960s and are much valued today for their methodological orientation and comparative data (see, e.g., Anderson 1964, 1968; Ossenberg 1969). Works of that genre have continued in Canadian skeletal studies (see, e.g., Cybulski 1992; Pfeiffer *et al.* 1989; Saunders and Lazenby 1991; Williamson and Pfeiffer 2003), but there is also an emphasis on methodology and problem-oriented research (see, e.g., Katzenberg *et al.* 1995; Saunders *et al.* 1995), topical issues (Hartney 1981; Skinner 1994; Walker 1978) and regional syntheses (Cybulski 2006; Keenleyside 2006).

Education and training

In addition to the University of Calgary in Alberta (M.A. Katzenberg) and McMaster University in Hamilton, Ontario (the late S.R. Saunders), outstanding doctoral programmes in physical anthropology (skeletal biology or bioarchaeology) are available at Simon Fraser University (Vancouver), the University of Alberta (Edmonton), the University of Manitoba (Winnipeg), the University of Western Ontario (London), the University of Toronto (Ontario), and the Université de Montréal (Québec). Additionally, the University of Victoria (British Columbia), Trent University (Peterborough, Ontario), and Memorial University of Newfoundland (St. John's) offer Master's degrees.

National human skeletal collections are housed in the Canadian Museum of Civilization (Gatineau, Québec) and they are generally available for study by qualified researchers and graduate students.

ARCHAEOLOGICAL HUMAN REMAINS AND LEGISLATION

Archaeological legislation

Canada is a huge country, the second largest in the world after Russia, with a land mass of close to ten million sq. km. It extends east to west from the Atlantic to the Pacific for a distance of about 9000 km, and covers six time zones. The Arctic Ocean forms a third coastline, with the tip of Ellesmere Island, Canada's northernmost land mass, situated within 800 km of the North Pole (Natural Resources Canada 2009).

Given this immense geography, most of which is habitable, one might wonder just how archaeological sites and the study of human skeletal remains could be managed. There is, in fact, no federal (i.e. Government of Canada) legislation that deals specifically with archaeology and the study of human remains. Rather, archaeology is organized according to jurisdictional properties governed by Canada's ten provinces and three territories. Additionally, Parks Canada, a Government of Canada agency responsible for National Parks, National Park Reserves, National Marine Conservation Areas, National Landmarks and National Historic Sites, has developed policies and guidelines for archaeology and the discovery of human remains in those areas contingent upon provincial and territorial legislation.

Canada's ten provinces form the southern half of the country, while the territories (Nunavut, Northwest Territories and Yukon) comprise the northern portion. Each of the 13 jurisdictions has rules, regulations and laws for managing archaeological sites, and guiding principles and/or laws regarding human remains. They are essentially similar but specific pieces of legislation, and their names may vary. Where human burials and human remains are concerned, more than one legislative act and ministry (i.e. government department) may be responsible. For example, at least three pieces of legislation may be relevant for the excavation and study of human remains in the province of Ontario: the Coroner's Act, the Cemeteries Act (Revised) and the Ontario Heritage Act (Ontario Ministry of Culture 2009). Likewise, multiple acts with similar titles may potentially operate in other provinces and the territories (e.g. British Columbia Ministry of Tourism, Culture and the Arts 2009; Inuit Heritage Trust 2009; Prince of Wales Northern Heritage Centre 2009). In all cases, an archaeologist or bioarchaeologist wishing to excavate a site either as an industrial consultant or a research academic cannot do so without first obtaining a licence or permit. In order to obtain such permits, researchers must consult with individuals or groups who are likely to be directly affected by the archaeology, particularly in cases involving human burials.

HUMAN REMAINS AND LEGISLATION

Guiding principles

NAGPRA, the Native American Graves Protection and Repatriation Act, passed into law by the United States Congress in 1990, has had a significant impact on the excavation, study and curatorial custody of archaeological human remains in the United States of America. Despite a similar indigenous prevalence of archaeological sites in Canada and concern for ancient human burials, the country has not opted for comparable legislation.

If anything, Canada has an equivalent guiding principal in the form of a 1992 Task Force Report on Museums and First Peoples which resulted from workshops held in Ottawa, Canada's capital, in 1991, sponsored and hosted by the Canadian Museums Association and the Assembly of First Nations (Canadian Museums Association 1992). Significantly and importantly, the report encourages a cooperative rather than adversarial approach to the business of anthropology, archaeology, biological anthropology (bioarchaeology) and repatriation in Canada *vis-à-vis* indigenous peoples. To quote the online edition of the Canadian Encyclopedia, the Task Force on Museums and First Peoples has:

> ... provided great impetus to collaborations between Aboriginal communities and heritage institutions. The task force established an ethical framework and guidelines for the use of Aboriginal objects and representation of Aboriginal culture that have been very influential within Canada and abroad.
>
> *Canadian Encyclopedia 2009*

Twelve years previous to the workshops, however, the Canadian Association for Physical Anthropology (CAPA), now in its 37th year, advocated understanding and cooperation on the part of archaeologists and physical anthropologists in published guidelines on the excavation, treatment, analysis and disposition of human skeletal remains from archaeological sites in Canada (Cybulski *et al.* 1979).

The CAPA statement was based on established experience. Some investigators were exposed to cooperative and collaborative ventures with First Nations early in their graduate and professional careers. Dr Shelley Saunders, for example, worked with the Ojibway Beausoleil Band on Christian Island in Georgian Bay, Ontario, late in the 1960s and early 1970s (Saunders *et al.* 1974). Beginning in 1971, the present author became involved with bioarchaeology projects in British Columbia, where he has worked over the years with at least 12 different First Nations communities (see, e.g. Cybulski 1978, 1992). Four major field projects have enabled community members to observe at first hand both excavation and analytical procedures, effectively un-shrouding the presumptive mystery of archaeological and osteological work involving ancient human burials. While projects regularly involved community members as field crew personnel, 2007 identified community members as full collaborators in two studies (Cybulski *et al.* 2007; Malhi *et al.* 2007).

Others, as well, have carried out cooperative, community based, First Nations projects involving bioarchaeology in Canada. In 1999, Kevin Brownlee and Leigh Syms published their *Kayasochi Kikawenow, Our Mother from Long Ago*, excavated from an eroding lakeshore in northern Manitoba and studied with the participation of the local Cree First Nations community (Brownlee and Syms 1999). The following year saw publication by Owen Beattie and co-workers of the first research results on Canada's very own 'iceman', *Kwäday Dän Ts'inchii*, a successful analytical and reburial collaboration among the British Columbia Archaeology Branch, the Royal British Columbia Museum, the University of British Columbia and the Champagne and Aishihik First Nation of Yukon Territory (Beattie *et al.* 2000). In 2003, Susan Pfeiffer and Ron Williamson published their *Bones of the Ancestors: The Archaeology and Osteobiography of the Moatfield Ossuary*, a project undertaken in collaboration with the Six Nations Council of the Grand River in the province of Ontario (Williamson and Pfeiffer 2003).

All museums in Canada have policies concerning human remains. Our national institution, the Canadian Museum of Civilization in Gatineau, Quebec, holds human skeletal collections that may be researched. Its largest holdings, those pertaining to the Arctic, may be studied by visiting researchers in compliance with an agreement the museum has with the Inuit Heritage Trust Incorporated, an Inuit organization that deals specifically with issues of archaeology, ethnographic objects and archives in Nunavut Territory. In effect, research proposals are evaluated by both the museum and the Trust before study is permitted.

METHODS OF ANTHROPOLOGICAL ANALYSIS

The study of archaeological human skeletal remains in Canada follows method and theory currently favoured in North America and abroad. Newly discovered remains as well as extant collections are generally evaluated and documented in the context of procedures outlined in the textbooks of White (2000) and Katzenberg and Saunders (2008). The latter provides an especially comprehensive national perspective on contemporary skeletal studies, since the editors were trained and have been long based as faculty in Canadian universities.

CONCLUSION

Physical anthropology may be said to be in a new age in the study of ancient human burials and skeletal remains, certainly in Canada and hopefully in the rest of the world, that sees the continuation of studies 'in a respectful and dignified manner'. We are certainly in a new and wondrous age of analysis as well – that of ancient DNA research which can tell us so much more about the origin and evolution of *Homo sapiens* and offspring populations, ancestral-descendant relationships, and the origins and evolution of disease. The experience in Canada is that there is a genuine public interest in what bioarchaeologists do and a genuine interest in the heritage of its multicultural landscape.

USEFUL CONTACTS

More information is available through the Canadian Association for Physical Anthropology (website: www.capa-acap.info/) and the Canadian Archaeological Association (website: www.canadianarchaeology.com/).

BIBLIOGRAPHY

Anderson, J. E. (1964) 'The people of Fairty: an osteological analysis of an Iroquois ossuary', *National Museum of Canada Bulletin*, 193: 28–129.

——(1968) *The Serpent Mounds Site Physical Anthropology*, Occasional Paper 11, Art and Archaeology, Toronto: Royal Ontario Museum.

Beattie, O.B., Apland, B., Blake, E.W., *et al.* (2000) The Kwäday Dän Ts'ìnchí discovery from a glacier in British Columbia, *Canadian Journal of Archaeology*, 24: 129–47.

British Columbia Ministry of Tourism, Culture and the Arts (2009) *Archaeology*, Victoria: Government of British Columbia. Online. Available online at www.tca.gov.bc.ca/archaeology/ (accessed 10 March 2010).

Brownlee, K. and Syms, E.L. (1999) *Kayasochi Kikawenow Our Mother From Long Ago: An Early Cree Woman and Her Personal Belongings from Nagami Bay, Southern Indian Lake*, Winnipeg: Manitoba Museum of Man and Nature.

Canadian Encyclopedia (2009) *Art Galleries and Museums, Current Trends*. Available online at www.thecana dianencyclopedia.com/index.cfm?PgNm=TCE& Params = A1SEC816280 (accessed 30 August 2009).

Canadian Museums Association (1992) *Turning the Page: Forging New Partnerships between Museums and First Peoples*, A Task Force Report jointly sponsored by the Assembly of First Nations and the Canadian Museums Association, Ottawa.

Cybulski, J.S. (1978) *An Earlier Population of Hesquiat Harbour, British Columbia; A Contribution to Nootkan Osteology and Physical Anthropology*. Cultural Recovery Papers 1, Contribution No. 1 of the Hesquiat Cultural Committee, Victoria: Royal British Columbia Museum.

——(1992) *A Greenville Burial Ground: Human Remains and Mortuary Elements in British Columbia Coast Prehistory*, Archaeological Survey of Canada Mercury Series Paper 146, Gatineau: Canadian Museum of Civilization.

——(2006) 'Skeletal biology: Northwest Coast and Plateau', in D.H. Ubelaker (ed.) *Handbook of North American Indians, Vol. 3., Environment, Origins, and Population*, Washington: Smithsonian Institution.

Cybulski, J.S., McMillan, A.D., Malhi, R.S., *et al.* (2007) 'The Big Bar Lake Burial: Middle Period human temains from the Canadian Plateau', *Canadian Journal of Archaeology*, 31: 55–79.

Cybulski, J.S., Ossenberg, N.S. and Wade, W.D. (1979) 'Statement on the excavation, treatment, analysis and disposition of human skeletal remains from archaeological sites in Canada', *Canadian Review of Physical Anthropology*, 1: 32–36.

Hartney, P.C. (1981) 'Tuberculous lesions in a prehistoric population sample from southern Ontario', in J.E. Buikstra (ed.) *Prehistoric Tuberculosis in the Americas*, Evanston, IL: Northwestern University Archeological Program.

Inuit Heritage Trust (2009) *Legislation*. Available online at www.ihti.ca/english/legislation.html (accessed 10 March 2010).

Katzenberg, M.A. and Saunders, S.R. (2008) *Biological Anthropology of the Human Skeleton*, 2nd edn, Hoboken: Wiley-Liss.

Katzenberg, M.A., Schwarcz, H.P., Knyf, M., *et al.* (1995) 'Stable isotope evidence for maize horticulture and paleodiet in southern Ontario, Canada', *American Antiquity*, 60: 335–50.

Keenleyside, A. (2006) 'Skeletal biology: Arctic and Subarctic', in D.H. Ubelaker (ed.) *Handbook of North American Indians, Vol. 3: Environment, Origins, and Population*, Washington, DC: Smithsonian Institution.

Malhi, R.S., Kemp, B.M., Eshleman, J., *et al.* (2007) 'Mitochondrial Haplogroup M discovered in prehistoric North Americans', *Journal of Archaeological Science*, 34: 642–48.

Meiklejohn, C. (1997) 'Canada', in F. Spencer (ed.) *History of Physical Anthropology, Volume 1*, New York: Garland Publishing.

Melbye, F.J. (1982) 'Advances in the contribution of physical anthropology to archaeology in Canada: the past decade', *Canadian Journal of Archaeology*, 6: 55–64.

Melbye, F.J. and Meiklejohn, C. (1992) 'A history of physical anthropology and the development of evolutionary thought in Canada', *Human Evolution*, 7: 49–55.

Natural Resources Canada (2009) *The Atlas of Canada; FAQs about Canada*. Available online at http://atlas. nrcan.gc.ca/site/english/learningresources/facts/faq.html (accessed 10 March 2010).

Ontario Ministry of Culture (2009) *Engaging Aboriginal communities in archaeology. A draft technical bulletin for consultant archaeologists in Ontario*. Available online at www.culture.gov.on.ca/english/heritage/archaeology/ Aboriginal Engagement Bulletin - FINAL.pdf (accessed 10 March 2010).

Ossenberg, N.S. (1969) *Osteology of the Miller Site*, Occasional Paper 18, Art and Archaeology, Toronto: Royal Ontario Museum.

Pfeiffer, S.(1984) 'Paleopathology in an Iroquoian ossuary, with special reference to tuberculosis', *American Journal of Physical Anthropology*, 65: 181–89.

Pfeiffer, S., Dudar, C. and Austin, S. (1989) 'Prospect Hill: skeletal remains from a 19th-Century Methodist cemetery, Newmarket, Ontario', *Northeast Historical Archaeology*, 18: 29–48.

Popham, R.E. (1950) 'A bibliography and historical review of physical anthropology in Canada: 1848–1949', *Revue Canadienne de Biologie*, 9: 175–98

Prince of Wales Northern Heritage Centre (2009) *Cultural Places Program – Archaeology*. Available online at http://pwnhc.learnnet.nt.ca/programs/archaeology.asp (accessed 10 March 2010).

Saunders, S.R., Herring, D.A. and Boyce, G. (1995) 'Can skeletal samples accurately represent the living population they come from? The St. Thomas Cemetery Site, Belleville, Ontario', in A.L. Grauer (ed.) *Bodies of Evidence: Reconstructing History Through Skeletal Analysis*, New York: Wiley-Liss.

Saunders, S.R., Knight, D. and Gates, M. (1974) 'Christian Island: a comparative analysis of osteological and archaeological evidence', *Canadian Archaeological Association Bulletin*, 6: 123–62.

Jerome S. Cybulski

Saunders, S.R. and Lazenby, R. (eds) (1991) *The Links That Bind: The Harvie Family Nineteenth Century Burying Ground*, Occasional Papers in Northeastern Archaeology No. 5, Dundas: Copetown Press.

Skinner, M.F. (1994) 'Osseous treponemal disease: limits on our understanding', in O. Dutour *et al.* (eds) *L'Origine de la Syphilis en Europe avant ou après 1493?* 191–201. Paris: Éditions Errance.

Walker, E.G. (1978) 'The paleopathology of certain skeletal remains from Saskatchewan', *Napao, A Saskatchewan Anthropology Journal*, 8: 30–47.

White, T. (2000) *Human Osteology*, 2nd edn, San Diego: Academic Press.

Williamson, R.F. and Pfeiffer, S. (2003) *Bones of the Ancestors: The Archaeology and Osteobiography of the Moatfield Ossuary*, Mercury Series Archaeology Paper 163, Gatineau: Canadian Museum of Civilization.

United States of America

Douglas H. Ubelaker

INTRODUCTION: A BRIEF HISTORY AND CURRENT STATE OF PHYSICAL ANTHROPOLOGY IN THE USA

In the USA, the histories of skeletal recovery and analysis are closely intertwined. Many scholars (Buikstra 2006; Milner 2004) trace the roots of professional excavation of human remains to Thomas Jefferson (1743–1826) who served as the third president of the United States, between 1801 and 1809. Curious about the presence of mounds spotting the American terrain, Jefferson and others of that era launched excavations seeking information. Jefferson's efforts at mound archaeology yielded information on the secondary nature of the human bones found within and the presence of layers suggesting that deposits within the mounds were made at different time intervals (Jefferson 1954). His work documented that interpretations involving human remains are enhanced with contextual information only gleaned through careful excavation.

As archaeological efforts intensified in the ensuing decades, collections of human remains from known archaeological contexts began to grow. Key contributors during this period were Joseph Jones (1833–96), Washington Mathews (1843–1905) and Samuel Morton (1799–1851). Joseph Jones received his medical degree from the University of Pennsylvania in 1856 and served as the first health officer of Nashville, Tennessee, as well as a Confederate medical officer during the American Civil War. While in Nashville, he excavated various archaeological structures in the vicinity and published his analysis of the human remains, which included assessment of the evidence for syphilis (Jones 1876).

Born in Ireland, Washington Mathews (1843–1905) emigrated to the United States, received his medical degree in 1864 and then worked as a US Army surgeon. While on duty in the western United States, he developed a strong interest in American Indian issues, especially those involving the Hidatsa and Navajo. Through his medical training, he sustained interest in skeletal anatomy and disease. His approach to analysis incorporated archaeological information and assessment (Matthews *et al.* 1893).

Professor of anatomy at the University of Pennsylvania, Morton assembled an important comparative collection of human skulls from archaeological contexts. His major work focusing on this collection (Morton 1839) contributed to his assessment of worldwide population variation and classification.

Earnest A. Hooton (1887–1954) and Aleš Hrdlička (1869–1943) both represent key figures in the early history of physical anthropology (Howells 2006). Harvard University Professor Hooton published on American Indian samples and trained many students, who themselves became university professors and advanced the field considerably. As the first curator of physical anthropology at the Smithsonian Institution, Hrdlička conducted excavations but also made major methodological advances to put analysis on a sounder basis. Hrdlička also founded the *American Journal of Physical Anthropology* in 1918 and the American Association of Physical Anthropologists, which first convened in 1930 (Ubelaker 1999a). From the early work of these pioneers and others, the modern field of physical anthropology involving the excavation and analysis of human remains has evolved. As practised in the United States, bioarchaeology integrates information gleaned from both excavation and analysis to address key issues in anthropology (Buikstra and Beck 2006; Larsen 2001). Training of anthropologists involved in this research primarily takes place in university departments of anthropology where education focuses broadly on all areas of anthropology, including archaeology and social anthropology.

ARCHAEOLOGICAL HUMAN REMAINS AND LEGISLATION

State law and policy

Legislation focusing on the recovery and subsequent treatment of human remains is at the state level and is highly variable. Most states have long-standing laws protecting cemeteries and the deceased, aimed primarily to prevent illicit grave-robbing. More recently, many states have passed laws attempting to address specific problems related to excavations yielding human remains, especially those thought likely to involve American Indians.

In 1989, Ubelaker and Grant reported on their survey of state preservation officers in all 50 states in regards to laws relating to reburial or unmarked graves. State preservation officers are state employees who have responsibilities to maintain oversight of archaeological resources within the state. Eighteen state officers reported that such laws exist in their state and many of them addressed issues of disposition of remains following excavation. States with such laws include California, Delaware, Florida, Idaho, Iowa, Maine, Massachusetts, Minnesota, Mississippi, Missouri, Nebraska, New Hampshire, North Carolina, Oklahoma, Oregon, Tennessee, Washington and Wisconsin. States lacking reburial or unmarked grave laws deal with situations on a case by case basis in reference to existing broader laws and policy.

Although these laws vary considerably, in general they lay out procedures to follow when excavation or other disturbance is planned. Most laws require that excavation activities cease when human remains are found until proper authorities are contacted and the issues are resolved. These authorities are usually local law enforcement officers and/or the designated coroner or medical examiner. They must then determine the relative antiquity of the remains and, if possible, whether they are of American Indian origin or are affiliated with any other ethnic group. If the remains are determined to be of sufficient antiquity (50 years in Minnesota; 150 years in Iowa) then the State Archeologist must determine if they are likely to be American Indian. Since coroners and medical examiners are usually not fully trained to assess the antiquity of remains, they frequently consult anthropologists, especially forensic anthropologists.

If a determination is made that the remains appear to be of American Indian origin, although not of forensic interest, many laws establish advisory boards to assist authorities in contacting the proper descendents. These advisory boards also assist in determining what scientific analysis should be allowed and what the ultimate disposition of the remains will be. In at least one state (Wisconsin), the advisory board also has the responsibility to monitor known burial sites and to decide if permits should be issued allowing excavation. State laws vary considerably in the extent to which they allow potential excavation. It is important also to note that nearly all of these state laws address issues of excavation and treatment of remains after discovery and do not relate generally to remains already curated in museums and similar repositories. If a research oriented excavation is planned, the relevant state authorities should be contacted for necessary permissions. Identification of the contact person or office can itself be a research project, since these vary considerably among states.

State law also varies considerably in regard to allowing scientific study after excavation and the amount of time to do so. While five years are allowed for study in South Dakota, no specific time period is allowed in California where, if remains are thought by the coroner to be of American Indian origin, they are dispatched immediately to the Native American Heritage Commission for such a determination. Obviously, such arrangements beg the question 'if analysis is not allowed, on what basis was the determination made that the remains are of American Indian origin?'.

State laws also vary considerably in definitions of interested parties once determinations of affinity have been made. These definitions range from federally recognized tribes to lists of individuals known to have an interest in such issues. In effect, such formal recognition of interested parties positions them to argue that they have legal standing if disputes emerge.

Considerable variability also occurs in regard to the ultimate disposition of remains and who is in charge of carrying out that disposition. In general, the laws do not dictate an ultimate disposition but rather define the process by which such determinations are made.

If a decision is made in favour of burial, states vary in who has responsibility to carry out the procedure. Examples of this variation include contemporary tribal leaders (Minnesota), the archaeologist who received the permit to excavate (Idaho), or the State Archeologist (Iowa).

Martin (2008) provides a useful summary and discussion of United States court cases relating to issues of removal and re-interment of remains. These legal proceedings make a clear distinction between issues of the grave and those involving the interred body, a distinction that becomes clouded as time and decomposition merge the decedent with the soil. Each case is decided on its own merits and unique circumstances in consideration of applicable state laws. Standing, the connection of the litigating parties to the decedent is a common issue in these cases. Other key issues include the known desires of the decedent, spouse, family and friends, interests of the public and the condition of the grave.

Penalties for violation of the state laws vary from misdemeanor to felony, to include financial penalty and incarceration. Veilleux (2008) summarizes the rationale and nature of judicial awards for violation. Despite the general legal view that no property rights are attached to a dead body, court awards have been granted on the basis of improper trespass to the burial lot, damage or loss of the tombstone or associated materials, or breach of contract in cases involving cemetery owners. Arguments are made that the responsible individual or individuals have caused mental suffering to interested parties. The extent of court rewards reflect the standing of the litigants, the extent of injury, and if the conduct was wilful and malicious or negligent.

Federal legislation

Although state laws relate to cemetery preservation and excavation issues, two federal laws focus specifically on human remains curated in repositories. Although treated separately in the legal arena, excavation and curation are closely intertwined. Without excavation museum collections of that type would not exist. Once excavation occurs, curation becomes an immediate concern.

In 1989, Congress passed the National Museum of the American Indian Act (P.L. 101–85). This new federal law called upon the Smithsonian Institution in Washington, DC, to conduct a thorough inventory of its collections to determine which could be related to existing federally recognized tribes. If such a linkage was discovered, the particular tribe could request transfer to their custody. As a result of this legislation, over 3000 sets of remains have been transferred from Smithsonian curation (Buikstra 2006).

The following year (1990), the federal law referred to as the Native American Graves Protection and Repatriation Act (NAGPRA) was passed. This legislation requires all federal agencies and institutions that receive federal money, other than the Smithsonian Institution, to undergo a similar process in relation to collections of human remains. With this legislation, repositories are required to determine the 'cultural affiliation' of remains relying on the preponderance of diverse evidence (Buikstra 2006).

While these laws have stimulated dialogue among institutions curating human remains and the American Indian community, and renewed research attention on those collections, interpretation and implementation have offered challenges. Whereas some collections have included known individuals or remains related to known tribal groups, many others include remains whose affiliation with contemporary groups has proven difficult to define.

In an attempt to glean information needed to assess affiliation and document collections prior to transfer, institutions have initiated substantial study of human remains in repositories. Such data collection has been facilitated by attempts to standardize protocols (Buikstra and Ubelaker 1994), which has the dual effect of ensuring that useful data have been collected prior to transfer and facilitating comparative studies.

METHODS OF ANTHROPOLOGICAL ANALYSIS

The quality of the recovery and analysis of human remains continues to be enhanced by innovative research and technological development. While emerging methodology is produced and shared globally, key developments play an important role in guiding applications in the United States. These new approaches are too vast and complex to be discussed in detail here, but certainly they include new technological approaches to recovery, molecular analysis of biological distance and sex, three dimensional morphometric shape analysis, microscopic methods of age determination, sophisticated differential diagnosis of disease and greater awareness of the impact of human variation in interpretation.

Approaches to recovery

Although recovery efforts remain reliant on traditional archaeological approaches, technological assessments involving remote sensing are increasingly employed, especially in location and assessment prior to excavation. Ground-penetrating radar, measures of soil resistivity and assessment of soil magnetic patterns are all utilized with increasing frequency in recovery efforts (Cheetham 2005; Clark 2000; Dupras *et al.*, 2006). While selection of techniques to employ is site- and problem-specific, the necessary technology increasingly is available and growing in effectiveness.

Recovery methodology follows standard archaeological procedures with the addition of techniques developed especially for human remains. These procedures are summarized in texts by Ubelaker (1999b) and Cox *et al.* (2008). Sprague (2005) provides useful discussion of the complex terminology employed in the recovery of human remains.

Practices vary considerably in the expertise involved in the recovery of human skeletal remains. Ideally, excavations involving human remains should include personnel trained not only in archaeological methodology but also in human osteology. Experience has documented that more information is gained if ideal procedures and documentation are employed during recovery. Osteological expertise should include knowledge of pathological conditions, taphonomical features and burial terminology. Although some individuals possess all these skills, usually a team approach is called for to maximize information capture.

If human remains are encountered during the course of a planned archaeological excavation, then probabilities are high that qualified personnel will be on hand to ensure proper excavation and interpretation. However, many human remains are discovered accidentally by the public or during the course of forensic investigation. Employment of skilled personnel in those circumstances is largely tied to arrangements made by the local law enforcement team and/or the medico-legal system. Responsibility for investigation of human remains varies considerably but largely falls upon the local coroner or medical examiner. These professionals must determine the line of consultation that follows, dictated by both policy and state law.

Analysis of human remains

Molecular approaches to population affinity issues show great potential and increasingly produce valuable and unique data. While contamination concerns and difficulties extracting molecular evidence from ancient degraded samples remain, growth in initiatives and quality control procedures provides reason for optimism. Focusing mostly on analyses of ancient mitochondrial DNA, workers in the United States have addressed key issues of origins, regional population history, sex, relationships of individuals within cemetery samples and social organization (Stone 2006).

Morphological approaches to assessments of population affinities and origins have been enhanced considerably with new technology that facilitates three-dimensional shape analysis (Rohlf and Slice 1990; Slice 2005). Geometric morphometrics captures more information than previously possible using traditional measurement techniques yet retains the landmark positions enabling comparison if needed. This relatively new morphometric approach using three-dimensional landmarks retrieves more anatomical information and thus offers more sophisticated analysis than previously possible (Ross *et al.* 1999, 2004). Such analysis is especially promising in elucidating issues of biological distance, population affinities and origins.

Accurate and realistic estimates of age-at-death are critical in examining patterns of palaeo-demography, palaeopathology and most other aspects of bioarchaeological analysis. Recent advances in the general area include recognition of the value of utilizing multiple age indicators (Baccino *et al.* 1999; Bedford *et al.* 1993), applications of transition analysis and Bayesian statistics (Boldsen *et al.* 2002; Milner *et al.* 2008) and assessment of population variation in the ageing process (Schaefer and Black 2005). Emerging techniques of assessment of cementum formation (Wedel 2007; Wittwer-Backofen *et al.* 2004) and amino acid racemization in teeth (Ohtani and Yamamoto 2005; Ohtani *et al.* 2005) appear promising if methodological and taphonomic issues can be overcome. Isotopic studies continue to reveal valuable dietary information (Katzenberg 1992) and have considerable potential to elucidate geographic origins of individuals and patterns of migration (Beard and Johnson 2000; Ehleringer *et al.* 2008).

Interpretations of palaeopathology are strengthened by more sophisticated models of differential diagnosis, enhanced histological approaches and new molecular techniques. Although facing the usual problems of contamination and the challenges of working with degraded samples, researchers working in the molecular arena offer the potential of discovering the residual DNA of the infecting organism, moving diagnosis beyond the traditional caveats of assessing lesions in bone and tooth (Donoghue *et al.* 1999; Ubelaker *et al.* 2003).

Recent research also has documented the value of regional databases in a broad range of interpretive studies. Methodological studies have demonstrated the importance of considering human variation in assessing age at death, sex, stature and other variables (Prince and Ubelaker 2002; Schaefer and Black 2005; Scheuer and Black 2000; Ubelaker and Parra 2008). Comparative studies also have documented key regional variation in ancient patterns of skeletal biology in North America (Ubelaker 2006) and in the western hemisphere (Ubelaker and Newson 2002; Verano and Ubelaker 1992).

CONCLUSION

In the United States, recovery efforts are enhanced by technological advances and increasingly sophisticated methodology, but they are shaped by concern for repatriation issues and more general state laws and policies. Although repatriation legislation has resulted in transfer of remains from repositories, data collection prior to transfer potentially enables broad comparative studies as well as focused problem-oriented research. The growing scholarly interest in forensic anthropology positively impacts the more general field of physical anthropology in introducing new technology and unique information from the case experience. Research focusing on the recovery and analysis of human remains in the United States continues to be strong and increasingly interdisciplinary.

USEFUL CONTACTS

American Association of Physical Anthropologists. Website: http://physanth.org/
Indian Burial and Sacred Grounds Watch. Website: www.ibsgwatch.imagedjinn.com/learn/lawsstate.htm/
Update of compilation of state repatriation, reburial and grave protection laws. Website: www.arrowheads.com/burials.htm/

BIBLIOGRAPHY

Baccino, E., Ubelaker, D.H., Hayek, L.C., *et al.* (1999) 'Evaluation of seven methods of estimating age at death from mature human skeletal remains', *Journal of Forensic Sciences*, 44: 931–36.
Beard, B.L. and Johnson, C.M. (2000) 'Strontium isotope composition of skeletal material can determine the birth place and geographic mobility of humans and animals', *Journal of Forensic Sciences*, 45: 1049–61.
Bedford, M.E., Russell, K.F., Lovejoy, C.O., *et al.* (1993) 'Test of the multifactorial aging method using skeletons with known ages-at-death from the Grant Collection', *American Journal of Physical Anthropology*, 91: 287–97.
Boldsen, J.L., Milner, G.R., Konigsberg, L.W., *et al.* (2002) 'Transition analysis: a new method for estimating age from skeletons', in R.D. Hoppa and J.W. Vaupel (eds) *Paleodemography: age distribution from skeletal samples*, Cambridge: Cambridge University Press.
Buikstra, J. (2006) 'History of research in skeletal biology', in D.H. Ubelaker (ed.) *Handbook of North American Indians: Environment, Origins, and Population*, Volume 3, Washington, DC: Smithsonian Institution.
Buikstra, J.E. and Beck, L.A. (eds) (2006) *Bioarchaeology: The Contextual Analysis of Human Remains*, Boston: Academic Press.
Buikstra, J.E. and Ubelaker, D.H. (eds) (1994) *Standards for Data Collection from Human Skeletal Remains, Proceedings of a Seminar at The Field Museum of Natural History*, Fayetteville, AR: Arkansas Archeological Survey Research Series No. 44.
Cheetham, P. (2005) 'Forensic geophysical survey', in J. Hunter and M. Cox (eds) *Forensic Archaeology: Advances in Theory and Practice*, London: Routledge.

Clark, A. (2000) *Seeing Beneath the Soil: Prospecting Methods in Archaeology*, revised edn, London: Routledge.

Cox, M., Flavel, A., Hanson, I., et al. (2008) *The Scientific Investigation of Mass Graves: Towards Protocols and Standard Operating Procedures*, Cambridge: Cambridge University Press.

Donoghue, H.D., Ubelaker, D.H. and Spigelman, M. (1999) 'The use of paleomicrobiological techniques in a current forensic case', in G. Pálfi et al. (eds) *Tuberculosis: Past and Present*, Szeged: Golden Book Publisher and Tuberculosis Foundation.

Dupras, T.L., Schultz, J.J., Wheeler, S.W., et al. (2006) *Forensic Recovery of Human Remains: Archaeological Approaches*, Boca Raton: CRC Press.

Ehleringer, J.R., Bowen, G.J., Chesson, L.A., et al. (2008) 'Hydrogen and oxygen isotope ratios in human hair are related to geography', *Proceedings of the National Academy of Sciences of the United States of America*, 105: 2788–93.

Howells, W.W. (2006) 'History of craniometric studies: the view in 1975', in D.H. Ubelaker (ed.) *Handbook of North American Indians: Environment, Origins, and Population*, Volume 3, Washington, DC: Smithsonian Institution.

Jefferson, T. (1954) *Notes on the State of Virginia* [1787], New York: W.W. Norton.

Jones, J. (1876) *Explorations of the Aboriginal remains of Tennessee*, Smithsonian Contributions to Knowledge 22, Washington, DC: Smithsonian Institution.

Katzenberg, M.A. (1992) 'Advances in stable isotope analysis of prehistoric bones', in S.R. Saunders and M.A. Katzenberg (eds) *The Skeletal Biology of Past Peoples: Research Methods*, 105–20. New York: John Wiley and Sons.

Larsen, C.S. (ed) (2001) *Bioarchaeology of Spanish Florida: The Impact of Colonialism*, Gainesville: University Press of Florida.

Martin, R.F. (2008) 'Removal and reinterment of remains' [1952], *American Law Reports 2d*, 21: 472.

Matthews, W., Wortman J.L. and Billings, J.S. (1893) 'Human Bones of the Hemenway Collection in the U.S. Army Medical Museum at Washington, by Dr. Washington Matthews. […] with Observations on the Hyoid Bones of this Collection, by Dr. J. L. Wortman. Reports Presented to the National Academy of Sciences, with the Approval of the Surgeon-General of the United States Army, by Dr. John S. Billings', *Memoirs of the National Academy of Sciences*, 7: 141–286.

Milner, G.R. (2004) *The Moundbuilders: Ancient Peoples of Eastern North America*, New York: Thames & Hudson.

Milner, G.R., Wood, J.W. and Boldsen, J.L. (2008) 'Advances in paleodemography', in M.A. Katzenberg and S.R. Saunders (eds) *Biological Anthropology of the Human Skeleton*, 2nd edn, New York: John Wiley and Sons.

Morton, S.G. (1839) *Crania Americana: or, A Comparative View of the Skulls of Various Aboriginal Nations of North and South America; To Which Is Prefixed an Essay on the Varieties of the Human Species*, Philadelphia: J. Dobson.

Ohtani, S. and Yamamoto, T. (2005) 'Strategy for the estimation of chronological age using the aspartic acid racemization method with special reference to coefficient of correlation between D/L ratios and ages', *Journal of Forensic Sciences*, 50: 1020–27.

Ohtani, S., Abe, I. and Yamamoto, T. (2005) 'An application of D- and L-aspartic acid mixtures as standard specimens for the chronological age estimation', *Journal of Forensic Sciences*, 50: 1298–1302.

Prince, D.A. and Ubelaker, D.H. (2002) 'Application of Lamendin's adult dental aging technique to a diverse skeletal sample', *Journal of Forensic Sciences*, 47: 107–16.

Rohlf, F.J. and Slice, D. (1990) 'Extensions of the Procrustes method for the optimal superimposition of landmarks', *Systematic Zoology*, 39: 40–59.

Ross, A.H., McKeown, A.H. and Konigsberg, L.W. (1999) 'Allocation of crania to groups via the "New Morphometry"', *Journal of Forensic Sciences*, 44: 584–87.

Ross, A.H., Slice, D.E., Ubelaker, D.H., et al. (2004) 'Population affinities of 19th Century Cuban crania: implications for identification criteria in South Florida Cuban Americans', *Journal of Forensic Sciences*, 49: 11–16.

Schaefer, M.C. and Black, S.M. (2005) 'Comparison of ages of epiphyseal union in North American and Bosnian skeletal material', *Journal of Forensic Sciences*, 50: 777–84.

Scheuer, L. and Black, S. (2000) *Developmental Juvenile Osteology*, San Diego: Academic Press.

Slice, D.E. (2005) 'Modern morphometrics', in D.E. Slice (ed.) *Modern Morphometrics in Physical Anthropology*, New York: Kluwer Academic/Plenum Publishers.

Sprague, R. (2005) *Burial Terminology: A Guide For Researchers*, Lantham, MD: AltaMira Press.

Stone, A.C. (2006) 'Ancient DNA', in D.H. Ubelaker (ed.) *Handbook of North American Indians: Environment, Origins, and Population*, Volume 3, Washington D.C.: Smithsonian Institution.

Ubelaker, D.H. (1999a) 'Aleš Hrdlička's role in the history of forensic anthropology', *Journal of Forensic Sciences*, 44: 724–30.

——(1999b) *Human Skeletal Remains, Excavation, Analysis, Interpretation*, 3rd edn, Washington D.C.: Taraxacum.

——(ed.) (2006) *Handbook of North American Indians: Environment, Origins, and Population*, Volume 3, Washington, DC: Smithsonian Institution.

Ubelaker, D.H. and Grant, L.G. (1989) 'Human skeletal remains: preservation or reburial?', *Yearbook of Physical Anthropology*, 32: 249–87.

Ubelaker, D.H. and Newson, L.A. (2002) 'Patterns of health and nutrition in prehistoric and historic Ecuador', in R.H. Steckel and J.C. Rose (eds) *The Backbone of History: Health and Nutrition in the Western Hemisphere*, Cambridge, Cambridge University Press.

Ubelaker, D.H. and Parra, R.C. (2008) 'Application of three dental methods of adult age estimation from intact single rooted teeth to a Peruvian sample', *Journal of Forensic Sciences*, 53: 608–11.

Ubelaker, D.H., Spigelman, M., Donoghue, H.D., *et al.* (2003) 'Evaluation of evidence for tuberculosis', in D.H. Ubelaker and E.B. Jones (eds) *Human Remains from Voegtly Cemetery, Pittsburgh, Pennsylvania*, Smithsonian Contributions to Anthropology No. 46, Washington, DC: Smithsonian Institution.

Veilleux, D.R. (2008) 'Liability for desecration of graves and tombstones' [1989], *American Law Reports 4th*, 77: 108.

Verano, J.W. and Ubelaker, D.H. (eds) (1992) *Disease and Demography in the Americas*, Washington, DC: Smithsonian Institution.

Wedel, V.L. (2007) 'Determination of season at death using dental cementum increment analysis', *Journal of Forensic Sciences*, 52: 1334–37.

Wittwer-Backofen, U., Gampe, J. and Vaupel, J.W. (2004) 'Tooth cementum annulation for age estimation: results from a large known-age validation study', *American Journal of Physical Anthropology*, 123: 119–29.

Mexico/México

Lourdes Márquez Morfín and Ernesto González Licón

INTRODUCTION: A BRIEF HISTORY AND CURRENT STATE OF PHYSICAL ANTHROPOLOGY IN MEXICO

Physical anthropology, especially osteology, palaeopathology and bioarchaeology, has a long tradition in Mexico, due to more than 10,000 years of pre-Hispanic history in the country. From the earliest human occupation to the first villages and their cultivation techniques, the rise of socio-political complexity and the development of prime state societies, the cities of Teotihuacan, Monte Albán and the Aztec Empire with Tenochtitlan as its capital, pre-Hispanic cultures settled all around the Mexican territory and left behind the material evidence of thousand of villages, towns and cities. Multiple archaeological excavations since the 18th century have produced thousands of human remains corresponding to very ancient skeletons, from the first hunter-gatherers of the Americas to skeletons from historical periods. As result of this situation, osteology, as a common practice, developed a long time ago.

A few years after Mexican Independence, two important actions were taken by the government to protect the National Property in order to stop the looting of ancient buildings and artefacts and to prevent the illegal movement of these valuable objects outside the country. As a protection measure, in 1822 the 'Antiquities Conservatory' was established, which depended on the University; and in 1825 the National Museum was founded. Two years later the first archaeological legislation was promulgated. This was the antecedent of the following legislation related to the archaeological heritage. At the end of that century, in 1897, Mexican legislation declared that archaeological monuments and objects were National Patrimony. Nevertheless it was not until the 20th century, in 1939, that a specific legislation for archaeological excavation was promulgated. The legislation framework and methodology regarding the excavation, lifting, analysis and curation of ancient remains are regulated by the Instituto Nacional de Antropología e Historia or National Institute of Anthropology and History of Mexico (INAH). It was established on 3 February 1939 through the law Ley Orgánica del Instituto Nacional de Antropología e Historia, promulgated on 31 December 1938 in the Diario Oficial de la Federación. In that same year the National School of Anthropology and History (ENAH) was created under INAH's responsibility and sponsorship. Many others laws and decrees were promulgated in this effort to preserve and protect the National Heritage, but it was not until 1972 that a specific legislation for archaeological excavation was promulgated and still prevails today (García Barcena 1993). In 1996 a total of 155 archaeological sites opened to the public under INAH management. Although this may seem a lot, conservative estimates indicates a total of 200,000 to 250,000 archaeological sites in the country, from caves and temporal shelters to large cities such as Teotihuacan or Chichen Itza (Martínez Muriel 2002).

Asociación Mexicana de Antropología Biológica

The Asociación Mexicana de Antropología Biológica (AMAB – Mexican Association of Biological Anthropology) was created in 1980 and its members include most physical anthropologists in Mexico and colleagues from other countries in Latin America and Europe. AMAB organizes every two years the 'Juan Comas' Colloquium of Biological Anthropology. This event is attended not only by physical anthropologists, but also by specialists in other areas such as archaeology, the biomedical disciplines and the social sciences. The papers presented at these meetings have been published in a series called *Studies of Biological Anthropology* (*Estudios de Antropología Biológica*) since 1982.

The development of physical anthropology in Mexico can thus be divided into four stages: 'Antecedents' (1862–90), dominated by foreign colleagues from Europe and the United States impelled by capitalism and neocolonialism expansion; 'Formative' (1901–36), with research focused on the anthropometry of Indian groups, osteometry research techniques and the beginning of skeletal collections for museums; 'Consolidation' (1937–67), characterized by studies on racial identity, palaeopathology and artificial (cultural) cranial and dental modification; and finally a period of 'Diversification' (1968–81) in which there are theoretical and methodological assessments and a focus on biosocial approaches (López Alonso *et al.* 1993).

Recent research trends

The development of new techniques in biological and chemical sciences, such as the recovery and identification of DNA, have had a great influence in education and research at an international level in Mexico. Nowadays a variety of research areas take place in the training of physical anthropologists including the analysis of breeding patterns, kinship relations, the initial peopling of America, and aspects of migration through the study of the mitochondrial DNA (De la Cruz Laina *et al.* 2006; González *et al.* 2001; Román Berrelleza and Chávez 2006).

The reconstruction of diet and its repercussions on health by means of trace element or isotope analysis is a subject that is of interest in many investigations on Maya populations (Berriel 2002; Brito 2000; Rodríguez Suárez 2004). There are also diverse chemical studies on the Maya population to solve questions such as the origin of some individuals and aspects of migration, as is the case of one of the governors of Copán and others in Teotihuacan.

Another aspect that it is possible to emphasize among the new research tendencies and training of physical anthropologists is the multidisciplinary approach to research by integrating physical anthropology with other disciplines in order to answer the same objective. 'Children and childhood' is one of the new lines of research at ENAH. Infantile growth in the pre-Hispanic groups has been an interest of students participating in the investigation of past populations such as those from Tlatilco, Cuicuilco, Jaina, and San Gregorio (Márquez 1985; Márquez *et al.* 1998; Peña *et al.* 2007).

Gender studies have had an enormous relevance, mainly for ethnology and social anthropology, and only in the last decade have archaeology and physical anthropology become interested in this topic. Woman's role in prehistory and the pre-Hispanic world begins to acquire a place within research and among the courses that are provided at ENAH (Alfaro 2002; Del Castillo and Márquez 2006; González Licón and Terrones 2003; Márquez and Hernández 2003).

Another subject that has had great success recently in the ENAH, one that is reflected in postgraduate theses, is physical activity in ancient individuals (Bernal 2001; Giannisis 2004; Medrano 1999). The identification of muscular insertion markers has allowed an understanding of the processes and ways in which the populations of different regions in the world have adapted to the different subsistence economies within their economic, ecological and political context among others.

Education and training

In Mexico, the first anthropology courses were given at the Anthropology Department at the National School of Biological Sciences (Escuela Nacional de Ciencias Biológicas), which was created as part of the Instituto Politécnico Nacional in 1938. First-generation students were Eusebio Dávalos, Johanna Faulhaber and Concepción Uribe. The anthropology bachelor's degree programme consisted of a two-year course with common anthropology subjects and a specialization in physical anthropology or social anthropology, with later additional subjects including archaeology, ethnology and linguistics. The International School of Archaeology and Ethnology was established in 1911, sponsored by French and German universities as well as New York's Columbia University (USA); but functioned more as a research centre than a school and was closed in 1920. North American influence was predominant at the time (García Barcena 1993). The Escuela Nacional de Antropologia e Historia (ENAH) was formed in 1939 as part of the National Institute of Anthropology and History. It was located in the Museum of Anthropology in Mexico City (Faulhaber 1993). Anthropology programmes were designed by Mexican academic staff according to their general vision about anthropology. Four specialities were established, with compulsory common courses to be taken during the first, and part of the second, year.

In Mexico today, the ENAH is the only institution where it is possible to study for a bachelor's degree in physical anthropology. In 1996 a master's programme started. Currently there is a specific programme, which includes a master's course and a doctorate in physical anthropology, with the first generation starting a doctoral programme in 2004. The postgraduate programme in physical anthropology seeks for academic excellence, where the curriculum and the curricular model results on the new theoretical approaches to the discipline and methodology, which implies the explicit definition and the construction of new paradigms in anthropological osteology. These programmes constitute a milestone in the formation of Mexican physical anthropologists, as well as of students of other countries, since they allow quality and a high level of training and formation of specialists. The success of the postgraduate programme reflects of the number of physical anthropologists dedicated to anthropological osteology since 1996 and therefore the number of theses on the subject. This increase does not only occur in the physical anthropology programme but also in archaeology, whether at ENAH or other universities; but with ENAH staff supervising the postgraduate students. At the moment more than 20 postgraduate theses have been completed on studies of ancient populations (see, e.g., Del Castillo 2000; Favila 2004; Giannisis 2004; Gómez 1999; Hernández 2002; Murrillo 2001; Rodríguez Suárez 2004).

Forensic anthropology has increased in importance mainly in terms of the new job opportunities in the Procuraduría General de Justicia, a Federal Agency or its equivalent in Mexico City, or the job opportunities relating to Human Rights. This area requires the confluence of several specialities and a specific technical training in physical anthropology. ENAH started a forensic anthropology programme in 2008.

ARCHAEOLOGICAL HUMAN REMAINS AND LEGISLATION

Archaeological legislation

INAH regulates all aspects related to archaeological research in the country. The National Coordination of Archaeology (Coordinación Nacional de Arqueología) coordinates and develops several actions oriented to research, preservation and restoration of archaeological sites as well as educating the public. The Council of Archaeology (Consejo de Arqueología) regulates and approves all archaeological projects in the country. Projects have to be submitted in order to gain authorization to excavate or undertake archaeological work. Nobody can explore an archaeological or historical site without this specific authorization by the Council of Archaeology. This Council sanctions the projects of archaeological exploration and the regulation of the archaeological materials, including human bones, which must be preserved and curated in their respective research centre.

An archaeological excavation can only be directed by a professional archaeologist; the physical anthropologist can be involved but cannot get permission to excavate or to direct an excavation on their own. Moreover, their presence at an excavation site is not compulsory by law. Thus, it is not possible for a physical anthropologist to decide where and what to excavate, nor to direct projects relating to the excavation of human remains. The anthropologist must therefore be integrated into an excavation that is directed by an archaeologist. As a result, for many years courses on archaeological excavation techniques were never taught in the physical anthropology curriculum at ENAH. In fact the central problem, in general, was the lack of integral investigations with a common general goal and particular questions to be answered. The reason for this was that physical anthropologists did not ask the same questions as archaeologists were asking regarding the reconstruction of the past and past populations, raising a number of further research avenues and hypotheses.

HUMAN REMAINS AND LEGISLATION

INAH has as a basic function the responsibility to explore, excavate, analyse and curate all the human remains in the country. It also regulates all the scientific research related to archaeological material. Human remains are considered by the law as one of the most important archaeological remains. Skeletal collections are in the custody of several departments, including the Dirección de Antropología Física, located at the National Museum of Anthropology in México City. Also, INAH has delegations in every political state ('Centros INAH'), and they have jurisdiction of their own materials, which belong to this state. ENAH also has the custody of several skeletal collections.

INAH Departments dealing with human remains

The Dirección de Antropología Física (DAF – Direction of Physical Anthropology), INAH centres, ENAH and other anthropological institutions such as Instituto de Investigaciones Antropológicas de la Universidad Autónoma de México (UNAM) and the following universities, Universidad Veracruzana, Universidad de Yucatán, Universidad Autónoma de Guadalajara, Universidad de Las Americas, Universidad de Zacatecas, among others institutions, can manage the safekeeping of skeletal material for research purposes. Foreign institutions have also carried out archaeological research involving human remains in México. For example, foreign participation accounted for 19.5 per cent of the projects in 1996 and included in these projects were the participation of missions from France, Belgium, Spain, Central America, USA universities, Canadian universities and the New World Archaeological Foundation (García Barcena 1993: 27)

DAF, INAH centres and ENAH have their own regulations for the study of skeletal material and on institutional access to the laboratory spaces, the osteology deposits, the use of equipment and instruments, loans between institutions, sanctions, rights and obligations. In general the collections are classified by sites of origin. There are teaching materials, and skeletal collections are available for research. The scientist who wants to undertake research on the material has to justify the collections' use, submit a request for the loan of materials, the time required and the type of analysis to be undertaken. In addition, any photographic record of the materials, as well as radiographic studies, requires the consent of the manager of the laboratory in each of the above-mentioned institutions. At the end of the investigation, a complete report of the activities undertaken is compulsory, as well as a copy of any photographs and radiographs.

There is no common procedure for invasive research. Any type of analysis that involves destructive techniques without authorization is illegal; permission must be sought from the Council of Archaeology, the directors of projects or the institution where the remains are curated. Permission to send samples abroad are under control of the Council of Archaeology from whom permission should be sought.

Reburial of human remains

Mexico does not have any legislation regarding reburial of human remains. Excavated skeletal material is packed in especially designed boxes for their transportation to the INAH department. Commonly, physical anthropologists are selected and invited by the archaeologist to participate in the project, analyzing the osteological material. Sometimes, skeletal remains are sent to DAF or are stored in other institutions alongside others archaeological materials.

METHODS OF ANTHROPOLOGICAL ANALYSIS

Mexico is starting to collect reference skeletal samples, in common with other countries. There are some cemetery samples, for example, such as that from the rural town of San Nicolás Tolentino, as well as a collection at the faculty of medicine at UNAM. These collections have allowed for the development of methods for sex, age-at-death and stature (Genovés 1959, 1962; López Alonso 1971; Pompa y Padilla 1975). During the 1960s Santiago Genovés developed formulae for male and female stature estimation in pre-Hispanic populations, which is well known and applied around the world, and especially in México (Genovés 1967). Sub-adult age estimation has been another field of research and there are some published tables related to pre-Hispanic and colonial populations, which have used dental development and long bone length to estimate sub-adult age (Márquez 1985; Ortega 1998). Biomolecular research on DNA to identify sex has been applied to a skeletal sample in relation to the question of child sacrifice among the Aztecs (De la Cruz Laina *et al.* 2006).

CONCLUSION

Osteology research in Mexico is bound by archaeological investigations of the social, political, economic and historical context of the past. The amount, the quality and general characteristics of skeletal collections are determined by the policies of archaeological investigation, within the institutional policy of INAH. For decades the exploration of the known pre-Hispanic sites throughout our country has received great attention, with the main objectives being twofold: the exploration, restoration, consolidation, and preservation of the cultural heritage for its historical and ideological value; and the opening and diffusion of the monumental centres of the ancient cities, such as Palenque, Uxmal, Chichén Itza, Monte Albán, Teotihuacan and Tula among many others, to an increasing national and international tourism. This tendency to explore only the central parts of these monumental and ceremonial constructions means that the skeletal remains, our primary resource to study these populations, are not representative of most of the individuals that lived there. Usually, skeletal material is discovered accidentally during the investigation and conservation of the main monumental buildings at these sites. Thus, these isolated osseous remains can provide little information about general population parameters since they lack statistical representativeness for the whole group, not only in size, but also in relation to sex, age and social status.

In general terms, there was a theoretical separation between osteology and archaeology, which produced a lack of interpretation of the archaeological context and prevented any attempt to explain human variability within the biocultural processes in a certain social and historical environment. The type of research and its perspective have changed through time according to the theoretical and methodological approaches of the discipline.

Research on ancient populations is complex, and the way to approach it depends on the theoretical positions and the lines of research at every historical moment. At the end of the 1960s, criticism within physical anthropology arose in Mexico towards the study of past populations through skeletons. The controversy was centred as much in the prevailing positivism of those studies, as in the interpretative biological approach, for its fragmentary and reductionist nature. The influence of Marxism motivated the proposal of some colleagues to use historical materialism as a method of analysis (Dickinson and Murgía 1982; Peña Saint Martin 1982, 1984; Sandoval 1982, 1984). This prevailing thought in ENAH proposed a total change towards integral studies that did not fragment the reality they tried to study. The goal was to understand the multi-causality of human populations; their biological variability for every historical moment. Nevertheless this approach had little impact in Mexican publications of those days. At the beginning of the 1980s there were diverse positions to the study of osteology, which faced the challenge to move from mere descriptions to analysis and interpretation, to provide alternative explanations to the different problems, and by integrating both biological and socio-cultural elements (Márquez 1996: 215–38; 2003).

Some bibliographical reviews present half a century of study of the discipline (Montemayor 1971; Villanueva 1982). López *et al.* (1996) aimed at providing an account of the state of physical anthropology in Mexico at the end of the 20th century. The objective was to provide a critical balance about the subjects that form physical anthropological research. At the end of the 20th century there was an emergence of new topics within the discipline and an increase in the work on a variety of subjects including osteology.

Nowadays, Mexico brings a long tradition of the protection of the national heritage, in particular of archaeological materials but not necessarily of skeletal material, which has been neglected by many archaeologists. In spite of the historical and cultural value of human remains, there are no positions for physical anthropologists in the Council of Archaeology. It is necessary therefore to increase the awareness of the potential of human remains and of the preservation of osteological material among anthropologists working in Mexico. The AMAB and physical anthropology colleagues from INAH are discussing the matter, and hopefully they will change the current situation.

USEFUL CONTACTS

Escuela Nacional de Antropología e Historia. Website: www.enah.edu.mx/
Instituto Nacional de Antropología e Historia. Website: www.inah.gob.mx/

BIBLIOGRAPHY

Alfaro, M.E. (2002) 'Acercamiento a la vida cotidiana y actividades femeninas de un sector de la población colonial'. Análisis de los patrones de actividad, unpublished undergraduate dissertation, Escuela Nacional de Antropología e Historia.

Bernal, N. (2001) 'Condiciones de vida y salud en una población rural: caso Santa María Texcalac, Tlaxcala, siglos XVII y XVIII', unpublished undergraduate dissertation, Escuela Nacional de Antropología e Historia.

Berriel, R.E. (2002) 'Paleodieta de los mayas de Chac Mool, Quintana Roo', unpublished Master's thesis, Escuela Nacional de Antopología e Historia.

Brito, E.L. (2000) 'Análisis de la población prehispánica de Monte Albán a través del estudio de la dieta', unpublished PhD thesis, Universidad Nacional Autónoma de México.

De la Cruz Laina, I., Román Berrelleza, J.A. and Torre Blanco, A. (2006) 'La tecnología del ADN antiguo aplicada al estudio de los niños sacrificados en honor a Tlaloc', in L. López Luján, D. Carrasco and L. Cue (eds) *Arqueología e Historia del Centro de México. Homenaje a Eduardo Matos Moctezuma*, México: Instituto Nacional de Antropología e Historia.

Del Castillo, O. (2000) 'Condiciones de vida y salud de una muestra poblacional de la ciudad de México en la época colonial', unpublished Master's thesis, Escuela Nacional de Antropología e Historia.

Del Castillo, O. and Márquez, L. (2006) 'Mujeres, desigualdad social y salud en la ciudad de México durante el Virreinato', in L. Márquez Morfin and P. Hernández Espinoza (eds) *Salud y Sociedad en el México Prehispánico y Colonial*, México: CONACULTA.INAH.PROMEP.

Dickinson, F. and Murgía, R. (1982) 'Consideraciones en torno al objeto de estudio de la antropología física', *Estudios de Antropología Biológica*, 1: 51–64.

Faulhaber, J. (1993) 'Los inicios de la ENAH y la carrera de Antropología Física', in E.B. Cárdenas (ed.) *50 años. Memoria de la ENAH*, México: Instituto Nacional de Antropología e Historia.

Favila, H. (2004) *Condiciones de salud y estratificación social en la población prehispánica de Tlapizahuac*, México: Escuela Nacional de Antropología e Historia.

García Barcena, J. (1993) 'Balance y perspectiva de la Arqueología en México', in L. Arizpe and C. Serrano (eds) *Balance de la Antropología en América Latina y el Caribe*, México: UNAM.

Genovés, S. (1959) *Diferencias en el hueso coxal*, México: Universidad Autónoma de México.

——(1962) *Introducción al diagnóstico de la edad en restos óseos prehistóricos*, México: Instituto de Historia, Universidad Nacional Autónoma de México,

——(1967) 'Proportionality of long bones and their relation to stature among Mesoamericans', *American Journal of Physical Anthropology*, 26: 67–77.

Giannisis, D. (2004) 'Aspectos de la vida cotidiana de la población costera maya de Chac Mool, Quintana Roo, en el Posclásico (900 – 1550 d.C.)', unpublished Master's thesis, Escuela Nacional de Antropología e Historia.

Gómez, A. (1999) 'Estratificación social y condiciones de salud en Palenque, Chiapas, en el periodo Clásico Tardío. Un estudio bioarqueológico', unpublished Master's thesis, Escuela Nacional de Antroopología e Historia.

González, A., Márquez, L., Jiménez, J.C., *et al.* (2001) 'Founding Amerindian mitochondrial DNA lineage in ancient Maya from Xcaret, Quintana Roo', *American Journal of Physical Anthropology*, 116: 230–35.

González Licón, E. and Terrones, E. (2003) 'Género y desigualdad social entre los mayas de Chac-Mol, Quintana Roo durante el Posclásico, a través de sus prácticas funerarias', paper presented at the *XII Coloquio Internacional de Antropología Física 'Juan Comas'* (9–13 November 2003), Tlaxcala, Mexico.

Hernández, P. (2002) 'La regulación del crecimiento de la población en el México Prehispánico', unpublished PhD thesis, Escuela Nacional de Antropología e Historia.

López Alonso, S. (1971) 'La escotadura ciática mayor en la determinación sexual de restos óseos prehispánicos de México', *Anales del INAH*, 2: 31–41.

López Alonso, S., Serrano, C. and Lagunas, Z. (1993) 'Bosquejo histórico de la Antropología Física en México', in L. Arizpe and C. Serrano (eds) *Balance de la Antropología en América Latina y el Caribe*, México: UNAM.

López, S., Serrano, C. and Márquez, L. (eds) (1996) *La antropología física en México. Estudios de las poblaciones antigua y contemporánea*. Instituto de Investigaciones Antropológicas. Universidad Nacional Autónoma de México, México.

Márquez, L. (1985) 'Determinación de edad por medio de la longitud de huesos largos infantiles de población colonial mexicana', *Avances de Antropología Física*, 2: 147–58.

——(1996) 'Los estudios osteológicos en México. Evaluaciones y nuevas perspectivas', in S. López Alonso, C. Serrano Sánchez and L. Márquez Morfín (eds) *La antropología física en México. Estudios de las poblaciones antigua y contemporánea*, México: Instituto de Investigaciones Antropológicas, Universidad Nacional Autónoma de México.

——(2003) 'Balance de los estudios sobre condiciones de vida y salud de las poblaciones prehispánicas mesoamericanas', paper presented at the Primer Foro de Investigación de la Escuela Nacional de Antropología e Historia, México.

Márquez, L. and Hernández, P. (2003) 'La mujer en la prehistoria. Una perspectiva de género', *Estudios de Antropología Biológica*, 11: 473–85.

Márquez, L., Hernández, P. and Ortega, A. (1998) 'Crecimiento infantil en poblaciones prehispánicas', *Revista Salud Problema*, 3: 107–19.

Martínez Muriel, A. (2002) 'La investigación arqueológica en sitios monumentales', in R.D. Drenan and S. Mora (eds) *Investigación arqueológica y preservación del patrimonio en las Américas*, México: INAH.

Medrano, A. (1999) 'La actividad ocupacional y la persona social en San Gregorio Atlapulco-Xochimilco. Época prehispánica (1350–1521 d. C.)', unpublished Master's thesis, Escuela Nacional de Antropología e Historia.

Montemayor, F. (1971) *28 años de antropología*, México: Escuela Nacional de Antropología e Historia.

Murrillo, S. (2001) 'La vida a través de la muerte: estudio biocultural de las costumbres funerarias en el Temazcaltepec prehispánico', unpublished Master's thesis, Escuela Nacional de Antropología e Historia.

Ortega, A. (1998) 'La estimación de la edad en restos óseos subadultos mesoamericanos. Colección osteológica de San Gregorio Atlapulco, Xochimilco', unpublished undergraduate dissertation, Escuela Nacional de Antropología Física.

Peña, M.E., Hernández, P. and Márquez, L. (2007) 'Estatus de crecimiento y condiciones de salud en los niños de Jaina', in P. Hernández and L. Márquez (eds) *La población prehispánica de Jaina. Estudio osteobiográfico de 106 esqueletos*, México: INAH/ENAH.

Peña Saint Martin, F. (1982) 'Hacia la construcción de un marco teórico para la antropología física', *Estudios de Antropología Biológica*, 1: 65–73.

——(1984) 'Algunas reflexiones en torno a la Antropología Física', *Estudios de Antropología Biológica*, 2: 27–46.

Pompa y Padilla, J.A. (1975) 'Algunos caracteres morfológicos en pelvis de tlatelolcas prehispánicos', paper presented at the XLI Congreso Internacional de Americanistas, Ciudad de México.

Rodríguez Suárez, R. (2004) 'Paleonutrición de poblaciones extinguidas en Mesoamérica y Las antillas: Xcaret y el Occidente de Cuba', unpublished PhD thesis, Escuela Nacional de Antropología e Historia.

Román Berrelleza, J.A. and Chávez, X. (2006) 'The role of children in the ritual practices of the Great Temple of Tenochtitlan an the Great Temple of Tlatelolco', in T. Arden and S. R. Hutson (eds) *The social experience of Childhood in Ancient Mesoamerica*, Boulder, CO: University of Colorado Press.

Sandoval, A. (1982) 'Hacia una historia genealógica de la antropología física', *Estudios de Antropología Biológica*, 1: 25–50.

——(1984) 'Consideraciones sobre la pretendida articulación de lo biológico y lo social en Antropolofía física', *Estudios de Antropología Biológica*, 2: 15–26.

Villanueva, M.E. (1982) 'La antropología Física de los antropólogos físicos en México. Inventario bibliográfico (1930–79)', *Estudios de Antropología Biológica*, 1: 72–124.

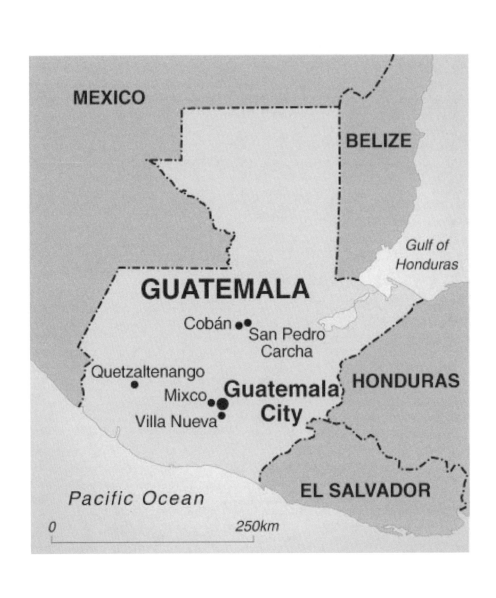

Guatemala

Lourdes Penados

INTRODUCTION: A BRIEF HISTORY AND CURRENT STATE OF PHYSICAL ANTHROPOLOGY IN GUATEMALA

The involvement of physical anthropologists in the study of skeletal remains in Guatemala is linked to the history of Maya archaeology and, in recent times, to the study of remains recovered from forensic settings. While the recovery of skeletal material was not the primary aim of the majority of archaeological projects, the excavations in the late 19th and early 20th centuries produced some of the largest samples, which were prime material for studies on prehistoric and historic Maya human osteology, mainly conducted by North American specialists. Recent projects have produced smaller samples as well and are usually used for specific studies on biological aspects and dietary habits of the ancient Maya.

However, there is a gap between the assessments of biological aspects of past and modern Guatemalan populations. Physical anthropology is still not included in any of the national universities' academic programmes, despite an increasing need for research and for the development of methods and local standards for the analysis of skeletal remains, particularly applied to remains recovered from forensic contexts related to the internal armed conflict that occurred in the country from 1960 until 1996.

The history of physical anthropology in Guatemala is mainly the history of Maya bioarchaeology.

During the 16th and 17th centuries, Spanish chroniclers recorded their observations about the cultures and customs of the aboriginal populations and, from time to time, they also included accounts and drawings of ancient cities they came across. One of those chroniclers, Francisco Antonio de Fuentes y Guzmán (1932–33) gave what is probably the first description of human skeletal findings in the east of Guatemala, when he narrated his encounter with a man who informed him that some bones had been discovered within a fine layer of soil, but when removed they disintegrated and turned into dust.

As a result of changes that occurred during the late 18th century in Europe, the Spanish Crown ordered a Royal Expedition to the 'New Spain'. This was the first academic and scientific expedition sent to Central America with the purpose of recording botanical, geological, ethnographical and palaeontological data. This campaign did not report any archaeological findings, but it opened the door to the flow of expeditions that followed.

Guatemala was not indifferent to the changes regarding knowledge, culture and humanity that took place during the 18th century. The academic institutions that were founded during the Colonial regime, such as the University of San Carlos, went through transformations that included the review of academic contents, the creation of the first natural history museum, and the incorporation of scientific studies which were free of religious influence (Gutiérrez 1996: 58).

After independence from Spain in 1821, and throughout the 19th century, the number of British and North American expeditions to Guatemala increased notably. Reports about ancient Mayan cities encouraged the Guatemalan government to carry out efforts to register and make topographic maps of all known archaeological sites. This marked the beginnings of the Guatemalan Archaeological Atlas (Gutiérrez 1996: 61). During the late 19th century many ethnographers from France, Germany, England, the United States and other places visited Guatemala to study the cultures of the Mayan groups, and published studies on topics such as traditional dances, languages, and religious customs. The development of Maya archaeology is rooted during those years.

In the 1840s, the North American writer and explorer John Stephens, along with British explorer Frederick Catherwood, visited the region and produced detailed descriptions and drawings of ancient Maya cities; some of these have now disappeared. It was Stephens who promoted the first collaboration with a physical anthropologist when he submitted his osteological findings to Dr Samuel George Morton, whose study stimulated the first discussion about the origin of the Maya and the Mayan collapse (Buikstra 1997: 222).

At the beginning of the 20th century, individual expeditions came to an end and gave way to large scientific projects sponsored by national and international institutions. Some of the most important archaeological projects involving the recovery of skeletal remains were those by the Harvard University Peabody Museum, with 12 expeditions between 1889 and 1915; the American Archaeology School of New Mexico, with four expeditions between 1910 and 1914; the joint projects between the American National History Museum of New York and the Washington Carnegie Institution, with 30 expeditions between 1914 and 1958; the Department of Middle American Research of Tulane (1925); the British Museum, with five expeditions in 1927; the Chicago Museum of Natural History, with three expeditions in the 1920s; the University of Pennsylvania, with seven expeditions in 1931; and the Proyecto Nacional Tikal between 1983 and 1985 (Gutiérrez 1996: 76; Wright 2002: 407).

During the 19th and 20th centuries prominent physical anthropologists such as Morton, Virchow, Hooton, Hrdlička, Comas and Stewart became involved in the analysis of Mayan remains. The topics of analysis varied from stature, sex and age-at-death to health status (Buikstra 1997: 222)

From the second half of the 20th century until today, archaeological projects have produced smaller skeletal samples (Danforth *et al.* 1997: 231–59), although burials are usually opportunistically found and recorded, and most of the time lifted by archaeologists who have only a general knowledge of osteology. Many of those remains still remain unanalysed and no records exist of their original context and conditions of recovery. In recent years, some projects in the Maya region, such as Copán, have been developed with the specific purpose of recovering skeletal remains (Webster 1997: 3); however, no such project has been carried out in Guatemala so far.

The research topics on bioarchaeology have varied throughout the years. During the 1930s there was an increase in physical anthropology publications based on Mayan samples, particularly those recovered by the Carnegie Institute projects, mostly on cranial deformation, dental modification and inherited anatomical features. Later on, during the 1960s, published works followed general trends in physical anthropology, moving towards health status and the linkage between diet and the Maya collapse. The study of disease attracted the attention of Samuel George Morton, Rudolph Virchow and Franz Boas as well (Buikstra 1997: 222). Secular trends in stature, and the relationship between a decrease in stature and nutritional stress associated with the Maya collapse, were studied by Haviland with the Tikal sample (Wright 2002: 407).

During the 1970s, Frank Saul's studies on pathology influenced future physical anthropology research as well. It is important to say that the studies of physical anthropologists at this time have been the basis of theoretical discussions and theories about the collapse of the Maya. More recently the study of Mayan diet has increased with the development of technology such as stable isotope analysis. There is also a rising interest in exploring the relation between archaeological findings and the interpretation of social and political changes (Buikstra 1997: 226).

Today, physical anthropology as a discipline is not part of the academic programme of any of the national universities. At the University of San Carlos there is one general osteology class, which is mandatory for archaeology students and optional for anthropology students. There is one mandatory biology course in the archaeology study programme at the Del Valle University as well (Universidad del Valle de Guatemala 2004). These facts are a drawback in terms of the interest that Guatemalan archaeologists and anthropologists have on the study of skeletal remains.

Skeletal collections

To this date, there are few collections available from ancient Maya sites. Guatemalan archaeologist Juan Carlos Pérez, Head of the Section of Prehispanic and Colonial Monuments in the Department of Cultural and Natural Patrimony at IDAEH (Instituto de Antropología e Historia de Guatemala, or The Guatemalan Anthropology and History Institute) (IDAEH 2006), has indicated that the skeletal remains that were recovered from archaeological excavations before the 1960s are kept in the general store at IDAEH (Pérez, *pers. comm.* 2009). However, it was only in 2008 that an inventory of this material was made. Mr Pérez had mentioned that there are no packaging and storage standard regulations regarding skeletal remains or other findings, therefore the caution that is taken depends on the people who are responsible for the archaeological excavation. It was his impression that many of the skeletal samples were severely damaged, some of them even destroyed (Pérez, *pers. comm.* 2009). Other samples that were recovered by projects after the 1960s are curated at the National Museum of Archaeology and Ethnology. There is a plan to inventory all these remains in the near future.

The excavations in Tikal, in the northern department of Petén, have produced one of the largest samples from the Classic Period (over 200 individuals). This sample is adequately preserved and stored and has been studied under the Tikal Osteology Project (Wright *et al.* 2000: 407) with the objective of producing a biocultural history of the site, as well as undertaking specific studies on the diet of the different social classes of the Maya from Tikal. More recently the skeletal sample was used in a study on the estimation of bone length from fragmented long bones, which have produced tables that are being used in modern forensic cases today (Wright and Vásquez 2003: 233). This latter study is a pioneer in terms of being the first attempt to produce local standards.

The forensic anthropology teams have small forensic samples as well. However, the access to these remains is restricted. There is a mutual project that is being developed between CAFCA (Centro de Análisis Forenses y Ciencias Aplicadas, or Centre for Forensic Analysis and Applied Sciences) (CAFCA 2010) and the Faculty of Medicine of the University of San Carlos, which is looking into accessing the remains that are periodically exhumed from local national cemeteries and are not claimed by relatives. The aim of the project is to create a national skeletal collection in order to develop local standards for use by the forensic teams that investigate human rights violations and also to promote the development of physical anthropology as a discipline. This project also aims to provide research material for academics from various disciplines, including archaeologists, anatomists and biologists among others (CAFCA 2007).

Forensic anthropology in Guatemala

Examination of skeletal remains in a medico-legal context, which is referred as forensic anthropology, is a subfield of physical anthropology. The aim of this discipline is identification and assistance in the clarification of criminal events. In the United States of America, the beginnings of forensic anthropology extend back to the 19th century with the intervention of academics in the resolution of criminal cases. It was through research that relevant physical anthropologists demonstrated what physical anthropology could provide for forensic cases (Ubelaker 2000: 42).

At the time of writing there have been recent continuous efforts to provide evidence of the massive human rights violations that occurred in Guatemala during the internal armed conflict. In 1992 the first forensic team was formed, the Forensic Anthropology Team of Guatemala (now the Forensic Anthropology Foundation of Guatemala, or FAFG). In 1997 two more teams were created, the Forensic Anthropology Team of the Human Rights Office of the Archbishop (ODHAG) and the Forensic Anthropology Team of the Centre for Human Rights Legal Action (CALDH). In 1998 the Diocese of El Quiche created a fourth forensic anthropology team solely to attend cases from that Department. In 1999 the Centre for Forensic Analysis and Applied Sciences (CAFCA) was formed, with forensic anthropology as one of its main objectives. Of all these, only two remain operational (see below) (Penados 2006: 17).

Despite the fact that most of the members of the teams come from an archaeological or anthropological academic background, the organizations have had to provide training in physical anthropology, forensic methods and forensic techniques. This has usually been done with the cooperation of foreign pathologists, physical or forensic anthropologists and other specialists. With a few exceptions, team members have not had access to postgraduate education specifically on physical or forensic anthropology. Although the demand for forensic anthropology investigations in the country focuses mostly on the recovery and identification of remains, the teams provide physical evidence and forensic reports to be used in courts of law. They also have collected significant amounts of data. These data provide an important resource not only for the understanding of the violations of human rights that occurred in the country but for the future development of physical anthropology (Penados 2006: 19).

ARCHAEOLOGICAL HUMAN REMAINS AND LEGISLATION

Archaeological legislation

The protection of all national cultural assets in Guatemala falls under the responsibility of the Ministry of Culture according to the Ley para la Protección del Patrimonio Cultural de la Nación (Law for the Protection of the National Heritage, Decree 26–97) (Ministerio de Cultura y Deportes 2004).

This law defines cultural heritage as 'all public or private assets which by law or by an authority are declared as related to palaeontology, archaeology, history, anthropology, art, science and technology, and general culture' (Article 2) [author's translation]. The law considers cultural assets of interest to palaeontology, archaeology, anthropology, science or technology, all findings that come from zoology, botany, mineralogy, anatomy and palaeontological collections; as well as the products of excavations or explorations, in land or under water, whether their recovery was authorized or not, as well as planned or unplanned palaeontological or archaeological activities (Article 3).

It is the General Director of the Natural and Cultural Heritage that has to give written authorization in order to carry out archaeological work, including underwater explorations if they are of palaeontological, archaeological or historical interest (Article 10). The procedure also includes an agreement where all findings belong to the state and are to be reported to IDAEH and taken there once the project is concluded.

HUMAN REMAINS AND LEGISLATION

It is not infrequent to discover human remains near churches and other colonial buildings. In such a case, Article 33 of the abovementioned Law indicates that, 'if cultural goods are fortituously found, the action that movitated the discovery must be suspended and the IDAEH must be notified'. It also states that IDAEH will 'evaluate the discovery and archaeologists or specialized technicians must take actions for the adequate recovery of the finding'.

The weaknesses regarding the enforcment of the laws that protect the cultural goods as well as the lack of general awareness of the importance of preserving national assets, including skeletal remains, often result in the destruction or inadequate removal of archaeological findings (Ajxup 1997: 134)

Based on the Accord on Identity and Rights of the Indigenous People, signed in Mexico in 1995 as part of the peace process (Congreso de la República de Guatemala 2008) in recent years, Mayan descendant groups have requested that all findings from archaeological projects be returned to them. This has been done with the cooperation and agreement of IDAEH, which requests that the findings are to be stored in a protected environment such as a local museum. Guatemalan archaeologist Juan Carlos Pérez, at IDAEH, has indicated that skeletal remains that have been returned have been reburied in local cemeteries (Pérez, pers. comm. 2009).

Skeletal remains of forensic interest

Between 1962 and 1996 Guatemala experienced one of the most violent internal armed conflicts in Latin America. Since the beginning of the 1990s, several families of those who disappeared have begun to demand the investigation of the violent events that occurred throughout that period. As a result of these requests, exhumations have been carried out by forensic anthropology teams, which between 1992 and the time of writing have altogether exhumed, analysed and returned approximately 5000 skeletons.

Given the large number of exhumations and the media coverage, there is more awareness of the implications involving the removal of possible criminal evidence. Therefore, it has become a generalized practice that whenever human remains are accidentally found, people should inform the local authorities or call the police. If the remains are buried in a context that does not seem historical or archaeological, then the authorities will usually contact one of the forensic teams that are still operational: the 'Forensic Anthropology Foundation of Guatemala' (Fundación de Antropología Forense de Guatemala, or FAFG) (FAFG 2010) or the team from CAFCA. These teams will assess and explore the area and recover the skeletal remains and any other relevant materials, as well as confirming whether the remains are of forensic interest or not. If, according to the anthropologist(s), they appear to be of forensic interest, then a formal investigation begins and the procedures to follow are those established in the guidelines approved in 2003 by the Attorney General (Ministerio Público de Guatemala 2003). This document outlines the laws concerning human remains in medico-legal contexts, as well as the uses, limitations and the purpose of forensic anthropology, the steps to take in a forensic anthropology investigation, and some specific matters regarding the investigation of human rights violations in Guatemala.

The National Institute of Forensic Sciences (Instituto Nacional de Ciencias Forenses, or INACIF) was created in 2006 with the aim of assisting in the administration of justice in the matter of forensic investigations (INACIF 2006). One of the first actions to be taken was the standardization of scientific procedures regarding evidence processing. An important development was the creation in 2008 of a Forensic Anthropology Section, responsible for the analysis of skeletal material from recent criminal cases, which resulted in the incorporation of two forensic anthropologists, one of them a former member of CAFCA and the other a former member of FAFG (INACIF 2008).

METHODS OF ANTHROPOLOGICAL ANALYSIS

Physical (including forensic) anthropologists apply standard international methods of anthropological analysis to the skeletal remains they recover, particularly the observation of changes in the pubic symphysis (Suchey and Katz 1998) and in the auricular surface of the ilium (Lovejoy *et al.* 1985) for adult age estimation. Epiphyseal union and dental development is employed for sub-adult age estimation. Sex is generally estimated by observing the morphology of the skull and pelvis (Krenzer 2006). Even though it is not a modern method, stature estimation is more commonly done with the application of the formulae developed by Santiago Genovés (1967), since the Mexican sample that he used shares similarities with the Guatemalan population.

The absence of modern skeletal collections is a serious limitation for the development of local standards. An effort was made by Krenzer (2006) to evaluate internationally recognized standards and write a compendium which includes those that are more applicable to Guatemalan modern samples. As mentioned earlier, one population-specific method for Guatemala is that developed to estimate the length of the bone in fragmented remains (Wright and Vásquez 2003: 233).

CONCLUSION

Despite the fact that the methods of physical anthropology have been consistently used in archaeological and forensic contexts in Guatemala, the development of physical anthropology as a discipline in Guatemala is still at an early stage. However, there are ongoing archaeological projects which continue to recover skeletal remains. Physical anthropologists and bioarchaeologists remain involved in the analysis and interpretation of skeletal findings to understand the fate of the ancient Maya as well as their relation with modern Guatemalan populations. The national skeletal collections that are still under the care of IDAEH remain available for research.

The forensic anthropology teams also continue their work, and there is a strong interest in systematizing the data that have been collected in the last decades. This will result in a valuable resource for scientific interpretation and furthermore for the wider understanding of the violent events that occurred in the country during the conflict, and might also encourage further research, whether it be forensic or not.

All these aspects grant a starting point for the advancement of the discipline and hopefully for the incorporation of physical anthropology into the academic programmes of Guatemalan national universities in the near future. Forensic anthropology teams are open to the involvement of specialists and also offer volunteer openings for students on graduate or postgraduate levels. CAFCA has a volunteer programme open to students on the postgraduate level in physical and forensic anthropology and other related fields. Students are given the opportunity to participate in excavations, analyse skeletal remains and develop scientific research.[1]

USEFUL CONTACTS

Guatemalan Institute of Anthropology and History. Website: www.mcd.gob.gt/
Centro de Análisis Forenses y Ciencias Aplicadas (CAFCA). Website: www.cafcaguatemala.org/
Fundación de Antropología Forense de Guatemala (FAFG). Website: www.fafg.org/

NOTE

1 For further information, contact CAFCA: cafca@cafcaguatemala.org.

BIBLIOGRAPHY

Ajxup, M. (1997) 'Juricidad de la arqueología guatemalteca', in J.P. Laporte and H. Escobedo (eds) *X Simposio de Investigaciones Arqueológicas en Guatemala, 1996*, Guatemala: Museo Nacional de Arqueología y Etnología.
Buikstra, J. (1997) 'Studying Mayan bioarchaeology', in S.L. Whittington and D.M. Reed (eds) *Bones of the Maya, Studies of Ancient Skeletons*, Washington, DC: Smithsonian Institution Press.
CAFCA (2007) 'Proyecto colección ósea de Guatemala', unpublished internal report.
——(2010) *Centro de Análisis Forenses y Ciencias Aplicadas*. Available online at www.cafcaguatemala.org (accessed 26 March 2010).
Congreso de la República de Guatemala (2008) 'Digital database', Peace Accords. Available online at www.congreso.gob.gt/Docs/PAZ/ (accessed 3 July 2009).
Danforth, M.E., Whittington, S. and Jacobi, K.P. (1997) 'An indexed bibliography of prehistoric and Early Historic Maya human osteology: 1839–1994', in S.L. Whittington and D.M. Reed (eds) *Bones of the Maya, Studies of Ancient Skeletons*, Washington, DC: Smithsonian Institution Press.
Escuela de Historia USAC (2005) *Guía informativa de la carreras de antropología*. Available online at http://escuelahistoria.usac.edu.gt/pdf/Guia_Antropologia_2005.pdf (accessed 30 June 2009).
——(2005) *Guía informativa de la carreras de arqueología*. Available online at http://escuelahistoria.usac.edu.gt/pdf/Guia_Arqueologia_2005.pdf (accessed 30 June 2009).
FAFG (2010) *Fundación de Antropología Forense de Guatemala*. Available online at www.fafg.org (accessed 26 March 2010).
Fuentes y Guzmán, F. (1932–33) *Recordación Florida. Vols. I-III*. Guatemala: Tipografía Nacional.
Genovés, S. (1967) 'Proportionality of the long bones and their relation to stature among Mesoamericans', *American Journal of Physical Anthropology*, 26: 67–78.
Gutiérrez, E. (1996) *Posiciones Teóricas en la Arqueología de Guatemala*, Guatemala: Instituto de Investigaciones Históricas, Antropológicas y Arqueológicas.
IDAEH (2006) *Instituto de Antropología e Historia de Guatemala*. Available online at www.mcd.gob.gt/ (accessed 26 March 2010).
INACIF (2006) *Ley Orgánica del Instituto Nacional de Ciencias Forenses*. Available online at www.inacif.gob.gt/docs/ley_organica.pdf (accessed 15 July 2009).
——(2008) *Memoria de Labores*. Available online at www.inacif.gob.gt/docs/Memoria_ Labores2008.pdf (accessed 15 July 2009).
Krenzer, U. (2006) *Compendio de Métodos Antropológico Forenses para la Reconstrucción del Perfil Osteo-Biológico, Vols. I to VIII*, Guatemala: CAFCA.
Lovejoy, C.O., Meindl, R., Przybeck, T. *et al.* (1985) 'Chronological metamorphosis of the auricular surface of the ilium: a new method for the determination of adult skeletal age at death', *American Journal of Physical Anthropology*, 68: 15–28.

Ministerio de Cultura y Deportes (2004) *Ley para la Protección del Patrimonio Nacional, Decreto 26–97 y Sus Reformas*, Guatemala: Ministerio de Cultura y Deportes.

Ministerio Público de Guatemala (2003) *Manual de Procedimientos para Investigaciones Antropológico Forenses en Guatemala*, Guatemala: Ministerio Público.

Penados, L. (2006) 'Human rights violations in Guatemala. Exploratory analysis of the results of forensic anthropology investigations in the Ixil area and Ixcan', unpublished MSc Research Project Report, University of Central Lancashire, UK.

Suchey, J. and Katz, D. (1998) 'Applications of pubic age determination in a forensic setting', in K. Reichs (ed.) *Forensic Osteology: Advances in the Identification of Human Remains*, Springfield, IL: Charles C. Thomas.

Ubelaker, D. (2000) 'Methodological considerations in the forensic applications of human skeletal biology', in M.A. Katzenberg and S.R. Saunders (eds) *Biological Anthropology of the Human Skeleton*, New York: Wiley-Liss.

Universidad del Valle de Guatemala (2004) *Plan de Estudios de Arqueología*. Available online at www.uvg. edu.gt/info-academica/u-academicas/cc-ss/licenciaturas/arqueologia/Arqueologia.pdf (accessed 30 June 2009).

Webster, D. (1997) 'Studying Maya burials', in S.L. Whittington and D.M. Reed (eds) *Bones of the Maya, Studies of Ancient Skeletons*, Washington, DC: Smithsonian Institution Press.

Whittington, S.L. and Reed, D.M. (eds) (1997) *Bones of the Maya, Studies of Ancient Skeletons*, Washington, DC: Smithsonian Institution Press.

Wright, L. (2002) 'The inhabitants of Tikal: a bioarchaeological pilot project', unpublished archaeological report for FAMSI.

Wright, L., Vásquez, M., Morales, M.A., *et al.* (2000) 'La bioarqueología en Tikal: resultados del primer año del Proyecto Osteológico Tikal', in J.P. Laporte *et al.* (eds) *XIII Simposio de Investigaciones Arqueológicas en Guatemala, 1999*, Guatemala: Museo Nacional de Arqueología y Etnología.

Wright, L. and Vásquez, M. (2003) 'Estimating the length of incomplete long bones: forensic standards from Guatemala', *American Journal of Physical Anthropology*, 120: 233–51.

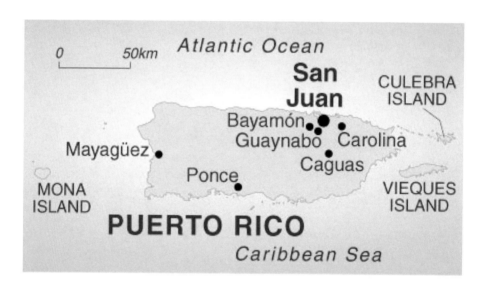

Puerto Rico/Borikén/Porto Rico

Myriam Llorens-Liboy and Milton Núñez

INTRODUCTION: A BRIEF HISTORY AND CURRENT STATE OF PHYSICAL ANTHROPOLOGY IN PUERTO RICO

Puerto Rico is a mountainous tropical island of 8,896 sq km with a population of about four million. It is the easternmost island of the Greater Antilles, with a maximum length and width of 111 km and 36 km respectively. In addition to the main island, Puerto Rican territory embraces a few smaller islands (Vieques and Culebra to the east; Mona, Monito and Desecheo to the west; Caja de Muertos to the south) and a number of barren islets and cays (Picó 1954).

Puerto Rico was discovered and annexed to the Spanish Crown by Columbus on 19 November 1493. At the time, the island was occupied by Arawak-speaking Taínos (Island Arawaks), who lived in a fairly developed chiefdom society. Only decades after the island's colonization had begun (1508), the indigenous population had plunged due to repeated epidemics and/or ill-treatment. The remaining survivors were eventually acculturated and assimilated by the Spaniards. In order to replace the declining Indian labour force, thousands of African slaves were brought to work in the mines and fields in the 16th century (Sauer 1966; Alegría 1999; Anderson-Córdova 1990, 2005).

The native Taíno called their island Borikén, but Columbus named it San Juan Bautista and it later came to be known as Puerto Rico (Coll 1970; Alegría 1999). Due to its strategic situation, the island had the potential of playing an important role as a sentinel of the Atlantic navigation routes and warehouse for the Spanish empire. However, its coasts, particularly its capital San Juan, suffered from repeated raids, first by Caribs from St Croix (Virgin Islands) and later by pirates, privateers and naval fleets from nations at war with Spain (Van Middeldyk 1903; Blanco 1947; Cifre de Loubriel 1964; Alegría 1981; Sonesson 1990; Alonso and Flores Román 1998; Rivera Fontán *et al.* 2003; Wells 2004; Reina Pérez 2007).

The last of such events was the invasion by US troops in connection with the Cuban–Spanish–American War on 25 July 1898. As a result, the United States annexed Puerto Rico, together with other Spanish colonies. Puerto Rico's first civil government was inaugurated on 1 May 1900, and 17 years later all Puerto Ricans received US citizenship through the Jones Act (Van Middeldyk 1903; Estades Font 1988; González Vales 2006). In addition to improvements in trade, education and health, these developments brought a series of systematic investigations by American archaeologists and anthropologists to the island, mainly in connection with the

Scientific Survey of Porto Rico and the Virgin Islands (see, e.g., Fewkes 1903, 1907; Boas 1916; Aitken 1917; Haeberlin 1917; Rainey 1933, 1940; Mason 1941; Rouse 1952a, 1952b). Of especial interest are Aitken's (1917) investigations of a funeral cave with 20 burials in the district of Caguana.

The decolonization process, which is marked by the first elected Governor in 1948 and the proclamation of Puerto Rico's Constitution and Commonwealth of Puerto Rico (Estado Libre Asociado) in 1952, gradually stirred new interest about the island's past. The publication of the work by American researchers on the island during the first half of the twentieth century may have also played a part (Gutiérrez Ortiz 1998) in encouraging Puerto Rican scholars to carry out their own investigations and to publish and study archaeology and anthropology abroad (see, e.g., de Hostos 1919, 1923a, 1923b, 1941, 1955; Alegría 1955, 1965; Alegría *et al.* 1955). The first local legislation concerning the protection of monuments and relics and human remains was introduced in the late 1960s.

During the Spanish colonial period, there were no systematic studies or attempts to protect aboriginal sites or their contents. They belonged, after all, to a culture that was foreign and unimportant to the Spanish settlers. During this time anyone could destroy any monuments or seize any relics from the aboriginal period. Swedish Pharmacist J.A. Hjalmarson, for example, was able to remove ten aboriginal crania from a Puerto Rican burial cave (Figure 50.1) and take them to Sweden in the 1850s (Gejvall and Henschen 1971; Núñez *et al.* 2009).

In the second half of the 19th century, however, a sense of romantic curiosity about the past of the Antillean aborigines seems to have developed among some *criollos* (ethnic Spaniards born in the colonies) and Europeans living in the island. This trend is reflected in Puerto Rico by the work of Alejandro Tapia y Rivera (1862), Enrique Dumont (1876), German born Leopold Krug (1876), Agustín Stahl (1889) and Cayetano Coll y Toste (1897, 1921). It is worth mentioning that there was a debate about the origin of syphilis between Stahl, who placed it in Europe, and Coll y Toste, who traced it to the Taíno. It now seems that the latter may have been right (cf. Estrada Torres 1990; Crespo Torres 2005a; Núñez *et al.* 2009). When American anthropologists began their Scientific Survey of Puerto Rico under the direction of Franz Boas in 1906, they relied heavily on the information collected by these and other local amateurs who had fallen in

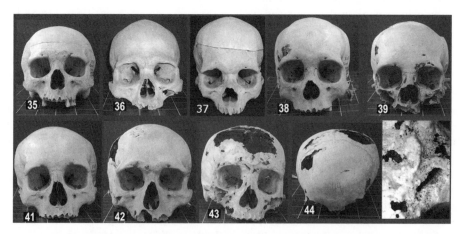

Figure 50.1 Nine of the ten aboriginal crania removed from a Puerto Rican burial cave and taken to Sweden in the 1850s

Source: Gejvall and Henschen 1971; Núñez *et al.*, 2009; photos: M. Núñez and M. Llorens-Liboy

love with Puerto Rico and its culture. Other scholars also wrote on Puerto Rico's past (see, e.g., Van Middeldyk 1903; Lovén 1935).

Anthropological research in Puerto Rico today

One of the main factors that has affected the development of archaeological investigations and, particularly, the analysis of ancient human remains in Puerto Rico is the lack of professionals and specialists among Puerto Rican nationals, which is a clear reflection of the colonial past (cf. Pagán-Jiménez 2004). Since only a few undergraduate courses in physical anthropology and archaeology are available on the island, any Puerto Rican wishing to obtain a university degree in these subjects must do so abroad. Obviously, this constitutes a strong limiting factor. The situation is partly a result of private or contract archaeology dictating the course of archaeological investigation on the island, as these commercial excavations do not result in scientific papers but only administrative reports. Moreover, the information retrieved by contract archaeologists is often patchy and is seldom published. They tend to give little importance to human remains, restricting their description to the distribution and position of the burials, age-at-death, sex and the artefacts associated with the remains. As an argument, Edwin Crespo Torres (2000, 2008) has stated that the only 57 publications on funerary practices and/or human osteology of populations from the whole of the Caribbean region had been published by the beginning of the 21st century.

To these publications could be added a few other articles dealing with human remains from the Caribbean and Puerto Rico published before the year 2000. For example, the article by Gejvall and Henschen (1971) on the anthropological analysis of eight aboriginal crania with possible syphilis from Puerto Rico (cf. Núñez *et al.* 2009); and the analysis of 17 Lucayans skeletons from eight Bahamian islands and comparing their stable isotope signatures with other coastal populations, including a Salaloid individual from the Hacienda Grande site on Puerto Rico (Keegan and DeNiro 1988). Also worth mentioning are L.C. Budinoff's (1991) osteological analysis of human remains from the Maisabel site in Puerto Rico, and José Oliver's (1999) article on the collagen and apatite analyses of human and animal bones from the Puerto Rican sites of Cueva de Juan Miguel (Figure 50.2) and the Doña Rosa shellmound.

A number of publications on physical anthropology have appeared since the year 2000. There was an anthropological study of the inhabitants of Cañabón (Rosario Fernández 2001) and several articles on mtDNA analyses both of skeletons from various archaeological sites in the Caribbean region (Lalueza-Fox *et al.* 2001, 2003, 2004) and of modern Puerto Ricans. The

Figure 50.2 Cave burial from the Juan Miguel Cave, in Barrio Caguana, Utuado, Puerto Rico
Source: Photography by J. Rivera-Fontán

latter research, based on 800 individuals from 28 localities throughout the island, revealed a rather mixed population with a high aboriginal component: 61.3 per cent Amerindian, 27.2 per cent African and 11.5 per cent European (Martínez Cruzado 2002; Martínez-Cruzado *et al.* 2001, 2005; Santory-Jorge *et al.* 2008). There have also been a few palaeopathological studies, including those on treponematosis (Crespo Torres 2005a; Núñez *et al.* 2009) and other lesions (Crespo Torres 2005b, 2008), in addition to some descriptions of various physical and bio-cultural traits of archaeological populations from Puerto Rico (see, e.g., Crespo Torres 2000, 2007; Stokes 2005).

A crucial development for the future of physical anthropology in Puerto Rico is the creation of the Forensic Anthropology and Bioarchaeology Laboratory at the Centre for Archaeological Investigations of the University of Puerto Rico (Centro de Investigación Arqueológica de la Universidad de Puerto Rico) in 2008. This centre is under the direction of Professor Edwin Crespo Torres and is dedicated to the study of material, including human remains, from Puerto Rican archaeological sites. Currently this brand-new facility is beginning the long process of assembling and arranging the archaeological and anthropological collections from the island.

The increase in physical anthropological research on the island during the last 20 years is a positive development. A growing number of Puerto Rican students are completing their PhDs in physical anthropology and/or archaeology and are doing research on human remains from the island. For example, Myriam Llorens-Liboy who, together with other graduate students from Barcelona and Stockholm and Professor Milton Núñez, is currently studying the possible evidence of treponematosis in a few Puerto Rican Taíno crania (Figure 50.1) currently housed at the Osteoarchaeological Laboratory at Stockholm University (Núñez *et al.* 2009). Once the Centre for Archaeological Investigations of the University of Puerto Rico is fully functional and prepared, it may be possible to repatriate the Puerto Rican crania that are now in Stockholm.

ARCHAEOLOGICAL HUMAN REMAINS AND LEGISLATION

Archaeological legislation

US annexation brought to Puerto Rico US federal laws that protected monuments and cemeteries on federal land, but the laws did not apply to those on private land. These remained unprotected until the late 1960s. In 1955 the Commonwealth of Puerto Rico (Estado Libre Asociado) passed Law 89, which called for the creation of the Instituto de Cultura Puertorriqueña (Institute of Puerto Rican Culture) to preserve, promote and divulge the cultural values of Puerto Rico. Subsequently, in the 1980s, the Institute was responsible for the creation of Laws 10 (1987) and 112 (1988) on cultural heritage. In the 1960s, national legislation made federal funds available for compulsory archaeological investigation prior to the exploitation of prehistoric and historic sites. In the 1970s, archaeologist Gus Pantel introduced a standard procedure based on the existing New York State Law, which called for a four-step procedure that included document inquiry (Phase Ia), field survey (Phase Ib), test pits (Phase II) and, depending on the site's importance, excavation (Phase III). The first two levels could be conducted by Puerto Rican amateurs who had completed some archaeology courses and appeared on a local register of qualified archaeologists; but the actual archaeological excavations could only be performed by archaeologists who held academic accreditation from the USA. Despite the good intentions, this legislation has regrettably led to the dominance of business-oriented contract archaeology. The guidelines connected with this first protection law are published in the Reglamento para la Radicación y Evaluación de Proyectos de Construcción y Desarrollo

(Regulation for the Allocation and Evaluation of Construction and Development Projects) by the Council for the Protection of the Archaeological Patrimony (Institute of Puerto Rican Culture 1992). Unfortunately, these rules do not quite apply to the portion of Vieques Island being used by the US Navy, and this situation has hindered the adequate investigation of about 65 per cent of this small but culturally-rich island with hundreds of prehistoric sites (Bonnet Benítez 1976; Chanlatte Baik and Narganes Storde 1979, 1983, 2003; Tronolone *et al.* 1984).

Further legislation concerning the conservation of cultural patrimony was passed by the Commonwealth of Puerto Rico (Estado Libre Asociado) in the 1980s: Law 111 dealing with the protection of caves, caverns and subterranean rivers (1985); Law 10 dealing with procedure of investigation and salvage of subaquatic archaeological sites (1987); and Law 112 dealing with the protection of terrestrial archaeological patrimony, including human remains (1988). There was also a 2003 amendment concerning the Consejo de Arqueología, which had been defined by Law 10 and established in 1990 (Institute of Puerto Rican Culture 2003). It calls for the creation of the Consejo de Arqueología Terrestre (Council of Terrestrial Archaeology), assigned to the Instituto de Cultura Puertorriqueña, with the task of enforcing all the previously mentioned laws, delineating the council's duty to:

> … make an inventory and to maintain a permanent and properly updated register of all the terrestrial materials, structures, and archaeological sites that have been found up to the date of the enacting of this law as well as those which come to be discovered later, including also those which are now part of collections and museums outside Puerto Rico …
>
> *Institute of Puerto Rican Culture 1992: 35 [free translation by the authors]*

The Legislation of the Commonwealth of Puerto Rico may be seen online at www.estado. gobierno.pr/Leyes_PR.htm/; and the regulations of the Institute of Puerto Rican Culture at www.icp.gobierno.pr/.

HUMAN REMAINS AND LEGISLATION

According to the current regulations, when human remains are found at an archaeological site, an accredited physical anthropologist must be summoned to perform a basic examination of the remains. If human remains are discovered at a place not known as an archaeological site, the Forensic Medicine Institute will determine first whether they are modern (i.e., less than 50 years old) or ancient. In the latter case, the Institute will contact Professor Edwin Crespo Torres, a forensic anthropologist who has served as consultant to the Institute since 1991. He will then carry out the pertinent analyses.

Some US federal laws apply also to Puerto Rico, namely the Code of Federal Rules (36 CFR 79) which deals with the protection and handling of archaeological collections and ancient human remains that are under the jurisdiction of the State Historical Preservation Office or SHPO (www.cr.nps.gov/aad/tools/36cfr79.htm). This office was created through Law 183 in 2000 and advises the Governor's Office and the Federal Agency concerning projects that require federal funds in accordance to 1966 Federal Law (P.L. 89–665), commonly known as the National Historic Preservation Act of 1966. On the other hand, the Native American Serious Protection and Repatriation Act (NAGPRA), enforced in the United States since 16 November 1990, does not apply on Puerto Rico.

METHODS OF ANTHROPOLOGICAL ANALYSIS

The first anthropological analysis that is carried out is to identify the age and sex of the individual, using the skull, pelvis and/or the long bones, using several methods. The methods that are used include the sequence of formation and dental eruption and ectocranial suture closure of the lateral-previous zone and the sutures of the vault; for sexing, the cranial capacity calculated by Pearson as well as markers such as the supraorbital crest, the protuberance of the glabella, the size of the mastoid process and the strength of the temporal line are used. Cranial measurements (*norm frontalis, norm lateralis, norm basilaris, norm occipitalis* and *norm verticalis*) are useful for determining facial characteristics. The points used consist of 37 absolute points distributed across the skull, of which 22 are used to establish facial characteristics, as stipulated in 1906 in the International Convention of Monaco to unify craniometric and cephalometric measurements.

Between 1960 and 1970, with the advent of the New Archaeology and Ecological Anthropology (Krigbaum 2008), the discipline began to change. The term bioarchaeology arose in 1972, coined by the British archaeologist Grahame Clark as a reference to zooarchaeology, and was redefined in 1977 by the North American physical anthropologist Jane Ellen Buikstra who, for first time, included human remains in the term (Crespo Torres 2000). Bioarchaeological studies can provide information on burial form and social organization, daily activities and division of labour, population size and density, population movement, genetic relations, diet and diseases (Korpisaari 2006).

CONCLUSION

It is lamentable that the importance of the skeleton within archaeology is not always fully realized in Puerto Rico. On many occasions it is still non-specialists (i.e., non-physical anthropologists) without basic knowledge of anatomy who carry out excavations and even at times the post-excavation analysis. As a result, descriptions of burials are often minimal or faulty and influence the quality of the final report when this information is combined with the osteological and palaeopathological data (Sánchez Astorga 2003).

It is hoped that, in the future, when the Laboratory of Forensic Anthropology and Bioarchaeology of the Archaeological Research Centre of the University of Puerto Rico (created recently in 2008) has been fully established and equipped (including laboratory and conservation facilities), Puerto Rican material that is now in different parts of the world will be returned through repatriation, in line with laws similar to the federal Law of Native American Graves Protection and Repatriation Act (NAGPRA).

USEFUL CONTACTS

Institute of Puerto Rican Culture. Website: www.icp.gobierno.pr/

ACKNOWLEDGEMENTS

We wish to thank the Council for Protection of the Archaeological Patrimony and Terrestrial of Puerto Rico, the Division of Terrestrial Archaeological at the Institute of Puerto Rican Culture (ICP) and the State Historic Preservation Office (SHPO) of Puerto Rico. We are also grateful to Juan Rivera Fontán, archaeology technician at the Institute of Puerto Rican Culture; to Dr Edwin Crespo Torres, of the Department of General Social Sciences, Director of the Centre of Archaeological Investigation of the University of Puerto Rico; and to Dr Jan Storå, of the Osteoarchaeology Laboratory of Stockholm University, for their collaboration and help.

BIBLIOGRAPHY

Aitken, R.T. (1917) 'Puerto Rican burial caves', *Proceedings of the Internacional Congreso of Americanists*, 19: 224–28.

Alegría, R.E. (1955) 'La tradición cultural arcaica antillana', in Sociedad Económica de Amigos del País (ed.) *Miscelánea de estudios dedicados al Dr. Fernando Ortiz por sus discípulos y amigos*, La Habana: Sociedad Económica de Amigos del País.

——(1965) 'On Puerto Rican archaeology', *American Antiquity*, 31: 246–49.

——(1981) 'Introducción', in M. Cárdenas-Ruiz (ed.) *Crónicas francesas de los indios Caribes*, San Juan: University of Puerto Rico Press.

——(1999) 'Apuntes en torno a las culturas aborígenes de Puerto Rico. Las fuentes para el estudio de nuestros aborígenes', in R.E. Alegría and E. Rivera Quiñones (eds) *Historia y cultura de Puerto Rico desde la época pre-colombina hasta nuestros días*, San Juan: Fundación Francisco Carvajal.

Alegría, R.E., Nicholson, H.B. and Wiley, G.R. (1955) 'The archaic tradition in Puerto Rico', *American Antiquity*, 2: 113–21.

Alonso, M.M. and Flores Román, M. (1998) *El Caribe en el siglo XVIII y el ataque británico a Puerto Rico en 1797*, San Juan: Publicaciones Puertorriqueñas.

Anderson-Córdova, K.F. (1990) 'Hispaniola and Puerto Rico: Indian acculturation and heterogeneity, 1492–1550', unpublished PhD thesis, Yale University.

——(2005) 'The aftermath of the conquest. The Indians of Puerto Rico during the early sixteenth century', in P.E. Siegel (ed.) *Ancient Borinquen. Archaeology and Ethnohistory of Native Puerto Rico*, Tuscaloosa: University of Alabama Press.

Blanco, E.T. (1947) *Los tres ataques británicos a la ciudad de San Juan Bautista de Puerto Rico: Drake 1595. Clifford 1598, Abercromby 1797*, San Juan Bautista: Cantero Fdez.

Boas, F. (1916) 'New evidence in regard to the instability of human types', *Proceedings of the National Academy of Sciences*, 2: 713–18.

Bonnet Benítez, J.A. (1976) *Vieques en la historia de Puerto Rico*, San Juan: Ortiz Nieves.

Budinoff, L.C. (1991) 'An osteological analysis of the human burials recovered from Maisabel: an Early Ceramic site on the North coast of Puerto Rico', in L.S. Robinson (ed.) *Proceedings of the 12th International Congress of the Association for Caribbean Archaeology*,12: 117–133, Association for Caribbean Archaeology: Martinique.

Chanlatte Baik, L.A. and Narganes Storde, Y.M. (1979) 'Excavaciones arqueológicas en Vieques', *Revista del Museo de Antopología. Historia y Arte de la Universidad de Puerto Rico*, 1: 55–59.

——(1983) *Catálogo Arqueología de Vieques*, Rio Piedras: Centro de Investigaciones Arqueólogicas, Universidad de Puerto Rico.

——(2003) 'Vieques: joya arqueológica del Caribe', *Diálogo antropológico*, 1: 5–8.

Cifre De Loubriel, E. (1964) *La inmigración a Puerto Rico durante el siglo XIX*, San Juan: Instituto de Cultura Puertorriqueña.

Coll, E. (1970) *Cayetano Coll y Toste. Síntesis de Estímulos humanos*, San Juan: Editorial Universitaria, Universidad de Puerto Rico.

Coll y Toste, C. (1897) *Prehistoria de Puerto Rico*, Bilbao: Editorial Vasco Americana.

——(1921) 'Vocabulario de palabras introducidas en el idioma español procedentes del lenguage indoantillano', *Boletín Histórico de Puerto Rico*, 8: 292–352.

Crespo Torres, E.F. (2000) '*Estudio comparativo biocultural entre dos poblaciones prehistóricas en la isla de Puerto Rico: Punta Candelero y Paso del Indio*', unpublished PhD thesis, Universidad Nacional Autónoma de México.

——(2005a) 'Evidence of Pre-Columbian treponematosis from Paso del Indio. An archaeological site on the island of Puerto Rico', in M.L. Powell and D.C. Cook (eds) *Myth of syphilis: The Natural History of Treponematosis in North America*, Gainsville: University Press of Florida.

——(2005b) 'La cultura huecoide y su conexión con la introducción de la práctica de la deformación cefálica intencional en las Antillas. Cultura La Hueca. Finca Sorcé, Barrio La Hueca. Vieques', in *Cultura La Hueca*, San Juan: Museo de Historia, Antropología y Arte y Centro de Investigaciones Arqueológicas/ Universidad de Puerto Rico: Recinto de Río Piedras, 57–65.

——(2007) 'La apariencia física de los indios de Borikén a través de sus restos humanos', *Instituto de Cultura Puertorriqueña*, 14: 3–9.

——(2008) 'Estudio paleopatológico comparativo entre dos sitios arqueológicos en la isla de Puerto Rico: Punta Candelero y Paso del Indio', in Instituto de Cultural Puertorriqueña (ed.) *5to encuentro de investigadores de arqueología y etnohistoria*, San Juan: Instituto de Cultura Puertorriqueña.

de Hostos, A. (1919) 'Prehistoric Porto Rican ceramics', *American Anthropologist*, 21: 376–99.

——(1923a) 'Anthropomorphic carvings from the Greater Antilles', *American Anthropologist*, 25: 525–58.

——(1923b) 'Three-pointed Stone Zemi or Idols from the West-Indies: an interpretation', *American Anthropologist*, 25: 56–71.

——(1941) 'Notes on West Indian hydrography in its relation to prehistoric migrations', in *Anthropological papers: Papers based principally on studies of the Prehistoric Archaeology and Ethnology of the Greater Antilles*, San Juan: Office of the Historian, Government of Puerto Rico, 30–53.

——(1955 [1936]) *Una Colección Arqueológica Antillana*, San Juan: First Federal Savings and Loan Association of Puerto Rico.

Dumont, E. (1876) *Investigaciones acerca de las antigüedades de la isla de Puerto Rico*, La Habana: Imprenta La Antillana.

Estades Font, M.E. (1988) *La presencia militar de Estados Unidos en Puerto Rico 1898–1918: Intereses estratégicos y dominación colonial*, San Juan: Ediciones el Huracán.

Estrada Torres, A. (1990) 'La sífilis en la historia de nuestra isla', *Boletín del Museo del Hombre Dominicano*, Año XVII, No. 23: 107–18.

Fewkes, J.W. (1903) 'Prehistoric Porto Rican pictographs', *American Anthropologist*, 5: 441–67.

——(1907) *The Aborigines of Porto Rico and the Neighboring Islands*, Washington, DC: Government Printing Office.

Gejvall, N.G. and Henschen, F. (1971) 'Anatomical evidence of Pre-Columbian syphilis in the West Indian Islands', *Beiträge zur Pathologie*, 144: 138–57.

González Vales, L.E. (2006) *Documentación de Puerto Rico en el Archivo General Militar de Madrid*, Madrid: Ministerio de Defensa de España. Asociación de Bibliotecarios. Museólogos y documentalistas (ANABAD)/Senado de Puerto Rico (cuatrienio 1996–2000).

Gutiérrez Ortiz, M. (1998) 'Reflexiones sobre la práctica arqueológica en Puerto Rico 1', *Actualidades Arqueológicas*, 19–20. Available online at http://swadesh.unam.mx/actualidades/actualidades/19y20/ Texto19y20/puertorico.html/.

Haeberlin, H.K. (1917) 'Some archaeological work in Porto Rico', *American Anthropologist*, 19: 214–38.

Institute of Puerto Rican Culture (1992) *Reglamento para la Radicación y Evaluación de Proyectos de Construcción y Desarrollo*, San Juan: Consejo para la Protección del Patrimonio Arqueológico.

——(2003) *Ley de protección del patrimonio Arqueológico Terrestre de Puerto Rico. Ley 112 del 20 de julio de 1988*, San Juan: Consejo para la Protección del Patrimonio Arqueológico Terrestre de Puerto Rico.

Keegan, W.F. and DeNiro, M.J. (1988) 'Stable carbon- and nitrogen-isotope ratios of bone collagen used to study coral-reef and terrestrial components of prehistoric Bahamian diet', *American Antiquity*, 53: 320–36.

Korpisaari, A. (2006) 'Death in the Bolivian high plateau. Burilas and Tiwanaku Society'. *BAR Internacional Series* 1536, Oxford.

Krigbaum, J. (2008) 'Bioarchaeology' in Deborah M. Pearsall (ed. in chief) *Encyclopaedia of archaeology*, Vol. 2 B–M, Elsevier, Academia Press, 924–27.

Krug, L. (1876) 'Indianische Alterthumer in Porto Rico', *Zeitschrift für Ethnologie*, 8: 428–35.

Lalueza-Fox, C., Calafell, F., Martínez-Fuentes, A.J., *et al.* (2004) 'Secuencias de DNA de restos pre-históricos de Cuba; reconstrucción del poblamiento del Caribe', in J.E. Egocheaga (ed.) *Biología de poblaciones humanas: diversidad, tiempo, espacio*, Oviedo: Universidad de Oviedo.

Lalueza-Fox, C., Gilbert, M.T., Martínez-Fuentes, A.J., *et al.* (2003) 'MtDNA from pre-Columbian Ciboneys from Cuba and the colonization of the Caribbean', *American Journal of Physical Anthropology*, 211: 97–108.

Lalueza Fox, C., Luna Calderón, F., Calafell, F., *et al.*. (2001) 'MtDNA from extinct Taínos and the peopling of the Caribbean', *Annals of Human Genetics*, 65: 137–51.

Lovén, S. (1935) *Origin of the Tainan Culture, West Indies*, Göteborg: Elanders boktryckeri.

Martínez Cruzado, J.C. (2002) 'The use of mitochondrial DNA to discover Pre-Columbian migrations to the Caribbean: results from Puerto Rico and expectations from Dominican Republic', *The Journal of*

Caribbean Amerindian History and Anthropology [Special Issue edited by Lynne Guitar]: 1–12. Available online at www.kacike.org/MartinezEnglish.html (accessed 16 April 2010).

Martínez-Cruzado, J.C., Toro-Labrador, G., Ho-Fung, V., *et al.* (2001) 'Mitochondrial DNA analysis reveals substantial Native American ancestry in Puerto Rico', *Human Biology*, 73: 491–511.

Martínez-Cruzado, J.C., Toro-Labrador, G., Viera-Vera, J., *et al.* (2005) 'Reconstructing the population history of Puerto Rico by means of mtDNA phylogeographic analysis', *American Journal of Physical Anthropology*, 128: 131–55.

Mason, J.A. (1941) 'A large archaeological site at Capá, Utuado, with notes on other Porto Rico sites visited in 1914–15', *Scientific Survey of Puerto Rico and the Virgin Island*, 18: 209–71.

Núñez, M., García-Guixé, E., Liebe-Harkort, C., *et al.* (2009) 'Treponematosis en cráneos aborígenes de Puerto Rico', in M.P. Cerdá and E. García-Prósper (eds) *Investigación histórica-médica sobre salud y enfermedades en el pasado*, Valencia: Grupo Paleolab and Sociedad Española de Paleopatología.

Oliver, J.R. (1999) 'Muestras para análisis de colágeno y apatita de huesos humanos y de animales (dieta humana)', *Proyecto arqueológico Utuado-Caguana 1999–2000*, Protocolo 4, Cueva de Juan Miguel (CAG-3) y conchero de Doña Rosa (U-44) (24 noviembre).

Oliver, J.R., Rivera Fontán, J.A. and Newsom, L.A. (1999) 'Arqueología del Barrio Caguana, Puerto Rico: resultados preliminares de las temporadas 1996–97', in J.A. Rivera Fontán (ed.) *Trabajos de Investigación Arqueológica en Puerto Rico*, Publicación Ocasional de la División de Arqueologia, San Juan: Instituto de Cultura Puertorriqueña.

Pagán-Jiménez, J.R. (2004) 'Is all archaeology at present a postcolonial one? Constructive answers from an eccentric point of view', *Journal of Social Archaeology*, 4: 200–13.

Picó, R. (1954) *Parte 1. Geografía física. Geografía de Puerto Rico*, Rio Piedras: Editorial Universitaria.

Rainey, F.G. (1933) 'Puerto Rican Archaeology', unpublished PhD thesis, Yale University.

——(1940) *Porto Rican Archaeology, Scientific Survey of Porto Rico and the Virgin Islands 18: 208, pt.1*, New York: New York Academy of Sciences.

Reina Pérez, P. (2007) 'Asedio a la ciudad de San Juan. Las ciudades se fortifican. Piratas y corsarios en aguas del Caribe. San Juan Bautista bajo el asedio de Inglaterra. Francia y Holanda', *El Nuevo Día, El Educador Gran Historia Ilustrada de Puerto Rico*, 7: 1–7.

Rivera Fontán, J.A., Cortes Santiago, H. and Olivencia Emeric, G. (2003) *Investigaciones arqueológicas en la fortaleza. Hallazgos y documentación de una sección de la Primera muralla de San Juan (1635–1640)*, San Juan: Programa de Arqueología y etnohistoria, Instituto de Cultura Puertorriqueña.

Rosario Fernández, J.C. (2001) 'Estudio de antropología física del Barrio Cañabón de Caguas. Historia y arqueología del Valle del Turabo. Universidad del Turabo', *Museo y Centro de Estudios Humanísticos*, 5: 23–31, San Juan: Municipio de Caguas and Johnson & Johnson.

Rouse, I. (1952a) 'Porto Rican Prehistory: Introduction; Excavations in the West and North', *Scientific Survey of Puerto Rico and the Virgin Islands*, Vol. 18: 307–460.

——(1952b) 'Porto Rican prehistory: excavations in the Interior, South and East', *Scientific Survey of Puerto Rico and the Virgin Islands*, 18: 463–578.

Sánchez Astorga, P. (2003) 'Antropología física para arqueólogos', Campillo, D. and Subirá, M.E. (eds) Colección. *Atlántica-Mediterránea de Prehistoria y Arqueología Social (RAMPAS)* 6, Universidad de Cádiz, 329–35.

Santory-Jorge, A.O., Avilés, L.A., Martínez-Cruzado, J.C., *et al.* (2008) 'The Paradox of the Puerto Rican Race: the interplay of racism and nationalism under U.S. colonialism', in A. Grant-Thomas and G. Orfield (eds) *Twenty-First Century Color Lines: Multiracial Change in Contemporary America*, Philadelphia: Temple University Press.

Sauer, C.O. (1966) *The Early Spanish Main*, Berkeley: University of California Press.

Schoeninger, M.J. (1989) 'Reconstructing prehistoric human diet', in T.D. Price (ed.) *The Chemistry of Prehistoric Human Bone. School of American Research Advanced Seminal Series*, Cambridge: Cambridge University Press.

Sonesson, B. (1990) *La Real Hacienda en Puerto Rico. Administración, política y grupos de presión (1815–1868), Monografías. Economía Quinto Centenario*, Madrid: Instituto de Cooperación Iberoamericana, Sociedad Estatal Quinto Centenario, Instituto de Estudios Fiscales.

Stahl, A. (1889) *Los indios borinqueños: estudios etnográficos*, San Juan: Imprenta de Acosta.

Stokes, A.V. (2005) 'Ceramic Age dietary patterns in Puerto Rico. Stable isotopes and island biogeography', in P.E. Siegel (ed.) *Ancient Borinquen. Archaeology and Ethnohistory of Native Puerto Rico*, Tuscaloosa: University of Alabama Press.

Tapia y Rivera, A. (1862) 'La palma del cacique: leyenda histórica de Puerto Rico', in *Ensayos literarios*, 170–205, La Habana: Imprenta del Tiempo.

Tronolone, C.A., Cinquino, M.A., Vandrey, C.E., *et al.* (1984) *Cultural Resource Reconnaissance Survey for the Vieques Naval Reservation*, Ecology and Environment, Inc., Report submitted to Department of the Navy, Atlantic Division, Naval Command of Norfolk Engineering Facilities. Copy at San Juan: the Office of Historical Conservation.

Wells, J.C. (2004) 'History and characterization of mortars in Spanish New World fortifications: A case study on El Castillo de San Cristóbal. San Juan. Puerto Rico', unpublished.MSc thesis, University of Pennsylvania. Available online at http://repository.upe nn.edu/hp theses/62/

Van Middeldyk, R.A. (1903) 'The History of Puerto Rico: from the Spanish discovery to the American occupation', in M.G. Brumbaugh (ed.) *Project Gutenberg*, University of Pennsylvania and First Commissioner of Education for Puerto Rico. Ebook #12272 (May 5 2004). Available online at www.gutenberg.org/files/12272/12272–78.txt; http://hdl.loc.gov/loc.gdc /lhbpr.08353/

BERMUDA
TURKS & CAICOS ISLANDS
DOMINICAN REPUBLIC
PUERTO RICO
BRITISH VIRGIN ISLANDS
US VIRGIN ISLANDS
ST CHRISTOPHER & NEVIS
ANTIGUA AND BARBUDA
GUADELOUPE
DOMINICA
MARTINIQUE
ST LUCIA
ST VINCENT & THE GRENADINES
BARBADOS
GRENADA
TRINIDAD & TOBAGO
BAHAMAS
MEXICO
CAYMAN ISLANDS
CUBA
JAMAICA
HAITI
ANGUILLA
MONTSERRAT
NETHERLANDS ANTILLES
ARUBA
BELIZE
HONDURAS
GUATEMALA
EL SALVADOR
NICARAGUA
COSTA RICA
PANAMA
VENE-ZUELA
GUYANA
FRENCH GUIANA
COLOMBIA
SURINAME
ECUADOR
BRAZIL
PERU
BOLIVIA
PARAGUAY
CHILE
URUGUAY
ARGENTINA
FALKLAND ISLANDS
SOUTH GEORGIA & THE SOUTH SANDWICH ISLANDS

South America

Paola Ponce

The following section (chapters 51–54) provides information on the history of physical anthropology and the legislation regarding the excavation and treatment of human remains in the countries of Argentina, Brazil, Chile and Uruguay. It also provides examples of repatriation of skeletal remains of Native American Indians from South America held until recent years in European institutions. Finally, brief information on the current methods used to analyse human remains within these countries is also provided.

The contributions from Argentina, Brazil, Chile and Uruguay have in common a number of issues of similar nature that are worth highlighting.

With regard to the history and the birth of physical anthropology, these countries shared a pre-scientific or pre-institutional stage of the discipline which started between the middle and end of the 19th century with the work of national and international researchers. These researchers usually had no anthropological backgrounds and were either naturalists, travellers or chroniclers who, for a number of reasons, became involved in the fascinating prehistory of South America.

The 20th century saw an important growth and advance of the discipline with the creation of research centres and academic institutions to study anthropology and related careers. It was at this time that a clear sense of national identity led to an emphasis on the importance of the prehistoric and historical heritage. Regulatory bodies were created and protectionist laws were enacted in order to regulate, for example, the excavation and recovery of human remains, the conditions under which foreign researchers could participate with national scientists, and the position regarding repatriation of human remains held in overseas institutions. Additionally, the military dictatorships that ruled these countries during the 1970s and 1980s had a direct and indirect impact on the development of physical anthropology. New scientific methods of analysis were adopted and applied to analyse the human remains of 'disappeared' and tortured civilians at the time that new laws were enacted that led to the excavation of mass graves in search of these remains.

Physical anthropology is today a science in its own right, taught in a number of national institutions, sometimes as an optional subject within archaeology. Despite the creation of new departments and laboratories, physical anthropology still faces a number of socio-political and economical factors that shroud its development. Among these are the lack of public interest and most importantly the lack of interest from national governments in providing research grants and funds for financial support. Along with these, and as some of the countries in this section have emphasized, the lack of national postgraduate opportunities in the form of Master's or Doctoral studies to specialize or grow further in the discipline, has made a number of students look for their further development in foreign institutions. Thus, despite recent efforts, new curricula will have to be created in order to accommodate the national requirements for better trained physical anthropologists who wish to further their degree studies.

With regard to the methods used to analyse human skeletal remains, a number of techniques, usually borrowed from other disciplines, have been applied and used by researchers. Although there does not seem to be consensus in terms of current methods used, the four countries have emphasized that most researchers seem to follow the standards proposed by Buikstra and Ubelaker for sexing, ageing and stature assessment. The application of newly adopted or developed methods is usually presented at national and international conferences, such as the Asociación Latinoamericana de Antropología Biológica, or ALAB (Association of Latin American Biological Anthropologists), that bring together specialists with similar interests within the fields of anthropology and archaeology.

The coordinator of this section would like to thank Marina Sardi, Sheila Mendonça de Souza, Eugenio Aspillaga, Bernardo Arriaza and Mónica Sans for their contributions.

Argentina

Marina L. Sardi

INTRODUCTION: A BRIEF HISTORY AND CURRENT STATE OF PHYSICAL ANTHROPOLOGY IN ARGENTINA

Descriptions about aboriginal populations that inhabited Argentina began in the 16th century, a few decades after the European conquest. However, it was during the 19th century that travellers and explorers, most of them of European origin, carried out more systematic studies. In the second half of the 19th century, when the Argentine state was not yet consolidated, the government looked to define its political frontiers by expanding its economic control over vast territories, as well as over aboriginal populations (Podgorny 1999, 2008; Podgorny and Lopes 2008). For this reason, the Argentine State organized military and scientific missions in order to increase the knowledge about its geography and human populations (Podgorny 1999, 2008; Podgorny and Lopes 2008; Farro 2009). The war against these aborigines, known as La Conquista del Desierto ('The Conquest of the Desert'), began in 1879 and resulted in thousands of native people being killed or captured.

Around this time, the Academia de Ciencias de Córdoba (Academy of Sciences of Córdoba), and Sociedad Científica Argentina (Argentine Scientific Society) were established, as well as the first museums with a positivist philosophical approach, for example the Museo de La Plata (Museum of La Plata) and the Museo Etnográfico Juan Bautista Ambrosetti (Juan Bautista Ambrosetti Ethnographic Museum). These museums served to consolidate anthropological activities (Carnese *et al.* 1992) and to house and expose natural and cultural objects recovered in scientific missions carried out by the Argentine government during the military campaigns (Podgorny 2008). Private exhibitions and museums, established some years later, also contributed to the increase in knowledge about American Indians (Podgorny and Lopes 2008).

All material recovered during previous years was organized as scientific collections that have been, until the present day, invaluable material for research. The majority of the collections belonged to native people from all over the Argentine territory. They increased in quantity over the years through different ways of acquisition, although the curation of some of these today may be regarded as non-ethical or questionable. For instance, those institutions also promoted the organizing of new missions, the buying and exchange of objects from private collectors or from other foreign institutions (e.g., from Brussels and Paris), in order to increase the diversity of their collections (Farro 2009). Several private collections were also donated

(Podgorny 2008). During 'The Conquest of the Desert', some people who accompanied the army kept the skulls of aborigines killed during the battles and even robbed the remains and grave goods of some Indians chiefs, such as those of Mariano Rosas, Chipitruz, Gherenal and Callfucura (Zeballos 1960). The skull was the only anatomical part exhumed during these military expeditions, and was later donated to the Museo de La Plata (Lehmann-Nitsche 1910). The Museo de La Plata, under the direction of Francisco P. Moreno, also held some people captured in 'The Conquest of the Desert'. The chiefs of some Patagonian populations, such as Inakayal, Sayeweke and Foyel, as well as their relatives, lived in this institution between 1885 and 1895 (Farro 2009). Some of them died in the museum, whereas others were returned to Patagonia. After their death, many anatomical parts, especially the brain and the skeleton, were incorporated into anthropological collections (Lehmann-Nitsche 1910).

Following the establishment of the first scientific institutions, further institutionalization of physical anthropology arose when the first courses were introduced. The first course in Anthropology was run by a German-born scientist, Professor Robert Lehmann-Nitsche, at the Universidad de Buenos Aires (University of Buenos Aires) in 1903 (Podgorny 2006). In 1905 and 1906, the first professorships were set up at the Universidad de Buenos Aires and the Universidad de La Plata, respectively, both organized by Lehmann-Nitsche. The first degrees in anthropology were established at these universities at the end of the 1950s (Carnese *et al.* 1992).

According to Carnese *et al.* (1992: 36), it was during the second half of the 19th century that biological anthropology began in Argentina as a separate discipline, independent from other natural sciences. Carnese *et al.* (1992) have divided the history of the discipline into three periods, according to the principal ideas that dominated the investigations. Between 1860 and 1920 studies were carried out by Argentine and foreign researchers and focused on human origins and descriptions of South American aborigines (Carnese *et al.* 1992; Marcellino 2002; Carnese and Pucciarelli 2007). The publication of anthropometric measurements had been a common activity since 1874 with Francisco Moreno, an Argentine explorer and naturalist (Podgorny 2006). The French school of anthropology, with the studies of Paul Broca, was influential. During this period, Darwinist theory was adopted and evolutionism gradually replaced creationist and catastrophist paradigms (Carnese *et al.* 1992). Florentino Ameghino made important contributions to anthropology and palaeontology, despite the fact that his theory about human origins in the Argentine Pampas was based on invalid evidence.

The period between 1920 and 1960 was dominated by diffusionist and typological paradigms (Carnese *et al.* 1992). Most studies consisted of skeletal descriptions, lacking in evolutionary explanation. When genetic studies developed, serological indicators were also incorporated into these 'catalogues' of human variation (Carnese *et al.* 1992; Carnese and Pucciarelli 2007).

Since 1960, biological anthropology has incorporated concepts derived from neo-Darwinism and molecular biology (Carnese and Pucciarelli 2007). Studies have focused on several issues, such as micro-evolutionary mechanisms, adaptation, environmental influences on growth and development of past and present populations, bioarchaeology, epidemiology and genetics, among others.

Anthropological studies have been published for more than a century; however, it was not until the end of the 1980s that a group of physical anthropologists from the Universidad de Buenos Aires, Universidad de La Plata, Universidad de Río Cuarto (University of Buenos Aires, University of La Plata and University of Río Cuarto), among others, started to meet together with the objective of unifying teaching methods and to exchange knowledge about their particular areas of study. Following on from these meetings, the First National Meeting of Biological Anthropology was organized in September 1993 at the Museo de La Plata. As a result of the success of this meeting, with more than 100 participants and 40 papers presented, it was decided to create the Asociación Argentina de Antropología Biológica or AABA (Association of Biological Anthropology of Argentina). In addition, it was decided to create a body that would document the home-grown scientific production, and thus the *Revista Argentina de Antropología Biológica*, or RAAB (*Argentinean Journal of Biological Anthropology*) was established. Since 1996, meetings of the AABA have been organized bi-annually and the RAAB is published annually and recently indexed in Latindex. More information can be found on the website of the Argentine Association of Biological Anthropology (www.fcnym.unlp.edu.ar/aabra/).

Biological anthropology has also been central in forensic science, mainly forensic anthropology and archaeology. In 1984 the Equipo Argentino de Antropología Forense, or EAAF (Argentine Forensic Anthropology Team) was created in order to investigate human rights violations in Argentina during the military government that ruled from 1976 to 1983. The EAAF is a non-governmental, non-profit making, scientific organization that conducts forensic investigations in Argentina and, since 1986, in around 30 countries throughout America, Asia, Africa and Europe. More information can be found on their website (www.eaaf.org/: EAAF 2009).

ARCHAEOLOGICAL HUMAN REMAINS AND LEGISLATION

Archaeological legislation

The national law 25,743 (2003) regulates the registration, permission and control of the Argentine archaeological and palaeontological heritage. This law does not make explicit mention of human remains. However, in Article 2 it defines what it considers to be archaeology and this definition includes human remains:

> The archaeological heritage is defined as movable and immovable property or remains regardless of its nature found on the surface, underground or within territorial waters that can provide information about the socio-cultural groups that have inhabited the country from pre-Colombian times to recent historical periods.
>
> *Ley 25,7434, Article 2 [author's translation]*

The Instituto Nacional de Antropología y Pensamiento Latinoamericano, or INAPL (National Institute of Anthropology and Latin American Thinking) is the national authority in charge of the application of the law. According to Article 6, it is the responsibility of each Province (the main territorial division in Argentina) to apply such law and it depends on each province to decide which organization has competence on this issue.[1] The competent provincial organization grants permits, organizes the registration of sites and collections and also applies sanctions to offenders.

In order to carry out an archaeological or palaeontological excavation it is necessary to obtain a permit. The government of each province or community grants permits that should contain the following information (Article 24): name of the scientific person and assistants who are participating in the excavation (with corresponding ID or passport number), name of the institution, map or topographical plan of the location for the proposed excavation, a research plan and its logistical capacity, specific work plan and a timetable for the excavation. For foreign researchers (Article 25) it is necessary, in addition, to have some link with a national scientific institution or Argentine university.

Excavations or removal of materials performed on archaeological or palaeontological sites without given permission will be considered an offence and will lead to confiscation of any material discovered (Article 39). If materials are discovered accidentally, it is necessary to inform the responsible authority of the province or the community; even the police if necessary (Articles 13 and 40).

HUMAN REMAINS AND LEGISLATION

According to the law, there are no guidelines or regulations regarding who can study human remains. When human remains are discovered by accident, regardless of their antiquity, they fall under the remit of the judicial system, after informing the police authorities. In the justice system, there is nothing that indicates that an anthropologist or archaeologist should intervene. On some occasions, forensic doctors may become involved, and in others, an archaeologist is called in from a research institution, such as the Argentine Forensic Anthropology Team (EAAF).

The competent authority of the province or the community can grant temporary loan of collections for research or exhibition inside or outside its jurisdiction (Article 21 and 50). The exchange, donation or barter of materials is not permitted (Article 52). However, the making of casts of materials and their sale is permitted (Article 53). Temporary or permanent permits for the moving of remains out of the country are granted by the INAPL.

National law 25,517 deals with human remains of indigenous people that are held in museums and public and private collections. In Article 3, it states that all scientific research that involves aboriginal communities and their heritage should have the express consent of such communities. Likewise, in Article 1, this law establishes that the human remains of aboriginal populations held in museums and public and private collections should be made available for any reclaim from the communities to which they belong. However, it does not specify the antiquity of the remains and the conditions under which they can be reclaimed, nor does it set out the criteria (geography, ethnicity or kinship) to be considered in carrying out restitution to a specific community.

Even though there are numerous claims made by the communities in Argentina, to date there has only been the restitution of the remains of two persons, held at the Museum of La Plata. In 1994, according to national law 23,940, the remains of Tehuelche Chief Inacayal were buried at Tecka, in the province of Chubut. In 2001, the skull of Mapuche/Ranquel Chief Mariano Rosas, known as Panquitruz Gner among his relatives, was returned to Leuvucó, in the province of La Pampa (national law 25,276), and was buried in a mausoleum.

In recent years, biological anthropologists and archaeologists have begun to work together with aboriginal communities that are close to areas where human remains are found. A recent example is the rescue and relocation of a burial found in the area of Sacanana, in the province of Chubut (Chiquichano *et al.* 2008). In 2003, during an environmental impact study carried out in Sacanana, a team of archaeologists discovered a funerary structure made of stones ('*chenque*'). In 2005, the Minister of Culture of the government of Chubut and the local indigenous communities decided to carry out the rescue and relocation to the land of one of the communities, with the active participation of all the parties involved. Prior to the relocation, a bioanthropological study of the remains was made, including sampling for radiocarbon dating, stable isotopes analysis and for DNA.

At the National Meeting in 2007, the AABA presented a document stating its position regarding human remains (Declaration of AABA in Relation to the Ethics of the Study of Human Remains 2007). This declaration points out that the scientific study of human remains is of interest to all humanity and cannot be replaced by other scientific approaches or by no science at all. As a result it is necessary to facilitate the restitution of remains of known individuals to communities to which they belong that are claiming them; other cases of reclamations will be the subject of special discussion and analysis and it is advisable to listen to any claims or opiniones relating to a public exhibit of human remains if requested by the communities to which they belong.

METHODS OF ANTHROPOLOGICAL ANALYSIS

In Argentina, there is no consensus about standards to be applied in the estimation of sex, age and stature. The main difficulty is that there are no local standards developed specifically for aboriginal populations, which is due to the lack of well documented reference samples.

During recent years, in order to unify methodological criteria, most researchers follow the standards proposed by Acsádi and Nemeskéri (1970) and those compiled by Buikstra and Ubelaker (1994). For age estimation, the standards most applied are those of Todd (1920), Brooks and Suchey (1990) and Lovejoy *et al.* (1985).

In order to estimate stature, the standards of Trotter and Gleser (1952; 1958) are followed and, in some cases, those of Fully (1956) and Genovés (1967).

USEFUL CONTACTS

Argentinian Association for Biological Anthropology. Website: www.fcnym.unlp.edu.ar/aabra/
Argentine Forensic Anthropology Team (Equipo Argentino de Antropología Forense) Website: www.eaaf.org/

ACKNOWLEDGEMENTS

The author is indebted to Paula Gonzalez for important contributions, and, with Paola Ponce and the editors of this book, for the invitation to contribute this chapter and for proof reading and correcting earlier versions. Susana Salceda, Gabriela Ghidini and Irina Podgorny made helpful comments. The Consejo Nacional de Investigaciones Científicas y Técnicas (CONICET, Argentina) and Universidad Nacional de La Plata financed this research.

NOTE

1 Provinces and competent organizations (for more details, see in http://www.inapl.gov.ar/renycoa/ orgaplic.html): Buenos Aires: Dirección Provincial de Patrimonio Cultural. Catamarca: Secretaría de Cultura, Dirección de Patrimonio Cultural. Chaco: Subsecretaría de Cultura, Comisión Provincial de Patrimonio Cultural y Natural. Chubut: Dirección General de Gestión, Investigación y Patrimonio Cultural. Córdoba: Subgerencia de Patrimonio y Museo. Corrientes: Subsecretaría de Cultura, Dirección de Bellas Artes y Patrimonio Cultural. Entre Ríos: Museo de Ciencias Naturales y Antropológicas 'Prof. Antonio Serrano'. Formosa: Dirección de Cultura. Jujuy: Secretaría de Turismo y Cultura, Coordinación de Patrimonio y Museo. La Pampa: Subsecretaría de Cultura. La Rioja: Secretaría de Cultura, Dirección de Patrimonio Cultural y Museos. Mendoza: Subsecretaría de Cultura, Dirección de Patrimonio Cultural. Misiones: Subsecretaría de Cultura. Neuquen: Secretaría de Estado de Cultura, Dirección General de Patrimonio Cultural. Río Negro: Dirección General de Cultura. Salta: Dirección General de Patrimonio Cultural, Subsecretaría de Cultura. San Juan: Subsecretaría de Cultura. Tucumán: Dirección de Patrimonio Histórico y Antropología. San Luis: Subprograma de Áreas Protegidas, Identidad Paisajística, Parques Urbanos y Forestación. Santa Cruz: Dirección del "Museo Regional Padre Jesus Molina". Santa Fe: Dirección Provincial de Patrimonio. Santiago Del Estero: Subsecretaría

de Cultura. Tierra del Fuego: Dirección de Ciencia y Tecnología, Secretaría de Promoción Económica y Fiscal. Ciudad Autónoma de Buenos Aires: Dirección General de Patrimonio.

BIBLIOGRAPHY

AABA (2009) *Asociación de Antropología Biológica Argentina*. Online. Available HTTP: <http://www.fcnym.unlp.edu.ar/aabra/> (accessed 17 March 2010).

Acsádi, G. and Nemeskéri, J. (1970) *History of Human Life Span and Mortality*, Budapest: Akadémiai Kiadó.

Brooks, S.T. and Suchey, J.M. (1990) 'Skeletal age determination based on the os pubis: a comparison of the Acsádi-Nemeskéri and Suchey-Brooks methods', *Human Evolution*, 5: 227–38.

Buikstra, J. and Ubelaker, D. (eds) (1994) *Standards for Data Collection from Human Skeletal Remains*, Fayetteville, AR: Arkansas Archaeological Survey Research Series No. 44.

Carnese, F.R., Cocilovo, J.A. and Goicoechea, A.S. (1992) 'Análisis histórico y estado actual de la Antropología Biológica en la Argentina', *Runa*, 20: 35–67.

Carnese, F.R. and Pucciarelli, H.M. (2007) 'Investigaciones antropobiológicas en Argentina, desde la década de 1930 hasta la actualidad', *Relaciones de la Sociedad Argentina de Antropología*, 32: 243–80.

Chiquichano, F., Sayhueque, C. and Dahinten, S. (2008) 'El rescate y relocalización del chenque de Sacanana (meseta centro-norte de la provincia de Chubut, Argentina)', *X Congreso de la Asociación Latinoamericana de Antropología Biológica, La Plata*. Available online at www.xalab.fcnym.unlp.edu.ar/index.php-action=simRELENTREANTROP.htm (accessed 17 March 2010).

Declaration of AABA in Relation to the Ethics of the Study of Human Remains (2007) *Ética del estudio de restos humanos*. Available online at www.fcnym.unlp.edu.ar/aabra/ (accessed 17 March 2010).

EAAF (2009) Argentine Forensic Anthropology Team. Available online at www.eaaf.org/ (accessed 17 March 2010).

Farro, M. (2009) *La formación del Museo de La Plata. Coleccionistas, Comerciantes, Estudiosos y Naturalistas Viajeros a Fines del Siglo XIX*, Rosario: Prohistoria Ediciones.

Fully, G. (1956) 'Une nouvelle méthode de détermination de la taille', *Annales de Médecine Légale*, 35: 266–73.

Genovés, S. (1967) 'Proportionality of the long bones and their relation to stature among mesoamericans', *American Journal of Physical Anthropology*, 26: 67–77.

Lehmann-Nitsche, R. (1910) *Catálogo de la Sección Antropología del Museo de La Plata*, Buenos Aires: Coni.

Lovejoy, C.O., Meindl, R.S., Pryzbeck, T.R., et al. (1985) 'Chronological metamorphosis of the auricular surface of the ilium: a new method for the determination of adult skeletal age at death', *American Journal of Physical Anthropology*, 68: 15–28.

Marcellino, A.J. (2002) *La Literatura Bioantropológica Argentina (1865–1995)*, Córdoba: Editorial Universidad Nacional de Córdoba.

Podgorny, I. (1999) 'La Patagonia como santuario natural de la ciencia finisecular', *Redes*, 6: 157–76.

——(2006). 'La Derrota del Genio. Cráneos y cerebros en la filogenia argentina', *Saber y Tiempo*, 5: 63–106.

——(2008) 'Momias que hablan. Ciencia, colección de cuerpos y experiencias con la vida y la muerte en la década de 1880', *Prismas, Revista de historia intelectual*, 12: 49–65.

Podgorny, I. and Lopes, M.M. (2008) *El Desierto en una Vitrina. Museos e Historia Natural en la Argentina, 1810–1890*, Mexico: Limusa.

Todd, T.W. (1920) 'Age changes in the pubic bone', *American Journal of Physical Anthropology*, 3: 285–334.

Trotter, M. and Gleser, G. (1952) 'Estimation of stature from long bones of American whites and Negroes', *American Journal of Physical Anthropology*, 10: 469–514.

——(1958) 'A re-evaluation of estimation of stature based on measurements taken during life and the long bones after death', *American Journal of Physical Anthropology*, 16: 79–123.

Zeballos, E. (1960) [1881] *Viaje al País de los Araucanos*, Buenos Aires: Hachette.

Brazil/Brasil

Sheila Maria Ferraz Mendonça de Souza

INTRODUCTION: A BRIEF HISTORY AND CURRENT STATE OF PHYSICAL ANTHROPOLOGY IN BRAZIL

In Brazil, as in other countries during the 19th century, archaeology and anthropology were non-vocational. Contributions from scientists from different areas helped to promote the importance of the prehistoric and historical heritage. In the first half of the 20th century Brazil was a young republic constructing its own values. It was during this period of profound national change, along with the joint effort provided by the sciences and arts to preserve the nation's heritage, that the first protection laws concerning archaeological sites were set up.

Due to the small number of professionals and institutions in Brazil it was only during the second half of the 20th century that the excavation, recovery and analysis of archaeological human remains were improved and finally became regulated. It was only during the 1970s that increased research, theoretical support and ethical principles really impacted on the control of research and curatorial activities.

The first to describe archaeological human bones in the country was Peter Lund, a palaeontologist working in Brazil in the first half of the 19th century (Lund 1950; Souza *et al.* 2006). His discoveries of the Lagoa Santa skeletons, one of the first discoveries of ancient fossils in the world, called attention to Brazil and the antiquity of settlement in our territory. Some internationally important names such as Rudolf Virchow exchanged letters and scientific opinions about the first mineralized bones from Lagoa Santa. Sören Hansen published scientific papers in 1883 on some of the skulls excavated by Lund, preserved in the Copenhagen museum.

However, the real beginning of physical anthropology in Brazil was in the 19th century when the Brazilian Emperor Peter II improved the scientific research at the Royal Museum. According to Schwarcz (1993), the strong links between Brazil and European countries helped to attract people such as Darwin and Broca to take part in the Museum committees as consultants. The first Brazilian Anthropological Exhibition including modern, as well as prehistoric skulls was opened in 1882. At this time, the person in charge of the Section of Anthropology, General Applied Zoology, Comparative Anatomy and Animal Palaeontology was João Baptista de Lacerda. Under the auspices of Peter II, Lacerda studied past and present Indian bones and discussed human evolution. He ran the first anthropology course in Brazil (Santos 2002). Many papers about the prehistoric human bones from Lagoa Santa and from the Brazilian shell mounds, or *sambaquis*, were published (Lacerda 1876). These remains date to around 11,000 BP. It was in the same museum, not an Imperial Museum any more but the Museu Nacional (National Museum), that anthropological studies have developed most in Brazil. Other institutions contributed more and more to the study of past human remains, but it was the Museu Nacional, today belonging to the Universidade Federal do Rio de Janeiro, that contributed to the longest period of scientific investigation and collection of human remains in this country (Santos 2002; Faria 2000).

According to Faria (2000), the history of physical anthropology in Brazil can be divided into three distinct periods. The first period was the formation period, from the 19th century to 1910. In the second period researchers turned their attention to modern groups and discussions about race and nationality and therefore little osteological research was undertaken on past populations. The third period starts in the 1930s. A number of important contributions in this period included the publication of the first edition of *Antropologia Física* ('Physical Anthropology') in Portuguese, by José Bastos D'Ávila (Ávila 1958) from the National Museum; the creation of new disciplines of anthropology at Brazilian Universities and the increasing interest in heritage and scientific research in all the anthropological fields.

Until the 1970s most of the osteological analysis, aimed at classifying human remains and testing their biological affinities, was based on osteometrics (Alvim 1963; Alvim and Seyferth 1971). The fields of osteometrics and osteology were considered very important for prehistoric studies during the 1970s in Brazil. The first Brazilian Manual of Craniometry and Craniology (Pereira and Alvim 1979) was published during that time. Adapting the more important technical standards from the German and French literature, and adding craniometrics based on radiological techniques, this manual has been used for both living and skeletonized individuals for decades. The second volume by the same authors, describing post-cranial osteometrics and osteology, was still in draft form when Marilia Carvalho de Mello e Alvim suddenly died in 1995, and it was never published. The use of multivariate analysis in osteometrics only became popular in Brazil after the contribution of Walter Neves, who in the 1980s brought the craniometric methods proposed by Howells (1973) to the study of cranial variation in Man.

At that time palaeopathology was still an isolated subject of interest to Ernesto de Mello Salles Cunha, a professor of dental pathology (Cunha 1959), who dedicated himself to the study of ancient skulls for almost two decades. The initial development of the studies of the health of past populations in Brazil and other countries by Brazilian professionals progressed after the 1970s, with the contribution of the present author among others (Ferraz 1977; Souza 1993; Souza *et al.* 2003; Lessa and Souza 2004; Wesolowski *et al.* 2007; Souza *et al.* 2008). Studies in epigenetics, palaeodemography and other fields were also progressively incorporated into the bioarchaeology of human remains. The field of skeletal biology was improved and new methods and techniques were introduced by subsequent generations of professionals, who helped to establish a new international network of South American, European and North American professionals. In some of the papers of the same period it is possible to confirm how the first professionals progressively incorporated new research lines (Alvim and Soares 1984; Uchoa and Alvim 1989). A rapid improvement in the academic activities in Brazil, especially at the graduate level, was fundamental to explaining the increasing number of specialized professionals in the field of bioarchaeology, and the substantial amount of scientific contribution to this field in the last few years (Buikstra and Beck 2006).

Currently there are two main groups of osteologists in Brazil. One is headed by Walter Neves, from the Universidade de São Paulo (University of São Paulo), and is dedicated to multivariate analysis, microevolution and the investigation into the settlement of the Americas (Neves 1989; Neves *et al.* 1999; Neves *et al.* 2005; Neves *et al.* 2007). The other group, headed by the present author and the team at the Fundação Oswaldo Cruz, Rio de Janeiro, is dedicated to bone and teeth palaeopathology and different kinds of mummified samples. The study of other remains such as coprolites and microresidues of food is also carried out by another group of specialists headed by Dr Adauto Araújo, at Fiocruz. Palaeogenetics, palaeonutrition, mobility and other subjects have also been developed in recent times, complementary to the investigation of the relationship between lifestyle, health and disease in the past. Funerary archaeology, as an important part of the study of human remains, has also been improved in Brazil in the last years. A few special projects on bioarchaeology were conducted by both groups in the last few decades, promising more and better interpretation of human remains in the near future.

The methodological changes of the last few decades have improved the study of human remains. Future analyses of the scientific field will hopefully define other important transitions to explain the history of Brazilian Anthropology. Osteology, supported by scientific improvements and laws, is developing fast.

Professional archaeology and physical anthropology

Archaeology today is recognized as a professional activity in Brazil, ruled by its own Ethical Code. The Sociedade de Arqueologia Brasileira, or SAB (SAB 2009), gathers hundreds of professionals and students. Only a few of those professionals are specialists dedicated to human remains.

Bioarchaeology in Brazil has always been more strongly connected to the biomedical field, but in recent decades it is getting closer to archaeology. More attention is dedicated to funerary and taphonomic aspects during the biological analysis of the remains.

Forensic anthropology is still a minor field of investigation, still waiting for substantial development. Only on some occasions is a forensic or physical anthropologist required to provide evidence in court. As a consequence, archaeological sites containing human skeletal remains are excavated by archaeologists with different expertises; to have a bioarchaeologist available on an archaeological site is seldom possible.

ARCHAEOLOGICAL HUMAN REMAINS AND LEGISLATION

Archaeological legislation

Today, archaeological sites are fully protected and the activities concerning the excavation of sites and the conservation of heritage and archaeological remains are under the supervision of the State (Soares 2007) through the main Federal institution, the Instituto do Patrimônio Histórico e Arqueológico Nacional, or IPHAN (National Institute of Historical and Archaeological Heritage). IPHAN (IPHAN 2009) was created in the 1930s and belongs to the Ministry of Culture of Brazil.

Heritage protection and archaeological policing are helped by the State and County authorities. Private institutions, and all Brazilian citizens, are also legally obliged to comply with the protection of archaeological sites under the Brazilian Constitution (Articles 215 and 216). Contrary to what happens in other countries, whatever is within the Brazilian soil belongs to the Brazilian Nation, not to any landowner. This legal disposition assures permanent protection to the archaeological sites against non-authorized excavation.

Some specific legal instruments protect archaeological sites. Law 25 (30/11/1937) and Law 3924 (26/07/1961) are the main instruments of heritage protection, and they specify that burial pits, graves, and cemeteries are among the protected sites. Sending archaeological material, human bones or any other archaeological evidence to another country is totally forbidden, except in very special conditions (for example, for authorized laboratory analysis that cannot be undertaken in Brazil; or travelling for temporary and authorized exhibitions in a foreign country). The projects and authorization for any archaeological research must follow the rules established by an IPHAN special document (Portaria 7, 1 December 1988). Any archaeologist representing public or private institutions must follow these instructions to obtain permission to excavate archaeological sites in Brazil. Foreign researchers can be authorized only when working in cooperation with Brazilian institutions. Non-vocational or amateur archaeology in Brazil is also completely forbidden.

Commercial archaeology (Caldarelli and dos Santos 1999–2000) started in Brazil in the 1980s, based on resolution 001 (23 January 1986) of the Conselho Nacional do Meio Ambiente, or CONAMA (National Council for the Environment), an organization that regulates and controls the environmental impact of engineering works such as roads, dams, and other large scale changes in the terrain. Archaeological surveys before the commencement of such works are obligatory, as well as evaluation and excavation to save endangered sites. Rescue of archaeological remains generally involves public and private universities and other academic institutions.

The archaeological survey, as well as the research, is ruled by two other IPHAN documents (Portaria 230 of 17 December 2002 and Portaria 28 of 31 January 2003).[1] Although it may be difficult to keep control of thousands of sites and hundreds of collections in such a big country as Brazil, the protection of our heritage has been improved in the last few decades, and the specific penalties for destruction of archaeological sites, cemeteries included, are detailed in Federal Law number 6514 (26 July 2008). Complete texts providing regulation of archaeological activities in Brazil can be found on the web (Arqueologia Brasil 2009).

HUMAN REMAINS AND LEGISLATION

The discovery of recent human skeletal remains is often placed on the border between forensic and archaeological interests, and the finding of mummified corpses or bones, for instance, may have either a forensic or an archaeological interest, depending on the case. A joint action of the heritage services and the legal authorities must be orchestrated to improve the decisions about the involvement of archaeologists in the excavation and analysis of human remains. In the absence of a clear protocol to deal with accidentally found human remains, it is necessary to consider the jurisprudence, technical information and professional experience to take decisions about cases that can be either forensic or archaeological.

Preservation of the historic urban cemeteries is a special concern for IPHAN, which has to consider their architectonic and urbanistic aspects. In respect of human remains, there is a contemporaneous body of laws ruling the rights and duties related to funerals, to the deceased and to their bodies (Silva 2000). It constitutes an intricate set of documents, not clearly connected to the anthropological field. A complex set of texts such as the Brazilian Constitution, the Civil Code and the Criminal Code, among other documents, rule on the subject of death. Osteological analysis of archaeological human remains is not compulsory in Brazil; instead, it is a matter of scientific choice.

No case of reburial of human remains has been registered in Brazil. Bones, as with other biological remains, are preserved in repositories at the museums and other academic institutions. It is compulsory to keep available inventories of the collections; the inventories are required to be sent to IPHAN, which keep files available to the public about the archaeological sites in the whole country.

METHODS OF ANTHROPOLOGICAL ANALYSIS

Most of the professionals in Brazil use their personal protocols for human remains, adapted mainly from the North American literature. As a general rule, since the 1990s the recommendations of Buikstra and Ubelaker (1994) for NAGPRA inventories were well accepted as a guideline for simplified description of age, sex, taphonomy, etc. The acceptance of those standards for different South American countries was formally recommended in a meeting of the Associação Latinoamericana de Antropologia Biológica, or ALAB (Latin American Association of Biological Anthropology), in Buenos Aires in 1996.

Stature estimation is based on the formulae proposed by Genovés (1967) and Trotter (1970) for American people. The long bone length of fragmentary remains is usually based on Steele and Bramblet (1988).

The curating of human bones generally follows the recommendations of UNESCO. A synthesis of curatorial recommendations for Brazilian archaeologists was published by Loredo (1994). Some manuals, such as Bass (1995), also provide guidelines for most of the bioarchaeologists in Brazil. Two additional papers were published here, providing additional information in Brazilian Portuguese for the archaeologists and physical anthropologists: Neves (1988) adapted the most important principles for curating archaeological skeletons, and Souza (1986) summarized instructions for the conservation and restoration of archaeological bones.

Well regulated professional training concerning the study of human remains is expected to be offered in the near future in Brazil. As the number of professionals dealing with human remains is continuously increasing, new conditions are created for professional development. The comparative experience of different countries and the peculiarities of our history and cultural traditions will certainly help to point us in future directions.

USEFUL CONTACTS

Society for Brazilian Archaeology. Website: www.sabnet.com.br/

NOTE

1 Portaria 241, of 19/11/1998, presents the form model to register archaeological sites in the Cadastro Nacional de Pesquisas Arqueológicas (National Archaeological Research Files), including basic bioarchaeological data.

BIBLIOGRAPHY

Ávila, J.B. (1958) *Antropologia Física*, Rio de Janeiro: Livraria e Ed. Agir.

Alvim, M.C. de M. e (1963) 'Diversidade morfológica entre os índios "Botocudo" do Leste brasileiro (Séc. XIX) e o Homem de Lagoa Santa', *Boletim do Museu Nacional – Antropologia/NS (Rio de Janeiro)*, 23: 1–70.

Alvim, M.C. de M. e and Seyferth, G. (1971) 'O femur na população do Sambaqui de Cabeçuda (Laguna), Estado de Santa Catarina, Brasil', *Boletim do Museu Nacional – Antropologia/NS (Rio de Janeiro)*, 24: 1–14.

Alvim, M.C. de M. e and Soares, MC. (1984) 'Incidência de traços não-métricos em material de sambaqui do acervo do Museu Nacional da Universidade Federal do Rio de Janeiro', *Revista de Arqueologia (Belém)*, 2: 3–12.

Arqueologia Brasil (2009) *As principais leis que regem o patrimônio arqueológico nacional.* Available online at www.arqueologiabrasil.com.br/arqueologia/leis.shtm (accessed 17 March 2010).

Bass, W. (1995) *Human Osteology. A Laboratory and Field Manual.*, Columbia, Mo: Archaeological Society (Special Publications No. 2).

Buikstra, J.E. and Beck, L.A. (2006) *Bioarchaeology. The Contextual Analysis of Human Remains*, New York: Academic Press.

Buikstra, J.E. and Ubelaker, D. (eds) (1994) *Standards for Data Collection from Human Skeletal Remains*, Fayetteville, AR: Arkansas Archaeological Survey Research Series No. 44.

Caldarelli, S.B. and dos Santos, M. de C.M.M. (1999/2000) 'Arqueologia de Contrato no Brasil', *Revista USP (São Paulo). Antes de Cabral: Arqueologia Brasileira*, 44: 52–73.

Cunha, E. de M.S. (1959) 'Patología odonto-maxilar do Homem do Sambaqui', *Revista Brasileira de Odontologia*, 17: 541–53.

Faria, L. de C. (2000) *Antropologia. Escritos Exumados: Dimensões do Conhecimento Antropológico*, Niterói: EDUFF.

Ferraz, S.M. (1977) 'Análise paleopatológioca de um cemitério indígena', *Nheengatu. Revista Brasileira de Arqueologia e Indigenismo (Rio de Janeiro)*, 1: 7–38.

Genovés, S. (1967) 'Proportionality of the long bones and their relation to stature among Mesoamericans', *American Journal of Physical Anthropology*, 26: 67–77.

Howells, W.W. (1973) *Cranial variation in man: a study of multivariate analysis of patterns of differences among recent human population*, Cambridge, Mass: Papers of the Peabody Museum of Archaeology and Ethnology 67.

IPHAN (2009) *Instituto do Patrimônio Histórico e Artístico Nacional.* Available online at www.iphan.gov.br (accessed 17 March 2010).

Lacerda Filho, J.B. de (1876) 'Contribuições para o estudo anthropológico das raças indígenas do Brasil. Nota sobre a conformação dos dentes', *Arquivos do Museu Nacional (Rio de Janeiro)*, 1: 77–83.

Lessa, A. and de Souza, S.M.F.M. (2004) 'Violence in the Atacama desert during the Tiwanaku period: social tension?', *International Journal of Osteoarchaeology*, 14: 374–88.

Loredo, W.M. (1994) *Manual de conservação em arqueologia de campo*, Rio de Janeiro: IBPH.

Lund, P.W. (1950) *Memórias sobre a paleontologia brasileira*, Rio de Janeiro: Instituto Nacional do Livro.

Neves, W.A. (1988) 'Uma proposta pragmática para cura e recuperação de coleções de esqueletos humanos de origem arqueológica', *Boletim do Museu Paraense Emilio Göeldi–Zoologia (Belém)*, 4: 3–26.

——(1989) 'Paleogenética dos grupos pré-históricos do litoral sul do Brasil (Paraná e Santa Catarina)', *Pesquisas (São Leopoldo)*, 43: 1–160.

Neves, W.A., Hubbe, M., Okomura, M.M.M., *et al.* (2005) 'A new early Holocene human skeleton from Brazil: implications for the settlement of the New World', *Journal of Human Evolution*, 48: 403–15.

Neves, W.A., Hubbe, M. and Pilo, L.B. (2007) 'Early Holocene human skeletal remains from Sumidouro Cave, Lagoa Santa, Brazil: history of discoveries, geological and chronological context, and comparative cranial morphology', *Journal of Human Evolution*, 52: 16–30.

Neves, W.A., Powell, J.F. and Ozolins, E.G. (1999) 'Extra-continental morphological affinities of Lapa Vermelha IV, Hominid I: A multivariate analysis with progressive numbers of variables', *Homo*, 50: 263–82.

Pereira, C.B. and Alvim, M.C. de M. e (1979) *Manual para estudos craniométricos e cranioscópicos*, Santa Maria: Universidade de Santa Maria.

SAB (2009) *Society for Brazilian Archaeology.* Available online at www.sabnet.com.br/ (accessed 17 March 2010).

Santos, R.V. (2002) 'Mestiçagem, degeneração e a variabilidade de uma nação: debates em antropologia física no Brasil (1870–1930)', in S. Pena (ed.) *Homo brasilis. Aspectos Genéticos, Linguísticos, Históricos e Sócioantropológicos da Formação do Povo Brasileiro*, Ribeirão Preto: Fumpec.

Schwarcz, L.M. (1993) *O Espetáculo das raças. Cientistas, instituições e questão racial no Brasil. 1870–1930*, Rio de Janeiro: Companhia das Letras.

Silva, J.A.F da (2000) *Tratado de Direito Funerário*, São Paulo: Método Editora.

Soares, I.V.P. (2007) *Proteção Jurídica do Patrimônio Arqueológico no Brasil*, Erechin: Habilis/Sociedade de Arqueologia Brasileira.

Souza, A.A.C.M. de (1986) 'Restauração de restos diretos e artefatos sobre ossos', *Clio(Recife)*, 8: 163–69.

——(1991) 'História da arqueologia brasileira', *Pesquisas (São Leopoldo)*, 46: 1–157.

Souza, S.M.F.M. de (1993) 'Paleopatologia humana de Santana do Riacho', *Arquivos do Museu de Historia Natural da UFMG*, 13: 129–60.

Souza, S.M.F.M. de, Carvalho, D.M. de, and Lessa, A. (2003) 'Paleoepidemiology: is there a case to answer?', *Memórias do Instituto Oswaldo Cruz*, 98: 21–27.

Souza, S.M.F.M. de, Reinhard, K.J. and Lessa, A. (2008) 'Cranial deformation as the cause of death for a child from the Chillon river valley, Peru', *Chungará (Arica)*, 40: 41–53.

Souza, S.M.F.M. de, Rodrigues-Carvalho, C., Silva, H., *et al.* (2006) 'Revisitando a discussão sobre o Quaternário de Lagoa Santa e o povoamento das Américas: 160 anos de debates científicos', in H. Silva and C. Rodrigues-Carvalho (eds) *Nossa Origem. O Povoamento das Américas, Visões Multidisciplinares*, Rio de Janeiro: Vieira and Lent.

Steele, D.G. and Bramblet, C.A. (1988) *The Anatomy and Biology of the Human Skeleton*, College Station: Texas A & M University Press.

Trotter, M. (1970) 'Estimation of stature from intact limb bones', in T.D. Stewart (ed.) *Personal identification in mass disasters*, Washington, DC: National Museum of Natural History.

Uchoa, D.P. and Alvim, M.C. de M. e (1989) 'Demografia esqueletal dos construtores do Sambaqui de Piaçaguera, São Paulo-Brasil', *Dédalo – Publicação Avulsa (São Paulo)*, 1: 455–72.

Wesolowski, V., Souza, S.M.F.M. de, Reinhard, K.J., *et al.* (2007) 'Gênulos de amido e fitólitosem cálculos dentários humanos: contribuição ao estudo do modo de vida e subsistência de grupos sambaquianos do litoral sul do Brasil', *Revista do Museu de Arqueologia e Etnologia*, 17: 191–210.

Chile

Eugenio Aspillaga Fontaine and Bernardo Arriaza

INTRODUCTION: BRIEF A HISTORY AND CURRENT STATE OF PHYSICAL ANTHROPOLOGY IN CHILE

As in many countries, physical anthropology in Chile had a number of stages prior to its institutionalization in academic groups and other centres of research, especially museums. These initial stages can be reduced in our country into two parts; the first being a historical or pre-scientific stage from the start of the European conquest of this part of the continent until the mid-19th century, in which chroniclers, travellers, naturalists and others made observations on human variation.

The second pre-institutional stage of physical anthropology, although with blurred boundaries, was comprised of not only the contributions of foreign naturalists such as Charles Darwin and other scientists, especially medical doctors and assistants to expeditions such as the French missions to Cape Horn, but also Chilean historians and other native or foreign professionals. This stage, which lasted until the middle of the 20th century, was characterized by an increasing interest in prehistory, ethnology, linguistics and other disciplines related to anthropology, which set up the basis for the relationship between archaeology and physical anthropology. Thus, for example, Darwin's observations about human groups from the extreme southern part of Chile were of limited value to physical anthropology; his theory, however, had an impact on Chilean intellectuals (Manríquez and Rothhammer 1997), stimulating academic discussion, including about the origins of indigenous populations.

In this second stage, some Chilean authors to highlight are Diego Barros Arana (1830–1907), José Toribio Medina (1852–1930), Aureliano Oyarzún (1858–1947), Carlos E. Porter (1867–1942) and Ricardo Latcham (1869–1943) among others, who raised an interest in the human populations that occupied Chile in the past. Among these contributors, the work of J.T. Medina is, as Orellana (1996) points out, the first relevant publication in anthropology (Rothhammer and Aspillaga 1997). Likewise, foreign authors based in Chile, such as Rodulfo Amando Philippi (1808–1904) and Francisco Fonck (1830–1912), produced important contributions. Similarly, the relevant work of the German archaeologist Max Uhle (1856–1944) should be highlighted, since he contributed to the consolidation of archaeological institutions in the country, started bioanthropological collections and promoted the Museum of Ethnology and Anthropology of Chile. Among his colleagues was the German anthropologist and priest Martín Gusinde (1886–1969), who was in Chile at the same time and carried out very important work on the ethnography and physical anthropology of the people of Tierra del Fuego (Rothhammer and Aspillaga 1997).

One of the scientists who took the first steps towards the consolidation of physical anthropology in this second stage and facilitated the change to academic institutionalization was the German pathologist and anatomist Carlos Henckel (1899–1984). He was hired by the Universidad de Concepción (University of Concepción) in 1929 and contributed two chapters on the physical anthropology of the Chilean aborigines in the *Handbook of South American Indian*, published by the Smithsonian Institute in 1950. He also published other works about the anatomical variation of indigenous Mapuches (Rothhammer and Aspillaga 1997). The same university also hired the German doctor Alejandro Lipschutz (1883–1980), who carried out one of the first studies on the blood groups, together with other medical records, of Fuegian populations.

A number of other disciplines such as medicine, odontology and different specialities of biology have contributed to the consolidation of physical anthropology in the country. It would be difficult to detail them here, but we can exemplify them by the contributions of the team working at the laboratory of physical anthropology at the Universidad Católica de Valparaíso (Catholic University of Valparaíso), directed by Atilio Almagiá; or with the work undertaken by different haematologists and many other specialists that have studied of human variation.

Physical anthropology was consolidated institutionally in 1954, with the creation of the Centro de Estudios Antropológicos de la Universidad de Chile (Centre for Anthropological Studies at the University of Chile), a body which, since its creation, integrated different branches of anthropology, including social anthropology, archaeology and physical anthropology. Among its members was Juan Munizaga, who decisively drove the discipline in the university sphere. He created the first professorship in the discipline when the centre was transformed into the Department of Anthropology of the University of Chile and was therefore the first school of anthropology in the country. In this way, Munizaga and many of his archaeology and biology students mainly, founded the discipline and widened its horizons throughout the country. Silvia Quevedo, in the Museo de Historia Natural de Santiago de Chile (Museum of Natural History of Santiago de Chile), Mario Castro on the Board of Museums, Patricio Urquieta in the Faculty of Odontology at the Universidad de Chile and others, including Eugenio Aspillaga, have continued the work started by Juan Munizaga.

In parallel with the above, Chilean and foreign geneticists produced important research work on various aspects of the genetic variation of different Chilean populations. Chilean researchers to highlight are Dr Ricardo Cruz-Coke, awarded the national science prize, Edmundo Covarrubias, Juan Pinto-Cisternas, Carlos Valenzuela, Hernán Palomino, Rafael Blanco and Francisco Rothhammer. The latter was responsible for increasing the collaboration between geneticists, archaeologists and physical anthropologists not only in Chile but also in the rest of South America. This led, in 1998, to the creation, in Santiago de Chile, *of the* Asociación Latinoamericana de Antropología Biológica, or ALAB (Association of Latin American Biological Anthropologists) (Rothhammer and Aspillaga 1997), a body which influenced the increasing status of the discipline. Today, the collaboration between human geneticists, biochemists, doctors and other specialists with physical anthropologists continues, extending beyond research and contributing to the formation of new generations of students.

As in the previous stages, foreign researchers continue to work in the country. Among these, we should mention Richard Schaedel (1920–2005) who, apart from his contribution to research, supervised and contributed to training anthropologists during his stay in the Centre of Anthropological Studies at the University of Chile. Another important collaborative work on mummies was carried out by the North American doctor and palaeopathologist Arthur C. Aufderheide (1922–), together with researchers from the Universidad de Tarapacá in Arica, including the physical anthropologist Bernardo Arriaza. Arriaza, together with Vivien Standen, started his career in physical anthropology with Marvin Allison, a North American pathologist working at the Archaeological Museum of San Miguel de Azapa (Museo Arqueológico San Miguel de Azapa 2009). He came to Chile with the Argentinean doctor Enrique Gerszten at the end of the 1970s to work alongside Juan Munizaga. The latter settled down in the city of Arica promoting research on palaeopathology within the region. It is also important to highlight the contribution of the Brazilian physical anthropologist María Antonieta Costa-Junqueira, who, over a number of years, contributed to research in the field for the Archaeological Museum of Le Paige, founded in 1957 in San Pedro de Atacama by a Belgium priest (Universitad Católica del Norte 2009). These two museums are considered today the centres with the largest osteological and mummified collections in the country.

Following the sad and painful period of violations of human rights carried out during the military dictatorship (1973–90) it became clear that there was a glaring lack of specialists in forensic anthropology and related research that would have allowed the standardization of methods and techniques of identification of human skeletal remains. This work had been started by Juan Munizaga at the end of the 1960s and was interrupted in 1979 by the dictatorship. In 1999, the Faculty of Social Sciences of the Universidad de Chile (Facultad de Ciencias Sociales 2009) started to regularly run an undergraduate course, specifically in physical anthropology, with a subject in forensic anthropology, which is still today the only one running in the country. From this date, students of anthropology, after completing a basic term of social sciences, can opt to specialize in one of the three branches that make up the Department of Anthropology: social anthropology, archaeology or physical anthropology. The last one is carried out in conjunction with the Faculty of Medicine and with academics from both faculties as well as odontology. The students are trained in the principle topics of physical anthropology, palaeopathology, bioarchaeology, human genetics, human palaeontology and forensic anthropology, among other subjects. Students learn the methods and techniques in use in the discipline, and they apply them in spheres as varied as geometric morphology and DNA studies. This training has allowed these students to become part of research teams in different parts of the country and to carry out their postgraduate studies overseas. This is complemented by Chilean researchers holding teaching positions overseas, such as Dr Maria Rosado Rowan who works at the University of Glassboro, NJ, USA, or René Bobe, who works in human palaeontology with a particular interest in the palaeoecology of African hominids. Baruch Arensburg, a Chilean researcher who has migrated to Israel (Department of Anatomy and Anthropology, Faculty of Medicine, Tel Aviv University) developed an excellent academic career in physical anthropology and comes regularly to visit Chilean institutions for teaching and lecturing purposes.

Today a number of universities have incorporated the teaching of physical anthropology among their disciplines, especially in the degrees of anthropology or similar sciences. Likewise a number of institutions have started to include graduates of this speciality within their teams. Nevertheless, research funds and grants to specialize in the discipline are limited. Similarly, not all museums where there are bioanthropological collections have a specialist on their staff, including such important museums as the National Museum of Natural History in Santiago de Chile (Museo Nacional de Historia Natural 2009).

Despite this and the number of other obstacles, the role that the physical anthropologist plays in archaeological excavations, as well as the situation with the collections directly related to the first settlers, the future of the discipline appears promising, with new generations facing novel research problems.

Finally, most physical anthropologists are today members of the Chilean Society of Archaeologists (SChA 2009) which gathers together hundreds of national and international professionals interested in Chilean archaeology and its heritage.

ARCHAEOLOGICAL HUMAN REMAINS AND LEGISLATION

Archaeological legislation

The excavation of cemeteries

A number of legal frameworks in Chile regulate the excavation of cemeteries, differentiating those of an archaeological nature from those historical cemeteries which are still in use, such as the Cementerio General de Santiago (General Cemetery of Santiago). Excavations in the former group are regulated by National Monuments Law 17,288 (1970), which in Article 1 states that:

> The national monuments that remain under the custody and protection of the state are the sites, ruins, constructions or objects of historical or artistic character, burials or cemeteries or other aborigine remains, artefacts or objects anthropo-archaeological, palaeontological or of natural formation, that exist below or on the surface of the national territory or in the submarine platform of the territorial waters and whose conservation is of historical, artistic or scientific interest ...
>
> *National Monuments Law 17,288 (1970), Article 1 [author's translation]*

In Article 21 of the same law, the definition of archaeological heritage simply refers to 'those Archaeological Monuments owned by the state are places, ruins, sites and anthropo-archaeological artefacts that exist on or below the surface of the national territory' [translation by Paola Ponce].

Palaeontological sites and artefacts are also included in this law (Section V, 'On Archaeological Monuments, Excavations and Scientific Research'). Under this section, the law also points out that no excavation of an archaeological site can be carried out without the express authorization of a central designated body that watches over the compliance of these rules, the Consejo de Monumentos Nacionales (Council of National Monuments). The Council is comprised of 20 representatives of various bodies of the state, curators of national museums and representatives of various civil bodies related to the national heritage. This body is presided over by the Minister of Education, with the Director of Libraries, Archives and Museums as the Executive Vice-President, and counting among its members a representative of the Chilean Society of Archaeology. A number of renowned archaeologists work in the aforementioned Council, although they have no qualified physical anthropologists on the permanent team. In addition, advisory boards, made up of local authorities, assist with the work of the Council in only three regions of the country. There exists, at present, a growing interest in the Council having more regional representatives to better manage their local heritage. This would have many advantages, although as it tends to divide up the collections, it makes the logistics necessary for adequate study and conservation more difficult due to the limitations on prevailing budgets.

Section V, already referred to above, also points out the conditions under which foreign scientists can excavate in Chile. These include, among others, the necessity for a Chilean counterpart, and support from an academic institution. Providing permission is obtained from the Council of National Monuments, a maximum of 25% of the discoveries made can be taken outside of the country on loan. Furthermore, this same Section V points out the sanctions for those who infringe the law and specifies the obligations to report accidental discoveries to the local government or the police. In this respect the law is modified by Law 20,021 that increases the penalties and specifies other situations.

The previous law, in which archaeology and palaeontology are referred to, is regulated by the 'Supreme Decree No 484, of 1990, of the Ministry of Education: Regulations on Excavations and Archaeological, Anthropological and Palaeontological surveys'. It contains specifications regarding who can excavate and under what circumstances and requirements. It also defines, according to the law, what can be defined as surveying and archaeological excavation, and also includes legislation on the state ownership of the cultural heritage and where it can be kept. From these regulations, we can highlight Articles 6 and 21.

Article 6 indicates that permits can only be granted to:

- Chilean researchers with archaeological, anthropological or palaeontological scientific training, as applicable, properly accredited, who have a research project and appropriate backing from an institution; and
- foreign researchers, providing they belong to a competent scientific institution and work in collaboration with a state scientific institution or a Chilean university.

Article 21 indicates that any artefacts or materials deriving from 'excavations and archaeological, anthropological and palaeontological surveys belong to the state', and that their 'possession will be assigned by the Council of National Monuments to whichever institution that can assure its conservation, exhibition and give easy access to researchers for its study'.

HUMAN REMAINS AND LEGISLATION

Articles 6 and 21 raise two points of interest for the excavation of human remains and where they can be subsequently held or curated. The first is in relation to the conditions that a researcher should fulfil to excavate remains. In practice, it should be a professional archaeologist who manages the excavation, limiting the work of the physical anthropologist to that of an assistant professional in charge of lifting the human remains. In addition, there is the requirement not only to ensure the authorization of the Council of National Monuments but also to have the support of an academic institution or museum and adequate funding. The second part is in relation to the destination of the remains, which is limited to museums and occasionally to universities and other institutions of a public nature that have adequate conditions for their conservation. As there are only a few institutions in the country that fulfil the above requirements, often this means that there is the risk that the remains stay in the custody of the regions where they were excavated.

In regard to indigenous cemeteries, the National Monuments Law 17,288 (1970) is complemented by the Indigenous Law 19,253. Section IV, entitled 'On the Indigenous Culture and Education', aims to provide a framework of respect, recognition and protection to the indigenous cultures and their heritage. Article 28(c) states that 'the excavation of historical indigenous cemeteries for scientific purposes must adhere to established procedures given by Law N° 17,288 and its rules, *with prior consent of the community involved*' [author's emphasis]. This law is complemented by the Supreme Decree No 392, in which Section III, 'On the Procedures for the Protection of the Historical Heritage of the Indigenous Cultures', expressly states in Article 14 that 'the consent for the excavation of indigenous cemeteries should be provided in advance by the community involved, … [and] will be expressed by means of a formal agreement adopted by the respective Indigenous Community'.

Other legislation that partly complements the above is Law 19,300 on the 'General Rules of the Environment' (1994). This was modified by Law 20,173 (2007) in which Article 11 states that:

> The projects or activities listed in the previous article require the production of an Environmental Impact Survey, if they generate or present at least one of the following effects, characteristics or circumstances: … (f) alteration of monuments, sites with

anthropological, archaeological or historical value or, in general, pertaining to cultural heritage.

Law 20,173 (2007), Article 11 [author's translation]

The above law and corresponding regulations are administered by the Comisión Regional o Nacional del Medio Ambiente (Regional or National Committee for the Environment) and they make up the basis of commercial archaeology in Chile. We will not expand on this further here, but none the less, as a result of its application, archaeological cemeteries are occasionally rescued, although generally speaking they are only partially excavated. A number of 'technical studies' are generated in this way that lead neither to a complete scientific work nor to a publication, and therefore these remains do not necessarily qualify for conservation in the long run and the appropriate recognition.

Other regulations that relate to the excavation of recent cemeteries are included in the second book of the Penal Code of the Republic of Chile about crimes and minor offences and their penalties. In Section VI, no. 15 'On Infractions of the Laws or Regulations Concerning Burials and Exhumations', Articles 320 to 322 express the conditions for an offence and the punishment for unauthorized exhumations. This legislation lies in the application of the Código Sanitario (Sanitary Code) (DFL No 725/67), which is related to the use and management of human remains for scientific research, and indicates the conditions and circumstances under which this is allowed (e.g., the necessity to seek authorization from relatives when required). The eighth book of this Code 'On Burials, Exhumations and Movement of Bodies' states, in Article 139, that 'a body cannot remain unburied for more than 48 hours, unless the National Health Service [Servicio Nacional de Salud] authorizes it, or unless the body has been embalmed or unless it is *necessary to carry out research of a scientific or judicial nature …* ' [author's emphasis]. In addition, in the ninth book entitled 'On the Use of Tissues or Body Parts of a Live Donor and the Utilization of Dead Bodies or Their Parts for Scientific or Therapeutic Purposes', Articles 146 and 147 regulate these aspects, allowing the University of Chile to organize a documented collection of skeletal remains with the objective of research in forensic anthropology.

In addition to the above, it has to be considered that crime legislation in Chile allows judges to order the exhumation of human remains, which on occasions is contrary to the heritage legislation. This type of action on the part of the judicial system has pre-eminence over the heritage legislation and sometimes results in human remains from archaeological contexts being referred to tribunals of the *Servicio* Médico Legal (Legal-Medical Service) or to technicians or experts nominated *ad-hoc* by a judge. This makes the final destination of such remains and all their contextual information uncertain. In this environment, the practice of the police and the judges underestimates the importance of investigating skeletons of an antiquity estimated at greater than 100 years, which in turn leads to the absence of appropriate criteria or scientific proceedings for their analysis.

Finally, it is important to consider other existent regulations that can affect the research of human remains in Chile. A reflection and a necessary dialogue remains pending in Chilean society with the different indigenous groups, in order to improve the regulatory framework that rules the study of human skeletal and mummified remains.

METHODS OF ANTHROPOLOGICAL ANALYSIS

In Chile, the bioarchaeological approach, along with as molecular studies and morphometric geometry, has shown rapid growth during recent decades. Chilean researchers do not have any specific methods for the analysis of their prehistoric populations, nor any specific reference book. However, the large majority of researchers working with human skeletal remains follow the standards of Buikstra and Ubelaker (1994) and Bass (1995) to determine their age, sex and pathology. Stature is often calculated using Genovés (1967) and Trotter and Gleser (1977).

In addition to these standard methods mentioned, it is necessary to highlight that in northern Chile naturally and artificially mummified remains are often found with their external genitalia. The work of Aufderheide and Rodríguez-Martín (1998) and Ortner and Putschar (1981) are often used to carry out palaeopathological analysis.

USEFUL CONTACTS

Department of Anthropology, University of Chile. Website: www.facso.uchile.cl/antropologia/ index.html/
Natural History Museum, Chile. Website: www.dibam.cl/historia_natural/

LEGISLATION

Links to important documents:

LEY N° 17.288, DE 1970: LEGISLACIÓN SOBRE MONUMENTOS NACIONALES: Available online at www.monumentos.cl/OpenDocs/asp/pagDefault.asp?boton=Doc50&argInstancia Id=50&argCarpetaId=&argTreeNodosAbiertos=()&argTreeNodoSel=&argTreeNodoActual/
DECRETO SUPREMO N° 484, DE 1990, DEL MINISTERIO DE EDUCACIÓN: REGLA-MENTO SOBRE EXCAVACIONES Y/O PROSPECCIONES ARQUEOLÓGICAS, ANTROPOLÓGICAS Y PALEONTOLÓGICAS: Available online at www.monumentos. cl/OpenDocs/asp/pagDefault.asp?boton=Doc50&argInstanciaId=50&argCarpetaId=19&arTree NodosAbiertos=(19)&argTreeNodoActual=19&argTreeNodoSel=19&argRegistroId=116/
REGLAMENTO DE VISITADORES ESPECIALES DEL CONSEJO DE MONUMENTOS NACIONALES: Available online at www.monumentos.cl/_temporal/4327/RESPALDOS/ Arquitectura/Mee/TODO%20WEB/CONTENIDOS_SITIO/Contenidos/QS/Visitadores/ Reglamento_VE_2009.pdf/
LEY INDÍGENA NO. 19.253: Available online at www.conadi.cl/documentos/Ley%20 Indigena%20v2008.pdf/
LEY NO. 19.300 SOBRE BASES GENERALES DEL MEDIO AMBIENTE: Available online at www.sinia.cl/1292/articles-26087_ley_bases.pdf/
CÓDIGO PENAL DE LA REPUBLICA DE CHILE. LIBRO II: Available online at www. servicioweb.cl/juridico/Codigo%20Penal%20de%20Chile%20libro2.htm/
CÓDIGO SANITARIO D.F.L. 725/67: Available online at www.minsal.cl/juridico/DFL_72 5_DE_1969.doc/

BIBLIOGRAPHY

Aufderheide, A. and Rodríguez-Martín, C. (1998) *The Cambridge Encyclopedia of Human Paleopathology*, Cambridge: Cambridge University Press.
Bass, W. (1995) *Human Osteology. A Laboratory and Field Manual*, Columbia, NY: Archaeological Society Special Publications no. 2.

Buikstra, J.E. and Ubelaker, D.H. (eds) (1994) *Standards for Data Collection from Human Skeletal Remains*, Fayetteville, AR: Arkansas Archaeological Survey Research Series No. 44.

Facultad de Ciencias Sociales (2009) *Departamento de Anthropología*. Available online at www.facso.uchile.cl/antropologia/index.html (accessed 17 March 2010).

Genovés, S. (1967) 'Proportionality of the long bones and their relation to stature among Mesoamericans', *American Journal of Physical Anthropology*, 26: 67–77.

Manríquez, G. and Rothhammer, F. (1997) *Teoría Moderna de la Evolución*, Santiago de Chile: Amphora Editores.

Museo Arqueológico San Miguel de Azapa (2009) *Departmento de Arqueología y Museología, Universidad de Tarpacá*. Available online at www.uta.cl/masma/ (accessed 17 March 2010).

Museo Nacional de Historia Natural (2009) *Museo Nacional de Historia Natural*. Available online at www.dibam.cl/historia_natural/ (accessed 17 March 2010).

Orellana, M. (1996) *Historia de la Arqueología en Chile*, Santiago: Bravo y Allende Editores.

Ortner, D. and Putschar, W. (1981) *Identification of Pathological Conditions in Human Skeletal Remains*, Smithsonian Contributions to Anthropology no. 28, Washington, DC: Smithsonian Institution Press.

Rothhammer, F. and Aspillaga, E. (1997) 'Chile', in F. Spencer (ed.) *History of Physical Anthropology*, London: Frank Spencer.

SChA (2009) *Sociedad Chilena de Arqueología*. Available online at www.scha.cl/ (accessed 17 March 2010).

Trotter, M. and Gleser, G. (1977) 'Estimation of stature from long limb bones of American Whites and Negroes', *American Journal Physical Anthropology*, 47: 355–56.

Universitad Católica del Norte (2009) *Museo Arqueológico Gustavo Le Paige*. Available online at www.ucn.cl/museo/ (accessed 17 March 2010).

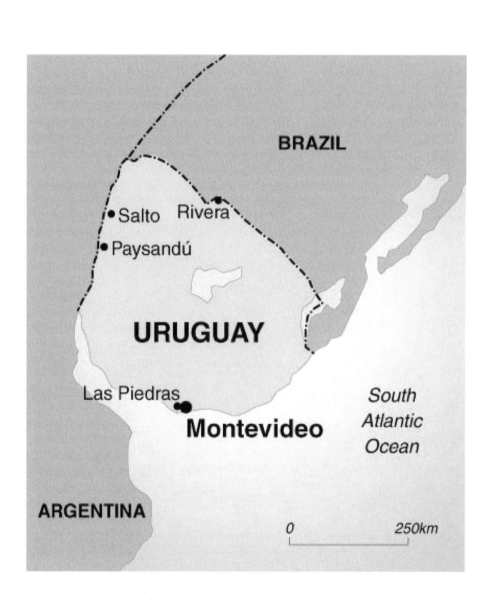

Uruguay

Mónica Sans

INTRODUCTION: A BRIEF HISTORY AND CURRENT STATE OF PHYSICAL ANTHROPOLOGY IN URUGUAY

The first findings of human remains within an archaeological context date to the end of the 19th century. Among these first brief and superficial studies undertaken by people with non-anthropological backgrounds, it is important to highlight the work performed by Figueira (1892). He described the appearance of human remains found in the burial mounds of the Department of Rocha, eastern Uruguay, as robust and of mid-size, and he also provided information on the cranial capacity and other cranial indices. These remains were later studied by the Argentine Luis María Torres (1911). During the first half of the 20th century various studies that included brief and anecdotal descriptions of human remains were published, the majority performed by amateur archaeologists. A milestone was marked by Muñoa (1954), a student of medicine, who provided a detailed description of the remains found by Figueira, within a diffusionist framework that predominated in the region. This study, performed by a self-taught person within this field, can be considered the first proper physical anthropology study because of its approach and characteristics.

The first Bachelor degree in Anthropological Sciences was created in Uruguay in 1976 at the Facultad de Humanidades y Ciencias, Universidad de la República (Faculty of Humanities and Sciences, University of the Republic) in Montevideo, which included a course in physical anthropology. At the beginning, because of the lack of professionals in the country, this course was run by a palaeontologist, a geneticist and an ethologist. Since 1985, the present author (M.S.) has been responsible for this course. In 1991, the Faculty was divided into two, one for Sciences and the other for Humanities, with Anthropological Sciences included within the second group. The following year, the section of Biological Anthropology was created, and in 2006 it was converted into a Department, with M.S. as the director of both. In 2000, the Laboratory of Biological Anthropology was set up, supported by the Department, which has three areas of research: ancient DNA, modern DNA and osteology.

After the consolidation of formal studies in anthropological sciences in the country, several bioarchaeological studies were carried out. These resulted from the interaction of physical anthropology and archaeology. Most of them were published in annals or compilations edited in the country. Among these it is important to highlight the work of Guidon *et al.* (1987),

Ministerio de Educación y Cultura (1994), López and Sans (1999), Durán Coirolo and Bracco (2000), Asociación Uruguaya de Arqueología (2001), and Beovide *et al.* (2004). An initial revision of the osteological remains present in collections was carried out in the 1980s by Sans (1988).

Education and training

Since its creation, the degree in Anthropological Sciences has had two branches: archaeology and social anthropology. Those interested in Physical or Biological Anthropology have to opt for one of these two branches and complement it with optional lectures that can be taken in other Faculties such as Human Evolution, Palaeontology and Genetics, all of them run in the Facultad de Ciencias (Faculty of Sciences). In addition, the Bachelor degree in Human Biology was created in 2004, supported by several faculties of the Universidad de la República with a flexible curriculum that allows a better selection of courses. This, in turn, constitutes a good option for those who wish to become involved in Biological Anthropology. It is necessary to say that the Universidad de la República is the only university in the whole country that provides diplomas in Anthropology or Biology.

Today those who dedicate themselves to Physical Anthropology have, therefore, a mixed background, in general with degrees in Archaeology, postgraduate degrees in Biology and specific courses from different parts of the world.

ARCHAEOLOGICAL HUMAN REMAINS AND LEGISLATION

Archaeological legislation

Law 14,040, which refers to the National Heritage, was enacted in Uruguay in 1971. This law created the Comisión del Patrimonio Histórico, Artístico y Cultural de la Nación (National Commission for Historical, Artistic and Cultural Heritage). It anticipated the fact that the country did not have many professional archaeologists and therefore the Commission included a representative from the Sociedad Amigos de la Arqueología (Society of Friends of Archaeology), although this situation changed later. Among other functions, the Commission is in charge of authorizing the investigation and evaluation of archaeological sites, as well as granting permits to carry out archaeological excavations in which human remains are expected or not expected to be found. Those interested in carrying out these investigations should present a project with information including the name of the institution, the region they want to study, the plan of work and the participants involved. In 1986, the regulations in Article 15 of this law were amended such that the project had to be signed by someone in possession of an academic degree in archaeology (it is understood that this would be from the Universidad de la República). The legislation does not mention specifically the excavation of different kinds of archaeological sites. Even if the presence of human remains is expected, an archaeologist can still present at the project for approval to the above mentioned Commission. At present, no experience in physical anthropology is required when the project is presented for approval by the Commission.

On occasion, particularly in the event of finding human remains, an archaeologist can request a physical anthropologist on site; however, this request does not take place generally until the post-excavation stage.

Law 14,040 also states that if archaeological remains are discovered while carrying out structural work, the work must stop and the Commission should be informed of the discovery. The archaeologists of the Commission will decide if it is necessary to take action to preserve the heritage.

HUMAN REMAINS AND LEGISLATION

In the case of an accidental discovery of human remains, whether this is during construction work or on the surface, the current practice is to inform the police. They in turn have to inform the Judiciary. Government employees such as anthropologists and doctors from the Instituto Técnico Forense (Technical Institute of Forensics), belonging to the Judiciary, will then analyse the findings and decide if this is a forensic case. From this point of view the borderline between a forensic and an archaeological case in Uruguay is 30 years, the maximum date necessary for a crime to expire.

The regulation of Law 14,040 (1972), mentions that archaeological artefacts unearthed by individuals or by private or public institutions are the property of the State. Human remains are evidently included; however, there is no special mention or disposition for them. Other more recent laws do not mention human remains, although some of them allude to the archaeological heritage. It is not permitted to take human remains (considered as 'palaeontological material') nor archaeological remains outside the country: Article 15 of Law 14,040 states that it is not permitted to take archaeological or palaeontological items belonging to the first settlers outside the country. It should be noted that, at the time of writing (February 2010), the National Commission for Historical, Artistic and Cultural Heritage is reviewing this law with the aim of introducing a new law in 2010; the archaeological details are being analysed by an *ad hoc* group made up mainly of archaeologists, and online discussion is open to all interested researchers.

In relation to the transportation of human remains within the country, as with any archaeological material, it is accepted that after being studied, the material has to be returned to the museum or original department that it came from, within the country.

The remains of the Charrúa chief Vaimaca Perú

In relation to human remains held outside Uruguay, the case of the Charrúa chief, Vaimaca Perú, provides an excellent example because this case encouraged the enactment of two laws, one related to his repatriation and the other for the possibility of studying his remains.

This native was one of the four Charrúa Indians taken prisoner to France in 1833. Vaimaca Perú passed away a few months after his arrival in Paris. His remains were analysed by local French anthropologists at the time and his skeleton was exhibited for many years and studied at Le Musée de L'Homme in Paris. In 2000, the Uruguayan Parliament approved Law 17,256 following the first repatriation claims ever made by one of the Uruguayan associations of indigenous descendents. The text established that 'it should be declared of national interest the location and later repatriation to the national territory of the Charrúa Indians who died in the Republic of France'. The same law established that human remains have to be buried in the National Pantheon. Although this Law referred to the remains of the four indigenous people, the location of only one of them, Vaimaca Perú, was known. In 2002, after negotiations with France, the remains of the chief were brought back to Uruguay and the following day were taken to the National Pantheon. The final resting place of the remains, as well as the possibility of their study, was a topic of debate among associations of the descendents of indigenous peoples as well as between them and academics. Finally, thanks to an agreement between the Ministerio de Educación y Cultura (Ministry of Education and Culture) and the Universidad de la República, an interdisciplinary team from the latter began the study, with the exception of DNA analysis, of the remains at the Pantheon within a short period of time.

Soon after the commencement of the study, one of the organizations of supposed indigenous descendents presented an appeal for legal protection that stopped the studies momentarily. In the court, the defence presented by the lawyers of the Ministry of Education and Culture as well as those of the Universidad de la República considered that, among other aspects, those who had appealed lacked legitimacy. This was in line with Article 4 of the Law 16,011 and Article 158 of the Civil Code that grants rights only to those who possess relatives in a direct line or secondary line until the fourth degree, which did not apply to the complainant. The examining magistrate and later the Court of Appeal considered that, according to the current legislation, the remains of Vaimaca Perú belonged to the state. The decision in favour of the Ministry of Education and Culture and the University was based on general public interest and based on the fact that the chief's remains were covered by Law 17,256 and that no human rights were violated. It is of interest to repeat one of the phrases of the judges:

> At least it could be said that legal documents help in conflicts of interest: on one hand, those representing the claiming Association would look forward to returning the remains of the chief so that he can rest in peace; and on the other hand, the general interest that, without ignoring the right to rest in peace, authorizes the studies of a scientific nature that allows it to shape and forge with no strings, no secrets and no mysteries, the identity of our People with the aim of being able to root and build our future destiny.
> *Definitive Judgement, 12 December 2002, dictated by the judges B. Minvielle, S. Klett and*
> *J.C. Chalar [author's translation]*

However, in 2004, two years after this judicial decision, the Parliament voted Law 17,767 that states that 'the carrying out of experiments and scientific studies on the human remains of the chief Vaimaca Perú is prohibited' [author's translation].

It should be noted that Uruguay is the only country in Latin America that does not have indigenous people who continue to live as separate ethnic groups. This generally means that at present there are no strong and valid claims such as those that exist in other countries of the continent. At the time of the Spanish conquests, Uruguay was occupied by two or three different groups, the biggest being the macro-ethnic Charrúa of possible Pampean origin. At the same time the Guaraní Indians, coming from the Amazon region, increased in number in historical times, in many cases as a direct consequence of the creation and later fall of the Jesuit Missions. It is also accepted that the extermination of the Charrúa Indians during the 19th century was a cultural and biological phenomenon and no indication was given to the fate of other ethnic groups, like the Guaraní Indians (Ministerio de Instrucción Pública 1925). Genetic studies have shown, however, the relative high frequency of indigenous genes in a country supposedly lacking in indigenous people. Indigenous autosomic contribution is up to 20 per cent of the population, and maternal contribution up to 62 per cent in certain regions of the country (Sans *et al.* 1997, Bonilla *et al.* 2004). During the 1980s some of the descendents of indigenous people began to gather together in different associations, some of them claiming their status as indigenous descendents or even directly indigenous. It is interesting to highlight that, in the large majority of cases, the descendents of indigenous people identified by means of mtDNA are not aware of it. Only 0.4 per cent of Uruguayan people declared themselves to be 'indigenous' or 'white-indigenous' in the population survey of 1996–97 (Instituto Nacional de Estadística 1997), whereas nearly 10 years later, 4.5 per cent stated that they possessed at least one indigenous ancestor (Instituto Nacional de Estadística 2006).

Human remains from the military dictatorship (1973–85)

One particular situation refers to the excavation of human remains of those who were detained and disappeared during the military dictatorship (1973–85). In 1986 the Law 15,848, Caducidad de la Pretensión Punitiva del Estado (Expiry of Punitive Aims of the State), was approved. In Article 4 the Law states that 'reported testimonies presented up to the date of enactment of the present law regarding the conduct of people allegedly arrested in military or police actions and disappeared as well as under-aged individuals allegedly kidnapped in similar conditions' will be made available. The Executive Power of the State must order the investigations aimed at the explanation of the facts.

In the last few years, the application of this law has led to the excavation of large areas in search of the remains of people who were arrested or who disappeared. Up to now, the remains of two persons have been found and identified. The investigations are led by a group of archaeologists from the Universidad de la República, thanks to an agreement between the University and the Executive Power of the State.

With regard to these cases, Uruguay has approved different international resolutions, such as that produced by the Convención Interamericana sobre Desaparición Forzada de Personas (Inter-American Convention on Forced Disappearance of People), ratified in 1996 by the country and incorporated into the National legislation by Law 17,347 in 2001. In addition, Law 18,026, enacted in 2006, is clear in stating that 'the crime of forced disappearance will be considered a permanent crime as long as the fate and whereabouts of the victim have not been established'. Therefore, until such crimes are resolved, there is no expiry date.

Human remains in other contexts

Another situation is exemplified by the archaeological excavation of old cemeteries. Very fragmented human remains were found in old estates belonging to the Iglesia del Santísimo Sacramento (Church of the Sacred Sacrament) in the city of Colonia, which was founded in 1680. This investigation was handled by a professional archaeologist from the Heritage Commission, with advice from a physical anthropologist. The legal framework was similar to that applied to other archaeological contexts.

Finally, at present no remains belonging to, for example, military events like the slaughter of Charrúa indigenous people that took place in the region of Salsipuedes in 1831, Guerra Grande (1839–1951) or the Civil War (events that took place during 1897–1904) have been found in the country. In the case of the British invasions (1806–7), human remains were found in the city centre of Montevideo belonging to this event but outside of an archaeological context. The police were informed and the remains were analysed by a forensic medical doctor.

METHODS OF ANTHROPOLOGICAL ANALYSIS

Uruguay does not have any specific methods for the analysis of its prehistoric population, nor any specific reference textbooks, with the exception of those proposed by Figueiro and Sans (2005) for sex estimation based on discriminant functions.

When the remains are particularly badly fragmented, a combination of methods developed for several populations is used. The team of Biological Anthropology in the Faculty of Humanities and Educational Sciences at the Universidad de la República has performed the majority of the analysis of human remains, not only from archaeological sites but also in public and private museums. The methods used today by this team, are as follows:

- Number of individuals, degree of completeness and state of preservation of the remains, as well as pathologies, are all kept on a recording form. This form was provided by the

Brazilian researcher Walter Neves. The estimations are based on Ubelaker (1978), Ortner and Putschar (1981), Krogman and İşcan (1986), Buikstra and Ubelaker (1994), Bass (1995) and Byers (2002).

- Sex estimation: qualitative methods are predominantly used, such as those proposed by Acsádi and Neméskeri (1970), as well as those listed in the above bullet point. Molecular methods created to assess sex have also been applied with limited success.

- Age estimation: whenever possible, the methods proposed by Meindl and Lovejoy (1985), Lovejoy *et al.* (1985), Meindl *et al.* (1985), and Brooks and Suchey (1990) that consider the pelvis and the skull in adults are applied, as well as those listed in the first bullet point. For sub-adults, a number of criteria are used, in particular those stated by Ubelaker (1978).

- Stature estimation: the formula proposed by Genovés (1967) is the one most commonly used. This formula was verified as adequate by applying it to the remains of the Charrúa Vaimaca Perú, whose height while alive was already known.

- Molecular studies: in 2000, the Laboratory of ancient DNA analysis was set up within the Departamento de Antropología Biológica. A number of mtDNA analyses have been carried out in prehistoric, historical and forensic cases from Uruguay and neighbouring countries. The work in the Laboratory keeps developing with the introduction of new techniques, in particular, DNA extraction from bones and hair.

USEFUL CONTACTS

Faculty of Humanities, University of the Republic (Universidad de la República). Website: www.fhuce.edu.uy/

Natural History and Anthropology National Museum. Website: www.mec.gub.uy/munhina/

BIBLIOGRAPHY

Acsádi, G. and Neméskeri, J. (1970) *History of Human Lifespan and Mortality*, Budapest: Akademiai Kiado.

Asociación Uruguaya de Arqueología (ed.) (2001) *Arqueología uruguaya hacia el fin del milenio. IX Congreso Nacional de Arqueología*, Montevideo: Gráficos del Sur.

Bass, W.W. (1995) *Human Osteology: A Laboratory and Field Manual*, 4th edn, Missouri: Missouri Archaeological Society, Special Publication No. 2.

Beovide, L., Barreto, I. and Curbelo, C. (eds) (2004) *X Congreso Uruguayo de Arqueología: La Arqueología Uruguaya ante los desafíos del nuevo siglo*, Montevideo: CD-ROM Multimedia Didáctico (ISBN 9974-7811-0-8).

Bonilla, C., Bertoni, B., González, S., *et al.* (2004) 'Substantial Native American ancestry in the population of Tacuarembó, Uruguay, detected using mitochondrial DNA polymorphisms', *American Journal of Human Biology*, 16: 289–97.

Brooks, S.T. and Suchey, J.M. (1990) 'Skeletal age determination based on the os pubis: a comparison of the Acsádi–Nemeskéri and Suchey–Brooks methods', *Human Evolution*, 5: 227–38.

Buikstra, J.E. and Ubelaker, D. (eds) (1994) *Standards for Data Collection from Human Skeletal Remains: Proceedings of a Seminar at the Field Museum of Natural History*. Fayetteville, AR: Arkansas Archaeological Research Series No. 44.

Byers, S. (2002) *Introduction to Forensic Anthropology: A Textbook* Boston, MA: Allyn and Bacon.

Durán Coirolo, A. and Bracco, R. (eds) (2000) *Arqueología de las Tierras Bajas*, Montevideo: Imprenta Americana.

Figueira, J.H. (1892) 'Viaje a San Luis' in Comisión de la Exposición Histórico-Americana (ed.) *El Uruguay en la exposición histórico-americana de Madrid*, Montevideo: Imprenta Dornaleche y Cía.

Figueiro, G. and Sans, M. (2005) 'Determinación de sexo y proporciones sexuales en la prehistoria del Uruguay', in *XI Congreso Nacional de Arqueología Uruguaya (Salto, Uruguay)*. Available online at www.fhuce.edu.uy/XICongresoArqueologia/ (accessed 17 March 2010).

Genovés, S.(1967) 'Proportionality of the Long Bones and Their Relation to Estature Among Mesoamericans', *American Journal of Physical Anthropology*, 26, 67–77

Guidon, N., Trakalo, R. and Armellino, A. (eds) (1987) *Misión de Rescate Arqueológico Salto Grande*, Montevideo: Banco de la República Oriental del Uruguay.

Instituto Nacional de Estadística (1997) *Encuesta Nacional de Hogares: Módulo raza 1996–1997*, Montevideo: Instituto Nacional de Estadística.

——(2006) *Encuesta Nacional de Hogares Ampliada: Flash temático ascendencia*, Montevideo: Instituto Nacional de Estadística.

Krogman, W.M. and İşcan, M.Y. (1986) *The Human Skeleton in Forensic Medicine*, Springfield, IL: Charles C. Thomas.

López, J.M. and Sans, M. (eds) (1999) *Arqueología y Bioantropología de las Tierras Bajas*, Montevideo: Facultad de Humanidades y Ciencias de la Educación, Universidad de la República.

Lovejoy, C.O., Meindl, R.S., Pryzbeck, T.R., *et al.* (1985) 'Chronological metamorphosis of the auricular surface of the ilium: a new method for the determination of adult skeletal age at death', *American Journal of Physical Anthropology*, 68: 15–28.

Meindl, R. and Lovejoy, C.O. (1985) 'Ectocranial suture closure: a revised method for the determination of skeletal age at death base on the lateral-anterior sutures', *American Journal of Physical Anthropology*, 68: 57–66.

Meindl, R.S., Lovejoy, C.O., Mensforth, R.P., *et al.* (1985) 'A revised method of age determination using the os pubis, with a review and tests of accuracy of other current methods of pubic symphyseal aging', *American Journal of Physical Anthropology*, 68: 29–45.

Ministerio de Educación y Cultura (ed.) (1994) *Aportes para el Conocimiento de la Prehistoria Uruguaya*, Montevideo: Graphis.

Ministerio de Instrucción Pública (ed.) (1925) *El Libro del Centenario del Uruguay de 1825–1925*, Montevideo, Capurro y Cía.

Muñoa, J. (1954) 'Contribuciones a la antropología física del Uruguay', *Anales del Museo de Historia Natural de Montevideo (2nd series)*, 6(4): 1–20.

Ortner, D. and Putschar, W. (1981) *Identification of Pathological Conditions in Human Skeletal Remains*, Washington, DC: Smithsonian Institution Press.

Sans, M. (1988) *Las poblaciones prehistóricas del Uruguay*, Montevideo: Facultad de Humanidades y Ciencias, Universidad de la República, Serie Avances de Investigación.

Sans, M., Salzano, F. M. and Chakraborty, R. (1997) 'Historical genetics in Uruguay: estimates of biological origins and their problems', *Human Biology*, 69: 161–70.

Torres, L. M. (1911) *Los Primitivos Habitantes del Delta del Paraná*, Buenos Aires: Imprenta Coni Hermanos.

Ubelaker, D.H. (1978) *Human Skeletal Remains: Excavation, Interpretation and Analysis*, Washington, DC: Taraxacum.

Israel/ישראל

Yossi Nagar

INTRODUCTION: A BRIEF HISTORY AND CURRENT STATE OF PHYSICAL ANTHROPOLOGY IN ISRAEL

Archaeology and anthropology in Israel attract great public and academic interest, since human history in this region spans some 1.5 million years. Being a bridge between three continents, this small land saw many wars, population changes, and rises of nations throughout its long history. Thirty thousand archaeological sites known to and controlled by the Israel Antiquities Authority (IAA), and mass development in a very small country, result in about 300 excavations each year. Human remains are found in about 10 per cent of the sites, representing every population that ever lived in Israel. These could be ancient hominids in prehistory; Cana'anites and Israelites in biblical times; inhabitants of the foreign empires controlling Israel, such as the Greeks, Romans, Byzantines and Arabs, and even the crusaders; and of course modern populations from the last millennium.

Israeli institutes

Several academic and public institutes are involved in anthropological research in Israel. These are listed below:

Tel Aviv University: A worldwide leading institution in this field. Several anthropologists study various aspects of physical anthropology in the Department of Anatomy and Anthropology, Sackler Faculty of Medicine, Tel Aviv. Courses in anatomy and anthropology are available for anthropology students (second and third degrees in physical anthropology). The university is also responsible for a large human bone collection, specializing in the local populations of this region, with special emphasis on prehistory. In the collection one can find skeletons of Neanderthals and Early *Homo sapiens*, Neolithic, Chalcolithic and historical populations, and these are continuously studied by anthropology students and visiting scholars from around the world. In a few years, all these skeletal remains are due to be stored in the National Collections of Natural History at the I. Meier Segals Garden for Zoological Research and the Botanic Gardens, Tel Aviv. More details can be found at the department's web site (Tel Aviv University Sacker Faculty of Medicine 2009).

Hebrew University, Jerusalem: Anthropological research takes place at the Laboratory of Bioanthropology and Ancient DNA, Faculty of Dental Medicine, Jerusalem. In recent years the number of researchers has declined; still, the university offers courses in physical anthropology for second and third degree students and cooperates with visiting scholars. The laboratory's website is at http://bioanthropology.huji.ac.il/

Israel Antiquities Authority (IAA): The IAA osteological laboratory is responsible for data collection and the study of bones found in the many excavations undertaken by the IAA or foreign institutions in Israel. The extent of the anthropological study is wide; however, it is limited by political constraints (discussed below). No skeletal collection is maintained, apart from a few prehistoric specimens that are on exhibition in the Rockefeller Museum. Description of ongoing projects can also be found at the IAA website at www.antiquities.org.il/

The National Center of Forensic Medicine: Institute of the Ministry of Health, with academic affiliation to the Sackler School of Medicine, Tel Aviv. The institute specializes in forensic anthropology; however, some studies on archaeological human remains are conducted from time to time.

ARCHAEOLOGICAL HUMAN REMAINS AND LEGISLATION

There are a number of laws in Israel in relation to archaeological human remains:

The Israeli Law: The Israeli law defines osteological remains as antiquities if they are 'zoological remains' before AD 1300 (Israel Antiquities Law 1978: Paragraph 1). In 1994 the Government's Legal Advisor, on the basis of an amendment to this law, did not agree to refer to human remains as 'zoological remains', hence they are not referred to as antiquities. This largely restricted the excavation of human remains and dramatically reduced the amount of bones unearthed. Since human remains are not considered antiquities, they are taken to reburial by representatives of the Ministry of Religious Affairs, forcing a shift to rapid data collection in the field, rather than a slow and thorough laboratory study.

The Jewish Orthodox Law: The Jewish religious law, the 'Halacha', discusses the issue of the treatment of bones in case a necessity arises, i.e. it treats the concept of 'salvage excavations'. It allows the movement of human bones from one place to another if the bones disturb public activities such as house building, road paving, etc. Shulkhan Aruch, a summary of Jewish codes from the early 16th century, still valid today, reads: 'A grave which disturbs the public, its transfer is permissible' (Karo 1575). This idea is based upon the common practice during the Hellenistic and Roman periods (Broshi *et al.* 1983). However, it is not accepted by a small and militant group of orthodox Jews called 'Athra Kaddisha', politically supported by religious MPs. Their aggressive opposition to the 'disturbance of the dead from their peaceful rest in the ground' caused by the excavation of graves, largely impedes anthropological research on ancient human remains (Nagar 2002). Although bones found in a Jewish context constitute but a small portion of the skeletal remains excavated each year, Athra Kaddisha opposes all such activities whatever the ethnicity of the dead.

IAA working procedures

Contrary to academic institutes, the IAA performs only salvage excavations and does not choose sites according to its academic preferences. Working procedures in the IAA must meet the law's demands. Therefore, whenever bones are found, a certified osteologist, physical anthropologist or zooarchaeologist on behalf of the IAA must classify them as human or non-human remains.

In case the bones are identified as human, their excavation can take place only upon approval by the administration of the IAA, following regulations made between the IAA and formal representatives of the Ministry of Religious Affairs. In many such cases, excavation of the bones (and sometimes the site itself) does not continue. In other cases, when an excavation does take place, the skeletal remains are sent for reburial after being studied on-site. The reburial is done by representatives of the Ministry of Religious Affairs; the IAA is not involved in any part of it. Therefore, most of the anthropological work is done in the field prior to reburial, and the anthropologist is especially skilled and equipped for that purpose.

Reburial statistics

According to IAA registrations, about 1000 boxes of human bones were sent for reburial between 1995 and 1997. The supposed ethnicity of the people in the relevant excavations is summarized in Table 55.1. Since then, a constant decrease in the number of boxes sent for reburial is registered each year, to a low point of 17 boxes in 2008. Restrictions posed upon the excavation of human bones must be the main cause for this dramatic decline.

Prehistoric remains

Prehistoric human remains, from the Neolithic period and earlier, are treated differently, and are stored and continuously studied at Tel Aviv University. The excavation of prehistoric human remains is usually made by trained anthropologists, followed by reconstruction of fragmentary bones and conservation using chemical agents such as Glyptol©. Selected publications of Israeli anthropologists on bones from prehistoric sites include Arensburg *et al.* (1990), Faerman *et al.* (1994), Hershkovitz *et al.* (1995), Rak *et al.* (1994), Smith (1972) and Smith and Horwitz (1997).

METHODS OF ANTHROPOLOGICAL ANALYSIS

Methodology used in the IAA

General methodology and data collection

Due to the political constraints, human bones are studied only on-site, and data collection is done in the field, rather than in the laboratory. The anthropological work is done either *in situ*, in case excavation of the bones is impossible, or in a field laboratory, when the bones that have been excavated are taken out. Radiocarbon or DNA sampling is subordinate to approval of the IAA management and not routinely done. In any case, the transportation of bones abroad is strictly forbidden.

Table 55.1 Number of boxes of bones sent for reburial in Israel (1995–97) and their supposed affiliation (%)

Year	Total	Jews	Christians	Muslims	Other or unknown
1995	480	9.4	16.0	10.6	64
1996	316	1.6	38.3	22.5	37.6
1997	220	9.0	13.0	50	28
Total	1016	7.0	22.0	23	48

Source: After Nagar 2002

Table 55.2 List of cranial measurements regularly recorded by the Israel Antiquities Authority

Maximum length (Glab-Opc.)	Bizygomatic breadth
Maximum breadth	Zygomaxillary angle
Biauricular breadth	Basion-Prosthion
Height Porion-Bregma	Basion-Nasion
Minimum frontal breadth	Malar height
Frontal chord	Foramen magnum length
Frontal angle	Foramen magnum breadth
Parietal chord	Palate breadth
Parietal angle	Palate length
Occipital chord	Palate depth at M1-M2
Occipital angle	Mandible
Basion-Bregma height	Maximum length
Glabella projection	Body length
Orbital breadth	Ramus height (vertical)
Orbital height	Ramus length (diagonal)
Interorbital breadth (maxillofrontale)	Ramus, minimum width
Biorbital breadth	Mandibular angle
Nasal height	Bicondylar breadth
Nasal breadth	Symphysial height
Naso-maxillofrontal subtense[1]	Height at M1-M2
Upper facial height (Nasion-Prosthion)	Width at mental foramen

Note: [1]After Gill *et al.* 1988

Due to the IAA's responsibility for the study and publication of ancient remains, data is collected systematically (see details below) and stored accordingly, to allow better and more reliable use of it long after the reburial of the remains. Close reliance on the most common anthropological literature is meant to reduce the effect of inter-observer error.

The reconstruction of age-at-death and the estimation of sex of an individual are the main basis of palaeodemography. Collection of data for determining the sex of adult individuals includes, when possible, skull and pelvic morphology, and relevant measurements of the femur and humerus. The interpretation of these is done following the common anthropological literature, as up-to-date as possible (most accepted methodologies were found applicable to Israeli populations). Collection of data relevant for age estimation includes as many parameters as possible, depending on the state of preservation of the remains. For infants and children the parameters recorded are usually: length measurements of long bones, tooth development and eruption stages, and closure of epiphyses (see, e.g., Hillson 1993; Johnston and Zimmer 1989). For adult individuals the parameters recorded are usually: dental attrition (following Hillson 1993), chronological changes in the pubic symphysis (Brooks and Suchey 1990), and development of vertebral osteophytes. These are complemented by as many methodologies as possible, according to the skeletal elements found. For this purpose, the osteologists at the IAA are always up to date with the relevant literature.

The age and sex profiles for each site are published in a report available to the excavator and kept in the IAA's anthropological archive. Most reports are in Hebrew; however, these data are usually later published within or alongside the final publication of the specific excavation in the IAA journal *'Atiqot.*

Skeletal morphology is described primarily by means of cranial measurements. For this purpose, a constant form has been devised, including 42 measurements of the vault, face and skull

Table 55.3 List of epigenetic traits regularly recorded by the Israel Antiquities Authority

Skull	Jaws	Postcranium
Metopic suture	Mylohyoid bridge	Humerus, septal aperture
Supraorbital foramen	Mandibular torus	Suprascapular foramen
Accessory infraorbital foramen	Mandible, M3 agenesis	Sacrum, spina bifida
Supratrochlear notch	Maxilla, M3 agenesis	Atlas, posterior bridge
Parietal foramen		Atlas, lateral bridge
Fronto-temporal articulation		Atlas, spina bifida
Foramen of Huschke		Atlas, incomplete fusion of the transverse process foramen
Ossicle at lambda		Axis, incomplete fusion of the transverse process foramen
Inca bone		
Condylar canal		

base, using the regularly accepted cranial measurement points (Table 55.2; methodology following Howells 1973). While preparing this list of mandatory measurements, care was taken to use measurements which do not repeat each other, and are necessary for the calculation of indices and angles, especially of the face, which was shown to be more biologically conservative than the shape of the vault. Data collection of skeletal morphology also includes constant recording of a battery of 22 epigenetic traits (Table 55.3), following Finnegan (1978) and Hauser and De Stefano (1989). Only traits with a substantial genetic basis were selected while constructing the mandatory list. Since epigenetic traits can be noticed in fragmentary bones as well (which is the situation in most of the cases), they become an important descriptive parameter of the investigated skeletal population.

The state of preservation of the bones, and the fact that data collection is done rapidly in the field, do not always allow for reliable description and recording of pathological conditions. Any pathology noticed is described in detail in the anthropological report. However, emphasis is given on some common pathological conditions, the presence or absence of which is recorded in every available sample. These include fractures and periostitis in the long bones, and *cribra orbitalia* and porotic hyperostosis in the crania. Since the absence of the common pathologies mentioned is also recorded, it is easier afterwards to calculate the true frequency of a pathology in a given population, when such is found, and to compare these frequencies between populations from different geographic areas.

Femoral oblique length is recorded whenever possible for the estimation of stature. Interpretation is based upon formulae presented by Feldesman *et al.* (1990).

Databases

A comprehensive anthropological database was established in the IAA in 1994. The database includes basic demographic, metrical and descriptive data of the ancient populations of the land of Israel. All data are taken using standardized criteria and methodologies as described earlier, most are preserved in a Microsoft Excel® file, user friendly and readily available for further study. Data accumulated thus far allow for a comprehensive biological description of the populations investigated, demographic and morphological comparisons between populations from various periods and geographical regions, and a large reference sample to be used by archaeologists and anthropologists studying ancient populations from other regions of the world.

Table 55.4. Selected sites, from various periods, with substantial anthropological remains

Period	Site	Geographic region	Remarks	Selected publications
Middle Paleolithic	Amud Cave	Lower Galilee	Neanderthals	Rak *et al.* 1994
Neolithic	Atlit Yam	Northern coast	Underwater Neolithic village	Hershkovitz and Galili 1990, Galili *et al.* 2005
	Kfar HaHoresh	Lower Galilee	Plastered skulls underneath floors	Goring Morris *et al.* 1995, 1998
	Yiftahel	Lower Galilee	In Neolithic village	Hershkovitz et al. 1986
Chalcolithic	Peq'iin	Upper Galilee	Large burial cave, large well-preserved sample	Lev-Tov *et al.* 2003, Nagar and Eshed 2001
	Kissufim Road	Negev Desert	Typical Negev cemetery	Zagerson and Smith 2002
Bronze Age	Assawir	Northern Samaria	Large EB burial caves	Nagar and Winocur, forthcoming
	Azor, Jericho, Megiddo, Arad	Various regions	Several Early Bronze sites from the southern Levant	Smith 1989
Classical periods	Tel-Hadid, Shoham	Shfela (central Israel)	Jewish burial sites	Nagar and Torgeë 2003
	Ein Gedi	Judean desert	Jewish burial sites	Arensburg *et al.* 1980
	Horvat Ma'aravim, Rehovot-in-the-Negev, Beer-Sheva	Negev desert	Various Nabatean sites	Nagar and Sonntag 2008
	Mamilla	Jerusalem	Christian burial cave	Nagar *et al.* 1999

Table 55.4 lists selected sites, from various periods, in which substantial anthropological remains have been found, analysed, and published accordingly.

CONCLUSION

The excavation and study of human skeletal remains in Israel is becoming more and more difficult. In spite of the political restrictions, which sometimes make it impossible, extensive and important work is undertaken by Israeli anthropologists. This is reflected in plenty of publications, whether descriptive (specific site analyses) or experimental in nature, and in the availability of over 400 anthropological reports. As excavation in the majority of the sites is conducted by the Israel Antiquities Authority, description of its working standards, as detailed above, is important.

Unfortunately, most human bones excavated in Israel are being reburied. Therefore, it is important to store recovered data in a computerized data bank, and to share it with anthropologist colleagues. Accordingly, fruitful cooperation with foreign investigators is welcomed by all the Israeli institutes mentioned above.

USEFUL CONTACTS

Israel Antiquities Authority (IAA). Website: www.antiquities.org.il/
Anatomy and Anthropology, Tel Aviv University Sacker Faculty of Medicine. Website: www. tau.ac.il/medicine/anatomy/anatomy_intro.html/

BIBLIOGRAPHY

Arensburg, B., Bar-Yosef, O., Belfer-Cohen, A., *et al.* (1990) 'Aurignacian and Mousterian Human Remains from Hayonim Cave, Galilee, Israel', *Paleorient*, 16: 107–9.

Arensburg, B., Goldstein, M.S., Nathan, H., *et al.* (1980) 'Skeletal remains of Jews from the Hellenistic, Roman, and Byzantine periods in Israel. I. Metric analysis', *Bulletins et Memoires de la Societé d'Anthropologie de Paris*, 7: 175–86.

Brooks, S. and Suchey, J.M. (1990) 'Skeletal age determination based on the os pubis: a comparison of Acsadi-Nemeskeri and Suchey-Brooks methods', *Human Evolution*, 5: 227–38.

Broshi, M., Barkai, G. and Gibson, S. (1983) 'Two Iron Age tombs below the western city wall, Jerusalem, and the Talmudic law of purity', *Cathedra*, 28: 17–32.

Faerman, M., Kharitonov, V., Batsevich, V., *et al.* (1994) 'A Neandertal infant from the Barakai Cave, Western Caucasus', *Journal of Human Evolution*, 27: 405–15.

Feldesman, M.R., Kleckner, J.G. and Lundy, J.K. (1990) 'Femur/stature ratio and estimates of stature in Mid- and Late-Pleistocene fossil hominids', *American Journal of Physical Anthropology*, 83: 359–72.

Finnegan, M. (1978) 'Non-metric variation of the infracranial skeleton', *Journal of Anatomy*, 125: 23–37.

Galili, E., Eshed, V., Gopher, A., *et al.* (2005) 'Burial practices at the submerged Pre-Pottery Neolithic C Site of Atlit-Yam, Northern Coast of Israel', *Bulletin of the American School of Oriental Research*, 339: 1–19.

Gill, G.W., Hughes, S.S., Bennett, B.A., *et al.* (1988) 'Racial identification from the midfacial skeleton with special reference to American Indians and Whites', *Journal of Forensic Sciences*, 33: 92–99.

Goring-Morris, N., Burns, R., Davidzon, A., *et al.* (1998) 'The 1997 season of excavations at the mortuary site of Kfar HaHoresh, Galilee, Israel', *Neo-Lithics*, 3: 1–4.

Goring-Morris, N., Goren, Y., Kolska, L.H., *et al.* (1995) 'Investigations at an Early Neolithic settlement in the Lower Galile: results of the 1991 season at Kefar HaHoresh', *'Atiqot*, 27: 46–48.

Hauser, G. and De Stefano, G.F. (1989) *Epigenetic Variants of the Human Skull*, Stuttgart: E. Schwei-zerbart'sche Verlagsbuchhandlung.

Hershkovitz, I. and Galili, E. (1990) '8000 year-old human remains on the sea floor near Atlit, Israel', *Human Evolution*, 4: 319–58.

Hershkovitz, I. Garfinkel, Y. and Arensburg, B. (1986) 'Neolithic skeletal remains at Yiftahel, area C (Israel)', *Paléorient*, 12: 73–81.

Hershkovitz, I., Spiers, M., Frayer, D., *et al.* (1995) 'Ohalo II – a 19,000 years old skeleton from a water-logged site at the Sea of Galilee', *American Journal of Physical Anthropology*, 96: 215–34.

Hillson, S. (1993) *Teeth*, Cambridge: Cambridge University Press.

Howells, W.W. (1973) *Cranial Variation in Man. Papers of the Peabody Museum of Archaeology and Ethnology*, Cambridge, MA: Harvard University Press.

Johnston, F.E. and Zimmer, L.O. (1989) 'Assessment of growth and age in the immature skeleton', in M.Y. İşcan and A.R. Kenneth (eds) *Reconstruction of Life From the Skeleton*, New-York: Alan R. Liss.

Karo, Y. (1575) *Shulkhan Arukh*, Chapter Yo're De'a, p.364.

Lev-Tov, N., Gopher, A. and Smith, P. (2003) 'Dental evidence for dietary practices in the Chalcolithic period: The findings from a burial cave in Peqi'in (Northern Israel)', *Paléorient*, 29: 121–34.

Nagar, Y. (2002) 'Bone reburial in Israel – legal restrictions and methodological implications', in C. Fforde *et al.* (eds) *The Dead and Their Possessions: Repatriation in Principle, Policy and Practice*, London: Routledge.

Nagar, Y. and Eshed, V. (2001) 'Where are the children? Age-dependent burial practices in Peqi'in', *Israel Exploration Journal*, 51: 27–35.

Nagar, Y. and Sonntag, F. (2008) 'Byzantine period burials in the Negev: anthropological description and summary', *Israel Exploration Journal*, 58: 79–93.

Nagar, Y., Taitz, C. and Reich, R. (1999) 'What can we make of these fragments? Excavation at "Mamilla" cave, Byzantine period, Jerusalem', *International Journal of Osteoarchaeology*, 9: 29–38.

Nagar, Y. and Torgeë, H. (2003) 'Biological characteristics of Jewish burial in the Hellenistic and Early Roman periods', *Israel Exploration Journal*, 53: 164–71.

Nagar, Y. and Winocur, E. (*forthcoming*) 'The skeletal remains from Assawir and Barkai South: recon-struction of some demographic parameters', in E. Yannai (ed.) *Ein Assawir. Excavations at a Protohistoric Site and Adjacent Cemeteries in the Coastal Plain, Israel*, Jerusalem: Israel Antiquities Authority.

Rak, Y., Kimbel, W.H. and Hovers, E. (1994) 'A Neandertal infant from Amud Cave, Israel', Journal of Human Evolution, 26: 313–24.

Smith, P. (1972) 'Diet and attrition in Natufians', *American Journal of Physical Anthropology*, 37: 233–38.

——(1989) 'The skeletal biology and paleopathology of Early Bronze Age populations in the Levant', in P. de Miroschedji (ed.) *L'urbanisation de la Palestine a l'age du Bronze Ancien*, Oxford: Archaeopress.

Smith, P. and Horwitz, L.K. (1997) 'Human skeletal remains from areas A and B at Yiftah'el', in E. Braun (ed.) *Yiftah'el. Salvage and Rescue Excavations at a Prehistoric Village in Lower Galilee, Israel. Antiquities Monographs*, Jerusalem: Israel Antiquities Authority.

Tel Aviv University Sacker Faculty of Medicine (2009) *Anatomy and anthropology*. Available online at www.tau.ac.il/medicine/anatomy/anatomy_intro.html/ (accessed 22 March 2010).

Zagerson, T. and Smith, P. (2002) 'The human remains', in G. Yuval and P. Fabian (eds) *Kissufim Road. A Chalcolithic Mortuary Site*, IAA Reports 16, Jerusalem: Israel Antiquities Authority.

MYANMAR

LAOS

Udon
Thani

THAILAND

Nakhon
Ratchasima

Bangkok

Nanthaburi

Samut
Prakan

CAMBODIA

Andaman
Sea

Gulf of
Thailand

0   300km

Thailand/ประเทศไทย

Siân Halcrow, Nancy Tayles, Natthamon Pureepatpong
and Korakot Boonlop

INTRODUCTION: A BRIEF HISTORY AND CURRENT STATE OF PHYSICAL ANTHROPOLOGY IN THAILAND

Over the past few decades Thailand has been in a development phase of archaeological and bioarchaeological research, with most of the legislation focused on circumventing the looting of cultural heritage and the illicit trading of cultural artefacts. There is no legislation relating specifically to archaeological human remains. National cultural policy in Thailand is designed to give power to and aid professional development of the local researchers in archaeology, such as through the mandatory co-directorship of all foreign research projects with Thai researchers, and the retention of excavated skeletal collections in Thailand. Ethical issues of dealing with human skeletal remains relate to Thai Buddhist beliefs and ritual.

The history of physical anthropology is relatively short in Thailand, due to the relatively late development of archaeology in the region and its sporadic nature (Higham 1989). Although human skeletal remains had been excavated from at least the 1930s (Quaritch Wales 1937, 1964), there was effectively no published research. The history of physical anthropology started relatively recently, with the first published works appearing in the 1960s by a Thai medical doctor, Dr Sood Sangvichien, a graduate from Chulalongkorn University, Bangkok. Dr Sood developed an interest in physical anthropology during his undergraduate years and in 1931–33 he was awarded a Rockefeller scholarship to study physical anthropology with Professors T. Wingate Todd and Wilton M. Krogman at Western Reserve University, Cleveland, Ohio, in the USA. His first publications were based on a sample of prehistoric human skeletal remains excavated as part of a joint Thai–Danish excavation from the site of Ban Kao, Kanchanburi province, western Thailand, in 1960–62. His primary interest was the origins of the Thai people and he first published two papers on the metric and non-metric affiliation of the Ban Kao skeletons (Sangvichien 1966a, 1966b), and ultimately a monograph on the sample (Sangvichien *et al.* 1969). Most of his later works on skeletal analysis from other sites were reports in Thai.

Western scholars have dominated physical anthropology in Thailand since the 1970s, when Michael Pietrusewsky, a Canadian physical anthropologist from the University of Hawai'i, worked on skeletal collections from three sites (Pietrusewsky 1974, 1982, 1984, 1988), and Associate Professor Philip Houghton, an anatomist from the University of Otago in New Zealand, supervised Thai archaeologist Warrachai Wiriyaromp in the 1980s for a Master's degree on a skeletal collection from a site in north east Thailand (Houghton and Wiriyaromp 1984; Wiriyaromp 1984). Successions of students of both Pietrusewsky (Michele Douglas) and Houghton (Nancy Tayles, Kate Domett, Siân Halcrow and Katharine Cox) have since completed PhDs, and most have established research projects in the country.

Praphid Phongmas (previously Choosiri) completed a Master's degree on non-metric traits from the prehistoric Thai site of Khok Phanom Di, at the University of Otago in New Zealand in the 1980s, and is now employed at the Fine Arts Department (FAD) in Bangkok. In the intervening years she has produced two books: *Introduction to Human Osteology* (Choosiri 1991) and *A Brief History of the Study of Human Skeletal Remains in Thailand* (Choosiri 1992), both in Thai, and has contributed to a monograph on early prehistoric human remains from Southern Thailand (Choosiri 1996). Dr Supaporn Nakbunlung of Chang Mai University gained a PhD at the University of Illinois in 1994 and has published on the dental anthropology of a Thai skeletal sample (Nakbunlung and Wathanawareekool 2004, 2008). Dr Vadhana Subhavan of the Museum of Prehistory, Siriraj University, has completed a PhD at the University of Witwatersrand, Johannesburg, on human remains identified as *Homo erectus* from Lampang province, northern Thailand.

Recently, young Thai physical anthropologists are being encouraged by both medically trained anatomists, such as Dr Sood's son, Dr Sanjai Sangvichien of the Department of Anatomy at Siriraj Hospital, and Dr Kamoltip Brown of the Faculty of Medicine, Khon Kaen University, and archaeologists such as Dr Rasmi Shoocongdej of Silpakorn University, Bangkok. Silpakorn University graduates Natthamon Pureepatpong and Korakot Boonlop have both completed Master's degrees on the topic of physical anthropology and have published papers (Boonlop, in press; Boonlop and Bubpha, in press; Pureepatpong 2006). Naruphol Wangthongchaicharoen is currently undertaking a Master's degree on the topic of physical anthropology and has produced a paper (Wangthongchaicharoen, in press). There are several skeletal reports in the grey literature or in local languages, including Boonlop and Wangthongchaicharoen (2006), Choosiri (1994, 1999) and Pureepatpong (2001).

Education and training

There are no specific programmes in Thailand for the study of human remains. Two of the present authors teach part-time: Pureepatpong at Silpakorn University, and Boonlop in archaeology and physical anthropology at other institutions. There are also other universities around the country with academics who teach human osteology, but all are medically trained, and not anthropologists. Occasional workshops and seminars in physical anthropology by Domett and present authors Tayles and Halcrow have been presented over the past ten years for Thai students and archaeological professionals. In 2006, a seminar on Thai physical anthropology was held at the Princess Maha Chakri Sirindorn Anthropology Centre in Bangkok, and proceedings from this conference have been published in Thai (Boonlop 2007).

A recent landmark publication is Oxenham and Tayles's book *Bioarchaeology of Southeast Asia* (Oxenham and Tayles 2006). This book includes an introductory chapter (Tayles and Oxenham 2006) which overviews bioarchaeological work in Thailand, along with other Southeast Asian countries, and Tayles *et al.* (in press) have completed a chapter on the history of palaeopathological research in Southeast Asia. Pietrusewsky and Douglas (2002: 220–22) include a description of several significant skeletal series from Thailand.

ARCHAEOLOGICAL HUMAN REMAINS AND LEGISLATION

Archaeological legislation

Legislation pertaining to archaeological remains is contained in the Act on Ancient Monuments, Antiques, Objects of Art and National Museums (1961, amended 1992) (referred to hereafter as the Act). Although it is not defined in the Act, the borderline between forensic and archaeological human remains is treated as 50 years BP (R. Thosarat, pers. comm.). However, the authors were unable to establish where this is specified. This is interesting as archaeological skeletons at around 50 years of antiquity may have close living relatives, but there are no specific documents that outline how this should be dealt with. If it is found that the individual has living relatives, the bones are given back to the family (R. Thosarat, pers. comm.).

The main purpose of the Act is to prohibit the trade of antiquities in response to the significant problem of looting and trade of archaeological artefacts. In the Act, human skeletal remains are not given separate consideration to cultural remains and are included in the definition of 'antique' (section 4):

> ... an archaic movable property, whether produced by man [sic.] or nature, or being any part of ancient monument or of human skeleton or animal carcass which, by its age or characteristics of production or historical evidence, is useful in the field of art, history or archaeology.
>
> *Act on Ancient Monuments, Antiques, Objects of Art and National Museums*
> *1961, amended 1992, Article 4 [authors' translation]*

Under section 24 of the Act, if antiques are found they are to be reported to the local authorities or the FAD. In response, a representative(s) of the FAD will inspect the area in which the antiques were reported (R. Thosarat, pers. comm.). There is no legislation or guidelines that relate specifically to the discovery of human remains in archaeological excavations.

HUMAN REMAINS AND LEGISLATION

In accordance with section 10 of the Act, it is compulsory for excavation plans to be approved by the Director-General of the FAD. However, there is no special licence needed for the excavation of human remains and any trained archaeologist can excavate them, without any training in biological anthropology. Although osteological analysis of human remains is not compulsory, local archaeologists see the value in doing so, and this analysis is generally carried out, at least at a minimal, purely descriptive, level.

For all archaeological investigations in Thailand (whether Thai led or Thai co-directed with foreigners), it is compulsory to have a trained archaeologist on site during excavation (R. Thosarat, pers. comm.). In accordance with section 10 of the Act, an appointed representative of the FAD may visit the site of excavation at any time. Generally, the Research Memorandum of Understanding for foreign co-directed archaeological projects stipulates that a representative from the FAD, or an appointed representative, is to be at the excavation at all times (R. Thosarat, pers. comm.).

Cultural heritage policy and retention of archaeological human remains

There is no specific legislation prohibiting the transportation of human skeletal remains from Thailand for research, and in the past whole archaeological skeletal collections excavated in the

1960s, 1970s and 1980s have been curated at institutions including the University of Otago, University of Nevada-Las Vegas, and University of Hawai'i.

However, during the past 20 years, foreign co-directed excavation projects have not been transporting human skeletal collections out of the country. Also, during this time some of the human skeletal collections that have been curated abroad (e.g., skeletal collections at the University of Otago) have been repatriated to Thailand, or arrangements for their repatriation are underway (e.g., the Ban Chiang skeletal collection at the University of Hawai'i). There are numerous reasons for the retention of the human skeletal collections in Thailand, including practical issues such as the cost and logistics of sending the remains overseas. However, probably the most significant factor is encouragement by the Thai government to promote local expertise in archaeology.

Over the past 40 years in Thailand, especially since the 1980s, there has been an increased emphasis on education in archaeology and therefore an increase in trained archaeologists. Since a 1981 National Cultural Policy announcement, with detailed guidelines following in 1986, there has been an increased cultural promotion effort (Office of the National Culture Commission 1986). These initiatives are designed to give more power/decisions to local people, and in the context of archaeology, to Thai archaeologists (Raksastaya 1997). The Policy Statement to Parliament in 1992 stated that the government will 'campaign to engage people, organizations, institutions and communities in activities relating to conserve, promote and propagate Thai arts and culture more actively' (Council of Ministers 1992: 37). This empowerment of local experts is implemented at numerous levels, including legislation, such as the Act and the National Research Council of Thailand Regulations on the Permission for Foreign (non-Thai) Researchers to Conduct Research in Thailand, B.E. 2550 (i.e. AD 2007). For example, the Regulations on the Permission for Foreign (non-Thai) Researchers to Conduct Research in Thailand, B.E. 2550 (article 9) stipulate that 'research involving a foreigner must be conducted jointly with a Thai researcher or consultant'. All foreign researchers must apply to the Office of the National Research Council of Thailand for a permit for research in the kingdom.

Section 26 of the Act states:

> Antiques and objects of art which are State property under the custody of the Department of Fine Arts shall not be kept in other place[s] than in the national museums. But in [the] case [where] it is unable or unsuitable to keep them in the national museums, they may be, subject to the permission of the Director-General [of the Fine Arts Department], kept in other museums, temples, or places belonging to the government.
>
> *Act on Ancient Monuments, Antiques, Objects of Art and National Museums 1961, amended 1992, Article 26 [authors' translation]*

A purpose-built storage facility for human remains excavated in Thailand is currently being constructed at the 12th National Office of the FAD in Phimai, northeast Thailand. It is planned that these facilities will be used to house several large Thai archaeological skeletal collections, such as those currently held in the National Museum in Phimai, as well as collections that will be repatriated to Thailand from the USA in the future. There is no specific legislation relating to the mode of transportation of archaeological human remains within Thailand to museums and other facilities for storage and study. A laboratory for the analysis of archaeological human skeletal remains is also located at the Princess Maha Chakri Sirindhorn Anthropology Centre in Bangkok.

Ethical issues in excavating and analysis of archaeological skeletal material

During the development of archaeological projects, full consultation with landowners and local communities by the FAD and other archaeologists is carried out (R. Thosarat, pers. comm.). For any excavation that is undertaken on privately owned land, the owner is compensated (R. Thosarat, pers. comm.). Before archaeological excavation commences the spiritual needs of the local Thais are met by the ceremonies which make merit to the spirits or to the ancestors (*sen wai phi* – make merit to the spirits, or *sen wai ban pa bu rute* – make merit to the ancestors) (Sparkes 2007).

Today Thai people cremate their dead as part of Buddhist practice, to release their spirits for re-birth. While they feel that prehistoric skeletons are their remote ancestors, death is only a passage to the next life, and the bones are not considered sacred. A telling example is the dis-interment in 2005 of more than 900 recent graves of Hmong people at Wat Tham Krabok in Saraburi, Thailand (University of Minnesota 2007). The Hmong are one of the many hill tribes from the mountainous regions of southern China and Southeast Asia. Hmong refugees from Laos have occupied this monastery since the 1970s. The disinterred bodies were then cremated in line with Buddhist Thai tradition. This caused much distress for the Hmong people as, according to their beliefs, and in contrast to Thai tradition, the burial place is sacred (University of Minnesota 2007). Although there were probably also underlying political issues between the Thai gov-ernment and this minority group in relation to the disinterment, this is a still a vivid example of the Thai Buddhist belief that the dead body is non-sacred. This view of human remains is also illustrated by the practice of looting of prehistoric grave goods, and the consequent damage to human skeletons, which occurs throughout Thailand and other countries in Southeast Asia. In these cases it seems that personal economic gain takes precedence over any ethical notions of respect for the skeletons.

Related to this non-sacred view of human remains is the establishment of open-air site museums, whereby sites are excavated and the burials left *in situ* (e.g., the Ban Prasat and Ban Chiang National Museums, northeast Thailand), which are popular with both Thai and foreign tourists.

The ethical issues of excavation and analysis of Thai human skeletons has been raised in a paper by an anonymous Thai author using the pen name of Artayok (2000). This paper argued that the excavation and analysis of human remains in Thailand (and elsewhere in the world) does not take into account spiritual and cultural beliefs associated with the dead. Pureepatpong (2000) responded to this paper, recounting her personal experiences with the analysis of human remains in Thailand. She stated that, contrary to the argument that human remains are dehu-manized, the main reason for the analysis of human bones is to understand their *life* in the past (Pureepatpong 2000). She went on to argue that it could be considered disrespectful for human skeletal remains to be left exposed in open-air site museums, as the bones tend to crack and fragment once exposed to humidity for a period of time. Pureepatpong also notes that the educa-tion of the local community is an important factor for ensuring preservation of archaeological human remains (Pureepatpong 2000).

The FAD is working with local communities to educate at the village level on the potential value of cultural heritage (Thosarat 2001). Also, since 1978, the Southeast Asian Ministers of Education Organization Regional Centre for Archaeology and Fine Arts (SEAMEO SPAFA) in Thailand has been working to raise awareness of south east Asia's heritage and to improve professionalism within the cultural sector. Dr Rasmi Shoocongdej has developed a cultural heritage management project at highland Pang Mapha, a small district in Mae Hong Son Province, northwestern Thailand. Dr Rasmi is working collaboratively with local communities in designing their own management plans for two site museums in the district, providing host/guide training to adults and children, and engaging in larger community archaeological education programmes (Figure 56.1).

Figure 56.1 Local children of Pang Mapha District, Mae Hong Son Province, northwestern Thailand, involved in a community archaeological education project at Tham Lod rock shelter site
Source: Photo courtesy Dr Rasmi Shoocongdej

METHODS OF ANTHROPOLOGICAL ANALYSIS

Most of the physical anthropology research on Thai samples makes use of internationally recognized standards, such as Buikstra and Ubelaker (1994). As noted, Choosiri (1991) has published osteological standards in Thai, but these standards are not based on Thai populations. There are, however, population-specific standards for stature, developed by Sanjai Sangvichien, based on cadaveric specimens from the Anatomy Department, Siriraj Hospital (Sangvichien *et al.* 1985; n.d.). Pureepatpong has also been collecting data on long bone metrics and stature from cadavers from Siriraj Hospital. Domett (2001: 29–30) and Halcrow *et al.* (2007) have given recommendations for sub-adult age estimation using dental methods. Forensic research by King *et al.* (İşcan *et al.* 1998; King 1999; King *et al.* 1998) on the sexual dimorphism of long bone metrics of Thai cadavers also have the potential to be used in the analysis of archaeological human remains. Schmitt (2004) undertook a blind test of two morphological methods of ageing on a modern Thai known age-at-death sample and found that for both methods that there was significant inaccuracy. Recently, Rooppakhun *et al.* (2009) have developed a logistic regression model for sex estimation from the skull using 3D CT analysis. Boonprakorb (1993) has completed a Master's thesis on Thai skeletal morphology, which is also used as a standard for cranial morphometric studies (see, e.g., Boonlop and Bubpha, in press).

CONCLUSION

The archaeological legislation in Thailand is aimed primarily at circumventing the looting of cultural heritage and the illicit trading of cultural artefacts. There is no legislation specifically governing archaeological human remains. The retention of archaeological human skeletal remains within Thailand for analysis is now the normal practice and the construction of purpose-built storage facilities for the remains indicates the development of concern for human remains as an archaeological resource.

LEGISLATION

Act on Ancient Monuments, Antiques, Objects of Art and National Museums (1961), last amended 5 April B.E. 2535 (1992). *Government Gazette* 109, Part 38.

USEFUL CONTACTS

Institutions

Office of the National Research Council of Thailand (NRCT), Office of International Affairs, 196 Phaholyothin Road, Chatuchak, Bangkok 10900, Thailand. Tel: +66 2 940 6369, +66 2 579 2690; Fax: +66 2 561 3049. Website: www.nrct.go.th/

Thai Fine Arts Department, Na Pra That Road, Bangkok 10200, Thailand. Tel: +66 2 2217811; Fax: +66 2 2217811. Website: www.finearts.go.th/

Silpakorn University, 31 Na Phralan Road, Phraborommaharatchawang Sub-District, Phra Nakhon District, Bangkok 10200, Thailand. Tel: +66 2 6236115–21; Fax: +66 2 2258991. Website: www.su.ac.th/index.asp/

Princess Maha Chakri Sirindorn Anthropology Centre, 20 Boromarachachonnani Road, Taling Chan, Bangkok 10170, Thailand. Tel. +66 2 8809429; Fax. +66 2 8809332. Website: www.sac.or.th/home.html/ (Thai); http://av.sac.or.th/SAC_E/index.html/ (English).

A physical anthropology database of Thai collections is under development by Korakot Boonlop and Sanjai Sangvichien (available online at www.sac.or.th/).

Southeast Asian Ministers of Education Organization Regional Centre for Archaeology and Fine Arts (SEAMEO SPAFA) Thailand, SEAMEO SPAFA Building, 81/1 Sri Ayutthaya Road, Samsen, Dusit, Bangkok 10300, Thailand. Tel: +66 2 2804022; Fax: +66 2 2804030. Website: www.seameo-spafa.org/

Anthropological societies

Indo-Pacific Prehistory Association. Website: http://arts.anu.edu.au/arcworld/ippa/ippa.htm/

European Association of Southeast Asian Archaeologists. Website: http://213.207.98.211/euraseaa12//

Southeast Asian Archaeology Scholarly Website (with bibliographic and skeletal databases): http://seasia.museum.upenn.edu/

The annual *Southeast Asian Bioarchaeological Newsletter* is edited by Kate Domett; email: kate.domett@jcu.edu.au

ACKNOWLEDGEMENTS

We would like to thank Dr Rachanie Thosarat for commenting on a draft of this chapter.

BIBLIOGRAPHY

Artayok, A. (2000) 'The "study" of human remains' [in Thai]. *Muang Boran*, 1: 5–8.

Boonlop, K. (ed.) (2007) *The Origins of Humanity: The Studies and Researches on Physical Anthropology in Thailand* [in Thai], Bangkok: Princess Maha Chakri Sirindhorn.

——(in press) 'Prehistoric people from Ban Chiang: a study of human skulls from excavation at Wat Pho Si Nai cemetery', in M. Klokke (ed.) *Proceedings of the 12th International Conference of the European Association of Southeast Asian Archaeologists*, Amsterdam: Amsterdam University Press.

Boonlop, K. and Bubpha, S. (in press) 'Prehistoric people from Ban Chiang: a physical anthropology perspective on a mainland Southeast Asian agrarian population', in N. Enfield and J. C. White (eds) *Dynamics of Human Diversity: The case of Mainland Southeast Asia*.

Boonlop, K. and Wangthongchaicharoen, N. (2006) 'Past, present, and future of physical anthropology in Thailand' [in Thai], *Muang Boran*, 32: 21–24. Anthropology Centre.

Boonprakorb, Y. (1993) 'The Northeastern Thai Skull: Physical Anthropology Studies', unpublished Master of Science thesis, Khon Kaen University.

Buikstra, J.E. and Ubelaker, D.H. (eds) (1994) *Standards for Data Collection from Human Skeletal Remains*, Fayetteville, AR: Arkansas Archaeological Survey Report No. 44.

Choosiri, P. (1991) *Introduction to Human Osteology* [in Thai], Bangkok: Sampanpanit.

——(1992) *A Brief History of the Study of Human Skeletal Remains in Thailand* [in Thai], Bangkok: Division of Archaeology, Fine Arts Department.

——(1994) *A Preliminary Report on Human Skeletal Analysis from Archaeological sites at Ban Tum and Ban Daeng Yai, Khon Kaen Province* [in Thai], Bangkok: Division of Archaeology, Fine Arts Department.

——(1996) 'An analysis of palaeopathological changes in the human skeletal remains from Southern Thailand', in S. Pookajorn (ed.) *Final Report of Excavations at Moh Kiew Cave, Krabi Province; Sakai Cave, Trang Province and Ethnoarchaeological Research of Hunter-Gatherer Group, So-called Mani or Sakai or Orang Koli at Trang Province*, Bangkok: Silpakorn University Press.

——(1999) 'Prehistoric men at Chaibadan' [in Thai], *Silpakorn Journal*, 42: 93–111.

Council of Ministers (1992) *Statement of Policy of the Council of Ministers* [in Thai] by Prime Minister Chuan Leekpai to the National Assembly, 21 October.

Domett, K.M. (2001) *Health in Late Prehistoric Thailand*, British Archaeological Reports International Series 946, Oxford: Archaeopress.

Halcrow, S.E., Tayles, N. and Buckley, H.R. (2007) 'Age estimation of children in prehistoric Southeast Asia: are the standards used appropriate?', *Journal of Archaeological Science*, 34: 1158–68.

Higham, C.F.W. (1989) *The Archaeology of Mainland Southeast Asia*, Cambridge: Cambridge University Press.

Houghton, P. and Wiriyaromp, W. (1984) 'The people of Ban Na Di', in C.F.W. Higham and A. Kijngam (eds) *Prehistoric Investigations in Northeastern Thailand*, British Archaeological Reports International Series 231, Oxford: Archaeopress.

İşcan, M.Y., Loth, S.R., King, C.A., *et al.* (1998) 'Sexual dimorphism in the humerus: a comparative analysis of Chinese, Japanese and Thais', *Forensic Science International*, 98: 17–29.

King, C.A. (1999) 'Sex determination from Thai tibiae', *Homo*, 50: 107–17.

King, C.A., İşcan, M.Y. and Loth, S.R. (1998) 'Metric and comparative analysis of sexual dimorphism in the Thai femur', *Journal of Forensic Sciences*, 43: 954–58.

Monkhonkamnuanket, N. (1992) *Ban Prasat: An Archaeological Site* [in Thai], Bangkok: Fine Arts Department.

Nakbunlung, S. and Wathanawareekool, S. (2004) 'Talking teeth: dental non-metric traits of wooden-coffin people in the Pang Ma Pha Cave Sites, Northwestern Thailand', *Bulletin of the Indo-Pacific Prehistory Association*, 24: 139–42.

——(2008) 'Whispering teeth: nutrition and health of wooden coffin people in the Pang Ma Pha Cave Sites, Northwestern Thailand', *Bulletin of the Indo-Pacific Prehistory Association*, 28: 84–87.

Office of the National Culture Commission (1986) *National Culture Policy and Guidelines on Protection, Promotion and Development of Culture* [in Thai], Bangkok: Kurusapa.

Oxenham, M.F. and Tayles, N. (eds) (2006) *Bioarchaeology of Southeast Asia*, Cambridge: Cambridge University Press.

Pietrusewsky, M. (1974) *Non Nok Tha. The Human Skeletal Remains from the 1966 Excavations at Non Nok Tha, Northeastern Thailand*, Dunedin: University of Otago.

——(1982) 'The ancient inhabitants of Ban Chiang: the evidence from the human skeletal and dental remains', *Expedition*, 24: 42–50.

——(1984) 'Pioneers of the Khorat Plateau: the prehistoric inhabitants from Ban Chiang', *Journal of the Hong Kong Archaeological Society*, 10: 90–106.

——(1988) *Prehistoric Human Remains from Non Pa Kluay, Northeast Thailand*, Dunedin: Department of Anthropology, University of Otago.

Pietrusewsky, M. and Douglas, M.T. (2002) *Ban Chiang, A Prehistoric Village Site in Northeast Thailand I: The Human Skeletal Remains*, Philadelphia: University of Pennsylvania Museum of Archaeology and Anthropology.

Pureepatpong, N. (2000) 'Perspectives on human skeletal analysis and proper treatment of human remains' [in Thai], *Muang Boran*, 1: 9–15.

——(2001) 'A preliminary report of an analysis of human skeletal remains from Muang Sema, Nakhon Ratchasima Province, Northeast Thailand' [in Thai], unpublished manuscript, Phimai, Nakhon Ratchasima, 12th Regional Office of the Thai Fine Arts Department.

——(2006) 'Recent investigation of early people (late Pleistocene to early Holocene) from Ban Rai and Tham Lod rock shelter sites, Pang Mapha district, Mae Hong Son Province, Northwestern Thailand', in E.A. Bacus *et al.* (eds) *Uncovering Southeast Asia's Past*, Singapore: NUS Publishing.

Quaritch Wales, H.G. (1937) 'Some ancient human skeletons excavated in Siam', *Man*, 37: 89–90.

——(1964) 'Some ancient human skeletons excavated in Siam: a correction', *Man*, 64: 121.

Raksastaya, A. (1997) 'A cultural policy for Thailand's national development', in B. Saraswati (ed.) *Integration of Endogenous Cultural Dimension into Development*, New Delhi: Indira Gandhi National Centre for the Arts.

Rooppakhun, S., Piyasin, S. and Sitthiseripratip, K. (2009) '3D CT craniometric study of Thai skulls relevance to sex determination using logistic regression analysis', in C.T. Lim and J.C.H. Goh (eds) *ICBME Proceedings 23*, Berlin: Springer.

Sangvichien, S. (1966a) 'Neolithic skeletons from Ban Kao, Thailand, and the problem of Thai origins', *Current Anthropology*, 7: 234–35.

——(1966b) 'A preliminary report on non-metrical characteristics of Neolithic skeletons found at Ban Kao, Kanchanaburi', *Journal of the Siam Society*, 54: 1–8.

Sangvichien, S., Sirigaroon, P. and Jorgensen, J.B. (1969) *Archaeological Excavations in Thailand, Volume III, Ban Kao: Neolithic Cemeteries in the Kanchanaburi Province. Part Two: The Prehistoric Thai Skeletons* (Vol. 3), Copenhagen: Munksgaard.

Sangvichien, S., Srisurin, V. and Wattanayingsakul, V. (1985) 'Estimation of stature of Thai and Chinese from the length of the femur, tibia and fibula', *Siriraj Hospital Gazette*, 37: 215–18.

Sangvichien, S., Srisurin, V., Wattanayingsakul, V., *et al.* (n.d.) 'Equations for estimation of the Thai's stature from the length of long bones (a preliminary report)', unpublished manuscript, Bangkok, Department of Anatomy, Faculty of Medicine, Siriraj Hospital, Mahidol Unviversity.

Schmitt, A. (2004) 'Age-at-death assessment using the os pubis and the auricular surface of the ilium: a test on an identified Asian sample', *International Journal of Osteoarchaeology*, 14: 1–6.

Sparkes, S. (2007) 'Rice for the ancestors: food offerings, kinship and merit among the Isan of Northeast Thailand', in M. Janowski and F. Kerlogue (eds) *Kinship and Food in South East Asia*, Copenhagen: Nordic Institute of Asian Studies.

Tayles, N., Halcrow, S.E. and Pureepatpong, N. *(in press)*. 'Southeast Asia', in J.E. Buikstra and C. Roberts (eds) *History of Paleopathology Pioneers, vol 3*, Oxford: University of Oxford Press.

Tayles, N. and Oxenham, M.F. (2006) 'Southeast Asian bioarchaeology: past and present', in M.F. Oxenham and N. Tayles (eds) *Bioarchaeology of Southeast Asia*, Cambridge: Cambridge University Press.

The National Research Council of Thailand (n.d.) *Regulations on the Permission for Foreign Researchers to Conduct Research in Thailand, B.E. 2550*.

Thosarat, R. (2001) 'Report from Southeast Asia', *Culture Without Context: The Newsletter of the Illicit Antiquities Research Centre* 8.

University of Minnesota (2007) *United Nations expert to hear testimony from Hmong families grave desecration in Thailand*. Available online at www1.umn.edu/urelate/newsservice/NS_details.php?release=081208_384 6& page=NS/ (accessed 7 July 2009).

Wangthongchaicharoen, N. (in press) 'Recently discovered infant jar burials from Wat Pho Srinai, Ban Chiang, northeastern Thailand', in M. Klokke (ed.) *Proceedings of the 12th International Conference of the European Association of Southeast Asian Archaeologists*, Amsterdam: Amsterdam University Press.

Wiriyaromp, W. (1984) 'The human skeletal remains from Ban Na Di: patterns of birth, health and death in Prehistoric North East Thailand', unpublished Master of Arts thesis, University of Otago.

Australia

Denise Donlon and Judith Littleton

INTRODUCTION: A BRIEF HISTORY AND CURRENT STATE OF PHYSICAL ANTHROPOLOGY IN AUSTRALIA

Human remains found in Australia range from Pleistocene Aboriginals to Europeans dating from 1788, to a mix of ancestries today. In recent times, the remains of Australians missing-in-action from wars offshore are also being recovered.

The term 'indigenous' is used here interchangeably with the term 'Aboriginal', but strictly speaking it refers to both Australian Aborigines and Torres Strait Islanders, as both are indigenous to Australia.

The history of physical anthropology in Australia falls into four phases.

Phase 1: 1788 – 20th century (pre-academic phase)

In this phase, physical anthropology in Australia grew out of the curiosity Europeans had for the culture and origins of the indigenous people. This is seen by observations of the physical characteristics of Australian Aborigines that are found in the journals of the early explorers. Captain James Cook, for example, made a number of observations on the physical appearance of the people (Beaglehole 1955). The idea of Aborigines as 'archaic' was taken up by many after the publication of Darwin's *On the Origin of Species* in 1859. It was generally assumed that Australian Aboriginals were typical of an early evolutionary stage of humans. Such ideas stimulated the excavation of Aboriginal graves and the collection of their skulls. For example, during the expedition of the *HMS Challenger* (1872–76), many Aboriginal skulls were collected and later studied in Britain by the anatomist Sir William Turner (1884). The early 'physical anthropologists' were in fact anatomists. Interest in the antiquity of the Aboriginal was further stimulated by the announcement of a possible Pleistocene skull, the Talgai skull, at the 1914 British Association for the Advancement of Science meeting by Edgeworth David and J. T. Wilson, professors of geology and anatomy respectively at the University of Sydney (David and Wilson 1914).

Phase 2: 1920s–1950s: academic beginnings

The first Department of Anthropology in Australia was established at the University of Sydney in 1925 with the first chair of Anthropology being A.R. Radcliffe-Brown (1926–30). The chair's role was to assist the government in the control, development and advancement of indigenous populations (Gray 2007). These early chairs, which included A.P. Elkin, were primarily social anthropologists but had training in physical anthropology. They were involved in collecting physical anthropological data on Australian Aborigines as well as on Aborigines from Papua New Guinea and the Solomon Islanders.

The Department of Anatomy at the University of Sydney produced some prominent physical anthropologists during this time, such as J.L. Shellshear, S.L. Larnach, A.A. Abbie and N.W.G. Macintosh, with Macintosh being the most dynamic force in physical anthropology during this period (Elkin 1978; Spencer 1997). These anatomists, who all studied comparative anatomy and who had an interest in human diversity, were well placed to collect the anatomical data that underpinned physical anthropology (Donlon 2009). Detailed anatomical descriptions were made of isolated Aboriginal crania such as Keilor (Wunderly 1943), Cohuna (Macintosh 1952a), and Talgai (Macintosh 1952b). The main interest of the early physical anthropologists was the origin of the Australian Aborigines and the routes of migration into Australia and the Pacific.

In 1926 in South Australia the Board for Anthropological Research was established. It sponsored over 40 anthropological expeditions between 1926 and 1976 to study Australian Aboriginal people. Frederick Wood-Jones, a British anatomist and physical anthropologist, was key founder of the Anthropological Society of South Australia in 1926, the first such society in Australia.

Also in the 1920s Andrew Arthur Abbie was appointed Elder Professor of Anatomy and Histology at the University of Adelaide. He undertook a number of research expeditions with the Board over the decade 1951–61, and published extensively on the physical anthropology of Aboriginal Australians.

In 1946 the Australian National University in Canberra was established. Although established later than many other universities in Australia, it was set up as a research-intensive university stuudying Australian as well as Asian and Pacific anthropology.

Phase 3: 1960s–1980s: Aboriginal burial excavations

The 1950s saw the introduction of radiocarbon dating, and this was followed by extensive excavations in the 1960s during which important remains such as the Lake Nitchie (Macintosh 1971), Mungo and Kow Swamp (Thorne 1975, 1976), Broadbeach (Haglund-Calley 1968) and Roonka remains (Pretty 1977) were excavated. Alan Thorne, a student of Macintosh, went on to the Australian National University where palaeoanthropology became an important focus of research (Kirk and Thorne 1976). This period also saw detailed descriptions of the cranial morphology of the Aborigines (Larnach and Macintosh 1970, 1971, 1973).

In 1961 the Australian Institute of Aboriginal Studies in Canberra in 1961 was established. Its aim was to undertake and promote Aboriginal studies, and this included physical anthropology. At the same time many of the seminal works on the anthropometry of living Aboriginal people were being published, with some stressing variation (Birdsell 1967) and others homogeneity (Abbie 1968). Archaeologists were beginning to show interest in burial practices (see, e.g., Hiatt 1969; Meehan 1971; Pardoe 1988).

In 1987 Charles Oxnard took up the Chair of Anatomy and Human Biology at the University of Western Australia. Oxnard has been very important for influencing the growth of physical anthropology, not only in Australia but worldwide, with his diverse interests ranging from primate anatomy and studies of form and function to morphometrics. He was responsible for setting up the Australasian Society for Human Biology (ASHB) and is an enthusiastic supporter of young researchers (Cartmill 2004).

Partly as a result of the Board for Anthropological research, the Departments of Anatomy and the Dental School at the University of Adelaide retained an interest and involvement in human ecology, resulting in a significant contribution by the Dental School in particular to aspects of dental anthropology and Aboriginal populations (Rogers *et al.* 2009), such as studies on dental eruption and development (Brown *et al.* 1979), attrition (Richards and Miller 1991) and sex determination (Townsend, Richards and Carroll 1982).

Phase 4: 1990s–present: non-Aboriginal research

Since 1984 many collections of Australian Aboriginal remains have been repatriated from museums and reburied, and control over access to collection for research has been given to indigenous people. An unexpected outcome of this has been the need to record remains *in situ* in order to prevent excavation (Hope and Littleton 1995a, 1995b). There has been a move away from research into Aboriginal remains to those of the other populations (Green 1990; Littleton 1992; Pietrusewsky 1990). Gender-based research began with the Women in Archaeology Conferences in Albury in 1991, and in Sydney in 1995 (Casey *et al.* 1998; Du Cros and Smith 1992).

In 1996, Maciej Henneberg was made Wood Jones Chair of Anthropological and Comparative Anatomy at the University of Adelaide. This is the first and only chair of physical anthropology in Australia,

> The discovery of *Homo floresiensis* at Flores in Indonesia in 2004 has stimulated great interest in human evolution in this region of the world, especially as the discovery team was a combined Australian/Indonesian team. Many of the earliest papers on the find were published by Australians.
>
> *Argue* et al. *2006; Brown* et al. *2004; Henneberg and Thorne 2004; Morwood* et al. *2004*

Commercial development activity, especially in the cities, has meant the disturbance of old European cemeteries. This has for the first time given physical anthropologists the opportunity to examine the remains of early European settlers (AustralArchaeology/Godden Mackay 1997; Donlon *et al.* 2009; Higginbotham *et al.* 2002; Lowe and Mackay 1992; Pate and Adams, 2000).

Recently there has been an explosion of interest in forensic anthropology, and physical anthropologists are now employed in most state mortuaries (Donlon 2008, 2009). During the 1990s and 2000s there has been a growing interest in the recovery and identification of Australians killed in action from the First and Second World Wars and the Vietnam War.

Milestones in the development of physical anthropology in Australia are summarized in Table 57.1.

Education and training

Physical anthropology has rarely been taught as a discipline in Australia but as part of anatomy programmes, and in the past practitioners have therefore been medical practitioners. It is only since the 1960s that physical anthropology has been taught to non-medical students. Forensic anthropology was introduced into anatomy and archaeology courses in the 1990s and 2000s. Today courses in forensic and physical/biological anthropology and osteology are offered within anatomy departments at the University of Sydney, the University of Adelaide, Bond University and the University of Western Australia, and within archaeology departments at the University of New England, Flinders University, and the Australian National University.

Table 57.1 Milestones in the development of physical anthropology in Australia

Date	Milestone	Location
1925	A.R. Radcliffe Brown, First Chair of Anthropology	University of Sydney, New South Wales
1926	South Australia Board for Anthropological Research	Adelaide, South Australia
1934	A.A. Abbie, Elder Professor of Anatomy and Histology	Adelaide South Australia
1961	Australian Institute of Aboriginal Studies set up	Canberra, ACT
1960s	Excavation of important Aboriginal burials and burial grounds	Queensland, New South Wales, Victoria and South Australia
1955–1972	N.W.G. Macintosh strong proponent of physical anthropology	University of Sydney, New South Wales
1987	Charles Oxnard appointed Professor of Anatomy and Human Biology	University of Western Australia, Perth
1987	Australasian Society for Human Biology	Australia–wide
1996	First Chair of Physical Anthropology: Wood Jones Chair of Physical Anthropology and Comparative Anatomy – Maceij Henneberg	University of Adelaide, South Australia
1990s–2000s	Excavation of large early European cemeteries	Adelaide, Sydney, Brisbane
2004	Discovery of *Homo floresiensis*	Flores, Indonesia
1990s–2000s	Inclusion of anthropologists into Department of Defence recovery teams for Australians missing in action	Europe, Papua New Guinea, Vietnam, Indonesia, Australia
1990s–2000s	Forensic anthropologists employed in most state mortuaries	Adelaide, Sydney, Perth, Melbourne, Hobart, Brisbane

Skeletal collections, laboratories and museums

All of the state and mainland territory museums in Australia hold collections of human skeletal remains. These collections consist mainly of Aboriginal remains with small collections of remains of Melanesians (mainly from Papua New Guinea). There are also very small collections of Polynesians, Asians and Europeans. The only museum which is fully dedicated to physical anthropology is the Shellshear Museum of Physical Anthropology and Comparative Anatomy at the University of Sydney. All Australian museums have policies to repatriate Aboriginal remains and are actively doing so. Permission to do research on Aboriginal remains requires consent from the relevant Aboriginal groups.

Research areas today

In Australia, research in physical anthropology focuses on Australian Aboriginal origins and dispersal, palaeoanthropology, forensic anthropology, palaeopathology, skeletal and dental variation, secular changes in body proportions and stable isotope analysis. Most research originates from university departments. Collections of Aboriginal remains in museums throughout Australia resulted mainly from the discovery of remains by members of the public but also by archaeological excavation. Such collections were investigated by various anthropologists and anatomists, mainly for their doctoral research. At the same time as interest was growing in physical, and especially forensic, anthropology in the 1990s, Aboriginal skeletal remains, which had typically been the source of much research, were becoming increasingly unavailable (Donlon 1994).

Professional associations

The primary association for physical anthropologists in Australia is the Australasian Society for Human Biology (ASHB), formed in 1987. It is a small society of a few hundred members, meets at a conference once a year, and publishes the proceedings of the ASHB. In addition, the *Journal of Comparative Human Biology* (HOMO) is the official journal for the society. Physical anthropologists who have an interest in archaeology generally belong to the Australian Archaeology Association, which publishes *Australian Archaeology*, and/or the Australasian Society of Historical Archaeologists, which publishes the *Australasian Journal of Historical Archaeology*. Physical anthropologists with a forensic bent usually belong to The Australian and New Zealand Forensic Science Society and some to the Australian Academy of Forensic Science, which publishes the *Australian Journal of Forensic Science*.

A relevant journal not associated with an association is *Archaeology in Oceania*, formally called *Archaeology and Physical Anthropology in Oceania*.

ARCHAEOLOGICAL HUMAN REMAINS AND LEGISLATION

Archaeological legislation

The law of Australia consists of the Australian common law (which is based on English common law), federal laws enacted by the Parliament of Australia, and laws enacted by each of the Parliaments of the six Australian states and two mainland territories. Laws passed by the Parliament of Australia, that is the Federal laws, apply to the whole of Australia.

The search for and excavation of human remains throughout Australia are subject to different laws depending on the state or territory in which the remains are situated. If they are ancient Aboriginal remains, then there are heritage laws governing their management. In addition they may also be subject to Federal laws. Non-Aboriginal remains of historic importance may be subject to a different set of heritage laws. Human remains of forensic interest are subject to the Coroners Act of that state or territory.

The legislation relevant to each state and territory is summarized in Table 57.2. Rather than go into detail for each of these, we give an overview and then we provide a detailed description of what happens in one state, New South Wales (NSW), and give case studies to illustrate how the legislation is applied.

Australian heritage laws exist at the national (Federal) level, and in each of the states and territories. It is these laws, and their associated regulations, that seek to protect and preserve the Australian nation's natural, cultural and historical heritage. At the same time they usually enable developers to apply for a permit or certificate to allow them to proceed with activities that might affect the indigenous heritage. Depending on the state or territory, indigenous and non-indigenous human remains may be dealt with under the same or different heritage legislation.

Federal heritage legislation

The Federal legislation which deals with indigenous remains is the Aboriginal and Torres Strait Islander Heritage Protection Act (1984). Section 20 of this act states: 'A person who discovers anything that he has reasonable grounds to suspect to be Aboriginal remains shall report his discovery to the Minister, giving particulars of the remains and their location.'

Also relevant is the Protection of Moveable Cultural Heritage Act 1986. Section 6 of this act protects 'objects relating to members of the Aboriginal race of Australia and descendants of the indigenous inhabitants of the Torres Strait Islands', and such objects cannot be exported from

Table 57.2 Legislation that should be consulted prior to the excavation of human skeletal remains in Australia

Jurisdiction	Coronial/Forensic	Heritage – Indigenous	Heritage – Non-indigenous
Australia-wide/ Federal	none	Aboriginal and Torres Strait Islander Heritage Protection Act 1984. Protection of Movable Cultural Heritage Act 1986	Protection of Movable Cultural Heritage Act 1986
States			
New South Wales	Coroners Act 1980 Law Enforcement (Powers and Responsibilities) Act 2002	National Parks and Wildlife Act 1974	Heritage Act 1977
Victoria	Coroners Act 2008	Aboriginal Heritage Act 2006	Heritage Act 1994
South Australia	Coroners Act 2003	Aboriginal Heritage Act 1988	Heritage Places Act 1993
Western Australia	Coroners Act 1996	Aboriginal Heritage Act 1972	Heritage of Western Australia Act 1993
Tasmania	Coroners Act 1995	Aboriginal Relics Act 1975	Heritage Act
Queensland	Coroners Act 2003	Aboriginal Cultural Heritage Act 2003 Torres Strait Islander Cultural Heritage Act 2003	Queensland Heritage and Other Legislation Amendment Bill 2007
Major mainland territories			
Northern territory	Coroners Act 2008	Aboriginal Sacred Sites Act 1989 Heritage Conservation Act 1991	Heritage Conservation Act 1991
Australian Commonwealth Territory	Coroners Act 1997	Heritage Act 2004 Heritage Objects Act 1991	Heritage Act 2004

Australia. This has the disadvantage of not allowing Aboriginal remains to undergo analysis (e.g., radiocarbon dating) outside Australia.

During the writing of this chapter, the Federal Heritage Minister, Peter Garrett, released a discussion paper for public comment on Australian laws to protect the indigenous heritage. The discussion paper proposes to reform legislation such as the Aboriginal and Torres Strait Islander Heritage Protection Act 1984. In particular it seeks to remove duplication of state and territorial protection for indigenous remains.

HUMAN REMAINS AND LEGISLATION

New South Wales heritage legislation controlling indigenous remains

The Department of Environment, Conservation, Climate Change and Water (DECCW) (formally known as the National Parks and Wildlife Service) is the government body responsible for protecting Aboriginal skeletal remains, and can issue permits for the excavation of those remains. The relevant legislation it administers is called the National Parks and Wildlife Act 1974. Section 90 of this act provides protection for all 'Aboriginal relics'. Relics include skeletal remains.

Thus, before Aboriginal skeletal remains are excavated, a permit must be obtained from the Director-General of the DECCW. The permit is granted only if the burial is in danger of being damaged, for example by building works or erosion. Substantial consultation with the local Aboriginal community is required. In addition, this Act protects all Aboriginal skeletal remains removed from their original location since 1967.

Section 88 of the Act also provides for relics to be removed to the custody and control of the Australian Museum Trust. The Australian Museum and all other museums have policies for consultation and return of relics and other cultural property to their traditional owners.

If police suspect remains are ancient Aboriginal then they must call the DECCW. The police are also responsible for arranging for an expert to examine the site and the remains. The Police Standard Handbook provides standard operations procedures for all NSW police officers to contact the DECCW and the local Aboriginal Land Council. They are then to send their documentation to the Coroner. If the remains have been determined to be Aboriginal and more than 100 years old then they are handed over to the DECCW or left *in situ* unless they are in danger of being destroyed or damaged, at which point a decision may be made to salvage.

There is often a problem with having the remains identified as of either forensic or historic nature. In many cases, ancient Aboriginal remains go to the mortuaries, where they may lie for long periods of time before being released. Given the history of the excavation and subsequent retention of Aboriginal remains in museums, this outcome may cause concern among Aboriginal communities. Some salvage excavations carried out by a combination of archaeologists, anthropologists and Aboriginal communities can reveal important information to all involved.

In April 2009 the Government announced the release of a draft Bill to amend the National Parks and Wildlife Act 1974. Due Diligence Guidelines relating to the proposed strict liability offence of harming Aboriginal objects have also been released. DECCW will be consulting with key stakeholder groups about the proposed changes.

Case study: the Narrabeen remains

This case study is typical of how indigenous remains are found and recovered in NSW. In 2007 a few bones were found beneath a bus stop near Narrabeen Beach in Sydney during excavation for electricity conduits. The police were called and they then contacted the Department of Forensic Medicine. A forensic pathologist and forensic anthropologist examined the bones. The partly mineralized nature of the bones and the morphology suggested they were almost certainly indigenous. The DECCW and the Metropolitan Aboriginal Land Council (in whose area the remains were located) were informed. The government department responsible for laying the conduit was then required to pay for a salvage excavation in order to remove the remains.

After obtaining a permit from the DECCW, an archaeologist and an anthropologist excavated the remains. They were astonished to find that the remains were those of an adult male who had a spear point embedded in a lumbar vertebra. The bones were later dated to 4000 years ago and are thought to be the first known case of death by ritual spearing in Australia (McDonald *et al.* 2007).

New South Wales heritage legislation controlling non-Aboriginal remains and some Aboriginal remains

Under the Heritage Act of NSW, 1977 (as amended 1987), it is illegal to disturb or excavate land to discover, expose or move a relic over 50 years old which relates to the settlement of New South Wales, not being an Aboriginal settlement, without an excavation permit under either Section 60 (when the relic is subject to a conservation order) or Section 140 (when the relic is not subject to a conservation order).

Historic non-Aboriginal skeletal remains are rarely found in the manner described in the previous section, as they are usually located in large cemeteries. In most cases such remains are excavated because of proposed developments on the site of the cemetery. Aboriginal graves which are more than 50 years old and are in public cemeteries are also protected under this Act. Guidelines for the management of skeletal remains found under the Heritage Act 1977 are discussed in a booklet published by the Heritage Office (Bickford *et al.* 1999).

Case study: Parramatta Convict Hospital

In 2006, during archaeological excavation of Parramatta Convict Hospital, a significant site from the days of early British settlement of Sydney, the remains of six prenatal skeletons were located. As the archaeologists were already operating under a Section 60 approval (the hospital being listed on the State Heritage Register), they obtained a variation to that approval based on the provision of information to the Heritage Office by outlining how they were proposing to excavate the skeletal remains and identifying the involvement of a physical anthropologist. The date of the remains in a grave was estimated to date between c.1795 and c.1810. European ancestry for two individuals has been indicated by mtDNA, making these of historical significance in this period of early Australian European settlement. The death and burial of these infants gives insight into late 18th- and early 19th-century attitudes to death and Australian colonial society.

Overview of Australian Coronial legislation

Coronial legislation exists at the State and Territorial levels but not at the Federal level. The various Coroners Acts are similar. However, some have sections which specifically deal with ancient Aboriginal remains.

NSW Coroners Act 1980

This is the act currently in use. A new Coroners Act is about to come into use at the time of writing. Neither acts deal with permission to excavate human remains except for the exhumation of remains (usually from cemeteries) for further examination or autopsy (Section 91 of the 1980 Act).

Section 19 of this act seeks to ensure that ancient Aboriginal remains are not disturbed unnecessarily. It states:

> A coroner does not have jurisdiction to hold an inquest concerning a death or suspected death unless it appears to the coroner that (or that there is reasonable cause to suspect that) the death or suspected death occurred within the last 100 years.
>
> *NSW Coroners Act 1980, Section 91*

When a body or a skeleton is discovered, the excavation is usually done by the police. Under the Law Enforcement (Powers and Responsibilities) Act 2002 Act no warrant is required if the body or skeleton is on public land (e.g., Crown land). If the police suspect there is a buried body on private land then they must apply for a court order from a magistrate to enter the premises and excavate. If the police suspect they know the location of a buried body it is becoming more common for them to request an archaeologist or anthropologist with archaeological training to direct the excavation. This is particularly so in sensitive cases such as the exhumation of murder victims or of Aboriginal people who died in custody, in order for a second autopsy to be carried out.

New South Wales Public Health Legislation

In all of the above excavations or exhumations there may be public health issues. This is particularly the case in exhumations of bodies recently buried.

The Public Health Act, 1991 and the Public Health Regulation 1991 are concerned with the protection of public health matters. The Act regulates the disposal of human remains, the conduct of mortuaries and crematoria, and issues relating to infectious diseases such as embalming, interment and exhumation (Section 82(2) (r)). The Regulation details conditions such as when shoring is required, the use of personal protective equipment, and the screening of graves from public view. In a few cases, large cemeteries such as Rookwood Necropolis have their own legislation which may impose conditions relating to exhumation.

The recovery of the remains of war dead

The last 20 years have seen a growing sentiment for the recovery of the remains of Australians missing in action from the First and Second World Wars and the Vietnam War. The Australian government does not actively seek out the locations of these remains; however, if there is compelling evidence that such remains have been located then the Australian government will investigate. Once excavated, remains from the First and Second World Wars are then reburied in the closest war cemetery, whether they are in Europe or Asia. In the case of Australian soldiers who died in Vietnam, they are repatriated to Australia where they are handed over to the families. In all of these excavations conducted offshore, the heritage and forensic requirements of those countries must be observed.

Occasionally, interested parties and potential relatives have made their own investigations and searches for those missing. These activities began in Papua New Guinea in the 1980s with the discovery of the Second World War Australian aircraft. Members of the defence forces were deployed in order to examine the wreckage and in some cases to search for and excavate human remains.

In 2009, the remains of a large number of the First World War Australian and British soldiers were excavated from a series of German-dug mass burial pits near the town of Fromelles in France. Again the Australian government had not actively searched for the remains, and the location was identified by interested members of the public. Currently, after all the analysis of the artefacts, the anthropological data and genetic analyses, attempts are being made to identify the remains so that they can have named headstones in the new Commonwealth War Graves Cemetery at a different site in Fromelles.

More recently, the Australian government has set up teams within the Department of Defence which include archaeologists and anthropologists, to make systematic recoveries of such remains.

METHODS OF ANTHROPOLOGICAL ANALYSIS

A growing issue for Australian practitioners concerns which standards to use for the recording of human remains. The routine work that involves many biological anthropologists in Australia working with local human remains centres around those issues of animal versus human bone, indigenous versus non-indigenous remains, historic versus modern remains. However, as can be imagined, the standard references used in practice have frequently originated from North America or Britain (see, e.g., Bass 2005). Needless to say their coverage of marsupial bones, which can be confused with human bones, is non-existent, while even references to Australian Aboriginal remains are rare. At the same time an analysis of casework from New South Wales (Donlon 2003) reveals that, while these are still issues, cases also involved people of Chinese and Vietnamese ancestry and people from near and remote Oceania (Melanesians and Polynesians). These are also populations for whom standard references can be of little value.

This diversity and the lack of publication of appropriate standards has become a greater problem over time as the diversity of Australia's inhabitants has increased, generations of physical anthropologists retire, and as the relevant collections have been repatriated or closed for access. There is, in fact, an extensive history of research on methods of sexing and identification of Australian Aboriginal remains (see, e.g., Davivongs 1963a, 1963b; Larnach 1978) but these references are to increasingly obscure journal articles or Honours or Master's theses which can be difficult to access. Moves such as that by the New South Wales National Parks and Wildlife Service to maintain a 'Skeleton Manual' serve to keep some of that information available, but the manual summarizes rather than containing the extensive information and referencing required in expert witness cases (Thorne and Ross 1986).

Reviewing and keeping well tested methods to the fore is important, but at the same time we also need to continue to question whether we should be devising standards that are more relevant for particular populations (see, e.g., Komar 2003; Ross and Königsberg 2002) or developing standards that are appropriate for a cross-section of Australia's current population. A specific example is the development of standards for dental age assessment. There are published data on specific populations, such as Australian Aboriginal people or people of European descent (Brown *et al.* 1979), but also Diamanti and Townsend (2003) have recently constructed a permanent dental eruption sequence which is based on a cross-section of living Australian children of diverse ancestries. As populations become increasingly admixed, it may be that the development of new standards has to adopt this approach as more closely approximating biological reality. Yet at the same time the importance of being able to identify indigenous from non-indigenous remains is always going to be significant beyond simple administration. That first stage of identification shifts the remains between jurisdictions, between responsible parties, and carries explicit cultural and spiritual significance (Cox *et al.* 2006). As Cox and colleagues, and Masters (2006), point out, a 'simple' identification of remains as indigenous or non-indigenous sets in train a sequence of events involving a range of bureaucracies and local groups.

CONCLUSION

Physical anthropology in Australia really only began to develop as a separate discipline in the 20th century. Today the subject is represented in most major universities, although usually on a small scale. Opportunities to study indigenous remains are very limited, unless consent can be obtained for access to museum collections. These limited opportunities are no doubt closely tied to the history of physical anthropology in Australia which has included the unlawful excavation of indigenous remains. Most studies of indigenous remains today are on a case-by-case basis of remains revealed as a result of salvage excavations. Recently there have been opportunities to study large numbers of remains from historic cemeteries. On an optimistic note, there is great interest in the scientific analysis of human skeletal remains whether they are archaeological or forensic.

USEFUL CONTACTS

Australasian Society for Human Biology (ASHB): *Proceedings of the Australasian Society for Human Biology*. Website: http://school.anhb.uwa.edu.au/ashb/

Australian Academy of Forensic Science (AAFS): *Australian Journal of Forensic Science*. Website: www.forensicacademy.org/index_two.htm/

Australian Archaeology Association (AAA): *Australian Archaeology*. Website: www.australianarchaeologicalassociation.com.au/

Australian and New Zealand Forensic Science Society Inc (ANZFSS). Website: www.anzfss.org.au/history.htm/

Australasian Society for Historical Archaeology (ASHA): *Australasian Journal of Historical Archaeology*. Website: www.asha.org.au/

Archaeology in Oceania. Website: www.arts.usyd.edu.au/publications/oceania/arch_oceania1.htm/

Useful websites concerning legislation

The Australasian Legal Information Institute (AustLII) provides free internet access to Australasian legal materials. The AustLII collection contains full-text databases of most Australian Court and Tribunal decisions and legislation. It also has a section on laws as they relate to indigenous heritage. Website: www.austlii.edu.au/

The Australian Government's Department of the Environment, Water, Heritage and the Arts has useful information on the protection of Australian heritage under Federal, State and Territory laws. Website: www.environment.gov.au/heritage/laws/indigenous/protection-laws.html/

ACKNOWLEDGEMENTS

Many thanks go to Ann Macintosh, John Ralston and Pip Rath for their comments.

BIBLIOGRAPHY

Abbie, A.A. (1968) 'The homogeneity of the Australian Aborigines', *Archaeology and Physical Anthropology in Oceania*, 3: 223–31.

Argue, D., Donlon, D., Groves, C., *et al.* (2006) '*Homo floresiensis*: Microcephalic, pygmoid, *Australopithecus* or Homo?', *Journal of Human Evolution*, 51: 360–74.

AustralArchaeology/Godden Mackay (1997) 'POW Project 1995, Randwick Destitute Children's Asylum Cemetery, Archaeological Investigation', unpublished report for Sydney Eastern Area Health Service and Heritage Council of NSW.

Bass, W.M. (2005). *Human Osteology: A Laboratory and Field Manual*, 5th edn, Columbia, Mo: Missouri Archaeological Society.

Beaglehole, J.C. (ed.) (1955) *The voyage of the Endeavour 1768–1771. The Journals of Captain James Cook on his voyages of discovery*, Cambridge: Hakluyt Society of the University Press.

Bickford, A., Donlon, D. and Lavelle, S. (1999) *Skeletal Remains: Guidelines for the Management of Human Skeletal Remains Under the Heritage Act 1977*, Sydney: NSW Heritage Office.

Birdsell, J.B. (1967) 'Preliminary data on the tri-hybrid origin of the Australian Aborigines', *Archaeology and Physical Anthropology in Oceania*, 2: 100–55.

Brown, P., Sutikna, T., Morwood, M.J., *et al.* (2004) 'A New Small-Bodied Hominin From The Late Pleistocene Of Flores, Indonesia', *Nature* 431: 1055–61.

Brown, T., Jenner, J., Barrett, M., *et al.* (1979) 'Exfoliation of deciduous teeth and gingival emergence of permanent teeth in Australian Aborigines', *Occasional Papers in Human Biology*, 1: 47–70.

Cartmill, M. (2004) 'Charles Oxnard: An appreciation', in F. Anapol *et al.* (eds) *Shaping Primate Evolution*, Cambridge: Cambridge University Press.

Casey, M., Donlon, D., Hope, J., *et al.* (eds) (1998) *Redefining Archaeology*, Canberra: ANU Press.

Cox, K., Tayles, N.G. and Buckley, H.R. (2006) 'Forensic identification of "race": the issues in New Zealand', *Current Anthropology*, 47: 869–74.

David, T.W.E. and Wilson, J.T. (1914) 'Preliminary communications on an Australian cranium of probable Pleistocene Age', paper presented at the 84th Meeting of the British Association for the Advancement of Science, Sydney, 1914.

Davivongs, V. (1963a) 'The pelvic girdle of the Australian Aborigine: sex differences and sex determination', *American Journal of Physical Anthropology*, 21: 443–56.

——(1963b) 'The femur of the Australian Aborigines', *American Journal of Physical Anthropology*, 21: 457–67.

Diamanti, J. and Townsend, G. (2003) 'New standards for permanent tooth emergence in Australian children', *Australian Dental Journal*, 48: 39–42.

Donlon, D. (1994) 'Aboriginal skeletal collections and research in physical anthropology: An historical perspective', *Australian Archaeology*, 39: 1–10.

——(2003) 'Diversity revealed: 10 years of anthropological casework based in New South Wales, Australia', Proceedings of the Australasian Society for Human Biology, Auckland. Abstract, *Homo-Journal of Comparative Human Biology*, 54: 151–52.

——(2008) 'Forensic anthropology in Australia: A brief history and review of casework', in M. Oxenham (ed.) *Forensic Approaches to Death, Disaster and Abuse*, Perth: Western Australia University Press.

——(2009) 'The Development and Current State of Forensic Anthropology: An Australian Perspective', in S. Blau and D. Ubelaker, D. (eds) *Handbook of Forensic Archaeology and Anthropology*, California: Left Coast Press.

Donlon, D., Casey, M., Haak, W., *et al.* (2009) 'Early colonial burial practices for perinates at the Parramatta convict hospital, NSW', *Australasian Historical Archaeology*, 26: 71–84.

Du Cros, H. and Smith, L. (eds) (1992) *Women in Archaeology: A Feminist Critique*, Canberra: Department of Prehistory, Research School of Pacific and Asian Studies, ANU Canberra.

Elkin, A.P. (1978) 'N.W.G. Macintosh and his work', *Archaeology & Physical Anthropology in Oceania*, 13: 85–142.

Freedman, L. (1964) 'Metrical features of Aboriginal crania from coastal New South Wales, Australia', *Records of the Australian Museum*, 26: 309–25.

Gray, G. (2007) *A Cautious Silence: The Politics of Australian Anthropology*, Canberra: Aboriginal Studies Press.

Green, M. (1990) 'Prehistoric cranial variation in Papua New Guinea', unpublished PhD thesis, The Australian National University.

Haglund-Calley, L. (1968) 'The Aboriginal burial ground at Broadbeach', *Mankind*, 6: 676–80.

Henneberg, M. and Thorne, A. (2004) 'Flores human may be a pathological *Homo sapiens*', *Before Farming*, 4: 2–4.

Hiatt, B. (1969) 'Cremation in Aboriginal Australia', *Mankind*, 7: 104–19.

Higginbotham and Associates (2002) 'Report on the archaeological excavation of the Cadia Cemetery, Cadia Road, Cadia, NSW, 1997–98', unpublished report for Cadia Holdings Pty Ltd.

Hope, J. and Littleton, J. (1995a) *Finding Out About Aboriginal Burials*, Murray–Darling Basin Aboriginal Heritage Handbooks 1, Sydney: Mungo Publications.

——(1995b) *Protecting Aboriginal Burial Sites*, Murray–Darling Basin Aboriginal Heritage Handbooks 1, Sydney: Mungo Publications.

Kirk, R.L. and Thorne, A.G. (eds) (1976) *The Origin of the Australians*, Canberra: Australian Institute of Aboriginal Studies.

Komar, D. (2003) 'Lessons from Srebrenica: the contributions and limitations of physical anthropology in identifying victims of war crimes', *Journal of Forensic Sciences*, 48: 713–16.

Larnach, S.L. (1978) *Australian Aboriginal Craniology*, Sydney: University of Sydney.

Larnach, S.L. and Freedman, L. (1964) 'Sex determination of Aboriginal crania from coastal New South Wales', *Records of the Australian Museum*, 26: 295–308.

Larnach, S.L. and Macintosh, N.W.G. (1966) *The craniology of the Aborigines of coastal New South Wales*, Oceania Monographs No 13, Sydney: University of Sydney.

——(1970) *The craniology of the Aborigines of Queensland*, Oceania Monographs No 15. Sydney: University of Sydney.

——(1971) *The mandible of the Aborigines of coastal New South Wales*, Oceania Monographs No 17. Sydney: University of Sydney.

Littleton, J. (1992) 'Articulating the past: An approach to prehistoric social composition', unpublished PhD thesis, Australian National University, Canberra.

Lowe, A. and Mackay, R. (1992) 'Old Sydney Burial Ground', *Australasian Historical Archaeology*, 10: 15–23.

Macintosh, N.W.G. (1952a) 'The Cohuna cranium: teeth and palate', *Oceania*, 23: 95–105.

——(1952b) 'The Talgai teeth and dental arch: remeasurement and restoration', *Oceania*, 23: 106–9.

——(1965) 'The physical aspects of man in Australia', in R. Berndt and C. Berndt (eds) *Aboriginal Man in Australia*, Sydney: Angus and Robertson.

——(1971) 'Analysis of an Aboriginal skeleton with a pierced tooth necklace from Lake Nitchie, Australia', *Anthropologie*, 9: 49–62.

Macintosh, N.W.G. and Larnach, S.L. (1973) 'A cranial study of the Aborigines of Queensland with a contrast between Australian and New Guinea crania', in R.L. Kirk (ed.) *The Human Biology of Aborigines of Cape York*, Canberra: AIAS.

McDonald, J., Donlon, D., Field, J., *et al.* (2007) 'The first archaeological evidence for death by spearing in Australia', *Antiquity*, 81: 877–86.

Masters, P. (2006) 'Time since death', unpublished MA thesis, University of Auckland, Auckland.

Meehan, B. (1971) 'The form, distribution and antiquity of Aboriginal mortuary practices', unpublished MA thesis, University of Sydney, Sydney.

Morwood, M.J., Soejono, R.P., Roberts, R.G., *et al* (2004) 'Archaeology and age of a new hominin from Flores in eastern Indonesia', *Nature*, 431: 1087–91.

Mulvaney, J. (1969) *The prehistory of Australia*, London, Thames and Hudson.

Pardoe, C. (1988) 'The cemetery as symbol. The distribution of prehistoric Aboriginal burial grounds in southeastern Australia', *Archaeology in Oceania*, 23: 1–16.

Pate, D. and Adams, W.H. (2000) 'News from the Pacific Rim. Excavation of St Mary's Anglican Cemetery, Adelaide, South Australia', *Palaeopathology Newsletter*, 111: 6–7.

Pietrusewsky, M. (1990). 'Cranial variation in Australian and Pacific populations', *American Journal of Physical Anthropology*, 82: 319–40.

Pretty, G. L. (1977) 'The cultural chronology of the Roonka Flat. A preliminary consideration', in R.V.S. Wright (ed.) *Stone tools as cultural markers: change, evolution and complexity*, Canberra: Australian Institute of Aboriginal Studies, 288—31.

Prokopec, M. (1979) 'Demographical and morphological aspects of the Roonka populations', *Archaeology and Physical Anthropology in Oceania*, 14: 11–26.

Richards, L.C. and Miller, S.L.J. (1991) 'Relationships between age and dental attrition in Australian Aboriginals', *American Journal of Physical Anthropology*, 84: 159–64.

Rogers, J.R., Townsend, G.C. and Brown, T. (2009) 'Murray James Barrett, dental anthropologist: Yuendumu and beyond', *HOMO Journal of Comparative Human Biology*, 60: 295–306.

Ross, A.H. and Königsberg, L.W. (2002) 'New formulae for estimating stature in the Balkans', *Journal of Forensic Sciences*, 47: 165–67.

Spencer, F. (1997) *History of Physical Anthropology: An Encyclopedia*, London: Taylor and Francis.

Thorne, A.G. (1975) 'Kow Swamp and Lake Mungo', unpublished PhD thesis, University of Sydney, Sydney.

——(1976) 'Morphological contrasts in Pleistocene Australians', in R.L. Kirk and A.G. Thorne (eds) *The Origin of the Australians*, Canberra: Australian Institute of Aboriginal Studies.

Thorne, A.G. and Ross, A. (1986) *The Skeleton Manual*, Sydney: NPWS and Police Aborigine Liaison Unit.

Townsend, G.C., Richards, L.C. and Carroll, A. (1982) 'Sex determination of Australian Aboriginal skulls by discriminant function analysis', *Australian Dental Journal*, 27: 320–26.

Turner, W. (1884) *Report on the human crania and other bones of the skeletons collected during the voyage of the H.M.S. Challenger Part I. Crania*, Challenger Report, Zoology, part 29.

Wood-Jones, F. (1931) 'The non-metrical character of the skull as criteria for racial diagnosis', *Journal of Anatomy*, 68: 323–30.

Wunderly, J. (1943) 'The Keilor fossil skull: anatomical description', *Memoirs of the National Museum of Victoria*, 13: 57–69.

Auckland
NORTH ISLAND
Tauranga
Hamilton
Tasman Sea
NEW ZEALAND
Palmerston North
Wellington
SOUTH ISLAND
Christchurch
South Pacific
Dunedin
STEWART ISLAND
0
250km

New Zealand/Aotearoa

Nancy Tayles and Siân Halcrow

INTRODUCTION: A BRIEF HISTORY AND CURRENT STATE OF PHYSICAL ANTHROPOLOGY IN NEW ZEALAND

This chapter will focus on the New Zealand Maori, the prehistoric inhabitants of New Zealand. Maori are Polynesians who settled the country about 1000 years ago from an unidentified location to the north, in Polynesia. They are the *tangata whenua*, literally 'the people of the land'. In early historic times, Europeans (principally British) and Asians (particularly Chinese, attracted to the goldfields in the first instance) settled in New Zealand, but clearly the Maori are the reason New Zealand physical anthropology is distinctive. We will also make some references to the Moriori, who are of the same Polynesian descent as the Maori but, early in the human settlement of New Zealand, migrated to a small group of islands east of New Zealand, the Chatham Islands (Wharekauri), where they became isolated for some centuries and so form a separate population.

Settlement of New Zealand by Europeans dates from approximately 200 years ago, and from the very first contact, the origin of Maori and Moriori in particular, and Polynesians in general, was a source of much interest and conjecture by Western scientists and anthropologists. Consequently the field of 'physical' anthropology (or 'biological anthropology' as it is now known locally) developed early in New Zealand's history, with the impetus of researching these origins. This fascination was primarily because of the very different physical appearance, social and cultural customs of Polynesians from those of the nearest neighbours in Melanesia and Australia (Forster 1996; Howe 2003). In the spirit of the times, not only did the research attempt to identify Polynesian origins but also to place them in human taxonomy. The methods used were those employed universally to categorize human populations from their skeletal remains, principally craniometrics (Buck 1938).

The methods of acquisition of the *koiwi tangata* (human skeletal remains) for research included what was perceived to be justified and ethical 'collecting', often from caves that were favoured by Maori as either primary or secondary burial sites; or they were sold to institutions by *Pakeha* (New Zealanders of European descent) or disaffected Maori. *Koiwi tangata* were also deliberately stolen from burial sites (King 1981). Museums created an international demand for Maori and Moriori skulls to add to their collections of examples of indigenous populations (Fforde and Hubert 2006). This occurred on a large scale, as exemplified by the ability of Mollison (1908) to collate published data from museum collections of over 275 Maori skulls, and Poll (1902) to prepare a similar collation from 100 skulls of Moriori. About half of the skulls included in these studies were deposited in museums in New Zealand and the remainder in Austria, France and Germany. This treatment of *koiwi tangata* in the 19th century was a reflection of the European attitude towards indigenous peoples at the time and is detailed elsewhere (Fforde and Hubert 2006; Tapsell 2005; Tayles 2009).

Those involved in this field included academic staff of the Medical School at the University of Otago, where the morphology and origin of Maori was among the first research topics, and accordingly a collection primarily but not exclusively of skulls was amassed from the late 19th century. This collection has formed the basis of over 60 publications and research theses, starting from the earliest description of cranial morphology by John Scott, Professor of Anatomy at the Medical School (1893). The only Maori researcher, Sir Peter Buck (also known as *Te Rangi Hiroa*), was active many decades ago. In 1925 he published a paper on the diet of prehistoric Maori that drew on evidence from the collection published by Scott (1893: 20). Apart from the inclusion of the skulls in the collection at Otago in publications seeking to categorize the Maori, other researchers were particularly interested in the prehistoric Maori dentition, which showed unusual patterns of wear and a lack of dental caries (Houghton 1978; Pickerill 1912; Taylor 1962a, 1962b, 1963, 1970, 1975). The most prolific researcher was much more recent. Associate Professor Philip Houghton was the first to provide a thorough description of the singular characteristics of the Maori and Moriori cranial and postcranial morphology (Houghton 1980, 1996). During the 1980s he and Professor Martin Kean, then Dean of the Otago Dental School, developed a theoretical basis for the cranial morphology (Kean and Houghton 1982, 1987, 1990; Houghton and Kean 1987), and Houghton also proposed an adaptive hypothesis to explain the distinctive Polynesian postcranial morphology (Houghton 1990, 1991a, 1991b, 1996).

For most Maori, the scientific expectation that morphology could act as a surrogate for genetic affiliation has no merit. Maori culture has a very strong oral tradition that not only documents the origins of their ancestors in the South Pacific but also documents the genealogy, the *whakapapa*, of individuals. This is an important aspect of being Maori, as *whakapapa* defines relationship to family (*whanau*), subtribe (*hapu*), tribe (*iwi*) and ultimately through ancestors (*tupuna*) to the land (*whenua*). The skeletal remains of *tupuna* are the physical embodiment of *whakapapa* (Ngai Tahu 1993) and are sacred. Strong emotional ties to *tupuna* mean that the idea of researchers handling *koiwi tangata* and storing them on museum shelves is abhorrent to Maori. Clearly the interests of Maori are of primary concern in research involving *koiwi tangata* in the 21st century.

The founding document of New Zealand, the Treaty of Waitangi, was drafted by representatives of the British Crown in 1840 on the grounds that there were benefits for both sides in the British establishing sovereignty over the country (Orange 2004). It was hastily translated into Maori, with the result that the English and Maori versions have some contentious differences, but the point relevant here is that 'Her Majesty the Queen of England confirms and guarantees to the Chiefs and Tribes of New Zealand the full exclusive and undisturbed possession of their Lands and Estates Forests Fisheries and other properties.'

This can be taken to include the remains of *tupuna*. Not only is there a moral and ethical duty not to disturb these remains; the Treaty provides a written contract between Maori and the Crown. The Treaty was clearly disregarded in many respects since 1840, not only in relation to *koiwi*, although the establishment of the Waitangi Tribunal in 1975 with the ability to hear claims for redress by 'any Māori or group of Māori who may have been prejudiced by laws and regulations or by acts, omissions, policies, or practices of the Crown since 1840 that are inconsistent with the principles of the Treaty of Waitangi' (Waitangi Tribunal 2009). Since then, numerous longstanding claims by Maori have been settled and the process is ongoing.

Clearly the spiritual, emotional, cultural and legal rights of Maori are now accepted as primary in the field of biological anthropology in New Zealand where prehistoric skeletal remains are involved.

The first formal actions taken to acknowledge what had happened to *koiwi tangata* since European settlement were initiated by Dr Maui Pomare, a member, and ultimately chair, of the National Museum Council 1978–92. During his time in office he pushed for the creation of a repository, known as a *Wahi Tapu* (place sacred to Maori), in the National Museum (now known as *Te Papa Tongarewa*) in Wellington, for the appropriate temporary storage of *koiwi tangata* held in the Museum collection until such time as provenance could be established and repatriation to appropriate *iwi* could be completed. In 2003, a Government Order in Council established a repatriation programme, with the Karanga Aotearoa Repatriation Research Committee, based at Te Papa, the Government Agent. The role of the Committee is to locate *koiwi* in international institutions and to negotiate their return to New Zealand (Te Papa, n.d.). This is an ongoing process (Tayles 2009).

With this current repatriation process, clearly the export of skeletal remains for research is not considered. The Protected Objects Act 1975 legislates the control of cultural items derived from an archaeological burial site, including scientific samples and organic remains. The Act places the regulation under the control of the Ministry for Culture and Heritage.

In relation to research on prehistoric skeletal remains within New Zealand, as the collections of any size are now under the control of *iwi*, permission for access for research must be made to them. Of relevance to international researchers, there is effectively no likelihood of access to acquire data purely for the purposes of using Maori as a comparative population in a worldwide study. Where there may be the possibility of determining evidence about the prehistoric Maori themselves that might be of interest to *iwi*, the question of access to *Koiwi* held in *Wahi Tapu* for research is as yet untested.

In 1993 the largest *iwi* in the South Island, Ngai ('Kai' in the local dialect) Tahu, developed a policy on *Koiwi Tangata* (Ngai Tahu 1993). They were the first *iwi* in New Zealand to do so. This policy iterates the rights of the *iwi* to manage the *koiwi* from their *rohe* (tribal area) under the Treaty of Waitangi. This policy has been accepted by regional museums within the *rohe*, which extends over much of the South Island of New Zealand, to the extent that *Wahi Tapu* have been established within the Otago Museum (Dunedin) and the Southland Museum and Art Gallery (Invercargill) in 1994 (Gillies and O'Regan 1994). The collection of *koiwi* from the Ngai Tahu *rohe* held in the University of Otago was transferred to the *Wahi Tapu* in the Otago Museum in 2003 under an agreement between the University and the *iwi*. Where the geographic origin of *koiwi tangata* in museum collections is known, the ultimate arbiters of the long-term disposition, whether retention in Museum *Wahi Tapu* or reburial, will be the local *runanga* (council, assembly). The policy recognizes the role of scientific investigation of *koiwi tangata* and reserves the right to control research access and to edit for reasons of cultural sensitivity any material proposed for publication, including illustrations. The policy is exclusive to Ngai Tahu, with no equivalent applicable to all *iwi*.

A relevant and significant recent event has been the reburial of a collection of human skeletal remains from an early prehistoric site, *Wairau Bar*, at the northern end of the South Island of New Zealand. These burials represent the earliest known prehistoric cemetery sample and were excavated over several decades in the mid-20th century. The collection represented about 40 individuals and had been held in the Canterbury Museum, Christchurch, New Zealand. Some research on the material had been published (Houghton 1975). The collection had been the subject of repeated requests for reburial by the local *iwi*, Rangitane, and in 2008 an agreement was reached between the *iwi* and the Museum, on the understanding that the skeletons would be first researched by biological anthropologists. The collection was transported to the University of Otago and the data collection, coordinated by Dr Hallie Buckley under a Memorandum of Understanding between Rangitane, Canterbury Museum and the University, was completed by early 2009. In April 2009 the *tupuna* were returned to Rangitane and the results of the research presented to the *iwi* before the *tupuna* were reburied at the site in watertight caskets, with appropriate ceremony. This is the first large-scale return and reburial of prehistoric Maori skeletal remains and therefore represents a seminal event in the history of biological anthropology in New Zealand. There is anecdotal evidence that conducting and presenting the research before reburial is altering attitudes of *iwi* towards science and scientific research.

ARCHAEOLOGICAL HUMAN REMAINS AND LEGISLATION

Archaeological legislation

The Historic Places Act 1993 is the principal legislation governing archaeology in New Zealand. Under the Act, the New Zealand Historic Places Trust (NZHPT) holds the right to issue permits for any archaeological site to be destroyed, damaged or modified (HPA (10:1)) including any archaeological excavation. The Act does not specifically refer to cemeteries or human remains, but these are subsumed within the broad definition of an archaeological site as 'any place in New Zealand that was associated with human activity that occurred before 1900; or may be able through investigation by archaeological methods to provide evidence relating to the history of New Zealand'.

HUMAN REMAINS AND LEGISLATION

This definition means that any cemetery or human remains dating from before 1900 is automatically deemed archaeological, but that there is the potential for more recent but historic finds to also be included. The Act requires that the NZHPT maintain a register that includes *wahi tapu*. These are defined as places 'sacred to Maori in the traditional, spiritual, religious, ritual or mythological sense', including burial places (*urupa*), places where human skeletal remains are kept, such as rock overhangs, caves or hollow trees.

Also relevant here are two other pieces of legislation. The Burial and Cremation Act 1964, administered by the Ministry of Health, requires that a disinterment licence be obtained from the local Public Health Unit to 'remove any body or the remains of any body buried in any cemetery, Maori burial ground, or other burial ground or place of burial'. The Coroner's Act 2006 requires that 'a person who finds a body in New Zealand must report that finding to a member of the police as soon as practicable'. The New Zealand Police have the responsibility to establish whether or not the site is a crime scene.

The NZHPT is currently producing a series of Archaeological Guidelines, the most recent of which is about *Koiwi Tangata*/Human Remains. This document details the process to be followed when human remains are discovered and provides precise steps to be followed by the finder, whether this is a member of the general public (including *tangata whenua*), a private land developer, a government department or local body employee during the course of their employment, or an archaeologist during the excavation of an archaeological site under an NZHPT permit. The NZHPT and New Zealand Police should immediately be notified. The first step is to determine whether or not the remains are human. If they are human, the second question is whether they are recent and therefore of forensic interest, or historic/prehistoric. If the latter, the local *iwi* should be advised. These Guidelines also provide guidance as to the appropriate temporary repository of any excavated remains, such as a museum, mortuary, a pathologist's laboratory or *marae* (Maori ceremonial and meeting place). It explicitly states that vehicles, offices or homes are inappropriate.

Where known burials are present in an area subject to an archaeological excavation permit or other disturbance, a disinterment licence will be required from the Ministry of Health under the Burial and Cremation Act. The Ministry requires the consent of the next of kin as well as a death certificate. In the case of cemetery excavation, this may require extensive community consultation. With historical burials, the potential difficulty in tracking down descendants and the inability to determine the cause of death is acknowledged. Where the burials predate 1900, an archaeological permit from the NZHPT will also be required.

The NZHPT is likely to require the involvement of a biological anthropologist to ensure that standard recording of material *in situ* takes place and that any exhumation is conducted in a manner that meets standard professional criteria. There is no legal requirement to have a bio-logical anthropologist on site, but it is recommended. A final repository for the remains must be identified prior to the commencement of the work.

Apart from the rights of *tangata whenua* where prehistoric burials are involved, New Zealand has been predominantly Christian since the arrival of the first Europeans. With historic burials or cemeteries, the interests of any Church community will be relevant, as in other European countries.

New Zealand archaeologists continued to excavate *koiwi tangata* until the 1970s (see, e.g., Leach and Leach 1979) but since then have not deliberately excavated known burials for research purposes. When burials are accidently uncovered in the course of archaeological excavations the local *iwi*, who will usually be aware of the excavation and will frequently be actively involved, will be advised and will usually undertake the immediate reburial as close as possible to the original site (see, e.g., Prickett 1990). More recently, there has been a move towards written agreements with relevant *iwi* before excavation begins, detailing the steps to follow should *koiwi* be disturbed (Allen *et al.* 2002).

Burials are often exposed accidently in situations other than archaeological excavations. New Zealand is a geologically active country with a long coastline. Much prehistoric settlement was coastal and so not infrequently burials are exposed by coastal erosion. There are therefore occasions when archaeological intervention is required or requested by the local *iwi* (see, e.g., Pischief 2002). Levelling or excavation of land for building or development is the other most frequent situation in which burials are disturbed, as recently occurred during the extension of a school building at Cook's Cove, Tolaga Bay, on the east coast of the North Island. The exposure of *Koiwi tangata* during the building works resulted in bioarchaeologists from the University of Otago collaborating with NZHPT in their excavation and reburial (Dominion Post 2007; New Zealand Historic Places Trust 2008). Dealing with this situation is not always as straightforward as it sounds, as archaeologists found recently during the development of a new runway at Auckland International Airport. First, identifying the appropriate *iwi*, and second, ensuring that those who come forward as representatives of that *iwi* are acceptable to all within the tribe, can be problematic. It is easy to create problems in this situation and care needs to be taken, which is not always practicable when there is pressure from developers to complete work quickly.

METHODS OF ANTHROPOLOGICAL ANALYSIS

The differentiation of Maori from non-Maori skeletons relies on the characteristic morphology of Polynesian skeletons, as described by Houghton (1996). The craniofacial morphology in particular is distinctive, with stereotypically high, straight-sided vaults that are pentagonal when viewed from a posterior or superior angle. The cranial base is flat with the effect that the face sits antero-inferiorly in relation to the neurocranium. The face is flat with a high nasal cavity and the maxillary alveolar processes inferior to the nasal cavity are short. The mandible has vertical rami, a short but high body, with a curved inferior border without an antegonial notch, known as a rocker jaw. Although there is variation from this stereotype, the combination of characteristics is readily identifiable in many skulls and indeed in many living Maori. The long bones also are generally robust, with consequent bowing of the shafts and more distinctive features such as an oval *fovea capitis* on the femur (Houghton 1980, 1996). These are generally identifiable in prehistoric remains but with historic (and increasingly with forensic) remains, intermarriage with non-Maori has reduced the frequency of conformity to the stereotype. Nevertheless, the ties that those who identify culturally as Maori retain with their *tupuna* means that they have strong spiritual connections with *koiwi tangata*, placing a duty of care on forensic anthropologists to make every effort to differentiate Maori from other ancestries (Cox *et al.* 2006). There are publications describing the characteristics of Polynesian skulls that implicitly include Maori but are not as directly applicable as Houghton's descriptions (Gill 1994; Howells 1989: 103).

For the estimation of age-at-death, internationally recognized standards (e.g., those detailed in Buikstra and Ubelaker 1994) are used for adults in the absence of any population specific alternative. This practice, of course, carries with it the limitations and potential for inaccuracy that arise when estimating age on any sample unrelated to the reference samples on which the methods were developed, but nevertheless can give a sense of relative age. Dental conditions in prehistoric Maori generally include extreme wear in many, but not all, cases, together with minimal caries but severe periodontal problems and frequent, multiple alveolar lesions arising from inflammation or infection. Where dental wear is used as an age indicator, this pattern needs to be kept in mind. For infants and children, again internationally recognized standards are applied. Although it is recognized that the dentition of Polynesians in general, including Maori, tends to develop early compared with dentition in Europeans (Te Moananui *et al.* 2008a, 2008b), and that skeletal development is completed earlier (Tonkin 1970), the differences are generally well within the error range of international standards.

Sex estimation for adults generally also relies on the international pelvic and cranial standards detailed in Buikstra and Ubelaker (1994), although the universal problem with the cranial standards of determining where on the scale the divisions between male, unknown and female fall applies. Watt (1974) reviewed the issue of sex estimation of the Maori skull, but her descriptions, primarily of the same indicators as the five in Buikstra and Ubelaker (1994) with the addition of the degree of 'development' of the temporal line and the cranial length to breadth ratio, are relative with no absolutes. Houghton and de Souza (1975) developed discriminant functions for sex estimation from long bone lengths. Murphy (1986, 1994, 1995, 2000, 2002a, 2002b, 2002c, 2005a, 2005b) applied the same technique to the bones of the pectoral and pelvic girdles and the foot. Dennison (1979) found no sexual dimorphism in the dentition.

For the estimation of stature, Polynesians generally, including Maori, have a high sitting height ratio with relatively short limbs. Houghton recognized these distinctive body proportions and developed stature equations for Maori (Houghton *et al.* 1975), although these have been critically reviewed in Littleton and Kinaston (2008; they also review methods for age, sex and ancestry over the wider South Pacific), with the suggestion that they are applicable only to male Maori, and with care.

CONCLUSION

The unique aspects of the study of human skeletal remains in New Zealand, variously known as physical anthropology, biological anthropology, bioarchaeology or human osteology, derive from the indigenous people, the Maori and Moriori. This chapter has therefore focused on the history of research about Maori and Moriori *koiwi tangata*, and described legislation most relevant to their skeletal remains, and methods used in their identification and description. There has been effectively no research on New Zealanders of other ancestry such as Europeans, Asians or the more recent migrants from the smaller islands of the South Pacific, in particular Polynesia.[1] Methods used to estimate the age, sex, stature and ancestry of Europeans and Asians, in both historic research and forensic situations, are clearly those applicable to those parts of the world. Polynesians from the Pacific islands share morphological characteristics with Maori, which means that their differentiation will clearly be an issue in forensic cases. Houghton (1996: 138) states that 'The Polynesian somatotype is remarkably homogeneous', a judgement that is supported genetically (see, e.g., Kayser *et al.* 2000; Underhill *et al.* 2001), and although the morphological homogeneity has been questioned (see, e.g., Pietrusewsky 1996: 344), the methods documented in this chapter are in general equally applicable to non-Maori Polynesians who are likely to have migrated to New Zealand.

USEFUL CONTACTS

New Zealand Historic Places Trust, Antrim House, 63 Boulcott Street,
Wellington 6011, PO Box 2629, Wellington 6140. Tel: +64 4 472–4341; Fax: +64 4 499–0699; email: information@historic.org.nz. Website: www.historic.org.nz/
New Zealand Archaeological Association, PO Box 6337, Dunedin North 9059. Website: www.nzarchaeology.org.nz/

Acts of Parliament

Burial and Cremation Act. 1964. No 75
Coroners Act. 2006. No 38
Historic Places Act. 1993. No 38
Protected Objects Act. 1975. No 41

NOTE

1 These people are known in New Zealand as 'Pacific islanders' or, more recently, collectively described as 'Pacifica'.

BIBLIOGRAPHY

Allen, H., Johns, D., Phillips, C., *et al.* (2002) '*Waahi ngaro* (the lost portion): strengthening relationships between people and wetlands in north Taranaki, New Zealand', *World Archaeology*, 34: 315–29.
Buck, P.H. (1925) 'The pre-European diet of the Maori', *New Zealand Dental Journal*, 20: 203–17.
——(1938) *Vikings of the Sunrise*, Philadelphia: Lippincott.
Buikstra, J.E. and Ubelaker, D.H. (eds) (1994) *Standards for Data Collection from Human Skeletal Remains*, Fayetteville, AR: Arkansas Archaeological Survey Research Series No. 44.
Cox, K., Tayles, N.G. and Buckley, H.R. (2006) 'Forensic identification of "race": the issues in New Zealand', *Current Anthropology*, 47: 869–74.
Dennison, K.J. (1979) 'Tooth size and sexual dimorphism in prehistoric New Zealand Polynesian teeth', *Archaeology and Physical Anthropology in Oceania*, 14: 123–28.

Dominion Post (2007) *Excavation uncovers burial site in Poverty Bay*. Available online at www.stuff.co.nz/national/46670/ (accessed 13 July 2009).

Fforde, C. and Hubert, J. (2006) 'Indigenous human remains and changing museum ideology', in R. Layton *et al.* (eds) *A Future for Archaeology*, Walnut Creek California: Left Coast Press.

Forster, J.R. (1996) *Observations Made During a Voyage Round the World*. N. Thomas *et al.* (eds) Honolulu, University of Hawai'i Press.

Gill, G.W. (1994) 'Craniofacial criteria in the skeletal attribution of race', in K.J. Reichs (ed.) *Forensic Osteology Advances in the Identification of Human Remains*, Springfield, IL: Charles C. Thomas.

Gillies, K. and O'Regan, G. (1994) 'Murihiku resolution of Koiwi Tangata management', *New Zealand Museums Journal*, 24: 30–31.

Houghton, P. (1975) 'The people of Wairau Bar', *Records of the Canterbury Museum*, 9: 231–46.

——(1978) 'Dental evidence for dietary variation in prehistoric New Zealand', *Journal of the Polynesian Society*, 87: 257–63.

——(1980) *The First New Zealanders*, Auckland: Hodder and Stoughton.

——(1990) 'The adaptive significance of Polynesian body form', *Annals of Human Biology*, 17: 19–32.

——(1991a) 'The early human biology of the Pacific: some considerations', *Journal of the Polynesian Society*, 100: 167–96.

——(1991b) 'Selective influences and morphological variation amongst Pacific *Homo sapiens*', *Journal of Human Evolution*, 21: 49–59.

——(1996) *People of the Great Ocean*, Cambridge: Cambridge University Press.

Houghton, P. and de Souza, P. (1975) 'Discriminant function sexing of human skeletal material in prehistoric New Zealand', *Journal of the Polynesian Society*, 84: 225–29.

Houghton, P. and Kean, M.R. (1987) 'The Polynesian head: a biological model for *Homo sapiens*', *Journal of the Polynesian Society*, 96: 223–47.

Houghton, P., Leach, B.F. and Sutton, D.G. (1975) 'Estimation of stature of prehistoric Polynesians in New Zealand', *Journal of the Polynesian Society*, 84: 325–36.

Howe, K.R. (2003) *The Quest for Origins: Who first Discovered and Settled New Zealand and the Pacific Islands?* Auckland: Penguin Books.

Howells, W.W. (1989) *Skull Shapes* and the *Map*. Papers of the Peabody Museum of Archaeology and Ethnology Harvard University Vol. 79, Harvard, MA: Harvard University Press.

Kayser, M., Brauer, S., Weiss, G., *et al.* (2000) 'Melanesian origin of Polynesian Y chromosomes', *Current Biology*, 10: 1237–46.

Kean, M.R. and Houghton, P. (1982) 'The Polynesian head: growth and form', *Journal of Anatomy*, 135: 423–35.

——(1987) 'The role of function in the development of human craniofacial form', *The Anatomical Record*, 218: 107–10.

——(1990) 'Polynesian face and dentition: functional perspective', *American Journal of Physical Anthropology*, 82: 361–70.

King, M. (1981) *The Collector Andreas Reischek – a Biography*, Auckland: Hodder and Stoughton.

Leach, B.F. and Leach, H.M. (eds) (1979) *Prehistoric Man in Palliser Bay*, New Zealand: National Museum of New Zealand Bulletin 21.

Littleton, J. and Kinaston, R. (2008) 'Ancestry, age, sex and stature: identification in a diverse space', in M. Oxenham (ed.) *Forensic Approaches to Death, Disaster and Abuse*, Sydney: Australian Academic Press.

Mollison, T. (1908) 'Contribution to the craniology and osteology of the Maoris' Reprint from *Zeitschrift für Morphologie und Anthropologie*, 11: 529–95. Translated by K.J. Dennison, 1976.

Murphy, A.M.C. (1986) 'Determination of sex in discriminant function analysis of New Zealand Polynesian pectoral girdles', *Proceedings of the University of Otago Medical School*, 64: 17–18.

——(1994) 'Sex determination of prehistoric New Zealand Polynesian clavicles', *New Zealand Journal of Archaeology*, 16: 85–91.

——(1995) 'Sex determination of prehistoric New Zealand Polynesian scapulae', *New Zealand Journal of Archaeology*, 17: 29–34.

——(2000) 'The acetabulum: sex assessment of prehistoric New Zealand Polynesian innominates', *Forensic Science International*, 108: 39–43.

——(2002a) 'Articular surfaces of the pectoral girdle: sex assessment of prehistoric New Zealand Polynesian skeletal remains', *Forensic Science International*, 125: 134–36.

——(2002b) 'The talus: sex assessment of prehistoric New Zealand Polynesian skeletal remains', *Forensic Science International*, 128: 155–58.

——(2002c) 'The calcaneum: sex assessment of prehistoric New Zealand Polynesian skeletal remains', *Forensic Science International*, 129: 205–8.

——(2005a) 'The articular surfaces of the hindfoot: sex assessment of prehistoric New Zealand Polynesian skeletal remains', *Forensic Science International*, 151: 19–22.

——(2005b) 'The femoral head: sex assessment of prehistoric New Zealand Polynesian skeletal remains', *Forensic Science International*, 154: 210–13.

Ngai Tahu (1993) '*Koiwi Tangata*', unpublished manuscript.

New Zealand *Herald* (2009) *Maori angry as burial site dug up*. Available online at www.nzherald.co.nz/maori/news/article.cfm?c_id=252& objected=1/ (accessed 13 July 2009).

New Zealand Historic Places Trust (2008) *Annual Report Purongo a Tau For the Year ending 30 June 2008*, New Zealand: Historic Places Trust. Available online at www.historic.org.nz/Publications/~/media/Corporate/Files/Publications/2008AnnualReport.ashx/ (accessed 19 June 2009).

New Zealand Historic Places Trust Pouhere Taonga (2010) Archaeological Guidelines Series No.8 Koiwi Tangata/Human Remains. New Zealand: Historic Places Trust. Available online at www.historic.org.nz/ProtectingOurHeritage/Archaeology/~/media/Corporate/Files/Archaeology/AGS8-KoiwiTangataHumanRemainsUpdated.ashx/ (accessed 25 March 2010).

Orange, C. (2004) *An Illustrated History of the Treaty of Waitangi*, Wellington: Bridget Williams.

Pickerill, H.P. (1912) 'Some pathological conditions found in the teeth and jaws of Maori skulls in New Zealand', *Proceedings of the Royal Society of Medicine, Section 5: Odontology*: 155–65.

Pietrusewsky, M. (1996) 'The Physical Anthropology of Polynesia: a review of some cranial and skeletal studies', in J. Davidson *et al.*(eds) *Oceanic Culture History Essays in Honour of Roger Green*, Dunedin: New Zealand Journal of Archaeology Special Publication.

Pischief, E. (2002) 'The *urupa* at Waimarama Hawke's Bay', *Archaeology in New Zealand*, 45: 59–65.

Poll, H. (1902) 'On Skulls and skeletons of the inhabitants of the Chatham Islands', Reprint from *Zeitschrift Für Morphologie und Anthropologie*, 5: 1–134. Translated by K.J. Dennison, 1992.

Prickett, N. (1990) 'Archaeological excavations at Raupa: the 1987 season', *Records of the Auckland Institute and Museum*, 27: 73–153.

Scott, J.H. (1893) 'Contribution to the osteology of the Aborigines of New Zealand and of the Chatham Islands', *Transactions of the New Zealand Institute*, 26: 1–64.

Tapsell, P. (2005) 'Out of sight, out of mind: human remains at the Auckland Museum – *Te Papa Whakahiku*', in R.R. Janes and G.T. Conaty (eds) *Looking Reality in the Eye: Museums and Social Responsibility*, Calgary: University of Calgary Press.

Tayles, N. (2009) 'Repatriation: a view from the receiving end, New Zealand', in M.E. Lewis and M. Clegg (eds) *Proceedings of the Ninth Annual Conference of the British Association for Biological Anthropology and Osteoarchaeology*, BAR International Series 1918, Oxford: Archaeopress.

Taylor, R.M.S. (1962a) 'The human palate', *Acta Anatomica Supplementum*, 49: 1–108.

——(1962b) 'Non-metrical studies in the human palate and dentition in Moriori and Maori skulls, Part I and II', *Journal of the Polynesian Society*, 71: 83–100 and 167–87.

——(1963) 'Cause and effect of wear of teeth', *Acta Anatomica*, 53: 97–157.

——(1970) 'Fern root planes', *New Zealand Dental Journal*, 66: 248–51.

——(1975) 'The significance of tooth wear in Polynesians', *Journal of the Dental Association of South Africa*, 30: 241–344.

Te Moananui, R., Kieser, J., Herbison, P., *et al.* (2008a) 'Advanced dental maturation in New Zealand Maori and Pacific Island children', *American Journal of Human Biology*, 20: 43–50.

——(2008b) 'Estimating age in Maori, Pacific Island and European children from New Zealand', *Journal of Forensic Science* 20: 43–50.

Te Papa (n.d.) *Karanga Aotearoa Repatriation Programme. Resource kit*, Wellington: Te Papa Tongarewa National Museum of New Zealand.

Tonkin, S. (1970) 'Height, weight and haemoglobin study of adolescent Maoris and Europeans', *New Zealand Medical Journal*, 72: 323–27.

Underhill, P.A., Passarino, G., Lin, A.A., *et al.* (2001) 'Maori origins, Y-chromosome haplotypes and implications for human history in the Pacific', *Human Mutation*, 17: 271–80.

Waitangi Tribunal (2009). Online resource. Available online at www.waitangi-tribunal.govt.nz/ (accessed 13 July 2009).

Watt, M. (1974) 'Sexing the Maori skull – a review', *New Zealand Archaeological Association Newsletter*, 17: 95–103.

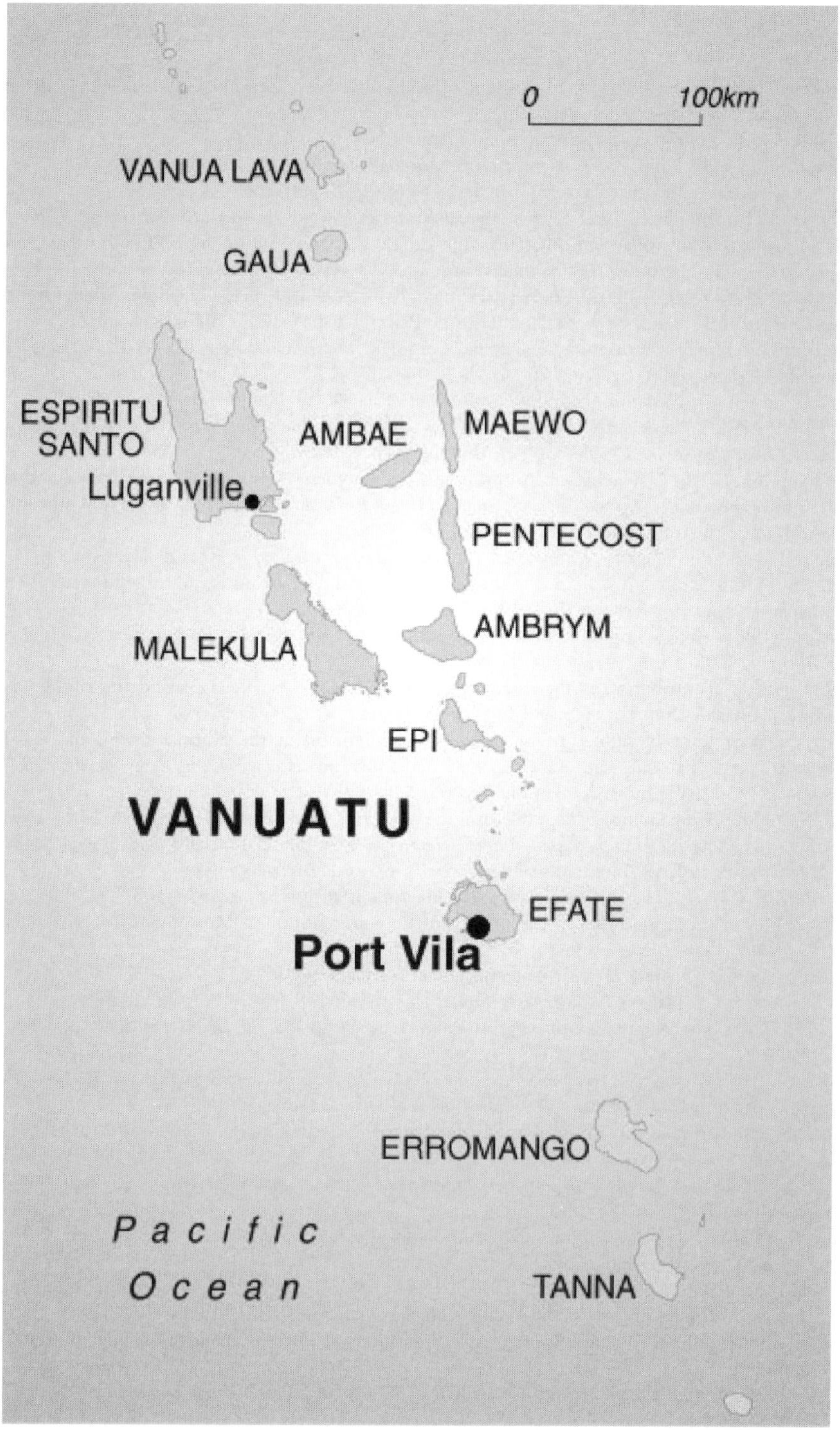

0
100km
VANUA LAVA
GAUA
ESPIRITU
SANTO
Luganville
AMBAE
MAEWO
PENTECOST
MALEKULA
AMBRYM
EPI
VANUATU
EFATE
Port Vila
ERROMANGO
Pacific
Ocean
TANNA

Vanuatu

Stuart Bedford, Ralph Regenvanu, Matthew Spriggs, Hallie Buckley
and Frédérique Valentin

INTRODUCTION: A BRIEF HISTORY AND CURRENT STATE OF PHYSICAL ANTHROPOLOGY IN VANUATU

The Republic of Vanuatu, located in the south west Pacific, comprises a total land area of 12,195 sq km, made up of 83 islands, 70 of which are inhabited (Figure 59.1). Vanuatu was a former colony of Britain and France, jointly run under a Condominium government and known during that period as the New Hebrides or *Nouvelles Hébrides*, until it gained its independence in 1980. The indigenous population (known as *ni-Vanuatu*) of about 220,000 today remains remarkably culturally and linguistically diverse (Bonnemaison *et al.* 1996; Siméoni 2009). Most of the population practise a subsistence lifestyle and live in kin-based groups on their ancestral lands, practising a range of traditional or *kastom* beliefs. As a small, developing nation, Vanuatu has limited financial resources and consequently government priorities are focused on supporting and developing basic infrastructure.

While the government is supportive of archaeological research it is not a priority area for funding, and as such there are limited government initiatives or opportunities for employment. Currently a single *ni-Vanuatu* archaeologist is employed at the Vanuatu Cultural Centre and Museum, the national institution responsible for the management of cultural heritage. There is legislation that was recently passed (National Heritage Preservation Act, 2008) which relates to the protection of archaeological sites, but there is no specific legislation or any detail in the current Act relating to archaeological practice or the excavation and analysis of human skeletal remains. While this situation is very different to most developed countries, Vanuatu has managed to establish a whole range of its own alternative approaches to the management of cultural heritage that combine both formal legislation and customary practice or *kastom*.

This chapter outlines the development of cultural heritage policy along with professional practice in relation to prehistoric human remains in Vanuatu, from its beginnings during the colonial period and through the transformations following independence. Two particular case studies are outlined which emphasize these developments. They are the Roi Mata site, a 400-year-old mass burial located on the small island of Retoka, Efate, and recently inscribed on the UNESCO World Heritage List, and the 3000-year-old Teouma Lapita cemetery, the oldest yet found in the Pacific. The Roi Mata site was excavated in 1967 (Garanger 1972), and excavation at the Teouma site began in 2004 and is on-going (Bedford *et al.* 2006). General public attitudes towards the excavation and analysis of human remains are also discussed.

Permission for archaeological research during the colonial period was given by relevant colonial authorities following presentation of an outline of proposed research and some evidence of the researcher's credentials. Research was undertaken independent of any monitoring arrangements or specific agreements detailing responsibilities or requirements. Local community support was often assumed, but was also essential, particularly when dealing with culturally sensitive sites and in more remote areas where colonial authority had limited influence.

The only pre-independence institution that focused on aspects of Vanuatu culture was the Port Vila Cultural Centre that was established in 1956 by the colonial administration as a conventional library and museum. Its primary function was to maintain its collections of books, documents and photos, and specimens related to natural history and ethnographic objects. For most of the period prior to Independence the Cultural Centre played a very limited role in any archaeological research that was being undertaken, although this began to change from 1977, when the first permanent curator, Kirk Huffman, was appointed (Bolton 2003: xvi–xviii).

Condominium government legislation in relation to archaeological sites was very limited, which was hardly surprising, considering a similar situation existed in the wider Pacific region, including Australia and New Zealand, at the time. In 1965 the Preservation of Sites and Artefacts Act was passed, but it was primarily designed to protect sites of cultural or artistic significance and to regulate the export of artefacts. There was no specific legislation or set of regulations relating to archaeological sites, or to prehistoric human remains, their excavation, analysis or curation.

Archaeological research began in Vanuatu in the early 1960s with a major Franco–American Project targeting the central and southern islands (Bedford 2006: 14–20). Earlier pioneering research in the neighbouring archipelagos of Fiji and New Caledonia had confirmed the antiquity of human occupation there and demonstrated the value of archaeological research in the western Pacific (Gifford 1951; Gifford and Shutler 1956). Vanuatu at this time remained an archaeological blank. Human remains were regularly encountered during this pioneering phase and, in the case of the work of José Garanger, they became one of the major defining aspects and legacy of his research in the colony (Garanger 1972). As was fairly standard practice at the time, no trained physical anthropologist was involved in the excavation of any of the human remains.

The Roi Mata burial

The archaeological programme undertaken by José Garanger in central Vanuatu (1963–67) was one of the more ambitious and successful projects ever carried out in the region, and Garanger's richly illustrated publication remains central to any discussion of the mortuary practice of the south west Pacific. His research focus was primarily the archaeological investigation of oral traditions that related to burials of chiefly figures on the islands of Retoka, off west Efate and Tongoa in the Shepherds Group (see Figure 59.1) (Garanger 1972, 1982). The Roi Mata burial on Retoka was particularly spectacular and corresponded with equally astonishing oral traditions relating to events that occurred around 1600 AD (revised dating from the present authors' research).

Chief Roi Mata was said to have arrived on Efate from the 'south', and is attributed with establishing peace and a matriclan system across Efate and the Shepherd Islands (Guiart 1973: 290–92). On his death, apparently from the effects of a customary competitive feast, his body lay in state at Feles Cave on the island of Lelepa before being taken back to his village of Mangaasi, located on the Efate mainland. Fearful of his sacred status and chiefly powers, it was decided that he, along with members of his court and family, should be buried on the nearby offshore island of Retoka, which was then abandoned by its small population.

Some 400 years later Garanger gained the confidence and permission of local communities to excavate the Roi Mata site with the agreement that, while skeletal remains could be exposed,

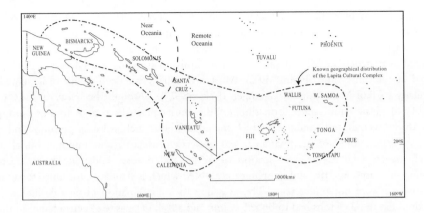

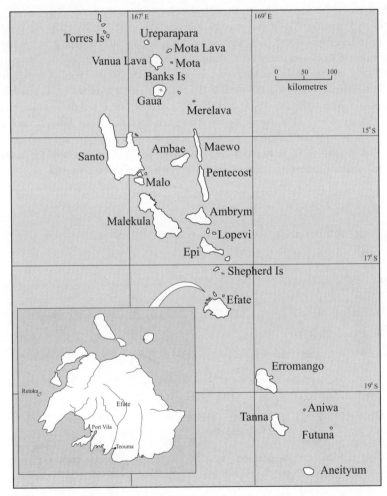

Figure 59.1 Vanuatu and the South West Pacific

they were not to be removed. Ultimately an area of about 104 sq m, centred around two upright flat stones, was meticulously excavated by Garanger and a local crew. Some 50 skeletons in total were exposed which were all drawn and photographed in detail. The skeleton identified as that of Roi Mata is surrounded by individuals, many buried in pairs, who were interred at the same time (Figure 59.2). Most individuals had been richly ornamented, and particularly so Roi Mata himself (Garanger 1972: 58–77). Through the excavations, Garanger was able to glean significant information on the burial practices related to this community dating to the second millennium AD which included aspects such as burial positions and orientation, the range and use of ornaments and associated artefacts, and multiple burial. Other research aspects such as the investigation of health and disease, body and bone treatment, recording of morphometrics and sampling for aDNA, which is standard procedure today in any such analysis, were not undertaken. This was due to a combination of factors, including the restriction that the skeletons had to be left *in situ*, and a lack of on-site expertise; and, in the case of aDNA, it was to be decades before such technology was even developed.

A number of other archaeologists carried out research in the archipelago up to and around the date of independence and, although none were specifically targeting burial sites, skeletal remains continued to be uncovered (for a summary see Valentin *et al.* 2009). These included 15 burials in a cave on Futuna Island in the south (Shutler and Shutler 1968), 4 burials in a cave at Mele on Efate Island (Ward and Houghton 1988, 1991), a single burial on Pakea Island, in the far north Banks Islands (Ward 1979: 5–15) and a chief's burial on the southernmost island, Aneityum (Spriggs 1997: 217). Again, as was the general practice at the time, no specialists were involved in excavating the remains. However, in contrast to the situation with the Roi Mata burials on Retoka, all of these remains were removed at the time and sent for study overseas, although full analysis and publication of any of them has yet to be achieved.

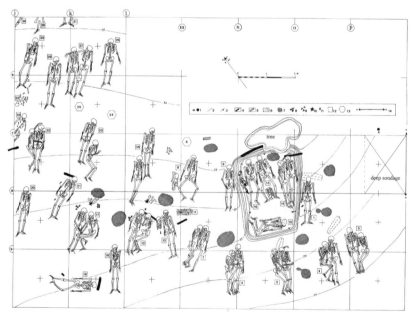

Figure 59.2 Plan of the Roi Mata burial, Vanuatu
Source: Garanger 1972

Transformations post-independence

Following independence in 1980, only limited archaeological research continued, and in 1985 the Vanuatu government imposed a moratorium on humanities-based research. With few exceptions, no expatriate fieldwork was undertaken for the next nine years (Bolton 1999, 2003). This was a period of consolidation and realignment for the newly named Vanuatu Cultural Centre (VCC) which, under national legislation, along with the associated supervisory body the Vanuatu National Cultural Council (VNCC), is responsible for the 'preservation, protection and development of various aspects of Vanuatu's cultural heritage'.

The VCC began to shift away from the conventional library and museum structure to a greater emphasis on working in the islands amongst indigenous communities to record and promote aspects of the country's cultural heritage or *kastom* (custom). This was facilitated and strengthened through the VCC's *filwoka* (fieldworker) system which had developed from the late 1970s (Regenvanu 1999; Tryon 1999). This network comprises volunteers across the country who are living within their own linguistic and cultural communities, and are selected by their various communities to document the culture and history of their own and neighbouring regions. This network offers a unique Vanuatu perspective and method on cultural heritage management where the emphasis is on local communities being fully involved and responsible for the implementation.

In addition to the strengthening of the *filwoka* network through the 1980s, the Vanuatu Cultural and Historic Sites Survey (VCHSS) was established in 1990, funded by the European Union. It was a separate but associated entity to the VCC and was a major boost to archaeology. Its aims were to build and maintain a database of sites of cultural, archaeological and historic significance; to conduct surveys to identify and document these sites; train ni-Vanuatu staff in techniques of survey, research planning and execution; consider and establish procedures for determining, assessing and responding to threats to sites; encourage and develop the study of archaeology and history of Vanuatu; and promote an awareness of its importance as part of the country's cultural heritage (Roe and Galipaud 1994). The VCHSS organized and undertook site surveys in conjunction with the locally-based VCC *filwokas* and local communities. Focus was generally on the recording of historical and cultural/*kastom* sites, particularly in areas where development was being planned. Surveys were carried out on many islands in the archipelago. While archaeological research projects involving targeted excavations were not a component of the work of the VCHSS, its distinctly ni-Vanuatu approach, style and perspective that developed over a number of years (Roe and Galipaud 1994; Roe *et al.* 1994) laid the foundations for collaborative archaeological research and training that was further developed following the lifting of the moratorium in 1994. With the completion and launch of the VCC Research Policy in 1994, the VNCC began issuing research permits, and research oriented archaeological projects were once again initiated (Regenvanu 1999).

ARCHAEOLOGICAL HUMAN REMAINS AND LEGISLATION

Archaeological legislation

It is the Vanuatu National Cultural Council (VNCC) that is responsible for research in Vanuatu under the laws of the Republic of Vanuatu. The VNCC defines and implements national research policies and priorities, and sponsors, regulates and undertakes programmes of research. As part of its regulatory function the VNCC determines whether foreign nationals can undertake research in Vanuatu in a given field of humanities research. All research proposals must receive the approval of the VNCC and any local community which is involved in the project.

Consultation with local communities, then, is a prerequisite to the submission of any research proposal. Other bodies that may have to be consulted, depending on the nature of the project, are provincial governments and the Area Council of Chiefs. The VNCC encourages the max-imization of opportunities for ni-Vanuatu and the involvement of indigenous scholars, students and members of communities associated with any particular research project. Suitable advisors and/or referees of relevant professional standing can be asked to help in the assessment of particular projects.

Further to the strengthening of protective legislation, in 2008 the old Preservation of Sites and Artefacts Act was modified and renamed the National Heritage Preservation Act, and it was subsequently passed in Parliament in May of the same year. It greatly strengthens the archaeological aspect of national heritage as it is now specifically mentioned.

HUMAN REMAINS AND LEGISLATION

There is still no detailed legislation outlining specifics dealing with prehistoric human remains. Rather, these aspects are dealt with on a project-by-project basis and are assessed during the permit application process. Detailed conditions relating to the excavation and study of human remains are often governed by decisions made by local communities. In some cases human remains can be transported overseas with the understanding that they are returned for long-term storage at the VCC. In other cases, communities want them to be returned to the site from where they were removed, to be reburied.

The Teouma Lapita cemetery

The Teouma Lapita site, located on the south coast of Efate Island, central Vanuatu (Figure 59.3) was found in January 2004 (Bedford et al. 2006, 2009). Excavations in July 2004 quickly revealed that the first use of the site was as a cemetery, and it was therefore not simply impor-tant at a local Vanuatu level but was the first real opportunity in more than 50 years of research to profile a group of Lapita people, pioneering colonizers who first settled the region from Vanuatu across to Samoa some 3000 years ago (Kirch 1997). The Teouma cemetery represents one of the very rare examples of a true pioneering population of the first one or two genera-tions of settlement of an island group anywhere in the world. It has also provided the first sig-nificant information on Lapita ritual and burial practices. The investigation of the site is being jointly run by the VCC and the Australian National University, with the collaboration of an international team of experts. The customary landowners are also involved in the excavations and have been supportive throughout, declaring that they had been completely unaware of any such site in this area.

Excavations undertaken over the first five field seasons have revealed a total of 60 burial features, with just over 80 individuals represented (Bedford et al. 2009). They have established that there was a wide range of burial practices and that mortuary ritual was a multi-faceted and lengthy on-going process, rather than a one-off event (Valentin et al. 2010). The burials were generally placed in shallow graves dug into the underlying tephra deposits amongst gaps in the uplifted reef and coral boulders on the upper part of the beach. There is evidence that suggests the manipulation of corpses prior to burial or at least during the early stages of decomposition, and that the graves were repeatedly visited. All the individuals had had their skulls, and often many other bones, removed during the extended mortuary procedure. Both primary and sec-ondary interments are in evidence (Bedford and Spriggs 2007). There is a wide array of burial

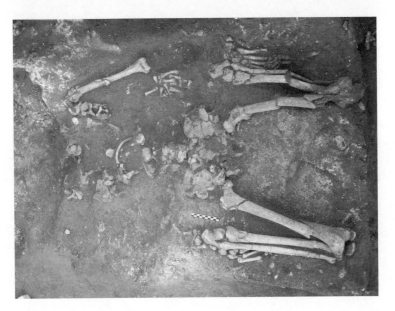

Figure 59.3a and b

positions, but most are laid out in a supine position, often with legs in a flexed or crossed position, possibly due both to particular burial practices and in some cases to the restricted space available.

All excavated skeletal material was transported overseas for specialist study, and that from the first three seasons has subsequently been returned to the VCC for long-term storage.

Ni-Vanuatu attitudes to the excavation of human remains

Traditional customs on many islands in Vanuatu involved extended funerary rites and the manipulation of skeletonized remains. These were practised in some areas until well after the

Figure 59.3c and d Excavation at the Teouma Lapita cemetery, Efate, Vanuatu

middle of the 20th century. Particularly well-known, because they are represented in several major ethnographic collections in foreign museums, are the *rambaramp* figures of southern Malakula, which involved the creation of a human sized mannequin of the dead person, involving overmodelling of the actual skull of the deceased with clay to replicate their facial features (Kaufmann 1996). Such *rambaramp* figures with overmodelled skulls are currently on public display in the Musée de Quai Branly in Paris.

Contemporary attitudes to the archaeological study of human remains vary across the archipelago, as one would expect in such a diverse nation as Vanuatu. There is generally a clear difference in attitude between the investigation of very ancient remains, such as those at Teouma, and more recent burials, often of known individuals, such as Roi Mata. These latter are also often implicated in claims to land ownership, itself the most sensitive issue in current local politics. Recent negotiations to investigate the grave said to be of Roi Mata's brother, Roy Muri, on Epi Island seemed to have been successful in gaining the support of the local community at the site. Investigation was prevented, however, when objections were raised by a family from the adjacent and culturally-related island of Tongoa who also claimed custodianship of the site. Their representations were made directly to the Vanuatu Cultural Centre, showing that there is general knowledge in the islands of who has control over such research.

That said, there are situations where investigation of comparatively recent remains is encouraged by local communities. Spriggs was asked by the then-chief of Anelcauhat village on Aneityum Island, in 1983, to investigate a chiefly grave on Aneityum that had been disturbed by pig-rooting. The grave was only a few hundred years old. Many years later, during a dispute over chiefly succession in the village, Spriggs was asked whether the grave was of a Polynesian 'usurper' who, in one oral tradition, was said to have seized the chiefship, or that of an indigenous Aneityumese. Evidence one way or the other could have been decisive in settling the chiefship of one particular family. He noted that the lack of a skull precluded easy identification one way or the other – the heads of high chiefs being traditionally removed for public veneration. He also explained that Polynesian-style ornaments in the grave could just as easily have been adopted as a fashion by the local population of the time, rather than being representative of actual Polynesian migrants. On another island there is interest in digging up the grave of a 'giant' mentioned in oral tradition: some believe that his stature would qualify the village for an entry in the Guinness Book of Records.

At the Teouma excavation, the ni-Vanuatu workforce is composed largely of young people from Eratap village, the traditional owners of the land on which the Lapita cemetery was found. Our observation is that they are quite relaxed about handling and washing human bones, and about the temporary storage in the village of these remains before they are sent overseas for analysis. The site is a major focus of school visits, with more than 1000 students from local schools visiting during one of the field seasons. The national newspapers, the *Daily Post* and the *Independent*, regularly show pictures of skeletons from the site in reports on the progress of the excavations. Local government officials and politicians often express polite interest and some-times even enthusiasm for the research. The team was honoured by an official visit from the President of Vanuatu, His Excellency Kalkot Matas Kelekele, during the 2005 field season. The most common question asked by visitors is always: Are these people our direct ancestors, or did we reach Vanuatu later? This is closely followed in popularity by questions about their stature, as it is a common belief in Vanuatu that people used to be taller in the past than today.

It is tempting to see this level of public interest as stemming from traditional attitudes to death, and to the ancestors as being present in some form or another – even if only in songs and stories. The often-complex funerary rituals of the recent past sometimes involved the handling and curation of skeletal elements, such as is evidenced by Teouma itself. The presence of the skulls of honoured persons in community men's houses and on public ceremonial plazas, or in frequently-visited burial caves, would have been a common sight not so long ago, and to some extent is so today in rural areas.

METHODS OF ANTHROPOLOGICAL ANALYSIS

Analysis in the field

The excavation of all burials from Teouma has been undertaken by physical anthropologists trained in both archaeological practice and human skeletal biology. Because of their involvement in the archaeological fieldwork, these specialists identify themselves as 'bioarchaeologists'. The methods of exposing and lifting the skeletons used in the field follow standard archaeological practice and specialist handling of bones, following protocols outlined by White and Folkens (2005) and Roberts (2009). Where possible, recording of age, sex, limb bone lengths and any gross pathology, such as fractures or osteophytes on the vertebrae, is carried out *in situ* before lifting of the bones. Extensive photography of the skeletons *in situ* is also an essential part of this stage of the recovery process.

The collection of *in situ* mortuary data at Teouma has followed the recommendations and terminology of Ubelaker (1989, 2002) and Sprague (2005). Aiming to reconstruct initial burial situations, the protocol and method of archaeothanatology or field anthropology elaborated by Duday (1990, 2006; Duday and Guillon 2006; Duday *et al.* 1990) has been used (see Valentin *et al.* 2009 for a detailed discussion). This methodology is now considered to be a fundamental component of mortuary analysis used in different sites around the world, including, for example, in Southeast Asia (Pautreau *et al.* 2004; Willis and Tayles 2009) and the Pacific Islands (Valentin *et al.* 2001).

Analysis in the laboratory

In the laboratory, internationally recognized standards have been used to assess aspects of skeletal biology including individual growth, age-at-death, sex, morphology, and health and disease (Table 59.1). The regression equations used for stature were developed specifically for use on individuals of Polynesian ancestry (Houghton *et al.* 1975). Although they are not necessarily appropriate for skeletal remains from Vanuatu, the same equations are extensively used by bioarchaeologists working on skeletal remains throughout the Pacific Islands. Long bone lengths are also used for comparative purposes for assessing relative size and growth within and between populations, which removes the possible biases of using population-specific regression equations for stature (Holliday and Ruff 2001). Preliminary analysis of the skeletal remains from the 2004–5 field seasons has already returned significant new information relating to the health, morphology, diet and migratory patterns of this colonizing population (Bentley *et al.* 2007; Buckley 2007; Buckley *et al.* 2008). Alas, early attempts at extracting aDNA have thus far not been successful.

CONCLUSION

It can be seen from the above discussion that, although there is no explicit legislation governing the excavation and curation of human remains in Vanuatu, there is strong national and local-community control over research of this kind. This is explicit both in the recently-updated legislation protecting cultural and historic sites and in the research policies of the Vanuatu National Cultural Council that governs all research in archaeology. These policies are particularly sensitive to the needs and wishes of local village communities in the islands, requiring extensive consultation through the *filwokas* network and involvement of local chiefs and landowners at all stages of the research. Such is the power of *kastom* that, even in the colonial period, when one would imagine that local views would not often have been taken into account, members of the community with responsibility for the Roi Mata burial site were active agents in permitting and setting limits to its investigation. What has changed in the most recent past is the public's knowledge of and interest in all aspects of archaeology, a process begun with the establishment of the Vanuatu Cultural and Historic Sites Survey in

Table 59.1 Methods used for assessing health parameters in the Teouma skeletal sample, Vanuatu

Health parameter	Characteristic	Method/bone or dental change	Interpretation/diagnosis	Sources
Body size	Adult stature	Long bone lengths	Achievement of growth potential and body size	Houghton, Leach *et al.* 1975; Buikstra and Ubelaker 1994
Oral health	Tooth attrition	Degree of dentine exposure (grades 1–8)	Age Dietary roughness	Molnar 1971; Hillson 1996
	Caries	Cavity in tooth; enamel or dentine or root	Diet	Hillson 2000
	Periodontal disease	Porosity and recession of alveolar bone	Oral infection	Hillson 1996; Tayles 1999
Disease parameter				
Activity-related	Osteoarthritis	Eburnation on one or more bone surfaces of synovial joints in the limbs and spine	Diagnostic of pathological loss of articular cartilage of joints due to osteoarthritis	Rogers, Waldron *et al.* 1987; Rogers and Waldron 1995
	Joint remodelling	Moderate to severe osteophyte formation (spiculated new bone formation extending beyond margins of joints) of synovial joint margins in the limbs	Remodelling of joints possibly in response to repetitive overuse	Tayles 1999
	Vertebral spondylosis	Ankylosis of corresponding osteophytes of adjacent vertebral bodies	Remodelling of joints possibly in response to repetitive overuse *but* may be related to spondyloarthropathies	Rogers *et al.* 1987; Rogers and Waldron 1995
Trauma	Bone fracture	Bony callus formation	Accidental or interpersonal violence	Lovell 1997; Ortner 2003
Periosteal reactions		Subperiosteal new bone formation and porosity on the shafts of long bones	Multiple causes; infection, trauma, metabolic disease (scurvy)	Aufderheide 1998; Ortner 2003

1990, and the direct involvement in excavations since 2004 of professional bioarchaeologists in the various joint projects between the Australian National University and the Vanuatu Cultural Centre that investigate human remains. This involvement has made an enormous difference to the standard of recording of individual burials in the field, and – following on from this – to the quality of the analyses performed subsequently and the conclusions drawn from them.

USEFUL CONTACTS

Vanuatu Cultural Centre. Website: www.vanuatuculture.org/

ACKNOWLEDGEMENTS

The Teouma Archaeological Project is a joint initiative of the Vanuatu Cultural Centre and The Australian National University, directed by Matthew Spriggs and Stuart Bedford, of the ANU, and Ralph Regenvanu, Director of the Vanuatu Cultural Centre until the end of 2006. Funding for the project since 2004 has been provided by the Australian Research Council, the Pacific Biological Foundation, a National Geographic Scientific Research Grant, the Department of Archaeology and Natural History and School of Archaeology and Anthropology at the ANU, the Snowy Mountains Engineering Corporation Foundation, and Mr Brian Powell. The laboratory research and travel of present author FV, for excavation of the skeletal remains, has been funded by CNRS, France. The laboratory research and travel of present author HB, for excavation of the skeletal remains, has been funded by research grants from The Royal Society of New Zealand Marsden Fund and the University of Otago. The support of the leaseholder, M. Robert Monvoisin, and family is acknowledged, as is the support and assistance of the traditional landowners and population of Eratap Village.

BIBLIOGRAPHY

Aufderheide, A. and Rodriguez-Martin, C. (1998) *Cambridge Encyclopedia of Human Paleopathology*, Cambridge: Cambridge University Press.

Bedford, S. (2006) *Pieces of the Vanuatu Puzzle: Archaeology of the North, South and Centre*, Canberra: Pandanus Press, The Australian National University. Terra Australis 23.

Bedford, S. and Spriggs, M. (2007) 'Birds on the rim: a unique Lapita carinated vessel in its wider context', *Archaeology in Oceania*, 42: 12–21.

Bedford, S., Spriggs, M. and Regenvanu, R. (2006) 'The Teouma Lapita site and the early human settlement of the Pacific Islands', *Antiquity*, 80: 812–28.

Bedford, S., Spriggs, M., Buckley, H., *et al.* (2009) 'The Teouma Lapita site, South Efate, Vanuatu: a summary of three field seasons (2004–6)', in P. Sheppard *et al.* (eds) *Lapita Antecedents and Successors*, Dunedin: New Zealand Archaeological Association Monograph Series.

Bentley, A., Buckley, H., Spriggs, M., *et al.* (2007) 'Lapita migrants in the Pacific's oldest cemetery: isotopic analysis at Teouma, Vanuatu', *American Antiquity*, 72: 645–56.

Bolton, L. (1999) 'Introduction', *Oceania*, 70: 1–8.

——(2003) *Unfolding the Moon*, Honolulu: University of Hawaii Press.

Bonnemaison, J., Huffman, K., Kaufmann, C., *et al.* (eds) (1996) *Arts of Vanuatu*, Bathurst: Crawford House Press.

Buckley, H. (2007) 'Possible gouty arthritis in Lapita-associated skeletons from Teouma, Efate Island, Central Vanuatu', *Current Anthropology*, 48: 741–49.

Buckley, H., Tayles, N., Spriggs, M., *et al.* (2008) 'A preliminary report on health and disease in early Lapita skeletons: possible biological costs of colonization', *Journal of Island and Coastal Archaeology*, 3: 87–114.

Buikstra, J. and Ubelaker, D. (eds) (1994) *Standards for Data Collection from Human Skeletal Remains*, Fayetteville, AR: Arkansas Archaeological Survey Research Series No. 44.

Duday, H. (1990) 'Observations ostéologiques et décomposition du cadavre: sépulture colmatée ou en espace vide', *Revue Archéologique du Centre de la France*, 29: 193–96.

——(2006) 'Archaeothanatolgy or the archaeology of death', in R. Gowland and C. Knüsel (eds) *Social Archaeology of Funerary Remains*, Oxford: Oxbow Books.

Duday, H., Courtaud, P., Crubézy, E., *et al.* (1990) 'L'anthropologie "de terrain": reconnaissance et interprétation de gestes funéraires', *Bulletins et Mémoires de la Société d'Anthropologie de Paris*, 2: 29–50.

Duday, H. and Guillon, M. (2006) 'Understanding the circumstances of decomposition when the body is skeletonised', in A. Schmitt *et al.* (eds) *Forensic Anthropology and Medicine. Complementary Sciences from Recovery to Cause of Death*, New Jersey: Humana Press.

Garanger, J. (1972) *Archéologie des Nouvelles-Hébrides: contribution à la connaissance des îles du centre*, Publications de la Société des Océanistes No.30, Paris: ORSTOM.

——(1982) *Archaeology of the New Hebrides. Contribution to the knowledge of the Central Islands*, Oceania Monograph 24.

Gifford, E.W. (1951) *Archaeological Excavations in Fiji*, Anthropological Records 13, Berkeley and Los Angeles: University of California Press.

Gifford, E.W. and Shutler, R. Jr. (1956) *Archaeological Excavations in New Caledonia*, Anthropological Records 18, Berkeley and Los Angeles: University of California Press.

Guiart, J. (1973) 'Le Dossier Rassemble', in J. Espirat *et al.* (eds) *Systèmes des titres dans les Nouvelles Hébrides Centrales, d'Éfate aux îles Shepherd*, Mémoires de l'Institut d'Ethnologie 10, Paris: Musée National d'Histoire Naturelle.

Hillson, S. (1996) *Dental Anthropology*, Cambridge: Cambridge University Press.

——(2000) 'Dental pathology', in M. Katzenburg and S. Saunders (eds) *Biological Anthropology of the Human Skeleton*, New York: Wiley.

Holliday, T. and Ruff, C. (2001) 'Relative variation in human proximal and distal limb segment lengths', *American Journal of Physical Anthropology*, 116: 26–33.

Houghton, P., Leach, B. and Sutton, D. (1975) 'The estimation of stature of prehistoric Polynesians in New Zealand', *Journal of the Polynesian Society*, 84: 325–36.

Kaufmann, C. (1996) 'The arts of Vanuatu: between traditional imagery and force of expression', in J. Bonnemaison *et al.* (eds) *Arts of Vanuatu*, Bathurst: Crawford House Press.

Kirch, P.V. (1997) *The Lapita Peoples. Ancestors of the Oceanic World*, Oxford: Blackwell.

Lovell, N. (1997) 'Trauma analysis in paleopathology', *Yearbook of Physical Anthropology*, 40: 139–70.

Molnar, S. (1971) 'Human tooth wear, tooth function and cultural variability', *American Journal of Physical Anthropology*, 34: 175–90.

Ortner, D. (ed.) (2003) *Identification of Pathological Conditions in Human Skeletal Remains*, San Diego: Academic Press.

Pautreau, J.-P., Monnais, P. and Doy-Asa (2004) *Bang Wang Hai: Excavations of an Iron-Age Cemetery in Northern Thailand*, Bangkok: Silkworm Press.

Regenvanu, R. (1999) 'Afterword: Vanuatu perspectives on research', *Oceania*, 70: 98–101.

Roberts, C. (2009) *Human Remains in Archaeology: A Handbook*, York: Council for British Archaeology.

Roberts, C. and Manchester, K. (1995) *The Archaeology of Disease*, New York: Cornell University Press.

Roe, D. and Galipaud, J.-C. (1994) *The Vanuatu Cultural and Historic Sites Survey: project description, evaluation and recommendations. Final Report*, Port Vila: The Vanuatu Cultural and Historic Sites Survey.

Roe, D., Regenvanu, R., Wadra, F. and Araho, N. (1994) 'Working with cultural landscapes in Melanesia: some problems and approaches in the formulation of cultural policies', in L. Lindstrom and G. White (eds) *Culture-Kastom-Tradition. Developing Cultural Policy in Melanesia*, Suva: Institute of Pacific Studies.

Rogers, J. and Waldron, T. (1995) *A Field Guide to Joint Disease in Archaeology*, Chichester: John Wiley and Sons.

Rogers, J., Waldron, T., Dieppe, P., *et al.* (1987) 'Arthropathies in palaeopathology: the basis of classification according to most probable cause', *Journal of Archaeological Science*, 14: 179–93.

Shutler, R. Jr. and Shutler, M.E. (1968) 'Archaeological excavations in Southern Melanesia', in I. Yawata and Y. Sinoto (eds) *Prehistoric Culture in Oceania, A Symposium*, Papers from the Eleventh Pacific Science Congress, Tokyo, Japan 1966, Honolulu: Bishop Museum Press.

Siméoni, P. (2009) *Atlas du Vanouatou (Vanuatu)*, Port Vila: Éditions Géo-consulte.

Sprague, R. (2005) *Burial Terminology*, Lanham, Md: Altamira Press.

Spriggs, M. (1997) *The Island Melanesians*, Oxford: Blackwell.

Tayles, N. (1999) *The Excavation of Khok Phanom Di: A Prehistoric Site in Central Thailand*, Volume 5. The People. Dunedin: The Society of Antiquaries of London Research Report 66.

Tryon, D. (1999) 'Ni-Vanuatu research and researchers', *Oceania*, 70: 9–15.

Ubelaker, D.H. (1989) *Human Skeletal Remains, Excavation, Analysis, Interpretation*, 3rd edn, Washington, DC: Taraxacum.

——(2002) 'Approaches to the study of commingling in human skeletal biology', in W.D. Haglund and M.H. Sorg (eds) *Advances in Forensic Taphonomy: Method, Theory and Archaeological Perspectives*, Boca Raton, Fa: CRC Press.

Valentin, F., Bedford, S., Buckley, H., *et al.* (2010) 'Lapita burial practices: evidence for complex body and bone treatment at the Teouma cemetery, Vanuatu, Southwest Pacific', *Journal of Island and Coastal Archaeology*, 5:1–24.

Valentin, F., Sand, C., Le Goff, I., *et al.* (2001) 'Burial practices at the end of the prehistoric period in Cikobia-i-ra (Macuata, Fiji)', in G.R. Clark *et al.* (eds) *The Archaeology of Lapita Dispersal in Oceania*, Terra Australis 17, Canberra: Pandanus Books.

Valentin, F., Spriggs, M., Bedford, S., *et al.* (2009) 'Une analyse diachronique des pratiques funéraires préhistoriques du centre du Vanuatu (région Efate-Shepherd)', *Journal de la Société des Océanistes*, 128: 39–52.

Ward, G.K. (1979) 'Prehistoric settlement and economy of a tropical small island environment: the Banks Islands, Insular Melanesia', unpublished PhD thesis, The Australian National University, Canberra.

Ward, G.K. and Houghton, P. (1988) 'The Mele burials: salvage excavation and skeletal analysis', unpublished manuscript.

——(1991) 'The Mele burials (Vanuatu): salvage excavations and biological relationships', *Indo-Pacific Prehistory Association Bulletin*, 11: 229–35.

White, T. and Folkens, P. (2005) *The Human Bone Manual*, Boston: Elsevier.

Willis, A. and Tayles, N. (2009) 'Field anthropology: application to burial contexts in prehistoric Southeast Asia', *Journal of Archaeological Science*, 3: 547–54.

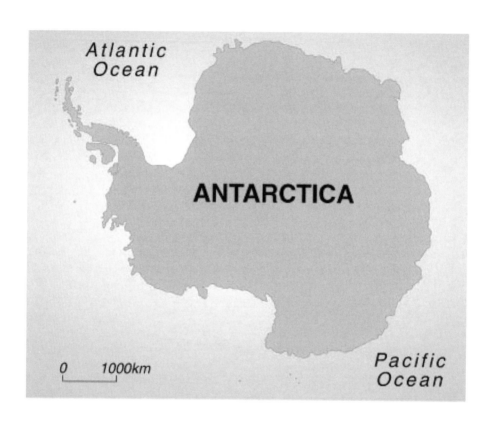

Antarctica

Michael Pearson

INTRODUCTION

Antarctica is unique in that the total history of human occupation of the continent is more or less known, and nearly all human burials there are of known persons. It is also unique in its administrative context, not being governed in the whole or in part by any single nation, but collegiately through an international agreement, the Antarctic Treaty. In this chapter I will focus on Antarctica as defined in the Antarctic Treaty – the area beneath 60 degrees south latitude. This encompasses the massive Antarctic continent and its nearby islands, which comprise an area considerably larger than the whole of Europe (14 million sq km compared with 10 million sq km). The various peri-Antarctic islands that litter the Southern Ocean north of 60 degrees south (Auckland, Bouvetoya, Campbell, Crozet, Gough, Heard and McDonald, Kerguelen, Macquarie, Prince Edward and Marion, South Georgia, and South Sandwich) are not dealt with here as they are all acknowledged as the territory of individual countries, whose domestic legal systems automatically apply to them.

The chapter outlines the history of human occupation of Antarctica, the surprisingly limited extent of human burials there, and the legal regime that would be applied in the case of the disturbance or removal of human remains.

HUMAN REMAINS IN ANTARCTICA: A BRIEF HISTORY

Antarctica has a very short human history. There is no evidence of human contact with or occupation of any part of Antarctica in prehistoric times. The most accessible part of Antarctica (the South Shetland Islands) is nearly 900 km south of Cape Horn across the Drake Passage, notorious for its severe weather and rough seas. It is extremely unlikely that a crossing would have been possible in traditional Amerindian watercraft, and, one would have to ask, for what purpose would such a voyage into icy seas be made?

The great British navigator James Cook and his crew were the first humans known to have crossed 60 degrees south latitude into what we now call Antarctica, in 1773. Cook sailed even further south, crossing the Antarctic Circle (66 degrees 33 minutes and 39 seconds south) three times and going on to 71 degrees and 10 minutes without seeing land (Beaglehole 1974, 315–18, 365).

Cook's journals reported the sighting of many seals at South Georgia Island in the far South Atlantic Ocean, triggering the development of a global sealing industry. The ship's captains involved in sealing were very active in extending the exploration in high latitudes in search of further prey. The first confirmed sighting of land south of 60 degrees south was by Captain William Smith in 1819 at the South Shetland Islands, just off the Antarctic mainland, leading to the area being visited and exploited by many sealers between 1819 and 1827 (Campbell 2000; Pearson and Stehberg 2006). Sealers died while working in the South Shetlands and were buried there, the first human remains on an entire continent. Exploration and scientific expeditions to Antarctica also followed in Cook's wake, starting with Bellinghausen's in 1819–21 (probably the first to sight the Antarctic mainland), and over the next two decades the expeditions of Foster, Weddell, Biscoe, Dumont d'Urville, Balleny, Wilkes and Ross and others followed (see Riffenburgh 2007; Gurney 1997, 2000; Howgego 2004). Some of these expeditions landed on Antarctic ice floes or land, but none buried their dead ashore.

Most readers are probably more familiar with the later land exploration of the continent during the so-called 'Heroic Era', which is generally taken to extend from 1895 to 1917. This was the period of the national expeditions of Scott, Nansen, Shackleton, Mawson, Borchgrevink, Nordenskjold, de Gerlache, von Drygalski, Filchner, Shirase, Charcot, Bruce and Bull, when men (and they were all men) for the first time voluntarily wintered on the frozen continent (though two sealing parties had done so involuntarily in 1820 and 1876). A number of members of these expeditions died, and were buried either on moving ice shelves or on land (see Riffenburgh 2007; Howgego 2006) (Table 60.1).

Whalers using fast steam whale-chasers were, from the 1890s onwards, able for the first time to chase whales in the Antarctic seas, operating from large factory ships moored in safe anchorages. Shore-based whaling factories were subsequently established in the South Shetland Islands (as well as on the sub-Antarctic South Georgia and Kerguelen Islands), operating at Deception Island in the South Shetlands 1912–38, and at Signy Island in the South Orkney Islands 1920–26 (see Tønnessen and Johnsen 1982). Small villages were established for the workers at the whaling stations, and those who died there were buried in adjacent cemeteries.

From the 1920s the exploration of Antarctica shifted, in part, to the air, with bases being set up by Richard Byrd and others to support inland flights. Britain, the USA, Australia and other nations carried out research and exploration in the 1930s and 1940s, and territorial claims began to be made over slices of Antarctica. But the real boom in human involvement with the continent started with the International Geophysical Year (IGY) in 1957–58, when 67 countries participated in scientific programmes and 12 nations constructed permanent scientific stations. The success of the IGY, together with the desire to deal peacefully with competing national territorial claims and to avoid Cold War disputes over the area, led to the development of the Antarctic Treaty, signed in 1959 by the 12 most active IGY nations (Argentina, Australia, Belgium, Chile, France, Japan, New Zealand, Norway, South Africa, the United Kingdom, the United States of America, and the former USSR). The Treaty has now been signed by 46 countries, leading to the establishment of over 50 scientific bases. Early in this modern phase of Antarctica's history a number of people died and were buried near scientific bases (Table 60.2), but in more recent decades the repatriation of bodies to their home country for burial has become standard policy for all countries operating there.

THE CONTEXT OF HUMAN REMAINS IN ANTARCTICA

In many cases the bodies of those killed in Antarctica were not buried. The bodies of those who fell down crevasses, or who died in moving pack ice along the shore, or from boats or planes at

Table 60.1 Human remains/burials in Antarctica up to the 1920s (not including bodies not recovered)

Location	Date	Skeletal/Burial details	Context
Cape Shirreff, Livingston Island, South Shetlands	1820s	Skull and other skeletal remains found on beach. Believed to date to the 1820s	Remains of an Amerindian female, believed to have been with sealers in the 1820s
Byers Peninsula, Livingston Island, South Shetlands	1820s	Burial site, believed to be 1820s, at Stackpole 2 site. The grave is a roughly rectangular collection of whale bones and stones on a moraine ridge behind a sealing beach	Located by Zarankin and Senatore, and thought to be a grave site, but not investigated archaeologically to test this
South Shetland Islands	1820–1880	Several burials of seamen and sealers reported, but burial sites not yet located	Archaeological survey of the islands is continuing and may locate further graves or skeletal material
Cape Adare	1899	Nicolai Hansen died on 14 October 1899 at Cape Adare, and following his dying request he was buried on the top of Cape Adare, in a grave excavated with the help of dynamite. A large boulder marks the head of the grave, with a cross and plaque attached, and the grave is outlined in white stones	Hansen was a zoologist on Borchgrevink's Southern Cross Expedition (1899–1900), the first party to intentionally overwinter in Antarctica
Paulet Island, Antarctic Peninsula	1903	Grave of Ole Kristian Wennersgaard, who died of heart disease 7 June 1903, aged 22. The grave is marked by a large mound of stone, and a wooden cross (now collapsed)	Due to the crushing of their ship in the Antarctic, the relief party for the Swedish Nordenskjöld expedition had to build a stone survival hut on Paulet Island. One crew member died, but the rest were rescued the following summer
Laurie Island cemetery, Scotia Bay, South Orkney Islands	1903–1959	Seven graves in a cemetery, the first being Alan Ramsay, ship's engineer, who died 6 August 1903. The graves are marked by mounds of stones and wooden crosses	The cemetery is at a weather station/scientific base, Ormond House, established by the Scottish Antarctic Expedition under W.S. Bruce in 1903
Whaler's Bay cemetery, Deception Island, South Shetlands	1908–1953	Cemetery for Norwegian whaling station, then British scientific base. About 40 Norwegian whalers and one British scientist buried there	Cemetery swept away by volcanic mud slide in 1969. Two crosses retrieved but all burials destroyed by scouring
Ross Ice Shelf	1912	The five members of the Scott party died on their return from the South Pole. Scott, Wilson and Bowers were buried in their tent on Ross Ice Shelf by a search party. Evans had been buried by Scott's party earlier, and Oates died on the shelf surface	All sign of the Scott party grave was buried by snow accumulation within a few years, and its location is no longer known

(Continued on new page)

Table 60.1 (continued)

Location	Date	Skeletal/Burial details	Context
Ross Ice Shelf	1916	Member of Shackleton's Ross Sea Party, the Reverend Arnold Patrick Spencer-Smith, died 9 March 1916. He was buried in the wrapped tent in a grave on the ice shelf, and a cross erected over it. The grave was quickly buried in snow and lost to sight	Spencer-Smith died during a desperately undersupplied depot-laying journey. The grave was quickly buried in snow and lost to sight. Two other members of the party died on sea ice and their bodies were never discovered
Signy whaling station, South Orkney Islands	1920–1926	Cemetery for whalers who died at the station. Five modern crosses exist, but total number of buried is not clear	Short-lived whaling station

sea, were often not able to be recovered. For example, of the 31 people who died on the British Falkland Islands Dependencies Survey (FIDS) and the subsequent British Antarctic Survey (BAS) expeditions between 1948 and 2003, the bodies of 21 could not be recovered, one was buried at sea, one was returned to Britain for burial, and only eight were buried in Antarctica (British Antarctic Survey 2009). Of the 17 people to have died on Australian expeditions since 1948, five are buried in Antarctica. It would appear that the bodies of all US nationals dying in Antarctica have been repatriated.

Bodies buried on moving ice shelves, such as the huge Ross Ice Shelf (Scott and Shackleton's 'Ross Ice Barrier'), have been progressively buried by snow and have moved north with the ice flow over the years, so they can no longer be located. For example, in 1912 the three last members of Scott's party (Scott, Bowers and Wilson) died in their tent on the return from the South Pole some 150 miles from the hut at Hut Point. Party member Edgar Evans had died earlier and had been buried in the ice shelf by the others, and 'Titus' Oates had walked away from the camp to a lonely death. When a search party eight months later found Scott's tent with the three dead men in it, they recovered their diaries and some personal effects, but left the bodies where they lay in the tent and built a snow cairn over it. Within a few years the snow level had built up over the cairn and their 'graves' were absorbed into the flat landscape of the ice shelf, gradually moving north.

No human skeletal remains have so far been found in excavated archaeological contexts in Antarctica. The oldest located skeletal material consists of a skull and parts of a femur found on the surface at Yamana Beach on Cape Shirreff, Livingston Island, in the South Shetland Islands by Chilean researchers. The skull was found in 1985, part of a femur was found nearby in 1987, and another in close proximity in 1991. A further archaeological survey was carried out at the site in 1993, but no further skeletal remains were found. The original samples were dated to approximately 175 years BP, and it was hypothesized, based on location, condition and context, that the fragments belonged to a single individual. DNA analysis was planned to determine whether this was the case, but results have not been seen by the present author (Torres 1992, 1999; Constantinescu and Torres 1995). The remains were interpreted after analysis as those of an Amerindian female aged in her 20s, brought to the site by sealers in the 1820s (Stehberg and Lucero 1996; Stehberg 2003).

The earliest burials, of sealers operating in the South Shetland Islands in the 1820s and later, are sometimes recorded in ships' journals. One such burial was discovered by Lieutenant Kendall (or Kendal) of HMS *Chanticleer* on Deception Island in 1829. Kendall's party found a

Table 60.2 Burials in Antarctica 1948–2008 (this table is not claimed to be definitive, and also does not include ashes returned to Antarctica for burial)

Name and circumstance of death	Date of death	Where buried
Oliver Burd and Michael C. Green. Killed in a hut fire	9 Nov 1948	Graves beneath cairns in the vicinity of the original hut, Hope Bay (former British base), now near Esperanza Station (Argentina)
Eric Platt, died of heart attack	10 Nov 1948	Grave at former British base at Admiralty Bay, King George Island. The cemetery, near Ferraz Base (Brazil), has three graves: two British and one Brazilian (died 1990)
Arthur H. Farrant	17 Nov 1953	Buried in whaler's cemetery, Deception Island, but cemetery destroyed by volcanic mud slide in 1969
Alan Sharman, fractured skull following a fall on rocks when out walking	23 April 1959	Grave at former British base at Admiralty Bay, King George Island
Hartley Robinson	7 July 1959	Buried on hill adjacent to Wilkes Station (former Australian base)
Walter Soto	1959	Last burial in the Scotia Bay cemetery on Laurie Island, South Orkneys (Argentinian base)
Eight Soviet, Czechoslovakian and GDR citizens, members of Soviet Antarctic Expeditions, killed by a fire at Mirnyy Station	3 August 1960	Cemetery on Buromskiy Island, near Mirnyy (USSR base)
Roger Filer, fell from cliff while doing ornithology work	13 Feb 1961	Grave on Pantomime Point, near Signy (South Orkney Islands) (British base)
Robert White	18 Oct 1963	Buried at West Arm overlooking Mawson Station (Australian base)
John F. Noel and Thomas J. Allan, died of exposure whilst sitting out a storm in a snow hole during field trip	June 1966	Graves within large stone cairn, above ground, on Flagstaff Hill, near the former British Stonington Island base
Reginald N. Sullivan, died during a field trip	22 July 1968	Buried on hill adjacent to Wilkes Station (former Australian base)
Kenneth Wilson	18 August 1972	Buried at West Arm overlooking Mawson Station (Australian base)
Geoffrey Cameron	24 March 1974	Buried at West Arm overlooking Mawson Station (Australian base)
Wlodzimierz Puchalski, filmmaker, died at Arctowski station	19 Jan 1979	Buried on a hill to the south of Arctowski station on King George Island (Polish base)
Name not available	1990	Brazilian expeditioner, killed in 1990, in the cemetery at Admiralty Bay, near Ferraz Base (Brazil)

number of relics of sealing parties, and the well-preserved body of a sailor in a rough coffin on the shores of the island's caldera harbour (Kendal 1831; Savours and McConnell 2007: 264). Kendall reported the discovery thus:

> Having observed a mound on the hill immediately above this cove, and thinking that something of interest might be deposited there, I opened it; and found a rude coffin,

the rotten state of which bespoke its having been long consigned to the earth, but the body had undergone scarcely any decomposition. The legs were doubled up, and it was dressed in the jacket and cap of a sailor, but neither they nor the countenance were similar to those of an Englishman. The stones were replaced, and a post erected, with a notice, in hopes of protecting this humble monument from further intrusion.

Kendal 1831: 66

The 14-year-old midshipman, Joseph Henry Kay, who accompanied Kendall, added that the coffin was discovered after they had 'cleared away the surface for 4 or 5 feet', and that it contained 'the body of a man in a red woollen shirt, in a high state of preservation, the features being very little distorted by time or decay' (Savours and McConnell 2007: 317). This description would seem to echo the condition of the remains of men from Franklin's last expedition, excavated on Beechey Island on the Northwest Passage in 1984 (Beattie and Geiger 1989).

Another burial site is shown on a rough chart of Blythe Bay, Desolation Island, one of the smaller islands in the South Shetland archipelago, drawn by the British sealer Captain Robert Fildes in 1821. This indicates a site located near a landing place on the island and labelled as 'Cooper's grave', but it is not clear if the grave was that of the ship's cooper or a seaman named Cooper (Fildes 1821).

In 1875 the Stonington (USA) sealer William Henry Appleman buried a crewman of the *Thomas Hunt*, who had been killed in a fall from the rigging, in a lonely grave marked only with a cairn of shingle rock on Low Island, the southernmost of the South Shetlands (Busch 1985: 210).

To date only one possible sealer's grave has been relocated in modern times. This is a site marked by a roughly rectangular collection of whale bones and stones on a moraine ridge behind a sealing beach on the Byers Peninsula, Livingston Island, and named 'Stackpole 2' by archaeologists Zarankin and Senatore (2007: 65) (Figure 60.1). Further work to correlate sealers' journals with surveyed sites may identify further graves in the future. Later graves of the whaling era, the Heroic era of exploration, and those associated with the later scientific bases, are usually of people whose names are known. Many have grave markers and memorials with their names on them (see Tables 60.1 and 60.2).

With the coming of the exploration parties of the Heroic Era, graves became memorials to expedition dead, and the locations of all graves are known and the occupants named. Other memorials were erected in memory of those whose bodies could not be recovered, or, as in the case of the Scott party and a member of Shackleton's Ross Sea party, who were buried on the distant moving ice shelf. The first Heroic Era grave, and the first named grave in Antarctica, is that of Nicolai Hansen at Cape Adare. Hansen was a Norwegian zoologist on Carsten Borchgrevink's Southern Cross Expedition (1899–1900), the first party to overwinter intentionally in Antarctica. Hansen died on 14 October 1899, and, in compliance with his dying request, was buried (with great effort) in a grave excavated with the use of dynamite on the high top of Cape Adare. A large boulder marks the head of the grave, with the grave itself outlined in white quartz stones. A cross and plaque are attached to the boulder (Figure 60.2).

In 1903 a member of another expedition was buried, this time a Swedish seaman, Ole Kristian Wennersgaard, a member of Otto Nordenskjöld's shipwrecked relief party which built a stone survival shelter on Paulet Island, off the tip of the Antarctic Peninsula. Wennersgaard died of heart disease on 7 June 1903, aged 22, and was buried some distance from the hut, a large stone cairn being built over his grave before his comrades were rescued the following summer (Figure 60.3).

Figure 60.1 Antarctica: Stackpole 2 grave

In the same year, 1903, the first death occurred at the Scottish research station set up by W.S. Bruce at Laurie Island in the South Orkney Islands. Alan Ramsay, the engineer of Bruce's ship the *Scotia*, was buried at the Scotia Bay cemetery, the first of seven burials to occur there, the last being in 1959.

The cemetery of the Norwegian whaling station, Hektor, on Whalers Bay, Deception Island in the South Shetlands, was used during the operation of the station from 1912 to 1938, though the first burial there was that of Nokard Davidsen, captain of the Newfoundland whale factory ship *Sobraon*, who fell overboard and drowned in 1908 (Headland 1989: 240). The cemetery was last used in 1953 for the burial of Arthur Farrant, who worked at the British scientific base that subsequently occupied the site. Some 40 whalers were buried at Hektor, making it the largest cemetery in Antarctica before it was destroyed in 1969 by a volcanic mud slide that scoured out the site and, it appears, deposited all the graves into the harbour. Two timber grave crosses now seen on the site appear to have been retrieved and re-erected adjacent to the original cemetery (Figure 60.4). It is possible that skeletal material from the cemetery was

Figure 60.2 Antarctica: Hanson's grave and cross

redistributed in disturbed deposits between the cemetery and the harbour, and might be encountered in future archaeological excavations, or might be exposed from the soil by erosion. Another cemetery was set up at the whaling station on Signy Island in the South Orkneys, which operated from 1920 to 1926 (see Tønnessen and Johnsen 1982). Five modern crosses mark the site today, but it is unclear how many were actually buried there.

The only burials in Antarctica between 1916 and 1946 appear to have been those at the two whaling stations, and at the Scotia Bay cemetery on Laurie Island. After the Second World

Figure 60.3 Antarctica: Paulet Island grave

Figure 60.4 Antarctica: Deception Island grave

War, as scientific and exploration activities built up, and particularly after the IGY programme in 1957–58, the number of casualties in Antarctica increased. Where bodies could be recovered they were either buried in marked graves or, in more recent years, repatriated, and it is unlikely that any will be studied in an archaeological context in the near future (see Table 60.2). A partial listing of Antarctic deaths is given by Stewart (1990, I: 243–44). Graves and cemeteries are located at several active and abandoned scientific bases of the post-Second World War era, including Mawson (Australia), Wilkes (USA and Australia), Base G Admiralty Bay (UK), Hope Bay (UK), Stonington (UK), Signy (UK), Arctowski (Poland) and Mirnyy (USSR) (Figures 60.5 and 60.6).

The largest loss of life in Antarctica occurred on 29 November 1979, when an Air New Zealand DC10 crashed into Mount Erebus, with the loss of 257 lives. All the bodies were retrieved and returned to New Zealand.

LEGAL CONTROLS OVER HUMAN REMAINS IN ANTARCTICA

The Antarctic legal system, like its human history, is unique. While parts of Antarctica were claimed as territory by seven nations during the first half of the 20th century (these being Argentina, Australia, the UK, Chile, France, New Zealand and Norway), no part of Antarctica

Figure 60.5 Antarctica: Crosses at Hope Bay 2

Figure 60.6 Antarctica: Graves, Wilkes 1986

was 'settled' by any nation, and claims of sovereignty were not developed and recognized internationally. Tension over the overlapping claims of the UK, Argentina and Chile grew during and immediately after the Second World War, when there was a series of belligerent actions such as the tit-for-tat demolitions of weather stations by the three nations in the South Shetland Islands, just off the Antarctic Peninsula. The growing heat was taken out of this territorial posturing in 1948, when Chile, Argentina and the UK notified each other that:

> in the present circumstances they [foresaw] no need to send warships south of Latitude 60° S during the 1948–49 Antarctic season, apart, of course, from routine movements such as have been customary for a number of years.
>
> *Headland 1989: 323*

This agreement was renewed annually through to 1956–57, and was subsequently made redundant by the parties signing the Antarctic Treaty.

The Antarctic Treaty

The Antarctic Treaty was signed in 1959 following the IGY, and came into force in 1961. The Treaty and documents relating to its operation are to be found on the website of the Scientific Committee on Antarctic Research (Scientific Committee on Antarctic Research 2009). The Treaty is a unique exercise in international cooperation, which sets aside or 'freezes' territorial claims for the duration of the Treaty, so no nation is recognized as having territorial rights on the continent, but existing claims are not disputed, and new ones cannot be made while the Treaty is in force. There is no 'Antarctic government' and no 'Antarctic citizens', but, rather, a transient population of scientists and workers who are governed by the laws of their own nation, and, by mutual agreement, by the conditions of the Antarctic Treaty. In the area south of 60 degrees south latitude, the Antarctic Treaty:

- specifies the area is to be used only for peaceful purposes and bans military activity such as manoeuvres, establishment of fortifications or military bases, and weapons testing;

- guarantees freedom of scientific investigation and cooperation as had been established during the IGY;
- requires the free exchange of plans for scientific programmes and personnel between countries, and scientific information and results;
- does not recognize, dispute, or establish territorial sovereignty claims, and specifies that acts undertaken during the operation of the Treaty are not to be used as a basis for asserting or refuting subsequent territorial claims, and no new claims are to be asserted while the treaty is in force;
- prohibits nuclear explosions or the disposal of radioactive wastes;
- specifies free access, including aerial observation, by any Treaty nation to any area and the open inspection of all stations, installations, and equipment, and requires advance notice of all activities undertaken by Treaty parties;
- allows for jurisdiction over individuals in Antarctica by their own states;
- requires that disputes be settled by the parties concerned through consultation and negotiation or, ultimately, by the International Court of Justice.

The Consultative Parties (those with active operations in Antarctica, which currently number 28) meet at least every two years to agree recommendations, allowing the nature of the treaty activities to evolve over time and to deal with issues as they arise. The recommendations of the Consultative Meetings become binding upon the ratification of the Consultative Parties, and are implemented through individual national legislation of the parties that are signatories of the Treaty (currently 46). A key set of recommendation, the Protocol on Environmental Protection (the Madrid Protocol), was agreed in 1991, coming into force on 14 January 1998 after delays in ratification by Japan and Russia. The Madrid Protocol establishes rigorous guidelines for, among other things, area protection and management, environmental impact assessment, conservation of flora and fauna, waste disposal and management, and prevention of marine pollution.

In 1972 the Consultative Parties agreed a process for the listing of Antarctic Historic Sites and Monuments, the protection of which was to be recognized by all parties. This list was compiled with no systematic inventory process and with no clear statement as to why the places should be considered historic. The list now numbers 76 places, including six of the graves/cemeteries detailed above.

The Madrid Protocol's Annex V sets up a system of Antarctic Specially Protected Areas (ASPA), and Antarctic Specially Managed Areas (ASMA), which can be used, among other things, to protect historic sites or monuments from unauthorized disturbance, either individually or as part of larger natural areas. Any Party, the Scientific Committee for Antarctic Research (SCAR) or the Commission for the Conservation of Antarctic Marine Living Resources (CAMLR) may propose an area for designation as an ASPA or ASMA by submitting a proposed Management Plan to the Antarctic Treaty Consultative Meeting. Some sealing sites in the South Shetlands are included within ASPAs (but see Pearson *et al.* 2009 for current problems with that system).

The application of legal regimes

The operation of the Antarctic Treaty means that no one nation is automatically responsible for the management of particular historic sites in Antarctica. In the case of the Heroic Era huts, being the Borchgrevink, Nordenskjöld, Mawson, Scott (x2) and Shackleton huts, the buildings themselves are the property of particular nations, and that largely determines who has responsibility. The same applies to later Antarctic bases and related field stations, and a number of countries, for example, have been undertaking clean-up activities at active and former bases to comply with the requirements of the Madrid Protocol. However, in the case of the 19th-century sealing sites in the South Shetland Islands, no national claims of ownership have been made for the individual sites or objects, and the Antarctic Treaty sets aside the overlapping claims of sovereignty over the islands maintained by the UK, Chile and Argentina. While archaeological research has been carried out by each of these countries, no serious conservation efforts have yet been initiated in the South Shetlands, and it remains to be seen if such work will be initiated by any of the Treaty parties independently, and whether other parties might object to (and hence veto) such unilateral work as overtly strengthening sovereignty claims.

The successful operation of the Antarctic Treaty regime relies on the mutual implementation of Antarctic Treaty Consultative Meeting (ATCM) recommendations, cooperative activities on the continent, the diplomatic setting aside of sometimes conflicting territorial claims, and the mechanisms for open inspection of national activities. Often, solutions to legal issues are negotiated ones.

The complexity of the legal systems applying in Antarctica can be seen by looking at one of the countries active in the area. Australia has been active in the Antarctic since 1911, and has enacted laws predating the Antarctic Treaty that still have application to Australia's administration of its activities. The Australian Antarctic Territory Act 1954 establishes a relatively complex legal regime for the area of the Australian Antarctic Territory (AAT), claimed by Australia but in abeyance under the Antarctic Treaty. The laws that apply in the AAT are drawn, in order of priority, from the following (Australian Antarctic Division. 2009):

- Commonwealth (Australian) laws which expressly apply to the AAT;
- Commonwealth Ordinances made specifically for the AAT;
- the laws, other than the criminal laws, of the Australian Capital Territory in so far as they are applicable to the AAT; and
- the criminal laws of the Jervis Bay Territory in so far as they are applicable to the AAT.

Key Australian legislation applying expressly to the AAT includes the Antarctic Treaty Act 1960 (giving force to the original Treaty obligations), the Antarctic Treaty (Environment Protection) Act 1980 (giving force to the Madrid Protocol), and the Antarctic Marine Living Resources Conservation Act 1981 (giving force to the Convention for the Conservation of Antarctic Marine Living Resources 1980).

In the case of human remains, the Australian Capital Territory (ACT) Coroners Act 1997 and the Criminal Code Harmonization Act 2005, which apply to Antarctica, require the reporting of a death to the police or coroner as soon as is practical after becoming aware of the death. This law is common to all Australian jurisdictions, and is applied, for example, when human skeletal material is excavated from or is found exposed by erosion from an archaeological deposit. Once it is determined that the remains are not modern, they are released for archaeological or indigenous cultural purposes (the latter usually being reburial).

Within the Treaty area, Australian law can apply to the actions of Australian citizens and Australian legal entities anywhere on the continent (and similarly the laws of other Treaty members apply to the citizens and activities of those countries), but such application would be a matter of diplomatic negotiation with other Treaty parties if they also had interest in a case, as is specified in the Treaty.

The control over archaeological work in Antarctica lies either with the nation owning or controlling the place being investigated, or in other localities with the nation for whom the researcher is undertaking the surveys or excavations. In the case, for example, of the Heroic Era huts or active or abandoned research bases, the physical remains are usually owned by a government, and it is that nation's archaeological control regime that would apply. In all other situations the nation supporting the research is expected to apply its own control mechanisms to parties whose activities it is sanctioning. In the case, for example, of the Chilean Museum's archaeological surveys and excavations in the South Shetland Islands, the lead archaeologist has to obtain permission from the Consejo de Monumentos Nacionales (National Monument Council), and all historical and archaeological remains and sites are protected under the Ley de Monumentos Nacionales no. 17.288. The National Monument Council issues the permit for the Museum to house and conserve returned artefacts and materials in the National Natural History Museum. This system applied to the human remains recovered at Cape Shirreff, referred to earlier.

In many countries the tightest archaeological controls are at the state/prefecture level, rather than resting with the national government. In these cases the nation undertaking or supporting archaeological research would be expected to issue a research permit relevant to the research that would guarantee that professional standards were applied and that artefacts recovered were lodged with a relevant public institution. Australia, for example, has no legislation at the national level to specifically control archaeological research, although at nationally registered historic sites (such as Mawson's Huts Historic Site in Antarctica), archaeology is coincidentally controlled through its more general heritage legislation. The Australian Government's Australian Antarctic Division (AAD) maintains a register of artefacts returned from Antarctica, and ensures that they are lodged with either the AAD or a public museum. Where specific protective requirements apply to a site under either the Australian National or Commonwealth Heritage Registers or an Antarctic Special Protected or Managed Area status under the Antarctic Treaty, archaeological permits would be issued in the context of the Management Plans that have to be developed for those sites. In all other situations the general requirement of the national environment legislation (The Environment Protection and Biodiversity Conservation Act 1999) would apply, that requires the Commonwealth to take no action that would diminish the values of the environment (which is defined as including heritage places) unless there was no 'feasible and prudent alternative', in which case any impact must be minimized. As archaeology would be an action that could diminish the heritage values of a site, the AAD is responsible for ensuring that permitted activities are professionally undertaken and the artefacts properly curated.

An interesting case that shows the complexity of the legal regime in Antarctica, and may have some bearing on how human remains might be dealt with in the future, is that of Australian Dr Rodney Marks, who died in May 2000 while wintering at the American Amundsen-Scott South Pole Station. The American base moves constantly with the ice, and is not actually at the pole but within the New Zealand-claimed sector known as the Ross Dependency. Dr Marks's death was attributed to natural causes by the medical staff of the US National Science Foundation and Raytheon, the contractor managing the base. However, as the deceased was not an American citizen, the body was released to the New Zealand coroner, presumably on the basis of New Zealand's claim to administrative control over matters not resolved by other nations in its 'territory'. Australia appears to have left the issue to New Zealand's coronial processes. An autopsy conducted in New Zealand indicated death from methanol poisoning, and an investigation was commenced. The coronial inquest dragged on for several years, and the coroner reported in 2008 that he found it unlikely that methanol had been ingested knowingly, but that there was also no evidence that it had been knowingly administered by another person (*ABC News* [Australia] 2008). The police investigating officer told the coroner in 2006 that the National Science Foundation and the contractor had consistently failed to cooperate with the investigation. The question left floating was whether the jurisdiction to determine the cause of death, and to take subsequent legal action, was the country running the base concerned or the country claiming territorial rights to the region. As one newspaper report put it, 'New Zealand considers the US base part of Antarctica's Ross Dependency, which it claims. But the US does not recognize the claim' (*Daily Telegraph* [UK]: 14 Dec 2006; *New Zealand Herald*: 14 Dec 2006). The coroner is reported as stating that 'the facts of the case and partial outcomes point to an urgent need to set comprehensive rules of investigation and accountability for deaths in Antarctica on a fair and open basis' (*ABC News* [Australia] 2008).

This case raises a number of questions relevant to considering how human remains identified in archaeological contexts might be dealt with in Antarctica. Who would have coronial control over the body, say, of a 19th-century sealer excavated in the South Shetlands? It may be possible to determine through context and historical documents whether the sealer was a US or UK citizen, but the site would be in an area claimed equally by the UK, Argentina and Chile. If the body was of an American, removed from an American sealing campsite, might the USA dispute through the treaty mechanism the right of an Argentinian or Chilean (or British, Spanish or Australian) archaeologist to take the remains to their own country for examination and storage? Would the researcher have to get clearance through the coronial system of their own country to legitimize their keeping the remains?

CONCLUSION

The answer to these questions will only be provided through the resolution of actual cases. This situation has not yet arisen in Antarctica, but undoubtedly it will, and the solution will probably be one reached with logic and international good will through the Antarctic Treaty system. But, as the Rodney Marks case demonstrates, the unique legal system applying to Antarctica allows for ambiguities that might only be resolved through trial and error.

ACKNOWLEDGEMENTS

I would like to acknowledge the input of a number of colleagues in developing the overview of burials in Antarctica: Michael Morrison (UK), Ruben Stehberg (Chile), Neville Ritchie (NZ), Elspeth Wishart (Australia), Susan Barr (Norway), Paul Chaplin (NZ), and Bruce Hull (Australia) all gave freely of their knowledge of burial sites and of the legal issues in Antarctica, for which I am most grateful. They cannot be blamed for what I have done with their information and advice.

BIBLIOGRAPHY

ABC News [Australia] (2008) *Broadcast 24 Sept 2008*. Transcript available online at www.abc.net.au (accessed 15 March 2010).

Australian Antarctic Division (2009) *Antarctic International Law*. Available online at www.aad.gov.au/default.asp?casid=3358 (accessed 2 February 2009).

Beaglehole, J.C. (1974) *The Life of Captain James Cook*, Stanford, Ca: Stanford University Press.

Beattie, O. and Geiger, J. (1989) *Frozen in Time: The Fate of the Franklin Expedition*, London: Grafton Books.

British Antarctic Survey (2009) *Deaths of FIDS and BAS staff in Antarctica*. Available online at www.antarctica.ac.uk/basclub/deaths.html> (accessed 2 February 2009).

Busch, B.C. (1985) *The War Against the Seals; A History of the North American Seal Fishery*, Montreal: McGill-Queen's University Press.

Campbell, R.J. (2000) *The Discovery of the South Shetland Islands: The Voyage of the Brig Williams 1819–1820 as Recorded in Contemporary Documents and the Journal of Midshipman C.W. Poynter*, London: Hakluyt Society.

Constantinescu, F. and Torres, D. (1995) 'Análisis bioantropológico de un cráneo humano hallado en cabo Shirreff, isla Livingston, Antártica', *Serie Científica del Instituto Antártico Chileno*, 45: 89–99.

Fildes, R. (1821) *Remarks Made During a Voyage to New South Shetland*, [UK] Public Records Office Series: Adm. 55, Admiralty and Secretariat. Log books etc. Supplementary, Series II, explorations: PRO AJCP reel 1599, piece 143.

Gurney, A. (1997) *Below the Convergence: Voyages Toward Antarctica 1699–1839*, New York: W.W. Norton & Co.

——(2000) *The Race to the White Continent: Voyages to the Antarctica*, New York: W.W. Norton & Co.

Headland, R.K. (1989) *Chronological List of Antarctic Expeditions and Related Historical Events*, London: Thornton Butterworth.

Howgego, R.J. (2004) *Encyclopedia of Exploration: 1800–1850*, Sydney: Hordern House.

——(2006) *Encyclopedia of Exploration: 1850–1940 the Oceans, Islands and Polar Regions*, Sydney: Hordern House.

Kendal, E.N. (1831) 'Account of the Island of Deception, one of the New Shetland Isles', *Journal of the Royal Geographical Society of London*, 1: 62–66.

Pearson, M. and Stehberg, R. (2006) 'Nineteenth century sealing sites on Rugged Island, South Shetland Island', *Polar Record*, 42: 335–47.

Pearson, M., Stehberg, R., Zarankín, A., *et al.* (2009) 'Conserving the oldest historic sites in the Antarctic: the challenges in managing the sealing sites in the South Shetland Islands', *Polar Record* 45: 1–8.

Riffenburgh, B. (2007) *Encyclopedia of the Antarctic*, London: Routledge.

Savours, A. and McConnell, A. (2007) 'Journal kept by midshipman Joseph Henry Kay during the voyage of HMS Chanticleer, 1828–31', in H.K. Beals *et al.* (eds) *Four Travel Journals: the Americas, Antarctica and Africa, 1775–1874*, London: The Hakluyt Society.

Scientific Committee on Antarctic Research (2009) *Antarctic Treaty system: an introduction*. Available online at www.scar.org/treaty (accessed 2 February 2009).

Stehberg, R. (2003) *Arqueología histórica antártica: Aborígenes sudamericanos en los mares subantárticos en el siglo XIX*, Santiago de Chile: Centro de Investigaciones Diego Barros Arana.

Stehberg, R.L. and Lucero, V. (1996) 'Excavaciones arqueológicas en playa Yámana, cabo Shirreff, isla Livingston, Shetland del Sur, Antártica', *Serie Científica del Instituto Antártico Chileno*, 46: 59–81.

Stewart, J. (1990) *Antarctica: An Encyclopedia*, Jefferson, NC: McFarland & Company.

Tønnessen, J.T. and Johnsen, A.O. (1982) *The History of Modern Whaling*, Canberra: C. Hurst & Co. and Australian National University.

Torres, D. (1992) '¿Cráneo indígena en cabo Shirreff? un estudio en desarrollo', *Boletín Antártico Chileno*, 11: 2–6.

——(1999) 'Observations on ca.175-year old human remains from Antarctica (Cape Shirreff, Livingston Island, South Shetlands)', *International Journal of Circumpolar Health*, 58: 72–83.

Zarankin, A. and Senatore, M.X. (2007) *Historias de un pasado en blanco: arqueología histórica antártica*. Belo Horizonte: Argumentum.

Concluding remarks

Nicholas Márquez-Grant and Linda Fibiger

As editors, we hope that this volume has achieved its main aim to provide a starting point for anyone wanting to undertake research on or work with human remains outside their country of origin, and to offer insights into different systems and practices within the discipline of physical anthropology.

Biological and physical anthropology have a long tradition on the European continent in particular, starting with studies of 'race' and the origins of man mainly during the 19th century, as well as seeing the beginnings of some extensive skeletal collections. A common trend has been noted with regard to the type of research questions and research methods (e.g., craniometry) prevalent in the early studies, the development of increasingly more varied palaeopathological studies, the consideration of the biocultural approach and the variety of new biomolecular techniques (such as stable isotope analysis) applied to many studies today. The wealth of bibliographical data included in this volume may also be of benefit to those researchers seeking comparative material, and the mention of a considerable number of skeletal collections may stimulate future research questions. Increasingly, there are a number of universities and courses that teach physical anthropology to students from a variety of backgrounds, at both undergraduate and graduate level.

The information on legislation regarding human remains, their excavation, curation and analysis, will undoubtedly be of help to commercial archaeological companies, museums, universities and freelance researchers who want to undertake work abroad. Many guidelines and standards governing the excavation, analysis and curation of archaeological human remains still operate at a local or national level and are very specific to a particular region. In many countries there certainly appears to be an increasing and appreciative need to involve and employ physical anthropologists as much as possible from the excavation stage onwards, but only government and heritage institutions can ensure that this need becomes a legislatively enforced requirement. It also appears crucial for anyone coming in from an outside institution to establish links with researchers and curators in the country of their proposed work and to pay special consideration to any sensitive issues specific to that country, whether religious, ethical or political that may have impeded the excavation, analysis or exhibition of archaeological human remains. The section on country-specific methods, while providing standardization and enabling comparison between assemblages, is clearly useful beyond the context of physical anthropology. In cases of missing people in a modern or forensic context, population-specific standards for age-at-death, sex and stature assessment are vital for victim identification.

We hope this handbook will be useful to anyone wishing to work with archaeological human remains abroad, and to those developing and dealing with human remains-related legislation. It is by no means the final product, and we sincerely hope that future editions will encompass an ever greater number of countries and chart the ongoing development of the discipline – towards one characterized by an increasingly international community of researchers who work, communicate and constantly improve physical anthropology beyond the constraints of political and geographical boundaries.

Appendix 1

British Overseas Territories

Karl Harrison

Despite the widespread return of the United Kingdom's former colonies to home rule throughout the 20th century (from the port of Weihaiwei returned to China in 1930, to the handing back of Hong Kong, again to China, in 1997), there remain a number of overseas states attached to British sovereignty (Table A1.1). In addition to the British Overseas Territories, there is also a separate classification of Crown Dependencies, which remain possessions of the British Crown (Table A1.2).

The nature of these territories and the reasons for their continued attachment to the British Crown or State are varied. The Crown Dependencies are physically close to Britain and retain feudal ties to the English Monarch, who retains the title Duke of Normandy. By contrast, the British Overseas Territories maintain attachments to Britain due to a number of factors: partial or full economic dependency, identification with the British nation state, and continuing strategic importance. This is particularly true of the island territories of the South Atlantic: Saint Helena, and the Falkland Islands. Both were originally formally settled to address direct strategic concerns: the guardianship of the exiled Napoleon in the case of Saint Helena, and the control of a waystation close to Cape Horn in the case of the Falklands. In the words of Secretary of State Viscount Castlereagh, speaking to Parliament in 1816: 'Our policy has been to secure the Empire against future attack. In order to do this we had acquired what in former days would have been thought romance – the keys of every great military position' (HC Deb (1st series) 1816).

Due to the complexities of individual legislature and the wealth of archaeological data, this chapter will not deal directly with the Crown Dependencies. Advice regarding the excavation of human remains can be sought from Jersey Heritage (www.jerseyheritage.org), Heritage Guernsey (www.heritageguernsey.com) or Manx National Heritage (www.gov.im/MNH) respectively. This chapter will instead focus on a sample of Overseas Territories in the Atlantic and Caribbean: Bermuda, the British Virgin Islands, the Falkland Islands and Saint Helena. It will become apparent throughout this discussion that legislation dealing directly with the excavation of human remains is scant, and frequently reliant on the precedent of English Statute and Common Law. Each of these Territories, however, exhibits a unique set of pressures on its respective environment, relating to tourism, population density or geographical isolation. Additionally, all have seen a growth of interest in the potential they offer for formal archaeological research. The exploitation of this potential will inevitably lead to greater pressure on

Table A1.1 Names and locations of British Overseas Territories

Name	Location
Anguilla	Caribbean
Bermuda	North Atlantic
British Antarctic Territory	Antarctica
British Indian Ocean Territory	Indian Ocean
British Virgin Islands	Caribbean
Cayman Islands	Caribbean
Falkland Islands	South Atlantic
Gibraltar (see Appendix 2)	Iberian peninsula
Montserrat	Caribbean
Pitcairn Island	Pacific
Saint Helena (including Ascension and Tristan da Cunha)	South Atlantic
South Georgia and the South Sandwich Islands	South Atlantic
Sovereign Base Areas of Akrotiri and Dhekelia	Mediterranean
Turks and Caicos Islands	Caribbean

Table A1.2 British Crown Dependencies

Name	Location
Bailiwick of Guernsey	English Channel
Bailiwick of Jersey	English Channel
Isle of Man	Irish Sea

existing legislative frameworks and a greater formal control over excavations, particularly where human remains are subject to disturbance and recovery.

BERMUDA

Bermuda is Britain's oldest remaining non-European outpost. In 1609 a storm drove Sir George Somers's *Sea Venture* from its course bound for Virginia and onto a reef, depositing 150 castaways on the uninhabited islands (Tucker 1975: 30). Located in the Atlantic, 900 km east of the US coast, Bermuda is comprised of over a hundred islands, of which 20 are inhabited (Aldrich and Connell 1998: 272). Like Saint Helena, Bermuda was at one time valued for its strategic importance in the Atlantic. As Saint Helena, Ascension Island and Tristan da Cunha were brought to greater government attention with the exile of Napoleon Bonaparte, so the ensuing peace in Europe facilitated the transport of troops and ships to the Americas, the rendezvous for which was Bermuda (Adkins and Adkins 2006: 404).

The change in emphasis from a European to an Atlantic theatre led the British government to purchase Ireland Island off Bermuda in 1809, for the construction of a naval dockyard. Of the 9000 convicts transported to Bermuda for the commissioned project, 2000 are recorded as having died on the islands, predominantly of yellow fever. Three locations were used for their burial. Until 1849 they were interred in the enlarged naval cemetery on Ireland Island itself. Between 1849 and 1854 they were then buried on nearby Watford Island. From 1854 onwards the Admiralty granted permission for yellow fever victims to be buried on Long Island, across the Dundonald Channel (Tucker 1975: 101–2).

Whereas the population of Saint Helena has historically been low, and today remains a scant 8000, Bermuda is reportedly the third most densely populated place on the planet, with a 2005 population estimate set at 68,500 people distributed over its 54 sq km of habitable area (Bermuda Online 2009). While such densities of population bring many challenges, they also facilitate the development of greater levels of legislative infrastructure. The government of Bermuda consists of a Governor, a Deputy Governor, a Cabinet and a bicameral legislative body, consisting of a Senate and a House of Assembly. The Bermudan system of government is a direct derivation of the 'Westminster model' of parliamentary democracy; while the House of Assembly has 36 elected members (one from each of Bermuda's constituencies), the Senate consists of 11 appointed members.

Two pieces of Bermudan legislation are of direct relevance to the excavation or exhumation of human remains within the islands: the Coroners Act and the Public Health Act.

Coroners Act 1938 (revised 1989)

The Governor of Bermuda is responsible for the appointment of two or more coroners for the islands, of which one would be appointed Senior Coroner. Under Bermudan law, it is a statutory offence to fail to notify the coroner of the discovery of a dead body. As in the English system, this notification generally occurs through the agency of the police. The Coroners Act lists no statute of limitations with regard to those remains liable to inclusion under the Act, and as such it must be assumed that the responsibility to establish whether remains are old enough to be beyond coronial interest and thus archaeological falls to the Coroners and their appointed officers.

Public Health Act 1949 (Revised 1989)

The Public Health Act serves to define lawful cemeteries and details the manner in which special licences for burial outside of these cemeteries might be applied for. In addition, it provides a legal framework for the disinterment of remains. The Chief Medical Officer is permitted to grant licences for disinterment in order that remains might be cremated, reburied or removed from Bermuda for disposal. In cases of archaeological excavation or forensic exhumation, the Governor is permitted to direct the recovery of human remains for the purposes of examination or the removal of samples for further analysis. Under the terms of the Public Health Act, any disinterment of human remains without suitable permissions results in the commission of an offence punishable by one year's imprisonment.

Archaeological legislation

In addition to the local statutory controls relating to the investigation, disposal and recovery of the deceased from identified lawful cemeteries on Bermuda, the islands also have a developed structure of planning consent, within which archaeological assessment plays a fundamental role. When a proposed development impacts upon a recognized Historic Protection Area or a Listed Building, the Development Application Board may require the completion of either an Archaeological Assessment, an Archaeological Management Plan, or both.

Under the terms of Bermudan planning law, an Archaeological Assessment need not feature excavation, and may be completed by means of a desktop survey based on archival research and historical photography resources. By contrast, the Archaeological Management Plan requires the prospective developer to commission a suitably qualified archaeologist to construct a strategy of cultural resource management.

The importance of tourism to Bermuda's economy, compounded by the development pressures exacerbated by such a densely concentrated population, highlights the need to preserve the cultural heritage of the islands. While much of the material history of Bermuda is characterized by shipwrecks along its coastline, there are also numerous recognized land-based heritage assets, such as the early timber fortifications on Paget and Governor's Islands. The Bermuda National Trust has conducted a number of excavations across the islands. Of particular interest in this context is the 2004 excavation of Watford Island Cemetery (Bermuda National Trust 2009). While the primary burial ground on Watford Island is the military cemetery used from 1853 to 1899, the nearby convict cemetery is located on unconsecrated ground.

Recently, an archaeological examination of Saint Peter's Church in Saint George's resulted in the discovery of remains believed to be those of George James Bruere, an 18th-century Governor of the colony. These remains were located beneath the floorboards of the church. While the coffin had disintegrated, Bruere's nameplate was found resting on the chest of the skeleton (Dale 2008). The discovery of Bruere's remains was preceded the week before by the location of two other sets of remains beneath the floor of Saint Peter's. One of these was believed to be those of Sir Jacob Wheate, Captain of *HMS Cerberus*, which sank on rocks off Castle Harbour in 1783 (Neil 2008).

THE BRITISH VIRGIN ISLANDS

The British Virgin Islands (BVIs) are made up of over 40 small islands in the Caribbean, of which some 15 are inhabited. While only cursory archaeological attention has been paid to the BVIs, their colonial history is a long one. Discovered by Columbus in 1493 and passed by Drake in 1580, the islands have a confused history of ownership. The main island of Tortola was settled by the Dutch in 1648, and then used by buccaneers until the British established governance by capturing the island in 1672. They then gradually annexed the surrounding islands up to 1733 (Coke 1811: 92). Quakers arrived in the BVIs in the early 18th century, where they founded colonies on the islands of Tortola and Virgin Gorda in 1727. Although Quakerism diminished on the islands in the late 18th century, it retains a historical influence through the early emancipation of slaves on Quaker plantations, and in material culture through the relict Quaker cemetery at Fat Hog's Bay on Tortola (Shepard and Shepard 1989: 88).

The legal system of the BVIs is a reflection of its complex past. Prior to 1773, law was extended to the territory from the legislature of the Leeward Islands, based on Antigua. Elements of this legal system survive, most notably the Common Law (Declaration of Application; Act Cap. 13, 1705). Much of the British Virgin Islands' domestic legislation today concerns the financial administration of the Territory. In addition to this, the constitution has passed through several revisions, the latest of which, the Virgin Islands Constitution Order 2006, reiterates the previously existing structure of the Legislative Council of the Territory consisting of a Speaker, an *ex-officio* Attorney General, and 13 elected members. It is interesting to note that a direct relationship has been drawn between the heritage of the British Virgin islanders and their legal system; the power to author their own laws has been seen as being central to BVI national identity (Maurer 2000: 227).

While there seems to be an overt link between the formulation of local laws and the identity of British Virgin islanders, this does not appear to extend to personification and identity following death, as there appears to be no direct consideration of a legal framework concerning the excavation of human remains. Despite this lack of direct legislation, it is clear that there is an established system of environmental impact assessment in operation in the Territory. During the completion of one such assessment survey, a plantation-era burial was uncovered in Belmont Park Grove, Tortola (Ecocerns 2006: 235).

Although a relatively large cemetery site has been excavated at the site of Tutu on the neighbouring US Virgin Islands (Righter 2002: 32), no similar project has yet been undertaken on the BVIs. Indeed, the excavation of a pre-Columbian settlement at Belmont on Long Bay by Peter Drewett of UCL is thought to be the first officially recognized archaeological excavation on the island of Tortola (Drewett 2003). Archaeological research conducted on the isolated atoll of Anageda in 1974 concentrated on middens of discarded conch shells (Saunders 2005: 7).

THE FALKLAND ISLANDS

The Falkland Islands, or Islas Malvinas, are located in the Atlantic, between 51 and 53 degrees south of the equator. They cover about 12,000 sq km, and are comprised of about two hundred islands, but two main ones dominate the archipelago: West Falkland and East Falkland (Gough 1992).

The Falklands have acted as an incidental base for whalers and sealers in the South Atlantic for centuries, and prior to that radiocarbon dates from charcoal sampled from blanket peat at Sapper Hill at least suggest the possibility of pre-colonial exploitation of the islands as early as 4780 ±80 BP (Buckland and Edwards 1998). The colonial history of the Falklands began with Bougainville's foundation of a French colony, Port Louis, on East Falkland in 1764. In 1765–66, the British founded their own colony on Saunders Island. The logic behind both of these settlements was the provision of a waystation for vessels rounding Cape Horn bound for or from the Pacific.

Following protests from Spain citing the terms of the Treaty of Tordesillas, by which the New World was divided in ownership between Spain and Portugal, both the French and British colonies were removed. Shortly after the grant of Argentine independence in 1810 the fledgling nation founded a new colony on the Falklands in 1829. The Argentine colony was short-lived, being destroyed by a US warship following a diplomatic argument over the seizure of whaling vessels. It was subsequently rebuilt, only for the resurgent colonists to revolt and kill their governor. At this point a British naval vessel returned to the Falklands to reassert the territorial claim that had not been surrendered following their withdrawal. The Falkland Islands were then recognized as a Crown Colony in 1840 (Aldrich and Connell 1998: 201).

The government of the Falkland Islands consists of a Governor who represents the Queen in the Islands, and a Chief Executive, which is comprised of eight elected representatives. As with the British Virgin Islands, a recent revision of the Falklands' constitution, the Falkland Islands Constitution Order 2003, enshrines roles for the various organs of state and the rights of individuals. There is no specific domestic statute or guidance covering the excavation or study of human remains.

Formal archaeological research of any kind has been very limited on the Falklands, but a number of exceptions are worthy of note. The first is underwater archaeology; the Falklands Wreck Survey Group advise the Falklands Government's Wrecks and Hulks Committee in assessing the level of protection required for the various shipwrecks around the islands (Eynon 1995). Second, the work of Dr Robert Philpott, who has conducted surveys of 18th- and 19th-century colonial settlements on the Falklands (Philpott 1996, 2007).

Contact [by the present author] with the Falkland Islands Museum and National Trust suggests that chance excavation of human remains has not as yet been an issue on the islands.

Initially, the opinion expressed through personal communications with the Museum suggested that such an eventuality was highly unlikely, given the uncertain nature of any pre-colonial settlement. It is clear, however, that sporadic marked burials exist on the islands, such as that of Matthew Brisbane, murdered in 1833, whose grave in Port Louis now stands in a farmstead (Wheeler 2004: 89). Further discussion revealed that early unmarked burials and informal cemeteries related to pre-formal colonization or early colonization attempts might well be present on the islands.

SAINT HELENA AND ASCENSION ISLAND

Saint Helena is an Overseas Territory located in the South Atlantic. While the administrative centre is located on the island of Saint Helena, the Territory also includes Ascension Island, located about 1300 km to the north, and the island group of Tristan da Cunha, 2500 km to the south. All three groups of islands were unoccupied on discovery, and their settlement was a testament to the growing strategic importance of waystations in the south Atlantic. All three groups also have in common their discovery during the Portuguese voyages of exploration: Saint Helena in 1502, Ascension in 1503 and Tristan da Cunha, named after its discoverer, in 1506.

The isolated nature of all of the islands has dominated the character of their settlement. From 1815 until his death in 1821, Napoleon Bonaparte was exiled on the island of Saint Helena. In order to ensure against his possible rescue by the French, both Ascension and Tristan da Cunha were deliberately garrisoned by the British in 1815 and 1816 respectively, although the garrison on Tristan was quickly abandoned in 1817 due to its great distance from Saint Helena and relative ineffectiveness in providing any form of security (Soodyall *et al.* 1997: 157). Following Napoleon, Saint Helena was a place of exile for Dinuzulu, the last formally recognized king of the Zulu, from 1890 to 1898 (Redding, 2006, 109). The isolation of Saint Helena was again put to use by the British in the detention of 5800 men and one woman during the Boer War between 1900 and 1904 (Royle 1998: 57). Most recently, the strategic importance of Ascension was again underlined during the Falklands Conflict, when in 1982 it acted as a crucial staging post for British forces in the South Atlantic.

As a British Overseas Territory, Saint Helena retains a reliance on English statute and common law, supplemented by local laws where appropriate. The legislative branch of the government is a unicameral council of 16 seats, occupied by a Speaker, three *ex-officio* members and 12 elected members. Recent correspondence with the Legal, Lands and Planning Department of the Government of Saint Helena via the Senior Assistant Secretary has served to confirm that no internal legislation exists to cover the excavation or exhumation of human remains. Rather, the local authorities would rely upon the English Law (Application) Ordinance 2001, whereby English statute could be applied in a Saint Helenan context.

Continued development of Saint Helena has prompted recent archaeological investigation, which has included the major project of installing an airport. In May 2008 a team of archaeologists was commissioned to conduct a survey, concentrating on three cemetery sites in the Rupert Valley area of the island. These cemeteries contained the remains of West African slaves freed at the Saint Helena depot between 1840 and 1865 (Schuler 2002).

Despite the small size, continuing relative isolation and general lack of a supporting domestic legislative framework, two case studies are worthy of further examination in relation to the topics of archaeological excavation and anthropological examination of human remains within the Territory.

The exhumation of Napoleon: 1840

Notwithstanding a general lack of legislation related to the excavation and recovery of human remains, Saint Helena was the site of one of the most famous exhumations of the modern era: that of Napoleon Bonaparte. The exhumation was undertaken to recover the remains of the Emperor and take them to France, as well as to allay some of the conspiracy theories rife in Paris, regarding the opinion that the coffin had been empty at Napoleon's burial.

Popular opinion regarding the fate of the Emperor's remains had been set for some time prior to the exhumation. As early as 1830, just 15 years after his death, a petition was presented to the French Chamber of Deputies, desiring that the government act to bring about the restitution of the Emperor's remains (L'Ardeche 1843: 4). The French government ultimately instructed their ambassador in London to request the exhumation and translation of the body of Napoleon in May 1840. It seems that permission was granted so rapidly by the British that it must surely have been an act of diplomatic importance. The reply of Melbourne's government was read to the Chamber of Deputies by the French Minister of the Interior, de Remusat:

> The government of her Britannic Majesty hopes that the promptitude of its reply will be regarded in France as a proof of its desire utterly to efface the national animosities which, during the life of the Emperor, armed England and France against each other. The government of her Britannic Majesty takes pleasure in believing that if such sentiments still exist in any quarter, they will be buried in the tomb in which the ashes of Napoleon are about to be placed.
>
> *l'Ardeche 1843: 4*

By this action of international policy, the first recorded exhumation of human remains on Saint Helena was formalized and granted legality as an act of diplomatic *force majeure* on the part of the British government. The cordial relations with which the project began were not to continue unchallenged and unencumbered, however. In much the same way, the physical tomb of Napoleon would not readily give up its charge. The Prince de Joinville, sailor-son of King Louis Philippe, was despatched in the *Belle Poule* to recover the remains of the Emperor. Despite his high billing in France, the prince was deeply unimpressed with the level of authority granted to him on arriving at Saint Helena: 'The Governor took upon himself the direction of the exhumation, and of all the ceremonies which were to take place on the English Territory' (Montholon 1847: 330).

The act of exhumation was planned for 15 September 1840, the 25th anniversary to the day of Napoleon's arrival on Saint Helena and the beginning of his Atlantic exile. Unfortunately, the resilience of the tomb stopped this plan. Despite the best efforts of the Royal Engineers under Captain Alexander, it took more than nine hours to break open the tomb and empty the vault of earth. While the snubbed de Joinville remained in splendid isolation on the *Belle Poule*, a cast of notaries attended the exhumation: Generals Bertrand and Gourgand, the Comte de Chabot, the Baron les Cases, the Abbé Coquereau, messieurs Marchand, Bertrand, St. Denis, Noreuraz, Pierron and Archambault (these last were three old servants of Napoleon), Captains Guyet and Doret, and Dr Guillard, Surgeon-Major of the *Belle Poule* (l'Ardeche 1843: 9). Bertrand had shared Napoleon's exile, and both Bertrand and Marchand had been present for the autopsy of the Emperor, 19 years before (Antommarchi 1825: 161).

The scale of funeral fittings festooned on the Emperor was as grandiose as might be expected, despite the isolated resting ground that Saint Helena had proved. Within the stone tomb was a sarcophagus of three integrated coffins of lead, wood and tin, measuring 2.56 m in length, 1.05 m broad and 0.76 m tall (Montholon 1847: 327). Freed from the sarcophagus, the body of Napoleon was exposed for two minutes: long enough for the assembled party to positively identify the well preserved corpse. The coffins were then resealed, with six layers of lead replacing the original four. Its 1200 kg load was then transported back to Saint Helena's main settlement, Jamestown. A total of 43 Royal Engineers guided the reinforced carriage over the rough, unmade roads.

Excavation at Comfortless Cove, Ascension, 2008

In March 2008 the author and forensic anthropologist Julie Roberts accompanied three members of the RAF Special Investigation Branch to Ascension, where arrangements had been made to locate and investigate a number of stone-built cairns on the island, thought to mark the graves of seamen (Yon 2008). The expedition was arranged as a formal archaeological excavation, with necessary levels of diligence and recording, but its primary aim was the training of military personnel in the search for and excavation of human remains. The excavation concentrated on a narrow cleft to the north of Comfortless Cove, where five cairns were arranged in close association.

A number of cemeteries had been foci of the posthumous erection of monuments in the Comfortless Cove area. The Bonetta Cemetery is thought to date from 1838 and contain the remains of those who died from yellow fever aboard the *HMS Bonetta*. The Trident Cemetery, located between Comfortless Cove and Pyramid Point, contains three marked but undated and unidentified graves within a wall of volcanic clinker (Packer 2002). Of the few sources gathering information on the naval cemeteries of Ascension, none suggest a date of origin for the five unmarked cairns found near to the Bonetta Cemetery (Anon. 2001). The cairns were photographed and planned, one of which (PP1) was subjected to removal and excavation, initially in half-section to reveal the presence of a burial, then subsequently completely. The single inhumation underlying the cairn was found to be in an extended supine position. No coffin was in evidence, but the body was tightly wrapped in a fibrous shroud or possibly a hammock, which was held secure around the remains with a crossed-over cord. The remains were photographed, drawn and described prior to being covered and the cairn rebuilt.

CONCLUSION

While they may be regarded as small and anomalous in international terms, the examples of the Territories detailed above have served to demonstrate how diverse they are as a group. Little could be said to unite the Overseas Territories, other than a shared colonial history, an ongoing connection back to Britain, and, in the context of this chapter, a predominantly simple legislative framework with regard to the excavation of human remains. In terms of the material history of these territories, many have only recently been subject to the attentions of a small number of professional archaeologists. As such, it is thought that broader understanding of the cultural past of these Territories would be facilitated by a greater degree of communication between the various interested archaeologists.

CITED LEGISLATION

Bermuda: Coroners Act 1938 (Revised 1989; Public Health Act 1949 (Rev. 1989).
British Virgin Islands: The Virgin Islands Constitution Order 2006; British Virgin Islands Common Law (Declaration of Application) Act 1705.

Falkland Islands: Falkland Islands Constitution Order 2003; Falklands Islands English Law (Application) Ordinance 2001.

Saint Helena: English Law (Application) Ordinance 2001a.

BIBLIOGRAPHY

Adkins, R. and Adkins, L. (2006) *The War for All the Oceans: From Nelson at the Nile to Napoleon at Waterloo*, London: Abacus.

Aldrich, R. and Connell, J. (1998) *The Last Colonies*, Cambridge: Cambridge University Press.

Anon. (2001) *Bonetta & Trident Cemeteries / Archer / Above Bonetta / Nr Comfortless Cove*. Unpublished manuscript held in the Ascension Island Archive, Georgetown, Ascension.

Antommarchi, F. (1825) *The Last Days of the Emperor Napoleon, Vol I*, London: Henry Colburn.

l'Ardeche, L. (1843) *History of Napoleon, Vol II*, New York: D. Appleton & Company.

Bermuda National Trust (2009) *Watford Cemetery, Somerset*. Available online at www.bnt.bm/Places_to_vi sit/watford_cemetery.php (accessed 16 March 2010).

Bermuda Online (2009) *Bermuda's Population*. Available online at www.bermuda-online.org/population. htm (accessed 16 March 2010).

Buckland, P. and Edwards, K. (1998) 'Palaeoecological evidence for possible pre-European settlement in the Falklands', *Journal of Archaeological Science*, 25: 599–602.

Coke, T. (1811) *A History of the West Indies. Volume 3*, London: A. Paris.

Dale, A. (2008) 'Centuries-old remains found beneath church', *Royal Gazette*, 12 August 2008.

Drewett, P. (2003) 'Belmont: Ball Games in the Prehistoric Caribbean', *Current World Archaeology*, 2.

Ecocerns (2006) *Environmental Assessment for Villa Paradiso (Tortola) Limited*. Available online at www. bvihcg.com/paper/smugglers_eia.pdf (accessed 16 March 2010).

Eynon, D. (1995) 'The Falklands Wreck Survey Group', *International Journal of Nautical Archaeology*, 24: 163–64.

Gough, B. (1992) *The Falkland Islands/Malvinas: The Contest for Empire in the South Atlantic*, London: Athlone Press.

HC Deb (1st series) (1816) Vol. 32 cc 1104.

Maurer, B. (2000) *Recharting the Caribbean: Land, Law and Citizenship in the British Virgin Islands*, Ann Arbor: University of Michigan Press.

Montholon, C. (1847) *History of the Captivity of Napoleon at St. Helena, Vol IV*, London: Henry Colburn.

Neil, S. (2008) 'Eighteenth Century governor's skeleton found under St. Peter's', *Royal Gazette*, 21 August 2008.

Government of the British Virgin Islands (2009) *Official Website of the Government of the Virgin Islands (U.K.)*. Available online at www.bvi.gov.vg (accessed 16 March 2010).

Packer, J.E. (2002) *A Concise Guide to Ascension Island, South Atlantic*, Ascension: Ascension Heritage Society.

Philpott, R.A. (1996) 'Port Egmont: the earliest British settlement in the Falkland Islands', *Post-Medieval Archaeology*, 30: 1–63.

——(2007) *The Archaeology of the Falkland Islands 1: The Early Falkland Islands Company Settlements: An Archaeological Survey*, Liverpool: Falkland Islands Museum & National Trust/National Museums Liverpool.

Redding, S. (2006) *Sorcery and Sovereignty: Taxation, Power and Rebellion in South Africa, 1860–1963*, Athens: Ohio University Press

Righter, E. (2002) *The Tutu Archaeological Village Site: A Multidisciplinary Case Study in Human Adaptation*, London: Routledge.

Royle, S.A. (1998) 'St Helena as a Boer prisoner of war camp, 1900–1902: Information from the Alice Stopford Green Papers', *Journal of Historical Geography*, 24: 53–68.

Saunders, N.J. (2005) *The Peoples of the Caribbean: An Encyclopedia of Archaeology and Traditional Culture*, Oxford: ABC-Clio.

Schuler, M. (2002) 'Liberated Central Africans in nineteenth century Guyana', in L. Heywood (ed) *Central Africans and Cultural Transformations in the American Diaspora*, Cambridge: Cambridge University Press.

Shepard, L. and Shepard, R. (1989) *Treasure Islands: A Guide to the British Virgin Islands*, London: Macmillan Caribbean.

Soodyall, H., Jenkins, T., Mukherjee, A., *et al.* (1997) 'The founding mitochondrial DNA lineages of Tristan da Cunha Islanders', *American Journal of Physical Anthropology*, 104: 157–66.

Tucker, T. (1975) *Bermuda: Today and Yesterday, 1503–1973*, London: R. Hale.

Wheeler, T. (2004) *The Falklands and South Georgia Island*, London: Lonely Planet.

Yon, G. (2008) 'Ascension: Specialist Police Wing Forensic Archaeology Team Visit', *The Islander*, 3 April 2008.

Appendix 2
Gibraltar

Kimberly Brown and Clive Finlayson

INTRODUCTION

Gibraltar is a small peninsula, 6 km long and with a maximum height of 426 m above sea level, situated at the southernmost tip of the Iberian Peninsula, sharing a land frontier with Spain. It is a self-governing British Overseas Territory with its own Parliament and elected government. Its judicial and police systems are modelled on those established in the United Kingdom.

This unassuming rock's abounding history has attracted international interest for centuries, and continues to this day to inspire various research projects. From its Jurassic origins, Neanderthal fossils, and Neolithic and Bronze Age settlements, to the turbulent upheavals of the 18th and 19th centuries, and its role as an important military base during the Second World War, Gibraltar offers an intact snapshot of its historical past.

A brief anthropological history of Gibraltar

The archaeological and palaeontological significance of this small peninsula had been recorded by as early as the 18th century (Boddington 1771; Mullens 1913). There are 10 recorded sites in Gibraltar with known Neanderthal occupation, as well as the discovery of two fossils in the 19th and 20th centuries.

The first of these fossils was discovered at a site known as Forbes' Quarry, on the North Face of the Rock in 1848, and is thought to be that of a woman because of its gracile features (Figure A2.1). The specimen was recovered during quarrying works at Forbes' Quarry and was presented by Lieutenant Edmund Flint to the Gibraltar Scientific Society on 3 March 1848. However, the significance of this skull was not realized and it remained undisclosed for another 16 years. During that time the specimen from the Neander Thal (Neander Valley, Germany) was discovered, eight years after the Gibraltar specimen, from which Neanderthals subsequently got their name. Had the significance of the Forbes' Quarry skull been appreciated sooner, we might have been referring to *Homo calpicus* today (Stringer 2000).

The second Neanderthal skull, that of a four-year-old child (Figures A2.2 and A2.3) found in association with Mousterian technology, was excavated by Dorothy Garrod in 1926 from a rock shelter known as Devil's Tower, again on the North Face and very close to the Forbes' Quarry site (Garrod *et al.* 1928). Therefore, with 10 Neanderthal sites and two fossils, packed within a

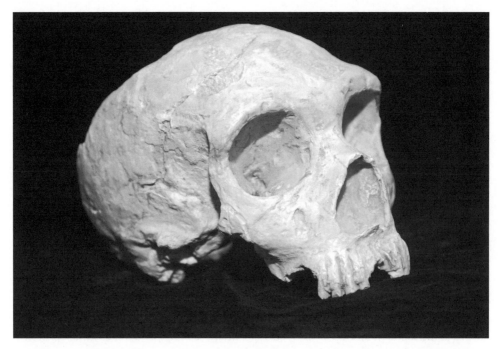

Figure A2.1 Fossil discovered at a site known as Forbes' Quarry, Gibraltar

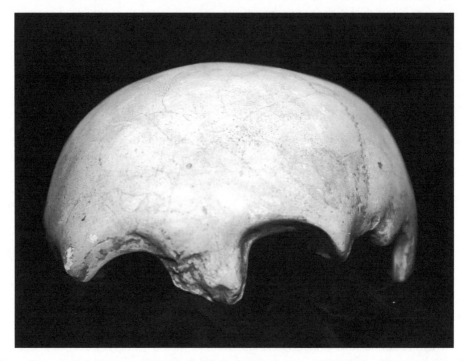

Figure A2.2 and A2.3 The second Neanderthal skull, that of a four-year-old child found in association with Mousterian technology, excavated by Dorothy Garrod in 1926 from a rock shelter known as Devil's Tower, Gibraltar

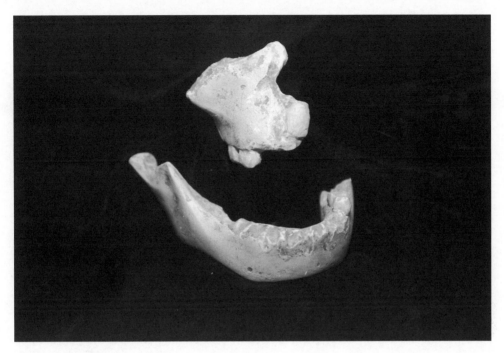

Figure A2.3 (continued)

6 km-long and 1 km-wide peninsula, it is quite possible that Gibraltar has one of the densest Neanderthal occupations in the whole of Europe, and as such is of major significance for the advancement of Palaeolithic archaeology.

Archaeological material relating to Gibraltar's recent prehistoric past was also recorded from as early at the mid-19th century (Busk 1869), from sites such as Genista 1, 2 and 3, St. Michael's, Martin's and Judge's Caves (Gutiérrez López *et al.* 2000). Some of the materials recovered are currently housed at the Gibraltar Museum, but the materials were recovered by the Gibraltar Society Cave Research Group, during the 1950s, 60s and 70s, and were unfortunately surface-collected using non-systematic excavation techniques, impeding any detailed further study.

The Gibraltar Caves Project was set up in 1989, in order to systematically investigate prehistoric sites around Gibraltar. This multi-disciplinary team is led by Professor Clive Finlayson, of the Gibraltar Museum, Professor Joaquín Rodríguez Vidal, from the University of Huelva, Spain, and Francisco Giles Pacheco, with Professor Chris Stringer, of the Natural History Museum, as scientific advisors to the project on palaeoanthopology. This team undertakes annual systematic archaeological investigations of cave sites around Gibraltar, researching the various different occupational events in Gibraltar from the Neanderthals to those of Modern Humans during the Upper Palaeolithic, Neolithic and beyond.

Recent archaeological investigations at sites such as Europa (formerly Rich Sands) and Bray's Caves revealed important Neolithic and Bronze Age horizons, respectively. Human remains were found in both caves, with a cranium being discovered from the Neolithic levels at Europa Cave. Bray's Cave, however, is of particular importance as it was used as a funerary site, which was revisited on numerous occasions. Three fairly complete skulls were recovered, together with post-cranial remains. However, various other cranial fragments would suggest more individuals were present. The burial site was revisited often, and the previous interment moved aside, in order to make room for more individuals. One such example of this secondary interment is the recovery of three cranial fragments found stacked one on top of the other *in situ* within the cave.

In its more recent past, Gibraltar has always been regarded as an important and strategic military post, and its possession has always been fought over by neighbouring military powers. Gibraltar has seen a total of 14 sieges (Fa and Finlayson 2006), as well as various cholera and yellow fever epidemics. These events resulted in high mortality rates between the 16th and 19th centuries, which, coupled with a reduced living space, often resulted in the use of impromptu burials and 'cemeteries' within the populated town area. This results therefore in unexpected discoveries of human remains within the city walls and areas which are outside of demarcated burial grounds, and which are otherwise unreported.

A more recent discovery was that of undisturbed human remains found under a garage, and close to two important military installations – the old Naval Hospital and the entrance to the tunnel systems known as Harley Street, at Europa Road. The bones were uncovered as a result of construction works at the site. The exposed stratigraphy did not, however, provide any clues as to the context in which the remains were buried. There were no obvious changes in the sediments surrounding the remains to suggest any recent pit or 'grave' cut. Therefore, at this stage, the only possible scenario was for the remains to predate the sedimentation layers at this site. The remains were found in complete articulation, extended and supine, with a SW/NE orientation, therefore confirming that this was the original deposition site, and that the remains had not formed part of a later infill. The remains were in particularly good condition, and a large proportion of the skeleton was recovered (Figure A2.4). However, the crucial areas of the body for identification (i.e., the skull and pelvis) were relatively damaged. The remains offered only three fragments of the pelvis, which made sex determination difficult. These fragments included part of the ischium, ilium and acetabulum (where the pelvis articulates with the femur), including part of the sciatic notch (Figure A2.5). The remains could not be conclusively sexed.

The long bones recovered from the site were studied for age estimation (after Herrmann *et al.* 1990). The upper limbs (humerus, radius and ulna) showed advanced stages of epiphyseal fusion indicating an estimated age range of 18–25. This age range took into account the different rate of maturity between males and females, as sex could not be determined conclusively. The lower limbs (femur, tibia and fibula) did however exhibit an earlier stage of fusion, with some of the epiphyses still unattached to the diaphyses. This constrained the age range to approximately 17–21.

Although only miscellaneous fragments of the skull and mandible were recovered, there was a peculiarity in a molar recovered with the remains, which may help indicate race. The lower first molar (M_1) recovered had three roots instead of the normal two (Figure A2.6). Although a small percentage of Caucasians can present with this trait, it is usually much more prominent in individuals of Mongoloid race, and is often used as an anthropological marker (Curzon 1973; Ferraz and Pecora 1992; Ming-Gene *et al.* 2007; Turner 2005).

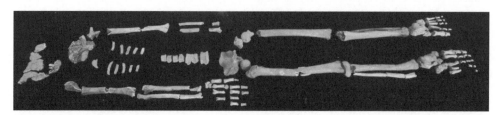

Figure A2.4 Naval Hospital site, Gibraltar. The remains were in particularly good condition, and a large proportion of the skeleton was recovered

Figure A2.5 Naval Hospital site, Gibraltar. Pelvic fragments including part of the ilium, ischium and acetabulum

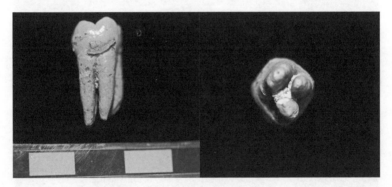

Figure A2.6 Naval Hospital site, Gibraltar. The recovered lower first molar (M$_1$) with three roots

Various items were also recovered in association with the remains, which would offer clues as to a possible date and context. A total of 23 copper alloy buttons and miscellaneous fragments were recovered from the site (Figure A2.7). The manufacturing techniques and materials used where quite common in 18th-century Britain. A bone button was also recovered (Figure A2.8). A clay pipe, commonly found in 19th-century deposits around Gibraltar, was also recovered with the remains (Figure A2.9).

The associated finds, the location of the remains next to the Naval Hospital and other military installations, as well as the possible Mongoloid origins of the individual, suggested the remains could possibly belong to a member of a Gurkha unit of the British army posted in Gibraltar. These were predominantly of Mongoloid race, and were actively used by the British army during the 19th century.

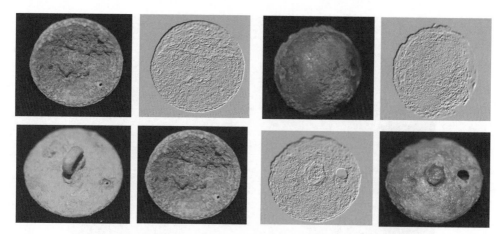

Figure A2.7 Naval Hospital site, Gibraltar. A total of 23 copper alloy buttons and miscellaneous fragments recovered from the site

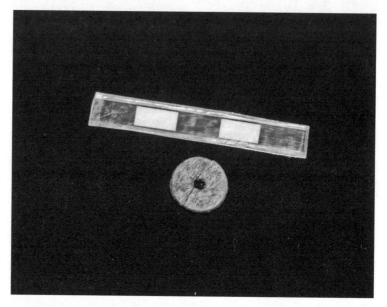

Figure A2.8 Naval Hospital site, Gibraltar. The bone button that was recovered

SCIENTIFIC RESEARCH IN GIBRALTAR

Scientific societies and the origins of the Gibraltar Museum

It was only in 1835 that the Gibraltar Scientific Society made the first proposal for the opening of a museum. There had been some research conducted prior to this, by naturalists such as the Rev. John White, during the late 18th and early 19th centuries, but Gibraltar's turbulent military history meant that prior to the 1830s the concept of establishing a research institution or museum would have not been entertained. By the end of the 18th century however, the Gibraltar Scientific Society had initiated its own museum, which became central to the Society's activities.

Figure A2.9 Naval Hospital site, Gibraltar. A clay pipe fragment, of the kind commonly found in 19th-century deposits around Gibraltar

In 1842, the society changed its name to the Museum Society and elected its first curator, a Mr Frembly, on 19 November 1836. The precise location of the museum is uncertain, but it seems to have been housed in rented accommodation and had a large collection of varied specimens.

By 1850, however, the meetings of the Gibraltar Museum Society became infrequent, and its first museum was lost. For over 35 years, Gibraltar was without a museum or intensive historical research. It was finally in 1930 that the Gibraltar Museum was finally founded, as a result of the initiative of the Governor, General Sir Alexander Godley, opening on 23 July 1930, and coinciding with the formation of the Gibraltar Society on 3 October 1929.

The museum was also backed by statute, with the Museum Ordinance, which was passed on 10 July 1931. This Ordinance related to 'Ancient Monuments and Antiquities' and provided for the management of the Gibraltar Museum, also catering for the protection of monuments and giving basic control over the export of archaeological finds from Gibraltar.

The outbreak of the Second World War, and the subsequent re-intensification of the military role of Gibraltar as a fortress, led to the suspension of the Gibraltar Museum Committee, the museum building being used during this time as a store. After the war, however, control of the museum and its activities slowly reverted to civilians.

Today, the Museum is an important research institution, with a team of professionally qualified individuals who are also members of the Gibraltar Government's Heritage Division, and who are thus involved in Gibraltar's wider heritage management issues.

LEGISLATION

The first legislation to be passed regarding the protection of Ancient Monuments and Antiquities in Gibraltar dates to 1931. However, this statute was very basic and only catered for monuments and historical artefacts. A more comprehensive piece of legislation, The Gibraltar Heritage Trust Ordinance, which encompassed the Gibraltar Heritage Trust, the Museum, as well as listed monuments and buildings, was passed in 1987 and revised in 1989.

The Ordinance established the Gibraltar Heritage Trust, a registered charity, as a statutory body entrusted with the preservation of Gibraltar's heritage. It also gave the Museum Curator a statutory responsibility with respect to the discovery of antiquities or other archaeological remains within Gibraltar. This ordinance (Gibraltar Heritage Act 1989) defined an 'antiquity' as:

(a) any object of historical, geographical, artistic, scientific or technical value or interest found or situated in Gibraltar (whether in or on the land or below the seabed), being older than fifty years; and
(b) any object that is declared under section 17 to be an antiquity; and
(c) any listed building, structure, site or land;

… and defined 'Gibraltar's heritage' as:

(a) buildings, structures, antiquities, works of art or craft, books, records and other chattels, wherever situated and being of historical, architectural, artistic, scientific or social interest in connection with Gibraltar; and
(b) areas of natural interest or beauty in Gibraltar along, where appropriate, with their animal and plant life;

This is the only legislation, to date, that encompasses all institutions in Gibraltar that help protect its heritage and antiquities.

Excavating human remains in Gibraltar

There is no specific law, statute or guideline regulating the recovery, processing, and repatriation of historical human remains found in Gibraltar. At present, any discovery of human remains is usually reported to the police, who then inform the Gibraltar Museum. The Museum archaeologist is usually then called to the site and asked to confirm whether the remains are indeed human and whether they are found in a historical context. With its limited land area, and its almost constant stream of new housing developments, Gibraltar has experienced a recent upsurge of new archaeological discoveries, most of them of unexpected human remains. Given Gibraltar's dense historical past, and its spatial confinements, it is not unusual to encounter unexpected human remains, especially within the city walls. This is most likely as a result of its turbulent recent past, with various sieges and plagues, as well as its important role as a military base during the Second World War.

The Museum is responsible for the recovery and recording of these remains, which are then incorporated into its collection, pending further study. In the event that the remains are removed from an existing burial ground, for example within church grounds, these are then recorded, studied, and eventually returned and reburied at a new location. However, most of these discoveries are made in areas outside of recorded consecrated land, which results in the remains not being able to be conclusively assigned to a particular religious belief.

Only on rare occasions, when the stratigraphy or the context in which the remains have been found are unclear or appear suspicious, are the police and the Coroner involved. One such case was the human remains found at Europa Road, as described earlier, as they bore similarities to an open suspected murder case which had occurred in Gibraltar in the 1980s. The Museum archaeologist assists the police and Scene of Crime officers in the correct and careful recovery of human remains, and in their identification. It also assists in confirming, by studying associated archaeological artefacts, the historical context of the human remains. This is particularly important in order to establish the possibility of criminal offence.

CONCLUSION

Archaeological and anthropological research in Gibraltar has developed over the years, and is now of international importance. Throughout the 19th and 20th centuries a lot of research was conducted, but unfortunately this was amateurish and at times caused more problems than it contributed to scientific investigation. The system as it stands at the moment, with the current cooperation between the relevant departments, namely the Gibraltar Museum, the Gibraltar Government and the Heritage Trust, as well as the current legislation, seems however to provide a much more systematic and positive working environment, with a common goal towards the conservation and recording of Gibraltar's heritage. The only amendment that might be needed would be to specifically address the issue of the exhumation of human remains and the issues of repatriation and reburial. But, as it stands, these are currently classified as archaeological remains, and are therefore dealt with by the current legislation.

The Gibraltar Museum, as custodian of all archaeology and antiquity, continues to work towards the understanding of Gibraltar's past, through its archaeological materials and its oral histories, and through its people.

USEFUL CONTACTS

Gibraltar Museum. Website: www.gibmuseum.gi/Welcome.html/

BIBLIOGRAPHY

Boddington, J. (1771) 'Account of some Bones found in the Rock of Gibraltar, in a Letter from John Boddington Esq.; to Dr William Hunter, F.R.S., with some Remarks from Dr Hunter in a Letter to Dr Matthew Maty, M. D. Sec. R. S'. *Philosophical Transactions of the Royal Society of London, 60*: 414–16.

Busk, G. (1869) 'On the caves of Gibraltar in which humans remains and works of art have been found', in *International Congress of Prehistoric Archaeology*, Transactions of the third session, Norwich 1868, 106–67, London.

Curzon, M.E J. (1973) 'Three-rooted mandibular permanent molars in English Caucasians', *Journal of Dental Research*, 52: 181.

Fa, D. and Finlayson, C. (2006) *The Fortifications of Gibraltar 1068–1945*, Oxford: Osprey Publishing.

Ferraz, J.A.B. and Pecora, J.D. (1992) 'Three-rooted mandibular molars in patients of Mongolian, Caucasian and Negro origin', *Brazilian Dental Journal*, 3: 113–17.

Garrod, D., Buxton, L., Elliot-Smith, G., *et al.* (1928) 'Excavation of a Mousterian Rock Shelter at Devil's Tower, Gibraltar', *Journal of the Royal Anthropological Institute*, 58: 33–113.

Government of Gibraltar (2009) *Gibraltar Heritage Act 1989*. Available online at www.gibraltarlaws.gov.gi/articles/1989–12o.pdf (accessed 11 September 2009).

Guitérrez López, J.M., Santiago Pérez, A., Mata Almonte, E., *et al.* (2000) 'Human occupation during the Neolithic and Bronze Age in cavities of the Rock of Gibraltar', in C. Finlayson *et al.* (eds) *Gibraltar During the Quaternary*, Gibraltar: Gibraltar Government Heritage Publications Monograph 1.

Herrmann, B., Grupe, G., Hummel, S., *et al.* (1990) *Prähistorische Anthropologie – Leitfaden der Feld-und Labormethoden*, Berlin: Springer.

Ming-Gene, T., Chi-Cheng Tsai, Ming-Jia Jou, *et al.* (2007) 'Prevalence of three-rooted mandibular first molars among Taiwanese individuals', *Journal of Endodontics*, 33: 1163–66.

Mullens, W.H. (ed.) (1913) *The Introduction to Fauna Calpensis (A Natural History of Gibraltar and Southern Spain) by John White*, London: The Selborne Society.

Stringer, C.B. (2000) 'Gibraltar and the Neanderthals 1848–1998', in C. Stringer *et al.* (eds) *Neanderthals on the Edge*, Oxford: Oxbow Books.

Turner, C.G. (2005) 'Three-rooted mandibular first permanent molars and the question of American Indian Origins', *American Journal of Physical Anthropology*, 34: 229–41.

Appendix 3

Burials related to recent military conflicts. Case studies from France

Michel Signoli and Guillaume de Védrines

INTRODUCTION

All research on human remains raises ethical questions. When those questions relate to mass graves and are associated with emblematic events of national and European history, the subject is even more sensitive from the perspective of the public opinion and political leaders.

The way the French law deals with the issue reflects how the society approaches the matter. Its analysis will lead to exciting and various thinking, where human dignity, legislation and the creation of the European Union overlap with a common value: the respect for the dead and for the living.

In the chapter on France (Michel *et al.*, this volume), the authors presented the legislation that rules the discovery and the study of human remains in France. In the present section we study a particular case: mass war graves. When the remains of a French soldier are found, what is their legal status? What happens when those remains are found outside French territory? What happens to the human remains of a foreign soldier found in France?

HUMAN REMAINS IN A MILITARY CONTEXT

In an archaeological context, for example a mediaeval cemetery, the discovery and the management of human remains tends to raise specific ethical problems. The remains bring back to us the memory of the past generations, and our duty of remembrance tends to become increasingly more important, as is shown by the requests (although still marginal) for reburial of the deceased by the local authorities.

The discovery of a more modern period grave, for instance from the 19th or 20th centuries, brings a pathos that is even more intense, because it refers to people who were living fewer than five generations from our own. Moreover, if this recent chronological context is related to an emblematic event, another memorial aspect adds to what we evoked previously.

The discovery, excavation and reburial of soldiers of the Great Army of Emperor Napoleon I in Vilnius, Lithuania, is an illustrative example and will be discussed later. Until the end of the 19th century, apart from a few exceptions, osteoarchaeologists dealt with the anonymous remains of men who died on a battle field and who did not have the status of '*Mort pour la France*'[1] ('Dead for France'). However, since the beginning of the 20th century, several legislative texts have changed the context.

Indeed, at the beginning of the First World War, several parameters changed our approach to human remains. On the one hand, the legal status of dead soldiers changed and since then they have been referred to as having died for France ('*Mort pour la France*'). This is a very special status that gives certain rights, whether the identity of the deceased is known or not. This status was retrospectively given to the soldiers who died during the Franco–Prussian conflict in 1870–71. On the other hand, the existence of a commemorative plaque, which has been used progressively since 1881 in the French army, provides a recognition and identification of the human remains and makes possible the restitution procedure of personal belongings to the relatives.

Because of these changes, the way that archaeological excavations are approached in these contexts is not in a traditional osteoarchaeological manner, but closer to forensic archaeology and anthropology. That is to say, the first objective of the excavation is not the understanding of the funerary rituals or the demographic aspect of the dead population, but it is to identify the individual and if possible the cause of death.

These parameters will result in practices and scientific approaches that will be slightly different from archaeology and related disciplines. As far as military burials are concerned, the historical, ideological and popular consideration is reinforced even more by the fact that the deceased have won the status of heroes, and by the immense sacrifice for the nation.

These positive legal dispositions determine the excavation practices and the status of these burials. We can note that these texts were corollary to a memorial and commemorative infatuation (Nora 1997; Ricœur 2000). Whatever the ethical choice and the sensitivity of anthropologists towards the recent past, their professional ethics impose respect for the biological record (i.e., for the skeletons or human remains), because they can be the 'object' of studies. The anthropologist Paul Ricœur proposed that, whether one intervenes as an osteoarchaeologist or as a forensic anthropologist, one can choose one philosophical approach or another, but whatever one's beliefs are, these biological remains will be part of one's discipline (Ricœur 2000).

The relationship with the past is never neutral and is always affected by subjective and ideological values. One can tend to a deferential position towards the past to such an extent that it can be the object of a cult and be overwhelming (Brossat 2003[2]). Conversely, by considering the present as the only reference, one can be irreverent by not considering the importance of the past. As far as we are concerned, we would aim for a balanced position, as explained by Paul Ricœur (2000): one should not incriminate the remembrance process. The problem is the abuse of commemoration and the appropriation of the 'mute words of the victims'.

DISCOVERY OF FOREIGN SOLDIERS IN FRANCE

During the First and Second World Wars, millions of soldiers of different nationalities died on French soil. As a response to the horror created by the wars, several nations tried to provide an adequate measure to the mass scale of death where dignity, memory and respect coexist.

In 1914, Sir Fabien Ware arrived in France as the head of a mobile unit of the British Red Cross. 'Saddened by the sheer scale of loss, Ware felt compelled to establish a system to ensure the final resting places of casualties would not be lost forever'.[3] In May 1917, the Imperial War Graves Commission was established by Royal Charter, with Edward, Prince of Wales, serving as President and Ware as Vice-Chairman. In 1949, Sir Fabien Ware died, but the Commonwealth War Grave Commission (CWGC) carried on his work.

Today, the mission of the CWGC is to ensure a continuous tribute to those who died on the battlefield. The CWGC is financed by several countries of the Commonwealth (the UK,

Australia, Canada, New Zealand, South Africa, India) and ensures the maintenance of the cemeteries for a perpetual period. 'By preserving the memory of the dead with simple dignity and true equality, the Commission hopes to encourage future generations to remember the sacrifice made by so many'.[4]

In France, the Regional Council for Veteran Affairs (Direction Régionales des Anciens Combattants) has the jurisdiction for such matters and the applicable legislation is the Code des pensions militaries d'invalidité et des victimes de la guerre. In 1951, the CWGC signed an agreement with the French state that allowed the CWGC the authority to manage and maintain the Commonwealth cemeteries in France. Over the years, the French state has allocated land for a perpetual period in order for the CWGC to construct the cemeteries. However, the Commission, which is an international organization by law, has to comply with French legislation, and therefore works closely with the French authorities.

When remains of soldiers from the two World Wars are found, the French police authorities contact the CWGC. From that moment the burial officer of the CWGC coordinates the procedure, and tries to collect associated artefacts which could help contribute to the victims' identification. The details are then registered and archived at the CWGC Headquarters in Maidenhead, UK. If the remains are German, the CWGC contacts the Volksbund Deutscher Kriegsgräberfursorge (VDK), which will arrange the collection of the remains. In any other cases, the CWGC tries to identify the remains. The archives are accessible to the public in order for people to do their own research. When it is not possible to identify the casualties, the information is recorded in the 'Memorial to the Missing'.

The Commission commemorates those who have died during the designated war years in service. The war years are considered to be from 4 August 1914 to 31 August 1921, and from 3 September 1939 to 31 December 1947. The CWGC also commemorates more than 67,000 Commonwealth civilians who died as a result of enemy action during the Second World War. Their names are listed on a Roll of Honour, housed near St George's Chapel in Westminster Abbey, London. Over the years, the CWGC has paid tributes to 1.7 million casualties on 23,000 sites in 150 countries.[5]

Usually it is not possible for families to claim remains. Every time the remains of soldiers are found, the CWGC funds the construction of a cemetery and named grave stones where possible. The CWGC's policy is different in its approach from the American one. Remains, after being registered and eventually identified, are buried as part of a collective memorial cemetery, on a site that is as close as possible to the place of the battle.[6] In France, there are more than 3000 cemeteries managed by the CWGC. The largest CWGC cemetery is located at Thiepval, where more than 72,000 soldiers are remembered.

During the 'Battle of Fromelles' (19–20 July 1916) more than 2000 Australian and 1500 English soldiers perished. In 2008, several mass graves were found, and the potential identification of some of the soldiers through a combination of artefactual evidence, anthropological data and DNA analysis provoked an immense emotion.

The CWGC tries to ensure a site-specific tribute to the dead, and encourages the participation of the general public. Recently, the CWGC organized a drawing competition for French, English and Australian children for the cemetery that is being built in Fromelles. A temporary fence was set up in Fromelles, until building of the cemetery was finished in 2010, and was decorated with these drawings. The initiative gave an educational dimension to the mission of the CWGC, and the contribution of the children brought a refreshing angle showing innocence and desire to learn. A link between the past and the present has been established, and the idea of cooperation between all nations involved (including Germany) in order to achieve remembrance and educational purposes was also promoted.

A CASE STUDY: VILNIUS, LITHUANIA

Human remains are often subject to identity or ideological appropriations, whatever the chronological distance of the event from the present day. If one considers that it is too early to deal with the mass war grave of the Second World War or the Algerian war, a relatively distant past is subject to a particularly ideological appropriation when mass graves ('inhumations multiples et simultanées'[7]) are found, for example, from the French Revolution. As part of preventive archaeological excavations in Le Mans, mass graves were discovered in the district of the Quinconces des Jacobins. The burials and the skeletal remains have not been completely examined scientifically; however, Jean-Claude Boulard, the Mayor of Le Mans, and Philippe de Villiers, President of the Vendée Regional Council, agreed to return the bodies of Vendéens to the Vendée region, so that the Vendée can pay the final tribute 'to these victims of the revolutionary barbarism, massacred while they were trying to reach their home'.[8] The symbolic representations depend on the social and ethnic preoccupations and on the mentalities of all the parties involved.

The discovery, excavation and the study of mass graves in Vilnius, Lithuania, generated preoccupation, as well as affective and ideological reactions, which still contribute to the Napoleonic epic. These reactions have been particularly significant, as they relate to an emblematic moment of the European saga: the Russian campaign.

In 2001, in the northern part of Vilnius called 'Siaures Miestelis', the city decided to start a programme of regeneration of urban wasteland (Signoli *et al.* 2008). On the right bank of the river Wilia, a military zone with a very restricted access had been set up since the end of the 19th century. This area was used in the course of history for accommodation by the Russians, Nazis and Soviet troops. The buildings were characterized by shallow foundations, which did not affect the archaeology beneath.

As part of the building work in 2001, many human bones were discovered during the excavation of a deep trench for the installation of a water tank. The first field evaluation indicated that these human remains had been buried in a mass grave. The analysis of the first artefacts found with the skeletons led osteoarchaeologists to identify these skeletons as the remains of individuals from the Napoleonic Great Army who disappeared during the retreat campaign from Russia during the winter of 1812–13.

The excavation of the burials was programmed for Spring 2002 by Lithuanian scientists including Rimantas Jankauskas, Professor of Anthropology at the University of Vilnius, and a representative of the History Department from the Lithuanian Ministry of Defence. The excavation of the mass grave in Vilnius was also part of a scientific research program of the CNRS,[9] which funded this project, with substantial financial help from the Université de la Méditerranée and the French Embassy in Vilnius. This first mission was an opportunity to initiate Franco–Lithuanian collaboration and to take a multidisciplinary approach on this site. Several other missions followed – October 2002: analysis of excavated bones in a laboratory; May–June 2003: initial stage of artefact analysis; October 2004: final study of the artefacts; and collaborations on other sites (Jankauskas *et al.* 2009).

From the French side, we (including present author M.S.) participated in this project for several reasons. As researchers, the main reason for our intervention was our increasing interest in the study of mass graves (sépultures multiples et simultanées) that has developed since the mid-1990s. Mass burials are the archaeological heritage of a period when the population of the time faced and had an abnormal experience of death. That exceptional context (high number of dead, administrative and economic chaos, etc.) had an impact on the techniques and procedures used during the treatment of the dead. The study of these mass burials through archaeological evidence allows us to understand how the living dealt with that abnormal experience of death.

Another reason for participation has been the interest of present author M.S. in plague-related burial assemblages, and the project in Vilnius provided an opportunity to develop our research on typhus epidemics. This research project was included in 2000 as part of the CNRS project mentioned above, and would take place at the site of the Battle of Borodino (also known as Moscowa[10]). Finally, due to the administrative difficulties of realizing an archaeological mission in Borodino, it was more realistic, at that time, to work on the Vilnius site. Contrary to the graves on the site in Moscowa, we were dealing in Vilnius with the context of a military retreat which took place in particularly difficult conditions, especially regarding the sanitary aspects (non-existent hygiene, limited supplies, exhaustion) and a favourable environment for the development of an epidemic caused by an ecto-parasite. A microbiological analysis of dental pulp was able to confirm the presence of typhus in several of the soldiers (Raoult *et al.* 2006).

But the site in Vilnius raised other questions. Who were the individuals who were buried there? Civilians? Soldiers? If soldiers, were they allies, Russians or both? It was quickly established that they were the remains of soldiers in the graves. For this reason, we also decided to participate in the project for the 'memory of the past'. The soldiers who were buried in those trenches were not all French, as they were part of the Twenty Nation Army, but they all died serving the *tricolore* flag. It was obvious that, if there were several scientific purposes that justified our mission, in memory of the dead, our work was also justified by the fact that we did not want any human remains to be left beneath a wastewater tank.

The site 'Siaures Miestelis' has the largest mass grave discovered to date. The historical context of the sample of the Twenty Nation Army provides a very original subject to study: a palaeodemographic picture of the young of the time. The archaeological evidence allows us to

Figure A3.1 Vault in which the soldiers found at 'Siaures Miestelis' in Lithuania are buried
Source: M. Signoli

further understand how a major demographic crisis in a military context was managed (not to mention the funerary rituals deployed after a battle). The conservation, restoration and study of thousands of artefacts provides a better understanding of the military units involved in this campaign. It also expands and improves museum collections (Vilnius Museum, Musée des Invalides), which have a relatively poor representation of this period.

As there were no individual plaques or markers, it was impossible to identify individuals in this case. It was also impossible to certify which individuals belonged to which regiment through the study of buttons, shoulder pads and historical archives, since the survivors took the uniforms from the dead throughout the campaign.

Since 2002, one member of the team has been called upon to react on several Internet forums, to explain our approach to several 'Napoleonic associations'. The objective was to stop inappropriate rumours, and to answer questions addressing what would become of the bodies.

Taking into account that this army was international and that it was not possible to identify the victims, both the political leaders and the scientists involved agreed that this 'Band of Brothers' should be buried in Lithuania.

Thanks to the help of the city of Vilnius, which donated the land, and the Napoleon Foundation, which provided funds for the construction of a vault (Figure A3.1), the reburial took place on 1 June 2003 during an official ceremony at the Antakalnis cemetery in Vilnius. We hope we found the best ethical solution regarding the remains of these soldiers. Even if the articles L 488 to L 492bis do not apply, they were many soldiers (altogether 3269 bodies) who paid with their lives to write one of the most emblematic pages of European history.

NOTES

1 The mention '*Mort pour la France*' is given in certain circumstances, following articles L 488 to L 492bis of the 'code des pensions militaires d'invalidité et des victimes de la guerre'.
2 There is no meaning to institute the past as an instance to which we owe duties, and in particular some duties of remembrance. As living adults or citizens, we do not owe anything in particular to the past. If that was the case, our life would be consumed by an obese memory, which would make us crazy, as Borges stated in a famous allegory.
3 www.cwgc.org
4 www.cwgc.org
5 www.cwgc.org
6 Mrs Corinne Rouillard (CWGC), personal communication.
7 It is the scientific expression that is used in French in order to define what the current language would describe as a mass grave, a communal grave, a catastrophic and crisis burial.
8 'Charniers de Vendéens au Mans: Les corps vont être rendus à la Vendée', Vendée Regional Council web site (www.vendee.fr), 14 April 2009.
9 "Aide à Projet Nouveau (A.P.N.)" of the CNRS: 'Caractérisation des crises démographiques, des archives historiques aux archives biologiques'. Programme managed by present author M. Signoli through a collaboration between several members of the U.M.R. 6578 CNRS/Université de la Méditerranée, the U.M.R. 5809 CNRS/Université de Bordeaux I, the U.P.R.E.S. A-6020 CNRS/Université de la Méditerranée, University Jozsef Attila (Szeged, Hungria), INED and the Academy of Science of Russia.
10 Currently, several teams of Russian archaeologists work on several parts of the battlefield. Recently, the remains of a French general were discovered along with some medals, which belonged to General Caulaincourt, who died during the siege of the Grand Redoute.

BIBLIOGRAPHY

Brossat, A. (2003) Brèves réflexions sur l'injonction au souvenir, *INRP Philosophie de l'éducation. Mémoire et histoire. Réflexion, débats.*

Jankauskas, R., Rigeade, C., Barkus, A., *et al.* (2009) 'Le charnier de Tuskulėnai (Vilnius, Lituanie): un exemple d'étude archéo-médico-légale', in L. Buchet *et al.* (eds) *Vers une anthropologie des catastrophes*, Paris: APDCA, Antibes/INED.

Nora, P. (1997) 'Les Lieux de mémoire' (dir.), *Sous la direction de Pierre Nora*, Paris: Gallimard (Quarto).

Raoult, D., Dutour, O., Houhamdi, L., *et al.* (2006) 'Evidence for louse-transmitted diseases in soldiers of Napoleon's Grand Army in Vilnius', *Journal of Infectious Diseases*, 193: 112–20.

Ricœur, P. (2000) *La Mémoire, l'histoire, l'oubli*, Paris: Le Seuil.

Signoli, M., Vette, T., Dutour, O., *et al.* (2008) *Les Oubliés De La Retraite De Russie; Vilna 1812-Vilnius 2002*, Paris: Librairie Historique F. Teissedre.

Appendix 4

The Vatican City State/Status Civitatis Vaticanæ/ Stato della Città del Vaticano

Dario Piombino-Mascali

Archaeological remains found within the territories belonging to the Vatican are currently protected through a law created by the Papal Commission for the State of the Vatican City (Law no. 355, issued on 25 July 2001). Such legislation was conceived to guarantee the integrity and conservation of the heritage pertaining to the Vatican state and to its extraterritorial areas, as established by the Lateran Pacts (Acta Apostolicae Sedis, 1929). Although human remains are not mentioned, the present law includes all objects characterized by an artistic, historical, archaeological or ethnographic interest, and the relative regulation for temporary exportation. It is worth noting Article 33 of the original 1929 Lateran Concordat – revised in 1984 (see Article 12.2) – according to which the Holy See keeps control of the Christian Catacombs in Rome and the rest of Italy, thus maintaining the right to carry out excavations and transfer holy bodies.

USEFUL CONTACTS

The Vatican City State Website: www.vatican.va/

REFERENCE

Acta Apostolicae Sedis (1929) Inter Santam Sedem et Italiae Regnum Conventiones, Vol. 21 (6): pp. 209–295.

Index

excavation of 598–99; contacts 601; history of
physical anthropology in 595–97; legislation,
human remains and 599–600, 601; physical
anthropology in, current state of 595–97
Chimenos, E. *et al.* 432
Chiquichano, F., Sayhueque, C. and
Dahinten, S. 582
Chlorokosta, G., Hatzisavva, K. and
Xirotitis, N.I. 174
Chochol, Jaromír 115
Cholakov, S. 79
Choosiri, Praphid 624, 628
Christensen, Tina 131–36
Christian Catacombs 718
Chtetcov, V.P. 363
Chubynsky, P. 469
Chura, Alojz Ján 391
Cifre de Loubriel, E. 563
Cihlarž, Z. and Kešetović, R. 67
Çiner, R. 456
Civil Code in Belgium 56
Civil War graves in Spain 430
Clark, A. 536
Cleuvenot, E. and Houët, F. 261
Clevis, H. and Constandse-Westermann, T. 310
Code de Patrimonie in France 154
Code of Criminal Procedures in Kosovo 242
Cohen, M.N. and Armelagos, G. 370
Coke, T. 694
Coll, E. 563
Coll y Toste, Cayetano 564
Collection of Studies for National
Anthropology (Anthropological Commission
of Poland) 331
collections: anthropological collections in Portugal
346; first in Russia, history of creation of
364–67; modern tendencies towards collections
of human remains in Russia 367–68; museum
collections in Italy 223; in Turkey 459–60; *see
also* skeletal collections
Collegium Antropologicum (Croatia) 83
Collett, M. 515
colonial legislation in Australia 640
Comas, Juan 423, 554
Comfortless Cove, Ascension Island, excavation
at (2008) 698
Commission for the Prosecution of Crimes
against the Polish Nation 337
Commission to Preserve National Monuments
in Bosnia and Herzegovina 65
Commissions Interrégionales de la Recherche
Archéologique (CIRA), France 153
Committee of Missing Persons in Cyprus (CMP) 99
Common Law (Declaration of Application) Act
(1705), British Virgin Islands 694, 698
Congrès International d'Anthropologie
Archéologie Préhistorique, Lisbon (1880) 342

Conseil National de la Recherche Archéologique
(CNRA), France 153
Constantinescu, F. and Torres, D. 676
Constitution Order (2006), Falkland Islands
695, 699
Constitutional Affairs, UK Dept. of (DCA)
487, 488
contacts: Albania 7; Andorra 13; Argentina 583;
Armenia 28; Australia 643; Azerbaijan 39;
Belarus 43; Belgium 58; Bosnia and
Herzegovina 69; Brazil 591; Canada 528; Chile
601; Croatia 92; Cyprus 105; Czech Republic
124–27; Denmark 135; Egypt 498; Finland
146; France 158–59; FYRO Macedonia 271;
Germany 170–71; Gibralter 709; Greece 181;
Guatemala 559; Hungary 199; Iceland 207;
Ireland 218–19; Israel 619; Italy 229;
Kosovo 245; Lithuania 253; Luxembourg
261; Malta 283; Mexico 549; Monaco 301;
Montenegro 307; Netherlands 313–14; New
Zealand 653; Norway 326–27; Poland 339;
Portugal 349; Puerto Rico 568; Romania
359–60; Russia 371; Serbia 386; Slovakia
398–99; Slovenia 418; South Africa 509;
Spain 433; Sudan 520; Sweden 451–52;
Thailand 629; Turkey 464; Ukraine 476;
United Kingdom 489–90; United States 538;
Uruguay 610; Vanuatu 667
Convent voor Gemeentelijk Archeologen (CGA),
Netherlands 311
Conzato, A. and Rizzi, J. 222
Cook, Captain James 633, 673–74
Cook, D.C. 32n6
Coon, Carleton 3–4
Coppa, A. *et al.* 223
Coppa, Alfredo 222
Coppens, Yves 299
Corcione, M.A. 432
Coroners Act (1938, revised 1989) in Bermuda
693, 698
Corrain, C. and Capitano, M. 222
Correnti, V. 221
Costa Ferreira, António Aurélio da 344
Costa-Junqueira, María Antonieta 597
Costanzo, P. 297
Couttenier, M. 49
Covarrubias, Edmundo 596
Cowgill, L.W. and Hager, L.D. 457
Cox, K., Tayles, N.G. and Buckley, H.R.
642, 652
Cox, Katherine 624
Cox, M. and Mays, S. 416
Cox, M. *et al.* 536
Cózar, P. *et al.* 140
Further Note of the Craneology of the Lapps
(Schreiner, K.E.) 317
Crania Armenica (Bunak, V.V.) 22